ICPP 2005

Proceedings

2005 International Conference on Parallel Processing

14-17 June 2005

Oslo, Norway

Edited by

Wu-chun Feng and José Duato

Sponsored by

The International Association for Computers and Communications (IACC)

Simula Research Laboratory

The Research Council of Norway

The University of Oslo

In cooperation with

The Norwegian Computer Society

Los Alamitos, California

Washington • Brussels • Tokyo

Copyright © 2005 by The Institute of Electrical and Electronics Engineers, Inc.
All rights reserved.

Copyright and Reprint Permissions: Abstracting is permitted with credit to the source. Libraries may photocopy beyond the limits of US copyright law, for private use of patrons, those articles in this volume that carry a code at the bottom of the first page, provided that the per-copy fee indicated in the code is paid through the Copyright Clearance Center, 222 Rosewood Drive, Danvers, MA 01923.

Other copying, reprint, or republication requests should be addressed to: IEEE Copyrights Manager, IEEE Service Center, 445 Hoes Lane, P.O. Box 133, Piscataway, NJ 08855-1331.

The papers in this book comprise the proceedings of the meeting mentioned on the cover and title page. They reflect the authors' opinions and, in the interests of timely dissemination, are published as presented and without change. Their inclusion in this publication does not necessarily constitute endorsement by the editors, the IEEE Computer Society, or the Institute of Electrical and Electronics Engineers, Inc.

IEEE Computer Society Order Number P2380
ISBN 0-7695-2380-3
ISSN 0190-3918

Additional copies may be ordered from:

IEEE Computer Society
Customer Service Center
10662 Los Vaqueros Circle
P.O. Box 3014
Los Alamitos, CA 90720-1314
Tel: + 1 800 272 6657
Fax: + 1 714 821 4641
http://computer.org/cspress
csbooks@computer.org

IEEE Service Center
445 Hoes Lane
P.O. Box 1331
Piscataway, NJ 08855-1331
Tel: + 1 732 981 0060
Fax: + 1 732 981 9667
http://shop.ieee.org/store/
customer-service@ieee.org

IEEE Computer Society
Asia/Pacific Office
Watanabe Bldg., 1-4-2
Minami-Aoyama
Minato-ku, Tokyo 107-0062
JAPAN
Tel: + 81 3 3408 3118
Fax: + 81 3 3408 3553
tokyo.ofc@computer.org

Individual paper REPRINTS may be ordered at: reprints@computer.org

Editorial production by Danielle C. Martin

Cover art production by Joseph Daigle/Studio Productions

Printed in the United States of America by The Printing House

IEEE Computer Society
Conference Publishing Services
http://www.computer.org/proceedings/

Table of Contents

2005 International Conference on Parallel Processing (ICPP 2005)

Session 2B: Compilers and Languages

Session 2C: Applications

Session 3A: On-Chip Parallelism

Session 3B: Messaging

Session 3C: Virtual & Optical Networking

Keynote Address 2

Session 4A: Shared-Memory Computing

Session 4B: P2P Search & Discovery

Session 4C: Ad Hoc Networks

Session 5A: Network Performance and Features

Session 5B: Network-Based & Grid Computing

Panel Session

Keynote Address 3

Session 5C: Wireless & Mobile Computing

Session 6A: Higher-Level Network Operations

Session 6B: Services in P2P Systems

Session 6C: Communications Tools

Session 7A: Network Hardware

Session 7B: Peer-to-Peer Technology

Session 7C: Algorithms & Applications

Session 8A: Interconnection Networks

Session 8B: Cross-Node Clustering

Session 8C: Scheduling

Message from the General Co-Chairs

On behalf of the organizing committee we wish to welcome you to ICPP 2005 in Oslo. This is the second time in the long history of the conference that it is hosted in Europe, and we have worked hard to make this event as memorable as the one in Valencia in 2001.

The venue, this time, is the northernmost that this conference has ever seen. In order to benefit from the location, we have moved the date of the conference to mid June from its more traditional schedule in August or September. If the weather is with us, we hope to experience over 20 hours of sunlight each day, and if you have combined the trip to the conference with a vacation to the northern parts of Norway, you might even get to see sun at midnight.

The topic of the conference, parallel processing, has been through many phases. We believe that the field is now moving into an era of renewed interest. The increasing signs that Moore's law is coming to an end have made us realize that continued increase in computer performance depends on our ability to do efficient parallel processing on efficient parallel architectures. The increasing number of submissions for conferences in this area supports this view.

Throughout the preparations for this event we have enjoyed support from many people. We cannot mention all of them, but in particular we would like to thank professor Ming Liu for inviting us to take on this task. Secondly, we are sincerely grateful to the program co-chairs José Duato and Wu-chun Feng for their continuous encouragement and support. Thanks are also due to our sponsors Simula Research Laboratory, The University of Oslo, The Norwegian Computer Society and the Research Council of Norway.

The program committee has put together an exciting program for you, containing many reports of novel research of high quality, as well as several distinguished keynote speakers. The social events that go with these presentations will give you opportunities to enjoy the company of other researchers as well as enjoy the local specialties of Oslo. Hopefully the combination of the scientific program, the social events, the daylight and the atmosphere of Oslo will give you all a memory for life.

Enjoy the 34th ICPP in Oslo, Norway!

Olav Lysne and Lionel Ni

Message from the Program Co-Chairs

Welcome to the 2005 International Conference on Parallel Processing (ICPP-2005) and to the beautiful city of Oslo. It is our pleasure to present the proceedings for this conference, the oldest in the field of parallel processing and one of the leading forums for the presentation of forefront research in this field.

Recent trends in the evolution of computing systems clearly show that the performance of uniprocessor systems is reaching its ceiling, being limited by both heat dissipation and data dependencies. Therefore, there has been a renewed interest in parallel processing. As a consequence of this renewed interest and also thanks to the excellent work of the Publicity Co-Chairs, the number of submissions this year was significantly higher than in previous editions of this conference.

This year, the conference received 241 submissions from over 20 countries. Each submission was assigned to at least one of the 13 Vice Chairs (VCs) of the conference to obtain at least 3 reviews. Some interdisciplinary papers were assigned to two VCs to obtain reviews from two different perspectives. The meeting of the VCs was held in Raleigh on March 12, 2005 to discuss the submissions. The VCs thoroughly evaluated the papers, providing their own insights in addition to the reviews delivered by the corresponding PC members. Special attention was paid to papers with conflicting reviews, providing additional on-site reviews when necessary. Differences in harshness among areas were also considered in order to make a fair decision. The result is the outstanding technical program with the 69 papers contained in these proceedings. These papers present state-of-the-art work in both traditional and emerging areas of parallel processing, including architecture, compilers, algorithms and applications, resource management, tools, cluster and grid computing, mobile computing, peer-to-peer technology, multimedia and network services, just to name a few. We are thankful to all the authors who submitted their papers to the conference. We are also thankful to the members of the program committee and to the external reviewers for their efforts to read and evaluate the papers within such a short period of time. The high quality of the papers in these proceedings is a testament to the hard work and dedication of all the authors and of all the reviewers.

The achievement of a successful conference relies on many people, whose efforts and hard work must be acknowledged. Olav Lysne and Lionel Ni, the conference's General Co-Chairs, provided invaluable support, guidance and constant encouragement. The VCs, Angelos Bilas, Eduard Ayguade, Yavuz Oruc, Anand Sivasubramaniam, Daniel Reed, Allan Snavely, Hideharu Amano, Matt Mutka, Micah Beck, Dongyan Xu, Hank Dietz, Xiaodong Zhang, and Sudhakar Yalamanchili, all made a superb effort in forming the program committee and have all put in many hours of their valuable time to evaluate and discuss the submissions. Timothy Pinkston and Cho-Li Wang did a wonderful job of publicizing the conference and attracting a high number of submissions. Steve H. Lai and Makoto Takizawa provided guidance in selecting the best paper. Daniel Reed and Sue Gambill provided local arrangements for the meeting of the VCs in Raleigh. Nils Agne Nordbotten provided invaluable assistance with Confman, the tool we used to handle electronic submissions and reviews. Mark Gardner also provided valuable technical support during the PC meeting. Finally, Thomas Baldwin provided invaluable assistance in the production of these proceedings.

And last, and by no means least, we would like to express our gratitude to Professor Tse-yun Feng, Professor Ming T. Liu, and Professor Steve H. Lai for their support of this conference in particular, and of the field of parallel processing in general.

Wu-chun Feng and José Duato

Organizing Committee

General Co-Chairs

Olav Lysne, Simula Research Laboratory, Norway

Lionel Ni, Hong Kong University of Science and Technology, China

Program Co-Chairs

Wu-chun Feng, Los Alamos National Lab, USA

José Duato, Technical University of Valencia, Spain

Program Vice-Chairs

Architecture

Angelos Bilas, University of Crete and FORTH

Algorithms and Applications

Yavuz Oruc, Bilkent University, Turkey

Cluster Computing

Hank Dietz, University of Kentucky, USA

Compilers and Languages

Eduard Ayguade, Technical University of Catalonia, Spain

Network-Based/Grid Computing

Micah Beck, University of Tennessee, USA

OS & Resource Management

Anand Sivasubramaniam, Pennsylvania State University, USA

Peer-to-Peer Technology

Xiaodong Zhang, NSF & College of William and Mary, USA

Petaflop Computing

Daniel A. Reed, UNC & The Renaissance Computing Institute, USA

Tools

Allan Snavely, San Diego Supercomputer Center & University of California, San Diego, USA

Parallel Embedded Systems

Sudhakar Yalamanchili, Georgia Institute of Technology, USA

Multimedia

Dongyan Xu, Purdue University, USA

Network Services

Hideharu Amano, Keio University, Japan

Wireless & Mobile Computing

Matt Mutka, Michigan State University, USA

Workshops Co-Chairs

Tor Skeie, University of Oslo, Norway

Chu-Sing Yang, Nat'l Sun Yat-Sen University, Taiwan

Awards Co-Chairs

Ten H. Lai, The Ohio State University, USA

Makoto Takizawa, Tokyo Denki University, Japan

Publicity Co-Chairs

Timothy Pinkston, University of Southern California, USA

Cho-Li Wang, University of Hong Kong, China

International Liaison Co-Chairs

Jiannong Cao, Hong Kong Polytechnic University

P. Sadayappan, The Ohio State University, USA

Local Arrangements Chair

Siri Gulbrandsen, Norwegian Computer Society

Registration Chair

Anne Cathrine Modahl, University of Oslo

Steering Committee Co-Chairs

Tse-yun Feng, Pennsylvania State University, USA

Mike Liu, The Ohio State University, USA

Program Committee

Manuel E. Acacio, University of Murcia
Murcia Cevdet Aykanat, Bilkent University
David A. Bader, University of New Mexico
Alan Benner, IBM
Ricardo Bianchini, Rutgers University
Angelos Bilas, FORTH & University of Crete, Greece
Robert Brown, Duke University
Costas Busch, Rensselaer Polytechnic Institute
Gregory T. Byrd, Center for Advanced Computing and Communication
Roy Campbell, ARL
Rafael Casado, University of Castilla-La Mancha
Abhishek Chandra, University of Minnesota
Siddhartha Chatterjee, IBM Research
Songqing Chen, George Mason University
Will Cohen, Red Hat
Brian F. Cooper, Georgia Institute of Technology
Chita Das, Pennsylvania State University
Sajal Das, University of Texas-Arlington
Luiz Derose, Cray
John Feo, Cray
Randall Fisher, Penn State University
Hubertus Franke, IBM Research
Nobuo Funabiki, Okayama University
Mark K. Gardner, Los Alamos National Laboratory
Ananth Grama, Purdue University
Carsten Griwodz, University of Oslo
Manish Gupta, IBM Research
Mitchell Gusat, IBM Zurich
Reiner Hartenstein, TU Kaiserslautern
Mohamed Hefeeda, Simon Fraser University
Raymond Hoare, University of Pittsburgh
Chung-Hsing Hsu, Los Alamos National Laboratory
Adriana Iamnitchi, Duke University
Liviu Iftode, Rutgers University
Steven James, Linux Labs
Song Jiang, Los Alamos National Lab
Bill Johnston, Lawrence Berkeley National Laboratory
Christos Karamanolis, Hewlett-Packard Labs
Daniel S. Katz, Jet Propulsion Laboratory/California Institute of Technology
Pete Keleher, University of Maryland
Darren Kerbyson, Los Alamos National Laboratory
Chung-Ta King, National Tsing Hua University
Peter Kogge, Notre Dame
Markku Kojo, University of Helsinki
Kenji Kono, University of Electro-Communications
Nectarios Koziris, National Technical University of Athens
Ulrich Kremer, Rutgers University
Raj Krishnamurthy, IBM Zurich
Laurent Lefevre, INRIA/Ecole Normale Superieure de Lyon
Zhiyuan Li, Purdue University
Baochun Li, University of Toronto
Sung-Kyu Lim, Georgia Institute of Technology

Yunhao Liu, Hong Kong University of Science and Technology
Andrew Lumsdaine, Indiana University
Xiaosong Ma, North Carolina State University
Arthur Maccabe, University of New Mexico
Satoshi Matsuoka, Tokyo Institute of Technology
Tim Mattox, University of Kentucky
John May, Lawrence Livermore National Laboratory
Michael McCracken, University of California, San Diego
Philip McKinley, Michigan State University
Sam Midkiff, Purdue University
Andreas Moshovos, University of Toronto
Frank Mueller, North Carolina State University
Gilles Muller, Ecole des Mines de Nantes
Henry Newman, Instrumental
Vivek Pai, Princeton University
Dmitri Perkins, University of Louisiana at Lafayette
Fabrizio Petrini, Los Alamos National Labs
Timothy Pinkston, University of Southern California
Oscar Plata, University of Malaga
Francisco J. Quiles, University of Castilla-La Mancha
Rodric Rabbah, Michigan Institute of Technology
J. Ramanujam, Louisiana State University
Ana Ripoll, University of Barcelona
P. Sadayappan, The Ohio State University
Sartaj Sahni, University of Florida
Vikram A. Saletore, Intel
Luis Sarmenta, Ateneo de Manila University
Jenneifer Schopf, Argonne National Laboratory
Jonathan Shapiro, Michigan State University
Bo Shen, HP Labs
Kai Shen, University of Rochester
Beth Simon, University of San Diego
Mukesh Singhal, University of Kentucky
Vaidy Sunderam, Emory University
Martin Swany, University of Delaware
Chunqiang Tang, IBM T.J. Watson Research Center
Karen A. Tomko, University of Cincinnati
Fred Tracy, ERDC
Pedro Trancoso, University of Cyprus
Anand Tripathi, University of Minnesota
Chau-Wen Tseng, University of Maryland
Keith Underwood, Sandia
Uzi Vishkin, University of Maryland
William A. Ward, ERDC
Jon Weissman, University of Minnesota
Weng-Fai Wong, National University of Singapore
Dapeng Oliver Wu, University of Florida
Jie Wu, Florida Atlantic University
Zhen Xiao, AT&T Research
Li Xiao, Michigan State University
Jingling Xue, University of New South Wales
Yuanyuan Yang, The State University of New York at Stony Brook
Andy Yoo, Lawrence Livermore National Labs
Yanyong Zhang, Rutgers University
Yuanyan Zhou, University of Illinois at Urbana-Champaign
Michael Zink, University of Massachusetts at Amherst
Taieb Znati, University of Pittsburgh

Reviewers

Manuel E. Acacio
Juan L. Aragsn
Enrique Arias
MurciaCevdet Aykanat
David A. Bader
Rendong Bai
Alan Benner
Aurelio Bermudez
Ricardo Bianchini
Angelos Bilas
Robert Brown
Costas Busch
Gregory T. Byrd
Blanca Caminero
Roy Campbell
Rafael Casado
Phil Cayton
Abhishek Chandra
Siddhartha Chatterjee
Songqing Chen
Zhifeng Chen
Nikolaos Chrysos
Will Cohen
Brian F. Cooper
Loring Craymer
Sajal Das
Chita Das
Luiz DeRose
John Feo
Juan Fernandez
Randall Fisher
Annie Foong
Hubertus Franke
Nobuo Funabiki
Mark K. Gardner
Ismael Garcia-Varea
Pedro Garcia
Antonio Garrido
Robert van de Geijn
Chryssis Georgiou
Amitabha Ghosh
Vankata Giruka
Ananth Grama
Carsten Griwodz
Manish Gupta
Mitchell Gusat
Reiner Hartenstein
Mohamed Hefeeda
Ahmed Helmy
Wai Hong Ho
Raymond Hoare
Chung-Hsing Hsu
Adriana Iamnitchi
Liviu Iftode
Deborah Jackson
Steven James
Song Jiang
Bill Johnston
Christos Karamanolis
Daniel S. Katz
Pete Keleher
Darren Kerbyson
Chung-Ta King
Joe Tucek
Peter Kogge
Markku Kojo
Kenji Kono
Nectarios Koziris
Ulrich Kremer
Raj Krishnamurthy
Laurent Lefevre
Baochun Li
Huaizhi Li
Zhenmin Li
Zhiyuan Li
Sung-Kyu Lim
Shiding Lin
Yunhao Liu
Pedro Lopez
Shan Lu
Andrew Lumsdaine
Xiaosong Ma
John May
Arthur MacCabe
Satoshi Matsuoka
Tim Mattox
Gary McAlpine
Michael McCracken
Philip McKinley
Arif Merchant
Sam Midkiff
Andreas Moshovos
Frank Mueller
Gilles Muller
Richard Murphy
Henry Newman
Dapeng Oliver Wu
Luis Orozco
Vivek Pai
Lei Pan
Vivek Pandey
Dmitri Perkins
Fabrizio Petrini
Timothy Pinkston
Oscar Plata
Feng Qin
Francisco J. Quiles
Rodric Rabbah
J. Ramanujam
Rahul Ratan
Ana Ripoll
Antonio Robles
P. Sadayappan
Sartaj Sahni
Vikram A. Saletore
Jose Luis Sanchez
Luis Sarmenta
Jenneifer Schopf
Jonathan Shapiro
Bo Shen
Kai Shen
Manish Shukla
Beth Simon
Mukesh Singhal
Shanshan Song
Paul Springer
Jeff Squyres
Vaidy Sunderam
Martin Swany
Chunqiang Tang
Karen A. Tomko
Fred Tracy
Pedro Trancoso
Anand Tripathi
Chau-Wen Tseng
Keith Underwood
Alistair Veitch
Francisco J. Villa
Uzi Vishkin
Yongwei Wang
Jun Wang
Bill Ward
Jon Weissman
Weng-Fai Wong
Chuan Wu
Jie Wu
Li Xiao
Zhen Xiao
Jingling Xue
Sudhakar Yalamanchili
Chao-Tung Yang
Yuanyuan Yang
Andy Yoo
Bilal Zafar
Yanyong Zhang
Pin Zhou
Yuanyan Zhou
Feng Zhu
Qingbo Zhu
Ying Zhu
Michael Zink
Taieb Znati

Keynote Address 1

Session 1A: Unconventional Scheduling

SAREC: A Security-Aware Scheduling Strategy for Real-Time Applications on Clusters

Tao Xie, Xiao Qin, Andrew Sung
Department of Computer Science
New Mexico Institute of Mining and Technology
801 Leroy Place, Socorro, New Mexico 87801-4796
{xietao, xqin, sung}@cs.nmt.edu

Abstract

Security requirements of security-critical real-time applications must be met in addition to satisfying timing constraints. However, conventional real-time scheduling algorithms ignore the applications' security requirements. In recognition that an increasing number of applications running on clusters demand both real-time performance and security, we investigate the problem of scheduling a set of independent real-time tasks with various security requirements. We propose a security overhead model that is capable of measuring security overheads incurred by security-critical tasks. Further, we propose a security-aware scheduling strategy, or SAREC, which integrates security requirements into scheduling for real-time applications by employing our security overhead model. To evaluate the effectiveness of SAREC, we implement a security-aware real-time scheduling algorithm (SAREC-EDF), which incorporates the earliest deadline first (EDF) scheduling algorithm into SAREC. Extensive simulation experiments show that SAREC-EDF significantly improves overall system performance over three baseline scheduling algorithms (variations of EDF) by up to 72.55%.

1. Introduction

With rapid advances in processing power, network bandwidth, and storage capacity of commodity off-the-shelf PCs in recent years, clusters have increasingly become the most cost-effective and viable platforms for scientific applications [21][22]. It becomes crucial to take advantage of cluster systems, where nodes are interconnected through high-speed networks, e.g. Myrinet or fast Ethernet, to meet the needs of highly complex scientific problems [20].

Recently there have been some efforts devoted to development of real-time applications on clusters [16] [23][24]. Real-time applications depend not only on results of computation, but also on time instants at which these results become available [13]. The consequences of missing deadlines of hard real-time systems may be catastrophic, whereas such consequences for soft real-time systems are relatively less damaging.

In addition to satisfying timing constraints in real-time applications, security is usually required in many applications [2][10]. Today there exist a growing number of systems that have real time and security considerations, because sensitive data and processing require special safeguard and protection against unauthorized access. In particular, real-time applications running on clusters require security protections to completely fulfill their security-critical needs. However, conventional real time systems, which are developed to guarantee timing constraints while possibly posing unacceptable security risks, are not adequate for real-time applications with requirements of information security and assurance.

In recognition that an increasing number of applications on clusters demand both real-time capabilities and security, we proposed a security-aware scheduling strategy, or SAREC, which is intended to integrate security requirements into real-time scheduling for applications running on clusters. SAREC can achieve high quality of security for real-time applications while meeting timing constraints imposed by these applications.

The contributions of this paper include: (1) an analysis of security and real-time performance needs of various applications running on clusters; (2) a security overhead model used to quantitatively measure overhead posted by various security services and security levels; (3) an security-aware real-time scheduling strategy; (4) definition of security and real-time performance metrics to evaluate our approach; and (5) a simulator where the SAREC-EDF algorithm is implemented and evaluated.

The rest of the paper is organized in the following way. Section 2 includes a summary of related work in this area. Section 3 discusses the system architecture and task model with security requirements. Section 4 proposes a security overhead model. Section 5 presents the security-aware real-time scheduling strategy. Performance analysis of the SAREC-EDF algorithm is explained in Section 6. Section7 concludes the paper with summary and future research directions.

0190-3918/05 $20.00 © 2005 IEEE

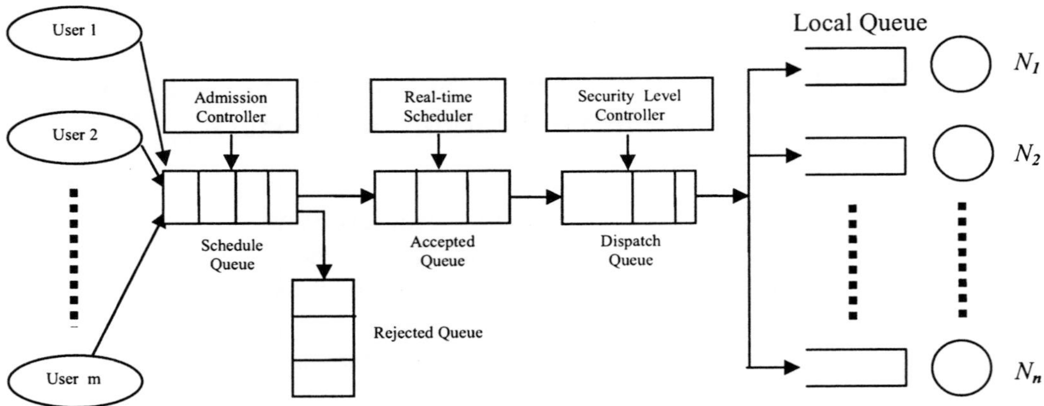

Figure 1. System model of the SAREC strategy.

2. Related work

Scheduling algorithms for clusters have been extensively studied in the past both experimentally and theoretically [29][31]. Subramani et al. incorporated a buddy scheme for contiguous node allocation into a backfilling job scheduler for clusters [29]. Vallee et al. proposed a global scheduler architecture that can dynamically change scheduling policies while applications are running on clusters [31]. However, these scheduling algorithms are not suitable for real-time applications, because there is no guarantee to finish real-time tasks in specified time intervals.

The issue of scheduling for real-time applications was previously reported in the literature, where various aspects of a complicated scheduling problem were addressed. In practice, real-time scheduling algorithms generally fall into two camps: static (off-line) [1] and dynamic (on-line) [7]. While many algorithms assume that real-time tasks are independent of one another [30], others schedule tasks with precedence constraints [1], which are represented by directed acyclic graphs. Conventional real-time scheduling algorithms such as Rate Monotonic (RM) algorithm [19], Earliest Deadline First (EDF) [28], and Spring scheduling algorithm [25] were successfully applied in real-time systems. However, most of existing real-time scheduling algorithms perform poorly for real-time and security-sensitive applications due to the oversight and ignorance of security requirements imposed by the applications.

Recently increasing attention has been drawn toward security-awareness in the context of clusters [3], because security has become a baseline requirement. Wright et al. proposed a security architecture for a network of computers bound together by an overlying framework used to provide users a powerful virtual heterogeneous machine [32]. Connelly and Chien proposed an approach to protecting tightly coupled, high-performance component communication [8]. Azzedin and Maheswaran integrated the notion of "trust" into resource management of a large-scale wide-area system [4]. However, the aforementioned security techniques are not appropriate for real-time applications due to the lack of ability to express and handle timing constraints.

Some work has been done to incorporate security into a variety of real-time applications [26]. George and Haritsa proposed concurrency control protocols to support applications with real-time and security requirements [12]. Ahmed and Vrbsky developed a secure optimistic concurrency control protocol that can make trade-offs between security and real-time requirements [2]. Our work is fundamentally different from the above approaches because they are focused on concurrency control protocols whereas ours is intended to develop a security-aware real-time scheduling strategy, which can meet security constraints in addition to real-time requirements of tasks running on clusters. In our previous study, we proposed a dynamic security-aware scheduling algorithm for a single machine [33]. Simulation results show that the proposed algorithm can improve system performance under a wide range of workload conditions.

3. Security and Real-Time Requirements

3.1. System Model

In this study, we consider the queuing architecture of an n-node cluster in which n identical nodes are connected via a high-speed network to process soft real-time tasks submitted by m users. Let $N = \{N_1, N_2, ..., N_n\}$ denote the set of identical nodes. The system model, depicted in Fig. 1, is composed of a security level controller, an admission controller, and a real-time scheduler where the earliest deadline first algorithm (EDF) is applied in our experiment. The function of the admission controller is to determine if an arriving task in the schedule queue can be accepted or not, whereas the security level controller is intended to maximize the security levels of admitted tasks.

A schedule queue used to accommodate incoming real-time tasks is maintained by the admission controller. If the incoming tasks can be scheduled, the admission controller will place the tasks in the accepted queue for further processing. Otherwise, the task will be dropped into the rejected queue. The real-time scheduler processes all the accepted tasks by its scheduling policy before transmits them into the dispatch queue, where the security level controller escalates the security level of the first task under two conditions: (1) the security level promotion will not miss its deadline; and (2) the security level promotion will not result in any accepted subsequent task to be failed. After being handled by the security level controller, the tasks are dispatched to one of the designated node $N_i \in N$ referred to as processing nodes for execution. The processing nodes, each of which maintains a local queue, can execute tasks in parallel.

3.2. Real-time tasks with security requirements

We consider a class of real-time systems where an application is comprised of a collection of tasks performed to accomplish an overall mission. It is assumed that tasks with soft deadlines are independent of one another. Each task requires a set of security services with various security levels specified by a user. Values of security levels are normalized to the range from 0 to 1. Note that the same security level value in different security services may have various meanings.

Suppose there is a task T_i submitted by a user, T_i is modeled as a set of rational parameters, e.g., $T_i = (a_i, e_i, f_i, d_i, l_i, S_i)$, where a_i, e_i, and f_i are the arrival, execution, and finish times, d_i is the deadline, and l_i denotes the amount of data (measured in KB) to be protected. e_i can be estimated by code profiling and statistical prediction [7]. Suppose T_i, requires q security services, $S_i = (S_i^1, S_i^2, \ldots, S_i^q)$, a vector of security level ranges, characterizes the security requirements of the task. S_i^j is the security level range of the jth security service required by T_i. Furthermore, the security value controller is intended to determine the most appropriate point s_i in space S_i, e.g., $s_i = (s_i^1, s_i^2, \ldots, s_i^q)$, where $s_i^j \in S_i^j$, $1 \le j \le q$.

A security-aware scheduler has to make use of a function to measure the security benefits gained by each admitted task. In particular, the security benefit of task T_i is quantitatively modeled as a security level function denoted by SL: $S_i \rightarrow \mathfrak{R}$, where $\mathfrak{R}$ is the set of positive real numbers: $SL(s_i) = \sum_{j=1}^{q} w_i^j s_i^j$, $0 \le w_i^j \le 1$ and $\sum_{j=1}^{q} w_i^j = 1$. (1)

Note that w_i^j is the weight of the jth security service for task T_i.

Let X_i be all possible schedules for task T_i, and $x_i \in X_i$ be a scheduling decision of T_i. x_i is a feasible schedule if (1) deadline d_i can be met, e.g., $f_i \le d_i$, and (2) the security requirements are satisfied, e.g., $\min(S_i^j) \le s_i^j \le \max(S_i^j)$. Given a real-time task T_i, the security benefit of T_i is expected to be maximized by the security level controller (See Fig. 1) under the timing constraint:

$$SB(x_i) = \max_{x_i \in X_i}\{SL(s_i(x_i))\} = \max_{x_i \in X_i}\left\{\sum_{j=1}^{q} w_i^j s_i^j(x_i)\right\}, \quad (2)$$

where the security level of the jth service $s_i^j(x_i)$ is obtained under schedule x_i, and $\min(S_i^j) \le s_i^j(x_i) \le \max(S_i^j)$. $\min(S_i^j)$ and $\max(S_i^j)$ are the minimum and maximum security requirements of task T_i.

A security-aware scheduler strives to maximize the system's quality of security, or security value, defined by the sum of the security levels of admitted tasks (See Equation 1). Thus, the following security value function needs to be maximized, subjecting to certain timing and security constraints:

$$SV(x) = \max_{x \in X}\left\{\sum_{i=1}^{p} y_i SB(x_i)\right\}, \quad (3)$$

where p is the number of submitted tasks, y_i is set to 1 if task T_i is accepted, and is set to 0 otherwise. Substituting Equation (2) into (3) yields the following security value objective function. Thus, our proposed security-aware scheduling algorithm makes an effort to schedule tasks in a way to maximize Equation (4):

$$SV(x) = \max_{x \in X}\left\{\sum_{i=1}^{p}\left(y_i \max_{x_i \in X_i}\left\{\sum_{j=1}^{q} w_i^j s_i^j(x_i)\right\}\right)\right\} \quad (4)$$

4. Security Overhead Model

Since security is achieved at the cost of performance degradation, it is fundamental to quantitatively measure overheads posed by various security services [17]. To enforce security in real-time applications while making security-aware scheduling algorithms practical, in this section we proposed an effective model that is capable of measuring security overheads experienced by tasks with security requirements. With the security overhead model in place, schedulers are enabled to be aware of security overheads, thereby incorporating the overheads into the process of scheduling tasks. Particularly, the model can be employed to compute the earliest start times and the minimal security overhead (see Equations 10 and 11). Without loss of generality, we consider three security services widely deployed in real-time systems, namely, encryption, integrity, and authentication. The security overhead model (described in section 4.4) consists of the following three overhead items (section 4.1~4.3).

4.1. Encryption Overhead

Encryption is used to encrypt real-time applications (executable file) and the data they produced such that a third party is unable to discover users' private algorithms embedded in the executable applications or understand the data created by the applications. Suppose the 3DES encryption algorithm is applied to a real-time cluster consisting of 100 MIPS machines. The time complexity of 3DES indicates an 800 bps (bit per second) encryption rate on a 100 MIPS machine [11]. Further, computation overhead caused by encryption is a linear function of the amount of data (input file size) to be protected [11]. As mentioned in Section 3.2, l_i (measured in KB) denotes the amount of data in task T_i needed to be protected. Let π_i^e (measured in milliseconds) be the CPU time spent in encrypting all data of T_i, and π_i^e is obtained by:

$$\pi_i^e = (l_i / 120 \text{ bytes})* 1.2 \text{ ms} = 10.24\, l_i \text{ ms} \tag{5}$$

Let s_i^e ($s_i^e \in [0,1.0]$) be the encryption security level. If 10% of data l_i has to be encrypted, the value s_i^e is set to 0.1. Similarly, setting the value of s_i^e to 1.0 indicates that all data must be encrypted. Given a task T_i with encryption security level s_i^e, the computation overhead for encryption is referred as c_i^e, which can be computed by Equation (6).

$$c_i^e(s_i^e) = \pi_i^e s_i^e, \text{ where } s_i^e \in S_i^e \tag{6}$$

Table 1. Hash Functions Used for Integrity

Hash Functions	s_i^g Security Level	$\mu^g(s_i^g)$ KB/ms
MD4	0.1	23.90
MD5	0.2	17.09
RIPEMD	0.3	12.00
RIPEMD-128	0.4	9.73
SHA-1	0.5	6.88
RIPEMD-160	0.6	5.69
Tiger	0.7	4.36
Snefru-128	0.8	0.75
Snefru-256	0.9	0.50

4.2. Integrity Overhead

Integrity services make it possible to ensure that no one can modify or tamper applications while they are executing on clusters. This can be accomplished by using a variety of hash functions [5]. Nine commonly used hash functions and their performance (evaluated on a 90 MHz Pentium machine) are shown in Table 1. Based on their performance, each hash function is assigned a corresponding security level in the range from 0.1 to 0.9. For example, level 0.1 implies that we use MD4, which is the fastest hash function among the alternatives. Level 0.9 means that Snefru-256 is employed for integrity, and Snefru-256 is the slowest yet strongest function among the competitors.

Let s_i^g be the integrity security level of T_i, and the computation overhead of the integrity service can be calculated using Equation (7), where l_i is the amount of data whose integrity must be guaranteed, and $\mu^g(s_i^g)$ is a function used to map a security level to its corresponding hash function's performance.

$$c_i^g(s_i^g) = l_i / \mu^g(s_i^g). \tag{7}$$

4.3. Authentication Overhead

Tasks must be submitted from authenticated users and, thus, authentication services are deployed to authenticate users who wish to access clusters [9][11][14]. Table 2 lists three authentication techniques: weak authentication using HMAC-MD5; acceptable authentication using HMAC-SHA-1, fair authentication using CBC-MAC-AES. Each authentication technique is assigned a security level s_i^a based on the performance. Thus, authentication overhead $c_i^a(s_i^a)$ is a function of security level s_i^a.

Table 2. Authentication Methods

Authentication Methods	s_i^a: Security Level	$c_i^a(s_i^a)$: Computation Time (ms)
HMAC-MD5	0.3	90
HMAC-SHA-1	0.6	148
CBC-MAC-AES	0.9	163

4.4. Security Overhead Model

Now we can derive security overhead, which is the sum of the three items above. Suppose task T_i requires q security services, which are provided in sequential order. Let s_i^j and $c_i^j(s_i^j)$ be the security level and overhead of the jth security service, the security overhead c_i experienced by T_i, can be computed using Equation (8). The security overhead of T_i with security requirements for the three services above is modeled by Equation (9).

$$c_i = \sum_{j=1}^{q} c_i^j(s_i^j), \text{ where } s_i^j \in S_i^j \tag{8}$$

$$c_i = \sum_{j \in \{a,e,g\}} c_i^j(s_i^j), \text{ where } s_i^j \in S_i^j \tag{9}$$

It is to be noted that $c_i^e(s_i^e)$, $c_i^g(s_i^g)$, and $c_i^a(s_i^a)$ in Equation (9) are derived from Equations (6)-(7) and Table 2. In section 5, Equation (9) will be used to calculated the earliest start times and minimal security overhead. (See Equations 10 and 11).

1.**for** each task T_i submitted to the schedule queue **do**
2. **for** each node N_j in the cluster **do**
3. Use **(10)** to computer $\text{es}_j(T_i)$,
4. Use **(11)** to obtain c_i^{min} of task T_i;
5. **if** $\text{es}_j(T_i) + e_i + c_i^{min} \le d_i$ **then**
6. Sort the security service weights, e.g., $w_i^{v_1} < w_i^{v_2} < w_i^{v_3}$, $v_l \in \{a,e,g\}, 1 \le l \le 3$;
7. **for** each security service $v_l \in \{a,e,g\}, 1 \le l \le 3$, **do**
8. $s_i^{v_l} = \min\{S_i^{v_l}\}$ /* Initialize the security value*/
9. **for** each security service $v_l \in \{a,e,g\}, 1 \le l \le 3$, **do**
10. **while** $s_i^{v_l} < \max\{S_i^{v_l}\}$ **do**
11. increase security level $s_i^{v_l}$;
12. Use **(9)** to calculate security overhead $c_i(N_j)$
13.(a) **if** $\text{es}_j(T_i) + e_i + c_i > d_i$ **or**
13.(b) $\exists T_k \in N_j, d_k > d_i$: $\text{es}_j(T_k) + e_i + c_i(N_j) > d_k$ **then**
14. decrease security level $s_i^{v_l}$; break;
15. **end while**
16. **end for**
17. $SL_i^j \leftarrow SL(s_i)$; /* Obtain the security level */
18. **else** $SL_i^j \leftarrow 0$; /* Set the security level to 0 */
19. **end for**
20. **if** $\exists N_j \in N : SL_i^j > 0$ **then**
21. $y_i \leftarrow 1$; /* Accept task T_i */
22. /* Optimize quality of security*/
Find node N_k for T_i, subject to: $SL_i^k = \max_{1 \le j \le n}\{SL_i^j\}$
23. dispatch task T_i to N_k based on the above schedule;
24. **else** $y_i \leftarrow 0$; /* Reject T_i */
25. **end for**
26.**end for**

Figure 2. The SAREC-EDF

5. The SAREC-EDF Algorithm

Now we are in a position to evaluate the effectiveness of SAREC by developing a novel security-aware real-time scheduling algorithm, or SAREC-EDF, which incorporates the earliest deadline first (EDF) scheduling algorithm into the SAREC strategy. The schedule of a task is feasible if the task is completed before its deadline. Hence, a task has a feasible schedule on a cluster if there exists at least one node, where a valid schedule is available for the task. More formally, this fact can be express by the following property. The earliest start time $\text{es}_j(T_i)$ can be computed by Equation (10).

$$\text{es}_j(T_i) = r_j + \sum_{T_k \in N_j, d_k \le d_i} \left(e_k + \sum_{l \in \{a,e,g\}} c_k^l(s_k^l) \right), \quad (10)$$

where r_j represents the remaining overall execution time of a task currently running on the *j*th node, and $e_k + \sum_{l \in \{a,e,g\}} c_k^l(s_k^l)$ is the overall execution time of task T_k whose deadline is earlier than that of T_i. Thus, the earliest start time of T_k is a sum of the remaining overall execution time of the running task and the overall execution times of the tasks with earlier deadlines. The minimal security overhead c_i^{min} of T_i can be efficiently calculated by the following equation.

$$c_i^{min} = \sum_{j \in \{a,e,g\}} c_i^j\left(\min\{S_i^j\}\right), \quad (11)$$

where $c_i^j\left(\min\{S_i^j\}\right)$ denotes the overhead of the *j*th security service when the minimal requirement is satisfied.

The SAREC-EDF algorithm is outlined in Figure 2. Before optimizing the security level of task T_i on N_j, SAREC-EDF attempts to meet the real-time requirement of T_i. This can be accomplished by calculating the earliest start time (use Equation 10) and the minimal security overhead of T_i (use Equation 11) in Steps 3 and 4, followed by checking if T_i can be completed before its deadline (see Step 5). If the deadline can not be met by N_j, Step 18 sets T_i' security level on N_j to 0, implying that T_i can not be allocation to node N_j. If no node can produce a feasible schedule for T_i, it is rejected by Step 24.

6. Simulation Studies

Using extensive simulation experiments based on real trace consisting of 29695 tasks, we compared SAREC-EDF against three baseline algorithms: SHMIN-EDF, SHMAX-EDF, and SHRND-EDF. These three algorithms are variations of the conventional EDF algorithm. For the sake of simplicity, throughout this section SAREC-EDF is referred to as SAREC. Similarly, the baseline algorithms are referred to as SHMIN, SHMAX, and SHRND, respectively. The baseline algorithms are described below.

(1) SHMIN: The admission controller intentionally selects the lowest security level of each security services required by an incoming task.
(2) SHMAX: The admission controller chooses the highest security level for each security requirement posed by an arriving task.
(3) SHRND: Unlike the above two baseline algorithms, SHRND randomly picks a value within the security level range of each service required by a task.

6.1. Simulator and Simulation Parameters

Table 3 summarizes the key configuration parameters of the simulated clusters used in our experiments. The parameters of nodes are chosen to resemble real-world workstations like Sun SPARC-20 and Sun Ultra 10.

We modified the traces used in [15] by adding deadlines for all tasks. The assignment of deadlines is controlled by the parameter β (We use Tbase for β in the following figures), which sets an upper bound on tasks' slack times. We use Equation (12) to generate T_i's deadline d_i.

$$d_i = a_i + e_i + c_i^{max} + \beta, \qquad (12)$$

where a_i and e_i are the arrival and execution times obtained from the traces. c_i^{max} is the maximal security overhead, which is computed by Equation (13).

$$c_i^{\max} = \sum_{j \in \{a,e,g\}} c_i^j\left(\max\{S_i^j\}\right) \qquad (13)$$

where $c_i^j\left(\max\{S_i^j\}\right)$ is the overhead of the jth security service for T_i with the maximal requirements being met.

Table 3. Characteristics of System Parameters

Parameter	Value (Fixed) - (Varied)
CPU speed	100 million instructions/second
β (Tbase)	(100 ms) – (100, 500, …, 60000ms)
Number of nodes	(64) – (8, 16, 32, 64, 96, 128, 256)
Mean size of data to be secured	50KB for short jobs, 500KB for middle jobs, 1MB for long jobs
Required security services	Encryption, Integrity and Authentication

The performance metrics by which we evaluate system performance include: *security value* (see Equation 4), *guarantee ratio* (measured as a fraction of total submitted tasks that are found to be schedulable), and *overall system performance* (defined as a product of security value and guarantee ratio).

6.2. Overall Performance Comparisons

To stress the evaluation, we assume that each task arrived in the cluster requires the three security services. Figure 3 shows the simulation results for these four algorithms on a cluster with 64 nodes where the CPU power is fixed at 100MIPS. We observe from Figure 3 (a) that SAREC and SHMIN exhibit similar performance in terms of guarantee ratio (the performance difference is less than 5%), whereas the SAREC noticeably outperforms SHMAX and SHRND. We attribute the performance improvement of SAREC to the fact that SAREC judiciously boosts the security levels of accepted tasks under the condition that the deadlines of the tasks are guaranteed, thereby maintaining relatively high guarantee ratios. Unlike SAREC, SHMAX and SHRND improve quality of security at the cost of missing deadlines.

Figure 3 (a) illustrates that the guarantee ratios of four algorithms increase with the increasing value of the deadline base. This is because the large deadline base leads to long slack times, which, in turn, make the deadlines more likely to be guaranteed. Figure 3 (b) plots security values of the four algorithms when the deadline base is increased from 0.1 to 60 ms. It reveals that SAREC consistently performs better, with respect to quality of security, than SHMIN and SHRND. When the deadlines are tight, the security values of SAREC are very close to those of SHMAX. However, SAREC significantly outperforms SHMAX when the deadline base becomes large. This is because that SAREC can accept for tasks compared with SHMAX. Interestingly, when the deadlines become loose, the performance improvements of SAREC over the three competitors are more pronounced. The results clearly indicate that clusters can gain more performance benefits from SAREC under the circumstance that real-time tasks have loose deadlines.

The overall system performance improvements achieved by SAREC are plotted in Figure 3(c). The first observation deduced from Figure 3(c) is that the value of overall system performance increases with the deadline base. This is because the overall system performance is a product of security value and guarantee ratio, which become higher when deadlines are loose. A second observation is that SAREC significantly outperforms the other alternatives. This can be explained by the fact that SAREC improves security values, while achieving higher guarantee ratio. Figure 3(c) indicates that the overall performance improvement achieved by SAREC becomes more pronounced when the deadlines are looser, implying that more performance benefits can be obtained for real-time tasks with large slack times.

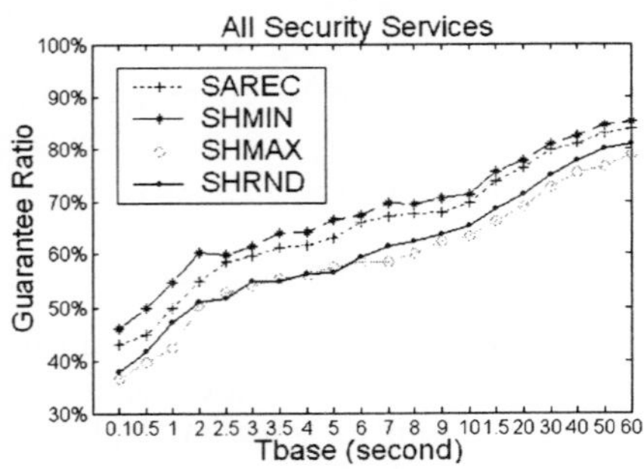

(a) Guarantee ratio

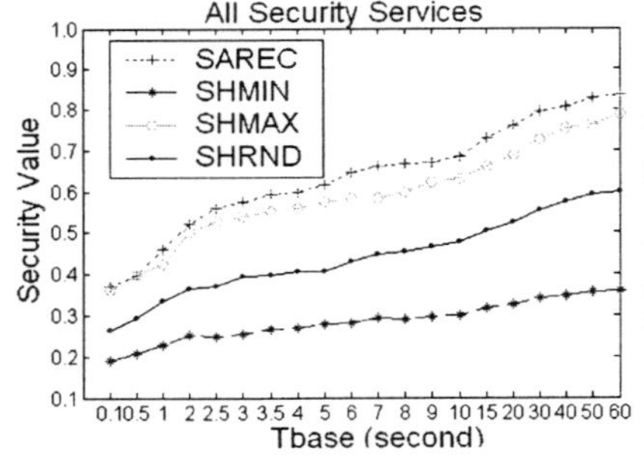

(b) Security value

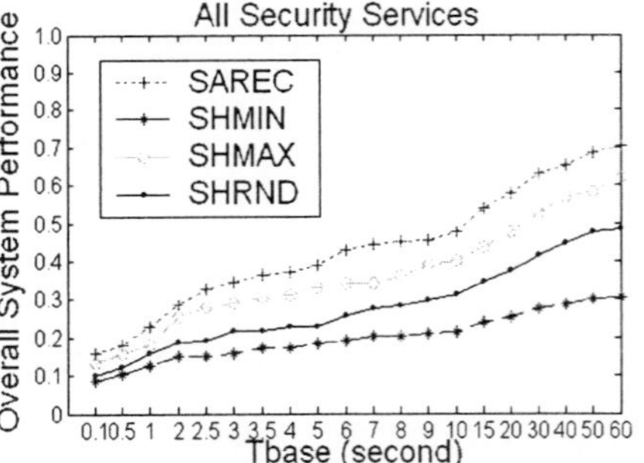

(c) Overall system performance

Figure 3. Simulation performance of four scheduling algorithms.

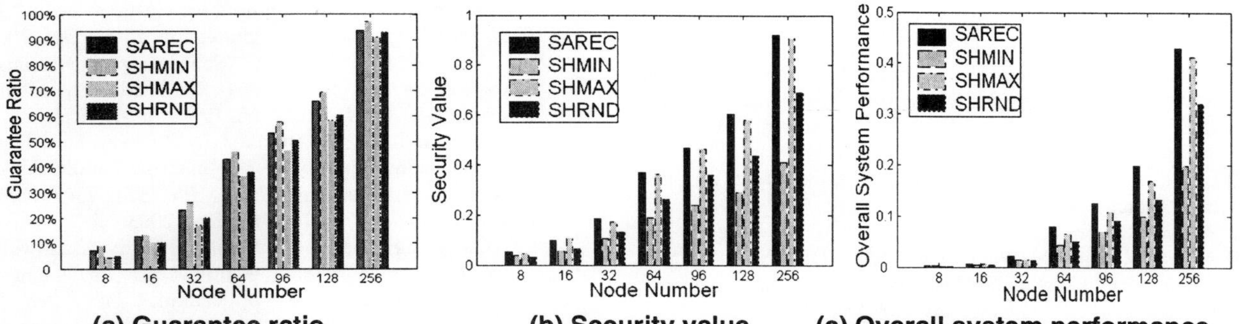

(a) Guarantee ratio **(b) Security value** **(c) Overall system performance**

Figure 4. Scalabilities of the four scheduling algorithms.

6.3. Scalability

This experiment is intended to investigate the scalability of the SAREC algorithm. We scale the number of nodes in a cluster from 8 to 256. Figure 4 plots the performances as functions of the number of nodes in the cluster. The results show that the SAREC approach exhibits good scalability.

Figure 5 shows the improvement of SAREC in overall system performance over the other three heuristics. It is observed from Figure 5 that the amount of improvement over SHMIN becomes more prominent with the increasing value of node number. This result can be explained by the conservative nature of SHMIN, which merely meets the minimal security requirements for tasks accepted by the cluster. Conversely, the amount of improvement over SHMAX decreases as the number of nodes increases. This is partially because SHMAX can guarantee the maximal security requirements of more accepted tasks when more nodes are available in the cluster. It is interesting to note that the trend of the improvement over SHRND is not monotonous, because SHRND randomly decides security levels for tasks.

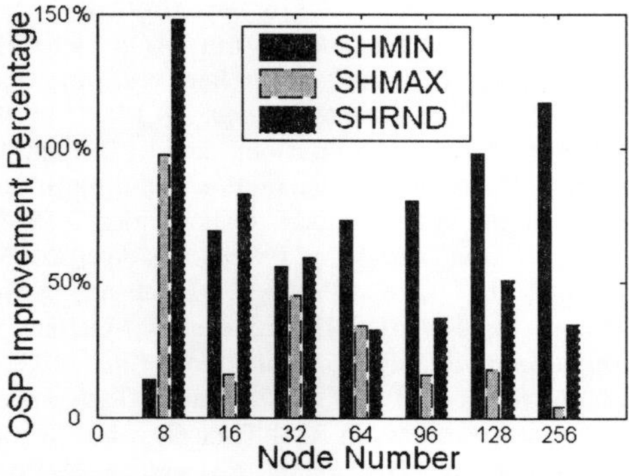

Figure 5. Impact of the number of nodes on the overall system performance improvement.

7. Summary and Future Work

In this paper, we presented a strategy SAREC for security-aware scheduling of real-time applications on clusters. This strategy is capable for the design of security-aware real-time scheduling algorithms like SAREC-EDF. To make security-aware scheduling algorithms practical, we also proposed a security overhead model to measure overheads of security services.

To evaluate the performance of our SAREC-EDF algorithm, we developed a trace-driven simulator and proposed two performance metrics: security value and overall system performance defined as the product of security value and guarantee ratio. Compared with three baseline algorithms, SAREC-EDF, on average, achieved improvement of 72.55%, 32.93% and 63.54%, respectively, in overall system performance. In addition, extensive experimental results show that compared with the three security-heuristic EDF algorithms above, SAREC-EDF consistently improves the overall system performance in terms of quality of security and system guarantee ratio under a wide range of workload characteristics and execution environments.

We qualitatively assigned security levels to the security services based on their respective security capacities. In our future work, we intend to investigate a quantitative way of reasonably specifying the security level of each security mechanism.

In this study we simply consider CPU time in the security overhead model. For future work, we will integrate multi-dimensional computing resources, e.g., memory, network bandwidth, and storage systems, into our model.

Acknowledgements

This work was partially supported by a start-up research fund (103295) from the research and economic development office of the New Mexico Tech and a DoD IASP Capacity Building grant.

References

[1] T.F. Abdelzaher and K.G. Shin., "Combined Task and Message Scheduling in Distributed Real-Time Systems," *IEEE Trans. Parallel and Distributed Systems*, Vol. 10, No. 11, Nov. 1999.

[2] Q. Ahmed and S. Vrbsky, "Maintaining security in firm real-time database systems," *Proc. 14th Ann. Computer Security Application Conf.*, 1998.

[3] A. Apvrille and M. Pourzandi, "XML Distributed Security Policy for Clusters," *Computers & Security Journal*, Elsevier, Vol.23, No.8, pp. 649-658, Dec. 2004.

[4] F. Azzedin, M. Maheswaran, "Towards trust-aware resource management in grid computing systems," *Proc. 2nd IEEE/ACM Int'l Symp. Cluster Computing and the Grid*, May 2002.

[5] A. Bosselaers, R. Govaerts and J. Vandewalle, "Fast hashing on the Pentium," *Proc. Advances in Cryptology*, LNCS 1109, pp. 298-312, Springer-Verlag, 1996.

[6] T. D. Braun et al., "A comparison study of static mapping heuristics for a class of meta-tasks on heterogeneous computing systems," *Proc. Workshop on Heterogeneous Computing*, pp.15-29, Apr. 1999.

[7] S. Cheng and Y. Huang, "Dynamic real-time scheduling for multi-processor tasks using genetic algorithm," *Proc. Ann. Int'l Conf. Computer Software and App.*, 2004.

[8] K. Connelly and A. A. Chien, "Breaking the barriers: high performance security for high performance computing," *Proc. Workshop on New security paradigms*, Sept. 2002.

[9] J. Deepakumara, H.M. Heys, and R. Venkatesan, "Performance comparison of message authentication code (MAC) algorithms for Internet protocol security (IPSEC)," *Proc. Newfoundland Electrical and Computer Engineering Conf.*, St. John's, Newfoundland, Nov. 2003.

[10] G. Donoho, "Building a Web Service to Provide Real-Time Stock Quotes," *MCAD.Net*, February, 2004.

[11] O. Elkeelany, M. Matalgah, K. Sheikh, M. Thaker, G. Chaudhry, D. Medhi, J. Qaddouri, "Performance analysis of IPSec protocol: encryption and authentication," *Proc. IEEE Int'l Conf. Communications*, pp. 1164-1168, 2002.

[12] B. George and J. Haritsa, "Secure transaction processing in firm real-time database systems," *Proc. ACM SIGMOD Conf.*, May, 1997.

[13] W. A. Halang, et al., "Measuring the performance of real-time systems," *Int'l Journal of Time-Critical Computing Systems*, 18, pp. 59-68, 2000.

[14] A. Harbitter and D. A. Menasce, "The performance of public key enabled Kerberos authentication in mobile computing applications," *Proc. of the 8th ACM Conf. Computer and Comm. Security*, pp. 78-85, 2001.

[15] M. Harchol-Balter and A. Downey, "Exploiting Process Lifetime Distributions for Load Balacing," *ACM Trans. Computer Systems*, vol. 3, no. 31, 1997.

[16] L. He, A. Jatvis, and D. P. Spooner, "Dynamic scheduling of parallel real-time jobs by modelling spare capabilities in heterogeneous clusters," *Proc. Int'l Conf. Cluster Computing*, pp. 2-10, Dec. 2003.

[17] C. Irvine and T. Levin, "Towards a taxonomy and costing method for security services," *Proc. 15th Annual Computer Security Applications Conference*, 1999.

[18] Z. Lan and P. Deshikachar, "Performance analysis of large-scale cosmology application on three cluster systems," *Proc. IEEE Int'l Conf. Cluster Computing*, pp. 56-63, Dec. 2003.

[19] C. L. Liu, J.W. Layland, "Scheduling Algorithms for Multiprogramming in a Hard Real-Time Environment," *Journal of the ACM*, Vol.20, No.1, pp. 46-61, 1973.

[20] X. Qin, H. Jiang, Y. Zhu, and D. R. Swanson, "Towards Load Balancing Support for I/O-Intensive Parallel Jobs in a Cluster of Workstations," *Proc. 5th IEEE Int'l Conf. on Cluster Computing*, pp.100-107, Dec. 2003.

[21] X. Qin and H. Jiang, "Improving Effective Bandwidth of Networks on Clusters using Load Balancing for Communication-Intensive Applications," *Proc. 24th IEEE Int'l Performance, Computing, and Communications Conf.*, Phoenix, Arizona, April 2005.

[22] X. Qin, "Improving Network Performance through Task Duplication for Parallel Applications on Clusters," *Proc. 24th IEEE Int'l Performance, Computing, and Communications Conference*, Phoenix, Arizona, April 2005.

[23] X. Qin, H. Jiang, D. R. Swanson, "An Efficient Fault-tolerant Scheduling Algorithm for Real-time Tasks with Precedence Constraints in Heterogeneous Systems," *Proc. 31st Int'l Conf. Parallel Processing*, pp.360-368. Aug. 2002.

[24] X. Qin and H. Jiang, "Dynamic, Reliability-driven Scheduling of Parallel Real-time Jobs in Heterogeneous Systems," *Proc. 30th Int'l Conf. Parallel Processing*, pp.113-122, Sept. 2001.

[25] K. Ramamritham, J. A. Stankovic, "Dynamic task scheduling in distributed hard real-time system," *IEEE Software*, Vol. 1, No. 3, July 1984.

[26] S. H. Son, R. Zimmerman, and J. Hansson, "An adaptable security manager for real-time transactions," *Proc. 12th Euromicro Conf. Real-Time Sys.*, pp. 63 – 70, June 2000.

[27] S. H. Son, R. Mukkamala, and R. David, "Integrating security and real-time requirements using covert channel capacity," *IEEE Trans. Knowledge and Data Engineering*, Vol. 12 , No. 6, pp. 865 – 879, Nov.-Dec. 2000.

[28] J. A. Stankovic, M. Spuri, K. Ramamritham, G.C. buttazzo, "Deadline Scheduling for Real-Time Systems – EDF and Related Algorithms," *Kluwer Academic Publishers*, 1998.

[29] V. Subramani, V., R. Kettimuthu, S. Srinivasan, J. Johnston, and P. Sadayappan, "Selective buddy allocation for scheduling parallel jobs on clusters," *Proc. IEEE Int'l Conf. Cluster Computing*, pp. 107 – 116, Sept. 2002.

[30] M.E. Thomadakis and J.-C. Liu, "On the efficient scheduling of non-periodic tasks in hard real-time systems," *Proc. 20th IEEE Real-Time Sys. Symp.*, pp.148-151, 1999.

[31] G. Vallee, C. Morin, J.-Y. Berthou, and L. Rilling, "A new approach to configurable dynamic scheduling in clusters based on single system image technologies," *Proc. Int'l Symp. Parallel and Distributed Processing*, April 2003.

[32] R. Wright, D. J. Shifflett, C. E. Irvine, "Security Architecture for a Virtual Heterogeneous Machine," *Proc. 14th Ann. Computer Security Applications Conf.*, 1998.

[33] T. Xie, A. Sung, and X. Qin, "Dynamic Task Scheduling with Security Awareness in Real-Time Systems", *Proc. Int'l Symp. Parallel and Distributed Processing, the 4th Int'l Workshop on Performance Modeling, Evaluation, and Optimization of Parallel and Distributed Sys.*, April 2005.

Multiprocessor Energy-Efficient Scheduling for Real-Time Tasks with Different Power Characteristics*

Jian-Jia Chen and Tei-Wei Kuo
Department of Computer Science and Information Engineering
Graduate Institute of Networking and Multimedia
National Taiwan University, Taipei, Taiwan, ROC
Email:{r90079, ktw}@csie.ntu.edu.tw

Abstract

In the past decades, a number of research results have been reported for energy-efficient scheduling over uniprocessor and multiprocessor environments. Different from many of the past results on the assumption for task power characteristics, we consider real-time scheduling of tasks with different power characteristics. The objective is to minimize the energy consumption of task executions under the given deadline constraint. When tasks have a common deadline and are ready at time 0, we propose an optimal real-time task scheduling algorithm for multiprocessor environments with the allowance of task migration. When no task migration is allowed, a 1.412*-approximation algorithm for task scheduling is proposed for different settings of power characteristics. The performance of the approximation algorithm was evaluated by an extensive set of experiments, where excellent results were reported.*

1 Introduction

With the advanced technology in VLSI circuit designs, many modern processors could now operate at various supply voltages, where different supply voltages lead to different processing speeds. Many computer systems, especially embedded systems, adopt not only voltage-scaling processors but also various energy-efficient strategies in managing their subsystems intelligently. Beside the energy-efficiency designs for battery-powered systems, how to reduce energy consumption for multi-processor systems, such as server farms, also receives a lot of attention in the past decade. As pointed out in [1], multiprocessor implementations of real-time systems could be more energy-efficient than uniprocessor implementations, due to the convex power consumption functions.

Energy-efficient scheduling is to derive a schedule for real-time tasks with minimization on the energy consumption such that the timing constraints can be met. The considerations of timing constraints in task scheduling significantly complicate the problems in energy-efficient scheduling. Uniprocessor energy-efficient scheduling problems have been widely explored, e.g., [2, 3, 10–12, 19]. The energy-efficient real-time task scheduling problems over multiprocessors are often $\mathcal{NP}$-hard. When all of the power consumption functions of tasks are the same, Chen, et al. [5, 18] proposed approximation algorithms to schedule frame-based tasks over multiprocessors with and without independent voltage scalings, where all the tasks share a common deadline and arrive at the same time. In [7, 8, 20], energy-efficient scheduling algorithms based on list heuristics were proposed to schedule real-time tasks with precedence constraints. Mishra, et al. [13] explored energy-efficient scheduling issues with the considerations of task communication delay.

This work is motivated by the energy-efficient scheduling of tasks in reality, where tasks often have different power characteristics [2, 11, 12]. The power consumption function of a task running at the processor speed s is of the form hs^α, where h and α are task and hardware dependent power characteristics, respectively ($0 < h$ and $2 \leq \alpha \leq 3$). The parameter setting of h in hs^α might depend on the software implementation and the execution path of each task, whereas the value of α might depend on the hardware design of the processors under considerations. The objective of this paper is to minimize the energy consumption of task executions under the given deadline constraint. We are interested in the scheduling of frame-based task sets, in which all the tasks are ready at time 0 and share a common deadline. When task migration is allowed, we propose an optimal real-time task scheduling algorithm with a time complexity $O(|\mathbf{T}| \log |\mathbf{T}|)$ for multiprocessor environments, where $\mathbf{T}$ is the set of real-time tasks under considerations. When task migration is not allowed, a polynomial-time approximation algorithm is proposed. The approximation ratio of the algorithm is shown being 1.412. The performance of the approximation algorithm was evaluated by an extensive set of experiments, where excellent results were reported.

*Support in parts by research grants from ROC National Science Council NSC-93-2752-E-002-008-PAE and NSC-93-2218-E-002-140.

0190-3918/05 $20.00 © 2005 IEEE

The rest of this paper is organized as follows: In Section 2, we define the system models and formulate the problem. Section 3 presents an algorithm for multiprocessor energy-efficient scheduling, when task migration is allowed. Our approximation algorithm to cope with systems which do not allow task migration is then presented in Section 4. Simulation results are shown in Section 5. Section 6 concludes this paper.

2 Formal Models and Problem Definitions

We are interested in energy-efficient scheduling of real-time tasks that are ready at time 0 and share a common deadline D over multiple homogeneous processors. Each task τ_i is characterized by its worst-case execution CPU cycles c_i and power consumption function $P_i()$:

$$P_i(s) = C_i V_{dd}^2 s, \quad (1)$$

where $s = \beta \frac{(V_{dd} - V_t)^2}{V_{dd}}$, and s, C_i, V_t, V_{dd}, and β denote the processor speed, the effective switch capacitance, the threshold voltage (the minimum voltage that can be supplied to the processor for correct functionality), the supply voltage, and a hardware-design-specific constant, respectively ($V_{dd} \geq V_t \geq 0$, $\beta > 0$, and $C_i > 0$) [4,17]. The value of the effective switch capacitance is highly related to the software implementations and the execution path of each task (which could be usually derived by profiling). Each power consumption function $P_i(s)$ can be phrased as $h_i \cdot s^\alpha$, where α is a hardware-dependent factor, and h_i is a parameter related to the corresponding task execution [3,9,12,15,19]. For example, when V_t is 0, h_i is C_i/β^2, and α is 3. h_i is a positive real number, and α is usually a real number between between 2 and 3 [12,15]. It is clear that the power consumption function is a strictly convex and increasing function of the processor speed when the processor speeds are non-negative numbers. In this paper, we assume that $P_i(s)$ is second-order differentiable.

Suppose that each processor could operate at a speed in $[0, \infty]$, and the speed of each processor could be adjusted independently from each another. We assume that the number of CPU cycles executed in a time interval is linearly proportional to the processor speed, and that the energy consumed for a processor in the execution of a task at the processor speed s for t time units is the multiplication of its corresponding power consumption at the speed s and t. Let the amount of CPU cycles completed for a task running at a speed s for t time units be the multiplication of s and t. Assume that the time and energy overheads required on speed/voltage switching be negligible. Since $P_i(s)/s$ is also a strictly convex and increasing function, an optimal schedule must execute each task $\tau_i \in \mathbf{T}$ entirely at a selected speed s_i [2,6]. Specifically, executing task τ_i at the speed s consumes $P_i(s)\frac{c_i}{s}$ amount of energy. The *energy consumption function* $E_i()$ of τ_i is defined as a function of the execution time t_i of τ_i: $E_i(t_i) = P_i(\frac{c_i}{t_i})t_i = h_i \cdot c_i^\alpha / t_i^{\alpha-1}$. Note that the energy consumption function of the execution time of τ_i is a strictly convex and *decreasing* function.

Problem Definition We consider energy-efficient scheduling with and without task migration in this work, where migration cost is assumed being negligible. No task is allowed to execute simultaneously on more than one processor. A *schedule* of a task set $\mathbf{T}$ is a mapping of the executions of the tasks in $\mathbf{T}$ to processors in the system with an assignment of processor speeds for the corresponding execution intervals of the tasks. A schedule is *feasible* if no task misses its deadline D, and no task is executed simultaneously on more than one processor. The energy consumption of a schedule S is denoted as $\Phi(S)$ which is the sum of the energy consumption of task executions in S. A schedule is optimal if it is feasible, and its energy consumption is equal to the minimum energy consumption of all feasible schedules. Two energy-efficient scheduling problems are defined, as follows:

Definition 1 *Multiprocessor Energy-Efficient Scheduling with Task Migration* (MEESM)

Consider a set $\mathbf{T}$ of independent tasks over M identical processors, where all tasks in $\mathbf{T}$ are ready at time 0 and share a common deadline D. Each task $\tau_i \in \mathbf{T}$ is associated with a computation requirement equal to c_i CPU-cycles and a power consumption function $P_i()$ of a given processor speed. The objective is to derive a schedule for $\mathbf{T}$ such that all of the tasks in $\mathbf{T}$ complete before D, the total energy consumption is minimized, where task migration among processors is allowed.

A variation of the MEESM problem without task migration could be defined similarly as follows:

Definition 2 *Multiprocessor Energy-Efficient Scheduling without Task Migration* (MEES)

The input, output, and objective of this problem are as the same as their counterparts of the MEESM problem, where no task migration among processors is allowed.

If the number of tasks in $\mathbf{T}$ is no more than the number of processors in the system, the executing of each task τ_i on a different processor from time 0 to D at the speed $\frac{c_i}{D}$ is an optimal schedule. For the rest of this paper, we only focus our discussions on the other case in which the number of tasks in $\mathbf{T}$ is more than the number of processors in the system. Since the MEES problem is $\mathcal{NP}$-hard even when all of the power consumption functions of the tasks are the same [5], we propose an efficient algorithm which finds an approximated solution with a worst-case guarantee on the energy consumption by adopting approximation algorithms [16].

3 An Optimal Algorithm When Task Migration is Allowed

In this section, we present an optimal algorithm for the MEESM problem. Since $P_i(s)/s$ is a convex and increasing function of the processor speed for every task τ_i in a given task set $\mathbf{T}$, there exists an optimal schedule that executes each task $\tau_i \in \mathbf{T}$ entirely at some speed s_i [2,6]. In the following discussions, we only consider schedules in which the entire duration of a task executes at the same speed.

Let $V = (t_1, t_2, \dots, t_{|\mathbf{T}|})$ be an assignment of execution times of tasks in $\mathbf{T}$, where t_i is a positive real number for every task $\tau_i \in \mathbf{T}$. The energy consumption of an assignment V of task execution times of $\mathbf{T}$ is defined as $\sum_{\tau_i \in \mathbf{T}} E_i(t_i)$. V is said feasible for $\mathbf{T}$ on M processors if the sum of execution times of all of the tasks in $\mathbf{T}$ is no greater than $M \cdot D$ (i.e., $\sum_{\tau_i \in \mathbf{T}} t_i \leq M \cdot D$), and t_i is no greater than D for every task τ_i in $\mathbf{T}$. Given a feasible schedule S_V of $\mathbf{T}$, it is clear that a feasible assignment V of task execution times can be derived by setting the execution time of task τ_i in V as that of τ_i in S_V. The energy consumption of V is equal to that of S_V. In the following lemma, we show that we can efficiently derive a feasible schedule S_V with the same energy consumption as that of a given feasible assignment V of execution times of tasks in $\mathbf{T}$. In other words, a feasible assignment V of execution times of tasks in $\mathbf{T}$ with the minimum energy consumption leads to an optimal schedule of $\mathbf{T}$ for the MEESM problem.

Lemma 1 *Given a feasible assignment V of execution times of tasks in $\mathbf{T}$, a feasible schedule S_V can be derived in $O(|\mathbf{T}|)$ such that the energy consumption of S_V is equal to that of V.*

Proof. We prove this lemma by constructing a feasible schedule S_V according to $V = (t_1, t_2, \dots, t_{|\mathbf{T}|})$:

- **Case 1:** If $\lceil \frac{\sum_{j=1}^{i-1} t_j}{D} \rceil = \lceil \frac{\sum_{j=1}^{i} t_j}{D} \rceil$, then execute τ_i on the $\lceil \frac{\sum_{j=1}^{i-1} t_j}{D} \rceil$-th processor from time $(\sum_{j=1}^{i-1} t_j \mod D)$ to $(\sum_{j=1}^{i} t_j \mod D)$.
- **Case 2:** If $\lceil \frac{\sum_{j=1}^{i-1} t_j}{D} \rceil \neq \lceil \frac{\sum_{j=1}^{i} t_j}{D} \rceil$, then execute τ_i on the $\lceil \frac{\sum_{j=1}^{i-1} t_j}{D} \rceil$-th processor from time $(\sum_{j=1}^{i-1} t_j \mod D)$ to D and on the $\lceil \frac{\sum_{j=1}^{i} t_j}{D} \rceil$-th processor from time 0 to $(\sum_{j=1}^{i} t_j \mod D)$.

Since $0 < t_i \leq D$ for all τ_i in $\mathbf{T}$ and $\sum_{\tau_i \in \mathbf{T}} t_i = MD$, the resulting schedule S_V above is a feasible schedule for the MEESM problem. Besides, it is clear that the energy consumption of S_V is equal to the energy consumption of V, since the execution time of task τ_i in $\mathbf{T}$ is t_i both in V and S_V. The time complexity is $O(|\mathbf{T}|)$ by taking the summation in an incremental manner. □

Moreover, the strict convexity of the energy consumption functions of tasks would not allow any processor being idle between time 0 and time D in an optimal schedule. In other words, an optimal schedule will always have some task executing between time 0 and time D on any of the M processors.

Lemma 2 *When $|\mathbf{T}| > M$, there exists an optimal schedule which executes some task at any time instant between time 0 and time D on each of the M processors.*

Proof. We prove this lemma by contradiction. Let S_V be an optimal schedule, in which S_V does not execute some task at some time instant between 0 and D on at least one of the M processors. Let $V = (t_1, t_2, \dots, t_{|\mathbf{T}|})$ be the assignment of execution times of $\mathbf{T}$ for schedule S_V. Therefore, we know that $\sum_{\tau_i \in \mathbf{T}} t_i < M \cdot D$. Since $|\mathbf{T}| > M$, there must be a task τ_j whose associated t_j is less than D in V. Stretching the execution time of τ_j as $\min\{D, MD - \sum_{\tau_i \in \mathbf{T} \setminus \{\tau_j\}} t_i\}$ results in a feasible assignment V' of execution times of tasks in $\mathbf{T}$. Because $E_j()$ is a strictly convex and decreasing function of the execution time of τ_j, the energy consumption of V' is less than that of V. By Lemma 1, there exists a *feasible* schedule whose energy consumption is less than S_V, which contradicts the optimality of S_V. □

Taking both Lemmas 1 and 2 into considerations at the same time, the MEESM problem can be formulated as a convex programming problem, as follows:

$$\begin{array}{ll} \text{minimize} & \sum_{\tau_i \in \mathbf{T}} E_i(t_i) \\ \text{subject to} & \sum_{\tau_i \in \mathbf{T}} t_i = M \cdot D \text{ and} \\ & 0 < t_i \leq D \quad \forall \tau_i \in \mathbf{T}. \end{array} \tag{2}$$

For the rest of this section, we will show that the optimal assignment of execution times of tasks in $\mathbf{T}$ described by Equation (2) can be determined in $O(|\mathbf{T}| \log |\mathbf{T}|)$ time by applying the Karush-Kuhn-Tucker optimality condition [14, §14] and a binary search strategy. After the optimal assignment of execution times of tasks in $\mathbf{T}$ is determined, Lemma 1 is applied to derive an optimal schedule for the MEESM problem.

In the following, we first obtain an optimal solution by ignoring the condition $t_i > 0$. After that, we show that $t_i > 0$ is satisfied for every task τ_i in $\mathbf{T}$ for the solution. To apply the Karush-Kuhn-Tucker optimality condition for concave programming, Equation (2) is reformulated as a concave programming problem, as follows:

$$\begin{array}{ll} \text{maximize} & \sum_{\tau_i \in \mathbf{T}} \bar{E}_i(t_i) \\ \text{subject to} & \sum_{\tau_i \in \mathbf{T}} t_i = M \cdot D \text{ and} \\ & t_i \leq D \quad \forall \tau_i \in \mathbf{T}, \end{array} \tag{3}$$

where $\bar{E}_i(t_i)$ is defined as $-E_i(t_i)$. The Karush-Kuhn-Tucker optimality condition for Equation (3) is to find a vector $(\lambda_1, \lambda_2, \dots, \lambda_{|\mathbf{T}|})$, a vector $(t_1^*, t_2^*, \dots, t_{|\mathbf{T}|}^*)$, and a constant λ such that

$$\begin{array}{l} \bar{E}_i'(t_i^*) - \lambda_i = \lambda, \quad t_i^* \leq D, \\ (t_i^* - D)\lambda_i = 0, \quad \lambda_i \geq 0, \end{array} \; \forall \tau_i \in \mathbf{T}, \text{ and} \quad \sum_{\tau_i \in \mathbf{T}} t_i^* = MD, \tag{4}$$

where $\bar{E}_i'()$ is the derivative of $\bar{E}_i()$. Since $\sum_{\tau_i \in \mathbf{T}} \bar{E}_i(t_i)$ is a concave function, and $\{t_j\}$ is a quasiconvex set for every $\tau_j \in \mathbf{T}$, setting $(t_1, t_2, \dots, t_{|\mathbf{T}|})$ as $(t_1^*, t_2^*, \dots, t_{|\mathbf{T}|}^*)$ is an optimal solution for the concave programming in Equation (3) [14, §14]. We will show that such a vector $(t_1^*, t_2^*, \ldots, t_{|\mathbf{T}|}^*)$ could be determined by the Lagrange multiplier technique. Let ℓ be an index, where $0 \leq \ell < M$. If the execution time of τ_i is set as D for $i = 1, 2, \ldots, \ell$, the concave programming in Equation (3) could be rephrased as

$$\begin{array}{ll} \text{maximize} & \sum_{i=\ell+1}^{|\mathbf{T}|} \bar{E}_i(t_i) \\ \text{subject to} & \sum_{i=\ell+1}^{|\mathbf{T}|} t_i = (M-\ell)\cdot D, \end{array} \tag{5}$$

by further ignoring the inequalities $t_i \leq D$ for $i = \ell + 1, \ldots, |\mathbf{T}|$.

Equation (5) could be solved by applying the Lagrange multiplier technique. Since $\bar{E}_i'(t_i) = (\alpha - 1)h_i c_i^\alpha t_i^{-\alpha}$, given an index ℓ, the conditions $\bar{E}_i'(t_i) = \bar{E}_j'(t_j)$ for all $\ell < i, j \leq |\mathbf{T}|$ for the Lagrange multiplier technique lead to

$$\frac{t_i^\alpha}{t_j^\alpha} = \frac{(\alpha-1)h_i c_i^\alpha}{(\alpha-1)h_j c_j^\alpha}, \quad \forall\, \ell < i, j \leq |\mathbf{T}|$$
$$\sum_{j=\ell+1}^{|\mathbf{T}|} t_j = (M-\ell)\cdot D.$$

Therefore, the optimal solution for Equation (5) is to assign $(t_{\ell+1}, t_{\ell+2}, \ldots, t_{|\mathbf{T}|})$ as $(t_{\ell+1}^*, t_{\ell+2}^*, \ldots, t_{|\mathbf{T}|}^*)$, where

$$\sum_{j=\ell+1}^{|\mathbf{T}|} t_{\ell+1}^* \frac{c_j}{c_{\ell+1}} \left(\frac{h_j}{h_{\ell+1}}\right)^{1/\alpha} = (M-\ell)D \tag{6a}$$

$$t_j^* = t_{\ell+1}^* \frac{c_j}{c_{\ell+1}} \left(\frac{h_j}{h_{\ell+1}}\right)^{1/\alpha}, \forall \ell+1 < j \leq |\mathbf{T}|, \tag{6b}$$

and the Lagrange multiplier λ^* is $\bar{E}_{\ell+1}'(t_{\ell+1}^*)$. As a result, the time complexity to derive the optimal solution of Equation (5) for an index ℓ is $O(|\mathbf{T}| - \ell)$.

It is clear that every t_j^* in $(t_{\ell+1}^*, t_{\ell+2}^*, \ldots, t_{|\mathbf{T}|}^*)$ derived from Equation (6) is greater than 0. Therefore, if each t_j^* in $(t_{\ell+1}^*, t_{\ell+2}^*, \ldots, t_{|\mathbf{T}|}^*)$ is no greater than D when $\ell = 0$, then assigning t_i as t_i^* for τ_i in $\mathbf{T}$ is an assignment of execution times with the minimum energy consumption. Therefore, we only have to consider the other case. For the rest of this section, let $\mathbf{T}$ be sorted by a *non-decreasing* order of $E_i'(D)$, where $E_i'()$ is the derivative of the energy consumption function $E_i()$. The following lemma helps to construct an assignment of execution times of tasks in $\mathbf{T}$ with the minimum energy consumption.

Lemma 3 *Suppose that every t_j^* in $(t_{\ell^*+1}^*, t_{\ell^*+2}^*, \ldots, t_{|\mathbf{T}|}^*)$ derived from Equation (6) is less than D for an index ℓ^*, and $\bar{E}_{\ell^*}'(D)$ is no less than $\bar{E}_{\ell^*+1}'(t_{\ell^*+1}^*)$, where $1 \leq \ell^* < M$. The assignment of t_i as D, for $i = 1, 2, \ldots, \ell^*$, and t_j as t_j^*, for $j = \ell^*+1, \ell^*+2, \ldots, |\mathbf{T}|$, would derive an assignment of task execution times with the minimum energy consumption.*

Proof. We prove this lemma by showing that all of the conditions in Equation (4) hold. It is clear that such an assignment satisfies $\sum_{\tau_i \in \mathbf{T}} t_i^* = MD$ and $0 < t_i^* \leq D$ for all τ_i in $\mathbf{T}$. Let λ be $\bar{E}_{\ell^*+1}'(t_{\ell^*+1}^*)$. For $j = \ell^*+1, \ell^*+2, \ldots, |\mathbf{T}|$, let λ_j be 0. For $i = 1, 2, \ldots, \ell^*$, let λ_i be $\bar{E}_i'(D) - \bar{E}_{\ell^*+1}'(t_{\ell^*+1}^*)$.

Algorithm 1 : BIN

Input: $(\mathbf{T}, D, M)$;
Output: An optimal schedule for the MEESM problem;

if $|\mathbf{T}| \leq M$ **then**
  return the schedule by executing each task τ_i in $\mathbf{T}$ at the speed $\frac{c_i}{D}$ on the i-th processor from time 0 to D;
sort $\mathbf{T}$ in a non-decreasing order of $E_i'(D)$;
$left \leftarrow 0$ and $right \leftarrow M$;
while $left < right - 1$ **do**
  $\hat{\ell} \leftarrow \lfloor (left + right)/2 \rfloor$;
  apply Equation (6) by setting ℓ as $\hat{\ell}$;
  if $\lambda > \bar{E}_{\hat{\ell}}'(D)$ **then**
    $right \leftarrow \lfloor (left + right)/2 \rfloor$;
  else
    $left \leftarrow \lfloor (left + right)/2 \rfloor$;
$\ell^* \leftarrow left$;
$V \leftarrow (t_1, t_2, \ldots, t_{|\mathbf{T}|})$ by setting t_i as D for $i = 1, 2, \ldots, \ell^*$ and t_j as t_j^* derived from Equation (6) for $j = \ell^*+1, \ell^*+2, \ldots, |\mathbf{T}|$;
return the schedule by applying Lemma 1 on V;

As a result, the equality $\bar{E}_i'(t_i^*) - \lambda_i = \lambda$ holds for every task τ_i in $\mathbf{T}$. Since $\mathbf{T}$ is sorted in a non-decreasing order of $E_i'(D)$, and $\bar{E}_i()$ is defined as $-E_i()$, we know that $\bar{E}_i'(D) \geq \bar{E}_j'(D)$ when $i < j$. Because of the condition $\bar{E}_{\ell^*}'(D) \geq \bar{E}_{\ell^*+1}'(t_{\ell^*+1}^*)$, we have

$$\bar{E}_i'(D) \geq \bar{E}_{\ell^*}'(D) \geq \bar{E}_{\ell^*+1}'(t_{\ell^*+1}^*),$$

for any $i = 1, 2, \ldots, \ell^*$. As a result, $\lambda_i = \bar{E}_i'(D) - \bar{E}_{\ell^*+1}'(t_{\ell^*+1}^*) \geq 0$ for $i = 1, 2, \ldots, \ell^*$. It is clear that all of the conditions in Equation (4) hold. □

By Lemma 3, an assignment of execution times with the minimum energy consumption for the MEESM problem can be derived in $O(M|\mathbf{T}| + |\mathbf{T}| \log |\mathbf{T}|)$ by setting ℓ from 0 to $M-1$ sequentially. Moreover, the following lemma helps the reducing of the time complexity to $O(|\mathbf{T}| \log |\mathbf{T}|)$ by a binary search on the setting of ℓ.

Lemma 4 *Suppose that every t_j^* in $(t_{\ell^*+1}^*, t_{\ell^*+2}^*, \ldots, t_{|\mathbf{T}|}^*)$ derived from Equation (6) is less than D for an index ℓ^*, and $\bar{E}_{\ell^*}'(D)$ is no less than $\bar{E}_{\ell^*+1}'(t_{\ell^*+1}^*)$, where $1 \leq \ell^* < M$. If $\ell^* < \hat{\ell} < M$, the Lagrange multiplier for Equation (5) by setting ℓ as $\hat{\ell}$ is strictly greater than $\bar{E}_{\hat{\ell}}'(D)$. If $\hat{\ell} \leq \ell^*$, the Lagrange multiplier for Equation (5) by setting ℓ as $\hat{\ell}$ is no greater than $\bar{E}_{\hat{\ell}}'(D)$.*

Proof. For notational brevity, let $\bar{t}_{\hat{\ell}+1}$ and $\bar{t}_{\hat{\ell}}$ be the values of $t_{\hat{\ell}+1}^*$ and $t_{\hat{\ell}}^*$ derived from Equation (6) by setting ℓ as ℓ^*, respectively. We consider the case when $\ell^* < \hat{\ell} < M$. As shown in Lemma 3, we know $\bar{E}_{\hat{\ell}+1}'(\bar{t}_{\hat{\ell}+1}) = \bar{E}_{\hat{\ell}}'(\bar{t}_{\hat{\ell}})$. When ℓ is set as $\hat{\ell}$, one can verify that $t_{\hat{\ell}+1}^*$ derived from Equation (6) is strictly less than $\bar{t}_{\hat{\ell}+1}$. Since $\bar{E}_j'()$ is a decreasing function of the execution time for any task τ_j in $\mathbf{T}$, we know

$$\lambda^* = \bar{E}_{\hat{\ell}+1}'(t_{\hat{\ell}+1}^*) > \bar{E}_{\hat{\ell}+1}'(\bar{t}_{\hat{\ell}+1}) = \bar{E}_{\hat{\ell}}'(\bar{t}_{\hat{\ell}}) > \bar{E}_{\hat{\ell}}'(D),$$

where λ^* is the Lagrange multiplier for Equation (5) by setting ℓ as $\hat{\ell}$, and the last inequality comes from the condition $\bar{t}_{\hat{\ell}} < D$. The other case can also be proved in a similar manner. □

Our proposed algorithm denoted as Algorithm BIN (shown in Algorithm 1) adopts the binary search strategy. After all, we conclude this section by showing the following theorem.

Theorem 1 *Algorithm* BIN *can derive an optimal schedule for the* MEESM *problem in* $O(|\mathbf{T}| \log |\mathbf{T}|)$.

Proof. It follows directly from Lemmas 1, 2, and 4. □

4 An Approximation Algorithm When Task Migration is not Allowed

In this section, we present an approximation algorithm for the MEES problem. Since the flexibility of task migration relaxes the constraint on the dis-allowance of task migration for the MEES problem, the energy consumption of the optimal schedule for the MEESM problem is no more than that of the optimal schedule for the MEES problem for the same task set $\mathbf{T}$ on M processors. Our proposed approximation algorithm first estimates a lower bound on the minimum energy consumption for the MEES problem by applying Algorithm BIN (presented in Section 3). Then, a feasible schedule of the MEES problem is derived by referring to the optimal schedule of the MEESM problem.

For the rest of this paper, let t_i^* denote the *estimated execution time* of task τ_i in $\mathbf{T}$, which is defined as the execution time of τ_i in the optimal solution derived from Algorithm BIN when task migration is allowed. The estimated execution times of tasks in $\mathbf{T}$ are then used to assign tasks onto these M processors. Let e_i^* be the *estimated energy consumption* of task τ_i when the execution time of τ_i is the estimated execution time of τ_i, i.e., $e_i^* = E_i(t_i^*)$. Let p_m denote the *load* on the m-th processor. The *load* of a processor is defined as the total amount of estimated execution time of the tasks assigned onto this processor. For notational brevity, let T_m denote the set of the tasks assigned onto the m-th processor. Our proposed algorithm shown in Algorithm 2 (denoted as Algorithm LEET) adopts the *Largest-Estimated-Execution-Time-First* strategy. That is, tasks are considered in a non-increasing order of their estimated execution time.

For notational brevity, for the rest of this paper, let $\mathbf{T}$ be a sorted set in a *non-increasing* order of the estimated execution time, i.e., $t_i^* \geq t_j^*$ if $i < j$. Algorithm LEET considers the tasks in the sorted order from τ_1 to $\tau_{|\mathbf{T}|}$. Once task τ_i is considered, τ_i is assigned onto the m-th processor whose current load is the smallest. (For the simplicity on presentation, we break ties by choosing the smallest index m. Actually, the analysis in the following still holds by breaking ties arbitrarily.) After the assignment of the tasks onto the M processors is done, we have to assign the execution times of these tasks to meet the timing constraint. For every task τ_i assigned onto the m-th processor, the execution time of τ_i is set as $t_i^* \frac{D}{p_m}$. After all, it is clear that the total execution time of the tasks assigned onto each processor is exactly equal to D. Since the processor speed is in $[0, \infty]$, executing the tasks assigned onto each processor one after one is a feasible schedule of the MEES problem. The time complexity of Algorithm LEET is $O(|\mathbf{T}| \log |\mathbf{T}|)$, which is dominated by applying Algorithm BIN, the sorting of the tasks, and the procedure to find the minimum p_m.

Algorithm 2 : LEET

Input: $(\mathbf{T}, D, M)$;
Output: A feasible schedule for the MEES problem;
let $(t_1^*, t_2^*, \ldots, t_{|\mathbf{T}|}^*)$ be the assignment of execution times of $\mathbf{T}$ by applying Algorithm BIN$(\mathbf{T}, D, M)$;
sort all tasks in $\mathbf{T}$ in a non-increasing order of their estimated execution times;
set $p_1, p_2, \cdots, p_M$ as 0, and $T_1, T_2, \cdots, T_M$ as ϕ;
for $i = 1$ to $|\mathbf{T}|$ **do**
  find the smallest p_m; (break ties by choosing the smallest index m)
  $T_m \leftarrow T_m \cup \{\tau_i\}$ and $p_m \leftarrow p_m + t_i^*$;
for $m = 1$ to $|M|$ **do**
  for each task $\tau_i \in T_m$ **do**
    $t_i' \leftarrow t_i^* \times \frac{D}{p_m}$;
return the schedule S_{LEET} which executes all of the tasks τ_i in T_m $(1 \leq m \leq M)$ at the speed c_i / t_i' on the m-th processor one after one;

In the following, we shall show the optimality of Algorithm LEET, i.e., that on the approximation ratio. For the simplicity of representation, the schedule derived from Algorithm LEET is denoted as S_{LEET} for task set $\mathbf{T}$. For notational brevity, let $\mathbf{T}'$ be a subset of $\mathbf{T}$, where $\mathbf{T}'$ consists of those tasks whose estimated execution times are strictly less than D. That is, $\mathbf{T}' = \{\tau_i \mid t_i^* < D, \forall \tau_i \in \mathbf{T}\}$. Moreover, let $\hat{\mathbf{T}}$ be the difference set of $\mathbf{T}$ from $\mathbf{T}'$, i.e., $\hat{\mathbf{T}} = \mathbf{T} \setminus \mathbf{T}'$. Note that the analysis in the rest of this section only focuses on the case that $|\mathbf{T}| > M$ since Algorithm LEET guarantees to derive an optimal schedule for the other case. Furthermore, this also implies that $\mathbf{T}'$ is not empty for the rest discussions. We will show that the approximation ratio of Algorithm LEET is $\frac{(\alpha-1)^{\alpha-1}(2^\alpha-1)^\alpha}{\alpha^\alpha(2^\alpha-2)^{\alpha-1}}$. Since the value of α is at most 3, and the approximation ratio is an increasing function on the value of α, the approximation ratio of Algorithm LEET is 1.412.

Before we proceed to prove the approximation ratio of Algorithm LEET, we first introduce some properties of the estimated energy consumptions and the estimated execution times of the tasks under considerations. In the following lemma, we show that the ratio of the estimated energy consumption to the estimated execution time of task τ_i is equal to that of task τ_j if both τ_i and τ_j are elements of $\mathbf{T}'$.

Lemma 5 *For any two tasks* $\tau_i, \tau_j \in \mathbf{T}'$, *the ratio of the estimated energy consumption to the estimated execution time of*

τ_i *is equal to that of* τ_j, *i.e.,* $\frac{e_i^*}{t_i^*} = \frac{e_j^*}{t_j^*}$.

Proof. It follows directly from the property of the Lagrange multiplier. By the definition of the task set $\mathbf{T}'$, t_i^* and t_j^* are both less than D. By Lemma 3 and Algorithm BIN, we have $-E_i'(t_i^*) = -E_j'(t_j^*)$. Therefore, we conclude this lemma by showing that

$$-(\alpha-1)h_i\frac{c_i^\alpha}{(t_i^*)^\alpha} = -(\alpha-1)h_j\frac{c_j^\alpha}{(t_j^*)^\alpha}$$

$$\Rightarrow \quad \frac{t_i^*}{t_j^*} = \frac{(t_j^*)^{\alpha-1}h_i c_i^\alpha}{(t_i^*)^{\alpha-1}h_j c_j^\alpha} = \frac{e_i^*}{e_j^*}.$$

□

If two processors are only assigned with some tasks in $\mathbf{T}'$ after all of the tasks are assigned in Algorithm LEET, we show that the ratio of the loads between these two processors is at most 2.

Lemma 6 *Suppose that the m^*-th and the $\hat{m}$-th processors are assigned with some tasks in $\mathbf{T}'$ such that p_{m^*} is the maximum and $p_{\hat{m}}$ is the minimum after all of the tasks are assigned onto processors in Algorithm* LEET, *then p_{m^*} is at most twice of $p_{\hat{m}}$.*

Proof. Since tasks are assigned onto the processor with the smallest load, and $|\mathbf{T}| > M$, it is clear that both p_{m^*} and $p_{\hat{m}}$ are greater than 0. For each task τ_i in $\hat{\mathbf{T}}$, Algorithm LEET assigns only τ_i onto a processor. Therefore, $\sum_{\tau_i \in \mathbf{T}'} t_i^* = (M - |\hat{\mathbf{T}}|)D$. Since $|\mathbf{T}'| > (M - |\hat{\mathbf{T}}|)$, we know $p_{m^*} \geq D$ and $p_{\hat{m}} \leq D$ by the pigeon hole principle. Because of the condition $t_i^* < D$ for every task τ_i in $\mathbf{T}'$, T_{m^*} consists of at least two tasks. Let the last task inserted into T_{m^*} be τ_r. When τ_r is considered in the first loop in Algorithm LEET (i.e., the **for** loop from Steps 4 to 6), there must be at least one task assigned onto the $\hat{m}$-th processor already, since τ_r is assigned onto the processor whose current load is the minimum. Let τ_q be the first task assigned onto the $\hat{m}$-th processor. Because Algorithm LEET assigns the tasks in a non-increasing order of the estimated execution times, we have $t_r^* \leq t_q^* \leq p_{\hat{m}}$. Furthermore, since τ_r is assigned onto the processor whose current load is the minimum, we know $p_{m^*} - t_r^* \leq p_{\hat{m}}$. By considering the above inequalities, we know $p_{m^*} \leq 2p_{\hat{m}}$. □

Besides, we need the following lemma to prove the approximation ratio of Algorithm LEET.

Lemma 7 *Suppose $f(x) = k \cdot (2x)^\alpha + (\hat{M} - k)x^\alpha$ for a positive number $\hat{M}$ and a non-negative number k, where $0 \leq k \leq \hat{M}$ and $2k \cdot x + (\hat{M} - k) \cdot x = \hat{M}$, then*

$$f(x) \leq \frac{(\alpha-1)^{\alpha-1}(2^\alpha-1)^\alpha}{\alpha^\alpha(2^\alpha-2)^{\alpha-1}}\hat{M}.$$

Proof. Since $2k \cdot x + (\hat{M} - k) \cdot x = \hat{M}$, we know $k = \frac{\hat{M} - \hat{M}x}{x}$. Therefore,

$$f(x) = \hat{M}(x^{\alpha-1}(2^\alpha - 1) + x^\alpha(2 - 2^\alpha)),$$

and the derivative of $f(x)$ is

$$f'(x) = \hat{M}((\alpha-1)x^{\alpha-2}(2^\alpha-1) + \alpha x^{\alpha-1}(2-2^\alpha)).$$

$f(x)$ is maximized at x^* when $f'(x^*) = 0$. By solving $f'(x^*) = 0$, we have $x^* = \frac{(\alpha-1)(2^\alpha-1)}{\alpha(2^\alpha-2)}$. As a result, we conclude that

$$f(x) \leq f(x^*) = \frac{(\alpha-1)^{\alpha-1}(2^\alpha-1)^\alpha}{\alpha^\alpha(2^\alpha-2)^{\alpha-1}}\hat{M}.$$

□

We conclude this section by showing that Algorithm LEET is a $\frac{(\alpha-1)^{\alpha-1}(2^\alpha-1)^\alpha}{\alpha^\alpha(2^\alpha-2)^{\alpha-1}}$-approximation algorithm for the MEES problem.

Theorem 2 *The approximation ratio of Algorithm* LEET *is* $\frac{(\alpha-1)^{\alpha-1}(2^\alpha-1)^\alpha}{\alpha^\alpha(2^\alpha-2)^{\alpha-1}}$.

Proof. Let O^* be the energy consumption for an optimal schedule for $\mathbf{T}$ of the MEES problem. Since the sum of the estimated energy consumption of all of the tasks in $\mathbf{T}$ is a lower bound on O^*, we know that $O^* \geq \sum_{\tau_i \in \mathbf{T}} e_i^*$. Let τ_r be some task in $\mathbf{T}'$. By Lemma 5, we have

$$O^* \geq \sum_{\tau_i \in \mathbf{T}} e_i^* = e_r^*/t_r^*(M - |\hat{\mathbf{T}}|)D + \sum_{\tau_i \in \hat{\mathbf{T}}} e_i^*.$$

For each task τ_i in $\hat{\mathbf{T}}$, Algorithm LEET assigns only τ_i onto a processor. Since we break ties by choosing the smallest index m in Algorithm LEET, the i-th processor is assigned with only task τ_i, where $0 < i \leq |\hat{\mathbf{T}}|$. For the m-th processor, where $m > |\hat{\mathbf{T}}|$, the energy consumption to execute task τ_i in T_m is equal to $e_i^*(\frac{p_m}{D})^{\alpha-1}$ in S_{LEET}, and the sum of the estimated energy consumption of the tasks in T_m is equal to $\frac{e_r^*}{t_r^*}p_m$ by applying Lemma 5. Therefore, we have

$$\begin{aligned}\Phi(S_{\text{LEET}}) &= \sum_{\tau_i \in \hat{\mathbf{T}}} e_i^* + \sum_{m=|\hat{\mathbf{T}}|+1}^{M} \frac{e_r^*}{t_r^*}p_m(\frac{p_m}{D})^{\alpha-1} \\ &= \sum_{\tau_i \in \hat{\mathbf{T}}} e_i^* + \sum_{m=|\hat{\mathbf{T}}|+1}^{M} \frac{e_r^*}{t_r^*}(\frac{p_m}{D})^\alpha D.\end{aligned}$$

The approximation ratio $\mathcal{A}$ of Algorithm LEET can be phrased as

$$\mathcal{A} = \frac{\Phi(S_{\text{LEET}})}{O^*} \leq \frac{\sum_{m=|\hat{\mathbf{T}}|+1}^{M}(\frac{p_m}{D})^\alpha}{M - |\hat{\mathbf{T}}|}, \tag{7}$$

where the inequality comes from the fact $\frac{a+b_1}{a+b_2} \leq \frac{b_1}{b_2}$ when $b_1 \geq b_2 > 0$ and $a \geq 0$. It remains to show that

$$\frac{\sum_{m=|\hat{\mathbf{T}}|+1}^{M}(\frac{p_m}{D})^\alpha}{M - |\hat{\mathbf{T}}|} \leq \frac{(\alpha-1)^{\alpha-1}(2^\alpha-1)^\alpha}{\alpha^\alpha(2^\alpha-2)^{\alpha-1}}. \tag{8}$$

Suppose that the m^*-th and the $\hat{m}$-th processors are assigned with some tasks in $\mathbf{T}'$ such that p_{m^*} is the maximum, and

$p_{\hat{m}}$ is the minimum. By Lemma 6, we have $2\frac{p_{\hat{m}}}{D} \geq \frac{p_{m^*}}{D} \geq \frac{p_m}{D} \geq \frac{p_{\hat{m}}}{D}$, for all $|\hat{\mathbf{T}}| < m \leq M$. Besides, by the convexity of $(\frac{p_m}{D})^\alpha$ of $\frac{p_m}{D}$ (i.e., the second order derivative of $(\frac{p_m}{D})^\alpha$ of $\frac{p_m}{D}$ is non-negative when $\frac{p_m}{D} \geq 0$) and the fact $p_{\hat{m}} \geq 2p_{\hat{m}} - p_m \geq 0$ for all $|\hat{\mathbf{T}}| < m \leq M$, we have

$$(\frac{p_m}{D})^\alpha \leq \frac{2p_{\hat{m}} - p_m}{p_{\hat{m}}}(\frac{p_{\hat{m}}}{D})^\alpha + (1 - \frac{2p_{\hat{m}} - p_m}{p_{\hat{m}}})(\frac{2p_{\hat{m}}}{D})^\alpha,$$

since $\frac{2p_{\hat{m}}-p_m}{p_{\hat{m}}}(\frac{p_{\hat{m}}}{D}) + (1 - \frac{2p_{\hat{m}}-p_m}{p_{\hat{m}}})(\frac{2p_{\hat{m}}}{D})$ is equal to $\frac{p_m}{D}$. Therefore,

$$\begin{aligned}\sum_{m=|\hat{\mathbf{T}}|+1}^{M} (\frac{p_m}{D})^\alpha &\leq \sum_{m=|\hat{\mathbf{T}}|+1}^{M} \frac{2p_{\hat{m}}-p_m}{p_{\hat{m}}}(\frac{p_{\hat{m}}}{D})^\alpha + (1 - \frac{2p_{\hat{m}}-p_m}{p_{\hat{m}}})(\frac{2p_{\hat{m}}}{D})^\alpha \\ &= k \cdot (\frac{2p_{\hat{m}}}{D})^\alpha + (M - |\hat{\mathbf{T}}| - k)(\frac{p_{\hat{m}}}{D})^\alpha,\end{aligned}$$

where $2k\frac{p_{\hat{m}}}{D} + (M - |\hat{\mathbf{T}}| - k)\frac{p_{\hat{m}}}{D} = (M - |\hat{\mathbf{T}}|)$, i.e., $k = \sum_{m=|\hat{\mathbf{T}}|+1}^{M}(1 - \frac{2p_{\hat{m}}-p_m}{p_{\hat{m}}})$. By applying Lemma 7 with the setting of $\hat{M}$ as $M - |\hat{\mathbf{T}}|$ and x as $\frac{p_{\hat{m}}}{D}$, we reach the conclusion. □

Corollary 1 *The approximation ratio of Algorithm* LEET *is* 1.412.

Proof. Since α is no greater than 3, and $\frac{(\alpha-1)^{\alpha-1}(2^\alpha-1)^\alpha}{\alpha^\alpha(2^\alpha-2)^{\alpha-1}}$ is an increasing function of α, the approximation ratio is bounded when $\alpha = 3$. □

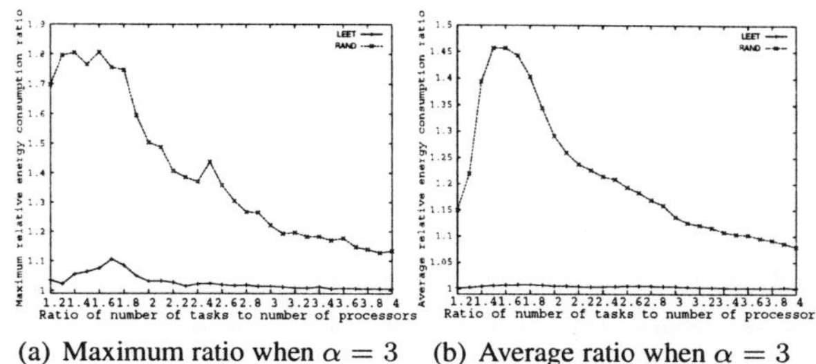

(a) Maximum ratio when $\alpha = 3$ (b) Average ratio when $\alpha = 3$

Figure 1. (a) and (b): maximum and average relative energy consumption ratios, respectively.

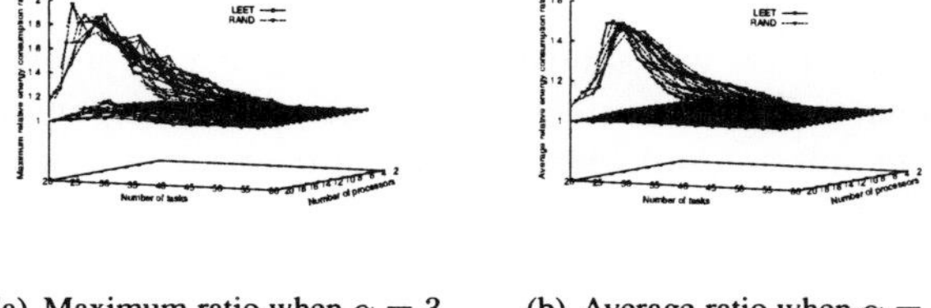

(a) Maximum ratio when $\alpha = 3$ (b) Average ratio when $\alpha = 3$

Figure 2. (a) and (b): maximum and average relative energy consumption ratios, respectively.

5 Performance Evaluation

In this section, we provide performance evaluation on the energy consumption of Algorithm LEET. Another algorithm, denoted as Algorithm RAND, which is very similar to Algorithm LEET, was simulated for comparison. The only difference between Algorithm RAND and Algorithm LEET is that tasks are not sorted before the assignment procedure in Algorithm RAND.

Workload Parameters and Performance Metrics The common deadline D of the tasks in a task set was set as 100 units of time in the simulations. For each task τ_i in $\mathbf{T}$, τ_i was characterized by two different parameters: the number of execution CPU cycles c_i and the coefficient h_i of the power consumption function of τ_i. c_i was generated uniformly in the range $(0, D]$. h_i was uniformly distributed in the range of 2 and 10. The exponent of the power consumption functions of the processor speed s was set as 3, i.e., $P_i(s) = h_i s^3$. We simulated two cases for different numbers of processors with different numbers of tasks. For the first case, we evaluated the algorithms for the effects on the ratio of the number of tasks to the number of processors. For a given ratio η of the number of tasks to the number of processors, the number of processors M was an integral random variable between 10 and 30, and the number of tasks was set as the floor of the multiplication of η and M, i.e., $\lfloor \eta \cdot M \rfloor$. For the other case, the number of processors ranged from 2 to 20, and the task-set size ranged from 21 to 60. Experimental results were conducted with 512 independent experiments for each parameter configuration.

The *relative energy consumption ratio* was adopted as the performance metric in our experiments. The relative energy consumption ratio for an input instance was defined as the energy consumption of the schedule derived by the algorithm to that of an optimal schedule with the allowance of task migration. As shown in Section 3, the energy consumption of an optimal schedule with the allowance of task migration can be derived in an efficient manner. Since the problem is $\mathcal{NP}$-hard, the performance metric *relative energy consumption ratio* aimed at the providing of an approximated index. When the results were for the average relative energy consumption ratio, their results were averaged. When they were for the maximum relative energy consumption ratio, the maximum value was returned.

Experimental Results For the evaluation of the effects on the ratio of the number of tasks to the number of processors, Figures 1(a) and 1(b) present the maximum and average relative energy consumption ratios for the simulated algorithms. The performance of Algorithm LEET was very close to that of the optimal solutions. The maximum and average relative energy consumption ratios for Algorithm LEET were less than 1.11 and 1.01, respectively. Furthermore, the maximum and average relative energy consumption ratios for Algorithm RAND were less than 1.82 and 1.46, respectively. When the ratio of the number of tasks to the number of processors was small, both of Algorithm LEET and Algorithm RAND might assign a task along with improper tasks on a processor. Such an assignment might result in a significant increase on the energy consumption of these tasks when the energy consumption for the other tasks were almost as the same as that in the optimal schedule. Such an observation explained why the maximum relative energy consumption ratios in Figure 1(a) decreased when the ratio of the number of tasks to the number of processors increased. However, when the ratio of the number of tasks to the number of processors was small, in most cases, most processors were assigned with only one task, and the assignment was almost as the same as that of an optimal schedule. Therefore, the average energy consumption ratio was relatively small when the ratio of the number of tasks to the number of processors was less than 1.5.

When the number of processors ranged from 2 to 20, and the task set size ranged from 21 to 60, Figure 2(a) (/Figure 2(b)) presents the maximum (/average) relative energy consumption ratios for the simulated algorithms. The performance of Algorithm LEET was again very close to the optimal solution. The maximum and average relative energy consumption ratios for Algorithm LEET were less than 1.084 and 1.01 respectively, where the maximum and average relative energy consumption ratios for Algorithm RAND were less than 1.941 and 1.485, respectively. The trends of the simulation results were similar to those in Figures 1(a) and 1(b). The results indicated that Algorithm LEET could derive effective schedules for the MEES problem.

6 Conclusion

This paper targets energy-efficient scheduling problems over homogeneous processors for real-time tasks with a common deadline. Different from the past work, we consider different parameter settings for the power consumption function $P_i(s)$ of the processor speed s for each task τ_i, i.e., $P_i(s) = h_i s^\alpha$, where the value of h_i depends upon the power characteristics of task τ_i and α is a hardware-specific constant ($2 \leq \alpha \leq 3$). We propose an optimal algorithm, when task migration is permitted, and an approximation algorithm, when task migration is not allowed. We show that the approximation ratio of the proposed approximation algorithm is $\frac{(\alpha-1)^{\alpha-1}(2^\alpha-1)^\alpha}{\alpha^\alpha(2^\alpha-2)^{\alpha-1}}$. Since the value of α is at most 3, the approximation ratio is at most 1.412. The proposed algorithm is evaluated by a series of simulation experiments, compared to a lower bound by allowing task migration. The performance of Algorithm LEET is very close to that of the optimal solutions. The results also indicate that Algorithm LEET could derive effective schedules for the MEES problem.

For future research, we will explore energy-efficient scheduling over multiple processors for periodic real-time tasks or tasks with arbitrary deadlines and arrival times.

References

[1] J. H. Anderson and S. K. Baruah. Energy-efficient synthesis of periodic task systems upon identical multiprocessor platforms. In *Proceedings of the 24th International Conference on Distributed Computing Systems*, pages 428–435, 2004.

[2] H. Aydin, R. Melhem, D. Mossé, and P. Mejía-Alvarez. Determining optimal processor speeds for periodic real-time tasks with different power characteristics. In *Proceedings of the IEEE EuroMicro Conference on Real-Time Systems*, page 225, 2001.

[3] N. Bansal, T. Kimbrel, and K. Pruhs. Dynamic speed scaling to manage energy and temperature. In *Proceedings of the 2004 Symposium on Foundations of Computer Science*, pages 520–529, 2004.

[4] A. Chandrakasan, S. Sheng, and R. Broderson. Lower-power CMOS digital design. *IEEE Journal of Solid-State Circuit*, 27(4):473–484, 1992.

[5] J.-J. Chen, H.-R. Hsu, K.-H. Chuang, C.-L. Yang, and A.-C. P. T.-W. Kuo. Multiprocessor energy-efficient scheduling with task migration considerations. In *EuroMicro Conference on Real-Time Systems (ECRTS'04)*, pages 101–108, 2004.

[6] J.-J. Chen, T.-W. Kuo, and C.-L. Yang. Profit-driven uniprocessor scheduling with energy and timing constraints. In *ACM Symposium on Applied Computing*, pages 834–840. ACM Press, 2004.

[7] F. Gruian. System-level design methods for low-energy architectures containing variable voltage processors. In *Power-Aware Computing Systems*, pages 1–12, 2000.

[8] F. Gruian and K. Kuchcinski. Lenes: Task scheduling for low energy systems using variable supply voltage processors. In *Proceedings of Asia South Pacific Design Automation Conference*, pages 449–455, 2001.

[9] S. Irani, S. Shukla, and R. Gupta. Algorithms for power savings. In *Proceedings of the Fourteenth Annual ACM-SIAM Symposium on Discrete Algorithms*, pages 37–46. Society for Industrial and Applied Mathematics, 2003.

[10] T. Ishihara and H. Yasuura. Voltage scheduling problems for dynamically variable voltage processors. In *Proceedings of the International Symposium on Low Power Electroncs and Design*, pages 197–202, 1998.

[11] W.-C. Kwon and T. Kim. Optimal voltage allocation techniques for dynamically variable voltage processors. In *Proceedings of the 40th Design Automation Conference*, pages 125–130, 2003.

[12] P. Mejía-Alvarez, E. Levner, and D. Mossé. Adaptive scheduling server for power-aware real-time tasks. *ACM Transactions on Embedded Computing Systems*, 3(2):284–306, 2004.

[13] R. Mishra, N. Rastogi, D. Zhu, D. Mossé, and R. Melhem. Energy aware scheduling for distributed real-time systems. In *International Parallel and Distributed Processing Symposium*, page 21, 2003.

[14] R. L. Rardin. *Optimization in Operations Research*. Prentice Hall, 1998.

[15] Y. Shin and K. Choi. Power conscious fixed priority scheduling for hard real-time systems. In *Proceedings of the 36th ACM/IEEE Conference on Design Automation Conference*, pages 134–139, 1999.

[16] V. V. Vazirani. *Approximation Algorithms*. Springer, 2001.

[17] M. Weiser, B. Welch, A. Demers, and S. Shenker. Scheduling for reduced CPU energy. In *Proceedings of Symposium on Operating Systems Design and Implementation*, pages 13–23, 1994.

[18] C.-Y. Yang, J.-J. Chen, and T.-W. Kuo. An approximation algorithm for energy-efficient scheduling on a chip multiprocessor. In *Proceedings of the 8th Conference of Design, Automation, and Test in Europe (DATE)*, pages 468–473, 2005.

[19] F. Yao, A. Demers, and S. Shenker. A scheduling model for reduced CPU energy. In *Proceedings of the 36th Annual Symposium on Foundations of Computer Science*, pages 374–382. IEEE, 1995.

[20] Y. Zhang, X. Hu, and D. Z. Chen. Task scheduling and voltage selection for energy minimization. In *Annual ACM IEEE Design Automation Conference*, pages 183–188, 2002.

Session 1B: Resource Allocation

A Utility-based Two Level Market Solution For Optimal Resource Allocation In Computational Grid

Li Chunlin, Li Layuan
Department of Computer Science, Wuhan University of Technology, Wuhan 430063,P.R.China
E-Mail: chunlin74@tom.com or jwtu@public.wh.hb.cn

Abstract

The paper presents a market oriented resource allocation strategy for grid resource. The proposed model uses the utility functions for calculating the utility of a resource allocation. This allows the integration of different optimization objectives into allocation process. This paper is target to solve above issues by using utility-based optimization scheme. We decompose the optimization problem into two levels of subproblems so that the computational complexity is reduced. Two market levels converge to its optimal points; a globally optimal point is achieved. Total user benefit of the computational grid is maximized when the equilibrium prices are obtained through the service market level optimization and resource market level optimization. The economic model is the basis of an iterative algorithm that, given a finite set of requests, is used to perform optimal resource allocation. The experiments show that scheduling based on pricing directed resource allocation involves less overhead and leads to more efficient resource allocation than conventional round robin scheduling.

Keywords: grid resource allocation, market, optimization, utility

1. Introduction

Computational grid is a high performance computational environment that is composed of heterogeneous resources spanning wide area networks and multiple administrative domains. Main problems in computational grid resource allocation are the ability to discover suitable services and resources and how to schedule separate tasks of an application on those resources in such a way as to maximize the user's benefits. The issues that grid allocation mechanism should address are as follows.1) efficient grid resource allocation to the different grid users taking into account their different needs and performance requirements; 2) the crucial notion of fairness; and 3) the issue of pricing the resources in such a way that the grid providers' revenue will be maximized if the grid users are allocated resource according to 1) and 2) above. The paper presents a market oriented resource allocation strategy for grid resource. The proposed model uses the utility functions for calculating the utility of a resource allocation. This allows the integration of different optimization objectives into allocation process. Future grid resource management and scheduling will highly rely on market-oriented methods to integrate the different objectives of grid providers and users. This paper is target to solve above issues by using utility-based optimization scheme. We decompose the optimization problem into two levels of subproblems so that the computational complexity is reduced.

Applying economic methods to grid and cluster computing field is an interesting subject that will yield more attention in grid research recently. There is already some research effort in this area. R. Buyya [19,21] have proposed and developed a distributed computational economy-based framework, called the Grid Architecture for Computational Economy (GRACE), for resource allocation and to regulate supply and demand of the available resources. Carsten Ernemann [22] addresses the idea of applying economic models to the scheduling task. To realize the full potential of Grid economy, the Gridbus project [4] has been developing technologies that provide end-to-end support for allocation of resources based on resource providers and consumers quality of service (QoS) requirements. R. Wolski [5] investigates 'G-commerce' computational economies for controlling resource allocation in Computational Grid settings. Above works don't give a comprehensive utility function, and aslo don't consider the global optimization of utility of all grid users and providers. In our proposed model, utility function is realistic and calculable. Moreover, we consider both grid users and grid provider's joint optimization by decomposing the grid resource allocation optimization into subproblems.

Utility function and economy model are also widely applied to communication network field. In [13], Yuan Xue *et al.* propose a price-based resource allocation model to achieve maximized aggregated utility of flows. They use maximal clique associated shadow prices for wireless channel access coordination. In [14] Yi Cui and

0190-3918/05 $20.00 © 2005 IEEE

Yuan Xue target the problem of optimal network resource allocation in overlay multicast. In [15] Nan Feng *et al* considered a radio resource management problem with user centric and network centric objectives. They used a utility function as the user-centric metric and for the network-centric counterpart. In [17], C. U. Saraydar *et al.* present a power control solution for wireless data in the analytical setting of a game theoretic framework where users maximize their utility. In [18], H. Yaiche *et al* present a game theoretic framework for bandwidth allocation for elastic services in high-speed networks. The framework is based on the idea of the Nash bargaining solution from cooperative game theory, which not only provides the rate settings of users that are Pareto optimal from the point of view of the whole system. In [20], Hong Jiang *et al* discuss the role of prices in combining user characterization, network resource allocation, and contract negotiation to form a complete connection establishment process. Such a process encourages network efficiency through distributed resource allocation among virtual circuits, circuit bundles, and virtual paths. In [23], Richard J. La *et al* investigate achieving the system optimal rates in the sense of maximizing aggregate utility in a communication network. This is done by decomposing the overall system problem into subproblems for the network and for the individual users by introducing a pricing scheme. The users are to solve the problem of maximizing individual net utility, which is the utility less the amount they pay. In [24], Jonathan Bredin *et al* formulate the hosts' resource-allocation problem as a game with the players being agents competing for a resource from a common server. They show how to compute the unique positive Nash equilibrium explicitly under perfect information when there are two or more players. In [26], M. A. Gibney *et al* present a market-based approach to call routing in telecommunications networks. System architecture is described that allows self-interested agents representing various network resources to coordinate their resource allocation decisions. In [27], O. Ercetin *et al* study the caching model in the framework of Content Delivery Networks. The objective is to minimize the user latency by intelligently distributing the content and serving the user requests from the most efficient surrogates. They use price-directed market based algorithms to achieve this goal. In [28], T. Eymann and M. Reinicke propose project CATNET that evaluates a decentralized mechanism for resource allocation in ALN, which is based on the economic paradigm of the Catallaxy, against a centralized mechanism using an arbitrator object. In [29], R. T. Maheswaran *et al* study a proportionally fair divisible auction to manage agents bidding for service from network and computational resources. In [30], Scott Jordan uses pricing to distribute the allocation of buffer and bandwidth at each node along a set of paths, with the goal of maximizing the total utility of all users in the network. Corresponding shadow costs associated with each resource and delay constraint are related to user's marginal utilities.

In this paper, we suggest that a market mechanism can enable resource allocation optimization in computational grid through distributed resource allocation among grid user, grid service and grid resource. Our approach is through the use of agents named user agents, resource agents and service agents. Negotiations between three types of grid agents would resolve service management, resource management; also address pricing and payments issues. These agents behave as intermediaries between users seeking a service (which may require access to a number of distributed resources) through grid service market and the many resources available in the grid resource market. These agents need to operate in an environment that consists of multiple grid service providers, multiple grid resource providers and where dynamic of users and resources behaviors, adds to the complexity of the distributed service environment. This paper investigates the interactions between agents representing users, services and resources to solve resource allocation optimization in computational grid. In order to reduce the computational complexity, we further decompose the grid resource allocation optimization into subproblems: grid user agent- grid service agent in service market and grid service agent-grid resource agent in resource market. Two market levels converge to its optimal points; a globally optimal point can be achieved.

2 Mathematical Model Of Optimal Grid Resource Allocation

2.1 Economic Agents in Two Level Markets

In microeconomics, a market is a model where numerous participants (suppliers and demanders) determine their own action and the price will automatically adjust to the equilibrium where the supply of the commodity equals to the demand. In our model, grid resource allocation optimization is distributed to and performed at two market levels: grid user agent-grid service agent in service market and grid service agent-grid resource agent in resource market (Fig.1). Interactions between the three agent types are mediated by means of market mechanisms. Two level markets maximize both user agents and resource agents' interests. The grid resource agents represent the economic interests of the underlying resources of the computational grid, the grid user agents represent the interests of grid user using the grid to achieve goals, and grid service agents act as both a buyer of grid resources and a seller of grid services for grid users. Service agents wish to buy resources cheaply from resource agents and sell services at a profit to grid users. To do this, they buy resources at a price less than earnings that they obtain from selling grid services to grid users. The service agent tries to maximize its profits by adjusting supplier role behavior on the basis of the feedback it receives from the service market, at the same time they try to buy the grid resource with lest budget through resource market.

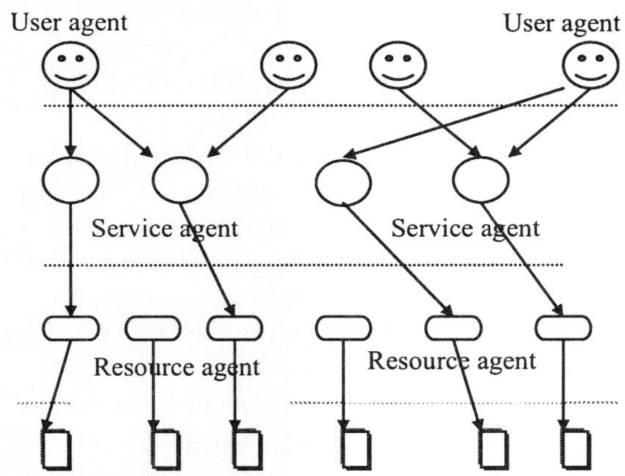

Fig.1 Grid agents in grid market

Grid resource agents sell the underlying resources of the grid through grid resource market. A grid service agent makes buying decisions within budget constraints to acquire computation resources. The service agent never sells a service for less than the cost paid to the grid resource agents to acquire suitable resources. Grid service agents buy computation resources solely on the basis of the most recent price information provide by grid resource agent. The service agent retains a vector of prices that it is willing to pay for resources. The grid service agent tries to maintain its resources at optimal units that are obtained through gradient climbing adaptation to the behavior of the resource market. The price paid for each resource agent should be as low as possible without failing to obtain the resource. Therefore the grid service agent makes a request for each resource that it needs separately. If a request was rejected, the grid service agent increases the price it will send to resource agent at the next negotiation. If a request was accepted, the grid service agent reduces the price it pays for that resource in subsequent negotiations. The Grid resource agents have varied computational resource capacity, and the computational resource capacity is shared among the grid service agents. The grid resource agents charge the service agents for the portion of the computational resource capacity occupies. We assume that the grid resource agents of a grid does not cooperate, probably due to high messaging and processing overheads associated with cooperative allocating. Instead, they act non-cooperatively with the objective of maximizing their individual profits [24,26]. The grid resource agents compete among each other to serve the service agents. The service agents do not collaborate either, and try to purchase as much computational resource as possible with the objective of maximizing their net benefit. The agents communicate by means of a simple set of signals that encapsulate offers, commitments, and payments for resources. In grid market mechanisms, resource agents set their prices solely on the basis of their implicit perception of supply and demand of grid resource at a given time. When a resource is scarce, grid service agents have to increase the prices they are willing to buy, when resource is enough, resource agents decrease the price at which they are willing to offer the resource. In our model, three types of agents perceive supply and demand in the market through price-directed market-based algorithm that will be described in section 4.

2.2 Formulation of Grid Resource Allocation Optimization

This section formulates the grid resource allocation problem into a two-level market model and proves that the equilibrium is the optimum; we can achieve the social optimal resource allocation in a distributed manner.

Assuming that the grid system knows its resource capacities and every user's utility function and grid service provider and grid resource provider's objective function, the grid system will be able to calculate the optimal resource allocation. Assume each grid user agent needs grid services owned by various grid service agents, and grid resources at grid resource layer to enable service agents complete jobs. Specifically, we assume grid user agent i can buy service y_i^j from service agent j, and service agent j buys resources x_j^l from resource agent l. If a service agent has a total service s_j available to users, then the service allocations must obey $s_j \geq \sum_i y_i^j$. c_l is the capacity of grid resource represented by grid resource agent l ,the corresponding resource allocation constraint is therefore $c_l \geq \sum_j x_j^l$. The completion time for grid user i to complete its nth job is $t_i^n = f(x_j^l, y_i^j, q_{in})$ where q_{in} is the size of ith user agent' s nth job. We assume that each grid user i can place an upper bound on the total completion time by $T_i \geq \sum^N t_i^n$ where N is the number of user's jobs. We assume that there are M types of services and that each user agent may need many types of services to complete a job. Assume that there is a set M = $\{1,2,\ldots M\}$ of different types of services that the grid allocates to grid user agent through the service market. Let u_i be the total payments of the jth user agent paid to m types of services where $u_i = \sum_M u_i^j$. N grid service agents compete for grid resources with the finite capacity. The resource is allocated through resource market, where the partitions depend on the relative payments sent by the grid service agents. We assume that each service agent j submits v_j^l to the grid resource agent l. Then, $v^l = [v_1^l......v_N^l]$ represents all payments of grid service agents for lth resource agent. We associate with each grid user a utility function $U(x_j^l, y_i^j)$, which depends on resource units allocated to service agent j by x_j^l that resource agent l allocates, and y_i^j that is the service obtained by grid user agent i from service agent j. The utility function $U(x_j^l, y_i^j)$ is defined as follows.

$$U(x_j^l, y_i^j) = -K(\sum_{n=1}^{N} t_i^n - T_i) - \sum_j u_i^j - \sum_l v_j^l \quad (2.1)$$

From the definition of $U(x_j^l, y_i^j)$ (2.1), grid user agent needs to complete a sequence of jobs in a specified amount of time, T_i, while minimizing the overhead accrued. The goal of each user agent is to complete its job while spending the least possible amounts of money. The user agent receives services or resources proportional to its payment relative to price of grid service and grid resource, we can get (2.2)

$$u_i^j = y_i^j \lambda_j, \quad v_j^l = x_j^l \beta_l \quad (2.2)$$

In (2.2), λ_j is the unit price of grid service j, β_l is the unit price of grid resource l. (2.1) can be reformulated as

$$U(x_j^l, y_i^j) = -K(\sum_{n=1}^{N} \frac{q_{in}}{x_j^l y_i^j} - T_i) - \sum_j y_i^j \lambda_j - \sum_l x_j^l \beta_l \quad (2.3)$$

The grid system performs total user benefit maximization under three constraints:

$$\text{(G)} \quad \begin{aligned} & \underset{x_j^l, y_i^j}{Max} \sum_{ij} U(x_j^l, y_i^j) \\ & \text{s.t. } c_l \geq \sum_j x_j^l, S_j \geq \sum_i y_i^j \\ & T_i \geq \sum_i t_i^n, x_j^l > 0, y_i^j > 0 \end{aligned} \quad (2.4)$$

The constraint implies that the aggregate resource units do not exceed the total capacity of grid resource, aggregate service units do not exceed the total grid service, and grid user should complete all its jobs under time limits. We can apply the Lagrangian method to solve such a problem. Let us consider the Lagrangian form of this optimization problem:

$$L(\lambda_j, \beta_l) = \sum_i U - \lambda_j(\sum_j y_i^j - S_j) - \beta_l(\sum_j x_j^l - c_l) - \gamma_i(\sum_i t_i^n - Ti) \quad (2.5)$$

$$x_j^l(\partial U / \partial x_j^l - \beta_l - \gamma_i \, \partial t_i^n / \partial x_j^l) = 0 \quad (2.6)$$

$$y_i^j(\partial U / \partial y_i^j - \lambda_j - \gamma_i \, \partial t_i^n / \partial y_i^j) = 0 \quad (2.7)$$

$$\beta_l(\sum_j x_j^l - c_l) = 0 \;\; \gamma_i(\sum_n t_i^n - T_i) = 0 \;\; \alpha_j(\sum_i y_i^j - S_j) = 0 \quad (2.8)$$

Where λ_j is the Lagrangian multiplier and also the unit price of grid service j. β_l is the Lagrangian multiplier and also the unit price of grid resource l, γ_i is the Lagrangian multiplier of grid user i. The system model presented by (2.4) is a nonlinear optimization problem with N_j decision variables. The resource allocation $\{x_j^l, y_i^j\}$ solves problem G (2.4) if and only if there exist a set of nonnegative shadow costs $\{\lambda_j, \beta_l, \gamma_i\}$ such that equations (2.6)-(2.8).

2.3 Service Market Level Optimization

Resource allocation optimization in computational grid is distributed to and performed at two market levels: grid user agent-grid service agent in service market and grid service agent-grid resource agent in resource market. At two levels, equilibrium prices can be reached and total user benefit can be locally maximized.

Grid User agent maximizes its own surplus given grid service's price policy λ_j and completion time constraint. Grid User agent optimization problem can be written as (2.9).

$$\text{(User)} \quad \begin{aligned} & Max\, U_{user}(u_i^j) \\ & \text{s.t. } T_i \geq \sum_n t_i^n \end{aligned} \quad (2.9)$$

The utility function $U_{user}(u_i^j)$ can be expressed as the following (2.10):

$$U_{user}(u_i^j) = -\sum_j u_i^j - K(\sum_{n=1}^{N} \frac{q_{in} \lambda_j}{u_i^j} - T_i) \quad (2.10)$$

Lagrangian for the user agent' s utility is $L(u)$ (2.11)

$$L(u_i^j) = -\sum_j u_i^j - K(\sum_{n=1}^{N} \frac{q_{in} \lambda_j}{u_i^j} - T_i) + \delta(T_i - \sum_n t_i^n) \quad (2.11)$$

Let $\partial L(u_i^j) / \partial u_i^j = 0$ to obtain (2.12)

$$u_i^j = ((K+\delta) q_{in} \lambda_j)^{1/2} \quad (2.12)$$

We obtain (2.13)

$$u_i^{j*} = (q_{in} \lambda_j)^{1/2} \frac{\sum_{k=1}^{N} (q_{ik} \lambda_k)^{1/2}}{T_i} \quad (2.13)$$

u_i^{j*} is the unique optimal solution to the optimization problem *User*. It means that grid user agent want to pay u_i^{j*} to grid service agent for needed service under completion time constraint.

In service market, grid service agent as a supplier maximizes its benefits; the optimization problem SP can be formulated as follows:

$$\text{(SP)} \quad \begin{array}{l} Max \sum u_i^j \log y_i^j \\ \text{s.t. } S_j \geq \sum_i y_i^j \end{array} \qquad (2.14)$$

In (2.14) y_i^j is the service sold to user agent *i* by service agent *j*. $\sum u_i^j \log y_i^j$ presents the revenue obtained by grid service agent *j* from grid user agents. Grid service agent can't sell service to user agent more than S_j, which is the upper limit of service presented by grid service agent *j*. The Lagrangian for *SP* problem is *L(y)*

$$\begin{aligned} L(y_i^j) &= \sum u_i^j \log y_i^j + \upsilon(S_j - \sum_i y_i^j) \\ &= \sum (u_i^j \log y_i^j - \upsilon y_i^j) + \upsilon S_j \end{aligned} \qquad (2.15)$$

We obtain y_i^{j*} (2.16)

$$y_i^{j*} = \frac{u_i^j S_j}{\sum_{k=1}^{n} u_k^i} \qquad (2.16)$$

y_i^{j*} is the unique optimal solution to the optimization problem *SP*. It means that grid service agent acting as provider want to allocate y_i^{j*} to grid user agent to maximize its revenue.

2.4 Resource Market Level Optimization

In the resource market for a given grid resource pricing policy, the service agent acts as a consumer which pays grid resource agent for available resources. The optimization problem (*SC*) can be written as (2.17).

$$(SC) \quad \begin{array}{l} Max U_{service}(v_j^l) \\ \text{s.t. } M_j^i - m \geq \sum_l v_j^l \end{array} \qquad (2.17)$$

In (2.17) the constraint is a budget constraint, which says that the aggregate sum of all costs of each service agent cannot exceed its budget that is represented by $M_j^i - m$. M_j^i is the money earned by service agent *j* from user agent *i*, $M_j^i = \lambda_j y_i^j$, m is net lest revenue earned by service agent. The utility function $U_{service}(v_j^l)$ can be expressed as the following (2.18):

$$U(v_j^l) = -K(\sum_{l=1}^{N} \frac{\beta_l}{v_j^l} + D) - \sum_l v_j^l \qquad (2.18)$$

The Lagrangian for the service agent is (2. 19).

$$L(v_j^l) = -K(\sum_{l=1}^{N} \frac{\beta_l}{v_j^l} + D) - \sum_l v_j^l - \varepsilon(\sum_l v_j^l - \theta_j^i) \qquad (2.19)$$

We can get (2.20)

$$v_j^l * = \frac{(\beta_l)^{1/2} \theta_j^i}{\sum_{k=1}^{N} \beta_k^{1/2}} = \frac{(\beta_l)^{1/2} (M_j^i - m)}{\sum_{k=1}^{N} \beta_k^{1/2}} \qquad (2.20)$$

v_j^{l*} is the unique optimal solution to the optimization problem *SC*, that is the amount of service agent want to pay to resource agent in the resource market.

In resource market, grid resource agent acts as supplier, its optimization problem can be formulated as follows:

$$(Resource) \quad \begin{array}{l} Max U_{resource} \\ \text{s.t. } c_l \geq \sum_j x_j^l \end{array} \qquad (2.21)$$

The utility function $U_{resource}(v_j^l)$ can be expressed as the following:

$$U_{resource} = \sum v_j^l \log(x_j^l + 1) \qquad (2.22)$$

In (2.22) x_j^l is resource capacity sold to grid service agent *j* by grid resource agent *l*. $\sum v_j^l \log(x_j^l + 1)$ presents the revenue obtained by grid resource agent *l* from grid service agents. The Lagrangian for *Resource* problem is *L(x)*

$$\begin{aligned} L(x_j^l) &= \sum v_j^l \log(x_j^l + 1) + \sigma(c_l - \sum_j x_j^l) \\ &= \sum (v_j^l \log(x_j^l + 1) - \sigma x_j^l) + \sigma c_l \end{aligned}$$

We can get

$$x_j^{l*} = \frac{v_j^l (c_l + n)}{\sum_{k=1}^{n} v_k^l} - 1 \qquad (2.23)$$

x_j^{l*} is the unique optimal solution to the optimization problem *Resource*. It means that grid resource agent allocate x_j^{l*} to grid service agent to maximize its revenue.

3 Distributed Algorithm Descriptions

The iterative algorithm that computes the price and resource allocation is described as follows.

Algorithm 1 Grid resource unit price calculation and resource allocation

Grid user agent at iteration *k*

(1)Receives from the grid service agent *j* the price λ_j which is calculated.

(2)Calculates its optimal service demand according to u_i^{j*} to maximize $U_{user}(u_i^j)$, and compute new service demand.

(3) Communicates new grid service demand $y_j(k+1)$ to grid service agents.

Grid service agent at iteration *k*

(1) Receives grid service demand $y_j(k)$ from grid user agents;

(2) Receives from the grid resource agent *j* the price β_j which is calculated.

(3) Computes a new service price according to the following formula

$$\lambda_j^{(k+1)} = \max\{\varepsilon, \lambda_j^{(k)} + \eta(y_j(k)\lambda_j^{(k)} - S_j)\}$$

Where $\eta > 0$ is a small step size parameter, *k* is iteration step. Let $\varepsilon > 0$ be a sufficiently small constant preventing prices to approach zero. It is consistent with the law of supply and demand: if the demand for grid service exceeds the capacity supply s_j, then the price $\lambda_j^{(k+1)}$ is raised; otherwise, the price is reduced;

(4) Calculates its optimal service demand according to v_i^{j*} to maximize $U_{service}(v_i^j)$, and compute new resource demand by.

(5) Communicates new price $\lambda_j^{(k+1)}$ to all grid service agents.

(6) Communicates new grid resource demand $x_j\ (k+1)$ to grid resource agents.

Grid resource agent at iteration *k*

(1) Receives grid resource demand $x_j(k)$ from grid service agents;

(2) Computes a new resource price according to the following formula

$$\beta_j^{(k+1)} = \max\{\varepsilon, \beta_j^{(k)} + \eta(x^j\ (k)\beta_j^{(k)} - C_j)\}$$

Where $x^j = \sum x_i^j$, if the demand for grid resource exceeds the capacity supply c_j, then the price $\beta_j^{(k+1)}$ is raised; otherwise, the price is reduced;

(3) Communicates new grid resource price $\beta_j^{(k+1)}$ to all grid service agents.

4 SIMULATIONS

This experiment is to study characteristics of price-directed distributed algorithm with Round-Robin algorithm in terms of task completion time and resource allocation efficiency. We use the BRITE generator to setup network topology. We choose the hierarchical topology model. We first generate an AS-level topology consisting of 5 nodes. Each node in the AS-level topology generates a router-level topology of 100 nodes. Therefore, the size of our experimental network is 500 nodes that are divided into four clusters. The nodes in each cluster vary from 30 to 150. The bandwidths of all links are uniformly distributed between 1 and 10 Mbps. Processor capacity varies from 10 to 100 per time unit, each node' computing delay varies from 1 to 20 per time unit. In our experiments the following parameters will be varied: grid nodes' load, the ratio of grid resources to all grid nodes, the network latency. We devise load factor of nodes from 0.05 to 0.9. The ratio of grid resources to all grid nodes is set from 0.01 to 0.5. Network latency varies from 0.001 to 0.1. During the time of experiment, grid resource requests are generated by the grid user agents. After this initial period, the number of tasks that is statistically expected to be generated during an interval of 100 time units is considered in the result. To allow grid task agents to complete tasks, an additional margin of 300 time units is provided. The initial value of the task price denoted by *P* varies from 10 to 300. Each measurement is run 6 times with different seeds. These experimental configurations are to bring up performance of resource allocation algorithm as many as possible. Completion times and resource allocation efficiency are two measurement criteria to measure in the experiment. Completion times measure the time observed by the grid client to access the requested grid resources and complete the task. It is influenced by the size of the grid, the available connections and bandwidth, and processor capacity, and processing delay. Resource allocation efficiency indicates the ratio of accepted grid resource requests to all sent grid resource requests. It is influenced by ratio of grid resources to all grid nodes, network latency, and processor capacity.

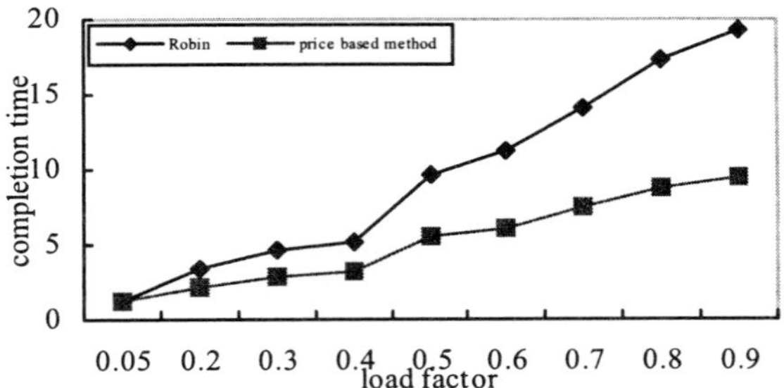

Fig.2 Completion time Vs load factor

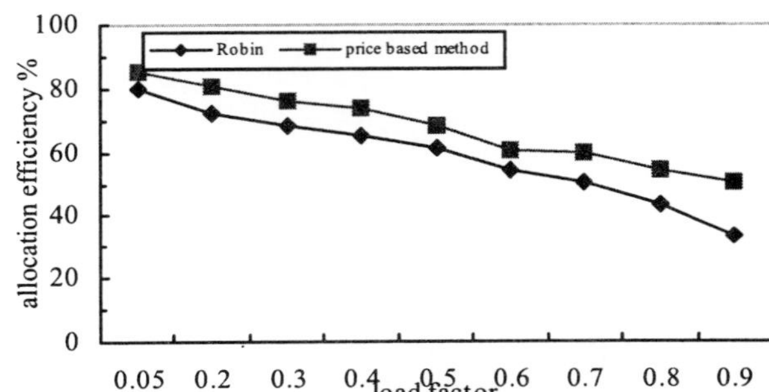

Fig.3 Resource allocation efficiency Vs load factor

First tow experiments are to measure effect of system load on completion times and allocation efficiency respectively. Load factor vary from 0.05 to 0.9. It can be seen from Fig.2 and Fig.3 that Price based strategy has better resource allocation efficiency and use less time to complete tasks when compared to the robin strategy especially at higher loads. Before load factor reach 0.5, two schemes perform well. When load factor reach 0.5, the completion time of Round-Robin increase sharply. After load factor reach 0.5, the completion time using price-directed allocation can be as much as 50% shorter than that using the Round-Robin allocation. The reason is that at low loads, the task entering the grid is less than grid resource available. In such case, the task can be accepted and executed at the same as is submission. However, at higher loads, priced based strategy selects the best available resource for a task, which in this case is the least loaded and therefore the fastest. It helps acquiring higher grid resource utility and revenues. Round-Robin performs worse because resources are allocated arbitrarily.

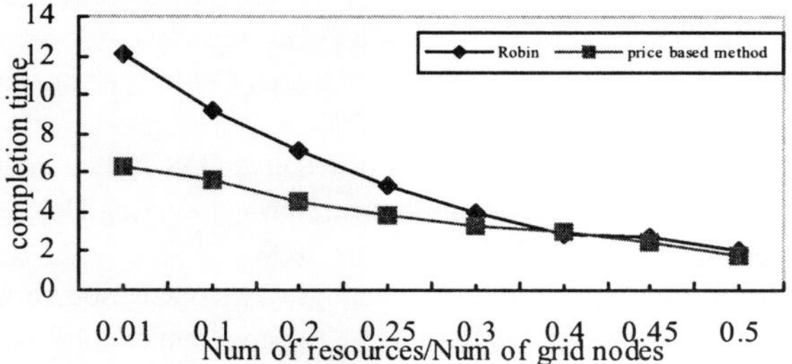

Fig.4 Completion time Vs the ratio of resources to all nodes

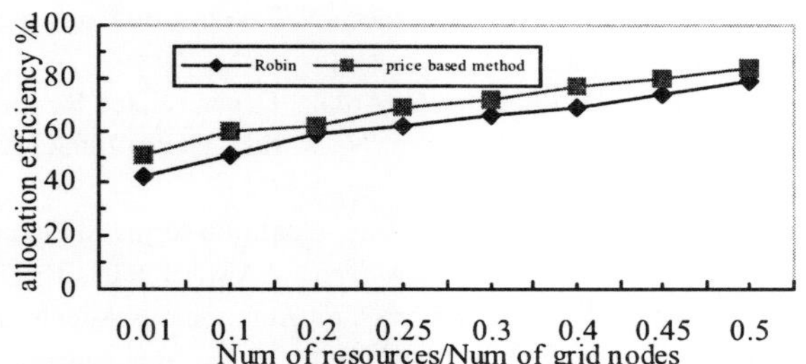

Fig.5 allocation efficiency Vs the ratio of resources to all nodes

The following tow experiments are to measure effect of ratio of grid resources to all grid nodes on completion times and allocation efficiency respectively. The ratio of grid resources to all grid nodes measures the relation of grid resource numbers to the total number of whole grid nodes. For price based allocation and Round-Robin allocation, the mean of the completion time goes down as the ratio of grid resources to all grid nodes is increased. The reason is that more grid resources are offered, less tasks need to wait for resource. As shown in Fig.4, with increasing the value of the ratio, the price-directed allocation outperforms the conventional Round-Robin allocation. Price-directed allocation and Round-Robin allocation present the good results when the value of the ratio is large. But, when the value of the ratio is smaller, Round-Robin allocation is decreasing quickly; the completion time using price-directed allocation can be as much as 30% shorter than that using the Round-Robin allocation. Round-Robin allocation takes more time to allocate appropriate resources. From the results in Fig.5, when the ratio of grid resources to all grid nodes is low, Resource allocation efficiency using price-directed allocation is as much as 11% larger than that using the Round-Robin allocation. With increasing the value of the ratio, price-directed allocation performs better than Round-Robin.

5 CONCLUSIONS

This paper presents a multi economic agent interaction scheme for resource allocation in computational grid. The proposed competitive market economy is described. It consists of three different types of agents: grid user agent, grid resource agents, grid service agents; and a two level grid market that is composed of a service market which regulates the prices based on benefits of service agent and user agent, and a resource market which is charged for service agent and resource agent. In order to solve the problem of heterogeneity in the grid, grid users' preferences and benefits of grid service provider and grid resource agent are summarized by means of their utility functions. This paper is target to solve resource allocation by using utility-based optimization scheme. We decompose the optimization problem into two levels of sub problems so that the computational complexity can be reduced.

ACKNOWLEDGMENTS

The work is supported by national Natural Science Foundation of China under grants (60402028), NSF of Hubei Province under grants (2003ABA041) and Wuhan Younger Dawning Foundation (20045006071-15).

References

[1] I. Foster and C. Kesselman, The Grid: Blueprint for a New Computing Infrastructure, Morgan Kaufmann, 1999.

[2] S. Chapin, J. Karpovich, A. Grimshaw. The legion resource management system. In: Proc. of the 5th Workshop on Job Scheduling Strategies for Parallel Processing, Springer Verlag, 1999, 162~178

[3] H. Casanova, G. Obertelli, F. Berman et al. The AppLeS parameter sweep template: User-level middleware for the grid. In: Proc. of Super Computing, Springer Verlag, 2000, 75~76

[4] The Gridbus Project: http://www.gridbus.org

[5] R. Wolski, J. Plank, J. Brevik, and T. Bryan, Analyzing Market-based Resource Allocation Strategies for the Computational Grid, International Journal of High-performance Computing Applications, Sage Publications, 2001,Vol 15(3), 258-281

[6] Li Chunlin, Li Layuan, Integrate Software Agents And CORBA In Computational Grid, Journal of Computer Standard and Interface, Elsevier, Vol 25/4, pp. 357-371, August, 2003

[7] Li Chunlin, Zhengding Lu, Li Layuan, Apply Market Mechanism to Agent-Based Grid Resource Management, International Journal of Software Engineering & Knowledge Engineering, World Scientific Publishing, Vol. 13/ 3, pp. 327-340, June, 2003

[8] Li Chunlin, Li Layuan, The Use Of Economic Agents Under Price Driven Mechanism In Grid Resource Management, Journal of Systems Architecture, Elsevier, Vol50/9, pp. 521-535,

September, 2004

[9] F. Kelly, A. Maulloo, and D. Tan. Rate control for communication networks: shadow prices, proportional fairness and stability. J. of Operational Res. Soc., 49(3):237–252, 1998.

[10] S. H. Low and D. E. Lapsley. Optimization flow control, I: Basic algorithm and convergence. IEEE/ACM Transactions on Networking, 7(6): 861–874, 1999.

[11] F. P. Kelly, Charging and Rate Control for Elastic Traffic, European Trans. on Telecommunications, vol. 8, pp. 33–37, 1997.

[12]J. Gomoluch and M. Schroeder.Market-based Resource Allo cation for Grid Computing: A Model and Simulation, 1st Interna tional Workshop on Middleware for Grid Computing (MGC200 3), Rio de Janeiro, Brazil, June 2003.

[13]Yuan Xue, Baochun Li, Klara Nahrstedt. Price-based Reso urce Allocation in Wireless Ad Hoc Networks, in the Proceedin gs of the Eleventh International Workshop on Quality of Service (IWQoS 2003), Lecture Notes in Computer Science, Springer Verlag, Vol. 2707, pp. 79-96, Monterey, CA, June 2-4, 2003.

[14]Yi Cui, Yuan Xue, Klara Nahrstedt, Optimal Resource Allo cation in Overlay Multicast, Proc. of IEEE ICNP 2003, Novem ber 2003.

[15]Nan Feng, Siun-Chuon Mau, and Narayan B. Mandayam, P ricing and Power Control for Joint Network-Centric and User-C entric Radio Resource Management, CISS'2002, Princeton, NJ, March, 2002

[16] D. Bertsekas, Nonlinear Programming, 2nd ed., Athena Scientific, 1999.

[17] C. U. Saraydar, N. B. Mandayam, and D. J. Goodman, Efficient power control via pricing in wireless data networks, IEEE Trans. Commun., vol. 50, no. 2, pp. 291–303, Feb 2002.

[18]H. Yaiche, R. Mazumdar, and C. Rosenberg, A Game Theor etic Framework for Bandwidth Allocation and Pricing in Broad band Networks, IEEE/ACM Transactions on networking, Vol8/5,pp: 667 – 678, October 2000.

[19] R. Buyya, D. Abramson, J. Giddy, Nimrod/G: An Architecture for a Resource Management and Scheduling System in a Global Computational Grid, International Conference on High Performance Computing in Asia-Pacific Region (HPC Asia 2000), Beijing, China. IEEE Computer Society Press, USA, 2000.

[20] H. Jiang, Scott Jordarn, A Pricing Model for High Speed Networks with Guaranteed Quality of Service, *IEEE InfoCom*, March 1996, pp. 888-895.

[21] R. Buyya, J. Giddy, D. Abramson, A Case for Economy Grid Architecture for Service-Oriented Grid Computing, 10th IEEE International Heterogeneous Computing Workshop (HCW 2001), In conjunction with IPDPS 2001, San Francisco, California, USA, April 2001.

[22] Carsten Ernemann, Economic Scheduling in Grid Computing. In Proc of 8th International Workshop Job Scheduling Strategies for Parallel Processing, Lecture Notes in Computer Science, UK, July 24, 2002,128-152

[23] Richard J. La and V. Anantharam, Utility-based rate control in the Internet for elastic traffic, IEEE/ACM Trans. on Networking, vol. 10, no. 2, pp. 272–286, 2002.

[24]Jonathan Bredin, Rajiv T. Maheswaran, Cagri Imer ,A Gam e-Theoretic Formulation of Multi-Agent Resource Allocation. I n Proceedings of the Fourth International Conference on Autono mous Agents, Barcelona, May, 2000

[25] Li Layuan, Li Chunlin, A distributed QoS-Aware multicast routing protocol, Acta Informatica, Springer-Verlag Heidelberg, Vol 40/3, pp. 211 – 233,November 2003

[26]M. A. Gibney and N. R. Jennings, Dynamic Resource Alloc ation by Market-Based Routing in Telecommunications Networ ks, Proc. 2nd Int. Workshop on Multi-Agent Systems and Telec ommunications (IATA-98), Paris, France, 102-117,1998

[27] O. Ercetin, L. Tassiulas, Market Based Resource Allocation for Content Delivery in the Internet, IEEE Trans. on Computers, Vol 52 /12, Dec 2003

[28]T. Eymann, M. Reinicke, O. Ardaiz, Decentralized Resourc e Allocation in Application Layer Networks,CCGrid'2003, May, 12th-15th, 2003. Tokyo, Japan.

[29]R. T. Maheswaran and T. Basar. Coalition formation in pro portionally fair divisible auctions. Proc. AAMAS 2003, The Se cond International Joint Conference on Autonomous Agents and Multi Agent Systems, July 14-18, 2003, Melbourne, Australia.

[30] Scott Jordan, Pricing of Buffer and Bandwidth in a Reservation-Based QoS Architecture, IEEE International Conference on Communications,ICC'03, Ancourage, Alaska, May 2003, pp. 1521- 1525

Two-tier Resource Allocation for Slowdown Differentiation on Server Clusters

Xiaobo Zhou Yu Cai C. Edward Chow Marijke Augusteijn
Department of Computer Science
University of Colorado at Colorado Springs, CO 80933, USA
Corresponding author: Xiaobo Zhou, zbo@cs.uccs.edu

Abstract

Slowdown, defined as the ratio of a request's queueing delay to its service time, is accepted as an important quality of service metric of Internet servers. In this paper, we investigate the problem of providing proportional slowdown differentiation (PSD) services to various applications and clients on cluster-based Internet servers. We extend a closed-form expression of the expected slowdown of a popular Internet workload model with a typical heavy-tailed service time distribution from a single server mode to a server cluster mode. Based on the closed-form expression, we design a two-tier resource allocation approach, which integrates a dispatcher-based node partitioning scheme and a server-based dynamic process allocation scheme. We evaluate the two-tier resource allocation approach via extensive simulations and compare it with an one-tier node partitioning approach. Simulation results show that the two-tier approach can provide fine-grained PSD services on cluster-based Internet servers. We implement the two-tier approach on a cluster testbed. Experimental results further demonstrate the feasibility of the approach in practice.

1 Introduction

Due to the openness and dynamics of the Internet, the past few years have seen an increasing demand for provisioning of different levels of quality of service (QoS) to meet changing system configuration and resource availability and to satisfy different application and client requirements [3, 4, 10, 13, 16, 18, 19, 20]. A desirable property of an Internet server is that a request's queueing delay depends on its service time in a linear fashion [8]. For example, a request for a job twice as long as some others will spend time on the average twice as long in the server. Performance metric slowdown, defined as the ratio of a request's queueing delay to its service time, reflects this need. Both queueing delay and response time are major performance metrics on the server side. But they are not suitable to compare requests that have very different resource demands. Actually, clients are likely to anticipate short delays for "small" requests, and are willing to tolerate long delays for "large" requests [6]. A high slowdown also indicates the system is heavily loaded. Slowdown or its variant is being used as a fundamental performance metric in recently designed QoS-aware systems [2, 6]. For instance, in [6], the author proposed a task assignment mechanism for dispatching tasks with heavy-tailed size distribution to hosts of a cluster to minimize the mean slowdown of the jobs. Although the size-based QoS-aware resource management is able to ensure that small requests experience small slowdowns, none of the systems can guarantee quantitative quality spacings among request classes in terms of slowdown.

The proportional differentiation model [4] states that QoS metrics of certain classes of aggregated requests should be proportional to their differentiation parameters, independent of their workloads. It is accepted as an important relative Differentiated Services model [11] and is applied in the proportional delay and loss rate differentiation in packet forwarding and dropping [4, 7]. It is also adopted for server-side service differentiation [10, 18, 19]. We proposed a proportional slowdown differentiation (PSD) model on individual Internet servers [18]. Its objective is to maintain slowdown ratios between request classes according to their pre-specified differentiation parameters. In this paper, we investigate the problem of provisioning PSD services on cluster-based Internet servers.

The cluster-based network services are increasingly deployed on the Internet due to the inherent scalability and cost-effectiveness of cluster architectures. A server cluster also provides a new resource allocation granularity, server node, for service differentiation. We design a two-tier resource allocation approach for PSD services provisioning. Figure 1 depicts its infrastructure. Tier-1 scheme is to dynamically partition the server nodes into a number of sets (called sub-clusters). Differentiation priorities assigned to classes are observed by providing differentiated processing rates with node partitioning. One sub-cluster handles one request class in FCFS discipline. To provide fine-grained

0190-3918/05 $20.00 © 2005 IEEE

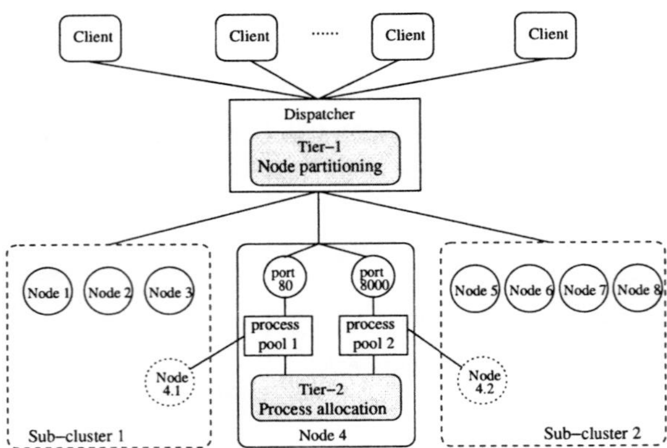

Figure 1. Two-tier resource allocation.

PSD services, one node or multiple nodes may have to be shared by different classes. Tier-2 scheme is to dynamically allocate resource units on an individual server, processes, to handle requests of different classes. Figure 1 shows a two-class differentiation scenario, where a node is shared between two classes by tier-2 resource allocation.

The problem of provisioning PSD services on cluster-based Internet servers is important, because 1) the proportional model is a widely accepted differentiation model; 2) slowdown is a key QoS metric on the server side; and 3) cluster is a popular and scalable platform. It is challenging because in order to meet the need of quantitative differentiation, a closed-form expression of expected slowdown with respect to resource allocation on a server cluster is required. The tier-1 and tier-2 resource allocation schemes must be integrated to provide fine-grained PSD services. We are concerned with the scenario where the interarrivals meet Poisson distribution and the workload is heavy-tailed, in specific, meeting a bounded Pareto distribution as it is characteristic of many empirically measured Internet workloads [1, 6]. The workload is referred to as an $M/G_P/1$ model. We extend the expected slowdown expression in a closed analytic form from a single server mode to a server cluster mode. Based on the closed-form expression, we design the two-tier resource allocation approach for PSD provisioning on a server cluster. We build a simulation model to evaluate the differentiation predictability and controllability of the approach. We further implement the two-tier resource allocation approach on a cluster testbed to verify the feasibility of the approach in practice.

The structure of the paper is as follows. Section 2 reviews related works. Section 3 gives the slowdown expression for an $M/G_P/1$ workload on a server cluster. Section 4 presents the two-tier resource allocation approach. Section 5 focuses on the performance evaluation. Section 6 presents the design and implementation issues. Section 7 concludes the paper with remarks on future work.

2 Related Work

The proportional differentiation model has been extensively studied in packet scheduling with respect to packet delay, packet loss, and connection bandwidth; see [4, 7, 15] for representative approaches. The work in [10] demonstrated that some approaches developed for proportional delay differentiation (PDD) on networks can be tailored for PDD provisioning on Internet servers. However, those approaches are not applicable to PSD provisioning because slowdown is not only dependent on a job's queueing delay but also on its service time, which varies significantly depending on the requested services [18]. There are efforts on priority-based request scheduling with admission control for response time differentiation [3, 14]. Incoming requests were categorized into the appropriate queues and executed according to their strict priority levels [3] or adaptive priority levels [14]. The results showed that higher priority classes receive less response time than lower classes. However, the quality spacings between classes cannot be quantitatively guaranteed. In [18], we proposed a processing rate allocation strategy for PSD provisioning on individual Internet servers. We used virtual servers in performance simulation. In this paper, we extend the slowdown modeling from a single-server mode to a server-cluster mode. We further design and implement a two-tier application-level approaches for providing fine-grained PSD services.

In [20], stretch factor, a variant of slowdown, was adopted as the performance metric for differentiation provisioning in a server cluster. The work adopted an $M/M/1$ queueing model to guide dispatcher-based node partitioning optimization. The work implicitly applied processor sharing discipline for the modeling of stretch factor. However, in a single queue, a realistic scheduling discipline is FCFS. More importantly, recent Internet workload measurements indicate that for many Internet applications the exponential distribution is a poor model for service time distribution and that a heavy-tailed distribution is more accurate [1, 6].

In [13], the authors proposed and designed a sound integrated resource management framework that provides flexible service quality specification, efficient resource utilization, and service differentiation for cluster-based Internet services. The work introduced an interesting metric, quality-aware service yield, to combine the overall system efficiency and individual service response time in one model. As the work in [20], it chose exponentially distributed arrival intervals and service times for modeling and performance evaluation. In this paper, we investigate the problem of PSD provisioning with a popular heavy-tailed traffic pattern. Simulation aside, we also design and implement the two-tier resource allocation approach on a cluster testbed to verify its feasibility in practice.

3 Slowdown Modeling on a Server Cluster

Predictability and controllability are two basic requirements of service differentiation. Predictability requires that higher priority classes receive better or no worse service quality than lower priority classes, independent of the class load conditions. Controllability requires that a scheduler contain a number of controllable parameters that are adjustable for the control of quality spacings between classes. For quantitatively predictable and controllable differentiation, we need to have a closed form expression of slowdown with respect to resource allocation on cluster-based servers. We consider a popular heavy-tailed distribution, bounded Pareto distribution, for modeling service time distribution on Internet workload characteristics [1, 6]. The bounded Pareto distribution with respect to job size x is characterized by three parameters: α, the shape parameter; k, the shortest possible job; and p, the upper bound of jobs. As in [6], the probability density function is defined as:

$$f(x) = \frac{1}{1-(k/p)^\alpha}\alpha k^\alpha x^{-\alpha-1} \qquad \alpha, k > 0, k \leq x \leq p.$$

Since α, k, and p are parameters of the bounded Pareto distribution, we define a function $\mathcal{K}(\alpha,k,p) = \frac{\alpha k^\alpha}{1-(k/p)^\alpha}$. The probability density function $f(x)$ is rewritten as:

$$f(x) = x^{-\alpha-1}\mathcal{K}(\alpha,k,p) \qquad \alpha, k > 0, k \leq x \leq p. \quad (1)$$

From (1), we have:

$$\begin{aligned} E[X] &= \int_k^p f(x)x\,dx \\ &= \begin{cases} \frac{\mathcal{K}(\alpha,k,p)}{\mathcal{K}(\alpha-1,k,p)} & \text{if} \quad \alpha \neq 1; \\ (\ln p - \ln k)\mathcal{K}(\alpha,k,p) & \text{if} \quad \alpha = 1. \end{cases} \quad (2) \\ E[X^2] &= \int_k^p f(x)x^2\,dx = \frac{\mathcal{K}(\alpha,k,p)}{\mathcal{K}(\alpha-2,k,p)}. \quad (3) \\ E[X^{-1}] &= \int_k^p f(x)x^{-1}\,dx = \frac{\mathcal{K}(\alpha,k,p)}{\mathcal{K}(\alpha+1,k,p)}. \quad (4) \end{aligned}$$

According to Pollaczek-Khinchin formula [8], we derived a closed-form expression of the expected slowdown in an $M/G_P/1$ workload on a single Internet server [18]. That is, let W be a job's queueing delay, and S be a job's slowdown, we have

$$E[S] = E[W] \cdot E[X^{-1}] = \frac{\lambda E[X^2]E[X^{-1}]}{2(1-\lambda E[X])}, \quad (5)$$

where the arrival process has rate λ and X denotes the bounded Pareto service time density distribution on the server. The slowdown formula follows from the fact that W and X are independent from a FCFS queue where requests of a class are processed by using FCFS discipline.

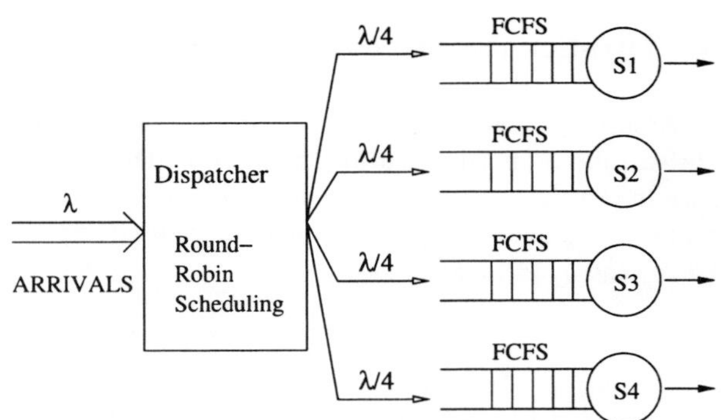

Figure 2. Round-Robin dispatching.

In the following, we further extend the closed-form expression of slowdown from the single-server mode to the server-cluster mode. Figure (2) illustrates a typical dispatching scheme, Round-Robin, which is one of the task assignment policies commonly proposed and deployed in clusters of servers [5, 9]. Jobs are assigned to hosts in a cyclical fashion with the kth job being assigned to Host $k mod m$, where m is the number of servers in the cluster. The policy equalizes the expected number of jobs at each host. There are other popular task dispatching disciplines, including Random, Shortest-Queue, and Least-Work-Remaining. We consider Round-Robin here because simplicity is an important property of any load-sharing scheme, as concluded by Eager *et al.* in [5] when they studied three approaches to load sharing in distributed servers. Relatively high overheads can outweigh the advantages of more complex schemes. Note that we do not want to compare different schemes for load sharing in this work. Like the Least-Work-Remaining task assignment scheme deployed in [6], Round-Robin scheme is also not applicable in the stateful e-Commerce applications while locality-aware request routing mechanisms support the session integrity [12]. As previous work in [6, 18], our work considers stateless jobs in the differentiation. When using Round-Robin dispatching policy, the arrival process at each server in the cluster has rate λ/m.

According to (5), we have

Lemma 1. *Given an $M/G_P/1$ queue on a cluster of m homogeneous FCFS servers, where λ denotes the arrival rate and X denotes the bounded Pareto service time density distribution on any of the servers. Let S_j be a job's slowdown on an individual server j ($1 \leq j \leq m$). By the use of Round-Robin task assignment on the dispatcher, the expected slowdown $E[S_j]$ is calculated as*

$$E[S_j] = \frac{\lambda E[X^2]E[X^{-1}]}{2(m-\lambda E[X])} \qquad 1 \leq j \leq m. \quad (6)$$

4 Two-tier Resource Allocation

Assuming incoming requests are classified into N classes, the proportional differentiation model aims to ensure the quality spacing between class i and class j to be proportional to certain pre-specified differentiation parameters δ_i and δ_j [4]; that is,

$$\frac{q_i}{q_j} = \frac{\delta_i}{\delta_j} \qquad 1 \leq i, j \leq N,$$

where q_i and q_j are the QoS factors of class i and class j, respectively. The PSD model aims to control the ratios of the average slowdown of classes based on their differentiation parameters $\{\delta_i, i = 1, \ldots, N\}$. Specifically, the PSD model requires that the ratio of average slowdown between class i and j is fixed to the ratio of the corresponding differentiation parameters

$$\frac{E[S_i]}{E[S_j]} = \frac{\delta_i}{\delta_j} \qquad 1 \leq i, j \leq N. \tag{7}$$

The differentiation predictability property requires that higher classes receive better service, i.e., lower slowdown. Without loss of generality, we assume class 1 is the "highest class" and set $0 < \delta_1 < \delta_2 < \ldots < \delta_N$.

Let M be the number of servers in the cluster and m_i be the number of server nodes assigned to a sub-cluster for processing the requests of class i. Then, we have

$$\sum_{i=1}^{N} m_i = M \qquad 0 < m_i \leq M\,. \tag{8}$$

For feasible resource allocation, we must ensure the system utilization constraint $\sum_{i=1}^{N} \lambda_i E[X] < M$. That is, the total processing requirement of the N classes of traffic is less than the processing capacity of the cluster.

According to Lemma 1, the set of (7), in combination with the constraint (8), lead to a linear equation system. It follows

$$m_i = \lambda_i E[X] + \frac{\tilde{\lambda}_i (M - E[X] \sum_{i=1}^{N} \lambda_i)}{\sum_{i=1}^{N} \tilde{\lambda}_i} \tag{9}$$

where $\tilde{\lambda}_i = \lambda_i/\delta_i$, the normalized arrival rate. The first term of (9) ensures that the sub-cluster allocated for handling requests of the corresponding class will not be overloaded. The second term means that the remaining capacity of the cluster is proportionally allocated to different classes according to their scaled arrival rates with respect to their differentiation parameters.

Lemma 1 assumes a round-robin task assignment among the homogeneous servers in a sub-cluster. According to (9), the number of servers in a sub-cluster is often not an integer. For example, in a two-class 8-node scenario, the calculated m_1 and m_2 by (9) could be 3.4 and 4.6, respectively. The tier-1 dispatching mechanism adopts a weighted round-robin (WRR) scheduling discipline to assign incoming requests of a class to servers of its corresponding sub-cluster. For instance, the weight to four servers of sub-cluster 1 is 1, 1, 1, and 0.4. The weight to five servers of sub-cluster 2 is 1, 1, 1, 1, and 0.6. The tier-2 resource allocation mechanism aims to achieve proportional resource sharing on the shared server. It dynamically changes the number of processes allocated to process pools for handling different request classes according to changing workloads while ensuring the ratio of resource allocations [17].

According to Lemma 1, the expected slowdown of class i, $E[S_i]$, is calculated as:

$$E[S_i] = \frac{\delta_i E[X^2] E[X^{-1}] \sum_{i=1}^{N} \tilde{\lambda}_i}{2(M - E[X] \sum_{i=1}^{N} \lambda_i)}. \tag{10}$$

5 Performance Evaluation

5.1 Simulation Model

In this section, we investigate the impact of the two-tier resource allocation approach on proportional slowdown differentiation in a server cluster. We built a simulator which consisted of a number of request generators, waiting queues, an arrival rate predictor, a request dispatcher, and a number of servers. Figure 3 outlines its structure. The arrival rate predictor estimated a class's workload every sampling period. A sampling period was set to the processing time of one thousand requests of mean job size. A moving window with window size of five sampling periods was adopted for workload prediction. The tier-1 node partitions and tier-2 process allocations were calculated according to (9). In the cluster, some servers were dedicated to handling requests from a specific request class, while some others were shared by multiple request classes. The dispatcher used WRR scheduling discipline to assign incoming requests to corresponding sub-clusters. In each of the shared servers, a number of task servers was simulated to handle requests of corresponding classes. As in [20], we compare the two-tier approach with an one-tier approach that relies on dynamic node partitioning but there is no tier-2 process allocation module. Another node partitioning approach is to assign a fixed number of servers to each class. The partitioning is static and obviously it cannot adapt to fluctuating workload conditions. Such kind of static node partitioning approaches cannot achieve proportional slowdown differentiation when workload is changing. Thus, it is omitted here.

The request generators produced requests with exponential interarrival distributions and bounded Pareto size distributions by using GNU scientific library. Each request was dispatched to a server (or a task server) and was processed

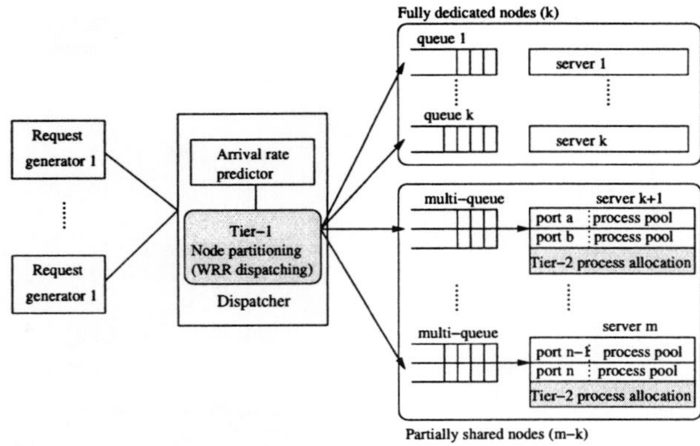

Figure 3. Structure of the simulation model.

using FCFS discipline. In the simulation, different traffic classes may have different arrival rates. But they have the same job size distribution [18]. In the following, we first study the effectiveness of the two-tier resource allocation in achieving proportional slowdown differentiation in long term. Simulation parameters were set as follows. The shape parameter (α) of the bounded Pareto distribution was set to 1.5 as suggested in [4]. The lower bound (k) and upper bound (p) were set to 0.1 and 100, respectively [6]. The number of servers in the cluster was 8. We then conduct the sensitivity study of the approaches with respect to their short-term behaviors, differentiation variances, and the impact of the number of nodes in the cluster on differentiation performance.

5.2 Effectiveness of the Two-tier Approach

In the service differentiation context, the number of classes is limited, which is normally two or three [11, 20]. We first examine the slowdown differentiation due to two resource allocation approaches, *i.e.,* two-tier and one-tier, by the use of a two-class workload. Figure 4 depicts average slowdown ratios with the 95% confidence intervals at different workload conditions. The target slowdown ratios between two classes $\delta_b : \delta_a$ is $2 : 1$. It shows that the achieved slowdown ratios due to two resource allocation approaches are always larger than 1, which means that the differentiated services are always predictable. That is, high priority classes receive better or "no worse" services than lower priority classes. The figure also shows that the two-tier approach achieves desirable proportionality of slowdown differentiation at various workload conditions. On the other hand, the one-tier approach based on node partitioning observes frequent and large slowdown ratio oscillations. This is because the node partitions calculated by (9) are rounded to integer numbers. The lack of tier-2 process allocation mechanism results in coarse-grained slowdown differentiation.

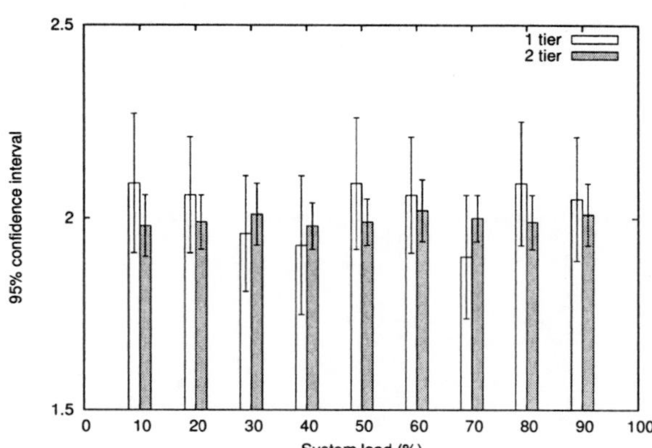

Figure 4. Two-class differentiation.

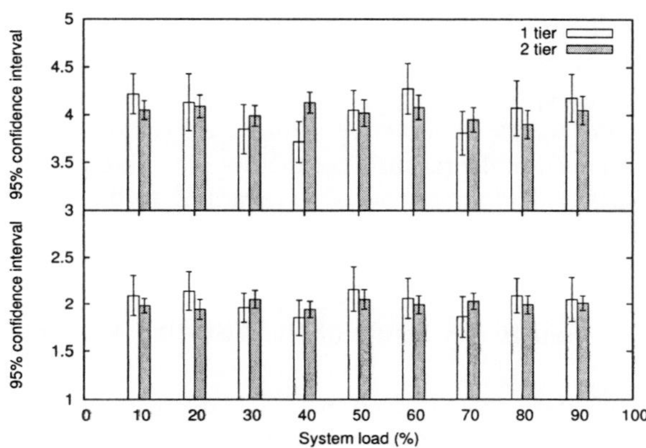

Figure 5. Three-class differentiation.

Figure 4 also shows that the two-tier approach significantly outperforms the one-tier approach not only in terms of the mean slowdown ratio, but in terms of the size of the confidence intervals. This demonstrates the robustness of the two-tier approach.

We then investigate the differentiation problem by the use of a three-class workload. Figure 5 depicts the achieved slowdown ratios with the 95% confidence intervals at different system workload conditions. The target slowdown ratios among three classes $\delta_c : \delta_b : \delta_a$ is $4 : 2 : 1$. In the case of three-class scenarios, a server may be shared by more than two classes and more than one server may be shared by multiple classes. From the figure, we can observe that the two-tier can achieve desirable proportionality of slowdown differentiation with respect to both the mean slowdown ratio and the size of confidence intervals.

In the simulation above, the arrival rate ratios of classes (A to B in the two-class scenario, and A to B to C in the three-class scenario) were set to be the same as their differentiation weight ratios. We conducted a wide ranger of

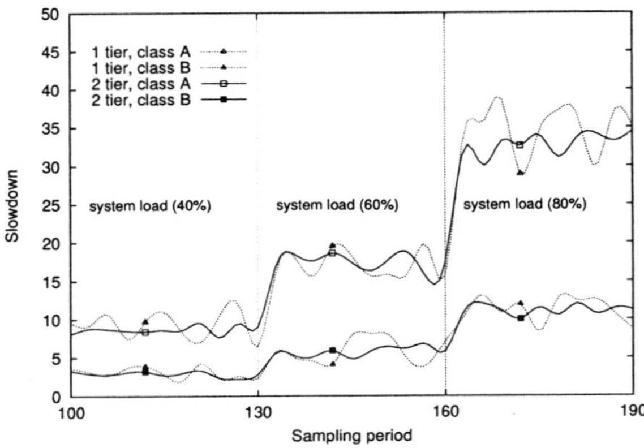

Figure 6. A short-term view of slowdown.

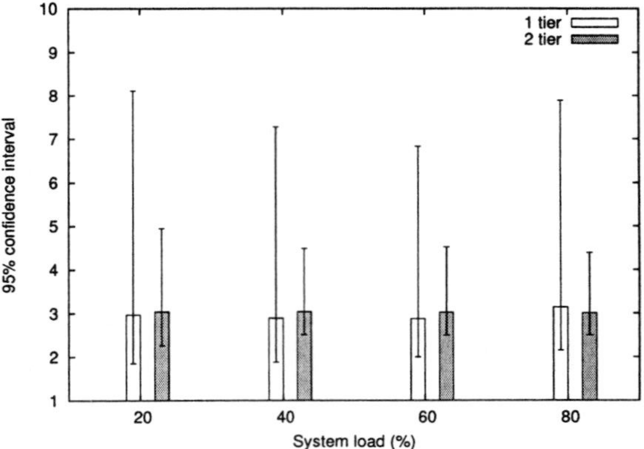

Figure 7. Variance of the proportionality.

sensitivity analyses. We varied the arrival rate ratios of the classes and the differentiation weight ratios of the classes. As it is expected, the proportional differentiation is independent of workload of classes. While we do not have space to present all of the results, note that we did not reach any significantly different conclusion regarding to the slowdown differentiation proportionality achieved by the two-tiered resource allocation approach.

5.3 Sensitivity Study of the Two-tier Approach

We have demonstrated that the two-tier resource allocation approach can achieve desirable proportional slowdown differentiation in long term with respect to the mean slowdown ratios. Now we want to investigate the sensitivity of the approach under different workload conditions. We conducted simulation using a two-class workload with target slowdown ratio $\delta_b : \delta_a = 3 : 1$. Figure 6 shows a short-term view of the slowdown of requests of the two classes in the sampling periods due to the two resource allocation approaches, when the system workload is low (40%), moderate (60%), and high (80%), respectively. The simulation was run for 100 sampling periods for warming up and then the data was collected for 30 sampling periods at each of three workload conditions. Obviously, we can observe that the two-tier approach achieves more consistent differentiation results during different sampling periods at various workload conditions.

Figure 7 further quantitatively depicts the variance of the differentiation proportionality due to the two approaches. At each of the four workload conditions (20%, 40%, 60%, 80%), we conducted simulations using a two-class workload with the target slowdown ratio $\delta_b : \delta_a = 3 : 1$. The upper line is the 95th percentile; the bar is the mean; and the lower line is the 5th percentile. We can observe that the two-tier approach can significantly reduce the variance generated by the one-tier approach. For example, when the workload is 40%, difference between the 95th and the 5th percentile is 1.98 and 5.4, and the mean is 3.04 and 2.89, due to the two-tier approach and the one-tier approach, respectively. At 80% workload condition, the difference between 5th and 95th is 1.89 and 5.74, and the mean is 3.01 and 3.14, due to the two-tier approach and the one-tier approach, respectively. The better proportionality in terms of the mean slowdown ratio has already been depicted by Figures (4) and (5). It is the small variance degree that further justifies the superiority of the two-tier resource allocation approach. We can conclude that the tier-2 process allocation mechanism deployed at the shared servers significantly contributes to the small variance degree of the proportional slowdown differentiation.

Figure 8 depicts the achieved mean slowdown ratio with the 95% confidence intervals due to two approaches when the number of servers in the cluster varies from 4 up to 20. Obviously, the performance of the two-teir approach is almost not affected by the number of nodes. On the other hand, the performance of the one-tier approach improves as the number of nodes in the cluster increases. This can be explained by the fact that as the number of nodes increases, the node partitioning itself can achieve finer granularity of resource allocation. It is obvious as the number of nodes goes up to infinity, there is no need to have the tier-2 process allocation mechanism.

6 Design and Implementation

We implemented the two-tier resource allocation approach on a Linux 2.6 system. The cluster testbed consists of four machines (PIII 600MHz, 256MB RAM) as request generators, one machine (PIII 1GHz, 516MB RAM) as the dispatcher of the cluster, and eight machines (PIII 600MHz, 256MB RAM) as cluster nodes. The machines are connected with 100Mbps Ethernet.

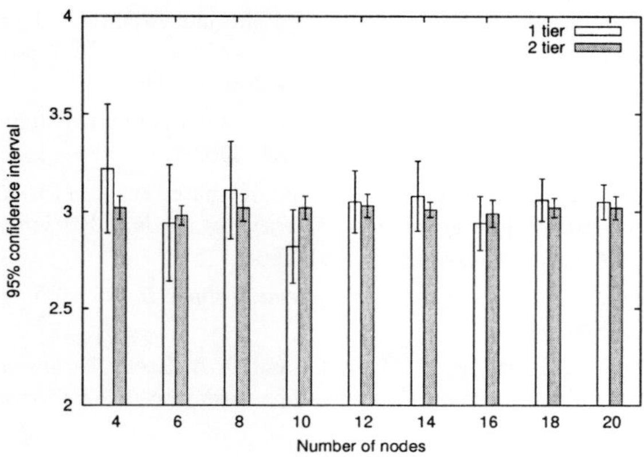

Figure 8. Impact of the number nodes on PSD.

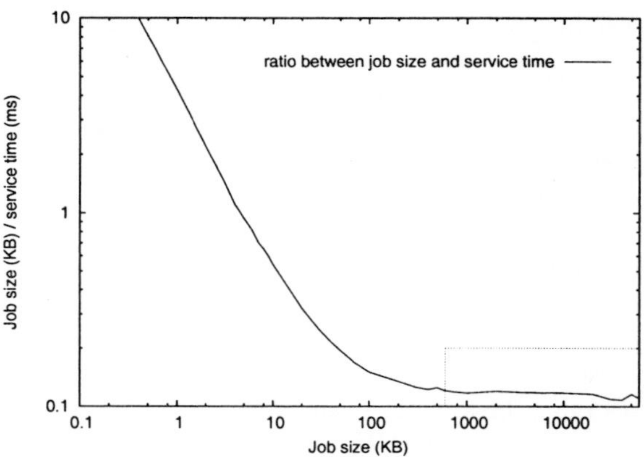

Figure 9. Service time vs. job size.

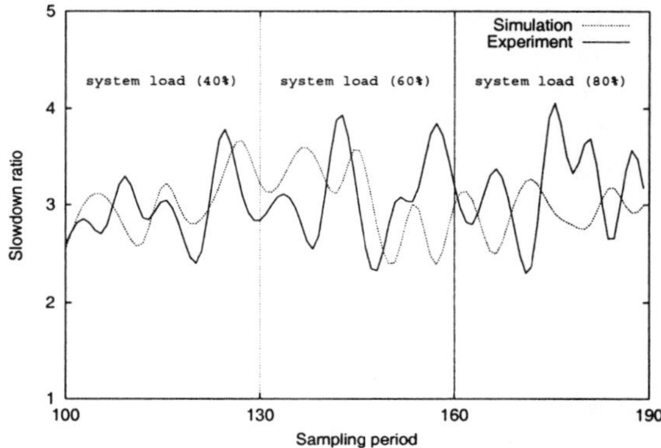

Figure 10. Experiment vs. simulation results.

We used enhanced Httperf to generate Http requests for a $M/G_P/1$ workload. We modified the Linux Virtual Server for the request dispatcher. In the dispatcher, a classifier module determines a request's class type according to its header information (e.g., port number). A node allocation module obtains the arrival rate of each class and calculates the node partitions according to (9). The dispatcher then assigns requests belonging to the same class to the cluster nodes in the corresponding sub-cluster using the weighted round-robin scheduling discipline. We deployed Apache Web Server 1.3.29 on each cluster node. The cluster nodes process the incoming Http requests, record their response time, and calculate the achieved slowdown. In a two-class scenario, one node may be shared by two classes. Note that every child process in Apache Web server is considered to be identical. We implemented an application-level dynamic process allocation approach on the shared node so as to achieve the fractional node partitions by controlling the number of child processes that a class is allocated. We also implemented several TCP/IP socket programs on the dispatcher and on the cluster nodes so that they can exchange information such as node partitions and achieved average slowdown on each node.

The implementation requires that the workload to meet the $M/G_P/1$ model, *i.e.*, the Poison distribution of arrival time and the bounded Pareto distribution of service time. In the simulation, service time of a request is often assumed to be proportional to the size of the requested job. However, in reality, the service time of a job is often not strictly linear to its size. Figure 9 depicts the relationship between the service time of a job on a cluster node and its size. We observed that when the job size is between 500 KB to 60 MB, the ratio between the job size and the service time is nearly linear. Therefore, we used the files in that size range to generate the $M/G_P/1$ workload in the experiment.

Figure 10 depicts the achieved slowdown ratio due to the two-tier resource allocation approach by simulation and by experiment based on the implementation, respectively. It shows the differentiation results of a two-class workload with target slowdown ratio ($\delta_b : \delta_a = 3 : 1$) when the system workload is low (40%), moderate (60%), and high (80%), respectively. Compared to the results due to the simulation, the experiment based on the implementation observes larger slowdown ratio oscillations and scales. This is explained by the fact that the generated workload in the experiment does not strictly meet the $M/G_P/1$ model. However, the experiment results overall are still around the target ratio. This demonstrates the feasibility of the two-tier resource allocation approach in achieving cluster-based PSD services in practice.

7 Conclusion

Slowdown is an important performance metric on Internet servers because it takes into account both the delay and the service time of a request simultaneously. There are few research work for proportional slowdown differentiation (PSD) services on the server side, while proportional delay differentiation has been studied extensively both on the network side and on the server side. In this paper, based on a popular Internet traffic model with a typical heavy-tailed service time distribution, we extended a closed form expression of the expected slowdown from a single server mode to a server cluster mode using a simple and scalable weighted round-robin scheduling discipline on the dispatcher. we designed a two-tier resource allocation approach to provide PSD services in a server cluster. Simulation results have shown that the approach can achieve the PSD services on cluster-based servers. We also implemented the approach in a cluster testbed. Experimental results showed that the approach is effective and practical.

As in [6, 18], this work assumed that the jobs assigned to server clusters were stateless. Our future work will be on providing PSD services to stateful applications like e-Commerce on server clusters, where both Round-Robin and Least-Remaining-Work dispatching disciplines are not applicable to support session integrity.

Acknowledgement

This material is based on research sponsored by the Air Force Research Laboratory, under agreement numbers FA9550-04-1-0239 and F49620-03-1-0207. The U.S. Government is authorized to reproduce and distribute reprints for Governmental purposes notwithstanding any copyright notation thereon. The views and conclusions contained herein are those of the authors and should not be interpreted as necessarily representing the official policies or endorsements, either expressed or implied, of the Air Force Research Laboratory or the U.S. Government.

The authors would also like to thank Network Information and Space Security Center (NISSC) for providing support in the work.

References

[1] M. Arlitt, D. Krishnamurthy, and J. Rolia. Characterizing the scalability of a large Web-based shopping system. *ACM Trans. on Internet Technology*, 1(1):44–69, 2001.

[2] C. Chekuri, A. Goel, S. Khanna, and A. Kumar. Multi-processor scheduling to minimize flow time with ϵ resource augmentation. In *Proc. of ACM Symp. on Theory of Computing (STOC)*, pages 363–372, 2004.

[3] X. Chen and P. Mohapatra. Performance evaluation of service differentiating Internet servers. *IEEE Trans. on Computers*, 51(11):1,368–1,375, 2002.

[4] C. Dovrolis, D. Stiliadis, and P. Ramanathan. Proportional differentiated services: Delay differentiation and packet scheduling. In *Proc. ACM SIGCOMM*, 1999.

[5] D. Eager, E. Lazowska, and J. Zahorjan. Adaptive load sharing in homogeneous distributed systems. *IEEE Trans. on Software Engineering*, 12(5):662–675, 1986.

[6] M. Harchol-Balter. Task assignment with unknown duration. *Journal of ACM*, 29(2):260–288, 2002.

[7] Y. Huang and R. Gu. A simple fifo-based scheme for differentiated loss guarantees. In *Proc. of the Int'l Workshop on Quality of Service (IWQoS)*, 2004.

[8] L. Kleinrock. *Queueing Systems, Volume II*. John Wiley and Sons, 1976.

[9] T. T. Kwan, R. E. McGrath, and D. A. Reed. Ncsa's world wide web server: Design and performance. *IEEE Computer*, 28(11):68–74, 1995.

[10] S. C. M. Lee, J. C. S. Lui, and D. K. Y. Yau. A proportional-delay diffserv-enabled Web server: admission control and dynamic adaptation. *IEEE Trans. on Parallel and Distributed Systems*, 15(5):385–400, 2004.

[11] K. Nichols, V. Jacobson, and L. Zhang. A two-bit differentiated services architecture for the internet. *IETF RFC 2638*, 1999.

[12] V. S. Pai, M. Aron, G. Banga, M. Svendsen, P. Drusche, W. Zwaenepoel, and E. Nahum. Locality-aware request distribution in cluster-based network servers. In *Proc. 8th Int'l Conf. on Architectural support for programming languages and operating systems*, 1998.

[13] K. Shen, H. Tang, T. Yang, and L. Chu. Integrated resource management for cluster-based Internet services. In *Proc. of USENIX OSDI*, pages 225–238, December 2002.

[14] M. M. Teixeira, M. J. Santana, and R. H. C. Santana. Using adaptive priority scheduling for service differentiation QoS-aware Web servers. In *Proc. IEEE 23rd Int'l Conf. on Performance, Computing, and Communications (IPCCC)*, pages 279–285, 2004.

[15] J. Wei, C.-Z. Xu, and X. Zhou. A robust packet scheduling algorithm for proportional delay differentiation services. In *Proc. of IEEE Globecom, Vol.2*, pages 697–701, 2004.

[16] Q. Zhang, E. Smirni, and G. Ciardo. Profit-driven service differentiation in transient environments. In *Proc. 11th IEEE/ACM Int'l Symp. on Modeling, Analysis and Simulation of Computer Telecommunications Systems*, 2003.

[17] X. Zhou, Y. Cai, G. K. Godavari, and C. E. Chow. An adaptive process allocation strategy for proportional responsiveness differentiation on Web servers. In *Proc. IEEE 2nd Int'l Conf. on Web Services (ICWS)*, pages 142–149, July 2004.

[18] X. Zhou, J. Wei, and C.-Z. Xu. Processing rate allocation for proportional slowdown differentiation on Internet servers. In *Proc. IEEE 18th Int'l Parallel and Distributed Processing Symp. (IPDPS)*, pages 88–97, April 2004.

[19] X. Zhou and C.-Z. Xu. Harmonic proportional bandwidth allocation and scheduling for service differentiation on streaming servers. *IEEE Trans. on Parallel and Distributed Systems*, 15(9):835–848, 2004.

[20] H. Zhu, H. Tang, and T. Yang. Demand-driven service differentiation for cluster-based network servers. In *Proc. IEEE INFOCOM*, pages 679–688, 2001.

Session 1C: Overlays

Design and Implementation of Overlay Multicast Protocol for Multimedia Streaming

Thilmee M. Baduge Akihito Hiromori Hirozumi Yamaguchi Teruo Higashino
Graduate School of Information Science and Technology
Osaka University
1-5 Yamadaoka, Suita, Osaka 565-0871, JAPAN
{thilmee, hiromori, h-yamagu, higashino}@ist.osaka-u.ac.jp

Abstract

In this paper, we propose a new protocol called Shared Tree Streaming (or STS in short) protocol that is designed for interactive multimedia streaming applications. STS is a decentralized protocol that constructs a shared tree called s-DBMDT (sender-dependent Degree-Bounded Minimum Diameter Tree) as an overlay network that involves all the participants of the application. For a given set of nodes where some of them are senders, s-DBMDT is a spanning tree where the maximum delay on the tree from those senders is minimized and the degree constraint on each node is held. We believe that this is the first approach that defines s-DBMDT construction problem and presents a distributed protocol for the purpose. Our performance evaluation is based on experiments in both simulated networks and real networks that strongly shows the efficiency and usefulness of STS protocol.

1 Introduction

Recent innovation of the Internet has brought us several *interactive group communication* models. Especially recent applications may require multimedia-based group communication methods such as whiteboard, audio and streaming video. It is a common consensus that we need multicast solutions for group communication and IP multicast is not suitable for such a purpose because it is designed for large-scale content distribution. Instead, overlay multicast solutions have had a lot of attentions where application nodes (end systems, referred to as simply *nodes* in this paper) are connected by unicast channels and consequently form tree-like virtual networks (overlay networks) among them.

A lot of research efforts have been dedicated so far to deploy overlay multicast. They are classified into the following three categories based on their policies to generate overlay topologies, (i) mesh-first approaches like [1, 2], (ii) tree-first approaches like [3, 4, 5, 6, 7] and (iii) other approaches like [8]. In Ref. [7], we have taken a tree-based approach and have presented a protocol called MODE (Minimum-delay Overlay tree construction by DEcentralized operation). MODE aims at minimizing maximum delay (referred to as *diameter*) between any pair of nodes under the degree-constraints given by the nodes, assuming interactive applications where every node can be a potential sender. Some techniques for constructing Degree-Bounded Minimum Delay (or Diameter) Trees (DBMDTs) have been proposed [4, 5, 7], considering the maximum delay of overlay trees and the bandwidth constraints around nodes. Unfortunately none of those methods has considered the following several important features of interactive *multimedia* applications such as video conferencing.

First, such an application may have several sources. These sources are subject to change, but are not changed so frequently. For example, in video-conferencing, pictures of some primary persons should be continuously delivered to the other audience. In such an application, we would like to efficiently build a tree where the maximum delay *from the current senders* is minimized satisfying the degree bounds of nodes. Hereafter, for a given set of senders, such a tree is called *sender-dependent DBMDT* and denoted as *s-DBMDT*. Fig. 1 shows an example that explains the difference between DBMDT and s-DBMDT. For a given complete graph that represents an overlay network in Fig. 1(a), DBMDT is a spanning tree which involves all the nodes of the graph and has a minimum diameter, as shown in Fig. 1(b). In this case, the diameter path is *b-a-c-e* (or *d-a-c-e*) of delay 5. Here, let us suppose that currently only nodes a and e, which are shown by the meshed circles in the figures are senders. In this case, considering the fact that only these nodes send data and others are receivers, s-DBMDT in Fig. 1(c) achieves smaller maximum delay 4 (*a-e-c*) from those senders, while 5 (*e-c-a-b* or *e-c-a-d*) in DBMDT of Fig. 1(b).

Secondly, considering practical aspects of interactive multimedia applications, we need to identify incapable hosts and prevent them from staying in the center of s-DBMDT, since

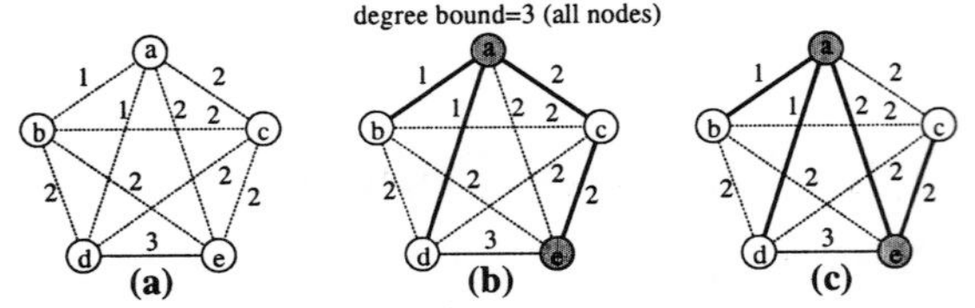

(a) An Overlay Network (b) DBMDT (dia.=5,s-dia.=5)
(c) s-DBMDT (dia.=5,**s-dia.=4**)

Figure 1. DBMDT and s-DBMDT on Overlay Networks

those hosts may delay or drop packets due to limitation of network bandwidth or processing power to forward packets, or instability of hosts. Similarly, we should provide a reasonable way to allow each host to determine an appropriate degree bound, since the capability overflow of such a host may also cause packet delay or dropping at the host.

In this paper, we propose a new protocol called *Shared Tree Streaming (or STS in short)* protocol that constructs s-DBMDT adaptively in a decentralized heuristic manner. We also design and implement a Java middleware based on STS protocol. Compared with the existing literatures, our contribution can be summarized in to the following two points. First, we define a new problem that is well-suited to multimedia interactive applications and design a new decentralized protocol for the problem. Secondly, we have designed and implemented an adaptation mechanism that is needed for multimedia streaming on overlay shared trees. Our performance evaluation is based on experiments in both simulated networks and real networks that strongly shows the efficiency and usefulness of our protocol.

2 Shared Tree Streaming (STS) Protocol

First, we give the definition of a Degree-Bounded Minimum Diameter Tree (DBMDT)[7]. Let $G = (V, E)$ denote a given undirected complete graph where V denotes a set of nodes and E denotes a set of potential overlay links which are unicast connections between nodes. Also let $d_{max}(v)$ denote a degree bound of each node $v \in V$ (the maximum number of overlay links attached to v), and let $h(i, j)$ denote the delay of each overlay link $(i, j) \in E$. DBMDT is a spanning tree T of G where the *diameter* of T (the maximum delay on T) is minimum and the degree of each node $v \in V$ (denoted as $d(v)$) does not exceed $d_{max}(v)$.

Based on the above, we define a sender-dependent DBMDT (s-DBMDT) introduced in this paper as follows. For a given $G = (V, E)$ and a given set $S \subseteq V$ of senders, s-DBMDT is a spanning tree T of G where the maximum delay from the senders in S is minimum and $d(v) \leq d_{max}(v)$ where $v \in V$. The maximum delay from the senders is called *sender-dependent diameter* and denoted by *s-diameter*.

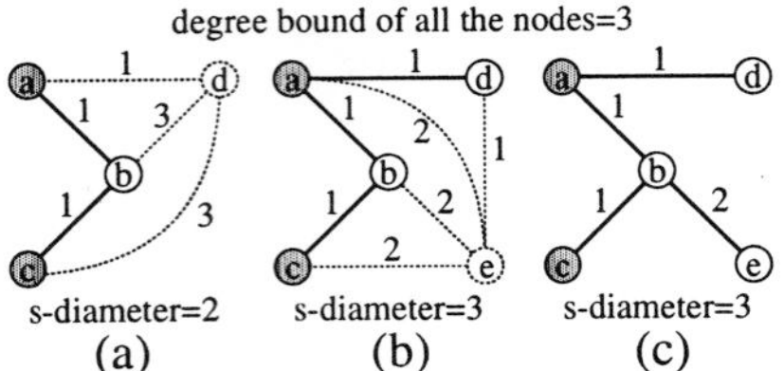

Figure 2. Join Procedure

The DBMDT construction problem has been proved to be NP-hard [4]. The DBMDT construction problem is a special case of our s-DBMDT construction problem where $S = V$. Therefore, we need an efficient heuristic algorithm for the problem.

2.1 Minimizing Maximum Delay from Senders

The proposing protocol, *Shared Tree Streaming (STS) protocol*, consists of two main procedures, join and repair. The join procedure makes a new joining node connect to a node which positions the joining node "closest to the senders" of the current tree in order to prevent the new node from making the s-diameter longer. The repair procedure is activated when a node on the current tree leaves (or suddenly disappears) and it connects appropriate intermediate nodes in the isolated sub-trees to make a new tree with a shorter s-diameter. To execute the above procedures in decentralized manner, each node in our STS protocol autonomously collects the information about the current sender nodes and diameter paths of the sub-trees that will appear by neighboring node's leaving. This information collection is executed periodically to keep up with the status changes of the tree (e.g. location of sender nodes and diameter paths of the sub-trees). This will be explained in Section 3.3. In this subsection, we explain how the two procedures keep the s-diameter as small as possible, satisfying the given degree bounds of nodes.

[Join Procedure Outline]: For a new joining node u, the join procedure never changes the current form of the tree, but lets the new node u connect to such a node (say v) where the maximum delay from the senders to the new joining node u (*i.e.* a candidate for the s-diameter of the consequent tree) is minimum. Note that node v must be such a node that has at least one residual degree.

Fig. 2 shows an example where senders are denoted by meshed circles. We assume that the degree bounds of all the nodes are 3. In Fig. 2(a), we have a tree involving three nodes a, b and c where a and c are senders. Also the s-diameter of the tree is 2. Let us assume that a node d wants to join the tree, and the dotted lines in Fig. 2(a) represent the measured delay between the new node d and the existing nodes on the tree. Consequently, node d is connected to node a since the maximum delay from senders a and c becomes 3 (Fig. 2(b)) and it is the minimum in all the possible connecting positions.

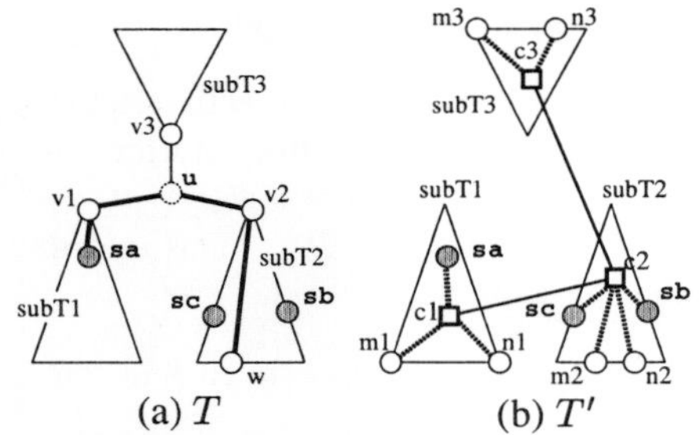

(a) T (b) T'

	path	type
1.	longest path from s_a in $subT_1$	(i)
2.	s_a-c_1-c_2-m_2	(ii)
3.	s_a-c_1-c_2-c_3-m_3	(ii)
4.	longest path from s_b in $subT_2$	(i)
5.	s_b-c_2-c_1-m_1	(ii)
6.	s_b-c_2-c_3-m_3	(ii)
7.	longest path from s_c in $subT_2$	(i)
8.	s_c-c_2-c_1-m_1	(ii)
9.	s_c-c_2-c_3-m_3	(ii)

(c) Candidates for s-diameter path of T'

Figure 3. Repair Procedure

And the subsequent joining nodes (*i.e.* node e in Fig. 2(c)) also follow the same method.

[Repair Procedure Outline]: Whenever a node's disappearance occurs, the disconnected sub-trees are repaired by the repair procedure. At that time, we try to shorten the s-diameter of the repaired tree, by connecting the *core nodes* of the isolated (disconnected) sub-trees. Here, let m and n be the both end nodes of the diameter path (*not s-diameter path*) of a tree t. The *core node* of t is a node whose maximum delay from the nodes m and n is minimum in all the nodes of t. This means that the core node is located on the "center" of the diameter path. Here, we will explain why such a procedure can make the s-diameter of the repaired tree shorter. An example is shown in Fig. 3 where the senders are s_a, s_b and s_c and represented by meshed circles. In tree T of Fig. 3(a), let us assume that its s-diameter path is s_a-v_1-u-v_2-w and a new node u leaves the tree. By the leave of node u, the tree T is partitioned into three sub-trees $subT_1$, $subT_2$ and $subT_3$, and they are connected through their core nodes c_1, c_2 and c_3 (denoted by squares) and reorganized into a new tree T' as shown in Fig. 3(b) (there are some possibilities to connect among the core nodes and this figure shows one of them). In this case, the s-diameter of T' is either of (i) the maximum delay from a sender to a node *within the same sub-tree*, or (ii) the maximum delay from a sender to a node on a *different sub-tree*. We enumerate all the candidates for the new diameter path in Fig. 3(c) along with their classification of the above type (i) or (ii). We note that m_i and n_i are both ends of the diameter path of $subT_i$ and without loss of generality we assume that delay of path c_i-m_i on the tree, denoted by $L(c_i, m_i)$, is always equal to or larger than $L(c_i, n_i)$.

Obviously, if a path of type (i) (either path 1, 4 or 7 in Fig. 3(c)) becomes the s-diameter path of T', the s-diameter is equal to or smaller than that of T. Otherwise, one of the paths of type (ii) becomes the s-diameter path of T'. Here we can say that for any sub-tree $subT_i$, the following inequality, $L(s_i, c_i) \leq L(c_i, n_i) \leq L(c_i, m_i)$, always holds where L is the delay of the path between two nodes on the tree[1]. The above inequality suggests that for any path of type (ii), the delay from a sender to the core node on the same sub-tree is not larger than the half of the diameter of the sub-tree. Also on another sub-tree, the delay from its core node to an end of the diameter path on the sub-tree is the half of the diameter of the sub-tree. Consequently, the diameter of T' may be equal to or less than the sum of halves of the diameters of the two sub-trees plus the delay between the core nodes. Here, the half of the diameter of a sub-tree of T is always smaller than the half of the diameter of the original tree T. Therefore, this may shorten the s-diameter compared with T in many cases even though it depends on the delay between the core nodes. To make it easy to understand, let us compare our strategy with the simple one where we simply connect the neighboring nodes of u (*i.e.* v_1, v_2 and v_3). This procedure makes the new s-diameter almost equal to that of T with a high possibility, since the maximum delay paths from the neighboring nodes v_1, v_2 and v_3 remain as they are, and they may again be a part of the s-diameter path of the repaired tree.

We note that the above description is valid for the case that the leaving node u is on the s-diameter path of T. For the case that node u is not on the s-diameter path of T, the s-diameter of T' is not smaller than that of T. This is because the s-diameter path of T is preserved in an isolated sub-tree as it is, and thus it remains in T'. However, we think that the s-diameter of T' is not changed from T in most cases.

As a whole, we can expect the s-diameter to be smaller when nodes leave.

3 Design of STS Protocol

3.1 Join Procedure Design

A new node which wants to join the current tree first sends a *query message* to a well-known node on the tree to ask the address of the *center node* of the tree. The *center node* of a tree is a node whose maximum delay from the senders is the minimum. Intuitively, the accepter-node that makes the maximum delay from the senders to the new node minimum seems to be located near the center node of the current tree. Therefore, we start searching the accepter-node from the center node. To do this, in our STS protocol, we assume that each node can know the center node of the current tree (thus any node can be a well-known node). We also assume that each node knows the maximum delays from all the senders. The way of this information collection will be explained later in Section 3.3.

[1]This is obvious since $L(c_i, n_i) + L(c_i, m_i)$ is the diameter (the maximum delay) of $subT_i$.

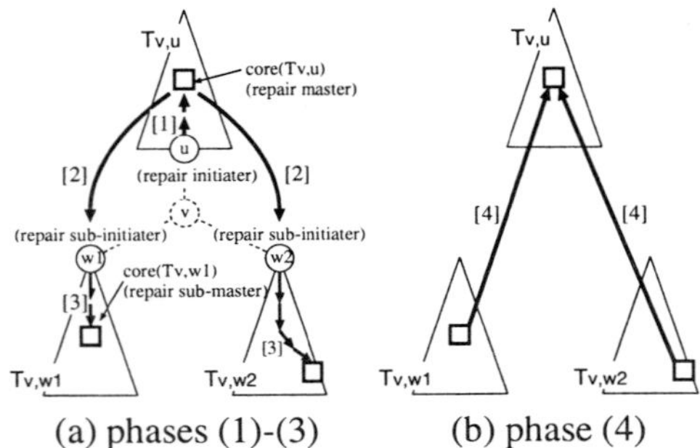

(a) phases (1)-(3) (b) phase (4)

Figure 4. Repair Procedure

Once the joining node receives the reply from the well-known node, it sends a *connection request message* to the center node. Then, the center node sends a *connection permission message* to the joining node only if its residual degree is not zero. At the same time, it broadcasts the connection request message to its neighboring nodes of the tree. In response to the reception of the connection request message, each neighboring node acts in the same way as the center node. Therefore the connection request message is delivered on the tree to all the nodes. Here, to prevent the joining node from receiving a large number of connection permission messages, a maximum hop count from the center node can be assigned to the connection request message.

The new joining node can know the maximum delay from the senders to each responded accepter-node, by making the connection permission message contain those information. Then, by knowing the delay to each accepter-node (this can be measured using *ping* for instance), the joining node can choose the accepter-node that minimizes the maximum delay from the senders to itself.

3.2 Repair Procedure Design

Hereafter, for a pair of two adjacent nodes v and w on the tree T, let $T_{v,w}$ denote the sub-tree rooted at node w and isolated by node v's disappearance. Suppose that the *sub-tree information* of $T_{v,w}$ contains the IDs and network addresses of (i) w, (ii) w's neighbors except v and (iii) the core node of $T_{v,w}$ (denoted as $core(T_{v,w})$). We assume that each node, say u, has the sub-tree information of $T_{v,w}$ for every pair of v and w where v is a neighboring node of u and w is a neighboring node of v including u. We also assume that for adjacent two nodes, parent-child relationship on the tree is pre-defined. Each node autonomously collects necessary sub-tree information by the information collection procedure described in Section 3.3.

Under the assumptions above, we present the design of the repair procedure as follows. For simplicity of discussion, we explain the repair procedure for a single node's disappearance without considering other nodes' disappearances.

The procedure repairs the tree for node v's disappearance in the following four phases (Fig. 4). In Fig. 4, we assume that node u is the parent node of node v.

(1) The parent node u of node v activates the repair procedure and sends all the sub-tree information of T_{v,w_j} (w_j is one of the child nodes of v, $1 \leq j \leq d(v) - 1$) to the core node $core(T_{v,u})$ of $T_{v,u}$. This information passing is done along the tree.

(2) $core(T_{v,u})$ sends its address to each w_j directly.

(3) Then each w_j sends the address of $core(T_{v,u})$ to its core node $core(T_{v,w_j})$ (*i.e.* sub-tree T_{v,w_j}'s core node). This information passing is done along the tree.

(4) Now each $core(T_{v,w_j})$ knows the address of $core(T_{v,u})$, so it connects itself to $core(T_{v,u})$. If $core(T_{v,u})$ or $core(T_{v,w_j})$ has no residual degree, it delegates its role to its closest node with some residual degree. After this phase (4), the core nodes exchange their sub-tree information with their neighboring nodes to prepare for future node disappearance.

By this procedure, the core nodes or their neighboring nodes get connected to each other. One may think that this procedure contains redundant operations (for example, we can directly send sub-tree information between the neighboring nodes of v and the core nodes in phases (1) and (3)), and that the sub-tree information contains unused data such as the neighboring nodes' information of the root node. This redundancy is necessary to prepare for another disappearance occurs during the procedure, but due to limitation of space, we omit the discussion of validation in case of simultaneous occurrence of multiple disappearances. Readers may refer to Ref. [7] to see analogous idea for the validation.

3.3 Information Collection

In STS protocol, all the nodes periodically collect the information required to execute join and repair procedures by message exchange along the current tree. We assume that there exists a node that never disappears, for example, the first member node or a well-known node. Such a node is called the *root node* [2]. The root node starts the information collection in the *collection phase* for every (regular) interval by broadcasting *synchronization messages* on the current tree. Obviously, the number of synchronization messages is $n - 1$ where n is the number of nodes on the current tree. A non-leaf node enters the collection phase if it has received a synchronization message from its parent and has sent synchronization messages to all its children. A leaf node does not send synchronization messages. Instead, when it receives a synchronization message, it enters the collection phase and replies a *collection*

[2]This is not an essential assumption. By giving a unique ID to each node, a new root node can be found autonomously by using a distributed algorithm for the leader election when the current root node has disappeared.

message to its parent. Each non-leaf node in the collection phase acts as follows. Whenever it receives collection messages from all the neighboring nodes except one neighboring node (say x), it sends a collection message to node x. Each node u leaves the collection phase if node u has received a collection message from every its neighboring node v and has sent a collection message to v. This means that in the collection phase, $2(n-1)$ collection messages are exchanged on the tree. So, totally, the number of messages required for the collection of the current status is only $3(n-1)$, that is, only three messages are exchanged on each link of the tree.

Hereafter we will explain how the information required by join and repair procedures are collected by collection messages. The information that each node x must hold are, (i) The ID and address of the center node of the current tree , (ii) The maximum delay from the senders to node x and (iii) The sub-tree information of $T_{y,z}$ for every pair of y and z where y is a neighboring node of x and z is a neighboring node of y . Note that the sub-tree information of $T_{y,z}$ contains the IDs and network addresses of z, z's neighboring nodes and the core node of $T_{y,z}$ ($core(T_{y,z})$).

And the following auxiliary information are needed to calculate the sub-tree information of $T_{x,y}$. (i). $dia(T_{x,y})$: the diameter of $T_{x,y}$, (ii). $L(T_{x,y})$: the maximum delay of $T_{x,y}$ from y, (iii). $H(T_{x,y})$: the maximum delay path of $T_{x,y}$ from y. The delay of each link on the path is also included and (iv). $S(s, T_{x,y})$: the path from a sender s in $T_{x,y}$ to y. The delay of each link on the path is also included.

We let each node (say v) be responsible for calculating the sub-tree information of $T_{u,v}$ for every its neighbor u. For this purpose, we let the collection message sent from v to u have the following information. (i). $dia(T_{u,v})$, $L(T_{u,v})$, $H(T_{u,v})$ and $S(s, T_{u,v})$ (for each sender s in $T_{u,v}$), (ii). the sub-tree information of $T_{u,v}$ and (iii). the sub-tree information of $T_{v,w}$ for each w (except u) of the neighboring node of v. Now we show that node v can calculate the above information if it receives the collection messages from all the neighboring nodes except u (let W denote the set of neighboring nodes of v except u). First, the parameters $dia(T_{u,v})$, $L(T_{u,v})$, $H(T_{u,v})$ and $S(s, T_{u,v})$ (for each sender s in $T_{u,v}$) can be defined as follows.

$$\begin{aligned}
dia(T_{u,v}) &= \max_{w,x,y \in W} \{dia(T_{v,w}),\ L(T_{v,x}) + \\
&\qquad h(v,x) + L(T_{v,y}) + h(v,y)\} \\
L(T_{u,v}) &= \max_{w \in W} \{L(T_{v,w}) + h(v,w)\} \\
H(T_{u,v}) &= [v]@H(T_{v,w_o}) \quad (w_o \in W \text{ where } w_o \\
&\qquad \text{maximizes } L(T_{u,v})) \\
S(s, T_{u,v}) &= [v]@S(s, T_{v,w}) \quad (\forall w \in W \text{ where} \\
&\qquad S(s, T_{v,w}) \text{ is not empty})
\end{aligned}$$

Note that $h(x, y)$ is the link delay on the tree. The equation for $dia(T_{u,v})$ comes from the definition of the diameter. The diameter of $T_{u,v}$ is the maximum value of (i) the diameters of its sub-trees and (ii) the sum of the two longest depths from node v. The others are straightforward.

Secondly, regarding the sub-tree information of $T_{u,v}$, the IDs and network addresses of v and v's neighbors are known by v. Therefore, $core(T_{u,v})$ can be defined as follows.

$$core(T_{u,v}) = \begin{cases} core(T_{v,w}) \quad (\text{if } dia(T_{u,v}) = dia(T_{v,w}) \\ \qquad \text{where } w \in W) \\ \\ \text{center of } rev(H(T_{v,x}))@[v]@H(T_{v,y}) \\ \quad (\text{if } dia(T_{u,v}) = L(T_{v,x}) + h(v,x) + \\ \quad L(T_{v,y}) + h(v,y) \text{where } x, y \in W) \end{cases}$$

Here "rev" is the reverse function of a given path.

Thirdly, the sub-tree information of $T_{v,w}$ is included in the collection message from w.

From the above, we have proved that each node v can calculate the content of the collection message to be sent to node u. Assuming those information, we show that any node, say x, can calculate the information that node x must hold, listed previously in this section. The center node and maximum delay from the senders can be calculated by all the $S(s, (T_{x,*}))$ included in the received collection messages. Also the sub-tree information of $T_{y,z}$ is directly included in the collection message from y to x. Consequently, we have proved that every node can obtain the required information after the collection phase.

4 Implementation of STS Protocol as Java Middleware

We have implemented our protocol as a Java based middleware called STS/J. Due to limitation of space, we only present our degree bound adaptation mechanism implemented in STS/J, which is an important functionality for media streaming on overlay networks.

Theoretically, we have shown importance of s-DBMDT for interactive multimedia applications in previous sections. Here, we focus on practical aspects of multimedia streaming on a tree. Practically, it is difficult to determine an appropriate degree for each node. It is theoretically simple, since usually an end host has only one network interface, and all the overlay links attached to the host uses this interfaces. Therefore, the upper bound of the degree bound $d_{max}(v)$ of node v is determined by $d_{max}(v) \leq \frac{N}{\sum_{s \in S} B_s}$ where N is the bandwidth of the network interface and B_s is the bitrate transmitted from a sender s. However, the actual bandwidth of network interface, especially wireless network interface, changes from time to time. Therefore, the degree bound should be adapted according to the network status.

Here, we adopt the following scheme for each node v. We denote the set of the neighboring nodes of v by W and the

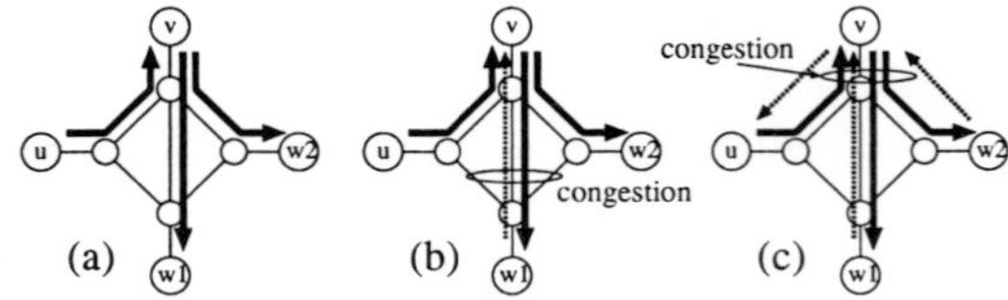

(a) Physical network and overlay tree.
(b) Congestion occurs on a remote link of node v.
(c) Congestion occurs on the local link of node v.

Figure 5. Adaptation Mechanism

neighboring node which sends a stream to v by u. Thus node v relays the stream to the nodes in $W - \{u\}$ (Fig. 5(a)). Our implementation uses RTP and RTCP, and if a node detects loss or jitter of packets, it sends receiver reports to its upstream. In Fig. 5, streams are represented by thick arrows, while RTCP reports are represented by dotted arrows. In the figure, the underlying network is shown where small circles represent physical routers and big ones represent end hosts.

- If node v receives an RTCP receiver report from only one node (or some nodes) $w \in W - \{u\}$, node v determines that network congestion happens not on the local link (*i.e.* network interface) but on a remote link on the unicast path between v and w (Fig. 5(b)). In this case, node v sends *compulsory leave message* to node w to let it leave and rejoin the tree.
- If node v receives an RTCP receiver report from each node in $w \in W - \{u\}$ and also node v sends an RTCP receiver report to node u, node v determines that network congestion happens on the local link (Fig. 5(c)). In this case, node v ignores the compulsory leave message from node u, and sends compulsory leave messages to some nodes in $w \in W - \{u\}$ to let them leave and rejoin the tree. This is done to dissolve the congestion on the local link of node v by decreasing its current degree. After that, node v sets its degree bound $d_{max}(v)$ to the adjusted degree to prevent itself from accepting other neighbors.
- If node v continues stable states for a while, it increments its degree bound.

5 Experiments

5.1 Simulation Experiments

We have implemented our STS protocol on ns-2 to evaluate the enhancement against our previous work MODE[7]. In our experiments, networks with 400 physical nodes have been generated and used as underlying networks. We have selected 200 nodes, including both wireless and wired nodes, as overlay participant nodes. In the simulation, we have set the initial end-to-end delay (overlay link delay) to vary between 10ms to 200ms for both wired and wireless nodes, while setting the wireless nodes to change their end-to-end delay up to 300ms during the simulation.

Considering practical situations, we have prepared the following scenario that simulates a real-time session in collaborative applications such as a video-based meeting or groupware. Note that we set the interval between collection phases to 60 seconds. The initial degree bound was set to 5 for all the nodes. The scenario is as follows. (i) The session period is 300 seconds. (ii) Each of 200 nodes joins the session only once and eventually leaves the session. (iii) Within the first 30 seconds, about 60 nodes join the session. (iv) From 30 seconds to 270 seconds, additional joins are processed. Also some existing nodes leave the session. The collection phases starts at 30, 90, 150, 210 and 270 seconds successively. (v) After 270 seconds, no node joins and about 40 nodes leave the session.

[Diameter and Sender-Dependent Diameter]: We have measured (a) the diameters and (b) sender-dependent diameters (s-diameters) at every one second for STS and MODE. According to the goals of those two protocols, we can expect that STS could achieve smaller s-diameters, but a bit larger diameters than MODE. Fig. 6 shows the results. We can figure out that the s-diameter of STS is smaller (Fig. 6(b)). On the other hand the diameter of STS remains larger than MODE according to Fig. 6(a). Note that the diameter is not dominant on the streaming as long as one of the sender nodes play the role of streaming source.

The average diameters and s-diameters were 651, 364 successively for STS and 585, 480 successively for MODE in milliseconds. They were measured performing simulations for 10 different sessions, where each followed the above scenario. According to those results, we can again say that STS can support multimedia applications better than MODE.

[Control Traffic]: The control traffic is shown in Fig.7. The highest traffic amount has been generated around 30 seconds (around the first collection phase) as the number of nodes has reached to top. Even taking this peak value (350kbit) together with the number of nodes in the session at that time (90 nodes approximately), the average traffic amount on a single node can be calculated as 4kbit/sec. We can say this value (4Kbps/node as maximum) is small enough for streaming applications which usually consume several hundreds of Kbps.

[Join/Repair Procedure Overhead]: The time required for join and repair procedures explained in Section 3 was 930 and 790 milliseconds successively. According to these results, the time required for restoration of isolated trees (repair time) remains less than 1 second, which can be considered small enough for multimedia streaming. The time required for the join procedure (join time) here is larger than the repair time. Here we have set the connection permission message timeout (the time each joining node waits to receive connection permission messages before it selects the best position to connect) large enough (0.6[s]) to receive as more as connection permission messages. So the join time holds a larger value

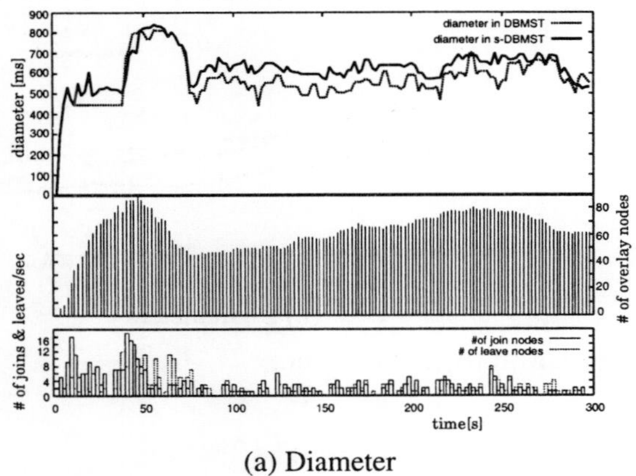

(a) Diameter

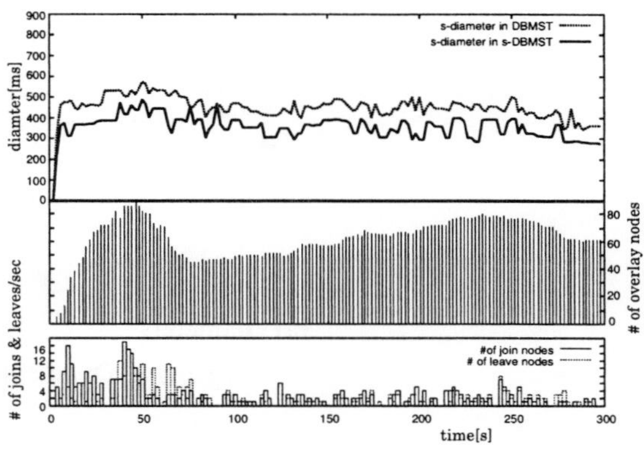

(b) Sender-Dependent Diameter (S-diameter)

Figure 6. Dynamics of (a) Diameters and (b) S-diameters

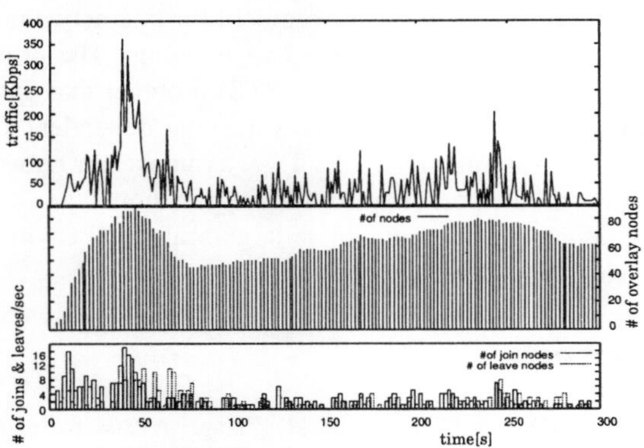

Figure 7. Control Traffic (Total kbits on tree per each second)

(0.93[s]), but this value is considered reasonable enough as time required for bootstrapping.

5.2 Experiments on Real Networks

We have used 8 machines placed in the same LAN (100Base-TX) and run 4-6 processes on each machine to emulate 40 user nodes. Here, we made each process keep the packets for a certain time period before forwarding, if the forwarding target is located in the same machine where that process runs. In this way, we could prevent the link-delay between the nodes located in the same machine from being too small. The scenario is as follows. All nodes join the tree before streaming video so that they can be ready to receive the initial frame of the stream. It includes some information to decode and play video such as its resolution and frame rate. Throughout the session, the streaming-source changes it's position through the sender nodes. During the streaming, 3-5 nodes are set to leave in every interval between collection phases. The period is of 60 seconds. Here the link delays vary from 10[ms] to 100[ms] and the initial degree bound for each node is 4. Each node's degree bound is dynamically changed to enhance the media

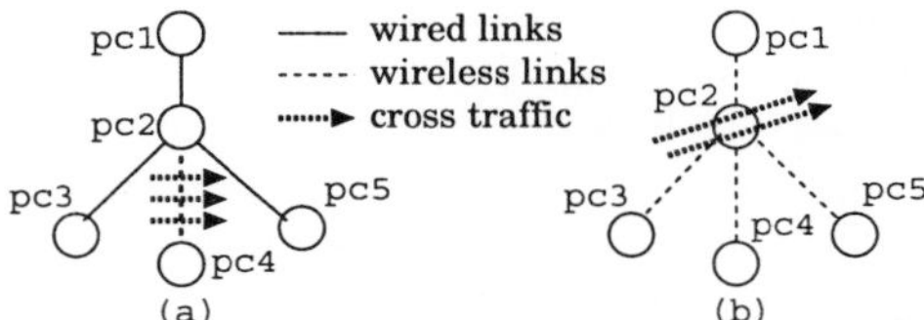

Figure 9. Degree Adaptation Experiment

delivery performance on the tree as described in Section 4. And also, we set STS to select its sender nodes increasingly with the total node count in a manner to make the senders, which includes the initial node as well, occupy 20% of the entire nodes.

[Diameters and S-Diameters]: We have measured the dynamics of diameters and s-diameters. We have used the same scenario for 10 cases each of which has different locations for sender nodes, and have measured the average for every 25 seconds. The measured variance is shown in Fig. 8. We can see that the diameter of STS is held higher than that of MODE (Fig. 8-(a)). But s-diameter, which counts more in multimedia streaming, is held smaller in STS according to the results shown in Fig. 8-(b).

[Degree Adaptation]: We have checked whether the degree adjustment strategy described in Section 4 works well. For that we have set the 2 scenarios shown in Fig. 9 which illustrates a part of the overlay nodes (machines) we used and the 802.11b wireless links. Fig. 9-(a) represents a case, where a congestion occurs on a unicast link between 2 nodes, and Fig. 9-(b) is another case, where a congestion occurs on the physical network link connected to a node. For each of these cases we have used a 256 Kbps media stream as the multicast media and a wireless node to make the congestions. And also the lower threshold of the bitrate, below which a node detects that a network congestion has occurred, has been set to -20% (205 Kbps) of the stream's real bitrate.

In the first case, we have generated some additional traffic across the link between $pc2$ and $pc4$. Then we could see node $pc2$ has detected the congestion on the down link to $pc4$,

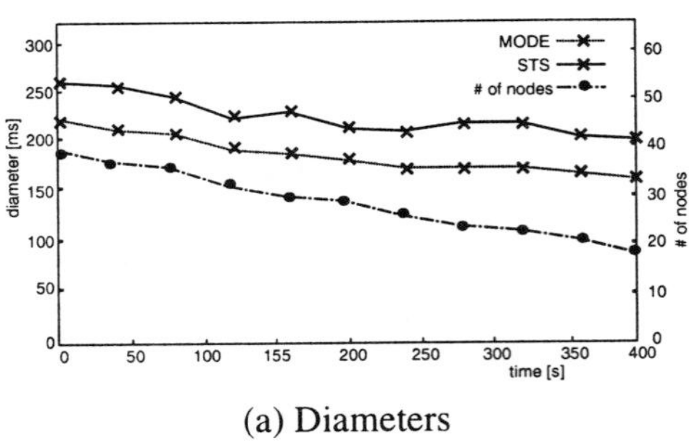

(a) Diameters

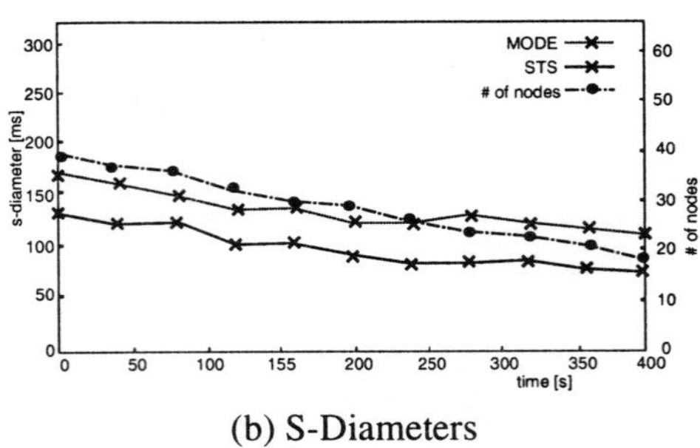

(b) S-Diameters

Figure 8. Dynamics of (a) Diameters and (b)S-Daimeters

where it has sent a compulsory-leave message to $pc4$. Then $pc4$ has successfully left and rejoined the session. In the second case, we have generated a separate process which requires some additional traffic, which is enough to make a congestion on the physical network link, on $pc2$. Here we have found that nodes $pc1$ and $pc2$ have detected that downward links are congested, after receiving RTCP reports from their child nodes. Then $pc2$ has sent a compulsory-leave message to $pc3$ and $pc4$ (these are randomly selected to occupy around 50% of the total connection count, in our experiments). Here, the forcibly disconnected nodes, which are subjected to follow the ordinary join procedure, has rejoined to the tree after 1.28 second average value. And the isolated sub-tree, which was located under the forcibly disconnected node, has reconnected to the tree after average 0.43 milliseconds following the ordinary repair procedure.

[Time Required for Join/Repair Procedures]: We have measured the time required to complete the join and repair procedures. The average and maximum values of them were 1212 and 1415 milliseconds for join and 318 and 734 milliseconds for repair successively. We can confirm that the time required for a repair procedure is small even in the worst case. Considering the fact that the repair procedure completes less than in one second, we do not have serious distortion in playback of received video. Here, the time for join procedures remains higher. This is because we have made each joining node wait at least 1 second before making a link to the tree. It allows a node to receive as many permission messages as possible (see Section 3.1). This contributes to let the joining node connect to more closer node to the center node.

Currently STS nodes convey each multimedia data packet to the corresponding neighbor nodes without using the cache (the ring buffer) to support the real-time video conferences. But, readers may understand that STS can be simply modified to adapt applications requiring a higher quality playback (*i.e.*lower jitter, less stream loss) by using the ring buffer, where the jitter can be made lower and the data loss in subtree restoration process can be get to zero or to a negligible value.

6 Concluding Remarks

In this paper, we have stated design and implementation of an overlay multicast protocol for interactive multimedia applications including media streaming. The protocol is called Shared Tree Streaming (STS) protocol that constructs a shared tree called *s-DBMDT* (sender-dependent Degree-Bounded Minimum Diameter Tree) as an overlay network that involves all the participants of the application.

Evaluating STS protocol on large-scale, real environments such as PlanetLab is part of our future work.

References

[1] Y. H. Chu, S. G. Rao, and H. Zhang. A case for end system multicast. In *Proc. of ACM SIGMETRICS*, 2000.

[2] Y. Nakamura, H. Yamaguchi, A. Hiromori, K. Yasumoto, T. Higashino, and K. Taniguchi. On designing end-user multicast for multiple video sources. In *Proc. of 2003 IEEE Int. Conf. on Multimedia and Expo (ICME2003)*, pages III497–500, 2003.

[3] D. Pendarakis, S. Shi, D. Verma, and M. Waldvogel. ALMI: An application level multicast infrastructure. In *Proc. of 3rd Usenix Symp. on Internet Technologies and Systems*, 2001.

[4] S.Y. Shi, J.S. Turner, and M. Waldvogel. Dimensioning server access bandwidth and multicast routing in overlay networks. In *Proc. of ACM NOSSDAV 2001*, 2001.

[5] S. Banerjee, C. Kommareddy, K. Kar, S. Bhattacharjee, and S. Khuller. Construction of an efficient overlay multicast infrastructure for real-time applications. In *Proc. of IEEE INFOCOM 2003*, 2003.

[6] R. Cohen and G. Kaempfer. A unicast-based approach for streaming multicast. In *Proc. of IEEE INFOCOM 2001*, 2001.

[7] H. Yamaguchi, A. Hiromori, T. Higashino, and K. Taniguchi. An autonomous and decentralized protocol for delay sensitive overlay multicast tree. In *Proc. of 24th IEEE Int. Conf. on Distributed Computing Systems (ICDCS2004)*, pages p 662–669, 2004.

[8] S. Banerjee, B. Bhattacharjee, and C. Kommareddy. Scalable application layer multicast. In *Proc. of ACM SIGCOMM 2002*, pages 205–217, 2002.

Embedding a Cluster-Based Overlay Mesh in Mobile Ad hoc Networks without Cluster heads

Amit Banerjee Chung-Ta King Hung-Chang Hsiao

Department of Computer Science
National Tsing Hua University
Hsinchu, Taiwan, 300
amit@pads1.cs.nthu.edu.tw
{king, hchsiao}@cs.nthu.edu.tw

Abstract

One strategy to tackle the complexity and scalability issue in large-scale mobile ad hoc networks (MANETs) is to use extra layers of abstraction. A common tactic is to group the nodes in the network into clusters. The clusters and the paths between them constitute an extra layer of overlay abstraction. To maintain the overlay structure, a head node is often elected in each cluster. The head nodes form a backbone to provide, among other things, passages from one cluster to another. Nonetheless, the use of dedicated head nodes also creates problems such as load and power imbalance. In this paper, we investigate the feasibility of building a cluster-based overlay mesh on MANETs without using cluster heads. Without head nodes, the challenge is in maintaining the overlay structure and performing inter-cluster routing. We will examine one possible scheme through simulation.

1. Introduction

Mobile ad hoc networks (MANETs) [13] can be viewed as a bandwidth-constrained multi-hop topology comprised of nodes that can change their positions dynamically. For large scale MANETs, a common strategy to tackle their complexity and scalability is to use extra layers of abstraction. One way to providing abstraction is to cluster the nodes in the network. The clusters and the paths between them constitute an overlay abstraction, whereby operations such as multicasting and resource discovery can be performed. The overlay structure is especially useful for MANETs having nodes without geometric information.

To maintain the overlay structure, a head node is often elected in each cluster. All the nodes within the cluster maintain route information to the head node. The inter-cluster routings are through the head nodes. The cluster heads can be viewed as forming a backbone to provide passages from one cluster to another. The backbone helps in reducing the implementation complexity and increasing the scalability of the system. This scheme will be referred to as Cluster-Based With Head Overlay (CWHO) in this paper.

Although CWHO is simple and works well in many situations, it has a number of shortcomings, e.g. load and power imbalance, head node failure, extra traffic to/from the head nodes, etc. This is mainly due to the added responsibility assigned to the cluster heads, which may have limited resources such as bandwidth and power. In addition, the intermediate nodes that connect them may be mobile, leading to unreliable communication. These nodes also suffer from excessive resource consumption for relying messages. Apart from all these constrains, there are cost factors involved for the selection and maintenance of the cluster heads and the backbone, as well as the reliability issue due to header failure and mobility.

In this study, we are interested in the following questions:

- Is it feasible to build a cluster-based overlay mesh on MANETs without cluster heads? The challenge is to provide backbone functionality in a clustered network with a flat structure in each cluster. In this paper, we are especially interested in the important issues of maintaining the overlay structure and performing inter-cluster routing, under node mobility.
- What will be the performance of such an overlay in terms of the delivery ratio, average hop counts, or the control packets for maintenance?

* This work was supported in part by the Ministry of Education, Taiwan, under Grant NSC 93-2752-E-007-004-PAE and also in part by Institute for Information Industry, Taiwan, under the Grant 93A0145SB

To answer these questions, we examine in this paper one possible scheme for a cluster-based overlay mesh without using the head nodes. It will be referred to as Cluster-Based WithOut Head Overlay (CWOHO). The basic idea is to distribute the mesh structure to all the nodes in the system and thus any node can trigger inter-cluster routing. In essence, all the nodes in a cluster play the role of the cluster head; there is no node in the cluster with added responsibility. If the overlay topology is quite stable, this approach may work well. This is in contrast with the CWHO approach, in which a node needs to reach the cluster head first to perform any inter-cluster routing.

Since we focus on the inter-cluster routing in this paper, we will not address how a request arriving to a cluster is handled. We consider this issue very much application as well as implementation specific. Flooding within a cluster will always be an option.

We provide simulation-based performance study for the above two approaches. We mainly focus on data delivery ratio, hop count and the control packets overhead. The goal is to understand the implementation and to see whether they utilize their mesh structure efficiently.

The rest of the paper is organized as follows: In section 2, we discuss the related works regarding the construction of the ad hoc overlays. In section 3, we examine one possible scheme for CWOHO, and followed by a brief description for CWHO. In section 4, we provide the simulation-based performance evaluation for comparing both schemes. Finally, we conclude our discussion with conclusion and future works in section 5.

2. Related Works

Overlays are constructed for the implementation of various applications on top of MANETs, such as multicasting and location management. Performance of such applications depends on the performance of the overlay. Applications [1] built on ad hoc networks with GPS enabled nodes can utilize the geographic information to simplify the implementation. For environments where the nodes do not have such information, we need to construct an overlay for such applications. In this section we review several overlays that are built on MANETs.

Cluster-based overlays on MANETs divide the system into clusters and select cluster heads within each cluster. In CBRP [5], the cluster heads keeps information about the members of its cluster, and also maintains a cluster adjacency table that contains information about the neighboring clusters. Non-cluster nodes maintain a neighbor table containing the route information to their cluster head. The topology formed by interconnecting these cluster heads is used for routing. Cluster heads act as a gateway for routing between clusters.

Multicasting using backbone-based approach constructs an overlay by selecting core nodes through some distributed algorithms. In MCEDAR [2], a distributed minimum dominating set (MDS) algorithm for CORE selection is proposed. There are various protocols proposed [3,4] for selecting the core nodes for virtual backbone. The core nodes are connected to from a mesh structure, e.g., mgraph in MCEDAR, which acts as an overlay. Selection of a subset of nodes in the system can also be done using the connected dominating set [6,7].

Approaches mentioned above construct an overlay by selecting a subset of nodes from the system and by maintaining the interconnections between them. Other approaches proposed for forming an overlay is to employ the distributed hash table (DHT) on ad hoc networks. In [16], it integrates the DHT abstraction by integrating Pastry [15] and DSR [14] at the network layer to map the logical namespace of DHT to the physical namespace used by the MANET routing protocol.

Another approach for constructing an overlay is to construct a virtual coordinate system to replicate the real coordinate system [8,9]. In [9], an algorithm called Self-Positioning Algorithm (SPA) is used to position the nodes within the network area. It uses Time of Arrival (TOA) to obtain the range between mobile devices to build a network coordinate system. The approach proposed in [8] uses two designated bootstrap nodes and the perimeter nodes to construct a virtual coordinate space. The nodes uses the inter perimeter distance to compute their normalized coordinates.

3. Cluster-Based Overlay

In this section, we consider the cluster-based mesh overlays and present one possible way of performing CWOHO and CWHO. A cluster can be defined as a group of physically interconnected nodes. A cluster X is considered connected to a cluster Y if there exits at least one border node in X that has at least one of its neighbors belonging to Y. A border node provides the required interconnection of a cluster with other clusters. A mesh can be formed by interconnecting the neighboring clusters.

We can group the nodes in various ways [2,5]. To simplify the presentation we consider partitioning the clusters into geographic grids, where each grid is identified by the cluster identifier, ClusterId. Nodes have the information of the ClusterId of the cluster in which it belongs or has moved into. This can be done using periodic beckon information.

3.1 Cluster-Based Without Head Selection Overlay (CWOHO)

A key operation in CWOHO is to identify the border nodes of a cluster. This can be done as follows: Nodes in the system periodically collect the information about its one hop neighbors by broadcasting a small ReqNghInfo packet. All the neighbors in response to ReqNghInfo packet send their information back using the NghInfo packet. The NghInfo packet contains the ClusterId in which the node belongs. This information is used to determine if the node is the border node to the cluster in which it belongs. Each node periodically checks the NghInfo packets it received, and determines if it has the information of a node belonging to the neighboring clusters. A node acts as a border node if it has received the NghInfo packet from its neighbor having a different ClusterId. For example, as shown in Figure 1, we consider two clusters with ClusterId 501 and 231. Each node is represented by a unique NodeId. Node 34 acts as the border node for the cluster 501, since it has received the NghInfo packet form its neighbor node 45 which belongs to a different cluster having the ClusterId 231.

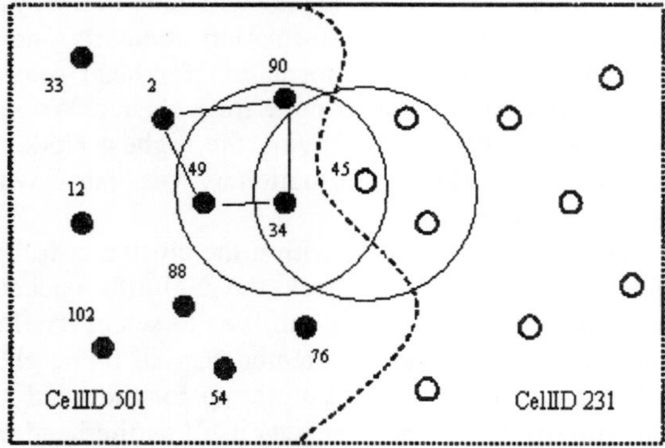

Figure 1. Construction of neighboring cluster routing table for CWOHO.

Each node in the cluster maintains a routing table containing information of its next hop neighbor. The table can be used to reach the neighboring clusters with the least hop count. It is created as follows:

```
if (border node) {
    Broadcast the neighboring cluster (with
    ClusterId say 'X') information within the same
    cluster with number of hops set to 1.
}

/* Node A receiving the broadcast information from
node B compares the hop count through node B (say
n+1) and the 'MinHops' in the Routing Table for
clusterId X (say m) */
```

```
if (Packet is for its present cluster) {
  if (n+1 = m) {
    if (Node B is present in the routing table for
    clusterId X)
      Update the timestamp value.
    else
      Insert a new entry for node B in the routing
      table for clusterId X
  }
  else if (n+1 < m) {
    Drop all the entries in the Routing Table for
    clusterId X and insert node B with MinHops
    n+1.
  }
  else {
    Drop the packet and return.
  }
  Replicate the packet by incrementing the hop
  count by 1.
}
```

Figure 2. The algorithm for constructing the routing table in CWOHO.

The border nodes of a cluster broadcast the neighboring cluster information to all the nodes in the cluster, using the NbdClusterInfo packet. The NbdClusterInfo packet contains the information of ClusterId and HopCount (equal to 1), which is the number of hops required to reach the neighbor cluster. The NbdClusterInfo packet is dropped if the packet belongs to a different cluster or if the node has received the packet from its neighbor having a larger hop count. A node on receiving the NbdClusterInfo packet from its next hop neighbor increments the hop count (say n) by 1 and checks its routing table if it has the information for the same neighboring cluster, say X. Let m be the minimum hop count for the neighboring cluster X presented in the routing table.

- If m < (n+1), then the packet is dropped as the routing table has the information for the same cluster with a fewer number of hops,
- else if m > (n+1), the node has received a better route with fewer hop count, hence all the information in the routing table for the cluster is dropped and the new information with fewer hop count is added in the routing table,
- else m = (n+1), the next hop neighbor is added for the corresponding neighboring cluster if it is not already present in the routing table; else the timestamp is incremented.

In Figure 2, we provide a pseudo code for the construction of the routing table. A routing table can have more than one next hop neighbor leading to a neighboring cluster. Table 1 shows an example of the routing table for node 2 corresponding to Figure 1.

CellID	*MinHops*	*NextHopNgh*	*TimeStamp*
231	2	49	XXXX
		90	YYYY
...	...	...	...

Table 1. Routing table for node 2.

The routing table is periodically updated depending on the timestamp value. A next hop neighbor is deleted from the routing table if the timestamp reaches a certain predefined threshold value. This situation occurs when a node has not received the NbdClusterInfo packet from its neighbor for the corresponding ClusterId. The ClusterId entry is removed from the routing table if there exits no next hop neighbor leading to the corresponding cluster. This situation can occur if the cluster has no border node acting as an intermediate between the two.

In addition to the routing table, each node also maintains the mesh structure. The MeshInfo packet contains the information of the cluster's connectivity with its neighboring clusters. Each node in the cluster has the information of all its neighboring clusters in its routing table (see Table 1). Figure 3 shows the algorithm for the construction of the mesh structure.

1) Check if (MeshInfo_TimeOut == TRUE), for the present cluster (say X)

- *Using 'Routing Table' update the mesh structure for the present cluster, X.*
- *Broadcast the neighboring cluster information for cluster X, to all the nodes using MeshInfo packet*

2) Received MeshInfo packet

- *Update the timestamp and the neighboring cluster information in the mesh structure for cluster X using MeshInfo packet*

Figure 3. The algorithm for constructing a mesh structure in CWOHO

The connectivity of the clusters with the neighboring clusters is broadcasted to all the nodes in the system. This broadcasting is initiated by a node in the cluster depending upon the timestamp value. Each node in the cluster periodically checks the timestamp value in the mesh structure it maintains, for the cluster in which it belongs. If the timestamp reaches a predetermined threshold, the neighboring cluster information in the mesh structure is updated using its routing table. This information is then broadcasted to all the nodes in the system. A node receiving the 'MeshInfo' packet updates its mesh structure and the timestamp value for the corresponding cluster. The number of the broadcasted 'MeshInfo' packets for a cluster is less than the number of nodes in the cluster. A cluster is considered a dead cluster if it has not received any MeshInfo from the cluster, within certain predefine time interval. Each node periodically checks and removes the information for the dead clusters from the mesh structure.

We next discuss the inter cluster routing strategy. A node initiating a data packet checks the mesh structure to determine the path to reach the destination cluster. In this implementation, the path information connecting the source and the destination clusters is attached to each data packet by the initiating node using its mesh structure. The path information is read by each intermediate node to determine the next hop neighbor for reaching the next neighboring cluster in the path. This is determined by comparing the node's own ClusterId with the path information.

3.2 Cluster-Based With Head Selection Overlay (CWHO)

For comparison purpose, we present in this section one possible scheme for the cluster-based overlay with head approach (CWHO). Again, each node in the system periodically collects the information about its one-hop neighbors. We use this information for head selection and determining the border node for a cluster. We select a node within the cluster having the highest NodeId as the head node. Head information is associated with a timestamp value.

Head node is selected within the cluster as follows: Each node periodically check the NghInfo packets it received from its neighbors and tries to select itself as a head node if its NodeId is greater than all its neighbors in the same cluster and if timestamp for the head node has expired. After a node selects itself as the head node it broadcasted the information within the clusters in the 'HeadInfo' packet containing its NodeId. The packet is dropped by an intermediate node if it has the head information having NodeId greater than that present in the 'HeadInfo' packet or else it updates its own information and replicates the information again within the cluster. As the 'HeadInfo' packet traverses within the cluster, each intermediate node construct its 'RouteToHead' table, including the next hop neighbor having the least hop count, as shown for the formation of the routing table in the implementation above.

Nodes also maintain a 'RouteToNbdCluster' table containing downstream route information to the neighbor cluster starting from the head node. This table is constructed as follows: A border node of the cluster periodically sends 'NbdClusterInfo' packets containing the neighboring cluster Information to the head node. A next hop neighbor on receiving the 'NbdClusterInfo' packet inserts the downstream route information in its

RouteToNbdCluster Table. This table contains the information such as next hop NodeId from whom it received the NbdClusterInfo packet and the corresponding ClusterId contained in the 'NbdClusterInfo' packet. This table shows the next hop neighbor in the downstream path starting from the head node which can be used to reach the neighboring cluster. The role of this table is similar to that of the routing table in CWOHO, as both are used for routing the information to the next hop neighbor to reach the neighboring cluster. Again each node periodically updates its RouteToNbdCluster table using a timestamp value.

Using the 'RouteToNbdCluster', the head node periodically determines its connected neighbors and sends this information to the head nodes of all the clusters using a 'MeshInfo' packet. Similar to the previous implementation, this information represents the connectivity with its neighboring clusters.

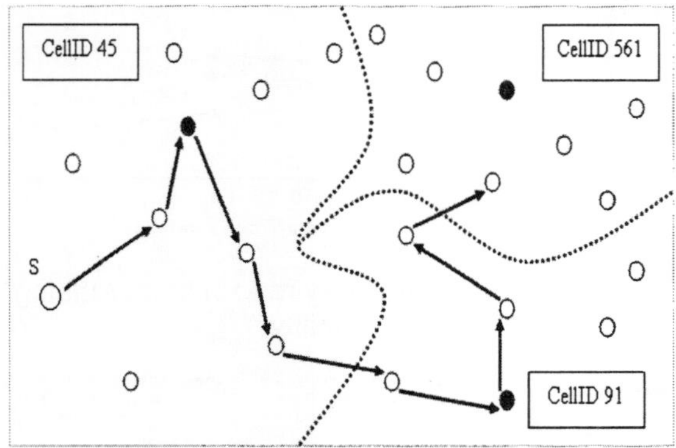

Figure 4. Routing in CWHO.

Since the mesh structure is maintained by the head node of each cluster, the inter cluster data routing takes place through the head nodes. A non-head node, initiating a data packet, uses its RouteToHead table to deliver the data packet to the head node of the cluster in which it belongs. As in the previous implementation, the head node attaches the path information to the data packet using the mesh structure, and the packet is routed towards the neighbor cluster using the 'RouteToNbdCluster' table. Since the root of the downstream route information for each neighboring cluster is maintained at the head node, the data passes through the head node of each intermediate cluster included in the path information.

A path failure occurs if path information is present in the data packet but there exits no neighbor in the RouteToNbdCluster table for forwarding the data packet. In such a case, a non-head node can strip off the path information from the data packet and deliver the packet back to the head node of its cluster for determining other paths to route the data packet to the destination.

An example of the routing strategy followed in CWHO is shown in Figure 4. In this figure, there are 3 clusters with ClusterId – 45, 91 and 561. The head node in each cluster is represented by a dark solid circle. It shows the data path followed when a non-head node S wants to deliver a data packet to the cluster 561.

4. Performance Evaluation

In this section we provide a simulation-based study to compare the performance of the two cluster-based mesh overlay schemes. We use the GloMoSim [10] simulator for the following evaluation. At the physical layer, GloMoSim uses a comprehensive radio model that accounts for noise power, signal propagation and reception.

In the following simulation, we use a network field size of 1000m X 1000m, containing 100 mobile nodes. All the nodes follow the random way mobility model [12] with speed ranging from 1 m/s to 20 m/s. To avoid the initial unstable phenomenon in the random waypoint model [11,12], we let the nodes move for 900 seconds before starting any network traffic [13], which lasts for 1500 seconds for each simulation run. The total number data item consider is 1000 each of 512 bytes.

We consider the following metrics to compare the performances of the two overlays:

1. Data Delivery Ratio: This is the ratio of the successful delivery of the data packets to the total number of the data packet created.
2. Average hop count: The average hop count of successful data delivered to the destination.
3. Average Control packet: The average control packets

We evaluate the above metrics by varying various parameters such as: the number of clusters, the mobility and the pause time. Each of the above stated metrics are measured by changing the maximum path as 1, 3 and 5, allowed for delivering the data packet to the destination cluster. As mentioned in the algorithm above, path 1 is the delivery of the data packet to the destination cluster in the first attempt without any path failure. Similarly, 3 and 5 are the maximum number of attempts to deliver the data packet to the destination cluster. We will provide details of the different parameters chosen along with our discussion of each experiment below.

4.1 Effects on Number of Clusters

The first simulation is to understand the effect of group size on both implementations. We fix the mobility of nodes and the pause time to 1–20 m/sec and 60 seconds respectively and increase the number of clusters as follows: 2, 4, 6, 8, 12, 16, 20, 25.

Figure 5 shows the data delivery ratio by increasing the number of clusters. In both implementations, the data delivery rate decreases with the increase in the number of clusters in the system. The data delivery ratio for CWOHO is greater than that of CWHO. Also, increasing the paths does not improve the data delivery ratio for CWHO, whereas there is a raise in the data delivery ratio for CWOHO as the maximum path number increases from 1 to 3. The data delivery ratio does not show the same stride when the maximum path is raised from 3 to 5 for CWOHO. The increase in the data delivery ratio for the maximum path 3 and 5 for the number of clusters 20 and 25 is due to the better cluster partitioning, i.e. decreasing the cluster size reduces partitioning of the clusters.

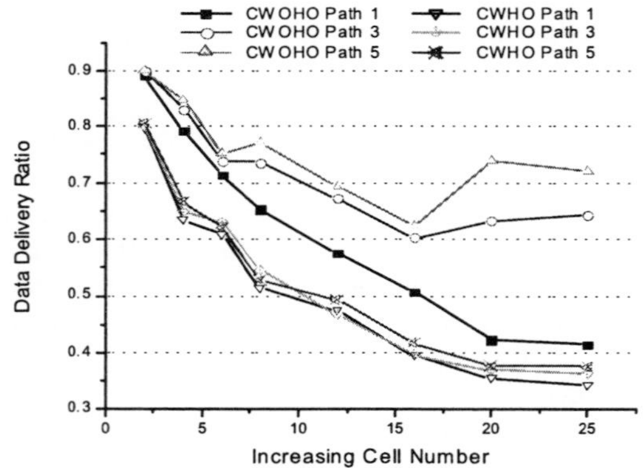

Figure 5. Data delivery ratio with increasing number of clusters.

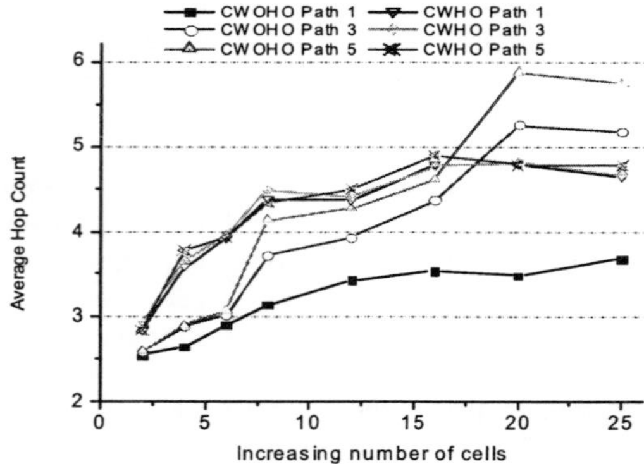

Figure 6. Average hop count with increasing number of clusters.

Figure 6 shows the average hop count. For both cases, the average hop count increases with increasing number of clusters. In addition, as the size of the clusters decrease, and the number of data packets reaching distant destination cluster increases. As a result, the hop count increases with the increase in the number of clusters. The increase in the average hop count for CWOHO from 1 to 3 shows the increase in the data packet reaching distant destination clusters due to better cluster connectivity.

4.2 Performance versus Increased Mobility

We design this performance evaluation to study the effect of increasing the mobility of the nodes with fixed pause time and fixed number of clusters. For this performance evaluation, we fix the number of clusters to 25 and the pause time 60 sec, and study the performance by changing the mobility of the nodes. We maintain the minimum mobility to 1 m/sec and change the maximum mobility of each node as follows (in m/sec): 2, 4, 8, 12, 16, 20.

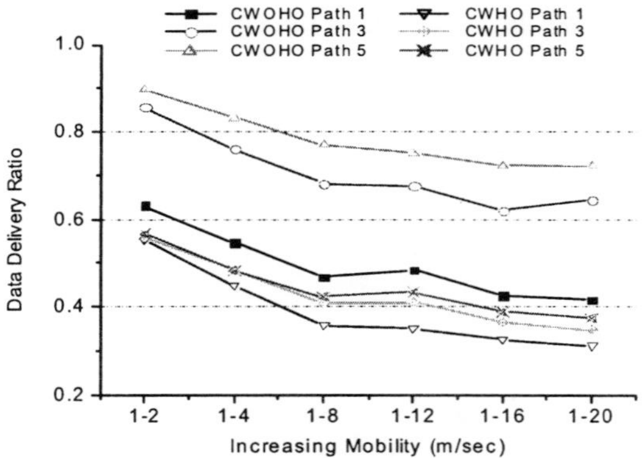

Figure 7. Data delivery ratio with increasing Mobility.

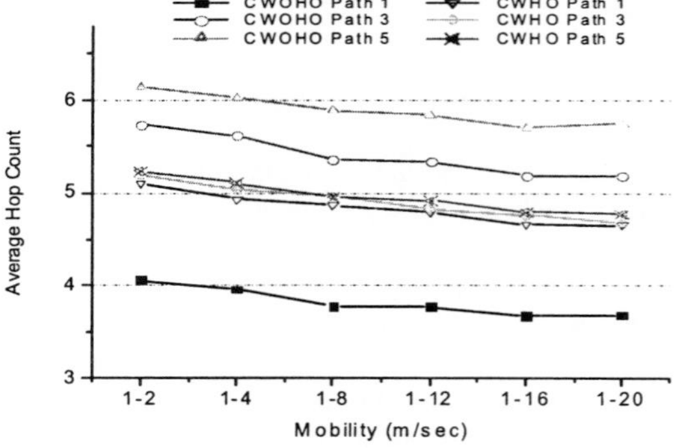

Figure 8. Average hop count with increasing mobility.

Figure 7 shows the data delivery ratio decreases with the increase in the mobility of the nodes for both the implementation. As above, the data delivery ratio does not show a significant improvement for CWHO with the increase in the number of paths, as seen for CWOHO. For comparison of the both, if we choose a maximum path as 3, the percentage of data delivery with mobility for CWOHO varies from, 60% to 85% where as for CWHO, it varies from 35% to 58% with the decrease in the mobility. Hence there exits a significant difference in the percentage of the data delivered with mobility.

Figure 8 shows a decrease in the average hop count in both cases with an increase in the mobility of the nodes. This shows that with the increase in the mobility of the nodes the data delivery failure occurs for data packets belonging to the distant destination clusters, thus reducing the average hop count.

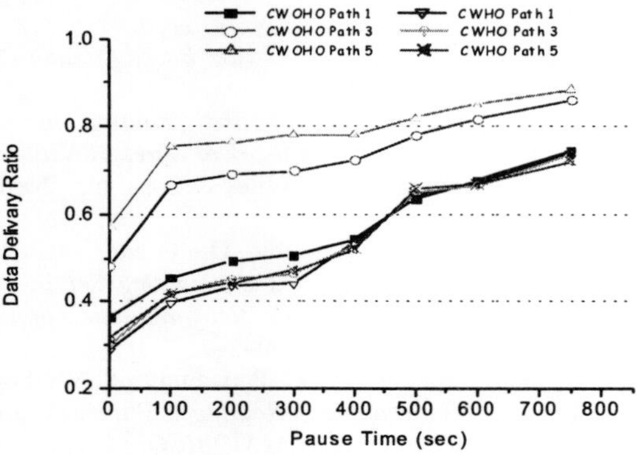

Figure 9. Data delivery ratio with increasing pause time.

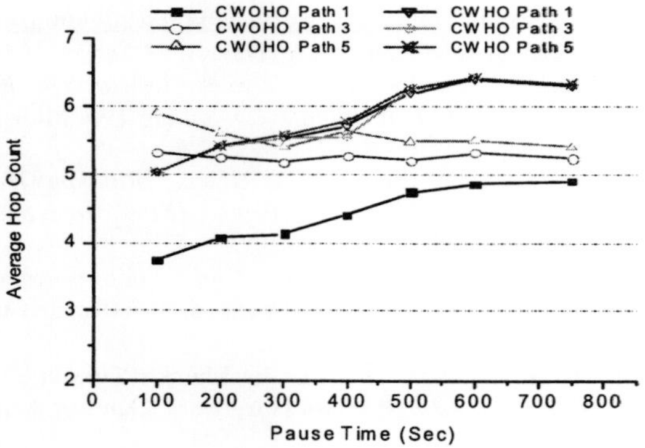

Figure 10. Average hop count with increasing pause time.

4.3 Performance versus Increased Pause Time

In this performance study, we study the effect of increasing the pause time in the system. For this performance evaluation we fix the number of clusters to 25 and mobility of the nodes 1-20 m/sec and change the pause time of the nodes as follows (in sec): 0, 100, 200, 300, 400 500, 600, 750.

Figure 9 shows the increase in the data delivery ratio with the increase in the pause time for both the implementation. The data delivery ratio for CWOHO is greater than that of CWHO. For maximum path 3, the data delivery ratio varies from 30% - 75% for CWHO and from 47% - 85% for CWOHO. Also for CWHO, the increase in the data path does not show a significant increase in the data delivery ratio as seen for CWOHO. The average hop count increases as shown in Figure 10 for CWHO, with the increase in the stability in the system there exits an increase in the data packet reaching the distant destination, hence the increase in the data delivery ratio in Figure 9. In the case CWOHO, the average hop count shows a similar behavior for the maximum path-1, but maintains a uniform hop count for path-3 and path 5 with the increase in the pause time, even with the increase in the data delivery ratio due to the increase in the stability in the system. It shows that with the increase in the maximum number of paths and the pause time data packets reach distant clusters with similar average hop count.

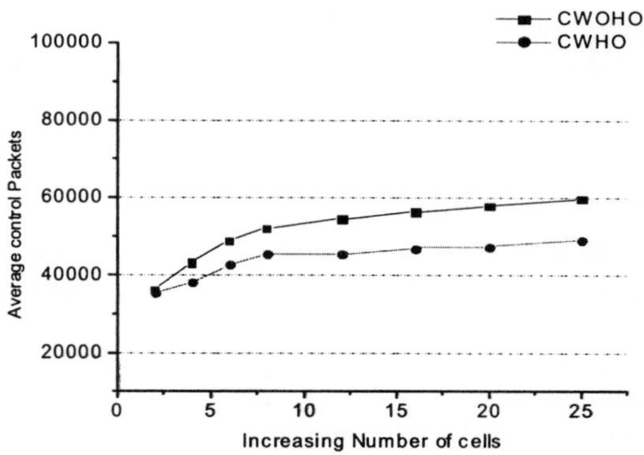

Figure 11. Average control packets with increasing number of clusters.

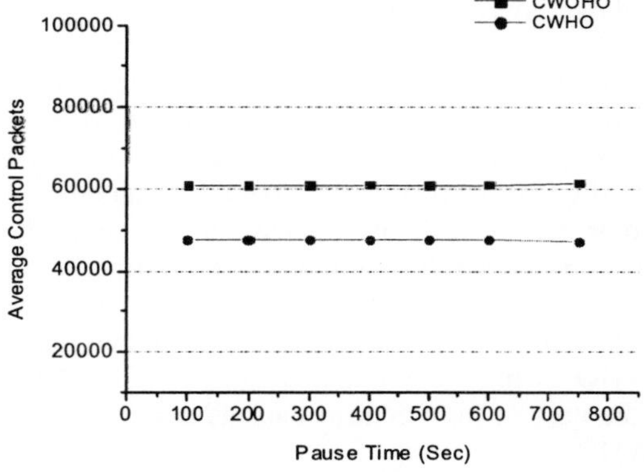

Figure 12. Average control packets with increasing pause time/mobility.

4.4 Average Control Packets

We compare the average control packets needed by both the implementation for the study of the data delivery ratio and the average hop counts in our above performance evaluation. An average is taken between the maximum paths 1, 3 and 5 selected for all the above performance evaluation.

Figure 11 shows the increase in the number of the average control packets in both the case with the increase in the number of clusters in the system. An increase in the control packets in CWHO with the increase in the number of clusters is due to the increase in the number of head nodes and hence increasing the number of the control packets for head selection, maintenance and mash maintenance. Similarly for CWOHO, the increase in the number of clusters increases the number of control packets for the maintenance of the neighboring cluster and the mesh formation. Figure 12 shows the average control packets required by increasing the pause time and the mobility of the nodes. Since in both the implementation the control packets are triggered by the nodes periodically based on a timestamp value, the average control packets remains more or less the same to the change in mobility or the pause time.

5. Conclusions

In this paper, we consider building a cluster-based overlay mesh in MANET without using cluster heads. The nodes in the ad hoc environment are grouped into clusters depending upon their physical connectivity. The interconnectivity of the clusters through border nodes forms a mesh structure which can be either be maintained by selecting a particular node within the cluster as is done in Cluster-Based with head Overlay (CWHO) or the information can be distributed to all the nodes in the system as is done in Cluster-Based without head overlay (CWOHO).

We examine one possible implementation for each of the two approaches and perform a simulation-based evaluation. Our performance evaluation demonstrates that the data delivery ratio for CWOHO is greater than that of CWHO. Also, in CWOHO the data delivery ratio also increases with the increase in the number of the paths i.e. the number of attempts for delivering the data packet to the destination cluster. This signifies that the mesh structure in CWOHO is better utilized than that of CWHO. A high data delivery ratio for CWOHO comes at the cost of high control packets compared to that of CWHO.

Future work includes a study for the various aspects related to dynamic cluster formation on ad hoc network and to integrate with our proposed CWOHO implementation. We also plan to implement various applications on top of CWOHO.

References

[1] S. Ratnasamy, B. Karp, S. Shenker, D. Estrin, R. Govindan, L. Yin, F. Yu, "*Data-Centric Storage in Sensornets with GHT - A Geographic Hash Table*," *Mobile Networks and Applications*, Aug. 2003.

[2] P. Sinha, R. SivaKumar and V. Bharghavan, "*MCEDAR: Multicast Core-Extension Distributed Ad Hoc Routing*," *Proc. IEEE WCNC*, Sept., 1999.

[3] C. Jaikaeo and C-C. Shen, "*Adaptive Backbone-Based Multicast for Ad hoc Networks*," *Proc. IEEE ICC*, New York, NY, 2002.

[4] M. Gerla, C-C.Chiang and L. Zhang, "*Tree Multicast Strategies in Mobile, Multihop Wireless Networks*," *ACM Mobile Networks and Applications*, Vol. 4, 1999, pp 193-207.

[5] M. Jiang, J. Li, Y.C. Tay, *Cluster Based Routing Protocol*, IETF Draft, August 1999.

[6] Jie Wu, "*Dominating-set-based Routing in Ad hoc Wireless Networks*," *Handbook of Wireless Networks and Mobile Computing*, John Wiley & Sons, Inc., New York, NY, 2002.

[7] P.J. Wan, K.M. Alzoubi, O. Frieder, "*Distributed Construction of Connected Dominating Set in Wireless Ad Hoc Networks*," *Mobile Networks and Applications*, Volume 9, Issue 2, April 2004.

[8] A. Rao, S. Ratnasamy, C. Papadimitriou, S. Shenker, I. Stoica, "*Geographic Routing Without Location Information*," *Proc. of ACM MOBICOM*, 2003.

[9] S. Capkun, M. Hamdi, J.-P. Hubaux, "*GPS-free Positioning in Mobile Ad hoc Networks*," *Proc. of 34th Hawaii International Conference on System Sciences* (HICSS-34), Volume 9, p.9008, January, 2001.

[10] GloMoSim : http://pcl.cs.ucla.edu/project/glomosim/

[11] T. Camp, J. Boleng, and V. Davies, "*A Survey of Mobility Models for Ad Hoc Network Research*," *Wireless Communication & Mobile Computing* (WCMC), Vol 2, no. 5, pp 483-502, 2002.

[12] J. Yoon, M. Liu, and B. Nobel, "*Random Waypoint Considered Harmful*," *Proc. IEEE Infocom*, San Francisco, CA, 2003.

[13] C. Perkins, "*Mobile Ad hoc Networking Terminology*," *Internet Draft*, draft-ietf-manet-term-00 (October 1997).

[14] D. B. Johnson and D. A. Maltz, "*Dynamic Source Routing in Ad Hoc Wireless Network*," Kulwer Academic, 1996.

[15] A. Rowstron and P. Druschel, "*Pastry: Scalable, Distributed Object Location and Routing for Large-scale Peer-to-peer Systems*," *Proc. of Middleware*, November 2001.

[16] H. Pucha, S.M. Das and Y. Charlie Hu, "*Ekta: An Efficient DHT Substrate for Distributed Applications in Mobile Ad Hoc Networks*," *Proc. of the 6th IEEE Workshop on Mobile Computing Systems and Applications* (WMCSA), December 2004.

Session 2A: Processor Architecture

Exploring Processor Design Options for Java-Based Middleware

Martin Karlsson and Erik Hagersten
Uppsala University
Department of Information Technology
P.O. Box 325, SE-751 05
Uppsala, Sweden
{martink, eh}@it.uu.se

Kevin E. Moore and David A.Wood
University of Wisconsin
Department of Computer Sciences
210 W. Dayton St.
Madison, WI 53706
{kmoore, david}@cs.wisc.edu

Abstract

Java-based middleware is a rapidly growing workload for high-end server processors, particularly Chip Multiprocessors (CMP). To help architects design future microprocessors to run this important new workload, we provide a detailed characterization of two popular Java server benchmarks, ECperf and SPECjbb2000. We first estimate the amount of instruction-level parallelism in these workloads by simulating a very wide issue processor with perfect caches and perfect branch predictors. We then identify performance bottlenecks for these workloads on a more realistic processor by selectively idealizing individual processor structures. Finally, we combine our findings on available ILP in Java middleware with results from previous papers that characterize the availibility of TLP to investigate the optimal balance between ILP and TLP in CMPs.

We find that, like other commercial workloads, Java middleware has only a small amount of instruction-level parallelism, even when run on very aggressive processors. When run on processors resembling currently available processors, the performance of Java middleware is limited by frequent traps, address translation and stalls in the memory system. We find that SPECjbb2000 differs from ECperf in two meaningful ways: (1) the performance of ECperf is affected much more by cache and TLB misses during instruction fetch and (2) SPECjbb2000 has more memory-level parallelism.

Keywords: Java, Middleware, workloads, ILP, CMP, Characterization

1 Introduction

The rapid rise of electronic commerce and Internet-delivered computing services has triggered explosive growth in the use of middleware. Simultaneously, Java has gained popularity as the programming environment of choice for Internet server software. Java-based middleware hosts the Internet presence of some of the world's largest companies in industries from financial services to airlines, making Java-based middleware one of the primary workloads for multiprocessor servers today.

The continued decrease in transistor size and the increasing delay of wires relative to transistor switching speeds has led to the development of chip multi-processors (CMPs) [2][23][27]. The introduction of CMPs presents new challenges and trade-offs to computer architects. In particular, architects must now strike a balance between allocating more resources to each processor against the number of processors on a chip. The proper balance of resources devoted to parallelism at the instruction level and parallelism at the tread level depends on the application. Previous studies have explored the limits to thread-level parallelism (TLP) and characterized the multiprocessor memory system behavior of Java middleware [13][14]. Here, we investigate the limits to instruction-level parallelism (ILP) and combine our findings with insights to TLP from previous papers to explore the design space of CMPs.

In this paper, we present a detailed characterization of two popular Java server benchmarks, ECperf and SPECjbb2000 (JBB). Where ECperf, also has been repackaged with only minor changes and released as SPECjAppServer2001 and SPECjAppServer2002. ECperf closely resembles commercially deployed Internet applications—it is a distributed system with clients, middleware and database all running separately. JBB emulates a 3-tiered application in a single process by simulating clients, and a database in the same Java virtual machine (JVM) as the middleware.

We attempt to classify Java middleware as a workload by comparing the behavior of ECperf to that of two other important commercial workloads, on-line transaction processing (OLTP) and static web serving (APACHE), and to several SPEC benchmarks. We also compare and contrast the behaviors of ECperf and JBB to see how well the simple

0190-3918/05 $20.00 © 2005 IEEE

JBB approximates the more complicated ECperf.

We find that the behavior of ECperf is similar to that of other commercial workloads. Like OLTP and APACHE, ECperf exhibits limited ILP, even on aggressive processors. On very aggressive processors, its performance is limited by address translation and frequent traps. We notice two substantial differences between ECperf and JBB. JBB, like the SPEC CPU2000 benchmarks, is not limited by misses in the instruction cache or ITLB, and JBB has more memory-level parallelism.

The rest of this paper is organized as follows: Section 2 describes our simulation methodology. Section 3 presents the level of instruction-level parallelism (ILP) present in the workloads and identifies several limiting factors. Section 4 analyzes the bottlenecks present in a realistic microprocessor. Section 5 discusses how our results from sections 3 and 4 might influence architects seeking to optimize per-chip performance of Java middleware on a CMP. Section 6 outlines some related work in workload characterization. We present our conclusions in Section 7.

2 Methodology

All of the results in this paper were generated with full-system execution-driven simulation. We used full-system simulation because the operating system makes up a substantial portion of the runtime for our commercial workloads. Execution-driven simulation allowed us to model hardware that would be impossible to build. In particular, we simulated several processor configurations with one feature "idealized," or made perfect.

2.1 Workloads

To better understand the characteristics of our two Java server workloads, we compared them to two other commercial workloads, APACHE and OLTP, and four benchmarks from the SPEC2000 suite [25]. Table 1 presents a description of each application and the input parameters we used to run them. We ran both of our Java workloads on Sun's Hotspot 1.4.1 Server JVM and all of our workloads on Solaris 8.

Benchmark	Description
ECperf	ECperf is a middle-tier benchmark designed to test the performance and scalability of a real 3-tier system. ECperf models an on-line business using a "Just-In-Time" manufacturing process (products are made only after orders are placed and supplies are ordered only when needed). It incorporates e-commerce, business-to-business, and supply chain management transactions.
SPECjbb2000	SPECjbb2000 is a server-side Java benchmark that models a 3-tier system, focusing on the middle-ware server business logic and object manipulation. The benchmark includes driver threads to generate transaction as well as an object tree working as a back-end. Our experiment use 24 driver threads (1.5 per processor) and 24 warehouses (with a total data size of approximately 500MB).
APACHE	Static Web Content Serving: Apache with SURGE. We use Apache 2.0.43 configured to use a hybrid multi-process multi-threaded server model with 64 POSIX threads per server process. Our experiments use a hierarchical directory structure of 80,000 files (with a total data size of approximately 1.8 GB) and a modified version of the Scalable URL Reference Generator (SURGE [1]) to simulate 6400 users (400 per processor) with an average think time of 12ms.
OLTP	On-Line Transaction Proccessing: DB2 with a TPC-C like workload. The TPC-C benchmark models the database activity of a wholesale supplier. Our OLTP workload is based on the TPC-C v3.0 benchmark using IBM's DB2 v7.2 EEE database management system. Our experiments simulate 256 users (16 per processor)without think time. The simulated users query a 5GB database with 25,000 warehouses stored on eight raw disks and a dedicated database log disk.
SPEC CPU2000	We have chosen four benchmarks, GCC, BZIP, PERLBMK and MCF, from the SPEC CPU 2000 Integer suite [25]. GCC is an compilation with an aggressively optimized C compiler. BZIP is a compression and decompression of a TIFF image, a program binary, and a source tar file. PERLBMK is an PERL interpretor running a scripts for mail generation. MCF is a combinatorial optimization of a vehicle depot scheduling problem.

Table 1. Benchmark descriptions.

2.2 Simulation Environment

For our simulations, we used the Simics full-system simulator [17]. Simics is an execution-driven functional simulator that models a SPARC V9 system accurately enough to run Solaris 8 unmodified. To model the timing of complex out-of-order processors we extend Simics with the Timing-first simulator, TFsim [20], and a detailed memory hierarchy simulator [19]. TFsim is a detailed timing simulator that models an out-of-order processor loosely based on the MIPS R10000 [28].

2.3 Measuring Performance Cost in Out-Of-Order Processors

In order to isolate the ILP limiting effects of various processor and memory system structures, we selectively idealize processor structures to approximate the cost of various aspects of instruction processing. The cost of a structure is defined as the difference between the performance with that structure idealized, or made perfect, and the performance of the base machine. Instead of measuring the costs of each structure individually, for simplicity, we measure the sum of the costs of various structures by idealizing structures such as caches and branch predictors in succession.

Our methodology allows us to model both perfect caches and perfect branch prediction on otherwise realistic processors. We model perfect branch prediction by recording the direction or target of all branches in a branch trace. We use separate traces for perfect branch direction prediction and perfect branch target prediction so that our timing simulator can execute arbitrarily far down a mispredicted branch capturing wrong-path effects. This separation enables us to distinguish the effect of idealizing the branch target buffer (BTB), return address stack (RAS) and the directional branch predictor. When simulating a perfect cache, which always hits, we still model each access throughout the memory hierarchy, which allows us to maintain approximately the same cache behavior in the unified lower levels of the memory hierarchy.

3 Limits on Instruction-Level Parallelism

Many modern microprocessors use out-of-order processing, branch prediction, non-blocking caches and other techniques to execute independent instructions in parallel. The number of instructions that can be executed in parallel is limited both by the characteristics of the workload and the resources available in the processor. In this section, we first estimate the amount of ILP available in each workload by eliminating as many constraints as possible in the hardware. This provides a generous estimate—albeit not a hard limit—of the speedup that can be achieved by increasing the size and complexity of each processor core. Next, we identify specific limitations on ILP in Java middleware.

3.1 Estimating the Level of ILP

To estimate the practical limit of ILP in these workloads, we simulate a 64-issue uniprocessor with both perfect caches and perfect branch prediction (i.e., the branch prediction is always correct and all memory accesses hit in the L1 cache). Our simulated processor has a five-stage pipeline, a 1024-entry reorder Buffer and infinite load/store queues. We measure the number of instructions executed per cycle (IPC) while increasing the size of the issue window.

Even this idealized processor is unable to exploit more than a small amount of ILP in any of our commercial workloads. As shown in Figure 1 (a), issue windows larger than 64 entries benefit only one of our commercial workloads, OLTP, on which performance peaks at a window size of 256 entries. Furthermore, much of the ILP exploited by our idealized processor is due to its unattainable perfect memory hierarchy. To isolate the effect of memory accesses on ILP, we simulate 2-cycle 4-way 32 KB L1 data cache, an 18-cycle 8-way 1 MB L2 cache and a 250-cycle memory latency.[1] Note that the instruction cache and branch predictor are still perfect. Comparing Figure 1 (a) and Figure 1 (b) highlights the effect of replacing the perfect memory sytem with a more realistic memory hierarchy. Performance improvement from increasing the window size is almost completely eliminated for all of the commercial workloads. Only PERL and BZIP continue to benefit from large instruction windows when memory accesses are modeled.

[1]This is the same memory system configuration as for the medium core shown in Table 6.

3.2 Traps: An ILP Limitation

Frequent traps, limit the benefits of large windows in out-of-order processors running Java middleware. On ECperf, we measured an average of 4.8 traps per 1000 instructions, which means that for a machine with a 1024-entry issue window there are, on average, more than 4 instructions that will cause a trap or exception in the window. Since exceptions are commonly detected at commit stage and usually require a pipeline flush, the cost of exceptions can be quite significant for processors with large issue windows. The effect of traps on ILP is not limited to Java workloads. We also find that the two applications whose performance scales the least with the issue window scaling, Apache and MCF, show some of the highest trap frequencies.

As shown in Table 2, the most frequent types of traps in Java workloads are TLB misses and register window spill/fill exceptions. Although the most common traps in our experiments are SPARC-specific—software-handled TLB misses and register window spill and fill traps—we believe that large instruction footprints and deep call stacks are inherent to Java middleware and will be an ILP limitation on other architectures as well.

Throughout this paper we have simulated a software-managed 128-entry four-way set-associative instruction and data TLB's and eight register windows. Unfortunately, since the TLB's and the register windows are part of the architected state in the SPARC architecture, our current simulator infrastructure does not allow us to idealize them.

	DTLB	ITLB	Spill/Fill	Trap	Total
ECperf	0.99	2.08	1.73	0.04	4.84
JBB	0.22	0.07	0.13	0.05	0.47
OLTP	0.92	1.00	1.47	0.07	3.47
APACHE	1.99	0.43	2.38	0.13	4.94
GCC	0.01	0.00	0.06	0.00	0.07
BZIP	0.03	0.00	0.00	0.00	0.03
PERL	0.06	0.00	0.30	0.00	0.37
MCF	8.50	0.00	0.00	0.00	8.50

Table 2. The number of traps/exceptions taken per 1000 retired instructions

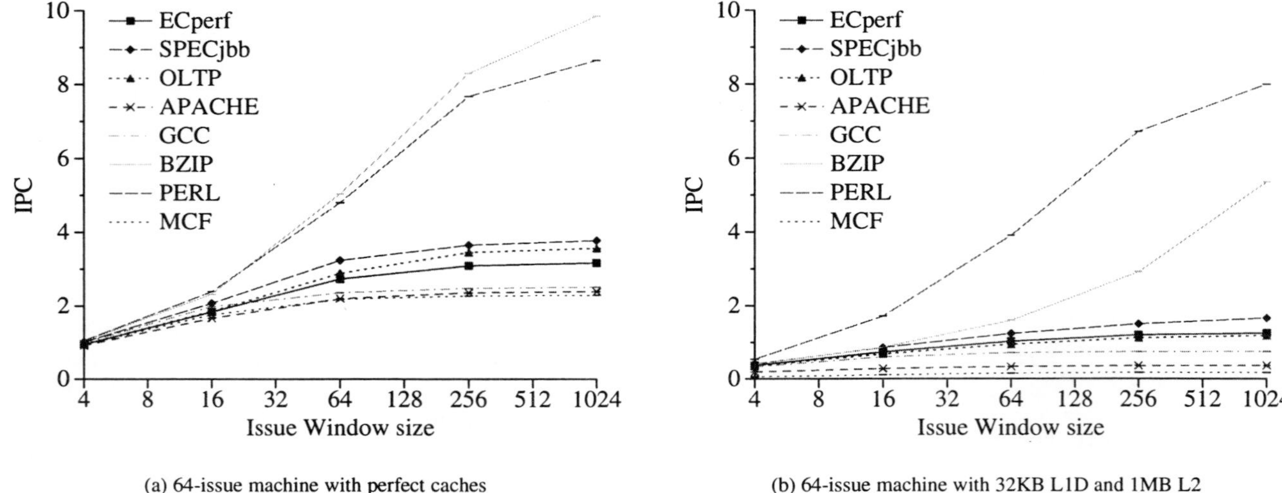

(a) 64-issue machine with perfect caches

(b) 64-issue machine with 32KB L1D and 1MB L2

Figure 1. Estimating the available amounts of instruction level parallelism with and without a perfect data cache.

3.2.1 TLB Misses

TLB misses, especially ITLB misses, place a significant limitation on the ILP in ECperf. We observe an ITLB miss rate on ECperf (2.08 misses per 1000 instructions) that is twice as high as the miss rate for OLTP and roughly five times as that for APACHE. Since ITLB misses are extremely hard to overlap both with software or hardware managed TLBs, we identify the ITLB performance as a significant bottleneck to single-thread performance. We find that the DTLB miss rate for ECperf is on par with OLTP, which is known to have a significant execution stall time due to DTLB misses.

One optimization that improves the performance of TLBs for workloads with large instruction and data sets is the use of large pages. Our JVM, HotSpot 1.4.1, includes support for Intimate Shared Memory (ISM), a Solaris API that supports the use of 4 MB pages (normal pages in Solaris are 8 KB). In our configurations, however, HotSpot uses these pages for the heap, but not for code compiled with its just-in-time compiler. Therefore, when running ECperf, the DTLB has a much greater reach than the ITLB. Solaris 9 contains a new API, MPSS, which replaces ISM [21]. When run on Solaris 9, HotSpot uses MPSS to create large pages for both code and heap. We anticipate that we will see fewer ITLB misses in ECperf when we update our configuration to Solaris 9.

The negative pipeline effects from software handling of DTLB misses can be reduced by hardware managed TLB's or by inlining exception handlers, which avoids pipeline flushes and allows independent instructions to complete out of order with the faulting instruction as proposed by Jaleel and Jacob [11]. Alternatively, Zilles et al. [29] propose using idle threads in an multithreaded processor to handle exceptions thereby avoiding squash and re-fetch of the instructions following the faulting instruction. Note, however, that neither of these approaches can reduce the penalty of an ITLB miss.

3.2.2 Register Window Manipulation

We observe a substantial amount of spill/fill traps in ECperf, APACHE and OLTP. The register windows in the Sparc architecture cause spill/fill traps when the call stack depth exceeds the number of available register windows—the processors we simulate have 8 register windows. Although register windows are specific to SPARC, the call stack behaviour that generates spill/fill traps could also limit performance in a flat register architecture, where register content is manually saved on the stack between procedure calls. Given the Call/Return frequencies observed in our Java workloads, it is likely that several procedure calls would be in-flight at the same time, leading to artificial dependencies on the stack pointer, which could severly reduce the benefits of large out-of-order windows.

Moreover, if multiple procedure calls at the same call depth are in flight simultaneously, they will reuse the same stack space. Hence loads and stores associated with the first call will access the same stack addresses as loads and stores of the second call. If these accesses are executed out of order they may violate memory ordering rules leading to costly replay traps. Such traps, however, could potentially be avoided with memory dependence prediction [22][6].

In Java, performance inhibitors such as frequent traps, can be addressed in the virtual machine software as well as in the hardware. We propose one such optimization based on the following observation. We find that in ECperf the JVM only uses spill_1 traps, which spills a single register window. We also note that for 50% of the spill traps, three or more spill_1 traps occur in a row before a fill trap happens. The SPARC architecture provides different spill/fill traps for spilling/filling multiple register windows at a time. For example, the Ultrasparc III can spill or fill one, three or six register windows at a time. Our results indicate that 99 % of the spill traps in ECperf occur from only 15 different user-level instructions. If these trap locations could be indentified and changed statically or dynamically to spill_3 traps, the number of pipeline-disrupting spill traps could be decreased by a third. We observe the same behavior for fill traps as well.

3.3 MLP and Memory System Impact

Memory-level parallelism (MLP) is an important workload characteristic because it measures the ability of the processor to overlap the latency of multiple cache misses. As latencies continue to increase, the importance of exploiting MLP becomes more and more important.

We estimate the amount MLP in our workloads by counting the number of outstanding cache misses each time a cache miss occurs. We perform these measurements using our most aggressive processor (1024-entry issue window) from Section 3.1 and Figure 1 (b) in order to maximize the MLP.

Since the number of outstanding misses may vary significantly during execution, we present the maximum number of outstanding cache misses recorded during various fractions of the total misses in addition to the average number of outstanding misses. Table 3 shows the highest number of outstanding misses during the 95% and 99% of misses with the least number of already outstanding misses—e.g. for ECperf the 99% column indicates that only 1% of the misses occurred when more than 5 L1 data cache misses were already outstanding.

All of the commercial benchmarks except OLTP exhibit a similar level of MLP. On average, OLTP has 8% more outstanding L2 misses than JBB and 20% more than ECperf. For the commercial workloads six MSHR's for the L1 data cache would be sufficient during 99% of the execution of all the commercial workloads.

	L1 Data Cache			L2 Unified Cache		
	95%	**99%**	**Avg.**	**95%**	**99%**	**Avg.**
ECperf	2	5	1.73	2	5	1.71
JBB	3	5	1.99	3	5	1.91
OLTP	3	6	1.69	4	11	2.06
APACHE	3	5	1.53	3	5	1.52
GCC	1	1	1.57	0	1	1.44
BZIP	15	38	5.30	9	31	4.39
PERL	0	1	1.43	0	1	1.43
MCF	3	16	4.82	3	16	4.69

Table 3. Estimating the degree of memory level parallelism. Maximum number of outstanding misses recorded for 95 and 99% of the miss events with a 1024 entry issue window.

4 Bottleneck Analysis

In order to find, quantify and isolate the limitations to ILP for a more realistic machine, we measured the IPC while idealizing structures like caches and branch predictors. In this section, we model a more conservative 3-issue processor, with a single load/store unit. We select this conservative design because our ILP limitation study in Section 3 reveals that even a processor with a very high issue width and large instruction window is unable to exploit any significant degree of ILP for our Java workloads. We also find that even more modest increases in issue width produce only small performance improvements over our 3-issue processor—e.g. an 8-issue processor with 2 load/store units only gave a 21% speedup for ECperf.

The simulated machine has the baseline memory system (2 cycle 4-way 32 KB L1 caches and an 18-cycle 8-way 1 MB L2 cache). Our baseline branch predictor are comprised of a 2.5 KB YAGS directional predictor [8], a 256-entry cascaded indirect predictor [7] and a 16-entry return-address stack [12].

For the experiments in this section, we also extend the pipeline depth to 16 stages to more accurately model pipeline effects. Our choice of 16 stages is a result of a simplistic optimal pipeline depth analysis similar to the one described by Hartstein et al. [10]. We determine the optimal pipeline depth by measuring the time per instruction while we increase the pipeline depth by scaling the decode, schedule and execute stages linearly—i.e., we add one additional stage at a time to each phase. In our model, a 22-stage pipeline minimizes the time per instruction. However, we conservatively choose to model a 16-stage pipeline because the improvement from 16 to 22 was negligible.

We measured the cost of branch mispredictions and

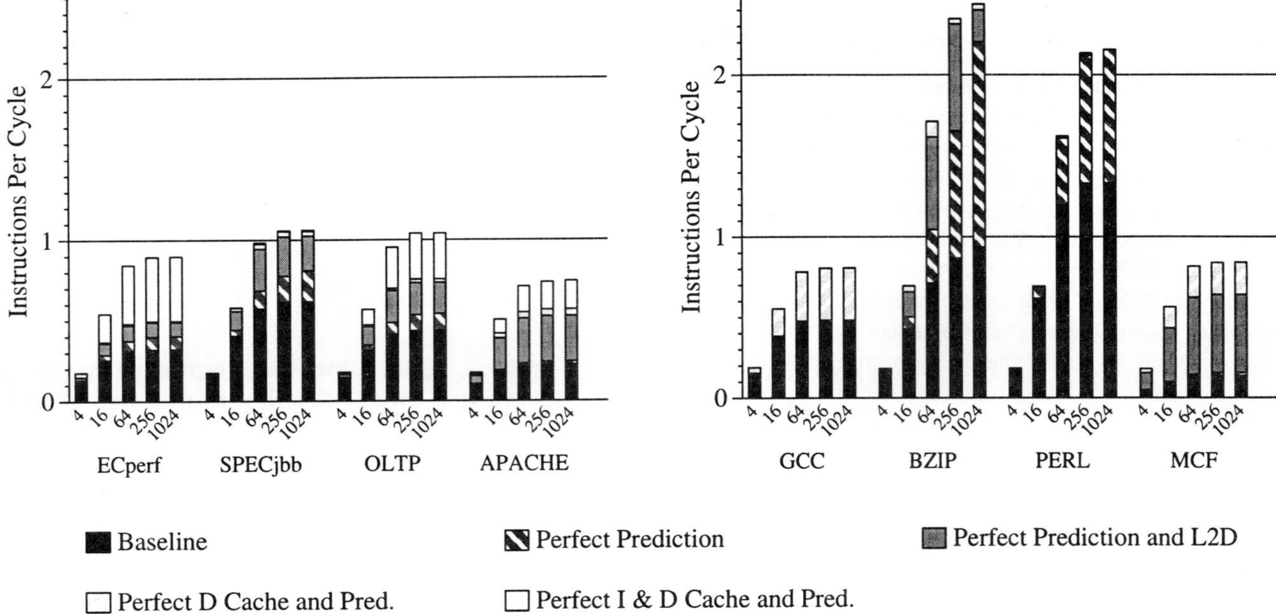

Figure 2. Performance improvements when idealizing certain structures compared to a 3-issue baseline configuration (Medium core), while scaling the issue window.

misses to the instruction and data caches by comparing the performance of our baseline machine to a similar machine with that one particular feature (a branch predictor or cache) made perfect. For example, we measure the cost of data misses to the unified L2 cache by simulating a perfect second-level cache[2] for all data accesses.

Figure 2 displays the performance improvement derived from idealizing more and more structures. Starting with a baseline design and then first idealize the branch predictors and then idealizing more and more of the memory hierarchy. The height of the bar represents the performance obtained when all structures are perfect.

4.1 Performance Effect of Cache Misses

We find that the performance of ECperf is more dependent on the instruction cache than any of our other benchmarks, which matches the high instruction cache miss rate reported by Karlsson et al. [13]. For ECperf, idealizing the L2 data accesses produces a considerable performance improvement. Idealizing the L1 data cache in addition, however, does not improve performance any further. We also observe that increasing the size of the instruction window beyond 64 entries does not significantly improve performance on either our baseline or idealized processors for any of our commercial applications. However, the SPEC applications BZIP and PERLBMK continue to benefit from larger instruction windows.

[2]Note that a perfect cache is not the same as an infinite cache as a perfect cache hits even for cold miss.

Figure 2 illustrates the degree to which each structure limits ILP for a particular workload, however, it does not indicate how much those limitations can be reduced by improving the structure. In order to test the feasibility of improving the caches, we measure the relative performance improvement of achievable optimizations such as doubling the cache size or associativity.

	L1 Data Cache		L1 Instr Cache	
Application	64KB	8-w	64KB	8-w
ECperf	0%	0%	0%	0%
JBB	0%	0%	0%	0%
OLTP	0%	0%	1%	0%
APACHE	2%	2%	3%	2%
GCC	0%	0%	0%	0%
BZIP	0%	0%	0%	0%
PERL	0%	0%	0%	0%
MCF	0%	0%	0%	0%

Table 4. Performance improvement over a 64-entry issue window baseline configuration when doubling cache size or associativity.

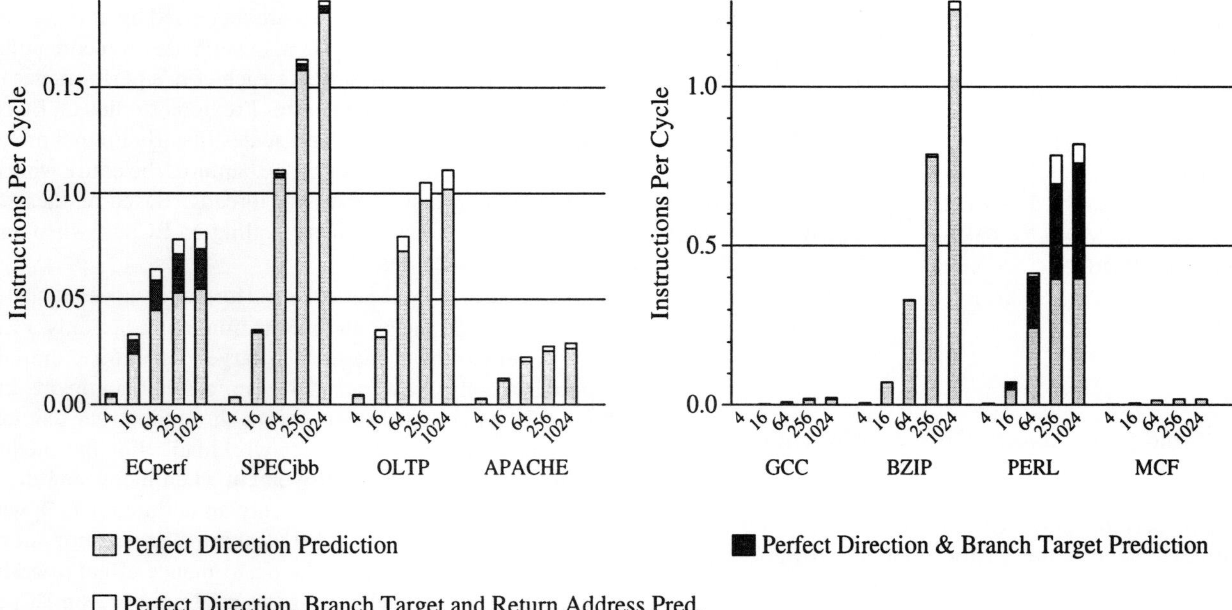

Figure 3. Performance improvement with perfect branch predictions structures compared to a 3-issue baseline configuration. Note this is a scaled up breakdown of the perfect prediction improvement stack from Figure 2.

Not surprisingly, doubling the size and associativity of the caches substantially reduces the cache miss rate. For example, when doubling the cache size, the number of data cache misses for ECperf and OLTP are reduced by 17% and 16% respectively. However, Table 4 shows that there is no corresponding improvement in performance for any application except APACHE. This lack of performance improvement indicates that L1 cache misses are not a primary bottleneck for these workloads running on our baseline processor.

4.2 Performance Effect of Branch Prediction

Modern processors use several different mechanisms to predict the instruction stream, including branch direction prediction, branch target prediction and return address prediction. We investigate breakdown the cost of several common types of mispredictions by measuring the effect of idealizing different types of predictors over our baseline branch predictor configuration.

As we can see in Figure 3, the bulk of the prediction cost in performance for all workloads is due to mispredictions of conditional branches. For ECperf, also perfecting the branch target buffer and return address stack yields a noticeable performance improvement. The same observation can be made for PERL. Perfect prediction improves the relative performance of ECperf by 21%, which is more than any of the other commercial benchmarks.

	Branch Predictors			
Application	Direction	BTB	RAS	All Perfect
ECperf	4%	0%	0%	21%
JBB	2%	0%	0%	19%
OLTP	6%	0%	0%	18%
APACHE	5%	2%	2%	11%
GCC	1%	0%	0%	5%
BZIP	1%	0%	0%	46%
PERL	3%	2%	0%	35%
MCF	0%	0%	0%	11%

Table 5. Performance improvement over a 64 entry issue window baseline configuration when doubling predictor sizes.

As above, we estimate how much of the possible performance improvement is attainable with realistic hardware by measuring the overall IPC improvement over the baseline when doubling the size of the different predictors. For all applications, especially the commercial ones, we observe significant gains from doubling the direction predictor. Doubling the BTB or the RAS only improves performance for APACHE and PERL.

Processor Core	LARGE	MEDIUM	SMALL
Fetch/Issue/Commit	8	3	1
Branch Pred.	10KB	2.5KB	0.6KB
BTB	1024	256	64
Return Address Stack	32	16	8
Mispred. Penalty	13	13	13
L1 I-Cache (4-way)	64KB	32KB	16KB
L1 D-Cache (4-way)	64KB	32KB	16KB
L1 Latency (I & D)	3 cycles	2 cycles	2 cycles
L2 Unified (8-way)		1MB	
L2 Latency		18 cycles	
Memory Latency		250 cycles	

Table 6. Processor Core configurations.

For ECperf, despite a 10% decrease in the BTB misprediction rate, we observe no noticeable improvement in performance. We hypothesize that this discrepancy is is due to the fact that programmers and compilers often put save and restore instructions in the delay slot of call and return instructions. When a spill or fill trap occurs on such an instruction, the pipeline is flushed. Therefore, any mispredictions immediately preceding the trap will have little or no effect on performance.[3]

5 Chip Multiprocessor Trade-offs

In order to make a back-of-the-envelope estimation of the CMP design that is best suited for Java-middleware workloads, we compare the performance of three processor configurations (small, medium and large) that represent different ILP vs. TLP design points. We measure the performance of each processor with three different L2 cache sizes. The relative performance improvement from each increase in processor size provides a rough estimate of the amount of additional chip area or power consumption that may be justified by the corresponding increase in throughput.

Our three processor configurations, large, medium and small, are described in Table 6. The medium core parameters were selected based on our earlier findings to represent a modestly aggressive processor in terms of single-thread performance, and relatively small in order to fit as many as possible on a die. It has the baseline memory system and branch predictor configurations. The small and large core designs was chosen as reference points in terms of single-thread performance and size.

The large and medium cores have issue windows with 128 and 32 entries, respectively, while the small core is single-issue and in-order. The issue width and the size of the L1 caches and predictors are increased by at least a factor 2 between each core. We also simulate each core with 1, 2 and 4 MB caches to observe each core's performance dependence on the L2 cache size. Previous studies on ECperf have shown both that ECperf scales linearly up to 8 processors and that a few MB of cache captures the entire working set [13][14] when shared by 8 threads. Based on these observations, we assume linear scaling on ECperf when comparing CMP designs.[4]

For ECperf, we notice a performance speedup of 2.5 times between the small and medium core, but only a 21% improvement from medium to large. Therefore, the large core can consume at most 21% more area than the medium core for it to be as efficient from a throughput-per-chip-area standpoint for this particular workload. For the medium core, we note a 14% improvement when increasing the L2 size from 1MB to 2MB, but only an additional 11% when increasing from 2MB to 4MB. Taking the area trade-off one step further, we compare the performance effect of adding cores instead of cache. For the medium core on ECperf, this implies that since we assume linear scaling when increasing the number of cores. Increasing the L2 cache size from 2MB to 4MB must increase the area by no more than 11% to be more beneficial than adding additional cores for ECperf.

When power is taken into consideration, cache would be favored instead of cores since caches consume significantly less power (both in terms of leakage and dynamic power) than processor cores. Adding cache can also reduce memory bandwidth consumption, which could become a major performance limitation in large CMPs as more cores on a die will lead to fewer available pins per core.

6 Related Work

Several previous papers have also analyzed Java workloads. Li and John identify the large number of branch sites in Java programs as the cause of poor branch prediction on these workloads [15]. Luo and John present an analysis of two Java server benchmarks (JBB and VolanoMark). They find that Java server workloads have poor instruction cache behavior and high ITLB miss rates [16]. Shuf et al. observe that prefetching is ineffective on Java workloads due to high TLB miss rates. Other studies characterize the memory system behavior of Java server workloads [4][5][13][18][26].

Many previous papers have studied the behavior of other commercial workloads. For example, Barroso et al. studied the memory system of an OLTP workload [3]. Redstone

[3]We assume an aggressive trap mechanism that does not squash the delay slot on a misprediction.

[4]Note that the linear scaling assumption does not hold for SPECjbb2000, APACHE and OLTP, since their dataset is larger than the simulated L2 cache sizes leading to potentially negative L2 sharing effects. We include them as uniprocessor performance reference points.

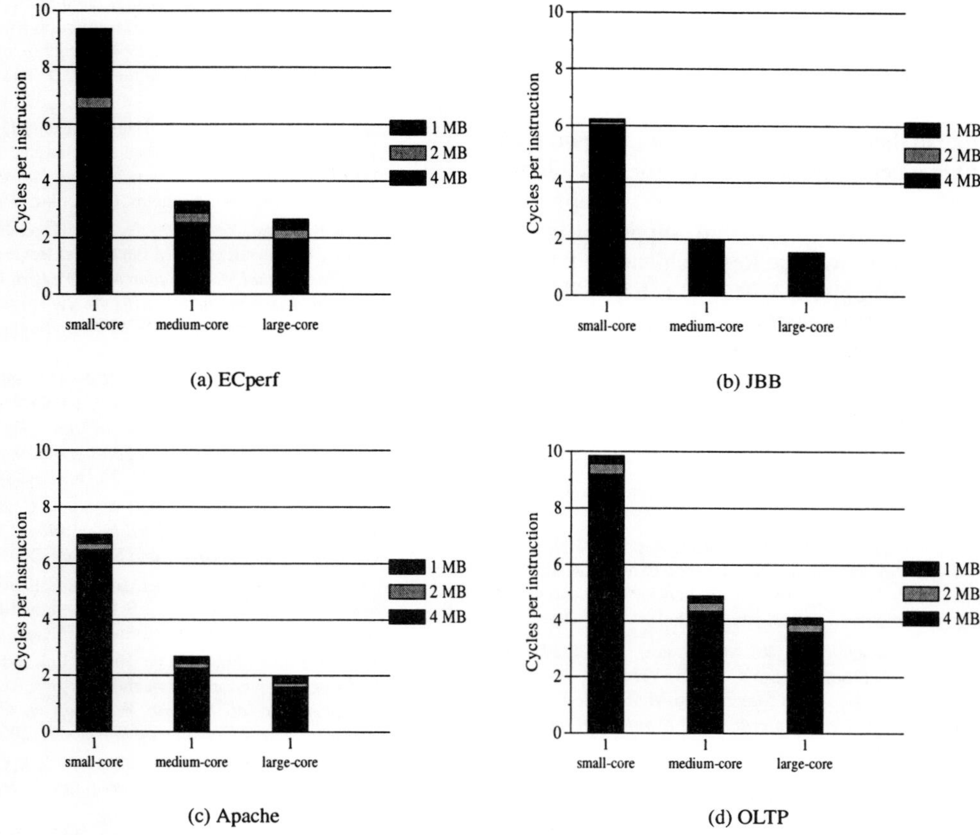

Figure 4. Chip trade-offs, Large cores vs. smaller cores and cores vs. cache

et. al. studied the operating system behaviour on an SMT architecture using APACHE [24].

Ekman and Stenström studied the performance and power impact of issue-width in CMP cores using the SPLASH-2 benchmark suite [9] and found that CMP designs with fewer wider-issue cores perform as well with a comparable power consumption as designs with larger numbers of smaller cores.

7 Conclusions

Java middleware is an important and growing workload for server processors. This paper is the first to characterize this emerging workload using the step-by idealization of processor structures. We use this technique to illustrate the behavior of ECperf and JBB. We offer greater insight into the behavior of our Java workloads by comparing them to other well-known commercial workload and to several of the widely studied SPEC benchmarks.

We find that, at the processor level, Java middleware behaves much like other well known commercial workloads—ILP is limited by memory system stalls, branch mispredictions and frequent traps. For ECperf, as for other commercial workloads, instruction fetch is a potential performance bottleneck. Overall performance is limited by instruction cache and TLB misses for ECperf, OLTP and APACHE. Improving ITLB performance, perhaps by using large pages for Just-In-Time compiled code, is essential to the effective utilization of aggressive processors on ECperf.

For ECperf, we find that a modestly aggressive medium-size processor core achieves very close to the performance obtained by a more aggressive core. Our most aggressive processor achieved only an 21% speedup over our medium-size core despite having twice the issue width, amount of L1 cache and branch predictor state. Extremely simple processors, on the other hand, sacrifice a significant amount of easily exploitable ILP. Our medium-size processor outperformed a simple in-order processor by a factor of 2.5. Therefore, we believe that from a performance-per-engineer-year, performance-per-mm2 and performance-per-watt point of view modestly aggressive processor cores may be the best CMP design choice for Java middleware.

8 Acknowledgments

We would like to thank Håkan Zeffer, Greg Wright, Carl Mauer, Alaa Alameldeen and Milo Martin for valuable input and feedback on this work. This work is supported in part by the PAMP research program, supported by the Swedish Foundation for Strategic Research and by the National Science Foundation (CDA-9623632, EIA-9971256, EIA-0205286, and CCR-0324878), a Wisconsin Romnes Fellowship (Wood), and donations from Intel Corp. and Sun Microsystems, Inc. Dr. Wood has a significant financial interest in Sun Microsystems, Inc.

References

[1] Paul Barford and Mark Crovella. Generating Representative Web Workloads for Network and Server Performance Evaluation. In *Proceedings of the 1998 ACM Sigmetrics Conference on Measurement and Modeling of Computer Systems*, pages 151–160, June 1998.

[2] L. Barroso, K. Gharachorloo, R. McNamara, A. Nowatzyk, S. Qadeer, B. Sano, S. Smith, R. Stets, and B. Verghese. Piranha: A Scalable Architecture Based on Single-Chip Multiprocessing. In *Proceedings of the 27th Annual International Symposium on Computer Architecture*, 2000.

[3] Luiz A. Barroso, Kourosh Gharachorloo, and Edouard Bugnion. Memory System Characterization of Commercial Workloads. In *Proceedings of the 25th Annual International Symposium on Computer Architecture*, pages 3–14, 1998.

[4] Harold W. Cain, Ravi Rajwar, Morris Marden, and Mikko H. Lipasti. An Architectural Evaluation of Java TPC-W. In *Proceedings of the Seventh IEEE Symposium on High-Performance Computer Architecture*, pages 229–240, 2001.

[5] Nirut Chalainanont, Eriko Nurvitadhi, Kingsum Chow, and Shih-Lien Lu. Characterization of L3 Cache Behavior of Java Application Server. In *Seventh Workshop on Computer Architecture Evaluation using Commercial Workloads (CAECW-7)*, 2004.

[6] George Z. Chrysos and Joel S. Emer. Memory Dependence Prediction Using Store Sets. In *Proceedings of the 25th Annual International Symposium on Computer Architecture (ISCA'98)*, pages 142–153, 1998.

[7] Karel Driesen and Urs Hölzle. Accurate indirect branch prediction. In *Proceedings of the 25th annual international symposium on Computer architecture*, pages 167–178. IEEE Computer Society, 1998.

[8] A. N. Eden and T. Mudge. The YAGS branch prediction scheme. In *Proceedings of the 31st Annual ACM/IEEE International Symposium on Microarchitecture*, pages 69–77. IEEE Computer Society Press, 1998.

[9] M. Ekman and P. Stenström. Performance and Power Impact of Issue-width in Chip-Multiprocessor Cores. In *Proceedings of International Conference on Parallel Processing (ICPP)*, 2003.

[10] A. Hartstein and T. R. Puzak. The Optimum Pipeline Depth for a Microprocessor. In *Proceedings of the 29th Annual International Symposium on Computer Architecture (ISCA'01)*, pages 7–13, 2002.

[11] A. Jaleel and B. Jacob. In-line interrupt handling for software-managed TLBs. In *Proceedings. 2001 International Conference on Computer Design*, pages 62–67, Sept 2001.

[12] Stephan Jourdan, Tse-Hao Hsing, Jared Stark, and Yale N. Patt. The Effects of Mispredicted-Path Execution on Branch Prediction Structures. In *Proceedings of the 1996 Conference on Parallel Architectures and Compilation Techniques (PACT '96)*, page 58. IEEE Computer Society, 1996.

[13] M. Karlsson, K. Moore, E. Hagersten, and D. A. Wood. Memory System Behavior of Java-Based Middleware. In *Proceedings of the Ninth International Symposium on High Performance Computer Architecture (HPCA-9)*, Anaheim, California, USA, February 2003.

[14] Martin Karlsson, Kevin Moore, Erik Hagersten, and David Wood. Memory Characterization of the ECperf Benchmark. In *Proceedings of the 2nd Annual Workshop on Memory Performance Issues (WMPI 2002), held in conjunction with the 29th International Symposium on Computer Architecture (ISCA29)*, Anchorage, Alaska, USA, May 2002.

[15] Tao Li, Lizy Kurian John, and Jr. Robert H. Bell. Modeling and Evaluation of Control Flow Prediction Schemes Using Complete System Simulation and Java Workloads. In *10th IEEE International Symposium on Modeling Analysis Simulation of Computer and Telecommunications Systems (MASCOTS'02)*, October 2002.

[16] Yue Luo and Lizy Kurian John. Workload Characterization of Multithreaded Java Servers. In *IEEE International Symposium on Performance Analysis of Systems and Software*, 2001.

[17] P. S. Magnusson, M. Christensson, D. Forsgren J. Eskilson, G. Hllberg, J. Hgberg, A. Moestedt F. Larsson, and B. Werner. Simics: A Full System Simulation Platform. *IEEE Computer*, February 2002.

[18] Morris Marden, Shih-Lien Lu, Konrad Lai, and Mikko Lipasti. Memory System Behavior in Java and Non-Java Commercial Workloads. In *Proceedings of the Fifth Workshop on Computer Architecture Evaluation Using Commercial Workloads*, 2002.

[19] Milo M. K. Martin, Daniel J. Sorin, Mark D. Hill, and David A. Wood. Bandwidth Adaptive Snooping. In *HPCA*, pages 251–262, 2002.

[20] Carl J. Mauer, Mark D. Hill, and David A. Wood. Full-system timing-first simulation. In *Proceedings of the 2002 ACM SIGMETRICS international conference on Measurement and modeling of computer systems*, pages 108–116. ACM Press, 2002.

[21] Sun Microsystems. Performance documentation for the java hotspot vm. http://java.sun.com/docs/hotspot/ism.html.

[22] Andreas Moshovos. *Memory Dependence Prediction*. PhD thesis, University of Wisconsin-Madison, 1998.

[23] Kunle Olukotun, Basem A. Nayfeh, L. Hammond, K. Wilson, and K.-Y. Chang. The Case for a Single-Chip Multiprocessor. In *Proceedings of the Seventh International Conference on Architectural Support for Programming Languages and Operating Systems*, 1996.

[24] Joshua A. Redstone, Susan J. Eggers, and Henry M. Levy. An analysis of operating system behavior on a simultaneous multithreaded architecture. *SIGPLAN Not.*, 35(11):245–256, 2000.

[25] SPEC. SPEC cpu2000 Page. http://www.spec.org/osg/cpu2000/.

[26] Lawrence Spracklen, Yuan Chou, and Santosh G. Abraham. Effective Instruction Prefetching in Chip Multiprocessors for Modern Commercial Applications. In *Proceedings of the 11th International Symposium on High Performance Computer Architecture (HPCA-11)*, 2005.

[27] M. Tremblay, J. Chan, S. Chaudhry, A. W. Conigliam, and S. S. Tse. The MAJC architecture: a synthesis of parallelism and scalability. *IEEE Micro*, 20(6):12–25, 2000.

[28] Kenneth C. Yeager. The MIPS R10000 Superscalar Microprocessor. *IEEE Micro*, 16(2):28–40, April 1996.

[29] Craig B. Zilles, Joel S. Emer, and Gurindar S. Sohi. The Use of Multithreading for Exception Handling. In *Proceedings of the 32nd Annual IEEE/ACM International Symposium on Microarchitecture*, pages 219–229, November 1999.

A Vector-μSIMD-VLIW Architecture for Multimedia Applications

Esther Salamí and Mateo Valero *
Computer Architecture Department
Universitat Politècnica de Catalunya, Barcelona, Spain
{esalami,mateo}@ac.upc.es

Abstract

Media processing has motivated strong changes in the focus and design of processors. These applications are composed of heterogeneous regions of code, some of them with high levels of DLP and other ones with only modest amounts of ILP. A common approach to deal with these applications are μSIMD-VLIW processors. However, the ILP regions fail to scale when we increase the width of the machine, which, on the other hand, is desired to achieve high performance in the DLP regions. In this paper, we propose and evaluate adding vector capabilities to a μSIMD-VLIW core to speed-up the execution of the DLP regions, while, at the same time, reducing the fetch bandwidth requirements. Results show that, in the DLP regions, both 2 and 4-issue width Vector-μSIMD-VLIW architectures outperform a 8-issue width μSIMD-VLIW in factors of up to 2.7X and 4.2X (1.6X and 2.1X in average) respectively. As a result, the DLP regions become less than 10% of the total execution time and performance is dominated by the ILP regions.

1 Introduction

As technology evolves, the number of transistors to be included on a single chip will continue increasing [40]. To take benefit of these additional resources, most of the traditional techniques focus on exploiting more *Instruction Level Parallelism* (ILP) [28].

Superscalar processors are the most traditional ILP implementation for the general purpose domain. However, it is widely assumed that current superscalar processors cannot be scaled by simply fetching, decoding and issuing more instructions per cycle [17]. Branches, the instruction cache bandwidth, the instruction window size, the register file and the memory wall are some of the aspects that currently limit the scalability of superscalar processors. And, even if these problems could be overcome with future technology, the performance results would not pay off the amount of chip area and power and the design effort required [27].

Very Long Instruction Word (VLIW) processors are another form of exploiting ILP that requires less hardware complexity. The compiler and not the hardware is responsible for identifying groups of independent operations and packaging them together into a single VLIW instruction [9]. The first generation of VLIW processors were successful in the scientific domain [4, 29], and it has also been the architecture of choice for most media embedded processors [26, 38, 37]. However, some relevant facts, such as code compatibility and non-deterministic latencies, have contributed to the belief that VLIW processors are not appropriate for the general-purpose domain. At present, a revival of the VLIW execution paradigm is observed. HP and Intel have recently introduced a new style of architecture known as *Explicitly Parallel Instruction Computing* (EPIC) [35] and a specific architecture implementation: the *Itanium Processor Family* (IPF) [36]. EPIC retains compatibility across different implementations without the complexity of superscalar control logic.

Another kind of parallelism that can be found in programs is *Data Level Parallelism* (DLP) (or *Single Instruction Multiple Data* (SIMD)) [10]. The DLP paradigm tries to specify with a single instruction a large number of operations to be performed on independent data words. Traditionally, this kind of parallelism has been successfully exploited in the supercomputing domain by vector [31, 3, 39] and array [13, 30] processors. However, during the last decade, the increasing significance of media processing has motivated a great interest in exploiting sub-word level parallelism (also called μSIMD parallelism) [25]. In the general purpose domain, these changes have been very straightforward with the inclusion of multimedia extensions such as SSE [15] or Altivec [24]. This is also a form of DLP in which short data are packed into a single register and opera-

*This work has been supported by the Ministry of Science and Technology of Spain and the European Union (FEDER funds) under contract TIC2001-0995-C02-01 and TIN2004-07739-C02-01, and by the European HiPEAC network of Excellence. We also acknowledge the Supercomputing Center of Catalonia (CESCA) for supplying the computing resources for our research.

0190-3918/05 $20.00 © 2005 IEEE

tions are carried out simultaneously on the different register elements. A third way of exploiting DLP comes from the combination of the previous two [6, 18, 20]. These architectures adapt to typical multimedia patterns by extending the scope of vectorization to two dimensions.

In the media domain, μSIMD-VLIW processors have been widely proposed [12, 26, 38, 8], as they are able to exploit DLP by means of the μSIMD operations and ILP by the use of wide-issue static scheduling. But, although media applications are usually characterized by high amounts of DLP, there is also a significant part of code that exhibits only modest amounts of ILP, thus taking little benefit from increasing the processor resources. And, even though VLIW processors are simpler than superscalar designs, very high issue rates require decoding more operations in parallel and complicate the register files, which clearly increases power consumption.

In this paper, we propose and evaluate a new architecture that includes vector operations in a μSIMD-VLIW processor to exploit the DLP typical of multimedia kernels in a more efficient way and with lower fetch bandwidth requirements. Although a quantitative analysis on power consumption is out of the scope of this paper, it is widely assumed that vector architectures contribute to increase power efficiency [2, 20]. Initial results for a reduced number of benchmarks were first presented in [34]. Apart from a more extensive evaluation, additional contributions also include a thorough description of the architecture and of the static scheduling of vector operations.

The rest of the paper is organized as follows. Section 2 defines the concept of scalar and vector regions and evaluates their scalability separately. Section 3 overviews the Vector-μSIMD-VLIW architecture and discusses the main compilation issues. Section 4 describes the modeled architectures and the simulation framework. Next, section 5 presents quantitative data such as speed-up and operation per cycle rates. Finally, the last section summarizes the main conclusions.

2 Scalar and Vector Regions

Most media applications consist on a set of algorithms that process streams of data in a pipeline fashion. Furthermore, the same set of operations are performed over the elements inside the stream. Therefore, media kernels exhibit high amounts of DLP [7]. On the other hand, there is also a significant portion of code that is difficult to vectorize. That is some protocol related processing overhead such as first order recurrences, table look-ups and non-streaming memory patterns with large amounts of indirections. Therefore, a real media program is composed of heterogeneous regions of code with highly variable levels of parallelism: some of them with high amounts of DLP and the other ones with only modest amounts of ILP. We will refer to those regions that can be vectorized with the term of *Vector Regions* and to the remaining non-DLP regions of code with the term of *Scalar Regions*.

Table 1. Vector regions

Benchmark	%Vect	Vector Regions
JPEG_ENC	29.56 %	RGB to YCC color conversion Forward DCT Quantification
JPEG_DEC	18.46 %	YCC to YCC color conversion H2v2 up-sample
MPEG2_ENC	52.29 %	Motion estimation Forward DCT Inverse DCT
MPEG2_DEC	23.11 %	Form component prediction Inverse DCT Add block
GSM_ENC	18.66 %	LTP parameters Autocorrelation
GSM_DEC	0.91 %	Long term filtering

In order to evaluate the scalar and vector regions separately, we have marked the start and end point of the most computational intensive vector regions in the source codes. These regions generally correspond to one or two levels of nested loops plus some previous initializations. Table 1 lists the selected benchmarks, the parts of each program that have been considered as vector regions, and the percentage of the execution time they represent in a 2-issue width μSIMD-VLIW architecture. These benchmarks are representative programs of image, audio and video, all from the UCLA *Mediabench* suite [22].

Figure 1 shows the speed-up of 2, 4 and 8-issue width μSIMD-VLIW architectures over the 2-issue width μSIMD-VLIW (see section 4 for details about methodology and processor configurations). The dashed lines represent the speed-up in the vector/scalar regions over the vector/scalar regions of the 2-issue width architecture. The solid lines refer to the speed-up in the full application.

From the graphs, it can be observed that, except for the *gsm_enc*, the scalar regions fail to scale above 4-issue width. While increasing the width of the architecture from 2 to 4 provides an average speed-up of 1.24X in the scalar regions, moving from 4 to 8-issue only introduces a small 1.03X performance improvement. As far as the vector regions is concerned, they exhibit potential to benefit from wider issue scheduling, but this parallelism could be exploited in a more efficient way by conventional DLP oriented techniques. Furthermore, even though the vector regions scale up to 3.19X for the *jpeg_dec* application (2.49X in average),

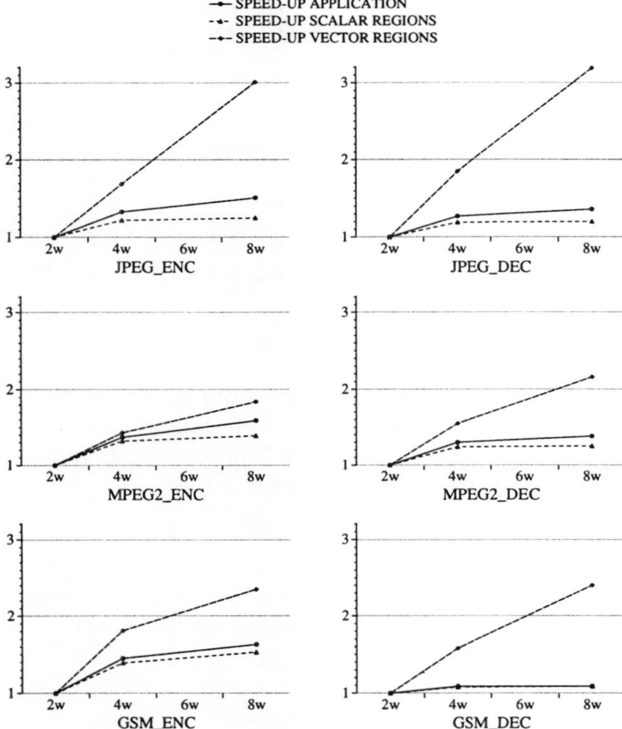

Figure 1. Scalability of scalar and vector regions in μSIMD-VLIW architectures

the vectorization percentage is low (24 % in average) and the lack of scalability in the scalar regions (1.28X in average) limits the performance of the complete application.

In any case, the actual performance achieved is very far from the theoretical peak performance and do not pay off the hardware complexity inherent in very aggressive architectures. We claim that Vector-μSIMD extensions arise as a better candidate to invest in, as they clearly reduce the fetch pressure, simplify the control flow and memory access, and speed-up the performance of the vector regions without detrimental effects over the scalar part.

3 Adding Vector Units to a VLIW processor

3.1 Vector-μSIMD ISA Overview

Our Vector-μSIMD ISA is based on the *Matrix Oriented Multimedia* (MOM) extension [6]. It can be viewed as a conventional vector ISA where each operation is a MMX-like operation. But it does not include costly vector operations, such as conditional execution, gathers or scatters.

It provides vector registers of 16 64-bit words each, vector load and vector store operations to move data from/to memory to/from the vector registers, and a set of computation operations that operate on vector registers. Since each word can pack either eight 8-bit, four 16-bit or two 32-bit items, each vector register can hold a matrix of up to 16x8 elements. The architecture also provides 192-bit packed accumulators similar to those proposed in the MDMX multimedia extension. Additionally, two special registers are required to control the execution of vector operations: the vector length register and the vector stride register.

As far as terminology is concerned, we reserve the term *operation* to refer to each independent machine operation codified into a VLIW *instruction*. Each vector operation executes so many *sub-operations* as the vector length dictates. Finally, as the maximum vector length is 16 and each sub-operation can operate on either eight 8-bit, four 16-bit or two 32-bit items, a vector operation can perform up to 16x8 *micro-operations*.

3.2 The Vector-μSIMD-VLIW Architecture

Figure 2 shows the main components of the proposed architecture. Essentially, it is a VLIW processor with the addition of a vector register file, one or more vector functional units, and a modified cache hierarchy specially targeted to serve vector accesses. Both, the vector register file and the vector functional units can be clusterized in independent vector lanes. This can be achieved with relatively simple logic by replicating the functional units, splitting each vector register across each lane and assigning each functional unit to a certain lane. The different elements of a vector register are interleaved across lanes, allowing all lanes to work independently. From the point of view of implementation, a vector register file scales better than a μSIMD one, due to the organization in lanes, which reduces the number of ports per cluster. For aggressive configurations, a vector register file can provide larger storage capacity with similar area cost and less access time [5]. In this work, we use four independent vector lanes. As our vector lengths are relatively short, a larger number of lanes would not pay off.

The Vector-μSIMD-VLIW architecture also includes a simple accumulator register file and adds limited connection between the lanes to be able to perform the last series of accumulation in a reduction operation. Only one of the lanes needs to read and write the source and destination packed accumulator. This lane is the responsible for performing the last reduction.

We use a *vector cache* [27] in the second level of the memory hierarchy. The vector cache is a two-bank interleaved cache targeted at accessing stride-one vector requests by loading two whole cache lines (one per bank) instead of individually loading the vector elements. Then, an interchange switch, a shifter, and a mask logic correctly align the data. Scalar accesses are made to the L1 data cache, while

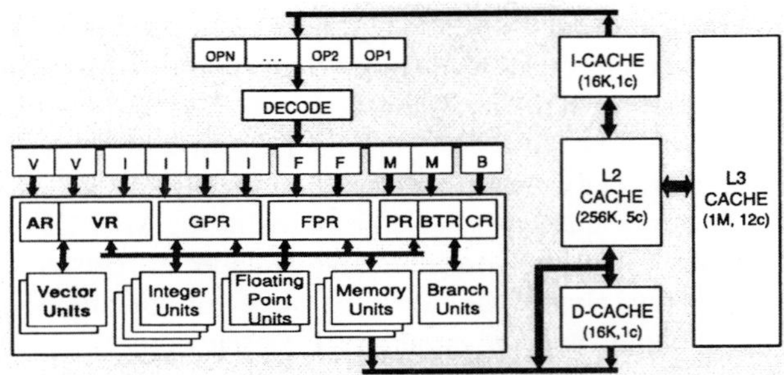

Figure 2. Vector-μSIMD-VLIW architecture

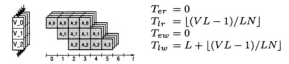

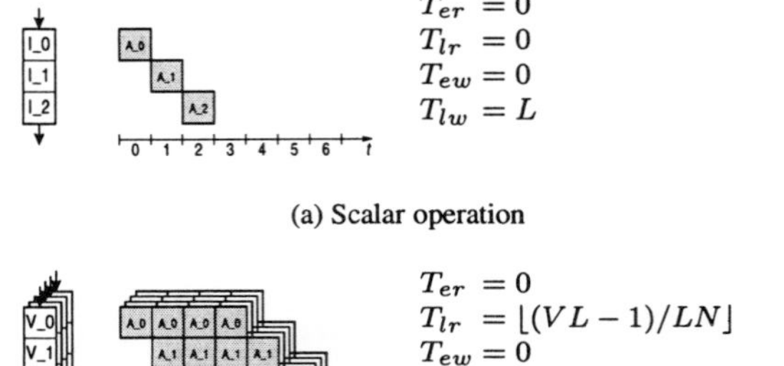

$T_{er} = 0$
$T_{lr} = 0$
$T_{ew} = 0$
$T_{lw} = L$
(a) Scalar operation
$T_{er} = 0$
$T_{lr} = \lfloor (VL-1)/LN \rfloor$
$T_{ew} = 0$
$T_{lw} = L + \lfloor (VL-1)/LN \rfloor$

(b) Vector operation

Figure 3. Latency descriptors (*Ter* = earliest read, *Tlr* = latest read, *Tew* = earliest write, *Tlw* = latest write, *L* = flow latency, *VL* = vector length, *LN* = vector lanes)

vector accesses bypass the L1 to access directly the L2 vector cache. If the L2 port is $B \times 64$-bit wide, these accesses are performed at a maximum rate of B elements when the stride is one, and at 1 element per cycle for any other stride. A coherency protocol based on an exclusive-bit policy plus inclusion is used to guarantee coherency.

3.3 Compilation Issues

The Achilles' heel of the proposed architecture is, obviously, the compiler; but nowadays there are compilers that allow basic autovectorization for μSIMD architectures, and the same compiler techniques could be used to generate Vector-μSIMD code. As we do not have a reliable compiler at our disposal yet, we have used emulation libraries to hand-write μSIMD and Vector-μSIMD code to evaluate the approach, and the compiler replaces the emulation functions calls by the corresponding operation.

From the VLIW point of view, new register files and functional units have been added, and some extra considerations must be taken into account by the scheduler, which is the module that needs the most detailed information about the target architecture, as it is responsible for assigning a schedule time to each operation, subject to the constraints of data dependence and resource availability. For every input and output operand, an earliest and a latest read and write latency must be specified respectively [1]. Figure 3.a depicts the execution of a 3 cycles fully-pipelined scalar operation. In this example, the source registers are read sometime during the first cycle after the initiation of the operation, and the result is written at the end of three cycles.

In the case of a vector operation, these values also depend on the vector length (VL) and on the number of parallel vector lanes (LN). As up to LN sub-operations are initiated per cycle, the last input operand will be read at $\lfloor (VL - 1)/LN \rfloor$, and the last output will be written at $L + \lfloor (VL - 1)/LN \rfloor$, being L the latency of one sub-operation (see Figure 3.b). The number of parallel vector lanes is a fixed parameter from the architecture and it is known at compile time; but the vector length is variable for each operation, and will be dynamically set. Fortunately, the vector length register is usually initialized with an immediate value, and a simple data flow analysis is able to provide the right value to the compiler. In the few cases in which the vector length is not known at compile time, the compiler must assume the maximum vector length (16) in order to ensure correctness. Note that, for a vector unit with four parallel lanes, the penalty to pay would be three extra cycles at worst (that is, if the vector length turns out to be four or less).

The same latency descriptors are taken for vector memory operations, but replacing the number of vector lanes by the width of the L2 port (in elements). As it was mentioned in Section 3.2, in the proposed architecture, the execution time of a vector memory operation also depends on the stride. For simplicity, our compiler schedules all vector memory operations as having a stride of one and hitting in the L2 vector cache, and the processor stalls at run-time if either of the two assertions is not true.

On the other hand, providing a register file which supports concurrent acceses to the same vector register, the compiler can do chaining [31] of two vector operations with a dependence on a vector register operand by just scheduling the second one before the first operation has completed execution.

3.3.1 Code Example

Figure 4 shows the scheduling of a vector code generated by the compiler for a 2-issue width VLIW architecture with two vector units and a wide 4x64 bit port to the vector cache. Latencies are 2 cycles for the vector units and 5 cycles for the vector cache. This code is taken from the *dist1* function in the *mpeg2_enc* application, and computes the *sum of absolutes differences* (SAD) between two blocks of $8x16$ pixels. It is assumed that registers $R1$ and $R2$ keep the initial address of the blocks, and lx is the stride between consecutive rows. As the registers are 64 bit wide, and the stride between rows is not one, we need two vector registers to keep each block. The SAD operation is implemented using a packed accumulator that allows parallel execution over the vector elements. Finally, the values packed in the accumulators are reduced and the final result is stored.

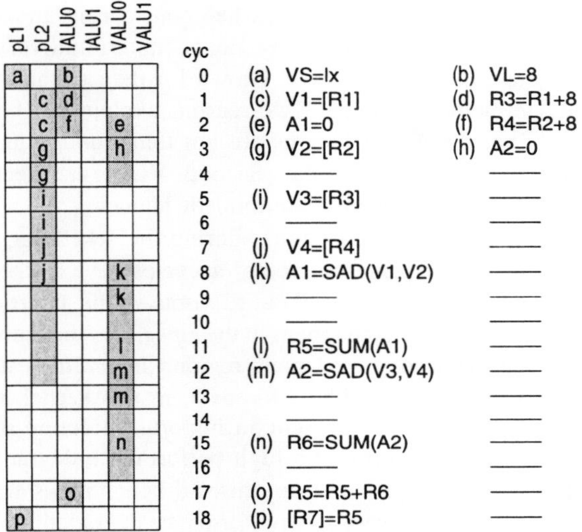

Figure 4. Scheduling of motion estimation for a 2-issue Vector-μSIMD-VLIW processor

It can be observed that this kernel is memory bound and, in fact, the second vector unit is not used at all, as the second SAD operation (m) must wait for the data being loaded from memory and cannot be scheduled earlier. Chaining is performed between the vector loads (g) and (j) and the vector SAD operations (k) and (m) respectively. Note also that the vector loads are scheduled as having a stride of one, that is, as if they will produce four elements by cycle. As this assumption is not true, the processor will be stalled at run-time, thus incurring in a great penalty in performance, as we will see in the evaluation section.

Note that the two innerloops in the scalar version have been totally eliminated, and the Vector-μSIMD architecture only needs to decode 16 operations to process one complete block, in front of the 172 operations required in the μSIMD versions of code.

4 Methodology

4.1 Compilation and Simulation Framework

For our experiments we have used *Trimaran* [21]. Trimaran is a compiler infrastructure for supporting state of the art research in compiling for ILP architectures. The system is currently oriented towards EPIC architectures. To expose sufficient ILP it makes use of advanced techniques such as Superblock [14] or Hyperblock[23] formation. The architecture space is characterized by HPL-PD [19], a parameterized processor architecture.

Our internal release of the compiler also includes *Pcode* Interprocedural Pointer Analysis [11] and Cost Effective Memory Disambiguation [32]. Therefore, our scalar versions of code include memory disambiguation (inherent in the vector versions), which introduces an average performance speed-up of 1.32X (for a 8-issue width architecture) over the same codes compiled with the public release of Trimaran. We have used emulation libraries to hand-write the applications with μSIMD and Vector-μSIMD extensions. The compiler has been modified to detect the emulation functions calls and replace them by the related low level operations. Both, the compiler and the HPL-PD machine description have been enhanced with the new operations, register files and functional units. The simulator has also been extended to include the new ISAs and a detailed memory hierarchy.

4.2 Modeled Architectures

We have evaluated 2, 4 and 8-issue width VLIW and μSIMD-VLIW architectures and two different 2 and 4-issue width Vector-μSIMD-VLIW configurations. Table 2 summarizes the general parameters of the ten architectures under study. In order to support the high computational demand of multimedia applications, our configurations are quite aggressive in the number of arithmetic functional units. Latencies are based on those of the *Itanium2* processor [16].

The μSIMD-VLIW architecture includes 64-bit registers together with functional units able to operate on up to eight 8-bit items in parallel. This extension provides 67 opcodes fairly similar to Intel's SSE [15] integer opcodes. Note that the vector architectures are not balanced against the same issue width VLIW or μSIMD-VLIW architectures because we consider them as an alternative to wider issue processors. For example, the arithmetic capability of the 2-issue Vector2 and the 4-issue Vector1 configurations is comparable to that of the 8-issue μSIMD configuration, not to the 2 or 4-issue μSIMD.

The first level data cache is a 16 KB, 4-way set associative cache with one port for the reference 2-issue width

Table 2. Processor configurations

Resource	VLIW 2 / 4 / 8 w	+μSIMD 2 / 4 / 8 w	+Vector1 2 / 4 w	+Vector2 2 / 4 w
Int regs	64 / 96 / 128	64 / 96 / 128	64 / 96	64 / 96
SIMD regs	–	64 / 96 / 128	20 / 32 x16	20 / 32 x16
Acc regs	–	–	4 / 6	4 / 6
Int units	2 / 4 / 8	2 / 4 / 8	2 / 4	2 / 4
SIMD units	–	2 / 4 / 8	1 / 2 x4	2 / 4 x4
L1 ports	1 / 2 / 3	1 / 2 / 3	1	1 / 2
L2 ports	–	–	1 x4	1 x4

architecture. We consider pseudo-multi-ported caches for the configurations with greater number of ports. There is a 256KB vector cache in the second level and a 1MB cache in the third level. Latencies are 1 cycle to the L1, 5 cycles to the L2, 12 cycles to the L3 and 500 cycles to main memory. We have not simulated the instruction cache since our benchmarks have small instruction working set. The compiler schedules all memory operations assuming they hit in the cache and the processor is stalled at run-time in case of a cache miss or bank conflict.

5 Evaluation

5.1 Speed-up in Vector Regions

Figure 5.a shows the performance speed-up obtained in the vector regions with perfect memory simulation. By perfect memory we consider that all accesses hit in cache, but with the corresponding latency. That is, all scalar accesses are served after 1 cycle of latency and all vector accesses in the Vector configurations go to the L2 and take 5 cycles plus the additional cycles to serve all vector data elements (which slightly favours the VLIW and μSIMD-VLIW configurations). For each architecture, the graph shows the speed-up of the vector regions over the execution time of the vector regions in the 2-issue width VLIW architecture.

As it was to be expected, both μSIMD and Vector architectures clearly outperform the same issue VLIW architecture. The 2-issue width Vector2 architecture outperforms the same width μSIMD architecture in a factor ranging from 3.0X to 6.2X (4.4X in average). Furthermore, the 8-issue μSIMD is outperformed by both, the 2-issue Vector2 in a factor of up to 2.6X (1.7X in average), and the 4-issue Vector2 in a factor of up to 4.0X (2.3X in average).

We also observe that half of the benchmarks do not take much benefit of increasing the number of vector units (that is, when going from Vector1 to Vector2). This is because they have vector regions similar to the *motion estimation* example explained in section 3.3, with very short vector lengths and small loops. Examples of this include the *form component prediction* and the *add block* regions in the MPEG2 decoder and the *calculation of the long term parameters* in the GSM encoder. On the contrary, other benchmarks shuch as the JPEG encoder and decoder, whose vector regions are characterized by larger vector lengths (ex. *color conversions* or *upsampling*) and/or larger loop sizes (ex. *DCT*'s), exhibit a significant improvement in performance when the number of vector units is doubled.

Figure 5.b shows the speed-up of the vector regions again, but with the simulation of the memory hierarchy. We observe that the Vector architectures exhibit the highest performance degradations when considering a realistic memory system. This fact may seem counterintuitive, since vector architectures are well known for their capability to tolerate memory latency. Two reasons explain this behavior. First, the vector lengths are not long enough to take benefit of this characteristic. Second, VLIW architectures are very sensitive to non-deterministic latencies.

As it was explained before, during the scheduling, the compiler assumes that all vector accesses have a stride of one, and the processor stalls at run-time if this assertion is not true. That is what happens in the *mpeg2_enc* benchmark, in which the stride of the main region (the *motion estimation*) is the image width. Moreover, in this kernel, these memory operations represent an important fraction of the overall code, resulting in a high performance degradation (close to 200%). Apart from this, all benchmarks exhibit high hit ratios and very low performance degradation when considering realistic memory.

5.2 Speed-up in Complete Applications

Figure 6 shows the speed-up for complete applications. As it was to be expected, the benchmark that exhibits the highest performance improvement is the *mpeg2_enc* (up to 4.74X speed-up for the 4-issue Vector2). Even though there are other benchmarks (such as *gsm_enc*) with similar (or even greater) speed-ups in the vector regions, the impact in the overall performance is not so significant, due to the low vectorization percentage. The 4-issue Vector2 architecture slightly outperforms the 8-issue μSIMD in all the applications (1.03X in average). Note also that the 4-issue Vector1 configuration achieves, in average, the same performance than the 8-issue μSIMD, with only one port to the first level cache and two vector units.

The gap between the different architectures decrease with the issue width of the machine. For example, while the 2-issue Vector2 exhibits a factor of 1.22X of performance improvement (in average) over the 2-issue μSIMD, the 4-issue Vector2 only outperforms the 4-issue μSIMD in a 1.14X. That makes sense, as a wide enough μSIMD-VLIW architecture is able to exploit as ILP the parallelism

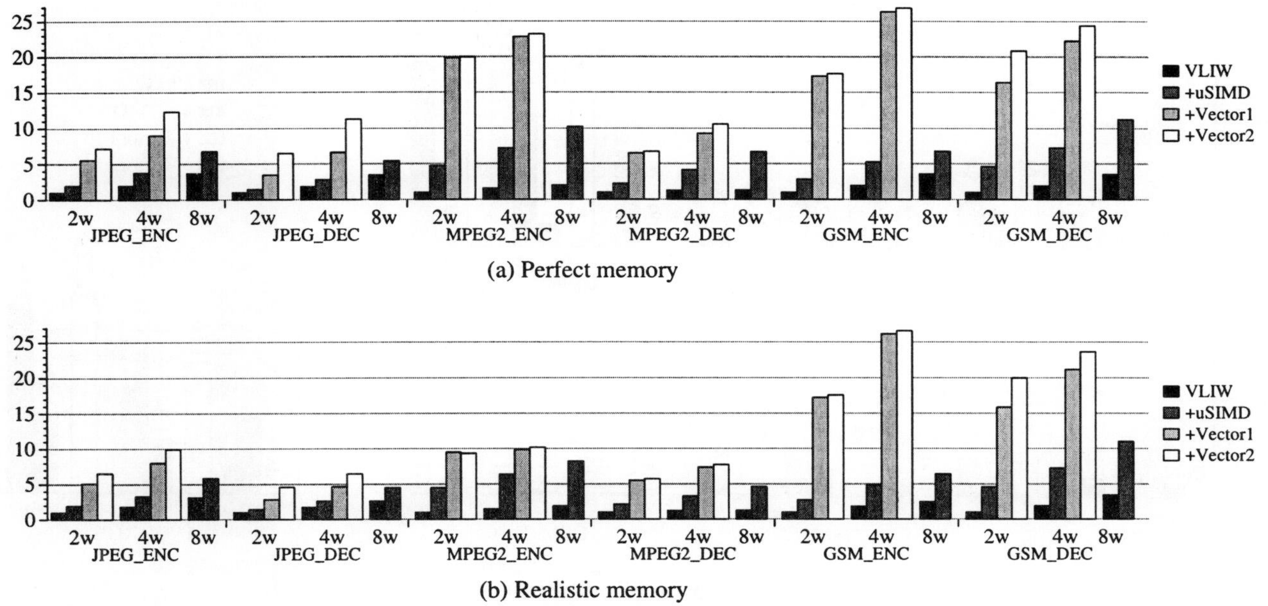

(a) Perfect memory

(b) Realistic memory

Figure 5. Speed-up in vector regions

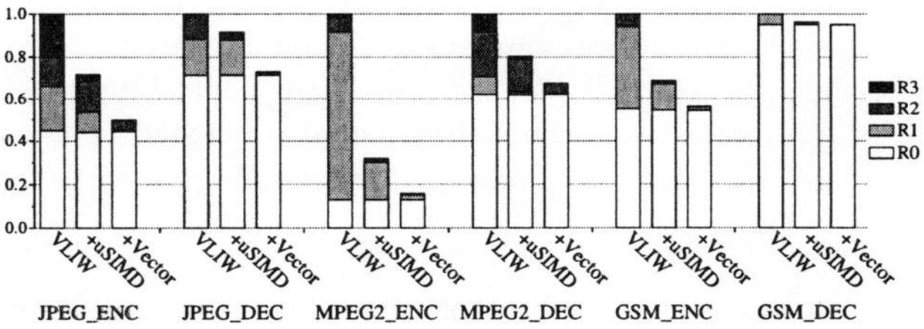

that the Vector-μSIMD-VLIW exploits as DLP.

On the other hand, the vector regions only represent a 40% of the total execution time in the 2-issue VLIW architecture. When most of the available DLP parallelism is exploited via multimedia extensions, the remaining scalar part becomes the bottleneck. In the 4-issue Vector2 architecture, the vector cycles represent less than 10% of the overall execution time (except for the *mpeg2_enc*). By the Amhdal Law, further improvements in the execution of the vector regions would be imperceptible in the complete application.

5.3 Operations per Cycle

Figure 7 shows the dynamic operation count normalized by the dynamic operation count of the base VLIW architecture. We have distinguished the contribution of each region. Regions from $R1$ to $R3$ are the fractions of code that have been vectorized in the μSIMD and Vector versions in the same order they are listed in Table 1 (for example, in *mpeg2_enc*, $R1$ accounts for the motion estimation and $R2$ and $R3$ for the forward and inverse two dimensional DCT). Region $R0$ always refers to the remaining scalar part.

The results confirm that the μSIMD and Vector-μSIMD versions of code require to execute much less operations than the scalar versions. This may not seem so obvious if we take into account that these versions are sometimes based on algorithms that require to execute much more operations [33].

As can be observed, the Vector architecture executes an average of 84% fewer operations in the vector regions than the μSIMD (19% fewer in the complete application). The obvious reason is that Vector architectures can pack more micro-operations into a single operation (up to 81.10 for the *jpeg_dec* application and 38.78 in average). Moreover, there is an additional reduction on the number of operations involved in the loop-related control. This reduction in the number of operations to fetch and decode also translates into a decrease in power consumption.

Figure 7. Normalized operation count

Table 3 shows the average number of operations per cycle for the scalar and vector regions of code separately. It confirms our belief that the non-vector regions of code do not benefit from scaling the width of the machine above 4 issue width. Fetching 1.84 operations per cycle does not pay off the hardware complexity of a 8-issue width architecture. For the μSIMD and Vector-μSIMD versions we also show the average number of micro-operations executed per cycle. The Vector-μSIMD ISA obtains the highest speed-ups by exploiting more data parallelism in the vector regions (up to 14.00 micro-operations per cycle) and with the low-

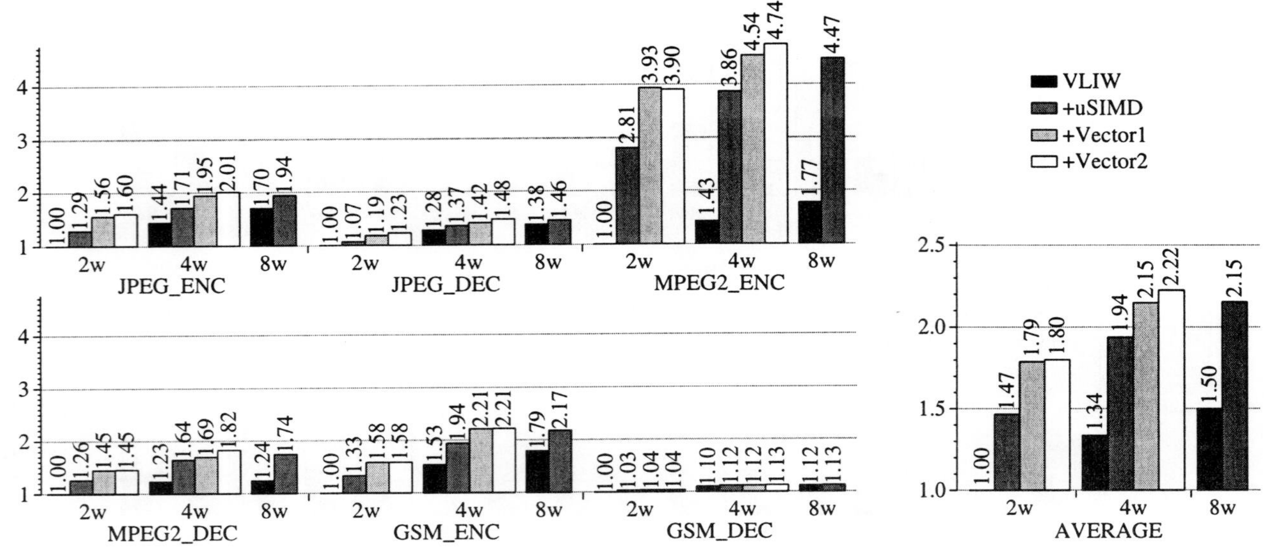

Figure 6. Speed-up in complete applications

est fetch bandwidth requirements (just 1.37 operations per cycle), making it an ideal candidate for embedded systems, where high issue rates are not an option. However, for wide issues, the μSIMD ISA exhibits more flexibility to benefit from wide static scheduling and also reaches significant micro-operations per cycle rates, but at a higher cost.

Table 3. ***OPC*** **= operations per cycle,** ***μOPC*** **= micro-operations per cycle,** ***SP*** **= speed-up**

	Scalar regs		Vector regs			Application		
	OPC	SP	OPC	μOPC	SP	OPC	μOPC	SP
2w VLIW	1.44	1.00	1.80	1.80	1.00	1.59	1.59	1.00
+μSIMD	1.44	1.00	1.78	4.68	2.88	1.52	2.32	1.47
+Vector1	1.44	1.00	0.87	7.91	9.33	1.36	2.12	1.79
+Vector2	1.44	1.00	0.98	10.10	10.61	1.37	2.15	1.80
4w VLIW	1.77	1.24	3.03	3.03	1.66	2.14	2.14	1.34
+μSIMD	1.78	1.24	2.95	7.80	4.62	1.98	3.05	1.94
+Vector1	1.71	1.20	1.24	11.64	12.87	1.63	2.55	2.15
+Vector2	1.76	1.23	1.37	14.00	14.09	1.69	2.64	2.22
8w VLIW	1.84	1.28	4.54	4.54	2.47	2.42	2.42	1.50
+μSIMD	1.84	1.29	4.47	12.07	6.76	2.18	3.38	2.15

6 Conclusions

The actual performance achieved by very wide issue VLIW architectures is very far from the theoretical peak performance and do not pay off the related hardware complexity. By analyzing the scalability of the scalar and vector regions of code separately, we have shown that the scalar regions do not benefit from increasing the width of the machine above 4-issue width. On the other hand, the kind of parallelism found in the vector regions could be exploited in a more efficient way by means of SIMD execution.

To exploit the data parallelism inherent in the vector regions, we have proposed the addition of one or more vector units together with a vector register filer and a wide port to the L2 that provides the bandwidth required by the vector regions. This extension can be viewed as a conventional short vector ISA where each element is operated in a MMX-like fashion. This enhancement has a minimal impact on the VLIW core and provides high performance in the vector regions for low issue rates.

We have evaluated the proposed architecture for complete applications of audio, video and image processing and compared it againts a VLIW architecture with and without μSIMD extensions. In the vector regions, a 4-issue width Vector-μSIMD-VLIW architecture outperforms the 8-issue μSIMD-VLIW architecture in a factor of up to 4.2X (2.1X in average). Furthermore, a 4-issue architecture with only one port to the first level cache and two vector units achieves, in complete applications, similar performance to that of the 8-issue μSIMD-VLIW.

On the other hand, it has been seen that Vector-μSIMD-VLIW architectures do not perform well in front of non stride-one memory references and exhibit the highest performance degradations when considering a realistic memory system, mainly due to the high sensitivity of VLIW architectures to non-deterministic latencies. Future research must be done to improve the memory hierarchy and to test more flexible scheduling techniques.

References

[1] S. Aditya, V. Kathail, and B. R. Rau. Elcor's machine description system: Version 3.0. Technical Report HPL-98-128, Information Technology Center, 1998.

[2] K. Asanovic, J. Beck, B. Irissou, B. Kingsbury, N. Morgan, and J. Wawrzynek. The t0 vector microprocessor. In *Hot Chips VII*, pages 187–196, August 1995.

[3] V. Bongiorno and G. Shorrel. Cray sv1, sv1e, sv1ex – overview, 2000. http://www.cray.com/products/systems/.

[4] R. P. Colwell, R. P. Nix, J. J. O'Donnell, D. B. Papworth, and P. K. Rodman. A vliw architecture for a trace scheduling compiler. *IEEE Trans. on Computers*, C-37(8):967–979, August 1988.

[5] J. Corbal. *N-Dimensional Vector Instruction Set Architectures for Multimedia Applications*. PhD thesis, UPC, Departament d'Arquitectura de Computadors, 2002.

[6] J. Corbal, R. Espasa, and M. Valero. Exploiting a new level of dlp in multimedia applications. In *Proceedings of the 32nd Int. Symp. on Microarchitecture*, pages 72–79, 1999.

[7] K. Diefendorff and P. Dubey. How multimedia workloads will change processor design. *IEEE Computer*, 30(9):43–45, Sept 1997.

[8] P. Faraboschi, G. Brown, J. A. Fisher, G. Desoli, and F. Homewood. Lx: a technology platform for customizable VLIW embedded processing. In *Proc. of the 27th Int. Symp. on Computer Architecture 2000*, pages 203–213, June 2000.

[9] J. A. Fisher. Trace scheduling: A technique for global microcode compaction. *IEEE Trans. on Computers*, C-30:478–490, July 1981.

[10] M. Flynn. Some computer organizations and their effectiveness. *IEEE Trans. on Computing*, C–21(9):948–960, 1972.

[11] D. M. Gallagher. *Memory Disambiguation to Facilitate Instruction-Level Parallelism Compilation*. PhD thesis, University of Illinois, 1995.

[12] L. Gwennap. Majc gives vliw a new twist. *Microprocessor Report*, 13(12):12–15, September 1999.

[13] R. M. Hord. *The Illiac IV, the first supercomputer*. Computer Science Press, 1982.

[14] W. W. Hwu, S. A. Mahlke, W. Y. Chen, P. P. Chang, N. J. Warter, R. A. Bringmann, R. G. Ouellette, R. E. Hank, T. Kiyohara, G. E. Haab, J. G. Holm, and D. M. Lavery. The superblock: An effective technique for vliw and superscalar compilation. *Supercomputing*, 7:229–248, 1993.

[15] Pentium iii processor: Developer's manual. Technical report, Intel, 1999.

[16] Intel. Intel itanium2 processor reference manual for software development and optimization, 2004. http://developer.intel.com/design/itanium2/manuals/.

[17] M. Johnson. *Superscalar Microprocessor Design*. Prentice-Hall, Englewood Cliffs, New Jersey, 1991.

[18] B. Juurlink, S. Vassiliadis, D. Tcheressiz, and H. A. Wijshoff. Implementation and evaluation of the complex streamed instruction set. In *Proceedings of the International Conference on Parallel Architectures and Compilation Techniques*, pages 73–82, September 2001.

[19] V. Kathail, M. Schlansker, and B. R. Rau. Hpl-pd architecture specification: Version 1.1. Technical Report HPL-93-80(R.1), Hewlett–Packard Lab., 2000.

[20] C. Kozyrakis. A media-enhanced vector architecture for embedded memory systems. Technical Report CSD-99-1059, UCB, 27, 1999.

[21] H. P. Lab., R.-I. Group, and I. Group. Trimaran user manual, 1998. http://www.trimaran.org/docs.html.

[22] C. Lee, M. Potkonjak, and W. H. Mangione-Smith. Mediabench: A tool for evaluating and synthesizing multimedia and communicatons systems. In *Proceedings of the 30th Int. Symp. on Microarchitecture*, pages 330–335, 1997.

[23] S. A. Mahlke, D. C. Lin, W. Y. Chen, R. E. Hank, and R. A. Bringmann. Effective compiler support for predicated execution using the hyperblock. In *Proceedings of the 25th Int. Symp. on Microarchitecture*, pages 45–54, Dec. 1992.

[24] H. Nguyen and L. K. John. Exploiting SIMD parallelism in DSP and multimedia algorithms using the altivec technology. In *Proceedings of the International Conference on Supercomputing*, pages 11–20, 1999.

[25] A. Peleg and U. Weiser. Mmx technology extension to the intel architecture. *IEEE Micro*, 16(4):42–50, 1996.

[26] Trimedia tm-1300. http://www-us3.semiconductors.com/.

[27] F. Quintana, J. Corbal, R. Espasa, and M. Valero. Adding a vector unit on a superscalar processor. In *Proc. of the International Conference on Supercomputing*, pages 1–10, 1999.

[28] B. R. Rau and J. A. Fisher. Instruction-level parallel processing: history, overview, and perspective. *The Journal of Supercomputing*, 7(1-2):9–50, 1993.

[29] B. R. Rau, D. W. L. Yen, W. Yen, and R. A. Towle. The cydra 5 departmental supercomputer. *IEEE Computer*, 22(1):12–35, January 1989.

[30] S. F. Reddaway. Dap-a distributed array processor. In *Proceedings of the 1st annual symposium on Computer architecture*, pages 61–65. ACM Press, 1973.

[31] R. Russel. The cray-1 computer system. *Comunications of the ACM*, 21(1):63–72, January 1978.

[32] E. Salamí, J. Corbal, C. Alvarez, and M. Valero. Cost effective memory disambiguation for multimedia codes. In *Proc. of the Int. Conf. on Compilers, Architecture, and Synthesis for Embedded Systems*, pages 117–126, 2002.

[33] E. Salamí, J. Corbal, R. Espasa, and M. Valero. An evaluation of different dlp alternatives for the embedded media domain. In *Proceedings of the 1st Workshop on Media Processors and DSPs*, pages 100–109, November 1999.

[34] E. Salamí and M. Valero. Initial evaluation of multimedia extensions on vliw architectures. In *Proceedings of the 4th international workshop on Systems, Architectures, Modeling, and Simulation*, pages 403–412, July 2004.

[35] M. S. Schlansker and B. Raw. Epic: Explicitly parallel instruction computing. In *IEEE Computer*, pages 37–45, February 2000.

[36] H. Sharangpani and K. Aurora. Itanium processor microarchitecture. *IEEE Micro*, 20(5):24–43, September 2000.

[37] TI. TMS320C62XX family, 1999. http://www.ti.com/sc/-docs/products/dsp/tms320c6201.html.

[38] Introducing tigersharc, 1999. http://www.analog.com/new/-ads/html/SHARC2.

[39] A. van der Steen and J. Dongarra. The nec sx-5, 2001. http://www.top500.org/ORSC/2001.

[40] A. Yu. The future of microprocessors. *IEEE Micro*, 16(6):46–53, 1996.

Design Tradeoffs for BLAS Operations on Reconfigurable Hardware *

Ling Zhuo and Viktor K. Prasanna
Department of Electrical Engineering
University of Southern California
Los Angeles, California 90089-2562, USA
{lzhuo, prasanna}@usc.edu

Abstract

Numerical linear algebra operations are key primitives in scientific computing. Performance optimizations of such operations have been extensively investigated and some basic operations have been implemented as software libraries. With the rapid advances in technology, hardware acceleration of linear algebra applications using FPGAs (Field Programmable Gate Arrays) has become feasible. In this paper, we propose FPGA-based designs for several BLAS operations, including vector product, matrix-vector multiply, and matrix multiply. By identifying the design parameters for each BLAS operation, we analyze the design tradeoffs. In the implementations of the designs, the values of the design parameters are determined according to the hardware constraints, such as the available area, the size of on-chip memory, the external memory bandwidth and the number of I/O pins. The proposed designs are implemented on a Xilinx Virtex-II Pro FPGA.

1 Introduction

Numerical linear algebra, particularly the solution of linear systems of equations, linear least square problems, eigenvalue problems and singular value problems, is fundamental to most scientific applications. As it is often the most computationally intensive part of such applications, the performance improvement of numerical linear algebra has always been of interest to researchers. Certain basic operations, such as the vector and matrix operations, have been implemented as libraries. Such libraries provide highly optimized routines for linear algebra operations [11].

Despite the abundant research in software acceleration of basic linear algebra operations, to the best of our knowledge, we are not aware of any of their hardware acceleration. Due to the low density of earlier hardware devices used in embedded systems, few floating-point operators can be implemented on those devices. However, with the advances in technology, these devices have become much more powerful. In particular, a state-of-the-art Field Programmable Gate Array (FPGA) device contains millions of gates so that many floating-point units can be configured on it. In addition, the current FPGA fabrics provide large amount of on-chip memory as well as abundant I/O pins. Some researchers have suggested that FPGAs can be highly competitive with microprocessors with respect to both peak performance and sustained performance for linear algebra applications [16, 20]. Meanwhile, vendors have begun to use FPGAs for high performance computing. For example, Cray [3] and SRC Computers [15] have developed high end computers that employ FPGAs as application accelerators.

On the other hand, FPGAs also pose new challenges in implementing (floating-point) BLAS operations. Limitations in the available resources, such as the number of slices, the size of on-chip memory and the number of I/O pins, impose multiple constraints on architectural design. These constraints, as well as the inherent characteristics of BLAS operations, result in various design tradeoffs. In this work, we focus on the design tradeoff analysis for BLAS operations. We choose the vector product from level 1 BLAS, matrix-vector multiply from level 2 BLAS, and matrix multiply from level 3 BLAS. To the best of our knowledge, the design tradeoffs analyzed in this paper have not been discussed for level 1 or level 2 BLAS operations on FPGAs. For level 3 BLAS operations, we extend our work in [20]. Although our work is not dependent on the data representation, we consider IEEE-754 double-precision numbers throughout the paper, as this representation is widely used in scientific computations [8].

For each BLAS operation, we analyze its inherent characteristics, such as the number of floating-point operations and I/O operations required, and identify various design parameters. By exploring the design space, we analyze the design tradeoffs among area, latency and size of on-chip memory needed by the design. Based on the analysis, we

*Supported by the United States National Science Foundation under award No. CCR-0311823 and in part by award No. ACI-0305763.

propose an FPGA-based design for each BLAS operation so as to achieve the optimal latency under the given hardware resources. The optimizations we employ are generic. Thus, they can be applied to various FPGA devices.

For both the vector product and the matrix-vector product, we propose a tree-based design. For the matrix multiply, we employ a linear array of Processing Elements (PEs). Block algorithms are employed to reduce the requirements on the memory bandwidth. The design for each BLAS operation is characterized through various parameters, such as the number of floating-point units and the block size. The parameters can be tuned according to various hardware resource constraints, which include the available area, the size of on-chip memory, and the number of I/O pins. We implemented our proposed designs using Xilinx ISE 6.2i [18], with Xilinx Virtex-II Pro XC2VP40 as our target device. For all of the designs, the area increases linearly with the number of floating-point units used. Moreover, the latency decreases almost proportionally with the number of floating-point units, if adequate memory bandwidth is provided. On the other hand, the size of on-chip memory needed and the memory bandwidth required by the designs are determined by both the number of floating-point units and the block size.

The rest of the paper is organized as follows. Section 2 introduces the background and the related work. Section 3 proposes our designs for the BLAS operations. Section 4 presents and analyzes the performance of our designs. Section 5 concludes the paper.

2 Background and Related Work

Scientific Computing on FPGAs

Field-Programmable Gate Arrays (FPGAs) are a form of programmable logic. They offer design flexibility like software, but with time performance closer to Application Specific Integrated Circuits (ASICs) [2]. An FPGA device consists of an array of logic blocks (*slices*) whose functionality is determined through programmable configuration bits. These logic blocks are connected using a set of routing resources that are also programmable. Thus, mapping an appropriate design to FPGAs consists of determining the functions to be computed by the logic blocks, and using the configurable routing resources to connect the blocks.

State-of-the-art FPGA devices also contain large amount of on-chip memory. including the memory that can be realized by the logic blocks and the embedded memory blocks called Block RAMs (BRAMs). Besides the on-chip memory, FPGA-based designs also have access to external memory through I/O pins. Throughout this paper, our analysis is based on this generic FPGA and (external) memory computing model. We assume that for each operation, the input data are initially stored in the external memory, and the size of the data can be larger than the on-chip memory.

In the past, FPGAs were mainly used for integer and fixed-point applications. However, with the advances in technology, FPGAs are now feasible to be used for a much broader range of applications, including those requiring floating-point operations. Floating-point units with various precisions have been designed [6]. FPGA-based architectures also have been proposed for computationally intensive applications [14].

Recently, high end computers have been built with FPGAs serving as application accelerators. Examples include the SRC MAPstation [15] and the Cray XD1 [3]. These computers combine general-purpose computing systems with reconfigurable hardware. The general-purpose microprocessors and the FPGAs share memory with each other. In these computers, FPGA-based designs have access to large external memory and high bandwidth interconnect.

BLAS

The set of Basic Linear Algebra Subprograms, which is commonly referred to as BLAS [11], has been used in a wide range of software including LINPACK [4]. BLAS provide building block routines for performing basic vector and matrix operations. Optimizations for the BLAS library on general-purpose processors include loop unrolling, register blocking and cache blocking [17]. Since many of the optimizations are platform specific, ATLAS was proposed which automatically generates and optimizes numerical software for processors with deep memory hierarchies and pipelined functional units [17].

Although BLAS and ATLAS have been widely accepted and used by the scientific computing community, building libraries of hardware implementations for linear algebra operations has not been well studied. There have been some researches on FPGA-based implementations of linear algebra applications. However, some of them consider fixed-point arithmetic only [1, 10]; while others only discuss one floating-point BLAS operation [20, 5]. The only prior work that considers FPGA-based implementations of operations from all BLAS levels is conducted by Underwood et al [16]. In that work, the authors examine the potential capacity of FPGAs in performing floating-point BLAS operations, and compare the computing capacity of FPGAs with general-purpose processors. Although some architectures are proposed for BLAS operations in [16], the performance results are mainly based on estimation. Moreover, in [16], only the number of I/O pins is considered as a constraint. However, as we show in Section 4, the available area and on-chip memory of the device can also constrain the performance of the designs. In contrast to [16], we provide design tradeoffs analysis based on multiple hardware resource constraints. In addition, we discuss techniques to reduce the requirement on memory bandwidth.

3 FPGA-based Designs for BLAS

In our work, we adopt a parameterized approach for basic linear algebra operations on FPGAs. For each BLAS operation, we identify the design parameters and analyze the resulting design tradeoffs. Note that the analysis in this section does not consider the implementation issues, such as the routing complexity and the target device. We employ the following mathematical notation throughout the paper:

- u, v, x, y: vectors of length n. Each vector can be either a column vector or a row vector, according to the context.
- A, B, C: $n \times n$ matrices, with elements a_{ij}, b_{ij}, c_{ij} $(i, j = 0, \ldots, n-1)$
- α: pipeline delay of the floating-point adder
- w, w_j: number of bits in a floating-point word and a column index, respectively
- k, l: number of floating-point multiplications and floating-point additions that can be performed in each clock cycle, respectively
- bw: number of data words (double precision floating-point) that are input/output in each clock cycle
- m: total size of on-chip memory needed by the design
- T: number of clock cycles needed to complete the BLAS operation
- T_{comp}: number of clock cycles needed for floating-point computations
- $T_{I/O}$: number of clock cycles needed for input/output

3.1 Level 1 BLAS

Level 1 BLAS are the specification and implementation of subprograms for scalar and vector operations. In this paper, we consider product of a row vector and a column vector, which can be formulated as:

$$u \times v = \sum_{i=0}^{n-1} u_i v_i$$

A. BLAS Operation Analysis: For the vector product, the minimum number of I/O operations is $2n + 1$, and n floating-point multiplications as well as n floating-point additions need to be performed. We can easily identify k and l as the design parameters, because they affect T_{comp}. Since there is no data reuse in this operation, no on-chip memory is needed by the design. To reduce the latency, we can overlap T_{comp} and $T_{I/O}$. Furthermore, we can overlap the floating-point multiplications and additions. Therefore, the lower bound on the latency of the operation (in cycles) is derived as follows:

$$T \geq \max(T_{comp}, T_{I/O}) \geq \max(\max(\frac{n}{k}, \frac{n}{l}), \frac{2n+1}{bw}))$$

B. Architecture: To achieve the lower bound, $k = l$ and $k \approx \frac{bw}{2}$. Thus we propose an architecture which consists of identical number of floating-point adders and multipliers. The floating-point adders and multipliers are pipelined so that additions, multiplications and I/O operations can be overlapped. Moreover, pipelining for the adder and multiplier results in high clock speed.

During each clock cycle, each multiplier reads one element from each of the two vectors, and multiplies these two floating-point numbers. An adder tree is employed to sum up the outputs of the multipliers. When $k < n$, we need an additional adder to sum up the outputs of the adder tree. Thus, we use k adders, including the $k - 1$ adders in the adder tree and the additional adder. If we ignore the clock cycles used to fill the multiplier and the adder pipelines, the effective latency of the architecture is $T = \frac{n}{k}$.

The adder tree in the architecture yields one output in each clock cycle. Thus, the task of the additional adder is to reduce sets of sequentially delivered floating-point values. However, the pipelining in the floating-point adder can cause read-after-write data hazards during the reduction. This problem has been investigated in [19] and [13]. Therefore, we replace the additional adder outside the adder tree using a reduction circuit proposed in [13]. This reduction circuit can reduce a series of inputs of arbitrary length. It employs two floating-point adders and $\Theta(\lg(s))$ buffer size for s sequential inputs. Let $T_{red}(s)$ denote the time to complete the reduction. As shown in [13], $T_{red}(s) = \Theta(s)$. The characteristics of the reduction circuit are presented in Section 4.

The architecture for the vector product is shown in Figure 1. The effective latency of the design is

$$T = \frac{n}{k} + T_{red}(\frac{n}{k}) = \Theta(\frac{n}{k}) \quad (1)$$

To achieve this latency, the design performs $2k + 1$ I/O operations during each clock cycle, that is, $bw = 2k + 1$. The number of I/O pins used is $(2k + 1)w$.

3.2 Level 2 BLAS

In level 2 BLAS, we select the matrix vector multiply, which is formulated as:

$$y = Ax, y_i = \sum_{j=0}^{n-1} a_{ij} x_j \quad (i = 0, 1, \ldots, n-1)$$

A. BLAS Operation Analysis: In the matrix-vector multiply, the total number of floating-point operations is $2n^2$.

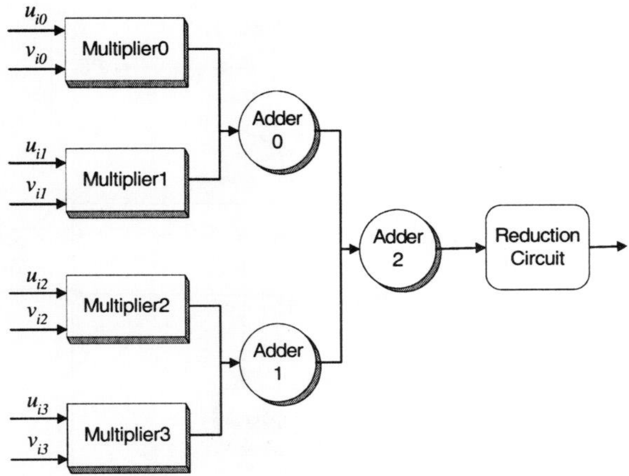

Figure 1. Architecture for vector product ($k = 4$)

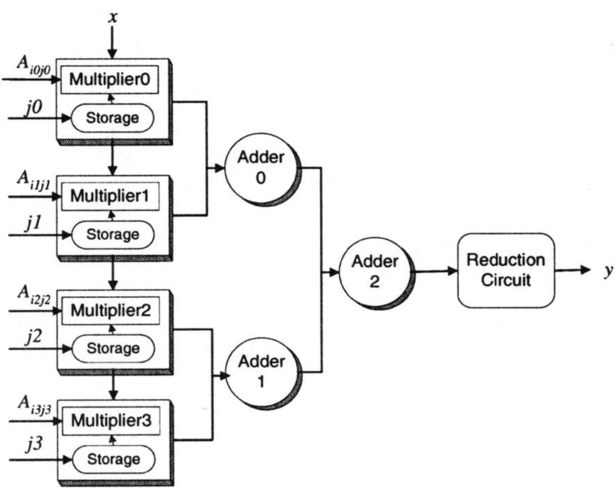

Figure 2. Architecture for matrix-vector product ($k = 4$)

As in the case of the vector product, we identify k and l as the design parameters. However, in this operation, each element in x can be reused n times. If we do not store any element of x in the architecture, the total number of I/O operations is $2n^2$.

To partially reduce the I/O costs, we use block matrix-vector multiply. Thus, a new parameter, b, needs to be introduced. Without loss of generality, we assume n is a multiple of b. In the blocked version, A is partitioned into $\frac{n}{b}$ blocks of columns, with each block of size $n \times b$. Similarly, x is partitioned into $\frac{n}{b}$ blocks of size $b \times 1$. We denote the blocks using A^g and x^g, respectively ($g = 0, 1, \ldots, \frac{n}{b} - 1$). For each block matrix-vector multiply $A^g \times x^g$, A^g and x^g need to be read from and the results need to be written to the external memory. Therefore, the total number of I/O operations with block size b equals $\frac{n}{b} \times (nb+b+n) = n^2 + \frac{n^2}{b} + n$.

We set $k = l$ to reduce T_{comp}. The lower bound on the latency of the operation can be derived as follows:

$$T \geq \max(T_{comp}, T_{I/O}) \geq \max(\frac{n^2}{k}, \frac{n^2 + \frac{n^2}{b} + n}{bw})$$

The above equation shows a design tradeoff between the block size and the I/O time, even though asymptotically the I/O time is $\frac{n^2}{bw}$. The smaller is the block size, the more I/O operations are required; and vice versa. Another tradeoff exists between the storage size and the data access time. If we only store one copy of x^g in the architecture, $m = b$. However, since each BRAM on FPGAs only has two I/O ports, reading k distinct values from the BRAM takes multiple clock cycles. On the other hand, if x^g is duplicated at each multiplier, each multiplier can access the needed data in each clock cycle. However, the size of on-chip memory needed by the design (m) increases to kb.

B. Architecture: Based on the design tradeoffs, we propose an architecture for the matrix-vector multiply, as shown in Figure 2. This architecture is very similar to the architecture for the vector product, except that each multiplier is attached to a local storage. The local storage stores a copy of x^g. Initially, the storage is loaded with x^0. During the computation, the multiplier reads one element from A^g in each clock cycle, then uses the column index to find the corresponding x^g element from its local storage, and finally multiplies these two numbers. To reduce the latency, the initialization of block x^g is overlapped with the computations of $A^{g-1} \times x^{g-1}$ ($g = 1, \ldots, \frac{n}{b} - 1$).

When $b > k$, one row in A^g is further partitioned into $\frac{b}{k}$ sub-rows which are fed into the architecture in order. A reduction circuit is used in the architecture to accumulate the sums of the sub-rows.

To generate the final y, we also need to accumulate the results generated by $A^0 \times x^0$, $A^1 \times x^1$, ..., $A^{\frac{n}{b}-1} \times x^{\frac{n}{b}-1}$. For each y element, such intermediate results are generated every n clock cycles. Since the typical value of α is less than 20 and is usually much smaller than n, an additional floating-point adder suffices for such accumulation.

The effective latency of our design is:

$$\begin{aligned} T &= (b+k) + (\tfrac{n \times b}{k} + k) \times (\tfrac{n}{b} - 1) + \tfrac{n \times b}{k} + T_{red}(\tfrac{b}{k}) \\ &= \tfrac{n^2}{k} + \tfrac{nk}{b} + b + T_{red}(\tfrac{b}{k}) \\ &= \Theta(\tfrac{n^2}{k}) \end{aligned} \quad (2)$$

To achieve the latency, the design needs to perform $bw \approx k + \frac{k}{b}$ floating-point I/O operations during each clock cycle. The number of I/O pins used is $k(w + w_j) + 2w$ because:

each multiplier reads one element of A and its column index in each clock cycle; the first multiplier reads one element of x per clock cycle for initialization. Note that we can reduce the number of I/O pins used by using a counter to keep track of the column index. The total size of on-chip memory needed by the design is $m = kb$.

3.3 Level 3 BLAS

The last BLAS operation we consider in this paper is dense matrix multiply, from level 3 BLAS. This BLAS operation is formulated as:

$$C = AB, c_{ij} = \sum_{q=0}^{n-1} a_{iq}b_{qj} \quad (i, j = 0, 1, \ldots, n-1)$$

A. BLAS Operation Analysis: Each element of A and B can be used n times, and the total number of floating-point operations is $2n^3$. Since there is lots of data reuse in the matrix multiply, m, the size of on-chip memory needed by the design becomes an important design parameter. We use *I/O complexity* to refer to the total number of I/O operations performed by an algorithm. It has been proven [7] that the I/O complexity of any implementations of the usual matrix multiply algorithm is $\Omega(\frac{n^3}{\sqrt{m}})$, when $\Theta(1) \leq m \leq \Theta(n^2)$.

Again we set $k = l$ to optimize T_{comp}. The lower bound on the latency of matrix multiply is:

$$T \geq \max(T_{comp}, T_{I/O}) \geq \max(\frac{n^3}{k}, \frac{n^3/\sqrt{m}}{bw}) \quad (m \leq n^2) \tag{3}$$

Thus, tradeoffs exist among the number of PEs, the total size of on-chip memory, and the required memory bandwidth. Based on Equation 3, following cases arise for various values of k and m:

- **Case 1:** $k \geq n, m = n^2$
- **Case 2:** $k \geq n, m < n^2$
- **Case 3:** $k < n, m = n^2$
- **Case 4:** $k < n, m < n^2$

In our prior work, we have proposed an architecture for Case 1: $\frac{n^2}{s}$ $(1 \leq s \leq n)$ PEs are connected in a linear array [20]. Each PE contains one floating-point multiplier, one floating-point adder and local storage of s words. During each clock cycle, n PEs are performing steps of the matrix multiply, while the other PEs wait for data. The required memory bandwidth is 3 words per clock cycle. The total size of on-chip memory needed is $m = \frac{n^2}{s} \times s = n^2$. Since $1 \leq s \leq n$, this design considers the case $k \geq n$. However, for FPGA-based implementations of floating-point matrix multiply, the condition $k \geq n$ is usually hard to satisfy. Due to the complexity of the floating-point units, only tens of floating-point units can be configured on an FPGA device, while n can be large. Moreover, n^2 can be much larger than the total size of on-chip memory on FPGAs. Hence the requirement $m = n^2$ will be difficult to meet. Thus, we do not consider Case 2 and Case 3 in this paper.

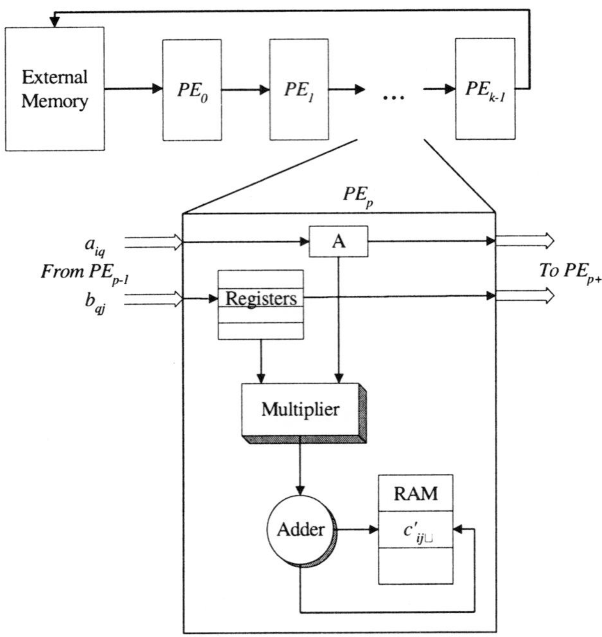

Figure 3. Architecture for matrix multiply

B. Architecture: In this paper, we extend our previous work [20] to Case 4: k can be smaller than n, and m can be smaller than n^2. Another contribution of this design is that we take the memory bandwidth into account in our analysis. For a given k and m, we are able to minimize the required memory bandwidth.

The architecture is shown in Figure 3, and the algorithm is shown in Figure 4. In the architecture, there are k PEs connected in a linear array. Each PE consists of one floating-point multiplier, one floating-point adder, local storage of size $\frac{m}{k}$, and $\frac{2\sqrt{m}}{k}$ registers. The PEs are labeled from left to right, as $PE_0, PE_1, \ldots, PE_{k-1}$. PE_0 reads A and B from the external memory. PE_{k-1} writes the final elements of C to the memory.

In the design, we are actually performing block matrix multiply where the block size is $\sqrt{m} \times \sqrt{m}$. The blocks are denoted as A^{gz} and B^{zh}, where $g, z, h = 0, 1, \ldots, \frac{n}{\sqrt{m}} - 1$. Without loss of generality, we assume n is a multiple of $\sqrt{m}$, and $\sqrt{m}$ is a multiple of k.

In our design, for each block matrix multiply $A^{gz} \times B^{zh}$, A^{gz} is read in column-major order, while B^{zh} is read in row-major order. PE_p, $p = 0, \ldots, k-1$, is in charge of computing the columns p, $(k+p)$, ..., $((\frac{\sqrt{m}}{k} - 1)k + p)$ of C^{gh}. Before the computation starts, the first row of B^{zh} is read into the architecture. As these $\sqrt{m}$ numbers traverse the linear array, PE_p, $p = 0, \ldots, k-1$, stores the pth, $(k+p)$th, ..., $((\frac{\sqrt{m}}{k} - 1)k + p)$th numbers into its registers. Afterwards, every $\frac{\sqrt{m}}{k}$ clock cycles, one element of A^{gz} and one element of B^{zh} are read into the architecture. As a_{iq} passes through a PE, it is multiplied with every element of B stored in the PE whose row index is q. The intermediate results for C^{gh} are denoted as c'_{ij}, and are stored in the local storage of the PEs.

During the computation, the value of c'_{ij} is updated every $\frac{m}{k}$ cycles. If $\frac{m}{k} > \alpha$, there is no data hazard. Otherwise we need to either decrease k to increase $\frac{m}{k}$, or replace the floating-point adder in each PE with a reduction circuit.

As in the matrix-vector multiply, the intermediate results of C need to be accumulated. The effective latency for each block matrix multiply, T', equals $(\frac{\sqrt{m}}{k})^3 = \frac{m\sqrt{m}}{k}$. Thus, every T' clock cycles, an intermediate result of C is generated. Since T' is usually much larger than α, we can simply use a floating-point adder for the accumulation.

{block matrix multiply}
for $PE\ p = 0$ to $k-1$ (in parallel) **do**
  if $p = j \mod k$ **then**
    copy b_{qj} to a register
  end if
  if $q = 1$ (the first row of B block) **then**
    shift b_{qj} right to PE_{p+1}
  else
    shift b_{qj}, a_{iq} right to PE_{p+1}
    for every $b_{qj'}$ in the registers **do**
      $c'_{ij'} <= c'_{ij'} + a_{iq} \times b_{qj'}$
    end for
  end if
end for

Figure 4. Algorithm for matrix multiply

In our design, $\frac{n^3}{\sqrt{m}}$ block matrix multiplies are performed. Thus, the total latency of our design is:

$$\begin{aligned} T = & \sqrt{m} + (\frac{n}{\sqrt{m}})^3 \times \frac{m\sqrt{m}}{k} \\ = & \sqrt{m} + \frac{n^3}{k} \\ = & \Theta(\frac{n^3}{k}) \end{aligned} \quad (4)$$

To achieve the latency, 2 words are read from and 1 word is written to the external memory every $\frac{\sqrt{m}}{k}$ cycles. Thus, $bw = \Theta(\frac{k}{\sqrt{m}})$. According to [7] and Equation 4, the memory bandwidth required by our design is minimum for a given m. The number of I/O pins needed is $3w$.

4 Performance Analysis and Discussion

4.1 Experimental Setup

To understand the tradeoffs, we used Xilinx ISE 6.2i [18] and Mentor Graphics ModelSim 5.7 [12] development tools in our experiments. Our target device is Xilinx Virtex-II Pro XC2VP40 [18], which contains 19392 slices, about 3 Mbit on-chip memory and 804 I/O pins. This is a typical state-of-art FPGA device at the time of writing.

The building blocks used in our designs include floating-point adder, floating-point multiplier, and reduction circuit. In all of the designs, the implementation of the building blocks has no effect on the architecture or the control logic of the designs. These blocks can be independently designed and then plugged into any of our designs, with no or few modifications to the design. Table 1 gives the characteristics of these blocks, whose implementation details can be found in [6, 13]. Note that our floating-point units comply with the IEEE-754 double-precision format [8].

In our experiments, we first determine the range for each design parameter based on the hardware resource constraints. Then we vary the values of the parameters, and measure the area and clock speed of the designs after place and route. The latency and the required memory bandwidth are calculated based on the clock speed and the analysis in Section 3. Suppose the clock speed is f MHz, the latency is calculated as $\frac{T}{f} \times 10^{-6}$ second; the required memory bandwidth is $bw \times 64 \times f$ Mb/s. Next, we discuss the tradeoffs in determining the values of the parameters for each operation. In all the experiments, the problem size n is set as 2048, so that the input data for matrix-vector multiply and matrix multiply cannot be stored in the on-chip memory of the FPGA device.

4.2 Performance Analysis

Level 1 BLAS For the vector product, the only parameter is k, the number of floating-point multiplications that can be performed in each clock cycle. Since each multiplication needs two 64-bit numbers, the range of k is determined by the number of available I/O pins. For the target device, $k \leq 5$. In the design, the control logic occupies less than 5% of the total area. Thus, as shown in Figure 5, when k increases from 1 to 5, the area of the design increases linearly. The clock speed of the design is limited by that of the reduction circuit, and remains 170 MHz (Table 1). Hence the latency of the design decreases proportionally as k increases. The memory bandwidth required by the design also increases linearly with k (figure not shown due to space limitation). Thus, k causes tradeoff among area, latency and required memory bandwidth. Larger k leads to smaller latency, but requires more area and higher memory bandwidth.

Table 1. Characteristics of 64-bit Floating-Point Units and Reduction Circuit

	Adder	Multiplier	Reduction Circuit
Number of Pipeline Stages	19	12	-
Number of Slices	933	910	3313
Achievable Clock Speed(MHz)	200	205	170

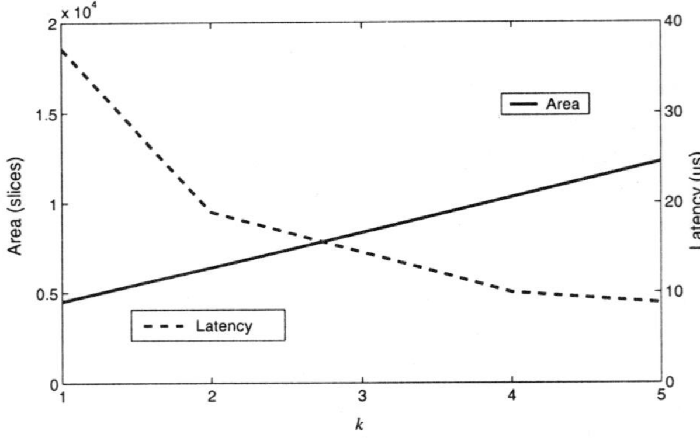

Figure 5. Area and latency for vector product ($n = 2048$)

Level 2 BLAS For the matrix-vector multiply, we need to tune both k and b. The range of k is determined by the total size of available area and the area of the floating-point adders, the floating-point multipliers and the reduction circuit. For the target device, $k \leq 8$. The range of b is determined by the size of on-chip memory on the FPGA device. For simplicity, we set the storage constraint as 1 Mbit, and vary b from 256 to 2048 words. We use BRAMs on the FPGAs as the local storage in the design. Note that BRAMs occupy few additional slices. The area of the design increases linearly with k, similar as in Figure 5. According to Equation 2, T depends on both k and b. However, Figure 6(a) shows that the latency is primarily determined by k. When k is fixed, the latency varies little as b increases. This is because when $n \gg k$ and $b \gg k$, $\frac{nk}{b} + b + T_{red}(\frac{b}{k})$ is negligible compared to $\frac{n^2}{k}$.

Each point in Figure 6(a) has a corresponding point in Figure 6(b) which indicates the memory bandwidth required to achieve the optimal performance. Figure 6(b) shows that the required memory bandwidth increases linearly with k. Thus, as in the case of the vector product, k causes tradeoffs among area, latency and required memory bandwidth.

Note that with current FPGA fabrics, k is usually in the order of tens, while n can be much larger. Therefore, although block matrx-vector multiply can reduce the number of memory accesses, a large block size does not decrease the latency or the required memory bandwidth. On the other hand, the total size of on-chip memory needed in the design increases with k as well as b (figure not shown due to space limitation). Thus, when determining the value of b, a small block size is preferred.

Level 3 BLAS In the design for the matrix multiply discussed in Section 3, k is actually equal to the number of PEs. The maximum value of k is determined by the total size of available area and the area of the PEs. Each PE contains one floating-point adder, one floating-point multiplier, some BRAMs and a control unit. In contrast to the control logic of the entire design, this unit is in charge of the routing and the control circuitry inside one PE. Our experiments show that the control unit occupies less than 30% of the area of the PE. For the target device, $k \leq 8$. As in the other two design, the area of the design increases linearly with k, as shown in Figure 7(a).

Different from the other two designs, the size of on-chip memory needed by the design, m, is a design parameter for matrix multiply. $\sqrt{m} \times \sqrt{m}$ is the block size for block matrix multiply. In our experiments, we vary m from 16^2 words to 128^2 words.

Since the reduction circuit is not used in this design, the clock speed of the design is not limited by it. Instead, the clock speed of the design decreases as k increases due to the increasing routing complexity. However, Figure 7(b) shows that the latency still decreases proportionally with k. This is because the decrease in the clock speed is not as fast as the decrease in T. In particular, when k increases from 1 to 8, the degradation in the clock speed is less than 10%. Figure 7(b) also shows that the latency is not affected by $\sqrt{m}$. According to Equation 4, this is because when $n \gg k$ and $n \gg \sqrt{m}$, $\sqrt{m}$ is negligible compared to $\frac{n^3}{k}$. However, the required memory bandwidth is dependent on both k and m, as shown in Figure 7(c). The larger the k, the higher the required memory bandwidth. On the other hand, larger $\sqrt{m}$ reduces the requirement on the memory bandwidth.

As in the case of the other two operations, k causes tradeoff among area, latency and required memory bandwidth for matrix multiply. Another tradeoff exists between the required on-chip memory and the required memory bandwidth.

In our experiments, using 18428 slices, 1 Mbit of on-chip memory, 192 I/O pins and a memory bandwidth of 2.1 Gb/s, our design for 64-bit matrix multiply can

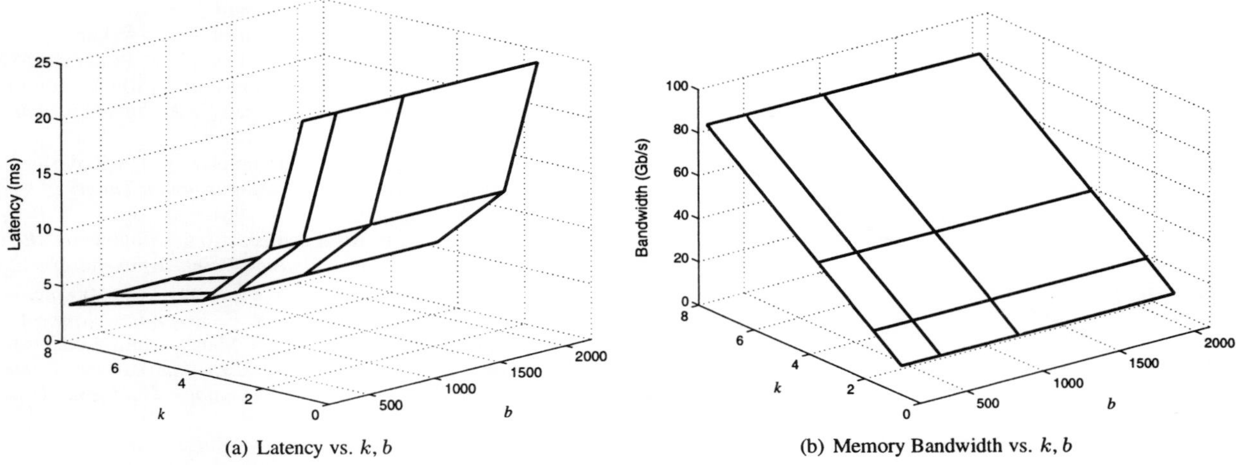

(a) Latency vs. k, b

(b) Memory Bandwidth vs. k, b

Figure 6. Performance analysis for matrix-vector multiply ($n = 2048$)

achieve 2.8 GFLOPS. This performance compares favorably with general-purpose processors. For example, a Xeon processor-based platform at 3.2 GHz with 1 MB L3 cache achieves 5.5 GFLOPS performing 64-bit matrix multiplication, while a 3-GHz Pentium 4 processor with 512 KB L2 cache achieves 5.0 GFLOPS [9]. These numbers are obtained by executing Intel Math Kernel Library [9]. This library not only employs common software optimizations such as loop unrolling and cache blocking, but also exploits the features of the Intel processors through specific optimizations. Note that our design is not optimized with respect to area or clock speed. In addition, no device specific optimizations were performed in our design.

We next compare the GFLOPS performance of our design for matrix multiply with the peak performance of the target device. In an ideal situation, the control logic occupies no slices; each floating-point unit (adder/multiplier) performs one floating-point operation during every clock cycle. A Xilinx Virtex-II Pro XC2VP40 can be configured to include at most 10 floating-point adders and 10 floating-point multipliers; the maximum clock speed of the design is 200 MHz. These estimations are based on the floating-point units in Table 1. Therefore, the peak performance of the device is $2 \times 10 \times 200$ MFLOPS = 4 GFLOPS. Our design achieves 70% of the peak performance, using only 33% of the on-chip memory.

5 Conclusion

We have proposed optimized FPGA-based implementations for the vector product, matrix-vector multiply and matrix multiply. Various design parameters were identified for each BLAS operation, and the resulting design tradeoffs were analyzed. The parameters include the number of floating-point units, the size of on-chip memory needed by the design and the block size. We implemented our designs on a Xilinx Virtex-II Pro XC2VP40 FPGA device. The performance results show that using more floating-point units in a design leads to smaller latency, but requires more area and higher memory bandwidth. The block size causes tradeoffs between the size of on-chip memory needed and the required memory bandwidth for matrix-vector multiply and matrix multiply. However, the block size has little effect on the latency of these two operations. In all of our proposed designs, the performance increases proportionally with the available hardware resources. We are now optimizing the floating-point units to further improve the GFLOPS performance of the designs. In the future, we plan to implement our designs for BLAS library on FPGA-augmented computers, such as Cray XD1 [3] and the MAPstation of SRC [15]. We also plan to extend our FPGA-based linear algebra library, by proposing designs for more linear algebra applications.

References

[1] D. Benyamin, W. Luk, and J. Villasenor. Optimizing FPGA-based Vector Product Designs. In *Proc. of the IEEE Symposium on FPGAs for Custom Computing Machines*, Napa Valley, CA, April 1999.

[2] K. Compton and S. Hauck. Reconfigurable Computing: A Survey of Systems and Software. *ACM Computing Surveys*, 34(2):171–210, June 2002.

[3] Cray Inc. `http://www.cray.com/`.

[4] J. Dongarra, J. Bunch, C. Moler, and G. Stewart. *LINPACK Users' Guide*. Society for Industrial and Applied Mathematics, 1979.

[5] Y. Dou, S. Vassiliadis, G. Kuzmanov, and G. Gaydadjiev. 64-bit Floating-Point FPGA Matrix Multiplication. In

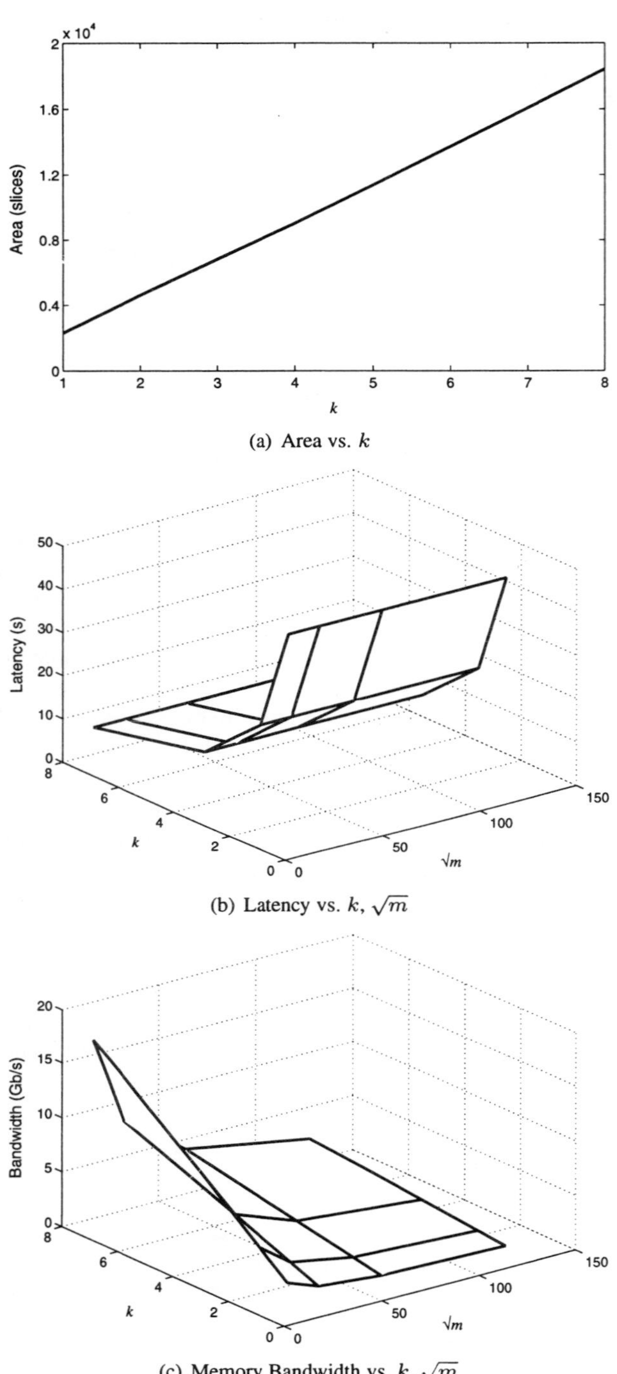

(a) Area vs. k

(b) Latency vs. k, $\sqrt{m}$

(c) Memory Bandwidth vs. k, $\sqrt{m}$

Figure 7. Performance analysis for matrix multiply ($n = 2048$)

Proc. of the 13th International Symposium on Field Programmable Gate Arrays, California, USA, February 2005.

[6] G. Govindu, L. Zhuo, S. Choi, and V. K. Prasanna. Analysis of High-Performance Floating-Point Arithmetic on FPGAs. In *Proc. of the 11th Reconfigurable Architectures Workshop*, New Mexico, USA, April 2004.

[7] J. Hong and H. Kung. I/O Complexity: The Red Blue Pebble Game. In *Proc. of ACM Symposium on Theory of Computing*, Wisconsin, USA, May 1981.

[8] Institute of Electrical and Electronics Engineers. *IEEE 754 Standard for Binary Floating-Point Arithmetic*. IEEE, 1984.

[9] Intel. http://www.intel.com.

[10] J. W. Jang, S. Choi, and V. K. Prasanna. Area and Time Efficient Implementation of Matrix Multiplication on FPGAs. In *Proc. of The First IEEE International Conference on Field Programmable Technology*, California, USA, December 2002.

[11] C. Lawson, R. Hanson, D. Kincaid, and F. Krogh. Basic Linear Algebra Subprograms for FORTRAN usage. *ACM Transaction on Mathematical Software*, 5(3):308–323, 1979.

[12] Mentor Graphics Corp. http://www.mentor.com/.

[13] G. R. Morris, L. Zhuo, and V. K. Prasanna. High-Performance FPGA-Based General Reduction Methods. In *Proc. of 10th IEEE Symposium on Field-Programmable Custom Computing Machines*, April 2005.

[14] R. Scrofano and V. K. Prasanna. Computing Lennard-Jones Potentials and Forces with Reconfigurable Hardware. In *Proc. of International Conference on Engineering of Reconfigurable Systems and Algorithms*, June 2004.

[15] SRC Computers, Inc. http://www.srccomp.com/.

[16] K. D. Underwood and K. S. Hemmert. Closing the Gap: CPU and FPGA Trends in Sustainable Floating-Point BLAS Performance. In *Proc. of 2004 IEEE Symposium on Field-Programmable Custom Computing Machines*, California, USA, April 2004.

[17] R. C. Whaley, A. Petitet, and J. J. Dongarra. Automated empirical optimization of software and the ATLAS project. *Parallel Computing*, 27(1–2):3–35, 2001.

[18] Xilinx Incorporated. http://www.xilinx.com.

[19] L. Zhuo, G. R. Morris, and V. K. Prasanna. Designing Scalable FPGA-Based Reduction Circuits Using Pipelined Floating-Point Cores. In *Proc. of the 12th Reconfigurable Architectures Workshop*, Colorado, USA, April 2005.

[20] L. Zhuo and V. K. Prasanna. Scalable and Modular Algorithms for Floating-Point Matrix Multiplication on FPGAs. In *Proc. of the 18th International Parallel & Distributed Processing Symposium*, New Mexico, USA, April 2004.

Session 2B: Compilers and Languages

Tuning High Performance Kernels through Empirical Compilation *

R. Clint Whaley
Dept. of Computer Science
Florida State University
whaley@cs.fsu.edu

David B. Whalley
Dept. of Computer Science
Florida State University
whalley@cs.fsu.edu

Abstract

There are a few application areas which remain almost untouched by the historical and continuing advancement of compilation research. For the extremes of optimization required for high performance computing on one end, and embedded systems at the opposite end of the spectrum, many critical routines are still hand-tuned, often directly in assembly. At the same time, architecture implementations are performing an increasing number of compiler-like transformations in hardware, making it harder to predict the performance impact of a given series of optimizations applied at the ISA level. These issues, together with the rate of hardware evolution dictated by Moore's Law, make it almost impossible to keep key kernels running at peak efficiency. Automated empirical systems, where direct timings are used to guide optimization, have provided the most successful response to these challenges. This paper describes our approach to performing empirical optimization, which utilizes a low-level iterative compilation framework specialized for optimizing high performance computing kernels. We present results showing that this approach can not only provide speedups over traditional optimizing compilers, but can improve overall performance when compared to the best hand-tuned kernels selected by the empirical search of our well-known ATLAS package.

1 Introduction and Related Work

For high performance computing on one end, and embedded computing at the opposite extreme, many critical routines are still hand-tuned (often directly in assembly) in order to achieve the required efficiency. It is very rare indeed that the hand-tuner in question applies a technique that is unknown to the compilation community. In almost every case, this hypothetical hand-tuner is applying transformations that are well understood, but is either optimizing for an architecture upon which compilers are not yet well-tuned (and may never be well-tuned), or is applying the techniques in ways that compilers either cannot (due to imperfect analysis) or purposely avoid (for instance, because the technique causes a slowdown in many cases).

This problem is exacerbated in high performance computing, where compute needs mandate usage of parallel machines. If the serial kernels upon which the computation is based fail to achieve adequate efficiency, this inefficiency results in the need to utilize more processors to solve the problem, which in turn leads to greater bottlenecks due to increased parallelization costs (eg., greater communication and implementation time). Therefore, any serial weakness is greatly magnified when parallelization is considered, and thus it becomes even more critical that the computational kernels used by the HPC application achieve the greatest percentage of peak possible.

At the same time, Moore's law has ensured that not only does new hardware come out in release cycles too short for compiler writers to keep pace, it has also resulted in architectures that implement many compiler-like transformations in hardware (eg., dynamic scheduling, out-of-order execution, register renaming, etc.). Due to this trend, the ISA available to the compiler writer becomes more and more like a high-level language, and thus the close connection between the instructions issued by the compiler, and the actions performed by the machine, is lost. This phenomenon makes it increasingly difficult to know a priori if a given transformation will be helpful, and almost impossible to be sure when it is worth applying a transformation that yields benefits only in certain situations. The most extreme example of this is embodied in the x86 architecture, whose non-orthogonal CISC instruction set has, to the frustration of many compiler writers, become the most widely-used ISA in general-purpose computing.

Even when the ISA is kept relatively close to the actual hardware, building models for each machine that instantiate all of the characteristics that affect optimization at this level is almost intractable. Even if a model could be created that was sophisticated enough to account for the in-

*This research was supported in part by National Science Foundation grants CIA-0072043, CCR-0208892, and CCR-0812493.

0190-3918/05 $20.00 © 2005 IEEE

teractions between all levels of cache, the pipelines of all relevant functional units, and all shared hardware resources required by a given operation, it is often the case that much of the required data is proprietary, or due to unforeseen resource interactions, unknown even to the hardware vendor.

These problems, taken together, have led to the implementation of empirically tuned packages, such as ATLAS [17, 16] and FFTW [5, 10]. The central idea behind these packages is that since it is dif£cult to predict a priori whether or by how much a given technique will improve performance, one should try a battery of known techniques on each performance-critical kernel, obtain accurate timings to assess the effect of each transformation of interest, and retain only those that result in measurable improvements for this *exact* system and kernel. This approach allows for a much greater degree of specialization than can be realistically achieved in any other fashion. For instance, it is not uncommon for empirical tuning of a given kernel on two basically identical systems, varying only in the type or size of cache supported, to produce tuned implementations with signi£cantly different optimizational parameters, and it is almost always the case that varying the kernel results in widespread optimization differences.

These empirically tuned packages have succeeded in achieving high levels of performance on widely varying hardware, but in a sense they are still very limited compared to compilation technology. In particular, they are tied to particular operations within given libraries, and are therefore not of great assistance in optimizing other operations that nonetheless require similar levels of performance. It is therefore no surprise that the compiler community has begun to evaluate the scope for using empirical techniques in compilation. Empirical techniques have greater overhead than more conventional feedback-generating schemes such as pro£ling, and thus are poorly suited for general compilation (unless a more targeted and less empirical approach is used, as in [12]). Therefore, most research in empirical compilation concentrates on one of these narrow areas to which we previously alluded. Sometimes this leads to library-oriented compiler research, as in the well-known SPIRAL work [9, 11], and sometimes it is more compiler-centric, but strongly oriented to an area such as embedded systems [7, 13] or high performance computing [4, 2]. These efforts, which should help automate building the libraries that drive high performance computing, are thus tools that can be leveraged in even higher-level compilation efforts, such as [6].

1.1 Our Contribution

The long-range goal of our research is to eliminate the need for hand-tuning in our area of interest, high performance computing. Our approach to this research is to utilize an empirical and iterative compilation framework to £rst enhance, and then (in some cases) replace, the kernel-speci£c techniques presently used in ATLAS. This work addresses two key weaknesses in the approach we employed in developing ATLAS: (1) ATLAS's optimization are kernel speci£c, and (2) Oftentimes the native compiler prevents ATLAS from achieving full performance in a portable manner. Many of the aforementioned researchers are performing related research using other packages (eg., SPIRAL, FFTW, etc.), but our approach is the £rst of which we are aware to perform all transformations at a low level in the backend (many researchers instead generate code in high level languages, just as ATLAS does), and at the same time actually have the search as part of the compiler (many projects put the search in the library generator). Working at the low level allows us to exploit the extremely architecture-speci£c features (eg., SIMD vectorization, CISC instruction formats, pipeline resource limitations, etc.) that are required to squeeze the last few percent of performance from an ISA, while in keeping the search in the compiler, we hope to generalize it enough to tune almost any ¤oating point kernel.

One of the key contributions of this research is in where we focus the work, which is guided by our experience in developing ATLAS. So many papers have discussed search techniques that many researchers have come to believe that fast searches are the primary barrier to solving the problems inherent in this level of tuning. Our own ATLAS work directly contradicts this, in that it still uses the simplest of search techniques, and yet is one of only a handful of such efforts that is both freely available as software and also produces reasonable results on real-world architectures. It is our experience that a simple but intelligently designed search (as described in Section 2.3) reduces the problem of search to a low order term, and thus it does not make sense to make it the focus of the work.

In this paper we discuss our iterative and empirical compilation framework, iFKO [15] (iterative Floating Point Kernel Optimizer). We provide an overview of how it operates, and the set of transformations it presently supports. In order to show that empirical tuning can be effective on even the most well-understood and easily analyzed operations, we £rst concentrate on the simplest kernels ATLAS provides, the Level 1 BLAS [8] (see Section 3.1 for details). One of the surprising contributions of this paper is that even on simple loops such as these, empirical application of even a modest set of well-known compiler transformations can lead to performance improvements greater than those supplied by the best native compiler. Due to its ubiquity and the extreme separation between its ISA and its actual hardware (which makes empirical techniques uniquely attractive), we have chosen the x86 as our initial architectural target. We show that even in this early stage of development, iFKO produces code on average better than the hand-tuned codes chosen by ATLAS's empirical search (we are not aware of any other group who has shown this to be the case on actual kernels on real-world machines, using a completely automated framework) ; in those few cases where iFKO fails to provide the fastest implementation, we describe the transformation that the hand-tuned code utilized to get the best kernel, so it is clear whether or not the technique can be eventually be generalized into our compilation framework.

2 iFKO Implementation Details

If the supported transforms fail to supply performance equivalent to that gained by hand-tuning, our target community will probably not employ an automated approach. Therefore, we must make the effect of each transformation, and the interaction between transformations, as optimal as possible, and so it is better to do a limited number of transformations very well than to support many transformations that do not fully realize their potential. With this narrow and deep focus in mind, Section 2.1 provides a high-level overview of the entire framework, Section 2.2 describes the optimizing compiler component, while Section 2.3 outlines the current search implementation.

2.1 Anatomy of an Iterative and Empirical Compiler

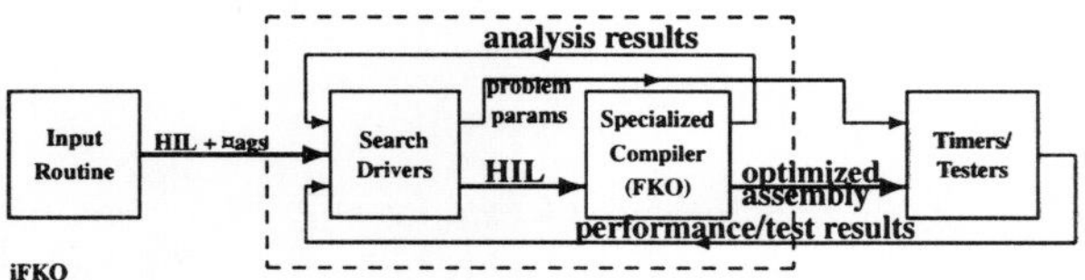

Figure 1. Overview of our Empirical and Iterative Compilation System

Figure 1 shows the basic outline of our empirical and iterative compilation system. Just as in a traditional compiler, iFKO is provided with a routine to be compiled, and perhaps some user-selected compiler ¤ags. iFKO is composed of two components: (1) a collection of search drivers and (2) the compiler specialized for iterative empirical ¤oating point kernel optimization (FKO).

The search £rst passes the input kernel to be optimized to FKO for analysis. FKO then provides feedback to the master search based on this analysis. The analysis phase together with any user input essentially establishes the optimization space to be searched, and the iterative tuning is then initiated. For each optimization of interest that takes an empirically tuned parameter (eg., the unrolling factor in loop unrolling), the search invokes FKO to perform the transformation, the timer to determine its effect on performance, and the tester to ensure that the answer is correct (unnecessary in theory, but useful in practice).

Input can be provided both by mark-up in the routine itself, and by ¤ag selection from the user. These inputs can be used to place limits on the search, as well as to provide information specialized for an individual usage pattern (such as whether the operands are pre-loaded in cache, the size of the problem to time, etc.). Note that iFKO has intelligent defaults for these values, so such user direction is optional. The 'HIL' in Figure 1 stands for high-level intermediate language, and is the language (specialized for ¤oating point kernel optimization) which FKO accepts as input.

2.2 Floating Point Kernel Optimizer (FKO)

The heart of this project is an optimizing compiler called FKO, which has been specialized for empirical optimization of ¤oating point kernels. Our focus on these kernels affects not only our choice of optimizations, but also our input language. Unlike a traditional compiler, FKO must also communicate its analysis to the search program, as described in Section 2.2.2.

In general, one of the main strengths of empirical optimization is that all known techniques can by tried, even ones that may cause signi£cant slowdown in some cases, since the search can keep only the successful optimizations. Therefore FKO eventually needs to have an incredibly diverse battery of transformations, which will result in an expanding optimization space, which in turn will require sophisticated search techniques. Compared with those available to an experienced hand-tuner (and thus to the set of techniques we would ultimately like to implement) FKO presently has a very tractable number of optimizations, which are split into two types. FKO has *fundamental* transformations, which are applied only one time and in a known order (thus easing the extra analysis required for some of these optimizations), and these techniques are outlined in Section 2.2.3. The second class consist of the *repeatable* transformations, discussed in Section 2.2.4, which may be applied multiple times and in almost any order. In order to present an overview of the entire work, we provide only a brief outline of each transformation here, due to space limitations.

2.2.1 Input Language (HIL)

Our input language is kept close to ANSI C in form, so that the task of kernel implementation is comparable to writing a reference implementation in languages such as ANSI C or Fortran 77 (common kernel languages). However, we wanted to keep it simple enough so that we can concentrate on back-end optimization, as well as to specialize it to some degree for our problem domain. Therefore, we provide an opportunity for user mark-up that can provide information that is normally discovered (if it can be determined at all) by extensive front-end analysis. For the simple operations surveyed in this paper, the only mark-up used was the identi£cation of the loop upon which to base the iterative search (iFKO could optimize all inner loops this way, but this could potentially cause insupportable slowdown in tuning more complex kernels, and so we require that a loop be ¤agged as important before it is empirically tuned).

Although our input language resembles ANSI C, its usage rules are closer to Fortran 77, which has a more performance-centric design. For instance, aliasing of output arrays is disallowed unless annotated by mark-up. A detailed description of the input language is beyond the scope of this paper, but Section 3.2.1 shows example loops written in our HIL (high-level intermediate language) that correspond to the ANSI C loops surveyed in Section 3.1.

2.2.2 Analysis and Communication with the Search

Unlike a normal compiler, a compiler used in an iterative search needs to be able to communicate key aspects of its analysis of the code being optimized, as this strongly affects the optimization space to be searched. Currently, FKO reports architecture information such as the numbers of available cache levels and their line sizes. More importantly, it reports kernel-speci£c information such as the loop (if any) identi£ed for tuning in the iterative search. For this loop, it then reports the maximum safe unrolling, and whether it can be SIMD vectorized. For each scalar and array accessed in the loop, the analysis further reports its type, sets and uses. Finally, the analysis returns a list of all scalars that are valid targets for accumulator expansion (see Section 2.2.3), and all arrays that are valid targets for prefetch (by default any array whose references increment with the loop, but the user can override this behavior, for instance for arrays known to be already in cache, using mark-up).

2.2.3 Fundamental Transformations

This section outlines the fundamental optimizations presently supported by FKO, in the order in which they are applied. For each such transformation, we list an abbreviation which is used in the paper to refer to this optimization. *SIMD Vectorization* [3] (**SV**): transforms the loop nest (when legal) from scalar instructions to vector instructions. This typically results in the same number of instructions in the loop, but its effect on loop control and computation done per iteration is similar to unrolling by the vector length (4 for single precision, 2 for double). *Loop Unrolling* [1] (**UR**): duplicates the loop body (avoiding repetitive index and pointer updates) N_u times. Since it is performed after SIMD vectorization, when vectorization is also applied the computational unrolling is actually $N_u * veclen$. *Optimize Loop Control* (**LC**): rearranges loop indexing (when possible) to avoid (on some architectures) unnecessary loop branch comparisons, or to exploit such features as specialized counter registers. *Accumulator Expansion* (**AE**): In order to avoid unnecessary pipeline stalls, **AE** uses a specialized version of scalar expansion [1] to break dependencies in scalars that are exclusively the targets of ¤oating point adds within the loop.

The next fundamental transformation is *prefetch* (**PF**). This transformation can prefetch any/all/none of the arrays that are accessed within the loop, select the type of prefetch instruction to employ, vary the distance from the current iteration to fetch ahead, as well as provide various simple scheduling methodologies. Prefetches are scheduled within the unrolled loop because many architectures discard prefetches when they are issued while the bus is busy, and so they can be an exception to the general rule that modern x86 architectures are relatively insensitive to scheduling (due to their aggressive use of dynamic scheduling, out-of-order execution, register renaming, etc.). Note that prefetching one array can require multiple prefetch requests in the unrolled loop body, as each x86 prefetch instruction fetches only one cache line of data.

Our £nal fundamental transformation is *non-temporal writes* (**WNT**), which employs non-temporal writes on the speci£ed output array. These are writes that contain a hint to the caching system that they should not be retained in the cache, though how this hint is used varies strongly by architecture.

2.2.4 Repeatable Transformations

Repeatable transformations can not only be applied multiple times, but are typically applied in a series (or optimization block) which is repeated while they are still successfully transforming the code. This is useful for synergistic optimizations (eg., register allocation and copy propagation). All of these operations may be applied to a scope (a set of basic blocks, typically a given loop nest or the entire function). When applied to each loop nest level in turn, scoping ensures that inner-loop resource needs are fully satis£ed before outer loops are considered, which is critical in ¤oating point code, where long-running loops are the typical case. Most of FKO's repeatable transformations are fairly standard (though in some we have added a few re£nements to specialize them for ¤oating point optimization), and are discussed in [1].

We support repeatable transformations for improving register usage and control ¤ow. In register usage optimization, we support two types of register allocation and several forms of copy propagation. We also perform several peephole optimizations that exploit the fact that the x86 is not a true load/store architecture (relatively important when the

ISA has only eight registers, but the underlying hardware may have more than a hundred). Finally, we perform branch chaining, useless jump elimination, and useless label elimination, which, when applied together, merges basic blocks (critical after extensive loop unrolling).

2.3 Iterative Search

Finding the best values for N_T empirically tuned transformations consists of £nding the points in an N_T dimensional space that maximize performance (thus the phrase "searching the optimization space"). There are several ways of performing this search, including simulated annealing and genetic algorithms. We currently use a much simpler technique, a modi£ed line search. In a pure line search, the N_T-D problem is split into N_T separate 1-D searches, where the starting points in the space correspond to the initial search parameter selection (in our case, FKO defaults). Obviously, this approach results in a very poor search of the space by volume. However, since we understand the properties of these transformations, we are able to select reasonable start values for the search, and because we understand many of the interactions between optimizations, we are able to relax the strict 1-D searches to account for interdependencies (eg., when two transformations are known to strongly interact, do a restricted 2-D search). Application of this knowledge to the line search algorithm provides what is in essence a de facto expert system / search hybrid. In this sense, much of the high-level knowledge that in¤uences model-driven compilation may be moved into the search (where heuristics and architectural assumptions are replaced with empirical probes, of course), rather than being lost as when the search is based purely on geometry. With these straightforward modi£cations, line searches are quite effective in practice (ATLAS, one of the most successful empirical projects, still uses a modi£ed line search), even though they are completely inadequate in theory.

The present iterative search varies only the fundamental optimizations. Our search takes FKO's optimization defaults for its initial values. If we de£ne L as the line size of the £rst prefetchable cache, and L_e as the number of elements of a given type in such a line (for example, if $L = 32$ bytes, L_e would be 4 for a double precision scalar, 8 for a single precision scalar, or 2 for a SIMD vector of either type), then the initial values for the search (and thus the defaults for FKO) are: **SV**='Yes', **WNT**='No', **PF**(type,dist) = ('prefetchnta', $2 \times L$), **UR**=L_e, **AE**='No'.

3 Experimental Results

This section presents and analyzes results on two of today's premier x86 implementations, and is organized in the following way: Section 3.1 outlines the ¤oating point kernels that are being optimized, Section 3.2 discusses version and timing methodology information, and Section 3.3 discusses some key points about the presented results. When we have had to concentrate on one machine due to space limitations, we have retained the the timings for the Intel machine, as it supplies the fairest comparison against Intel's compiler, even though it is not our best platform. For instance, for the omitted in-L2 Opteron timings, the two best tuning mechanisms are iFKO followed by FKO, and icc-tuned kernels run on average at 68% of the speed of iFKO-tuned code.

3.1 Surveyed Routines

The general domain of this research is ¤oating point kernels, but this paper focuses on the Level 1 BLAS. The Level 1 BLAS are vector-vector operations, most of which can be expressed in a single for-loop. These operations are so simple that it would seem unlikely that empirical optimization could offer much bene£t over model-based compilation. One of the key contributions of this initial work is that we show that even on such well-understood and often-studied operations as these, empirical optimization can improve performance over standard optimizing compilers.

Most Level 1 BLAS have four different variants depending on type and precision of operands. There are two main types of interest, real and complex numbers, each of which has double and single precision. In this work, we concentrate on single and double precision real numbers. The Level 1 BLAS all operate on vectors, which can be contiguous or strided. Again, we focus on the most commonly used (and optimizable) case £rst, the contiguous vectors. For each routine, the BLAS API pre£xes the routine name with a type/precision character, `s` meaning single precision real, and `d` for double precision real. Since `iamax` involves returning the index of the absolute value maximum in the vector, the API puts the precision pre£x in this routine as the second character rather than the £rst (i.e., `isamax` or `idamax` rather than `ddot` or `sdot`). There are quite a few Level 1 BLAS, and so we study only the most commonly used of these routines, which are summarized in Table 1.

Note that the performance of the BLAS are usually reported in MFLOPS (millions of ¤oating point operations per second), but that some of these routines actually do no ¤oating point computation (eg., `copy`). Therefore, the FLOPs column gives the value we use in computing each routine's MFLOP rate.

3.2 Methodology and Version Information

All timings were done with ATLAS version 3.7.8, which we modi£ed to enable vectorization by Intel's C compiler, icc. Most of the loops in ATLAS are written as '`for(i=N; i; i--)`' or '`for(i=0; i!=N; i++)`' and icc will not vectorize either form, regardless of what is in the loop. Once we experimentally determined that this loop formulation was preventing icc from vectorizing any of the target loops, we simply modi£ed the source of the relevant routines to '`for(i=0; i<N; i++)`', which icc successfully vectorizes.

We report numbers for two very different high-end x86 architectures, the Intel Pentium4E and AMD Opteron. Further platform, compiler and ¤ag information is summarized in Table 2 (for the pro£le build and use phases, the appropriate ¤ags were suf£xed to those shown Table 2.) The ATLAS Level 1 BLAS kernel timers were utilized to generate all performance results. However, we enabled ATLAS's assembly-coded walltimer that accesses hardware performance counters in order to get cycle-accurate results. Since walltime is prone to outside interference, each timing was repeated six times (on an unloaded machine), and the minimum was taken. Because these are actual timings (as opposed to simulations), there is still some ¤uctuation in performance numbers despite these precautions, and so we additionally ran each install three times and chose the best.

3.2.1 Input Routines

With the exception of `iamax`, the computational loops of the ANSI C reference implementations are precisely those given in Table 1. The input routines given to FKO were the direct translations of these routines from ANSI C to our HIL (i.e., high level optimizations were not applied to the source). For instance, Figure 6(a) shows the translation of the `dot` routine into our HIL. The exception to this strictly corresponding mapping is the `iamax` routine. Our HIL does not yet support scoped ifs, and so it was originally coded for all compilers (in the appropriate language) as shown in 6(b), which, absent code positioning transformations, is the most ef£cient way to implement the operation. However, this formulation of `iamax` depressed performance signi£cantly for icc, while not noticeably improving gcc's performance, and so we utilized the more straightforward implementation for these compilers.

3.3 Analysis

Figures (2,3,4) report the percentage of the best observed performance provided by the following six methodologies: **gcc+ref**: Performance of ANSI C reference implementation compiled by gcc. **icc+ref**: Performance of ANSI C reference implementation compiled by icc. **icc+prof**: Performance of ANSI C reference implementation, using icc and pro£ling. Pro£ling was performed with tuning data identical to the data used in timing. **ATLAS**: The best kernel found by ATLAS's empirical search, installed with both icc and gcc. ATLAS empirically searches a series of implementations, which were laboriously written and hand-tuned using mixtures of assembly and ANSI C, and contain a multitude of both high and low-level optimizations (eg., software pipelining, prefetch, unrolling, scheduling, etc.). When ATLAS has selected a hand-tuned all-assembly kernel (as opposed to the more common ANSI C routine with some inline assembly for performing prefetch), the routine name is suf£xed by a * (eg., `dcopy` becomes `dcopy*`). This is mainly of interest in that hand-tuning in assembly allows for more complete and lower-level optimization (eg. SIMD vectorization, exploitation of CISC ISA features, etc.). **FKO**: The performance of the kernel when compiled with FKO using default transformation parameters (i.e., no empirical search). **iFKO**: The performance of the kernel when iterative compilation is used to tune FKO's transformation parameters.

For each kernel, we £nd the mechanism that gave the best kernel performance, and all other results are divided by that number (eg. the method that resulted in the fastest kernel will be at 100%). This allows for the relative bene£t of the various tuning mechanisms to be evaluated. This comparison is done for each studied kernel, and we add two summary columns. The second-to-last column (AVG) gives the average over all studied routines, and the last column (VAVG) gives the average for the operations where SIMD vectorization was successfully supplied; in practice, this means the average of all routines excluding `iamax`, which neither icc nor iFKO automatically vectorize.

On all studied architectures and contexts, iFKO provides the best performance on average, better even than the hand-tuned kernels found by ATLAS's own empirical search. However, in several individual hand-tuned cases, iFKO loses decidedly. Primarily, this occurs in `iamax`, where the hand-tuned assembly vectorizes the loop, but neither iFKO nor icc can do so automatically. It is a topic for further research to see if we can £nd a way to vectorize such loops generally and safely in the compiler. The only other routine where iFKO is signi£cantly slower is in P4E/`dcopy`, where the hand-tuned assembly uses a technique called block fetch [14]. This technique can be performed generally and safely in a compiler, and we are planning to add it to FKO.

iFKO is slightly slower (just barely above clock resolution) on out-of-cache Opteron `scopy`, and this is due to FKO generating an extra integer operation per loop iteration. FKO presently does not exploit the opportunity to use x86 CISC indexing to index both arrays using a register, which avoids an additional pointer increment at the end of the loop. The summary here is that, given a few optimizations that we understand and plan to add, we would lose only on `iamax`, and further research is required to determine if we can £nd a general way to vectorize this operation as well (it seems almost certain that we can overcome this problem in a narrow way, for instance by having the user supply us with markup indicating how to address the dependency).

Table 3 shows the best parameters that were found by our empirical search for each platform/context. Section 2.2.3 de£nes the abbreviations used in the headings, and Section 2.3 provides the default values used by FKO. The prefetch parameters have both instruction type (INS) and distance in bytes (DST). For each type of prefetch instruction, the search chooses between those available on the machine, and they are reported using the following abbreviations: `tX`: SSE temporal prefetch to cache of level $X+1$ (eg., `prefetcht0`, `prefetcht1`, etc.); `nta`: SSE non-temporal prefetch to the level of supported cache nearest the CPU (`prefetchnta`), or `w`: 3DNow! prefetch for write (`prefetchw`). Figure 7 shows, as a percentage of FKO's speed, the results of empirically tuning these parameters (i.e. the speedup of iFKO over FKO, *not over code in which a given transformation has not been applied*). For each BLAS kernel, we show a bar for each architecture (p4e/opt) and context (ic: in-L2 cache, oc: out of cache). Each bar shows the total speedup over FKO, and how much tuning each transformation parameter contributed to that speedup. For instance, on average over all operations, architectures and contexts, empirically tuning [WNT, PF DST, PF INS, UR, AE], provided speedups of [2, 26, 3, 2, 5]%, respectively, resulting in the empirically-tuned kernels on average running 1.38 times faster than our statically-tuned kernels. The prefetch results are of particular interest, in that they are relatively dif£cult to to model accurately, and provide the greatest speedup on average.

One of the most important observations from these tables is how variable these parameters are: they vary depending on operation, precision, architecture, *and* context. This suggests that any model that captures this complexity is going to have to be very sensitive indeed. Note that while empirical results such as these can be used to re£ne our understanding of relatively opaque interactions (eg., competing compiler and hardware transformations), which in turn allows for building better theoretical models, one of the great strengths of empirical tuning is that full understanding of why a given series of transformations yielded good speedup is not required in order to achieve that speedup.

In addition to the general variability, we can examine how parameters can change based on either the architecture or context of the operation. When we vary the architecture, of course, empirical methods shine, particularly when the compiler has not yet been (or will never be) fully tuned to the new platform (eg. Intel compiler on AMD platform). Here we see the strength of empirical tuning over even aggressive pro£ling: notice that for both `swap` and `axpy`, **icc+prof** is many times slower than than **icc+ref** in Figure 3. This is because non-temporal writes (**WNT**) can improve performance anytime the operand doesn't need to be retained in the cache on the P4E. On the AMD Opteron, however, non-temporal writes result in signi£cant overhead unless the operand is write only (as in the Y vector of `copy`). Icc's pro£ling detects that the loop is long enough for cache retention not to be an issue, and blindly applies **WNT**, whereas the empirical tuning tries it, sees the slowdown, and therefore does not use it.

In addition to adapting to the architecture, empirical methods can be utilized to tune a kernel to the particular context in which it is being used. Figure 4 and Table 3 show such an example, where the adaptation is to having the operands in-L2-cache. This changes the optimization set fairly widely, including making prefetch much less important, and **WNT** a bad idea. Prefetch is still useful in keeping data in-cache in the face of con¤icts, and so we see it provides greater bene£t for the "noisier" (bus-wise) routines such as `swap`. In-cache, computational optimizations become much more important. One such is transformation is accumulator expansion (**AE**), which on the P4E accounts for an impressive 41% of `sasum` speedup in-cache, while only improving performance by 2% for out-of-cache.

Since all results discussed so far are relative to the best tuning method, it is easy to lose track of the relative performance of the individual operations. Therefore, Figure 5(a) shows the the speed of these operations in MFLOPS, computed as discussed in Section 3.1. Note MFLOPS is a measure of speed, so larger numbers indicate better performance. All timings in this £gure deal only with iFKO (on average, the best optimizing technique). Basically, the more bus-bound an operation is, the worse the performance. For example, ASUM, which has only one input vector, and no output vectors, is always the fastest routine, with single precision (half the data load for same amount of FLOPs) always faster than double precision. Similarly, Figure 5(b) shows the speedup of the in-L2 cache P4E timings over the out-of-cache performance. One of the most interesting things about this graph is that it provides a very good measure of how bus-bound an operation is, even after prefetch is applied: If the kernel tuned for in-cache usage is only moderately faster than the kernel when tuned in out-of-cache timing, the main performance bottleneck is clearly not memory.

An interesting trend to notice in surveying these results in their entirety is that the more bus-bound an operation is, the less prefetch improves performance. The reason for this seeming paradox is in how prefetch works: prefetch is a latency-hiding technique that allows data to be fetched for later use while doing unrelated computation. If the bus is always busy serving computation requests, there is no time when the prefetch can be scheduled that doesn't interfere with an active read or write, and most architectures simply ignore prefetch instructions in this case. This is why operations such as `swap` or `axpy` get relatively modest bene£t. Since prefetch optimization is one of our key strengths for out-of-cache usage on these routines, this is also why iFKO does much better on the Opteron than on the P4E (when compared against all tuning mechanisms, including icc): the Opteron, having a slower chip and faster memory access, is less bus bound, and so there is more room for empirical improvement using this key optimization.

4 Summary and Conclusions

We have shown how empirical optimization can help adapt to changes in operation, architecture, and context. We have discussed our approach to empirical compilation, and presented the framework we have developed. We have shown that even on simple, easily analyzed loops that many would expect to be fully optimized by existing compilers, empirical application of well-understood transformations provides clear performance improvements. Further, even though our current palette of optimizations is limited compared to that available to the hand-tuner, we have presented results showing that this more fully automated approach results in greater average performance improvement than that provided by ATLAS's hand-tuned (and empirically selected) Level 1 BLAS support. Note that our initial timings show iFKO already capable of improving even Level 3 BLAS performance more than icc or gcc, but due to the lack of outer-loop specialized transformations (which we plan to add) we are presently not competitive with the best Level 3 hand-tuned kernels. Therefore, as this framework matures, we strongly believe that it will serve to generalize empirical optimization of ¤oating point kernels, and that it will vastly reduce the amount of hand-tuning that is required for high performance computing. Finally, it appears certain that an open source version of such a framework will be a key enabler of further research as well. For example, just as ATLAS was used to provide feedback into model-based approaches [18], iFKO will provide an ideal platform for tuning and further understanding the models used in traditional compilation, while a fully-featured FKO will provide a rich test bed for research on fast searches of optimization spaces.

References

[1] D. F. Bacon, S. L. Graham, and O. J. Sharp. Compiler transformations for high-performance computing. *ACM Comput. Surv.*, 26(4):345–420, 1994.

[2] P. Diniz, Y.-J. Lee, M. Hall, and R. Lucas. A case study using empirical optimization for a large, engineering application. In *International Parallel and Distributed Processing Symposium*, 2004. CD-ROM Proceedings.

[3] F. Franchetti, S. Kral, J. Lorenz, and C. Ueberhuber. Ef£cient utilization of simd extensions. Accepted for putblication in *IEEE special issue on Program Generation, Optimization, and Adaptation*, 2005.

[4] M. Frigo. A Fast Fourier Transform Compiler. In *Proceedings of the ACM SIGPLAN Conference on Programming Language Design and Implementation (PLDI '99), Atlanta, GA*, 1999.

[5] M. Frigo and S. Johnson. FFTW: An Adaptive Software Architecture for the FFT. In *Proceedings of the International Conference on Acoustics, Speech, and Signal Processing (ICASSP)*, volume 3, page 1381, 1998.

[6] K. Kennedy, B. Broom, A. Chauhan, R. Fowler, J. Garvin, C. Koelbel, C. McCosh, and J. Mellor-Crummey. Telescoping languages: A system for automatic generation of domain languages. Accepted for publication in *IEEE special issue on Program Generation, Optimization, and Adaptation*, 2005.

[7] T. Kisuki, P. Knijnenburg, M. O'Boyle, and H. Wijsho. Iterative compilation in program optimization. In *CPC2000*, pages 35–44, 2000.

[8] C. Lawson, R. Hanson, D. Kincaid, and F. Krogh. Basic Linear Algebra Subprograms for Fortran Usage. *ACM Trans. Math. Softw.*, 5(3):308–323, 1979.

[9] M. Pushel, J. Moura, J. Johnson, D. Padua, M. Veloso, B. Singer, J. Xiong, F. Frenchetti, A. Cacic, Y. Voronenko, K. Chen, R. Johnson, and N. Rizzolo. Spiral: Code generation for dsp transforms. Accepted for putblication in *IEEE special issue on Program Generation, Optimization, and Adaptation*, 2005.

[10] See page for details. FFTW homepage. `http://www.fftw.org/`.

[11] See page for details. SPIRAL homepage. `http://www.spiral.net/`.

[12] S. Triantafyllis, M. Vachharajani, N. Vachharajani, and D. I. August. Compiler optimization-space exploration. In *International Symposium on Code Generation and Optimization*, pages 204–215, 2003.

[13] P. van der Mark. Iterative compilation. Master's thesis, Leiden Institute of Advanced Computer Science, 1999.

[14] M. Wall. Using Block Prefetch for Optimized Memory Performance. Technical report, Advanced Micro Devices, 2002.

[15] R. C. Whaley. *Automated Empirical Optimization of High Performance Floating Point Kernels*. PhD thesis, Florida State University, December 2004.

[16] R. C. Whaley and A. Petitet. Atlas homepage. `http://math-atlas.sourceforge.net/`.

[17] R. C. Whaley, A. Petitet, and J. J. Dongarra. Automated empirical optimization of software and the ATLAS project. *Parallel Computing*, 27(1–2):3–35, 2001. Also available as University of Tennessee LAPACK Working Note #147, UT-CS-00-448, 2000 (cmttwww.netlib.org/lapack/lawns/lawn147.ps).

[18] K. Yotov, X. Li, G. Ren, M. Garzaran, D. Padua, K. Pingali, and P. Stodghill. A comparison of empirical and model-driven optimization. Accepted for publication in *IEEE special issue on Program Generation, Optimization, and Adaptation*, 2005.

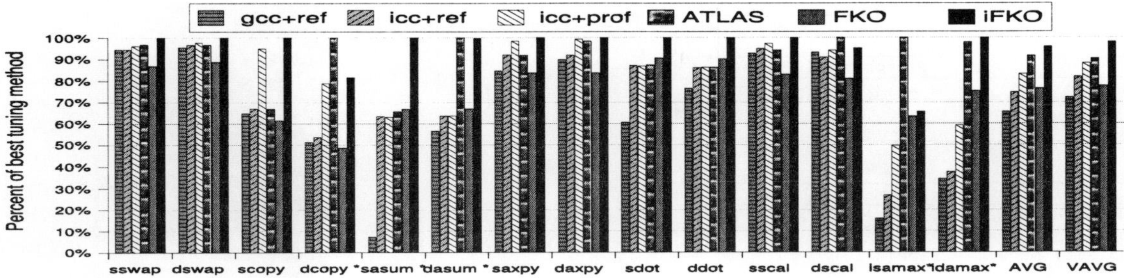

Figure 2. Relative speedups of various tuning methods on 2.8Ghz P4E, N=80000, out-of-cache

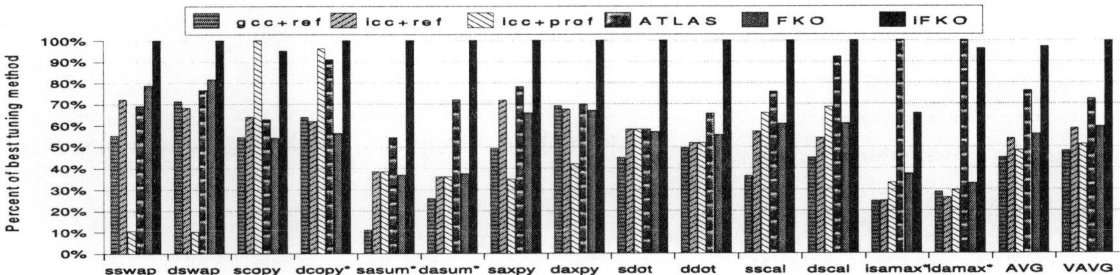

Figure 3. Relative speedups of various tuning methods on 1.6Ghz Opteron, N=80000, out-of-cache

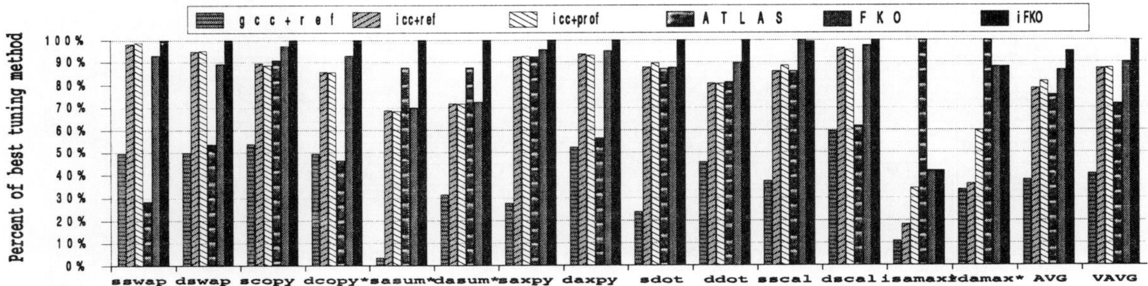

Figure 4. Relative speedups of various tuning methods on 2.8Ghz P4E, N=1024, in-L2 cache

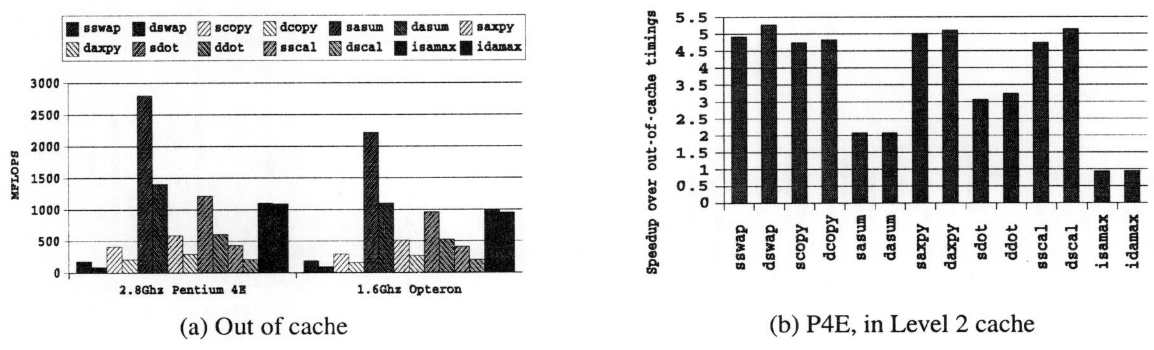

(a) Out of cache

(b) P4E, in Level 2 cache

Figure 5. Relative BLAS performance results

NAME	Operation Summary	FLOPs
swap	`for (i=0; i < N; i++) {tmp=y[i]; y[i]=x[i]; x[i]=tmp}`	N
scal	`for (i=0; i < N; i++) y[i] *= alpha;`	N
copy	`for (i=0; i < N; i++) y[i] = x[i];`	N
axpy	`for (i=0; i < N; i++) y[i] += alpha * x[i];`	$2N$
dot	`for (dot=0.0,i=0; i < N; i++) dot += y[i] * x[i];`	$2N$
asum	`for (sum=0.0,i=0; i < N; i++) sum += fabs(x[i])`	$2N$
iamax	`for (imax=0,maxval=fabs(x[0]), i=1; i<N; i++){ if (fabs(x[i]) > maxval) { imax = i; maxval = fabs(x[i]); } }`	$2N$

Table 1. Level 1 BLAS summary

PLATFORM	COMP	FLAGS
2.8 Ghz P4E (Pentium 4E)	icc 8.0	-xP -O3 -mp1 -static
	gcc 3.3.2	-fomit-frame-pointer -O3 -funroll-all-loops
1.6 Ghz Opt (Opteron)	icc 8.0	-xW -O3 -mp1 -static
	gcc 3.3.2	-fomit-frame-pointer -O3 -O -mfpmath=387 -m64

Table 2: Compiler and ¤ag information by platform

```
LOOP i = 0, N
LOOP_BODY
   x = X[0];
   y = Y[0];
   dot += x * y;
   X += 1;
   Y += 1;
LOOP_END
```

(a) dot loop

```
   LOOP i = N, 0, -1
   LOOP_BODY
      x = X[0];
      x = ABS x;
      IF (x > amax)
         GOTO NEWMAX;
ENDOFLOOP:
         X += 1;
   LOOP_END
   RETURN imax

NEWMAX:
   amax = x
   imax = N-i
   GOTO ENDOFLOOP;
```

(b) amax loop

Figure 6: Relevant portion of HIL implementation

	P4E, out-of-cache				Opteron, out-of-cache				P4E, in-L2 cache			
BLAS	SV: WNT	PF X INS:DST	PF Y INS:DST	UR: AE	SV: WNT	PF X INS:DST	PF Y INS:DST	UR: AE	SV: WNT	PF X INS:DST	PF Y INS:DST	UR: AE
sswap	Y:Y	none:0	nta:1920	1:0	Y:N	nta:1536	nta:1024	1:0	Y:N	t0:512	t0:1152	2:0
dswap	Y:Y	none:0	nta:1024	4:0	Y:N	nta:960	nta:512	1:0	Y:N	none:0	nta:1792	4:0
scopy	Y:Y	none:0	none:0	2:0	Y:Y	none:0	none:0	1:0	Y:N	nta:1408	nta:1536	2:0
dcopy	Y:Y	none:0	none:0	2:0	Y:Y	none:0	none:0	1:0	Y:N	nta:1408	nta:128	2:0
sasum	Y:N	nta:1024	n/a:0	5:5	Y:N	t0:1664	n/a:0	4:4	Y:N	nt0:896	n/a:0	16:2
dasum	Y:N	nta:1024	n/a:0	5:5	Y:N	nta:1920	n/a:0	4:4	Y:N	nta:1536	n/a:0	16:2
saxpy	Y:Y	t0:640	t0:1152	1:0	Y:N	nta:1984	nta:2048	4:0	Y:N	nta:512	nta:512	32:0
daxpy	Y:Y	nta:1152	nta:256	1:0	Y:N	nta:832	nta:448	1:0	Y:N	t0:1152	t0:384	32:0
sdot	Y:N	nta:1536	nta:384	3:3	Y:N	nta:1984	nta:1088	2:2	Y:N	nta:512	nta:768	64:4
ddot	Y:N	nta:1152	nta:384	3:3	Y:N	t0:1536	t0:576	3:3	Y:N	nta:1664	nta:1536	64:4
sscal	Y:Y	nta:1024	n/a:0	1:0	Y:N	nta:640	n/a:0	1:0	Y:N	nta:768	n/a:0	8:0
dscal	Y:Y	nta:1536	n/a:0	1:0	Y:N	nta:1536	n/a:0	1:0	Y:N	nta:1664	n/a:0	8:0
isamax	N:N	t0:768	n/a:0	8:0	N:N	nta:768	n/a:0	16:0	N:N	nta:56	n/a:0	32:0
idamax	N:N	nta:1280	n/a:0	8:0	N:N	nta:1920	n/a:0	32:0	N:N	t0:128	n/a:0	32:0

Table 3. Transformation parameters by architecture and context

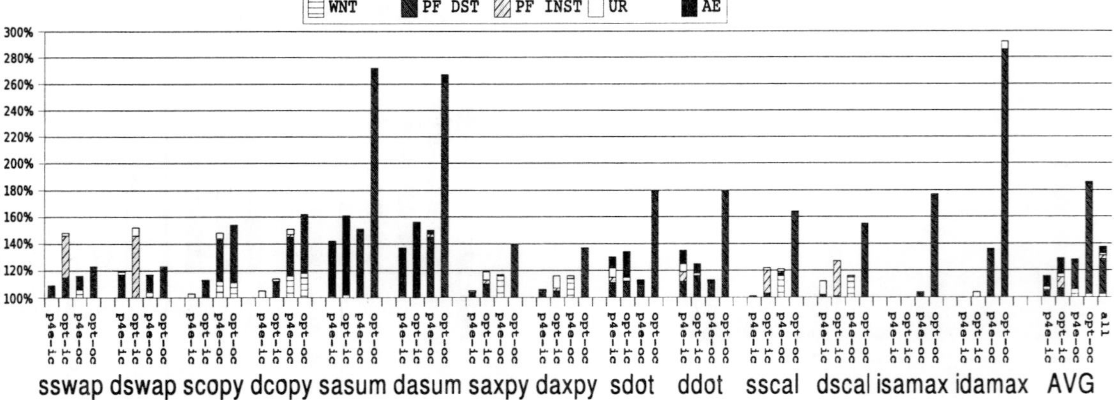

Figure 7. Percent of FKO performance by transform due to empirical search

A Novel Approach for Detecting Heap-based Loop-carried Dependences*

A. Tineo, F. Corbera, A. Navarro, R. Asenjo, and E.L. Zapata
Dpt. of Computer Architecture, University of Málaga,
Complejo Tecnologico, Campus de Teatinos, E-29071. Málaga, Spain.
{tineo,corbera,angeles,asenjo,ezapata}@ac.uma.es

Abstract

The problem of data dependences in pointer-based codes is crucial to various compiler optimizations. The approach presented in this paper focus on detecting data dependences induced by heap-directed pointers on loops that access dynamic data structures. Knowledge about the shape of the data structure accessible from a heap-directed pointer, provides critical information for disambiguating heap accesses originating from it. Our approach is based on a previously developed shape analysis that maintains topological information of the connections among the different nodes (memory locations) in the data structure. As a novelty, our approach carries out abstract interpretation of the statements being analyzed, annotating memory locations with read/write information. This information will be later used in a very accurate dependence test which we describe in this paper. We also discuss its application to three different programs: the sparse matrix-vector product, mst *from Olden and* twolf *from the SPEC CPU2000 suite.*

1 Introduction

Optimizing and parallelizing compilers rely upon accurate static disambiguation of memory references, i.e. determining at compile time if two given memory references always access disjoint memory locations. Unfortunately the presence of alias in pointer-based codes makes memory disambiguation a non-trivial issue. An alias arises in a program when there are two or more distinct ways to refer to the same memory location. The problem of calculating pointer-induced aliases, called pointer analysis, has received significant attention over the past few years [11], [3]. Pointer analysis can be divided into two distinct subproblems: stack-directed analysis and heap-directed analysis. We focus our research in the latter, which deals with objects dynamically allocated in the heap. An important body of work has been conducted lately on this kind of analysis. A promising approach to deal with dynamically allocated structures consists in explicitly abstracting the dynamic store in the form of a bounded graph. In other words, the heap is represented as a storage shape graph and the analysis tries to capture some shape properties of the heap data structures. This type of analysis is called *shape analysis* and in this context, our research group has developed a powerful shape analysis framework [2].

The approach presented in this paper focus on detecting data dependences induced by heap-directed pointers on loops that access pointer-based dynamic data structures. Particularly, we are interested in the detection of the loop-carried dependences (henceforth referred as LCDs) that may arise between the statements in two iterations of the loop. Knowledge about the shape of the data structure accessible from heap-directed pointers, provides critical information for disambiguating heap accesses originating from them, in different iterations of a loop, and hence to provide that there are not data dependences between iterations.

Until now, the majority of LCDs detection techniques based on shape analysis [3], [6], use as shape information a coarse characterization of the data structure being traversed (Tree, DAG, Cycle). One advantage of this type of analysis is that it enables faster data flow merge operations and reduces the storage requirements for the analysis. However, it also causes a loss of accuracy in the detection of the data dependences, specially when the data structure being visited is not a "clean" tree, contain cycles or is modified along the traverse.

Our approach, on the contrary, is based on a shape analysis that maintains topological information of the connections among the different nodes (memory locations) in the data structure. In fact, our representation of the data structure provides us a more accurate description of the memory locations reached when a statement is executed inside a loop. Moreover, as we will see in the next sections, our shape analysis is based on the abstract interpretation of the program statements over the graphs that represent the data structure at each program point. In other words, our ap-

*This work was supported in part by the Ministry of Education of Spain under contract TIC2003-06623.

0190-3918/05 $20.00 © 2005 IEEE

proach does not relies on a generic characterization of the data structure shape in order to prove the presence of data dependences. The novelty is that our approach symbolically executes the statements of the loop being analyzed, and let us annotate the real memory locations reached by each statement with read/write information. This information will be later used in order to find LCDs in a very accurate dependence test which we describe in this paper. In addition, we discuss the behavior and effectiveness of our test when applied to some sample programs. For these experiments we considered the sparse matrix by vector product and benchmark programs like *mst* from the Olden suite [1] and *twolf* from the SPEC CPU2000 suite [9]. In the light of these experiments and in the context of real applications, we believe that our approach provides more accurate results when compared to previous techniques while the analysis times are still reasonable.

Summarizing, the goal of this paper is to present our compilation algorithms which are able to detect LCDs in loops that operate with pointer-based dynamic data structures, and to discuss their applicability. The rest of the paper is organized as follows: Section 2 briefly describes the key ideas under our shape analysis framework. With this background, in Section 3 we present our compiler techniques to automatically identify LCDs in codes based on dynamic data structures. Next, in Section 4 we summarize some of the previous works in the topic of data dependences detection in pointer-based codes. In Section 5 we discuss the application of our test to some realistic programs. Finally, in Section 6 we conclude with the main contributions and ideas for future work.

2 Shape Analysis Framework

The algorithms presented in this paper are designed to analyze programs with dynamic data structures that are connected through pointers defined in languages like C or C++. The programs have to be normalized in such a way that each statement dealing with pointers contains only simple access paths. This is, we consider six simple instructions that deal with pointers: `x = NULL`, `x = malloc`, `x->field = NULL`, `x = y`, `x->field = y` and `x = y->field`, where `x` and `y` are pointer variables and `field` is a field name of a given data structure. More complex pointer instructions can be built upon these simple ones and temporal variables. We have used and extended the ANTLR tool [10] in order to automatically normalize and preprocess the C codes before the shape analysis.

Basically, our analysis is based on approximating by graphs (Reference Shape Graphs, RSGs) all possible memory configurations that can appear after the execution of a statement in the code. By *memory configuration* we mean a collection of dynamic structures. These structures comprise several memory chunks, that we call *memory locations*, which are linked by references. Inside these memory locations there may be several fields (data or pointers to other memory locations). The pointer fields of the data structure are called *selectors*. In Fig. 1 we can see a particular memory configuration which corresponds with a single linked list. Each memory location in the list comprises the `val` data field and the `nxt` selector (or pointer field). In the same figure, we can see the corresponding RSG which capture the essential properties of the memory configuration by a bounded size graph. In this graph, the node $n1$ represent the first memory location of the list, $n2$ all the middle memory locations, and $n3$ the last memory location of the list.

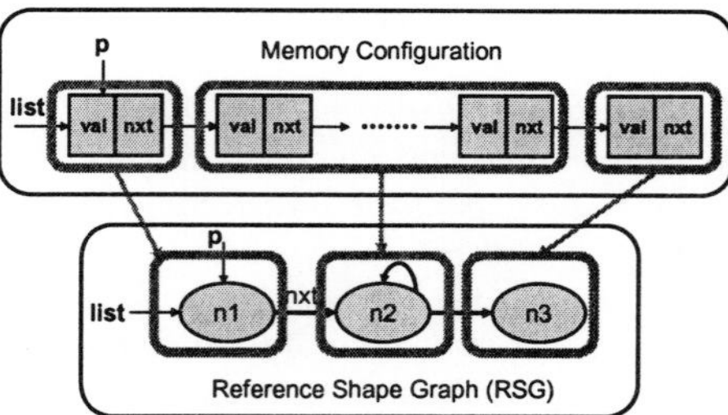

Figure 1. Working example data structure and the corresponding RSG.

Basically, each RSG is a graph in which nodes represent memory locations which have similar reference patterns. To determine whether or not two memory locations should be represented by a single node, each one is annotated with a set of properties. Now, if several memory locations share the same properties, then all of them will be represented (or summarized) by the same node ($n2$ in our example). These properties are described in [2].

Each statement of the code may have associated a set of RSGs, in order to represent all the possible memory configuration at each particular program point. In order to generate the set of RSGs associated with each statement (or in other words, to move from the "memory domain" to the "graph domain" in Fig. 1), a **symbolic execution** of the statements of the program over the graphs is carried out. In fact, each program statement transforms the graphs to reflect the changes in memory configurations derived from the statement execution. The **abstract semantic** of each statement states how the execution of the statement must transform the graphs [2]. This abstract interpretation is carried out iteratively for each statement until we reach a fixed point in which the resulting RSGs associated with the statement does not change any more. All this process is illustrated by the example of Fig. 2, where we can see how the statements of the code which builds a single linked list are symbolically executed until a fixed point is reached.

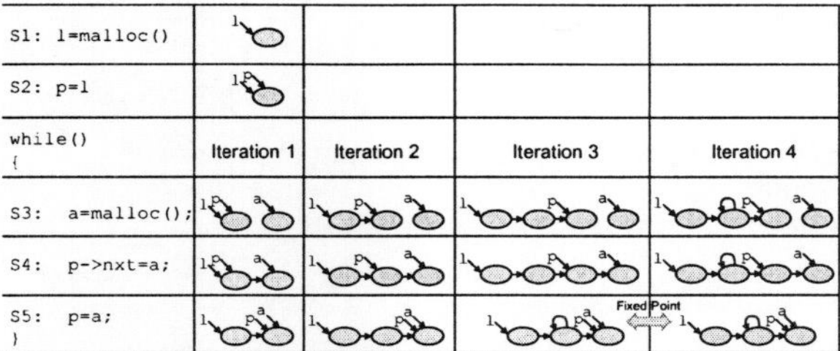

Figure 2. Building an RSG for each statement

3 Loop-Carried Dependence Detection

As we have mentioned, we focus on detecting the presence of LCDs on loops that traverse heap-based dynamic data structures. Two statements in a loop induce a LCD, if a memory location accessed by one statement in a given iteration, is accessed by the other statement in a future iteration, with one of the accesses being a write access.

Our method tries to identify if there is any LCD in the loop following the algorithm that we outline in Fig. 3. Let's recall that our programs have been normalized such that the statements dealing with pointers contain only simple access paths. Let's assume that statements have been labeled. The set of the loop body simple statements (named SIMPLESTMT) is the input to this algorithm.

Summarizing, our algorithm can be divided into the following steps:

1. Only the simple pointer statements, S_i, that access the heap inside the loop are annotated with a **Dependence Touch**, `DepTouch`, directive. A Dependence Touch directive is defined as `DepTouch(AccPointer, AccAttrS`$_i$`, AccField)`. It comprises three important pieces of information regarding the access to the heap in statement S_i: i) The **access pointer**, `AccPointer`: is the stack declared pointer which access to the heap in the statement; ii) The **access attribute**, `AccAttS`$_i$: identifies the type of access in the statement (ReadS$_i$ or WriteS$_i$); and iii) The **access field**, `AccField`: is the field of the data structure pointed to by the access pointer. For instance, an `S1: aux = p->nxt` statement should be annotated with `DepTouch(p, ReadS1, nxt)`, whereas the `S4: aux3->val = tmp` statement should be annotated with `DepTouch(aux3, WriteS4, val)`.

2. The **Dependence Groups**, are created. A Dependence Group, $DepGroup_g$, is a set of access attributes fulfilling two conditions: a) all the access attributes belong to Dependence Touchs with the same access field (g) and with access pointers of the same data type; and b) at least one of these access attributes is a WriteS$_i$. In other words, a $DepGroup_g$ is related to a set of statements in the loop that may potentially lead to a LCD, which happens if: i) the analyzed statement makes a write access (WriteS$_i$) or ii) there are other statements accessing to the same field (g) and one of the access is a write. We outline in Fig. 4 the function `Create_Dependence_Groups`. It creates Dependence Groups, using as an input the set of Dependence Touch directives, DEPTOUCH. Note that it is possible to create a Dependence Group with just one WriteS$_i$ attribute. This Dependence Group would help us to check the output dependences for the execution of S_i in different loop iterations. As we see in Fig. 4 the output of the function is the set of all the Dependence Groups, named DEPGROUP.

Associated with each $DepGroup_g$, our algorithm initializes a set called $AccessPairsGroup_g$ (see Fig. 3). This set is initially empty but during the analysis process it may be filled with the pairs named **access pairs**. An access pair comprises two ordered access attributes. For instance, a $DepGroup_g$ = {`ReadS`$_i$, `WriteS`$_j$, `WriteS`$_k$} with an $AccessPairsGroup_g$ comprising the pair <ReadS$_i$,WriteS$_j$> means that during the analysis the same field, g, of the same memory location may have been first read by the statement S_i and then written by statement S_j, clearly leading to an anti-dependence. The order inside each access pairs is significant for the sake of discriminating between flow, anti or output dependences. The set of all $AccessPairsGroup$'s is named ACCESSPAIRSGROUP.

3. The shape analyzer is fed with the instrumented code. As we have mentioned, the shape analyzer is described in detail in [2] and briefly introduced in Section 2. In this step, our algorithm calls the `Shape_Analysis` function whose inputs are the set of simple statements SIMPLESTMT, the set of DepTouch directives, DEPTOUCH, and the set of Dependence Groups, DEPGROUP. The output of this function is the final set ACCESSPAIRSGROUP. In Fig. 5 we outline the necessary extension to the shape analysis presented in [2] in order to deal with the dependence analysis.

Let's see more precisely how the `Shape_Analysis` function works. The simple statements of the loop body are executed according to the program control flow, and each execution takes the graphs from the previous statement and modifies it (producing a new set of graphs). When a statement S_j, belonging to the analyzed loop and annotated with a DepTouch directive, is symbolically executed, then the access pointer of the statement, `AccPointer`, points to a node, n, that has to represent a single memory location. Each node n of an S_j's RSG graph, has a **Touch Set** associated with it, $TOUCH_n$. The `DepTouch` directive is also interpreted by the analyzer leading to the updating of that $TOUCH_n$ set.

This TOUCH set updating process can be formalized as follows. Let be
`DepTouch(AccPointer,AccAttS`$_j$`,AccField)`
the Dependence Touch directive attached to sentence S_j. Let's assume that AccAttS$_j$ belongs to a Dependence

```
fun LCDs_Detection (SIMPLESTMT)
1.  ∀ S_i ∈ SIMPLESTMT that accesses the heap
         Attach(S_i, DepTouch(AccPointer,AccAttS_i,AccField));
2.  DEPGROUP = Create_Dependence_Groups(DEPTOUCH);
    ∀ DepGroup_g ∈ DEPGROUP
         AccessPairsGroup_g = ∅ ;
3.  ACCESSPAIRSGROUP = Shape_Analysis(SIMPLESTMT, DEPTOUCH, DEPGROUP);
4.  ∀ AccessPairsGroup_g ∈ ACCESSPAIRSGROUP
         Dep_g = LCD_Test(AccessPairsGroup_g);
    if ∀ g, Dep_g == NoDep then
         return(NoLCD);
    else
         return(Dep_g);
    endif;
end
```

Figure 3. Our dependences detection algorithm.

```
fun Create_Dependence_Groups(DEPTOUCH)
 DEPGROUP = ∅;
 ∀ DepTouch(AccPointer_i,AccAttS_i,AccField_i) ∈ DEPTOUCH
    if [(AccAttS_i == WriteS_i) or
    ∃ DepTouch(AccPointer_j,AccAttS_j,AccField_j) being j ≠ i /
    (AccField_i == AccField_j) and (TYPE(AccPointer_i) == TYPE(AccPointer_j)) and
    (AccAttS_i == WriteS_i or AccAttS_j == WriteS_j)] then
       g = AccField_i;
       if ∄ DepGroup_g ∈ DEPGROUP then
          DepGroup_g = {AccAttS_i}; DEPGROUP = DEPGROUP ∪ {DepGroup_g};
       else
          DepGroup_g = DepGroup_g ∪ {AccAttS_i};
       endif;
    endif;
return(DEPGROUP);
```

Figure 4. `Create_Dependence_Groups` function.

Group, $DepGroup_g$. Let n be the node pointed to by the access pointer, `AccPointer`, in the symbolic execution of the statement S_j. Let be $\{AccAttS_k\}$ the set of access attributes which belongs to the $TOUCH_n$ set, where k represents all the statements S_k, which have previously touched the node. $TOUCH_n$ could be an empty set. Then, when this node is going to be touched by the above mentioned `DepTouch` directive, the updating process that we show in Fig. 5 takes place.

As we note in Fig. 5, if the $TOUCH_n$ set was originally empty we just append the new access attribute AccAttS_j of the `DepTouch` directive. However, if the $TOUCH_n$ set does already contains other access attributes, $\{AccAttS_k\}$, two actions take place: first, an updating of the $AccessPairsGroup_g$ associated with the $DepGroup_g$ happens; secondly, the access attribute AccAttS_j is appended to the $TOUCH_n$ set of the node, i.e., $TOUCH_n = TOUCH_n \cup \{AccAttS_j\}$.

The algorithm for updating the $AccessPairsGroup_g$ is shown in Fig. 5. Here we check all the access attributes of the statements that have touched previously the node n. If there is any access attribute, AccAttS_k which belongs to the same $DepGroup_g$ that AccAttS_j (the current statement), then a new access pair is appended to the $AccessPairsGroup_g$. The new pair is an ordered pair $<\text{AccAttS}_k, \text{AccAttS}_j>$ which indicates that the memory location represented by node n has been first accessed by statement S_k and later by statement S_j, being S_k and S_j two statements associated with the same dependence group, and so a conflict may occur. Note that in the implementation of an $AccessPairsGroup_g$ there will be no redundancies in the sense that a given access pair can not be stored twice in the group.

4. In the last step, our `LCD_Test` function will check each one of the $AccessPairGroup_g$ updated in step 3. This function is detailed in the code of Fig. 6. If an $AccessPairGroup_g$ is empty, the statements associated with the corresponding $DepGroup_g$ does not provoke any LCD. On the contrary, depending on the pairs comprised by the $AccessPairsGroup_g$ we can raise some of the dependence patterns provided in Fig. 6, thus LCD is reported.

We note that the `LCD_Test` function must be performed for all the $AccessPairGroups$ updated in step 3. When we verify for all the $AccessPairGroups$, that none of the dependence patterns is found, then our algorithm informs that the loop does not contain LCD dependences (NoLCD) due to heap-based pointers.

3.1 An example

Let's illustrate via a simple example how our approach works. Fig. 7(a) represents a loop that traverses the data structure of Fig. 1. This is, this loop is going to be exe-

```
fun Shape_Analysis(SIMPLESTMT, DEPTOUCH, DEPGROUP)
 ...
 ∀ S_j ∈ SIMPLESTMT
    ...
    if DepTouch(AccPointer,AccAttS_j,AccField) attached to S_j then
       AccessPairsGroup_g = TOUCH_Updating(TOUCH_n, AccAttS_j, DepGroup_g);
    endif;
    ...
return(ACCESSPAIRSGROUP);

fun TOUCH_Updating(TOUCH_n, AccAttS_j, DepGroup_g)
 if TOUCH_n == ∅ then /* The Touch set was originally empty */
    TOUCH_n = {AccAttS_j}; /* just append the new access attribute */
 else /* The Touch set was not empty */
    AccessPairsGroup_g = AccessPairsGroup_Updating(TOUCH_n, AccAttS_j, DepGroup_g);
       /* update the access pairs group set */
    TOUCH_n = TOUCH_n ∪ {AccAttS_j}; /* append the new access attribute */
 endif;
return(AccessPairsGroup_g);

fun AccessPairsGroup_Updating(TOUCH_n, AccAttS_j, DepGroup_g)
 ∀ AccAttS_k ∈ TOUCH_n
    if AccAttS_k ∈ DepGroup_g then /* AccAttS_k and AccAttS_j ∈ DepGroup_g */
       AccessPairsGroup_g = AccessPairsGroup_g ∪ {<AccAttS_k,AccAttS_j>};
          /* A new ordered pair is appended */
    endif;
return(AccessPairsGroup_g);
```

Figure 5. `Shape_Analysis` **function extension,** `TOUCH_Updating` **and** `AccessPairsGroup_Updating` **functions.**

```
fun LCD_Test(AccessPairsGroup_g)
 if <WriteS_i,ReadS_j> ∈ AccessPairsGroup_g
   then return(FlowDep); /* Flow dep.   */
 if <ReadS_i,WriteS_j> ∈ AccessPairsGroup_g
   then return(AntiDep); /* Anti dep.   */
 if <WriteS_i,WriteS_j> ∈ AccessPairsGroup_g
   then return(OutputDep); /* Output dep.   */
 if <WriteS_i,WriteS_i> ∈ AccessPairsGroup_g
   then return(OutputDep); /* Output dep.   */
 endif
return(NoDep); /* no LCD detected */
```

Figure 6. LCD test.

```
p = list;
while (p->nxt != NULL)
{
  tmp = p->val;
  p->nxt->val = tmp;
  p = p->nxt;
}
```

(a)

```
p = list;
while (p -> nxt != NULL)
{
S1: tmp = p->val; DepTouch(p, ReadS1, val);
S2: aux = p->nxt; DepTouch(p, ReadS2, nxt);
S3: aux->val = tmp; DepTouch(aux, WriteS3, val);
S4: p = p->nxt; DepTouch(p, ReadS4, nxt);
}
```

(b)

Figure 7. (a) Loop traversal of a dynamic data structure; (b) Instrumented code.

cuted after the building of the linked list data structure due to the code of Fig. 2. In the loop, the statement `tmp = p->val` read a memory location that has been written by `p->nxt->val = tmp` in a previous iteration, so there is a LCD between both statements.

In order to automatically detect this LCD, we use an ANTLR-based preprocessing tool that atomizes the complex pointer expressions into several simple pointer statements which are labeled, as we can see in Fig. 7(b). For instance, the statement `p->nxt->val = tmp;` has been decomposed into two simple statements: S2 and S3. After this step, the SIMPLESTMT set will comprise four simple statements.

Next, by applying the first step of our algorithm to find LCDs, the `DepTouch` directive is attached to each simple statement in the loop that accesses the heap, as we can also appreciate in Fig. 7(b). For example, the statement `S2: aux = p->nxt` has been annotated with the `DepTouch(p, ReadS2, nxt)`, stating that the access pointer is p, the access attribute is `ReadS2` (which means that the S2 statement makes a read access to the heap) and finally, that the read access field is `nxt`. This first step of our method have been also implemented with the help of ANTLR.

Next we move on to the second step in which we point out that statements S1 and S3 in our code example meet the requirements to be associated with a dependence group: both of them access the same access field (`val`) with pointers of the same type (`p` and `aux`), being S3 a write access. We will define this dependence group as $DepGroup_{val}$={ReadS1, WriteS3}. Besides, the associated $AccessPairsGroup_{val}$ set will be, at this point, empty. Therefore, after this step, DEPGROUP = $\{DepGroup_{val}\}$ and ACCESSPAIRSGROUP = $\{AccessPairsGroup_{val}\}$.

Let's see now how step 3 of our algorithm proceeds. As we have mentioned, Fig. 1 represents the only RSG graph of the RSGs set at the loop entry point. Remember that our analyzer is going to symbolically execute each of the statements of the loop iteratively until a fixed point is reached. This is, all the RSG graphs in the RSGs set associated with each statement will be updated at each symbolic execution and the loop analysis will finish when all the graphs in all the RSGs do not change any more.

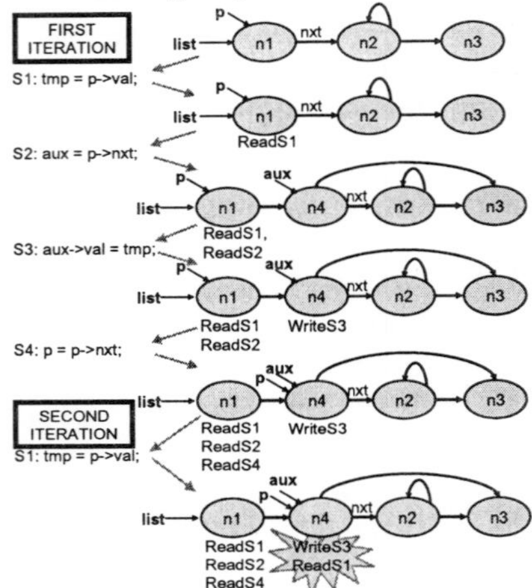

Figure 8. Initial RSG at loop entry and resultant RSG graphs when executing statements.

Now, in the first loop iteration, the statements S1, S2, S3 and S4 are executed by the shape analyzer. The resultant RSG graphs when these statements are symbolically executed, taking into account the attached `DepTouch` directives, are shown in Fig. 8. Executing S1 will produce that the node pointed to by `p` (n_1) is touched by `ReadS1`. When executing S2, `aux = p->nxt` will produce the materialization of a new node (the node n_4), and the node pointed to by `p` will be touched by `ReadS2`. Next, the execution of S3 will touch with a `WriteS3` attribute, the node pointed to by `aux` (n_4). Finally, the execution of S4 will touch with a `ReadS4` attribute the node n_1, and then `p` will point to node n_4.

In the second loop iteration, when executing S1 over the RSG graph that results from the previous symbolic execution of S4, we find that the node pointed to by `p` (now node n_4) is touched by `ReadS1`. When touching this node, the `TOUCH_Updating` function detects that the node has been previously touched because $TOUCH_{n4}$ ={WriteS3}. Since the set is not empty, the function will call to the `AccessPairsGroup_Updating` function. Now, this function will check each access attribute in the $TOUCH_{n4}$ set, and it will look for a dependence group for such access attribute. In our example, WriteS3 is in the $DepGroup_{val}$. In this case, since the new access attribute that is touching the node (ReadS1) belongs to the same dependence group, a new access pair is appended to the $AccessPairsGroup_{val}$= {<WriteS3, ReadS1>}. This fact is indicating that the same memory location (in this case the field val in node n_4) has been reached by a write access from statement S3, followed by a read access from statement S1.

The shape analyzer follows, iteratively, the symbolic execution of statements in the loop until a fixed point is reached. The resultant RSG graph is shown in Fig. 9. We also get at the end of the analysis that $AccessPairsGroup_{val}$= {<WriteS3, ReadS1>}.

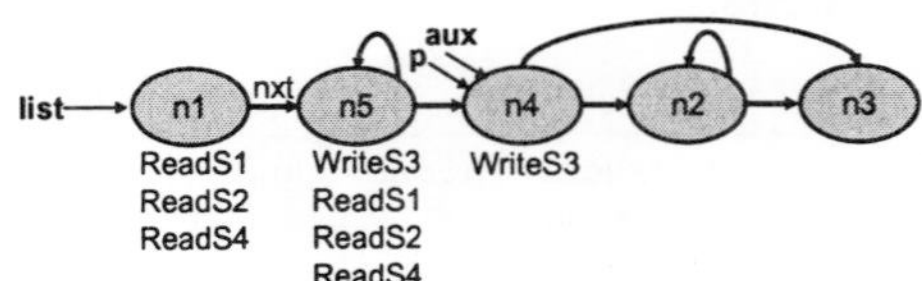

Figure 9. Resultant RSG when the fixed point is reached. The TOUCH sets are illustrated.

Our algorithm applies now the fourth step: the LCD test (Fig. 6). Our LCD test reports a `FlowDep` (flow dependence), because the only access pair group, $AccessPairGroup_{val}$ in the ACCESSPAIRSGROUP set, contains a <WriteS3, ReadS1> pair. As we see, our dependences detection algorithm accurately captures the LCD that appears in the loop.

4 Related work

Some of the previous works on dependences detection on pointer-based codes, combine dependence analysis techniques with pointer analysis [4], [7], [5]. The focus of these techniques is on identifying dependences at the function-call level and they do not consider the detection in the loop context, which is the goal in our approach.

More recently, some authors [3], [6] have proposed dependence analysis tests based on shape analysis in the context of loops that traverse dynamic data structures, and these approaches are more related to our work. For instance, Ghiya and Hendren [3] proposed a test for identifying LCDs that relies on the shape of the data structure being traversed

(Tree, DAG or Cycle), as well as on the computation of the access paths for the pointers in the statements being analyzed. On the other hand, Hwang and Saltz proposed a new technique to identify LCDs in programs that traverse cyclic data structures [6]. This approach automatically identifies acyclic traversal patterns even in cyclic (Cycle) structures. For this purpose, the compilation algorithm isolates the traversal patterns from the overall data structure, and next, it deduces the shape of these traversal patterns (again Tree, DAG or Cycle). Once they have extracted the traversal-pattern shape information, dependence analysis is applied to detect LCDs. One limitation of these approaches is that they are just able to analyze loops that navigate data structures in a "clean" tree-like traverse.

We differ from previous works in that our technique let us annotate the memory locations reached by each heap-directed pointer with read/write information. This feature let us analyze quite accurately loops that traverse and modify generic heap-based dynamic data structures. Our algorithm is able to identify accurately the dependences that appears even in loops that navigate (and modify) complex structures in traversals that contain cycles, as we have demonstrated in [8]. Besides we can successfully discriminate among flow, anti and output dependences which is vital in optimizing and parallelizing compilers. The previous works were unable to compute that information. Our goal here is to put our analysis to work with larger codes and to study the applicability of our method to real programs.

5 Experimental results

We have implemented all the algorithms presented in this paper. We have tested our prototype implementation on several small examples (see [8]). In order to prove the effectiveness of our method on larger C programs, we have considered 3 codes. The first one is a custom-made program that represents the kernel of typical real world applications which deal with dynamic data structures: the sparse matrix-vector product. It is available through our website[1]. The last two programs were taken from well established benchmarks, *mst* from the Olden suite [1] and *twolf* from the SPEC CPU2000 suite [9].

For these tests, we focused our analysis on certain loops that carry a significant amount of execution time. That information was gathered through profiling. At a first stage, the programs were digested by our preprocessing tool based on ANTLR to discard statements not involved in heap accesses and to mark the useful statements with `DepTouch` information. At this point of development, interprocedural analysis is not yet supported so, as a temporal solution, inlining of functions was performed. Besides, some manual adjustments were needed in order to fully adapt the input code to the test dependence module. However, it should be noted that the method itself is fully automatic. Table 1 shows some statistics for the tests, run in a Pentium IV 2.8GHz with 256MBytes. The measured **Times** include the underlaying shape analysis. In addition, the times take into account the analysis of the statements that create the data structures which are accessed in the analyzed loops. In fact, **No. Stmt.** represents the number of simple statements of the analyzed input code, including the statements of the studied loop as well as the statements for the corresponding data structures creation. **No. It.** represents the number of iterations that our method needs to reach a fixed point. **No. Graphs** is the number of RSG graphs generated for each code, including the temporal graphs that may appear during a statement execution, whereas **Graphs/Stmt.** represents the RSG graphs per statement ratio.

Our first program computes the product of a sparse matrix by a sparse vector. We apply our analysis to the loop that computes the product. In this loop, the elements of the output data structure are created while the matrix and the input vector are traversed. For the studied loop, the analysis determines that there is no dependence because the nodes that are read (those from the matrix and the input vector) are different in every iteration from the nodes that are written (those from the output vector). Thus, the method reports `NoDep`, therefore the loop could be parallelized. As we see in Table 1, the analysis time is reasonable even though the number of RSG graphs generated during the analysis, and the number of iterations to find the fixed point are high.

Our next code, *mst* is a program from the Olden benchmark suite. In *mst*'s data structure there is an array of vertexes. Each of them holds a hash table that must store information about every other vertex. The profiling of the code discovered that more than 85% of the execution time was spent in an inner loop of the `AddEdges` function. So we select that loop for the study with our tool. In that loop, hash tables for the nodes are populated with information about every other node. It is undecidable at compile-time the order of writing for the entries in the hash tables, so all kind of dependences arise (flow, anti, output). The method reports all these dependences and the statements for which each dependence appears. This latter information is very important to improve data-cache performance. We see in Table 1 that this is the code for which the number of generated RSG graphs and the number of iterations to reach the fixed point are the smallest. As a consequence, the analysis time is significantly short.

The last code considered is *twolf*, from SPEC CPU2000. It is considerably larger in size than the previous programs (roughly 20,000 lines of code). Profiling was performed to find the most computationally expensive loops. We found that the loop contained in the `new_dbox_a` function consumed more than 30% of the execution time, so we focused

[1] http://www.ac.uma.es/~asenjo/research/codes.html

Program	Time	No. Stmt.	No. It.	No. Graphs	Graphs/Stmt.
`matrix-vector`	1 min 44 sec	120	315	170450	1420
`mst`	0.7 sec	62	70	3314	53
`twolf`	5 min 51 sec	154	149	112803	732

Table 1. Time and other measures for the codes.

our analysis in that loop. On the other hand, *twolf*'s data structure is more complicated than those from the previous examples. For the studied loop, 3 dynamic interconnected structures are involved. A list is traversed reading values to index another list. The elements of the indexed list are then processed to compute some values. It is possible to access the same elements in different iterations of the list, so dependences arise again and the method reports all of them accurately. The results for this code (Table 1) are very telling. It is the biggest code, but it is not the one with the highest number of generated RSG graphs. In fact, the ratio of RSGs per statement is smaller than for the matrix-vector code. As a consequence, the number of iterations to reach the fixed point is smaller than in the matrix-vector case. However, the analysis time is the worst. The reason is due to the complex nature of the `twolf`'s RSG graphs. We have verified that the majority of the nodes in the `twolf`'s graphs, are heavily connected with each other, what produces an important time consumption every time that internal operations of the shape analysis take place (materialization of nodes, summarization of nodes, comparison of graphs, etc.). This observation tell us that optimization of these internal operations of the shape analysis tool must be addressed.

Summarizing, these results have shown us that a smaller number of graphs per statement will need less iterations to reach the fixed point. But this is not a guarantee that the analysis times will be smaller. Another surprising result is that although the number of generated graphs is very high, we think that the times are still reasonable. Let's keep in mind that our approach is able to provide very accurate data dependence information in the context of real codes which traverse and modify generic and complex heap-based data structures. One key aspect of our method is that it allows elements of the data structure to be created inside the traversals (like in the matrix-vector product), as well as conveniently distinguish between flow, anti and output dependences, which is basic for doing data-cache optimizations. Let's recall that all these aspects are left out in every other approach we know. In short, the results have been promising, but at this stage, we think that this kind of analysis is suitable for analyzing only selected parts of the code, for instance the computationally most expensive loops, as we have done in these experiments.

6 Conclusion and Future Work

We have presented a compilation technique that is able to identify LCDs in loops that traverse and modify general pointer-based dynamic data structures. Our main contribution is that we have designed a LCD test that let us extend the scope of applicability to any program that handle any kind of dynamic data structure. Moreover, our dependence test let us discern accurately the type of dependence: flow, anti, output. We have conducted some tests that prove it can be useful for real-life programs. However, more work is necessary in order to optimize the internal operations of the shape analyzer to achieve a faster test.

References

[1] M. C. Carlisle and A. Rogers. Software caching and computation migration in olden. In *ACM Symposium on Principles and Practice of Parallel Programming (PPoPP)*, July 1995.

[2] F. Corbera, R. Asenjo, and E. Zapata. A framework to capture dynamic data structures in pointer-based codes. *Transactions on Parallel and Distributed System*, 15(2):151–166, 2004.

[3] R. Ghiya, L. J. Hendren, and Y. Zhu. Detecting parallelism in c programs with recursive data strucutures. In *Proc. 1998 International Conference on Compiler Construction*, pages 159–173, March 1998.

[4] S. Hortwitz, P. Pfeiffer, and T. Repps. Dependence analysis for pointer variables. In *Proc. ACM SIGPLAN'89 Conference on Programming Language Design and Implementation)*, pages 28–40, July 1989.

[5] J. Hummel, L. J. Hendren, and A. Nicolau. A general data dependence test for dynamic, pointer-based data structures. In *Proc. ACM SIGPLAN'94 Conference on Programming Language Design and Implementation)*, pages 218–229, June 1994.

[6] Y. S. Hwang and J. Saltz. Identifying parallelism in programs with cyclic graphs. *Journal of Parallel and Distributed Computing*, 63(3):337–355, 2003.

[7] J. R. Larus and P. N. Hilfinger. Detecting conflicts between structure accesses. In *Proc. ACM SIGPLAN'88 Conference on Programming Language Design and Implementation)*, pages 21–34, July 1988.

[8] A. Navarro, F. Corbera, R. Asenjo, A. Tineo, O. Plata, and E. Zapata. A new dependence test based on shape analysis for pointer-based codes. In *The 17th International Workshop on Languages and Compilers for Parallel Computing (LCPC '04)*, West Lafayette, IN, USA, September 2004.

[9] S. P. E. C. (SPEC). *SPEC CPU2000 V1.2 Documentation*, 2000. http://www.spec.org/cpu2000/docs/.

[10] T.J.Parr and R. Quong. ANTLR: A predicated-LL(k) parser generator. *Journal of Software Practice and Experience*, 25(7):789–810, July 1995.

[11] R. P. Wilson and M. S. Lam. Efficient context-sensitive pointer analysis for C programs. In *Proc. ACM SIGPLAN'95 Conference on Programming Language Design and Implementation*, pages 1–12, La Jolla, California, June 1995.

Enabling Loop Fusion and Tiling for Cache Performance by Fixing Fusion-Preventing Data Dependences

Jingling Xue[†]and Qingguang Huang[†]
School of Computer Science and Engineering
University of New South Wales
Sydney, NSW 2052, Australia

Minyi Guo
School of Computer Science and Engineering
The University of Aizu
Fukushima 965-8580, Japan

Abstract

This paper presents a new approach to enabling loop fusion and tiling for arbitrary affine loop nests. Given a set of multiple loop nests, we present techniques that automatically eliminate all the fusion-preventing dependences by means of loop tiling and array copying. Applying our techniques iteratively to multiple loop nests yields a single loop nest that can be tiled for cache locality. Our approach handles LU, QR, Cholesky and Jacobi in a unified framework. Our experimental evaluation on an SGI Octane2 system shows that the benefit from the significantly reduced L1 and L2 cache misses has far more than offset the branching and loop control overhead introduced by our approach.

1 Introduction

Due to the ever-widening performance gap between processors and memories, loop tiling or blocking [6, 16] remains an important optimisation in improving cache performance. However, loop tiling is applicable to perfect loop nests only. Unfortunately, dense matrix kernels often contain multiple, imperfectly nested loops over the same data. Figure 1 shows the four important kernels, LU with partial pivoting, QR, Cholesky and Jacobi, which are among the frequently used in scientific applications.

To enable an imperfect loop nest to be tiled, the compiler may apply transformations such as loop fusion and loop distribution to turn parts of the nest into some perfect loop nests [15] and then apply loop tiling to tile the individual perfect loop nests. However, these transformations are mostly dependence-preserving and are thus frequently inapplicable since the data dependences in the program would otherwise be violated. Several recent attempts aim at providing a more systematic treatment to the problem of tiling imperfect loop nests. They have tackled the problem from different angles with varying degrees of success, resulting in the special-purpose techniques for array factorisations [2] and stencil computations [12] as well as the general-purpose techniques for arbitrary loop nests based on data shackling [8] and iteration space transformations [1].

This paper presents a new general-purpose approach to tiling imperfect loop nests from yet a different perspective. Our key motivation can be stated as follows. Many dense kernel programs include multiple loops iterating over the same data. Often the most computations in such a kernel are carried out in a set of loops, which cannot be tiled directly since they are imperfectly nested. In Figure 1, each kernel contains one such a nest as highlighted by $*$'s. But fusing the loops where the most computations are performed with the others and then tiling the fused loops will greatly improve cache performance. Unfortunately, the fused program is generally incorrect due to the existence of some fusion-preventing dependences. We observe that in *real* programs, the "trouble spots" that prevent loop fusion can be relatively few. We are motivated to fix these fusion-preventing dependences so that the fixed program is correct. We eliminate the fusion-preventing flow and output dependences by applying loop tiling (which subsumes loop unrolling and unroll-and-jam [17]) to the appropriate loop nests in the fused program. We eliminate all the fusion-preventing anti-dependences by inserting array copy operations wherever appropriate.

Our approach creates loop tiling candidate nests aggressively. As a result, more conditionals (due to code sinking) and loop control overhead (due to tiling) may be introduced into the transformed codes. Our experimental evaluation on an SGI Octane2 system shows that our approach generates simple tiled codes and achieves performance speedups across varying problem sizes on an SGI Octane2 computer system. The benefit from the significantly reduced L1 and L2 cache misses has far more than offset the branching and loop control overhead incurred.

The rest of this paper is organised as follows. Section 2 describes the class of programs considered by this work. Section 3 presents our methodology for tiling imperfect loop nests. In particular, Section 3.1 presents an algorithm for fusing multiple perfect loop nests. Section 3.2 discusses how to apply this algorithm iteratively to a program to yield larger perfect loop nests. Section 4 presents and analyses our experimental results for the four kernels shown in Figure 1. Section 5 compares with the related work. Section 6 concludes by discussing some future work.

[†]This work is supported by an ARC Grant DP0452623.

0190-3918/05 $20.00 © 2005 IEEE

```
*do k=1, N
    temp=0
    m=k
    do i=k, N
      d= A(i,k)
      if (abs(d).GT.temp)
        temp=abs(d)
        m=i
    if (m.NE.k)
      do j=k, N
        temp=A(k,j)
        A(k,j)=A(m,j)
        A(m,j)=temp
    do i=k+1, N
      A(i,k)=A(i,k)/A(k,k)
*   do j=k+1, N
*     do i=k+1, N
        A(i,j)=A(i,j)-A(i,k)*A(k,j)
```

(a) LU (with pivoting)

```
*do i=1, N
    norm=0
    do j=i, N
      norm=norm+A(j,i)*A(j,i)
    norm2=sqrt (norm)
    asqr=A(i,i)*A(i,i)
    A(i,i)=dsqrt(norm-asqr+(A(i,i)-norm2)^2)
    do j=i+1, N
      A(j,i)=A(j,i)]/A(i,i)
    do j=i+1, N
      X(j,i)=0
      do k=i, N
        X(j,i)=X(j,i)+A(k,i)*A(k,j)
*   do j=i+1, N
*     do k=i+1, N
        A(k,j) = A(k,j)-A(k,i)*X(j,i)
```

(b) QR

```
*do k=1, N
    A(k,k)=dsqrt(A(k,k))
    do i=k+1, N
      A(i,k)=A(i,k)/(A(k,k)
*   do j=k+1, N
*     do i=j, N
        A(i,j)=A(i,j)-A(i,k)*A(j,k)
```

(c) Cholesky

```
*do t=0, M
*   do i=2, N-1
*     do j=2,N-1
        L(j,i)=(A(j,i-1)+A(j-1,i)
             + A(j+1,i)+A(j,i+1)*0.25
    do i=2, N-1
      do j=2, N-1
        A(j,i)=L(j,i)
```

(d) Jacobi

Figure 1. Four frequently used kernels in dense matrix computations.

2 Program Model

Our approach is applicable to all affine loop nests. In general, all loop bounds are required to be affine since the loops with non-affine bounds are difficult to fuse. However, some non-affine if-conditional or array subscript expressions may be allowed (as long as our algorithm given in Figure 2 can successfully compute the required dependences and eliminate all fusion-preventing dependences). For example, we can handle the LU program given in Figure 1, which contains a data-dependent test in line 6.

All programs are given in the FORTRAN-like syntax. In Figure 1, Jacobi is the classic program for solving PDEs by explicit method. The other three kernels are taken from [7] except that the scalar m in LU is not array-expanded here. Note that QR given here has been simplified in [7] with some inessential statements removed.

3 Approach

Given a program in the form of an imperfect loop nest, our approach applies loop fusion inside out to the program to create larger and larger perfect loop nests, and eventually one single perfect loop nest if desired. During this process, all the fusion-preventing dependences are eliminated automatically by means of loop tiling and array copying. The resulting perfect loop nests can be tiled in the normal manner. Section 3.1 gives an algorithm for fusing multiple perfect loop nests, which is the key to our approach. Section 3.2 describes how to apply this algorithm to a program iteratively to obtain increasingly larger perfect loop nests.

3.1 Fusing Multiple Perfect Loop Nests

The problem of fusing multiple perfect loop nests is solved in more or less the same way as the special case when two perfect loop nests are to be fused.

The fusion of two perfect loop nests is legal iff all dependences from the first (i.e., the lexically earlier) nest to the second nest are not reversed in the fused program [17, p. 315]. The dependences that are reversed are known as the *fusion-preventing dependences*. There are three kinds of fusion-preventing dependences: flow (i.e., write before read) dependences, output (i.e., write before write dependences) and anti- (i.e., read before write) dependences.

Suppose we are given two perfect loop nests that are to be fused in a certain way. The two nests may not have the same loop bounds in a common dimension or even the same number of loops. The violated dependences are fixed as follows. We first compute the fusion-preventing dependences between the two nests. We then eliminate the fusion-preventing flow and output dependences automatically by applying loop tiling to the first loop nest. Finally, we eliminate the fusion-preventing anti-dependences by inserting array copy operations inside the second loop nest. The resulting program is a perfect loop nest and can thus be tiled for locality improvement.

In the case of more than two nests, our algorithm first applies loop tiling bottom-up across all the loop nests to eliminate the fusion-preventing flow and output dependences. We then insert array copy operations to eliminate all the fusion-preventing anti-dependences.

Suppose there are K perfect loop nests:

$$
\begin{array}{ll}
\mathcal{L}_1: & \text{do } I_1 = L_{1,1}, U_{1,1} \\
 & \quad \vdots \\
 & \quad \text{do } I_{n_1} = L_{1,n_1}, U_{1,n_1} \\
 & \qquad BODY_1(I_1, \ldots, I_{n_1}) \\
\vdots & \\
\mathcal{L}_K: & \text{do } I_K = L_{K,1}, U_{K,1} \\
 & \quad \vdots \\
 & \quad \text{do } I_{n_K} = L_{K,n_K}, U_{K,n_K} \\
 & \qquad BODY_K(I_1, \ldots, I_{n_K})
\end{array}
\tag{1}
$$

where the loop bounds of each loop nest are assumed to be affine. Two different loop nests may not have the same loop bounds in a common dimension or even the same number of loops.

Let IS_k be the n_k-dimensional iteration space of the k-th loop nest $\mathcal{L}_k$. Let $n = \max\{n_k \mid 1 \leqslant k \leqslant K\}$. If the dependences in the program (1) are ignored for the moment, it is always possible to fuse the K nests into one perfect loop nest whose n-dimensional iteration space is:

$$IS = \{(I_1, \ldots, I_n) \mid \forall\, 1 \leqslant i \leqslant n : L_i \leqslant I_i \leqslant U_i\} \tag{2}$$

The fusion transformation consists of finding an injective mapping from IS_k to IS for every loop nest $\mathcal{L}_k$:

$$F_k : IS_k \mapsto IS \tag{3}$$

The fused program becomes one single perfect loop nest:

$$
\begin{array}{l}
\text{do } I_1 = L_1, U_1 \\
\quad \vdots \\
\quad \text{do } I_n = L_n, U_n \\
\qquad \text{if } (I_1, \ldots, I_n) \in F_1(IS_k) \\
\qquad\quad BODY_1(F_1^{-1}(I_1, \ldots, I_n)) \\
\qquad\quad \vdots \\
\qquad \text{if } (I_1, \ldots, I_n) \in F_K(IS_K) \\
\qquad\quad BODY_K(F_K^{-1}(I_1, \ldots, I_n))
\end{array}
\tag{4}
$$

For many real dense matrix programs, IS is typically the same or slightly larger than the iteration space of the loop nest that carries out the most computations in a program (e.g., the loop nests highlighted by $*$'s in Figure 1). The iteration space of $\mathcal{L}_k$ such that $k < n$ is often embedded at a boundary of IS. Its exact placement may not be critical to our approach for two reasons. First, fusing a loop nest that carries out the most computations with the other loop nests enables this "important" loop nest to be tiled so that the overall cache performance of the program is improved. Second, whichever placement is used, our approach can always turn the fused loop nest into a correct program.

The loop fusion used for obtaining the fused program (4) may be illegal. Figure 2 gives an algorithm for fixing all the fusion-preventing dependences so that the fixed program has the same input/output behaviour as the original program (1).

The following notations (with some from [20]) are used:

$I, I', I'', \ldots$:an iteration vector in IS
$\prec$:lexicographic "less than" operator
$[R]$:set of iteration vectors at which reference R is accessed
$R(I)$:subscript expression when the loop variables have the values specified by I
$R_1(I) \overset{sub}{=} R_2(I')$:subscripts of $R_1(I)$ and $R_2(I')$ are equal
$Writes_A(k)$:all write references of A in $\mathcal{L}_k$
$Reads_A(k)$:all read references of A in $\mathcal{L}_k$

Let A be an arbitrary but fixed array in the program (1). When we transform (1) to (4) by loop fusion, the fusion-preventing dependences, i.e., the dependences that are violated are characterised precisely by the following sets:

- $WW_A(k, k')$ gives the output dependences of A that prevent $\mathcal{L}_k$ and $\mathcal{L}_{k'}$ from being fused, where $k < k'$:

$$
\begin{array}{l}
WW_A(k, k') = \{(I, I') \mid \\
\quad R \in Writes_A(k) \wedge I \in [R] \\
\quad \wedge\, R' \in Writes_A(k') \wedge I' \in [R'] \\
\quad \wedge\, I' \prec I \wedge R(I) \overset{sub}{=} R'(I')\}
\end{array}
\tag{5}
$$

- $WR_A(k, k')$ gives the flow dependences of A that prevent $\mathcal{L}_k$ and $\mathcal{L}_{k'}$ from being fused, where $k < k'$. This set is defined exactly as $WW_A(k, k')$ except that $Writes_A(k')$ in $WW_A(k, k')$ is replaced by $Reads_A(k')$.

- $RW_A(k, k')$ gives the anti-dependences of A that prevent $\mathcal{L}_k$ and $\mathcal{L}_{k'}$ from being fused, where $k < k'$:

$$
\begin{array}{l}
RW_A(k, k') = \{(I, I', \alpha(R')) \mid \\
\quad R \in Reads_A(k) \wedge I \in [R] \\
\quad \wedge\, R' \in Writes_A(k') \wedge I' \in [R'] \\
\quad \wedge\, I' \prec I \wedge R(I) \overset{sub}{=} R'(I')\}
\end{array}
\tag{6}
$$

where $\alpha(R')$ indicates that the reference R' is the LHS of the $\alpha(R')$-th assignment in the loop nest $\mathcal{L}_{k'}$. This component is useful in imposing an execution order for different writes executed at the same iteration in $\mathcal{L}_{k'}$.

1 **ALGORITHM:** *FixDeps*
2 **INPUT:** The fused program (4), denoted P
3 **OUTPUT:** A program, P'', with the same input/output behaviour as the original program (1)
4 P' = *ElimWW_WR*(P)
5 P'' = *ElimRW*(P')
6 Insert more coping operations to simplify the if conditionals introduced in lines 46 – 48

7 **ALGORITHM:** *ElimWW_WR*(P)
8 Let $\mathcal{V}$ be the set of all variables in P
9 $P_1 := P$
10 for $k = K-1, 1$
11   // compute the WW and WR dependences
12   for every array A in $\mathcal{V}$
13   for $k' = k+1, K$
14   Compute $WW_A(k,k')$ and $WR_A(k,k')$ in P_{K-k}
15   $WW_A(k) := \bigcup_{k'=k+1}^{K} WW_A(k,k')$
16   $WR_A(k) := \bigcup_{k'=k+1}^{K} WR_A(k,k')$
17   $W(k) := \bigcup_{A\in\mathcal{V}}(WW_A(k) \cup WR_A(k))$
18   if $W(k) = \emptyset$ then GOTO line 34
19   // compute the tile size to tile $\mathcal{L}_k$
20   $D_1 := W(k)$
21   for $i = 1, n$
22     $d_i = \max\{I_i - I'_i \mid (I,I') \in D_i\}$ // $\max\emptyset =_{def} 0$
23     $D_{i+1} := D_i \setminus \{(I,I') \mid \forall\,(I,I') \in D_i : I_i - I'_i > 0\}$
24   Let m be the largest value such that $d_{m+1} = \cdots = d_n = 0$
25   Let $(T_1,\dots,T_m)$ be a legal tile size for the outermost loops of $\mathcal{L}_K$ such that $\forall\, 1 \leqslant i \leqslant m : T_i > d_i$
26   Set $T_{m+1} = \cdots = T_n = 1$
27   // generate the tile code for $\mathcal{L}_k$
28   Let $(O_1,\dots,O_n)$ be the lexicographic minimum of *IS*
29   Let $\mathcal{T}$ be the tiling transformation, $\mathcal{T} : F_k(IS_k) \mapsto \mathbb{Z}^{2n}$
    $\mathcal{T}(I_1,\dots,I_n) = (O_1 + \lfloor\frac{I_1-O_1}{T_1}\rfloor, \dots, (O_n + \lfloor\frac{I_n-O_n}{T_n}\rfloor, I_1,\dots,I_n)$
30   Let $(I_1,\dots,I_n,J_1,\dots,J_n)$ be the loop variables of tiled $\mathcal{L}_k$
31   Let $P_t(I_1,\dots,I_n) \leqslant p_t$ be the inequalities defining the tiles
32   Let $P_e(I_1,\dots,I_n,J_1,\dots,J_n) \leqslant p_e$ specify the points in a tile
33   Replace the following code for $\mathcal{L}_k$ in (4)

    if $(I_1,\dots,I_n) \in F_k(IS_k)$
      $BODY_1(F_k^{-1}(I_1,\dots,I_n))$

  by:

    if $P_t(I_1,\dots,I_n) \leqslant p_t$
      The $J_1,\dots,J_n$ loops for enumerating
        points in $P_e(I_1,\dots,I_n,J_1,\dots,J_n) \leqslant p_e$ in $\prec$
        if $(J_1,\dots,J_n) \in F_k(IS_k)$
          $BODY_k(F_k^{-1}(J_1,\dots,J_n))$

34   $P_{K-k+1} := P_{K-k}$ (tiled if not from line 18)
35 return P_K

Figure 2. An algorithm for fixing all the fusion-preventing data dependences.

Our algorithm *FixDeps* has two main procedures. The *ElimWW_WR* procedure applies loop tiling to the fused loop nests (4) so that all WW_A and WR_A sets are empty. The *ElimRW* procedure applies array copying so that all RW_A sets are empty. Both procedures are discussed below.

3.1.1 *ElimWW_WR*: Loop Tiling

The basic idea is to apply loop tiling iteratively bottom-up across the K loop nests starting from the second last loop nest. By tiling $\mathcal{L}_{K-1}$, we make sure that $\mathcal{L}_{K-1}$ and $\mathcal{L}_K$ can be fused without violating any flow and output dependences from $\mathcal{L}_{K-1}$ to $\mathcal{L}_K$. By tiling $\mathcal{L}_{K-2}$, we ensure that $\mathcal{L}_{K-1}$, $\mathcal{L}_{K-2}$ and $\mathcal{L}_K$ can be fused without violating any flow and output dependences from $\mathcal{L}_{K-2}$ to $\mathcal{L}_{K-1}$ and $\mathcal{L}_K$. This process is repeated until $\mathcal{L}_1$ is processed.

36 **ALGORITHM:** *ElimRW*(P)
37 Let $\mathcal{V}$ be the set of all variables in P
38 for every array A in $\mathcal{V}$
39   for $k = K-1, 1$
40   for $k' = k+1, K$
41   Compute $RW_A(k,k')$
42     $\overline{RW}_A(k) := \bigcup_{k'=k+1}^{K}\{(I',k',s') \mid (I,I',s') \in RW_A(k,k')\}$
43   Compute $\min_{\prec} \overline{RW}_A(k)$ (see Section 3.1.2)
44   Introduce a new copying array for A, $H_{A,k}$, whose size is specified by $|\min_{\prec} \overline{RW}_A(k)|$
45   Insert the following copy operations at the beginning of the loop body of $\mathcal{L}_{k+1}$

      if $(I,k',s') \in \min_{\prec} \overline{RW}_A(k)$
        $H_{A,k}(f_{R'}(I)) = A(f_{R'}(I))$

    where $A(f_{R'}(I))$ is the LHS of the s'-th assignment in $\mathcal{L}_{k'}$
46   for every read reference R of form $A(f_R(I))$ in $Reads_A(k)$
47       $C_R := I \in [R] \wedge k' > k \wedge R' \in Writes_A(k') \wedge I' \in [R'] \wedge I' \prec I \wedge R(I) \stackrel{sub}{=} R'(I')$
48   Replace $A(f_R(I))$ by:

        if $I \in C_R$
          $H_{A,k}(f_R(I))$
        else
          $A(f_R(I))$

Figure 2. An algorithm for fixing all the fusion-preventing data dependences (Cont'd).

As a loop invariant at the beginning of the loop in line 10, all the fusion-preventing flow and output dependences in the loop nests $\mathcal{L}_{k+1},\dots,\mathcal{L}_K$ of the fused program (4) have been eliminated. In lines 11 – 17, $W(k)$ is computed to be the set of all flow and output dependences from $\mathcal{L}_k$ to $\mathcal{L}_{k+1},\dots,\mathcal{L}_K$. These are the WW and WR dependences that are violated when $\mathcal{L}_k$ is fused with $\mathcal{L}_{k+1},\dots,\mathcal{L}_K$. In lines 19 – 24, we find the outermost m loops in $\mathcal{L}_k$ that carry all the dependences in $W(k)$. These are the loops to be tiled to eliminate all the violated dependences in $W(k)$. However, $(d_1+1,\dots,d_m+1)$ computed in line 22 may not be a legal tile size if the dependences within $\mathcal{L}_k$ are also taken into account. Thus, in line 25, a legal tile size is found based also on the dependences within $\mathcal{L}_k$ [18, 19]. A legal tile size always exists. For example, $(N_1,\dots,N_m)$ is always legal, where N_i is the maximum number of points in the i-th dimension of $F_k(IS_k)$. In lines 25 – 26, the tile size $(T_1,\dots,T_n)$ for tiling $\mathcal{L}_k$ is selected. In lines 27 – 33, the tiled code for $\mathcal{L}_k$ is generated in the standard manner [18, 19]. Finally, in line 34, the tiled program becomes the program that will be used when $\mathcal{L}_{k-1}$ is tiled.

Theorem 1 *All the fusion-preventing flow and output dependences in the original program (1) are eliminated in the program P' generated by* ElimWW_WR.

3.1.2 *ElimRW*: Array Copying

The basic idea is to make use of array copying to eliminate all the fusion-preventing anti-dependences. The order in which the loop nests are processed in line 39 is not significant. In lines 40 – 41, we compute all the fusion-preventing anti-dependences from $\mathcal{L}_k$ to $\mathcal{L}_{k+1}, \dots, \mathcal{L}_K$. To insert copy operations correctly, we must know the earliest iteration at which an anti-dependence is violated. In line 42, we identify each write access by not only the iteration at which the access is executed but also the loop nest that contains the write reference as well as the assignment whose LHS is that write reference. In line 43, we compute $\min_{\prec} \overline{RW}_A(k)$. Let the specifying constraint for this set be $\mathcal{P}(I, (I', k', s'))$. This set is defined as follows:

$$\begin{array}{l} \min_{\prec} \overline{RW}_A(k) = \{(I', k', s') \mid \mathcal{P}(I, (I', k', s')) \\ \quad \wedge \nexists (I'', k'', s'') \text{ s.t. } (I'', k'', s'') \prec (I', k', s') \\ \quad \wedge \mathcal{P}(I, (I'', k'', s''))\} \end{array} \quad (7)$$

If all constraints in $\mathcal{P}(I, (I', k', s'))$ are affine, $\min_{\prec} \overline{RW}_A(k)$ can be computed parametrically (in terms of I) using the PIP [4] or Omega Calculator [11].

$\min_{\prec} \overline{RW}_A(k)$ contains the earliest writes at which some anti-dependences are violated in the program P' generated by *ElimWW_WR*. In line 48, we insert the copy statements to copy the old values of A at these iterations just before they are overwritten. In lines 43 – 45, we make sure that the copied values are used correctly only at the iterations defined by the predicate C_R in line 47.

The elimination of the fusion-preventing anti-dependences relies on the fact that all the fusion-preventing flow and output dependences have been eliminated.

Theorem 2 *The program P'' generated ElimRW has the same input/output behaviour as the original program (1).*

The number of copying arrays introduced for an existing array depends only on the number of fused loop nests. If array expansion [5] is used to eliminate output and anti-dependences, the amount of extra space introduced often depends on the problem size. For example, a 2-D array of size $N \times N$ is often expanded into a 3-D array of size $N \times N \times N$. In our case, the worst-case scenario is $N \times N \times L$, where L is the number of loop nests in the program. In addition, the following optimisations are often possible.

If all write references for an array A are located in one loop nest, then at least one copying array for A is required.

Theorem 3 *Let A be an array in the input program P' to ElimRW. If the write references of A are all contained in one loop nest only, then the copying arrays that may be introduced for A by ElimRW can be combined into one array.*

This theorem leads directly to the following result.

Theorem 4 *If the input program P' to ElimRW is free of output dependences between different write references, then the copying arrays $H_{A,2}, \dots, H_{A,K}$ that may be introduced for an existing array A can be combined into one array.*

3.2 Fusing Arbitrary Loop nests Program-wise

We can apply our algorithm *FixDeps* to a program to form increasingly larger perfect loop nests inside out. If desired, a single perfect loop nest can be eventually created.

Let us apply our algorithm to the four kernels given in Figure 1. By applying code sinking, we obtain the fused programs given in Figure 3. In each case, all perfect loop nests fused are numbered. Note that the last iteration of the `k` loop in LU has been peeled. Otherwise, loop peeling can be applied after our algorithm has been applied.

It is straightforward to fix the fusion-preventing dependences for these kernels to obtain the final programs given Figure 4. For LU, $WR_m(2,3) \neq \emptyset$. The final program is obtained by tiling the `i` loop with a tile size of `N`. The treatment of QR is similar. Since $WR_{norm}(2,3) \neq \emptyset$, the `k` loop for the loop nest 2 has been tiled by a tile size of `N`. The fused program for Cholesky is already legal. Finally, the anti-dependences in Jacobi are violated by loop fusion since $RW_A(1,2) \neq \emptyset$. These anti-dependences are fixed by array copying. We have applied some optimisations to copy more boundary values of `A` to simplify the if conditionals introduced in line 48 of *ElimRW*. The array L can be eliminated since $L(j,i)$ can be replaced by a scalar.

No extra memory space is introduced for these kernels.

4 Experiments

We evaluate this work using the four kernels given in Figure 1 on an SGI Octane2 with a 600MHz MIPS R14000A processor running IRIX64 6.5. Both L1 and L2 data caches are 2-way associative with LRU replacement. The L1 data cache has a size of 32KB with a line size of 32B while the L2 (unified) cache has a size of 2MB with a line size of 128B. Our SGI Octane has 3GB of RAM.

For each kernel, `seq` denotes its sequential program and `tiled` its tiled version. The tiled programs are obtained from the fused codes given in Figure 4 as follows. For LU and Cholesky, the outermost `k` loop is tiled. For QR, the outermost `i` and `j` loops are tiled. For Jacobi, we first apply $\left[\begin{smallmatrix}1&0&0\\1&1&0\\1&0&1\end{smallmatrix}\right]$ to skew the three loops in the fused code and then permute the time loop to the innermost position. Moving the time loop inside enables the temporal reuse carried by the loop to be exploited. Finally, all the three loops are tiled. Note that code sinking introduces some if conditionals into the fused programs given in Figure 3. In the tiled codes, the effect of code sinking is undone as much as possible.

All the kernels are tiled for the L1 data cache only. We have experimented with two tile-size-selection algorithms to compute the tile sizes for different problem sizes, `LRW` from Wolf and Lam [13] and `PDAT` from Panda *et al.* [10]. `LRW` computes the largest square tile such that the number of self-interferencing cache misses for one array reference is minimised. `PDAT` uses the fixed tile size $\sqrt{\frac{K-1}{K}C}$, where C is the size of the L1 data cache and K is its associativity on the underlying machine. For each of the four kernels, the performance curves obtained using `LRW` and `PDAT` almost

```
do k=1, N-1
   do j=k+1, N
     do i=k, N
    (1) if (i.EQ.k.AND.j.EQ.k+1)
          temp=0
          m=k
    (2) if (j.EQ.k+1)
          d=A(i,k)
          if (abs(d).GT. temp)
            temp=abs(d)
              m=i
    (3) if (j.EQ.k+1)
          if (m.NE.k)
            temp=A(k,i)
            A(k,i)=A(m,i)
            A(m,i)=temp
    (4) if (j.EQ.k+1)
          if (i.GE.k+1)
            A(i,k)=A(i,k)/A(k,k)
    (5) if (i.GT. k)
          A(i,j)=A(i,j)-A(i,k)*A(j,k)
temp=0
m=k
d= A(N, N)
   if (abs(d).GT. temp)
     temp=abs(d)
     m=N
```

(a) LU

```
do i=1, N
  do j=i, N
    do k=i, N
  (1) if (j.EQ.i.AND.k.EQ.i)
        norm=0
  (2) if (j.EQ.i)
          norm=norm+A(k,i)*A(k,i)
  (3) if (j.EQ.i.AND.k.EQ.i)
        norm2=sqrt(norm)
        asqr=A(i,i)*A(i,i)
        A(i,i)=dsqrt(norm-asqr+(A(i,i)-norm2)^2)
  (4) if (j.GE.i+1.AND.k.EQ.i)
        A(i,j)=A(i,j)/A(i,i)
  (5) if (j.GE.i+1.AND.k.EQ.i)
        X(j,i)=0
  (6) if (j.GE.i+1)
        X(j,i)=X(j,i)+A(i,k)*A(i,k)
  (7) if (j.GE.i+1.AND.k.GE.i+1)
       A(j,k)=A(j,k)-A(i,k)*X(j,i)
```

(b) QR

```
do k=1, N-1
  do j=k+1, N
     do i=j, N
    (1) if(i.EQ.j.AND.j.EQ .k+1)
          A(k,k)=sqrt(A(k,k))
    (2) if(j.EQ.k+1)
          A(i,k)=A(i,k)/A(k,k)
    (3) A(i,j)=A(i,j)-A(i,k)*A(j,k)
A(N,N)=sqrt(A(N,N))
```

(c) Cholesky

```
do t=0, M
  do i=2, N-1
    do j=2,N-1
  (1) L(j,i)=(A(j,i-1)+A(j-1,i)
             + A(j+1,i)+A(j,i+1)*0.25
  (2) A(j,i)=L(j,i)
```

(d) Jacobi

Figure 3. The fused versions of the four kernels given in Figure 1.

always coincide. Therefore, all the results presented here for tiled codes are obtained using PDAT only.

All the sequential and tiled programs are in ANSI C and compiled by the SGI MIPSpro compiler (version 7.4) at O3. For tiled codes, the compiler switch "LNO:blocking=off" is further used to disable loop tiling by the SGI compiler. (The sequential programs are equivalent to those in Figure 1 once the differences in storage order are considered.)

The Jacobi kernel has two problem size parameters, M and N, while each of the other three kernels has one problem size parameter, N. In our experiments, we have fixed $M = 500$ for Jacobi. For all the four kernels, we choose N from 200 to 2500 at multiples of 238. This captures some pathological cases about cache misses that might occur at some problem sizes [14]. All arrays are double arrays. So an array of size 512×512 fills up the 2MB L2 cache on our SGI Octane2 system. Therefore, we are able to investigate the impact of both L1 and L2 data caches on performance for all the four kernels. In our experiments, only one of the two processors in our SGI machine is used.

Figure 5 illustrates the performance improvements of the four kernels on the SGI Octane2 system. The speedups of LU range from 0.98 to 2.80, the speedups of QR range from 0.57 to 2.28, the speedups of Cholesky range from 1.11 to 4.27 and the speedups of JacobI range from 2.16 to 7.51. In all the cases, our tiled codes are simple and achieve good performance speedups consistently at all problem sizes.

Due to space limitations, we present only the performance analysis results obtained using the SGI *perfex* tool for Cholesky (abbreviated to CHOL). We measure the improved data reuse in terms of reduced L1 and L2 data cache misses, the branching overhead introduced by code sinking

```
do k=1, N-1
   do j=k+1, N
      do i=k, N
         if (i.EQ.k.AND.j.EQ.k+1)
            temp=0
            m=k
            do P=k, N
               d=A(P,k)
               if (abs(d).GT.temp)
                  temp=abs(d)
                  m=P
         if (j.EQ.k+1)
            if (m.NE.k)
               temp=A(k,i)
               A(k,i)=A(m,i)
               A(m,i)=temp
         if (j.EQ.k+1)
            if (i.GE.k+1)
               A(i,k)=A(i,k)/A(k,k)
         if (i.GT. k)
            A(i,j)=A(i,j)-A(i,k)*A(j,k)
 temp=0
 m=k
 d= A(N, N)
   if (abs(d).GT.temp)
      temp=abs(d)
      m=N
```

(a) LU

```
do i=1, N
   do j=i, N
      do k=i, N
         if (j.EQ.i.AND.k.EQ.i)
            norm=0
            do P=i,N
               norm=norm+A(i,P)*A(i,P)
         if (j.EQ.i.AND. k.EQ.i)
            norm2=sqrt(norm)
            asqr=A(i,i)*A(i,i)
            A(i,i)=dsqrt(norm-asqr+(A(i,i)-norm2)^2)
         if (j.GE.i+1.AND. k.EQ.i)
            A(i,j)=A(i,j)/A(i,i)
            X(j,i)=0
         if (j.GE.i+1)
            X(j,i)=X(j,i)+A(i,k)*A(i,k)
         if (j.GE.i+1.AND. k.GE.i+1)
          A(j,k)=A(j,k)-A(i,k)*X(j,i)
```

(b) QR

```
do k=1, N-1
   do j=k+1, N
      do i=j, N
         if(i.EQ.j.AND. j.EQ .k+1)
            A(k,k)=sqrt(A(k,k))
         if(j.EQ.k+1)
            A(i,k)=A(i,k)/A(k,k)
         A(i,j)=A(i,j)-A(i,k)*A(j,k)
A(N,N)=sqrt(A(N,N))
```

(c) Cholesky

```
do k=2,N-1
   H(k,1)=A(k,1)
   H(1,k)=A(1,k)
   H(k,N)=A(k,N)
   H(N,k)=A(N,k)
do t=0, M
   do i=2, N-1
     do j=2,N-1
        L(j,i)=(H(j,i-1)+H(j-1,i)
                  + A(j+1,i)+A(j,i+1)*0.25
        H(j,i)=A(j,i)
        A(j,i)=L(j,i)  // L(j,i) to be replaced by a scalar
```

(d) Jacobi

Figure 4. The fused codes given in Figure 3 with all the fusion-preventing data dependences fixed.

in terms of increased branches resolved and mispredicted, and loop control overhead (due to mainly tiling) in terms of extra instructions introduced.

Figures 6 – 8 present our measurements obtained by *perfex*. The typical L1 and L2 cache miss cycles for both sequential and tiled programs are compared in Figure 6. Note that the vertical axis is drawn in the log scale. The minimum and maximum costs for an L1 data cache miss are 10.00 cycles and 14.00 cycles, respectively. Due to the out-of-order execution, the *typical cost* is 9.92 cycles. The typical, minimum and maximum costs for an L2 data cache miss are 162.55, 166.41 and 196.51 cycles, respectively. By enabling loop fusion and tiling, our approach has reduced significantly L1 and L2 cache misses (as a whole). Relative to the reduced cache miss cycles shown in Figure 6, the branching overhead is small as illustrated in Figure 7. Each "resolved" curve represents the number of resolved conditionals, which also represents the number of cycles typically consumed since it takes one cycle to resolve a conditional branch. Each "mispredicted" curve represents the number of cycles typically consumed by mispredicted branches; it is five times as many as the number of mispredicted branches since the typical cost for one misprediction is 5 cycles. Finally, Figure 8 illustrates the total instruction increases in the tiled codes due to code sinking, fusion and tiling. The relatively large increases in dynamic instruction counts are

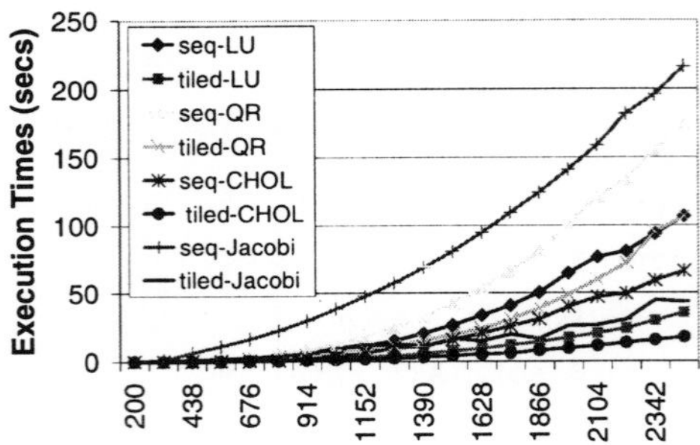

Figure 5. Performance improvements.

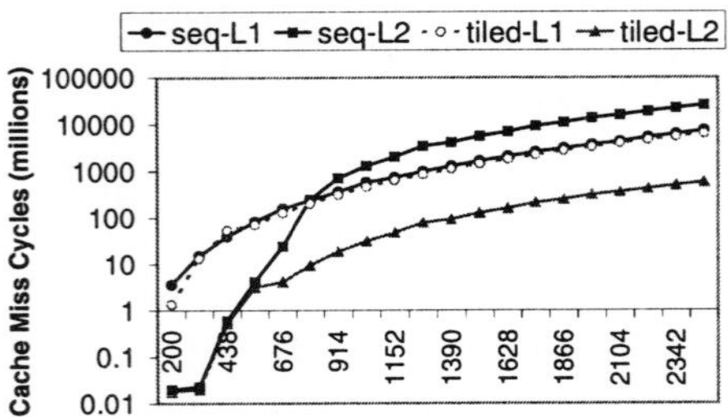

Figure 6. The typical miss cycles caused by L1 and L2 data cache misses for CHOL.

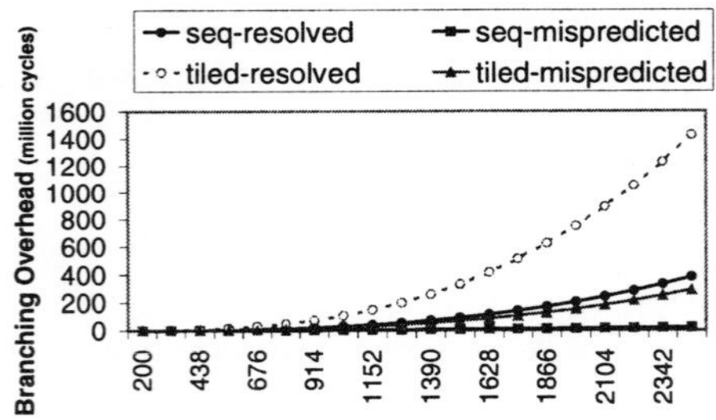

Figure 7. The typical cycles caused by branch resolutions and mispredictions for CHOL.

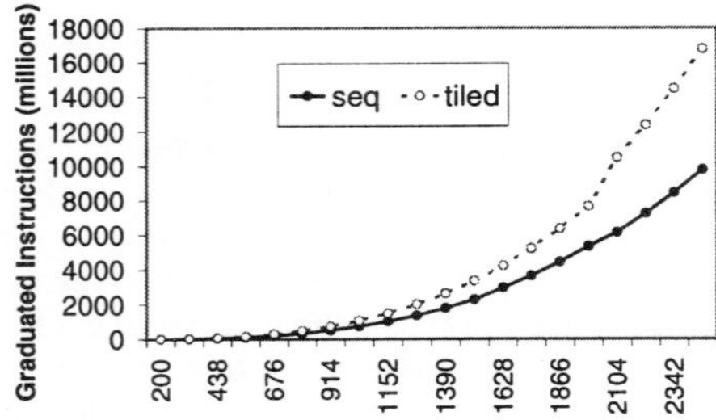

Figure 8. Graduated instructions for CHOL.

observed at all problem sizes. However, the extra instructions introduced are all integer operations (e.g., loads, stores and conditionals), which each take usually one cycle to execute. On the other hand, eliminating one single L2 data cache miss saves typically at least (typical L2 miss penalty - typical L1 miss penalty) = 162.55 – 9.92 = 152.63 cycles. By comparing Figure 6 with Figures 7 and 8, we see clearly that the benefit from the improved data reuse has far outweighed the cost due to branching and loop control overheads, resulting in performance speedups for Cholesky at all the problem sizes.

Figures 6 shows that our method may impact L1 and L2 cache misses differently for different kernels. While being almost equally effective for reducing both L1 and L2 misses in QR and Jacobi (not shown here), our method is far more effective in reducing L2 misses for LU and Cholesky.

Unlike the other three kernels, the tiled code for Jacobi is more efficient than the sequential version. Fusing the two loop nests in the sequential code results in one single perfect loop nest. In the tiled code, no extra conditionals are introduced. By fusing the two loop nests in the sequential code, we have also reduced the number of array loads in the tiled code by an average of 40.9%. The net effect is an average of 3.4% reduction in the the number of instructions executed in the tiled code. The speedups of JacobI are the mostly impressive, ranging from 2.16 to 7.51. Based on the performance analysis for Jacobi, we may be able to achieve better speedups for the other kernels if we can reduce the performance overheads as illustrated in Figure 8.

5 Related Work

Carr and Lehoucq [2] introduce some special-purpose techniques for tiling matrix factorisations: LU with and without pivoting, Cholesky and QR. They conclude that LU with partial pivoting and QR given in Figure 1 are not blockable based on dependence information alone. They show how the compiler can generate tiled codes for these two kernels by applying pattern matching for LU with pivoting or starting with a different algorithm for QR. We can generate tiled codes for these two kernels starting from the programs given in Figure 1 based on the dependence information only.

Song and Li [12] describe special-purpose techniques for tiling stencil computations. They transform Jacobi into a perfect loop nest by applying odd-even array copying to remove anti- and output dependences. Our approach eliminates flow and output dependences by loop tiling and anti-dependences by array copying for any affine loop nests. In the case of Jacobi, we obtain a single loop nest by applying array copying only. The tiled code is simple and achieves good performance speedups on three different architectures.

Kodukula *et al.* [8] describe a data shackling approach that is applicable to both perfect and imperfect loop nests. As they mention, their approach cannot handle stencil codes such as Jacobi and Gauss-Seidel. Ahmed *et al.* [1] present an approach to improving data reuse in any affine loop nests by means of iteration space transformations. They embed the iteration spaces of different loop nests in a program into a common iteration space such that the resulting program exhibits better data reuse. The embedding process must ensure that all dependences in the original program are pre-

Method	LU	QR	Cholesky	Jacobi
Matrix Factorisations [2]	√	√	√	×
Stencil Computations [12]	×	×	×	√
Data Shackling [8]	√	√	√	×
Iteration Space Transforms [8]	×	×	√	√
This Work	√	√	√	√

Table 1. A comparison of five methods in terms of their ability in handling the four kernels given in Figure 1.

served. As a result, the dimensionality of the common iteration space may be larger than that of any existing iteration space in the original program. In this case, the effectiveness of tiling the resulting program becomes problematic. As they mention, their approach cannot handle LU with pivoting and QR. Recently, Menon *et al.* [9] discuss exclusively how to carry out automatic restructuring of codes such as LU with pivoting by symbolic analysis. In contrast, we attempt to solve the problem of tiling imperfect loop nests from a different angle. We allow arbitrary loop nests to be fused but we remove all the fusion-preventing dependences by applying loop tiling and array copying automatically.

Table 1 provides a comparison of our work with the previous research efforts in terms of their capability in handling the four important kernels in scientific computations. Our approach is the only one that can handle both matrix factorisations and stencil computations in a unified framework.

6 Conclusion

This paper presents a new approach to improving data reuse in imperfect loop nests. The basic idea is to fuse the loop nests in a program into larger perfect loop nests and then eliminate all the fusion-preventing dependences so that the resulting program is correct. The perfect loop nests formed can be tiled for improved cache performance. We eliminate the fusion-preventing flow and output dependences by means of automatic loop tiling and the fusion-preventing anti-dependences by means of automatic array copying. Our approach is applicable to affine loop nests as well as some non-affine ones including LU with pivoting as an important example. In comparison with some existing techniques as shown in Table 1, our approach can handle the four important kernels shown in Figure 1 for both matrix factorisations and stencil computations in a unified framework. Our approach is simple and generates simple tiled code for these four kernels. The tiled codes achieve consistently good performance improvements as validated by our experiments on an SGI Octane2 high-performance computer system. The benefit from the significantly reduced L1 and L2 cache misses has far more than offset the branching and loop control overhead introduced by our

One future work is to generalise loop distribution (which is the inverse of loop fusion) to make it more widely applicable. Another is to to develop a cost model for guiding our and other transformations for locality enhancement in whole programs.

References

[1] N. Ahmed, N. Mateev, and K. Pingali. Synthesizing transformations for locality enhancement of imperfectly-nested loop nests. In *14th international conference on Supercomputing*, pages 141–152. ACM Press, 2000.

[2] S. Carr and R. B. Lehoucq. Compiler blockability of dense matrix factorizations. *ACM Trans. Math. Softw.*, 23(3):336–361, 1997.

[3] C. Ding and K. Kennedy. Improving effective bandwidth through compiler enhancement of global cache reuse. In *15th International Parallel & Distributed Processing Symposium*, page 38. IEEE Computer Society, 2001.

[4] P. Feautrier. Parametric integer programming. *Operations Research*, 22:243–268, 1988.

[5] P. Feautrier. Dataflow analysis for array and scalar references. *Int. J. of Parallel Programming*, 20(1):23–53, Feb. 1991.

[6] F. Irigoin and R. Triolet. Supernode partitioning. In *15th Annual ACM Symposium on Principles of Programming Languages*, pages 319–329, San Diego, California., Jan. 1988.

[7] I. Kodukula. *Data-centric Compilation*. PhD thesis, Cornell University, 1998.

[8] I. Kodukula, N. Ahmed, and K. Pingali. Data-centric multilevel blocking. In *ACM SIGPLAN '97 Conference on Programming Language Design*, pages 346–357, 1996.

[9] V. Menon, K. Pingali, and N. Mateev. Fractal symbolic analysis. *ACM Trans. Program. Lang. Syst.*, 25(6):776–813, 2003.

[10] P. R. Panda, H. Nakamura, N. D. Dutt, and A. Nicolau. Augmenting loop tiling with data alignment for improved cache performance. *IEEE Transactions on Computers*, 48(2):142–149, 1999.

[11] W. Pugh. The Omega test: A fast and practical integer programming algorithm for dependence analysis. *Comm. ACM*, 35(8):102–114, Aug. 1992.

[12] Y. Song and Z. Li. New tiling techniques to improve cache temporal locality. In *ACM SIGPLAN'99 Conference on Programming Language Design and Implementation (PLDI'99)*, pages 215–228, May 1999.

[13] M. Wolf and M. Lam. A data locality optimizing algorithm. In *ACM SIGPLAN'91 Conference on Programming Language Design and Implementation (PLDI'91)*, pages 30–44, Jun. 1991.

[14] M. E. Wolf and M. S. Lam. A data locality optimizing algorithm. In *ACM SIGPLAN'91 Conf. on Programming Language Design and Implementation*, Jun. 1991.

[15] M. E. Wolf and M. S. Lam. A loop transformation theory and an algorithm to maximize parallelism. *IEEE Trans. on Parallel and Distributed Systems*, 2(4):452–471, Oct. 1991.

[16] M. J. Wolfe. More iteration space tiling. In *Supercomputing '88*, pages 655–664, Nov. 1989.

[17] M. J. Wolfe. *High Performance Compilers for Parallel Computing*. Addison-Wesley, 1996.

[18] J. Xue. On tiling as a loop transformation. *Parallel Processing Letters*, 7(4):409–424, 1997.

[19] J. Xue. *Loop Tiling for Parallelism*. Kluwer Academic Publishers, Boston, 2000.

[20] H. Zima. *Supercompilers for Parallel and Vector Computers*. Frontier Series. Addison-Wesley (ACM Press), 1990.

Session 2C: Applications

Integrated Performance Monitoring of a Cosmology Application on Leading HEC Platforms

J. Borrill, J. Carter, L. Oliker, D. Skinner
Computational Research Division
Lawrence Berkeley National Laboratory
Berkeley, CA 94720
{jdborrill,jtcarter,loliker,dskinner}@lbl.gov

R. Biswas
NAS Division
NASA Ames Research Center
Moffett Field, CA 94035
rbiswas@mail.arc.nasa.gov

Abstract

The Cosmic Microwave Background (CMB) is an exquisitely sensitive probe of the fundamental parameters of cosmology. Extracting this information is computationally intensive, requiring massively parallel computing and sophisticated numerical algorithms. In this work we present MADbench, a lightweight version of the MADCAP CMB power spectrum estimation code that retains the operational complexity and integrated system requirements. In addition, to quantify communication behavior across a variety of architectural platforms, we introduce the Integrated Performance Monitoring (IPM) package: a portable, lightweight, and scalable tool for effectively extracting MPI message-passing overheads. A performance characterization study is conducted on some of the world's most powerful supercomputers, including the superscalar Seaborg (IBM Power3+) and CC-NUMA Columbia (SGI Altix), as well as the vector-based Earth Simulator (NEC SX-6 enhanced) and Phoenix (Cray X1) systems. In-depth analysis shows that in order to bridge the gap between theoretical and sustained system performance, it is critical to gain a clear understanding of how the distinct parts of large-scale parallel applications interact with the individual subcomponents of HEC platforms.

Keywords: Cosmic Microwave Background, MADCAP, Altix Columbia, Earth Simulator, X1 Phoenix, Power3 Seaborg, parallel performance characterization

1 Introduction

The Cosmic Microwave Background (CMB) is a snapshot of the Universe when it first became electrically neutral some 400,000 years after the Big Bang. The tiny anisotropies in the temperature and polarization of the CMB radiation are sensitive probes of cosmology, and measuring their detailed statistical properties has been a high priority in the field since its serendipitous discovery in 1965. Since these anisotropies are $O(10^{-5})$ in temperature and $O(10^{-7})$ or less in polarization, and are imprinted on a background that has been cooled by the expansion of the Universe to only 2.7 K today, harnessing the extraordinary scientific potential of the CMB requires precise measurements of the microwave sky at high resolution. The progressive reduction of the resulting datasets, first to a pixelized sky map, then to an angular power spectrum, and finally to cosmological parameters, is a computationally intensive endeavor. The problem is exacerbated by an explosion in dataset sizes as cosmologists try to make more and more accurate measurements of the CMB. High-end computing (HEC) has become an essential part of CMB data analysis, and the effective use of such resources requires a detailed understanding of their performance under the demands of real CMB data analysis algorithms and implementations.

CMB data analyses have typically been performed on superscalar-based commodity microprocessors due to their generality, scalability, and cost effectiveness. However, two recent innovative parallel-vector architectures — the Earth Simulator (ES) and the Cray X1 — promise to narrow the growing gap between sustained and peak performance for many classes of scientific applications. In addition, the new Columbia system at NASA, constructed in just four months and continuously operational during the build, brings an unprecedented level of computational power at a fraction of the cost of typical supercomputers. In order to characterize what these platforms offer scientists that rely on HEC, it is imperative to critically evaluate and compare them in the context of demanding scientific applications [2, 3, 4, 5].

In this work, we present MADbench, a lightweight version of the Microwave Anisotropy Dataset Computational Analysis Package (MADCAP) CMB power spectrum estimation code [1] that retains the operational complexity and integrated system requirements. We compare the performance of MADbench on the ES (NEC SX-6 enhanced) and Phoenix (Cray X1) against those obtained on Columbia (SGI Altix) and Seaborg (IBM Power3). To quantify communication behavior

Table 1. Architectural specifications of the Power3, Altix, ES, and X1

Platform	CPU/ Node	Clock (MHz)	Peak (GF/s)	Mem BW (GB/s)	Peak (bytes/flop)	MPI Lat (usec)	Netwk BW (GB/s/CPU)	Bisection BW (bytes/flop)	Network Topology
Power3	16	375	1.5	0.7	0.47	16.3	0.13	0.087	Fat-tree
Altix	2	1500	6.0	6.4	1.1	2.8	0.40	0.067	Fat-tree
ES	8	500	8.0	32.0	4.0	5.6	1.5	0.19	Crossbar
X1	4	800	12.8	34.1	2.7	7.3	6.3	0.088	2D torus

across this spectrum of architectures, we developed and utilized the Integrated Performance Monitoring (IPM) package: a portable, lightweight, and scalable tool for effectively extracting MPI message-passing overheads. In-depth analysis shows that in order to bridge the gap between theoretical and sustained system performance, it is critical to gain a clear understanding of how the distinct parts of large-scale parallel applications interact with the individual subcomponents of HEC platforms.

2 Target HEC Platforms

We begin by briefly describing the salient features of the four parallel HEC architectures that are examined here (Table 1 presents a summary). Note that the vector machines have higher peak performance and better system balance than the superscalar platforms. The ES and X1 have high memory bandwidth relative to peak CPU speed (bytes/flop), allowing them to more effectively feed the arithmetic units. Additionally, the custom vector interconnects show superior characteristics in terms of measured inter-node MPI latency [6, 9], point-to-point messaging (network bandwidth), and all-to-all communication (bisection bandwidth) — both in raw performance and as a ratio of peak processing speed. Overall, the ES appears to be the most balanced system, while the Altix shows the best architectural characteristics among the superscalar platforms.

2.1 Seaborg (Power3)

The Power3 was first introduced in 1998 as part of IBM's RS/6000 series. Each 375 MHz processor contains two floating-point units (FPUs) that can issue a multiply-add (MADD) per cycle for a peak performance of 1.5 Gflop/s. The Power3 has a pipeline of only three cycles, thus using the registers very efficiently and diminishing the penalty for mispredicted branches. The out-of-order architecture uses prefetching to reduce pipeline stalls due to cache misses. The CPU has a 32KB instruction cache, a 128KB 128-way set associative L1 data cache, and an 8MB four-way set associative L2 cache with its own private bus. Each SMP node consists of 16 processors connected to main memory via a crossbar. Multi-node configurations are networked via the Colony switch using an omega-type topology. In this model, disk I/O uses the switch fabric, sharing bandwidth with message-passing traffic. The Power3 experiments reported here were conducted on Seaborg, the 380-node IBM pSeries system running AIX 5.1 and operated by Lawrence Berkeley National Laboratory (LBNL). The distributed filesystem was configured with 16 GPFS servers, each with 32GB of main memory that can be used to cache files and metadata. The total size of the filesystem was 30TB, with a block size of 256KB.

2.2 Columbia (Altix 3000)

Introduced in early 2003, the SGI Altix 3000 systems are an adaptation of the Origin 3000, which use SGI's NUMAflex global shared-memory architecture. Such systems allow access to all data directly and efficiently, without having to move them through I/O or networking bottlenecks. The NUMAflex design enables the processor, memory, I/O, interconnect, graphics, and storage to be packaged into modular components, called "bricks." The primary difference between the Altix and the Origin systems is the C-Brick, used for the processor and memory. This computational building block for the Altix consists of four Intel Itanium2 processors (in two nodes), local memory, and a two-controller ASIC called the Scalable Hub (SHUB). Each SHUB interfaces to two CPUs in one node, along with memory, I/O devices, and other SHUBs. The Altix cache-coherency protocol is implemented in the SHUB that integrates both the snooping operations of the Itanium2 and the directory-based scheme used across the NUMAflex interconnection fabric. A load/store cache miss causes the data to be communicated via the SHUB at a cache-line granularity and automatically replicated in the local cache.

The 64-bit Itanium2 architecture operates at 1.5 GHz and is capable of issuing two MADDs per cycle for a peak performance of 6.0 Gflop/s. The memory hierarchy consists of 128 FP registers and three on-chip data caches (32KB L1, 256KB L2, and 6MB L3). The Itanium2 cannot store FP data in L1, making register loads and spills a potential source of bottlenecks; however, a relatively large register set helps mitigate this issue. The superscalar processor implements the Explicitly Parallel Instruction set Computing (EPIC) technology where instructions are organized into 128-bit VLIW bundles.

The Altix platform uses the NUMAlink3 interconnect, a high-performance custom network in a fat-tree topology that enables the bisection bandwidth to scale linearly with the number of processors. All Altix experiments reported here were performed on the 10,240-processor Columbia system running 64-bit Linux version 2.4.21, the world's second-most powerful supercomputer [8] located at NASA Ames Research Center. The Columbia experiments used a 6.4TB parallel XFS filesystem with a 35-fiber optical channel connection to the CPUs.

2.3 Earth Simulator

The vector processor of the Earth Simulator (ES) uses a dramatically different architectural approach than conventional cache-based systems. Vectorization exploits regularities in the computational structure of scientific applications to expedite uniform operations on independent data sets. The 500 MHz ES processor (an enhanced version of the NEC SX-6) contains an 8-way replicated vector pipe capable of issuing a MADD each cycle, for a peak performance of 8.0 Gflop/s. The processors contain 72 vector registers, each holding 256 64-bit words. For non-vectorizable instructions, the ES has a 500 MHz scalar processor with a 64KB instruction cache, a 64KB data cache, and 128 general-purpose registers. The four-way superscalar unit has a peak of 1.0 Gflop/s (an eighth of the vector performance) and supports branch prediction, data prefetching, and out-of-order execution.

Like traditional vector architectures, the ES vector unit is cache-less; memory latencies are masked by overlapping pipelined vector operations with memory fetches. Each SMP contains eight processors that share the node's memory. The ES is the world's third-most powerful supercomputer [8], and consists of 640 SMP nodes connected through a custom single-stage crossbar. This high-bandwidth interconnect topology provides impressive communication characteristics, as all nodes are a single hop from one another. The 5120-processor ES runs Super-UX, a 64-bit Unix operating system based on System V-R3 with BSD4.2 communication features. Each group of 16 nodes has a pool of RAID disks (720GB per node) attached via fiber channel switch. The filesystem used for our tests is SFS, with a block size of 4MB. Each node has a separate filesystem, in contrast to the other architectures studied here. As remote access is not available, the reported experiments were performed during the authors' visit to the ES Center and by ES Center collaborators in late 2004.

2.4 Phoenix (X1)

The Cray X1 combines traditional vector strengths with the generality and scalability features of modern superscalar cache-based parallel systems. The computational core, called the single-streaming processor (SSP), contains two 32-stage vector pipes running at 800 MHz. Each SSP contains 32 vector registers holding 64 double-precision words, and operates at 3.2 Gflop/s peak for 64-bit data. The SSP also contains a two-way out-of-order superscalar processor running at 400 MHz with two 16KB instruction and data caches. Like the SX-6, the scalar unit operates at 1/8-th the vector performance, making a high vector operation ratio critical for effectively utilizing the underlying hardware.

The multi-streaming processor (MSP) combines four SSPs into one logical computational unit. The four SSPs share a 2-way set associative 2MB data Ecache, a unique feature that allows extremely high bandwidth (25–51 GB/s) for computations with temporal data locality. MSP parallelism is achieved by distributing loop iterations across each of the four SSPs. An X1 node consists of four MSPs sharing a flat memory, and large system configurations are networked through a modified 2D torus interconnect. The torus topology allows scalability to large processor counts with relatively few links compared with fat-tree or crossbar interconnects; however, this topological configuration suffers from limited bisection bandwidth. All reported X1 results were obtained on Phoenix, the 256-MSP system running UNICOS/mp 2.4 and operated by Oak Ridge National Laboratory (ORNL). This machine has four nodes available for I/O, each of which is connected to a RAID array using fiber channel arbitrated loop protocol. Data transfer from a batch MSP must travel over the interconnect to one of the I/O nodes. The filesystem used in this study is a 4TB XFS filesystem, with a block size of 64KB.

3 Integrated Performance Monitoring

Integrated Performance Monitoring (IPM) is a portable performance profiling infrastructure that binds together communication, computation, and memory information from the tasks in a parallel application into a single application-level profile. IPM provides a lightweight portable mechanism for workload-wide parallel profiling that does not require user intervention and scales to thousands of processors. As the application executes on the parallel platform, IPM records a per-process profile of computation and communication using a small fixed memory footprint and very low CPU overhead. When the application terminates, a report of the aggregate profile is generated. In this work, IPM was used on all the target architectures as a probe of the amount of communication. There are other ways one can obtain this information within a procedural context. For example, MPIP [10] is a name-shifted profiling library that records the call stack for each MPI call. Cur-

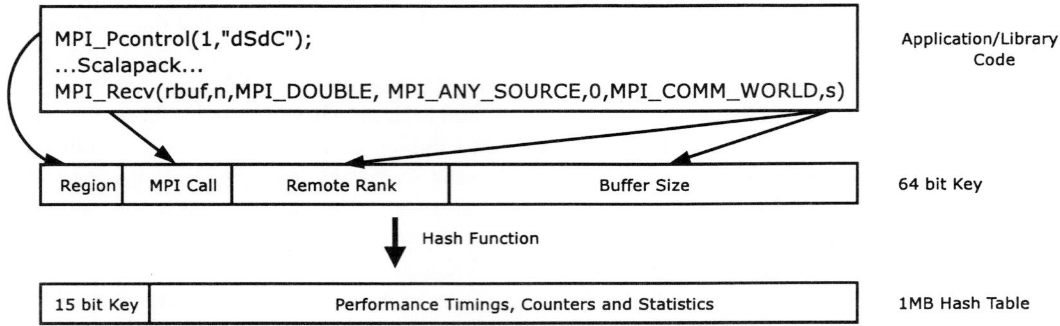

Figure 1. Program control flow from the application through MPI to the IPM layer

rently, determining the call stack on a variety of architectures presents a technical challenge we chose to avoid.

The basic mechanism by which IPM operates is the name-shifted profiling interface specified in the MPI standard. Name-shifted profiling wrappers have been widely used [7] to determine the nature of communication within parallel codes. The entry point to each MPI call is replaced with another that wraps a call to the PMPI entry point. `MPI_Pcontrol` is called directly from the application to mark the code region to be profiled. The profile is stored in a hash table that is keyed off the region, MPI call, message size, and the rank to which the message was sent or received (in the case of point-to-point communications). Figure 1 shows a schematic of this process. We are thus able to compute basic statistics like average, minimum, and maximum for the times that each rank spends in an MPI call for every buffer size. For point-to-point calls, we also track the other rank involved in the communication and thereby determine the topological character of the communication.

The principal benefit of using IPM is that it provides sufficient contextual clarity to separately analyze the communication in each of the distinct computational steps within MADbench. Since each functional component has a specific algorithmic or data movement role in the overall calculation, having region-specific timings allows one to compare measurements with estimates derived analytically or from microbenchmarks. Analyses of parallel performance that treats the application as a whole does not provide this level of detail. Because MADbench uses ScaLAPACK extensively, IPM also provides insights into the communication primitives used by an otherwise opaque library call.

To ensure that IPM accurately measures communication time, we investigated the different implementations of ScaLAPACK across the target machines. Since IPM records the time spent in MPI calls, we must know that all communication is done via MPI or that non-MPI communication is negligible. For the architectures studied here, we were able to verify this either by checking directly with vendor documentation or by testing with platform-specific profiling tools (PAT, ftmpirun, etc.). Phoenix and ES spend negligible time in non-MPI communication within ScaLAPACK, while the Seaborg and Columbia implementations are based entirely on MPI.

In the current work, we use IPM strictly for determining information about communication occurring within the MADbench code. No analysis of data obtained from hardware performance counters was conducted. The present analysis can be extended by investigating the distribution of message sizes, communication topology, and hardware performance counters occurring within each of the code regions and across architectures. We currently lack the right tools for fully analyzing the performance profiles generated by IPM. In future, we plan to expand the scope and level of detail by such analysis.

4 MADbench Overview

The MADCAP CMB angular power spectrum estimator uses Newton-Raphson iteration to locate the peak of the spectral likelihood function. This involves calculating the first two derivatives of the likelihood function with respect to the power spectrum coefficients C_l (since the CMB is azimuthally symmetric, the full spherical harmonic basis can be reduced to include the l-modes only). For a noisy pixelized CMB sky map $d_p = s_p + n_p$ (data is signal plus noise) and pixel-pixel correlation matrix $D_{pp'} = S_{pp'}(C_l) + N_{pp'}$, the log-likelihood that the observed data comes from some underlying set of C_l is

$$\mathcal{L}(d_p|C_l) = -\frac{1}{2}\left(d^T D^{-1} d + \mathrm{Tr}[\ln D]\right)$$

whose first two derivatives with respect to the C_l are

$$\frac{\partial \mathcal{L}}{\partial C_l} = \frac{1}{2}\left(d^T D^{-1}\frac{\partial S}{\partial C_l}D^{-1}d - \mathrm{Tr}\left[D^{-1}\frac{\partial S}{\partial C_l}\right]\right)$$

$$\frac{\partial^2 \mathcal{L}}{\partial C_l \partial C_{l'}} = -d^T D^{-1}\frac{\partial S}{\partial C_l}D^{-1}\frac{\partial S}{\partial C_{l'}}D^{-1}d + \frac{1}{2}\mathrm{Tr}\left[D^{-1}\frac{\partial S}{\partial C_l}D^{-1}\frac{\partial S}{\partial C_{l'}}\right]$$

yielding a Newton-Raphson correction to an initial guess of the spectral coefficients

$$\delta C_l = \left[\frac{\partial^2 \mathcal{L}}{\partial C_l \partial C_{l'}} \right]^{-1} \frac{\partial \mathcal{L}}{\partial C_{l'}}$$

Typically, the data has insufficient sky coverage and/or resolution to obtain each multipole coefficient individually, and so we bin them instead, replacing C_l with C_b.

Given the size of the pixel-pixel correlation matrices, it is important to minimize the number of matrices simultaneously held in memory; the MADCAP implementation is constrained to have no more than three matrices in core at any one time. It's operational steps, and their scalings for a map with NPIX pixels and NMPL multipoles in NBIN bins, are:

1. Calculate the signal correlation derivative matrices $\partial S/\partial C_b$; complexity is O(NMPL × NPIX^2).
2. Form and then invert the data correlation matrix $D = \sum_b C_b\, \partial S/\partial C_b + N$; complexity is O(NPIX^3).
3. For each bin, calculate $W_b = D^{-1}\partial S/\partial C_b$; complexity is O(NBIN × NPIX^3).
4. For each bin, calculate $\partial \mathcal{L}/\partial C_b$; complexity is O(NBIN × NPIX^2).
5. For each bin-bin pair, calculate $\partial^2 \mathcal{L}/\partial C_b \partial C_{b'}$; complexity is O(NBIN^2 × NPIX^2).
6. Invert the bin correlation matrix $\partial^2 \mathcal{L}/\partial C_b \partial C_{b'}$ and calculate the spectral correction δC_b; complexity is O(NBIN^3).

Note that steps 4–6 are computationally subdominant as NBIN << NMPL << NPIX.

All pixel-pixel correlation matrices are ScaLAPACK block-cyclic distributed, so each processor carries a unique subset of the rows and columns of each matrix. All I/O is performed in terms of this distribution, with each processor writing its subset of the full matrix to its own file. This has the advantage of simplicity when the matrices need to be read back in, and avoids any problems with the ES's distributed filesystem. However, since the reading or writing of a matrix now involves all processors simultaneously trying to perform their own I/O, there is the possibility for significant contention. This is minimized by restricting the actual number of processors performing concurrent I/O to a user-specified fraction of the total, implemented using a simple token-passing scheme. The specified fraction can be different for reading (RMOD) and writing (WMOD), and numerical experiments are performed to optimize the values of these parameters — as well as the ScaLAPACK block size (BSIZE) — on each architecture.

The full MADCAP spectral estimator includes a large number of special-case features, from preliminary data checking to marginalization over foreground templates, that dramatically increase the size and complexity of the code without altering its basic operational structure. For simplicity, we have therefore developed a stripped-down version, called MADbench, expressly designed for benchmarking that preserves all the computational challenges of the problem while removing extraneous bells and whistles. MADbench consists of three functions: dSdC, invD, and W, that respectively perform the dominant steps 1–3 above. (W also performs a slightly simplified version of the subdominant steps 4–6 to confirm code correctness.) In order to understand the overall performance, it is useful to lay out the overall sequence of calculation, communication, and I/O for each function:

dSdC For each bin b, calculate the local subset of the $\partial S/\partial C_b$ matrix using Legendre recursion and write it to disk. This function involves neither communication nor reading. The innermost loop of the recursion had to be rewritten to take advantage of the vector architectures.

invD For each bin b, read in the local subset of the $\partial S/\partial C_b$ matrix and weighted-accumulate it to build the local subset of the data correlation matrix D; invert this by Cholesky decomposition and triangular solution using the ScaLAPACK pdpotrf and pdpotri routines. This function involves no writing.

W For each bin b, read in the local subset of the $\partial S/\partial C_b$ matrix and perform the dense matrix-matrix multiplication $W_b = D^{-1}\partial S/\partial C_b$ using the ScaLAPACK pdgemm routine. This function again requires no writing. Note that the multiplications are entirely independent of one another; we therefore compare two implementations: the first proceeding as above, and the second introducing a level of gang-parallelism, with NGANG of the $\partial S/\partial C_b$ matrices each being remapped to a different subset of the processors using the ScaLAPACK pdgemr2d function and all of the processor-gangs then simultaneously calling pdgemm.

5 Parallel Performance Results

MADbench requires six parameters to be specified. Two set the size of the run (NPIX and NBIN), and one the degree of gang-parallelism (NGANG). The other three parameters (RMOD, WMOD, and BSIZE) need to be tuned for each architecture and were set as follows: Seaborg (4,1,128), Columbia (1,1,32), ES (1,1,64), and Phoenix (1,1,128). We ran MADbench on P = 16, 64, and 256 processors on all architectures, and on P = 1024 where possible (Seaborg and ES). In each case, the number of bins was fixed at NBIN = 16, and the number of pixels chosen to keep the total data volume per processor constant, NPIX = 5000×P/16. Each configuration was run with no gang-parallelism (NGANG = 1), and then only W was rerun with NGANG = 16. Each experiment was repeated several times, with the best runtimes reported.

5.1 Overall Performance

We first give a high level overview of MADbench performance on the architectures described in Section 2 for a variety of problem sizes. In the next subsection (Section 5.2), we increase the level of detail by conducting similar performance analyses within the context of each important functional component (dSdC, invD, and W) that constitutes MADbench. In a broad sense, MADbench spends almost all of its time calculating, communicating, or reading/writing data to disk. We identify the time associated with each of these activities as CALC, MPI, and I/O in the remainder of this paper. We add another metric, called LBST, which measures load balancing including synchronization time. When proceeding from one functional component to the next, we impose a barrier in order to have a well-defined boundary between the phases. LBST records the time when all processes do not reach these barriers at exactly the same time.

It is useful to identify the runtimes associated with each of these four broad categories to most directly understand which subsystems of a computing platform are stressed during the course of a calculation. As the problem size and concurrency increase, we expect changes in the relative fraction of time spent in I/O, MPI, CALC, and LBST to provide the clearest indication of the nature of the scaling bottlenecks present in MADbench.

Ultimately, however, the absolute timings are the most important factor when making architectural performance comparisons. Table 2 shows the execution times for each functional component of MADbench for various processor counts on each of the four platforms. For all but the very smallest problem size (P = 16), the ES shows the best absolute performance in terms of time-to-solution (Phoenix outperforms the ES for P= 16). In terms of percentage of theoretical peak performance (% TPP), Seaborg demonstrates the best results except for P = 1024 when the ES is superior.

We now focus on the scaling of I/O, MPI, CALC, and LBST timings for each architecture. Figure 2 shows the relative amount of time spent in each of these activities.

On Seaborg, the relative amount of time spent in I/O decreases as the problem size and concurrency increase. However, the I/O time actually increases more than threefold as P grows from 16 to 1024. This shows that while there is contention for the I/O resource, it is not sufficient to impact code scalability significantly. The relative amounts of time spent communicating (MPI) and computing (CALC) remain constant for P = 64, 256, and 1024. Since Seaborg is composed of 16-way SMPs, the MPI time for P = 16 is misleading because no data movement occurs over the switch. CALC is the predominant activity; this is understandable given the relatively slow (375 MHz) CPUs in this SP cluster.

Table 2. Overall MADbench performance

Platform	P	Time (s) dSdC	invD	W	TOTAL	% TPP TOTAL
Seaborg (Power3)	16	42.9	36.5	311.2	390.6	45.0
	64	44.5	60.1	608.8	713.4	49.0
	256	56.1	107.7	1209.9	1373.7	50.7
	1024	121.3	214.8	2466.7	2802.8	49.6
ES (SX-6 enhanced)	16	23.8	43.8	63.3	130.9	25.2
	64	28.9	48.9	98.9	176.7	37.1
	256	29.2	58.6	173.9	261.7	49.9
	1024	31.8	94.5	321.4	447.7	58.3
Phoenix (X1)	16	3.1	9.2	45.5	57.8	35.6
	64	51.8	106.0	86.1	243.9	16.8
	256	1029.3	379.0	421.4	1829.7	4.5
Columbia (Altix)	16	58.2	7.2	163.2	228.6	19.2
	64	117.2	14.1	306.6	437.9	19.9
	256	483.4	23.8	409.4	916.6	19.0

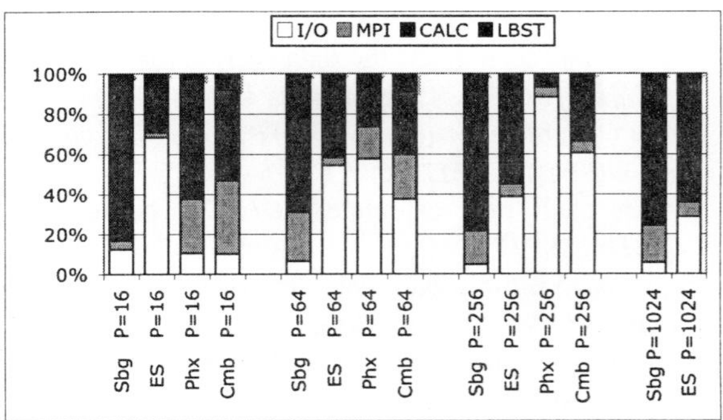

Figure 2. Relative timings for MADbench

On the ES, the I/O timings do not increase appreciably with concurrency. The filesystems on the ES are semi-local RAID arrays attached to each 128 CPUs. Since the I/O resources scale with concurrency, the performance trend makes sense. As with Seaborg, the relative amount of time spent in I/O decreases as the problem is scaled up. This however comes at the cost of not having a parallel filesystem. In calculations where external data must be read in, the staging time of datasets to the different filesystems could become a significant bottleneck. The overall trends in MPI and CALC are smooth functions of concurrency. The amount of MPI time increases dramatically (10x) between 16 and 1024 tasks, but represents only a small fraction of total time. CALC increases by a factor of 6x over the same range but doubles its contribution to the overall runtime.

On Phoenix, the trends seen in CALC, MPI, and I/O are smooth functions of concurrency. For this X1 architecture, the scaling of I/O becomes the predominant bottleneck at about P = 64. It is unclear to the authors what is the expected level of I/O parallelism for this machine. From our measurements, it appears that a scaling threshold in I/O has been crossed or that the manner in which MADbench performs I/O interferes with the filesystem. The primary contribution to the I/O time was from writing and synchronizing at the barrier following the writes. This is consistent with the presence of a limit to the number of simultaneous parallel writes and thus a serialization in I/O for large problem sizes.

Unlike the other platforms, the trends are not as smooth on Columbia. For some runs, we observe the MPI time to decrease with increasing problem size. This is clearly unexpected and the variation in these timings is under investigation. For instance, although all calculations were performed on the same 512-way SMP, it is unclear whether the placement of tasks was done in a consistent fashion by the OS. However, results demonstrate that I/O is the predominant component of runtime at and above 256-way runs. As with Phoenix, most of the I/O time is spent in writing data within dSdC. We note that a significant (3.6x) increase in I/O occurs between P = 16 and 64. Since there are 35 independent links to the filesystem in use, it is possible that the number of channels to disk had become saturated.

5.2 Performance of Individual Functions

The detailed performance of MADbench is better understood by separately examining each of the functional components of the code.

dSdC Table 3 presents the timing breakdowns for dSdC. Results show that for P = 64, the ES achieves the highest raw performance, approximately 1.5x, 1.8x, and 4x faster than Seaborg, Phoenix, and Columbia, respectively. Due to the weak scaling nature of the problem, CALC remains roughly constant as concurrency increases, with Phoenix showing the fastest values; however, ES attains the best CALC TPP (19.0%) followed by Phoenix (16.5%), Seaborg (6.7%) and Columbia (2.7%). The original dSdC implementation relied on fine-grained recursive computations that prevented effective vectorization. A customized version was therefore developed for the ES and X1 so that at each recursion a large batch of angular separations is computed in the inner loop, allowing high vector performance. This, coupled with their superior memory bandwidth characteristics lead to the significantly higher performance of the vector architectures over the superscalar machines.

In terms of dSdC's I/O behavior (dominated by data writing), all systems show significant performance degradation at the highest concurrencies — except for ES whose local filesystem is insensitive to the degree of parallelism. This is particularly true for Phoenix and Columbia where performance drops precipitously for 256 processors, resulting in I/O bandwidth of only 0.2 Mb/s/P and 0.4 Mb/s/P, respectively.

Table 3. Detailed timings for dSdC

Plat-		Time (s)				Mb/s/P	% TPP	
form	P	LBST	I/O	CALC	TOT	BW	TOT	CALC
Sbg	16	3.3	9.7	29.9	42.9	20.6	4.7	6.7
	64	4.1	11.1	29.3	44.5	18.0	4.5	6.8
	256	4.1	22.2	29.8	56.1	9.0	3.6	6.7
	1024	4.6	86.9	29.8	121.3	2.3	1.6	6.7
ES	16	0.1	21.7	2.0	23.8	9.2	1.6	19.2
	64	0.1	26.8	2.0	28.9	7.5	1.3	19.0
	256	0.1	27.1	2.0	29.2	7.4	1.3	18.9
	1024	0.7	29.1	2.0	31.8	6.9	1.2	18.5
Phx	16	0.1	1.6	1.4	3.1	124.2	7.6	16.6
	64	0.1	50.3	1.4	51.8	4.0	0.5	16.5
	256	0.1	1027.8	1.4	1029.3	0.2	0.0	16.3
Cmb	16	17.6	21.3	19.3	58.2	9.4	0.9	2.6
	64	18.4	80.4	18.4	117.2	2.5	0.4	2.7
	256	1.0	464.1	18.3	483.4	0.4	0.1	2.7

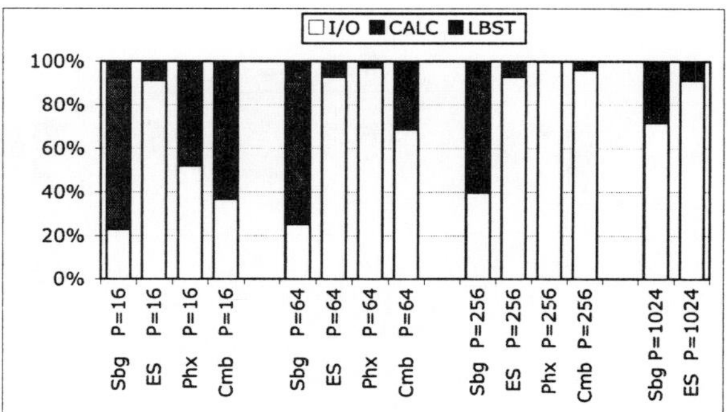

Figure 3. Relative timings for dSdC

Finally, the LBST metric (computational load imbalance) shows a non-trivial cost for the superscalar systems, accounting for approximately 15% of the total overhead on Seaborg and Columbia for the 64-processor case; the vector systems are mostly unaffected.

Figure 3 shows the relative performance breakdown of dSdC for each platform. These results clearly demonstrate that at high concurrencies, the relative I/O cost increasingly dominates the overall runtime. Note, however, that on the ES, the ratio between computation and I/O remains roughly constant due to the local filesystem.

invD The breakdown of invD runtime components are shown in Table 4. Since this function performs dense linear algebra operations, CALC is expected to grow linearly with increasing numbers of processors and pixels, while I/O requirements remain constant. Columbia shows the best overall performance in terms of total runtime and TPP, followed by ES, Seaborg, and Phoenix. For example, for P = 64, Columbia achieves a total TPP of 24.6% compared to only 1.5% on Phoenix. Since the numerical kernel of invD is computationally inten-

Table 4. Detailed timings for invD

Platform	P	Time (s) MPI	I/O	CALC	TOT	Mb/s/P BW	% TPP TOT	CALC	MPI+CALC
Sbg	16	4.3	21.0	11.0	36.5	9.5	19.0	63.0	45.2
	64	19.7	22.6	17.7	60.1	8.9	23.1	78.3	37.1
	256	50.5	23.7	33.3	107.7	8.5	25.8	83.4	33.1
	1024	109.4	40.4	64.7	214.8	5.0	25.9	85.8	31.9
ES	16	0.8	41.0	2.0	43.8	4.9	3.0	65.1	47.3
	64	1.8	43.3	3.8	48.9	4.6	5.3	68.0	46.4
	256	3.7	47.3	7.6	58.6	4.2	8.9	68.4	46.2
	1024	7.6	71.7	15.1	94.5	2.8	11.0	69.2	45.9
Phx	16	5.0	2.4	1.8	9.2	84.7	8.9	45.7	12.0
	64	13.8	89.1	3.1	106.0	2.2	1.5	51.7	9.6
	256	41.4	331.7	5.9	379.0	0.6	0.9	55.6	6.9
Cmb	16	3.4	1.1	2.6	7.2	180.2	24.0	67.6	28.9
	64	8.5	1.2	4.3	14.1	166.7	24.6	81.1	27.2
	256	13.3	1.0	9.4	23.8	210.5	29.1	73.8	30.6

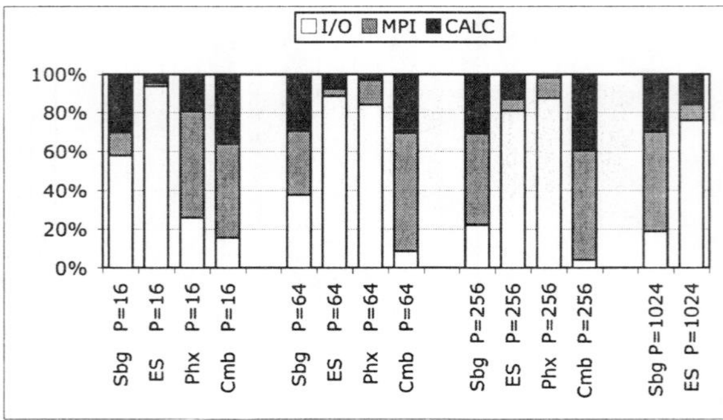

Figure 4. Relative timings for invD

sive, all architectures sustain a high CALC TPP: for P = 64, Columbia achieves 81.1% of peak, compared with 78.3%, 68.0%, and 51.7% on Seaborg, ES, and Phoenix, respectively. Thus, for this functional component of MADbench, the superscalar architectures outperform the vector systems in computational efficiency.

In terms of MPI costs, the high-performance single-stage switch of the ES shows the lowest runtime requirements: 4.7x, 7.6x, and 11x lower than the communication overhead of Columbia, Phoenix, and Seaborg, respectively. The read-dominated I/O overhead varies greatly among the architectures. Columbia shows the most impressive performance, approximately 20x, 36x, and 75x higher than Seaborg, ES, and Phoenix. Note that for P = 256, Phoenix's I/O bandwidth diminishes to only 0.5 Mb/s/P. The source of these large discrepancies is primarily due to memory caching that affects read/write rates differently on each platform.

Figure 4 presents the relative cost of invD components for each of the studied architectures. Observe that on the vector systems, I/O is responsible for a significant fraction of the total runtime, while the MPI overhead is relatively negligible. The opposite is true with the superscalar systems, which show relatively low I/O overheads compared with the MPI requirements. Finally, note that the computational requirements consume a roughly constant fraction of overhead for each architecture regardless of processor count.

W Table 5 presents the breakdown of timing components for W. Overall, the vector architectures achieve higher performance than the superscalar systems. For example, for P = 64, Phoenix is approximately 1.1x, 3.6x, and 7x faster than ES, Columbia, and Seaborg, respectively. However, ES achieves the highest overall TPP at 63.2% while Columbia shows the lowest at 27.2%. Like invD, W performs dense linear algebra calculations and therefore achieves high CALC TPP across all architectures. ES shows the most impressive results for the numerical computation, sustaining over 92% of peak, compared with 69% or less on the other platforms.

Both MPI and I/O shows similar performance characteristics to that of invD, since it is also comprised of dense algebra calculations. The ES once again achieves the lowest communication overhead, while the relatively old switch technology of Seaborg results in the highest MPI time. Columbia demonstrates impressive I/O (read dominated) characteristics, sustaining over 215 Mb/s/P for P = 64: 1.6x, 20x, and 28x faster than Phoenix, ES, and Seaborg, respectively. However, for P = 256, both Phoenix and Columbia show anomalously slow I/O behavior, achieving only 0.8 Mb/s/P and 2.2 Mb/s/P.

The relative breakdown of costs for W is presented in Figure 5. These results show that, due to the large computational requirements, the MPI and I/O overheads represent a small fraction of the total runtime — thereby allowing high sustained performance across all architec-

Table 5. Detailed timings for W

Platform	P	Time (s) MPI	I/O	CALC	TOT	Mb/s/P BW	% TPP TOT	CALC	MPI+CALC
Sbg	16	13.1	17.5	279.5	311.2	11.4	53.6	59.6	57.0
	64	79.3	18.2	509.2	608.8	11.0	54.8	65.5	56.6
	256	180.2	18.9	1008.3	1209.9	10.6	55.1	66.1	56.1
	1024	413.4	30.5	2019.5	2466.7	6.6	54.1	66.0	54.8
ES	16	2.7	26.6	33.9	63.3	7.5	49.4	92.1	85.4
	64	5.5	26.0	67.4	98.9	7.7	63.2	92.8	85.7
	256	12.3	27.2	134.4	173.9	7.4	71.9	93.0	85.2
	1024	25.3	27.5	268.5	321.4	7.3	77.8	93.1	85.1
Phx	16	10.8	2.0	31.2	45.5	100.5	42.9	62.6	46.5
	64	24.7	1.5	58.4	86.1	130.7	45.4	66.8	47.0
	256	49.2	257.0	113.7	421.4	0.8	18.5	68.7	48.0
Cmb	16	81.3	0.4	80.4	163.2	500.0	25.5	51.8	25.8
	64	155.2	0.9	149.1	306.6	215.1	27.2	55.9	27.4
	256	40.3	91.6	276.1	409.4	2.2	40.7	60.4	52.7

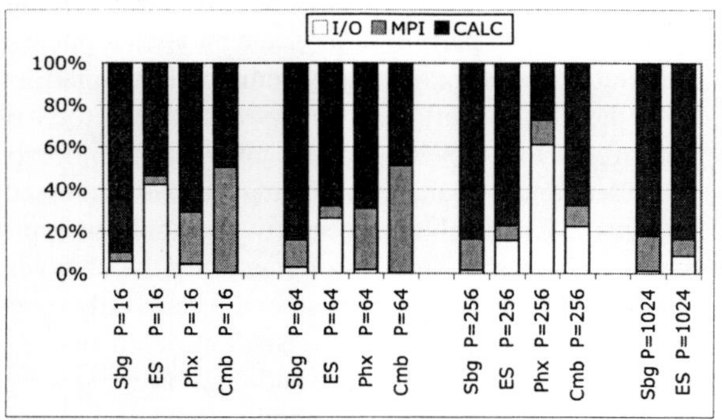

Figure 5. Relative timings for W

tures for this phase of the MADbench calculation.

5.3 Performance with Multi-Gang

In this section, we analyze the trade-offs inherent in the multi-gang strategy. As mentioned in Section 4, the function W can operate in two modes: either all of the processors work on each matrix-matrix multiplication in turn, or the processors divide into `NGANG` gangs and each gang independently performs `NBIN/NGANG` multiplications. Increasing the data density in this fashion should increase the efficiency of this step, but since the matrices are initially block-cyclically distributed over the whole processor grid, they must be redistributed over the gang processor grid before multiplication. The relative efficiency between single- and multi-gang approaches is therefore a trade-off between the benefit of the faster multiplication and the cost of the remapping.

Table 6 and Figure 6 show the absolute and relative timings for W using 16 gangs (with the remap times for the 1-gang runs shown in parentheses of Table 6). Compared to Figure 5 (single gang W performance), observe that the MPI time drops considerably on all architectures, as expected. In addition, it is clear that the CALC time changes by only a small amount. This is because the optimized `dgemm` algorithm performs well over a large range of matrix sizes.

The relative I/O cost shows no overall pattern, but depends on the architecture. Within W, the amount of I/O is identical in the single- and multi-gang cases; however, the interleaving of I/O and calculation is changed. For the 1-gang runs, one matrix is read and then multiplied; whereas for the 16-gang runs, all the matrices are read in and remapped, and only then are all 16 multiplies performed simultaneously. On Seaborg, there is a modest increase in I/O time when going to 16 gangs at all concurrencies. On the ES, I/O varies only slightly. Phoenix and Columbia show only a small change for P = 16 and 64, but large changes at P = 256. In the case of Phoenix,

Table 6. Detailed timings for W using 16 gangs (and remap cost for 1-gang runs)

Plat-form	P	Time (s) MPI	I/O	CALC	REMAP	RTOT	% TPP RTOT	CALC	MPI+CALC
Sbg	16	0.0	23.7	207.3	50.4 (9.6)	281.5	59.2	80.4	80.4
	64	13.8	20.8	509.3	74.4 (10.5)	618.3	53.9	65.4	63.7
	256	30.9	36.0	1016.9	193.6 (11.6)	1277.3	52.2	65.6	63.6
	1024	83.8	43.7	2005.1	246.1 (26.1)	2378.7	56.1	66.5	63.8
ES	16	0.0	23.7	31.4	19.6 (12.8)	74.6	41.9	99.7	99.7
	64	0.5	24.6	66.8	25.5 (15.6)	117.4	53.2	93.6	92.8
	256	1.9	24.7	133.3	35.1 (31.9)	195.0	64.1	93.8	92.4
	1024	7.1	24.8	266.4	61.6 (51.8)	359.8	69.5	93.9	91.4
Phx	16	0.0	0.9	23.3	7.9 (1.9)	32.0	61.0	83.9	83.9
	64	4.3	2.0	54.9	7.2 (3.2)	68.5	57.1	71.1	65.9
	256	17.1	303.5	110.9	73.3 (38.2)	504.7	15.5	70.4	61.0
Cmb	16	0.0	1.0	50.4	15.8 (1.0)	67.2	62.0	82.7	82.7
	64	12.0	1.6	161.4	24.6 (1.0)	199.6	41.7	51.6	48.1
	256	12.7	7.6	313.0	— (—)	—	—	53.2	51.2

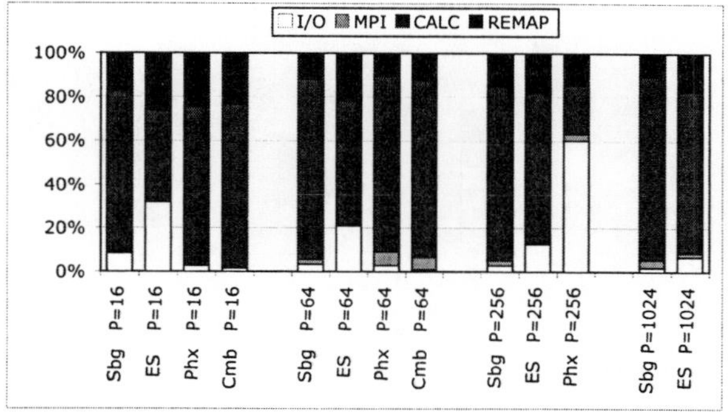

Figure 6. Relative timings for W (16 gangs)

the I/O seems generally very sensitive at P = 256; in the case of Columbia, the cause of the difference is unknown at this time.

The remapping is performed using the ScaLAPACK routine `pdgemr2d`. (The ScaLAPACK remapping function on Columbia failed for P = 256; SGI engineers are currently addressing this problem.) For simplicity, and to maintain a consistent mapping of the data in memory, the routine is called even in the single-gang case. However the current implementation of `pdgemr2d` takes no advantage of potential simplifications, but always assumes the worst case data-remapping scenario. It is thus extremely slow, as evidenced by the parenthetical 1-gang timings in Table 6, where the remappings are equivalent to each processor performing 17 completely local 12.5Mb memcopies — over 51 seconds on 1024 processors of the ES! Given this, we are in the process of developing a custom remapping function which will considerably reduce the overhead of this phase for both single- and multi-gang simulations.

6 Summary and Conclusions

In this paper, we presented MADbench, a synthetic benchmark that preserves the full computational complexity of the underlying scientific application. We tested the performance of its computation, communication, and I/O modules both individually and collectively on four of the world's most powerful supercomputers.

Figure 7 illustrates the percentage of theoretical peak performance obtained on each architecture, using 16 gangs in W. Each entry actually consists of four overlayed bars showing the percentage of peak achieved by considering (i) the total runtime, (ii) all but the remapping time, (iii) all but the remapping and I/O times, and (iv) all but the remapping, I/O, and MPI times. (Note that the 256-processor Columbia run is missing the white bar since the remapping function failed.)

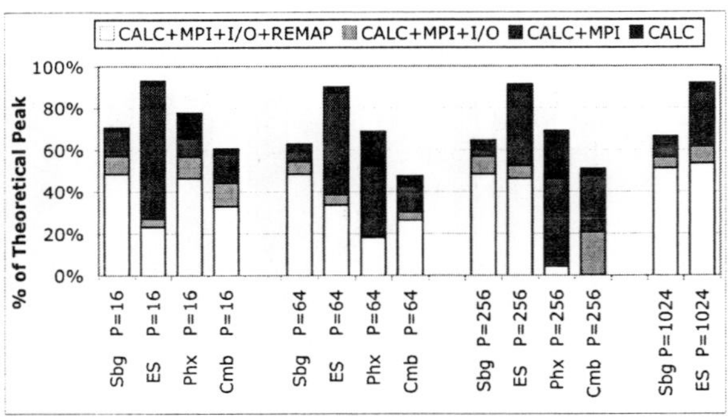

Figure 7. Percentage of peak performance for MADbench with 16-gang parallelism

A more perceptive way to interpret Figure 7 is that the height of the light grey bars reflects the relative cost of remapping, dark grey the relative cost of I/O, and black the relative cost of MPI. From this perspective, I/O is a minor issue for Seaborg, but a significant factor for the ES at all concurrencies, for Phoenix 64-way or more, and for Columbia 256-way. The I/O cost for increasing parallelism is broadly flat for Seaborg, significantly decreasing for the ES (reflecting its slow but perfectly scalable filesystem), but dramatically increasing for Phoenix and Columbia. It is also apparent that MPI constitutes a small overhead for all but Phoenix where it is significant and increases with concurrency.

We also introduced a new performance profiling tool, called IPM, and showed that it can be used successfully on a wide variety of computational platforms to extract useful performance data. In particular, we were able to identify the ScaLAPACK function `pdgemr2d` as a bottleneck in our algorithm.

A more general conclusion of this work is that greater clarity in the application context and overall specificity of performance timings greatly benefit understanding of how the distinct parts of large-scale parallel applications interact with the major subsystems of HEC platforms. It is therefore insufficient to report only the total runtime for a full-blown scientific application and expect to understand its parallel performance. As witnessed in Figures 2-7, the achieved performance will not approximate that seen in simple computational kernels which model only the compute phase and often vastly overestimate sustained performance. Such in-depth analysis is critical in first understanding and then bridging the gap between theoretical and sustained parallel performance.

Acknowledgments

The authors thank the ESC for providing access to the ES, and ORNL for access to the X1. The authors are grateful to Yoshinori Tsuda, David Parks, and Michael Wehner for collecting much of the latest ES data. All authors from LBNL were supported by the Office of Advanced Scientific Computing Research in the DOE Office of Science under contract DE-AC03-76SF00098.

References

[1] J. Borrill. MADCAP: The Microwave Anisotropy Dataset Computational Analysis Package. In *5th European SGI/Cray MPP Wkshp.*, 1999.

[2] T. Dunigan Jr., M. Fahey, J. White III, and P. Worley. Early evaluation of the Cray X1. In *SC2003*, 2003.

[3] K. Nakajima. Three-level hybrid vs. flat MPI on the Earth Simulator: Parallel iterative solvers for finite-element method. In *6th IMACS Intl. Symp. on Iterative Methods in Scientific Computing*, 2003.

[4] L. Oliker, R. Biswas, J. Borrill, A. Canning, J. Carter, M.J. Djomehri, H. Shan, and D. Skinner. A performance evaluation of the Cray X1 for scientific applications. In *6th Intl. Mtg. on High Performance Computing for Computational Science*, pages 219–232, 2004.

[5] L. Oliker, A. Canning, J. Carter, J. Shalf, D. Skinner, S. Ethier, R. Biswas, M.J. Djomehri, and R. V. der Wijngaart. Performance evaluation of the SX-6 vector architecture for scientific computations. *Concurrency and Computation; Practice and Experience*, 17(1):69–93, 2005.

[6] ORNL Cray X1 Evaluation. http://www.csm.ornl/~dunigan/cray.

[7] R. Rabenseifner. Recent advances in Parallel Virtual Machine and Message Passing Interface. In *6th European PVM/MPI Users' Group Mtg.*, volume LNCS 1697, pages 35–42, 1999.

[8] Top500 Supercomputer Sites. http://www.top500.org.

[9] H. Uehara, M. Tamura, and M. Yokokawa. MPI performance measurement on the Earth Simulator. Technical Report 15, NEC R&D, 2003.

[10] J. Vetter and A. Yoo. An empirical performance evaluation of scalable scientific applications. In *SC2002*, 2002.

First Evaluation of Parallel Methods of Automatic Global Image Registration Based on Wavelets

Haifang ZHOU Xuejun YANG
Hengzhu LIU
School of Computer
National University of Defense Technology
Changsha, Hunan, 410073, China
Email: haifang_zhou@sina.com

Yu TANG
School of Electronic Technology
National University of Defense Technology
Changsha, Hunan, 410073, China
Email: yutang18@sina.com

Abstract

With the increasing importance of multiple multiplatform remote sensing missions, fast and automatic integration of digital data from disparate sources has become critical to the success of these endeavors. Firstly, an overview of development of automatic and parallel global image registration is given. And then, based on the analyses of existing three parallel methods of wavelet-based global registration, a new parallel strategy is proposed. Moreover, towards the quantitative evaluation, first results of the intercomparision of four parallel global registration algorithms are presented in theory and in experiments.

1. Introduction

Image registration is defined as the process that determines the most accurate match between two or more images acquired at the same or at different times by different or identical sensors. Digital image registration is very important in many applications of image processing, such as medical imagery, robotics, visual inspection, and remotely sensed data processing [1][2]. Our work mostly faces to remote sensing applications, for which parallel automated image georegistration has become a highly desirable technique.

New remote sensing systems will generate enormous amounts of data representing multiple observations of the same features at different times or/and by different sensors. Also, with the new trend of smaller missions, these sensors will be spread over multiple platforms. The Earth Observing System (EOS), for example, daily produces massive amounts of data approaching 1 terabyte per day [3]. As a result, on the one hand, automatic registration methods will become indispensable for such tasks as data fusion, navigation, achieving super-resolution or optimizing communications rates between spacecraft and ground systems. On the other hand, due to the computational intensive requirement of the registration process and the large amount of image data to be registered, parallel method is needed to sustain such demands. Automatic parallel image registration using high-performance parallel computers does not only provide fast and scalable execution, but also allows larger problems to be solved by utilizing aggregated memory capacity.

However, our investigations have shown that there are only limited and inconclusive studies of parallel image registration. One important reason is the most common registration approach is not suitable for the automatic processing of a large number of data, for it needs repetitively interactive operation to extract accurate control points (CPs) from both images to compute the final mapping function. There are studies of automatic CPs-based registration methods, but missing or spurious CPs make these methods more difficult and less reliable, so unpractical. Global registration[4], however, is an approach that dose not rely on point-to-point matching of CPs, whose mapping function is computed globally over the images, therefore easy to be automatically processed. One of the disadvantages of global registration is it is computationally expensive, but fortunately parallel solutions just can solve this problem. In this paper, we will focus on parallel methods for global registration, with an emphasis on the computational speed.

0190-3918/05 $20.00 © 2005 IEEE

2. Related works

2.1. Related research on global registration

Among the global methods [5-13], the mapping function is either found by correlation or by optimization, in the spatial or in the frequency domain. When in the spatial domain, correlation or optimization is performed either in the original data or on edge gradient data. Another method proposed in [5] involves the computation of a "Hough accumulator" for all the transformations matching edge segments or vectors linking feature points.

Moreover, some recent research [2][4][10][14-16] has focused on the use of wavelets for global image registration. The wavelet transform generates a multi-resolution representation of image data. The choice of using wavelets is justified by the following reasons: 1) Using such multi-resolution data, the size of the search data can be reduced, and higher accuracies with higher speeds are achieved than a full search at full resolution; 2) Wavelet-based multi-resolution preserves most of the important features of the original data even at a low resolution, but also eliminates weak features in higher resolution; 3) it can be implemented very easily on a parallel computer. With the emphasis on the computational speed and the ability of the developed techniques to handle multi-sensor data, we are brought to the utilization of multi-resolution wavelet transforms in our work.

2.2. Related research on parallel registration

Due to the computationally expensive requirement of image registration some researchers have looked into applying parallel processing to help speed up the registration process. A parallel image registration based on a global GA model was proposed in [17] using a 5-processor transputer-based computer. However, only one medical image data was used in their experiment. Based on the multi-resolution wavelet (MRW) technique, LeMoigne presented a fine-grain parallel algorithm for the MasPar SIMD (Single Program Multiple Data) architecture [18]. Substantial computational savings have been reported. Unfortunately, the fine-grain MRW is not applicable to modern MIMD architectures. Based on the GA-based image registration presented in [19], a hardware-based parallel image registration algorithm was proposed by Turton [20] for computer vision. The algorithm was fine grain and was implemented in the hardware. In more recent work, [4], [21] and [22] presented coarse-grain parallel algorithm for wavelet-based global registration, and the method in [22] was also combined with GA model.

The above review of parallel image registration indicates that the developed work was quite limited in scope; there is little previous research work on coarse-grain parallel algorithms for general-purpose high-performance computers. The rest of this paper provides an in-depth survey and dedicated design of applicable parallel methods for wavelet-based global registration and evaluates their performances on popular class of parallel computer systems using existing remote sensing data. Towards quantitative evaluation, existing parallel algorithms for wavelet-based global image registration are described firstly; and then, a new parallel strategy is proposed followed by complexity analyses and comparison of all these parallel methods; in the end, first results of their evaluation are presented for different datasets.

3. Overview of wavelet-based global image registration

We assume that any *input image* is being registered relative to a known *reference image*. According to [1], image registration can be viewed as the combination of four components: 1) Feature space, the set of characteristics used to perform the matching and which are extracted from reference and input data; 2) Search space, the class of potential transformations that establish the correspondence between input image and reference image; 3) Search strategy, which is used to choose which transformations have to be computed and evaluated; 4) Similarity metric, which evaluates the match between input image and transformed reference image for a given transformation chosen in the search space.

As to the wavelet-based global image registration, wavelet coefficients form the feature space; and only rigid transformations are considered as search space in most application; the search strategy follows the multi-resolution approach provided by the wavelet decomposition. In our experiments, the search space is composed of 2-D rotations and translations; and cross correlation measure is used as similarity metric. So far, the process of global image registration based on wavelets can be described as following: after performing the wavelet decomposition of both reference and input images, at the each level of decomposition, the wavelet-compressed version of reference image is transformed using different combinations of rotation and translations; for each transformation cross correlation between the input image and the transformed reference image is computed; the transformation corresponding to the maximum of cross correlation is the best transformation at current level, and becoming the center of a next level search scope that is reduced and refined. The iterative search starts from the smallest wavelet image towards the larger size images, and the final registration transformation is found at the full resolution image. See [4] for more details on this serial process.

4. Existing parallel algorithms and a new parallel strategy

4.1. Special concepts and mathematical notations

For clear and consistent presentation, some concepts and notations are given in this section. 1) *M*: the image size, short for $M \times M$. 2) *N*: the number of processors/nodes in a parallel computer system, where $N \geq 1$. 3) *Mapping parameter*: the parameter that describes one type of transformation. E.g., the mapping parameter of rotation is $\theta \in [\theta_1, \theta_2]$. 4) *Solution*: the mapping function that is used to match input and reference images, which is denoted by $(p_1, p_2, \ldots, p_k)$, where $p_i (i = 1, \ldots, k)$ is different *mapping parameter*, and $p_i \in \Omega_i$ (Ω_i is the range of p_i). i.e., a solution is composed of one or more mapping parameters. 5) *S*: search space composed of all solutions, and $S = \{(p_1, p_2, \ldots, p_k) \mid p_1 \in \Omega_1, p_2 \in \Omega_2, \ldots, p_k \in \Omega_k\}$. 6) *R*: the number of solutions in search space, i.e. $|S| = R$.

4.2. Existing parallel algorithms

From the description of section 3, wavelet-based global registration searches best solution in search space of each level of decomposition. Based on the fact that each correlation computing for possible solutions is independent, the existing parallel algorithms [4][21][22] can be formulated based on the relationship between the number of solutions (*R*) and how they are distributed over a number of processors (*N*). There are three types of parallel method previously: 1) Parameter-Parallel (PP); 2) Image-Parallel (IP); 3) Hybrid-Parallel (HP).

4.2.1. Parameter-Parallel (PP). The basic idea of PP is "copying images but distributing parameters". At the beginning of PP, every node in parallel system owns the whole reference image and input image. In the case that $R \geq N$, let $q = \lfloor R/N \rfloor$ and $r = R\%N$, where % denotes that *R* leaves *r* modulo *N*. At each level of decomposition, if $r = 0$, each processor is allocated *q* correlations to compute (mapping parameter is different for every correlation). In this case, the load is divided perfectly. If $r \neq 0$, the remainder correlations are distributed only to the first *r* processors. In this case, load imbalance is introduced in the parallel execution, as only *r* processors will be busy during the last parallel correlation computation. At the end of each level, a global reduction step is needed to find the best registration solution, also a broadcast operation to scatter the result globally for next level of search. It is easy to find out that PP is unworkable in the case that $R < N$.

4.2.2. Image-Parallel (IP). The basic idea of IP is "copying parameters but distributing images". Contrary to PP, in IP, input and reference images are divided into *N* row sub-images respectively, and each sub-image contains M^2/N pixels. In this case, each processor becomes only concerned with correlation computations that belong to its row sub-image for all *R* solutions. Obviously, the load is balanced. However, extra communication and computation is introduced into global reduction step at each level of decomposition for integrating the medium correlation data over the same image, so IP is not suitable for the case that the amount of solutions (*R*) is large.

4.2.3. Hybrid-Parallel (HP). To cure the disadvantages of PP and IP mode, a hybrid method, HP is proposed naturally. There are three circumstances for HP: 1) If $R < N$, the algorithm performs in IP mode; 2) If $R \geq N$ ($q = \lfloor R/N \rfloor$, $r = R\%N$) and $r = 0$, the algorithm performs in PP mode; 3) If $R \geq N$ but $r \neq 0$, the algorithm first performs in PP mode where *q* solutions are assigned to each processor, and then the remainder *r* correlations are computed using IP mode, i.e. each processor need processing *q* correlations for whole images and *r* correlations for the local sub-images ($1/N$ of original image). To note that, at the highest level of decomposition, the wavelet-decomposed image is small (usually using 4 or more levels wavelet-decomposed images). The application of the HP at this level may not make significant improvement because *q* could be large enough to make the parallel execution time of the remaining correlations relatively negligible. However, as successive refinements start in the intermediate levels, the balancing of the remainder becomes of great important.

In our experiments, HP excels PP and IP in the most cases, but we also find that the performance of HP sometime decreases with the increasing of N. This often happens when $r \neq 0$ and M is not very large. After in-depth analysis, the reason is found out that the overhead introduced by IP for r remaining correlations counteracts the benefit from load balance. That is to say, the IP stage in HP mode is efficient only when the computation to communication ratio is high enough. To achieve this goal, we should make sub-image dealt with by each processor as large as possible but amount of correlations as small as possible during the IP stage. Based on above discussion, a new parallel mode or strategy, GP is proposed for better results.

4.3. Group-Parallel (GP): a new parallel strategy

There are also three circumstances in GP mode, and the first two cases are same as HP. In the third case, for the remainder r correlations, N processors are divided into r groups. Let g denotes the number of processors in groups, where $g = \lfloor N/r \rfloor + 1$ for the first $N\%r$ processors and $g = \lfloor N/r \rfloor$ for the rest. Every group is responsible for one of the r correlations. IP mode is performed in group, while PP mode is performed among the groups. Therefore, in GP mode, each processor needs processing q correlations for whole images and only one correlation for the local sub-images ($1/g$ of original image). Compared with HP, the sub-images distributed to each processor is enlarged but allocated correlations are decreased ($q+1$ per processor, not $q+r$). Two reduction steps are needed, with one for integrating the medium data from processors in each local group, and another for global reduction to find best registration.

It is reasonable to predict that GP is the best strategy for its lower overhead, load balance and adaptability. The next two sections give the intercomparison of these four parallel methods from theory and experiments. However, the fact is that GP is conditionally best one, but it synthetically excels other methods by overall evaluations.

5. Complexity analyses

No previous work did quantitative evaluation for existing parallel methods of global registration. Here we give the complexity analysis of above four parallel strategies firstly. We use the LogGP as a computation model for analyzing these parallel algorithms on distributed memory machines. The complexity of algorithm will be evaluated in terms of two measures: the computation time T_{comp} and the communication time T_{comm} . For communication time, let t_α denotes startup time for a message, and t_β stands for transfer time per word. In addition, let n denote levels of wavelet decomposition, and a solution includes T mapping parameters denoted by $(p_1, p_2, \ldots, p_T)$. There are R solutions in the search space at each level of decomposition. Original image size is M and the parallel system has N processors/nodes.

5.1. PP

Because computing the cross correlation of two images needs gray values of all pixels in input and reference image, the complexity for one solution is linear with amount of pixels, e.g., $O(M^2)$ at the full resolution image level. Considering the case that $R\%N \neq 0$ ($q \cdot N + r = R$), at the ith ($i = 0, \ldots, n$) level of wavelet decomposition, the computational complexity of the first r processors is $O((q+1) \cdot M^2/4^i)$, and that of the rest is $O(q \cdot M^2/4^i)$. Consequently, the computation cost of the ith level in PP mode is:

$$T^i_{comp} = O((q+1) \cdot M^2/4^i) = \frac{1}{4^i} O(\frac{R \cdot M^2}{N} + \frac{(N-r) \cdot M^2}{N}) \quad (1)$$

In PP mode, there are two communication steps, one of which is reduction and another is broadcast. The transferred data contain T mapping parameters and one correlation. Therefore, the communicational complexity of the ith level is: $T^i_{comm} = O(2t_\alpha + 2t_\beta \cdot (T+1) \cdot N)$. In addition, there are some global operations for finding maximum of correlations, which is linear with N and denoted by $T^i_g = O(N)$.

In sum, the overall parallel executing time T_N in PP mode is: (for the worst case that $R\%N \neq 0$)

$$T_N = T_{comp} + T_{comm} + T_g = \sum_{i=0}^{n} T^i_{comp} + \sum_{i=0}^{n} T^i_{comm} + \sum_{i=0}^{n} T^i_g = \sum_{i=0}^{n} \frac{1}{4^i} O(\frac{R \cdot M^2}{N} + \frac{(N-r) \cdot M^2}{N}) + O(2(n+1) \cdot (t_\alpha + t_\beta(T+1)N)) + O((n+1) \cdot N) \quad (2)$$

There is $\sum_{i=0}^{n}\frac{1}{4^i}<\frac{4}{3}$, so formula (2) can be simplified as following:

$$T_N = O(\frac{R\cdot M^2}{N} + n\cdot t_\alpha + n\cdot t_\beta \cdot T\cdot N + n\cdot N + \frac{(N-r)\cdot M^2}{N}) \quad (3)$$

5.2. IP

In IP mode, each processor should deal with all R solutions but only be faced with two sub-images whose size is $1/N$ of original images or wavelet-compressed images at each level. Therefore, the computational complexity of the ith $(i=0,\ldots,n)$ level in IP mode is:

$$T_{comp}^{i} = \frac{1}{4^i}O(R\cdot(\left\lfloor\frac{M^2}{N}\right\rfloor+1)) = \frac{1}{4^i}O(\frac{R\cdot M^2}{N}+\frac{(N-M^2\%N)\cdot R}{N}) \quad (4)$$

And also there are two communication steps same as PP, but in reduction step extra R medium data of correlations over sub-images must be packed into messages for global computation of the final correlations over whole images. So the communication cost of the ith level is: $T_{comm}^{i} = O(2t_\alpha + t_\beta\cdot(T+R)\cdot N)$. Accordingly, the computational complexity of global operations is increased for processing the R medium data, then $T_g^i = O(R\cdot N)$. In sum, the overall parallel executing time T_N in IP mode is:

$$\begin{aligned} T_N &= \sum_{i=0}^{n}\frac{1}{4^i}O(\frac{R\cdot M^2}{N}+\frac{(N-M^2\%N)\cdot R}{N}) \\ &\quad + O(2n\cdot t_\alpha + n\cdot t_\beta\cdot(R+T)\cdot N) + O(n\cdot R\cdot N) \\ &= O(\frac{R\cdot M^2}{N} + n\cdot t_\alpha + n\cdot t_\beta\cdot T\cdot N + n\cdot t_\beta\cdot R\cdot N \\ &\quad + n\cdot R\cdot N + \frac{(N-M^2\%N)\cdot R}{N}) \end{aligned} \quad (5)$$

Comparing (4)(5) with (1)(3), although computation complexity of IP is lower than PP, its communication overhead and global computation cost is much more than PP, so still can not benefit from load balance. The advantage of IP is it is workable in any cases and needs less memory.

5.3. HP

HP is combination of PP and IP, so it is easy to deduce the complexity formula of HP refer to above presentation. The computational complexity of the ith $(i=0,\ldots,n)$ level in HP mode is:

$$T_{comp}^{i} = \frac{1}{4^i}O(\frac{R\cdot M^2}{N}+\frac{(N-M^2\%N)\cdot r}{N}) \quad (6)$$

The communication cost of the ith level is: $T_{comm}^{i} = O(2t_\alpha + t_\beta\cdot(T+r)\cdot N)$, and the computational complexity of global operations is $T_g^i = O(N\cdot r)$. The overall parallel executing time T_N in HP mode is:

$$\begin{aligned} T_N &= \sum_{i=0}^{n}\frac{1}{4^i}O(\frac{R\cdot M^2}{N}+\frac{(N-M^2\%N)\cdot r}{N}) \\ &\quad + O(2n\cdot t_\alpha + n\cdot t_\beta\cdot(r+T)\cdot N) + O(n\cdot r\cdot N) \\ &= O(\frac{R\cdot M^2}{N} + n\cdot t_\alpha + n\cdot t_\beta\cdot T\cdot N + n\cdot t_\beta\cdot r\cdot N \\ &\quad + n\cdot r\cdot N + \frac{(N-M^2\%N)\cdot r}{N}) \end{aligned} \quad (7)$$

Comparing (7) with (3), HP can benefit from load balance and achieve better performance as long as M is large enough and network performance is not very low.

5.4. GP

GP is different from HP in the IP stage, where original images are divided into g ($g=\lfloor N/r\rfloor$) parts not N parts and each processor only deals with one correlation. Therefore, the complexity of the IP stage in GP mode is $\frac{1}{4^i}O(\frac{M^2}{g})=\frac{1}{4^i}O(\frac{M^2}{\lfloor N/r\rfloor})$. There are two cases when discussing the computational complexity of the ith $(i=0,\ldots,n)$ level in GP mode:

1)If $N\%r=0$, then $T_{comp}^{i} = \frac{1}{4^i}O(\frac{R\cdot M^2}{N})$.

2) If $N\%r\neq 0$, then $\frac{1}{4^i}O(\frac{M^2}{\lfloor N/r\rfloor})<\frac{1}{4^i}O(\frac{r\cdot M^2}{N-r})$.

There is $\frac{1}{4^i}O(\frac{r\cdot M^2}{N-r})=\frac{1}{4^i}O(\frac{r\cdot M^2}{N}+\frac{r^2\cdot M^2}{N\cdot(N-r)})$, so

$$T_{comp}^{i} < \frac{1}{4^i}O(\frac{R\cdot M^2}{N}+\frac{r^2\cdot M^2}{N\cdot(N-r)}) \quad (8)$$

The process of communication is a little complicated, including two-step hierarchical reduction and a broadcast operation, the cost of which is $T_{comm}^{i} = O(3t_\alpha + t_\beta\cdot(T\cdot N+(N/r)\cdot r+T\cdot N)) < O((2T+1)\cdot N)$. In addition, the computational complexity of global operations is $T_g^i = O(N+r+1)\le O(2N)$. Considering the first case that $N\%r = 0$, the overall parallel executing time T_N in GP mode is:

$$T_N = \sum_{i=0}^{n} \frac{1}{4^i} O(\frac{R \cdot M^2}{N}) + O(3n \cdot t_\alpha + n \cdot t_\beta (2T+1) \cdot N + 2n \cdot N) \quad (9)$$
$$= O(\frac{R \cdot M^2}{N} + n \cdot t_\alpha + n \cdot t_\beta \cdot T \cdot N + n \cdot N)$$

Obviously, GP will get the best performance when $N\%r = 0$ compared with the other three parallel strategies. For the case of $N\%r \neq 0$, which method has the shortest executing time is determined by the combination of several factors such as *R*, *M*, *N* and network capability. These theoretical conclusions can direct us to choose the most suitable parallel mode in real applications.

6. Results of the evaluation

6.1. General comparison

Based on above theoretical analyses, the comprehensive intercomparison of these four parallel strategies for wavelet-based global image registration can be summarized in Table 1.

Table 1. Intercomparison of four parallel strategies (*n'*=*n*+1)

Strategy	PP	IP
Degree of Parallel	*R*	*N*
Load balance	Imbalance	Balance
Comm. times	$2 \cdot n'$	$2 \cdot n'$
Comm. amount	$O(n' \cdot T \cdot N)$	$O(n' \cdot R \cdot N)$
Global operations	$O(n' \cdot N)$	$O(n' \cdot R \cdot N)$
Memory requirement	$O(\frac{4}{3} M^2)$	$O(\frac{4M^2}{3N})$
Adaptability	Limited	Limited

Strategy	HP	GP
Degree of Parallel	*N*	*N*
Load balance	Balance	Negligible Imbalance
Comm. times	$2 \cdot n'$	$3 \cdot n'$
Comm. amount	$O(n' \cdot (T + r) \cdot N)$	$O(n' \cdot T \cdot (N + r))$
Global operations	$O(n' \cdot (N \cdot r + N + r))$	$O(n' \cdot (N + r + 1))$
Memory requirement	$O(\frac{4}{3} M^2)$	$O(\frac{4}{3} M^2)$
Adaptability	Good	Very Good

From Table 1, we can conclude that GP excels other methods by overall evaluations although it is conditionally the best one in complexity.

6.2. Experimental results

For comparison, we implement these parallel algorithms on two parallel computers, CL and YH. CL is a Cluster system with 16 nodes. Each node is equipped with Pentium4-2G CPU and 512MB local storage. All nodes are connected by the 100Mb/s Ethernet. YH is a massively parallel computer with MIMD architecture. YH has 32 processors with 1GB local storage for each processor. Speed of YH CPU is valued as 1.66 gigaflops/sec. Topology of network is fat tree, and point-to-point bandwidth is 1.2Gb/s. Various remotely sensed images with different size (*M*=256/512/1024/2048/3072) are used for testing.

Figure 1 shows the registration result of a pair of test images, in which Figure 1(c) is the output of the transformed input image matched with reference image by mapping function.

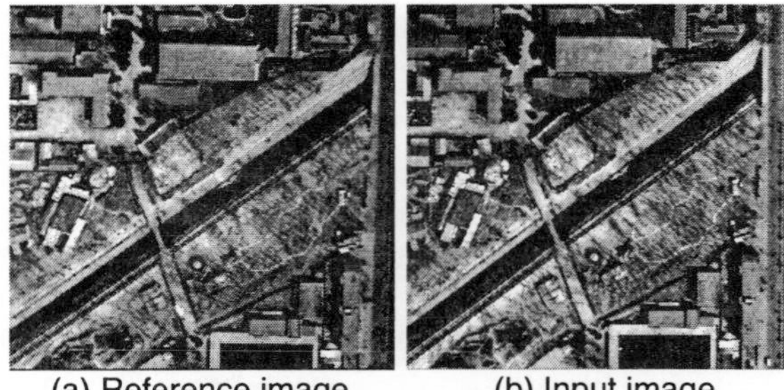

(a) Reference image (b) Input image

(c) Output image after registration

Figure 1. Registration result of test images

Figure 2 to Figure 3 gives the comparison of speedups achieved by four parallel algorithms with different datasets (image size *M* changes from 512 to 3072) on our parallel platforms, CL and YH.

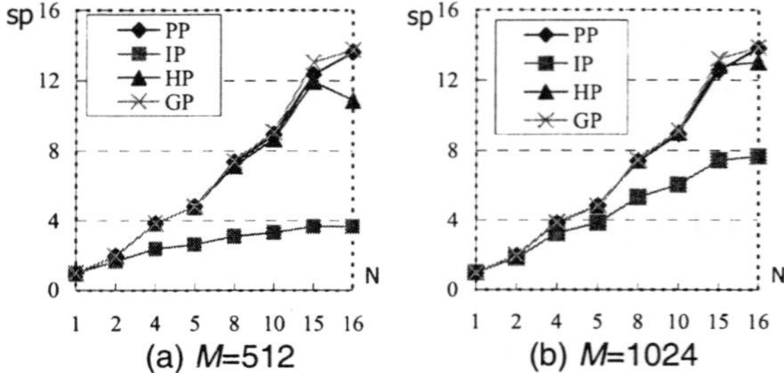

(a) *M*=512 (b) *M*=1024

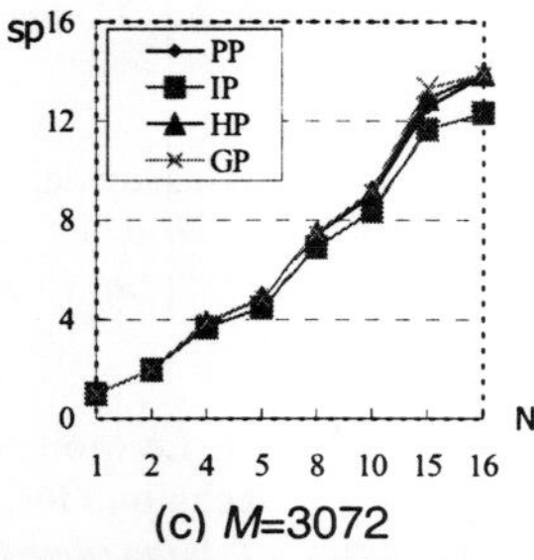

(c) M=3072

Figure 2. Speedups of four algorithms achieved on CL with different datasets

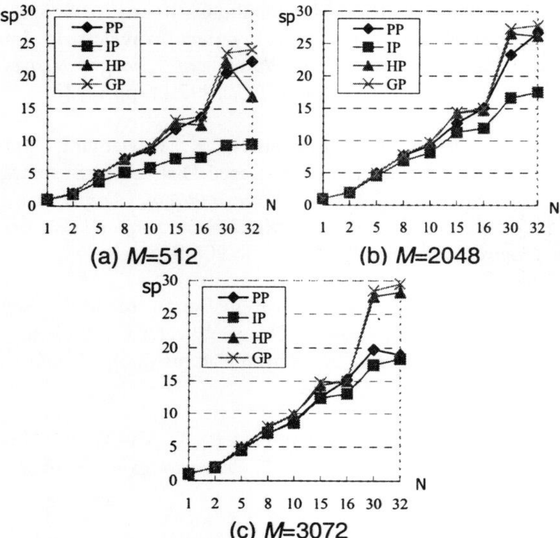

(a) M=512 (b) M=2048

(c) M=3072

Figure 3. Speedups of four algorithms achieved on YH with different datasets

From Figure 2 and Figure 3 we can do some comparisons as following: 1) the performance of all algorithms achieved on YH is better than that on CL. The main reason is that the network performance of YH is higher than CL. Because the communication overhead is a significant factor to affect performance of these algorithms, the speedup curves on YH can reflect the features of four algorithms more clearly. 2) The performance of IP is lowest, but with the increase of image size the speedup of IP goes up rapidly when the computation to communication ratio is high enough to get benefit from load balance. 3) The performance of PP, HP and GP approximates to each other, especially on CL. But when M reaches 3072 on YH, the speedup of PP is decreased when N is over 30 (Figure 3(c)). This justifies the above theoretical analyses that the imbalance of the remainder correlation computation can not be negligible when M is large and the network of system is more efficient. We also find that the performance of HP is even lower than PP with the increasing of N when M is not very large. It is because that the improvement of HP over PP through load balance is counteracted by introduced overhead at some cases. However, GP achieves better performance in most cases, which indicates that our optimization is effective.

7. Conclusion

We have given an overview of development of automatic global image registration. And since both the need for image registration and the amount of data are growing tremendously, the implementation of automatic image registration methods on high-performance computers needs to be investigated. Based on analyses of existing three parallel methods of wavelet-based global registration, a new parallel strategy is proposed. Then, first evaluations of these four types of parallel wavelet-based registration methods have been presented in theory and in experiments.

Future work will include the study of combination of global registration and CPs-based methods with emphasis on both speed and accuracy. Automatic registration of remotely sensed data is a very complex problem, and as stated in [4], we feel that only a future system that integrates multiple automated registration techniques will be able to address such a task for multiple types of remote sensing data.

Acknowledgment

The authors would like to acknowledge the support of Grid Project sponsored by China ministry of education under the grant No.CG2003-GA00103. The authors would also like to thank Dr. J. Le Moigne for sharing her knowledge and expertise.

References

[1] L. Brown, "A survey of image registration techniques", *ACM Computing Surveys*, 24 (4), 1992, pp.325–375.

[2] J. Le Moigne, W. Xia, T. El-Ghazawi, "Towards an Intercomparison of Automated Registration Algorithms for Multiple Source Remote Sensing Data", In the *Proceeding of the first image registration workshop, NASA/GSFC*, 1997.11.

[3] M. Kafatos, L. Bergman, R. Chinman, T. El-Ghazawi, S. Nittel, L. Olsen, and X. S. Wang, "Data exchanges and interoperability in distributed Earth science information systems". In *proceedings of 11th International Conference on Scientific and Statistical Database Management*, Cleveland, Ohio, USA, 1999.7.

[4] J. Le Moigne, W.J. Campbell, R.F. Cromp, "An automated image registration technique based on the correlation of wavelet features". *IEEE Transaction on Geoscience and Remote Sensing*, 40(8), 2002, pp.1849-1864.

[5] G. Stockman, S. Kopstein, and S. Bennett, "Matching images to models for registration and object detection via clustering", *IEEE Transaction on Pattern Analysis and Machine Intelligence*, PAMI-4(3), 1982, pp.229–241.

[6] M. Irani, S. Peleg, "Improving resolution by image registration", *Computer Vision, Graphics and Image Processing*, 53(3), 1991, pp.213–239.

[7] R.L. Allen, F.A. Kamangar, E.M. Stokely. "Laplacian and orthogonal wavelet pyramid decompositions in coarse-to-fine registration", *IEEE Transaction on Signal Processing*, 41(12): 1993, pp.3536–3541.

[8] J.-C. Olivo, J. Deubler, C. Boulin. "Automatic registration of images by a wavelet-based multiresolution approach", *in Proceeding of SPIE Wavelet Applications in Signal and Image Processing III*, San Diego, CA, 1995.7.

[9] R.C. Hardie, K.J. Barnard, E.E. Armstrong. "Joint MAP registration and high-resolution image estimation using a sequence of undersampled images", *IEEE Transaction on Image Processing*, 6(12), 1997, pp.1621–1633.

[10]P. Thévenaz, U.E. Ruttimann, M. Unser, "A pyramid approach to sub-pixel registration based on intensity". *IEEE Transaction on Image Processing*, 7(1), 1998, pp.27–41.

[11]Q.S. Chen, M. Defrise, F. Deconinck, "Symmetric phase-only matched filtering of Fourier–Mellin transforms for image registration and recognition". *IEEE Transaction on Pattern Analysis and Machine Intelligence*, 16(12), 1994, pp.1156–1168.

[12]H. Shekarforoush, M. Berthod, J. Zerubia, "Subpixel image registration by estimating the polyphase decomposition of the cross-power spectrum", *in Proceedings of Computer Vision Pattern Recognition*, 1996, pp.532–537.

[13]R.J. Althof, M.G. J Wind, J.T. Dobbins, "A rapid and automatic image registration algorithm with subpixel accuracy", *IEEE Transaction on Medical Imagine,* 16(6), 1997, pp.308–316.

[14]J. Pinzon, S. Ustin, C. Castaneda, J. Pierce, "Image Registration by Non-Linear Wavelet Compression and Singular Value Decomposition", *in Proceedings of IRW, NASA/GSFC,*1997.11, pp.1-6.

[15]S. Chettri, W. Campbell, J. Le Moigne, "A Scale Space Feature Based Registration Technique for Fusion of Satellite Imagery", *in Proceedings of ImageRegistration Workshop (IRW97), NASA/GSFC*, 1997.11, pp.29-34.

[16]L. Fonseca, B.S. Manjunath, C. Kenney, "Scope and Applications of Translation Invariant Wavelets to Image Registration", *in Proceedings of ImageRegistration Workshop (IRW97), NASA/GSFC,* 1997.11, pp.13-28.

[17]M. Ozkan, J.M. Fitzpatrick, K. Kawamura, "Image Registration for a Transputer-Based Distributed System", *In proceedings of the 2nd International Conference on Industrial & Engineering Applications of AI & Expert Systems* (*IEA/AIE-89*), 1989.6, pp.908-915.

[18]J. LeMoigne, "Parallel Registration of Multi Sensor Remotely Sensed Imagery Using Wavelet Coefficients", *In Proceedings 1994 SPIE Wavelet Applications Conference*, Orlando, 1994, pp.432-443.

[19]J.M. Fitzpatrick, J.J. Grefenstette, D. Van-Gucht, "Image registration by genetic search", *Proceedings of Southeastcon 84,* 1984, pp.460-464.

[20]B. Turton, T. Arslan, D. Horrocks, "A hardware architecture for a parallel genetic algorithm for image registration", *In Proceedings of IEEE Colloquium on Genetic Algorithms in Image Processing and Vision*, 1994.10, pp.111-116.

[21]T. El-Ghazawi, P. Chalermwat, "Wavelet-based image Registration on parallel computers", *In SuperComputing'97: High Performance Networking and Computing: Proceedings ACM/IEEE,* 1997.11.

[22]P Chalermwat, "High performance automatic image registration for remote sensing", [Ph.D. Thesis], George Mason University, Fairfax, Virginia, 1999.

Parallel Algorithm and Implementation for Realtime Dynamic Simulation of Power System

Wei Xue, Jiwu Shu, Yongwei Wu, and Weimin Zheng
Dept. of C.S., Tsinghua Univ., Beijing, 100084, P.R.China
{xuewei, shujw, wuyw, zwm-dcs}@tsinghua.edu.cn

Abstract

As power systems continue to develop, realtime simulation and on-line dynamic security analysis using parallel computing are becoming increasingly important. This paper presents a novel multilevel partition scheme for parallel computing based on power network regional characteristics and describes the design and implementation of a hierarchical Block Bordered Diagonal Form (BBDF) algorithm for power network computation. Some optimization schemes are also proposed to reduce the computing and communication time and to improve the scalability of the program. The simulation results of a large network having 10188 nodes, 13499 branches, 1072 generators and 3003 loads show that the proposed algorithms and schemes running on a cluster system with 12 CPUs can provide a 15 times faster speed than the single CPU one, to satisfy the realtime simulation requirements for large scale power grids.

1. Introduction

Power system dynamic simulation is a powerful tool in power system research. With the development of power system scale, the computation tasks are increasingly becoming heavier and more complex. Traditional sequential computation is inadequate for on-line dynamic security analysis and realtime simulation. Thus, the key to realizing the realtime dynamic simulation of large scale power systems is to find new simulation algorithms and parallel software with high performance computers.

Research on parallel algorithms and their application in dynamic simulation has become well developed in the last 15 years [1][2]. Kron proposed the domain decomposition method to accomplish large scale power system simulation, which was considered as the genesis of the research in this field [3]. This was an exciting idea and gave a new impulse to the research ardor in this field. Up to now, there have been many research topics related to parallel dynamic simulation algorithm and its implementation of power system [4]-[13]. The research has developed in two directions, spatial parallelism and time parallelism. Spatial parallel algorithms, including the partition method and parallel factoring algorithm, take a time-domain integration method and break each time step computation down into sub-tasks among processors. As a coarse granularity parallel algorithm, the partition method is simple to apply, and can achieve higher efficiency on distributed architecture, while the parallel factoring scheme is better on shared memory machines. In order to achieve better performance on more processors, solutions using the simultaneous multiple time steps such as the waveform relaxation method and the parallel-in-time Newton algorithm, have been introduced into parallel dynamic simulations. These time parallel algorithms enlarge the size of problems solved simultaneously and effectively improve the speed of simulations. However, it is difficult to achieve a large degree of parallelism while maintaining a high convergence rate. Another limiting factor hindering efficient parallelism is that more invalid computations may be brought into the simulation when random events happen in the computation's time window. Recently, the wide use of scalable cluster systems, which have high performance and low cost, has made parallel and distributed realtime dynamic simulation possible for large scale power systems. The research on cluster-based parallel algorithms for dynamic simulations has become a new hotspot in this field [4][11][12][13].

For cluster system, this paper presents a multilevel partition scheme based on power network regional characteristics. This partition scheme enhances the quality of the solutions and decreases the computation time of parallel dynamic simulation. This paper also proposes an improved spatial parallel algorithm including a hierarchical Block Bordered Diagonal Form power network algorithm, which uses message-passing and share-memory models simultaneously. At the same time some optimization schemes to reduce computation and communication time are also presented in this paper. The numerical results of two

0190-3918/05 $20.00 © 2005 IEEE

actual power networks show that the new algorithm on cluster system can run much faster than the realtime dynamic process, and simulations using this algorithm can meet the requirement of on-line dynamic simulation for future nationwide power grid in China.

2. Computing model for power system dynamic simulation

To accomplish the task of power system dynamic computation, a set of Differential Algebraic Equations must be solved.

$$\begin{gathered} \dot{\mathbf{X}} = f(\mathbf{X}, \mathbf{V}) = \mathbf{A}\mathbf{X} + \mathbf{B}u(\mathbf{X}, \mathbf{V}) \\ 0 = \mathbf{I} - Y(\mathbf{X}) * \mathbf{V} \end{gathered} \quad (1)$$

In (1), the nonlinear differential equations describe the dynamic characteristics of the power devices and the second nonlinear equations present the restriction of the power network, where **X** is the state vector of individual dynamic devices; **I** is the vector of current injected from the devices into the network; **V** is the node voltage vector; Y(**X**) is the complex sparse matrix, which is not constant with time; and u is the function of **X** and **V**.

The most common used sequential algorithm for dynamic simulation is the interlaced alternating implicit approach (IAI algorithm). The IAI algorithm uses a trapezoidal rule as its integration method, and solves differential equations and algebraic equations alternately and iteratively, which not only maintains the advantages of the implicit integration approach, but also has modeling and computing flexibility.

At present, the time consumed for dynamic simulation increases super-linearly as the power system's size increases. The performance of sequential dynamic simulation is not adequate for realtime simulation of large scale power grids. Its limitations will be increasingly serious as the nationwide power grid continues to develop. Therefore, it is very important to study practical parallel algorithms and software.

3. Parallel algorithm for dynamic simulation

As well known, successful parallel algorithm must accord with the characteristics of parallel system. This brings more difficulties in the design and implementation of parallel algorithm. Because cluster system has higher communication cost, the coarse granularity IAI algorithm proposed in [6][9] is regarded as the most effective one of known parallel algorithms implemented on cluster system. In this paper, the complete solution to parallel dynamic simulation is studied. In which, an improved parallel algorithm based on IAI algorithm is proposed. This algorithm makes contribution to the bottleneck of the partition scheme, performs more optimizations in implementation on cluster system and get higher performance than that in [6][9]. Meanwhile, a new task scheduling scheme is presented to leverage the conflict between load balancing and communication reduction, and to insure the validity of parallel computing at the same time.

3.1. Novel multilevel partition scheme for dynamic computation

The strategy for dispatching computation tasks to processors in the parallel algorithm of dynamic simulation focuses on how to separate the power network and devices into several sub-areas. To solve this problem, the following principles should be considered simultaneously:

1. Minimization of the connections between different sub-areas.
2. Maintaining an equal computational load for every sub-area.

Since power device is related to only one of the network nodes and its computation is independent with each other, the most difficult part of task scheduling is the power network decomposition.

On the one hand, power system is a large scale network with connections related to geographical positions. The problem of network decomposition can be changed into the graph partition problem, which is well developed in HPC field [14]. However, if graph partition algorithm is used simply, more communication will be introduced into the parallel simulation [15]. Meanwhile, more time will be consumed in the partition phase. On the other hand, because power system develops with the regional network connection, the connections in regional network are much tighter than those between regions. So partition based on this regional characteristic of power network can reduce the communication cost in parallel simulation, while it maybe introduces more load imbalance [15].

In this paper, to integrate the advantages of graph partition algorithm and the partition method based on power network regional characteristic, a multilevel network partition scheme is presented. There are three phases in this new scheme: the coarsing phase, the multi-level partitioning phase and the refining phase.

During the coarsing phase, aggregating the nodes in the same province or region successively decreases the size of the power network graph. The partition problem of power network is formulated into a weighted graph partition problem. In which, the weights of vertex and edge represent the computation load of the sub-network in the vertex and the amount of communication between sub-networks respectively. According to network coasing, the latter partition algorithm can identify the weak connections in power network easily and effectively. The time consumed in partition process is also reduced sharply.

In the multi-level partitioning phase, the derived small weighted graph is broken down into a specific number of sub-graphs with graph partition algorithm. Because the small derived graph limits the freedom in partitioning and may bring more load imbalance in final solution, the multi-level scheme is proposed to evaluate the quality of partition results, decompose the sub-area with the maximum computation load and partition the new graph again. This process will not pause until optimal solution is found. The objective function used is shown below.

$$\min F(p) = \underset{i=1,\dots,p}{Max}(CompCost_i) + CompCost_B \quad (2)$$

In (2), CompCosti (i=1,…,p) is the computation of the sub-area i; CompCostB is the computation of the boundary system described below. In the evaluation function, the sum of CompCosti and CompCostB represents the total computation in the critical path and also the overall time consumed in the parallel simulation. It is noted that more communication occurs between sub-tasks, more computation will be introduced into the boundary system. So the influence of communication has been taken into account by CompCostB.

After the weighted graph partition, the results have to be applied to the original network. Further refinement and adjustment are performed to improve the quality of partition results.

Here, the flow chart of the multilevel partition scheme based on the regional characteristic of power network is shown as below.

Step 1 Establish the multilevel model of the power network
- Establish the power network model in grid level, province level, region level, station level and so on

Step 2 Network Coarsing
- 2.1 Decide the reasonable level of network coarsing with partition number
- 2.2 Reduce network
- 2.3 Compute the vertex weights and edge weights of the derived graph

Step 3 Graph partitioning
- 3.1 Graph partitioning with the multilevel recursive bisection algorithm
- 3.2 Evaluate the results of partition. If the result of objective function is bigger than that of previous partition, terminate the successive partition process and the final result is the previous one, then goes to Step 4; otherwise, go to Step 3.3
- 3.3 Split the sub-area with the maximum computation load, and go to Step 3.1

Step 4 Refine Results
- 4.1 Identify the isolated node sets by topo analysis
- 4.2 Analyze the connections of the nodes in the boundary system
- 4.2 Refine the network partition.

3.2. New hierarchical BBDF algorithm for power network computation

According to the power system's characteristics, the corresponding differential equations for dynamic device such as the generator are only related to one of the network nodes. The differential part of (1) can be put into connected sub-areas, and divides into the corresponding processor to compute simultaneously. Therefore, the parallel computation of linear power network equations is the key of the dynamic process simulation. Furthermore, new events occurring during the simulation result in a rapid increase in the computation in dynamic simulation, including adjusting admittance matrix, rebuilding factors and renewal of node voltages.

Based on cluster system, the network equations are reformed in the Block Bordered Diagonal Form [16], as shown in (3). The following equations are for two sub-areas as previously described.

$$\begin{bmatrix} \mathbf{Y} & \mathbf{M'} \\ \mathbf{M} & \mathbf{Z} \end{bmatrix} \begin{bmatrix} \mathbf{U} \\ \mathbf{I} \end{bmatrix} = \begin{bmatrix} \mathbf{I}_p \\ 0 \end{bmatrix} \quad (3)$$

In which,

$$\mathbf{M} = \begin{bmatrix} \mathbf{M}_{CF-1p} & \mathbf{M}_{CF-2p} & & & & \\ & & \mathbf{M}_{CF-1n} & \mathbf{M}_{CF-2n} & & \\ & & & & \mathbf{M}_{CF-1z} & \mathbf{M}_{CF-2z} \end{bmatrix}$$

$$Y = \begin{bmatrix} Y_{1p} & & & & & \\ & Y_{2p} & & & & \\ & & Y_{1n} & & & \\ & & & Y_{2n} & & \\ & & & & Y_{1z} & \\ & & & & & Y_{2z} \end{bmatrix}, \quad \mathbf{U} = \begin{bmatrix} \mathbf{U}_{1p} \\ \mathbf{U}_{2p} \\ \mathbf{U}_{1n} \\ \mathbf{U}_{2n} \\ \mathbf{U}_{1z} \\ \mathbf{U}_{2z} \end{bmatrix}$$

$$I_p = \begin{bmatrix} I_{1p} \\ I_{2p} \\ 0 \\ 0 \\ 0 \\ 0 \end{bmatrix}, \quad M' = \begin{bmatrix} M_{1p-CF} & & \\ M_{2p-CF} & & \\ & M_{1n-CF} & \\ & M_{2n-CF} & \\ & & M_{1z-CF} \\ & & M_{2z-CF} \end{bmatrix}$$

$\mathbf{Z} = \mathbf{Z}_{CF}$, $\mathbf{I} = \mathbf{I}_{CF}$

where the subscripts 1 and 2 represent the sub-area number, and the subscripts p, n, z represent the positive, negative, and zero sequence networks respectively. $\mathbf{Y_{1p}}$, $\mathbf{Y_{2p}}$, $\mathbf{Y_{1n}}$, $\mathbf{Y_{2n}}$, $\mathbf{Y_{1z}}$ and $\mathbf{Y_{2z}}$ are the admittance matrices of three (positive, negative and zero) sequence networks respectively. $\mathbf{Z_{CF}}$ is the impedance matrix for cutting branches (the branches between different sub-areas) and fault branches, and also the coefficient matrix of boundary equations in the BBDF computation. **M** and **M'** are the associated matrices between **Y** and **Z** respectively.

According to the parallel scheme used in BBDF equations, the limiting factor hindering parallelism is the solution of the boundary system, which is the sequential part in the whole parallel algorithm. With the increase of sub-areas, the time required to complete the boundary equations and the time spent on communication between processors increase sharply. This paper presents a hierarchical BBDF power network algorithm to enhance the computing efficiency of boundary equations. This algorithm introduces the BBDF parallel scheme into boundary equations recursively. The coefficient matrix of the boundary system are reordered by positive, negative, and zero sequence parts of cutting branches in front of fault branches, as described in (4):

$$\begin{bmatrix} \mathbf{Y}_{Tp} & & & \mathbf{N}_{Tp} \\ & \mathbf{Y}_{Tn} & & \mathbf{N}_{Tn} \\ & & \mathbf{Y}_{Tz} & \mathbf{N}_{Tz} \\ \mathbf{N}_{pT} & & & \\ & \mathbf{N}_{nT} & & \mathbf{Y}_F \\ & & \mathbf{N}_{zT} & \end{bmatrix} \quad (4)$$

In which, $\mathbf{Y_{Tp}}$, $\mathbf{Y_{Tn}}$ and $\mathbf{Y_{Tz}}$ are the three sequence node admittance matrices for cutting branches; $\mathbf{Y_F}$ is the admittance matrix for fault nodes; and $\mathbf{N_{Tp}}$, $\mathbf{N_{Tn}}$, $\mathbf{N_{Tz}}$, $\mathbf{N_{pT}}$, $\mathbf{N_{nT}}$ and $\mathbf{N_{zT}}$ are the associated matrices. Because some fault forms have invalid impedance matrices, an admittance matrix is adopted in (4).

Boundary equations are much smaller than network equations. And most of their computations focus on reforming the boundary equations and factoring the coefficient matrix when events happen. A dynamic multithread scheme is used to solve the boundary equations, which is more effective for clusters that consist of multi-processor machines (SMP-Cluster). When this hierarchical network equation algorithm is applied to dynamic simulations, it not only dramatically improves the efficiency and gains, but also enhances the scalability of the program.

3.3. Parallel Algorithm for Dynamic Simulation

In the simulation, a large system represented by (1) is broken into N subsystems based on the partition scheme. N subsystems are respectively assigned to N processors for computing; for example, the k-th subsystem is processed by the processor P_k (k=1, 2,..., N). Each subsystem is calculated independently with the solutions of the boundary system. Then the solution to the boundary equations comprises the computation results for each subsystem. This process is repeated until convergence is reached, as described in the following flow chart.

Initialization;
For TimeStep = 1,..., MaxTimeStep (Simulaton Loop)
  For Iter = 0,..., MaxIters (Simulation Loop)
  Parallel Simulation by Processor P_1, ..., P_N
  Include new events in subsystem k;
    Solve the differential equations of subsystem k with the trapezoidal rule:

$$\dot{X}_k = f(X_k, V_k) = AX_k + Bu(X_k, V_k);$$

   Compute the current injected into subsystem k: $I_k(X_k, V_k)$;
   Check local convergence of subsystem k:

$$\left\| \frac{I_{kt} - I_{k(t-1)}}{I_{k(t-1)}} \right\| < \varepsilon_I, t - iteration \text{ number};$$

   Solve vector, matrix corrected in subsystem k:

$$\begin{cases} \Delta Y_{km} = (M_{CF-km} Y_{km}^{-1} M_{km-CF})^{-1} \\ \Delta I_{kp} = \Delta Y_{kp} M_{CF-kp} Y_{kp}^{-1} I_{kp} \end{cases}, m = p, n, z;$$

   Communication collection between processors;
   Global convergence checking;
   If convergence is reached, break iteration loop;
   Solve boundary systems:

$$\begin{bmatrix} Y_{Tp} & & & N_{Tp} \\ & Y_{Tn} & & N_{Tn} \\ & & Y_{Tz} & N_{Tz} \\ N_{pT} & & & \\ & N_{nT} & & Y_F \\ & & N_{zT} & \end{bmatrix} \begin{bmatrix} U_{Cp} \\ U_{Cn} \\ U_{Cz} \\ U_{Fp} \\ U_{Fn} \\ U_{Fz} \end{bmatrix} = \begin{bmatrix} I_{Tp} \\ \\ \\ I_{Fp} \\ \\ \\ \end{bmatrix} + \sum_{m=1}^{k} \Delta I_{kp}$$

   Comm. for scattering boundary system solution;
   Check partial convergence in subsystem k:

$$\left\| \frac{I_{km-CF,t+1} - I_{km-CF,t}}{I_{km-CF,t}} \right\| < \varepsilon_I, t - \text{iteration number};$$

   Solve the node voltages in subsystem k;

$$U_{km} = Y_{km}^{-1} \begin{pmatrix} I_{km} - M_{km-CF} \Delta Y_{km} * \\ (M_{CF-km} Y_{km}^{-1} I_{km} - U_{km-CF}) \end{pmatrix},$$

   where $m = p, n, z$;

```
    End Parallel Simulation;
    End For iter (End Simulation Loop);
    Compute computation results of subsystem k;
    Collect and put output data into realtime database;
    Get new events from the outer system;
  End For TimeStep (End Simulation Loop);
  End Simulation.
```

The convergence checking scheme on parallel architecture is more complex than that on sequential systems because it has to take into account the cooperation of the computing processes. We employ a new global convergence checking scheme to improve the computation's efficiency, as follows:

1. Relative deviation of currents injected is regarded as variable to check convergence. One communication can be saved in every iteration by this scheme. And the computation has the similar convergence rate and numerical accuracy to the traditional voltage convergence checking scheme.
2. In every subsystem, convergence is checked locally. If local convergence occurs, the corresponding process informs the control process (the same as the process for computing the boundary system) with a local convergence flag instead of with the new corrected vector. Then this subsystem waits for the global convergence flag or the new solutions of the boundary equations. If global convergence is reached, the simulation enters into the next time step; if not, whether the local computation is performed or not depends on the partial convergence checking.
3. The control process collects the local convergence flags from all subsystems. After the global convergence is checked, the results are sent to each subsystem. If global convergence is not reached, the boundary equations have to be solved once more.

In addition, some optimization schemes are developed to reduce the time spent on computing and communication, and to improve the scalability of the program presented in this paper.

Firstly, there are two iteration loops in the IAI algorithm. The inner one, to solve nonlinear network equations, is broken in this algorithm in order to cancel invalid substitutions. And numerical tests prove that our algorithm's results are as accurate as those of the traditional IAI algorithm.

Secondly, during the simulation, state variables of dynamic devices, injected currents, and node voltages of the positive sequence network have to be updated in every iteration. Nevertheless it is not necessary to compute the negative or zero sequence network equations in subsystems and boundary systems. So the variables of negative or zero sequences in subsystems and boundary equations are solved only once in every time step. Furthermore, different schemes for computing faults are used for different fault forms, such as canceling the zero sequence network computation when inner-phase faults happen only.

4. Test results

In this study, two power systems shown in Table 1 have been tested on a SMP Cluster. In the cluster, each node is a SMP computer and has 4 Intel Xeon PIII700MHz CPUs and 1 gigabyte of memory. The communication medium between SMP nodes is Myrinet with a bandwidth of 2.56Gb/s. The software environments are Redhat Linux 7.2 (kernel version 2.4.7-10smp), MPICH-1.2.1..7 and gm-1.5pre4.

Table 1. Network information for two power systems

System		Case 1	Case 2
Scale	number of nodes	706	10188
	number of branches	1069	13499
	number of generators	88	1072
	number of loads	459	3003

The detail computation models including 5 order generator model, typical exciter and governor model, and induction motor model, are concerned [17] for all test cases. An A-phase fault on single 220kV branch is assumed for Case 1, the fault occurs at 0s, and the branch trips at 0.16s. It is a typical non-symmetric fault case. A three-phase fault on 500kV branch is assumed for Case 2, the fault occurs at 0s, and the branch trips at 0.08s. It is a serious symmetric fault case with numerical difficult. In the simulations, the fixed time step 0.01s is used, and the simulation time is 10s. The convergence tolerance is 10^{-4} pu. For all the test cases, the same complier flags are used as well as the code tuning schemes.

The partition results using the multilevel scheme are listed in Table 2.

In the figures below, Sp stands for speedup, which is the ratio of the time required for parallel simulations with partitions to the time required for sequential simulations without partitions. SV stands for the simulation velocity, which is the ratio of the actual running time of the power grid dynamic process to the simulation time on cluster system for the same power grid case. And the efficiency is expressed as E=Sp/P, where P is the number of CPUs.

Table 2. Results of the partition scheme for two power systems

Network	Partition number	Max/Min[1]	CutBrn[2]
Case 1	2	422/284	4
	4	301/121	7
	6	149/75	17
	8	119/68	34
Case 2	2	5258/4930	2
	4	3205/762	6
	8	2004/628	9
	10	1374/762	19
	12	1143/694	27
	16	1116/305	42
	20	1088/156	40

4.1. The validity of our algorithm

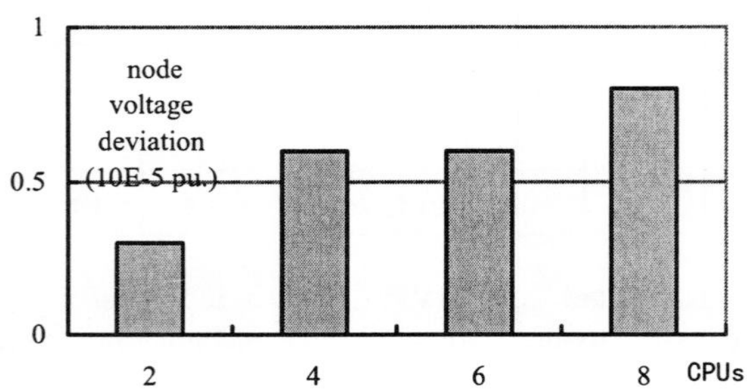

Fig. 1. Maximal deviation of node voltage using our algorithm and PSASP (PSASP is regarded as the standard software)

For Case 1, Fig.1 shows the maximum deviation of node voltage between the parallel program presented in this paper and the software named PSASP. PSASP is the standard sequential software package developed by EPRI China, which is widely used for power system simulation [18].

According to Fig.1, the maximum deviation of node voltage between our algorithm and PSASP is less than 10^{-5} pu. It proves that our algorithm is accurate and feasible.

4.2. Performance of our algorithm

Fig 2 and 3 show the speedups and simulation velocity of the parallel computing for case 1 and case 2.

[1] Max/Min: the ratio of the number of nodes in the maximal partition to the number in the minimal partition.

[2] CutBrn: the number of branches between sub-areas.

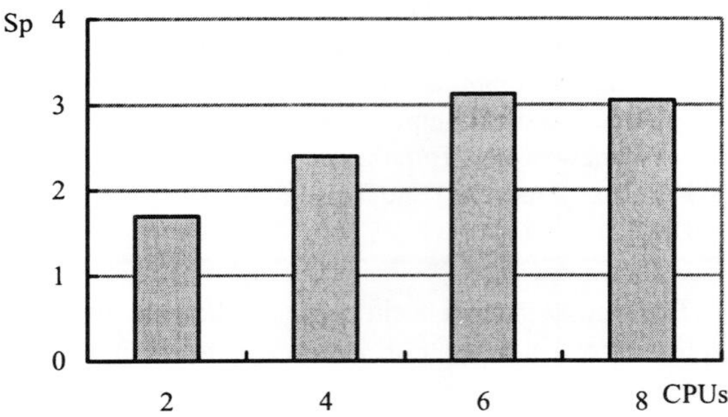

Fig. 2 Speedups of Case 1

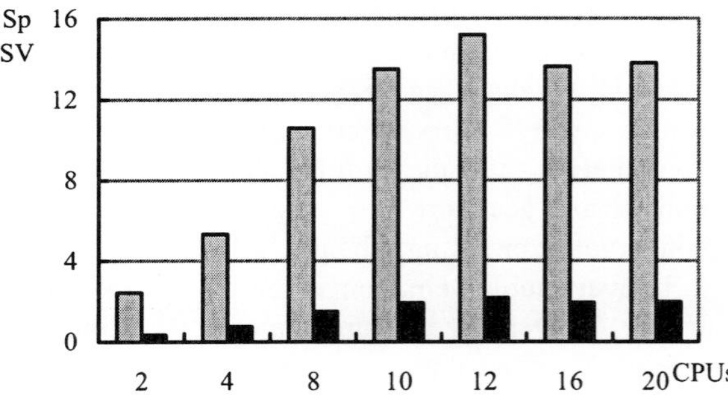

Fig. 3 Speedups and SV of Case 2 (left for Sp)

Comparing the results of the two cases shown in figures, the following conclusions can be drawn.

1. The high speedups and parallel efficiency are achieved in two actual power networks and even some super-linear speedups are achieved in Case 2 for so-called "cache effect". These results suggest that the parallel algorithm proposed in this paper is efficient and practical, and can be used for realtime power system simulations.
2. The dynamic process simulations run faster than the realtime process for two large scale power systems. For example, when single CPU is used in Case 2, simulation carried out with single CPU is not adequate for the requirement of realtime simulation. So parallel processing is necessary to improve the simulation velocity. When 12 CPUs are used for parallel computation in Case 2, the simulation velocity reaches 2.2, only 45% of the actual dynamic process time, and about 15 times faster than that on single CPU. These prove that the partition scheme and the hierarchical parallel algorithm for dynamic simulation are very efficient.
3. The speedups of parallel simulations become saturated with the increase of sub-areas and computing processors. 6 processors for Case 1 and 12 processors for Case 2 are being used when the

speedup and the simulation velocity reach the maximum. From Case 1 to Case 2, the optimal partition number and speedup increase with the increase of power system size. It should be noted that the algorithm presented in this paper is scalable.

4.3. Performance comparison between our algorithm and known BBDF algorithm

For Case 1, The performance comparison between our hierarchical BBDF algorithm and the algorithm proposed in [6][9] is shown in Fig.4. When computing the speedups, the same sequential time is used in both algorithms. Meanwhile the same partitions and cluster system are used in these two programs as well as the same complier flags.

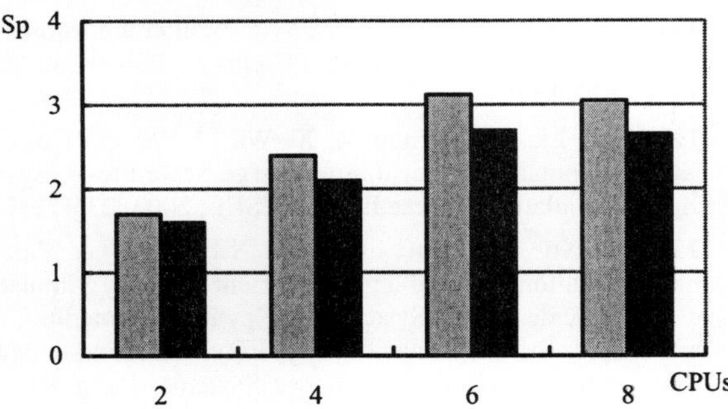

Fig. 4 Performance comparison using the hierarchical BBDF algorithm and the algorithm in [6][9] (left for our algorithm)

As shown in Fig.4, the hierarchical BBDF algorithm proposed in this paper can gain higher performance than the coarse granularity IAI algorithm in [6][9]. More partition number used, higher speedups are achieved. When 6 CPUs are used, the two algorithms both get the optimal performance. It's also found that the performance advantage of our algorithm to the algorithm in [6][9] reaches the maximum with 6 CPUs. The optimal speedup of our algorithm is 3.12, which is about 16% higher than that of the algorithm proposed in [6][9]. This is due to communication reduction and the optimizations of boundary system computation in our algorithm. Therefore, it can be concluded that our algorithm is superior to the well-known coarse granularity algorithm.

4.4. Performance comparison between our partition scheme and METIS

Table 3. Comparison of the multilevel scheme and the algorithm in METIS

Partition number	Multilevel scheme		METIS algorithm	
	Max/Min	CutBrn	Max/Min	CutBrn
2	5258/4930	2	5102/5086	2
4	3205/762	6	2552/2535	18
8	2004/628	9	1284/1266	64
10	1374/762	19	1035/1008	78
12	1143/694	27	861/835	79
16	1116/305	42	644/621	121
20	1088/156	40	531/496	140

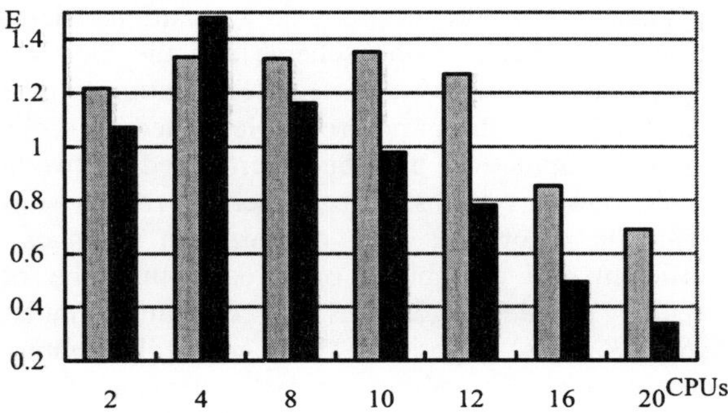

Fig. 5 Performance comparison using the multilevel partition algorithm and the GRAPH partition algorithm in METIS (left for our algorithm)

Table 3 lists the partition results of Case 2 using the multilevel scheme and the recursive bisection method in METIS [19]. It should be noted that the different partition parameters have been tested for METIS algorithm in these cases and the best results are shown here. Furthermore, the simulation performance comparison of the multilevel partition scheme and the algorithm in METIS is shown in Fig.5 and our hierarchical spatial algorithm is used to simulate the dynamic process for two partition methods.

Table 3 shows that the multilevel partition scheme gets much less cutting edges than the recursive bisection algorithm in METIS, but leads to more imbalance between sub-areas. The results in Fig.5 suggest that in the most cases the multilevel scheme achieves higher efficiency in dynamic simulations on cluster system and its performance does not noticeably suffer from the imbalance of sub-areas. With 2 partitions, the multilevel partition scheme gets higher efficiency because of the more accurate workload model of sub-network. Furthermore, higher efficiency is achieved with the increase of partition number. With 12 CPUs, the efficiency of our algorithm is about 63% higher than that of METIS. Therefore, it can be concluded that the multilevel partition scheme fits our cluster-based spatial algorithm well, especially when more CPUs are used. The multilevel partition scheme and the hierarchical algorithm give an integrated solution to parallel dynamic simulation and can get very satisfying results.

5. Conclusion

This paper proposes a multilevel partition scheme based on power network regional characteristics and a hierarchical Block Bordered Diagonal Form power network algorithm. The algorithm uses message-passing and share-memory models simultaneously. Optimization schemes such as convergence checking are also presented to improve the simulation efficiency. The multilevel partition scheme and the hierarchical spatial algorithm give an integrated solution to parallel dynamic simulation and are implemented on a cluster system. Simulations have been performed for two large scale power systems. The numerical results suggest that the algorithms and optimization schemes are efficient and scalable. Compared with some other spatial parallel algorithms for dynamic simulation [6][20], this algorithm has markedly improved performance. This algorithm, with adequate efficiency and scalability, is a feasible selection for the realtime dynamic simulation of China's future nationwide power grid.

Acknowledgement

This work was supported in part by Intel ACP, the National Natural Science Foundation of China (Grant No. 60433040 and 60473101), and the National Key Basic Research and Development Program of China (Grant No. 2004CB318205).

References

[1] Daniel J. Tylavsky, A. J. Bose, Parallel processing in power systems computation, IEEE Trans. On PWRS, 1992, 7(2), 629-638.

[2] J. S. Chai, A. J. Bose, Bottlenecks in parallel algorithms for power system stability analysis, IEEE Trans. On PWRS, 1993, 8(1), 9-15.

[3] G.Kron, Diakoptics – the piecewise solution of large scale systems, MacDonald, London, 1963.

[4] W. Xue, J. W. Shu, X. F. Wang, W. M. Zheng, Advance of parallel algorithm for power system transient stability simulation, Journal of system simulation, 2002, 14(2), 177-182.

[5] IEEE Committee Report. Parallel processing in power systems computation. IEEE Trans. on Power Systems, 1992, 7(2): 629-638.

[6] I.C.Decker, D.M.Falcao, E.Kaszkurewicz. Conjugate gradient methods for power system dynamic simulation on parallel computers. IEEE Trans. on PWRS, 1996,11(3), 1218-1227

[7] M. La Scala, G. Sblendorio, A. Bose, J. Q. Wu. Comparison of algorithms for transient stability simulations on shared and distributed memory multiprocessors. IEEE Trans. on Power Systems, 1996, 11(4), 2045-2050.

[8] G. Aloisio, M. A. Bochicchio, M. La Scala, R. Sbrizzai. A distributed computing approach for realtime transient stability analysis. IEEE Trans. on Power Systems, 1997, 12(2), 981-987.

[9] K.W.Chan, R.C.Dai, C.H.Cheung. A coarse grain parallel solution method for solving large set of power systems network equations. 2002 international conference on power system technology, 2002.Volume: 4: 2640 -2644

[10] A. H. Jorge, R. M. Jose Real time network simulation with PC-Cluster. IEEE Trans. on power systems, 2003, 18(2), 563-569.

[11] Y. L. Li, X. X. Zhou, Z. X. Wu, Parallel algorithms for transient stability simulation on PC cluster. PowerCon 2002, vol.3, 1592-1596.

[12] Y. L. Li, X. X. Zhou, Z. X. Wu, A Parallel Complex Fault Computation Algorithm for Large Scale Power System Digital Simulation. Proceedings of CSEE, 2003, 23(12), 1-5

[13] W. Xue, J.W.Shu, J.F.Yan, X.F.Wang, A Parallel Implementation for Real-Time Transient Stability Simulation of Large Scale Power System. In: Keyue Ma Smedley, eds. Proceedings of the Seventh IASTED International Multi-Conference on Power and Energy Systems. Palm Springs, Feb.24-26, 2003. 133-137

[14] Kirk Schloegel. George Karypis. Vipim Kumar. Graph Partitioning for High Performance Scientific Simulations. CRPC Parallel Computing Handbook. Morgan Kaufmann, 2000

[15] Jiwu Shu, Wei Xue, Weimin Zheng, An Optimal Partition Scheme of Transient Stable Parallel Computing in Power System, Automation of Electric Power Systems, 2003, 27(19), 6-10.

[16] A. Torralba, Three methods for the parallel solution of a large, sparse system of linear equations by multiprocessors, International journal of energy systems, 1992, 12(1), 1-5.

[17] EPRI China, Power System Analysis Software Package, Fundamental database user manual, 2001.

[18] Cheng Hua, Xu Zheng, Comparison of mathematical models for transient stability calculation in PSASP and PSS/E and corresponding calculation results, Power system teconology, 2004, 28(5), 1-4.

[19] K. George, V. P. Kumar, METIS-a software package for partitioning unstructured graphs, partitioning meshes, and computing fill-reducing orderings of sparse matrices, version 4.0 [EB/OL], http:// www.cs.umn.edu/~karypis, 1998,9.

[20] M. Nagata, N. Uchida, Parallel processing of network calculations in order to speed up transient stability analysis, Electrical Engineering in Japan, 2001, 135(3), 26-36.

Session 3A: On-Chip Parallelism

Heuristics for Profile-driven Method-level Speculative Parallelization

John Whaley and Christos Kozyrakis
Computer Systems Laboratory
Stanford University
{jwhaley,kozyraki}@stanford.edu

Abstract

Thread level speculation (TLS) is an effective technique for extracting parallelism from sequential code. Method calls provide good templates for the boundaries of speculative threads as they often describe independent tasks. However, selecting the most profitable methods to speculate on is difficult as it involves complicated trade-offs between speculation violations, thread overheads, and resource utilization. This paper presents a first analysis of heuristics for automatic selection of speculative threads across method boundaries using a dynamic or profile-driven compiler. We study the potential of three classes of heuristics that involve increasing amounts of profiling information and runtime complexity. Several of the heuristics allow for speculation to start at internal method points, nested speculation, and speculative thread preemption.

Using a set of Java benchmarks, we demonstrate that careful thread selection at method boundaries leads to speedups of 1.4 to 1.8 on practical TLS hardware. Single-pass heuristics that filter out less profitable methods using simple speedup estimates lead to the best average performance by consistently providing a good balance between over- and under-speculation. On the other hand, multi-pass heuristics that perform additional filtering by taking into account interactions between nested method calls often lead to significant under-speculation and perform poorly.

1 Introduction

With uniprocessors running into fundamental ILP and VLSI limitations [1], single-chip multiprocessors (CMPs) provide a realistic path towards scalable performance using the ever-growing transistor budgets [13, 15, 11]. The problem now becomes how to best utilize the parallel resources on the chip. Manually writing explicitly programs is a tedious and error-prone task for the average programmer.

Thread-level speculation (TLS) is an effective approach for extracting suitable levels of parallelism from sequential code for CMPs [18, 16]. With TLS, the processor executes computational tasks in parallel, optimistically assuming that sequential semantics will still be preserved. Special hardware detects if the assumption is violated and initiates re-execution of any offending tasks. TLS is particularly attractive because it relieves the programmer and the compiler of proving independence between threads and placing locks to orchestrate accesses to shared data.

Parallel execution with TLS requires that speculative threads are identified in the code. One option is to have the programmer manually select speculative threads [17]. Alternatively, a dynamic or profile-driven compiler can automatically select the optimal set of speculative threads in a sequential program given runtime information collected from previous runs. In this case, the programmer must only write an ordinary sequential program and all legacy source code can reap the benefits of TLS support in CMP systems.

This paper presents a first analysis of practical heuristics that allow a profile-driven compiler to automatically select speculative threads in a sequential program. We focus on method calls that describe independent tasks within a program. Limit studies have shown that there are significant amounts of method-level parallelism in common applications [16, 21]. Several researchers have exploited method-level parallelism with TLS hardware. Yet, to our knowledge, this work is the first to describe, tune, and evaluate a comprehensive set of heuristics that compiler writers can employ in order to extract method-level speculative parallelism. The heuristics presented here are complementary and fairly orthogonal to the well-studied compiler techniques for speculative parallelization of loops [23, 7].

The main contributions of this work are:

- We describe three classes of heuristics that use increasing amounts of profiling information and involve increasing runtime complexity. Simple heuristics rely on straight-forward measurements such as the method runtime. Single-pass heuristics filter methods that are unlikely to be profitable using estimates of speedup and runtime savings. Multi-pass heuristics remove additional methods by considering the interactions between nested method calls. Several heuristics allow for speculation to start at intermediate method points, nested speculation, and speculative thread preemption.
- We evaluate the performance potential of these heuristics with Java applications running on a simulated CMP with TLS support. The heuristics lead to speedups of 1.4 to 1.8 over sequential execution on a single processor, which is 80% to 95% of the performance possible when using an ideal oracle. We also show that the worst case buffering requirements by the selected speculative threads are less than 16 Kbytes,

0190-3918/05 $20.00 © 2005 IEEE

which is reasonable for both current and future CMP designs.

- We demonstrate that single pass heuristics achieve the best average performance as they provide a reasonable balance between under- and over-speculation. Multi-pass heuristics often lead to under-speculation and mediocre performance gains due to the complexity of the interactions between nested method calls.

The rest of the paper is structured as follows. In section 2 we give an overview of method-level speculation and the challenges it involves. Section 3 presents the investigated heuristics. We explain the experimental methodology in section 4. Section 5 presents the evaluation results. Section 6 discusses related work and Section 7 concludes.

2 Method-Level Speculation Overview

TLS targets parallelism in sequential programs by dividing the code into threads to be speculatively executed in parallel. Since the program is not explicitly written for parallel execution, the TLS system must preserve the original sequential semantics. The hardware tracks all memory addresses that threads write or read and detects when a less speculative thread writes to an address that a more speculative thread has already read. This is a violation of sequential semantics and causes the younger thread and all other more speculative threads to be squashed and restarted [8]. In this study, we always restart threads at the beginning of their execution. A more aggressive model would be to restart them at the first instruction causing the violation [22], but this requires significant hardware complexity.

A complete TLS compiler should select speculative threads from both loops and method calls in the sequential code in a complementary manner. Loop-level thread selection is a well-studied topic [23, 5, 7]. In this paper, we focus on thread selection at method boundaries. There are two reasons why method calls are well-suited for speculation. First, methods are used by programmers to divide the code into separate units of computation. Although it is not always the case, separate methods frequently perform independent tasks. Second, method calls communicate primarily through memory with only a small and well-defined number of parameters or return values going through registers. Hence, there is little need for analysis of the liveness of register-allocated variables when creating speculative threads [23].

2.1 Speculation Model

Our model for method-level speculation is to optimistically execute the code following a method return while the called method is still executing as shown in Figure 1. Speculation leads to speedups when no violations occur (Figure 1.c), but it may also cause slowdowns in the case of violations and re-executions (Figure 1.d). At method return the only state communicated through registers is the return value. We use value prediction to allow speculation on non-void methods, which is especially beneficial for methods that return an error code, as they typically return a constant on successful program runs.

We do not always initiate speculation at the beginning of a method call. Instead, the speculative thread may be forked at any point within the method body. Hence, speculative threads that would otherwise violate if they were forked at the beginning of the method can start later in the method, so that the read in the speculative thread will happen after the write in the non-speculative thread. This technique requires no additional hardware or software support beyond normal method speculation as the values to start the speculative thread are easily available in the caller's and/or callee's stack frame. We use the term *fork point* for the location in the method where speculation starts. The *join point* is right before the method return in order to accommodate methods with multiple callers. When the join point is reached, the non-speculative thread finishes and the speculative thread executing beyond the method return becomes non-speculative (or less speculative).

Finally, our model allows for nested speculation. A speculative thread can fork more speculative threads when it reaches a fork point. Any additional threads are strictly nested within the thread that forked them. This happens automatically due to the nested nature of method calls and returns in imperative programming languages.

2.2 Challenges of Method-Level Speculation

TLS leads to maximum benefits if the selected speculative threads are very likely to be independent and each includes a non-trivial amount of work. Such a selection assigns processors with useful threads that will not lead to violations. It also minimizes the impact of the overheads associated with forking, joining, and restarting threads.

Thread selection at method-level boundaries involves several challenges. Unlike with loop-based speculation, speculative threads from method calls are dissimilar, which makes it difficult to evaluate the likelihood of violations. Furthermore, threads may have arbitrary lengths with some of them being particularly long and some of them being particularly short. A long running thread is more likely to violate, which is particularly wasteful if it happens towards the end of the thread execution. On the other hand, a short speculative thread may not have sufficient work to amortize the cost associated with starting and stopping the thread in a modern system.

Long threads can be problematic even without violations. TLS hardware must retire speculative threads in sequential order. It is possible that a long running thread can delay several shorter, more speculative threads that have completed their execution but cannot retire. Consequently, precious hardware resources may be unavailable for new threads. This problem can be lessened by hardware support for multiple speculative buffers per CPU, but this can be fairly expensive to implement. A long running speculative thread may also overflow the available buffer space for speculative writes. In this case, the TLS hardware will have to stall this thread until it becomes non-speculative. In other words, long threads may lead to unnecessary serialization.

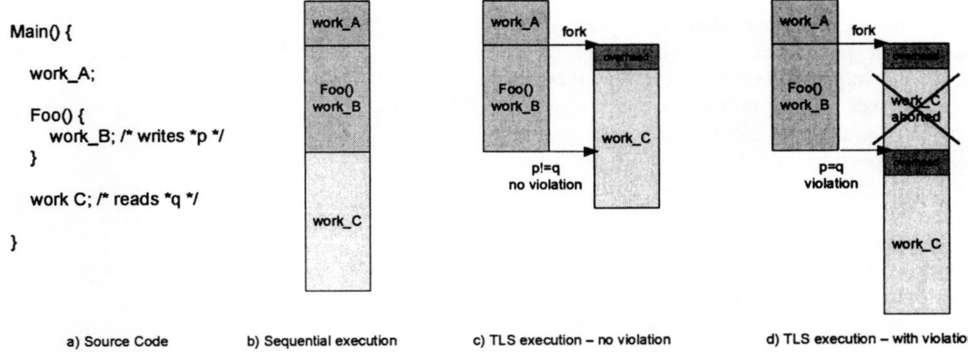

Figure 1. Example of method-level TLS. In (b), Foo() and the subsequent code (work_C) execute sequentially. In (c), the code executes in parallel without violations because the two pointers p and q are not aliased. In (d), speculation results into a dependency violation and re-execution because the p and q are aliased.

3 Heuristics

A dynamic or profile-driven compiler can select profitable methods for speculation using runtime information about the application behavior. Profiling data is the key to overcoming the challenges of method-level speculation in ways that a static compiler is unlikely to match. An ideal selection is accurate with high probability and fast to make. Both features depend on the amount of runtime data the compiler employs and the number of passes it must make over the data before reaching a decision.

We investigate a set of heuristics that allow a profile-driven compiler to select profitable fork points for method-level speculation. All heuristics attempt to select speculative threads with low probabilities of violations, which is the key performance issue. The heuristics do not attempt to minimize buffer space requirements for the speculative threads. Nevertheless, our experimental methodology tracks the maximum buffer requirements for each heuristic, which provides an understanding of the tradeoffs between buffer size and performance.

We categorized our heuristics into three classes based the amount of runtime information they use and the complexity involved in their decisions. *Simple heuristics* are the most straightforward. They determine fork points with a simple analysis of information such as sequential runtime or dynamic count of stores for each method. The simplistic analysis can often lead to over-speculation. *Single-pass heuristics* attempt to eliminate some unprofitable selections by estimating the potential speedup or runtime savings by speculating at each method call. They involve a single-pass over the addresses accessed by the method and the code beyond its return point. *Multi-pass heuristics* are the most complex. They attempt to filter even more inappropriate selections by adjusting the speedup expectations when nested speculation is used. These heuristics require multiple passes over the profile data. The number of passes is bounded by the depth of the method call graph. Single-pass and multi-pass heuristics allow for speculation to start at points other than the very beginning of a method.

This work focuses on describing the idea and evaluating the potential of the heuristics through simulation. Their exact implementation in a specific compiler is beyond the scope of this paper. Nevertheless, the runtime information necessary can be collected during a profiling stage using hardware with address analysis capabilities [24, 3]. Then, the heuristics can be implemented dynamically by a service thread [10] or off-line using traditional profile-driven compilation techniques.

3.1 Simple Heuristics

Runtime Heuristic (SI-RT): This heuristic speculates on all methods with an average runtime between a minimum (MIN) and a maximum (MAX) threshold. The idea is to find methods that do enough work to amortize the speculation overhead, but are not too likely to cause violations and load imbalance. The only information needed is the average runtime of each method under consideration, which is trivial to collect using hardware counters. The drawback is that method runtime is only loosely correlated to the likelihood of violations between speculative threads.

Store Heuristic (SI-SC): This heuristic speculates on methods with a total dynamic count of stores less than a maximum (MAX) threshold. The rationale is that methods with low store counts are unlikely to cause many violations. The dynamic store count can also be monitored using hardware counters. This heuristic also suffers from the problem that dynamic store count is only somewhat correlated to violations, since it does not capture the overlap between the write sets of different threads. Additionally, by selecting methods with low numbers of stores, there is a hazard of choosing methods that are too short.

3.2 Single-Pass Heuristics

Best Speedup Heuristic (SP-SU): This heuristic speculates on methods that are predicted to lead to relative speedup above a determined threshold (THRES). We define speedup as the ratio of the sequential execution time for the method and its subsequent code over the time necessary to execute the two in parallel. For the subsequent code, we assume a portion with average runtime equal to that of the method itself. Like all single-pass heuristics, this heuristic allows the fork point to be placed at the first point within the method that eliminates violations in the subsequent code. SP-SU requires a single pass over the address stream for the method and its subsequent code in order to place the fork point. The addresses for the method are examined in reverse order. It also requires an estimate of average runtimes for the relative speedup calculation. Its major shortcoming is that it is possible for very short methods to score very highly in terms of speedup. The corresponding threads may prevent longer methods with smaller relative speedups but larger contributions to the overall runtime from running.

Most Cycles Saved Heuristic (SP-CS): This heuristic targets a shortcoming of SP-SU by speculating on methods which are predicted to save the largest number of cycles when executed speculatively. Instead of dividing the sequential runtime by the predicted parallel runtime, we simply subtract them. Then, we speculate on all methods with a predicted number of saved cycles greater than a threshold (THRES). The fork point is placed so that the predicted probability of violation is less than a selected ratio (RATIO). The idea here is that, eventually, we are really trying to trim from the runtime as many clock cycles as possible. The complexity and runtime information needed for this heuristic are identical to that for SP-SU.

3.3 Multi-Pass Heuristics

Simple and single-pass heuristics assume that the speculation decision for one method call is independent of the decision for all other methods. With nested speculation, the decision to speculate on a specific method depends on the decision for any parent methods in the call graph. The multi-pass heuristics explore these interactions by making multiple passes over the profiling data. With each pass, the decision for a specific method is reflected upon the information used to decide for its children in the following pass. Multi-pass heuristics attempt to limit over-speculation that may result from double-counting the potential benefits of speculation for both parent and child methods. Their main drawback is the additional complexity of the multiple passes.

The usefulness of the multi-pass mechanism is illustrated in Figure 2. We initially select to speculate on `Foo` using the first set of fork/join points. We will execute the work in `Foo` (`work_A`, `work_B`, and `work_C`) in parallel with (`work_D`). Next, we consider whether to speculate on `Bar`. With the single-pass heuristics, we would make the decision in isolation. We would consider the potential speedup if we executed the work in `Bar` (`work_B`) in parallel with the work after it ends (`work_C` *and* `work_D`). The multi-pass heuristics take into account that the code after the end of `Foo` (`work_D`) has already been selected for speculation. Hence, the decision for `Bar` will consider the speedup from executing in parallel `work_B` and `work_C`.

Best Speedup Heuristic with Parent Info (MP-SU): This heuristic builds upon SP-SU. Each method is evaluated for its predicted relative speedup and the one with the best speedup is chosen for speculation. Then, we revisit each of its child methods and adjust the runtime of their speculative region to take into account that the code following the parent method will be executed speculatively as well. After all of the children methods are adjusted, the predicted relative speedups are calculated again, the method with the best speedup is chosen for speculation, and the process repeats for its own children. The process continues until no methods remain with a predicted speedup greater than the selected threshold (THRES). Despite the additional passes and complexity, the information required by MP-SU is identical to that for its single-pass equivalent.

```
Foo(){
   /* fork point 1*/
   work_A;

   Bar(){
      /* fork point 2*/
      work_B;
   }

   /* join point 2*/
   work_C;
}

/* join point 1*/
work_D;
```

Figure 2. Illustration of a nested speculation.

Most Cycles Saved Heuristic with Parent Info (MP-CS): This heuristic builds on SP-CS. We start with the method which saves the largest number of cycles above the selected threshold (THRES) and has a predicted violation rate below the selected ratio (RATIO). Then we update the number of cycles expected to save by speculating on any of its child methods and repeat the whole process. By relying on clock cycles saved, MP-CS hopefully selects useful methods that are significant contributors to the overall execution time.

Most Cycles Saved Heuristic with No Nesting (MP-CSNN: Similar to MP-CS, this heuristic speculates first on the method that can save the largest number of cycles. It only selects methods with a predicted number of saved cycles greater than a threshold (THRES) for which the predicted violation rate is less than a determined ratio (RATIO). Once a method is selected, its children are immediately excluded from selection for speculation in the multi-pass process. In other words, this heuristic disallows nested speculation to completely eliminate the potential pitfall of double-counting the benefits. While MP-CSNN uses multiple passes as well, it is faster to implement than MP-SU and MP-CS as it quickly disqualifies many methods.

4 Experimental Methodology

This section summarizes the CMP model, benchmarks, and tools used to evaluate the potential of the heuristics. The evaluation of TLS hardware alternatives or compiler implementation issues is beyond the scope of this paper.

4.1 CMP Architecture Model

The CMP architecture includes four Pentium III processors (3-way out-of-order CPU). Each processor includes 32-KByte L1 instruction and data caches. The processors access a shared, on-chip, 256-KByte L2 cache over a cache-coherent bus. The L2 bus allows inter-processor commu-

Benchmark	Description
compress	Lempel-Ziv compression
jack	Java parser generator
javac	Java compiler from the JDK 1.0.2
jess	Java expert shell system
mpeg	Mpeg layer 3 audio decompression
raytrace	Raytracer that works on a dinosaur scene
barnes	Hierarchical N-body solver
water	Simulation of water molecules

Figure 3. The Java benchmarks used in this study.

nication and detection of inter-thread dependencies during TLS execution. Four processors are sufficient for this evaluation because limit studies for method-level speculation have shown that few applications can attain more than a 4x speedup [16]. Additionally, most upcoming CMPs will include 2 to 4 processors.

We assume that each processor includes a infinite store buffer that tracks speculative updates at word granularity during TLS execution. Store buffers are drained when a speculative thread becomes non-speculative. For the results in Section 5, we use a single speculative buffer per processor. We have performed experiments with double-buffering as well, which lead to similar results from the point of the heuristics, hence we omit them for brevity. We set the overhead for forking, retiring, or squashing a speculative thread to 70 clock cycles, which is a reasonable estimate for a CMP with hardware support for coarse-grain TLS [9, 6].

4.2 Benchmarks and Simulation Tools

We used a large set of Java benchmarks because Java is an object-oriented language which favors a large number of method calls that could stress our heuristics. In addition, a virtual machine with just-in-time compilation capabilities is a good place for implementing the heuristics for method-level speculative parallelization. For brevity, we only present the results for the 8 most representative benchmarks shown in Figure 3. The first six belong to the SpecJVM98 suite, while the remaining two are Java versions of SPLASH-2 benchmarks.

We use trace-driven simulation for our evaluation. First, we run benchmarks on native Pentium hardware with instrumentation code and produce a detailed trace. We run each benchmark multiple times within the same execution to eliminate JIT overheads and use a large heap space to avoid interference from the garbage collector. The trace includes method markings (calls/returns) and the addresses for all loads and stores. It also includes a timestamp for each address that represents the cycle count in the native run. Timestamps are used to account for timing events unrelated to inter-thread communication (e.g. non-memory instructions). They are re-calibrated to remove the instrumentation overhead before using traces for analysis.

The main evaluation tool is a trace analyzer that performs two tasks. First, it analyzes the trace to select the methods to speculate on according to the studied heuristic. As part of this process, the analyzer averages profiling data from the multiple invocations of each method. For each selected method, its fitness according to the heuristic is entered into a scoreboard structure for later use. The fitness is expressed as a number from 0 to 1 (higher is better). Next, the analyzer simulates the execution of the specific trace on the CMP architecture. This step involves parsing the behavior of loads and stores in the memory hierarchy of the 4-processor CMP while taking into account the overhead of forking, retiring, and squashing threads identified in the previous step. Detailed statistics are maintained for the outcome of speculation and the utilization of the four processors.

The analyzer also models speculative thread preemption, which is used to avoid performance loss due to excessive imbalance. Short threads can tie up processor and buffer resources while waiting for longer, less speculative threads to retire. This may prevent other, more profitable, speculative threads from being forked. The preemption technique uses the scoreboard information. When a method fork is reached and no processor is available, its fitness is compared to that of the currently running threads. If some of the running threads have lower fitness and are more speculative than the one about to be forked, we squash the one with the lowest fitness and fork the new thread. For nested speculation, we adjust the fitness of the child under consideration by multiplying with that of the parent method. Currently, we do not adjust the fitness of running threads based on their execution time so far. When a thread completes, we adjust its fitness in the scoreboard to reflect whether it has successfully retired or was squashed due to a violation. This preemption technique can be implemented in the TLS runtime that controls thread forking without a significant increase in fork overhead.

Finally, we can select the methods that the trace analyzer considers based on the expected support for return value prediction in the CMP architecture. We currently model three types of prediction: none, single value, and perfect. "None" does not speculate on any non-void method. "Single value" only speculates on methods that return a single value throughout the execution of the program (e.g. an error code). "Perfect" allows for speculation on any method and assumes that its return value can be perfectly predicted. We discuss the interaction of the heuristics with return value prediction in Section 5.

The trace-based methodology allows for fast, high-accuracy simulations. The traces contain all the data needed to simulate the memory system behavior such as L1 and L2 hits/misses, inter-processor communication, and dependency violations. For non-memory instructions, we assume that their timing is the same as in the native runs and do not simulate their execution. Parallel execution changes the latency of certain loads (inter-processor transfers or L2 hits instead of L1 misses) and those may affect some non-memory instructions. Still, out-of-order processors can tolerate the latency of on-chip accesses. Only off-chip accesses (L2 misses) cause significant changes in the behavior of the processor [12]. For the benchmarks we studied, the 256-KByte L2 cache is large enough to hold their working set at all times, hence there is no difference in L2 misses between parallel and sequential execution. The speed advantage of our methodology was critical during the tuning phase of the heuristics, which required thousands of simulations for parameter sweeps.

4.3 Oracle Heuristic

As an extra comparison target, we have implemented a perfect oracle for selecting speculative threads. The oracle allows us to measure the maximum method-level parallelism available in these applications. Such a heuristic is impossible to implement in a practical system. The oracle has the following properties. It can make a separate decision for each individual invocation of a method. The fork points selected always lead to correct speculation (no violations). There is no overhead for forking or retiring threads. Effectively, the oracle heuristic is only limited by true dependencies between methods. The implementation of the oracle relies on the fact that the analyzer has access to the whole execution trace for each benchmark and includes the architecture model.

5 Evaluation

This section presents the evaluation of the thread selection heuristics on the simulated 4-way CMP system.

5.1 Heuristic Tuning

Before we apply the heuristics to the benchmarks and compare the performance they deliver, we needed to determine the optimal parameter values to be used with each heuristic. To accomplish this, we ran sweeps of all of the parameter values for each of the heuristics. Due to space considerations, we only present the results for some of the sweeps for the jess benchmark using the SI-RT, SP-SU, MP-SU, and MP-CS heuristics in Figure 4. Jess was fairly representative of the behavior we saw with most benchmarks during parameter tuning. Figure 4 presents both speedups over sequential execution and violation counts.

The SI-RT heuristic achieved the best results with the MIN and MAX runtime parameters chosen to be 10^3 cycles and 10^7 cycles respectively. The SI-SC heuristic generally performed best with a MAX threshold set to 10^5 store accesses. The parameters indicate that relatively large speculative threads are often needed to hide thread overhead and avoid load imbalance.

The SP-SU heuristic achieved the greatest speedup when the THRES value for the predicted relative speedup is set as low as possible (1.2 to 1.001). This suggests that this heuristic is very conservative in its selection, and when it is used, its threshold should be very low to allow it to be more aggressive. The MP-SU heuristic, on the other hand, achieved its greatest results with the THRES value set considerably higher, at 1.4. Even though the multi-pass heuristics are always more conservative than their single-pass equivalents when cycles saving are used, this is not always the case when speedups are concerned. The SP-CS and the MP-CS heuristics achieve their best results when the threshold value (THRES) is approximately 10^5, and when minimum predicted success rate of speculation is approximately 0.3. In other words, the allowed violation ratio (RATIO) is 0.7.

Figure 4 also shows the effect of the return value prediction method used with the trace-based simulations for method-level speculation. For the SP-SU and MP-SU heuristics, we present the speedup with the three supported prediction schemes. Speculating only on functions that are declared to return void severely limits the effectiveness of method-level speculation as most functions return some value. Adding speculation for functions that always return the same value gets us almost as much benefit as perfect return value prediction. This is due to the high frequency of virtually static error codes and the fact that in many cases the return value of a method is not used at all. Furthermore, our heuristics tend to select large methods for speculation, which rarely return anything but an error code. For most other benchmarks, the speedup difference between constant and perfect value prediction is even smaller. Since we are evaluating the potential of the speculation heuristics, the remainder of the numbers we present assume perfect return value prediction.

5.2 Heuristics Analysis

Figure 5 shows the speedup achieved using each of the proposed heuristics with the parameters values identified in the previous section. The speedups are relative to the execution time of the original sequential code for each benchmark. The first observation is that all practical heuristics lead to positive speedups. They are able to identify profitable threads that lead to sufficient useful parallelism to hide the speculation overheads. The maximum speedup achieved with the heuristics ranges from 1.4 to 1.8. This is a significant improvement over an out-of-order processor, especially for hard integer applications like javac and jess. For some of the lowest performing benchmarks such as raytrace and water, there is additional loop-level, speculative parallelism one can extract. Nevertheless, loop-level TLS is beyond the scope of this paper. It is also interesting to compare the practical heuristics to the perfect oracle. The maximum speedup with the heuristics is within 80% to 95% of the oracle speedup, which incurs no violations and no thread overhead. The result suggests that the proposed heuristics are quite effective.

Figure 5 also allows us to compare the different heuristics. While there is not single obvious winner across all benchmarks, some heuristics perform noticeably better than others. In general, the single-pass heuristics (SP-SU and SP-CS) perform as well or better than both simple and multi-pass heuristics. The multi-pass heuristics are more conservative in their selection of speculation candidates, and therefore suffer from under-speculation. The simple heuristics suffer from over-speculation for certain benchmarks. Still, simple heuristics are consistently better than multi-pass heuristics which suggests that over-speculation is better than under-speculation. Another interesting observation is that the Most Cycles Saved heuristics (SP-CS, MP-CS, MP-CSNN) tend to perform slightly better than their Best Speedup counterparts (SP-SU, MP-SU). This confirms our expectation that the absolute number of cycles saved is more important than the relative speedup of each speculative method candidate. Overall, the SP-CS heuristic (single-pass most cycles saved with no parent info) exhibits the best average performance.

Figure 6 analyzes the behavior of speculative threads

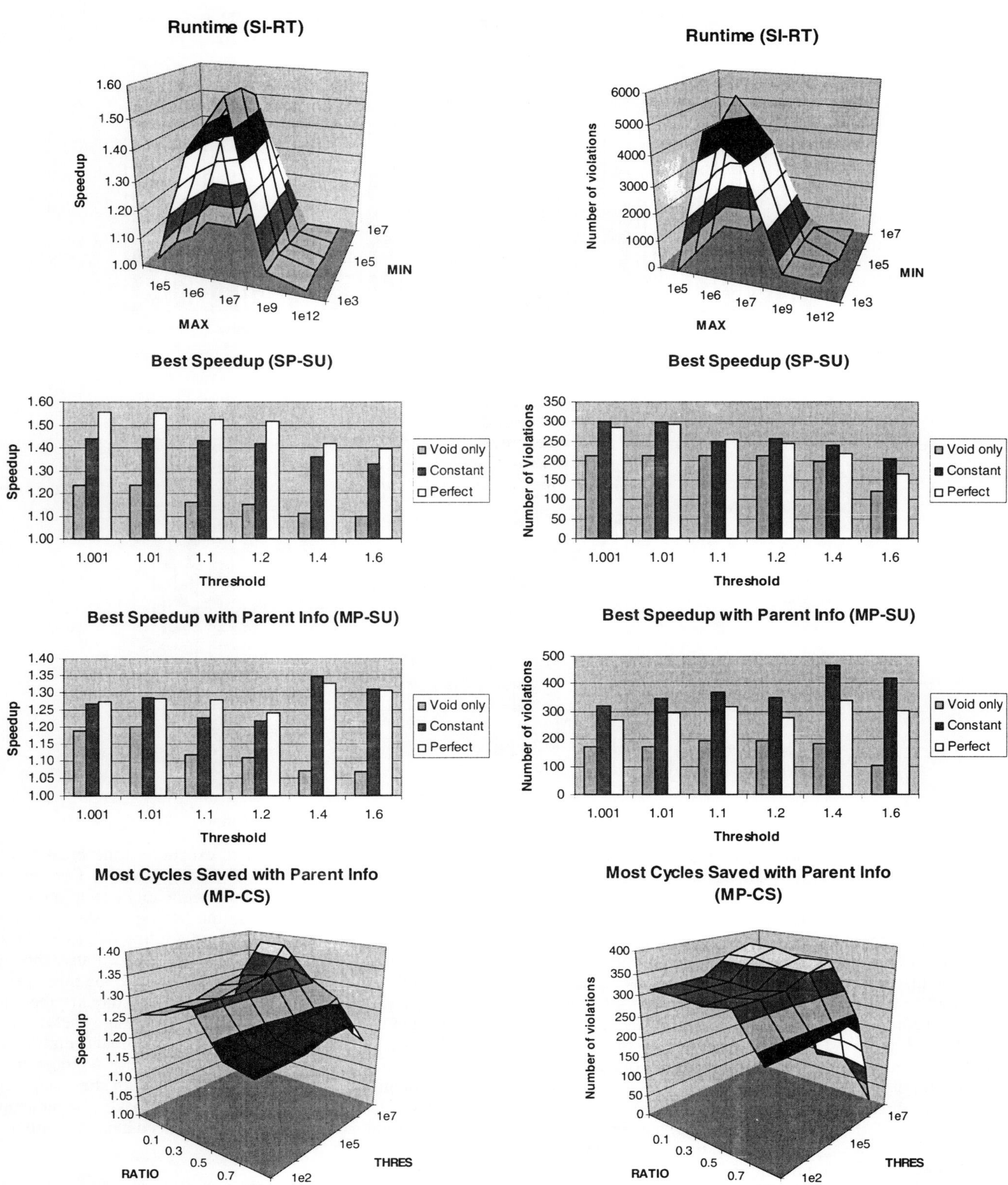

Figure 4. Results of the parameter sweep on the jess benchmark. The graphs on the left present speedups over sequential execution, while the graphs on the right present the number of violations.

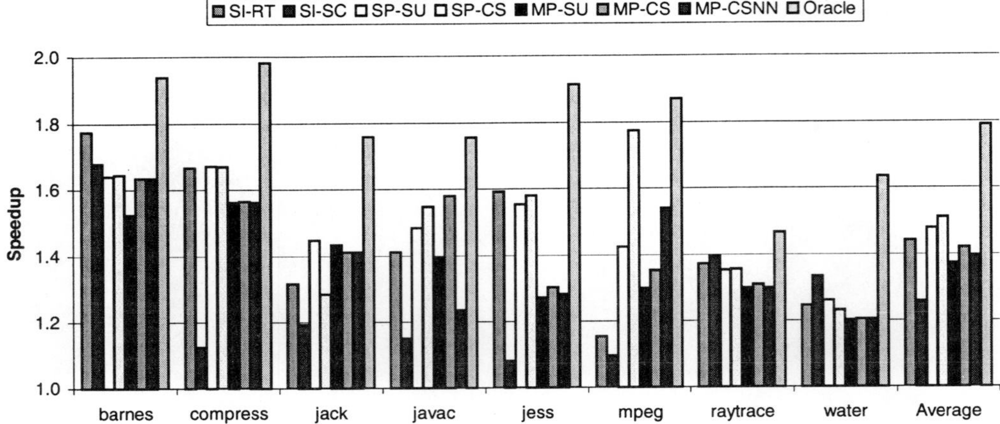

Figure 5. Overall speedups for each benchmark and heuristic.

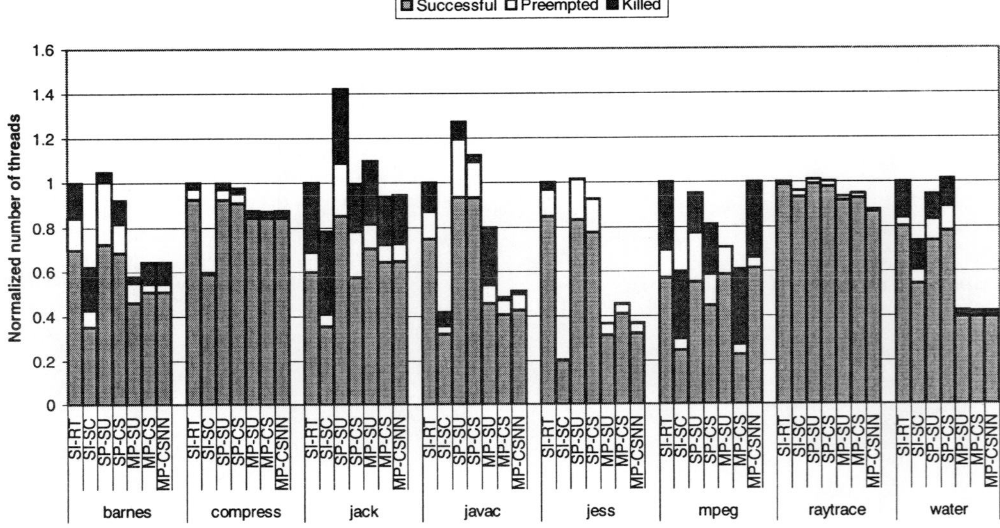

Figure 6. The breakdown of speculative threads generated for each benchmark.

forked with each heuristic. The height of each bar (total number of threads) is normalized to the number of speculations performed by the simple runtime heuristic SI-RT. Each bar is split into three sections: threads that completed successfully, threads that were preempted by another speculative thread considered more profitable at the time, and threads that were squashed due to violations. Single-pass and multi-pass heuristics tend to be more conservative than simple heuristics in terms of forking threads. For benchmarks like jack and mpeg, the selectivity in speculation is positive as it eliminates some of the violating threads of the simple heuristics without affecting significantly the profitable threads. For benchmarks like water or jess, on the other hand, the selectivity may lead to excessive underspeculation. This is particularly true for the multi-pass heuristics. A large number of preempted threads has no effect on performance (e.g. jack, javac, and mpeg). If processors are idling, it is not harmful to start a speculative thread on them even if it is likely that it will be preempted soon.

Figure 7 shows the average execution time breakdown across the 4 processors in the CMP system[1]. The height of each bar is normalized to the sequential execution time. Each bar has three segments: the time spent doing useful work on successful threads, the time idling due to the lack of speculative threads or due to a nested speculative thread reaching the end of a speculative region, and the time spent on work wasted due to thread violations, thread preemptions, and speculation overheads. The average useful time is always 25% of original time as we take initial useful work in the sequential program and split it across 4 processors. The amount of wasted time correlates with the complexity of the heuristic. Simple heuristics have a significant wasted component, which more advanced heuristics are of-

[1]Because Figure 7 provides an average across all four CPUs, the time it presents does not always correlate to the speedups in Figure 5. If two processors are making progress while the rest are idling, the speedup is two, while the average time breakdown shows an even break between idle and useful time.

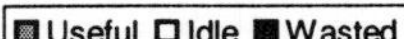

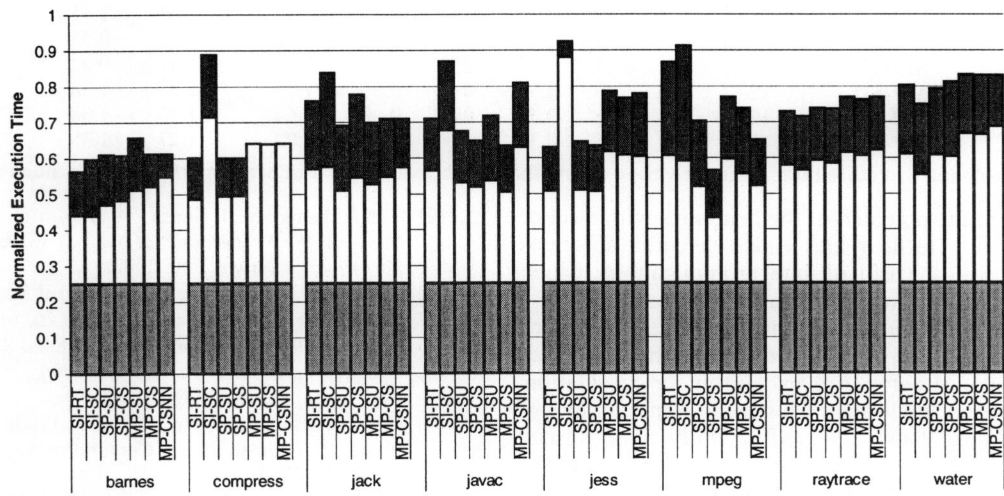

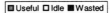

Figure 7. The breakdown in execution time for each benchmark and heuristic. The y-axis is normalized to the execution time of the sequential benchmark. Each bar is broken up into useful time, idle time, and wasted time.

ten able to eliminate, as seen with the barnes benchmark. However, in some cases the multi-pass heuristics simply increase the idle time due to under-speculation without making a significant change to the wasted time (e.g. compress). The single-pass heuristics achieve the best balance of under-speculation (idle time) and over-speculation (wasted time).

Figure 8 shows the maximum store buffer size required for speculative execution with each heuristic. We track speculative updates at word granularity both for buffering and violation detection purposes. The data suggest that a buffer size of 16 Kbytes per processor would be sufficient for all benchmarks with all heuristics. This buffer requirement can be easily met by the first level for both current and future CMP designs. Certain heuristics such as SI-RT require significantly less speculative buffering and can be fully satisfied with a couple of Kbytes. If the store buffer capacity is limited in a specific TLS implementation, a compiler may want to use a heuristic like SI-RT in order to avoid buffer overflows which cause significant performance loss due to serialization or main memory accesses [8].

6 Related Work

There has been significant research on TLS since the original proposal [18]. Most of the work has focused on hardware issues, while evaluations have mostly focused on loop-level parallelism [9, 14, 6, 19]. Compiler support for TLS has also focused on loops as a primary source for speculative threads [23, 7]. JRPM uses hardware supported profiling and heuristics to automatically select speculative threads from loops [3, 5]. A similar system could be used to implemented the heuristics discussed in this paper.

The potential of method-level speculation have been studied by [16, 21]. The heuristics used in these studies to select speculation points are fairly simple compared to our heuristics. Warg et al. examined a heuristic based solely on minimum runtime [22], which is similar to our SI-RT heuristic. Our work examines a much wider variety of heuristics. The speedups in [22] are not directly comparable to ours due to the different assumptions about the hardware systems. First, they assume a single-issue, in-order machine with perfect, one-cycle, memory access, while we assume an out-of-order processor with a cache hierarchy. They also assume multiple speculative buffers per CPU in the system. Hence, the reported speedups in [22] are much higher than ours but probably less realistic. Chen et al. investigated method-level speculation in a JVM environment [4], but selected all speculation points by hand.

The Multiscalar and SpMT compilers [20, 2] take advantage of both loop-level and method-level speculation. They operate at a basic block granularity as they use special hardware support for fine-grain parallelism. Their heuristics use profiling data such as dynamic instruction count. They do not compare the heuristics used to any others (or a perfect oracle) and provide little insight to how to tune them for performance. Our work is complementary to these studies as we evaluate alternative heuristics for thread selection. However, our work focuses on method-level speculation only.

7 Conclusions

TLS allows sequential code to benefit from the upcoming CMP chips. To realize this potential, we need compilers capable of selecting speculative threads that maximize the benefits of TLS while minimizing its performance overheads. This paper presented and analyzed a set of heuristics for automatic selection of speculative threads at method boundaries by a dynamic or profile-driven compiler. The heuristics involve increasing amounts of profiling information and selection complexity. As heuristics get more complex, the goal is to filter out methods that are unlikely to lead to profitable speculation.

	barnes	compress	jack	javac	jess	mpeg	raytrace	water
SI-RT	0.31	0.18	0.39	2.05	0.26	0.76	1.64	0.20
SI-SC	12.02	6.47	0.19	3.51	0.15	13.02	1.64	1.45
SP-SU	8.11	6.48	0.39	1.08	0.30	13.02	1.64	0.55
SP-MC	0.31	6.48	0.39	2.57	0.30	15.29	1.64	0.22
MP-SU	12.01	6.48	0.39	0.30	0.30	1.27	1.27	1.38
MP-CS	12.02	6.48	0.39	0.30	0.30	1.64	1.27	1.38
MP-CSNN	12.02	6.48	0.39	2.57	0.30	13.02	1.27	1.38

Figure 8. Speculative store buffer size for various combinations of heuristics and benchmarks. All the values are Kbytes.

We evaluated the potential of the heuristics with a set of Java applications. The heuristics lead to execution speedups of 1.4 to 1.8 even for difficult integer applications, which is within 80% to 96% of the performance possible with a perfect oracle. We demonstrated that single-pass heuristics lead to the best average performance by consistently providing a good balance between over- and under-speculation. On the other hand, multi-pass heuristics often lead to significant under-speculation and are frequently outperformed by the simple heuristics. The buffering requirements of the generated speculative threads are reasonable for current and future CMP designs.

References

[1] V. Agarwal et al. Clock rate versus IPC: the End of the Road for Conventional Microarchitectures. In *the Proceedings of the Intl. Symposium on Computer Architecture*, June 2000.

[2] A. Bhowmik and M. Franklin. A General Compiler Framework for Speculative Multithreading. In *the Proceedings of the Symposium on Parallel Architectures and Algorithms*, June 2002.

[3] M. Chen and K. Olukotun. TEST: A tracer for extracting speculative threads. In *the Proceedings of the Intl. Symposium on Code Generation and Optimization*, Mar. 2003.

[4] M. K. Chen and K. Olukotun. Exploiting Method-Level Parallelism in Single-Threaded Java Programs. In *the Proceedings of the Intl. Conference on Parallel Architectures and Compilation Techniques*, Oct. 1998.

[5] M. K. Chen and K. Olukotun. The Jrpm System for Dynamically Parallelizing Java Programs. In *the Proceedings of the Intl. Symposium on Computer Architecture*, June 2003.

[6] M. Cintra et al. Architectural Support for Scalable Speculative Parallelization in Shared-Memory Multiprocessors. In *Proceedings of the Intl. Symposium on Computer Architecture*, June 2000.

[7] J. Dou and M. Cintra. Compiler Estimation of Load Imbalance Overhead in Speculative Parallelization. In *the Proceedings of the Intl. Conference on Parallel Architectures and Compilation Techniques*, Oct. 2004.

[8] M. Gatzaran et al. Tradeoffs in Buffering Memory Sate for Thread-Level Speculation in Multiprocessors. In *the Proceedings of the Intl. Symposium on High Performance Computer Architecture*, Feb. 2003.

[9] L. Hammond et al. Data Speculation Support for a Chip Multiprocessor. In *the Proceedings of the Symposium on Architectural Support for Programming Languages and Operating Systems*, Oct. 1998.

[10] T. Heil and J. Smith. Relational Profiling: Enabling Thread Level Parallelism in Virtual Machines. In *the Proceedings of the Intl. Symposium on Microarchitecture*, Dec. 2000.

[11] R. Kalla. Simultaneous Multi-threading Implementation in POWER5. In *the Conference Record of Hot Chips 15 Symposium*, Aug. 2003.

[12] T. Karkhanis and J. Smith. A Day in the Life of a Cache Miss. In *the Proceedings of the 2nd Workshop on Memory Performance Issues*, June 2002.

[13] P. Kongetira. A 32-way Multithreaded Sparc Processor. In *the Conference Record of Hot Chips 16*, Aug. 2004.

[14] P. Marcuello and A. González. Clustered Speculative Multithreaded Processors. In *the Proceedings of the Intl. Conference on Supercomputing*, June 1999.

[15] C. McNairy. Montecito: The next Product in the Itanium Processor Family. In *the Conference Record of Hot Chips 16*, Aug. 2004.

[16] J. T. Oplinger et al. In Search of Speculative Thread-Level Parallelism. In *the Proceedings of the Intl. Conference on Parallel Architectures and Compilation Techniques*, Oct. 1999.

[17] M. K. Prabhu and K. Olukotun. Using Thread-Level Speculation to Simplify Manual Parallelization. In *the Proceedings of the Conference on Principles and Practices of Parallel Programming*, June 2003.

[18] G. S. Sohi et al. Multiscalar Processors. In *the Proceedings of the Intl. Symposium on Computer Architecture*, June 1995.

[19] J. G. Steffan et al. A Scalable Approach to Thread-Level Speculation. In *the Proceedings of the Intl. Symposium on Computer Architecture*, June 2000.

[20] T. N. Vijaykumar and G. S. Sohi. Task Selection for the Multiscalar Architecture. *Journal of Parallel and Distributed Computing*, 58(2):132–158, Aug. 1999.

[21] F. Warg and P. Stenstrom. Limits on Speculative Module-Level Parallelism in Imperative and Object-Oriented Programs on CMP Platforms. In *the Proceedings of the Intl. Conference on Parallel Architectures and Compilation Techniques*, Sept. 2001.

[22] F. Warg and P. Stenstrom. Improving Speculative Thread-Level Parallelism Through Module Run-Length Prediction. In *the Proceedings of the Int. Parallel and Distributed Processing Symposium*, 2003.

[23] A. Zhai et al. Compiler Optimizatoin for Scalar Value Communication Between Speculative Threads. In *the Proceedings of the Intl. Symposium on Architectural Support for Programming Languages and Operating Systems*, Oct. 2002.

[24] G. Zilles and G. Sohi. A Programmable Co-Processor for Profiling. In *the Proceedings of the Intl. Symposium on High Performance Computer Architecture*, Jan. 2001.

A Complexity-Effective Simultaneous Multithreading Architecture

Carmelo Acosta † Ayose Falcón ‡ Alex Ramirez † Mateo Valero †

† Departament d'Arquitectura de Computadors
Universitat Politecnica de Catalunya –Barcelona, Spain
{cacosta, aramirez, mateo}@ac.upc.edu

‡ Barcelona Research Office
HP Labs
ayose.falcon@hp.com

Abstract

Different applications may exhibit radically different behaviors and thus have very different requirements in terms of hardware support. In Simultaneous Multithreading (SMT) architectures, the hardware is shared among multiple running applications in order to better profit from it. However, current architectures are designed for the common case, and try to satisfy a number of different application classes with a single design. That is, current designs are usually overdesigned for most cases, obtaining high performance, but wasting a lot of resources to do so.

In this paper we present an alternative SMT architecture, the Heterogeneously Distributed SMT (hdSMT). *Our architecture is based in a novel combination of SMT and clustering techniques in a heterogeneity-aware fashion. The hardware is designed to match the heterogeneous application behavior with the statically and heterogeneously partitioned resources. Such a design is aimed for minimizing the amount of resources wasted to achieve a given performance rate. On top of our statically partitioned architecture, we propose an heuristic policy to map threads to clusters so that each cluster matches the characteristics of the running threads and overall hardware usage is optimized.*

We compare our hdSMT architecture with a monolithic SMT processor, where all threads compete for the same resources, and with a homogeneous clustered SMT, where resources are statically and equally partitioned across clusters. Our results show that hdSMT architectures obtain an average improvement of 13% and 14% in optimizing performance per area over monolithic SMT and homogeneously clustered SMT respectively.

Keywords - SMT, CMP, Clustering, Complexity-Effective, Heterogeneity-Awareness, Mapping Policies.

1 Introduction

The needs of today's multi-programmed workloads put pressure on microprocessor design towards high-performance and high-throughput machines. Thus, new approaches have arisen aimed at such a multithreaded scenario, improving traditional superscalar processor capabilities. Simultaneous multithreading (SMT) [20, 18, 19] and chip multiprocessors (CMP) [11, 6] are two of these approaches. The first one evolves the traditional superscalar architecture by sharing all the processor resources among more than one running thread. The latter relies on simpler cores, replicating them on a single chip and allocating running threads to these cores. Each one represents a different approach to optimize the performance that a fixed transistor budget can produce: A big machine where every resource is shared versus several simpler machines where the sharing locality is restricted. But they also imply a commitment: the single thread high-performance of SMT, at a complexity cost, against the low complexity but limited single-threaded performance of CMP. However, there is also a wide spectrum in between SMT and CMP approaches as we vary the amount of shared resources on chip [4].

As the number of transistors on chip increases, the issue of how to employ them to achieve the highest performance potential gets renewed importance. The design complexity has to remain under reasonable costs while it achieves the highest performance potential. But achieving high levels of both performance and throughput from a given hardware budget at a reasonable complexity cost is not an easy task. Employing the additional resources to simply stretch traditional structures, such as instruction queues, is not conducive towards building highly pipelined processors with short clock periods. Besides, power and thermal considerations also have to be taken into account since future microprocessors' designs are likely to be limited by them. In this sense, the reduced complexity of the CMP approach combined with the resource exploitation capacity of the SMT approach seems an appealing alternative.

General-purpose designs treat applications homogeneously, although not all applications have the same behavior. In fact, we can find a huge inter-application heterogeneity in current multi-programmed workloads, which can be measured in terms of memory misses, branch mispredictions or instruction level parallelism (ILP) among others. This heterogeneity results sometimes in applications executed using an amount of resources and power that is not cost-effective with the performance obtained. The techniques applied in SMT processors to reduce the contention over shared resources between conflictive applications [17, 5] can help to face up this heterogeneity in application behavior. However, instead of helping to reduce the design complexity they even increase it. In the CMP approach, each running application is assigned to one of the homogeneous cores in which the hardware has been partitioned. The design complexity is kept low at the cost of a static limitation to the hardware that each application can use, equal for all applications. By making the hardware conscious of this inter-application heterogeneity, or heterogeneity-aware, we could keep design complexity reasonably low without losing too much performance. The central insight behind a heterogeneity-aware design is giving each application access to a cost-effective amount of resources.

In this paper, we propose the *Heterogeneously Distributed Simultaneous Multithreading (hdSMT)* architecture, a novel heterogeneity-aware SMT architecture that combines SMT and clustering techniques. We review the open issue of on chip resource distribution and propose a simultaneous multithreading processor in which all the pipeline stages but the fetch stage have been heterogeneously clustered —pipelined from now on—, making up a multipipeline SMT processor. Besides the fetch engine, all the pipelines share the memory subsystem —including L1 caches— and the register file. Consequently, the single-thread performance is not hampered by a memory or register file static distribution as could happen in a CMP processor. In this architecture the heterogeneity of the typical software that will be executed on the processor is analyzed and mirrored itself in the hardware. Thus, the heterogeneous behavior of the running applications is matched with the heterogeneous hardware, mapping software needs to heterogeneously partitioned hardware resources. This hardware configuration also allows reducing the contention between conflictive threads as occurs in SMT processors. Thus, the application-to-pipeline matching process also intends to put conflictive threads in different pipelines, in order to reduce a counterproductive interaction.

2 The hdSMT Architecture

The foundations of the hdSMT architecture are comprised of a threefold combination of well known principles and techniques: *SMT*, *clustering*, and *heterogeneity-awareness*. An hdSMT processor proposes a multithreaded alternative that lays on the spectrum that extends in between SMT and CMP processors. As evaluated in [4], there are multiple possible hardware configurations in between SMT and CMP processors, as we vary the amount of resources shared among the execution cores. However, the heterogeneity in applications' behavior makes vary the hardware requirements among different applications. This heterogeneity may turn the evenly clustered approaches in [4] into not optimal. To better profit from the available hardware it should be heterogeneously clustered and the applications appropriately matched with the clusters according to their needs. The hdSMT architecture maximizes the available hardware budget by taking into account the heterogeneity in this way.

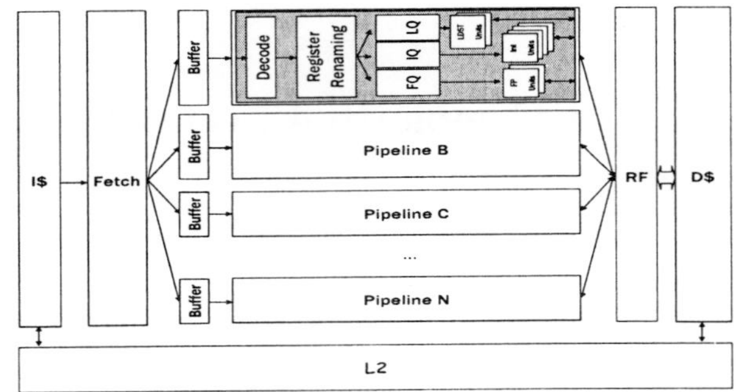

Fig. 1. The hdSMT Architecture.

The hdSMT architecture overview is depicted in Fig. 1. As in a conventional SMT processor, all threads share the caches, register file, and fetch engine. However, the rest of the pipeline stages and resources are arranged in heterogeneous clusters (or pipelines). So, each pipeline comprises all the pipeline stages of the conventional processor but the fetch stage. Each pipeline also has got its own private instruction queues, renaming map tables and functional units. The size and number of these resources may vary from pipeline to pipeline. Additionally, each thread's instructions are stored in a private reorder buffer (ROB), one per thread.

In this clustered multithreaded architecture, entire threads are assigned to pipelines according to heterogeneity. This implies that there are no dependencies between instructions in different clusters, since all instructions from a single thread are mapped to the same pipeline. The heterogeneity-aware fetch engine strives to match both the needs of each running application and the interaction among each application with the heterogeneously distributed hardware. This software-hardware mapping is performed each time the job scheduler of the operating system selects a new bunch of active threads. The whole subsequent execution of the workload is done according to this mapping. We describe more in detail the mapping policy in Section 2.1.

The number of hardware contexts and width of each pipeline may vary from pipeline to pipeline. So, an hdSMT microarchitecture may be comprised of both narrow single-threaded and wide multithreaded pipelines, as well intermediate pipelines. Depending on the resource needs of each application and the interaction between application behavior, more than one application may be mapped to a single pipeline. This distribution of the hardware contexts along the chip can be profited to turn off idle pipelines whenever the number of running applications does not reach the number of hardware contexts. This is also applied in the Heterogenous Multi-Core architecture [7], turning off idle heterogeneous cores. The main difference of our proposal in this sense is that we can still use the whole budget of physical registers and memory space to improve the performance of the running applications, since they are shared by all pipelines.

Notice that multipipeline-awareness in hdSMT uncovers new fetch policies not available in conventional SMT processors. The shared fetch engine is limited by the number and width of the instruction cache ports. However, the number of instructions that each pipeline accept per cycle may vary from pipeline to pipeline. In order to decouple the fetch engine from the characteristics of each specific pipeline it feeds, some small buffers are added before each pipeline (see Fig. 1). Thus, the fetch engine inserts in-order the fetched instructions at its own rate while each pipeline extracts in-order instructions according to its width. The fetch policy takes into account these buffers in order to appropriately balance the instructions fetched among the pipelines. Depending on the pipeline set characteristics, this may result in a wider global decode bandwidth since all pipelines are fed from their private buffer each cycle.

2.1 Mapping policies in hdSMT

The impact of static partitions of the hardware may be either productive or counterproductive depending on the resource partitioned. Thus, as showed in [12], while statically partitioning instruction queues provides good performance, an static division of the issue bandwidth has a negative impact on throughput.

In order to avoid this penalty, the hardware in the hdSMT architecture is heterogeneously distributed and a thread-to-pipeline mapping policy is applied. The success in avoiding this negative effect will depend on the ability of the mapping policy to map high-performing threads to wide pipelines, to profit from their wide issue bandwidth.

In this work we have used a simple profile-based heuristic policy that uses the memory behavior of each thread to do the mapping. By means of profile information, the active threads are arranged by the number of data cache misses and assigned to the pipelines. The full mapping process is as follows:

1. Arrange all active threads by the number of data cache misses in a list (T). The first thread in T is the one with the lesser number of misses.
2. Arrange all pipelines by their width in a list (P). The first pipeline in P is the widest one.
3. Map the first thread in T to the first pipeline in P.
4. If this is the first assignment, and there are more available hardware contexts than active threads then remove the top of the list P.
5. Remove the top of the list T.
6. If all the hardware contexts of the pipeline in the top of the list P are busy then remove the top of the list P.
7. If list T is not empty continue in step 3.

Regarding interaction among applications, it is assumed that applications with a similar number of data cache misses behave similarly and therefore can share a single pipeline. Thus, the negative scenario in which applications with a bad memory behavior hinder applications with a good memory behavior is avoided. In this sense, our mapping policy assumes that adjacent applications in the list T behave similarly and consequently could share a single pipeline.

In order to match each application with the appropriate pipeline, our mapping policy makes this simple assumption: the number of data cache misses of an application is inversely proportional to the pipeline width required. The more data cache misses occurred during an application execution, the more resources will be held by that application while each miss is resolved. By doing so, we expect to match each application with the most appropriate pipeline, that is the one in which it is obtained the highest performance but involving the lowest resource budget.

3 Area Cost Model

In this work we evaluate different microarchitectures, which involve different hardware budgets. Since comparing the results produced by microarchitectures with different amount of resources may be quite unfair, we need some complexity measurement to guide this evaluation. Quantifying complexity is a tricky task and giving a single and comparable measurement is even harder to accomplish. In this paper we follow a quite generalized approach and use the area (in mm^2) of the processor as a metric of its "complexity". Although complexity is not proportional to area in all cases, it gives a quite accurate idea of the resultant complexity and is reasonably easy to be measured.

To estimate the area of each configuration we employ the *Karlsruhe Simultaneous Multithreaded Simulator* [14, 15, 16]. On top of this area estimation tool we develop our area cost model. Since both hdSMT and SMT approaches share the same register file and caches, we have removed them from the model to simplify the results. However, since in hdSMT these resources are shared among all pipelines, the additional logic cost is taken into account. It is added to the execution core of each pipeline, as additional hardware for data access. The hdSMT fetch engine also needs some additional logic. Although its characteristics are similar to the SMT one, multipipeline support requires some extra logic. Taking into consideration Burns and Gaudiot work in quantifying SMT layout overhead [1, 2], we have extrapolated single to multipipeline environment area overhead from single to multithreading environment. So we have estimated the area overhead of the execution core within each pipeline in a 10%. The conventional SMT fetch engine area overhead, when applied to a hdSMT multipipeline environment, has been estimated in a 20%.

In our evaluation, we use four different models of pipeline, named *M8*, *M6*, *M4*, and *M2*. The number in each model name gives a hint of the amount of resources it has been devoted. Our conventional monolithic SMT baseline processor is represented by the M8 model. The remainder models represent pipelines with reduced resources budget with respect to the baseline. The functional units are among the private resources of each pipeline. In order to choose the most appropriate number of functional units for each pipeline, we evaluated the performance obtained as we reduced them, starting from the baseline model (M8). With all other resources changed to the pipeline new values, in each case it was chosen the number of functional units that kept the slowdown below the 2%.

Our area cost model considers the total area as the sum, for all constituent pipelines, of the instruction fetch, decode, dispatch, execution core, and instruction completion stages plus the decode, dispatch, and completition queues. In hdSMT and homogeneously clustered SMT configurations, comprised of combinations of M6, M4, and M2 models, only one instruction fetch stage is included in the total area calculus. In Fig. 2.(a) the amount of resources devoted to each pipeline model is shown. Additionally, we have assumed a per-thread 256-entry ROB in all configurations, both SMT and hdSMT. In Fig. 2.(b) we show the area estimation of each model according to our area cost model. All estimations have been made in 0.18 μm, as in [1], to ease our area overhead extrapolations. Notice that in Fig. 2.(b) M6, M4, and M2 pipelines are accompanied by an instruction fetch stage a 20% bigger than the baseline (M8) one. Each of them represent in fact an hdSMT processor with a single pipeline, the one measured in each case.

Finally, as shown in Fig. 2.(a), our SMT baseline (M8) is not able to execute more than four threads. Although adding additional hardware contexts increases the total area of an SMT processor, as Burns and Gaudiot evaluate in [1], we assume no additional area overhead for this model when adding two additional hardware contexts; in order to execute workloads of six threads on it.

	M8	M6	M4	M2
Hardware Contexts	4	2	2	1
Max. Instr./cycle	8	6	4	2
Max. Threads/cycle	2	2	2	1
Queues (IQ/FQ/LQ)	64	32	32	16
Integer Func. Units	6	4	3	1
FP Func. Units	3	2	2	1
LD/ST Units	4	2	2	1

a) Resources.

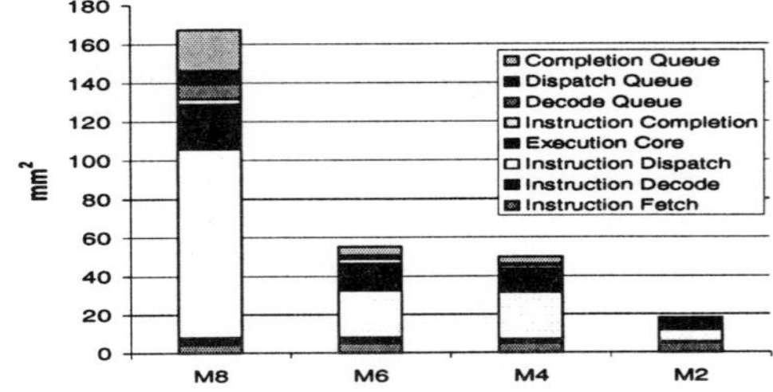

b) Area estimation.

Fig. 2. Pipeline models.

4 Simulation Setup

We use a trace driven SMT simulator derived from SMT-SIM [18]. The simulator consists of our own trace driven front-end and an improved version of SMT-SIM's back-end, that provides multipipeline support among others. Both the monolithic SMT and the multipipeline configurations have an 8 stage pipeline depth. Our simulator also permits execution along wrong paths by having a separate basic block dictionary in which information of all static instructions is contained.

As mentioned earlier in Section 3, we use four different models of pipelines: M8, M6, M4, and M2. Our monolithic SMT baseline processor is represented by model M8. Additionally to model characteristics shown in Fig. 2.(a), the baseline configuration, used in both monolithic and multipipeline configurations, is shown in Table 1. Besides, since hdSMT requires additional logic to handle multipipeline register file sharing we duplicate the number of cycles required by register reads/writes in hdSMT configurations. Thus, register reads/writes have a latency of 1 cycle in case of a monolithic SMT processor as against the 2 cycle latency of the hdSMT processors.

In our experiments, we adopt the FLUSH [17] fetch policy for the baseline (M8) case. This fetch policy, built on top of ICOUNT 2.8 [19], predicts an L2 miss every time a load spends more cycles in the cache hierarchy than needed to access the L2 cache. In case of L2 miss, the instructions after the L2 missing load are flushed, and the offending thread is stalled until the load is resolved. Thus, the resources used by the offending thread are freed and it does not compete

Branch Predictor	perceptron (4K local, 256 perceps)
BTB	256 entries, 4-way associative
RAS*	256 entries
ROB Size*	256 entries
Rename Registers	256 regs.
L1 I-Cache	64KB, 2-way, 8 banks
L1 D-Cache	64KB, 2-way, 8 banks
L1 lat./misspenalty	3/22 cyc.
L2 Cache	512KB, 2-way, 8 banks
L2 latency	12 cyc.
Main Memory Latency	250 cyc.
I-TLB/D-TLB/TLB missp.	48 ent. / 128 ent. / 300 cyc.

Table 1. Simulation parameters (resources marked with * are replicated per thread)

for new resources until the load is resolved. This allows the other threads to proceed while the stalled thread is waiting for the outstanding cache miss.

In all other cases, we adopt the L1MCOUNT fetch policy, a variant of the DCache Warn fetch policy [3]. This fetch policy keeps track of the number of inflight loads. Threads are arranged by the number of inflight loads they have and given fetch priority accordingly. Threads with fewer number of inflight loads have priority. In case of equal number of inflight loads, threads allocated to wider pipelines have priority over those in narrower pipelines. Finally, in case of pipeline coincidence, the ICOUNT 2.8 policy is applied. Regardless of the fetch policy, all simulations are limited to 8 instructions fetchable per cycle, from a maximum of 2 threads. In order to decouple the shared fetch engine from each pipeline characteristics, we have put a buffer between the fetch engine and each pipeline (see Fig. 1). The size of these buffers is 32 entries, for M6 and M4 pipeline models, and 16 entries, for M2 pipeline model.

We use the SPEC2000 integer benchmark suite. From them, we have collected traces of the most representative 300 million instruction segment of each benchmark, following the idea presented in [13]. Each program is compiled with the *-O2 -non_shared* options using DEC Alpha AXP-21264 C/C++ compiler and executed using the reference input set. Tables 2 and 3 show the workloads used in our simulations. We have used workloads including 2, 4, and 6 threads. Workloads are classified according to the characteristics of the included benchmarks: with high instruction-level parallelism (ILP), with bad memory behavior (MEM), or a mix of both (MIX). Due to the characteristics of SPECint2000, with few benchmarks that are really memory bounded, MEM workloads are only feasible for 2 and 4 threads.

In each experiment, we strictly focus on the period of time in which all the initial threads share the processor. The objective in each case is evaluating the behavior of each microarchitecture with workloads of two, four and six threads. This means that each simulation finishes as soon as one thread contained in the evaluated workload finishes executing 300 million instructions.

Wld	Benchmarks	T	Wld	Benchmarks	T
2W1	eon, gcc	I	4W1	eon, gcc, gzip, bzip2	I
2W2	crafty, bzip2	I	4W2	crafty, bzip2, eon, gzip	I
2W3	gap, vortex	I	4W3	gap, vortex, parser, crafty	I
2W4	mcf, twolf	M	4W4	mcf, twolf, vpr, perlbmk	M
2W5	vpr, perlbmk	M	4W5	vpr, perlbmk, mcf, twolf	M
2W6	vpr, twolf	M	4W6	gzip, twolf, bzip2, mcf	X
2W7	gzip, twolf	X	4W7	crafty, perlbmk, mcf, bzip2	X
2W8	crafty, perlbmk	X	4W8	parser, vpr, vortex, twolf	X
2W9	parser, vpr	X	4W9	vpr, twolf, gap, vortex	X

Table 2. Two and four threaded workloads (I=ILP, M=MEM, X=MIX)

Wld	Benchmarks	T
6W1	gzip, gcc, crafty, eon, gap, bzip2	I
6W2	gcc, crafty, parser, eon, gap, vortex	I
6W3	gzip, vpr, mcf, eon, perlbmk, bzip2	X
6W4	vpr, mcf, crafty, perlbmk, vortex, twolf	X

Table 3. Six threaded workloads.

4.1 Microarchitectures and Metrics

In our experiments, we evaluate several multipipeline microarchitectures, both homogeneously and heterogeneously distributed. All these multipipeline microarchitectures are implementations of the hdSMT architecture[1]. In Fig. 3 we show the area estimation of all microarchitectures evaluated. Beneath each area estimation appears the microarchitecture name, which stands for the number and type of pipeline models involved. So, the 2M4+2M2 microarchitecture is comprised of 2 pipelines of type M4 plus two pipelines of type M2 (see Fig. 2 for specific details of each pipeline type). From left to right, the first microarchitecture (M8) in Fig. 3 represents our monolithic SMT baseline. The next two microarchitectures (3M4 and 4M4) are homogeneous clustered hdSMT microarchitectures. Finally, the last three microarchitectures represents the truly hdSMT microarchitectures. According to Fig. 3, all but two microarchitectures (4M4 and 1M6+2M4+2M2) require less area than the monolithic SMT baseline. That is, they are "simpler" than the SMT baseline.

For each microarchitecture we evaluate its performance (IPC) for all workloads. However, since each microarchitecture has a different resource budget and consequently a different performance potential, we also take into account the complexity involved. In order to make a fairer comparison we combine the performance and the complexity of each microarchitecture in a single metric. Thus, in this paper we also provide results measured in Performance per Area, which is obtained by dividing the resulting performance of a microarchitecture by its area (in mm^2). This additional metric allows to evaluate the "complexity-effectiveness" of each microarchitecture.

[1] Although the homogeneous ones do not obey the hdSMT principle of heterogeneous distribution of resources.

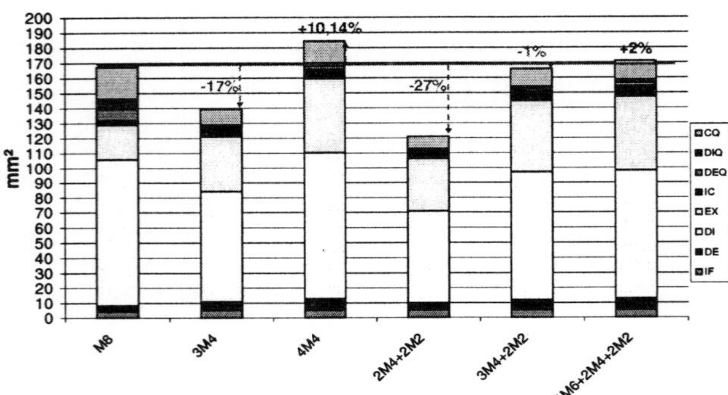

Fig. 3. Area estimation of evaluated microarchitectures.

5 Simulation Results

In this section, we evaluate and compare monolithic SMT, homogeneously distributed hdSMT, and heterogeneous distributed hdSMT processors. For each workload, three measurements are given. First, the BEST result, obtained using an oracle thread mapping policy, gives the maximum performance of the microarchitecture. Second, the HEUR result gives the performance obtained by the microarchitecture using the heuristic thread mapping policy presented in Section 2.1. Finally, the WORST result gives the performance obtained by the microarchitecture in case of applying in each case the worst possible thread-to-pipeline mapping. Special cases are the baseline (M8) and the two-threaded workloads of homogeneous distributions (3M4 and 4M4). Since the baseline is not multipipelined, no thread-to-pipeline mapping policy is needed and so only one measurement is given. In two-threaded workloads, when all pipelines are of the same sort the three measurements (BEST, HEUR, WORST) coincide.

Fig. 4 shows the raw performance results (measured in IPC) for all microarchitectures evaluated. In each case, the harmonic mean of all workloads of a same type and size is shown. These results point out that, although some hdSMT results are quite similar to SMT baseline ones, the hdSMT results are exceeded by the SMT baseline ones in some cases. Comparing the baseline (M8) and best-performing hdSMT (1M6+2M4+2M2) means, we got baseline speedups over hdSMT of 5%, 4% and 15% in ILP, MEM, and MIX workloads respectively. In the first two cases, the mean performance of hdSMT is not quite bad considering that the hdSMT microarchitecture is able to execute up to 8 threads while the resource budget of the baseline (M8) in fact is not able to execute more than 4 threads (as mentioned in Section 3). Nevertheless, the ability to flush and re-execute instructions of the baseline is crucial in the MIX scenario. Although this is the general trend, notice that hdSMT is able to outperform the SMT baseline in the six-threaded ILP workload scenario (see Fig. 4.(a)).

The previous results strictly take into consideration the performance that each microarchitecture obtains executing the given workloads. However, each microarchitecture involves a different amount of resources; and a different power consumption among others. To make a fairer comparison we show in Fig. 5 the Performance per Area results for all microarchitectures evaluated. Again, the harmonic mean of all workloads of a same type and size is shown. From these results, we can infer that the hdSMT architecture achieves higher performance per area ratios than the monolithic SMT architecture, that is, better relative results than SMT using fewer resources. Comparing the baseline (M8) and best-performance-per-area hdSMT (2M4+2M2) means, we got hdSMT improvements over the SMT baseline of 15%, 18% and 10% in ILP, MEM, and MIX workloads respectively.

Regarding the homogeneous (3M4, 4M4) or heterogeneous distribution (2M4+2M2, 3M4+2M2, 1M6+2M4++2M2) of hdSMT processors, results in Figs. 4 and 5 point out that heterogeneous distributions are better than homogeneous ones. Thus, for each case there is a heterogeneous distribution that overcomes, both in terms of absolute performance and performance per area, all homogeneous distributions.

From all previous results it can also be inferred that the thread-to-pipeline mapping policy is a crucial factor in hdSMT architecture. This can be noticed by comparing the BEST and HEUR results in Figs. 4 and 5. As an example, notice that the 2M4+2M2 hdSMT microarchitecture obtains the highest performance per area ratios in all but the four-threaded MEM workload case. In that case, although the oracle mapping policy obtains a 9% improvement over the baseline, the heuristic accuracy drops to 76%, resulting in a worse result than the baseline. From Figs. 4 and 5 it is also noticeable that the effectiveness of the mapping policy depends on the specific hdSMT microarchitecture. Thus, while the heuristic applied in this work achieves 92% and 96% accuracy in 2M4+2M2 and 1M6+2M4+2M2 microarchitectures respectively, its accuracy drops to a 88% in 3M4+2M2 microarchitecture.

To summarize, our results point out that the hdSMT achieves its goal of minimizing the amount of wasted resources. In this sense, it obtains a 13% and 14% improvement in optimizing performance per area over monolithic SMT and homogeneously clustered SMT, respectively. Regarding to raw performance, monolithic SMT obtains in mean a 6% speedup over hdSMT. Nevertheless, hdSMT obtains in mean a 7% raw performance speedup over homogeneously clustered SMT. Finally, the results also indicate that the thread-to-pipeline mapping policy plays a very important role in hdSMT.

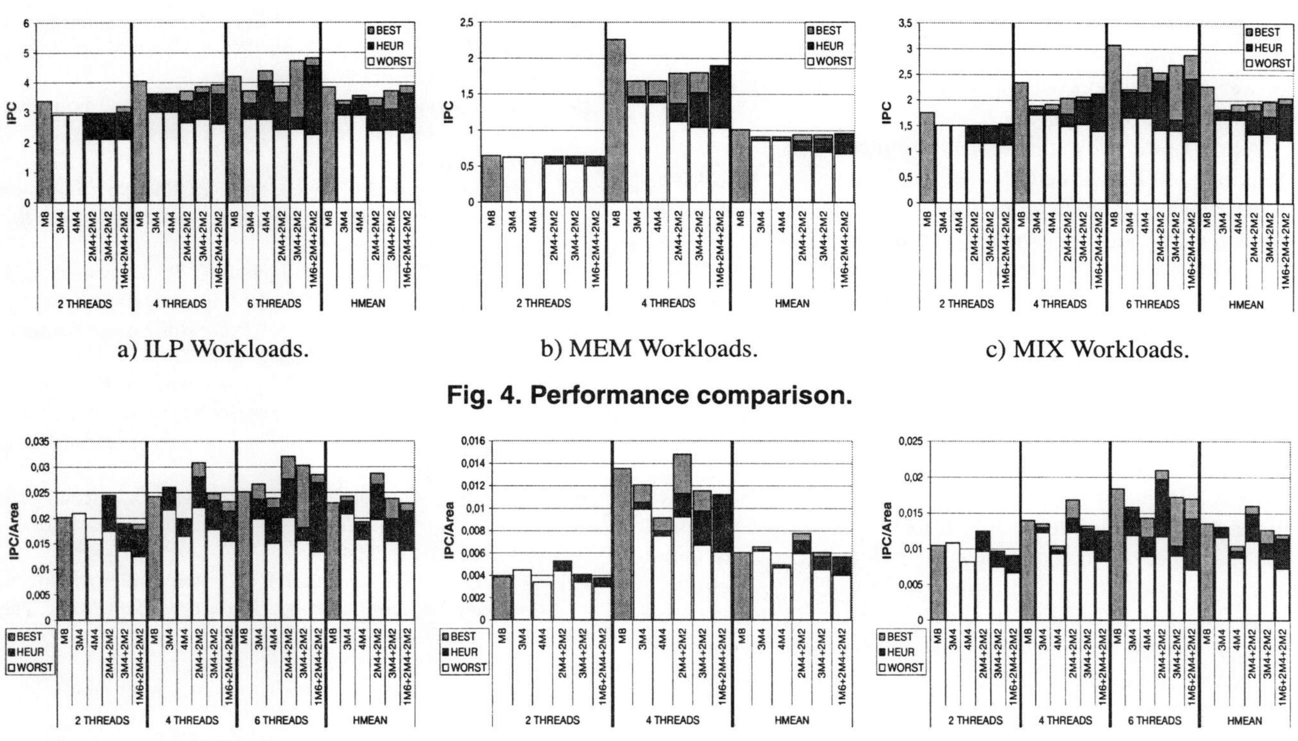

a) ILP Workloads. b) MEM Workloads. c) MIX Workloads.

Fig. 4. Performance comparison.

a) ILP Workloads. b) MEM Workloads. c) MIX Workloads.

Fig. 5. Performance per Area comparison.

6 Related Work

Kumar et al. propose in [8] the Heterogeneous Multicore processor, a CMP processor comprised of heterogeneous cores. In this proposal, matching the inter-application heterogeneity with the statically partitioned hardware is, as in hdSMT, a prime issue. The main difference between them comes from their CMP/SMT inclinations. So, in case of few applications running on the processor, split resources accross CMP cores as physical registers and L1 caches are wasted in a Heterogeneous Multicore processor. On the contrary, an hdSMT can still utilize these resources to improve the performance of the running applications.

Putting aside heterogeneity-awareness, we find in the literature some prior work that study the combination of clustering and SMT techniques. Collins and Tullsen explore in [4] the relation between clustering and SMT. They show that the synergistic combination of the two techniques minimizes the IPC impact of the clustered architecture, and even permits more aggressive clustering of the processor than is possible with a single-threaded processor. In contrast, the hdSMT approach explores the benefits of a heterogeneous clustering to obtain high performance at a reduced complexity cost. Raasch and Reinhardt quantify in [12] the performance impact of resource partitioning policies in SMT machines, focusing on the execution portion of the pipeline. They found out that for storage resources, such as the instruction queue, statically allocating an equal portion to each thread provides good performance, in part by avoiding starvation. In contrast, they also showed that static division of issue bandwidth has a negative impact on throughput. SMTs ability to multiplex bursty execution streams dynamically onto shared functional units contributes to its overall throughput. As we have shown in this paper, a heterogeneous partition of issue bandwidth can be possitive if it is appropriatily matched with the heterogeneous needs of the running applications. The hdSMT approach also differs from these prior studies in the granularity applied in the cluster distribution. Notice that in hdSMT entire threads are assigned to pipelines, instead of the instruction level applied in these studies. So, dependent instructions are always executed in the same cluster, avoiding additional latencies and complexity.

Other proposals are more concerned in reducing the power consumption by means of the clustering technique. Thus, Latorre et al. [9] propose a multithreaded clustered microarchitecture as a way to deal with power consumption and wire delay problems. In this microarchitecture an evenly clustered front-end maps running threads to an evenly clustered back-end where the instructions are executed. This clustering also extends to resources such as L1 caches and register file, that are spread out the different clusters. Lee and Gaudiot also propose in [10] a symmetric, dual unified cluster SMT architecture as a way of reducing power consumption without significantly reducing its performance and throughput.

As far as we know, the hdSMT architecture is the first alternative SMT architecture in which the hardware is heterogeneously clustered in order to reduce the amount of wasted resources. By an appropriate matching of the heterogeneous applications with the heterogeneously distributed hardware, hdSMT achieves a better utilization of a reduced hardware budget, resulting in a better performance per area ratio.

7 Conclusions

The heteregeneity among application behaviors turns current architectures overdesigned for most cases, obtaining high performance but wasting a lot of resources to do so. In this paper we have presented the Heterogeneously Distributed Simultaneous Multithreading (hdSMT) architecture, an SMT alternative in which the running threads are mapped to a heterogeneosly clustered hardware according to this heterogeneity. The results obtained in this work indicate that hdSMT reduce this waste of resources at reduced budget, obtaining a 13% and 14% improvement in optimizing performance per area over monolithic SMT and homogeneously clustered SMT, respectively.

In hdSMT, the thread-to-pipeline mapping policy is a prime concern. In this work, we have presented a simple profile-based heuristic policy that achieves a 92% average accuracy. Raw performance results also point out that, in future hdSMT implementations, this mapping should probably be made dynamically in order to better adapt to the dynamic changes in program behaviour during execution.

Acknowledgements

This work has been supported by the Ministry of Education of Spain under contract TIN2004–07739–C02–01, CEPBA and the HiPEAC European Network of Excellence. Carmelo Acosta is also supported by the Ministry of Science and Technology of Spain grant BES–2002–0015.

References

[1] J. Burns and J.L. Gaudiot. Quantifying the SMT Layout Overhead - Does SMT Pull its Weight? In *Proc. of HPCA-6*, pages 109–120, 2000.

[2] J. Burns and J.L. Gaudiot. SMT Layout Overhead and Scalability. *IEEE Transactions on Parallel and Distributed Systems*, 13(2):142 – 155, February 2002.

[3] F. J. Cazorla, E. Fernández, A. Ramirez, and M. Valero. DCache Warn: An I-Fetch policy to increase SMT efficiency. In *Proc. of IPDPS-18*, pages 24–34, 2004.

[4] J. D. Collins and D. M. Tullsen. Clustered multithreaded architectures – Pursuing both IPC and cycle time. In *Proc. of IPDPS-18*, pages 46–57, 2004.

[5] A. El-Moursy and D. H. Albonesi. Front-end policies for improved issue efficiency in SMT processors. In *Proc. of HPCA-9*, 2003.

[6] L. Hammond, B. A. Nayfeh, and K. Olukotun. Single-chip multiprocessor. In *IEEE Computer Special Issue on Billion-Transistor Processors*, 1997.

[7] R. Kumar, K. Farkas, N. P. Jouppi, P. Ranganathan, and D. M. Tullsen. Single-ISA Heterogeneous Multi-Core Architectures: The Potential for Processor Power Reduction. In *Proc. of MICRO-36*, 2003.

[8] R. Kumar, D. M. Tullsen, P. Ranganathan, N. P. Jouppi, and K. I. Farkas. Single-ISA heterogeneous multi-core architectures for multithreaded workload performance. In *Proc. of ISCA-31*, 2004.

[9] F. Latorre, J. González, and A. González. Back-end Assignment Schemes for Clustered Multithreaded Processors. In *Proc. of ICS-18*, 2004.

[10] S. W. Lee and J. L. Gaudiot. Clustered microarchitecture simultaneous multithreading. In *Proc. of EuroPAR-9*, pages 576–585, 2003.

[11] K. Olukotun, B. A. Nayfeh, L. Hammond, K. Wilson, and K. Chang. The case for a single-chip multiprocessor. In *Proc. of ASPLOS-7*, 1996.

[12] S. E. Raasch and S. K. Reinhardt. The Impact of Resource Partitioning on SMT Processors. In *Proc. of PACT-12*, 2003.

[13] T. Sherwood, E. Perelman, and B. Calder. Basic block distribution analysis to find periodic behavior and simulation points in applications. In *Proc. of PACT-10*, pages 3–14, 2001.

[14] U. Sigmund, M. Steinhaus, and T. Ungerer. On Performance, Transistor Count and Chip Space Assessment of Multimedia-enhanced Simultaneous Multithreaded Processors. In *Proc. of MTEAC-4*, 2000.

[15] M. Steinhaus, R. Kolla, J. L. Larriba-Pey, T. Ungerer, and M. Valero. Transistor Count and Chip-Space Estimation of SimpleScalar-based Microprocessor Models. In *Proc. of WCED-2*, 2001.

[16] M. Steinhaus, R. Kolla, J. L. Larriba-Pey, T. Ungerer, and M. Valero. Transistor Count and Chip-Space Estimation of Simulated Microprocessors. In *T. R. UPC-DAC-2001-16, UPC*, 2001.

[17] D. M. Tullsen and J. A. Brown. Handling long-latency loads in a simultaneous multithreaded processor. In *Proc. of MICRO-34*, 2001.

[18] D. M. Tullsen, S. Eggers, and H. M. Levy. Simultaneous multithreading: Maximizing on-chip parallelism. In *Proc. of ISCA-22*, 1995.

[19] D. M. Tullsen, S. J. Eggers, J. S. Emer, H. M. Levy, J. L. Lo, and R. L. Stamm. Exploiting choice: Instruction fetch and issue on an implementable simultaneous multithreading processor. In *Proc. of ISCA-23*, 1996.

[20] W. Yamamoto and M. Nemirovsky. Increasing superscalar performance through multistreaming. In *Proc. of PACT*, 1995.

Construction and Compression of Complete Call Graphs for Post-Mortem Program Trace Analysis

Andreas Knüpfer, Wolfgang E. Nagel
Center for High Performance Computing (ZHR)
TU Dresden, Germany
E-mail: {knuepfer|nagel}@zhr.tu-dresden.de

Abstract

Compressed Complete Call Graphs (cCCGs) are a newly developed memory data structure for event based program traces. The most important advantage over linear lists or arrays traditionally used is the ability to apply lossy or lossless data compression. The compression scheme is completely transparent with respect to read access, decompression is not required. This approach is a new way to cope with todays challenges when analyzing enormous amounts of trace data. The article focuses on CCG construction and compression, querying and evaluation are briefly covered.

Keywords: Performance Analysis, Tracing, Data Structures, Data Compression

1 Introduction to cCCGs

Compressed Complete Call Graphs are a very sophisticated and efficient approach to store program trace data in main memory at analysis time. Against the general conception there are alternative ways over the plain linear data structures usually employed. Linear lists or arrays that hold trace events in temporal order are quite efficient nonetheless. However, there is not much room for optimizations.

Complete Call Graphs (CCGs) represent the whole function call hierarchy of a serial or parallel program. All additional information (record types) are appended to that tree data structure, usually as leaf nodes. As the main advantage over the traditional linear trace data structures CCGs have the ability to map equal or similar sub-structures onto one another, i.e. replace multiple redundant instances by references to a single object. This resembles common data compression schemes but cCCGs allow this data compression to be transparent to read access operations, i.e. there is no decompression necessary. The entire compression scheme is tailored towards the need of trace analysis, it is in this form not suitable for trace time data compression.

As a result, cCCGs allow compression ratios of 200 : 1 and better are possible. Unlike general purpose compression tools it is capable of lossy compression, too. Of course, deviations and errors arising are controllable. First, compression reduces the memory requirements of trace analysis tools dramaticly. Second, new evaluation algorithms emerge which are more convenient and more efficient than those for traditional linear data structures. All algorithms profit from the smaller memory footprint, some provide additional performance advantages that can reduce the computational effort proportionally to compression result.

The following sections provide a detailed presentation of CCGs, their construction and compression. Actually, both aspects are closely incorporated in order to avoid unnecessary temporary memory requirements. However, the discussion is separated for sake of understanding. It is focused on optimized algorithms, analyzes their computational complexity and demonstrates practically achievable compression ratios. Finally, a short outlook is given towards cCCG evaluation algorithms. However, this is not supposed to be the main focus of this paper but is covered by a separate paper [4] and by a previous survey article [11].

2 Specification

As the name indicates a *Complete Call Graph* is basically a graph of function calls of a program. In contrast to common *Call Graphs* [7, 8] it is not summarized to a mapping of caller to called functions but *complete*, i.e. contains every instance of every function call as a node. The main structure is defined by the function call hierarchy. Other kinds of information are appended as special (leaf) nodes.

Following the procedural programming paradigm this results in a tree graph for a sequential program resp. a set of trees for a parallel program. The reason why it hasn't been named *Complete Call Trees* in the first place will become

0190-3918/05 $20.00 © 2005 IEEE

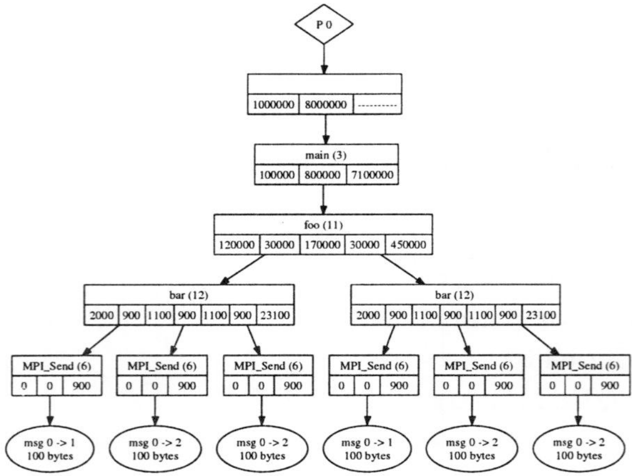

Figure 1. This uncompressed example shows a Complete Call Graph of an example function call hierarchy including some message events which are appended as leaf nodes. Note that time is expressed as durations instead of time stamps. See Figure 3 for the compressed counterpart.

apparent in the Compression chapter. Basically, the tree property will be abandoned, which states that every graph node has not more than a single parent node. None of the proposed algorithms will rely on that property in order to allow uniform handling of compressed and uncompressed CCGs. Figure 1 provides an example CCG from a sequential program trace. It contains a hierarchy of function calls and a number of MPI message send events. Timing information is provided not as time stamps like usual in trace analysis [15] but in form of time durations. This is as expressive as time stamp information but has substantial advantages for compression (see below).

Construction Algorithm

Like traditional memory data structures for trace data trace files contain a linear stream of trace records sorted by time stamps. The CCG construction algorithm described here transforms this linear data structure into a graph structure. CCG construction is done for every process of a trace separately, i.e. separate graphs are created for every process or thread independently.

The construction algorithm works straight forward and is quite simple: On arrival of an function enter event a new node is created and appended to the current active node as most recent child. Then, it is made the new active node.

For function leave events the actual active node is finalized. This implies that all children are present and have been finalized before[1]. Thus, at finalization all information concerning the node itself and the whole associated sub-tree are present. In particular all time stamp information are present. Thus, the trivial transformation from time stamps to time durations is performed at this stage. For all event types producing leaf nodes the distinction into enter and leave resp. creation and finalization time can be omitted.

Finalization time is also the occasion to perform the actual data compression. This is achieved on a node by node basis. See Section 3 for further details.

The CCG construction resembles a call stack replay of a program trace. Thus, the memory requirements for CCG construction is $O(d)$, i.e. proportional to the call stack depth[2] d. The computational effort is $O(N)$ with the number of events N.

Branching Factor

Applying the construction algorithm described above will produce a CCG that is a perfect image of the function call hierarchy. This serves the intention of CCGs which is to represent trace data. However, this is unfavorable with respect to graph algorithms in general. A very important criterion for tree graphs is the *branching factor*, i.e. the maximum number of children per node.

Looking at unmodified CCGs of typical programs and especially HPC programs the branching factors found are unbounded. Usually, *wide* nodes with very high numbers of children descend from functions containing child calls inside a loop. Thus, child counts from 1000 to 1000000 and above are not rare.

On behalf of tree graph algorithms and computational complexity an arbitrary branching factor is a severe disadvantage. For example the computational complexity for a tree search operation is $O(d \cdot b)$ where d is the tree depth and b the branching factor. Last but not least the compression scheme will profit from a bounded branching factor as Section 3 explains.

In order to adapt CCGs to fixed branching factors without restriction in application to real world program traces so called *artificial nodes* are introduced. That are nodes not representing a function call by themselves but a part of another function call. Now, nodes with more than $b = const.$ children will be split up into a set of artificial nodes. Artificial nodes are arranged in a tree again such that a arbitrary number of child nodes can be carried in a tree of artificial nodes with child count $\leq b$ each. Figure 2 shows an example node with $> b$ children before and after splitting.

[1]This follows from the procedural programming paradigm: If a function enter event lies inside a parent function P then the according function leave event must be contained in P as well.

[2]Of course, this doesn't contain the memory requirements for storing the whole CCG. Here, the finalized nodes are simply ignored like they are deleted right away.

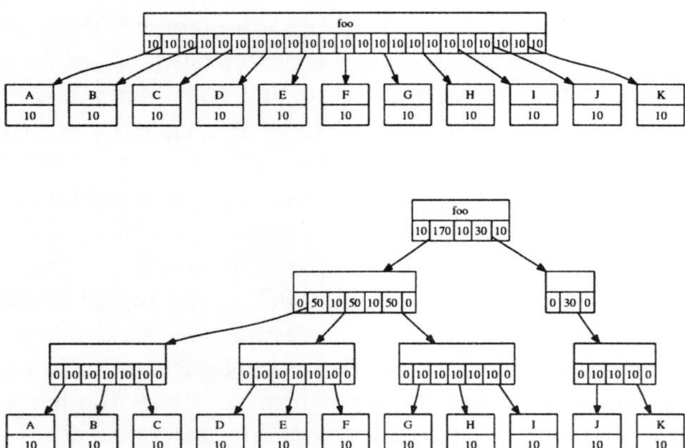

Figure 2. An example node without splitting (above) an the result after on-the-fly splitting (below). The child nodes might represent arbitrary sub-trees which might equal/similar. Note that the artificially introduced nodes (those without labels) can be subject to compression whereas inside the unsplit parent node compression is impossible.

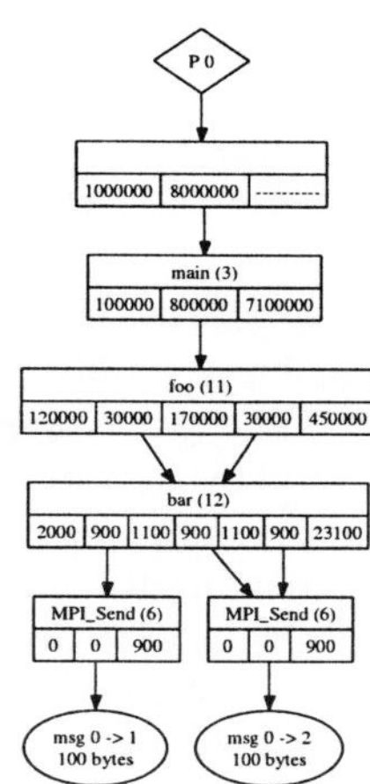

Figure 3. Compressed counterpart to the example of Figure 1. It contains only 8 nodes instead of 17 and provides the exact same information, without deviations due to lossy compression.

With respect to tree graph data structure theory it would be desirable to generate a perfectly balanced tree of artificial nodes. This could be achieved with a straight forward algorithm. However, this requires the total child count to be known when splitting. Yet, the total child count is not available before finalization time, i.e. when the very last child node has been added. This is problematic for high child counts. Storing such huge nodes as a whole requires a lot of temporary memory and node compression cannot start before splitting.

For that reasons the algorithm developed for splitting wide nodes will not result in a balanced tree of artificial nodes but in a minimum depth tree. Minimum depth trees are nearly as good as balanced trees with respect to computational complexcity for common traversal algorithms. In particular, they are guaranteed to have the same minimal depth than their balanced counterparts. Unlike those they can be constructed node by node without knowledge of the final node count.

The on-the-fly algorithm for splitting nodes works like follows: Every parent node P keeps a list of its current children. Furthermore, it assigns a *level* to every child. When a new child node is added the initial level is 0.

Early stage splitting takes place upon appending new children to a node. Whenever any level l contains b entries, those nodes are removed and transfered to a newly created artificial node A. Then, node A is added to the next higher level $l + 1$. At the same time A might be subject to node compression. That means parts of the original node can be compressed while the node itself is not completely constructed yet!

Late stage splitting occurs on node finalization. All nodes of equal level are turned into a new artificial node regardless of the number of entries $e \leq b$. The temporary memory requirements for keeping child nodes is now $O(b \cdot \log n)$ with the branching factor b and the total child count n. This is substantially less than the $O(n)$ memory requirements for creating a balanced tree.

In Figure 2 there is a comparison of an plain wide node with the tree of artificial nodes resulting from splitting.

3 Compression

All performance critical programs that are subject to detailed analysis and optimization necessarily contain loops[3]. Inside loops identical portions of code are executed multiple times. From a very general point of view one would expect those identical code segments to produce equal or similar sequences in the event trace. At the first glance truly equal segments seem far too optimistic but they are not unlikely. For an impression of a compressed CCG see Figure 3 which represents the same trace as in Figure 1.

For data compression purposes those inherent redundancy of traces CCGs is most suitable. The basic idea is to replace n repeated sub-trees that are equal or similar with

[3]Otherwise the programmer as well as the compiler would spend much more time on the code than execution.

a reference to a single instance saving the $n - 1$ remaining copies. Of course, this violates the unique parent property of tree graphs as mentioned before. However, all construction and evaluation algorithms can be adapted not to rely on this property at all.

This compression scheme involves identification of CCG sub-trees that are equal resp. similar with respect to some comparison operators. This task is generally known as clustering. There are algorithms to compute optimal clustering for a given set of samples and advanced heuristic algorithms to produce nearly optimal results. For our purposes a less expensive approach is used. The first reason for this is of the enormous computational complexity of more advanced algorithms. The second and most important reason is the temporary memory requirement which is about the size of the uncompressed CCG. Both would be unacceptable.

The actual compression works on a node by node basis: After finalization of every node it is checked if there is a equal resp. similar node among all previously seen nodes. That involves all nodes from the current process trace and from traces of parallel processes. While the CCG construction works separately for parallel process traces, the compression facilities share the set of recognized nodes in order to improve compression ability even more.

As a crucial part of clustering the sub-tree comparison operator is implemented in a very efficient way such that it has a constant computational complexity regardless of the total size of the sub-tree. This is achieved by focusing on the sub-trees root node alone, i.e. not traversing the whole sub-tree. This is feasible if the child node references of the two nodes in question are required to be pairwise equal. From the fact that two root nodes are similar and all direct children are equal follows that the whole sub-trees are regarded similar. Thus one might be replaced by a reference to the other. For this optimization to be applicable the child nodes must already be compared and replaced - otherwise they cannot be equal. That means child nodes must be handled before their parents. Accidently, this is the exact order node finalization is performed according to the procedural programming paradigm! So this optimization fits most naturally into the CCG construction. Figure 4 demonstrates the recursive comparison and replacement of nodes.

When comparing two graph nodes there are some properties that one wants to match exactly and some scalar values where a certain deviation is acceptable. For example a function id must not be altered since it would destroy the meaning of the node. Yet, a time stamp resp. a time duration may be changed by a few ticks[4] without altering the overall result of any evaluation notably.

Those two types are called *hard* and *soft properties*. While hard properties must simply match in order to fit, soft properties tolerate a certain error range which is to be defined by the user explicitly.

With the division to hard and soft properties the search for a replacement node can be accelerated. A naive approach would search all n existing nodes for a possible match. The resulting computational complexity of $O(n)$ per node would be unacceptable.

An optimized version divides the comparison of hard and soft properties. From all hard properties a hash value is generated which enables the algorithm to select a subset of candidates with constant effort $O(1)$, assuming all existing nodes are kept in a suitable data structure. Only for those candidates the soft properties have to be checked. Since the comparison of soft properties involves a tests if a number of values lie inside the allowed error intervals there is no hashing technique applicable but ever representant has to be tested separately. Assumed all $n = h \cdot s$ nodes available are arranged in h groups of s elements where every group has identical hard properties. Then the over-all effort for searching a representant node is just $O(s)$. This composes from $O(1)$ effort for selecting of the right group, $O(s)$ for testing all group entries with $O(1)$ effort for each sub-tree comparison (see above).

The check for the allowed error interval can be performed locally (to the graph nodes) for all but one of the soft properties. Time stamp information plays a special role. The first constraint is that time durations must not be altered more than a certain relative error, e.g. 1%, 10% or 100%. This can easily be ensured by checking the atomic time durations as stored in the graph nodes. Then it will automaticly apply to any duration between any two time stamps of a process.

The second and special requirement is that *time stamps* must not be altered more than a certain absolute number of ticks. Since time stamps have to be recomputed from time duration values of several nodes in the hierarchy, this cannot be tested locally. However, this issue can be solved by propagating absolute errors of a sub-tree to the parent node which then is allowed to consume the remaining allowed error. Thus, it is guaranteed that the over-all error for any sub-tree won't exceed the allowed limit. Experiments showed that this error propagation should be done with interval arithmetic rather than scalar error values. Interval arithmetic allows cancellation of errors with opposite sign which scalar arithmetic cannot achieve - see Figure 4.

Compression Results

To underline the usefulness and success of our new approach this section demonstrates some experimental results. As test data a number of existing trace files were selected which range from small sized examples to rather huge test cases. All traces originate from parallel real-world HPC programs. Among them there are the IRS [1] bench-

[4]ticks: units of timer resolution.

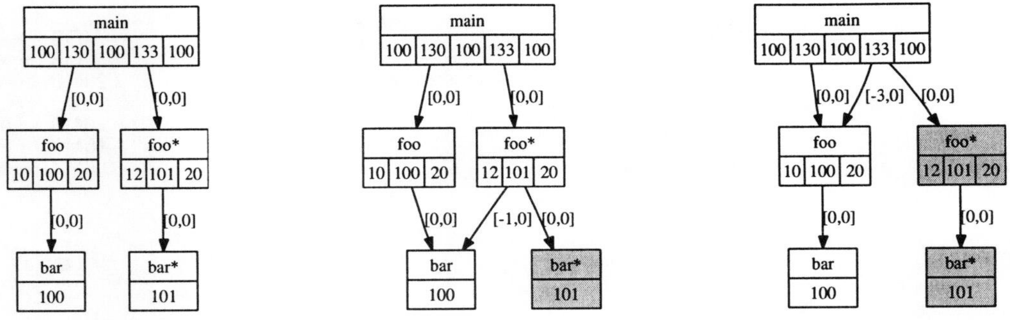

Figure 4. Successive compression in a CCG. The first graph (left) shows the uncompressed subtree. After the finalization of node `bar*` it is found to be compatible with node `bar` and replaced by a reference (middle). Note the slight difference in run-times: the deviation arising from this is propagated to the parent node as a deviation interval `[-1,0]`. After finalizing `foo*` it is replaced by a reference to `foo` as both reference the same child node (right). The deviation interval `[-3,0]` applies to the whole subtree below `foo`.

mark from ASCI Purple (4 GB), a parallel dynamic three-dimensional Delaunay mesh manipulation code (1.5 GB) and a Computational Fluid Dynamics solver [16] (28 MB).

The following experiments show the influence of the error bound parameters on the compression ratios R_M and R_N. Only for time information deviations are tolerated, i.e. timing is regarded as soft property, everything else are hard properties. Deviations in time are restricted in two ways. First, time stamps t must not be altered more than T_{abs} ticks:

$$|t - t'| \leq T_{abs} \tag{1}$$

Second, time durations (differences between two arbitrary timestamps) must not be changed more than a certain percentage T_{rel}:

$$d = t_{j+1} - t_j, \qquad \left|\frac{d' - d}{d}\right| \leq T_{rel} \tag{2}$$

The maximum branching factor for all test cases was set to 10 which is a moderate value.

There are two metrics to measure the success of the cCCG approach. First, the *memory compression ratio* focuses on the plain memory requirements:

$$R_M := \frac{M_0}{M_C} \tag{3}$$

where M_0 is the total size of the uncompressed CCG and M_C the size after compression. This means higher values of R_M stand for better compression. Because of optimized encoding an uncompressed CCG requires roughly the same memory as the trace file[5].

[5]This applies to the VTF3 binary trace format with $\pm 50\%$.

As the left hand side of Figure 5 shows there are compression ratios ranging from 1.7 to over 100 achievable depending on the error intervals and the different examples. Mind that even for zero error intervals there are compression ratios from 1.7 to 2.7! So without accepting any error in timing data the memory requirements drop to approx. half. With wider error bounds R_M raises up to 262!

The second metric to apply to CCG counts the graph nodes in an uncompressed CCG versus the count in the compressed counterpart. As the graph nodes are of different size depending on node type and child count this is not proportional to the memory compression ratio. The *nodes compression ratio* is defined as

$$R_N := \frac{N_0}{N_C} \tag{4}$$

with the node counts for uncompressed CCGs N_0 and for the compressed counterpart N_C. This metric roughly expresses the effort necessary when accessing the graph nodes which concerns node search for compression itself. That correctly implies that compression becomes faster as it produces higher node compression ratios! Furthermore, R_N is a hint for acceleration of many typical cCCG evaluation algorithms which are briefly mentioned in Section 4.

The right hand side of Figure 5 shows the R_N for the same examples as for R_M before. Now, there are results from 2.3 up to 9.8 for the zero error case. For higher errors the values R_N grow to 11 up to 1260! These enormous compression ratios relate directly to speedup of some evaluation algorithms. This means such an algorithm is R_N times faster on a cCCG than on an uncompressed CCG. Furthermore, this estimation doesn't take the additional speed-up from the reduced memory footprint into account!

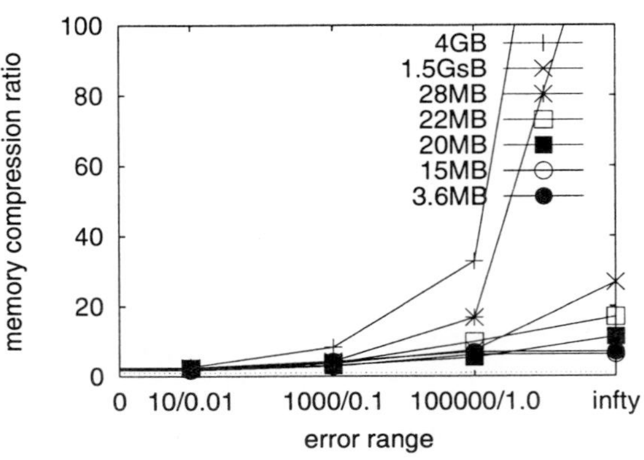

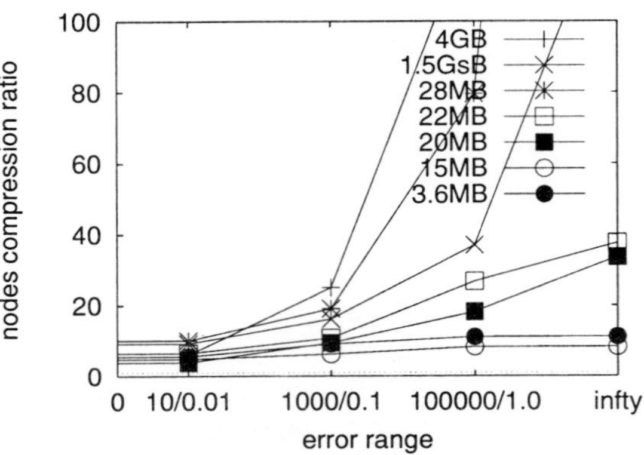

Figure 5. Compression ratios achieved for some example traces of different size with varying error intervals. The left hand side shows the memory compression ratio, the 4GB example reaches a compression ratio of about $262:1$ at maximum. The right hand side shows the nodes compression ratio where the 4GB case grows to more than $1260:1$ maximum compression. The error bounds are given as pairs of the absolute time stamp threshold and the relative duration threshold T_{abs}/T_{rel}.

All in all the compression ability is very much dependent from the trace in question, esp. the inherent redundancy and regularity. As a rule o thumb bigger traces allow better compression because there is a higher potential for more repetitions of equal trace segments. Furthermore, as expected the compression ability grows with more relaxed error bounds. However, neither R_M nor R_N are strictly monotonic growing with wider error bounds. Because no optimal clustering is applied, an example to prove the opposite can be constructed even though it is very unlikely to occur.

Input and compression speed combined reaches from 150,000 to 850,000 records per second on the test workstation (AMD Athlon 64 3200+, 2GB RAM). Of course, this is notably slower than raw record input which usually performs at hard disk speed. If the initial compression effort seems unacceptable for certain applications there is an alternative solution, though. By a serialization and restore scheme the actual compression can be performed beforehand as a batch processing. The resulting CCG can be serialized to a file of special format, then. Reading and restoring this compressed CCG from file requires minor computational effort and is as fast as raw file input. Yet, this precompression requires the compression parameters to be determined early.

Error bounds always need to be selected appropriately for different analysis tasks. For fine grained analysis of function calls absolute error bounds of 0 to 100 and relative error bounds of 0 to 5% are surely acceptable. For coarse grained statistical analysis of run times error bounds of 1000 to 100,000 ticks and 10% to 100% might be sufficient. For example this would allow $1\mu s$ to $0.1ms$ of time stamp deviation on a 1 GHz processor. For other analysis tasks even larger or infinite timing error bounds are feasible. Because all hard properties are unchanged, queries about the call tree, the order of function calls, the number of calls per function, message order and message sizes, etc. are unchanged by lossy compression.

Note that traditional tools that require to load an entire trace into main memory would not be capable of handling very large files at all. The $4GB$ example (Figure 5) would not have been accessible by such tools on the test workstation nor would it fit into 32 bit address space! From this perspective a storage approach that can be adapted to deliver slightly inaccurate results instead of none is most desirable.

Influence of Branching Factor

Besides the error parameters whose effects on compression has been shown before there is the branching factor that causes a very interesting influence. That is to say, it has an opposite impact on R_M and R_N. While this might seem suprising at first glance, it is indeed the expected behavior.

In general, a smaller branching factor b produces more but smaller nodes. Smaller nodes have a higher probability that a replacement is found than larger nodes. This is clearly apparent when every child is regarded as a possible cause of mismatch between a pair of nodes. Furthermore, if a wide node contains a mismatch compression is inhibited. The same mismatch on a set of smaller nodes won't prevent compression completely, i.e. some unaffected nodes might still be replaced - compare Figure 2. Together, the reduced size of the nodes, a higher number of nodes and a higher replacement probability result in a better R_M.

For R_N the reduced node size is not taken into account

but only the higher number of nodes. Furthermore, every wide node is turned into a tree of artificial nodes. This tree of depth d degenerated to a vertical list of d nodes if maximum compression is assumed. For smaller b the tree depth d is higher. In all, this makes R_N grow for higher b.

With this opposite influence to R_M and R_N the branching factor b can be used to tune compression for memory consumption or for node count according to actual needs. However, mind that R_N is only one estimate for effort of evaluation algorithms.

4 Overview of Querying cCCGs

When compression is concerned there is always the question about decompression. However, with cCCGs this is not a separate process prior to data access like with other data compression schemes. Rather, read access is more or less the same for uncompressed and compressed Complete Call Graphs.

First, one can freely navigate in the graph structure. Based on this, a linear iterator facility can be created which traverses a process graph in temporal order. This resembles the traditional access method for linear data structures. By this means, all traditional evaluation procedures can be transfered to cCCGs. Of course, they will profit from the reduced memory footprint of cCCGs but keep their original computational complexity.

Second, new algorithms can be designed to fit cCCGs in particular. Most importantly this involves fast search algorithms. Additionally, statistical summaries of node properties can be computed in a divide & conquer fashion. Both, iterative and recursive approaches are possible and shared memory parallelization is applicable.

A third concept that fits in very nicely is caching of intermediate results. Whenever node is evaluated for any property of its associated sub-tree the result can be cached for later use. Various caching strategies can be applied. Caching not only makes sense when there are repetitive queries which are frequently found in interactive trace analysis indeed. Also see the example in Figure 6.

Much more important is the effect of caching for compressed CCGs. Whenever a node is referenced multiple times the according intermediate result needs to be computed only once. For all repetitions the value is provided from cache with $O(1)$ effort. With comnplete caching the nodes compression ratio R_N correlates to the speed-up of evaluation quite accurately.

For example, see Figure 3 again, where node `bar` is referenced by `foo` twice. For the first occasion the sub-tree below `bar` needs to be evaluated. On the second occasion the prior result can be re-used. Thus, only 8 nodes need to be accessed instead of 17 for the uncompressed counterpart.

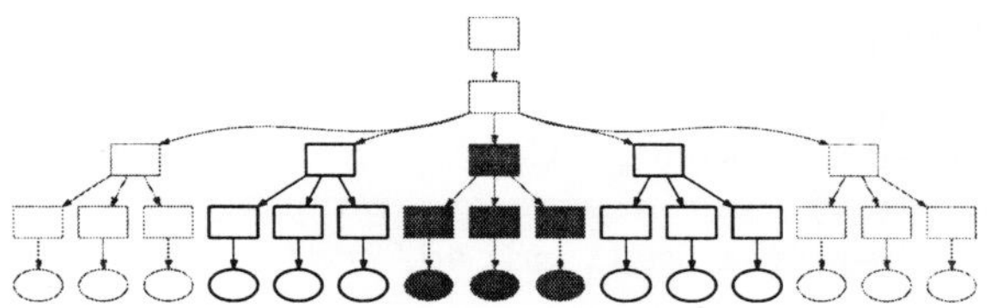

Figure 6. Schematic diagram of a CCG with three successive queries. An initial query involves all nodes. Intermediate results are cached. The first successive query concerns the middle nodes (bold and filled). The intermediate result for the top level nodes can be taken from cache, all remaining nodes need not to be re-evaluated. A second successive query watches the innermost nodes (filled) only and profits from cached values, too. Such successive queries happen frequently when zooming step-by-step from global overview to detail view.

A paper about cCCG evaluation algorithms has been published separately in order to handle it as elaborately as appropriate [4]. Another survey article [11] comprises both, construction and evaluation.

5 Conclusion

The presented work is part of research focusing on analysis of very large trace data sets. On one hand, this involves contributions to efficient trace data encoding and trace file compression [10]. On the other hand, this concerns interactive trace data evaluation and visualization. It is connected with the well known Vampir tool [5] as well as its parallel successor Vampir NG [6]. The latter has been extended as a prototype using the cCCGs data structure internally in order to show the feasibility of the cCCG approach [3].

Further traditional and well known tools of HPC performance analysis are DeWiz [12], TAU [13] and EARL [17] that have been examined and compared for their data structure design. Other approaches for trace data reduction can be found in [14] which identifies spacial similarities in parallel streams of trace data but no temporal ones. Finally, there is a lot of literature about compression of memory reference traces, for example [2, 9]. That much simpler type of traces is necessary for simulation of memory hierarchies, caches, TLBs etc.

References

[1] IRS Benchmark Code. `http://www.llnl.gov/asci/platforms/purple/rfp/benchmarks/limited/irs/`.

[2] A. Agarwal and M. Huffman. Blocking: Exploiting spatial locality for trace compaction. In *Proc. ACM SIGMETRICS 1990*, pages 48–57, 1990.

[3] A.Knüpfer, H.Brunst, and W.E.Nagel. High Performance Trace Visualization. In *13th Euromicro Conference on Parallel, Distributed and Network-based Processing*, Lugano, Switzerland, Feb. 2005.

[4] A.Knüpfer and W.E.Nagel. New Algorithms for Performance Trace Analysis based on Compressed Complete Call Graphs. In *Proceedings of ICCS 2005*, Atlanta/Georgia/USA, May 2005.

[5] H. Brunst, H.-Ch. Hoppe, W.E. Nagel, and M. Winkler. Performance Otimization for Large Scale Computing: The Scalable VAMPIR Approach. In *Proceedings of ICCS2001, San Francisco, USA*, LNCS 2074, page 751. Springer, May 2001.

[6] Holger Brunst, Wolfgang E. Nagel, and Allen D. Malony. A Distributed Performance Analysis Architecture for Clusters. In *IEEE International Conference on Cluster Computing, Cluster 2003*, Hong Kong, China, December 2003. IEEE Computer Society.

[7] Susan L. Graham, Peter B. Kessler, and Marshall K. McKusick. gprof: a Call Graph Execution Profiler. In *SIGPLAN Symposium on Compiler Construction*.

[8] David Grove and Craig Chambers. An Assessment of Call Graph Construction Algorithms. `http://citeseer.nj.nec.com/grove00assessment.html`, 2000.

[9] Scott F. Kaplan, Yannis Smaragdakis, and Paul R. Wilson. Trace Reduction for Virtual Memory Simulations. In *ACM SIGMETRICS International Conference on Measurement and Modeling of Computer Systems*, 1999.

[10] Andreas Knüpfer. A New Data Compression Technique for Event Based Program Traces. In *Procceedings of ICCS 2003 in Melbourne/Australia, Springer LNCS 2659*, pages 956 – 965. Springer, Heidelberg, June 2003.

[11] Andreas Knüpfer and Wolfgang E. Nagel. Compressible Memory Data Structures for Event Based Trace Analysis. *Future Generation Computer Systems by Elsevier*, 2005. [accepted for publication].

[12] Dieter Kranzlmüller, Michael Scarpa, and Jens Volkert. Dewiz - A Modular Tool Architecture for Parallel Program Analysis. In *Euro-Par 2003 Parallel Processing, Proc. 9th International Euro-Par Conference*, volume LNCS 2790, pages 74–80, Klagenfurt, Austria, August 2003. Springer-Verlag.

[13] Allen D. Malony and Sameer Shende. Performance Technology for Complex Parallel and Distributed Systems. *Quality of Parallel and Distributed Programs and Systems*, 2003.

[14] O. Y. Nickolayev, P. C. Roth, and D. A. Reed. Real-Time Statistical Clustering for Event Trace Reduction. *The International Journal of Supercomputer Applications and High Performance Computing*, 11(2), 1997.

[15] S. Seidl. VTF3 - A Fast Vampir Trace File Low-Level Library. personal communications, May 2002.

[16] W. Wienken, J. Stiller, and U. Fladrich. A Finite-Element Based Navier-Stokes-Solver for LES. In *Proceedings of the Parallel CFD 2002 Conference*, Kansai Science City, Japan, May 2002.

[17] F. Wolf and B. Mohr. EARL - A Programmable and Extensible Toolkit for Analyzing Event Traces of Message Passing Programs. Technical report, Forschungszentrum Jülich GmbH, April 1998. FZJ-ZAM-IB-9803.

Session 3B: Messaging

A Preliminary Analysis of the MPI Queue Characterisitics of Several Applications

Ron Brightwell Sue Goudy Keith Underwood
Sandia National Laboratories*
PO Box 5800
Albuquerque, NM 87185-1110

E-mail: {rbbrigh, spgoudy, kdunder}@sandia.gov

Abstract

Understanding the message passing behavior and network resource usage of distributed-memory message-passing parallel applications is critical to achieving high performance and scalability. While much research has focused on how applications use critical compute related resources, relatively little attention has been devoted to characterizing the usage of network resources, specifically those needed by the network interface. This paper discusses the importance of understanding network interface resource usage requirements for parallel applications and describes an initial attempt to gather network resource usage data for several real-world codes. The results show widely varying usage patterns between processes in the same parallel job and indicate that resource requirements can change dramatically as process counts increase and input data changes. This suggests that general network resource management strategies may not be widely applicable, and that adaptive strategies or more fine-grained controls may be necessary for environments where network interface resources are severely constrained.

1. Introduction

There are many challenges to running an application on a large-scale, distributed-memory massively parallel processing (MPP) machine. Much attention has been directed toward understanding the performance and scalability of applications. This focus has been on understanding and characterizing resource usage including host processors, memory, and, to a limited extent, the network. The goal of most performance analysis tools is to provide the insight necessary to insure that an application is using important resources to its maximum benefit. Every effort is made to find the appropriate strategies for management of processor cycles, the memory subsystem, and the network. The performance and scalability of an application is largely determined by how well these resources can be used as the scale of the system increases.

While significant effort has been directed toward understanding the usage of host processors and memory, there is relatively little effort aimed at understanding and characterizing network resource usage, and network interface resources in particular. Networks are typically measured in terms of micro-benchmarks that demonstrate the maximum performance potential in idealized situations. Although this set of micro-benchmarks has been extended to enable measurements of network performance using typical application scenarios, there is currently little understanding or published researched of what typical scenarios really are.

Even as the struggle to understand the behavior of real-world applications continues, networks are requiring greater resources. New bus technologies, such as PCI Express and HyperTransport, have enabled lower latencies than were previously possible, and advanced signaling technology has led to a significant increase in network bandwidth. To leverage performance increases, network interfaces have increased in processing power and memory capacity. As network interfaces become more complex and the number and type of resources associated with the network continues to increase, the general lack of understanding also increases. In order to address this problem, the amount of effort directed toward understanding network resource usage will need to be similar to that currently being put into gathering, analyzing, and obtaining insight from host processing and memory resources.

*Sandia is a multiprogram laboratory operated by Sandia Corporation, a Lockheed Martin Company, for the United States Department of Energy's National Nuclear Security Administration under contract DE-AC04-94AL85000.

U.S. Government Work Not Protected by U.S. Copyright

This paper presents an initial analysis of the network interface processing and memory requirements of several real-world applications. There are two important impacts of this analysis. First, this type of data can be beneficial from an application performance standpoint. The application may be modified to better match a fixed resource management scheme, or, conversely, a more efficient management scheme can be employed to meet the needs of the application. Second, this type of data can be extremely beneficial for designing future networks and network interfaces.

The rest of the paper is organized as follows. In the next section, we provide additional background information, which is followed in Section 3 by a description of our approach to characterizing network resource usage. In Section 4, we describe the platform from which our data has been collected and provide details about the applications that were used. Results and analysis of the collected data are presented in Section 5. The important conclusions of this study are discussed in Section 6. Section 7 discusses this work in the context of similar studies, and Section 8 provides an overview of future work on this topic.

2. Background

2.1. Placement and Management of Network Resources

Network resources and their associated management strategies have continued to evolve throughout the existence of distributed memory MPP platforms. In early MPPs, such as the Intel Paragon[13], the operating system allocated and managed network resources. Accessing the network required an application to invoke the operating system. The operating system managed buffer space, implemented flow control protocols, and allocated other resources (such as message descriptor handles for identifying asynchronous transfers). When a resource was exhausted, the operating system had to allocate new resources or recover used ones. For example, an application using the NX message passing interface had a (fixed) maximum number of outstanding message receive descriptors. A process that tried to exceed this limit would block until a transfer completed and a previously allocated descriptor was freed.

Research on these early platforms led to new strategies for dealing with network resources. For example, a fundamental part of the Puma [19] lightweight kernel research at Sandia National Laboratories and the University of New Mexico is the Portals network API [6]. Portals moves nearly all of the networking resources into the application's address space and provides building blocks that can be assembled to handle many different types of protocols. By moving resources to the user-level, the application is only constrained by the amount of its memory that it wants to dedicate to networking. It also controls how much processing will be needed to handle messaging requests. This strategy has several benefits. The size of the Puma kernel is fixed and does not change as a process allocates and consumes more network resources, and the complexity of the kernel is significantly reduced.

Recent networking technology has shifted the placement of network resources and requires a reexamination of resource usage and management strategies. Network interfaces now have processor and memory resources dedicated to handling network activities; however, these resources are significantly less capable than the resources on the host. The embedded processors used on current-generation high-performance network interfaces are at least an order of magnitude slower than typical host processors, and the amount of on-board memory is one to four orders of magnitude smaller than host memory.

This arrangement is prevalent in large and extreme scale systems. ASCI Q (over 8000 processors) uses the Quadrics network[14], which handles many networking tasks using a user programmable thread processor on the NIC. Numerous large clusters[2, 1] use the Quadrics or Myrinet network (which also has a processor on the NIC). The Red Storm supercomputer, a joint project between Cray, Inc., and Sandia, has over 10,000 processors[3, 8] and uses a custom network designed by Cray. The network interface for Red Storm has a 500 MHz PowerPC and 384 KB of on-board memory, while the host node has a 2.0 GHz AMD Opteron and 2 GB of main memory. Thus, the network interface is tightly constrained in memory resources and somewhat constrained in processing resources. Even the 65,000 node IBM Blue Gene/L supercomputer must consider the allocation of resources to networking as it uses a similar architecture to the Intel ASCI Red machine[20] currently deployed at Sandia. In this architecture, two processors (700 MHz PowerPC 440 processors on Blue Gene/L and 333 MHz Pentium II processors on ASCI Red) share main memory and share access to the network(s). Network resource usage will significantly impact how application and network processing is divided between the processors.

2.2. MPI Network Resources

Although the high-performance networks in large-scale distributed-memory machines are often used for other traffic (e.g. I/O traffic), MPI is typically the most important service to analyze in terms of resource usage. This importance arises from two factors. First, MPI typically has the biggest influence on the network performance of an application. Second, MPI is often the only service that is primarily controlled by the user rather than the system. That is, MPI is the only network service where the application programmer is largely in charge of behavior at *both* the sender and the receiver. Other services involve system-level components that provide the opportunity to tightly control resource allocation and management.

Different networks require different levels of host computation to process MPI messages. For example, one network may require a host processor to setup and monitor network DMA activity, while another network may completely decouple the host processor from the network, and avoid any host processor involvement in data transfers. Since characteristics of this type are highly network dependent, we have taken a more general approach to characterizing MPI processor resources by analyzing message queue data.

Conceptually, MPI implementations have two message queues — one that contains a list of outstanding receive requests (the posted receive queue) and one that contains a list of messages that arrived without a posted receive request (the early arrival or unexpected queue). The posted receive queue must be traversed when a message arrives. For most implementations, which represent this queue with a linear list[1], the processing time grows with the length of the queue [21]. Likewise, the unexpected queue must be traversed whenever a receive request is posted. The MPI implementation must atomically check the unexpected queue for a matching message before the request is added to the posted receive queue. Again, traversing this (typically) linear list requires processing resources.

There are several ways in which an MPI implementation can consume memory. Networks typically have a finite number of send and receive requests that can be allocated. In some cases, implementations must use sophisticated credit-based schemes for efficiently managing network transfer requests. Implementations also need to set aside memory for buffering unexpected messages. This memory resource is probably the biggest single concern for any MPI implementor. Since most implementations send short messages eagerly to optimize for latency, situations like an N-to-1 communication pattern can quickly exhaust the buffer space for unexpected messages.

3. Approach

In this section, we describe how we have instrumented the MPICH [12] implementation of MPI to gather information about MPI network resource usage. We chose to instrument MPICH because it is the supported production MPI implementation on our target platform, which is described in detail in the following section. This allowed us to leverage existing application configuration and build environments.

[1]Other data structures (such as hashing) are occasionally used, but many of them can be foiled by applications that wildcard the source and message tag fields in an `MPI_Recv`.

The MPICH implementation has an abstract device interface (ADI) [11] that provides a network transport layer with the functions necessary to implement MPI semantics. In particular, the posted receive queue and unexpected message queue are linked lists that are managed by the ADI code. These linked lists are not usually manipulated by the underlying transport layer, because the ADI abstracts the implementation of these queues.

For example, the ADI provides a function call, `MPID_Msg_arrived()`, for the transport layer to use to signal the arrival of a message. This function traverses the posted receive queue to see if there is a matching receive posted. If so, it removes the entry from the queue and proceeds. If not, it enqueues information about the new message in the unexpected queue. In order to measure the average number of times the posted receive queue is searched, we increment a counter when `MPID_Msg_arrived()` is called. Inside this function call, we also increment another counter each time a queue entry is inspected.

This function call was also used to track the number of unexpected and expected messages. At each invocation of the function, a counter is incremented based on the type of message. In order to have more detail about short versus long messages, we traced the code further down into the device-specific transport layer (ch_gm) and inserted counters there.

The unexpected queue must be searched each time an MPI receive is posted. The MPICH ADI function, `MPID_Search_unexpected_queue_and_post()`, searches through the unexpected queue looking for a matching message. If no match is found, the receive is added to the posted receive queue. If a match is found, the unexpected message is dequeued and the receive is processed. This function calls another ADI function that searches the unexpected queue. We simply increment a counter each time this function is called, and increment another counter each time an unexpected queue entry is inspected.

We also profiled the queue management utility functions in the MPICH ADI to keep track of maximum queue length (for each queue). Each time an entry is enqueued, we increment a length counter associated with the queue. Likewise, this counter is decremented each time an entry is dequeued. Each time a new entry is enqueued, we inspect the length counter to maintain its maximum value.

In order to allow applications to access these counters and maximum values, they were implemented as global variables. This approach allows them to be initialized without an explicit function call and allows them to be exported to the application easily. The MPICH ADI is not multithreaded, so the global values are only manipulated by a single thread of execution.

The data was collected through the MPI profiling interface and written to a file. We defined our own `MPI_Finalize()` routine to record the values and gather them to rank 0, which opens a text file and writes them out for each rank. This eliminates the need to modify applications. We simply re-link the code with the profiling code and the instrumented MPI library.

The overhead of instrumenting MPICH this way is negligible. The additional computation needed for this instrumentation is insignificant, especially for unexpected messages, which are already in the low-performance path. For a posted message, the computation and logic operations are performed after the message has been received, so the additional computation does not impact the transfer of the data. To reduce variability, we ran each test four times and report the average of the runs. Each run was made on the same set of compute nodes for each of the different processor counts.

Because the determination of expected and unexpected messages and the implementation of MPI message queues are specific to each MPI implementation, and possibly specific to each transport layer within an MPI implementation, general instrumentation strategies, such as those used for performance analysis, are not sufficient. There is an ongoing effort to standardize some of this information in a way that application developers as well as tool implementors can use, which we describe in Section 7.

4. Platform and Applications

All tests were run on the Vplant machine at Sandia National Laboratories. Vplant is a Linux cluster with approximately 320 compute nodes composed of Intel Pentium-III and Pentium-4 processors. These experiments were run on dual-processor Pentium-4 Xeon nodes running at 2.0 GHz. Each node has 1 GB of main memory and a Myrinet-2000 [4] network interface. The nodes are connected in a Clos topology. Vplant was running a Linux 2.4.18 kernel, GM version 1.6.4, and MPICH/GM version 1.2.4..11. All of our runs used only one process per node. A number of production applications were evaluated on the experimental platform, including LAMMPS, CTH, and ITS.

4.1. LAMMPS

LAMMPS is a classical molecular dynamics (MD) code designed to simulate systems at the atomic or molecular level[17, 16, 18]. Typical applications include simulations of proteins in solution, liquid-crystals, polymers, zeolites, or simple Lenard-Jones systems. It runs on any parallel platform that supports the MPI message-passing library [2].

This study presents data from the *Bead-Spring Polymer Chains* input deck. This is a simulation of a simple system with molecular bonds. Two types of idealized, 50-length, bead-spring polymer chains using different bead sizes are simulated along with some free monomers. The polymer chains first push off from each other for 10000 timesteps and then equilibrate for 10000 timesteps. The simulated system includes 810 atoms and runs for 20000 timesteps.

[2]This text adapted with permission from `http://www.cs.sandia.gov/~sjplimp/lammps.html`.

4.2. CTH

CTH is a multi-material, large deformation, strong shock wave, solid mechanics code developed at Sandia National Laboratories. CTH has models for multi-phase, elastic viscoplastic, porous and explosive materials. Three-dimensional rectangular meshes; two-dimensional rectangular, and cylindrical meshes; and one-dimensional rectilinear, cylindrical, and spherical meshes are available. It uses second-order accurate numerical methods to reduce dispersion and dissipation and to produce accurate, efficient results. CTH is used extensively within the Department of Energy laboratory complexes for studying armor/anti-armor interactions, warhead design, high explosive initiation physics, and weapons safety issues.

CTH has two fundamental modes of operation: with or without adaptive mesh refinement (AMR). Adaptive mesh refinement changes the application properties significantly and is useful for only certain types of input problems. Therefore, we have chosen one AMR problem and one non-AMR problem for analysis. The non-AMR input was the traditional *2 Gas* problem which is simplistic, but provides a comparison with previous studies[5]. The AMR input was a representative production run.

4.3. ITS

The Integrated TIGER Series (ITS) is a suite of codes to perform Monte Carlo solutions of linear time-independent coupled electron/photon radiation transport problems. It can simulate problems with or without the presence of macroscopic electric and magnetic fields in multi-material, multi-dimensional geometries. Individual particles are tracked with independent particle histories. Thus, particle transport is assumed to be a linear process in which individual particles do not interact with each other, or alter the medium in which they transport. The ITS data is from an input deck used in a production run.

5. Results and Analysis

In this section, we provide an analysis of the data by looking at trends. We are less concerned with exact queue resources that a particular application uses, but rather are interested in the relationship between queue resources and various parameters, such as the size of the job, the input data, the distribution across ranks, and the correlation of real application data to popular benchmarks.

5.1. Unexpected Messages

An unexpected message is a message that arrives before a matching receive has been posted. Unexpected messages can cause a significant amount of performance degradation. Unexpected short messages are typically stored in buffers that are managed by the MPI library and copied into the user buffer once a matching receive is posted. Too many unexpected short messages can cause the MPI library to exhaust the space alloacated to store them. Unexpected long messages are typically not buffered at the receiver. Rather, a rendezvous protocol is used to buffer the message in place at the sender. When a matching receive is posted, the receiver takes steps necessary to transfer the data from the sender. By their nature, unexpected long messages do not realize the full bandwidth performance of the network.

Unexpected messages are considered to be the "slow path" because they remain in the unexpected queue for an indeterminate amount of time. Unexpected short messages also have large memory resource requirements to accommodate the buffering of the entire message at the receiver. Figure 1 shows the proportion of messages that falls into each of four categories: expected long, expected short, unexpected long, and unexpected short. Unexpected short messages are clearly quite common in the real applications that were evaluated while unexpected long messages were very uncommon. ITS demonstrates the worst case behavior with the proportion of unexpected short messages appearing to scale linearly with the number of processes in the job. In all of the cases, it is clear that unexpected messages must be handled quickly and that significant memory will be needed to buffer unexpected short messages.

5.2. Queue Lengths

One of the greatest limitations of most modern network interface hardware is the extremely limited amount of memory on the card. As such, the maximum length of the posted receive queue and the unexpected message queue have significant implications for the feasibility of message offload. Figure 2 shows the maximum search length and maximum overall length for the posted receive and unexpected message queues. The maximum queue length is an indication of the amount of memory resources required to store the queue. These results indicate that, even for relatively small numbers of processors, the maximum length of both the posted queue and the unexpected queue are within the limits of the memory that a modern NIC would support; however, the results also indicate several potential problems. The posted queue length of the AMR version of CTH increases with the number of processes in the job. Similarly, the unexpected queue results for the non-AMR version of CTH and LAMMPS appear to scale linearly. This is potentially more significant since the unexpected queue is an order of magnitude longer than the posted queue.

These results also show the disparity between rank 0 and the rest of the ranks in the job. Removing rank 0 from the results, the maximum length of the unexpected queue drops dramatically. This can probably be attributed to the fact that most applications use rank 0 as the root of collective operations. This data indicates that uniform allocation of resources across all ranks may not be optimal.

5.3. Search Length

The search length of a queue is the number of queue entries that are traversed in a given search. While long queues have implications for the amount of memory required for NIC offload, the portion of those queues that are searched has a significant impact on the processing power needed by the NIC. Search length also affects the real latency seen by applications.

Figure 2 shows the maximum search length for these applications. This data reveals many interesting properties. There are several cases for both queues where the maximum search length is the entire length of the queue. This makes sense for the unexpected queue, where a matching entry may not be in the queue when a receive is posted. It is more disconcerting to see that several applications search the entire length of the posted receive queue to find a match. These results seemingly discourage, for example, an offload implementation of the MPI matching semantics where a small portion of the posted receive queue is buffered in NIC memory and the remainder of the queue is traversed by accessing host memory from the NIC.

Figure 3 shows the average search depth of the posted and unexpected queues. Compared to the maximum value, the average traversal of the posted receive queue is extremely small. This is also true for the unexpected queue, except for the ITS application. In this case, the impact of search length at rank 0 is significant. The disparity between maximum search length and average search length is also likely to introduce variability into the execution time of a time step (the time between synchronization points). This type of variability is the key symptom of the "rogue OS effect"[15], which leads to significantly longer applications execution times. This type of variability will also prove to be one of the major limiting factors in scaling from 10,000 to 100,000 nodes.

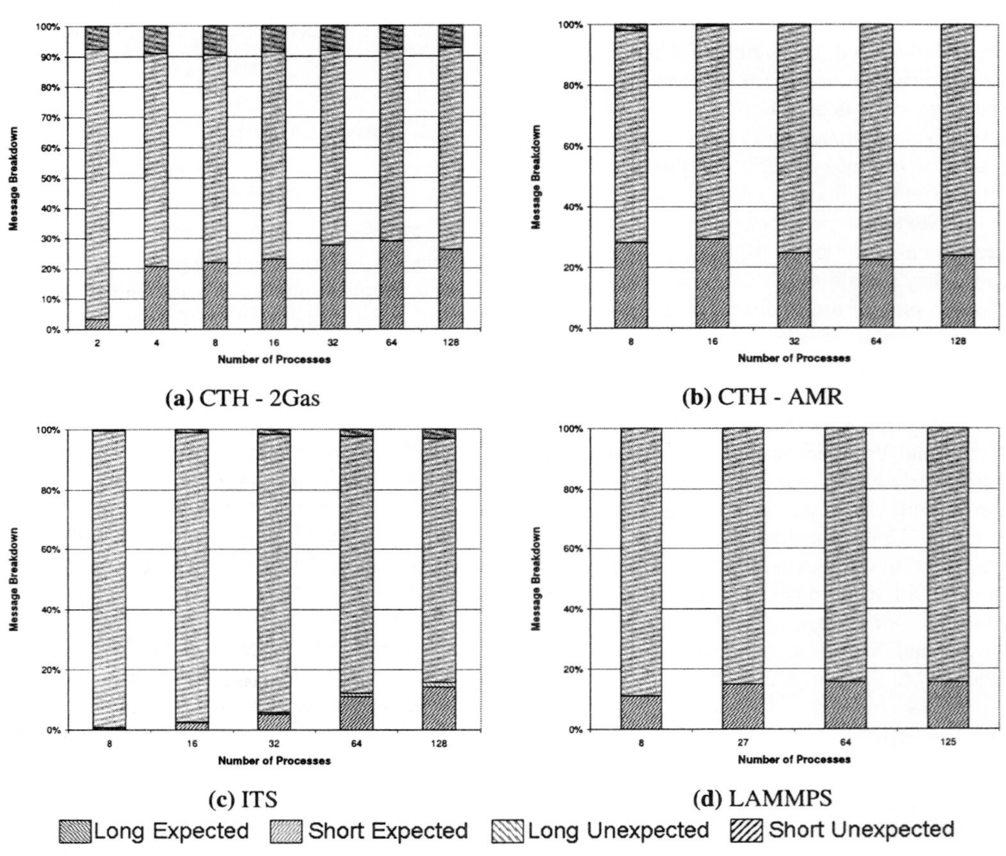

Figure 1. Breakdown of messages by expected/unexpected and long/short properties for applications

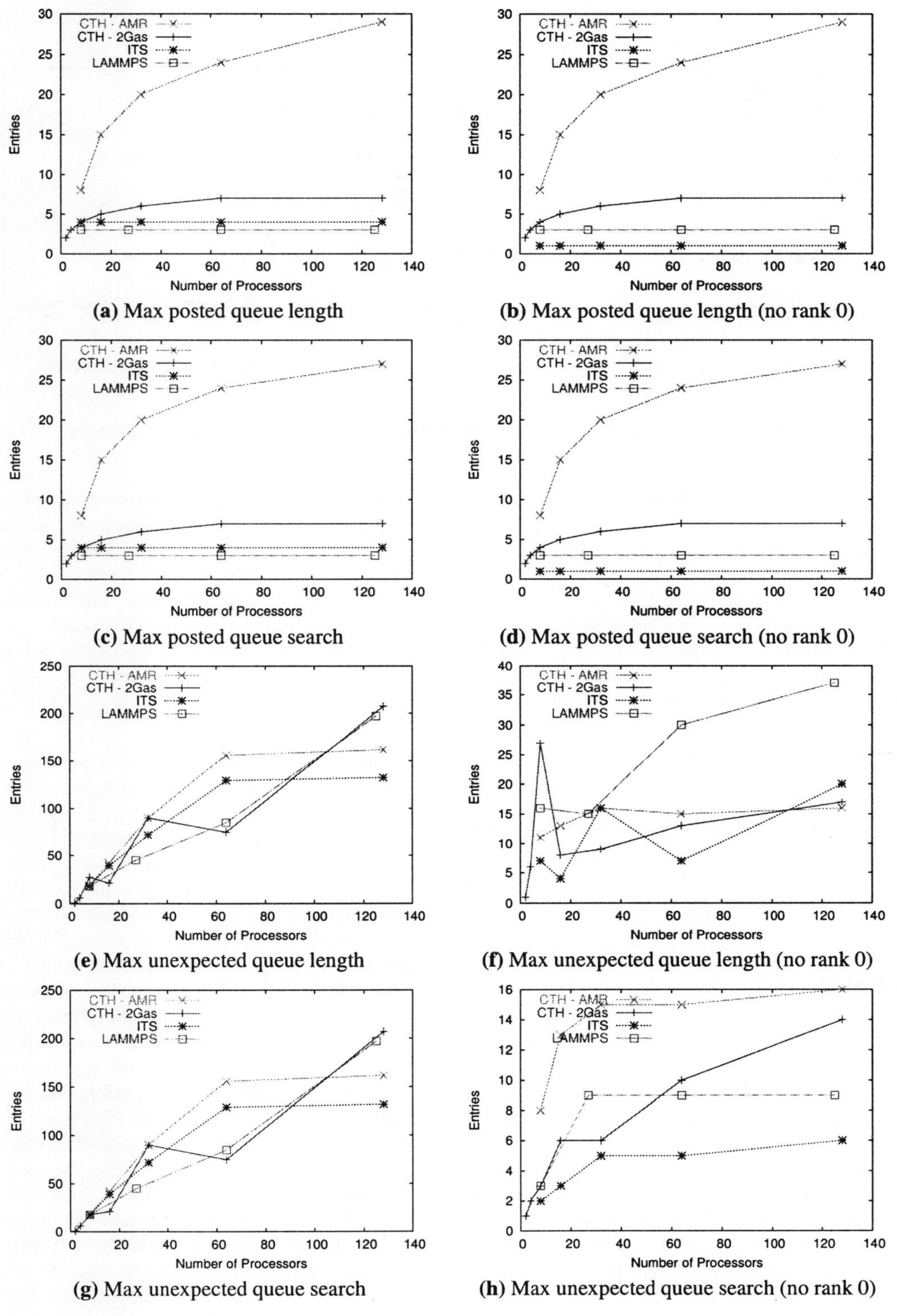

(a) Max posted queue length

(b) Max posted queue length (no rank 0)

(c) Max posted queue search

(d) Max posted queue search (no rank 0)

(e) Max unexpected queue length

(f) Max unexpected queue length (no rank 0)

(g) Max unexpected queue search

(h) Max unexpected queue search (no rank 0)

Figure 2. Maximum length and search depths of the posted and unexpected message queue

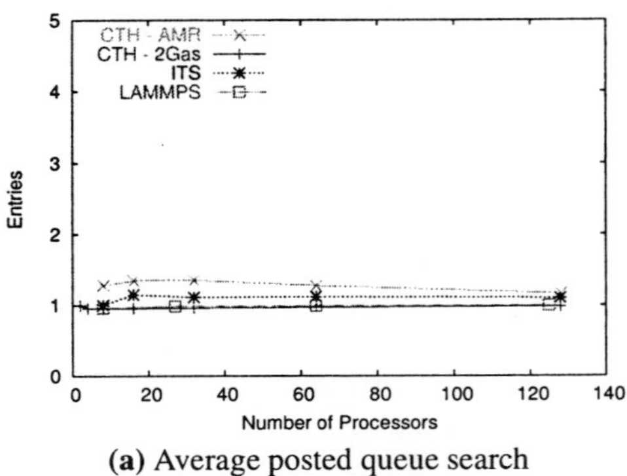

(a) Average posted queue search

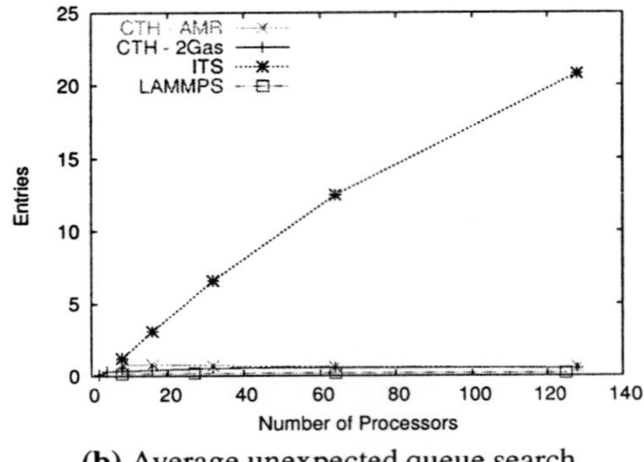

(b) Average unexpected queue search

Figure 3. Average search depth of the posted and unexpected queues

5.4 Comparison to Benchmarks

We now compare the results of these applications with results of the NAS Parallel Benchmark (NPB) suite [9] previously published in [7]. Our experience with real applications thus far shows very little correlation with the behavior of the NPB suite in terms of expected and unexpected messages. In contrast, there is more correlation in the queue behaviors of real applications and the NPB suite. In this case, only the measurements without rank zero are compared. Most of the real applications (like most of the NPB) have small maximum queue lengths, but some are related to the number of nodes. The key difference is that the growth in length for applications appears to be related to $log(P)$ while the growth for the benchmarks appears to be related to P. Similarly, the search behavior of the benchmarks is correlated with, but not identical to, the behavior of the real applications.

6. Conclusions

This paper presented an initial analysis of the message passing behavior of four real application scenarios in terms of the resource usage and resource requirements. The results indicate that, in many cases, certain MPI resource requirements scale with the number of processes. The growth (with process count) of the unexpected queue and the growth in the percentage of messages which are short and unexpected requires that both significant memory and significant processing be dedicated to MPI. Unfortunately, these patterns vary across applications in a way that indicates that a generalized resource management scheme may be inappropriate. Moreover, the usage patterns within one job (specifically for rank 0) vary widely indicating that a single, static resource management scheme may be insufficient even within a single job. These results were compared to the NAS parallel benchmark suite, which was studied using the same analysis techniques. We found that the degree of correlation between the message passing behavior of the NPB suite and Sandia's applications varied based on the parameters being measured. The behavior of the NPB suite appears to be a reasonable first approximation of real applications, but is not truly representative.

7. Related Work

There is a significant amount of work in the area of parallel application performance analysis. However, we know of no work that collects, analyzes, or uses MPI unexpected messages or MPI queue information as a basis to characterize performance, scalability, or network resource usage.

Most performance analysis tools for MPI use the MPI profiling interface to gather message tracing and timing information. Since unexpected messages are not exposed in the MPI programming interface, this information is not available to the profiling layer. Many of the issues with unexpected messages that we described in this paper have motivated work on a portable interface for exposing low-level MPI implementation details, such as unexpected messages, to application developers and performance tool developers. This interface, called PERUSE [10], is currently being explored by a number of organizations in the MPI research community. This work emphasizes the need to be able to capture low-level MPI performance information to assist in characterizing application message passing requirements.

In addition to performance analysis, there is also a significant amount of work that characterizes the message passing behavior of applications and application benchmarks in an attempt to understand or predict how well they will scale. Example of this type of analysis can be found in [22] and [23]. As with performance tools, this analysis does not consider the impact or effect of unexpected messages or queue lengths, largely because this information is not easily attainable.

8. Future Work

This initial analysis provided answers to some important questions regarding MPI queue behavior for real applications. However, several important questions remain.

We expect that some of our results are platform dependent and that various apsects of a system may have a significant impact on MPI queue usage. For example, the cluster from which our results have been gathered is highly unbalanced in terms of computation to network bandwidth. A platform that provides significantly more network bandwidth may behave much differently. We intend to explore the degree to which these types of system parameters impact MPI queue usage. One system aspect that we intend to explore in depth is the impact of scale. While 128 processors is a significant number, it is well short of the several thousand that we expect for the typical application running on Red Storm.

The approach to instrumentation that we presented is this paper is straightforward. More advanced techniques may be necessary to truly capture the level of detail necessary for performance optimizations or to help develop adaptive strategies for network interface resource allocation and management. In particular, we would like to examine the distribution of MPI queue search data rather than just examining average data over the entire run of an application.

References

[1] http://www.lanl.gov/projects/pink/.

[2] http://www.llnl.gov/linux/mcr/.

[3] R. Alverson. Red Storm. In *Invited Talk, Hot Interconnects 10*, August 2003.

[4] N. J. Boden, D. Cohen, R. E. F. A. E. Kulawik, C. L. Seitz, J. N. Seizovic, and W.-K. Su. Myrinet: A gigabit-per-second local area network. *IEEE Micro*, 15(1):29–36, Feb. 1995.

[5] R. Brightwell, H. E. Fang, and L. Ward. Scalability and performance of CTH on the Computational Plant. In *Proceedings of the Second International Workshop on Cluster-Based Computing*, May 2000.

[6] R. Brightwell, W. Lawry, A. B. Maccabe, and R. Riesen. Portals 3.0: Protocol building blocks for low overhead communication. In *Proceedings of the 2002 Workshop on Communication Architecture for Clusters*, April 2002.

[7] R. Brightwell and K. D. Underwood. An analysis of NIC resource usage for offloading MPI. In *Proceedings of the 2004 Workshop on Communication Architecture for Clusters*, Santa Fe, NM, April 2004.

[8] W. J. Camp and J. L. Tomkins. Thor's hammer: The first version of the Red Storm MPP architecture. In *In Proceedings of the SC 2002 Conference on High Performance Networking and Computing*, Baltimore, MD, November 2002.

[9] R. F. V. der Wijngaart. NAS parallel benchmarks version 2.4. Technical report, October 2002.

[10] R. Dimitrov, A. Skjellum, T. Jones, B. de Supinski, R. Brightwell, C. Janssen, and M. Nochumson. PERUSE: An MPI performance revealing extensions interface. Presented at the Sixth IBM System Scientific Computing User Group, August 2002.

[11] W. Gropp and E. Lusk. *MPICH ADI Implementation Reference Manual*. Mathematics and Computer Science Division, Argonne National Laboratory, October 1994.

[12] W. Gropp, E. Lusk, N. Doss, and A. Skjellum. A high-performance, portable implementation of the MPI message passing interface standard. *Parallel Computing*, 22(6):789–828, September 1996.

[13] Intel Corporation. Paragon XP/S product overview, 1991.

[14] F. Petrini, W. chun Feng, A. Hoisie, S. Coll, and E. Frachtenberg. The Quadrics network: High-performance clustering technology. *IEEE Micro*, 22(1):46–57, January/February 2002.

[15] F. Petrini, D. J. Kerbyson, and S. Pakin. The case of the missing supercomputer performance: Identifying and eliminating the performance variability on the ASCI Q machine. In *Proceedings of the 2003 Conference on High Performance Networking and Computing*, November 2003.

[16] S. J. Plimpton. Fast parallel algorithms for short-range molecular dynamics. *Journal Computation Physics*, 117:1–19, 1995.

[17] S. J. Plimpton. Lammps web page, July 2003. http://www.cs.sandia.gov/ sjplimp/lammps.html.

[18] S. J. Plimpton, R. Pollock, and M. Stevens. Particle-mesh ewald and rRESPA for parallel molecular dynamics. In *Proceedings of the Eighth SIAM Conference on Parallel Processing for Scientific Computing*, Minneapolis, MN, Mar. 1997.

[19] L. Shuler, C. Jong, R. Riesen, D. van Dresser, A. B. Maccabe, L. A. Fisk, and T. M. Stallcup. The Puma operating system for massively parallel computers. In *Proceeding of the 1995 Intel Supercomputer User's Group Conference*. Intel Supercomputer User's Group, 1995.

[20] S. R. W. Timothy G. Mattson, David Scott. A TeraFLOPS Supercomputer in 1996: The ASCI TFLOP System. In *Proceedings of the 1996 International Parallel Processing Symposium*, 1996.

[21] K. D. Underwood and R. Brightwell. The impact of MPI queue usage on message latency. In *Proceedings of the International Conference on Parallel Processing (ICPP)*, Montreal, Canada, August 2004.

[22] J. S. Vetter and F. Mueller. Communication characteristics of large-scale scientific applications for contemporary cluster architectures. In *16th International Parallel and Distributed Processing Symposium (IPDPS'02)*, pages 27–29, April 2002.

[23] F. Wong, R. Martin, R. Arpaci-Dusseau, and D. E. Culler. Architectural requirements and scalability of the NAS parallel benchmarks. In *Proceedings of the SC99 Conference on High Performance Networking and Computing*, November 1999.

LiMIC: Support for High-Performance MPI Intra-Node Communication on Linux Cluster *

Hyun-Wook Jin Sayantan Sur Lei Chai Dhabaleswar K. Panda

Department of Computer Science and Engineering
The Ohio State University
{jinhy, surs, chail, panda}@cse.ohio-state.edu

Abstract

High performance intra-node communication support for MPI applications is critical for achieving best performance from clusters of SMP workstations. Present day MPI stacks cannot make use of operating system kernel support for intra-node communication. This is primarily due to the lack of an efficient, portable, stable and MPI friendly interface to access the kernel functions. In this paper we attempt to address design challenges for implementing such a high performance and portable kernel module interface. We implement a kernel module interface called LiMIC and integrate it with MVAPICH, an open source MPI over InfiniBand. Our performance evaluation reveals that the point-to-point latency can be reduced by 71% and the bandwidth improved by 405% for 64KB message size. In addition, LiMIC can improve HPCC Effective Bandwidth and NAS IS class B benchmarks by 12% and 8%, respectively, on an 8-node dual SMP InfiniBand cluster.

1. Introduction

Cluster based computing systems are becoming popular for a wide range of scientific applications owing to their cost-effectiveness. These systems are typically built from Symmetric Multi-Processor (SMP) nodes connected with high speed Local Area Networks (LANs) or System Area Networks (SANs) [6]. A majority of these scientific applications are written on top of Message Passing Interface (MPI) [2]. Even though high performance networks have evolved and have very low latency, intra-node communication still remains order of magnitudes faster than network. In order to fully exploit this, MPI applications usually run a set of processes on the same physical node.

To provide high performance to MPI applications, an efficient implementation of intra-node message passing becomes critical. Although several MPI implementations [3, 12] provide intra-node communication support, the performance offered is not optimal. This is mainly due to several message copies involved in the intra-node message passing. Every process has its own virtual address space and cannot directly access another process's message buffer. One approach to avoid extra message copies is to use operating system kernel to provide a direct copy from one process to another. While some researchers have suggested this approach [7, 15, 12], their efforts fall short because of several design limitations and the lack of portability.

In this paper, we propose, design and implement a portable approach to intra-node message passing at the kernel level. To achieve this goal, we design and implement a Linux kernel module that provides an MPI friendly interface. This module is independent of any communication library or interconnection network. It also offers portability across the Linux kernels. We call this kernel module as LiMIC (**Li**nux kernel module for **M**PI **I**ntra-node **C**ommunication).

InfiniBand [1] is a high-performance interconnect based on open standards. MVAPICH [3] is a high-performance implementation of MPI over InfiniBand. MVAPICH is based on the Abstract Device Layer of MPICH [8]. To evaluate the impact of LiMIC, we have integrated it into MVAPICH. Our performance evaluation reveals that we can achieve a *405%* benefit in bandwidth and *71%* improvement in latency for 64KB message size. In addition, we achieve an overall improvement of 12% with HPCC Effective Bandwidth on an 8-node InfiniBand cluster. Further, our application level evaluation with the NAS benchmarks, Integer Sort, reveals a performance benefit of 10%, 8%, and 5% executing classes A, B, and C, respectively, on an 8-node cluster.

The rest of this paper is organized as follows: Section 2 describes existing mechanisms for intra-node communication. In Section 3, we discuss limitations of previous kernel-based approaches and suggest our solution, LiMIC. Then we discuss the design challenges and implementation issues of LiMIC in Section 4. We present performance evaluation results in Section 5. Finally, this paper concludes in Section 6.

* This research is supported in part by Department of Energy's grant #DE-FC02-01ER25506, National Science Foundation's grants #CCR-0204429 and #CCR-0311542 and a grant from Mellanox, Inc.

0190-3918/05 $20.00 © 2005 IEEE

2. Existing Intra-Node Communication Mechanisms

2.1. NIC-Level Loopback

An intelligent NIC can provide a NIC-level loopback. When a message transfer is initiated, the NIC can detect whether the destination is on the same physical node or not. By initiating a local DMA from the NIC memory back to the host memory as shown in Figure 1(a), we can eliminate overheads on the network link because the message is not injected into the network. However, there still exist two DMA operations. Although I/O buses are getting faster, the DMA overhead is still high. Further, the DMA operations cannot utilize the cache effect.

InfiniHost [11] is a Mellanox's second generation InfiniBand Host Channel Adapter (HCA). It provides internal loopback for packets transmitted between two Queue Pairs (connections) that are assigned to the same HCA port.

2.2. User-Space Shared Memory

This design alternative involves each MPI process on a local node, attaching itself to a shared memory region. This shared memory region can then be used amongst the local processes to exchange messages. The sending process copies the message to the shared memory area. The receiving process can then copy over the message to its own buffer. This approach involves minimal setup overhead for every message exchange.

Figure 1(b) shows the various memory transactions which happen during the message transfer. In the first memory transaction labeled as 1; the MPI process needs to bring the send buffer to the cache. The second operation is a write into the shared memory buffer, labeled as 3. If the block of shared memory is not in cache, another memory transaction, labeled as 2 will occur to bring the block in cache. After this, the shared memory block will be accessed by the receiving MPI process. The memory transactions will depend on the policy of the cache coherency implementation and can result in either operation 4a or 4b-1 followed by 4b-2. Then the receiving process needs to write into the receive buffer, operation labeled as 6. If the receive buffer is not in cache, then it will result in operation labeled as 5. Finally, depending on the cache block replacement scheme, step 7 might occur. It is to be noted that there are at least two copies involved in the message exchange. This approach might tie down the CPU with memory copy time. In addition, as the size of the message grows, the performance deteriorates because vigorous copy-in and copy-out also destroys the cache contents.

This shared memory based design has been used in MPICH-GM [12] and other MPI implementations such as MVAPICH [3]. In addition, Lumetta et al. [10] have dealt with efficient design of shared memory message passing protocol and multiprotocol implementation.

3. Kernel-Based Solution, Its Limitations, and Our Approach

3.1. Kernel-Based Memory Mapping

Kernel-based memory mapping approach takes help from the operating system kernel to copy messages directly from one user process to another without any additional copy operation. The sender or the receiver process posts the message request descriptor in a message queue indicating its virtual address, tag, etc. This memory is mapped into the kernel address space when the other process arrives at the message exchange point. Then the kernel performs a direct copy from the sender buffer to the receiver application buffer. Thus this approach involves only one copy.

Figure 1(c) demonstrates the memory transactions needed for copying from the sender buffer directly to the receiver buffer. In step 1, the receiving process needs to bring the sending process' buffer into cache. Then in step 3, the receiving process can write this buffer into its own receive buffer. This may generate step 2 based on whether the buffer was in cache already or not. Then, depending on the cache replacement policy, step 4 might be generated implicitly.

It is to be noted that the number of possible memory transactions for the Kernel-based memory mapping is always less than the number in User-space shared memory approach. We also note that due to the reduced number of copies to and from various buffers, we can maximize the cache utilization. However, there are other overheads. The overheads include time to trap into the kernel, memory mapping overhead, and TLB flush time. In addition, still the CPU resource is required to perform a copy operation.

There are several previous works that adopt this approach, which include [7, 15]. However, their designs lack portability across different networks and deny flexibility to the MPI library developer. To the best of our knowledge, no other current generation MPI implementations provide such a kernel support.

3.2. Our Approach: LiMIC

It is to be noted that the kernel-based approach has the potential to provide efficient MPI intra-node communication. In this paper we are taking this approach, providing unique features such as portability across various interconnects and different communication libraries. This section sharply distinguishes our approach and design philosophy from earlier research in this direction. Our design principles and details of this approach are described in Section 4.

Traditionally, researchers have explored kernel based approaches as an extension to the features available in user-

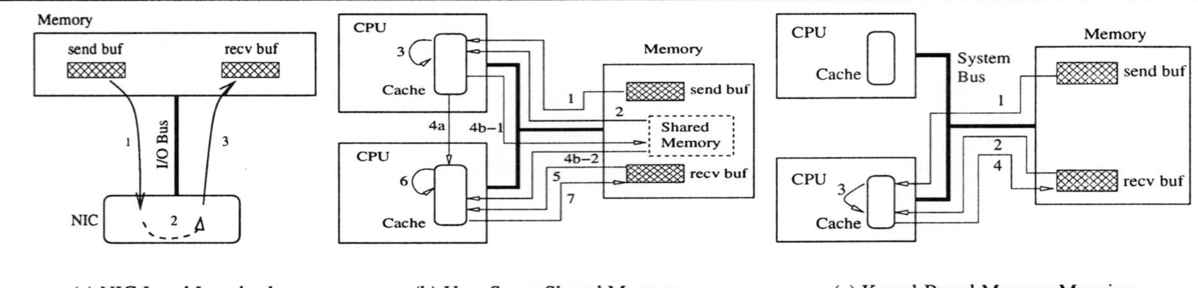

(a) NIC-Level Loopback (b) User-Space Shared Memory (c) Kernel-Based Memory Mapping

Figure 1. Memory Transactions for Different Intra-Node Communication Schemes

level protocols. A high level description of these earlier methodologies is shown in Figure 2(a). As a result, most of these methodologies have been non-portable to other user-level protocols or other MPI implementations. In addition, these earlier designs do not take into account MPI message matching semantics and message queues. Further, the MPI library blindly calls routines provided by the user-level communication library. Since some of the communication libraries are proprietary, this mechanism denies any sort of optimization-space for the MPI library developer.

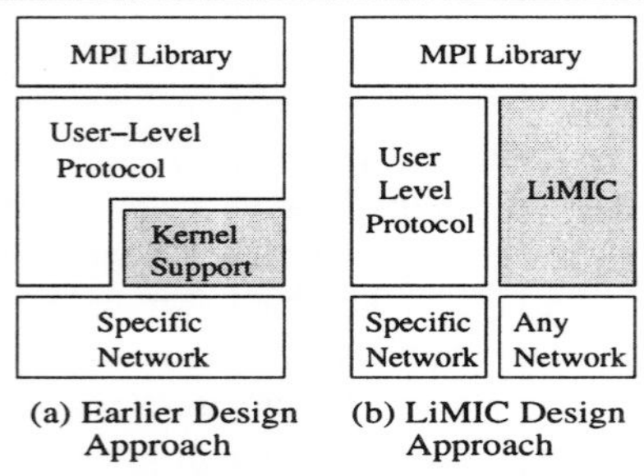

(a) Earlier Design Approach (b) LiMIC Design Approach

Figure 2. Kernel Support Design Approaches

In order to avoid the limitations of the past approaches we look towards generalizing the kernel-access interface and making it MPI friendly. Our implementation of this interface is called LiMIC (Linux kernel module for MPI Intra-node Communication). Its high level diagram is shown in Figure 2(b). We note that such a design is readily portable across different interconnects because its interface and data structures are not required to be dependent on a specific user-level protocol or interconnect. Also, this design gives the flexibility to the MPI library developer to optimize various schemes to make appropriate use of the one copy kernel mechanism. For instance, LiMIC provides flexibility to the MPI library developer to easily choose thresholds for the hybrid approach with other intra-node communication mechanisms and tune the library for specific applications. Such flexibility is discussed in [5]. As a result, LiMIC can provide portability on different interconnects and flexibility for MPI performance optimization.

4. Design and Implementation Issues

4.1. Portable and MPI Friendly Interface

In order to achieve portability across various Linux systems, we design LiMIC to be a runtime loadable module. This means that no modifications to the kernel code is necessary. Kernel modules are usually portable across major versions of mainstream Linux. The LiMIC kernel module can be either an independent module with device driver of interconnection network or a part of the device driver. In addition, the interface is designed to avoid using communication library specific or MPI implementation specific information.

In order to utilize the interface functions, very little modification to the MPI layer are needed. These are required just to place the hooks of the send, receive and completion of messages. The LiMIC interface traps into the kernel internally by using the `ioctl()` system call. We briefly describe the major interface functions provided by LiMIC.

- `LiMIC_Isend(int dest, int tag, int context_id, void* buf, int len, MPI_Request* req)`: This call issues a non blocking send to a specified destination with appropriate message tags.
- `LiMIC_Irecv(int src, int tag, int context_id, void* buf, int len, MPI_Request* req)`: This call issues a non-blocking receive. It is to be noted that blocking send and receive can be easily implemented over non-blocking and wait primitives.
- `LiMIC_Wait(int src/dest, MPI_Request* req)`: This call just polls the LiMIC completion queue once for incoming sends/receives.

As described in Section 3.2, we can observe that the interface provided by LiMIC does not include any specific information on a user-level protocol or interconnect. The interface only defines the MPI related information and has an MPI standard similar format.

4.2. Memory Mapping Mechanism

To achieve one-copy intra-node message passing, a process should be able to access the other processes' virtual address space so that the process can copy the message to/from the other's address space directly. This can be achieved by memory mapping mechanism that maps a part of the other processes' address space into its own address space. After the memory mapping the process can access mapped area as its own.

For memory mapping, we use `kiobuf` provided by the Linux kernel. The `kiobuf` structure supports the abstraction that hides the complexity of the virtual memory system from device drivers. The `kiobuf` structure consists of several fields that store user buffer information such as page descriptors corresponding to the user buffer, offset to valid data inside the first page, and total length of the buffer. The Linux kernel exposes functions to allocate `kiobuf` structures and make a mapping between `kiobuf` and page descriptors of user buffer. In addition, since `kiobuf` internally takes care of pinning down the memory area, we can easily guarantee that the user buffer is present in the physical memory when another process tries to access it. Therefore, we can take advantage of `kiobuf` as a simple and safe way of memory mapping and page locking.

Although the `kiobuf` provides many features, there are several issues we must address in our implementation. The `kiobuf` functions provide a way to map between `kiobuf` and page descriptors of target user buffer only. Therefore, we still need to map the physical memory into the address space of the process, which wants to access the target buffer. To do so, we use the `kmap()` kernel function. Another issue is a large allocation overhead of `kiobuf` structures. We performed tests on `kiobuf` allocation time on our cluster (Cluster A in Section 5) and found that it takes around $60\mu s$ to allocate one `kiobuf`. To remove this overhead from the critical path, LiMIC kernel module preallocates some amount of `kiobuf` structures during the module loading phase and manages this `kiobuf` pool.

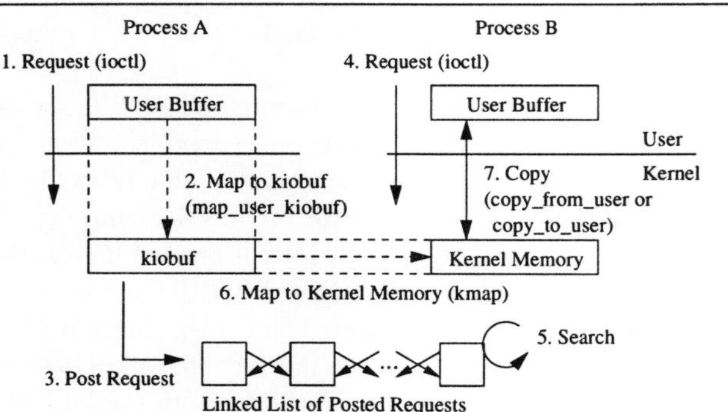

Figure 3. Memory Mapping Mechanism

Figure 3 shows the internal memory mapping operation performed by LiMIC. When either of the message exchanging processes arrives, it issues a request through `ioctl()` (Step 1). If there is no posted request that can be matched with the issued request, the kernel module simply saves information of page descriptors for the user buffer and pins down it by calling `map_user_kiobuf()` (Step 2). Then, the kernel module puts this request into the request queue (Step 3). After that when the other message partner issues a request (Step 4), the kernel module finds the posted request (Step 5) and maps the user buffer to the kernel memory by calling `kmap()` (Step 6). Finally, if the process is the receiver, the kernel module copies the data from kernel memory to user buffer using `copy_to_user()`, otherwise the data is copied from user buffer to kernel memory by `copy_from_user()` (Step 7). The data structures in the kernel module are shared between different instances of the kernel executing on the sending and receiving processes. To guarantee consistency, LiMIC takes care of locking the shared data structures.

4.3. Copy Mechanism

Since the copy needs CPU resources and needs to access pinned memory, we have to carefully decide the timing of the message copy. The message copy could be done in either of the three ways: copy on function calls of receiver, copy on wait function call, and copy on send and receive calls.

In this paper we suggest the design where the copy operation is performed by send and receive functions (i.e., `LiMIC_Isend` and `LiMIC_Irecv`) so that we can provide better progress and less resource usage. In addition, this approach is not prone to skew between processes. The actual copy operation is performed by the process which arrives later at the communication call. So, regardless of the sender or receiver, the operation can be completed as soon as both the processes have arrived. In addition, only the first process is required to pin down the user buffer.

4.4. MPI Message Matching

There are separate message queues for messages sent or received through the kernel module. This is done to allow portability to various other MPI like message queues. So, in general the LiMIC does not assume any specific message queue structure. MPI messages are matched based on *Source*, *Tag* and *Context ID*. Message matching can also be done by using wild cards like `MPI_ANY_SOURCE` or `MPI_ANY_TAG`. LiMIC implements MPI message matching in the following manner:

- **Source in the same node**: In this case, the receive request is directly posted into the queue maintained by LiMIC. On the arrival of the message, the kernel instance at the receiver side matches the message based on the source, tag and context id information and then it passes the buffer into user space.

- **Source in a different node**: In this case, LiMIC is no longer responsible for matching the message. The interface hooks provided in the MPI should take care of not posting the receive request into the kernel message queue.
- **Source in the same node and `MPI_ANY_TAG`**: As in the first case, the receive request is not posted in the generic MPI message queue, but directly into the LiMIC message queue. Now, the matching is done only by the source and context id.
- **`MPI_ANY_SOURCE` and `MPI_ANY_TAG`**: In this case, the source of the message might be on the same physical node but also it can be some other node which is communicating via the network. So the receive request is posted in the MPI queue. Then the MPI internal function that senses an arrival of message checks the send queue in the kernel module as well by using a LiMIC interface, `LiMIC_Iprobe`, and performs message matching with requests in the MPI queue. If the function finds a message which matches the request, the function performs the receive operation by calling the LiMIC receive interface.

Some specialized MPI implementations offload several MPI functions into the NIC. For example, Quadrics performs MPI message matching at the NIC-level [13]. The LiMIC might need an extended interface for such MPI implementations while most of MPI implementations can easily employ LiMIC.

5. Performance Evaluation

In this section we evaluate various performance characteristics of LiMIC. As described in section 2, there are various design alternatives to implement efficient intra-node message passing. MVAPICH [3] version 0.9.4 implements a hybrid mechanism of User-space shared memory and NIC-level loopback. The message size threshold used by MVAPICH-0.9.4 to switch from User-space shared memory to NIC-level loopback is 256KB. In this section, we use a hybrid approach for LiMIC, in which User-space shared memory is used for short messages (up to 4KB) and then Kernel-based memory mapping is used to perform an one copy transfer for larger messages. The choice of this threshold is explained below in section 5.1. However, it is to be noted that each application can set a different threshold as discussed in Section 3.2. Here on, all references to MVAPICH-0.9.4 and LiMIC refer to the hybrid designs mentioned above. In addition, we also provide performance results for each of the individual design alternatives, namely, User-space shared memory, NIC loopback, and Kernel module.

We conducted experiments on two 8-node clusters with the following configurations:

- **Cluster A:** SuperMicro SUPER X5DL8-GG nodes with dual Intel Xeon 3.0 GHz processors, 512 KB L2 cache, PCI-X 64-bit 133 MHz bus
- **Cluster B:** SuperMicro SUPER P4DL6 nodes with dual Intel Xeon 2.4 GHz processors, 512 KB L2 cache, PCI-X 64-bit 133 MHz bus

The Linux kernel version used was 2.4.22smp from kernel.org. All the nodes are equipped with Mellanox InfiniHost MT23108 HCAs. The nodes are connected using Mellanox MTS 2400 24-port switch. Test configurations are named (2x1), (2x2), etc. to denote two processes on one node, four processes on two nodes, and so on.

First, we evaluate our designs at microbenchmarks level. Second, we present experimental results on message transfer and descriptor post breakdown. Then we evaluate the scalability of performance offered by LiMIC for larger clusters. Finally, we evaluate the impact of LiMIC on NAS Integer Sort application kernel.

5.1. Microbenchmarks

In this section, we describe our tests for microbenchmarks such as point-to-point latency and bandwidth. The tests were conducted on Cluster A.

The latency test is carried out in a standard ping-pong fashion. The latency microbenchmark is available from [3]. The results for one-way latency is shown in Figures 4(a) and 4(b). We observe an improvement of 71% for latency as compared to MVAPICH-0.9.4 for 64KB message size. The results clearly show that on this experimental platform, it is most expensive to use NIC-level loopback for large messages. The User-space shared memory implementation is good for small messages. This avoids extra overheads of polling the network or trapping into the kernel. However, as the message size increases, the application buffers and the intermediate shared memory buffer no longer fit into the cache and the copy overhead increases. The Kernel module on the other hand can reduce one copy, hence maximizing the cache effect. As can be noted from the latency figure, after the message size of 4KB, it becomes more beneficial to use the Kernel module than User-space shared memory. Therefore, LiMIC hybrid uses User-space shared memory for messages smaller than 4KB and the Kernel module for larger messages.

For measuring the point-to-point bandwidth, a simple window based communication approach was used. The bandwidth microbenchmark is available from [3]. The bandwidth graphs are shown in Figures 4(c) and 4(d). We observe an improvement of 405% for bandwidth for 64KB message size as compared to MVAPICH-0.9.4. We also observe that the bandwidth offered by LiMIC drops at 256KB message size. This is due to the fact that the cache size on the nodes in Cluster A is 512KB. Both sender and receiver buffers and some additional data cannot fit into the cache beyond this message size. However, the bandwidth offered by LiMIC is still greater than MVAPICH-0.9.4.

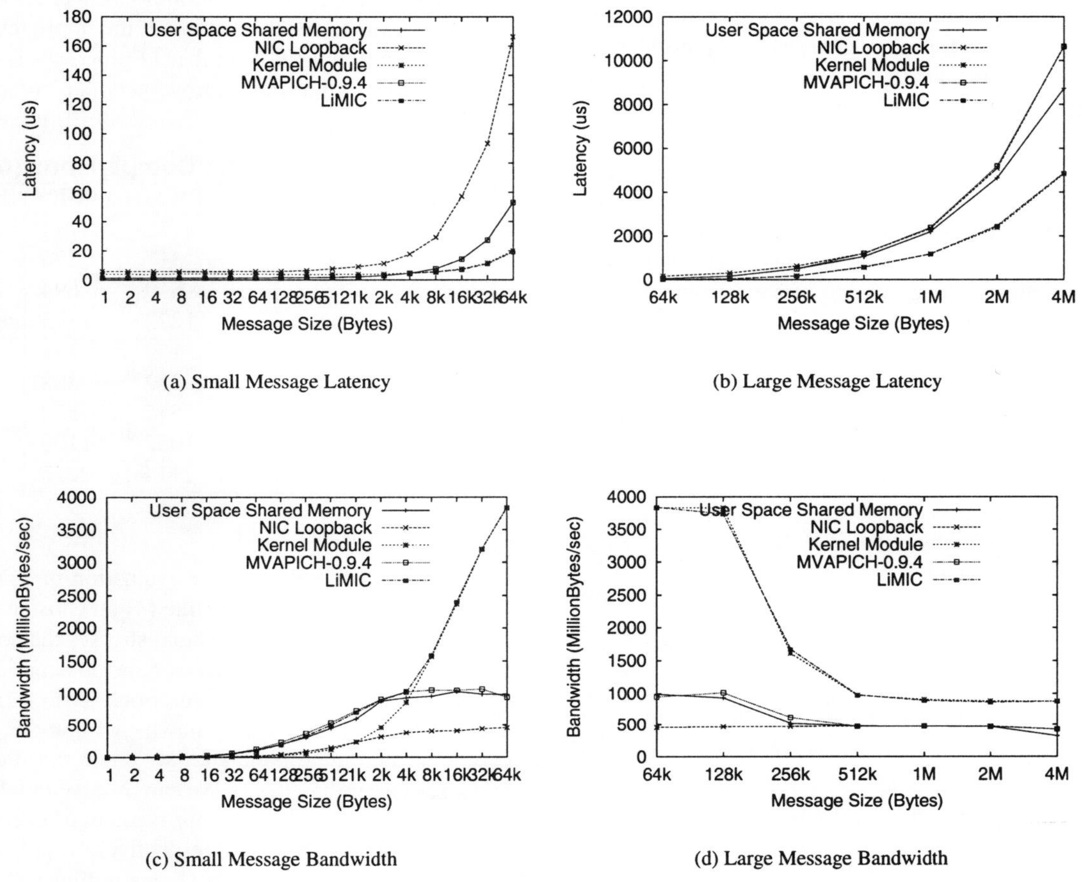

(a) Small Message Latency

(b) Large Message Latency

(c) Small Message Bandwidth

(d) Large Message Bandwidth

Figure 4. MPI Level Latency and Bandwidth

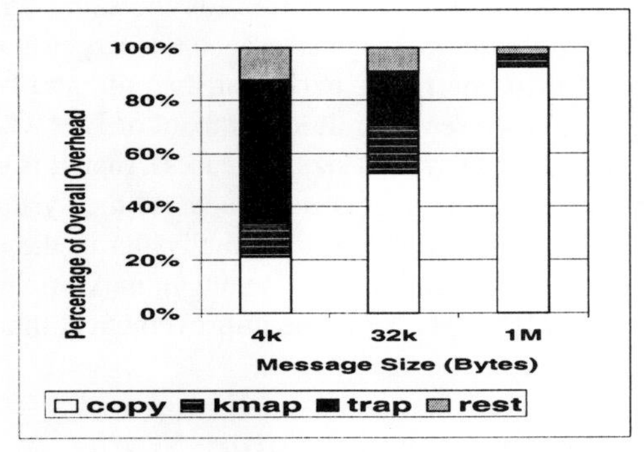

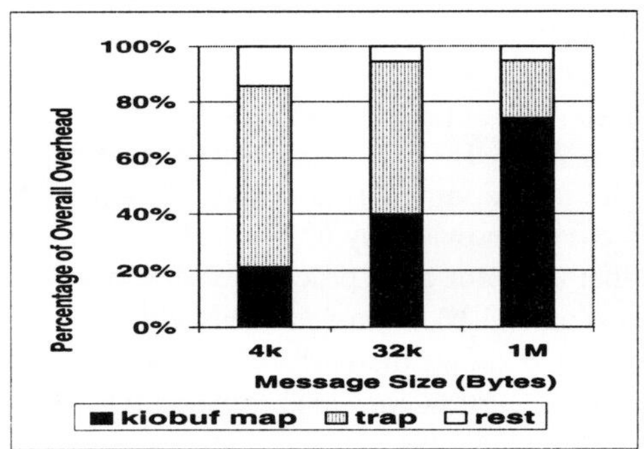

(a) Message Transfer Breakdown

(b) Descriptor Post Breakdown

Figure 5. LiMIC Cost Breakdown (Percentage of Overall Overhead)

5.2. LiMIC Cost Breakdown

In order to evaluate the cost of various operations which LiMIC has to perform for message transfer, we profiled the time spent by LiMIC during a ping-pong latency test. In this section, we present results on the various relative cost breakdowns on Cluster A.

The overhead breakdown for message transfer in percentages is shown in Figure 5(a). We observe that the message copy time dominates the overall send/receive operation as the message size increases. For shorter messages, we see that a considerable amount of time is spent in the kernel trap (around $3\mu s$) and around $0.5\mu s$ in queueing and locking overheads (indicated as "rest"), which are shown as 55% and 12% of the overall message transfer overhead for 4KB message in Figure 5(a). We also observe that the time to map the user buffer to the kernel address space (using `kmap()`) increases as the number of pages in the user buffer increases.

The overhead breakdown for descriptor posting in percentages is shown in Figure 5(b). We observe that the time to map the `kiobuf` with the page descriptors of the user buffer forms a large portion of the time to post a descriptor. It is because the `kiobuf` mapping overhead increases in proportional to the number of pages. This step also involves the pinning of the user buffer into physical memory. The column labeled "rest" indicates again the queuing and locking overheads.

5.3. HPCC Effective Bandwidth

To evaluate the impact of the improvement of intra-node bandwidth on a larger cluster of dual SMP systems, we conducted effective bandwidth test on Clusters A and B. For measuring the effective bandwidth of the clusters, we used b_eff [14] benchmark. This benchmark measures the accumulated bandwidth of the communication network of parallel and distributed computing systems. This benchmark is featured in the High Performance Computing Challenge benchmark suite (HPCC) [9].

Table 1 shows the performance results of LiMIC compared with MVAPICH-0.9.4. It is observed that when both processes are on the same physical node (2x1), LiMIC improves effective bandwidth by 61% on Cluster A. It is also observed that even for a 16 process experiment (2x8) the cluster can achieve 12% improved bandwidth.

The table also shows the performance results on Cluster B. The results follow the same trend as that of Cluster A. It is to be noted that the messages latency on User-space shared memory and Kernel module depends on the speed of CPU while the NIC-level loopback message latency depends on the speed of I/O bus. Since the I/O bus speed remains the same between Clusters A and B, and only the CPU speed reduces, the improvement offered by LiMIC reduces in Cluster B.

In our next experiment, we increased the number of processes as to include nodes in both Clusters A and B. The motivation was to see the scaling of the improvement in effective bandwidth as the number of processes is increased. It is to be noted that the improvement percentage remains constant (5%) as the number of processes is increased.

Table 1. b_eff Results Comparisons (MB/s)

Cluster	Config.	MVAPICH	LiMIC	Improv.
A	2x1	152	244	61%
	2x2	317	378	19%
	2x4	619	694	12%
	2x8	1222	1373	12%
B	2x1	139	183	31%
	2x2	282	308	9%
	2x4	545	572	5%
	2x8	1052	1108	5%
A & B	2x16	2114	2223	5%

5.4. NAS Integer Sort

We conducted performance evaluation of LiMIC on IS in NAS Parallel Benchmark suite [4] on Cluster A. IS is an integer sort benchmark kernel that stresses the communication aspect of the network. We conducted experiments with classes A, B and C on configurations (2x1), (2x2), (2x4), and (2x8). The results are shown in Figure 6. Since the class C is a large problem size, we could run it on the system sizes larger than (2x2). We can observe that LiMIC can achieve 10%, 8%, and 5% improvement of execution time running classes A, B, and C respectively, on (2x8) configuration. The improvements are shown in Figure 7.

To understand the insights behind the performance improvement, we profiled the number of intra-node messages larger than 1KB and their sizes being used by IS within a node. The results with class A are shown in Table 2. We can see that as the system size increases, the size of the messages reduces. The trend is the same on classes B and C while the message size becomes larger than class A. Since LiMIC performs better for medium and larger message sizes, we see overall less impact of LiMIC on IS performance as the system size increases. Also, it is to be noted that since the message size reduces as the system size increases, the message size eventually fits in the cache size on (2x8) configuration. This results in maximizing the benefit of LiMIC and raising the improvement at the (2x8) system size as shown in Figure 7.

6. Conclusions and Future Work

In this paper we have designed and implemented a high performance Linux kernel module (called LiMIC) for MPI intra-node message passing. LiMIC is able to provide MPI friendly interface and independence from proprietary communication libraries and interconnects.

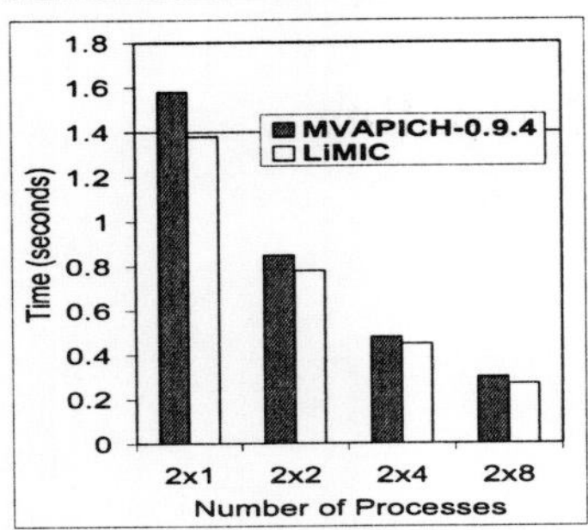

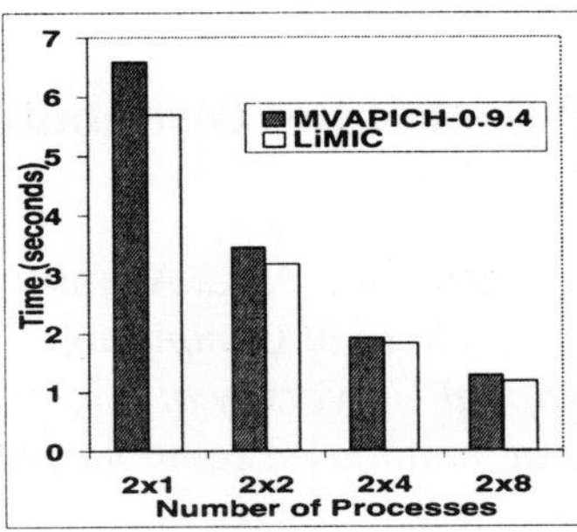

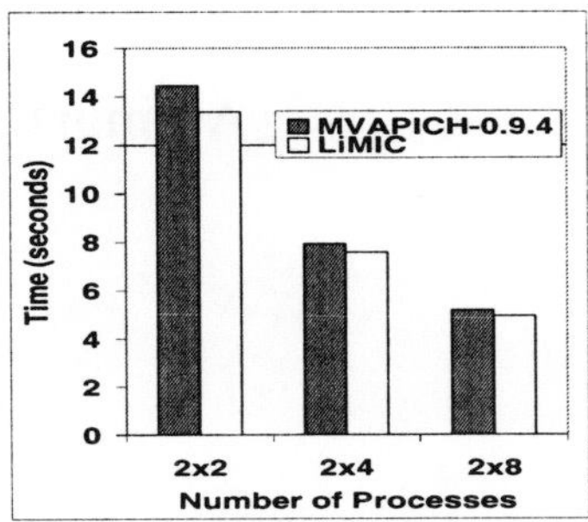

Figure 6. IS Total Execution Time Comparisons: (a) Class A, (b) Class B, and (c) Class C

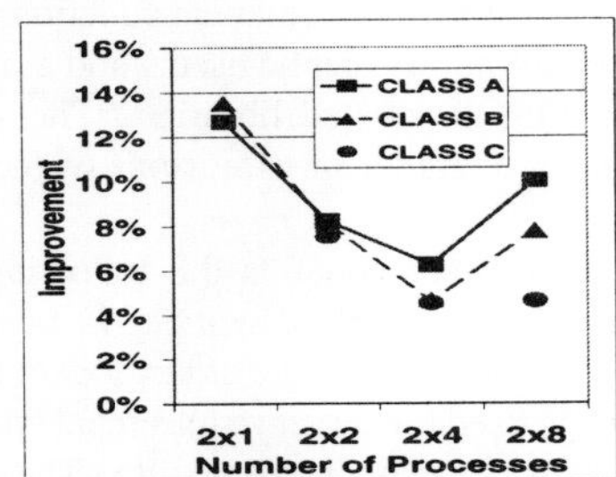

Figure 7. IS Performance Improvement

Table 2. Intra-Node Message Size Distribution for IS Class A

Message Size (Bytes)	2x1	2x2	2x4	2x8
1K-8K	44	44	44	44
32K-256K	0	0	0	22
256K-1M	0	0	22	0
1M-4M	0	22	0	0
4M-16M	22	0	0	0

To measure the performance of LiMIC, we have integrated it with MVAPICH. Through the benchmark results, we could observe that LiMIC improved the point-to-point latency and bandwidth up to 71% and 405%, respectively. In addition, we observed that employing LiMIC in an 8-node InfiniBand cluster, increased the effective bandwidth by 12%. Also, our experiments on a larger 16-node cluster revealed that the improvement in effective bandwidth remains constant as the number of processes increased. Further, LiMIC improved the NAS IS benchmark execution time by 10%, 8%, and 5% for classes A, B, and C respectively, on an 8-node cluster.

As future work, we plan to enhance LiMIC to achieve zero-copy intra-node communication by using the copy-on-write and memory mapping mechanisms.

References

[1] InfiniBand Trade Association. http://www.infinibandta.com.

[2] MPI: A Message-Passing Interface Standard. http://www.mpi-forum.org/docs/mpi-11-html/mpi-report.html.

[3] MPI over InfiniBand Project. http://nowlab.cis.ohio-state.edu/projects/mpi-iba/.

[4] D. H. Bailey, E. Barszcz, J. T. Barton, D. S. Browning, R. L. Carter, D. Dagum, R. A. Fatoohi, P. O. Frederickson, T. A. Lasinski, R. S. Schreiber, H. D. Simon, V. Venkatakrishnan, and S. K. Weeratunga. The NAS Parallel Benchmarks. *The International Journal of Supercomputer Applications*, 5(3):63–73, Fall 1991.

[5] L. Chai, S. Sur, H.-W. Jin, and D. K. Panda. Analysis of Design Considerations for Optimizing Multi-Channel MPI over InfiniBand. In *CAC 2005*, 2005.

[6] J. Duato, S. Yalamanchili, and L. Ni. *Interconnection Networks: An Engineering Approach.* The IEEE Computer Society Press, 1997.

[7] P. Geoffray, C. Pham, and B. Tourancheau. A Software Suite for High-Performance Communications on Clusters of SMPs. *Cluster Computing*, 5(4):353–363, October 2002.

[8] W. Gropp, E. Lusk, N. Doss, and A. Skjellum. High-performance, portable implementation of the MPI Message Passing Interface Standard. *Parallel Computing*, 22(6):789–828, 1996.

[9] Innovative Computing Laboratory (ICL). HPC Challenge Benchmark. http://icl.cs.utk.edu/hpcc/.

[10] S. S. Lumetta, A. M. Mainwaring, and D. E. Culler. Multi-Protocol Active Messages on a Cluster of SMP's. In *SC '97*, 1997.

[11] Mellanox Technologies. Mellanox InfiniBand InfiniHost MT23108 Adapters. http://www.mellanox.com, July 2002.

[12] Myricom Inc. Portable MPI Model Implementation over GM, 2004.

[13] F. Petrini, W. Feng, A. Hoisie, S. Coll, and E. Frachtenberg. The Quadrics Network: High Performance Clustering Technology. *IEEE Micro*, 22(1):46–57, January-February 2002.

[14] R. Rabenseifner and A. E. Koniges. The parallel communication and I/O bandwidth benchmarks: beff and beffio. http://www.hlrs.de/organization/par/services/models/mpi/b_eff/.

[15] T. Takahashi, S. Sumimoto, A. Hori, H. Harada, and Y. Ishikawa. PM2: High Performance Communication Middleware for Heterogeneous Network Environments. In *SC 2000*, 2000.

A Smart TCP Socket for Distributed Computing

Shao Tao, A. L. Ananda
School of Computing
National University of Singapore
{shaot, ananda}@comp.nus.edu.sg

Abstract

The middle-ware in distributed computing coordinates a group of servers to accomplish a resource intensive task; however, without resource monitoring, the server selection algorithms will not be sophisticated enough to provide satisfying results at all time. This paper presents a smart TCP socket library using server workload feedback to improve selection techniques. Users are able to specify server requirements by using a predefined meta language. Monitoring components such as the server probes and monitors are in charge of monitoring the server resource usage, network metrics and performing security measurements. Based on the user's request and available server resources, the user request handler called wizard will recommend the most suitable servers to user applications. The centralized and the distributed modes are both provided so that the socket library can be adapted to both small distributed systems and a large scale GRID.

1. Introduction

The standard TCP socket library provides a rich set of functions for the network application development. With the growth of distributed applications on the networks, the traditional socket library shows a few limitations in functionality. Most distributed applications consider networked servers as abstracted grouped computation services accessible through sockets, without concerning about the names or location of the servers. However, in the conventional TCP socket library, users can only select servers by giving their domain names or IP addresses. When the addressed server fails, the application will not be able to switch to alternative servers even if they can provide identical services. Applications may have different requirements for various system resources at different intensity levels. There is not yet a standard interface available to inform the socket library about what kind of servers are desirable for a particular task.

The smart TCP socket library is developed to address the above issues. It implements the status-aware server selection schemes at the application level. A meta language is provided to define server requirements, with numerous parameters and predefined mathematical functions available. A convenient client library can be used stand alone or combined with existing distributed libraries. The structure is highly flexible for upgrades or extensions of the key components.

The rest of the paper contains the following sections. Section 2 introduces the related works. In Section 3, we will look at the architecture of the smart socket library and the meta language used for server requirement specification. Section 4 contains the experiment results. The conclusion and recommendations for the future work are presented in Section 5.

2. Related Works

Improvements to the distributed computing environment can be achieved from various projects, including system probing tools, distributed libraries, task schedulers and large scale grid middle-wares. The *Trust Agent*[1] from Cisco Systems is a probing tool, which interacts with softwares installed in the local machine to report information like system version, patch level and infection records of computer viruses. *Pathload*[2] uses an end-to-end technique to measure the available network bandwidth by sending periodic packet streams. *MPI*(Message Passing Interface)[3] defines an MPI standard to support efficient process communication in a heterogeneous environment. The *PVM*[4] library enables the user program to spawn multiple processes within a server cluster and provides inter-communication among these processes. It includes the programming interfaces for data exchange, server monitoring and process management. A detailed comparison of MPI and PVM is given in Geist's work[5]. The *Globus* Alliance project[6] started with a goal of "enabling the application of Grid concepts to scientific and engineering computing". It provides a Globus toolkit for building Grids and Grid applications efficiently. The *Condor*[7] project developed a set of utilities for resource monitoring, task scheduling and process migration. It uses *classad*(Classified Advertisement)[8] to represent the char-

0190-3918/05 $20.00 © 2005 IEEE

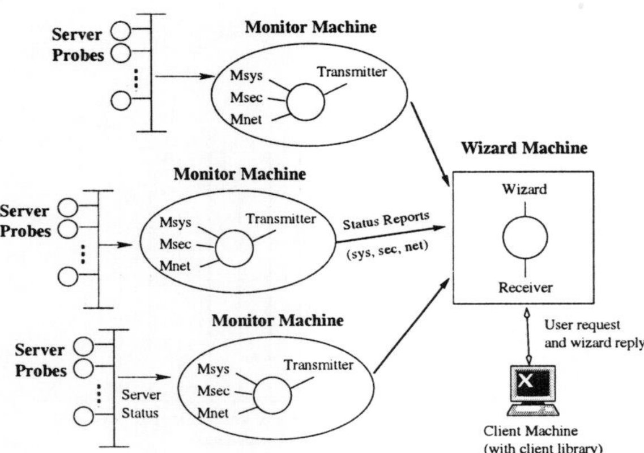

Figure 1. The Smart Socket Library

acteristics of the available servers and user tasks. The task scheduler executes user tasks on the best matched servers.

Compared with previous works, the smart TCP socket library is an attempt to improve distributed computing at the socket layer. Active probing is used to monitor the server workload, network metrics and security information. A meta language similar to *classad* is implemented for specifying server requirements. Through the smart socket library, user applications can claim the servers by telling the workload features of qualified servers and networks instead of domain names or IP addresses. The library components can run in the centralized mode for small distributed systems and switch to the distributed mode when operating over sparsely located server clusters. It is fully compatible with some existing distributed libraries such as PVM.

3. Design Issues

The smart socket library consists of eight components. Fig. 1 depicts the interactions among these components. Each server cluster has one dedicated monitor machine. Each server has a *server probe* installed for probing the hardware configurations and workload status. The probing results, called server status reports, are transmitted back to the *system monitor* running on the monitor machine. Besides the *system monitor*, there are a *network monitor*, a *security monitor* and a *transmitter* running on each monitor machine. The *network monitor* measures the network metrics and the *security monitor* checks the security levels of each server. The *transmitter* transfers the status reports collected by the three monitors to the *receiver* on the wizard machine. User queries are handled by the *wizard* program, which compares the server reports and the user's requirement to select qualified servers. User applications use the *client library* to interact with the *wizard* program, in order for passing the requirement contents and retrieving the list of recommended servers.

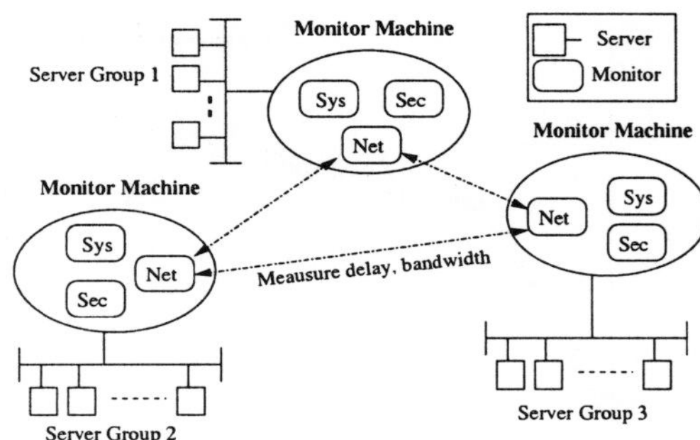

Figure 2. Operations of Network Monitor

Table 1. Server Status Entries

Entries	File	Meaning
load_1, load_5, load_15	/proc/loadavg	system load
user, nice, system, idle	/proc/stat	CPU time usage
total, used, free	/proc/meminfo	memory usage
allreq, rreq, rblocks wreq, wblocks	/proc/stat	disk IO activity
name, rbytes, rpackets tbytes, tpackets	/proc/net/dev	network interface IO

3.1. Server probe and system monitor

The server probe scans through the */proc*[9] entries in the Linux system for sever workload including CPU/memory usage, disk/network activities and average system load. The scanned parameters and */proc* entries are listed in Table. 1.

The probed parameters are combined into one server status report and sent to the system monitor in a UDP message. Before transmission, all numerical values will be converted to the string format to avoid endian issues. This allows machines with different hardware architectures to be monitored correctly. The system monitor stores each updated server report into a shared memory space on the monitor machine.

3.2. Network monitor and security monitor

If the client machine is located close to one of the server groups, the network performance of the client application will be mainly determined by the links between various server groups. The network monitor in each server group probes the network paths linking to other monitor machines for the network metrics information including the available bandwidth and the network delay. Fig. 2 gives a scenario of three network monitors. As each server cluster has one monitor machine running, all network paths interconnecting every two server clusters will be probed.

The network delay represented in Formula. 1 is used to estimated the available network bandwidth. The network delay T for a probing packet is determined by the available bandwidth B, the packet size S, the system/network overhead O_{sys}/O_{net} and the initialization speed of the network

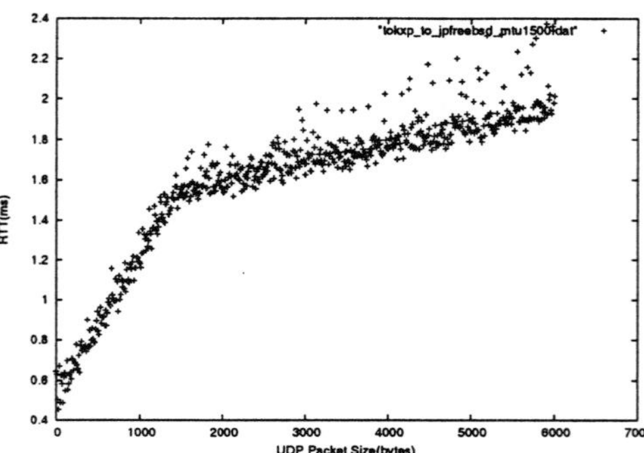

Figure 3. Network Delay and Packet Size

interface R_{init}. Two probing packets with unreachable destination ports are sent out to trigger the ICMP messages from the remote host. The time between the moment we send out a probing packet and the moment when the ICMP message comes back is measured as the network delay. Assuming the packet sizes are S_1 and S_2 and the network delays are measured as T_1 and T_2, the estimated bandwidth B' is calculated as $\frac{S_2 - S_1}{T_2 - T_1}$.

$$T = \begin{cases} \frac{S}{B} + \frac{S}{R_{init}} + O_{sys} + O_{net}, & \text{if } S < MTU \\ \frac{S}{B} + \frac{MTU}{R_{init}} + O_{sys} + O_{net}, & \text{if } S \geq MTU \end{cases} \quad (1)$$

The factor R_{init} was discovered during the network delay experiments. The sample given in Fig. 3 illustrates that the round trip delay is not strictly linearly proportional to the packet size for a given network path. The slope of the delay over the packet size has a dramatic change as the packet size S approaches the MTU(maximum transfer unit) of the physical network interface. Another six sets of experiments have been done between machines in the same network segment and from hosts in Singapore to hosts located in USA and Tokyo, all showing similar effects.

The estimated bandwidth B' is calculated as the inverse of the slope in the delay plots. If sizes of the probing packets $S_1, S_2 < MTU$, we will have $\frac{1}{B'} = \frac{1}{B} + \frac{1}{R_{init}}$ according to Formula. 1. This means when the probing packet sizes are less than the MTU value, the estimated bandwidth value B' will be less than the actual available bandwidth B and network interface initialization speed R_{init}.

Therefore, we propose the following rules for selecting the probing packet size: The packet size should be small to reduce overhead but larger than the MTU. The packet sizes S_1 and S_2 should generate the same number of fragments. The difference between S_1 and S_2 should be large enough to provide sufficient resolution in the network delays T_1 and T_2. Fig. 4 shows the series of measurement results by using various probing sizes on the same network, where the MTU value is 1500 bytes. The last set of probing yields the best estimation, as it most closely follows the proposed criteria.

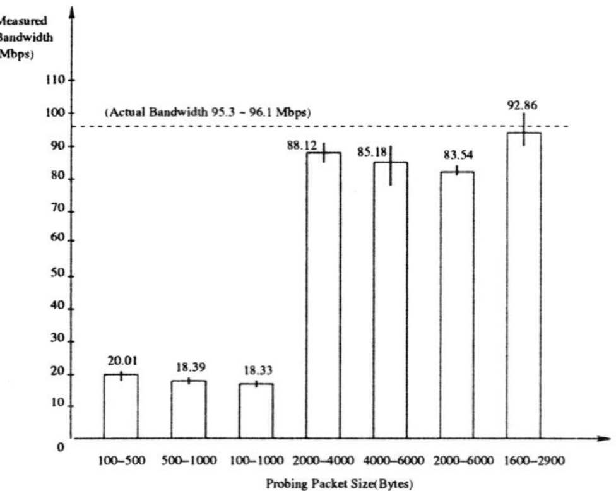

Figure 4. Bandwidth Measurements using various Packet Sizes

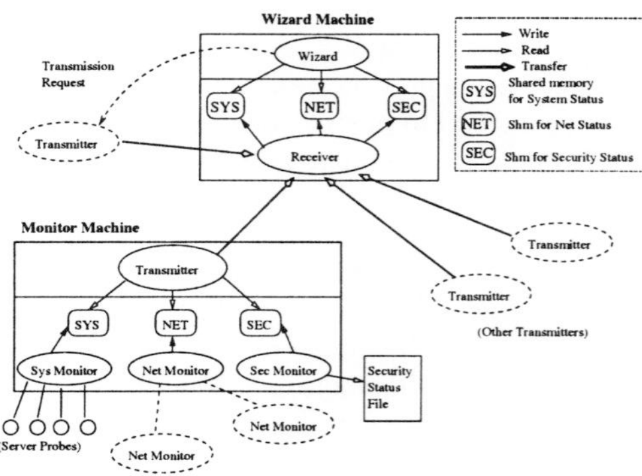

Figure 5. Interactions between the transmitter and receiver

The security monitor scans through the security log file for the security levels of all servers in the cluster. The security level is a number indicating how secure a server is. In later works, more sophisticated security mechanisms can be applied to replace the primitive implementation.

The network status reports and security status reports collected by the network monitor and security monitor are stored into the shared memory space in the monitor machine for the *transmitter* to access.

3.3. Transmitter and receiver

The *transmitters* and *receivers* work together to transfer the complete status information from the monitor machines to the wizard machine as demonstrated in Fig. 5.

Besides the transmitter, the monitor machines also contains the system monitor, the network monitor, and the security monitor. Each monitor stores the status reports into a separate shared memory region. The records are copied

User Query:	seq num	server num	option	requirement	
Wizard Reply:	seq num	server num	server-1	....	server-n

Figure 6. User Query and Wizard Reply

out by the *transmitter* from the memory space and sent out directly in the binary format. TCP protocol is deployed for the transmission between transmitters and receivers. The format of the message is `[type, size, data]`. The `type` field tells the type of the record being transmitted, which can be *sys*, *net* or *sec*. The `size` field is the number of records in the message. The `data` field contains the actual status reports in the binary format.

Transmitters can work in either the centralized mode or the distributed mode. In the centralized mode, transmitters send the updated status reports to the receiver at a regular interval. In the distributed mode, transmitters remain in the listening state, until an update request from the *wizard* arrives. The *wizard* program triggers the update transmission from all transmitters, once the user issues a new query.

For each incoming update from transmitters, the *receiver* creates the corresponding data structure to store the information and updates the contents in the respective memory space. In this way, the *receiver* can maintain identical shared memory contents as what the transmitters have, such that the *wizard* program can access the status reports as if they were generated locally.

3.4. Wizard and client library

The *wizard* program works as a daemon, which processes user queries from the *client library* sequentially. It returns a list of qualified servers in the reply message. In order to reduce the overhead, both the query and the reply messages are encapsulated in UDP packets.

The structures of the query and reply are shown in Fig. 6. In the query message, the *seq num* field is a random number generated by the client library to identify the current user query. The *server num* field contains the number of servers requested by the user. The *option* field uses a number to indicate the additional options. The last field *requirement* contains the detailed server requirement in the string format. For a wizard reply, the *seq num*, *server num* fields will be the same as the ones in the request message. The last field in the reply message is the address list including all qualified servers returned to the client.

The server requirement in the user query is presented by using a meta language derived from examples in Brian's book[10]. The meta language contains the following five types of elements:

- *variable*: Variables are character string tokens. There are four types of variables: *server-side, user-side, temp, undefined.* Users can use the predefined 22 server-side variables to describe requirements on the server workload and network metrics. For example, the statement `host_system_load1<0.5` indicates that a server is qualified if the system load in the last one minute is less than 0.5. User-side variables are provided for users to give their preference on some particular servers. The statement `user_denied_host=10.0.1.2` tells the *wizard* to avoid the server with an IP address equal to "10.0.1.2". The third type of variables are temporary variables, which are defined locally in the requirement statements and used for intermediate steps. Any *temp* variable without a value is considered as an *undefined* variable.

- *number*: Numbers are crucial to the requirement description, as most of the predefined parameters have numerical values. All numbers in requirement statements are converted into `double` type for processing.

- *netaddr*: A *netaddr* variable represents the network address of a host in the format of either domain name or IP address. For example, both "dummy.somedomain.net" and "10.0.0.1" are classified as *netaddr* type.

- *operator*: Operators are classified into two categories: non-logical and logical. Non-logical operators include =, +, -, ×, / and ^ (exponential function). The result of a non-logical operator is numerical. Logical operators include >, <, >=, <=, ==, ! =, &&(AND), and ||(OR). A logical operator returns a boolean value, either `true` or `false`.

- *build-in*: Build-in functions are the mathematical functions that can be understood by the *wizard* program, such as sin(), cos(), log() and sqrt(). These build-in functions can help users to write complex statements.

A server requirement may contain multiple statements with each statement in a single line. Each statement/line is also called an *expression* or *expr* in short. The *expr* can be in one of the following four formats:

- `number` or `netaddr` or `variables`: The basic element for an expression can be a number, a variable or a *netaddr* value.

- `<build-in>(expr)`: The build-in functions can be applied to an expression and return a numerical value.

- `(expr)`: Users can use parentheses `()` to change the operation precedence in a statement.

- `<expr> <op> <expr>`: Users are allowed to write nested expressions by using an *operator* to join two *expressions*. The operator can be either logical or non-logical. If the main operator of an expression is logical, the statement is called a logical statement. Otherwise, it is a non-logical statement. For example, "$(a + b) < c$" is a logical statement and "$a + (b < c)$" is non-logical. A server is qualified if all the logical statements return `true` under its workload features.

The operation procedure of the *client library* contains the following three steps:

1. The client library reads the server requirement from the user's input file. A sample of input is displayed below:

```
# server status
host_system_load1 < 1
host_mem_used <= 250
host_cpu_free >= 0.9
# network metric
host_network_tbytesps < 1024*1024
# user preference
user_denied_host1 = 192.168.1.100
user_preferred_host1 = abc.some.net
```

   This requirement makes use of four server-side variables and two user-side variables. The first four statements are logical statements. The statement with a leading "#" is considered as a comment, ignored by the *wizard* during processing.

2. The client library generates a random number to identify a user query. The identification number, the number of servers required, the option value and the requirement details are packed into one UDP message as shown in Fig. 6 and forwarded to the *wizard* program.

3. Once the user query is sent, the client library will wait for the reply from the *wizard*. A timer is used to monitor any time out events. If the reply fails to come back with the time limit, an error will be returned to the application. If the reply is returned successfully, the client library will try to make a connection to the service port of each server in the candidate list. The connected sockets are returned to the application. The user application is responsible for the further usage of the sockets.

4. Experiment Results

All components in the smart socket library were implemented on a Pentium-4 2.4GHz PC installed with Debian Linux 3.0 and gcc 2.95. The topology of the testbed network is shown in Fig. 7. All the 11 machines are located in the Communication and Internet Research Lab(CIR), NUS. Host *sagit* and *lhost* are Pentium-3 866MHz workstations.

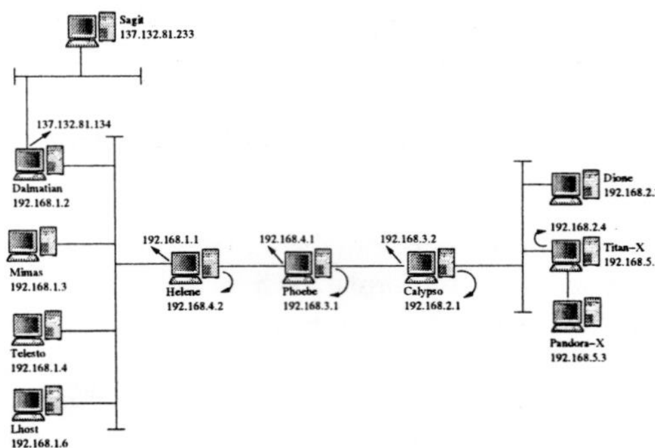

Figure 7. Experiment Network Topology

Host *dalmatian* and *dione* are Pentium-4 2.4GHz PCs. The rest 7 machines run on Pentium-4 CPUs ranging from 1.6GHz to 1.8GHz. All machines run on the Linux system with 100Mbps Ethernet connections.

Two distributed programs were developed to test the smart socket library, a distributed matrix multiplication program named *matrixp* and a massive downloading program named *massd*. The program *matrixp* divides the original input into small blocks and assigns each block to a candidate server for calculation. The program *massd* retrieves different parts of a data file from multiple servers simultaneously in order for higher throughput. The execution time of *matrixp* and the average throughput achieved by *massd* can serve as the metrics to evaluate the effectiveness of the smart sockets.

The experiments based on *matrixp* and *massd* are explained in the following subsections.

4.1. Experiments for matrixp

Four sets of matrix multiplication experiments were conducted to compare the execution time without and with the assistance of the smart socket library, including 2 vs 2, 4 vs 4, 6 vs 6 under zero workload and 4 vs 4 under non-zero workload. Each set uses 2 servers, 4 servers, 6 servers and 4 servers respectively. Without the smart socket library, the servers were selected by a random function. The matrix dimension is 1500×1500 and each matrix element is a *double* floating number.

The benchmarking test was conducted to measure the computational power of the eleven machines. As shown in Fig. 8, the P3 866MHz and P4 2.4GHz machines have better performance than the rest seven P4 1.6~1.8GHz machines for the *matrixp* program.

2vs2 without workload. In this experiment, 2 servers were selected to compute a matrix with a dimension of 1500×1500 by using 600×600 blocks. With the help of the smart socket library, users can ask for the fastest servers for this CPU intensive task. The server requirement contains a statement `bogomips>4000` to select the two P4 2.4GHz

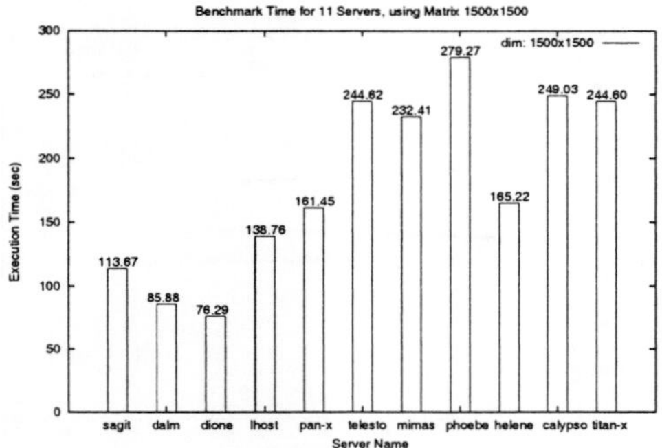

Figure 8. Matrix Multiplication Benchmark

Table 2. matrixp: 2vs2 under zero workload

Item\Library	Random	Smart Lib
Matrix Size	1500×1500, blk=600	1500×1500, blk=600
No. of Servers	2	2
Requirement	(none)	cpu_bogomips>4000 cpu_free>0.9 mem_free>5
Server List	(5 random sets)	dione, dalmatian
Avg Time(sec)	81.08	61.94

servers. The details of the experiment is given in Table. 2. The execution time for the two server groups were 81.08 seconds by using the random function and 61.94 seconds with the smart library. The execution time was reduced by 23.06%.

4vs4 without workload. Four servers were selected to compute the same 1500×1500 matrix with a block size of 200×200. From the benchmarking step, users have the knowledge that P3 866MHz and P4 2.4GHz machines have better performance than P4 1.6~1.8GHz machines. We use the requirement statement `bogomips>4000 || bogomips<2000` to select only those machines into the server pool. Table. 3 shows that the execution time dropped from 63.18 to 52.70 seconds after the smart library was enabled.

6vs6 without workload. In the third experiment, the *user_denied_host* option was used to avoid the 5 slowest servers in the server pool. The details are given in Table. 4. The execution time was reduced by 8.3% only. The low improvement was caused by the increased communication overhead with 6 servers working for the single task. There is also a large overlap between the servers selected randomly and those chosen by the smart library, which further shortened the gap in performance.

4vs4 with workload enabled. To evaluate the effectiveness of the library under non-zero workload, 7 servers with P4 1.6~1.8GHz CPU were used to form the server pool. Three servers were chosen to run the *super_pi*[11] program as the busy servers, including *helene*, *telesto* and *mimas*. A busy server has a CPU usage ranging from 0% to 100% and a memory usage of over 150 MBytes. The average system

Table 3. matrixp: 4vs4 under zero workload

<table>
<tr><th>Item\Library</th><th>Random</th><th>Smart Lib</th></tr>
<tr><td>Matrix Size</td><td>1500×1500, blk=200</td><td>1500×1500, blk=200</td></tr>
<tr><td>No. of Servers</td><td>4</td><td>4</td></tr>
<tr><td>Requirement</td><td>(none)</td><td>(cpu_bogomips>4000 ||
cpu_bogomips<2000)
cpu_free>0.9
mem_free>5</td></tr>
<tr><td>Server List</td><td>(5 random sets)</td><td>dalmatian, dione,
sagit, lhost</td></tr>
<tr><td>Avg Time(sec)</td><td>63.18</td><td>52.70</td></tr>
</table>

Table 4. matrixp: 6vs6 under zero workload

Item\Library	Random	Smart Lib
Matrix Size	1500×1500, blk=200	1500×1500, blk=200
No. of Servers	6	6
Requirement	(none)	cpu_free>0.9 mem_free>5 denied_host1=telesto denied_host2=mimas denied_host3=phoebe denied_host4=calypso denied_host5=titan-x
Server List	phoebe, lhost, calypso telesto, helene, pandora-x	dalmatian, dione, sagit pandora-x, lhost, helene
Avg Time(sec)	46.90	43.02

load remains above 1. Four servers were used to compute the result matrix.

Without the workload feedback, the random function selects servers blindly. The smart socket library was used to avoid the busy servers, thus the performance was tuned to be optimal. In the best case, a random function can select the best servers for the task and the performance will be competitive to the smart library. However, in general cases the random function will provide sub-optimal results. Tables. 5 shows a comparison of the worst case scenario for the random function. After the smart was used, the execution time was reduced from 90.93 to 66.72 seconds, with an improvement of 26.6%.

4.2. Experiments for massd

The massive downloading program *massd* downloads data from multiple servers simultaneously. In the experiments, 6 servers were chosen as the file servers, divided into two groups: *mimas*, *telesto*, *lhost* in group-1 and *dione*, *titan-x*, *pandora-x* in group-2. All machines in the same group were assigned the same network bandwidth by *rshaper*[12] in the range from 0 Mbps to 10 Mbps randomly. The group with the higher bandwidth is called the fast server group; the other group is the slow server group. By using the smart socket library, with requirements on the network bandwidth enabled, users can select servers from the fast group for data transmission at higher throughput.

For comparison, 3 sets of experiments were performed with 1, 2 and 3 file servers used in each set. The total amount of data to transmit is 50000 KBytes and the block size is 100 KBytes.

Table 5. matrixp: 4vs4 with workload

Item\Library	Random	Smart Lib
Matrix Size	1500×1500, blk=200	1500×1500, blk=200
No. of Servers	4	4
Requirement	(none)	cpu_free>0.9 mem_free>5 system_load1<0.5
Server List	mimas, calypso, helene, telesto	calypso, phoebe, titan-x, pandora-x
Avg Time(sec)	90.93	66.72

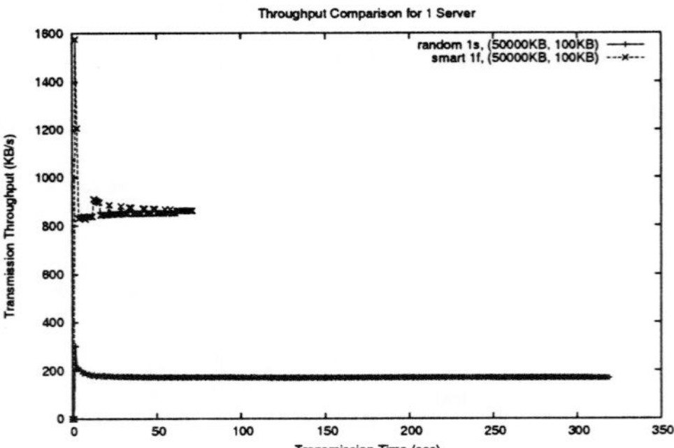

Figure 9. Experiment for *massd*: 1vs1

massd using 1 server. Group-1 was assigned a bandwidth of 6.72 Mbps and group-2's bandwidth was 1.33 Mbps. The random function selected host *pandora-x* from group-2. With requirement *monitor_network_bw>6*, only servers with a bandwidth larger than 6 Mbps were used by the smart socket library. The throughput comparison in Fig. 9 shows that the random function had an average throughput of 170 KBps, while the smart socket library achieved a throughput of 860 KBps.

massd using 2 servers. When two servers are required, 3 types of choices are possible for the random function: 2 slow servers, 1 slow server plus 1 fast server and 2 fast servers. When the random function chooses only the optimal servers, the performance will match the smart socket library. In other cases, the smart library will provide better results. We call the first 2 sub-optimal selections random set-1 and random set-2. The optimal selection made by the smart socket library is called the smart set. The performance of the two random sets is compared with the selection of the smart socket library in Fig. 10.

In this experiment, group-1 bandwidth was 5.01 Mbps and group-2 bandwidth was 7.67 Mbps. The first random set achieved an average throughput of 660 KBps and the second random set had a throughput of 795 KBps. Both are lower than what we got by using the smart socket library, which is 994 KBps.

massd using 3 servers. In the last set of experiments, 3 file servers were used, with 4 possible combinations - four groups of servers with 0, 1, 2 and 3 fast servers in each. We call the four combinations random set-1, random set-2, random set-3 and the smart set(the same as the optimal random set).

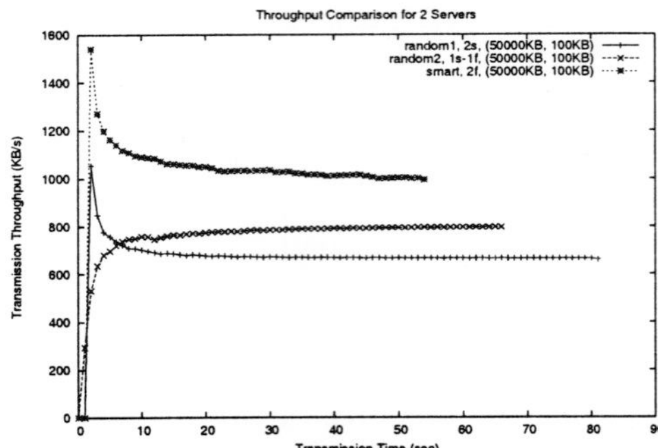

Figure 10. Experiment for *massd*: 2vs2

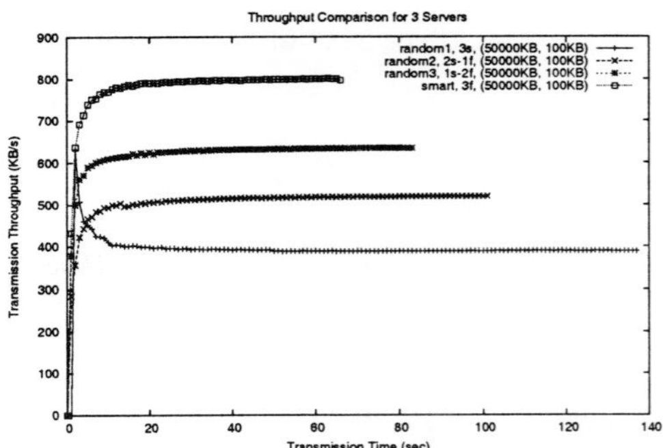

Figure 11. Experiment for *massd*: 3vs3

The bandwidth was set to 5.99 Mbps for server group-1 and 2.92 Mbps for server group-2. With requirement *monitor_network_bw>5*, the smart library used all the 3 servers from group-1, the fast server group. Fig. 11 illustrates the results for the four server combinations. The throughput values are 387 KBps, 520 KBps, 634 KBps and 796 KBps for random set-1, random set-2, random-3 and the smart set.

The above experiment results demonstrate that compared with random server selection, better performance can be achieved by the smart socket library in general cases. As appropriate server requirements are crucial for selecting the optimal servers, users of the smart library should be familiar with the relationship between the server hardware configuration, workload status and application performance.

5. Conclusion and Future Work

This paper presents a smart TCP socket library for distributed computing with high level programming interfaces. The server selection is implemented based on resource monitoring and server requirements. A meta language is defined for the requirement specification with abundant variables available, covering server workload, network metrics and security information. Server probes are used to provide instant reports for appropriate task allocation. The framework is expandable such that new elements for server selection, network measurements and security checking can be imported conveniently. This library is highly compatible with other distributed utilities.

For future development, we have the following ideas: Better network monitoring[13] and security monitoring[14] techniques can be deployed to improve the accuracy of probing results. A *examiner* program[15] can be developed to classify user applications into various categories, allowing the *wizard* to use preset requirement templates for automatic server selection. Workload parameters can be added or removed from the status reports dynamically to facilitate different requirements. An enhanced meta language parser can be developed to handle user queries on individual servers as well as server groups.

6. Acknowledgement

We would like to thank Mr. Chan Mun Choon, Teo Yong Meng and Gary Tan from School of Computing, NUS for providing insightful comments to this project. We would also like to thank Venkatesh of the CIR Lab, NUS for the support during the experimental network setup.

References

[1] "Cisco NAC: The Development of the Self-Defending Network", *http://www.cisco.com/warp/public/cc/so/neso/sqso/csdni_wp.htm*, Cisco Systems, Inc. 2004.

[2] Manish Jain, Constantinos Dovrolis, "Pathload: a measurement tool for end-to-end available bandwidth", PAM 2002.

[3] "The Message Passing Interface (MPI) standard", MCS Division, Argonne National Laboratory, *http://www-unix.mcs.anl.gov/mpi/*.

[4] "Parallel Virtual Machine", Computer Science and Mathematics Division, Oak Ridge National Laboratory, *http://www.csm.ornl.gov/pvm/pvm_home.html*, 2004.

[5] G. A. Geist, J. A. Kohl and P. M. Papadopoulos. "PVM and MPI: a Comparison of Features", May 30, 1996.

[6] "Globus Alliance", *http://www.globus.org/*.

[7] "Condor Project", CS Department, UW-Madison, *http://www.cs.wisc.edu/condor/*.

[8] Rajesh Raman, Miron Livny, and Marvin Solomon. "Matchmaking: Distributed Resource Management for High Throughput Computing", HPDC-98, 1998.

[9] Erik(J. A. K) Mouw. "Linux Kernel Procfs Guide", *http://www.kernelnewbies.org/documents/kdoc/procfs-guide/lkprocfsguide.html*, 2001.

[10] Brian W. Kernighan and Rob Pike. "The UNIX Programming Environment", Prentice Hall, 1984.

[11] "Super PI", Kanada Laboratory, *http://pi2.cc.u-tokyo.ac.jp/*.

[12] Allessandro Rubini, "rshaper", *http://ar.linux.it/software/*, Nov 2001.

[13] Manish Jain and Constantinos Dovrolis. *"End-to-End Available Bandwidth: Measurement Methodology, Dynamics, and Relation with TCP Throughput"*, ACM SIGCOMM 2002, Pittsburgh PA USA, 2002.

[14] "Remote OS detection via TCP/IP Stack Finger-Printing", *http://www.insecure.org/nmap/nmap-fingerprinting-article.html*, Fyodor, 1998.

[15] A. M. Alkindi, D. J. Kerbyson, E. Papaefstathiou and G. R. Nudd. "Run-time Optimisation Using Dynamic Performance Prediction", High Performance Computing and Networking, LNCS, Vol. 1823, Springer-Verlag, May 2000, pp. 280-289.

Session 3C: Virtual & Optical Networking

Constructing Battery-Aware Virtual Backbones in Sensor Networks

Chi Ma
Dept. of Computer Science

Yuanyuan Yang and Zhenghao Zhang
Dept. of Electrical and Computer Engineering

State University of New York, Stony Brook, NY 11794, USA

***Abstract*—A critical issue in wireless sensor networks is to construct energy efficient virtual backbones for routing, broadcasting and data propagating. The Minimum Connected Dominating Set (MCDS) has been proposed as a backbone to reduce power dissipation and prolong network lifetime. However, we find that an MCDS cannot guarantee maximum network lifetime as it does not consider the battery discharging behavior. Recent study in battery technology reveals that the discharging of a battery is not linear. Batteries tend to discharge more power than needed, and reimburse the over-discharged power later if they have sufficiently long recovery time. In order to optimize network performance and construct an energy efficient virtual backbone in sensor networks, battery-awareness should be considered. In this paper we first study the mathematical battery discharging model and provide a simplified battery model suitable for implementation in sensor networks. We then introduce the concept of battery-aware connected dominating set (BACDS) and show that in general the BACDS can achieve longer lifetime than the MCDS. Then we show that finding a minimum BACDS (MBACDS) is NP-hard and give a distributed approximation algorithm to construct the BACDS. The resulting BACDS constructed by our algorithm is at most $(8+\Delta)opt$ size, where Δ is the maximum node degree and *opt* is the size of an optimal BACDS. The time and message complexities of the algorithm are $O(n)$ and $O(n(\sqrt{n}+\log n+\Delta))$, respectively, where n is the number of nodes in the network. The simulation results show that the BACDS constructed by our algorithm can save a significant amount of energy and achieve up to 30% longer network lifetime than the MCDS. To the best of our knowledge, this is the first work considering battery-awareness in the construction of connected dominating sets.**

Keywords: sensor networks, connected dominating sets, energy efficiency, battery models, battery-awareness, battery-aware connected dominating sets.

I. Introduction

A sensor network is a distributed wireless network which is composed of a large number of self-organized unattended sensor nodes [1], [2], [12]. A typical function of sensor networks is to collect data in a sensing environment. Usually the sensed data in such an environment is routed to a sink, which is the central unit of the network [6]. Although a sensor network does not have a physical infrastructure, a virtual backbone can be formed by constructing a *Connected Dominating Set (CDS)* [7], [8] in the network for efficient packet routing, broadcasting and data propagating.

In general, a sensor network can be modeled as a graph $G=(V,E)$, where V and E are the sets of nodes and edges in G, respectively. A CDS is a connected subgraph of G where all nodes in G are at most one hop away from some node in the subgraph. A node in the CDS is referred to as a *dominator*, and a node not in the CDS is referred to as a *dominatee*. There has been a lot of work that dedicates to construct a *Minimum Connected Dominating Set (MCDS)* which is a CDS with a minimum number of dominators. Unfortunately, finding such an MCDS in a general graph was proven to be NP-hard [9]. So was in a *unit disk graph* (UDG) [10], where nodes have connections only within unit distance. Approximation algorithms were proposed to construct CDS, see, for example, [3]. The CDS computed by these algorithms has at most $8opt_{MCDS}$ size, where opt_{MCDS} is the size of the MCDS.

The research was supported in part by NSF grant numbers CCR-0207999 and ECS-0427345 and ARO grant number W911NF-04-1-0439.

Although previous CDS construction algorithms achieve good results in terms of the size of the CDS, a minimum size CDS does not necessarily guarantee the optimal network performance from an energy efficient point of view. The MCDS model assumes that the battery discharging of a sensor node is linear, in other words, the energy consumed from a battery is equivalent to the energy dissipated in the device. However, recent study on battery behavior reveals that, unlike what we used to believe, batteries tend to discharge more power than needed, and reimburse the over-discharged power later if they have appropriate rests [13]. The process of this reimbursement is referred to as *battery recovery*. In this paper we will present a mathematical battery discharging model, which is independent of battery chemistry. This model can accurately model the battery discharging/recovery behavior with on-line computable functions for implementing in wireless ad hoc networks. Based on this model we will introduce *Battery-Aware Connected Dominating Set (BACDS)* and show that the BACDS can achieve better network performance than the MCDS.

The rest of the paper is organized as follows. In Section II we discuss some background and related work to place our work in context. We study the mathematical battery model in details and present a simplified model suitable for sensor network applications in Section III. Section IV first gives the BACDS model along with its performance comparison with the MCDS model, then presents a distributed approximation algorithm to construct the BACDS. We also analyze the performance of the algorithm and give an upper bound on the size of the BACDS obtained in this section. Finally, we give simulation results in Section V, and concluding remarks in Section VI.

II. Background and Related Work

Before constructing the battery-aware CDS, in this section, we provide some background on battery models.

The most commonly used batteries in wireless devices and sensors are nickel-cadmium and lithium-ion batteries. In general, a battery consists of cells arranged in series, parallel, or a combination of both. Two electrodes: an anode and a cath-

0190-3918/05 $20.00 © 2005 IEEE

ode, separated by an electrolyte, constitute the active material of each cell. When the cell is connected to a load, a reduction-oxidation reaction transfers electrons from the anode to the cathode. To illustrate this phenomenon, Fig. 1 shows a simplified symmetric electrochemical cell. In a fully charged cell (Fig. 1(a)), the electrode surface contains the maximum concentration of active species. When the cell is connected to a load, an electrical current flows through the external circuit. Active species are consumed at the electrode surface and replenished by diffusion from the bulk of the electrolyte. However, this diffusion process cannot keep up with the consumption, and a concentration gradient builds up across the electrolyte (Fig. 1(b)). A higher load electrical current I results in a higher concentration gradient and thus a lower concentration of active species at the electrode surface [11]. When this concentration falls below a certain threshold, the electrochemical reaction can no longer be sustained at the electrode surface and the charge is unavailable at the electrode surface (Fig. 1(e)). However, the unused charge is not physically "over-consumed," but simply unavailable due to the lag between the reaction and the diffusion rates. If the battery current I is reduced to zero or a very small value, the concentration gradient flattens out after a sufficiently long time, reaching equilibrium again (Fig. 1(c)). The concentration of active species near the electrode surface following this recovery period makes unused charge available again for extraction (Fig. 1(d)). We refer to the unused charge as *discharging loss*. Effectively recovering the battery can reduce the concentration gradient and recover discharging loss, hence prolong the lifetime of battery (Fig. 1(f)). Experiments on nickel-cadmium battery and lithium-ion battery show that the discharging loss might take up to 30% of the total battery capacity [5]. Hence, precisely modeling battery behavior is essential for optimizing system performance in sensor networks.

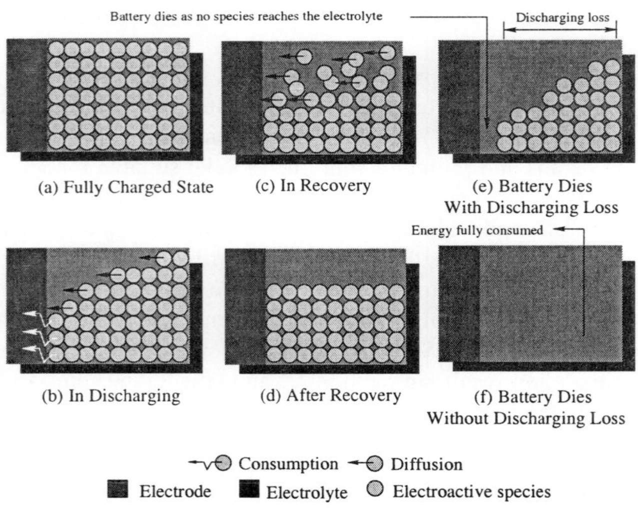

Fig. 1. Battery operation at different states.

Researchers have developed high-level mathematical models that capture the battery behavior and are independent of battery chemistry [5], [13]. An analytical battery model was proposed in [5], however, this model requires long computing time and large pre-computed look up tables. We therefore provided a discrete time battery model in [13] with on-line computable functions. This model splits the time into discrete time slots with a fixed slot length and is suitable for packetized ad hoc networks. We will discuss this model in more detail in Section III.

III. Battery Discharging Models

The battery discharging model presented in [13] is an on-line computable model for general ad hoc wireless networks. In this section, we further reduce the computational complexity to make it implementable in sensor networks. We assume that a battery is in discharging during time $[t_{begin}, t_{end}]$ with current I. The consumed power α is calculated in [13] as

$$\begin{aligned} \alpha = & \; I \times (t_{end} - t_{begin}) \\ + & \; I \times \frac{\pi^2}{3\beta^2} \times \left(e^{-\beta^2(t-t_{end})} - e^{-\beta^2(t-t_{begin})}\right) \end{aligned} \quad (1)$$

where t is the current time and β is a constant parameter. The right hand side of (1) contains two components. The first term, $I \times (t_{end} - t_{begin})$, is simply the energy consumed in device during $[t_{begin}, t_{end}]$. The second term is the discharging loss in $[t_{begin}, t_{end}]$ and it decreases as t increases. The constant β (> 0) is an experimental chemical parameter which may be different from battery to battery. In general, the larger the β, the faster the battery diffusion rate is, hence the less the discharging loss.

In ad hoc networks, current I is a continuous variable for various applications, such as operating systems, multimedia transmission, word processing and interactive games. However, in sensor networks, the simple sensing and data propagating activities of sensor nodes may only require several constant currents. We define the constant currents of dominator nodes and dominatee nodes as I_d and I_e, respectively. A dominator needs to keep active and listen to all channels at all times. Compared with I_d, the I_e of a dominatee is very low. We divide the sensor lifetime into discrete time slots with slot length δ. In each time slot the battery of a node is either as a dominator ($I = I_d$) or a dominatee ($I = I_e$). From (1) we have

$$\zeta_n(t) = I_n \times \frac{\pi^2}{3\beta^2}(e^{-\beta^2(t-n\delta)} - e^{-\beta^2(t-(n-1)\delta)}) \quad (2)$$

where I_n is either I_d or I_e, and t is the current time.

We can see that $\zeta_n(t)$ is recovered gradually in the following $(n+1)_{th}, (n+2)_{th}, \ldots$ slots until t. It should be mentioned that discharging loss $\zeta_n(t)$ is only a potentially recoverable energy. At time t the gross discharging loss energy of this battery is

$$\zeta(t) = \sum_{i=1}^{m} \zeta_i(t) \quad (3)$$

where $m = \lfloor t/\delta \rfloor$. The lower the $\zeta(t)$, the better the battery is recovered. To be aware of the battery recovery status, $\zeta(t)$ needs to be calculated at each slot. However, the computation can be simplified by observing that $\zeta_i(t)$ decreases

TABLE 1
THE MAXIMUM SIZE OF THE RECOVERY TABLE ($\beta = 0.4$)

c / I_d	$1200mA$	$800mA$	$400mA$	$100mA$
$200mA$min	1	2	3	4
$400mA$min	2	3	3	5
$600mA$min	3	3	4	6
$800mA$min	3	4	5	6

exponentially as t increases. Naturally, $\zeta_i(t)$ can be ignored if $\zeta_i(t)$ is less than a small amount of power c, where c is the power to transmit a single packet. We introduce κ_i as $\zeta_i(\kappa_i\delta) < c < \zeta_i((\kappa_i - 1)\delta)$, that is, after $t = \kappa_i\delta$, $\zeta_i(t)$ is ignored. We have

$$\kappa_i = \left\lceil \frac{1}{\beta^2\delta} \log \frac{\pi^2(1 - e^{-\beta^2\delta})}{3\beta^2 c/I_i} \right\rceil \tag{4}$$

where $I_i = I_d$ or I_e. We maintain κ_i in a recovery table. At the m_{th} slot if $\kappa_i < (m - i)$, which indicates that $\zeta_i(m\delta) < c$, then this entry i is removed from the table.

Introducing this recovery table has several advantages and is also feasible for sensor networks. First, we can reduce the computational complexity of battery-awareness. Only the remained entries in the table are used for computing $\zeta(t)$. Now (3) can be rewritten as

$$\zeta(t) = \sum_j \zeta_j(t) \tag{5}$$

where entry j is the entry remained in the recovery table. Second, we can reduce the complexity of table maintenance. In order to check whether an entry needs to be removed, rather than calculating $\zeta_i(t)$ for every i at each time, we only need to read κ_i from the table and compare it with m. Because κ_i is computed once, maintaining the recovery table is simple. Third, the size of the table is feasible for sensor memory. According to (4) and (5), the total entries in the recovery table are no more than $\lceil \frac{1}{\beta^2\delta} \log \frac{\pi^2(1-e^{-\beta^2\delta})}{3\beta^2 c/I_d} \rceil$. For various possible values of I_d and c of sensors, Table 1 shows the maximum number of entries in a recovery table ($\beta = 0.4$). Considering that the memory capacity of today's sensor node is typically larger than 512KB [4], it is acceptable to store and maintain such a recovery table in sensor memory. Thus, we can reduce the computational complexity by maintaining a recovery table on a sensor node with a feasible table size.

In summary, in this section we use the battery model to achieve battery-awareness by capturing its recovery $\zeta(t)$. The lower the $\zeta(t)$, the better the sensor node is recovered at time t. We introduce the recovery table to reduce the computational complexity. We also show that maintaining such a table is feasible for today's sensor nodes. Next we apply this battery model to construct the BACDS to prolong network lifetime.

IV. BATTERY-AWARE CONNECTED DOMINATING SET

In this section we first introduce the concept of battery-aware connected dominating set (BACDS), and show that the BACDS can achieve better network performance. Then we provide a distributed algorithm to construct BACDS in sensor networks.

A. Battery-Aware Dominating

Let the sensor network be represented by a graph $G = (V, E)$ where $|V| = n$. For each pair of nodes $u, v \in V$, $(u, v) \in E$ if and only if nodes u and v can communicate in one hop. The maximum node degree in G is Δ. Each node v is assigned a unique ID_v. $P_{residual}(v)$ is v's residual battery power. $P_{threshold}$ is the threshold power adopted in CDS construction algorithms. $\zeta^v(t)$ is the discharging loss of v at time t. For any subset $U \subseteq V$, we define $\zeta^U_{max} = \max\{\zeta^v(t) | v \in U\}$.

Next we explain how to use the battery model to construct an energy-efficient dominating set in a sensor network. Intuitively, longer network lifetime can be achieved by always choosing the "most fully recovered" sensor nodes as dominators. For a graph $G = (V, E)$ at time t, we define a BACDS as a set $S_B (\subseteq V)$ such that

$$S_B \text{ is a CDS of } G \text{ and } \zeta^{S_B}_{max} = \min\{\zeta^S_{max} | S \text{ is a } CDS \text{ of } G\} \tag{6}$$

An optimal BACDS is a BACDS with a minimum number of nodes and is denoted as MBACDS. For notational convenience, we let

$$\zeta^{BACDS} \equiv \min\{\zeta^S_{max} | S \text{ is a } CDS \text{ of } G\} \tag{7}$$

BACDS can achieve better performance than MCDS since it balances the power consumption among sensor nodes. Table 2 gives the outline of the MCDS and BACDS algorithms for forming a virtual backbone in a sensor network, where node i is qualified to be selected as a dominator as long as its residual battery power $P_{residual}(i)$ is no less than the threshold power $P_{threshold}$.

We conducted simulations to compare the two algorithms. Fig. 3 shows the simulated lifetime under BACDS and MCDS models for the network in Fig. 2. At the beginning all nodes are identical with battery capacity $C = 4.5 \times 10^4 mA$min and $\beta = 0.4$. The discharging currents are $I_d = 900mA$ and $I_e = 10mA$. An MCDS is chosen as $Set_1 = \{C, D, F, G\}$. Since MCDS does not consider the battery behavior, Set_1 remains as the dominator until the power of all nodes in Set_1 drops to a threshold $0.1 \times 10^4 mA$min. After that another MCDS is chosen as $Set_2 = \{A, B, E, H\}$. After Set_2 uses up its power, no node in the network is qualified as a dominator. The total network lifetime is 56min (Fig. 3).

On the other hand, in the BACDS model a CDS is formed by the nodes with minimum $\zeta(t)$s. The network reorganizes the BACDS for every δ time. Suppose at the beginning the BACDS is still $Set'_1 = \{C, D, F, G\}$. After $\delta = 10$min the power of nodes in Set'_1 is reduced to $2.1 \times 10^4 mA$min. At this time, a new BACDS is chosen as $Set'_2 = \{A, B, E, H\}$ (Fig. 2). During the next 10min, Set'_2 dissipates the power to $2.1 \times 10^4 mA$min while Set_1 recoveries its nodes' power from $2.1 \times 10^4 mA$min to $3.35 \times 10^4 mA$min. Then the BACDS is organized again. As shown in Fig. 3, the total

TABLE 2

OUTLINE OF MCDS AND BACDS ALGORITHMS FOR FORMING A VIRTUAL BACKBONE

MCDS Algorithm
Repeat
Every node i with $P_{residual}(i) \geq P_{threshold}$
  is marked as *qualified*
All other nodes are marked as *unqualified*
Call *MCDS Construction Algorithm* for all qualified nodes
If successful, use the MCDS constructed as the backbone
Otherwise report 'no backbone can be formed' and exit
Until Some dominator j has $P_{residual}(j) < P_{threshold}$

BACDS Algorithm
Repeat
Every node i with $P_{residual}(i) \geq P_{threshold}$
  is marked as *qualified*
All other nodes are marked as *unqualified*
Call *BACDS Construction Algorithm* for all qualified nodes
If successful, use the BACDS constructed as the backbone
Otherwise report 'no backbone can be formed' and exit
Until δ time has elapsed
  or some dominator j has $P_{residual}(j) < P_{threshold}$

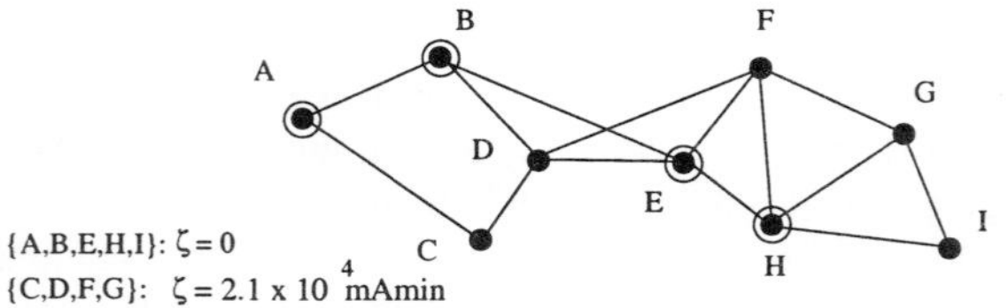

Fig. 2. The battery-aware connected dominating set (BACDS) for a network $t = 10$min. The $\zeta^i(t)$ for each node i is listed above.

network lifetime in the BACDS model is 69 mins, which is 23.2% longer than the MCDS model.

We have seen that BACDS can achieve longer lifetime than MCDS. Next we will consider the BACDS construction algorithm.

B. Formalization of BACDS Construction Problem

The BACDS construction problem can be formalized as: given a graph $G = (V, E)$ and $\zeta^i(t)$ for each node i in G, find an MBACDS. For simplicity, we use ζ to denote $\zeta(t)$ in the rest of the paper. First, we have a theorem regarding the NP-hardness of the problem.

Theorem 1: Finding an MBACDS in G is NP-hard.

Proof. Consider a special case that all nodes in G have the same ζ values. In this case, finding an MBACDS in G is equivalent to finding an MCDS in G. Since the MCDS problem is NP-hard, the MBACDS problem is also NP-hard. ■

Now since the MBACDS construction is NP-hard, we will construct a BACDS by an approximation algorithm. By definition, the BACDS to be constructed, S_B, must satisfy the following two conditions: (i) $\zeta_{max}^{S_B} = \zeta^{BACDS}$; (ii) S_B is a CDS of G. Also, the size of S_B should be as small as possible.

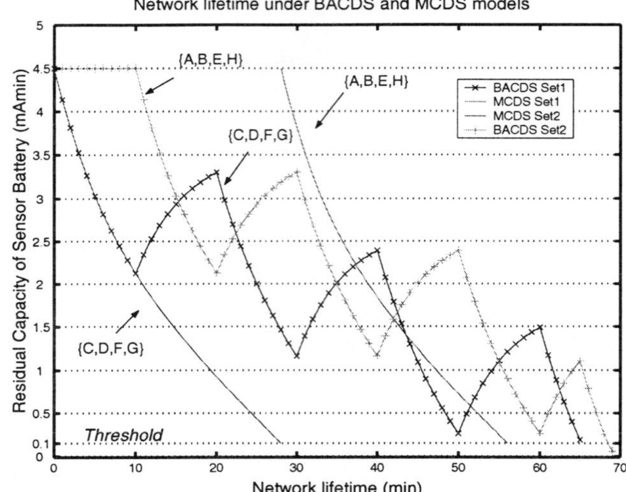

Fig. 3. The sensor network in Fig. 2 achieves longer lifetime using the BACDS model than the MCDS model. The results were simulated with the battery discharging model. In this case the network lifetime is prolonged by 23.2% in the BACDS model.

Our algorithm is designed to find a set to satisfy these conditions. To satisfy condition (i), the algorithm finds a subset SET^+ in G, such that for any subset $S'(\subseteq SET^+)$, $\zeta_{max}^{S'} \leq \zeta^{BACDS}$. We will prove that, as long as a set $S'(\subseteq SET^+)$ is a CDS of G, we can guarantee that $\zeta_{max}^{S'} = \zeta^{BACDS}$.

To satisfy condition (ii), the algorithm will find two sets: CDS^+ and COV, both in SET^+. $CDS^+(\subseteq SET^+)$ is an MCDS of SET^+. $COV(\subseteq SET^+)$ is a cover of $V - SET^+$, which dominates all the nodes in $V - SET^+$. We will prove that $SET^0 = COV \bigcup CDS^+$ is the BACDS we want. The detailed algorithm will be presented in the next subsection. Table 3 gives an outline of the BACDS construction algorithm.

TABLE 3

THE OUTLINE OF THE BACDS CONSTRUCTION

1. Find a subset SET^+ in G
2. Construct a subset COV in SET^+ /* COV covers the nodes in $V - SET^+$ */
3. Construct a subset CDS^+ in SET^+ /* CDS^+ is the CDS of SET^+ */
$SET^0 = COV \bigcup CDS^+$ is a BACDS

We now show that $SET^0 = COV \bigcup CDS^+$ is indeed a BACDS.

Theorem 2: $SET^0 = COV \bigcup CDS^+$ is a BACDS.

Proof. We first define SET^+ as

$$SET^+ = \{v \in V | \zeta^v \leq \zeta^{BACDS}\} \quad (8)$$

We know that CDS^+ is a CDS of SET^+ and COV dominates the nodes in $V - SET^+$. To prove $SET^0 =$

$COV \bigcup CDS^+$ is a BACDS, we need to show that set SET^0 is a connected dominating set of G, and $\zeta_{max}^{SET^0}$ is minimized.

First, we show that SET^0 is connected. Because $COV \subseteq SET^+$, every node in COV is at most one hop away from CDS^+. Also, since CDS^+ is connected, $SET^0 = COV \bigcup CDS^+$ is connected.

Second, we prove that SET^0 is a dominating set of G. Since CDS^+ is a CDS of SET^+, all nodes in SET^+ are dominated by CDS^+. Also, since all nodes in $V - SET^+$ are covered by COV, $SET^0 = COV \bigcup CDS^+$ is a dominating set of G.

Finally, we show that $\zeta_{max}^{SET^0}$ is minimized, i.e. $\zeta_{max}^{SET^0} = \zeta^{BACDS}$. Since $SET^0 \subseteq SET^+ = \{v \in V | \zeta^v \leq \zeta^{BACDS}\}$, we have $\zeta_{max}^{SET^0} \leq \zeta^{BACDS}$. However, SET^0 is also a CDS of G. Thus $\zeta_{max}^{SET^0} \geq \zeta^{BACDS}$. Therefore, $\zeta_{max}^{SET^0} = \zeta^{BACDS}$, and we have proved that $SET^0 = COV \bigcup CDS^+$ is a BACDS. ■

In summary, in this subsection we have shown that we can construct a BACDS by finding three subsets SET^+, COV and CDS^+ step by step. Then $SET^0 = COV \bigcup CDS^+$ is a BACDS. Next we will give the algorithms to construct SET^+, COV and CDS^+.

C. A Distributed Algorithm for BACDS Construction

Our algorithm for BACDS construction consists of three procedures for constructing SET^+ and COV in G. In the algorithm, we use $N(v)$ to denote the set of neighbor nodes of v. each node is colored in one of the three colors: black, white and gray. $N_{black}(v), N_{white}(v)$ and $N_{gray}(v)$ are the sets of black, white and gray neighbors of v, respectively. Also we use sets $list_{gray}(i)$ and $list(i)$ to store the neighbor information for node i.

First we consider the construction of SET^+. To find SET^+, we do the following: the ζ^i of each node i in G is collected in the sink; then the sink calculates $\zeta_{max}^{SET^+}$ and broadcasts it in a beacon; on receiving the beacon, all nodes with $\zeta^i \leq \zeta_{max}^{SET^+}$ form set SET^+. The procedure is described in Table 4. Initially, all nodes in G are colored gray. Then the algorithm colors some gray nodes black. In the end, the set of black nodes is SET^+.

Note that in SET^+ finding procedure, the sink collects information from sensors only once, and broadcasts the $\zeta_{max}^{SET^+}$ in a single beacon. The overhead of information collecting and broadcasting is minimum.

Since $COV (\subseteq SET^+)$ is a cover of $V - SET^+$, to find COV, we only need to consider the nodes which are one hop away from $V - SET^+$. We use SET^- to denote these nodes. SET^- is defined as

$$SET^- = \{v \in SET^+ | \exists u \in (V - SET^+), (u, v) \in E\} \quad (9)$$

Now we construct COV from SET^-. COV can be obtained as follows. Initially, $COV = \emptyset$, $S_1 = (V - SET^+)$. Then, for node $v \in S_1$ with the lowest ID number, add all nodes $u \in SET^-$ to COV, where u and v are one hop neighbors. Then we remove $N(u) \cap S_1$ from S_1. Repeatedly doing

TABLE 4

SET^+ FINDING PROCEDURE

All nodes in G are colored gray
Each gray node i in the network does the following
begin
  Broadcast a packet which includes its ID_i
  Receive neighbors' IDs
  Calculate ζ^i
  Route a packet with $(ID_i, ID_{N(i)}, \zeta^i)$ to the sink
  Listen to the beacon for $\zeta_{max}^{SET^+}$
  if $\zeta^i \leq \zeta_{max}^{SET^+}$ **then** node i is colored black
end

The sink does the following
  begin / Calculate* $\zeta_{max}^{SET^+}$ **/*
  Collect packets from sensor nodes
  $S_0 := \{\zeta^i | i = 1, 2, \ldots, n\}$
  $S_1 := \emptyset$
  repeat
    $S_2 :=$ {those nodes with the smallest ζ in S_0}
    $S_0 := S_0 - S_2$
    $S_1 := S_1 \cup S_2$
  until S_1 is a CDS **or** $S_0 = \emptyset$
  if S_1 is a CDS **then**
    $\zeta_{max}^{SET^+} := \zeta_{max}^{S_1}$
    Broadcast $\zeta_{max}^{SET^+}$ in a beacon
  end if
  else report 'no CDS can be found'
  end
$SET^+ :=$ {black nodes}

TABLE 5

SET^- FINDING PROCEDURE

$SET^- := \emptyset$
Each node $i \in SET^+$ does the following
begin
if $\exists j \in N(i)$ and $j \in (V - SET^+)$ **then**
$SET^- := SET^- \cup \{i\}$
end

so until S_1 is empty. Then we obtain set COV. The localized procedure for finding COV from SET^- is described in Table 6. There are three colors used to color a node: white, black and gray. Initially, nodes in SET^- are colored white, and nodes in $V - SET^+$ are colored gray. Then the procedure colors some white nodes black. In the end, the set of black nodes is the COV. Four messages are used: *addblack*, *black*, *remove* and *update*.

Our algorithm only requires at most 2-hop information to construct the COV. We now prove the correctness of the *COV Finding Procedure*. We will show that the COV found by this procedure is a cover of $V - SET^+$. We will also give an upper bound on the size of set COV.

Lemma 1: Set COV found by *COV Finding Procedure*

TABLE 6

COV FINDING PROCEDURE

1. Each node in $SET^{-} \bigcup (V - SET^{+})$ does the following
2. *begin*
3. Nodes in SET^{-} are colored white
4. Nodes in $V - SET^{+}$ are colored gray
5. $COV := \emptyset$
6. Each gray node i broadcasts ID_i
to its white neighbors $N_{white}(i)$
7. Each white node j adds the received IDs
to a set $list_{gray}(j)$ and broadcasts $list_{gray}(j)$
to its gray neighbors $N_{gray}(j)$
8. Each gray node i does the following
9. *begin*
10. Receive all $list_{gray}(N_{white}(i))$
11. $list(i) := \bigcup list_{gray}(N_{white}(i))$
12. **while** $list(i) \neq \emptyset$ **do**
13. **if** $ID_i = \min\{id | id \in list(i)\}$ **then**
14. Broadcast *addblack* to $N_{white}(i)$
15. $list(i) := \emptyset$
16. **else if** *black* message is received **then**
17. broadcast *remove* to $N_{white}(i)$
18. $list(i) := \emptyset$
19. **else if** $update(k)$ message is received **then**
20. $list(i) := list(i) - \{k\}$
21. **end while**
22. *end*
23. Each white node j does the following
24. *begin*
25. **while** $list_{gray}(j) \neq \emptyset$ **do**
26. **if** *addblack* message is received **then**
27. Color itself black
28. $list_{gray}(j) := \emptyset$
29. Broadcast *black* to $N_{gray}(j)$
30. **else if** *remove* message is received from k **then**
31. Broadcast $update(k)$ to $N_{gray}(j)$
32. $list_{gray}(j) := list_{gray}(j) - \{k\}$
33. **end while**
34. *end*
35. *end*
$COV := \{\text{black nodes}\}$

covers $V - SET^{+}$. Its size $|COV|$ is at most Δopt_c, where Δ is the maximum node degree of G and opt_c is the size of an optimal cover.

Proof. By contradiction. Suppose when the *COV Finding Procedure* terminates, there exists a gray node i which is not covered by COV. It indicates that $N(i) \cap COV = \emptyset$, which means $N(i) \cap SET^{-}$ is not colored black. Since $N(i) \cap SET^{-}$ is not colored black, all nodes in $N(i) \cap SET^{-}$ should receive *remove* messages from i, otherwise their $list_{gray} \neq \emptyset$ and the procedure does not terminate. However, i broadcasts *remove* message if and only if one of its white neighbors is colored black. Thus, $N(i) \cap COV \neq \emptyset$, which is a contradiction. Hence COV is a cover.

Now we consider the size of COV. Initially COV is empty, and we add some nodes to it in later steps. We will show that: (i) at each step, at least one node, which belongs to the optimal cover, is added to COV; and (ii) at each step, at most $\Delta - 1$ extra nodes, which do not belong to the optimal cover, are added to the COV. By combining (i) and (ii), we obtain that $|COV|$ is at most Δopt_c, where opt_c is the size of an optimal cover.

We first consider (i). According to the algorithm, at each step, node i sends *addblack* messages to $N_{white}(i)$. Therefore, there are at most Δ nodes added to COV in each step. Among the Δ nodes there must exist at least one node which is in the optimal cover, because an optimal cover has to cover node i. Next we consider (ii). Since among the Δ nodes added to COV there are at least one node belonging to the optimal cover, each time we add at most $\Delta - 1$ extra nodes not belonging to the optimal cover to COV. Thus, $|COV|$ is at most Δopt_c. ■

Now we prove that the *COV Finding Procedure* can finally terminates, i.e. all $list_{gray}(j)$ and $list(i)$ will finally be empty. We also give the time complexity of *COV Finding Procedure*.

Lemma 2: All $list_{gray}(j)$ and $list(i)$ will finally be empty. *COV Finding Procedure* has time complexity of $O(n - |SET^{+}| + |SET^{-}|)$.

Proof. First, we show that $list_{gray}(j)$ will finally be empty. Suppose there is a white node j where $list_{gray}(j) \neq \emptyset$. Without loss of generality, we have a node $u_1 \in list_{gray}(j)$ with the lowest ID. In this procedure u_1 is the node that colors j black. If u_1 does not send *addblack* to j, there must be a node $u_2 \in list(u_1)$ such that $ID(u_1) > ID(u_2)$. Then if u_2 does not broadcast *addblack*, there must be a node $u_3 \in list(u_2)$ such that $ID(u_2) > ID(u_3)$, and so on. Then we have $ID(u_1) > ID(u_2) > ID(u_3) > \cdots$. Since there are a finite number of nodes, there must exist a node, u_k, such that $ID(u_k) = \min\{id | id \in list(u_k)\}$. The node u_k should send *addblack*, which indicates that finally $list_{gray}(j)$ should be empty.

Second, we show that $list(i)$ will finally be empty. By Lemma 1, each gray node i is finally covered by some black node, which indicates that all gray nodes received *black* messages. Therefore, finally $list(i)$ will be $\emptyset$. In this procedure, because it colors at least one node black in each step, the time complexity is $O(n - |SET^{+}| + |SET^{-}|)$. ■

Now we consider the CDS^{+} construction. We can adopt any existing MCDS construction algorithm for this purpose. Since the MIS-based algorithm in [3] achieves the best performance in terms of its set size and time and message complexities, we adopt this algorithm here. This algorithm is a UDG based algorithm. However, our BACDS constructing algorithm is not restricted to a UDG. In fact, we can employ any other general graph based MCDS algorithm to construct CDS^{+}. The complete algorithm for finding a BACDS is given in Table 7. In the next subsection, we will analyze the performance of our BACDS construction algorithm, and give

TABLE 7

THE ALGORITHM FOR FINDING A BACDS IN GRAPH G

begin
call SET^+ *Finding Procedure* for G
call SET^- *Finding Procedure* for SET^+
call *COV Finding Procedure* for SET^-
call CDS^+ *Finding Algorithm for* SET^+
$SET^0 := COV \bigcup CDS^+$
end

an upper bound on the size of SET^0.

D. Complexity Analysis of the Algorithm

In this subsection we analyze the approximation ratio, the time complexity and the message complexity of the algorithm. We use opt, opt_{MCDS}, opt_c, and $opt^{SET^+}_{MCDS}$ to denote the sizes of MBACDS in G, MCDS in G, the minimum cover in SET^- and the minimum CDS^+ in SET^+, respectively.

Theorem 3: The size of SET^0 is at most $(8+\Delta)opt$. The time complexity and the message complexity of the algorithm is $O(n)$ and $O(n(\sqrt{n}+\log n+\Delta))$, respectively, where n is the number of nodes in G.

Proof. First, we consider the size of SET^0. Note that $MBACDS \cap SET^-$ is a cover and $|MBACDS| = opt$. It indicates that

$$opt_c \leq |MBACDS \cap SET^-| \leq opt \quad (10)$$

Since we have proved in Lemma 1 that $|COV| \leq \Delta opt_c$, we have

$$|COV| \leq \Delta opt \quad (11)$$

We employ the MIS based CDS finding algorithm for CDS^+ construction. It can obtain a CDS^+ with a size of at most $8opt^{SET^+}_{MCDS}$. Thus,

$$|CDS^+| \leq 8opt^{SET^+}_{MCDS} \quad (12)$$

Because constructing an MBACDS needs to consider the extra battery parameter, the size of the MBACDS is no less than opt_{MCDS}. Thus we have

$$opt_{MCDS} \leq opt \quad (13)$$

Clearly, the size of a minimum CDS^+ in SET^+ is at most opt_{MCDS} because it needs to consider extra nodes in $V - SET^+$. Thus,

$$opt^{SET^+}_{MCDS} \leq opt_{MCDS} \quad (14)$$

By (12), (14) and (13) we obtain

$$|CDS^+| \leq 8opt \quad (15)$$

Therefore from (11) and (15) we have

$$|SET^0| = |COV \cup CDS^+| \leq (8+\Delta)opt$$

Now we analyze the complexity of the algorithm. Our algorithm consists of three phases: SET^+ and SET^- constructions, COV construction and CDS^+ construction. In the first phase, to find SET^+ and SET^-, each node only needs to propagate their messages to the sink and wait for a beacon. A node needs at most $\sqrt{n}$ hops to relay a message to the sink. Hence the time complexity for sending the message and receiving a beacon are $O(\sqrt{n})$ and $O(1)$, respectively. The time complexity of the second phase is $O(n-|SET^+|+|SET^-|)$ as Lemma 2 shows. The complexity of the third phase is $O(|SET^+|)$. Therefore, the total time complexity of the algorithm is $O(n)$.

Now we consider the number of messages transmitted. In the first phase, the total number of messages relayed in the network is at most $O(n\sqrt{n})$. The beacon has $O(1)$ message complexity. At the beginning of the second phase, to set up the lists, all white nodes and gray nodes need to send $|SET^-|$ and $n-|SET^+|$ messages, respectively. After that, all the gray nodes send at most $|SET^-|$ *addblack* messages and $\Delta|SET^-|$ *remove* messages. All the white nodes send at most $\Delta(n-|SET^+|)$ *update* messages, and all the black nodes send no more than $|SET^-|$ *black* messages. Thus, in the second phase, there are totally at most $O(n\Delta)$ messages. If we employ the algorithm in [3], the message complexity in the third phase is $O(n+n\log n)$. Hence, the total message complexity of our algorithm is $O(n(\sqrt{n}+\log n+\Delta))$. ■

V. SIMULATION RESULTS

We conducted extensive simulations to evaluation the network performances under the BACDS model and MCDS model. We simulated the network lifetime under different models. Our simulation results show that the BACDS achieves longer network lifetime. we also compare the set sizes of SET^0 and MBACDS. The simulation results verify the upper bound of SET^0 in Theorem 3.

We first compare the network lifetime achieved by MCDS and BACDS. We generated a sensor network with $n = 100$ randomly deployed nodes. The communication radius is $r = 1$. Any pair of nodes are connected if and only if their distance is shorter than r. We let $d = 6$ be the average degree of nodes, where d indicates the density of the network. Each sensor node i is associated with a discharging loss value ζ^i $(i \leq n)$. ζ^i is uniformly randomly distributed in $[0, 2\times10^4](mA\text{min})$. For simplicity, we assume that initially the available power of node i is $C_i = 4.5\times10^4 mA\text{min}$ and $\beta_i = 0.4$ as in the example of Fig. 3. The discharging currents are $I_d = 900mA$ and $I_e = 10mA$, respectively.

Fig. 4 shows the number of active nodes decreases with respect to the lifetime. Four models: no-CDS, MCDS, MBACDS and SET^0 are implemented. A network without a CDS infrastructure terminates at 30min as all its nodes use up their power. MCDS achieves about 83min total lifetime. MBACDS organizes its dominators every 10min. The lifetime is prolonged by up to 52% in MBACDS model. SET^0 is the BACDS constructed by our algorithm. It obtains a lifetime prolonged up to 30%.

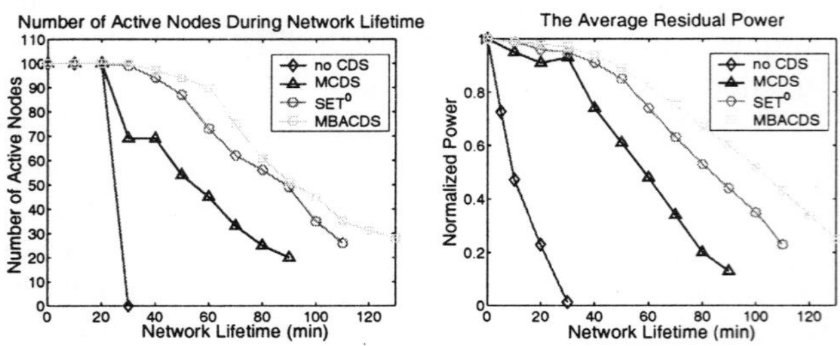

Fig. 4. Comparing the network lifetime and the average power per node under different models.

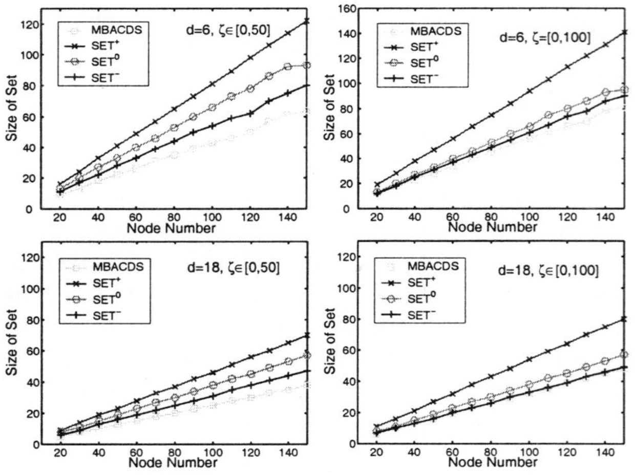

Fig. 5. The size of constructed sets with different ζ and d.

We also note that MBACDS terminates with more nodes remained in the network. This is because MBACDS balances the power consumption of each nodes, thus more nodes are preserved in the network. We compare the available power per sensor node under different models in Fig. 4. In this comparison, the average power is the total available power of the network over the number of active nodes. The average power is normalized. MBACDS achieves higher average power during the lifetime. It should be mentioned that at 30min the average power of MCDS suddenly increases. This is because many of its dominators suddenly die at that time. Consequently, the average power increases as the total number of nodes decreases.

We also implemented our BACDS construction algorithm to verify the upper bound on the set size. The size of the generated network is $n = 20, \ldots, 140$. Four sets are compared: SET^+, SET^-, SET^0 and MBACDS. Fig. 5 compares the sizes of these sets with different node degree d and discharging loss ζ. It shows that as d increases, the sizes of MBACDS and SET^0 are reduced. This is due to the larger degree of the dominators. While as ζ increases its distribution space from $[0, 50]$ to $[0, 100]$, the sizes of MBACDS and SET^0 increase. The results verify the upper bound of SET^0 in Theorem 3.

VI. Conclusions

In this paper we have constructed battery-aware virtual backbones in sensor networks to improve the network performance. We first gave a simplified battery model to accurately describe the battery behavior. Then by using the battery model, we introduced the BACDS model and showed that the minimum BACDS can achieve longer lifetime than the MCDS. We also provided a distributed approximation algorithm to construct the BACDS in general graphs. The simulation results show that our model can achieve 30% longer lifetime in sensor networks.

References

[1] I. F. Akyildiz, W. Su, Y. Sankarasubramaniam and E. Cayirci, "A Survey on Sensor Networks," *IEEE Communications Magazine*, Aug. 2002, pp. 102-114.

[2] G.J. Pottie, W.J. Kaiser, "Wireless Integrated Network Sensors," *Communications of the ACM*, vol. 43, no. 5, pp. 551-558, May 2000.

[3] K.M. Alzoubi, P.-J. Wan and O. Frieder, "Distributed Heuristics for Connected Dominating Sets in Wireless Ad hoc Networks", *J. of Communications and Networks*, vol. 4, no. 1, Mar. 2002.

[4] A. Mainwaring, J. Polastre, R. Szewczyk, D. Culler and J. Anderson, "Wireless Sensor Networks for Habitat Monitoring", *ACM Wireless Sensor Networks and Applications (WSNA)*, Sept. 2002.

[5] D. Rakhmatov and S. Vrudhula, "Energy Management for Battery-Powered Embedded Systems", *ACM Transactions on Embedded Computing Systems*, vol. 2, no. 3, pp. 277-324, Aug. 2003.

[6] K. Sohrabi, J. Gao, V. Ailawadhi and G.J. Pottie, "Protocols for Self-Organization of a Wireless Sensor Network," *IEEE Personal Communication*, Oct 2000.

[7] S. Butenko, X. Cheng, D.-Z.Du and P.M. Pardalos,"On the Construction of Virtual Backbone for ad Hoc Wireless Networks," *Cooperative Control: Models, Applications and Algorithms*, pp.43-54, Kluwer Publishers, 2003.

[8] T. W. Haynes, S. T. Hedetniemi and P. J. Slater, *Fundamentals of Domination in Graphs*," Marcel Dekker, 1998.

[9] T. S. Rappaport, *Wireless Communications*," Prentice Hall, 1996.

[10] B.N. Clark, C.J. Colbourn and D.S. Johnson, "Unit Disk Graphs," *Discrete Mathematics*, vol. 86, pp. 165-177, 1990.

[11] M. Doyle, T. F. Fuller and J. Newman, "Modeling of Galvanostatic Charge and Discharge of the Lithium/Polymer/Insertion Cell." *J. Electrochemical Soc.* vol. 140, no. 6, 1993, pp. 1526-1533.

[12] C. Ma, M. Ma and Y. Yang, "Data-Centric Energy-Efficient Scheduling in Densely Deployed Sensor Networks," *Proc. of IEEE ICC 2004*, Paris, France, 2004.

[13] C. Ma and Y. Yang, "Battery Aware Energy Efficient Routing in Wireless Ad Hoc Networks," SUNY Stony Brook, CEAS Technical Report #817, October 2004.

Provisioning Virtual Private Networks in the Hose Model with Delay Requirements

Lei Zhang, Jogesh Muppala, Samuel Chanson
Dept. of Computer Science, Hong Kong Univ. of Science and Technology
Clearwater Bay, Kowloon, Hong Kong
{zhanglei, muppala, chanson}@cs.ust.hk

Abstract

Virtual Private Networks (VPN) provide a cost-effective means of meeting the communication needs among several sites. The hose model for VPN configuration alleviates the scalability problem of the pipe model by reserving bandwidth for traffic aggregates instead of between every pair of endpoints. Existing studies on quality of service (QoS) guarantees in the hose model deal only with bandwidth requirements. In this paper we enhance the hose model to specify delay requirements between endpoints. Three categories of algorithms, namely the pipe mesh, the multiple source-based trees, and the shared tree approaches, are then proposed for VPN provisioning. We investigate methods of implementing the shared tree approach to meet the delay requirements with low provisioning cost and small computation overhead.

1. Introduction

Two popular models have been proposed for supporting QoS in Virtual Private Networks (VPNs): the "pipe" model [2] and the "hose" model [4]. The hose model has good characteristics such as flexibility, multiplexing gain and ease of specification [5]. In [4], a hose is realized with a source-based tree resulting in a factor of 2 to 3 in capacity savings over the pipe model. In [7], the hoses are implemented with a single shared tree and the algorithms attempt to optimize the total bandwidth reserved on the edges of the tree. In [6] the bandwidth efficiency of the hose model was studied, where the over-provisioning factor is evaluated in networks with various sizes and node densities. In [3], a multi-path provisioning approach was proposed.

However, no work on the hose model has considered delay, which is becoming important in VPNs with delay-sensitive applications such as Voice over IP [9]. In this paper we enhance the hose model to support delay requirements at the VPN endpoints. We propose three approaches for the enhanced hose model: the pipe mesh approach, the multiple source-based trees approach, and the shared tree approach. For the shared tree approach we consider the following questions: (1). How to make the shared tree support the delay requirements? (2). How to achieve high statistical multiplexing gain given that the delay requirement is satisfied? (3). How to reduce the computational overhead? The first issue is solved by formulating a minimum diameter Steiner tree (MDStT) problem. The second problem is proved to be NP-hard and we use heuristics to build trees with low provisioning cost. The third issue is tackled by a pruning technique.

The rest of the paper is structured as follows. The enhanced hose model, supporting both delay and bandwidth requirements, is described in Section 2. Section 3 presents three approaches for the enhanced hose model and discusses their advantages and disadvantages. The three problems with the the shared tree approach are further studied in Sections 4, 5, and 6 respectively. Simulation results comparing the performance of the proposed algorithms are presented in Section 7. Finally, Section 8 concludes the paper.

2. The Enhanced Hose Model

We model the network as a graph $G = (V, E)$ where V is the set of nodes and E is the set of bidirectional links connecting the nodes. Each link (i, j) is associated with two QoS metrics – the bandwidth capacity L_{ij} and the delay D_{ij}. The delay value of a path is defined as the sum of the delay values of all links along the path.

The VPN specification in the hose model includes [7]: (1) A subset of the nodes $P \subseteq V$ corresponding to the VPN endpoints, and (2) for each node $i \in P$, the

This work described in this paper has been supported by the Research Grants Council of Hong Kong SAR, China (Project No. HKUST6177/04E)

0190-3918/05 $20.00 © 2005 IEEE

associated ingress and egress bandwidths B_i^{in} and B_i^{out}, respectively. Note that the terms "ingress" and "egress" are taken with respect to the VPN endpoints. This model can be enhanced to include a delay requirement in two ways: (1) Associate a delay requirement D_i with each node i, which specifies the maximum delay from this node to every other node in the VPN, or (2) Group applications that use the VPN into different delay classes characterized by their end-to-end delay requirements that must hold between every pair of end points. We adopt the latter approach in this paper.

The network identifies a set of delay classes; each class j is characterized by its end-to-end delay requirement D_j, $j = 1 \ldots L$. Without loss of generality, we order the L delay classes as: $D_1 < D_2 < \ldots < D_L$. In practice, these delay classes are obtained by measuring the characteristics of typical applications over the VPN. For each class j, with a delay constraint D_j, we need to find the corresponding ingress and egress bandwidth requirements $B_{i,j}^{in}$ and $B_{i,j}^{out}$ at each $i \in P$.

Therefore, the VPN specification in the enhanced hose model consists of the following three components: (1) A subset of the nodes $P \subseteq V$ corresponding to the VPN endpoints, (2) For each delay class j, the delay requirement D_j, which specifies the maximum end-to-end delay allowed between any pair of VPN endpoints, (3) For each $i \in P$ and each D_j, the associated ingress and egress bandwidths $B_{i,j}^{in}$ and $B_{i,j}^{out}$, respectively.

For clarity of presentation, the provisioning of one specific delay class, with its given delay requirement D and the associated ingress and egress bandwidths B_i^{in} and B_i^{out} for each VPN endpoint i, is discussed subsequently. The provisioning a VPN network can be viewed as provisioning each of the L delay classes.

3. Implementing the Enhanced Hose Model

Three general approaches for implementing the enhanced hose model are considered: (1) The "pipe mesh" approach, (2) The "multiple source-based trees" approach, and (3) The "shared tree" approach. The "pipe mesh" approach [4] implements the hoses with a mesh of pipes between the VPN endpoints. This can be viewed as the traditional pipe model and is included mainly for comparison purposes. The second approach builds a source-based tree to implement each hose of the VPN endpoints. A total of $|P|$ source-based trees are needed. The third approach uses a single shared tree for all the hoses in the VPN.

3.1. Pipe Mesh

In this approach a hose is implemented by a mesh of pipes between ingress and egress routers of the VPN. For a pipe from ingress i to egress j, $\min(B_i^{out}, B_j^{in})$ of bandwidth is reserved on each link along the path.

In order to minimize the reserved bandwidth for a pipe, we need to minimize the number of hops without violating the delay constraint D. We call this the Delay-Constrained Min-Hop Problem, which is a special case of the Delay-Constrained Least-Cost Problem when all the link costs are equal to 1. The problem is solvable by the Constrained Bellman-Ford (CBF) algorithm [13], which finds independent Min-Hop paths from a source to a set of destinations subject to delay constraints. The provisioning cost of the pipe mesh is the sum of bandwidth reservations of all links.

3.2. Multiple Source-Based Trees

In this approach, we use $|P|$ source-based trees to realize the hoses, one tree per hose. For a given source based tree T rooted at the VPN endpoint i, we denote by T_v the connected component of T containing node v when link (u, v) is deleted from the tree. In this case, the traffic passing through link (u, v) can only originate from i to the other endpoints in T_v. The traffic that i can send is bounded by B_i^{out}, and the traffic that T_v can receive cannot exceed $\sum_{j \in P \cap T_v} B_j^{in}$. Thus the bandwidth reserved for link (u, v) of T is given by $C_T(u, v) = min\{ B_i^{out}, \sum_{j \in P \cap T_v} B_j^{in} \}$. Therefore, the total bandwidth reserved for tree T is given by Eq. (1):

$$C_T = \sum_{(u,v) \in T} C_T(u,v) . \qquad (1)$$

In the above equation only links directing away from i need to be considered. This is because the source-based tree is only used to send traffic from i to the other VPN endpoints. Therefore, if link (u, v) is a link in tree T directing away from i, no bandwidth needs to be reserved on (v, u). Since we are interested in minimizing the total bandwidth reserved for tree T, the problem of computing the optimal source-based tree for endpoint i can be expressed as follows:

Optimal Delay-Constrained Source-Based Tree Problem: Given a set of VPN endpoints P with their associated ingress and egress bandwidths and the delay requirement D, compute a source-based tree T rooted at endpoint i whose leaves are the other VPN endpoints. The objective is to minimize C_T while satisfying the delay requirement, $\max_{j \in P \setminus i} delay(i, j) \le D$.

Theorem 1: The Optimal Delay-Constrained Source-Based Tree Problem is NP-hard. (See [14] for proof.) ■

We select the QDMR algorithm proposed in [8] to construct the source-based trees. QDMR is a fast and scalable heuristic for generating low-cost delay-bounded multicast trees. The total bandwidth reserved using multiple source-based trees can be calculated by adding the bandwidth reserved for each tree.

3.3. Shared Tree

This approach implements the $|P|$ hoses with a single shared tree. The tree structure is used because it is scalable and simplifies routing and restoration. Furthermore, a shared tree allows the bandwidth reserved on a link to be shared by the traffic between the two sets of VPN endpoints connected by the link.

For a given shared tree T, we denote by T_u/T_v the connected component of T containing node u/v when link (u, v) is deleted from the tree. Note that the traffic passing through link (u, v) can only originate from the endpoints in T_u and terminate at the endpoints in T_v. The traffic that endpoints in T_u can send is bounded by $\sum_{j\in P\cap T_u} B_j^{out}$, and the traffic that T_v can receive cannot exceed $\sum_{j\in P\cap T_v} B_j^{in}$. Thus the bandwidth to be reserved on link (u, v) of T is given by $C_T(u, v) = min\{ \sum_{j\in P\cap T_u} B_j^{out}, \sum_{j\in P\cap T_v} B_j^{in} \}$. The total bandwidth reserved for tree T is therefore given by formula (2):

$$C_T = \sum_{(u,v)\in T} C_T(u,v) . \quad (2)$$

Note that unlike eq. (1), where only the links directing away from the root of the tree are counted, all links in the tree (in both directions) are considered in eq. (2). Since we are interested in minimizing the total bandwidth reserved for tree T, the problem of computing the optimal shared tree can be formulated as:

Optimal Delay-Constrained Shared Tree Problem: Given a set of VPN endpoints P with their associated ingress and egress bandwidths and the delay requirement D, compute a shared tree T connecting all the VPN endpoints with the objective of minimizing C_T while satisfying the delay requirement, $\max_{i,j\in P} delay(i, j) \le D$.

Theorem 2: The Optimal Delay-Constrained Shared Tree Problem is NP-hard (See [14] for proof) ■

Compared to the previous two approaches, the shared tree approach makes the best use of statistical multiplexing to reduce the provisioning cost. Only one tree is needed for the whole VPN with p hoses. The simulation results in Sec. 7.2 justify this, showing a significant reduction in provisioning cost. Furthermore, routing along the shared tree is simple and restoration of the tree structure is easy.

We develop heuristics for the Optimal Delay-Constrained Shared Tree Problem using a center based shared tree approach. The procedure can be divided into three phases as follows:

Phase 1: The graph is examined to identify a set of candidate centers satisfying the delay requirement. The set is called the Candidate Center Set (CCS).

Phase 2: The Candidate Center Set is pruned to reduce the computation overhead of the heuristic. Depending on the need to control overhead, the set can be unchanged, partially-pruned, or totally pruned. By "totally pruned", we mean the set is reduced to only one candidate center after pruning.

Phase 3: Trees that do not violate the delay requirement D are constructed for each of the nodes in the pruned Candidate Center Set. The tree with the minimum reserved bandwidth is chosen.

Three problems are of interest: (1). In Phase 1, how to make the shared tree support the most stringent delay requirements? (2). In Phase 2, how to reduce the computation overhead as far as possible by pruning without incurring additional provisioning cost? (3). In Phase 3, how to achieve high statistical multiplexing gain given a specific candidate center? These three problems are solved in sections 4, 5, and 6 respectively.

4. Meeting the Delay Requirement

In this section, we first propose two heuristics, namely the RC and DC heuristics to find all candidate centers satisfying the delay requirement. These two heuristics cannot guarantee a feasible tree will be found when the delay requirement is too stringent. We solve this by formulating the minimum diameter Steiner tree problem and propose a new algorithm MDStT.

4.1. The Radius Constrained (RC) Heuristic

The radius r for node v is defined as the largest least-delay value from v to the VPN endpoints. The RC heuristic includes a node c in the candidate center set if its radius r satisfies $r \le D/2$. This guarantees that the maximum delay between any two VPN endpoints along the least-delay tree rooted at c cannot exceed twice the radius, i.e., D. Therefore, a shared Steiner tree is constructed to span the p endpoints with c as the center.

4.2. The Diameter Constrained (DC) Heuristic

The diameter d for node v is defined as the sum of the two largest least-delay values from v to the VPN endpoints. Note that this definition of the diameter for a node is different from the definition of the diameter for a tree in Section 4.3. The DC heuristic includes a node c in the candidate center set if its diameter d satisfies the delay requirement D ($d \le D$). If the condition is satisfied, the delay between any two VPN endpoints along the least-delay tree rooted at node c does not violate the delay requirement D.

4.3. Optimal Solution: The MDStT Algorithm

The above two heuristics, while fast and simple, cannot guarantee finding a feasible tree even if one exists. In the example given in Figure 1, the delay requirement among the VPN endpoints ($P_1 - P_4$) is 50. Nevertheless, the RC and DC heuristics are only able to support a delay requirement up to 58 with the candidate center located at Q_2 with a radius value of 29. This already violates the delay requirement. Figure 1(c), shows a feasible tree satisfying the requirement.

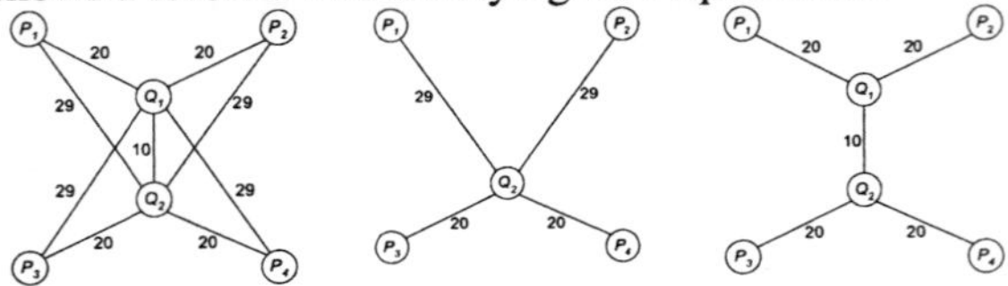

(a) Network topology (b) Shortest path tree by the DC heuristic (c) The feasible tree

Figure 1. Problem with the RC and DC heuristics. Only link delays are displayed.

We define the diameter of a Steiner tree connecting the VPN endpoints as the maximum delay between any two endpoints. Then the minimum delay requirement that can be supported by the shared tree can be found by finding the minimum diameter Steiner tree.

Mathematically, the minimum diameter Steiner tree (MDStT) problem can be formulated as follows:

Minimum Diameter Steiner Tree problem: Let $G = (V, E)$ be an undirected graph, where V is the set of nodes, and E the set of links. A subset of nodes $P \subseteq V$ represents the set of target destinations. Also let $|V| = n$ and $|E| = m$ and $|P| = p$. Suppose each link $e \in E$ is associated with a nonnegative weight d_e. A Steiner tree is a subgraph $T(V', E')$ of G which is a tree and $P \subseteq V'$. The diameter $D(T)$ of T is defined as the longest of the shortest paths in T among all node pairs in P. The *Minimum Diameter Steiner Tree* (MDStT) Problem is to find a Steiner tree of G with the minimum diameter.

We first prove that MDStT problem is equivalent to the absolute subset 1-center problem of a general graph. An absolute subset 1-center of a graph $G = (V, E)$ with respect to a subset $P \subseteq V$ is a point x (on a link or at one of the nodes) which represents the position at which the greatest distance from x to any destination in P is minimized. Note that the distance from x to a given destination in P is defined as the length of the shortest path (with respect to link weights) connecting them.

We let $A(G)$ denote the continuum set of points on the edges of G. For any point x in $A(G)$, which may or may not be a vertex of G, and a destination node $v \in P$, we let $d_G(x, v)$ denote the length of a shortest path in G between x and v. For each x in $A(G)$ define $F(x) = max_{v \in P}\, d_G(x, v)$. The *absolute subset 1-center* problem (AS1CP) in graph G is to find a location x which minimizes $F(x)$. A point x^* in $A(G)$ is an absolute subset 1-center for subset P in G if the function F attains its minimum at x^*.

Theorem 3: Let x* be an absolute subset 1-center of P in G and let T(x*) be a shortest path tree connecting x* to all nodes in P. Then T(x*) is a minimum diameter Steiner tree connecting all nodes in P. (See [14] for proof.)■

We develop our MDStT algorithm based on the algorithms for the absolute center problem [1]. The main idea is to identify a local absolute subset 1-center for each link in the graph. The global absolute center can be found by selecting the optimal one from the $|E|$ local centers. The local center is defined as the point minimizing $F(x)$ among every possible point on the link. To find the local center for a specific link (A, B), the functions from any point x to VPN endpoints $F_i(x)$ are first computed. Then $F(x)$ can be obtained by taking the upper envelope of these $F_i(x)$, $i= 1, 2, \ldots, |P|$. The local center is easily identified as the point minimizing $F(x)$.

The MDStT algorithm finds the minimum diameter Steiner tree in a general graph, and hence supports the lowest delay requirement using a tree structure in the enhanced hose model. Given the distances from the nodes to all VPN endpoints, the RC and DC heuristics need only $O(|V|)$ time to identify the center, compared to $O(|E|\, p + |V| p \log p)$ of the optimal MDStT algorithm which is more expensive. The following theorem shows that the RC and the DC heuristics are 2-approximations of the optimal MDStT algorithm with respect to the minimum delay requirement supported.

Theorem 4: The diameters of the trees constructed by the RC heuristic and the DC heuristic are at most twice the diameter of the minimum diameter Steiner tree constructed by the MDStT algorithm. (See [14] for proof.)■

5. Lowering Provisioning Cost

Phase 1 finds a set of candidate centers satisfying the delay requirement D. This set consists of network nodes if RC and DC heuristics are used, but will contain only one virtual node if the MDStT algorithm is used, which is the absolute center identified for the minimum diameter Steiner tree. The objective of Phase 2 is to build a low-provisioning-cost tree rooted at a specific candidate center. Four types of trees are considered in this work.

5.1. Least Delay Tree

The Least-delay (LD) Tree uses the least-delay tree rooted at the center to connect the VPN endpoints. The delay values from the center to the VPN endpoints are minimized in this case. Because of the way the candidate center is chosen, the delay requirement D will always be satisfied. However, no effort is made to minimize the total bandwidth reserved.

5.2. QDMR (QoS Dependent Multicast Routing) Tree

The QDMR tree [8] tries to minimize the number of hops in the constructed tree in order to reduce the bandwidth reserved. The delay constraint from the center to any of the VPN endpoints is set to $D/2$.

5.3. LCLD (Least Cost Least Delay) Tree

The third variation is to construct a LCLD tree [11]. Given a center c, each VPN endpoint v tries to connect to the center using its LCLD path. The LCLD path from VPN endpoint v to the center c goes along the Min-Hop path as long as the delay bound $D_{shared} = D/2$ is not violated. It then switches to the Least-Delay path from the current node to the center when going further along the Min-Hop path would violate the constraint. Switching to the least-delay path from the current node will satisfy the delay constraint and would not cause backtracking.

Theorem 5: The shared tree constructed using the LCLD approach is loop free and satisfies the delay requirement D. (See [14] for proof.) ■

5.4. BFS (Breadth-First-Search) Tree

The LCLD tree can reduce the provisioning cost as shown by simulation results in Sec. 8. However, going along the min-hop path and switching to the least-delay path may not always be the best choice. The Breadth-First-Search (BFS) tree first finds independent delay-constrained min-hop (DCMH) paths from the center to the endpoints using the CBF algorithm [13]. Then these DCMH paths are merged to form the final BFS tree.

A by-product of this merging procedure is that there may be loops resulting from simple union of these DCMH paths. Therefore, we need to form an induced graph by the union of the paths, and perform a final round of the shortest-path algorithm from the center to the VPN endpoints in the induced graph. This procedure would eliminate all loops and leave only a Steiner tree spanning the VPN endpoints.

6. Reducing Computation Overhead

In large networks with relatively loose delay requirements, the number of candidate centers obtained in Phase 1 may be quite large. This will cause high computation overhead in Phase 3. The objective of Phase 2 is to reduce the number of candidate centers in the CCS, thereby reducing the computation overhead in Phase 3. Let us denote the minimum radius of the centers in the CCS by r_{min}. The radius of each candidate center v in the original CCS is checked to see if $|r-r_{min}|\leq\delta r_{min}$, where δ is a predefined threshold. Candidate centers failing to satisfy the condition are deleted from the set. If δ is set to the extreme value 0, the CCS will be pruned to only one candidate center with the minimum radius. If computation overhead is not a major concern, or the number of centers obtained in Phase 1 is small, Phase 2 can be omitted and all nodes in the original candidate center set are used in Phase 3.

7. Simulation Results

We conducted a number of simulation experiments to measure the performance of the three approaches described in Section 3 and the algorithms proposed for the shared tree approach in Sections 4, 5, and 6. The results show that the shared tree approach is able to support a given delay requirement with a scalable tree structure at lower reserved bandwidth compared to the other two approaches. Given the advantages of the shared tree approach, we further study the performance of its various implementation alternatives.

7.1. Network Topologies

Two sets of topologies were used in our simulations. The first set is taken from the Rocketfuel project [10]. Among all the topologies, we selected four tier-1 ISP topologies as listed in Table 1 below. They represent real-world toplogies. The link delays of these topologies were computed based on their geographical distances. The setting of delay values is reasonable since transmission delay and queueing delay values are very small in these ISP backbone networks.

Table 1. Rocketfuel ISP topologies used in the simulations.

	Name	Tier	Dominant Presence	Degree	# of nodes
701	UUNet	1	US	2569	83
209	Qwest	1	US	887	58
1239	Sprint	1	US	1735	52
7018	ATT	1	US	1490	115

The second set was randomly generated using the Waxman Model [12]. Since we can easily control the size of the topologies, we use them to study the effect of network size on algorithm performance. In this model, the nodes are placed on a 3000×2400 Km^2 plane, roughly the size of the USA. The probability for two nodes to be connected by a link decreases exponentially with the Euclidean distance between them according to the following probability function:

$$P_e(u,v) = \rho \exp[-l(u,v)/(L\theta)] \quad (3)$$

where L is the maximum distance between any two nodes in the network and $l(u, v)$ is the distance between u and v. The parameter θ controls the ratio of short links to long links, while the parameter ρ controls the average node degree of the network. A large value of θ increases the number of long links, and a large value of ρ results in a large average node degree. In the experiments, θ and ρ were set at 0.15 and 2.2 respectively. These values were selected to obtain random networks which closely resemble real networks. Like the Rocketfuel topologies, the link delay values of the random networks were calculated according to their geographic distances. Link capacities were randomly chosen from one of the three: OC3, OC12, and OC48.

For both sets of topologies, the VPN endpoints were randomly selected from the network nodes. The number of VPN endpoints was set to be 10% of the total number of nodes in the network unless explicitly specified. The bandwidth requirement of each VPN endpoint was uniformly chosen between 2 and 100 Mbps. A parameter r is associated with each endpoint, representing the ratio between the ingress and egress bandwidth requirements. This asymmetry ratio varies from 1 to 256 in our simulation experiments. The delay requirement of the endpoints was generated uniformly between 20*ms* and 100*ms*. Each simulation result given below is the average of 10 rounds of experiments.

7.2. Efficiency of the Shared Tree Approach

The performance of the pipe mesh approach, the multiple source-based tree approach, and the shared tree approach were compared. Moreover, the effect of varying the network size and the number of VPN endpoints on performance was also investigated. In our study, the provisioning cost (the total bandwidth reserved) and the minimum delay requirement that can be supported were used as performance indices. The second metric is of interest because it describes the ability of meeting stringent delay requirements.

Minimum delay requirement supported

Figure 2 shows the minimum delay requirement that can be supported using each of the three approaches. We used both rocketfuel and random topologies. The name of the random topologies indicates the number of nodes in the network (e.g., "ran100" is a random topology with 100 nodes). The number of VPN endpoints in the networks is fixed at 10% of the total number of nodes. The first three bars are the three variations of the shared tree approach, with different methods of forming the candidate center set in phase 1. The last bar shows the performance of the pipe-mesh approach and the multiple source-based trees approach.

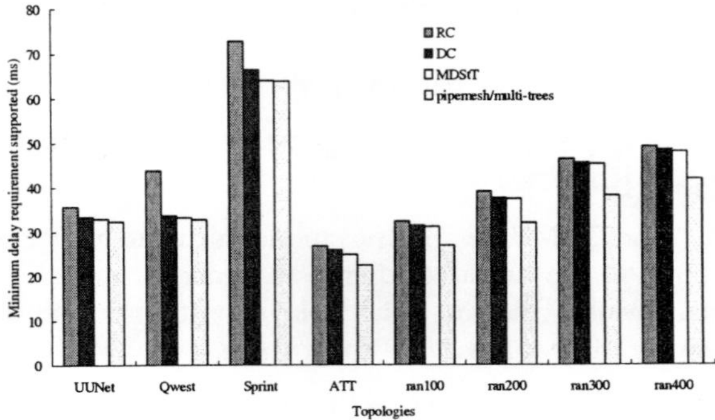

Figure 2. Minimum delay requirements supported by the approaches.

From the figure, the following observations can be made. First, the pipe-mesh approach and the multiple source-based trees approach perform identically with respect to supporting the minimum delay requirement. This is because when the delay requirement is stringent, the source-based trees are identical to the least-delay trees. These two approaches support smaller delay requirements than the shared tree approach. Second, the minimum delay requirement supported by the shared tree approach is higher than the other two approaches, although the difference is not large, especially for real-world topologies.

Total bandwidth reserved

Figure 3 shows the provisioning costs of the three approaches. The network parameter settings were the same as before. For each network configuration, the delay requirement is chosen randomly from [20, 100*ms*] as long as all three approaches can find feasible solutions. For the shared tree approach, we used the LD tree in phase 2. The shared tree approach exhibits better performance than the other two approaches, reducing the provisioning cost by a factor of 2 or more for a wide range of network parameters.

7.3. Meeting Delay Requirements

Figure 2 also shows the minimum delay requirement that can be supported using the three technologies in phase 1 of the shared tree approach. The MDStT algorithm supports the minimum delay requirement that can be supported by a tree structure. This provides a lower bound for the RC and DC heuristics. The performance of the two heuristics is also near-optimal although they are only 2-approximations in theory. In most cases, the DC heuristic performs close to the optimal MDStT algorithm. This suggests that the DC heuristic is a good choice in phase 1 since it is fast and yields near-optimal tree diameters.

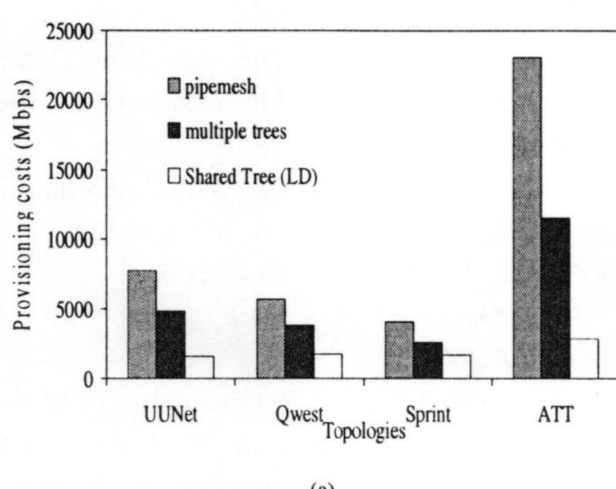

(a)

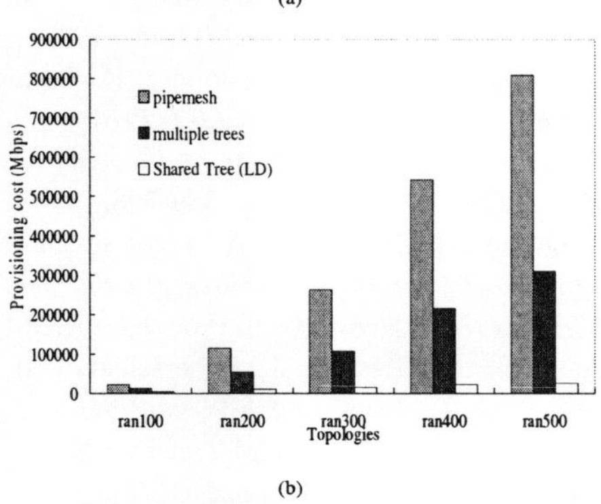

(b)

Figure 3. The provisioning costs of the approaches.

7.4. Lowering Provisioning Cost

The performance of the four implementation techniques in Phase 3, i.e., LD tree, QDMR tree, LCLD tree, and BFS tree, is exhibited in Figure 4. For each network configuration, the minimum delay requirement D_{min} that the four heuristics can support was the same. The delay requirements had to be carefully selected to show the different performance of the heuristics. If it is too small, the latter three trees will be very similar to the LD tree. If it is too large, the delay constraint will be meaningless and the LCLD tree and the BFS tree will become the min-hop tree, which definitely reserves less bandwidth than the LD tree approach. In Figure 4, the delay requirement was set to $1.15 \times D_{min}$. The results show that using the LCLD tree and the BFS tree in Phase 3 needs less bandwidth reservation than using either the LD tree or the QDMR tree. The difference is small for rocketfuel topologies. This is because the sizes of these topologies are small, which leaves less room for LCLD and BFS trees to go along alternative paths other than least-delay paths. The same is true with the randomly generated graph "ran100". When the network size increases, we see obvious advantage of LCLD and BFS trees over LD and QDMR trees.

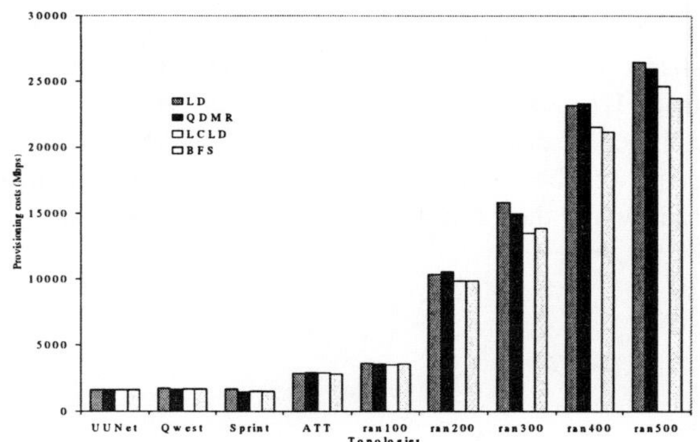

Figure 4. The provisioning costs of the four heuristics of the shared tree approach.

7.5. Reducing Computation Overhead

The pruning technique in Phase 2 is a compromise between performance and overhead. Table 2 depicts the relation between provisioning cost and the threshold δ used to prune the set. The table also shows the number of centers left in the CCS when the value of δ increases. We used one of the rocket fuel topologies, the Sprint topology in the simulation. Delay requirements are set at 1.5 of the minimum value supported by the shared tree approach. The DC heuristic is used in Phase 1 and the LCLD trees are used in Phase 2.

When δ was 0, only 1 center was left in the CCS. When δ was increased to 0.18, 12 out of 36 candidate centers were left in the pruned set. This means we only need to build 12 trees in Phase 3 instead of 36 if the set is not pruned, and these 12 trees already give optimal provisioning cost. Further increasing the value of δ and including more nodes in the set did not improve the cost. This leads to the conclusion that a small δ (< 0.2) can significantly reduce the computation overhead without sacrificing much provisioning cost. In most cases, the overhead would be around 1/3 of the original.

Table 2. Performance of the pruning technique

δ	0	0.1	0.18	0.2	0.4	0.8
Number of centers	1	11	12	14	23	36
Provisioning cost	1408	1098	1061	1061	1061	1061
Overhead over non-pruning	2.8%	31%	33%	39%	64%	100%
Excessive cost	32.7%	3.5%	0	0	0	0

7.6. Asymmetric Ingress-Egress Bandwidth Requirements

In real networks, the ingress and egress bandwidth requirements are not necessarily the same. Using the same experiment settings as [7], we model this asymmetry with an asymmetry ratio r, which defines the ratio between the ingress/egress bandwidth requirements. Figure 5, shows the provisioning cost of the four heuristics with different tree types for the shared tree approach as the asymmetry ratio increased from 1 to 256. The number of nodes was 200 and the number of endpoints was fixed at 5. The provisioning costs of the heuristics increase with the asymmetry ratio while their relative ranking remains the same.

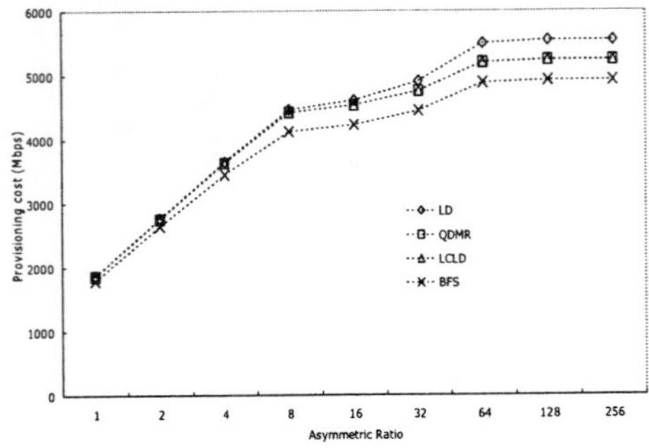

Figure 5. Effect of asymmetry ratio.

8. Conclusions

We extend the original hose model to incorporate delay requirements. Three approaches, namely the "Pipe Mesh" approach, the "Multiple Source-based Trees" approach, and the "Shared Tree" approach are proposed for provisioning VPNs in the enhanced model. For the "Shared Tree" approach, because of its scalability and ease of routing and restoration, several heuristics are developed using different techniques to implement the three phases in constructing the tree.

Simulation is used to evaluate the performance of the approaches. The "Pipe Mesh" approach satisfies the most stringent delay requirements, but requires more bandwidth to be reserved than the other approaches. The "Multiple Source-Based Trees" approach reserves less bandwidth than the "Pipe Mesh" approach since statistical multiplexing can be used within each of the trees, especially at the roots. The "Shared Tree" approach requires the least total bandwidth to be reserved, but the minimum delay requirement that can be supported is higher than the other two approaches.

The results suggest that the "Shared Tree" approach can be tuned to improve performance. In Phase 1, we obtain the minimum delay requirement that a tree can support by transforming it into the MDStT problem. The RC and DC heuristics are 2-approximations of MDStT algorithm and yield near-optimal tree diameters. In Phase 3, the LCLD and BFS trees require less total bandwidth to be reserved than the L trees and the QDMR trees. Finally, the pruning threshold δ in Phase 2 can be tuned to control the computation overhead while still yielding near-optimal provisioning cost.

References

[1] R. Cunnighame-Greene, The Absolute Center of a Graph, *Discrete Applied Mathematics,* 7 (1984), pp. 275-283.

[2] B. Davie, and Y. Rekhter. *MPLS Technology and Applications.* San Mateo, CA: Morgan Kaufmann, 2000.

[3] T. Erlebach, M. Ruegg, *Optimal Bandwidth Reservation in Hose-Model VPNs with Multi-Path Routing,* INFOCOM 2004.

[4] N. G. Duffield, P. Goyal, A. Greenberg, P. Mishra, K. K. Ramakrishnan, and J. E. van der Merwe, *A Flexible Model for Resource Management in Virtual Private Networks,* In Proc. ACM SIGCOMM, 1999. pp. 95-108.

[5] A. Gupta, A. Kumar, J. Kleinberg, R. Rastogi, and B. Yener, *Provisioning a Virtual Private Network: A Network Design Problem for Multicommodity Flow,* In Proc. ACM STOC, 2001. pp. 389-398.

[6] A. Juttner, I. Szabo, and A. Szentesi, *On Bandwidth Efficiency of the Hose Resource Management Model in Virtual Private Networks,* In Proc. INFOCOM 2003.

[7] A. Kumar, R. Rastogi, A. Silberschatz, and B. Yener, *Algorithms for Provisioning Virtual Private Networks in the Hose Model,* IEEE/ACM Trans. on Networking, vol. 10, issue 4, August 2002. pp. 565-578.

[8] I. Matta, and L. Guo, *QDMR: An Efficient QoS Dependent Multicast Routing Algorithm, In Journal of Communications and Networks,* Real-time Technology and Applications Symposium, 1999. pp. 213-222.

[9] P. P. Mishra, H. Saran, *Capacity Management and Routing Policies for Voice over IP Traffic, IEEE Network,* vol. 14, no. 2, pp. 20-27, March/April 2000. pp. 20-27.

[10] Rocketfuel project, Computer Science and Engineering, Univ. of Washington. http://www.cs.washington.edu/research/networking/rocketfuel/.

[11] H. F. Salama, D. S. Reeves, and Y. Viniotis, *A Distributed Algorithm for Delay-Constrained Unicast Routing,* IEEE/ACM Trans. on Networking, vol. 8, issue 2, April 2000. pp. 239-250.

[12] B. M. Waxman, *Routing of Multipoint Connections,* IEEE Journal on Selected Areas in Communications, vol. 6, issue 9, December 1988. pp. 1617-1622.

[13] X. Yuan, *On the Extended Bellman-Ford Algorithm to Solve Two-constrained Quality of Service Routing Problems,* in ICCN'99, Oct. 1999.

[14] L. Zhang, J. Muppala and S. T. Chanson, *Provisioning Virtual Private Networks in the Hose Model with Delay Requirements,* Tech. Rep. HKUST-CS05-07, Dept. of Computer Science, HKUST, 2005.

On Mapping Multidimensional Weak Tori on Optical Slab Waveguides

Ramachandran Vaidyanathan* Karthik Sethuraman
Department of Electrical & Computer Engineering
Louisiana State University, Baton Rouge, LA 70803-5901, USA
{vaidy,ksethu}@ece.lsu.edu

Abstract

Optics is acknowledged as the most viable means to meet the bandwidth needs of future interconnects. While the optical medium can easily deliver huge bandwidths, this bandwidth is difficult to harness; this is because of engineering and technological constraints associated with accommodating a large number of high-speed lasers and photodetectors within a small confine. We consider the problem of mapping weak multidimensional tori on optical slab waveguides. Our approach uses the fact that not all edges of a weak topology are used simultaneously; it uses this fact to employ a single laser/detector to work in multiple capacities at different times. We introduce the notion of aggregates to capture the cost of mapping a topology by our approach. We derive a non-trivial lower bound on this cost for a class of mappings and construct mappings, all of which surpass a naive method and some of which match the lower bound.

1. Introduction

It is expected that in the near future CMOS-based transistors will be capable of supporting data rates of around 20 Gbps [12]. At these (and even lower) data rates, the bandwidth of electrical interconnects is severely limited by RC delay and frequency dependent losses such as skin effect and dielectric loss [5]. Other considerations such as signal distortion, crosstalk and reflections also come into play at these high data rates. Furthermore, in structures such as buses in which multiple taps are made to a wire, capacitive loading limits the rate at which data can be transmitted reliably [1]. Thus, there is a wide gap between the data rates electrical interconnects can deliver and the computing needs of the future. The promise of optical interconnects in filling this gap is well recognized. Indeed, optical communication has been studied at various levels of the computing system hierarchy ranging from long haul fibers (for example [6]), to communications over much shorter distances such as board-level/backplane buses inter-chip/module connections and intra-chip integrated optics (for example [5]). Optics has also been used to implement traditional topologies such as the k-ary n-cubes (including special cases and variants), and reconfigurable models [2, 8, 9, 11].

In this paper we consider optical interconnects over short distances and used within small confines, for example at the board, interchip or backplane levels. Such interconnects are usually based on slab waveguides, multimode fibers or free-space optics. In this setting the "system bandwidth" is often constrained by the speed of light sources (lasers) and photodetectors and the size of the optical apparatus needed to insert and extract the signal from the medium (slab or fiber in a waveguided system, or air in a free-space optical system). The optical medium itself is relatively unconstrained, and often has a much higher "medium bandwidth" than what the electrical and optical components can deliver within the constraints of available technology. For example, a slab waveguide about a mm^2 in cross section can very easily carry over 10,000 100-Gbps channels (at different modes and wavelengths [1]), provided these 10,000 high-speed signals can be inserted into and extracted from the slab. If one factors in size, cost and other engineering constraints involved with inserting and detecting the signals, the figure is likely to be at most 50 10-Gbps channels with current technology [12]. The medium bandwidth (1000 Tera bps in this illustration) is much higher than the system bandwidth (0.5 Tera bps).

This paper addresses the problem of bridging this gap between the medium and system bandwidths. Broadly speaking, the idea is to reduce the size of the system by using the fact that not all edges of an interconnection topology are employed simultaneously. Put differently, for a given system size, this allows for a larger sized topology (requiring more channels) to be mapped on to the optical medium. More specifically, we examine the problem of implementing a "weak" d-dimensional torus topology on an optical system using a slab waveguide. Informally, a weak topol-

*Supported in part by the US. National Science Foundation under grant CCR-0310916.

0190-3918/05 $20.00 © 2005 IEEE

ogy is one in which at any given point in time, each node (or processor) receives information from at most one of its neighbors and sends information to at most one of its neighbors [7, 10]. Many useful algorithms run on such weak models. Our approach exploits this slack to reduce the number of lasers and detectors as well as the cost and size of the optical apparatus. The idea is to map edges of the topology to channels of the waveguide so that a single tunable laser can transmit on several channels (each at a different time) and a single photodetector can detect several channels (that are used at different times).

Let $\mathcal{G} = (\mathcal{V}, \mathcal{E})$ be an N-node, directed graph representing a weak interconnection topology; as usual, nodes represent processors and edges represent communication links; mapping the topology entails assigning each edge of $|\mathcal{E}|$ to a channel of the slab waveguide. Assuming $\mathcal{G}$ to be strongly connected, $N \leq |\mathcal{E}| \leq N(N-1)$. For any processor $p \in \mathcal{V}$, let $\delta_o(p)$ and $\delta_i(p)$ denote its out-degree and in-degree, respectively. At any given time, at most N of the edges are in use (no more than one transmission and reception per processor). Therefore, any mapping of the topology requires at least one laser and one photodetector per processor or a total of N lasers and N photodetectors. At the other extreme, processor p does not need more than $\delta_o(p)$ lasers and $\delta_i(p)$ photodetectors, resulting in a total of at most $\sum_{p\in\mathcal{V}} \delta_i(p) = \sum_{p\in\mathcal{V}} \delta_o(p) = |\mathcal{E}|$ lasers and $|\mathcal{E}|$ photodetectors. That is, the total number of lasers and photodetectors can each be between N and $|\mathcal{E}|$. For a topology that is not very sparse, this gap between N and $|\mathcal{E}|$ can be large.

For an N-processor, d-dimensional torus, a naive mapping uses as many as $2dN$ lasers and $2dN$ detectors. All the mappings presented in this paper use N photodetectors, the smallest number possible, and which reduces optical hardware as described later. For a 1-dimensional torus (or a ring), our mapping uses at most $N + 2$ lasers. For a d-dimensional torus (where $d > 1$), our mapping employs $2N\left(d - 1 + \frac{1}{L}\right)$ lasers, where $L \geq N^{\frac{1}{d}}$. We also derive a non-trivial lower bound to show that a weak d-dimensional torus (with $d \geq 2$) that uses N detectors must use at least $2N(d-1) + 2$ lasers. Thus, our result exceeds the lower bound only by the quantity $\frac{2N}{L} - 2$. For some cases, $L = N$ and our mapping is optimal.

Although our results are directed towards slab waveguides, many elements are relevant to fiber-based and free-space optical systems as well. To our knowledge, ours is the first method that approaches the problem of reducing the gap between the system and medium bandwidths by tuning the mapping. Our approach does not use devices properties and, consequently, its advantages independently add on to benefits from advances in device technology.

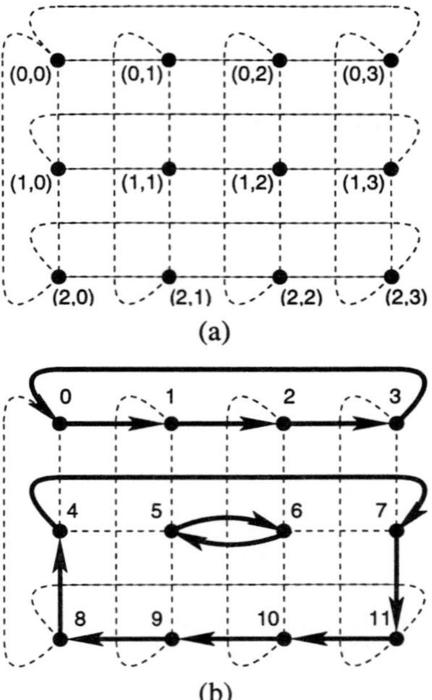

Figure 1. A weak 3×4 torus communication.

2. Preliminaries

2.1. Weak Multidimensional Torus

For integers $d \geq 1$, $0 \leq i < d$ and $N_i \geq 2$, an $N_0 \times N_1 \times \cdots \times N_{d-1}$ *d-dimensional* torus is a directed graph with $N = \prod_{i=0}^{d-1} N_i$ nodes and edges as described below. Let each vertex v be indexed $(v_0, v_1, \cdots, v_{d-1})$, where $0 \leq v_j < N_j$, for each $0 \leq j < d$. There is a directed edge from vertex v to vertex $w = (w_0, w_1, \cdots, w_{d-1})$ iff there is a dimension $0 \leq k < d$ such that $v_k = (w_k \pm 1)(\text{mod } N_k)$ and for all $j \neq k$, $\quad v_j = w_j$.

Figure 1(a) shows a 3×4 2-dimensional torus. Each vertex of a d-dimensional torus has $2d$ outgoing edges and $2d$ incoming edges. If $N_j = 2$ for some dimension, then the two dimension-j edges of a vertex v are to the same point (as $v_j + 1 \equiv v_j - 1$ (mod 2)). In general, we will assume that each dimension has a size of at least 3.

Consider a N-processor parallel processing system[†] with set $\mathcal{V} = \{p_0, p_1, \cdots, p_{N-1}\}$ of processors and connected by a topology represented by a directed graph $\mathcal{G} = (\mathcal{V}, \mathcal{E})$.

[†]We assume that each edge (communication link) of the system is a 1-bit link. This assumption is without loss of generality as the ideas developed in this paper readily extend to higher link widths.

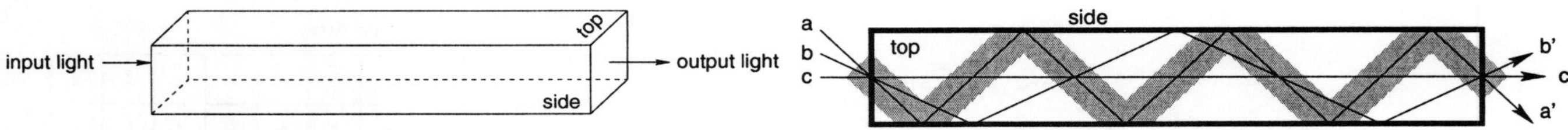

Figure 2. A simple slab waveguide.

Figure 3. MDM in a slab.

Definition 1 A *communication* among the processors of a topology $\mathcal{G} = (\mathcal{V}, \mathcal{E})$ is any non-empty subset of $\mathcal{E}$. A communication $\mathcal{S} \subseteq \mathcal{E}$ is a *weak communication*, iff every pair of distinct directed edges, $e = (p_i, p_j), e' = (p_{i'}, p_{j'}) \in \mathcal{S}$, satisfies $p_i \neq p_{i'}$ and $p_j \neq p_{j'}$. A *weak topology* is one in which every communication is weak. ■

In a weak communication, a processor sends at most one message and receives at most one message in step. Figure 1(b) shows a weak communication on a 3×4 torus.

2.2. Slab Waveguides

An *optical slab waveguide* is a piece of transparent material (of appropriate geometry) through which light can be transmitted. As in an optical fiber, the light is confined within a slab by total internal reflection. The main difference between a fiber and a slab is in their cross-section dimensions; a slab is generally much larger with a cross-section area in the order of a mm^2. This higher area allows light to be transmitted in many modes[‡] within the slab. In contrast, fibers are usually single-mode waveguides; indeed, this single mode feature is indispensable for transmission over large distances, but is not needed for interconnects over short distances such as those considered in this paper. We distinguish a slab from a multimode waveguide by assuming that a slab's geometry is designed to preserve modes. That is, if two signals are transmitted in separate modes, then they can be received separately. This allows one to employ *mode-division multiplexing* (or MDM) [1] to multiplex signals in different modes on the same slab.

To make these ideas more concrete we discuss them in the setting of a simple slab waveguide shaped as a rectangular parallelepiped (henceforth, referred to simply as the slab) shown in Figure 2. Though many waveguide geometries are possible (for example see Feldman *et al.* [1]), the slab in Figure 2 captures all the waveguide properties needed for our discussion.

The slab can multiplex information independently in several modes and wavelengths. To understand how the slab performs mode-division multiplexing it is useful to view it from the "top" (see Figure 3). This figure shows three signals (labeled a, b and c) that are transmitted in different modes (angles relative to the axis) that are still separated at the output of the slab (shown as a', b' and c'). The light, as viewed from the top of the slab, is collimated to preserve the modes during transmission. In contrast, the light (as viewed from the side of the slab) need not be collimated. Using MDM only on the "top plane" of the slab provides room for demultiplexing hardware—see Figure 4.

A slab that is about 1 mm wide in the top view can easily support a few hundred distinct modes (sufficiently separated to be useful in practice [1]). In addition (and independently of MDM) it can also distinguish channels by their wavelength (wavelength division multiplexing or WDM [6]). (Dense Wavelength Division Multiplexing or DWDM is used today to transmit around 80 channels in a fiber). Thus, the slab can carry several thousand *channels*, each with a unique wavelength and mode combination. In general if M modes and W wavelengths are possible, then the slab has MW channels.

Input and Output Optics: Typically, light is inserted into the slab by lasers. The output of a laser must be collimated (for MDM) and inserted at the appropriate mode (angle). The cost and size of the input optics is determined primarily by the number of lasers.

At the output, the channels must be demultiplexed into spatially separated spots, each incident on a photodetector. Figure 4 shows a schematic of the output optics. The output optical hardware consists of two main parts in series that are responsible for demultiplexing wavelengths and modes. These demultiplexers separate the information (along different dimensions) into spots of light on a detector plane. By placing photodetectors on these spots, the signals can be detected and sent to the appropriate processors. For an M-mode, W-wavelength system, the detector plane can be viewed as an $M \times W$ channel array, representing MW channels. Note that adjacent rows (resp., adjacent columns) of the channel array correspond to adjacent modes or MDM angles (resp., adjacent wavelengths). The cost and size of the output optics depends to a large extent on the demultiplexer hardware and the number of detectors used.

3. Mapping Topologies on a Slab Waveguide

Each channel of the slab corresponds to a unique mode and wavelength combination. The task is to suitably map each edge of the given topology to a channel.

Let the modes and wavelengths be ν_u (for $0 \leq u < M$) and λ_v (for $0 \leq v < W$). That is, MW channels are

‡For this paper, each mode corresponds to an angle at which light is inserted into the waveguide. For more details see, for example, Fowles [3].

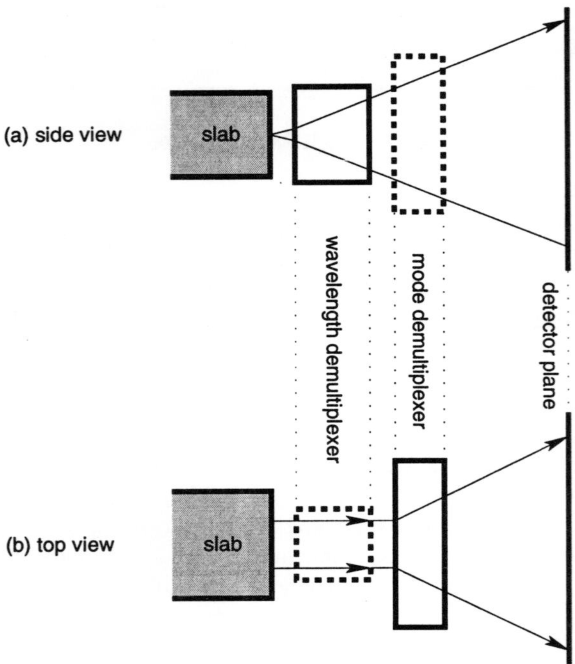

Figure 4. A schematic of the demultiplexing of signals on the slab.

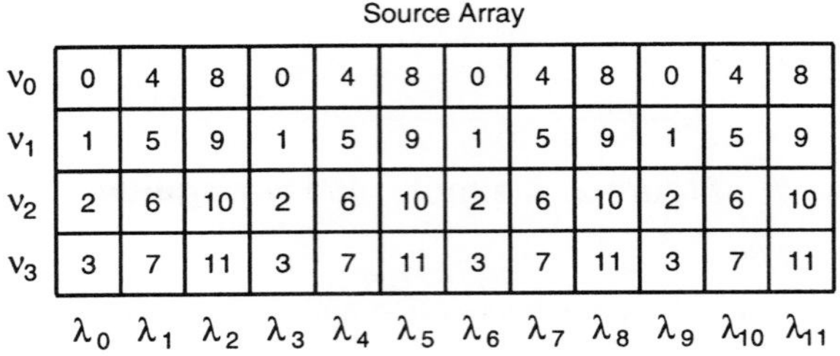

Source Array

	λ_0	λ_1	λ_2	λ_3	λ_4	λ_5	λ_6	λ_7	λ_8	λ_9	λ_{10}	λ_{11}
v_0	0	4	8	0	4	8	0	4	8	0	4	8
v_1	1	5	9	1	5	9	1	5	9	1	5	9
v_2	2	6	10	2	6	10	2	6	10	2	6	10
v_3	3	7	11	3	7	11	3	7	11	3	7	11

Destination Array

	λ_0	λ_1	λ_2	λ_3	λ_4	λ_5	λ_6	λ_7	λ_8	λ_9	λ_{10}	λ_{11}
v_0	1	8	11	8	5	4	3	0	9	4	7	0
v_1	0	1	10	5	4	1	2	9	8	9	6	5
v_2	10	5	6	3	10	11	6	7	2	1	2	9
v_3	7	4	3	2	3	10	11	6	7	0	11	8

Figure 5. Mapping 1

available. We will specify the mapping using two $M \times W$ arrays called the source and destination arrays and denoted by *Src* and *Dst*, respectively. Each element of these arrays is a processor index $0 \leq i < n$. If an edge (p_i, p_j) from processor p_i to processor p_j is mapped to a channel with mode ν_u and wavelength λ_v, the entry $Src(u, v)$ at row u and column v of the source (resp., destination) array is i, and similarly, $Dst(u, v) = j$.

For example, consider the torus shown in Figure 1 that has 12 processors and 48 directed edges. Figures 5 and 6 show the source and destination arrays corresponding to two different mappings of these edges that use 4 modes and 12 wavelengths; for now ignore the ovals in Figure 6.

We now introduce the notion of aggregates that are used to define the cost of a mapping. Consider a fixed mapping of edges of the weak topology to channels of the slab.

Definition 2 Let C be a set of channels of the slab. For any processor index $0 \leq i < N$, the doublet (C, i) is called a *source (resp., destination) mode aggregate* iff the following conditions hold.

(a) $\forall(\nu_u, \lambda_v), (\nu_{u'}, \lambda_{v'}) \in C, \quad \nu_u = \nu_{u'}$; that is, all channels of C have the same mode.

(b) Let $0 \leq v < v' < W$. If $(\nu_u, \lambda_v), (\nu_u, \lambda_{v'}) \in C$, then $\forall v''$ with $v < v'' < v, \quad (\nu_u, \lambda_{v''}) \in C$; that is, the channels of C have adjacent wavelengths.

(c) If $(\nu_u, \lambda_v) \in C$, then $Src(u, v) = i$; that is, an entry of the source (resp., destination) array corresponding to a channel of C contains the value i.

Similarly, (C, i) is called a *source (resp., destination) wavelength aggregate* iff

(a) all channels of C have the same wavelength,

(b) the channels of C have adjacent modes and

(c) an entry of *Src* (resp., *Dst*) corresponding to a channel of C has value i. ■

The source and destination arrays of Figure 6 show mode and wavelength aggregates, respectively. An aggregate (C, i) is *trivial* iff C contains only one processor index. An aggregate (C, i) is maximal iff there is no other aggregate (C', i) such that $C \subset C'$. All the circled aggregates of Figure 6 are maximal and non-trivial. The four uncircled aggregates in the source array of this figure are both trivial and maximal.

The significance of a source mode aggregate (C, i) is that a single tunable laser controlled by processor p_i can generate signals for all the channels of C. Since all entries of the source array corresponding to channels of C contain index i, each channel of C has processor p_i as source. For a weak topology, only one of these channels can be used at a time. Therefore, a single laser can take turns to tune to different (adjacent) wavelengths. The fact that these wavelengths are adjacent makes this tuning feasible[§]. For example, consider

[§]Currently, tunable lasers are expensive and their ability to change wavelengths quickly is limited. However, this work establishes the formalism needed to exploit the possibility of reusing components across channels.

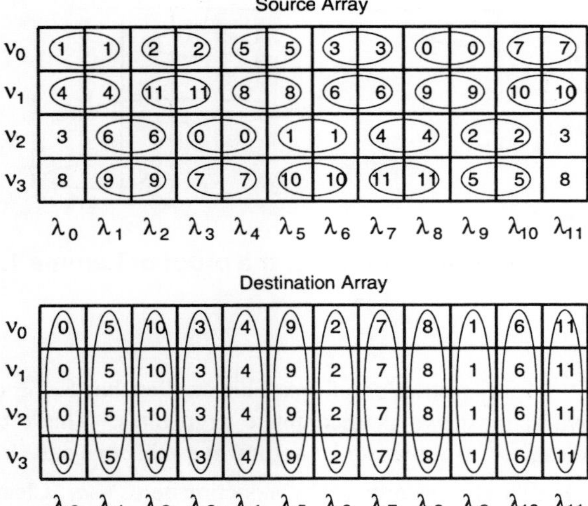

Figure 6. Mapping 2 (for a 3×4 torus)

the aggregate in the top left corner of the source array of Mapping 2 (Figure 6). Here a tunable laser of processor p_1 tunes between wavelengths λ_0 and λ_1. The laser itself is positioned to transmit in mode ν_0. We assume that a tunable laser can tune rapidly between wavelengths in the aggregate. A source wavelength aggregate (C, i) has a similar interpretation, if the laser can switch between the modes of the channels in C.

At the destination array, a mode or wavelength aggregate (C, i) has a similar interpretation. A single photodetector covering all the spots corresponding to C suffices to detect information destined for processor p_i. Tuning (to a mode or a wavelength) is not necessary; an inactive channel has no light and therefore, a logical OR of the signals of all channels in the aggregate provides the correct value at any fixed communication step. The leftmost aggregate in the destination array of Figure 6 corresponds to a single photodetector that detects all channels destined for p_0.

The above example presents another interesting aspect of the mapping. Note that all the destination aggregates cover all four modes. This obviates the need to separate the modes. That is, the mode demultiplexing hardware shown in Figure 4 is no longer needed. Indeed, modes need not be distinguished at the source.

We now state some assumptions.

1. For any vertex v of the graph, define its in-degree $\delta_i(v)$ (resp., out-degree $\delta_o(v)$) to be the number of incoming (resp., outgoing) edges of v. Define the in-degree D_i (resp., out-degree D_O) of the graph to be $\max\{\delta_i(v) : v \in \mathcal{V}\}$ (resp., $\max\{\delta_o(v) : v \in \mathcal{V}\}$). Define the degree D of the graph to be $\max\{D_i, D_o\}$. For an N-node topology, we will assume that the source and destination arrays are $D \times N$ arrays. That is, the mapping will use D modes and N wavelengths. For a d-dimensional torus $D = 2d$. In Section 6 we touch upon the possibility of using different numbers of wavelengths and modes.
2. We will assume that each column of the $D \times N$ destination array forms a single wavelength aggregate as shown in Figure 6. This obviates the need for mode demultiplexing and requires N detectors (the smallest number possible for an N-node topology).

Definition 3 Let $\mathcal{G}$ be an N-node graph with degree D. A *standard mapping* for $\mathcal{G}$ is one that uses $D \times N$ arrays such that each column of the destination array is covered by a single aggregate.

Mapping 2 (Figure 6) is a standard mapping, whereas Mapping 1 (Figure 5) is not. In this paper we will only consider standard mappings.

Cost of a Mapping: Because all mappings we consider are standard, the number of detectors is the best possible (N) and the output optics is considerably simplified. Thus, the cost of a standard mapping is directly related to the number of lasers used. From the earlier discussion, the number of lasers equals the number of maximal aggregates in the source array. Mapping 1 of Figure 5, a non-standard mapping uses 48 lasers and 48 photodetectors, whereas Mapping 2 (Figure 6), a standard mapping, employs only 26 lasers and 12 detectors. It also obviates the need for mode demultiplexing. Thus, the manner in which edges of the topology are mapped to channels of the slab can have a big impact on the cost and complexity of the system.

4. Cost Lower Bounds for Mapping Weak Tori

In this section we derive non-trivial lower bounds on the cost of a standard mapping of a d-dimensional, N-processor, weak torus on a slab waveguide. Here the arrays *Src* and *Dst* will be of size $2d \times N$, with rows and columns numbered $0, 1, \cdots, d-1$ and $0, 1, \cdots, N-1$, respectively. We assume that each dimension has size ≥ 3. This is only to avoid sticky situations presented by multiple edges.

For brevity, we state many of the results without proof; details can be found in Sethuraman [4]

Theorem 1 *A standard mapping of an N-node, 1-dimensional, weak torus (ring) requires N detectors and at least $2\left\lceil \frac{N}{2} \right\rceil$ lasers.*

Proof outline: It can be shown that all non-trivial source aggregates of a standard mapping are mode aggregates. Since each node of a ring has out-degree of 2, each processor index appears exactly twice in the array *Src*. Therefore,

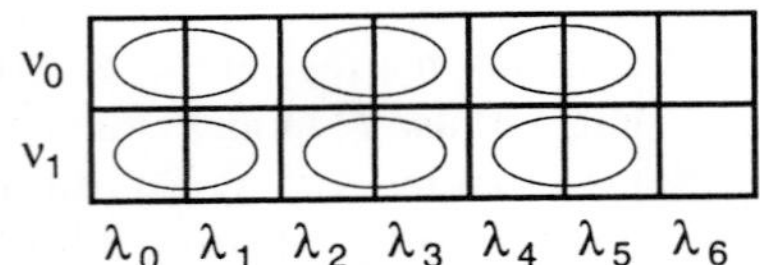

Figure 7. Example for the proof of Theorem 1

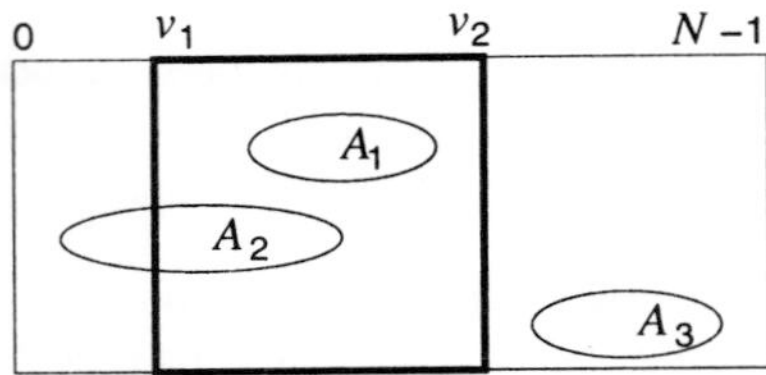

Figure 8. A restriction of an array.

all source aggregates have a size of at most 2. If N is even, all $2N$ elements of *Src* can be covered by $N = 2\lceil\frac{N}{2}\rceil$ non-trivial aggregates. For odd N, at least two of the entries must have trivial aggrgates (see Figure 7), giving a total of $2 + 2\left(\frac{N-1}{2}\right) = 2\lceil\frac{N}{2}\rceil$ aggregates (or lasers). ■

Definition 4 Let X be a source or destination array. For any $0 \le v_1 \le v_2 < N$, the $[v_1, v_2]$-*restriction* of X is the part of X consisting only of columns $v_1, v_1+1, \cdots, v_2$.

Figure 8 shows a $[v_1, v_2]$-restriction of an array. Let X be a source or destination array and let Y be a $[v_1, v_2]$-restriction of X. An aggregate of X that lies entirely within Y is called a *complete aggregate* of Y (for example, aggregate A_1 of Figure 8). An aggregate of X that lies partially within Y is called an *incomplete aggregate* of Y (for example, aggregate A_2 of Figure 8). An incomplete aggregate must cross at least one of the two borders (columns v_1 and v_2) of Y. If it crosses column v_1 (resp., column v_2), then it is called a v_1-incomplete aggregate (resp., v_2-incomplete aggregate); aggregate A_2 of Figure 8 is a v_1-incomplete aggregate.

Lemma 1 *For $d \ge 2$, $0 \le v_1 \le v_2 < N$, and a standard mapping of an N-processor, d-dimensional, weak torus, let S_{v_1,v_2} be a $[v_1, v_2]$-restriction of the array Src. Then,*

(a) *If S_{v_1,v_2} contains n_1 v_1-incomplete aggregates, then $n_1 \le 2$.*

(b) *If S_{v_1,v_2} contains n_2 v_2-incomplete aggregates, then $n_2 \le 2$.*

(c) *S_{v_1,v_2} contains at least $2(v_2 - v_1)(d-1) + 2d - (n_1 + n_2)$ complete aggregate.*

Proof: As observed earlier, all non-trivial aggregates of S_{v_1,v_2} are mode aggregates. If $v_1 = 0$, then S_{v_1,v_2} has no v_1-incomplete aggregate. If $v_1 \ge 1$, then it can be shown that there can be at most two non-trivial aggregates in the $[v_1 - 1, v_1]$-restriction of *Src*. This implies that S_{v_1,v_2} can have at most two v_1-incomplete aggregates. This establishes part (a) and a similar argument establishes part (b).

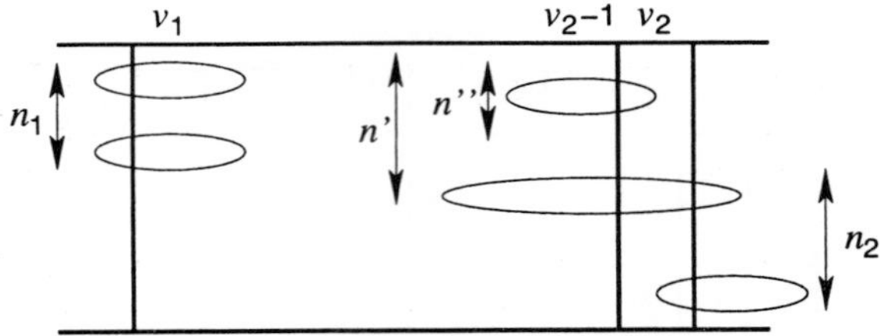

Figure 9. Illustration of the proof of Lemma 1.

For part (c) we proceed by induction on $v_2 - v_1$. Clearly, $0 \le v_2 - v_1 < N$. For $v_1 = v_2$, there is only one $2d$-element column in the restriction and at least $2d - (n_1 + n_2) = 2(v_2 - v_1)(d-1) + 2d - (n_1 + n_2)$ complete aggregates. Assuming part (c) to hold for any restriction of x columns (where $1 \le x < N$), consider the case where $v_2 - v_1 = x + 1 \ge 1$ (see Figure 9). Here $v_2 > v_1$.

With the induction hypothesis, let the $[v_1, v_2 - 1]$-restriction, S' of *Src* have n_1 v_1-incomplete aggregates, and n' $(v_2 - 1)$-incomplete aggregates. Therefore, S' has at least $2(v_2 - v_1 - 1)(d-1) + 2d - (n_1 + n')$ complete aggregates (that are also complete aggregates of S_{v_1,v_2}). Clearly, S_{v_1,v_2} has n_1 v_1-incomplete aggregates. Let it have n_2 v_2-incomplete aggregates. If any of the n' $(v_2 - 1)$-incomplete aggregates of S' does not become a complete aggregate of S_{v_1,v_2}, then it must also be a v_2-incomplete aggregate of S_{v_1,v_2}. Let $n'' \le n'$ of the $(v_2 - 1)$ incomplete aggregates of S' become complete aggregates of S_{v_1,v_2}. The $n' - n''$ incomplete aggregates of S_{v_1,v_2} are included in the n_2 v_2-aggregates of S_{v_1,v_2}. The number of complete aggregates in column v_2, not including the n'' mentioned above, is $2d - n_2 - n''$. So the total number of complete aggregates in S_{v_1,v_2} is $[2(v_2 - 1 - v_1)(d-1) + 2d - (n_1 + n')] + [n''] + [2d - n_2 - n'']$; the three terms represent the number of aggregates that are complete in S', incomplete in S', and those in column v_2, respectively. This quantity equals $2(v_2 - v_1)(d-1) + 2d - (n_1 + n_2) + (2 - n') \ge 2(v_2 - v_1)(d-1) + 2d - (n_1 + n_2)$, as $n' \le 2$ by part (b) of this lemma. ■

With $n_1 = n_2 = v_1 = 0$ and $v_2 = N - 1$ in Lemma 1, we have the following result.

Theorem 2 *For $d \ge 2$, a standard mapping of an N-processor, d-dimensional, weak torus, requires at least N detectors and at least $2N(d-1) + 2$ lasers.* ■

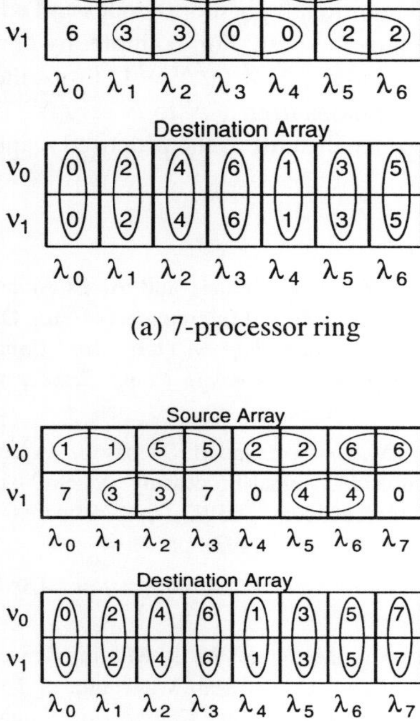

(a) 7-processor ring

(a) 8-processor ring

Figure 10. Mapping a ring.

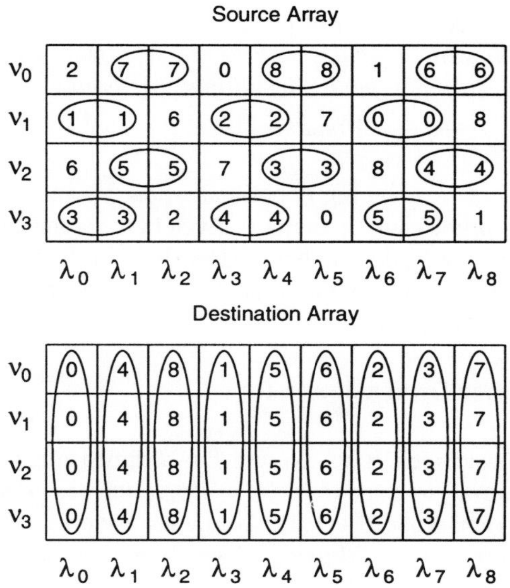

Figure 11. Mapping a 3×3 torus

5. Mappings for Multidimensional Tori

We now outline the mapping for a ring, 2-dimensional torus and multidimensional torus. We will specify the mapping by first assigning a processor index to each column of the array *Dst*; recall that in a standard mapping, each column of *Dst* forms a wavelength aggregate. Then we will specify element *Src*(u, v) by specifying which neighbor of *Dst*(u, v) it is.

5.1. 1-Dimensional Torus (Ring)

Figure 10 shows the tiling of aggregates in the *Src* and *Dst* arrays for rings with 7 and 8 processors.

Theorem 3 *An N-processor ring can be mapped on a slab with 2 modes and N wavelengths using N detectors (without mode demultiplexing hardware) and $N+2$ (resp., $N+1$) tunable lasers, if N is even (resp., odd).* ■

Remark: This mapping is optimal for odd N and within 2 of the optimal for even N.

5.2. 2-Dimensional Torus

Number the processors of the torus from 0 to $N-1$ in row major order (as in Figure 1(b)). For any processor i in row r and column c of the torus, its neighbors are defined by the functions f_0, f_1, f_2, f_3 as follows. Processor $f_0(i)$ is the left neighbor of i in row r and column $(c-1)(\text{mod } N_1)$ (consistent with the wraparound connections of the torus). Similarly, $f_1(i)$, $f_2(i)$ and $f_3(i)$ are the neighbors of i to its right, top and bottom, respectively. Figures 6 and 11 show the *Src* and *Dst* arrays for mapping 3×4 and 3×3 tori.

Let $I_N = \{0, 1, \cdots, N-1\}$. Consider the the function $\Delta : I_N \longrightarrow I_N$ described by the procedure below. Initialize $\Delta(0) \longleftarrow 0$. Proceed as described below until $\Delta(i)$ has been assigned for all indices $i \in I_N$. Let the procedure have just assigned $\Delta(j) \longleftarrow v$. Let k be the processor that is diagonally to the bottom-right of j (consistent with the wraparound connections of the torus). That is, $k = f_3(f_1(j))$. If $\Delta(k)$ has not yet been assigned, then set $\Delta(k) \longleftarrow v+1$; otherwise, pick the smallest ℓ such that $\Delta(\ell)$ has not been assigned and set $\Delta(\ell) \longleftarrow v+1$.

The function Δ is a permutation of the set I_N and, therefore, it partitions I_N into cycles. For positive integers a, b, let $\ell cm(a, b)$ denote their lowest common multiple. It can be shown that Δ partitions I_N into $\frac{N}{\ell cm(N_0, N_1)}$ cycles, each of size $\ell cm(N_0, N_1)$. This quantity will impact the cost of the mapping.

Columns v of *Dst* is assigned processor index i iff $\Delta(i) = v$. Let *Dst*$(u, v) = i$. If v is odd, then *Src*$(u, v) = f_{3-u}(i)$; if v is even, then *Src*$(u, v) = f_u(i)$. Each of the $\frac{N}{\ell cm(N_0, N_1)}$ cycles of Δ induces the pattern of aggregates shown in Figure 6 for the 3×4 torus.

Theorem 4 *An N-processor, $N_0 \times N_1$ torus can be mapped on a slab with 4 modes and N wavelengths using N detectors (without mode demultiplexing hardware) and $2N\left(1 + \frac{1}{\ell cm(N_0,N_1)}\right)$ tunable lasers.* ■

Remark: This mapping is optimal when N_0 and N_1 are relatively prime (see Theorem 2). Even in the worst case of $N_0 = N_1 = \sqrt{N}$, the number of lasers is $2N + 2\sqrt{N}$ which can be substantially smaller than $4N$, the number required with a naive mapping.

5.3. Higher Dimensional Tori

The basic idea is to express the d-dimensional torus (where $d > 2$) as a set of $N_2 N_3 \cdots N_{d-1}$ tori (each of size $N_0 \times N_1$) and proceed as in the 2-dimensional case. The *Src* and *Dst* arrays have $2d$ rows, of which only the first 4 are assigned as in the 2-dimensional case. This also specifies the entries of *Dst*. The remaining $2d - 4$ rows of *Src* are assigned arbitrarily.

Theorem 5 *For $d \geq 2$, an N-processor, $N_0 \times N_1 \cdots N_{d-1}$ torus can be mapped on a slab with $2d$ modes and N wavelengths using N detectors (without mode demultiplexing hardware) and at most $2N\left(d - 1 + \frac{1}{L}\right)$ tunable lasers, where $L = \max\{\ell cm(N_i, N_j) \ : \ 0 \leq i < j < N\}$.* ■

Remark: This mapping exceeds the lower bound of Theorem 2 by $\frac{2N}{L} - 2$. Since $L \geq \max\{N_i \ : \ 0 \leq i < d\} \geq N^{\frac{1}{d}}$, the deviation from the optimal is $\leq 2\left(N^{1-\frac{1}{d}} - 1\right) < 2(N(d+1) - 1)$, the deviation for a naive mapping.

6. Concluding Remarks

In this paper we have addressed the problem of bridging the gap between the system and medium bandwidths of optical interconnects. Specifically, our results are for mapping weak tori on slab waveguides. We have proposed the idea of aggregates to capture the cost of our mapping and derived a non-trivial lower bound on this cost. We have presented methods that are all less expensive than a naive mapping and some of which match the lower bound.

All the results of this paper have dual results in which *Src* and *Dst* are interchanged and/or modes and wavelengths are interchanged. For example, a standard mapping can also be viewed as one with N fixed-wavelength lasers and detectors that span across wavelengths at a fixed mode.

The standard mappings we have proposed always use N wavelengths and $2d$ modes. This somewhat restricts the choices available for the system designer. It is possible to use our results to trade modes off for wavelengths and vice versa (in many cases without any additional cost) [4].

This work opens up several possible directions of future research, including "non-standard mappings" and the introduction of additional (phantom) nodes and edges to the topology to reduce the cost. For example, by converting a $\sqrt{N} \times \sqrt{N}$ torus to a $\sqrt{N} \times (\sqrt{N} + 1)$ torus, the value of $\ell cm(N_0, N_1)$ increases from $\sqrt{N}$ to $N + \sqrt{N}$. This could substantially reduce the cost of the proposed mapping.

References

[1] M. Feldman, R. Vaidyanathan, and A. El-Amawy, "High Speed, High Capacity Bused Interconnects Using Optical Slab Waveguides," *Proc. Workshop on Optics and Comp. Science (Springer-Verlag Lecture Notes in Comp. Science vol. 1586)*, (1999), pp. 924–937.

[2] H. Forsberg, M. Jonsson, and B. Svensson, "A Scalable and Pipelined Embedded Signal Processing System Using Optical Hypercube Interconnects," *SPIE Opt. Networks Magazine*, vol. 4, no. 4, (July/August 2003), pp. 35–49.

[3] G. R. Fowles, *Introduction to Modern Optics*, Dover Publications, 2nd edition, 1989.

[4] K. Sethuraman "Mapping Weak Multidimensional Torus Communications on Opical Slab Waveguides," M.S. Thesis, Dept. of Electrical & Computer Engineering, Louisiana State University, (2005).

[5] E. Mohammed *et al.*, "Optical Interconnect System Integration for Ultra-Short-Reach Applications," *Intel Tech. J.*, vol. 8, issue 2, (May 2004), pp. 115–128.

[6] K. Noguchi, Y. Koike, H. Tanobe, K. Harada, and M. Matsuoka, "Field Trial of Full-Mesh WDM Network (AWG-STAR) in Metropolitan/Local Area," *J. Lightwave Tech.*, vol. 22, no. 2, (February 2004), pp. 329–336.

[7] C. G. Plaxton, "Load Balancing, Selection and Sorting on the Hypercube," *Proc. Symp. on Parallel Algs. and Arch.*, (1989), pp. 64–73.

[8] M. Raksapatcharawong and T. M. Pinkston, "Modeling Free-Space Optical k-ary n-Cube Wormhole Networks," *J. Parallel and Distrib. Comput.*, vol. 55(1), (1998), pp. 60–93.

[9] K. J. Symington, J. F. Snowdon, and H. Schroeder, "High Bandwidth Dynamically Reconfigurable Architectures using Optical Interconnects," *Proc. Int. Workshop on Field-Programmable Logic and Appls. (Springer-Verlag Lecture Notes in Comp. Science vol. 1673)*, (1999), pp. 411–416.

[10] R. Vaidyanathan and A. Padmanabhan, "Bus-Based Networks for Fan-in and Uniform Hypercube Algorithms," *Par. Comput.*, vol. 21, (1995), pp. 1807–1821.

[11] R. Vaidyanathan and J. L. Trahan, *Dynamic Reconfiguration: Architectures and Algorithms*, Kluwer Academic/Plenum Publishers (Series in Computer Science), January 2004.

[12] I. A. Young, "Introducing Intel's Chip-to-Chip Optical I/O Technology," *Technology@Intel Magazine*, (April 2004), www.intel.com/update/departments/initech/ito4o41.pdf.

Keynote Address 2

Session 4A: Shared-Memory Computing

Performance Evaluation of the SGI Altix 3700

Thomas H. Dunigan, Jr. Jeffrey S. Vetter Patrick H. Worley

Oak Ridge National Laboratory
Oak Ridge, TN, USA 37831
{dunigan,vetterjs,worleyph}@ornl.gov

Abstract

SGI recently introduced the Altix 3700. In contrast to previous SGI systems, the Altix uses a modified version of the open source Linux operating system and the latest Intel IA-64 processors, the Intel Itanium2. The Altix also uses the next generation SGI interconnect, Numalink3 and NUMAflex, which provides a NUMA, cache-coherent, shared memory, multi-processor system. In this paper, we present a performance evaluation of the SGI Altix using microbenchmarks, kernels, and mission applications. We find that the Altix provides many advantages over other non-vector machines and it is competitive with the Cray X1 on a number of kernels and applications. The Altix also shows good scaling, and its globally shared memory allows users convenient parallelization with OpenMP or pthreads.

1 Introduction

Computational requirements for many large-scale simulations and ensemble studies of vital interest to the Department of Energy (DOE) exceed what is currently offered by any U.S. computer vendor. As illustrated in the DOE Scales report [9] and the High End Computing Revitalization Task Force report [3], examples are numerous, ranging from global climate change research to combustion to biology.

IBM, HP, and an array of cluster vendors have dominated recent HPC procurements in the US. Their HPC systems are clusters of 2 to 32 processor SMP nodes connected with a high speed interconnect where applications use MPI to communicate between the SMP nodes. Both Cray and SGI have recently introduced systems that compare favorably with these clusters, and both Cray and SGI have a number of unique characteristics that are attractive for certain classes of applications. For example, both systems support globally shared memory where any processor can access any memory location in the global address space.

The SGI Altix system is a large shared memory system. Initial offerings were as large as 256 processors, and plans are for it to scale into the 1000s of processors. In contrast to previous SGI systems, the Altix uses a modified version of the open source Linux operating system and the latest Intel IA-64 processor, the Itanium2. The Altix also uses the next generation SGI interconnect, the NUMAlink3, which is the natural evolution of the highly successful interconnect used in previous generation SGI systems. For SGI, the Altix is a combination of traditional strengths (large SMP nodes and fast interconnects) and risk (new processors and new operating system).

This report describes the initial evaluation results collected on an SGI Altix system sited at ORNL. Results are also publicly available from the ORNL evaluation web site [7].

2 Evaluation Overview

The primary tasks of the evaluation project are to 1) determine the most effective approaches for using the SGI Altix, 2) evaluate benchmark and application performance, and compare with similar systems from other vendors, and 3) predict scalability, both in terms of problem size and in number of processors.

We employ a hierarchical approach to the evaluation, examining low-level functionality of the system first, then using these results to guide and understand the evaluation using kernels and compact or full application codes.

Standard benchmarks are used as appropriate to ensure meaningful comparisons with other system evaluations; however, the emphasis of our evaluation is studies of a number of different important DOE applications, as noted below.

The distinction here is that the low-level benchmarks, for example, message passing, and the kernel benchmarks are chosen to model important features of a full application. This is important in order

U.S. Government Work Not Protected by U.S. Copyright

to understand application performance and to predict scalability.

3 SGI Altix 3700 Overview

The initial offering of SGI Altix is a shared memory system made up of 2 processor nodes interconnected with the first implementation of the SN2 "scalable node architecture". This architecture supports 64 TB of addressable memory. At introduction, the SGI modification of Linux supported a single system image on up to 64 processors, but this increased to 256 processors during the course of the ORNL evaluation. Multiple Linux kernels reside in a Coherent Sharing Domain (CSD), which provides cache coherence for up to 512 processors. Multiple CSDs can reside within a single system, with the NUMAlink layer of SN2 providing high bandwidth and low latency communication within and between CSDs. Optimized communication libraries provide coherent access both within and between partitions defined by the OS images.

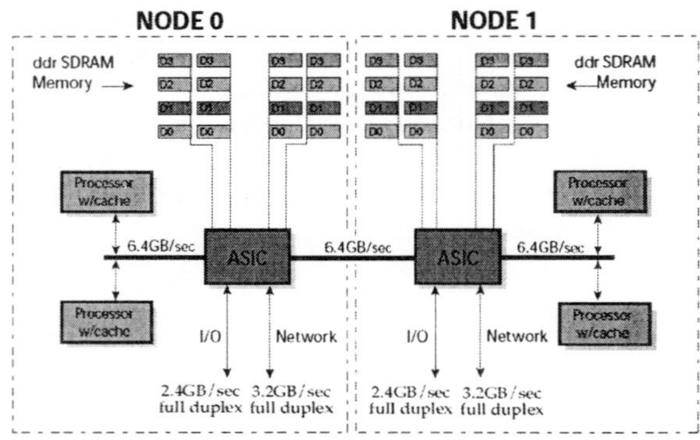

Figure 1: SGI Altix C-brick. *(Image courtesy of SGI.)*

Unlike commodity Linux clusters, SGI's cache-coherent, shared memory, multi-processor system is based on NUMAflex, a non-uniform memory access (NUMA) architecture, which has proven to be a highly-scalable, global shared memory architecture in SGI's Origin 3000 systems. In fact, the Altix 3000 uses many of the same components — called *bricks* — as the Origin. These bricks mount in racks and may be composed in various combinations to construct a system balanced for a specific workload. SGI offers several different types of bricks; Table 1 lists these bricks.

The Altix C-brick (Figure 1) consists of two nodes, each containing two Intel Itanium 2 processors with their own cache. These Altix C-bricks are different from those in the Origin because the Origin C-bricks contain MIPS processors, while the Altix C-bricks contain Itaniums. Custom ASICs -- called SHUBs – connect to the front-side buses of these processors. The SHUBs link the two processors to the memory DIMMs, to the I/O subsystem, and to other SHUBs via the NUMAflex interconnect. The SHUBs also interconnect the two nodes in a C-brick at the full bandwidth of the Itanium 2 front side bus (6.4 GB/sec).

Table 1: SGI Alix brick types.

Brick Type	Purpose
C-Brick	computational module housing CPUs and memory
M-Brick	Memory expansion module
R-Brick	NUMAflex router interconnect module
D-Brick	Disk expansion module
IX-Brick	Base system I/O module
PX-Brick	PCI-X expansion module

The global shared memory architecture, implemented through SGI's NUMAlink interconnect fabric, provides high cross-sectional bandwidth and allows performance scaling not usually obtained on commodity Linux clusters. While some coarse-grained applications scale well on Linux clusters, others need the high bandwidth and very low latency offered by a machine like the Altix. Still, users often feel that their applications are best implemented as shared-memory applications with OpenMP or pthreads using many processors.

Table 2: System configurations.

	SGI Altix	Alpha SC	IBM SP3	IBM SP4	Cray X1
Name	Ram	LeMieux	Eagle	Cheetah	Phoenix
Proc	Itanium 2	Alpha EV67	POWER3-II	POWER4	Cray X1
Interconnect	Numalink	Quadrics	Colony	Colony	Cray X1
MHz	1500	667	375	1300	800
Mem/Node	512GB	2GB	2GB	32GB	16GB
L1	32K	64K	64K	32K	16K (scalar)
L2	256K	8MB	8MB	1.5MB	2MB (per MSP)
L3	6MB	n/a	n/a	128MB	n/a
Proc Peak Mflops	6000	1334	1500	5200	12800
Peak mem BW	6.4 GB/s	5.2GB/s	1.6GB/s	51 GB/s/MCM	26 GB/s/MSP

The Altix shipped with a version of the Intel Madison Itanium2 processor running at 1.3 GHz. It was later upgraded with processors with a larger L3 cache and a clock rate of 1.5 GHz. This latter Itanium has 3 levels of cache: 32 KB L1 (1 clock latency), 256 KB L2 (5 clock latency), and 6 MB L3 (14 clock latency). The L3 cache can sustain 48 GB/sec bandwidth to/from the processor. The memory system utilizes commodity DDR SDRAM DIMMs, achieving 10+ GB/sec bandwidth per node. The interconnect topology is a dual plane, quad bristled fat tree, capable of 800 MB/sec per processor in a bisection bandwidth test for up to 32 processors, and 400 MB/sec per processor for more than 32 processors. Additional configuration and operational information is available at [6].

ORNL purchased a 256 processor Altix system with a total of 2 terabytes of shared memory, 12 TB of fiber channel attached disks, and a single system image (SSI) software needed to support 256 processors. The processors are 1.5 GHz Intel Madison Itanium2 processors with 6 MB of cache per processor. Initially, the system was configured to run 4 partitions of the Linux operating system. However, after working closely with SGI, the Altix is currently running a 256 processor single system image. Single applications run on all 256 processors using the NUMAlink interconnect for interprocessor communications between the multiple segments of the system.

This evaluation also includes comparisons to other systems examined by CCS. Table 2 and Table 3 outline these system configurations. Interested readers can find more information about these platforms at the CCS website [6].

Table 3: Experiment configurations.

Mnemonic	System	Programming model
X1-mpi	Cray X1 (Phoenix)	MPI
X1-ca	Cray X1 (Phoenix)	CoArray Fortran
Altix-mpi	SGI Altix (RAM)	MPI
Altix-omp	SGI Altix (RAM)	OpenMP
p690-mpi	IBM p690 (Cheetah)	MPI
p690-omp	IBM p690 (Cheetah)	OpenMP

4 Microbenchmarks

The objective of microbenchmarking is to characterize the performance of the underlying architectural components of the SGI Altix. Both standard benchmarks and customized benchmarks are used. The standard benchmarks allow component performance to be compared with other computer architectures. The custom benchmarks permit the unique architectural features of the Altix (e.g., large shared memory system utilizing Intel processors) to be tested with respect to the target applications. The architectural-component evaluation assesses the following:

- Arithmetic performance, including varying instruction mix.
- Memory-hierarchy performance, including three levels of cache and shared memory. These tests utilize both System V shared memory and the SHMEM primitives.
- Task and thread performance, including performance of thread creation, locks, semaphores, and barriers.
- Message-passing performance, including intra-node, inter-node, intra-OS image, and inter-OS image MPI performance of point-to-point and collective communication.
- OS and I/O performance.

Detailed microbenchmark data are available from [7]. For example, we used the EuroBen benchmark to evaluate hardware performance of add, multiply, divide, and square root, and the performance of the software intrinsics (exponentials, trigonometric functions, and logarithms). Other tests demonstrate how vector length and stride, compiler optimizations, and vendor scientific libraries affect performance. Figure 2 is a FORTRAN 1-D FFT from Euroben benchmarks. For this benchmark the Altix processor outperforms that of the IBM p690 and the Cray X1 for small to medium sized vectors.

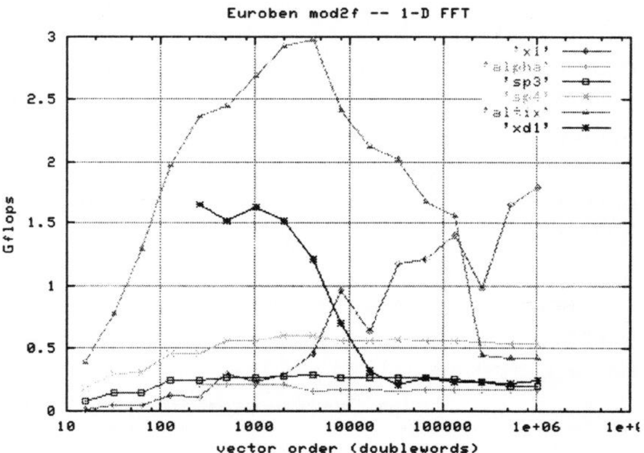

Figure 2: Euroben mod2f benchmark for 1-D FFT.

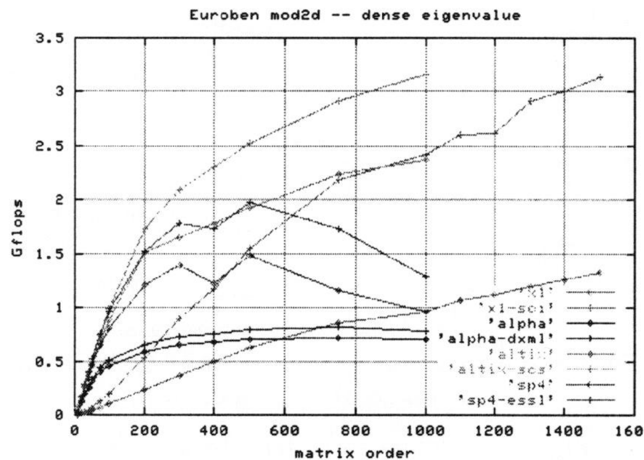

Figure 3: EuroBen mod2b benchmark for dense linear systems.

Our results also show that the Altix performs well on both sparse eigenvalue kernels and dense linear algebra kernels, achieving over 90% of peak for a matrix-matrix multiply (DGEMM). Figure 3 compares the performance of vendor math libraries for solving a dense linear system, demonstrating that the Altix is better than the IBM p690 and the Cray X1 for the middle range of matrix sizes.

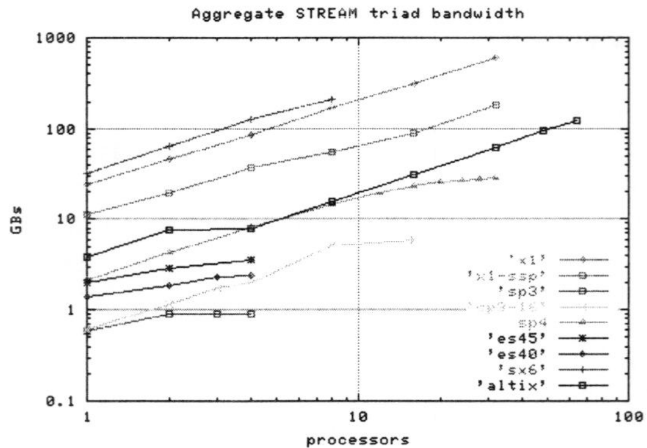

Figure 4: Aggregate STREAM triad bandwidth.

The STREAMS and MAPS benchmarks show the high memory bandwidth the Altix achieves, and Figure 4 shows how the memory performance scales with the number of processors. (See [5].)

Our communication tests include the standard benchmarks (ParkBench and Euroben-dm) to measure latency and bandwidth as a function of message size and distance, as well as custom benchmarks that reflect common communication patterns. The Altix MPI latency is only 1.1 microseconds (us) compared to 7 us on the Cray X1 and IBM p690 (Federation).

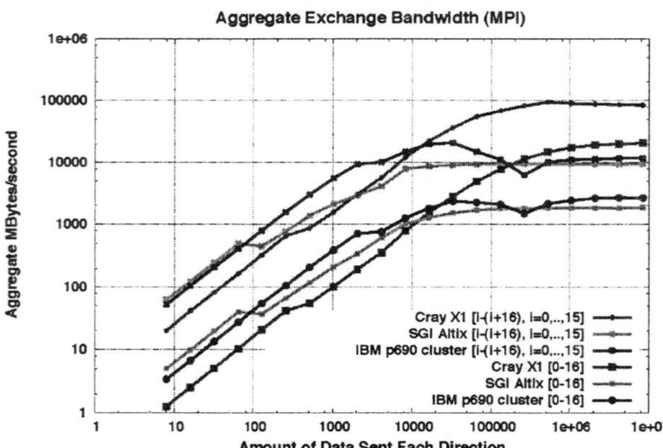

Figure 5: Aggregate Exchange Bandwidth (MPI) for distance of 16 processors.

Figure 5 compares the bandwidth when 2 processors a distance of 16 apart are exchanging messages using MPI and when 32 processors (16 pairs) are exchanging messages across the same distance. Figure 6 compares the bandwidth when 2 processors a distance of 64 apart are exchanging messages using MPI and when 128 processors (64 pairs) are exchanging messages. Note that on the IBM p690 cluster the first experiment is limited to processors in the same p690 shared memory node, while the second experiment requires communication across the HPS switch. Within the SMP node, the achieved IBM bandwidth is at least as good as that on the Altix.

In contrast, the Altix achieves much better aggregate bandwidth than the IBM when the IBM must communicate between p690s. While the Cray X1 achieves the best aggregate bandwidth for large messages, it reaches the same maximum for the two experiments, approximately 90 GBytes/sec. In contrast, the aggregate SGI bandwidth is still rising, achieving approximately 50% of the maximum X1 bandwidth in the second experiment. For small messages, the Altix achieves the best performance among the three systems.

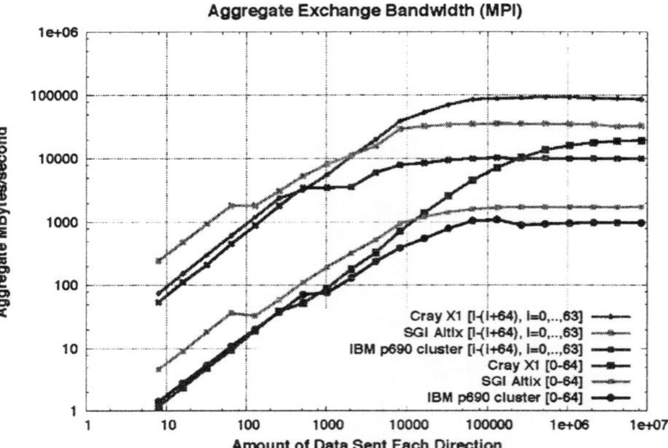

Figure 6: Aggregate Exchange Bandwidth (MPI) for distance of 64 processors.

Figure 7 and Figure 8 examine MPI communication performance as a function of physical distance between communicating processes. Except where noted, the cache is not invalidated before taking measurements. For small messages there is a performance advantage to communicating between physically neighboring processors, especially if in the same node. However, there is little performance sensitivity for larger distances.

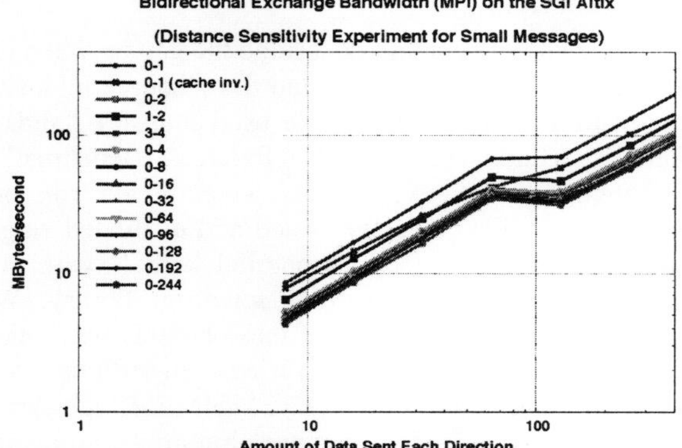

Figure 7: Distance sensitivity for small messages.

In contrast, exchanging large messages between processors in the same 2-processor node is more expensive than when exchanging between processors not in the same node. This effect shows up sooner with cache invalidation than without. Exchanging large messages between processors in the same C-brick, but not in the same node, shows the highest performance. As with small messages, large message performance is relatively insensitive (<20%) to distance once the separation is greater than 4. Experiments with cache invalidation show similar behavior, except as noted above.

Figure 9 and Figure 10 examine the same issue for simultaneous exchange. Unlike Figure 6, the metric here is bandwidth per process pair, not aggregate bandwidth. For small messages there is again little performance sensitivity to distances greater than 4, and performance degradation compared to the distance experiments is <20%. For large messages contention does occur, with the performance observed by a single pair halved for 4 simultaneous exchanges, and reduced to 25% of the former bandwidth for 32 simultaneous exchanges. Note, however, that the aggregate bandwidth continues to increase, especially as the number of pairs (and the distance) increases.

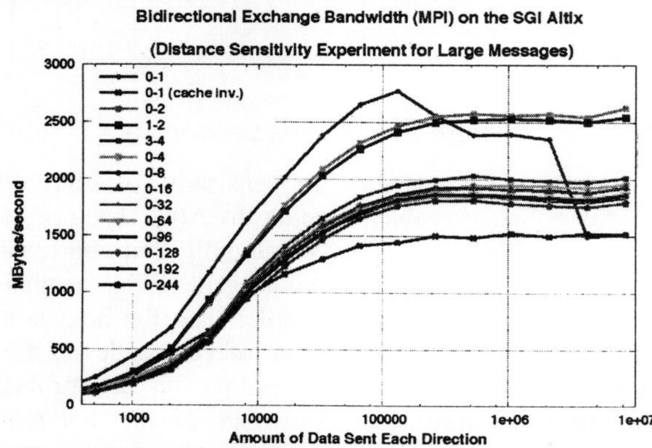

Figure 8: Distance Sensitivity for large messages.

Similar results hold when using SHMEM to implement the exchange instead of MPI. For small messages SHMEM performance is twice that of MPI, but sensitivity to distance and contention are qualitatively the same. For large messages SHMEM and MPI performance are nearly identical when the cache is invalidated first. However, without cache invalidation SHMEM performance is significantly better than MPI performance for all but the largest message sizes.

The exchange experiments were also used to determine the most efficient MPI communication protocol to use for an exchange. When enabling the SGI single copy MPI optimizations, which are automatically used with MPI_SENDRECV, protocols using MPI_ISEND and MPI_RECV are the most efficient, but MPI_SENDRECV is typically one of the better performers.

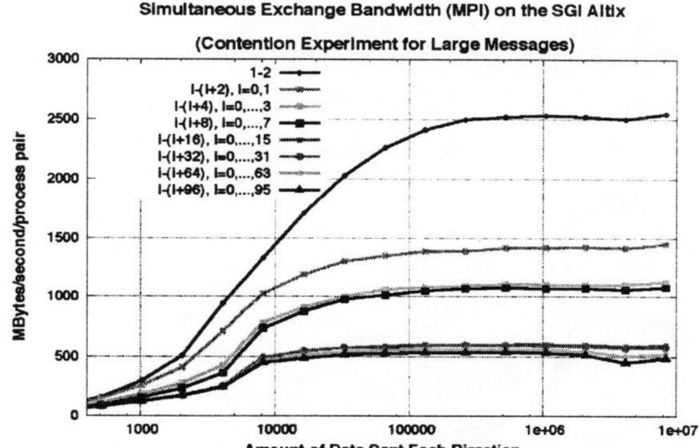

Figure 9: Contention for large messages.

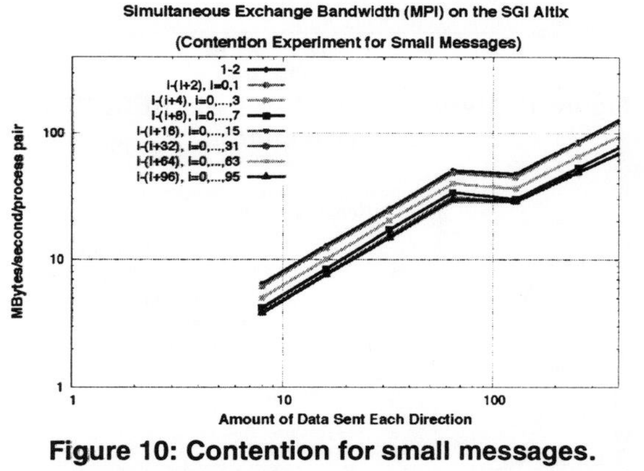

Figure 10: Contention for small messages.

When applications are scaled to larger processor counts or larger problems sizes, the ALLTOALLV and ALLREDUCE communication collectives are often the source of performance problems. The performance observed in the exchange experiments provides some information on the performance of the MPI_ALLTOALL collective.

Figure 11, Figure 12, and Figure 13 compare best-observed ("optimal") MPI_ALLREDUCE performance across a number of platforms for each of the three vector lengths. The Altix has the best MPI_ALLREDUCE for short vectors, but the Cray X1 has better performance for long vectors.

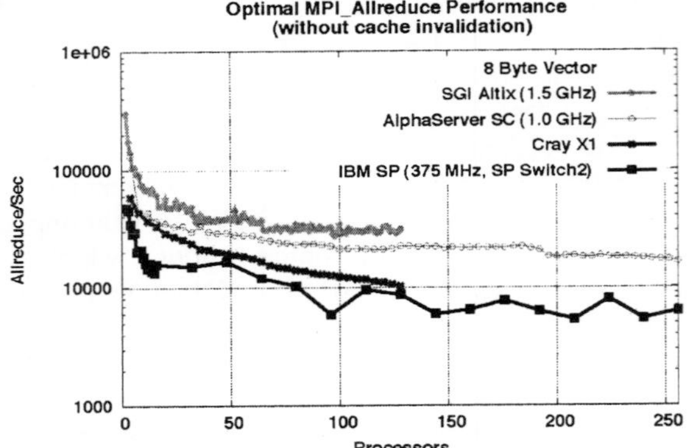

Figure 11: Performance of MPI_ALLREDUCE (8B) across platforms.

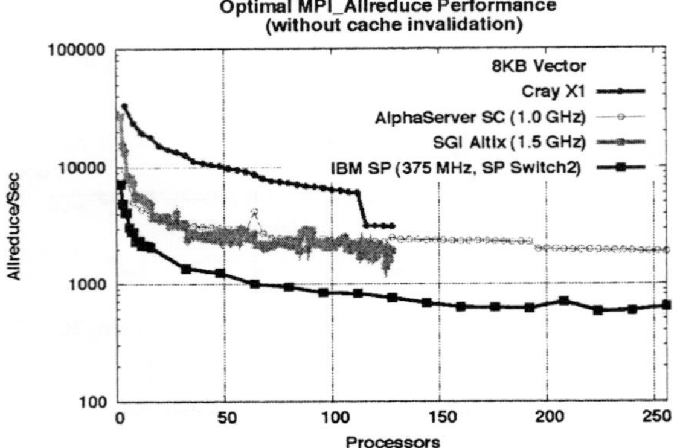

Figure 12: Performance of MPI_ALLREDUCE (8KB) across platforms.

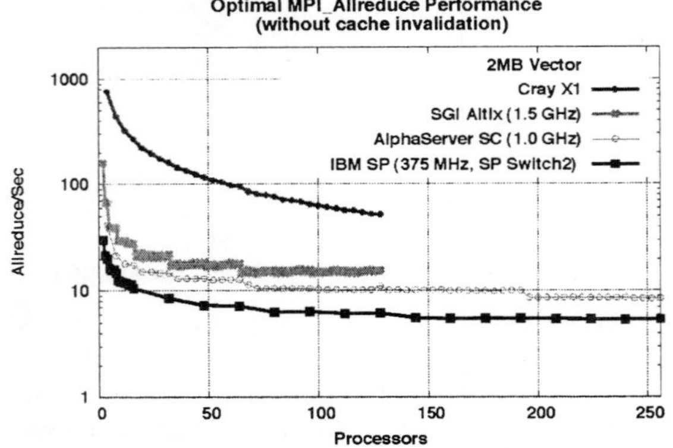

Figure 13: Performance of MPI_ALLREDUCE (2MB) across platforms.

5 Kernels

The kernel benchmarks bridge the gap between the low-level microbenchmarks and the resource intensive application benchmarking. We used industry-standard kernels (ParkBench, NAS Parallel Benchmarks, Euroben) as well as kernels that we extracted from our scientific applications. We tested and evaluated single processor performance and parallel kernels with and without the vendor's parallel scientific library. We compared the performance of these kernels with other architectures and have varied algorithms and programming paradigms (MPI, SHMEM, Co-Array Fortran, OpenMP). For example, Figure 14 compares the performance of the NAS multi-grid benchmark with various processor counts, architectures, and communication strategies.

We used a kernel representative of the dynamics algorithm found in the atmospheric component of the Community Climate System Model (CCSM) [1], the primary model for global climate simulation in the U.S. This kernel, the parallel spectral transform shallow water model (PSTSWM), supports different problem sizes, algorithms, and programming paradigms, and has been optimized on many parallel computer architectures. On the Altix we used PSTSWM to analyze compiler optimizations, evaluate math libraries, evaluate performance of the memory subsystem, compare programming paradigms, and compare performance with other supercomputers.

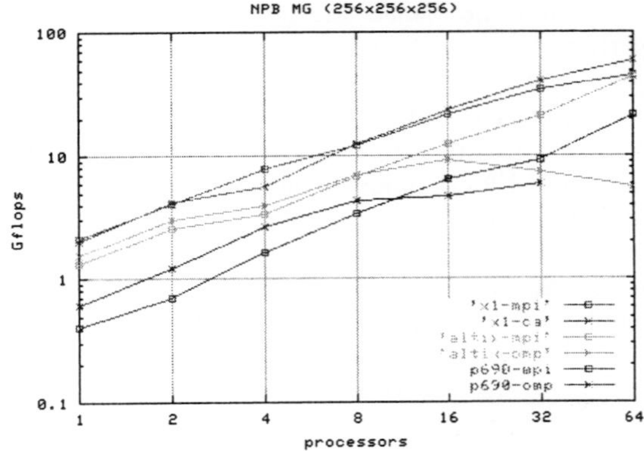

Figure 14: NPB MG benchmark.

Figure 15 describes the sensitivity of PSTSWM performance to problem size on the Altix. The problem sizes T5, T10, T21, T42, T85, and T170 are horizontal resolutions. Each computational grid in this sequence is approximately 4 times smaller than the next larger size. The X-axis is the number of vertical levels for a given horizontal resolution. Most of the problem coupling is in one or the other of the horizontal directions, and the vertical dimension simply controls the cache locality of certain phases of the computation. As the number of vertical levels increase, performance for the 4 largest problem sizes converges, slowly decreasing as the number of levels continues to increase. The performance curves look very similar to memory bandwidth curves used to illuminate the memory hierarchy, and we assume that the memory hierarchy is what is controlling the performance degradation as the number of vertical levels increases.

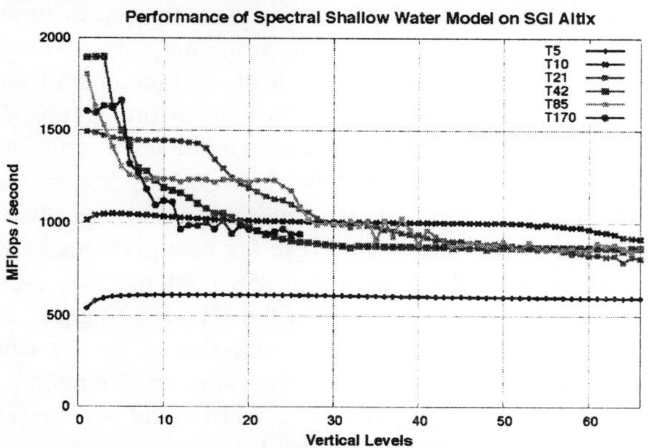

Figure 15: Sensitivity of PSTSWM performance to problem size on SGI Altix.

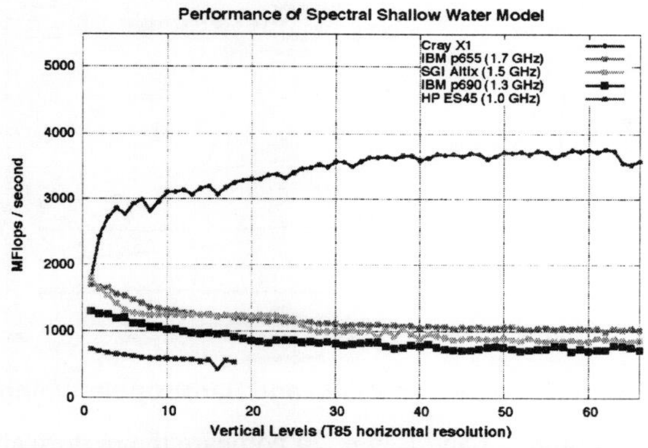

Figure 16: Performance of PSTSWM T85 across platforms.

Figure 16 compares the performance for the T85 problem on a number of HPC systems. These data show the advantage of the memory subsystem of the Cray X1 over that in the nonvector systems. However, the Altix performance holds its own compared to the other nonvector systems. These results are all for a single processor.

Figure 17 compares the performance for the different horizontal resolutions with 18 vertical levels when run on 1, 2, 4, ..., 128 consecutive processors simultaneously. Performance is identical when using 1 or 2 processors, or when using 32 processors when only every fourth processor is used. However, if all four processors in a C-brick are used, then there is contention for memory bandwidth and performance degrades for the larger problem sizes. This is the only situation where contention occurs, and performance does not continue to degrade as more processors are used.

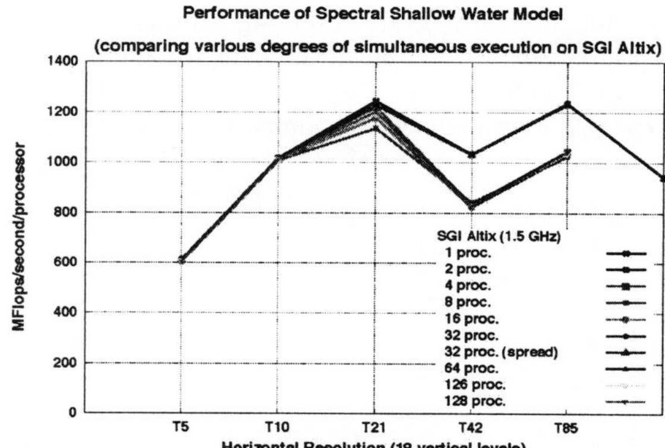

Figure 17: PSTSWM performance for different horizontal resolutions.

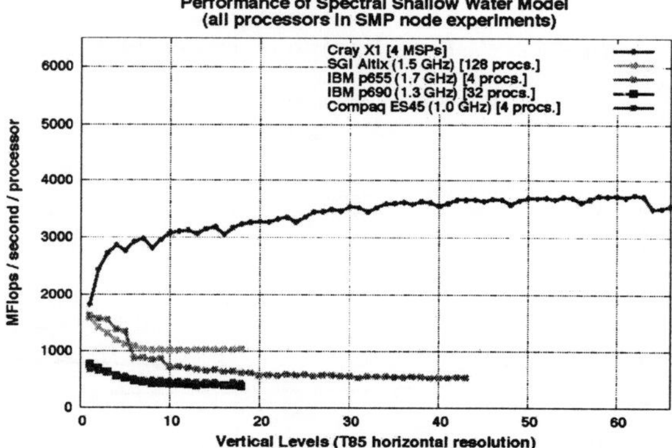

Figure 18: Effects of SMP node contention on PSTSWM.

Figure 18 compares the impact of contention when using all processors in an SMP node for problem T85 as the number of vertical levels increase. (For the Altix, data was collected on 128 consecutive processors in the larger system.) The Altix shows the least amount of performance degradation among the non-vector systems, indicating that the SGI memory subsystem scales very well for this type of memory contention benchmark.

6 Applications

Two aspects of application benchmarking are emphasized in these preliminary results, identifying peak achievable performance and inter-platform comparisons.

6.1 Climate – POP

The Parallel Ocean Program (POP) is an ocean modeling code developed at Los Alamos National Laboratory to take advantage of high-performance computer architectures. POP is used on a wide variety of computers for eddy-resolving simulations of the world oceans [4, 8] and for climate simulations as the ocean component of coupled climate models. For example, POP is the ocean component of CCSM [1].

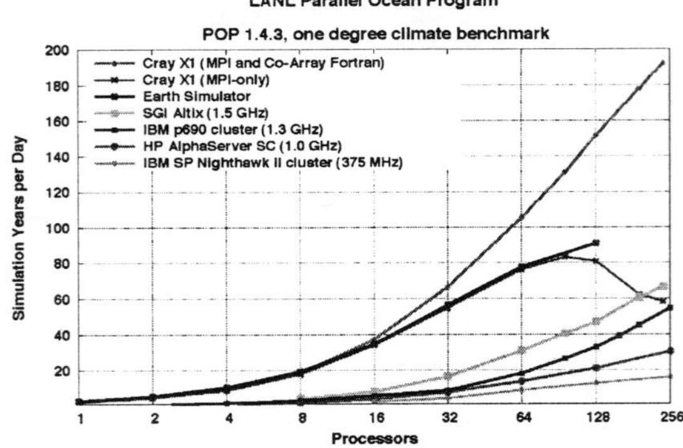

Figure 22: POP performance across platforms.

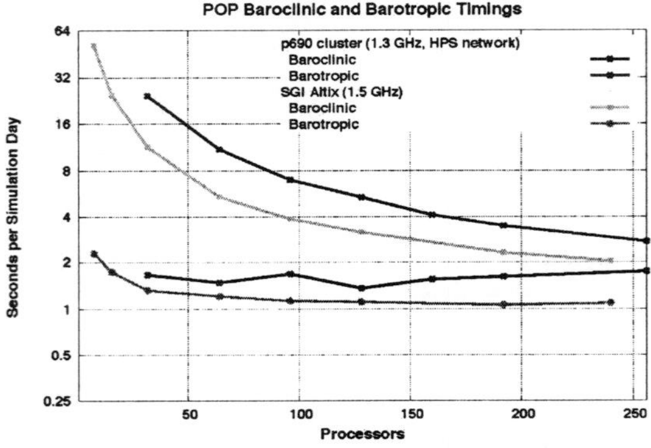

Figure 23: POP baroclinic and barotropic timings.

POP has proven to be a valuable tool for evaluating the scalability of HPC systems. It is comprised of two computational kernels, the baroclinic and the barotropic. POP parallelization is based on a two dimensional decomposition of the horizontal grid (leaving the vertical dimension undecomposed). Communication is required to update halo regions and to compute inner products in a conjugate gradient linear solver. The baroclinic phase scales very well on most platforms, with computation dominating communication until the processor count becomes large. In contrast the barotropic is dominated by a slowly converging iterative solution of a linear system used to solve a 2D elliptic problem. The linear system is solved using a conjugate gradient method, which requires halo updates to compute residuals and global reductions to compute inner products. The barotropic is very sensitive to communication latency, and the best that can be hoped is that the time spent in the barotropic does not grow with processor count for large processor counts.

Figure 22 compares the performance of POP for a relatively small benchmark using a computational grid with a one-degree horizontal resolution. This problem size is the same as used in current coupled climate model simulations. POP has been vectorized to run on the Cray X1 and the Earth Simulator, and different versions of the code were run on the vector and non-vector systems to produce the data in this figure. On the Altix, optimizations included empirical determination of optimal domain decompositions and tuning of certain of the communication protocols. While the vector systems were the best performers, the Altix showed the best performance of the non-vector systems and achieved 30% of the X1 performance. The Altix performance was better than that of the X1 when the X1 used only MPI. (An alternative implementation of POP using SHMEM instead of MPI did not improve POP performance on the Altix.)

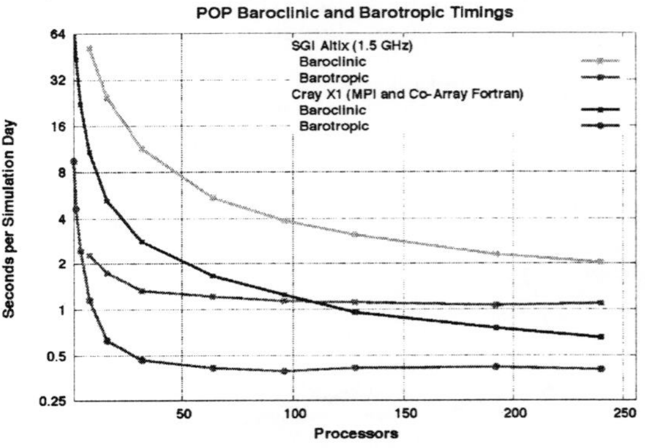

Figure 24: POP baroclinic and barotropoic timings.

Figure 23 and Figure 24 compare the performance of the Altix on the baroclinic and barotropic phases with that of the IBM p690 cluster and the Cray X1, respectively. The Altix has a 50-100% advantage over the IBM system in the computation-bound baroclinic phase, and the barotropic phase scales better on the Altix than on the p690 cluster. This benchmark is computation bound on both systems out to 248 processors. The Altix is 3 times slower than the X1 on both the baroclinic and the barotropic at 248 processors, but is scaling equally well on both.

6.2 Fusion – GYRO

GYRO is an Eulerian gyrokinetic-Maxwell solver developed by R.E. Waltz and J. Candy at General Atomics [2]. It is used to study plasma microturbulence in fusion research. GYRO uses the MPI_ALLTOALL command to transpose the distributed data structures and is more sensitive to bandwidth than to latency for large problem sizes.

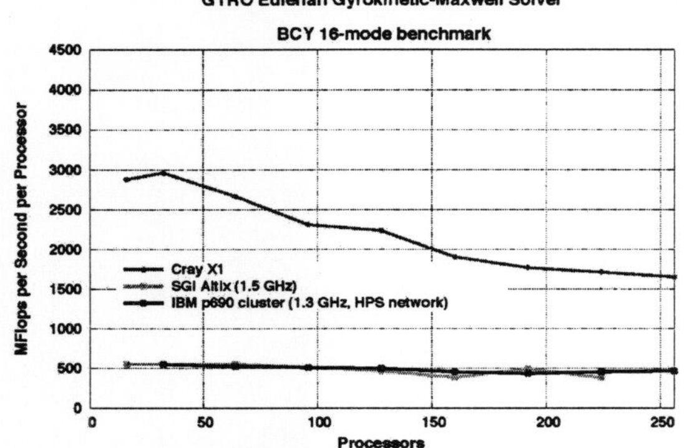

Figure 25: GYRO 16-mode performance across platforms.

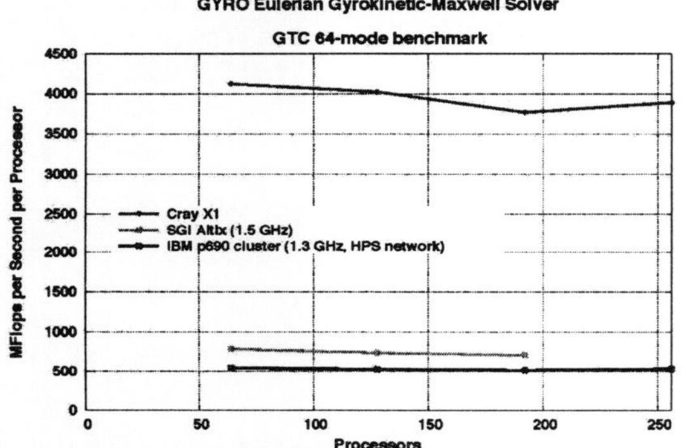

Figure 26: GYRO 64-mode performance across platforms.

Figure 25 and Figure 26 describe the per processor performance of two different benchmark problems: a small 16-mode problem labeled BCY and a large 64-mode problem labeled GTC. The metric, MFlops/sec/processor, is calculated using the same floating point operation count for each system, so performance between the different systems can be compared directly. This view of performance is useful in that it allows both raw performance and scalability to be displayed in the same graph.

Scalability on the non-vector systems is excellent for both benchmarks (and is also very good for the large benchmark on the Cray X1). Note, however, that while the Altix is 60% faster than the IBM on the GTC benchmark, it achieves essentially identical performance on the BCY benchmark.

Figure 27 depicts the fraction of the total time spent in MPI communication on each system for the two benchmark problems. Since the total time differs for each system, these values cannot be compared directly. However, it is clear that time spent in MPI_ALLTOALL is impacting performance on the Altix to a much greater degree than on the other systems. For example, on the X1, communication is never more than 10% of the execution time, and the small and large problem sizes demonstrate similar percentages. On the p690 cluster, communication is a much smaller percentage of the time for the large problem size, indicating that the computational complexity is increasing faster than the communication complexity (and that the IBM HPS switch is able to handle the increased bandwidth demands).

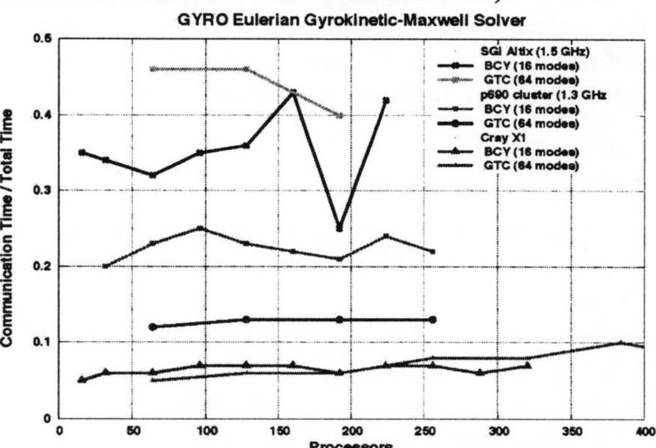

Figure 27: Communication fraction for GYRO.

In contrast, on the Altix the fraction of time spent in communication is higher for the larger benchmark, indicating that the interconnect is having difficulty communicating the large messages. It is unclear at this time whether there is a performance problem in the MPI_ALLTOALL or whether this is a limitation in the Altix network. The communication microbenchmarks indicated that the Altix network should support higher bandwidth rates than the IBM system. However, part of the MPI_ALLTOALL communicates within the p690 SMP node, and the IBM may have an advantage there.

7 Conclusions

In summary, the Altix provides many advantages over other non-vector machines and it is competitive with the Cray X1 on a number of representative kernels and applications. Across our measurements, three salient advantages to the Altix emerged. First, the latency for MPI operations is very low – on the order of 1.1 microseconds – inside an Altix node. This low latency contributes to good application scaling. Second, the Intel Itanium 2 processor and Altix memory subsystem provide notable performance advantages for computation when compared to other non-vector systems. The only systems in our study that exceeded the Altix's aggregate STREAM triad bandwidth were both vector systems: the Cray X1 and the NEC SX-6. Third, on numerous operations, such as DAXPY and FFT, the Altix actually outperforms the vector systems at short vector lengths. These advantages translated into good results for both raw performance and scaling on the applications that we examined. We are continuing our evaluations, porting, optimizing, and analyzing additional application codes and looking in detail at open issues such as hybrid MPI/OpenMP performance and alternative parallel programming paradigms such as SHMEM and UPC. The system software on the Altix is also continuing to mature, with a recent move to a new Fortran compiler with somewhat different performance characteristics.

Acknowledgements

This research was sponsored by the Office of Mathematical, Information, and Computational Sciences, Office of Science, U.S. Department of Energy under Contract No. DE-AC05-00OR22725 with UT-Batelle, LLC. Accordingly, the U.S. Government retains a nonexclusive, royalty-free license to publish or reproduce the published form of this contribution, or allow others to do so, for U.S. Government purposes.

References

[1] M.B. Blackmon, B. Boville *et al.*, "The Community Climate System Model," *BAMS*, 82(11):2357-76, 2001.

[2] J. Candy and R. Waltz, "An Eulerian gyrokinetic-Maxwell solver," *J. Comput. Phys.*, 186(545), 2003.

[3] High-End Computing Revitalization Task Force (HECRTF), "Federal Plan for High-End Computing," Executive Office of the President, Office of Science and Technology Policy, Washington, DC 2004.

[4] M.E. Maltrud, R.D. Smith *et al.*, "Global eddy resolving ocean simulations driven by 1985-1994 atmospheric winds," *J. Geophys. Res.*, 103:30825--53, 1998.

[5] J.D. McCalpin, *Stream Benchmarks*, http://www.cs.virginia.edu/stream, 2002.

[6] Oak Ridge National Laboratory, *Center for Computational Sciences*, http://www.ccs.ornl.gov, 2005.

[7] Oak Ridge National Laboratory, *Early Evaluation Website*, http://www.csm.ornl.gov/evaluation, 2005.

[8] R.D. Smith, M.E. Maltrud *et al.*, "Numerical simulation of the North Atlantic ocean at 1/10 degree," *J. Phys. Oceanogr.*, 30:1532-61, 2000.

[9] US Department of Energy Office of Science, "A Science-Based Case for Large-Scale Simulation," US Department of Energy Office of Science 2003, http://www.pnl.gov/scales.

Fast Barriers for Scalable ccNUMA Systems

Liqun Cheng and John B. Carter
School of Computing
University of Utah
50 South Central Campus Drive, Room 3190
Salt Lake City, UT 84112

{*legion, retrac*}@*cs.utah.edu*

Abstract

As multiprocessors systems become larger and larger and network latency rapidly approaches thousands of processor cycles, the primary factor in determining a barrier algorithm's performance is the number of serial network latencies it requires. Existing barrier algorithms require at least $O(\log N)$ round trip message latencies to perform a single barrier operation on an N-node shared memory multiprocessor. In addition, existing barrier algorithms are not well tuned in terms of how they interact with modern shared memory systems, which leads to an excessive number of message exchanges to signal barrier completion.

The contributions of this paper are threefold. First, we identify and quantify the performance deficiencies of conventional barrier implementations when they are executed on real (non-idealized) hardware. Second, we propose a queue-based barrier algorithm that has effectively $O(1)$ time complexity as measured in round trip message latencies. Third, we demonstrate how matching the barrier implementation to the way that modern shared memory systems operate can improve performance dramatically by exploiting a hardware write-update (PUT) mechanism for signaling. The resulting barrier algorithm only costs one serialized round trip message latency to perform a barrier operation across N processors. Using a cycle-accurate execution-driven simulator of a future-generation SGI multiprocessor, we show that with no special hardware support our queue-based barrier outperforms OpenMP's LL/SC-based barrier implementation by a factor of 7.9 on 256 processors. With hardware that supports a coherent PUT operation, our queue-based barrier outperforms OpenMP barriers by a factor of 94 and outperforms barriers based on SGI's memory controller-based atomic operations by a factor of 6.5 on 256 processors.

1 Introduction

The growing gap between processor and remote memory access times is impacting the scalability of many shared memory algorithms, especially synchronization operations. As a result, synchronization overhead has become a major obstacle to sustaining good application performance on scalable shared memory multiprocessors [3, 12, 23].

In this paper, we focus on analyzing and improving the performance of *barriers*, a synchronization operation often used in modern shared memory algorithms [2, 9, 16]. Barriers synchronize a large number of cooperating threads that repeatedly perform some work and then wait until all cooperating threads are ready to move on to the next computation phase, e.g., as follows:

```
for (i = 0; i < MAX; i++) {
    DoWork(thread_id);
    ...
    BarrierWait(barrier);
}
```

Figure 1 illustrates the timeline for a typical barrier operation. We define the time at which the first thread performs a `BarrierWait()` operation as the barrier start time. We define the time at which the last thread has been signaled that the barrier operation is complete

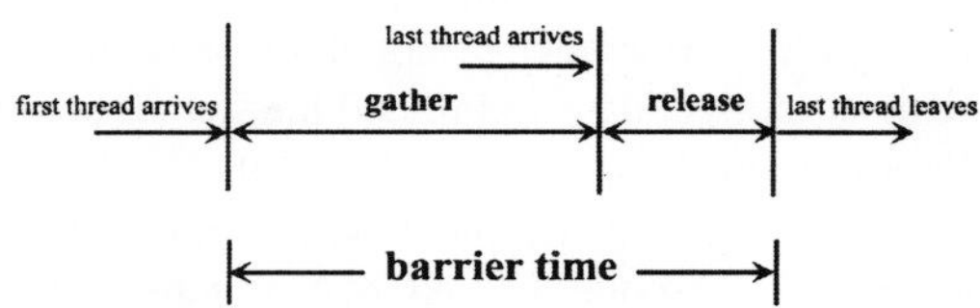

Figure 1. Timeline for a typical barrier

0190-3918/05 $20.00 © 2005 IEEE

(a) naive coding

```
atomic_inc( &gather_variable );
spin_until( gather_variable == num_procs );
```

(b) "optimized" version

```
int count = atomic_inc( &gather_variable );
if( count == num_procs-1 )
      release_variable = num_procs;
else
      spin_until( release_variable == num_procs );
```

Figure 2. Traditional barrier pseudo-code

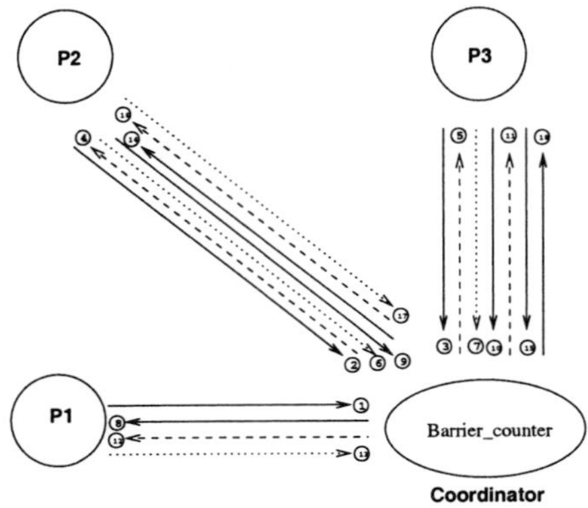

Figure 3. Traditional barrier

and returns from the `BarrierWait()` operation as the barrier completion time. The total time required to perform a single barrier operation is the difference between the barrier start time and the barrier end time. We divide this time into two components, the time during which each thread signals its arrival at the barrier, which we denote the *gather* phase, and the time it takes to convey to each thread that the barrier operation has completed, which we denote the *release* phase. Between the time when a thread signals its arrival at the barrier and the time that it is signaled that the barrier operation has completed, it can perform no other computation. To motivate the need to improve barrier performance we measured the time that it takes to perform a 32-thread OpenMP barrier operation on a 32-node Origin 3000. We found that in the time it takes to perform a 32-node barrier operation, the system could have executed 5.76 million FLOPS.

Traditionally, barriers are implemented by having each thread increment one or more barrier count variables located in shared memory, e.g., as illustrated in Figure 2. Barrier completion is signaled via a release flag [7] that each thread checks repeatedly until it indicates that all threads have arrived at the barrier. Traditional barrier implementations often suffer from contention during both the gather phase, when all of the processors atomically update the barrier count, and the release stage, when all of the processors read a release flag until it indicates barrier completion.

Figure 2(a) illustrates a naive barrier implementation where the count and signal variables are the same; threads waiting for the barrier operation to complete spin reading the count variable, which is updated each time a new thread reaches the barrier. On a scalable directory-based shared memory multiprocessor, this algorithm results in $O(N^2)$ coherence protocol messages being sent per barrier to invalidate and reload the shared count.

Figure 3 illustrates the source of these $O(N^2)$ coherence messages in a typical barrier implementation running on a 3-node CC-NUMA (cache coherence non-uniform memory access) multiprocessor system. Solid lines represent request and data messages, dashed lines represent intervention messages and dotted lines represent intervention replies. In the illustrated scenario, we assume that all three processors start with a read-only (shared) copy of the cache line containing `gather_variable` in their cache, and one thread on each node arrives at the barrier at approximately the same time. Each thread attempts to perform the `atomic_inc()` operation, which causes each processor to send a request to the home node of the barrier count variable asking that the other cached copies of the count be invalidated and the requesting node be given write access to the corresponding cache line (messages (1), (2), and (3)). Only the first request to arrive at the barrier variable's home memory controller will be granted write access (message (8)), which occurs only after the other processors have been sent invalidation messages (messages (4) and (5)) that have been acknowledged (messages (6) and (7)). The remaining two processors then compete for write access to the barrier count variable, which generates another round of invalidations and acknowledgements. As the figure shows, the simple algorithm barrier requires 18 messages before all three processors can increment the barrier count, plus a few more messages (not shown) for each processor to detect that the barrier count has reached its upper limit. Even worse, relatively few of these messages are *pipelined* (overlapped); each message round trip adds to the overall barrier completion time, which can lead to very poor performance.

Previous optimized barrier algorithms have sought to minimize contention and the number of messages required to synchronize in a number of ways. For example, Figure 2(b) illustrates a barrier implementation that uses separate count and signal variables for each thread [18]. However, as we show in Sections 2 and 3, previous algorithmic optimizations have not eliminated all sources of contention, and in some cases even lead to reduced performance on real shared memory systems.

In this paper, we present a novel barrier algorithm that is designed to perform well on real shared memory multiprocessors that employ write-invalidate protocols and can support only a limited number of outstanding cache misses by any particular processor. To eliminate contention for the single global barrier count variable, we employ an array of per-thread *signal flags*. Each thread participating in the barrier signals its arrival at the barrier by writing to its private flag variable in the global flag array, and then spins on a shared *release flag*. A separate coordinator thread continually examines the shared flags until they indicate that all threads have arrived at the barrier, at which time the coordinator updates the *release flag* to signal all threads that they may exit the barrier spin loop. To minimize inter-processor memory contention, the *signal flags* are allocated in separate cache lines (via array padding) in physical memory located on the coordinator node (via careful memory allocation)

Our barrier algorithm outperforms conventional barrier algorithms for several reasons. First, since each thread updates an independent *signal flag*, no invalidation and reload coherence protocol messages are generated due to inter-thread contention. Second, because each thread updates an independent *signal flag*, the coherence protocol messages needed to perform the updates can be pipelined (performed concurrently). If the round trip communication latency is much larger than the time it takes the coordinator's memory controller to respond to a single read or write request, which is increasingly the case in large-scale multiprocessors, O(N) protocol exchanges can be overlapped such that they occur in roughly O(1) time (as measured in round trip message latencies). Third, by using a single (separate) *signal flag*, as opposed to one signal flag per thread as proposed by some researchers [14], we avoid the problem that modern processors can only signal a limited number of processors at a time before the load-store unit runs out of Miss Status Handling Registers (MSHRs) and thus stalls the processor pipeline. As a result of these optimizations, our queue-based barrier algorithm with no special hardware support outperforms the baseline OpenMP barrier implementation by a factor of 7.9X on 256 processors.

Looking ahead to architectural features that have been proposed for future multiprocessors, we investigated the extent to which judicious use of write update protocols (or PUT operations) could improve both gather and release operations. A write update protocol can reduce the amount of coherence traffic required to update the value of a shared variable in a remote node by eliminating the invalidations and reloads that occur using a conventional write-invalidate shared memory coherence protocol. Using updates to signal barrier arrival and barrier completion, our optimized barrier algorithm can reduce the time required to synchronize N threads to a single message round trip, assuming round trip message latency dwarfs memory controller overhead, which is the limit of how fast a barrier operation can be performed.

The rest of the paper is organized as follows. We review various hardware and software barrier implementations in Section 2. In Section 3 we describe a variety of queue-based barrier implementations in detail. In Section 4 we present our simulation results, and in Section 5 we present our conclusions.

2 Background

A number of barrier implementations have been published over the years. The hardware barriers of Cray *et al.* are the fastest [2, 12, 21, 22]. While provably optimal in terms of performance, this approach is only feasible in a small scale system because it requires $N*(N-1)$ unidirectional wires on a N-node system. In addition to the high cost of dedicated wires, static hardware approaches cannot synchronize an arbitrary subset of threads and do not perform well when the number and identity of participants in a barrier change over time.

Most barrier implementations are software-based, but exploit whatever hardware synchronization support is provided on the particular platform. Many modern processors, including MIPS™ [8], Alpha™ [1], and PowerPC™ [13] rely on load linked / store conditional (LL/SC) instructions to implement atomic operations. In an LL/SC-based barrier implementation[8], each thread loads the barrier count into its local cache before trying to increase it atomically. Only one thread will succeed on the first try while the SCs on all other threads will fail. This process repeats itself as each new thread arrives at the barrier, until all participating threads have atomically increased the barrier count.

For this basic barrier algorithm, average barrier latency increases superlinearly with respect to the number of synchronizing threads because (i) round trip network latency increases as system size increases and (ii) contention for the single barrier count variable increases as the number of threads increases. In the worst case, when there is significant contention and thus frequent backoff-and-retry cycles, $O(N^2)$ round trip message latencies are required to complete the gather stage of the barrier operation. When contention is light, updates to the barrier count occur sequentially, resulting in $O(N)$ round trip message latencies to complete the gather stage of each barrier operation.

To signal barrier completion, each node participating in the barrier must receive an invalidation message and then reload the barrier count variable. These operations can be performed in parallel, so the number of serialized message latencies required during signaling is $O(1)$.

Overall, the best case time complexity of LL/SC-based barriers is $O(N)$ round trip message latencies, while the worst case complexity is $O(N^2)$. The average case is highly application dependent, and depends on the relative ratio of computation to synchronization and the average skew in completion time of each thread – the more skew, the less contention, although large amounts of skew can cause performance problems due to load imbalance.

Replacing the LL/SC try-retry loop with atomic *fetch-and-incr* instructions can eliminate failed SC attempts, thereby improving performance. Goodman *et al.*[3] propose *fetch-and-ϕ* as a generic hardware atomic primitive and Michael *et al.* [16] and Nikolopoulos *et al.* [17] demonstrate how these primitives can be used to reduce synchronization contention. These types of instructions are often referred to as *processor-side atomic operations*, because the data is loaded into the processor cache and modified there atomically. Although barriers implemented using processor-side atomic operations induce less serialization and scale better under heavy load, the global shared counter must be updated by every single thread, and every atomic update costs a round trip message latency, so the gather stage still has $O(N)$ time complexity. As a result, barriers implemented using processor-side atomic operations do not significantly outperform LL/SC-based barriers.

The NYU Ultracomputer [4, 9] implements a variety of atomic instructions in its memory controller. Further, it uses a combining network that tries to combine all loads and stores for the same memory location in the routers. Combining is useful only when barriers are global and accessed frequently, because the combining mechanism can slow down other requests in an attempt to induce opportunities to combine. In contrast, the SGI Origin 2000 [10] and Cray T3E [21] implement similar combining functionality, but do so at the barrier variable's home memory controller. This design eliminates the problems associated with combining in the router. We refer to these mechanisms as *memory-side atomic operations*. Compared to processor-side atomic operations, memory-side atomic operations simplify the processor pipeline and save system bus bandwidth. However, each atomic operation still requires a round trip across the network, which needs to be done serially.

Some researches have proposed using barrier trees to reduce synchronization contention and overlap communication in large-scale systems [6, 20, 24]. Barrier trees employ a hierarchy (tree) of barriers. Rather than centralize the barrier implementation through a single global barrier or coordinator, tree-based barrier algorithms divide the participating threads into modest-sized groups of threads that synchronize amongst themselves. If we assume the maximum fanout in the tree is M, both the gather and release stages can complete in $\lceil \log_M N \rceil * O(M)$ round trip latencies. A tree-based barrier on a large system is essentially a series of smaller barriers. For example, 256 threads could synchronize by employing a four-level barrier tree, with a fanout of four at each level in the tree. Since barrier operations at the same level of the tree can be done in parallel, the time required for this 256-thread barrier is only roughly four times that of a base 4-thread barrier.

Other techniques are proposed to address some issues on barrier imbalance. Fuzzy barriers [5] extend the barrier concept to include a region of statements that can be executed by a processor while it awaits synchronization. Alternatively, thrifty barriers [11] maximizes energy savings by turning processors that arrive early into low-power sleep states. Our barrier implementation is orthogonal and complimentary to these techniques.

The queue-based algorithm presented in the following section requires only $O(1)$ message round trips to synchronize N threads if the time for a given memory controller to perform N protocol operations is less than a single message round trip latency. As described above, this assumption holds true for reasonable sized values of N, but it does not hold for arbitrary sizes of N. For large values of N, a hybrid barrier solution employing barrier trees combined with our queue-based barriers for synchronization within a level of the barrier would perform best. Our algorithm improves the performance of individual subtree barrier synchronization, which allows us to increase the fanout in the tree and thereby reduce the height of the barrier tree.

Table 1 summarizes the time complexities of the various barrier solutions discussed above, including our proposed queue-based barrier algorithm, as measured in round trip message latencies.

3 Algorithms

In this section, we describe our queue-based barrier mechanism, starting with a simple version in Section 3.1, followed by a series of refinements in the subsequent subsections. We call our algorithms "queue-based" due to their similarity in spirit and data structures to Scott *et al.*'s queue-based spinlocks [15]. However, our queue-based barrier is quite different than simply implementing a barrier using queue-based spinlocks. A barrier could be implemented using two spin locks, one to protect the barrier count variable and another on which threads can block until the barrier operation completes. However, doing so requires every thread to acquire and release each lock once per barrier iteration, resulting in an $O(N)$ barrier time complexity.

Algorithm	Gather stage	Release stage	Total
LL/SC Average case	$O(N)$	$O(1)$	$O(N)$
LL/SC Worst case	$O(N^2)$	$O(1)$	$O(N)$
Atomic(Processor side)	$O(N)$	$O(1)$	$O(N)$
Atomic(Memory side)	$O(N)$	$O(1)$	$O(N)$
Barrier Tree	$O(\log N)$	$O(\log N)$	$O(\log N)$
Queue-based	$O(1)$	$O(1)$	$O(1)$

Table 1. Time complexity of various barrier implementation

3.1 Simple Queue-Based Algorithm

In our first queue-based barrier algorithm, we designate one node as the *coordinator* and allocate an array of flags, one per participating thread, in the coordinator's local physical memory. To eliminate false sharing, we pad the flag array such that each thread's flag variable resides in a separate cache line. When a thread arrives at the barrier and attempts to signal its arrival by updating its flag variable, its cache controller sends a READ_EXCLUSIVE coherence protocol message to the flag's home memory controller (on the coordinator node). Upon receiving the READ_EXCLUSIVE request, the home memory controller invalidates the (local) coordinator's processor cache (if necessary) and then supplies a writable copy of the cache line to the signaling thread. The *gather stage* of the barrier operation completes when the last thread sets its flag variable. Figure 4 depicts the coherence protocol messages exchanged during the gather phase of our simple queue-based algorithm. Note that each thread can update its flag variable effectively in parallel, since each processor's request is independent of the others and controller occupancy is low for reasonable-sized systems. This is illustrated in Figure 4 by the fact that messages 1a, 1b, and 1c can be pipelined. As a result, using an array of flag variables rather than a single global count reduces the effective number of round trip message latencies required for N threads to signal arrival from $O(N)$ to $O(1)$.

To determine when the barrier operation is complete, a coordinator thread sweeps through the flag array until it sees that all of the flags are set. This sweep requires $O(1)$ message round trips, because although the coordinator loads N cache lines containing flags from the corresponding remote processor caches, only the cache line load corresponding to the last thread to signal its arrival at the barrier impacts performance.

To determine when they are allowed to finish the barrier operation, each participating thread spins on a private flag variable, which the coordinator sets when all threads have arrived at the barrier. At first glance, this might appear to be an $O(1)$ operation, since the writes are all independent and thus can be pipelined. However, modern out-of-order processors can only support a

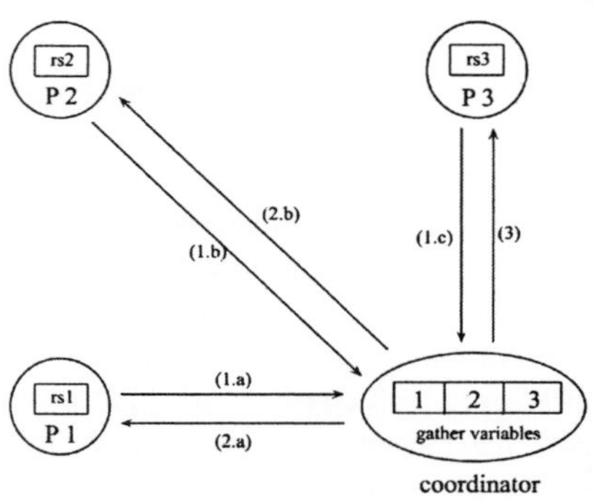

Figure 4. Simple Queue-based Barrier

modest number of outstanding memory operations. Processors have a limited number of Miss Handling Status Registers (MSHRs); if the processor accesses a cache line not present in its local cache when no MSHRs are available, the processor pipeline stalls. The impact of this architectural limitation is that the coordinator will only be able to pipeline k updates at a time, if k is the number of MSHRs for that processor.

Referring back to Figure 4, if the processor in question has only 2 MSHRs and thus can support at most 2 outstanding remote writes at a time, then the coordinator cannot issue the write request to P3 until one of the other updates (2a or 2b) completes. As a result, in this case the signaling phase takes two round trip latencies. In general, on a system that can support k outstanding remote writes, the coordinator needs at least $\lceil N/k \rceil$ round trip times to perform the signaling phase. This hardware constraint on performance is discussed in more detail in the following section.

The overall execution time of this queue-based barrier scheme is the sum of the gather stage ($O(1)$) and the release stage ($O(N/k)$), where k is the maximum number of pending writes the system can support. Consequently, due to the oft-overlooked restriction of the number of outstanding memory operations a single processor can have a time, the overall time complexity of this algorithm is $O(N)$. We refer to this algorithm as S-Queue (simple queue) throughout the rest of this paper.

3.2 Optimized Queue-Based Algorithm

Since the gather stage of our initial queue-based barrier algorithm is already an $O(1)$ operation, we focus on reducing the time complexity of the release stage. Actually, our baseline algorithm is $O(1)$ in terms of software operations, provided the coordinator can scan the flag array in $O(1)$ time. This holds true as long as the time constant for round trip message latencies dwarfs the time constant of local memory reads, which is true for practical system sizes.

As noted in the previous section, the problem with employing a separate signal flag for each participating thread is that the coordinator processor can only issue in parallel as many invalidation requests as it has MSHRs. Increasing the number of MSHRs, and thereby increasing the number of outstanding remote misses that can be tolerated, would clearly help alleviate this problem. However, Palacharla *et al.* [19] note that further increases in windows size, issue queue length, and the number of MSHR entries are not complexity effective.

Given the limited number of MSHRs in real processors, we must reduce the number of remote writes. Using a single global release variable for all participating threads eliminates the MSHR problem. A single write by the coordinator causes the coordinator's memory controller to issue N pipelined invalidation requests to invalidate the N remote cached copies of the cache line holding the flag variable. This burst of invalidations will be followed by N pipelined read requests as each participant re-reads the updated flag variable.

Figure 5 illustrates how the optimized algorithm works. After all participating threads have arrived at the barrier, they spin on locally cached copies of a shared global release variable. These copies are invalidated when the coordinator updates the value of the release variable, after which each thread reloads a copy. Since the round trips related to read contention for the shared release variable are pipelined by modern MESI protocols, the time complexity of the release stage drops to $O(1)$ in our optimized algorithm, again assuming protocol handling time is dwarfed by message latency.

Combined with the algorithm $O(1)$ for the gather stage described in Section 3.1, the resulting barrier time is reduced to $O(1)$ round trip message latencies. We refer to this algorithm as O-Queue (optimized queue) throughout the rest of this paper.

3.3 Simple Update Algorithm

The algorithm described in Section 3.2 provides an $O(1)$ round trip latency solution to the barrier problem, but its constant coefficients are not as low as (say) a hardware wired-AND barrier. In particular, during

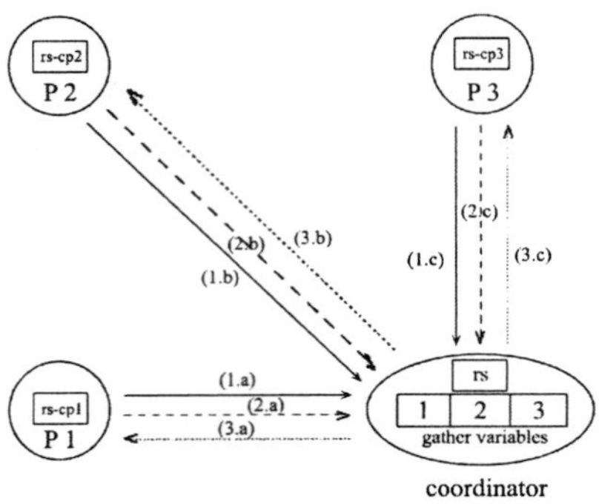

Figure 5. Optimized Queue-based Barrier

the gather phase each participating thread suffers a remote write miss when it attempts to update its flag variable, which results in N read-exclusive messages and N corresponding acknowledgements. During the release phase, the coordinator invalidates all N copies of the shared release flag variable (resulting in N invalidation messages and N acknowledgement messages), and then each of the N participating threads suffers a read miss (resulting in N read-shared messages and N data-return messages). Even though these coherence protocol messages are pipelined so that they are performed as three sets of N concurrent (pipelined) messages, the protocol described in Section 3.2 requires a minimum of three round trip message latencies per barrier synchronization. As round trip latencies approach 1000 processor cycles, this overhead limits barrier performance, especially for small configurations where the benefit of protocol message pipelining is small. In Sections 3.1 and 3.2 we developed algorithms that improved barrier latency by aggressively overlapping (pipelining) coherence message traffic. The problem we address in this and the following section is how to reduce the number of non-overlapped round trip message latencies that remain and how to reduce the number of coherence operations performed by the coordinator's memory controller.

We first consider how to reduce the performance impact of the two sets of round trip message latencies required for the coordinator to signal barrier completion. Recall that these two sets of round trip messages are for (i) the coordinator to invalidate all N shared copies of the barrier completion flag and then (ii) for each of the N participating threads to reload a shared copy of the flag. In conjunction with researchers at SGI, we are investigating the value of *write update* coherence protocols in scalable shared memory multiprocessors. The write update protocol we are investigating allows threads to perform either explicit coherent GET/PUT operations on cacheable shared data or to designate particular regions of memory as ones that should be kept coherent using a hardware write update coherence protocol. Our enhanced directory controller tracks coherence at the cache line level, as is the norm in existing scalable shared memory systems. When the home memory controller of a particular variable receives a GET request, it returns a coherent value of the target variable loaded either from local memory or a remote processor cache, depending on the state of the cache line. In response to a GET operation, the requesting node is not added to the cache line's list of sharers, and hence will not be informed of future modifications of the cache line. In response to a PUT operation, the home memory controller sends an update request to main memory and every processor that has a copy of line containing the target variable, where the modification is applied.

In our simple update-based barrier algorithm (S-Update), the coordinator uses PUTs to update the global release variable after the last thread reaches the barrier. Doing so eliminates one of the two round trips required to perform a release in the O-Queue algorithm described above. A secondary benefit of the use of PUTs is that they require smaller protocol messages (e.g., 8-bytes versus 32-128 bytes plus overhead to send a full cache line), which further improves performance.

3.4 Optimized Update Algorithm

In this section we consider how to improve the performance of the gather phase of our queue-based barrier implementation using PUTs. Recall that during the gather phase, each participating thread suffers a remote write miss when it attempts to update its flag variable, which causes the corresponding cache line to be invalidated from the coordinator's processor cache. When the coordinator subsequently tests the flag, it suffers a read miss and is forced to reload the cache line across the network. As described in Section 3.2, the round trip overhead of independent invalidate requests can be pipelined, but invalidation requests can queue up at the coordinator's directory controller. Since the coordinator is in the critical path of our barrier implementation, every delay it experiences impacts barrier performance. As such, high controller occupancy on the coordinator node induced by the N invalidations and subsequent N reloads performed during the gather phase can increase barrier latency by a non-negligible constant factor, especially in large configurations. This overhead can be reduced by having participating threads use PUTs to update the value of their private flag on the coordinator node, thereby eliminating an invalidation and reload cycle. As we report in Section 4 the judicious use of cache-coherent PUTs for signaling reduces the number of protocol messages that pass through the coordinator's network interface by 70%, which results in an additional 7.3X speedup compared even to our optimized queue-based barrier implementation. We refer to this algorithm as O-Update (optimized update) throughout the rest of this paper.

3.5 Summary

Figure 2(a) shows a naive barrier implementation, where `num_procs` is the number of participating threads. This design is inefficient because it spins on the gather variable directly, which as discussed in Section 1 can lead to significant contention problems and even in the best case requires $O(N)$ round trip message latencies to complete because the updates are effectively serialized.

A common optimization to this barrier implementation is to use a separate release flag, as shown in Figure 2(b). Instead of spinning on the barrier count variable, the optimized version loop spins on a separate release variable that is only updated when the last thread arrives at the barrier. Nikolopoulos *et al.* [18] report that spinning on a separate variable improves barrier performance by 25% over an implementation that spins directly on the barrier count for a 64-node barrier.

In our two basic queue-based barriers, an array of cache-line-aligned flags (one per thread) is allocated in the physical memory of a coordinator node. To signal arrival at the barrier, participating threads update their private slot in this array. The coordinator repeatedly sweeps through the array to determine when all participating threads have arrived at the barrier, which induces N remote read misses as it reloads the updated flag variables. However, in practice these misses and the induced message traffic are pipelined. Our two queue-based algorithms differ only in how the coordinator signals barrier completion to the waiting threads, either via private signal flags (S-Queue) or via a shared signal flag (O-Queue).

4 Evaluation

In this section we present details of our experimental methodology and results. We describe the simulation environment we employ for all experiments in Section 4.1 and compare the results of the various barrier implementations described earlier in Section 4.2

4.1 Simulator Environment

We use a cycle-accurate execution-driven simulator, UVSIM, in our performance study [25]. UVSIM models a hypothetical future-generation Origin 3000

Parameter	Value
Processor	4-issue, 48-entry active list, 2GHz
L1 I-cache	2-way, 32KB, 64B lines, 1-cycle lat.
L1 D-cache	2-way, 32KB, 32B lines, 2-cycle lat.
L2 cache	4-way, 2MB, 128B lines, 10-cycle lat.
System bus	16B CPU to system, 8B system to CPU
	max 16 outstanding L2C misses, 1GHZ
DRAM	16 16-bit-data DDR channels
Hub clock	500 MHz
DRAM	60 processor cycles latency
Network	100 processor cycles latency per hop

Table 2. System configuration.

architecture that we are investigating along with researchers from SGI. The simulated architecture supports a directory-based coherence protocol that supports both write invalidate and write update coherence protocols. The hardware write update protocol is implemented using implicit "GET/PUT" operations as described in Section 3.3. Each simulated node contains two next-generation MIPS microprocessors connected to a future-generation system bus. Also connected to the bus is a next-generation HUB chip, which contains the processor interface, memory controller, directory controller, network interface and IO interface.

Table 2 summarizes the major parameters of our simulated system. The simulated interconnect is based on SGI's NUMALink-4, which uses a fat-tree structure with eight children on each non-leaf router. The minimum-sized network packet is 32 bytes and we model a network hop latency of 50nsecs (100 cpu cycles). We do not model contention within the routers, but do model port contention on the hub network interfaces. We have validated our simulator by configuring it with parameters that match an Origin 3000 system and found that all predicted results for a wide set of tuning benchmarks are within 20% of the real machine, most within 5%. Key performance metrics, e.g., elapsed cycle counts and cache miss rates, are typically within 1%.

4.2 Results

In this section we report the relative performance of seven barrier implementations for 4-256 processors. All of the programs in our study are compiled using the MIPSpro compiler version 7.3 with an optimization level of -O2. We use OpenMP's barrier implementation for the SGI Origin 3000 as the baseline against which we compare all other barrier implementations. OpenMP's barrier is implemented using LL/SC instructions on the Origin 3000 system.

We compare the performance of six barrier implementations against the baseline OpenMP implementation. The first two alternative implementations replace the LL/SC instructions with conventional processor-side atomic fetch-and-inc instructions (*Atomic*) and SGI-specific memory-side atomic instructions (*MAO*).

In addition to these three conventional implementations of barriers, we consider four queue-based barriers: our basic queue-based barrier that uses separate flags for both signaling arrival at the barrier and completion of the barrier operation (*S-Queue*), a version that uses a single variable to signal barrier completion (*O-Queue*), and versions of both algorithms that employ updates (*S-Update* and *O-Update*, respectively).

All results reported herein correspond to 1001 barrier operations per thread. The first barrier is used simply to synchronize the start time of our measurements. The barrier time is measured as the time from when the first barrier operation completes until the last thread leaves the 1000th barrier.

Table 3 presents the normalized speedups of the six optimized barrier implementations compared to the baseline OpenMP LL/SC-based barrier implementation. We vary the number of threads that synchronize from 4 (i.e., 2 nodes) to 256 (i.e., 128 nodes). Columns 2 through 7 of Table 3 present the speedups of various optimized barrier implementations.

All of the optimized implementations noticeably outperform the baseline implementation. Of the algorithms that require only the basic hardware support that could be expected on any scalable shared memory multiprocessor (baseline, Atomic, S-Queue, and O-Queue), our optimized queue-based algorithm (O-Queue) performs 7.85 times faster than the baseline and approximately 5 times faster than any other algorithm for 256 processors. This demonstrates the importance of being aware of every source of protocol overhead and the problem of MSHR-induced stalls when designing a scalable barrier mechanism.

All three of the algorithms that require special hardware support (MAO, S-Update, and O-Update) perform well, although the value of avoiding MSHR-induced stalls (S-Update vs O-Update) is particularly important when protocol overhead is reduced by the use of updates. Overall, the O-Update algorithm significantly outperforms all other algorithms, outperforming the baseline implementation by almost a factor of 94 and its next closed competitor (MAO) by a factor of 6.5 on 256 processors.

Figure 6 presents a breakdown of the sources of performance improvement for the O-Update algorithm. Over half of the improvement comes from using updates. The remainder comes from having participating threads signal independent variables $O(N) \rightarrow O(N/K)$, using a single variable to signal barrier completion $O(N/K) \rightarrow O(1)$, and eliminating extraneous invalidates.

CPUs	Speedup over Baseline					
	Atomic	MAO	S-Queue	O-Queue	S-Update	O-Update
4	1.15	1.21	0.58	0.65	0.95	**5.43**
8	1.06	2.70	1.23	2.02	2.73	**18.04**
16	1.20	3.61	1.11	2.56	3.98	**25.04**
32	1.36	4.20	1.16	3.14	4.44	**31.71**
64	1.37	5.14	1.01	4.23	5.92	**43.59**
128	1.24	8.02	1.13	5.06	6.54	**44.39**
256	1.23	14.70	1.58	7.85	9.61	**93.96**

Table 3. Performance of different barriers.

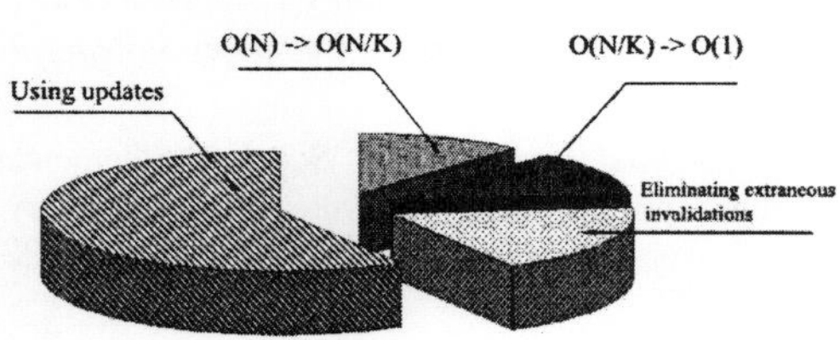

Figure 6. Improvement for 32P Barrier

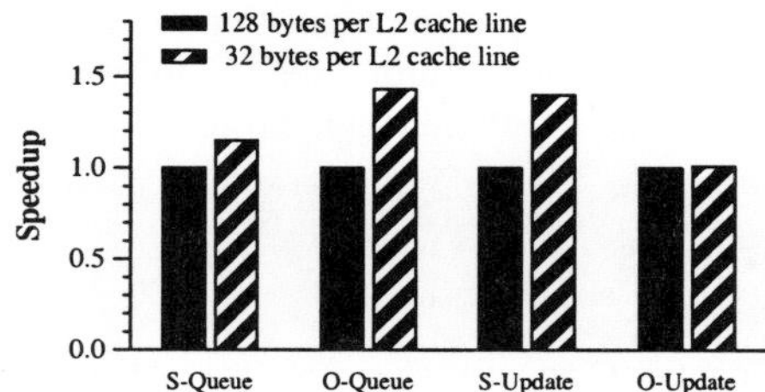

Figure 7. Bandwidth effect on Algorithm

4.3 Sensitivity to Bandwidth

As described in Section 3.4, controller occupancy at the coordinator can limit the performance of the queue-based barrier implementations. Essentially, when occupancy is high enough, the assumption that the overhead of handling individual protocol operations is negligible compared to a round trip message latency is no longer completely accurate. When this happens, the $O(N)$ protocol operations performed at the coordinator begin to lose their insignificance compared to the $O(1)$ round trip message latencies, resulting in a less scalable algorithm.

When the fraction of time spent handling protocol messages becomes significant compared to the inter-node communication overhead, a more precise formula for the performance of the various algorithms is $\tau + \frac{km}{\phi}$, where τ is the round trip message latency, m is size of a single request packet, k is the number of packets handled by the coordinator node, and ϕ is the network bandwidth on/off the coordinator node. We use bandwidth as our metric for coordinator controller occupancy because in practice it is the limiting factor for the rate at which the controller can handle the simple protocol messages induced by our barrier algorithms.

To investigate the extent to which controller occupancy impacted performance, we tested the sensitivity of our queue-based algorithm to cache line size, which in our experiments was the primary factor in determining how many bytes were sent on/off the coordinator node. For this experiment, we compared how the performance of the various algorithms changed when we reduced the L2 cache line size from 128 bytes to 32 bytes, which effectively decreases m by a factor of 4. As can be seen in Figure 7, reducing the L2 cache line size by a factor of 4 improves the performance of S-Queue, O-Queue, and S-Update by factors of 1.15, 1.43, and 1.40, respectively. The performance of O-Update algorithm was essentially unchanged. These results tell us that network bandwidth, and thus controller occupancy, had only a modest impact on performance even for the 256-processors barrier case.

5 Conclusions and Future Work

Efficient synchronization is crucial to the performance and scalability of applications running on large share memory multiprocessors. In this paper, we analyze a variety of existing barrier solutions and identify sources of unnecessary performance overhead when run on real shared memory hardware.

We propose a family of novel *queue-based barrier algorithms* that eliminate most sources of serialization found in existing barrier implementations. By aggressively exploiting pipelining and being aware of the limitations of modern processors , the resulting algorithms can perform an N-thread barrier operation in $O(1)$ message round trip latencies. For practical machine configurations, e.g., up to 256 processors, the $O(1)$ message round trip latencies dominate the $O(N)$ protocol operations performed by the memory controller on the coordinator node.

On a 256-processor system, our O-Update algorithm demonstrates a 94X speedup compared to the baseline LL/SC-based OpenMP barrier algorithm. Compared to other algorithms that exploit specialized machine features, O-Update outperforms algorithms that use memory-side atomic ops (MAO) by a factor of 6.5X and ones that employ processor-side atomic operations (Atomic) by a factor of 75X. The best queue-based algorithm that does not exploit special hardware features (O-Queue) outperforms the baseline OpenMP barrier implementation by a factor of 7.9X on 256 processors.

As part of our future work, we plan to determine the extent to which queue-based barrier algorithms can be combined with MAOs and barrier trees. Also, we plan to test the sensitivity of our algorithm to network latency and investigate what minimal set of hardware primitives is ideal to support efficient synchronization.

References

[1] Compaq Computer Corporation. Alpha architecture handbook, version 4, Feb. 1998.

[2] Cray Research, Inc. Cray T3D systems architecture overview, 1993.

[3] J. R. Goodman, M. K. Vernon, and P. Woest. Efficient synchronization primitives for large-scale cache-coherent multiprocessor. In *Proc. of the 3rd ASPLOS*, pp. 64–75, Apr. 1989.

[4] A. Gottlieb, R. Grishman, C. Kruskal, K. McAuliffe, L. Rudolph, and M. Snir. The NYU multicomputer - designing a MIMD shared-memory parallel machine. *IEEE TOPLAS*, 5(2):164–189, Apr. 1983.

[5] R. Gupta. The fuzzy barrier: a mechanism for high speed synchronization of processors. In *ASPLOS-III: Proc. of the third international conference on Architectural support for programming languages and operating systems*, pages 54–63. ACM Press, 1989.

[6] R. Gupta and C. Hill. A scalable implementation of barrier synchronization using an adaptive combining tree. *International Journal of Parallel Programming*, 18(3):161–180, June 1989.

[7] J. Hennessy and D. Patterson. *Computer Architecture: A Quantitative Approach.* Morgan Kaufmann, 2003.

[8] G. Kane and J. Heinrich. *MIPS RISC Architecture.* Prentice-Hall, 1992.

[9] C. Kruskal, L. Rudolph, and M. Snir. Efficient synchronization on multiprocessors with shared memory. *ACM TOPLAS*, 10(4):570–601, October 1988.

[10] J. Laudon and D. Lenoski. The SGI Origin: A ccNUMA highly scalable server. In *ISCA97*, pp. 241–251, June 1997.

[11] J. Li, J. F. Martínez, and M. C. Huang. The thrifty barrier: Energy-aware synchronization in shared-memory multiprocessors. In *International Symposium on High-Performance Computer Architecture (HPCA)*, Madrid, Spain, Feb. 2004.

[12] S. Lundstrom. Application considerations in the system design of highly concurrent multiprocessors. *IEEE Trans. on Computers*, C-36(11):1292–1390, Nov. 1987.

[13] C. May, E. Silha, R. Simpson, and H. Warren. *The PowerPC Architecture: A Specification for a New Family of Processors, 2nd edition.* Morgan Kaufmann, May 1994.

[14] J. Mellor-Crummey and M. Scott. Synchronization without contention. In *Proc. of the 4th ASPLOS*, pp. 269–278, Apr. 1991.

[15] J. M. Mellor-Crummey and M. L. Scott. Algorithms for scalable synchronization on shared-memory multiprocessors. *ACM Trans. on Computer Systems*, 9(1):21–65, Feb. 1991.

[16] M. M. Michael and M. L. Scott. Implementation of atomic primitives on distributed shared memory multiprocessors. In *Proc. of the First HPCA*, pp. 222–231, Jan. 1995.

[17] D. S. Nikolopoulos and D. S. Papatheodorou. Fast synchronization on scalable cache-coherent multiprocessors using hybrid primitives. In *Proc. of IPDPS*, pp. 711–720, 2000.

[18] D. S. Nikolopoulos and T. A. Papatheodorou. The architecture and operating system implications on the performance of synchronization on ccNUMA multiprocessors. *International Journal of Parallel Programming*, 29(3):249–282, June 2001.

[19] S. Palacharla, N. P. Jouppi, and J. E. Smith. Complexity-effective superscalar processors. In *ISCA*, pp. 206–218, 1997.

[20] M. Scott and J. Mellor-Crummey. Fast, contention-free combining tree barriers for shared memory multiprocessors. *International Journal of Parallel Programming*, 22(4), 1994.

[21] S. Scott. Synchronization and communication in the T3E multiprocessor. In *Proc. of the 7th ASPLOS*, Oct. 1996.

[22] S. Shang and K. Hwang. Distributed hardwired barrier synchronization for scalable multiprocessor clusters. *IEEE Trans. on Parallel and Distributed Systems*, 6(6):591–605, June 1995.

[23] Y. Solihin, V. Lam, and J. Torrellas. Scal-Tool: Pinpointing and quantifying scalability bottlenecks in DSM multiprocessors. In *International Conference on High Performance Computing and Communication (SC'99)*, Portland, Oregon, USA, Nov. 1999.

[24] P. Yew, N. Tzeng, and D. Lawrie. Distributing hot-spot addressing in large-scale multiprocessors. *IEEE Trans. on Computers*, C-36(4):388–395, Apr. 1987.

[25] L. Zhang. UVSIM reference manual. TR UUCS-03-011, University of Utah, May 2003.

Performance Evaluation of View-Oriented Parallel Programming

Z. Huang†, M. Purvis‡, P. Werstein†
†Department of Computer Science

‡Department of Information Science
University of Otago, Dunedin, New Zealand
Email:hzy@cs.otago.ac.nz, mpurvis@infoscience.otago.ac.nz, werstein@cs.otago.ac.nz

Abstract

This paper evaluates the performance of a novel View-Oriented Parallel Programming style for parallel programming on cluster computers. View-Oriented Parallel Programming is based on Distributed Shared Memory which is friendly and easy for programmers to use. It requires the programmer to divide shared data into views according to the memory access pattern of the parallel algorithm. One of the advantages of this programming style is that it offers the performance potential for the underlying Distributed Shared Memory system to optimize consistency maintenance. Also it allows the programmer to participate in performance optimization of a program through wise partitioning of the shared data into views. Experimental results demonstrate a significant performance gain of the programs based on the View-Oriented Parallel Programming style.

Key Words: Distributed Shared Memory, View-based Consistency, View-Oriented Parallel Programming, Cluster Computing

1 Introduction

A Distributed Shared Memory (DSM) system can provide application programmers the illusion of shared memory on top of message-passing distributed systems, which facilitates the task of parallel programming in distributed systems. However, programs using DSM are normally not as efficient as those using the Message Passing Interface (MPI) [12]. The reason is that message passing is part of the design of a MPI program and the programmer can finely tune the performance of the program by reducing the unnecessary message passing. As we know, message passing is a significant cost for applications running on distributed systems, which is also true for DSM programs. Since consistency maintenance for DSM [3, 10, 8] deals with the consistency of the whole shared memory space, there are many unnecessary messages incurred in DSM systems. Furthermore, the programmer cannot help reduce those messages when designing a DSM program.

Traditionally DSM programs are required to be data race free (DRF) using system provided synchronization primitives such as *lock_acquire*, *lock_release*, and *barrier*. If a DSM program has no data race through using those primitives, it is called a *properly-labelled* program [3]. However, properly-labelled DRF programs do not facilitate optimization such as data selection [8], which only updates part of the shared memory in consistency maintenance in DSM. Since DRF-oriented programming focuses on mutual exclusion and synchronization rather than data allocation, there is no communication channel in those programs for expert programmers to interact with the DSM system in terms of performance tuning. As a matter of fact, it is the optimal data allocation which can improve the performance of DSM applications.

To help DSM optimize its performance as well as to allow programmers to participate in performance tuning such as optimization of data allocation, we propose a novel View-Oriented Parallel Programming (VOPP) style for DSM applications.

The rest of this paper is organised as follows. Section 2 briefly describes the VOPP programming style. Section 3 discusses possible optimizations when a VOPP program is created or converted from an existing program. Section 4 compares VOPP with related work. Section 5 presents and evaluates the performance results of several applications. Finally, our future work on VOPP is suggested in Section 6.

0190-3918/05 $20.00 © 2005 IEEE

2 View-Oriented Parallel Programming (VOPP)

A *view* is a concept used to maintain consistency in distributed shared memory. It consists of data objects that require consistency maintenance as a whole body. Views are defined implicitly by the programmer in his/her mind or algorithm, but are explicitly indicated through primitives such as *acquire_view* and *release_view*. *Acquire_view* means acquiring exclusive access to a view, while *release_view* means having finished the access. However, *acquire_view* cannot be called in a nested style. For read-only accesses, *acquire_Rview* and *release_Rview* are provided, which can be called in a nested style. By using these primitives, the focus of the programming is on accessing shared objects (views) rather than synchronization and mutual exclusion.

The programmer should divide the shared data into views according to the nature of the parallel algorithm and its memory access pattern. Views must not overlap each other. The views are decided in the programmer's mind or algorithm. Once decided, they must be kept unchanged throughout the whole program. The view primitives must be used when a view is accessed, no matter if there is any data race or not in the parallel program. Interested readers may refer to [7, 6] for more details about VOPP and program examples.

In summary, VOPP has the following features:

- The VOPP style allows programmers to participate in performance optimization of programs through wise partitioning of shared objects (i.e. data allocation) into views and wise use of view primitives. The focus of VOPP is shifted more towards shared data (e.g. data partitioning and allocation), rather than synchronization and mutual exclusion.

- VOPP does not place any extra burden on programmers since the partitioning of shared objects is an implicit task in parallel programming. VOPP just makes the task explicit, which renders parallel programming less error-prone in handling shared data.

- VOPP offers a large potential for efficient implementations of DSM systems. When a view primitive such as $acquire\_view$ is called, only the data objects associated with the related view need to be updated. An optimal consistency maintenance protocol has been proposed based on this simplicity [5].

To support VOPP, a View-based Consistency (VC) model has been proposed and efficiently implemented [7, 5]. In this model, a view is updated when a processor calls *acquire_view* or *acquire_Rview* to access the view. Since a processor will modify only one view between *acquire_view* and *release_view*, which should be guaranteed by the programmer, we are certain that the data objects modified between *acquire_view* and *release_view* belong to that view and thus we only update those data objects when the view is accessed later. In this way, the amount of data traffic for DSM consistency in the cluster network can be reduced and thus the VC model can be implemented optimally [5]. The Sequential Consistency (SC) [11] of VOPP programs can also be guaranteed by the VC model, which has been proved in [7].

3 Optimizations in VOPP

Traditional DSM programs need to be converted into VOPP programs before being run on the VC model. The applications we have converted include Integer Sort (IS), Gauss, Successive Over-Relaxation (SOR), and Neural network (NN). These programs are used in our performance evaluation in Section 5.

IS ranks an unsorted sequence of N keys. The rank of a key in a sequence is the index value i that the key would have if the sequence of keys were sorted. All the keys are integers in the range [0, B_{max}], and the method used is bucket sort. The memory access pattern is very similar to the pattern of our sum example in Section 2. Gauss implements the Gauss Elimination algorithm in parallel. Multiple processors process a matrix following the Gaussian Elimination steps. SOR uses a simple iterative relaxation algorithm. The input is a two-dimensional grid. During each iteration, every matrix element is updated to a function of the values of neighboring elements. NN trains a back-propagation neural network in parallel using a training data set. After each epoch, the errors of the weights are gathered from each processor and the weights of the neural network are adjusted before the next epoch. The training is repeated until the neural network converges.

The task of conversion includes identifying exclusive views and inserting view primitives. During the conversion, the applications have been optimized using the following tips.

3.1 Local buffer for infrequently-shared or read-only data

In traditional DSM programs, shared data is accessed directly from the shared memory, no matter how frequently it is shared. Even some read-only data is put into the shared memory. This generous use of shared memory may unnecessarily cause the false sharing effect [8], which results from two or more processors accessing different data objects in the same page of DSM and unnecessary memory consistency maintenance. For some applications such as Gauss, shared data is read in by individual processors and is accessed by the same processor until the end of the program when final result has to be printed out. When we convert Gauss into the VOPP program, local buffers are used to keep the infrequently-shared data during processing. The shared data is divided into views for individual processors and each processor reads its view into a local buffer. The processing on the shared data is carried out on the local buffers by the processors. After the processing is finished, the data in the local buffers is copied back into the shared memory using view primitives. The pseudo-code is shown below.

```
acquire_view(proc_id);
copy from the view to loc_buffer;
release_view(proc_id);

for(i=0;i<max_iterations;i++){
   process data in loc_buffer;
}
acquire_view(proc_id);
copy from loc_buffer to the view;
release_view(proc_id);

barrier(0);
if(proc_id==0){
  for(j=0;j<nprocs;j++)
              acquire_Rview(j);
  read and print data in all views;
  for(j=0;j<nprocs;j++)
               release_Rview(j);
}
barrier(0);
```

We also optimized the NN application in this manner. The application trains a back-propagation neural network in parallel. The training data set is read-only and initially read into the shared memory for programming convenience. We divide the training data set evenly into *nprocs* views, where *nprocs* is the number of processors. The views are copied into local buffers for later processing. The pseudo-code is shown below.

```
acquire_view(proc_id);
copy from the view to loc_buffer;
release_view(proc_id);

while (not trained){
   train the network with data
              in loc_buffer;
   barrier(0);
   change the weights of the network;
   check the errors from the target;
}
```

By using the local buffers, the applications can avoid false sharing effect. Of course, there is an overhead of copying between the shared memory and the local buffers. If the processing on the local buffers is sustained for relatively longer time, the overhead is negligible and there is a performance gain due to the removal of the false sharing effect.

Even though the above optimizations can be done in traditional DSM programs, they are enforced in VOPP. Since *acquire_views* cannot be nested, infrequently-shared data have to be moved to local buffers so that frequently-shared data can be accessed at the same time.

3.2 Removal of barriers

In VOPP, barriers are only used for synchronization among processors and have nothing to do with access exclusion and consistency maintenance of DSM. The consistency maintenance and access exclusion are achieved automatically by the view primitives. In some traditional DSM programs, barriers are used for access exclusion instead of synchronization, in which case barriers can be removed in VOPP programs. Integer Sort (IS) has such a barrier that can be moved from inside a loop to outside.

3.3 Shared memory for frequently-shared data

Frequently-shared data is often mixed with infrequently shared data in traditional DSM programs. For example, the SOR program processes a matrix with multiple processors, each of which gets a portion of the matrix. Each processor works on its portion most of the time, but needs the border elements between portions from the portion of its neighbour processors after every iteration. Each portion of the matrix is not frequently shared except the border elements. However, the SOR program allocates a block of shared memory to the whole matrix and multiple processors directly access the shared memory, which causes the false sharing effect. The pseudo-code of the traditional SOR program is shown below.

```
processor 0 reads in the matrix
            into the shared memory;
barrier(0);
   //executed by each processor;
```

```
for(i=0;i<max_iterations;i++){
    read border elements
         from its neighbor's share;
    update its share of the matrix
         with the border elements;
    barrier(0);
}
read and print out the whole matrix;
```

In VOPP, we allocate a local buffer for the portion of the matrix of each processor, since it is not frequently shared. We use separate views for those border elements which are frequently shared. At the end of each iteration, border elements of the views are updated by copying them from the local buffers to their respective views. At the beginning of the next iteration, the border elements in the views are read by the corresponding processors. In this way, only the border elements of the views are passed between processors through the cluster network instead of other irrelevant elements of the same page. The pseudo-code is as below.

```
processor 0 reads in the matrix
             into the shared memory;
barrier(0);
acquire_view(proc_id);
read its share of the matrix
                 into a local buffer;
release_view(proc_id);
bdv = nprocs;
for(i=0;i<max_iterations;i++){
    acquire_view(bdv+prev_pid);
    read border elements from
          the previous processor;
     release_view(bdv+prev_pid);

    acquire_view(bdv+next_pid);
    read border elements from
          the next processor;
     release_view(bdv+next_pid);

     update the local buffer
           with the border elements;

    acquire_view(bdv+proc_id);
    update the border elements of
          the current processor;
     release_view(bdv+proc_id);
    barrier(0);
}
if(proc_id==0){
  for(j=0;j<nprocs;j++)
                 acquire_Rview(j);
  read and print the whole matrix;
  for(j=0;j<nprocs;j++)
                 release_Rview(j);
}
barrier(0);
```

The above optimization is again enforced by VOPP so that frequently-shared data can be accessed at the same time as the infrequently-shared data is accessed. Likewise there is an overhead of copying between the shared memory and the local buffers. However the overhead is negligible if the processing on the local buffers is sustained for relatively long time. Another overhead is the view primitives called in the loop, which will result in more messages than the traditional DSM program. However, there is a big performance difference between the barriers in VOPP and those in traditional programs. Barriers in VOPP simply synchronize the processors without any consistency maintenance, while barriers in traditional programs have to maintain the consistency of the shared memory. Maintaining consistency in barriers is a centralized way for consistency maintenance and becomes time-consuming when the number of processors increases. Even though there are many view primitives in the above VOPP program, consistency maintenance is optimally achieved by them in a distributed way. Therefore, overall the above VOPP program will still perform better than its traditional version, especially when the number of processors is large.

3.4 *acquire_Rview* for read-only data

Read-only views can be accessed with *acquire_Rview* and *release_Rview* in VOPP. Programmers can use them to improve the performance of VOPP programs, since multiple read-only accesses to the same view can be granted simultaneously, so that the waiting time for acquiring access to read-only views is very small. Programmers can use them to replace barriers and read/write view primitives (*acquire_view* and *release_view*) wherever possible to optimise VOPP programs. In NN, a global weight matrix is shared by all processors. After each iteration, the weight matrix is updated by every processor. At the beginning of each iteration, every processor needs to read the weight matrix to update the neural network. We use *acquire_Rview* to enable every processor to read the matrix concurrently rather than sequentially.

3.5 *merge_views* for merging views

When there is a need to rearrange the views at some stage in a program, *merge_views* can be used to update all views of every processor so that each processor has an up to date copy of the whole shared memory. This operation is expensive but convenient for programmers. However, we have not seen any program that has such a need so far.

3.6 Basic rule of thumb

The following basic rule of thumb can help VOPP programmers optimize view partitioning and parallel algorithms proactively: the more views are acquired, the more messages there are in the system; and the larger a view is, the more data traffic is caused in the system when the view is acquired.

4 Comparison with related work

VOPP is different from the programming style of Entry Consistency in terms of the association between data objects and views (or locks). Entry Consistency [2] requires the programmer to explicitly associate data objects with locks and barriers in programs, while VOPP only requires the programmer to implicitly associate data objects with views (in the programmer's mind). The actual association is achieved in view detection in the implementation of the VC model. Since the association is achieved dynamically, VOPP is more flexible than the programming style of Entry Consistency.

VOPP is also different from the programming style of Scope Consistency (ScC) in terms of the definition of the concepts of view and scope. Once determined by the programmer, views in VOPP are non-overlapped and constant throughout a program, while scopes in ScC can be overlapped and are merged into a global scope at barriers. Programs based on ScC are extended from the traditional DSM programs, i.e., lock primitives are normally used in programs while scope primitives such as *open_scope* are used only when required by memory consistency. However, in contrast to the traditional DSM programs, the focus of VOPP is shifted towards shared data (views) rather than synchronization and mutual exclusion.

VOPP is more convenient and easier for programmers than the message-passing programming style such as MPI [4], since VOPP is still based on the concept of shared memory (except the consistency of the shared memory is maintained according to views). Moreover, VOPP provides experienced programmers an opportunity to fine-tune the performance of their programs by carefully dividing the shared memory into views. Partitioning of shared data into views becomes part of the design of a parallel algorithm in VOPP. This approach offers the potential for programmers to make VOPP programs perform as well as MPI programs, which is the ultimate goal of our VOPP-based DSM system.

5 Experimental evaluation

In this section, we present our experimental results of several applications running on the following three DSM implementations: LRC_d, VC_d and VC_{sd}.

- LRC_d is a diff-based implementation of the Lazy Release Consistency (LRC) model [10]. It is the original implementation of LRC in TreadMarks [1], which uses diffs to represent modifications of a page.

- VC_d is our implementation of VC which uses diffs to represent modifications of a page. It uses the same implementation techniques (e.g. the invalidation protocol) as the LRC_d.

- VC_{sd} is our implementation of VC based on a diff integration scheme [5], which uses a single diff to represent modifications of a page and piggy-backs diffs of a view on the view acquiring message. It is an optimal implementation of VC and renders better performance for applications than other DSM implementations.

Since VC_d and LRC_d use the same implementation techniques, the performance advantage of VOPP over traditional DSM programs can be demonstrated by running applications on these two implementations. The overall performance advantage of VOPP (including the potential for an optimal implementation) can be demonstrated by comparing VC_{sd} with LRC_d.

All tests are carried out on our cluster computer called Godzilla. The cluster consists of 32 PCs running Linux 2.4, which are connected by a N-way 100 Mbps Ethernet switch. Each of the PCs has a 350 MHz processor and 192 Mbytes of memory. The page size of the virtual memory is 4 KB. Though our processors are relatively slow, a cluster with faster processors can more favorably demonstrate the advantage of the VC model. The reason is that VC significantly reduces data traffic of the network which is the bottle neck of a cluster with faster processors.

The applications used in our tests include Integer Sort (IS), Gauss, Successive Over-Relaxation (SOR), and Neural network (NN).

5.1 Integer Sort (IS)

The problem size of IS in our tests is ($2^{25} \times 2^{15}$, 40). Table 1 shows the statistics of IS running on 16 processors, which can typically demonstrate the performance of our applications.

	LRC_d	VC_d	VC_{sd}
Time (Sec.)	78.4	53.4	25.8
Barriers	682	682	682
Acquires	0	20,479	20,479
Data (GByte)	1.236	1.279	0.174
Num. Msg	123,994	180,207	80,387
Diff Requests	38270	38,398	0
Barrier Time (usec.)	34,492	5467	2211
Rexmit	114	14	0

Table 1: Statistics of IS on 16 processors

In the table, *Barriers* is the number of barriers called in the program; *Acquires* is the number of lock/view acquiring messages; *Data* is the total amount of data transmitted; *Num. Msg* is the total number of messages; *Diff Requests* is the number of diff requests; and *Barrier Time* is the average time spent on barriers; and *Rexmit* is the number of messages retransmitted. From the statistics, we find the number of messages and the amount of data transmitted in VC_d are more than in LRC_d, however VC_d is faster than LRC_d. The reason is two-fold. First, the barriers in LRC_d need to maintain consistency while those ones in VC_d do not. The consistency maintenance of barriers in LRC_d is normally time-consuming and centralized at one processor which can be a bottleneck. The consistency maintenance in VC_d is distributed among the processors through the view primitives. From the table, the average barrier time in LRC_d is 34,492 microseconds, while the average barrier time in VC_d is 5467 microseconds. Second, LRC_d has more message loss than VC_d according to the number of retransmissions ($Rexmit$ in the table). LRC_d has 114 retransmissions while VC_d only has 14 retransmissions. One message retransmission results in about 1 second waiting time. The above statistics demonstrate the distribution of data traffic in VOPP programs can help reduce message retransmissions and improve the performance of the VOPP programs. The table also shows the optimal implementation VC_{sd} has greatly reduced the amount of data and number of messages in the cluster network.

We have two VOPP versions of IS: one uses the same number of barriers as the original version (whose statistics have been shown above), and the other moves the barrier from inside the loop to outside (as we mentioned in Section 3.2). Table 2 shows the statistics of IS with fewer barriers.

	VC_d	VC_{sd}
Time (Sec.)	49.6	24.2
Barriers	122	122
Acquires	20,479	20,479
Data (GByte)	1.278	0.173
Num. Msg	163,420	63,586
Diff Requests	38,398	0
Barrier Time (usec.)	9891	5540
Rexmit	14	0

Table 2: Statistics of IS with fewer barriers on 16 processors

Comparing Table 2 with Table 1, it is not surprising to find that the VOPP version of IS with fewer barriers is significantly faster than its counterpart with more barriers.

Table 3 shows the speedups of IS running on 2, 4, 8, 16, 24, and 32 processors. From the table we find the speedups of VC_{sd} are significantly better than those of LRC_d. When the barrier is moved to outside the loop (refer to the row $VC_{sd}lb$) the speedups are further improved, especially when the number of processors becomes large.

	2-p	4-p	8-p	16-p	24-p	32-p
LRC_d	2	3.67	5.07	3.66	2.38	1.70
VC_{sd}	2	3.81	6.88	11.12	12.58	12.16
$VC_{sd}lb$	2	3.8	6.93	11.81	15.01	16.04

Table 3: Speedup of IS on LRC_d and VC_{sd}

5.2 Gauss

The matrix size of Gauss is 2048×2048 and the number of iterations is 1024 in our tests. The original *Gauss* program has the false sharing effect. The VOPP version has significantly improved the performance by removing the false sharing effect with local buffers. Table 4 shows the number of diff requests in VC_d is significantly smaller than that of LRC_d due to the removal of the false sharing effect.

	LRC_d	VC_d	VC_{sd}
Time (Sec.)	38.7	13.2	10.2
Barriers	1027	1028	1028
Acquires	0	17330	17295
Data (MByte)	255	21	20
Num. Msg	184517	119346	88521
Diff Requests	44145	15360	0
Barrier Time (usec.)	7080	3586	3610

Table 4: Statistics of Gauss on 16 processors

Even though there is an overhead for copying data between the shared memory and the local buffers (as mentioned in Section 3.1), there is a significant advantage by processing the data in the local buffers instead of in the shared memory. Due to the use of local buffers for infrequently-shared data, the work for consistency maintenance (e.g. diff requests) is greatly reduced and accordingly the amount of data and the number of messages are significantly reduced (refer to the rows $Data$ and $Num.Msg$ in Table 4).

Table 5 shows the speedups of LRC_d and VC_{sd}. The speedups of VC_{sd} is really impressive compared with those of LRC_d.

	2-p	4-p	8-p	16-p	24-p	32-p
LRC_d	1.9	3.08	3.5	2.5	1.84	1.44
VC_{sd}	1.98	3.75	6.55	9.42	9.13	8.3

Table 5: Speedup of Gauss on LRC_d and VC_{sd}

5.3 Successive Over-Relaxation (SOR)

SOR processes a matrix with size 4000×4000 and the number of iterations is 50 in our tests. Similar to *Gauss*, *SOR* has infrequently-shared data which mixes with frequently-shared data. The VOPP version uses local buffers for those infrequently-shared data to reduce the false sharing effect. Furthermore, it uses shared memory (a set of views) for those frequently-shared data such as the border elements. Due to the wise allocation of shared memory and local buffers, the amount of data transferred in the cluster network is very small and accordingly the VOPP program performs better than the original *SOR* program. Table 6 shows the amount of data transferred in LRC_d is 65.57 Megabytes while the amount in VC_d is reduced to 2.99 Megabytes. The number of messages in VC_d is also reduced.

	LRC_d	VC_d	VC_{sd}
Time (Sec.)	11.2	4.3	4.12
Barriers	102	102	102
Acquires	0	6030	6030
Data (MByte)	65.57	2.99	3.37
Num. Msg	45,471	33,144	21,152
Diff Requests	5907	5996	0
Barrier Time (usec.)	139,100	3738	3483

Table 6: Statistics of SOR on 16 processors

Another factor contributing to the better performance of the VOPP program is faster barrier implementation in VC (as mentioned in Section 3.3). From Table 6, the average barrier time in VC_d is 3738 microseconds, while the barrier time in LRC_d is 139,100 microseconds.

Table 7 shows that the speedups of the VOPP program running on VC_{sd} is greatly improved compared with the original program running on LRC_d.

	2-p	4-p	8-p	16-p	24-p	32-p
LRC_d	1.65	2.67	3.7	4.45	4.47	4.33
VC_{sd}	1.98	3.81	6.96	11.43	14.1	14.75

Table 7: Speedup of SOR on LRC_d and VC_{sd}

5.4 Neural Network (NN)

The size of the neural network in *NN* is $9 \times 40 \times 1$ and the number of epochs taken for the training is 235. The VOPP version of *NN* uses local buffers for infrequently-shared data and *acquire_Rview* for read-only data. The *acquire_Rview* for read-only data is very important for the VOPP program. Without it the major part of the VOPP program would run sequentially. Table 8 shows VOPP itself does not demonstrate any performance advantage in *NN* since VC_d sends more messages and data than LRC_d due to more view primitives used in the VOPP program. Thus VC_d is slower than LRC_d. However, the performance potential offered by VOPP to DSM implementation becomes larger when more view primitives are used. Table 8 shows VC_{sd} performs significantly better than LRC_d. The number of messages and the amount of data transferred in the cluster network are greatly reduced in VC_{sd} due to diff integration and diff piggy-backing.

	LRC_d	VC_d	VC_{sd}
Time (Sec.)	114	119.4	54.07
Barriers	473	473	473
Acquires	7520	22,371	22,371
Data (MByte)	335	376	64.7
Num. Msg	101,919	161,400	81,590
Diff Requests	31,228	39,900	0
Barrier Time (usec.)	122,324	147,389	13,141
Acquire Time (usec.)	2555	21,527	3872

Table 8: Statistics of NN on 16 processors

Table 9 presents the speedups of LRC_d and VC_{sd}. The table shows the speedups of the VOPP version of *NN* are significantly improved by VC_{sd}. In order to compare the performance of VOPP programs with MPI programs, we run the equivalent MPI version of *NN* on MPICH [4]. The speedups of the MPI version of *NN* is also shown in Table 9. The performance of the VOPP program is comparable with that of the MPI version on up to 16 processors. On more than 16 processors, the speedup of the VOPP program still keeps growing, though it is not as good as the MPI program. We will investigate the reason behind the performance difference between the VOPP program and the MPI program running on larger number of processors in the future.

	2-p	4-p	8-p	16-p	24-p	32-p
LRC_d	1.98	3.93	7.1	6.45	4.02	2.54
VC_{sd}	1.99	3.97	7.73	13.43	16.17	16.95
MPI	1.78	3.64	7.17	14.08	20.22	25.38

Table 9: Speedup of NN on LRC_d, VC_{sd} and MPI

6 Conclusions

This paper presents a novel VOPP programming style for DSM parallel programs on cluster computers. Several applications are converted and optimized based on the requirements of VOPP. Our experimental results demonstrate the significant performance advantage of VOPP and its great performance potential offered to DSM implementations. VOPP is based on shared memory and is easy for programmers to use. It only requires programmers to insert view primitives when a view is accessed. The insertion of view primitives can be automated by compiling techniques, which will be investigated in our future research. We will also investigate the reasons behind the performance difference between VOPP programs and MPI programs and will develop more efficient implementation techniques for the associated VC model. Our ultimate goal is to make shared memory parallel programs as efficient as message-passing parallel programs.

References

[1] Amza, C., Cox, A.L., Dwarkadas, S., Keleher, P., Lu, H., Rajamony, R., Yu, W., Zwaenepoel, W.: TreadMarks: Shared memory computing on networks of workstations. IEEE Computer 29 (1996) 18–28

[2] Bershad, B.N., Zekauskas, M.J.: Midway: Shared memory parallel programming with Entry Consistency for distributed memory multiprocessors. CMU Technical Report (CMU-CS-91-170) Carnegie-Mellon University (1991)

[3] Gharachorloo, K., Lenoski, D., and Laudon, J.: Memory consistency and event ordering in scalable shared memory multiprocessors. In: Proc. of the 17th Annual International Symposium on Computer Architecture (1990) 15–26.

[4] Gropp, W., Lusk, E., Skjellum, A.: A high-performance, portable implementation of the MPI message passing interface standard. Parallel Computing 22 (1996) 789–828

[5] Huang, Z., Purvis M., and Werstein P.: View Oriented Update Protocol with Integrated Diff for View-based Consistency. In: Proc. of the IEEE/ACM Symposium on Cluster Computing and Grid 2005 (CCGrid05), IEEE Computer Society (2005)

[6] Huang, Z., Purvis M., and Werstein P.: View-Oriented Parallel Programming on Cluster Computers. Technical Report (OUCS-2004-09), Dept of Computer Science, Univ. of Otago, (2004) (http://www.cs.otago.ac.nz/research/techreports.html)

[7] Huang, Z., Purvis M., and Werstein P.: View-Oriented Parallel Programming and View-based Consistency. In: Proc. of the Fifth International Conference on Parallel and Distributed Computing, Applications and Technologies (LNCS 3320) (2004) 505-518.

[8] Huang, Z., Sun, C., Cranefield, S., Purvis, M.: A View-based Consistency model based on transparent data selection in distributed shared memory. Technical Report (OUCS-2004-03) Dept of Computer Science, Univ. of Otago, (2004) (http://www.cs.otago.ac.nz/research/techreports.html)

[9] Iftode, L., Singh, J.P., Li, K.: Scope Consistency: A bridge between Release Consistency and Entry Consistency. In: Proc. of the 8th Annual ACM Symposium on Parallel Algorithms and Architectures (1996)

[10] Keleher, P.: Lazy Release Consistency for distributed shared memory. Ph.D. Thesis (Rice Univ) (1995)

[11] Lamport, L.: How to make a multiprocessor computer that correctly executes multiprocess programs. IEEE Transactions on Computers 28 (1979) 690–691

[12] Werstein, P., Pethick, M., Huang, Z.: A Performance Comparison of DSM, PVM, and MPI. In: Proc. of the Fourth International Conference on Parallel and Distributed Computing, Applications and Technologies (PDCAT03), IEEE Press, (2003) 476–482

Session 4B: P2P Search & Discovery

A C/S AND P2P HYBRID RESOURCE DISCOVERY FRAMEWORK IN GRID ENVIRONMENTS

Yili Gong*, + Wei Li* Yuzhong Sun* Zhiwei Xu†
*(Software Division, Institute of Computing Technology, Chinese Academy of Sciences, Beijing 100080)
+(Graduate School of the Chinese Academy of Sciences, Beijing 100039)
† (Institute of Computing Technology, Chinese Academy of Sciences, Beijing 100080)
gongyili@ict.ac.cn

Abstract

Resource discovery is crucial to efficient deployment of a grid system whose dynamic, heterogeneous characteristics make it difficult. In this paper, Vega Infrastructure for Resource Discovery (VIRD) is developed, then augmented with new features (i.e., some new algorithms) to build a C/S (client/server) and P2P (peer-to-peer) hybrid resource discovery framework. The three layered architecture of the VIRD is developed to make advantage of the physical and logical topologies of the Internet to facilitate resource discovery. With our simulations and theoretical analysis, it is proved that VIRD is of good scalability with respect to the sizes of the underlying backbone. Even when the resource density is low and the max TTL (time-to-live) is small, VIRD still achieves high search success rates in a small amount of hops. Compared with flooding and random walk algorithms via the same search success rates, VIRD outperforms them in both network traffic and response time.

1. Introduction

Resource discovery, a crucial part of a grid, refers to the process of finding satisfactory resources for user requests, including resource description, resource organization, resource lookup, and resource selection. Both dynamism and heterogeneity of a grid make resource discovery difficult.

The current resource discovery systems fall into two categories: centralized and distributed. Centralized resource management systems may have better lookup performance due to little network communication overhead, but may be of poor scalability and have a single point of failure. Distributed systems, such as peer-to-peer systems, usually are scalable, but having a barrier that the flat structure of peers does not make full use of the physical and logical topologies of the Internet. For example, users in a LAN may share similar interests; users may have faster access speeds to resources in the same MAN than to those in a different MAN; the traffic cost of users in LANs is faster and cheaper than that in the backbone. To make full use of these properties, in [1], we proposed the three-layer VIRD for the first time, however, giving no specific inter-domain routing algorithms and no experiments on the overall architecture. In this paper, VIRD is extended, and the intra-domain information update algorithm, the intra- and inter-domain request routing algorithms are completely given. In addition, theoretical analysis, and, simulations of VIRD in comparison with flooding and random walk algorithms are presented.

Regarding of the large quantity and variety of resources in grids, and the constant changes of their states and attributes, it is not enough to descript a resource by a simple string (ID), such as human unreadable hash values. Therefore the more expressive and user friendly attribute-value description is used. Users can use it to describe what they want, instead of where to find things.

By far, there exist no general standards and benchmarks for evaluating grid resource discovery systems. On users' behalf, this paper is interested in the success rate and the response time of request lookups. From the perspective of systems, the main interest goes to the network traffic. The simulation results prove that the response time almost keeps constant as the number of BGRNSes grows up. The inter-domain traffic does not grow exponentially with the size of the backbone network, which conforms to our theoretical analysis. Therefore VIRD is of good scalability with respect to the

This work is supported in part by the National Natural Science Foundation of China (Grant No. 69925205), the China Ministry of Science and Technology 863 Program (Grant No. 2002AA104310), and the Chinese Academy of Sciences Oversea Distinguished Scholars Fund (Grant No. 20014010).

0190-3918/05 $20.00 © 2005 IEEE

size of the backbone network. In addition, even with rather low resource density and small TTL_{max}, success rate of VIRD is still high. Our simulation also shows that VIRD outperforms flooding and random walk algorithms in both network traffic and response time.

VIRD presented in this paper makes three key contributions: (1) it integrates Client/Server and Peer-to-Peer architecture to make full use of the physical and logical topology of the Internet; (2) it provides an attribute-value based naming scheme for users to query resources in grids; (3) it performs better in both network traffic and response time than flooding and random walk under a given success rate.

The rest of this paper is organized as follows. Section 2 discusses some related grid and peer-to-peer resource discovery systems. The VIRD architecture and algorithms are presented in Section 4. Section 5 explains the simulation methodology, environment and results and Section 6 concludes.

2. Related Work

A lot of work has been done on the grid resource discovery. Matchmaker in Condor [3] uses a central server to match the attributes in the users' specification and those in the service providers' declaration. Such approach has a single point of failure and scales poorly. In Legion [4], Collections, the information databases, are populated with resource descriptions. The Scheduler queries the Collection and finds proper resources for applications. A few global Collections will prohibit the scalability of the system. Globus' MDS-2 [5] is a distributed resource information system: resource providers register to GIIS by the registration protocol; and users access the resource information in GIIS and GRIS by the enquiry protocol. But it does not work well when the number of resources grows and updates are common.

Peer-to-peer technologies, which have been recently popularized through file sharing applications, are divided into two categories: one is unstructured, such as Gnutella [2] and Freenet [6]; the other is structured, including Pastry [7], Tapestry [8], CAN [9] and Chord [10], etc. It is generally thought that the Gnutella protocol, which is based on broadcasting, is simple and robust, while puts heavy demand on the bandwidth and limits the scalability of the system. Both Gnutella and Freenet do not guarantee to find an existing object. In general, the structured systems have better lookup performance than the unstructured ones; they will obtain definite results within finite hops and keep scalability and autonomy as well. But because they are based on the prerequisite that every object has a unique ID and users know the IDs of the objects they want before hand, these methods lack adequate querying capability for complex resource queries.

INS [17] is a resource discovery and service location system for dynamic and mobile networks of devices and computers. INS is intended for small networks on the order of several hundred to a few thousand nodes. INS/Twine [18] is a peer-to-peer architecture for intentional resource discovery. The updating paths between resolvers may be across the whole network and the updating cost is a big problem. On the other side, Twine can do little for a category of queries whose every strand is popular.

A grid resource discovery model based on routing-forwarding is proposed and analyzed in [11]. The model may suffer from scalability problem because all the resource routers are equal peers and resource routing information need propagate across the whole network.

3. Design of VIRD

3.1. Overview

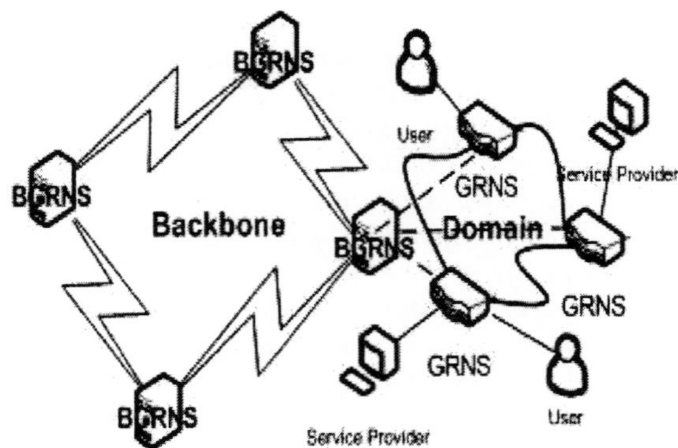

Figure 1. The VIRD architecture: backbone, domains and leaves.

A VIRD system is presented in Figure 1: the top level is the backbone consisting of BGRNSes (Border Grid Resource Name Server); the second level is domains and each domain consists of GRNSes (Grid Resource Name Server), and the bottom level is leaves which include all clients and resource providers.

BGRNS A BGRNS connects the backbone with one or more domains. It answers queries forwarded from GRNSes or other BGRNSes.

GRNS A GRNS not only knows the information about the resources registered to it, but that about all other resources in the same domain through information propagation. It also acts to queries according to its local information.

Service Provider A service provider reports its resource status periodically to its designated GRNS, i.e. the GRNS it connected to.

Client A client sends requests to a GRNS and receives responses. A host can be both a client and a resource provider.

3.2. Topology

As mentioned before, the motivation of VIRD is to utilize the physical and logical structure of the Internet. The topology of VIRD obeys the topology of the Internet, i.e. a user or a resource provider corresponding to a host, a GRNS corresponding to a router in a domain, and a BGRNS corresponding to a border gateway. A BGRNS should be a stable, well-connected server, and a GRNS is recommended to act as a gateway of a LAN. Some kind of cache may be implemented at a GRNS to use the fact that users in a LAN may share many common interests. The interconnections between the GRNSes and BGRNSes also follow those of the routers on the Internet. Thus it can be said that the communication latency of two neighboring BGRNSes or GRNSes is generally shorter than that of two which are not neighboring. This is a difference between VIRD and many overlay networks, such as peer-to-peer networks.

When a BGRNS starts up, it queries a well known site, which returns it with a list of BGRNSes according to its IP address. The BGRNS calculates the latency between itself and them, and chooses several nearest nodes to set up neighboring connections according to its own bandwidth and/or computing capacity. While a GRNS enters, it queries the site for a BGRNS of the domain it belongs to. Then it asks the BGRNS for a current graph of the GRNSes in that domain to calculate neighbors. We note that networking of nodes might put great influence on the performance of resource discovery algorithms. We are currently exploring the "best" topology for certain algorithms and how to construct it. Users or service providers may get their designated GRNS addresses from their system administrators like the way to get Internet connections. They can also get a list of GRNS addresses from some well known site and choose a nearest one by some *pings*.

3.3. Resource Naming

A lot of work has been done on resource naming or description, such as [3], [4], [17], [19] and [20]. VIRD implements a simple naming scheme, which specifies what resources users are looking for, instead of where to find them. The naming scheme is independent form VIRD and replaceable.

The naming scheme is to divide resources into classes and define attributes for every class. The syntax of our naming scheme in Backus-Naur Form, or BNF, is as follows.

```
<res_name> ::= (<class_name> | <class_id>) ["?" <specification>]
<class_name> ::= <string>
<class_id ::= <number>
<specification> ::= (<attribute> <cop> <value>) {<bop> (<attribute> <cop> <value>)}
<attribute> ::= <string>
<value> ::= <string> | <res_name>
<bop> ::= ">" | "=" | "<" | ">=" | "!=" |"<=" | include | exclude | satisfy
<cop> ::= AND | OR | NOT
```

The following resource name describes an instance of class ComputingRresource whose attribute OS is an instance of class OperatingSystem.

```
ComputingResource ? (CPU > "933MHz") AND (memory = "256M") AND (OS satisfy (OperatingSystem ? (type = "Linux") AND (version = "RedHat7.2")))
```

3.4. Intra-domain Information Updating

Intra-domain updating is to propagate resource information dynamically in a domain, while there is no information propagated between domains.

Resources refresh their attribute values periodically and GRNSes disseminate the information among the domain. Expired resources will automatically be eliminated after a timeout. This soft-state approach allows a fact that resources may join and leave the system without explicit de-registration.

A GRNS constructs a RSP (Resource State Package) periodically or when one or more of the following things happen: (1) a new neighbor comes or goes; or (2) the state of some registered resource changes. If no such things happen in a given time period, a GRNS should send an empty RSP to its neighbors to show its status, or its neighbors may think that it is down.

Each GRNS keeps track of the sequence number of its last RSP. When generating a new RSP, it will use the next number. At the same time, a GRNS will also keep all latest sequence numbers of other GRNSes' RSPs, and on receiving a RSP, it will compare the sequence number of the received RSP with the one of the same neighbor in its memory, if the former is bigger, the received RSP is newer and would be used to update the local routing table, or would be discarded.

3.5. Intra-domain Resource Discovery

On receiving a request from a user, a GRNS will check its local resources first. If there is a satisfactory resource, it will reserve the resource and return a handle for the resource. If no, it will search its resource table of the domain, if finding some, it will send an acknowledgement request to that resource's designated GRNS. If the acknowledgement fails for *Threshold* times; the requests will be forwarded to a corresponding BGRNS. In our simulation *Threshold* is set to 3.

3.6. Inter-domain Routing

The inter-domain routing algorithm of VIRD is based on the Gnutella protocol with some modification. To limit traffic in the backbone, and due to the fact that the information tends to be out of date because of the long distance between GRNSes in different domains, it is designed that a BGRNS does not store any information about resources in other domains. On the other hand, because BGRNSes are all dedicated servers, no anonymity and firewall problems are considered, the VIRD inter-domain routing algorithm is a little different from the Gnutella: a search response does not return to the requester along hops of the coming path, instead, the GRNS having the satisfactory resource responds to the initial GRNS directly. This modification may reduce the response time by half.

3.7. Performance Analysis

Table 1. Symbols and definitions.

Symbol	Definition
N	The number of nodes (BGRNSes) in the backbone network.
E	The number of edges in the backbone network.
δ	The diameter of the backbone network.
$\overline{d}$	The average outdegree of the nodes of the backbone network: $\overline{d} = 2E/N$.
$NN(h)$	The average number of nodes in a neighborhood of h hops.
N_r	The number of a kind of resources in the grid.
N_{domain}	The average number of nodes (GRNS) in a domain.
D_r	The resource density of a kind of resources, defined as $N_r/(N^* N_{domain})$.
p_{match}	The probability that a resource and a request match.
$p_{success}$	The probability that a request succeeds, i.e. at least one satisfactory resource is found.
TTL_{max}	The maximum allowed value of TTL (time-to-live).

Known from the work of Faloutsos et al [12] and that of Jovanovic [13], both the routers in the Internet (whose distribution VIRD also follows) and the nodes in the Gnutella system obey all the power-laws described in [12]. In next part we will use these conclusions to analytically characterize some attributes in VIRD. The symbols used are listed in Table 1.

First, we study the number of messages related to a single request. In the worst case, six messages (three acknowledge requests and corresponding acknowledge fail responses) are generated in a domain and then the request is forwarded to the backbone, after h hops all the messages time out and no satisfactory resource is found. At this time, the number of the generated inter-domain messages, N_{inter_msg}, is

$$N_{inter\_msg} \leq \overline{d} + \overline{d}^2 + \ldots + \overline{d}^h = \frac{\overline{d}\left(1 - \overline{d}^h\right)}{1 - \overline{d}} \qquad (1)$$

According to Lemma 2 in [12], the number of edges, E, of a graph, can be estimated as a function of the number of nodes, N, and the rank exponent, $\Re$:

$$E = \frac{1}{2(\Re+1)}\left(1 - \frac{1}{N^{\Re+1}}\right)N \qquad (2)$$

Substituting Equation 2 into $\overline{d} = \frac{2E}{N}$, it goes into

$$\overline{d} = \frac{1}{\Re+1}\left(1 - \frac{1}{N^{\Re+1}}\right) \qquad (3)$$

It can be seen that when $N \rightarrow +\infty$, $\overline{d} \rightarrow \frac{1}{\Re+1}$, i.e. $\overline{d}$ has a supremum as $\frac{1}{\Re+1}$. Bring this supremum into Equation 1, it turns into

$$N_{inter\_msg} \rightarrow \frac{1}{\Re}\left(1 - \left(\frac{1}{\Re+1}\right)^h\right) \qquad (4)$$

Thus in the worst case the number of messages generated by a single request is no more than $6 + \frac{1}{\Re}\left(1 - \left(\frac{1}{\Re+1}\right)^h\right)$, which is only related to h and has no direct relationship with N.

Next, let's quantify the hops, h. The average size of the neighborhood, $NN(h)$, within h hops as a function of the hop-plot exponent, H, for $h \ll \delta$, is

$$NN(h) = \frac{c}{N}h^H - 1 \qquad (5)$$

where $c = N + 2E$.

The probability that a request can find at least one matched resource in h hops is given by

$$p_{success} = 1 - \left(1 - p_{match}\right)^{D_r \times N_{domain} \times NN(h)} \qquad (6)$$

Substituting Equation 5 and $E = \frac{1}{2}\left(\overline{d} \times N\right)$ into this equation, h would be given by

$$h = \left[N\left(\frac{1}{1+\overline{d}}\right)\left(\frac{\ln(1 - p_{success})}{D_r \times N_{domain} \times \ln(1 - p_{match})} + 1\right)\right]^{\frac{1}{H}} \qquad (7)$$

Assuming h_{min} is the smallest integer which is no less than the number of the right side of Equation 4, if only $h \geq h_{min}$, the search success rate will be greater than $p_{success}$. From the above analysis, it can be seen that with a certain search success rate, increasing p_{match}, D_r and N_{domain} would decrease h_{min}. p_{match} depends on attributions of resources and requests, and their relationship, which can not be changed by a resource discovery system. On the other side, layering VIRD decreases the node number of the backbone and increases the node number in a domain, and in sequence decreases h_{min}. Of course, the node number of a domain can not be too big, and the issue of the size of a domain is discussed in [1]. In particular, from Equation 7 it is known that increasing $\overline{d}$ will decrease h_{min}, but at the mean time, it will increase the traffic that a request may bring to the network, and thus it is not desirable to decrease h_{min} by increasing $\overline{d}$.

Some people criticize Gnutella for not scaling well with the argument that if one wants to query a constant fraction of the Gnutella network, as the network grows, each node and network edge will be handling query traffic which is proportional to the total number of nodes in the network. But in reality, searching for a query is limited within a radius of TTL_{max}. To achieve a given search success rate, TTL_{max} should be set to h_{min}, which is proportional to $N^{\frac{1}{H}}$. In particular, because VIRD is made up of three layers and the flooding algorithm is only used in the backbone, the increase in the number of resources registered to a GRNS and the number of GRNSes in a BGRNS will have no influence on inter-domain searching performance except that it may increase the cost of searching the local routing table on BGRNSes.

4. Performance Evaluation

Flooding is optimal in delay for finding a resource among all unstructured P2P algorithms without respect to bandwidth limitation of underlying networks [21]. Regarding of the heavy traffic caused by flooding algorithms, random walk [21] are designed to supersede flooding algorithms in a bandwidth limited environment. Therefore we made a wide range of experiments to compare VIRD, flooding and random walk in terms of network traffic, response time and success rate by simulation.

We implemented a parameter-configurable, event-driven simulator, SimVIRD, by which we simulate our framework.

4.1. Assumptions

A resource discovery system is rather complicated and influenced by many factors. To simplify the problem, some assumptions are made: 1) because VIRD servers are more stable than nodes in a P2P network, transient nodes are not considered; 2) because running the simulator with different arguments may simulate different resources, at once only one kind of resource, computing resource, is simulated, and only one attribute of a resource, load, changes dynamically; 3) correspondingly, a request only queries a resource with load smaller than a certain value; 4) since it is implementation-specific and should be much smaller than the network latency, the processing time on a node is ignored; 5) it is assumed that the storage of a node is unlimited.

4.2. Metrics

Three metrics are considered. The former two are from the user's perspective, while the latter is from the system's perspective.

Response time ($T_{response}$): the time period from the point when a request arrives at its initial GRNS to the point when the first satisfactory resource is found. In VIRD when the resource is found, its designated GRNS will directly reply to the request's initial GRNS, while in Gnutella when the resource is found, the request will return along the coming path. To compare the resource discovery time, the response time is defined as the time to find the first qualified resource instead of that of returning to the client.

Request Success Rate: the percentage of satisfied requests of total request.

Traffic: system traffic ($Traffic_{sys}$), caused by propagating of system information and user traffic ($Traffic_{usr}$), caused by answering user requests. While for the flooding and random walk algorithms, only the latter traffic is incurred. Here the unit of traffic is the number of packages sent.

4.3. Inputs and Parameters

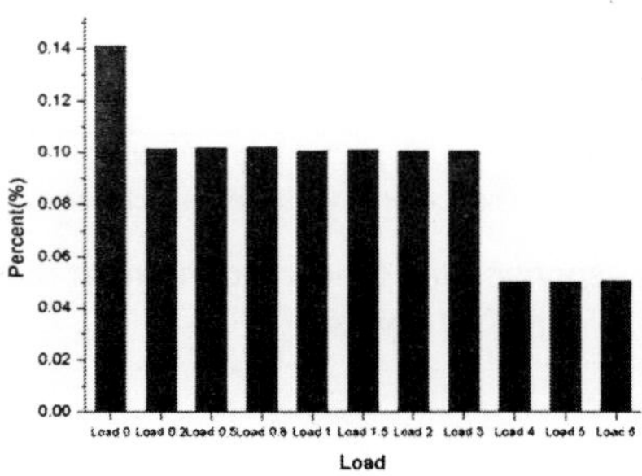

Figure 2. The distribution of the dynamic attribute, load.

The inputs of the simulations include:

Network topology: the networks of all domains and the backbone are generated by GridG [14], which extends the network generator, Tiers [15], and produces networks obeying the power laws of the Internet topology.

Resource distribution: the resources simulated are computing resources whose attributes are generated by GridG, including CPU number, CPU speed, memory size, etc, and a dynamically changing attribute, current load. It is assumed that resources are distributed across the network evenly. Resource density D_r is defined as

$$D_r = \frac{\text{Resource Number}}{\text{BGRS Number} \times \text{GRNS Number per Domain}}.$$

Distribution of resource's attribute, load: the distribution of the dynamic attribute, load, is shown in Figure 2, which is calculated from the initial state generated by GridG.

Resource dynamic attribute's change period (T_{res_change}): the dynamic attribute, load, changes every period of time and the result also follows the distribution shown in Figure 2.

Resource information update period (T_{update}): every resource information update period, a GRNS will propagate the new resource information to its neighbors.

Request period ($T_{request}$) and distribution: user requests arrive randomly every user request period. The content of the request is to search for a resource with load smaller than a certain value, which also follows the distribution of Figure 2.

Maximum TTL value (TTL_{max}): this is the system default maximum TTL value.

4.4. Results

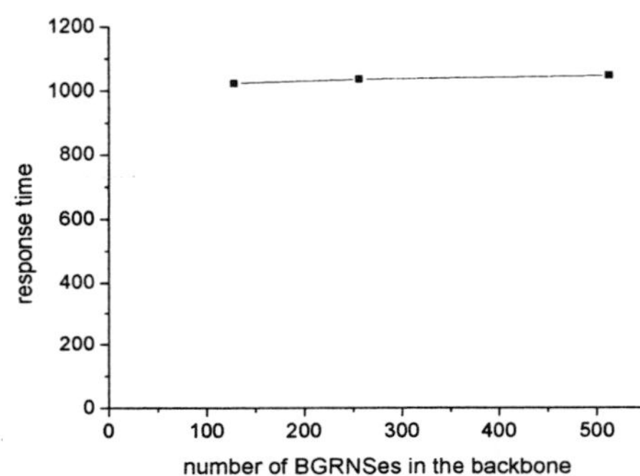

Figure 3. Response time function of number of BGRNSes in the backbone.

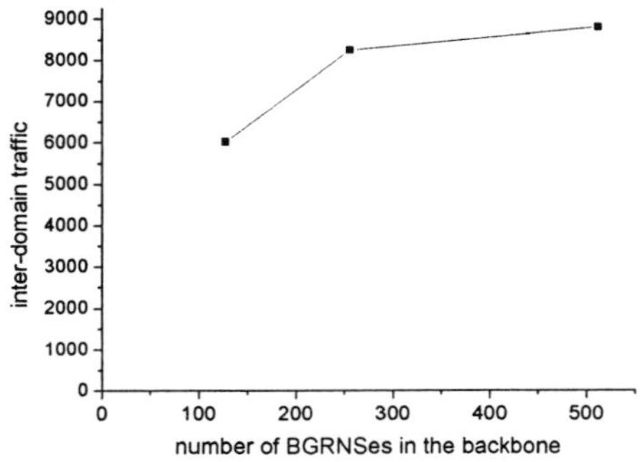

Figure 4. Number of inter-domain requests function of number of BGRNSes in the backbone.

Because some parameters in the simulation are randomly generated, every set of simulations repeats for 100 times and all results are averaged.

The influence of the ratio of T_{res_change} and T_{update} on the performance of intra-domain lookups has been demonstrated in [1]. Here we just set $T_{res\_change} = T_{update} = 100$ ms, $T_{request} = 1$ ms, the number of the GRNSes in a domain is 64, the number of the BGRNSes is 128, 256 and 512 separately, thus the total GRNS number is 8192, 16384 and 32768.

The first group of simulations is to show the request response time and the inter-domain request number under different size of the backbone network, where $TTL_{max} = 4$. From Figure 3, observe that the response time almost keeps constant as the growth of the network. From Figure 4, it can be seen that the inter-domain traffic does not grow with the size of the backbone network exponentially. These two sets of simulation results show that the VIRD architecture has good scalability according to the size of the backbone.

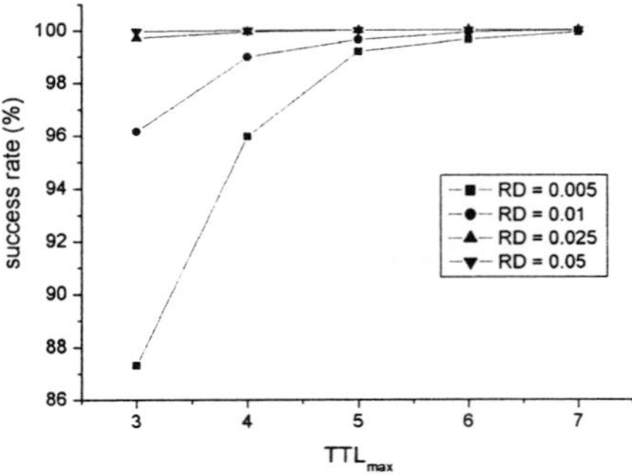

Figure 5. Success rate function of TTL_{max}.

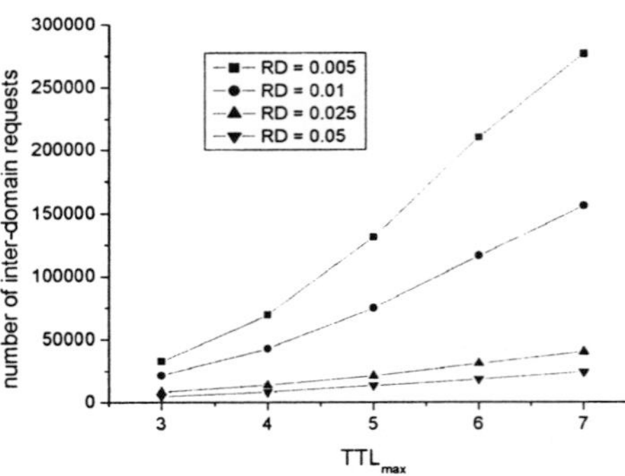

Figure 6. Number of inter-domain requests function of TTL_{max}.

The second group of simulations is about the success rate and the number of requests forwarded to the backbone under various resource densities and TTL_{max} values. The backbone used in this and following groups of simulation is a network with 256 BGRNSes, and every domain has 64 GRNSes, consequently there are 16384

GRNSes in total. From Figure 5, observe that with the same RD, the success rate grows as the TTL_{max} grows, and with the same TTL_{max}, the higher the RD, the higher the success rate. Further more, even with rather low RD and TTL_{max}, the success rate of VIRD is still high. Figure 6 presents the relationship between the TTL_{max} and the number of requests forwarded among the inter-domain network. It is obvious that with the increasing of the RD, the number of forwarded requests decreases. Combining the two figures together, observe that with $TTL_{max} = 5$, 6, and 7, the increase of the success rate is not very significant (because they are already very high), while the number of forwarded requests increases dramatically. Therefore the TTL_{max} of VIRD is set to 4 in later simulations.

The third group of simulations is to compare success rate, network traffic and response time of VIRD, flooding and random walk, where RD = 0.05. Random walk uses the checking method, which means that a walker periodically checks with the original requester before walking to the next node. A walker checks once at every fourth step along the way as indicated in [21], which strikes a good balance between the overhead of the checking messages and the benefits of checking.

The data in Figure 8 and Figure 9 are ratios to the values obtained at flooding $TTL_{max} = 7$ (abbreviated as F7), because most Gnutella systems set their default TTL_{max} as 7.

Figure 7 shows that the request success rate of VIRD with $TTL_{max} = 4$ (short for VIRD4) (99.99%) is higher than that of F11 (98.95%), while that of F7 is only 87.05%. The success rate of random walk with TTL = 1000 (abbreviated as RW1000) is 100%, but its response time is 9.24 times of that of F7 and the traffic is 1.68 times of that of F7 and 6.29 times of that of VIRD4. As mentioned before, the traffic of VIRD is composed of system traffic ($Traffic_{sys}$) and user traffic ($Traffic_{usr}$). As the number of requests arriving in a certain time unit increases, $Traffic_{usr}$ increases, while $Traffic_{sys}$ remains the same. Figure 8 shows that $Traffic_{usr}$ and the sum of $Traffic_{sys}$ and $Traffic_{usr}$ of VIRD4 are only 3.48% and 26.83% of that of F7, and only 0.30% and 2.31% of that of F11. From Figure 9, the response time of VIRD4 is 97.48% of that of F7, while it is 15.25% faster than F11. The response time of VIRD4 is higher than that of flooding with small TTL_{max} values (such as $TTL_{max} = 4$, 5 and 6), which is because the later systems only search in a small neighborhood, and their request success rates are very low (56.79%-81.03%), which are unacceptable for a grid resource discovery system. From this group of simulations, it can be seen that when VIRD4, F11 and RW300 have approximately same success rate, 99.99%, 98.95% and 98.89% respectively, the traffic of VIRD4 is 2.31% of that of F11 and 17.43% of that of RW300, and its response time is 84.75% of that of F11 and 10.55% of that of RW300. Random walk is proposed to reduce traffic in the sacrifice of response time, but VIRD performs better in both aspects: far less traffic and faster response time.

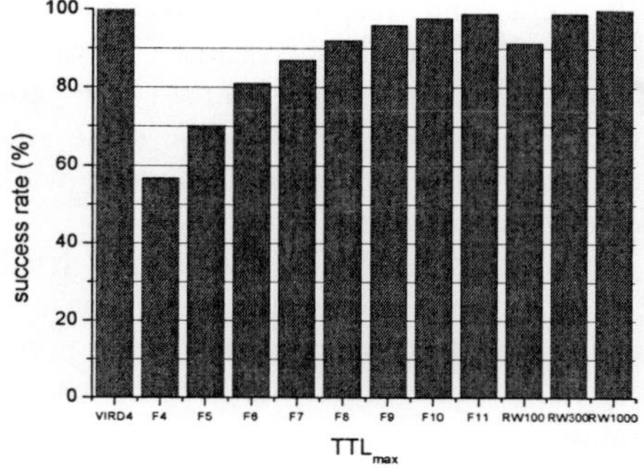

Figure 7. Success rate of VIRD, flooding and random walk under TTL_{max}. TTL for VIRD is 4, TTLs for flooding are from 3 to 11, and TTLs for random walk are 100, 300 and 1000.

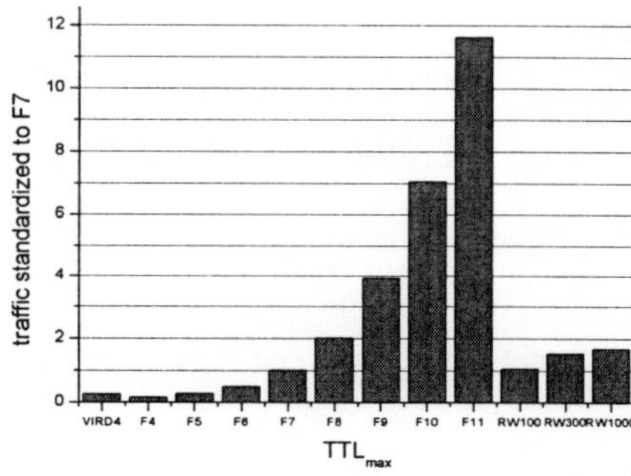

Figure 8. Network traffic of VIRD, flooding and random walk under TTL_{max}. TTLs for different approaches are the same with those in Figure 7.

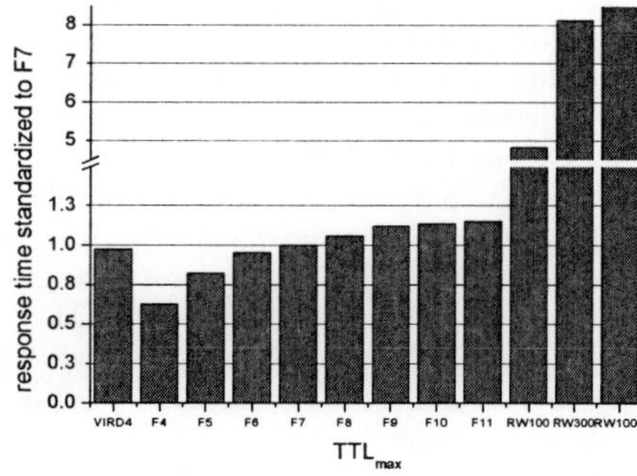

Figure 9. Response time of VIRD, flooding and random walk under TTL_{max}. TTLs for different approaches are the same with those in Figure 7.

5. Conclusion and Future work

This paper proposes a C/S and P2P hybrid resource discovery framework, VIRD, to make advantage of the physical and logical topologies of the Internet.

According to our simulations, VIRD is of good scalability regarding response time and inter-domain traffic. Even with rather low RD and TTL_{max}, the success rate of VIRD is still high. From the comparative simulations, it is shown that with the same success rate, VIRD outperforms flooding and random walk in both network traffic and response time.

On the other side, VIRD has some disadvantages. Even if there is satisfactory resource in the current grid, VIRD may fail to find it. From the user's point of view, high request success rate may compensate for this shortcoming.

The performance impact of the network topology and cache is not discussed in this paper, which will be our future work. Additionally, the automatic recovery from BGRNS failure will be discussed.

References

[1] Y. Gong, F. Dong, W. Li, Z. Xu. VEGA Infrastructure for Resource Discovery in Grids. Journal of Computer Science & Technology, vol. 18, No.4, pp.413-422, July 2003.

[2] Clip2, The Gnutella Protocol Specification v0.4 (Document Revision 1.2), http://www.clip2.com, June 2001.

[3] R. Raman, M. Livny, M. Solomon: Matchmaking: Distributed Resource Management for High Throughput Computing. Proc. of IEEE Intl. Symp. on High Performance Distributed Computing, Chicago, USA, 1998.

[4] S. J. Chapin, D. Katramatos, J. Karpovich, A. Grimshaw. Resource Management in Legion. Future Generation Computer System, Vol. 15, No. 5: pp. 583594, 1999.

[5] Czajkowski K, Fitzgerald S, Foster I, Kesselman C. Grid information services for distributed resource sharing. In Proceedings of the 10th IEEE International Symposium on High-Performance Distributed Computing (HPDC-10), IEEE Press, pp.181-194, Aug. 2001.

[6] I. Clarke, O. Sandberg, B. Wiley, and T. W. Hong. Freenet: A distributed anonymous information storage and retrieval system. In Workshop on Design Issues in Anonymity and Unobservability, pp. 311–320, ICSI, Berkeley, CA, USA, July 2000.

[7] A.Rowstron and P. Druschel. Pastry: Scalable, decentralized object location and routing for large-scale peer-to-peer system. In Proc. IFIP/ACM Middleware 2001, Heidelberg, Germany, Nov. 2001.

[8] B. Y. Zhao, J. D. Kubiatowicz, and A. D. Joseph. Tapestry: An infrastructure for faultresilient wide-area location and routing. Technical Report UCB//CSD-01-1141, U. C. Berkeley, April 2001.

[9] S. Ratnasamy, P. Francis, M. Handley, R. Karp, and S. Shenker. A scalable content addressable network. In Proc. ACM SIGCOMM'01, San Diego, CA, Aug. 2001.

[10] I. Stoica, R. Morris, D. Karger, M. F. Kaashoek, and H. Balakrishnan. Chord: a scalable peer-to-peer lookup service for Internet applications. In Proc. ACM SIGCOMM'01, SanDiego, CA, Aug. 2001.

[11] W. Li, Z. Xu, F. Dong and J. Zhang. Grid resource discovery based on a routing-transferring model. In Proceedings of the 3rd International Workshop on Grid Computing, pp.145-156, Baltimore, MD, 2002.

[12] Michalis Faloutsos, Petros Faloutsos, and Christos Faloutsos. On power-law relationships of the internet topology. In SIGCOMM, pp. 251-262, 1999.

[13] M. Jovanovic, F.S. Annexstein, and K.A. Berman. Modeling Peer-to-Peer Network Topologies through "Small-World" Models and Power Laws. In TELFOR, Belgrade, Yugoslavia, Nov. 2001.

[14] D. Lu, P. Dinda, Synthesizing Realistic Computational Grids, in Proceedings of Supercomputing 2003 (SC 2003), Phoenix, AZ, Nov. 2003.

[15] Doar M. A better model for generating test networks. IEEE Global Internet, pp. 86-93, 1996.

[16] S. J. Chapin. Distributed scheduling support in the presence of autonomy. In Proceedings of the 4th Heterogeneous Computing Workshop, IPPS, pages 22-29, April 1995, Santa Barbara, CA.

[17] W. Adjie-Winoto, E. Schwartz, H. Balakrishnan, J. Lilley. The design and implementation of an intentional naming system. In Proceedings of the ACM Symposium on Operating Systems Principles, pages 186-201, 1999.

[18] M. Balazinska, H. Balakrishnan, D. Karger. INS/Twine: A Scalable Peer-to-Peer Architect ure for Intentional Resource Discovery. In Proceedings of the International Conference on Pervasive Computing, Zurich, Switzerland, August 2002.

[19] Globus Project, The Globus Resource Specification Language RSL v1.0, http://www.globus.org/gram/rsl_spec1.html.

[20] O.Smirnova, Extended resource specification language, reference manual, http://www.nordugrid.org/documents/xrsl.pdf.

[21] Q. Lv, P. Cao, E. Cohen, K. Li, S. Shenker. Search and Replication in Unstructured Peer-to-Peer Networks. In Proceedings of the 16th ACM International Conference on Supercomputing (ICS'02), New York, USA, June 2002.

Differentiated Search in Hierarchical Peer-to-Peer Networks

Chen Wang, Li Xiao, Pei Zheng
Department of Computer Science and Engineering
Michigan State University
Email: {wangchen, lxiao, zhengpei}@cse.msu.edu

Abstract

Although the original intent of the peer-to-peer (P2P) concept is to treat each participant equally, heterogeneity widely exists in deployed P2P networks. In this paper, we suggest to improve the search efficiency of P2P network by utilizing the ***query answering heterogeneity****. Our proposed Differentiated Search (DiffSearch) algorithm can evolve an unstructured P2P network to a two-tier hierarchical structure, where peers with high query answering capabilities are grouped in the first tier, which has higher priority to be queried than the second tier. Because the query answering capability is extremely unbalanced among peers, a high query success ratio can be achieved by querying only a small portion of the network. The search traffic is dramatically reduced due to the shrunken search space. Our trace analysis and simulation show that the DiffSearch algorithm can save up to 60% of search traffic.*

1 Introduction

Peer-to-peer (P2P) networks are booming in today's network community because their fully distributed design makes them good candidates to build fault-tolerant file sharing systems that can well balance the load of file storage and transfer. However, the basic flooding approaches of unstructured P2P networks raise enormous concerns in their scalability.

In this paper we propose the Differentiated Search (DiffSearch) algorithm to improve the search efficiency of unstructured P2P networks by giving higher querying priority to peers with high querying reply capabilities. Our proposal is based on the observation [3, 12] that the query reply capabilities are extremely unbalanced among peers: 7% of peers in the Gnutella network share more files than all that other peers can offer, and 47% of queries are responded to by the top 1% of peers. The remarkable heterogeneity of peer's reply capability intrigues us to revisit the nature of P2P network: rather than all peers actively participate in file sharing, only a small portion of volunteering peers provide the majority of the service in P2P networks, and the rest of the peers are just free riders. In such a model, the basic flooding approach is like looking for a needle in a bottle of hay, since queries are forwarded by a large number of free riders without any contribution to search results. Instead of flooding, we propose the DiffSearch algorithm that gives service providers higher priorities to be queried. Under the DiffSearch algorithm, a few service providers (Ultrapeers) with high query answering capability form a service provider overlay, and the rest of all free riders connect to the service provider overlay as leaf nodes. Each query will be sent to the service provider overlay first. Only when the query fails in the service provider overlay, it will resort to the whole P2P network. It is also proposed in work [7] to improve the search efficiency by utilizing the content locality. In this paper, we further develop this idea by investigating how content-rich peers can be grouped and maintained in a spontaneous and dynamic network.

This paper makes three contributions to improve the performance of unstructured P2P networks: (1) We analyze the query/reply traces collected from the Gnutella network to investigate the phenomena of file sharing heterogeneity, and propose to utilize the heterogeneity to improve the search efficiency. (2) The DiffSearch algorithm proposed in this paper is a fully distributed approach. The two-tire hierarchical structure can be evolved from an ad hoc P2P network by the *localized* algorithm running on each peer without global knowledge. (3) A caching and redirecting mechanism is proposed to well balance the query load in ultrapeers according to their processing capacity.

The remainder of the paper is organized as follows: Section 2 presents an overview of the DiffSearch algorithm. Section 3 investigates the file sharing heterogeneity of P2P networks in detail. We illustrate how the two-tier hierarchical structure can be efficiently evolved by DiffSearch algorithm in Section 4. The performance improvement of the algorithm is evaluated in Section 5. Section 6 describes the related work, and a conclusion is drawn on Section 7.

This work was partially supported by the US National Science Foundation (NSF) under grant CCF-0325760.

0190-3918/05 $20.00 © 2005 IEEE

2 Overview of the DiffSearch Algorithm

We first redefine the criteria for ultrapeers. Current hierarchical design selects the ultrapeers by emphasizing their computing capability such as bandwidth, CPU power and memory space. In this paper, we argue that the content capacity, i.e. the number of files shared in a node, is also an important factor to decide if a hosting peer should be an ultrapeer. After aggregating peers sharing a large number of files into the ultrapeer overlay, good search performance can be achieved by only flooding a query within small searching space.

Based on the ultrapeer overlay which contains the main portion of shared files, we propose the DiffSearch algorithm. In the DiffSearch algorithm, a query consists of two round searches. In the first round search, the query is only sent to the ultrapeer overlay. If the first round search fails in the ultrapeer overlay, the second round search will be evoked to query the whole network. However, the prerequisite of the DiffSearch algorithm is that the ultrapeer overlay consisting of content rich peers is well formed in a P2P network. We show that the DiffSearch algorithm can be self-utilized to shape an ad hoc P2P network into a two-tier hierarchical structure which clearly separates the content rich ultrapeer overlay from the underlying network. We illustrate the ultrapeer overlay construction by a query example initiated from an individual peer. Suppose a DiffSearch query fails in the first round search, but succeeds in the second round, which implies two possible cases:

- The queried object is not shared by any ultrapeers, such that it can only be found by querying all the network.
- The queried object is shared by ultrapeers and some of replies in second round search are responded from ultrapeers, which implies that the failure of the first round search is caused by the incompleteness of the two-tier hierarchical structure: either because the leaf node is not connected to the ultrapeer overlay or the ultrapeer overlay is partitioned into multiple disjointed clusters. Otherwise, the query should have succeeded in the first round search in ultrapeer overlay.

In the second case, the incompleteness of the two-tier structure is detected and can be repaired by adding new connections between source peer and responding ultrapeers. Since any first round search failure due to the incompleteness of the hierarchical structure can be self-remedied by the DiffSearch algorithm, the two tier structure can be incrementally evolved from an chaotic status through the frequent search behavior initiated from abundant querying peers. Our experiment shows that the algorithm converges very fast and the two tier hierarchy structure can be evolved after each peer sends out about 20 queries in average.

A concern on the DiffSearch algorithm is that the load of file transfer will be unbalanced between ultrapeers and leaf nodes. Since ultrapeers have higher priorities to be queried, leaf nodes may have no chance to contribute their uploading bandwidth if they share the same files as ultrapeers. To solve the problem, we enhance the DiffSearch algorithm by uploading indices of leaf nodes to ultrapeers, such that the indices of all the shared files are searchable in the first round search. Since the ultrapeer overlay shares the majority of files, the cost of index operations is small, which is shown in our experiment.

We will start our investigation on the file sharing heterogeneity in the next section, which will be followed by a detailed discussion on DiffSearch algorithm later.

3 Heterogeneity of File Sharing

While a primary intent of the P2P concept is to blur the border between service providers and consumers and treat each participant equally, the heterogeneity is an inherent character of P2P systems. Peers vary in many aspects such as network bandwidth, CPU power and storage capacity. It is a natural choice that this heterogeneity be taken into account when designing P2P systems, such as Gia [4] and the flow control and topology adaption algorithm in [9]. Those algorithms try to balance the load among peers according to their bandwidth resources to maximize the system capacity. In contrast to the heterogeneity of the query process capability, the heterogeneity of query reply capability, observed in several studies [3, 12], has not been emphasized in P2P system design yet. To investigate the heterogeneity of peers' querying answering capabilities in detail, we implemented a Gnutella trace collector based on the Limewire servant. By hooking the log functionality to the Limewire servant, all the queries and responses passing by the trace collector are recorded. Aiming at collecting enough data within a short time, we intentionally set the collector as an ultrapeer with 100 neighbors. After one day of online time on Dec. 28th, 2003, 20 million queries were collected in a query trace file of 1.6Gbytes, and 5 million responses were collected in a response trace file of 670Mbytes. Because each query and its responses share the same GUID (Global unique ID), the query can be matched with its corresponding responses even if they are logged in two separated files.

The response distribution based on the response traces is illustrated in Figure 1. The peers are ranked by the descent order of the number of responses. Figure 1 shows a similar result as in [3], i.e. the top 1% of peers

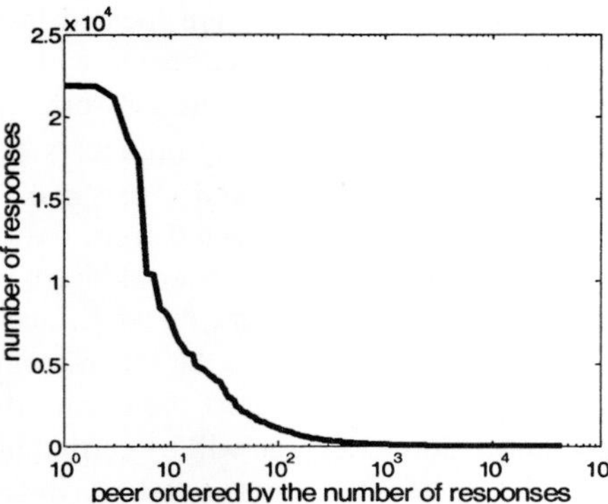

Figure 1 Response Distribution

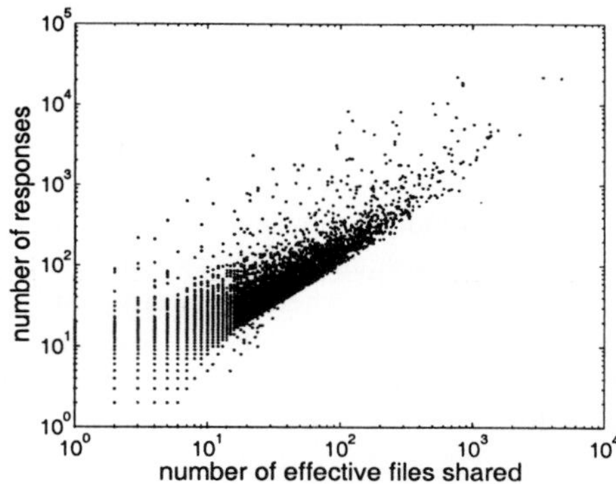

Figure 2 Correlation between Query Response and number of files

answers the main portion of queries. Such observation encourage the conjecture that if we could route all the queries to those top peers first, close to 90% of query traffic would be saved.

Peers vary in their query reply capabilities because of their file sharing heterogeneity. Basically query answering is the process of matching keywords with all the shared file names. As the number of shared files increases, the probability of successful matching should become higher. However, the investigation in [3] shows that there is weak correlation between query response and the number of shared files. Our explanation is that some useless files make no contribution to the query answering, i.e. some files are never used to answer the queries. If we only count the files which have been used to answer the queries, the number of responses do show correlation with the number of shared files to a greater extent. To distinguish those files from useless files, we define the files which have been used to answer the queries as *effective files*. The correlation between the number of responses and the number of effective files is illustrated in Figure 2. As we can see, the peers sharing more effective files has more tendency to answer queries.

4 DiffSearch Algorithm

Using the metric of *effective files* discussed above, the ultrapeers are self-aware by simply counting the number of shared files which have been visited before. As long as the number of visited files reaches the threshold, a peer can promote itself as a ultrapeer. In our DiffSearch algorithm, those peers should form an ultrapeer overlay and have higher priority to be queried. The challenge is how to find the ultrapeers and connect them into an overlay efficiently?

The basic objectives of our topology creation algorithm are: (1) each leaf node has at least one ultrapeer as a neighbor; (2) the ultrapeer overlay is a connected graph.

4.1 Finding Ultrapeers

For the first objective, the peer isolated from ultrapeers needs to find an ultrapeer as a neighbor. There are two basic approaches to find an ultrapeer. The first one is an *active approach,* in which the isolated peer sends out an "ultrapeer search" message in the way of flooding, and the ultrapeers respond back with their IP addresses. The second one is a *passive approach,* in which ultrapeers periodically publicize themselves to the P2P network, and the isolated peers can find ultrapeer by overhearing the publicizing message forwarded from its neighbors.

In the first approach, both the search message and response messages will cause tremendous overhead if all the isolated peers repeat the same process. Furthermore, the isolated peers will be overwhelmed by the response messages sent back from thousands of ultrapeers. In the second approach, the periodically publicized messages will also cause remarkable overhead, and the peer being publicized may be overwhelmed by the connection requests from a huge number of isolated peers, which will result in some heavily loaded ultrapeers.

To design an efficient topology creation algorithm, we suggest the principles below:

- To minimize the overhead, the topology creation message should hitchhike on other query/response messages on the way of free riding.
- The extreme asymmetric scenario, i.e. thousands of peers responding to or connecting to a single peer should be avoid.
- The incremental connections should be well load balanced among ultrapeers.

Following the above principles, we incorporate topology adjustment operations into the query/reply protocols of a current P2P network. One bit of data is appended to the reply message to indicate if the respondent is an ultrapeer. All the replies received by isolated peers will be checked and the IP addresses will be extracted from the message responses from ultrapeers. Because ultrapeers have high query answering capability, the isolated peers can find ultrapeers with high probability after sending out several queries. Besides, no extra message is required for the isolated peers to find the ultrapeers, the overhead is minimized by using only one bit of data in query replies. Furthermore, the isolated peer will not be overwhelmed since the number of replies is limited.

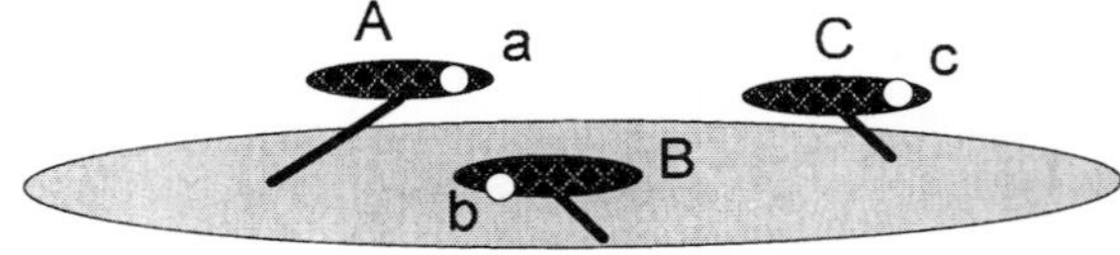

Figure 3 a hierarchical P2P network

4.2 Evolve an Ultrapeer Overlay

To guarantee that each peer in the ultrapeer overlay can be reached by the first round search in DiffSearch, all the peers in the ultrapeer overlay should form a connected topology. The basic approach is to detect all the separated clusters consisting of ultrapeers, and connect them with each other. Again, in a fully decentralized environment, a careful design is necessary to avoid too much overhead caused by the cluster detection.

All the separated clusters can be found if we flood the cluster detection message to the whole network. However, this flooding may be initiated by each peer due to the lack of a synchronization mechanism. Since each peer is uncertain if other peers will start the cluster detection, all the peers have to repeat the same operations. Furthermore, the cluster detection messages have to be periodically flooded since the connected overlay will be disjointed by the dynamic leaving of peers.

The P2P network can not tolerate the tremendous overhead caused by the detection message periodically flooded from all the peers. A minor improvement is that we can designate the bootstrapping sever to be responsible for the cluster detection. The redundant operations can be reduced while the bootstrapping sever may be overloaded.

To minimize the overhead of cluster detection, we follow the same design principles as finding ultrapeers, i.e. the peers' search operation will be reused by cluster detection. In our design, the cluster detection data is hitchhiked to the DiffSearch query message. As illustrated in Figure 3, the ultrapeer overlay is divided into three clusters. Suppose peer a fails to search keyword k in cluster A during the first round search of DiffSearch, which is caused by two possible reasons: (1) the keyword k is not shared by ultrapeers; (2) the file k is shared by ultrapeers but they are located in separated clusters B or C. For any case, peer a will initiate the second round search to the whole network. If the second round search is received by ultrapeers b and c in possession of file k, both b and c can make the conclusion that they are disconnected from the cluster A. Otherwise, the first round search would have received a successful response from peers b and c, and it is unnecessary for peer a to initiate the second round query. As long as peers b and c detect the cluster disconnection, the notification message will be carried back in the query replies made by peers b and c. Based on the notification and the IP addresses in the query replies, peer a will setup new connections with peers b and c, such that all the three disjointed clusters will be connected together. If the source peer a itself is not an ultrapeer, an ultrapeer from its neighbors will be picked up to set connections with peers b and c. If the peer a cannot find any ultrapeer in its neighbor list, peer a itself will be connected to peers b and c. In this case, peers b and c cannot be reached in the first round query just because peer a is isolated from the ultrapeer overlay.

The approach proposed above works in an incremental way. As the number of queries increases, the ultrapeer overlay will gradually evolve to a connected graph. Since the ultrapeers have higher probability to answer queries, the disjointed clusters can be detected with high probability. The simulation shows that the algorithm to connect disjointed clusters converges very fast.

One problem of the above algorithm is that the clusters B and C may be connected with each other. In this case, one connection from a to either b or c is enough to connect all the clusters. We hope the number of newly added connections can be minimized so that the duplicated query messages in the ultrapeers overlay can be reduced. To eliminate the redundant connection, peer a has to judge if peers b and c are in a connected graph. Again, the testing approach for peer b to flood a message to peer c is not encouraged. An alternative method is that peer a only make one connection with one of the two peers which has higher query answering capability. This conservative approach will slow down the convergence speed but reduce redundant connections.

4.3 Maintaining the Hierarchical Structure

From the above analysis, we show that all the overlay constructing operations can be finished by only using the search messages. If peer a is disconnected from the ultrapeer overlay, it will initiate the second round search, which may be responded by some ultrapeers with their IP addresses carried back in the query reply messages. In such a case, the disjointed clusters are detected and the notification will be sent back to source peer a. To hitchhike the overlay construction to the search messages, three bits need to be append to the original query and reply message. One bit is used in the query message to show whether the query is in the first round or second round. Two bits are used in the reply message to show whether the reply is from an ultrapeer and which round search the reply is responded to.

Due to the highly dynamic nature of P2P networks, the ultrapeer overlay may be broken by peers' ungraceful departure. However, as discussed earlier, the incompleteness of the two tier structure can be detected and repaired by ongoing queries of the DiffSearch. We show in our experiment that the DiffSearch approach is a self-maintained algorithm which can keep the network in a good shape even in an unstable environment.

5 Performance Evaluation

We implemented a trace-driven P2P network simulator in the message level to evaluate the DiffSearch algorithm. The metrics we evaluated are listed below:

Network Traffic: We use the total number of forwarded hops per query to measure the volume of network traffic incurred by each query.

Query Success Rate: Query success rate is the percentage of queries which is successfully responded by at least one query reply.

Overlay Query Success Rate: The Overlay Query Success Rate is the percentage of DiffSearch queries which can succeed in the first round search of DiffSearch.

Response Time: We define Response Time as the minimum number of hops for the query reply to be forwarded back to the source peer.

5.1 Configuration of the Simulation

Network Topology: A modified crawler is used to take a snapshot of the Gnutella network. By repetitively sending out the Ping message with TTL=2, the crawler can collect the topology information together with the number of files shared by each peer. The 10,000 peers are randomly picked up from the snapshot to form the network topology of our simulation.

File Distribution: The files are assigned to each peer according to the trace of query replies. All the files responded from the same IP addresses in the trace of query replies are assigned to the same peer in the simulation.

Query Distribution: The sequence of query keywords is extracted from the query trace file. The queries which have no correspondent replies in the query reply trace are filtered, such that any query is always solvable if all the peers in simulation are queried. Through this way, we set up a baseline to measure the query success rate. The filtered sequence of query keywords will be rebroadcast by the source peers randomly picked up from the simulated P2P network.

5.2 Performance Evaluation of DiffSearch

5.2.1 Convergence speed

Since the DiffSearch algorithm builds up the two tier hierarchical structure in an incremental way, the primary concern is how long it will take to create the structure. We use the query success rate in ultrapeer overlay to measure the convergence speed of the DiffSearch algorithm. First, we intentionally sent the queries to a set which consisted of all the ultrapeers. The testing results show that about 80% of queries can be answered by the set of ultrapeers, which means the DiffSearch algorithm can achieve 80% query success rate in ultrapeer overlay if the two-tier hierarchical structure evolved into a perfect shape.

In the following experiment, we construct the network topology based on the snapshot taken by our Gnutella crawler. Since the Pong messages collected by the crawler also contain the number of files shared by each peer, we approximately assign each node the same number of files as that collected by the crawler. The filenames are extracted from query reply traces recorded by our trace collector, and all the files shared by the same peer were assigned to the same node in our simulation. The queries were sent out from randomly selected nodes in the same sequence as that collected in the query trace. The simulation result is shown in Figure 4.

As we can see, with the number of queries increased, the query success ratio rises to 80%, which is close to the ratio under the ideal condition that the ultrapeer overlay is perfectly formed. The figure also shows that after each peer sends out about 20 queries, the ultrapeer overlay can be evolved to an ideal situation. The simulations above demonstrates that DiffSearch is an effective algorithm which can efficiently construct the two-tier hierarchical structure from a completely chaotic starting point. The algorithm converges very fast because of the node heterogeneity in P2P networks. As we have shown in the previous trace analysis, the query reply can be made by ultrapeers with high probability, such that the ultrapeers can be easily found by the DiffSearch algorithm and the ultrapeer overlay can be quickly formed.

5.2.2 Performance Improvement

The average network traffic per query is used to measure the query cost. The average query response time and the query success rate are used to measure the user perceived query quality, i.e. how long a user has to

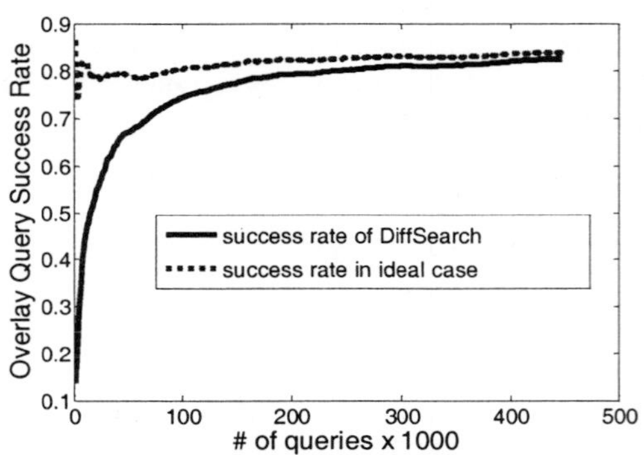

Figure 4 Overlay Success Ratio

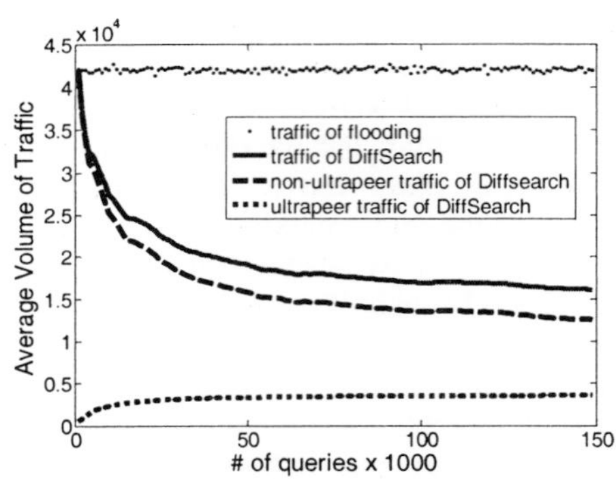

Figure 5 Average Traffic of DiffSearch

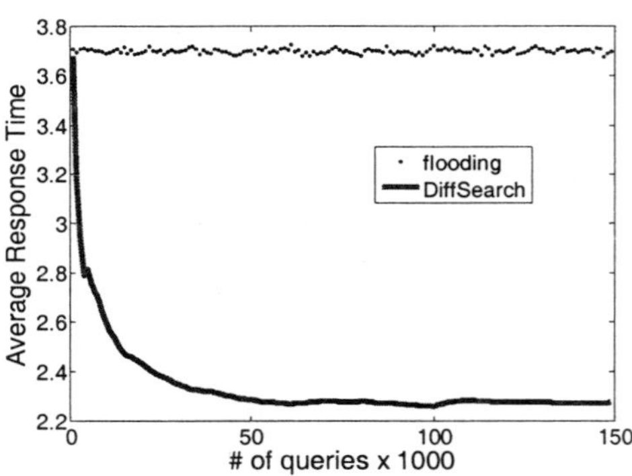

Figure 6 Average Response Time of DiffSearch

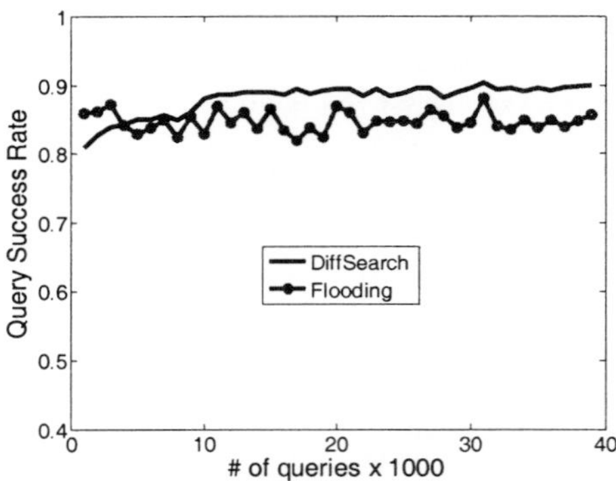

Figure 7 Query Success Rate Comparison

wait before a query result can be sent back to a querying node and how likely that a query can be solved. We compare the search performance of the DiffSearch algorithm with the flooding-based approach. The simulation results are shown in Figure 5, Figure 6 and Figure 7. The comparison shows that with the help of the DiffSearch algorithm, the average volume of traffic per query decreases from 42,000 hops to 16,000 hops. More than 60% traffic can be saved by utilizing the ultrapeer overlay. The DiffSearch algorithm can significantly reduce the query cost because 80% of the queries can be solved in the ultrapeer overlay which has a much smaller searching space than the whole network. Figure 5 also shows that the traffic incurred by the second round search consists of more than 80% of the cost, even though only 20% of the queries need to resort to the second round search. Since the second round search contributes the main portion of the overall cost, it is extremely important to improve the success rate in the ultrapeer overlay such that fewer queries need to resort to the costly second round search. We address this issue in a later discussion.

The average response time comparison is shown in Figure 6. The simulation result shows that the average response time decreases from 3.7 hops to 2.3 hops. The overall user perceived response time can be reduced by 40%. The DiffSearch algorithm can reduce the query response time because 80% of the queries can be solved in the ultrapeer overlay which has smaller diameter than the underlying network, such that most of the queries can be responded to within a shorter distance.

Figure 7 shows that the DiffSearch algorithm can also improve the query success rate, but to some limited extent. The DiffSearch algorithm can improve the query success rate, because the ultrapeer overlay creates shortcuts between ultrapeers and leaf nodes, such that more ultrapeers are within searching distance. However, the improvement is not so significant due to the small world property of P2P networks. The original flooding based search approach with a high time to live (TTL) value already has good coverage in the searching space.

5.2.3 Load Balance

However, the DiffSearch algorithm causes serious load balance problems that are demonstrated in two aspects:

(1) The query load is unbalanced between ultrapeers and leaf nodes.

(2) The query load is unbalanced among ultrapeers, and some of them may become hotspots.

We use the number of received messages per query to measure the query load of each peer. In a P2P network with tree-like topology, a query will be forwarded to each node at most once, while existent P2P networks are randomly formed by unsupervised peers, which creates link circles in the overlay topology. Due to a large number of link circles existing in a the P2P network overlay, a query may be forwarded to the same peer multiple times along different incoming connections. In such a case, the higher the number of neighbors a peer is connected to, the higher the number of messages the peer may receive for the same query. In two-tier hierarchical P2P networks, ultrapeers become central hubs connected by a large number leaf nodes. It is likely that ultrapeers may be overloaded by incoming query messages. To measure the query load of ultrapeers, we recorded the total number of messages received by each ultrapeer. The number of received messages per query equals the total number messages received divided by the total number of queries. To investigate the hierarchical topology's impact on query load of ultrapeers, we first used the flooding based search in the "flat" topology and calculated the number of received messages per query in each ultrapeer. After that, the same experiment was repeated using the DiffSearch algorithm in the hierarchical topology.

Figure 8 shows the ultrapeers' load comparison. Two results can be observed from the comparison:

- The average query load of ultrapeers in a hierarchical structure is much heavier than that in a flooding based P2P network.
- The load among ultrapeers is extremely unbalanced, varying from a maximum of 400 messages per query to a minimum of 3 message per query.

The ultrapeers are heavily loaded by query messages because of the asymmetry between ultrapeers and leaf nodes. The ratio between ultrapeers and leaf nodes is 2 to 100, which means one ultrapeer is connected by 50 leaf nodes in average. The large number of connections between ultrapeers and leaf nodes causes a serious problem in the second round search of the DiffSearch algorithm. Since the second round search floods queries to the whole network, the large number of connections between ultrapeers and leaf nodes results in duplicated queries being forwarded to the same ultrapeer multiple times. To alleviate the impact of connections between ultrapeers and leaf nodes on the query load, we distinguish the connections by marking the newly added connections which are created by the DiffSearch algorithm to form the ultrapeer overlay. The new connections are only used in the first round search, and ignored by the second round search. The consequence is that the ultrapeers work as ordinary nodes in the second round search since the newly added connections are virtually removed. The Figure 9 shows that after we applied the connection distinguishing solution to the DiffSearch algorithm, the query load of ultrapeers is significantly reduced.

The other unsolved problem is that the query load is extremely unbalanced among ultrapeers, which can be addressed by the caching and redirection solution we propose below. In a P2P network enhanced by caching and redirecting, a peer's current load status is distributed out together with the query reply message. Each ultrapeer overhears the passing by query reply messages and caches the IP addresses of other ultrapeers which are less loaded than itself. When a fully loaded ultrapeer cannot accommodate more incoming connection requests, it will redirect the requests to other ultrapeers in caching list. The same operation will be recursively applied until a capable candidate is found. To represent the query process capability of each peer in our simulation, we manually set a threshold as the maximum number of accepted incoming connections for each peer. Figure 9 also shows that query load is well balanced among ultrapeers after the caching and redirection solution is applied.

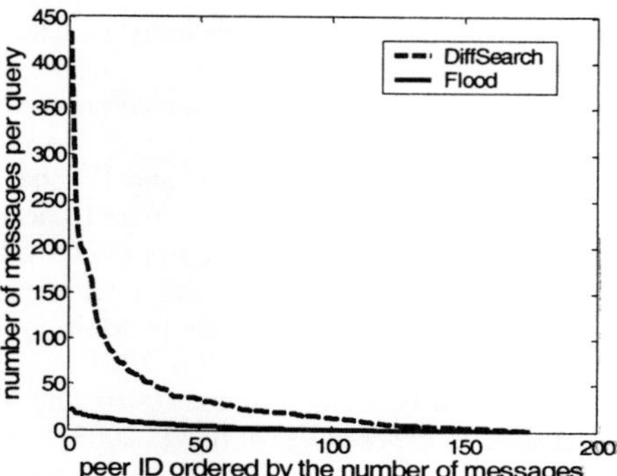

Figure 8 Unbalanced Load of Ultrapeers

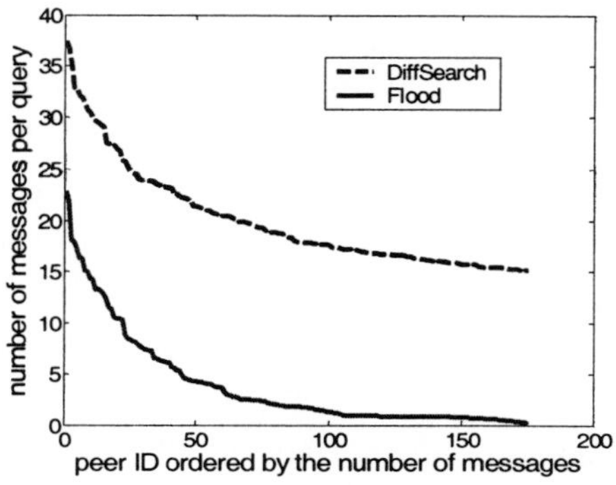

Figure 9 Load balance of Ultrapeers

6 Related Work

Many approaches have been proposed to improve the search efficiency of unstructured P2P networks. To take advantage of the query locality, the authors in [14] try to improve the search efficiency by setting up short-cut among peers which share the same query interest. Query reply caching is also proposed in [10, 13, 15] to reuse query replies cached in nearby peers. The CUP [11] algorithm try to control the flooding query/reply messages by register a peer's interest to its neighboring peers.

Random walk [6, 8] is suggested to avoid the exponential increased flooding traffic by selecting only several searching paths among peers.

The heterogeneity of P2P networks is observed in [3, 12]. Nevertheless, how to exploit the heterogeneity to improve system performance is not suggested in those works.

It is explicitly advocated in [9] to make Gnutella scalable by taking advantage of its heterogeneity. The Gia [4] proposes to control the query flow based on the peers' query processing capability. By assigning tokens to its neighbors, each peer will not be overloaded since the peer only accepts the queries 'traded with' tokens. All this work suggests to make use of the heterogeneous capability of query forwarding, instead of query answering.

The superiority of cluster-based P2P network and Supernode-based hierarchical P2P network is theoretically analyzed in [5] and [16]. However, how to efficiently evolve such a hierarchical structure has not been discussed yet.

Different from the self-maintained ultrapeers in DiffSearch, the Super nodes in KaZaA [2] depend on proprietary fixed infrastructure to construct and maintain the ultrapeer overlay. The Ultrapeers in Gnutella [1] are selected based on the metrics of bandwidth other than query answering capability, and there is no guarantee that the ultrapeers in the Gnutella network are formed as a connected overlay.

7 Conclusion and future work

In this paper, we propose the DiffSearch algorithm, a fully distributed approach which can evolve a two tier hierarchical structure from a spontaneously formed ad hoc P2P network. By hitchhiking the topology operations to query/reply messages, and prompting content-rich peers to the ultrapeer overlay, the DiffSearch algorithm can achieve significant performance improvement with a little overhead on topology and index operations. It is notable that the DiffSearch algorithm is orthogonal to many existing P2P optimization algorithms. For example, the random walk or DHT can still be applied in the ultrapeer overlay to further reduce the search traffic, which will be investigated in our future work.

References

1. The Gnutella protocol specification 0.6, http://rfc-gnutella.sourceforge.net/developer/testing/index.html
2. KaZaA, http://www.kazaa.com
3. E. Adar and B. A. Huberman, Free Riding on Gnutella, http://www.firstmonday.dk/issues/issue5_10/adar/
4. Y. Chawathe, S. Ratnasamy, L. Breslau, N. Lanham, and S. Shenker. Making Gnutella-like P2P Systems Scalable. in *Proceedings of SIGCOMM*. 2003.
5. B. Cooper and H. Garcia-Molina, SIL: Modeling and Measuring Scalable Peer-to-Peer Search Networks, http://dbpubs.stanford.edu:8090/pub/2003-12
6. C. Gkantsidis, M. Mihail, and A. Saberi. Random Walks in Peer-to-Peer Networks. in *Proceedings of INFOCOM*. 2004.
7. L. Guo, S. Jiang, L. Xiao, and X. Zhang, Fast and Low Cost P2P Searching by Exploiting Localities in Peer Community and Individual Peers. *Journal of Parallel and Distributed Computing*, 2005.
8. Q. Lv, P. Cao, E. Cohen, K. Li, and S. Shenker. Search and replication in unstructured peer-to-peer networks. in *Proceedings of the 16th ACM International Conference on Supercomputing*. 2002.
9. Q. Lv, S. Ratnasamy, and S. Shenker. Can Heterogeneity Make Gnutella Scalable? in *Proceedings of IPTPS*. 2002.
10. S. Patro and Y. C. Hu. Transparent Query Caching in Peer-to-Peer Overlay Networks. in *Proceedings of the 17th International Parallel and Distributed Processing Symposium (IPDPS)*. 2003.
11. M. Roussopoulos and M. Baker. Controlled Update Propagation in Peer-to-Peer Networks. in *Proceedings of the USENIX Annual Technical Conference*. 2003.
12. S. Saroiu, P. Gummadi, and S. Gribble. A Measurement Study of Peer-to-Peer File Sharing Systems. in *Proceedings of Multimedia Computing and Networking (MMCN)*. 2002.
13. K. Sripanidkulchai, The popularity of Gnutella queries and its implications on scalability, http://www2.cs.cmu.edu/~kunwadee/research/p2p/gnutella.html
14. K. Sripanidkulchai, B. Maggs, and H. Zhang. Efficient Content Location Using Interest-Based Locality in Peer-to-Peer Systems. in *Proceedings of INFOCOM*. 2003.
15. C. Wang, L. Xiao, Y. Liu, and P. Zheng. Distributed Caching and Adaptive Search in Multilayer P2P Networks. in *Proceedings of ICDCS*. 2004.
16. B. Yang and H. Garcia-Molina. Designing a Super-Peer Network. in *Proceedings of ICDE*. 2003.

A Hybrid Searching Scheme in Unstructured P2P Networks *

Xiuqi Li and Jie Wu
Department of Computer Science and Engineering
Florida Atlantic University
Boca Raton, FL 33431
{xli, jie}@cse.fau.edu

Abstract

The existing searching schemes in Peer-to-Peer (P2P) networks are either forwarding-based or non-forwarding based. In forwarding-based schemes, queries are forwarded from the querying source to the query destination nodes. These schemes offer low state maintenance. However, querying sources do not entirely have control over query processing. In non-forwarding based methods, queries are not forwarded, and the querying source directly probes its neighbors for the desired files. Non-forwarding searching provides querying sources flexible control over the searching process at the cost of high state maintenance. In this paper, we seek to combine the powers of both forwarding and non-forwarding searching schemes. We propose an approach where the querying source directly probes its own extended neighbors and forwards the query to a subset of its extended neighbors and guides these neighbors to probe their own extended neighbors on its behalf. Our approach can adapt query processing to the popularity of the sought files without having to maintain a large set of neighbors because its neighbors' neighbors are also in the searching scope due to the 1-hop forwarding inherent in our approach. It achieves a higher query efficiency than the forwarding scheme and a better success rate than the non-forwarding approach. To the best of our knowledge, the work in this paper is the first one to combine forwarding and non-forwarding P2P searching schemes. Experimental results demonstrate the effectiveness of our approach.

1. Introduction

Peer-to-Peer (P2P) networks have been widely used for information sharing. In such systems, all nodes play equal roles and the need of expensive servers is eliminated. P2P networks are overlay networks, where each overlay link is actually a sequence of links in the underlying network. P2P networks are self-organized, distributed, and decentralized. In addition, they can gather and harness the tremendous computation and storage resources on computers in the entire network. P2P networks can be classified as *unstructured*, *loosely structured*, and *highly structured* based on the control over data location and network topology [7]. In this paper, we are concerned with unstructured P2Ps because they are the most widely used systems in practice. In such systems, no rule exists that defines where data is stored and the network topology is arbitrary.

Searching is one of the most important operations in P2P networks. Most existing P2P searching techniques are based on *forwarding* [7]. In such schemes, a query is forwarded on the overlay from the querying source toward the querying destinations where the desired data items are located. The query forwarding stops when the termination condition is satisfied. Forwarding schemes offer low state maintenance. Each node only needs to keep a small number of neighbors. However, the querying source has no control over query processing. Once the query is forwarded, the querying source has no influence on the number of nodes that receive the query and in which order these nodes receive the query. Too many nodes are searched for popular data items while not enough nodes are examined for rare ones. Therefore, the forwarding-based approach does not offer query flexibility and has low query efficiency.

Recently, *non-forwarding* schemes were proposed in [2] [12]. In these approaches, queries are not forwarded. Instead, the querying source directly probes its neighbors for the data items it desires. Thus the querying source has full control over query processing. The extent of a search is determined by the querying source. For popular items, only a small number of nodes need to be searched. For rare items, a large number of nodes are queried. No resource is wasted to search for popular items. However, to find rare items, each node has to maintain (dynamically recruit) a large number of living neighbors because it relies solely

*This work was supported in part by NSF grants CCR 9900646, CCR 0329741, ANI 0073736, and EIA 0130806.

0190-3918/05 $20.00 © 2005 IEEE

on its own neighbors for finding a data item. The system has to either carry a large overhead to keep a large number of neighbors alive or leaves queries unsatisfied with a low state maintenance overhead because the number of living neighbors that a node is aware of is not enough for finding rare items.

In this paper, we seek to combine these two schemes to get their advantages while lowering their disadvantages. Our goals are to advocate the integration of both schemes, to explore different methods for integration, and to evaluate the integrated schemes. We propose an approach that is a unification of direct query probing and guided 1-hop forwarding. Given a query, the querying source directly probes its own extended neighbors for the desired files and forwards the query to a selected number of neighbors. These neighbors will probe their own extended neighbors on behalf of and under the guidance of the querying source and will not forward the query further. When the query termination condition is satisfied, the querying source terminates its own probing and the probing of its neighbors.

The main contributions of this paper are the following:

- We identify the necessity to integrate both the forwarding schemes and non-forwarding schemes into one approach.

- We devise a hybrid approach that combines both the forwarding and non-forwarding schemes. This hybrid approach achieves query flexibility, query efficiency, and query satisfaction without a large state maintenance overhead. To the best of our knowledge, this work is the first one to combine both schemes.

- We investigate different design tradeoffs in integrating the forwarding and non-forwarding approaches. These choices include constant integration and adaptive integration. We point out their pros and cons and offer some practical advice in applying them to real world systems.

- We put forward two new policies for recruiting new neighbors, called *Most Files Shared in Neighborhood (MFSN)* and *Most Query Results in Neighborhood (MQRN)*. The nodes with more files and more past query results in its neighborhood are recruited first.

- We evaluate our hybrid approach against both the forwarding schemes and non-forwarding schemes and demonstrate the performance improvement in our hybrid approach through simulations.

This paper is organized as follows. In Section 2, the forwarding and non-forwarding searching schemes in unstructured P2P networks are reviewed. In Section 3, the proposed hybrid approach is overviewed and contrasted with the forwarding and non-forwarding schemes. In Section 4, the details about the hybrid approach, such as action queue computation, different integration design choices including constant integration and adaptive integration, and state maintenance are discussed. In Section 5, the experimental setup and results are described. At the end, our work is summarized and a future plan is identified.

2 Related work

Most searching schemes in unstructured P2P networks are forwarding-based, including iterative deepening [11], local indices [11], k-walker random walk [8], modified random BFS [6], two-level k-walker random walk [5], directed BFS [11], intelligent search [6], routing indices based search [3], adaptive probabilistic search [9], and dominating set based search [13]. These schemes are different variations of flooding used in Gnutella [1]. They can be classified as deterministic or probabilistic [7].

In contrast, there are only two non-forwarding schemes for searching unstructured P2Ps in the research literature. The non-forwarding concept was first proposed in GUESS [2]. In this approach, each node fully controls the entire process of its own queries. Each node directly probes its own neighbors in a sequential order until the query is satisfied or until all neighbors have been probed. The query fails in the latter case. Each node uses a *link cache* to keep information about its neighbors, which includes the IP, the time stamp, the number of files shared, and the number of results from the most recent query. There is one entry for each neighbor in the link cache. These link cache entries are refreshed through periodic pings. In addition, to add new neighbors into the link cache, each node also requests that its neighbors select a certain number of their own link cache entries and return them in the pongs during the periodic pings.

Because of the overhead of link cache maintenance, the link cache size cannot be too large. To accommodate this problem, when a neighbor is probed during the processing of a query, it also returns some of its own link cache entries in a separate query pong message. These link cache entries are stored in another cache, called *query cache*. Each entry in the query cache has the similar content to that in the link cache. Some entries in the query cache may be moved to the link cache. However, the entries in the query cache is not maintained.

The performance of GUESS is improved in [12], which emphasizes the impacts of different design choices, called policies, in non-forwarding schemes. The policies are classified into five types: QueryProbe, QueryPong, PingProbe, PingPong, and CacheReplacement. For each policy type, many specific policies may be adopted. Five common policies, which include random (RAN), most recently used

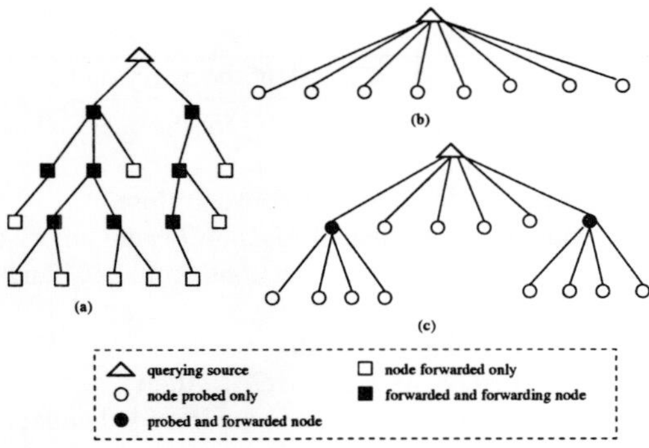

Figure 1. The three types of P2P searches. (a) forwarding based. (b) non-forwarding based. (c) hybrid.

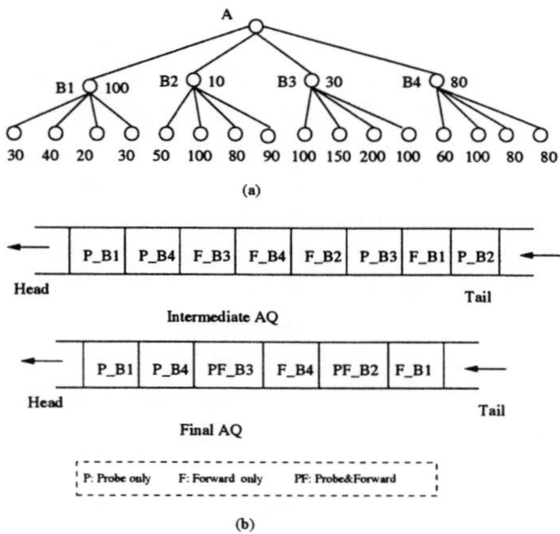

Figure 2. An example of action queue computation. (a) the querying source A and its 2-hop neighborhood, and the file distribution. (b) the computed action queue (the intermediate and final results).

(MRU), least recently used (LRU), most files shared (MFS), and most results (MR), are proposed for these policy types.

3 Outline of the hybrid search

Figure 1 illustrates the differences between the three types of searching approaches, forwarding based, non-forwarding based, and hybrid. In the figure, a node's children refer to some or all its neighbors in the P2P overlay. Forwarding-based searching can be regarded as a D-level tree rooted at the querying source as shown in Figure 1(a). D refers to the maximum TTL value. The querying source, denoted by a triangle, checks its local datastore and forwards the query to its children nodes. These children, denoted by solid squares, look up their local datastores and forward the query to their own children. This process continues until the search terminates successfully at a leaf node that is not at Level-D or the search fails at a leaf node that is at Level-D. It is observed that once the query is forwarded, the querying source cannot control how the nodes on this tree process the query. Each node just needs to maintain a small number of neighbors because nodes within D hops of the querying source are potentially in the searching scope.

Non-forwarding based searching is shown in Figure 1(b). It is a 1-level tree rooted at the querying source. The querying source directly probes its child nodes for the desired files. These children only search their local datastores and do not send the query further. The querying source terminates the search when the query is satisfied or when all its neighbors are probed. Only the querying source and its direct neighbors are involved in the processing of a particular query. Therefore, each node must maintain a sufficient number of live neighbors. These neighbors are dynamically recruited and updated via periodical ping-probes and ping-pongs.

The hybrid searching is illustrated in Figure 1(c). It is a 2-level tree rooted at the querying source. The querying source directly probes the nodes at Level-1 of the tree. In the mean time, it also forwards the query to the internal nodes at Level-1 and guides these nodes to probe the nodes at Level-2 on its behalf. The querying source terminates the search when the query is satisfied or when all its neighbors and its neighbors' neighbors are probed. The maximum searching scope for a query in this approach is the 2-hop neighborhood of the querying source.

Like the non-forwarding approach, a node in the hybrid approach maintains an extended neighbor set and dynamically recruits and updates this neighbor set via periodic ping-probes and ping-pongs. However, the hybrid approach can achieve the same or higher query satisfaction with less neighbors per node. Compared to the forwarding-based approach, the querying source in the hybrid approach can control the extent of the searching.

To combine the forwarding and non-forwarding smoothly, the hybrid search is implemented as follows. It considers three types of actions, *probing only*, *forwarding only*, *probing and forwarding*. *Probing only* means that the querying source probes its neighbors and these neighbors look up their local datastores. *Forwarding only* means that the querying source does not probe its neighbors but guides its neighbors to probe their own neighbors on its behalf. *Probing and forwarding* means the combination of the first two actions.

When processing a query, the querying source first ranks these three types of actions if performed on all its neighbors and organizes these actions into an *action queue*. Two examples of action queues are shown in Figure 2(b). The final AQ(Action Queue) contains six actions listed in the descending order of their ranks, probe node B_1, probe node B_4, probe and forward to node B_3, forward to node B_4, probe and forward to node B_2, and forward to node B_1. The querying source then takes actions in this queue in order. It can take actions at a constant rate of k_1 actions at once, which is called *constant integration.* It can also take actions at a variable rate depending on the rareness of the sought files, which is referred to as *adaptive integration.* The querying source terminates the entire searching process when the query is satisfied or when all actions in the queue have been taken.

The action ranking considers both the costs and gains of actions. The cost of an action is the time (in terms of the number of overlay hops) it takes for that action to be completed. The gain of an action is the estimated probability of that action for returning query results, which are determined by the system policies. These policies can also be used by the neighbors of the querying source for probing their own neighbors on behalf of the querying source.

To keep information about neighbors, each node actively maintains a *link cache.* There is one entry per neighbor. These entries are periodically updated (deleting dead entries, replacing existing entries using new entries) according to system policies. We propose two new policies, *Most Files Shared On Neighborhood (MFSN)* and *Most Query Results on Neighborhood (MQRN).*

4 The hybrid search

The hybrid search involves the querying source and its neighbors. The processing at these nodes is shown in Algorithm 1 and Algorithm 2. Given a query q, the querying source s first computes the action queue AQ based on the discussion in section 4.1. If constant integration is adopted, s takes the first k_1 actions in AQ at the same time. k_1 is a system parameter. P, F , or PF messsages are sent to the intended neighbors according to the action types. When v receives P or PF messages, it looks up its datastore and returns the query results if there is any. When v receives F or PF messages, it probes its own neighbors on behalf of s with k_2 neighbors per probe. k_2 is also a system parameter. If s receives any query result from a neighbor v, s stores that result. If adaptive integration is employed, follow the detailed algorithm in section 4.2. When q is satisfied, s stops its own probing and the probing performed by its neighbors on its behalf.

4.1 Action queue computation

The action queue is computed based on the gain/cost ratios of the actions if they are performed on the querying

Algorithm 1 The hybrid search at the querying source s

Compute the *action queue* AQ for the query q based on the description in section 4.1;
if the integration design is constant **then**
  while q is not satisfied AND AQ is not empty **do**
    remove the first k_1 actions from AQ and store them in the array ACT_k;
    for $i = 0$ to $k_1 - 1$ **do**
      if $ACT_k[i]$ is $ProbeOnly$ **then**
        send P message to the intended node;
      else if $ACT_k[i]$ is $ForwardOnly$ **then**
        send F message to the intended node;
        add this node to the set: $FWDed$;
      else
        send PF message to the intended node;
        add this node to the set: $FWDed$;
      end if
    end for
    if s receives query results from a neighbor v **then**
      store the query results in the array $QRes$;
      if v has probed all its neighbors **then**
        remove v from the set $FWDed$;
      end if
    end if
  end while
else
  call the algorithm $adaptive\_integration\_search$ in section 4.2;
end if
if q is satisfied **then**
  Order each node in $FWDed$ to stop probing on behalf of s;
end if

Algorithm 2 The hybrid search at the querying source s's neighbor v

if v receives a P message **then**
  v checks its local datastore and returns a query result to s if the result is found;
else if v receives a F message **then**
  v probes its own neighbors on behalf of s at the rate of k_2 nodes per probe;
else
  v checks its local datastore and returns a query result to s if the result is found;
  v probes its own neighbors on behalf of s at the rate of k_2 nodes per probe;
end if

source's neighbors. We intend to use the number of query results per hop as the gain/cost ratio. The cost of an action is the time (in terms of the number of overlay hops) taken for that action to be completed. The gain of an action is the estimated probability of that action for returning query results. This probability is computed based on the system policy on estimating nodes' query-answering ability. Possible policies are random (RAN), most recently used (MRU), most files (MF), and most query results (MR). The action queue computation algorithm varies according to the chosen system policy.

If the system policy is random, the action queue is a random sequence of $ProbeOnly$ actions on all neighbors of the querying source s followed by a random sequence of $ForwardOnly$ actions on those neighbors. If the system policy is most recently used, the action queue is a sequence of $ProbeOnly$ actions on s's neighbors, followed by a sequence of $FowardOnly$ actions on those neighbors. Both sequences are sorted in the descending order of the timestamp when s interacted with these neighbors regardless which party initiated the interation. No $Probe\&Forward$ action is involved in these two policies to reduce the query traffic.

If the system policy is most files, the action queue is computed according to Algorithm 3. The gain/cost ratio of a $ProbeOnly$ action on a neighbor v, denoted by $PGCR_v$, is computed using the following formula. $NumF_v$ represents the gain of the action. It is the number of files on node v. 2 is the cost of this action, 2 overlay hops.

$$PGCR_v = \frac{NumF_v}{2}$$

The gain/cost ratio of a $ForwardOnly$ action on a neighbor v, denoted by $FGCR_v$, is calculated according to the following formula. NB_v refers to the set of neighbors of node v. $NumF_u$ refers to the number of files on u. d_v represents the degree of node v. k_2 is the system parameter mentioned earlier. The gain of this action is the total number of files on v's neighbors. The cost of this action is the denominator where 1 means that it takes one hop for the querying source s to send a F message to v, $2d_v/k_2$ represents the time taken for v to finish probing all its neighbors at the rate of k_2 nodes per probe, d_v/k_2 denotes the time taken for v to return all query results found on its neighbors to s, and γ refers to the penalty weighting factor because probing and forwarding are considered together in action ranking.

$$FGCR_v = \frac{\sum_{u \in NB_v} NumF_u}{\gamma(1 + 2d_v/k_2 + d_v/k_2)}$$

If the system policy is most query results, the action queue computation is similar to that of most files. The only difference is that the number of files on node u and v are replaced by the number of query results for the most recent query on u and v respectively.

Algorithm 3 The action queue computation at the querying source s for policies MF and MR

compute the gain/cost ratios of the actions $ProbeOnly$ and $ForwardOnly$ if performed on each neighbor v;
sort these actions in the descending order of their gain/cost ratios and store the result in the linked list AQ.
if a node v exists such that the action $ForwardOnly\ to\ v$ precedes action $Probe\ v\ Only$ in AQ **then**
  replace the action $FowardOnly\ to\ v$ by $Probe\ v\ and\ Forward\ to\ v$;
  remove the action $Probe\ v\ Only$ from AQ;
end if

An example of action queue computation is shown in Figure 2 and Table 1. Suppose that the querying source A, its neighbors B_1, B_2, B_3, B_4, and its neighbors' neighbors are the same as that in Figure 2(a). The numbers next to each node refers to the number of files on that node. Assume that the system policy for estimating nodes' query-answering ability is most files, $k_2 = 2$, and $\gamma = 2$. We first consider the $ProbeOnly$ and $ForwardOnly$ actions if performed on each neighbor of A. The gain/cost ratios of these actions are illustrated in Table 1. Take node B_4 as an example. The gain/cost ratio of the action $Probe\ B_4\ only$ is $80/2 = 40$. The gain/cost ratio of the action $Forward\ to\ B_4\ only$ is

$$\frac{60 + 100 + 80 + 80}{2(1 + \frac{2*4}{2} + \frac{4}{2})} \doteq 23.$$

Then we sort these actions in the descending order of their gain/cost ratios and get the intermediate action queue as shown in Figure 2(b). Because $Forward\ to\ B_3\ only$ (F_B_3) action appears before $Probe\ B_3\ only$ (P_B_3) action in the intermediate AQ, they are combined into one action $Probe\ B_3\ and\ Forward\ to\ B_3$ (PF_B_3). Similarly the actions F_B_2 and P_B_2 are combined into the action PF_B_2. The final AQ is shown in Figure 2(b).

4.2 Integration design

We consider two ways to integrate forwarding and probing, *constant integration* and *adaptive integration*. In constant integration, the querying source s takes actions in the action queue at a constant speed (k_1 actions each time where k_1 is determined experimentally). In adaptive integration, s adjusts its action-taking progress according to the rareness of the sought files. The rarer, the more progressive. There are many options for adaptive integration. One simple example is to adjust the progress according to the following formula. α denotes the number of actions taken by s each time. α is initialized to α_0 and is increased by β actions for every $NumN$ nodes that have been searched since last update. $NumN$ serves as an update interval. $NumNSoFar$ is the total number of nodes that have been searched since the beginning of the query processing. α_0 and β will be determined experimentally. The neighbors of the querying source s must report their probing progress to s. The hybrid search in the case of adaptive integration is shown in Algorithm 4. The main difference is that s must initialize α before processing a query q and update α while processing q.

$$\alpha = \alpha_0 + \lfloor \frac{NumNSoFar}{NumN} \rfloor \beta$$

Algorithm 4 The *adaptive_integration_search* at the querying source s (called by Algorithm 1)

Initialize α;
while q is not satisfied AND AQ is not empty **do**
  remove the first α actions from AQ and store them in the array ACT_k;
  for $i = 0$ to $\alpha - 1$ **do**
    if $ACT_k[i]$ is *ProbeOnly* **then**
      send P message to the intended node;
    else if $ACT_k[i]$ is *ForwardOnly* **then**
      send F message to the intended node;
      add this node to the set: *FWDed*;
    else
      send PF message to the intended node;
      add this node to the set: *FWDed*;
    end if
  end for
  if s receives query results from a neighbor v **then**
    store the query results in the array $QRes$;
    if v has probed all its neighbors **then**
      remove v from the set *FWDed*;
    end if
  end if
  if the interval for updating α arrives **then**
    update α accordingly;
  end if
end while

4.3 Query probing

Both the querying source s and its neighbors perform probing during the processing of a query. The probing performed by s is considered together with forwarding in the action queue computation. This subsection dicusses the probing performed by s's neighbors on its behalf as a result of query forwarding. This probing is at the rate of k_2 nodes per probe. It is guided by the same system policy for estimating nodes' query-answering ability that was chosen in action queue computation.

Suppose that v is a neighbor of s. If the system policy is random, v randomly chooses k_2 of its own neighbors that have not been probed and probes these neighbors concurrently. If the system policy is most recently used, v selects k_2 of its own neighbors that have not been probed and have the latest timestamps among all of its unprobed neighbors. If the system policy is most files or most query results, v chooses k_2 unprobed neighbors that have the top number of files or top number of query results for the most recent query.

Node	ProbeOnly	ForwardOnly
B1	50	8.5
B2	5	23
B3	15	40
B4	40	23

Table 1. The gain/cost ratios of *ProbeOnly* and *ForwardOnly* actions if performed on A's neighbors.

Notation	Definition
IP	The IP address of B
TS	The last time when A and B interacts with each other
$NumFiles_P$	The number of files on B
$NumRes_P$	The number of query results for the last query found on B
$NumFiles_F$	The total number of files on B's neighbors
$NumRes_F$	The total number of query results for the last query found on B's neighbors

Table 2. The data structure of a link cache entry at node A for neighbor B.

4.4 The state maintenance

Like the non-forwarding based searching, each node uses a link cache to maintain information about neighbors. However, link cache entries in the hybrid approach have different content because a node needs to know the information about a neighbor and this neighbor's neighbors. Table 2 shows the data structure of the link cache entry for neighbor B at node A in the hybrid approach. It should be noted that the TS is updated no matter which party, A or B, initiates the interaction and what type of interaction is.

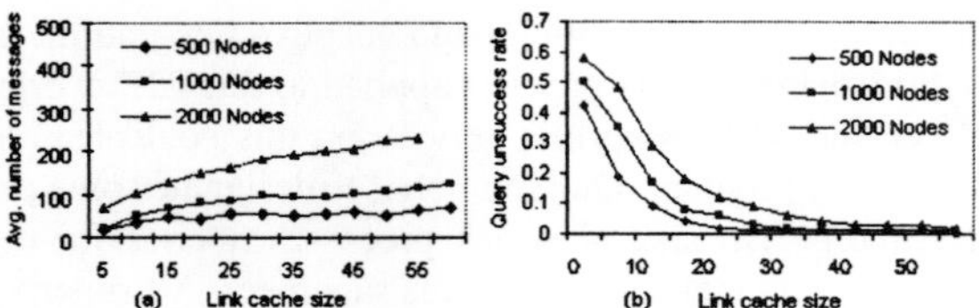

Figure 3. (a) The number of query messages per query. (b) The unsuccess rate in terms of the link cache size for the hybrid search.

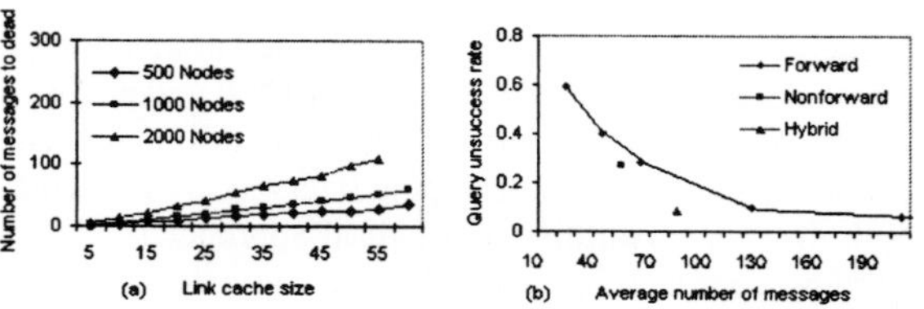

Figure 4. (a) The unsuccess rate in terms of the link cache size. (b) The query unsuccess rate in terms of the average number of messages per query of three approaches

The link cache is refreshed and updated through periodic pings. Each node periodically selects some of its neighbors and sends Ping messages to these neighbors. These neighbors reply with Pong messages that include the latest information about themselves and a selected number of entries in their own link cache. The ping interval is a system parameter. There are three types of system policies that specify how the periodic pings are conducted. They are Ping-Probe policy, PingPong policy, and CacheReplacement policy. The PringProbe policy specifies the neighbor selection rule for sending Pings. The PingPong policy is used to select neighbors to be included in the Pong when responding to a Ping. The CacheReplacement policy determines the rule for replacing existing entries by the new entries.

For each policy type, one of the seven specific policies may be chosen, random (RAN), most recently used (MRU), least recently used (LRU), most files shared on neighbor (MFS), most query results on neighbor (MR), most files shared in neighborhood (MFSN), and most query results in neighborhood (MQRN). The RAN, MRU, LRU, MFS, and MR are similar to those in the non-forwarding approach. The MFSN and MQRN are new policies proposed in this paper. The MFSN selects the neighbor that has the most shared files in its 1-hop neighborhood including that neighbor itself. The MQRN chooses the neighobr that returns the most query results for the last query, which counts the results found on that neighbor and the results found on that neighbor's neighbors.

5 Experimental Results

The performance of the hybrid approach is evaluated experimentally against the forwarding-based scheme and non-forwarding searching. Only the base-line policy *RAN* is implemented because of the time limitation. The performance measures are the average query success rate and the average number of query messages per query. A query is a search for a single document based on the document ID. A query is considered successful if at least *numDesiredResults* copies of the sought document are found.

We created a network of $numNodes$ nodes. The overlay for the forwarding approach is random graph with an average node degree of 4. For the non-forwarding and hybrid approach, each node's link cache is seeded with *cacheSeedSize* neighbors. Then the neighbors are dynamically extended/updated based on the *PingProbePolicy*, *PingPongPolicy*, and *CacheReplacementPolicy*. Both the document replication distribution and the query distribution is zipfian distribution. As suggested in [10], we let 10 percent of the documents have around 30 percent of the total stored copies and receive around 30 percent of total query requests.

To simulate the dynamic network, we let *pctNodesChanged* nodes die periodically. It is assumed that when a node dies, another new node is born and the dead node does not return to the system. Therefore the number of nodes in the system remains the same. We use the *random friend seeding policy* [4] to initialize the link cache of the new node. The new node introduces itself to nodes in its link cache at probability $introProb = 0.1$. Each node pings a fixed number of neighbors in the link cache at constant speed.

Figure 3 illustrates the impact of the different link cache sizes in networks of different scales for the hybrid approach. To isolate the effect of the link cache, we did not implement the query cache. As seen in Figure 3(a), the number of query messages per query increases as the link cache gets larger. The query unsuccess rate drops quickly as the link cache size increases as shown in Figure 3(b). When the link cache size is more than 30, the query unsuccess rate does not change much. Figure 4(a) explains the reason. More messages are sent to dead neighbors when the link cache size is larger. The networks at different scales show similar trends as the link cache size changes. These figures suggest that the appropriate values for the link cache are in the range of 15 to 30.

In Figure 4(b), we compare the hybrid approach to the forwarding and non-forwarding approach using the query unsuccess rate per average query cost (the number of query messages per query) in the network of 1000 nodes. The link cache sizes of the non-forwarding and hybrid approach are 100 and 20 respectively. The ping intervals are the same for both the non-forwarding and hybrid approaches. The forwarding approach has a fixed searching extent; the query unsuccess rate increases dramatically when the query cost is restricted. Both the hybrid approach and non-forwarding approach have smaller unsuccess rates than the forwarding approach at the same query cost due to query flexibility. When the state maintenance overhead is similar (ping at the same speed and pong size is the same), the hybrid approach can achieve a higher success rate than the non-forwarding approach. This is due to the 1-hop forwarding inherent in the hybrid approach. The searching scope of the hybrid approach includes more living neighbors. It should be noted that the higher success rate of the hybrid approach is achieved at a query cost higher than the non-forwarding approach but lower than the forwarding approach. In summary, the experimental results demonstrate that the hybrid approach combines the advantages of both the forwarding and non-forwarding approaches.

6. Conclusions

In this paper, we propose a hybrid searching scheme in unstructured P2P networks. It is a combination of probing and guided 1-hop forwarding. Given a query, the querying source probes its neighbors and forwards the query to its neighbors. These neighbors probe their own neighbors on behalf of and under the guidance of the querying source as a result of query forwarding. When the query is satisfied, the querying source terminates its own probing and the probing performed by its neighbors. To integrate the probing and forwarding smoothly, we compute an *action queue* which consists of *ProbeOnly*, *ForwardOnly*, and *Probe&Forward* actions sorted in the descending order of their gain/cost ratios. The querying source just takes actions in this queue at a constant rate or a variable rate that is adapted to the rareness of the sought data. We also propose two new policies for recruiting new neighbors, *Most Files Shared on Neighborhood (MFSN)* and *Most Query Results on Neighborhood (MQRN)*.

Compared to the forwarding-based scheme, hybrid searching is more flexible. It adapts the query processing to the popularity of sought files and does not waste resources when searching for popular files. Therefore hybrid searching has a higher query efficiency. Compared to the non-forwarding scheme, hybrid searching accomplishes a better query success rate without maintaining a more complex state. To the best of our knowledge, this is the first work to combine the forwarding and non-forwarding schemes.

In the future, we plan to do more experiments to evaluate different system policies and adaptive integration. The hybrid search in this paper is applied to flat P2P overlays. When the p2P network is very large, this could lead to a scalability problem. One solution is to designate some peers as superpeers, each of which processes queries for other regular peers that connects to this superpeer. All superpeers form an unstructured P2P sub-overlay. Hybrid searching can be applied to this P2P sub-overlay. We will evaluate this approach in the future.

References

[1] The gnutella protocol specification v0.4. Clip2 distributed search solutions, http://www.clip2.com.

[2] Guess protocol specification v0.1. http://groups.yahoo.com /group /the_gdf /files /Proposals /GUESS /guess_o1.txt.

[3] A. Crespo and H. Garcia-Molina. Routing indices for peer-to-peer systems. In *Proceedings of the 22nd International Conference on Distributed Computing (IEEE ICDCS'02)*, 2002.

[4] N. Daswani and H. Garcia-Molina. Pong cache poisoning in guess. In *Technical report, Stanford University*, 2003.

[5] I. Jawhar and J. Wu. A two-level random walk search protocol for peer-to-peer networks. In *Proceedings of the 8th World Multi-Conference on Systemics, Cybernetics and Informatics*, 2004.

[6] V. Kalogeraki, D. Gunopulos, and D. Zeinalipour-yazti. A local search mechanism for peer-to-peer networks. In *Proceedings of the 11th ACM Conference on Information and Knowledge Management (ACM CIKM'02)*, 2002.

[7] X. Li and J. Wu. *Searching techniques in peer-to-peer networks.* in Handbook of Theoretical and Algorithmic Aspects of Sensor, Ad Hoc Wireless, and Peer-to-Peer Networks, Edited by J. Wu, CRC Press, 2005.

[8] Q. Lv, P. Cao, E. Cohen, K. Li, and S. Shenker. Search and replication in unstructured peer-to-peer networks. In *Proceedings of the 16th ACM International Conference on Supercomputing (ACM ICS'02)*, 2002.

[9] D. Tsoumakos and N. Roussopoulos. Adaptive probabilistic search in peer-to-peer networks. In *Proceedings of 2nd International Workshop on Peer-to-Peer Systems (IPTPS'03)*, 2003.

[10] D. Tsoumakos and N. Roussopoulos. A comparison of peer-to-peer search methods. In *Proceedings of the 2003 International Workshop on the Web and Databases (WebDB'03)*, 2003.

[11] B. Yang and H. Garcia-Molina. Improving search in peer-to-peer networks. In *Proceedings of the 22nd IEEE International Conference on Distributed Computing Systems (IEEE ICDCS'02)*, 2002.

[12] B. Yang, P. Vinograd, and H. Garcia-Molina. Evaluating guess and non-forwarding peer-to-peer search. In *Proceedings of the 24th IEEE International Conference on Distributed Computing Systems (IEEE ICDCS'04)*, 2004.

[13] C. Yang and J. Wu. A dominating-set-based routing in peer-to-peer networks. In *Proceedings of the 2nd International Workshop on Grid and Cooperative Computing Workshop (GCC'03)*, 2003.

Session 4C: Ad Hoc Networks

BluePower – A New Distributed Multihop Scatternet Formation Protocol for Bluetooth Networks

Yuanrui Zhang*, Shu Liu*, Weijia Jia**, Xu Cheng*

*MicroProcessor R&D Center, Department of Computer Science, Peking University, China
**Department of Computer Engineering & IT, City University of Hong Kong, China
*{zhangyuanrui, liushu, chengxu}@mprc.pku.edu.cn
itjia@cityu.edu.hk

Abstract

Bluetooth is a promising local area wireless technology designed to establish both personal area and multihop ad hoc networks. In this paper, we present BluePower as a novel and practical distributed scheme for building large multihop scatternets based on device transmitting power. The protocol is executed at each node with no prior knowledge of network topology and constructs the topology simply by enabling each node to alternate between scatternet formation and communication. Different from existing solutions, our design integrates device mobility and network self-healing from partitions with topology formation. Besides, partial loop detection is applied to minimize the redundant links in the network. The simulation results show that BluePower has low scatternet formation latency, decent number of slaves per piconet, short average route length and small connection delay for nodes to establish the first communication links in dynamic environments.

1. Introduction

Bluetooth (BT) technology, originally introduced as short-range cable replacement, is emerging as one of the most promising enabling technologies to build inexpensive but large *ad hoc* networks.

According to the current BT specifications [1], when two devices come into each other's communication range (i.e., they become *neighbors*), one of them must assume the role of *master* of the communication while the other becomes its *slave*. This simple "one-hop" network is called a *piconet* and may include up to 7 slaves which can actively communicate with the master at the same time. If a master node has more than 7 slaves, some slave nodes have to be *parked* in an inactive state. To communicate with a parked slave node, a master node has to *unpark* it while possibly parking another slave. All the active slaves inside a piconet share the same 1-Mbps Frequency Hopping Spread Spectrum (FHSS) channel derived from the unique ID and BT clock of the master in a *time-division* multiplexing scheme, which is centrally controlled by the master.

The specifications [1] allow each device to assume multiple roles. A node can be a master in one piconet or a slave in multiple piconets. Nodes with multiple roles act as *bridges* between the adjacent piconets, resulting in a multihop ad hoc network called a *scatternet* (Figure 1). Time multiplexing must be used for a bridge node to switch between the piconets. Since two BT devices cannot communicate directly before a master-slave relation is set up, communications within a large-scale Bluetooth network have to be based on a scatternet.

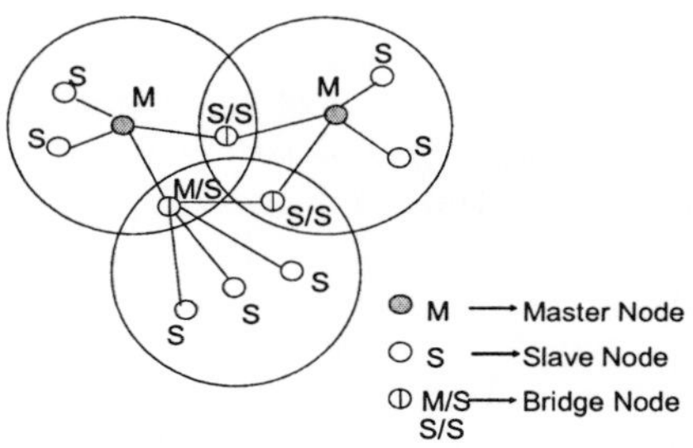

Figure 1. A Bluetooth scatternet

However, the specifications [1] do not indicate any method for scatternet formation. Many solutions have been proposed in the literature so far. The solution proposed in [7] is based on a leader election process to collect information at the leader, who then runs a centralized algorithm to assign the roles to all the

0190-3918/05 $20.00 © 2005 IEEE

others. A significant limitation is that the maximum number of nodes it can handle is limited to 36, which is not suitable for dynamic environments. To support dynamic features, two distributed procedures for the insertion and removal of a node in/from the scatternet is discussed in [10], but they are so complicated that a BT device is classified into 51 classes based on the device's physical characteristics, current role in the scatternet and the amount of traffic transmitted and received. A simpler TSF algorithm is given in [8]. It builds topologies incrementally by connecting nodes into a tree and heals partitions when they occur. The tree structure limits robustness and lacks efficiency in routing, and all the internal nodes in the tree are M/S bridges with overheads much higher than S/S types. Another incremental scheme presented in [12] is for multihop scenario. Like TSF, communication between nodes can be performed during scatternet formation, indicating a longer latency in order to guarantee the network connectivity. Other solutions for multihop topologies are presented in [2-6]. BlueTrees [2] also generates a tree-like scatternet, and applies a re-configuration procedure to bind the number of slaves per master. The solution could not work if network is not connected after device discovery phase, for it depends on the *blueroot* to start. The protocols BlueStars [3] and BlueNet [4] both begin the execution with device discovery and need not select any root node. However, the number of slaves in a piconet is not limited in [3] and the resulting scatternet connectivity is not guaranteed in [4]. A new protocol has been recently proposed in [5], termed BlueMesh. Similar to [2,3,4], with the complex implementation of neighbor discovery, device mobility is not allowed during scatternet formation. To support mobility, an additional adjustment protocol must be applied, such as the procedure proposed in [13].

In this paper, we present and evaluate a new scatternet formation protocol for multihop Bluetooth networks called *BluePower*. Based on device transmitting power, it can dynamically decide the roles of master and slave, and use Bluetooth's lower-layer primitives to detect potential nodes to form links. No neighbor discovery procedure or designed root is required to start. Unlike [2,3,4,5] that regard scatternet formation and device mobility as different issues, our protocol treats scatternet formation as a special case of network self-healing so that mobility is fully supported. Devices may arrive incrementally when forming a scatternet, or join and leave at any time without causing long disruptions in connectivity after the scatternet is formed. Contrary to [7], there is no limitation on the number of devices in the scatternet due to a loop elimination mechanism.

The rest of the paper is organized as follows. Section 2 explains the background information about Bluetooth link formation process. Section 3 presents our design and the detailed algorithms of BluePower. The simulation results are shown in section 4. Conclusions and future works are given in section 5.

2. Bluetooth link formation

The specifications [1] define the BT point-to-point connection establishment as a two-step procedure: *Inquiry* and *Page*. As described in [8], the goal of the Inquiry process is for a potential master to discover the existence of neighbors and collect enough information about their low-level states to establish frequency hopping connections within a subset. The goal of the Page process is to use the information gathered during the Inquiry process to establish bi-directional frequency hopping communication channels.

During the Inquiry process, a device enters either the *inquiry* or the *inquiry scan* state. Devices in the inquiry state repeatedly alternate between broadcasting short ID packets containing an Inquiry Access Code (IAC) and listening for responses. Devices in the inquiry scan state constantly listen for packets from those in the inquiry state and respond with a Frequency Hopping Sequence (FHS) packet when appropriate. Although all devices hop over dedicated frequencies, to minimize the neighbor discovery time, the BT Baseband specification [1] requires that the inquiry scan node hops at a much lower rate than the inquiry node to increase the probability of a handshake on the same frequency of the inquirer.

Multiple inquiry scan nodes can simultaneously receive messages from the same inquiry node. To avoid contention, each scanning node chooses a random backoff interval T_{rb} before responding with the signaling information when synchronizing with the inquirer again. If T_{sync} is the delay before two nodes can synchronize their frequencies, the time taken to complete the Inquiry process is given by:

$$T_{inq} = 2T_{sync} + T_{rb} \qquad (1)$$

A node remains in the inquiry state until a timeout period elapses, or the number of responses has reached a predefined value. If the number of responses is greater than zero, it enters the *page* state and uses the signaling information obtained during the inquiry state to send out trains of Device Access Code (DAC) packets. A node in the inquiry scan state periodically enters the *page scan* state. When receiving a DAC packet, it immediately acknowledges the sender with an FHS packet that carries all the required information for the sender to synchronize on its own frequency hopping sequence. Then, both nodes proceed to exchange necessary information to establish a link. Eventually, a piconet is formed with the node in the page state as the master and the node in the page scan state as its slave. This link formation process is illustrated in Figure 2.

The Page process is similar to the Inquiry process except that the paging node already knows the estimated clock value and address of the paged node. But there will still be some synchronization delay before the pager and the paged node can communicate. It will be most efficient for the two nodes in the Inquiry process to enter the Page process as soon as the inquiring node has received the inquiry response. If we define T_{pg} as the time taken to complete the Page process, then the least total time taken to establish a link between two nodes is:

$$T_{conn} = T_{inq} + T_{pg} \quad (2)$$

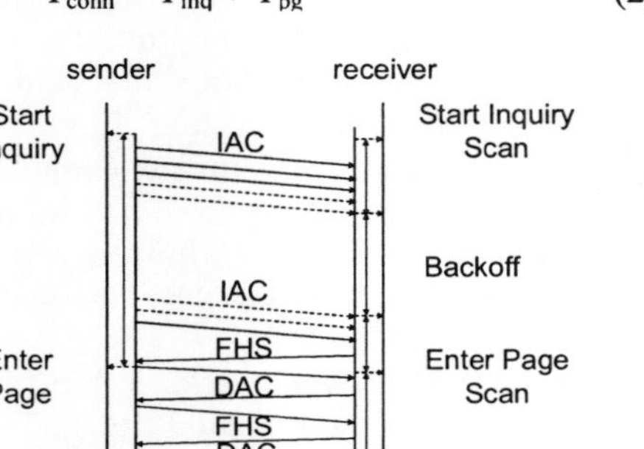

Figure 2. Bluetooth link formation process

3. BluePower scatternet formation protocol

3.1. Motivations of our protocol

We first introduce some basic principles for the design of our protocol:

P1 – Scatternet formation and network self-healing from partitions should be treated intrinsically the same as they recovery from topology changes.

Most schemes regard scatternet formation and network self-healing as two different issues. They often neglect device mobility when designing a scatternet formation protocol and provide an additional algorithm to adapt for dynamic environments. In fact, these two processes are intrinsically the same as they recovery from topology changes. Generally speaking, there are three cases to be considered:

1. Topology formation: all nodes arrive *en masse* over a relatively small window of time to construct topologies by forming piconets and interconnecting them via some bridges; they are individually free, or a part of them are connected into a piconet/scatternet.

2. Topology maintenance: in an already established network, a fraction of existing links are disconnected due to the movement of nodes or the weakness of some wireless channels. In this case, some original links are lost and new links need to be created to regain the network connectivity, even if no nodes really leave the region.

3. Topology reconstruction: nodes arbitrarily arrive or leave in an incremental fashion, such that there is a pre-constructed and relatively static "core" network that a new node will join. In this situation, algorithms for dynamic environments should be called in order to reconstruct the network. Similar to case 1, nodes may move individually or in the form of a group in a sub-network, such as a piconet.

Topology maintenance and reconstruction are both network partition healing process. Actually, topology formation can be viewed as a special case of self-healing, but from scratch given an initial set of BT devices. In any case, network needs recovery if topology changes happen. To satisfy all the situations, a solution is to make each node alternate between scatternet formation and communication repeatedly, allowing the incremental arrival and departure of nodes. The alternation should be executed at each node in a distributed fashion to avoid centralized management or periodical broadcasting over the whole network.

P2 – Network is constructed by combining the Bluetooth lower-layer primitives with device transmitting power.

Currently, most network formation algorithms are based on some kind of assumption, e.g. undefined symmetric link formation protocol [2-5,7,9,11], which is inconvenience or impossible for some practical applications. Instead, our design simply utilizes the Inquiry process to form scatternets without any additional procedure to gather the prior information about neighbors.

There are three critical issues of directly using the Inquiry process to design a protocol. The first question is how to initiate this process, i.e., which state a node should enter after power on. The second is how a node switches between the inquiry and inquiry scan states. The third is how long a node should remain in each state. They all have significant effects on the number of potential neighbors each node can discover and the final network connectivity.

Different from previous solutions [3,5,12], we solve these problems by combining the Inquiry process with device transmitting power. According to the specifications [1], a device is classified into 3 classes: Power Class 1 (PC1) device has the maximum output power of 100mW; Power Class 2 (PC2) has 2.5mW at most and Power Class 3 (PC3) has 1mW. To initiate the Inquiry process, when a free node comes online, it enters the inquiry state if it is a PC1 device, and enters inquiry scan state if it belongs to the other two classes. The node then switches strictly between the two states. The time lasting for each state is based on device power class: the node with higher transmitting power remains longer in the inquiry state so as to have a higher probability of becoming a master.

P3 – Roles are assigned to the two nodes when establishing a link based on transmitting power and adjacent link conditions.

The goal of scatternet formation is to determine the roles of all nodes in the network, especially carried out through the determination of which node acts as master and which acts as slave when establishing a link. In general, the node in the page mode becomes master and the node in the page scan mode becomes slave. However, constraints on the role that some nodes can have may exist, such as battery charge, traffic load, processing capabilities, adjacent links, transmitting power and so on. For instance, gateways to the fixed network that have great processing capabilities and infinite battery should be chosen as masters, while earphone devices are likely to act as slaves. Rather than using an abstract number to represent constrains [3,5], we impose two actual factors on the role when establishing a link: device transmitting power and adjacent links.

As to device transmitting power, the higher a node has, the more appropriate it is to act as master. Without loss of generality, we assume that a device's battery is in propositional to its transmitting power. Master nodes usually have many links to connect, thus they require more battery to switch between channels and require higher power to transmit to others.

If a node has already had more than one link, its adjacent links should be considered to determine which role it will act as when setting up a new link. For example, if a master of a piconet is connecting with a free node, the free node should join the piconet as a slave given less than 7 slaves already in that piconet. This can keep an adequate number of piconets and avoid excessive bridges. Similarly, a slave node prefers to remain as slave when forming new links. This preference can control the number of piconets and result in a decrease in the number of M/S bridges.

3.2. BluePower algorithm

BluePower is distributed with each node operating autonomously with local communication. At any time, each node in the network runs the same state-machine algorithm, switching between two states: scatternet formation (FORM) and communication (COMM). In the FORM state, the node attempts to rendezvous with its neighbors to form communication links, improving the scatternet connectivity. In the COMM state, the node is involved in the data communication with others in its connected component. After power on, every node enters FORM first to start topology formation, and then switches between the two states.

The time a node spends in FORM depends on three factors: the current number of links, *currLinks*; the maximum number of links a node can have, *MaxLinks*; and the maximum time a node can stay in FORM, T_{form}, whose optimal value was found through experiments and long enough to guarantee the scatternet connectivity. The time spent in COMM depends on the node's current total traffic volume to handle.

As *currLinks* increases, a node will spend less time in scatternet formation and more in communication. The intuition behind this is that if a node has many available links, it should spend more time trying to acquire more neighbors to improve the connectivity; when it already has many links, it should be essential for efficient data communication. In particular, if the node is free, it cannot perform any communication but stays in FORM, attempting to join a scatternet. If the node has achieved *MaxLinks* links, it cannot perform any scatternet formation but keeps on communicating with others in COMM.

When one of a node's links is torn down during communication, the node should first update its role to an appropriate type and then start scatternet formation immediately. Here, the loss of a link can be found by two ways: when a master is polling its slave, it can detect the loss given no reply from the slave; when a slave has not received any message from its master for some time, it may detect the loss of that master.

3.2.1. Scatternet formation algorithm. The FORM state consists of two sub-states: INQUIRY and INQUIRY SCAN, corresponding to the Bluetooth-specified states: *inquiry* and *inquiry scan*. Generally speaking, each node switches strictly between them. When two neighboring nodes rendezvous, they will enter the *page* and *page scan* mode respectively, trying to establish a communication link. The alternation of each node depends on the node's type rather than a random schedule [3,5,12]. In BluePower, we have defined three types of nodes represented by *F* (free), *M* (master), and *S* (slave). In the beginning, all free nodes with no connections to others have type *F*. After the first connection setup, an *F* node becomes either master or slave in a piconet with type *M* or *S* accordingly. We also assume that an S/S bridge has type *S* and an M/S bridge has type *M*.

Nodes of different types have different behaviors after entering the FORM state. For *F* nodes, since they have no links, transmitting power is the determinant factor. A PC1 node enters INQUIRY first, whereas the other two class nodes enter INQUIRY SCAN first. This indicates that free nodes with higher transmitting power will have greater probabilities of becoming masters. When in the INQUIRY sub-state, a PC1 node will remain for *3*U* period of time, a PC2 node will remain for *2*U*, and a PC3 node will remain for *1*U*. Contrarily, when in the INQUIRY SCAN sub-state, a PC1 node will remain for *1*U*, a PC2 node will remain for *2*U*, and a PC3 node will remain for *3*U*. Note that the higher transmitting power a free node has, the longer it will stay in INQUIRY. The unit length of time *U* is a random value picked from an interval before each node enters a sub-state each time. It is applied in order to avoid periodic synchronization effects and to expedite the scatternet formation process, and computed as:

$$U = \text{random}\,(U1[T_{conn}], U2[T_{conn}]) \qquad (3)$$

where *U1*, *U2* are the minimum and maximum experimental time taken to complete a connection process given by Eq.(2). Through our experiments, the current algorithm for the three power classes has the shortest delay to generate a connected topology.

Unlike *F* nodes, the alternation of *M* or *S* nodes mainly depends on the current neighbor link conditions. An *M* node enters INQUIRY first each time when starting FORM, whereas an *S* node enters INQUIRY SCAN first. When in the INQUIRY sub-state, the *M* node will remain for *(MaxLinks–currLinks)*2*U*, while the *S* node will remain for *1*U*. Contrarily, when in the INQUIRY SCAN sub-state, the *M* node will remain for *1*U*, and the *S* node will remain for *(MaxLinks– currLinks)*2*U*. We can notice that the time spent in INQUIRY for *M* and in INQUIRY SCAN for *S* is a function of *currLinks* in the sense that a node should reduce the time in the scatternet formation as *currLinks* increases. This can also prevent *M* or *S* nodes from running out of available links very quickly. Moreover, the design that *M* nodes behave oppositely to S, entering INQUIRY first and remaining longer in INQUIRY, conforms to P3 that a master node has greater probabilities to be master again when establishing new links while a slave node has more chances to be slave.

Here, we define *MaxSlaves* as the maximum number of slaves a master can have in a piconet in order to reduce the intra-piconet overhead, and *MaxPnets* as the maximum number of piconets a slave can join in order to minimize the inter-piconet overhead. Although an *M* or *S* node switches between the two sub-states, however, if its current number of slave links has reached *MaxSlaves* or its current number of master links has reached *MaxPnets*, the node will remain only in one correspondent state in order not to violate these regulations. We can guarantee that a node is able to meet at least one constrain in the FORM state by making the sum of *MaxSlaves* and *MaxPnets* greater than *MaxLinks*.

An *F* node will exit the FORM state when the pre-set timer T_{form} expires. An exception is that if the node gains at least one link within the timer, it should not quit FORM quickly but run as an *M* or *S* node accordingly. An *M* or *S* node will end the execution of FORM when T_{form} expires or the current number of links reaches *MaxLinks*. Notice that the *S* node may turn to *M* by acquiring a neighbor as its slave in the FORM state. In this situation, the *S* node will switch to the type *M* and run its procedure, without rescheduling the timer.

3.2.2. Communication algorithm. In the COMM state, the time a node spends for communication can be computed by:

$$T_{comm}=f_{comm}*currLinks*random(U1,\ U2) \qquad (4)$$

The variable f_{comm} is an average measurement of a node's communication load for each link. Result of f_{comm} **currLinks* implies the current total traffic volume for a node to handle, indicating how busy it is likely to perform its communication tasks. The other parameter is a random value, selected from a predefined interval and used to reduce the probability that neighboring nodes are all simultaneously in communication for a long time when a new node arrives. We can observe that T_{comm} mainly relies on a node's neighbor link conditions; therefore, as neighboring links change, the node should update *currLinks* and re-estimate f_{comm} in time.

3.2.3. Loop detections. It is true that the existence of loops can intensify the network; however, some loops should be eliminated to reduce redundant links. We only detect loops with 2, 3 and 4 links because of the tradeoff between network performance and scatternet formation efficiency. Elimination of 2-and 3-link loops can avoid forming further piconets inside a piconet. Elimination of 4-link loops can avoid having too many S/S bridges between the adjacent piconets. Eliminating loops with more than 4 links will be complicated that it may sacrifice the scatternet formation efficiency.

We have applied a simple solution: each node keeps the address of its connected one-hop and two-hop neighbors; any pair of nodes can detect loops by exchanging this information once a new link is established and break the link as soon as the loop is found. If the connection is accepted, two nodes will update their neighbor address information accordingly and then may switch the master/slave roles on the link in case that transmitting power of the slave is higher than that of the master. Not all 4-link loops can be detected due to the outdated information at each node. In dynamic environments, when a node notices the missing of its neighbor, it will delete the corresponding neighbor address information immediately.

4. Simulation results

To evaluate the effectiveness of BluePower, we have implemented it in "Blueware" [14], a network simulator extending with *ns-2* [15]. Although BluePower is designed according to device transmitting power and classifies a BT device into 3 groups, for simplicity, we only use PC3 nodes to simulate, with the maximum transmission radius of 10 meters. All nodes are randomly and uniformly located within a square of side L.

We have conducted our simulations in two different environments: 1) *en masse* arrivals, where nodes arrive simultaneously and no nodes leave, and 2) dynamic environments, where nodes arrive and leave in an incremental fashion after the network achieves a steady state.

For each environment, the number of BT nodes n has been varied in the range 10, 20, 30, … , 120, while L has been set to either 10 m or 20 m. This allows us to test our protocol over single-hop and multihop networks. Each data point in the figures is an average of 7 trials. We have compared BluePower with TSF [8] in the same simulator with $L = 10$. Because TSF assumes radio vicinity of all nodes, it cannot generate a connected scatternet with $L = 20$. All simulations are carried out with a typical set of parameters defined as *MaxLinks* = 8, *MaxSlaves* = 7, *MaxPnets* = 3, and T_{form} = 10 s. The parameter *MaxPnets* is chosen to be 3 because the simulations show that such a setting results in the best scatternet performance on the average, whereas other protocols always set it to 2 only to ensure that a node belongs to up to two piconets.

4.1. *En masse* arrivals

Figure 3 illustrates how long it takes to form a connected scatternet when nodes arrive simultaneously. As the number of arriving nodes increases, the scatternet formation delay decreases in BluePower, compared to the increase in TSF. In particular, the delay of BluePower tends to achieve a certain value lower than 3 s when $n \geqslant 30$ with $L = 10$, and lower than 6 s when $n \geqslant 40$ with $L = 20$, independent of the scatternet size. We give an intuition why these happen. First, as the number of nodes increases, the number of PC1 nodes may also increase. Recall that PC1 nodes enter the inquiry state at the beginning of the protocol, having a big chance to become a master, while PC2 and PC3 nodes behave oppositely. Therefore, if the number of master grows, the number of parallel links being formed will increase, leading to faster piconet formation; and the chance of slave nodes to continuously accept up to *MaxPnets* master links as S/S bridges will also increase, leading to faster piconet interconnection. Second, if the network has lower node density, it needs more time to generate a connected scatternet. That is why the delay with $L = 20$ is a little higher than with $L = 10$ in BluePower.

The average number of piconets generated for *en masse* arrivals is depicted in Figure 4. Although the curves of TSF and BluePower grow both linearly as a function of the network size, our protocol has better results.

A critical performance measure for scatternet is the number of bridges. A large number of them may translate into increased inter-piconet overhead and reduced throughput. Figure 5 has shown the average number of bridges as well as M/S bridges generated in TSF and BluePower respectively. As for bridges, it is found that TSF apparently outperforms BluePower as the scatternet size becomes larger, although they are comparable for scenarios involving less than 70 nodes. However, as for M/S bridges, BluePower has much fewer since all bridges are M/S type in TSF. This implies that the percentage of M/S bridges in BluePower is much lower and most of bridges are S/S type with smaller overheads. The results exactly match the expected outcome of our design.

Figure 6 plots the average number of slaves per piconet. We can observe that each master acquires no more than 5 slaves on average in BluePower, whereas the curve seems unfluctuating in TSF and never exceeds 2. Though the two algorithms can both guarantee that no piconet has more than 7 slaves, we consider that BluePower has a decent value. The reason is that fewer slaves per piconet will lead to more bridges, especially M/S bridges which may reduce network performance.

In Figure 7, the average number of links per node is clearly presented. The two BluePower curves increase slightly with n while the TSF curve remains stable, much lower and below 2. By comparing Figure 7 with Figure 6, we can infer that BluePower has a flat network structure in that the number of slaves per piconet is roughly equal to the number of links per node, around 3 for all network size. That is to say, S/S bridges achieve *MaxPnets* = 3 links on average. Thus, there is no "bottlenecks" with communication in BluePower, such as a root of a tree.

Independently of the particular routing protocol to be finally used, the shortest route length is a metric that gives a measure of how well a routing protocol can perform. Figure 8 depicts the average path length for all source and destination pairs. It is concluded that

TSF is much more sensitive to the number of nodes. We attribute this to the only one route between any pair of nodes in TSF. In contrast, the average path length in BluePower is independent of n because of its flat structure. The results in Figure 8 are commensurate with those in Figure 7 in that high average number of links per node will bring low average route length in the scatternet.

4.2. Dynamic environments

We have also evaluated the performance of BluePower with dynamic environments where nodes can join and leave arbitrarily. The link setup delay is defined as the time taken before a free node can establish its first communication link with others. This is an important metric since it gives a sense of how fast a node can talk to its first neighbor. Figure 9 represents the average delay for a free node to connect to the network when some nodes leave and then some arrive after the network reaches a steady state. The overall time scale of BluePower is smaller than TSF, except with $L = 20$ when $n \leqslant 30$. It is obvious that as the population of nodes increases, the delay gets smaller. This is due to the more chances of a free node to be found by neighbors who are performing topology discovery when it comes.

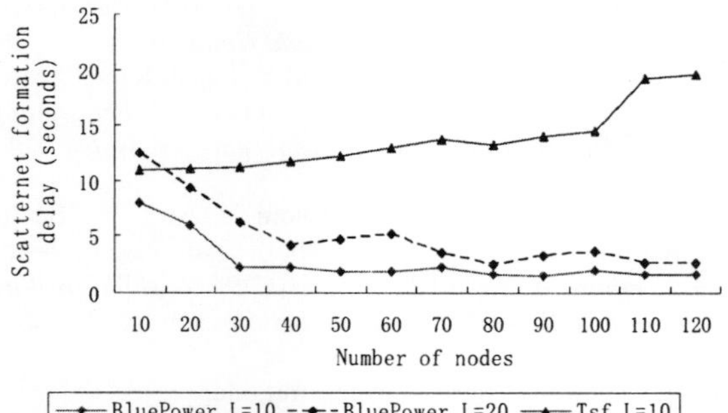

Figure 3. Scatternet formation delay

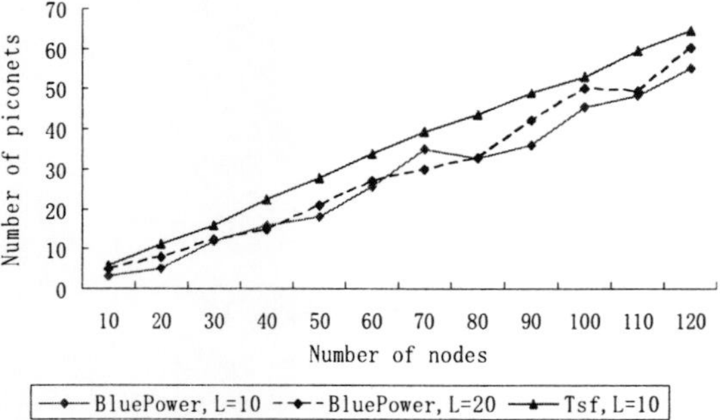

Figure 4. Average number of piconets

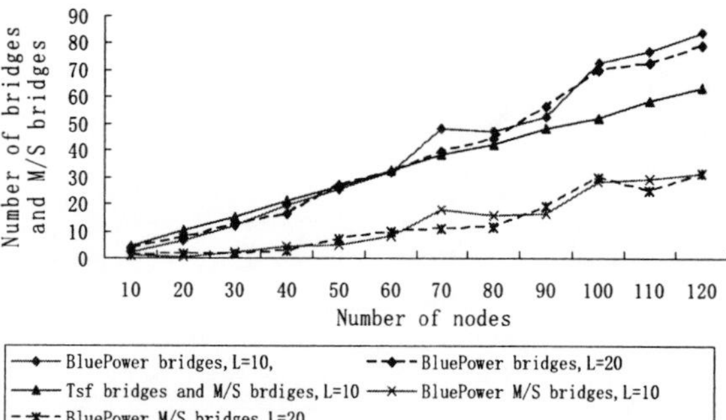

Figure 5. Average number of bridges and M/S bridges

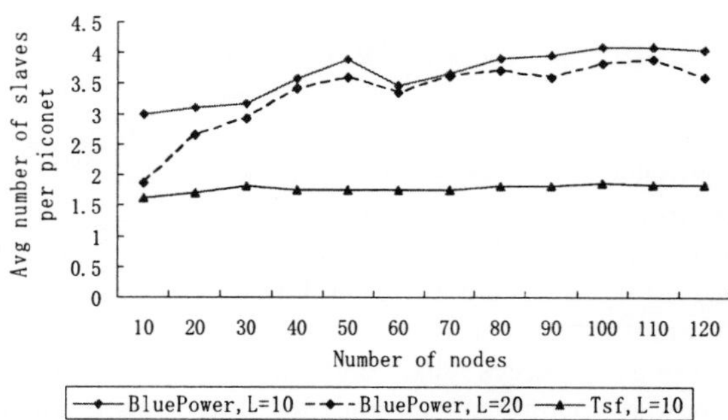

Figure 6. Average number of slaves per piconet

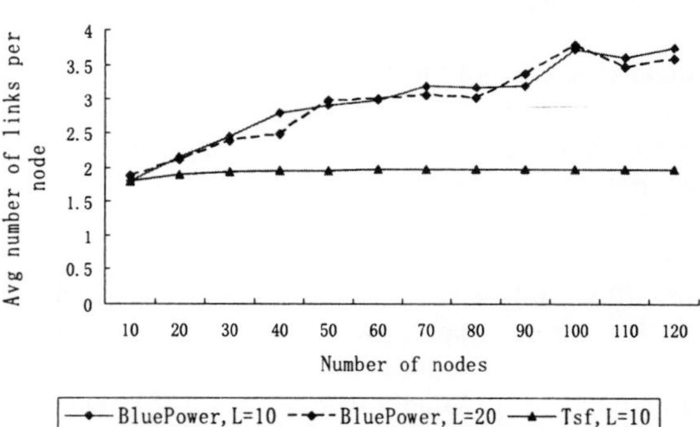

Figure 7. Average number of links per node

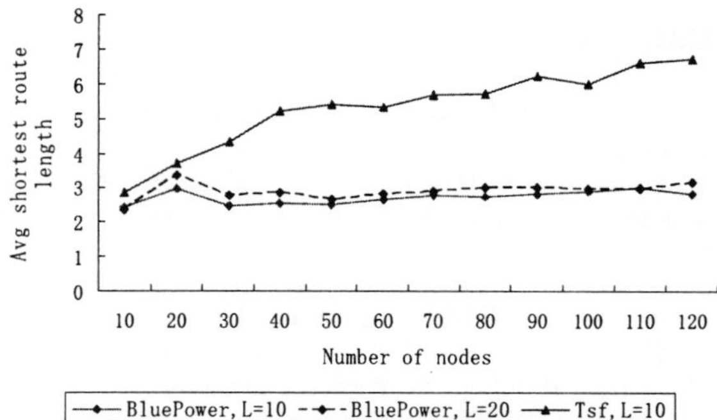

Figure 8. Average shortest route length

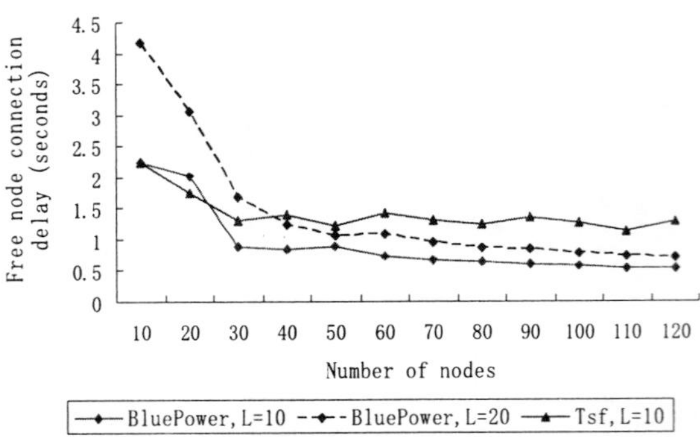

Figure 9. Link setup delay for free nodes to heal partitions

5. Conclusions and future work

In this paper, we have proposed an integrated approach for scatternet formation in Bluetooth environments. The design simply uses Bluetooth lower-layer primitives to construct scatternets according to device power and adjacent link conditions. A mobility model is presented in the perspective of topology changes that include topology formation, topology maintenance, and topology reconstruction. The protocol can adapt well to the cases whether all nodes are within communication range of each other or not. The simulation results have shown that BluePower makes scatternet formation with certain desirable characteristics: minimal delay to form a connected network, bounded number of slaves per piconet, short average path length around 3 and minimal connection delay for free nodes to join the network in dynamic environments. For future work, we will intensify the mobility study and take into account the "quality" of the resulting topology. Also, linking scheduling mechanism and routing protocol will be developed to collaborate with BluePower so that traffic latency can be measured accurately to investigate communication efficiency in the scatternet.

References

[1] Bluetooth SIG, "Specification of the Bluetooth System, Version 1.1", http:// www.bluetooth.com/

[2] G. Zaruba, S. Basagni, and I. Chlamtac, "BlueTrees – Scatternet Formation to Enable Bluetooth-based Personal Area Networks", *Proceedings of the IEEE International Conference on Communications*, ICC 2001, Helsinki, Finland, Vol. 1, 11-14 June 2001, pp. 273-277.

[3] C. Petrioli, S. Basagni, and I. Chlamtac, "Configuring BlueStars: Multihop Scatternet Formation for Bluetooth Networks", *IEEE Transactions on Computers 52(6)*, Special Issue on Wireless Internet, 2003, pp. 779-790.

[4] Z. Wang, R.J. Thomas, and Z. Haas, "BlueNet – a New Scatternet Formation Scheme", *Proceedings of the 35th Hawaii International Conference on System Science (HICSS-35)*, Big Island, Hawaii, January 2002, pp. 7-10.

[5] C. Petrioli, S. Basagni, and I. Chlamtac, "BlueMesh: Degree-constrained Multi-hop Scatternet Formation for Bluetooth Networks", *ACM/Kluwer Journal on Mobile Networks and Applications,* 9, Special Issue on Mobile Ad Hoc Networks, 2004, pp. 33-47.

[6] S. Basagni, R. Bruno, and C. Petrioli, "Comparative Performance Evaluation of Scatternet Formation Protocols for Networks of Bluetooth Devices", *ACM/Kluwer Journal on Mobile Networks*, 10, 2004, pp. 197-213.

[7] T. Salonidis, P. Bhagwat, L. Tassiulas, and R. Lamaire, "Distributed Topology Construction of Bluetooth Personal Area Networks", *Proceedings of the IEEE INFOCOM 2001*, April 22-26 2001, pp.1577-1586.

[8] G. Tan, A. Miu, J. guttag, and H. Balakrishnan, "Forming Scatternets From Bluetooth Personal Area Networks", *MIT Technical Report*, MIT-LCS-TR-826, October 2001.

[9] C. Law, A.K. Mehta, and K.-Y. Siu, "A New Bluetooth Scatternet Formation Protocol", *ACM/Kluwer Journal on Mobile Networks and Applications (MONET),* 8(5), Special Issue on Mobile Ad Hoc Networks, 2003.

[10] C.F. Chiasserini, M. Ajmone Marsan, E. Baralis and P. Garza, "Towards Feasible Topology Formation Algorithms for Bluetooth-based WPANs", *Proceedings of IEE HICSS-36 2003*, Big Island, Hawaii (6-9) January 2003.

[11] Alok Aggarwal, Manika Kapoor, Lakshmi Ramachandran, and Abhinanda Sarkar, "Clustering Algorithms for Wireless Ad Hoc Networks", *Proceedings of the 4th International Workshop on Discrete Algorithms and Methods for Mobile Computing and Communications*, 2000.

[12] Bin Zhen, Jonghun Park, and Yongsuk Kim, "Scatternet Formation of Bluetooth Ad Hoc Networks", *Proceedings of the 36th Hawaii International Conference on System Sciences*, 2003.

[13] Tadashi Sato, and Kenichi Mase, "A Scatternet Operation Protocol for Bluetooth Ad Hoc Networks", *Proceedings of the 5th International Symposium on Wireless Personal Multimedia Communications*, Oct. 2002, pp. 223-227.

[14] "Blueware", http://nms.lcs. mit.edu/ projects/bluew.

[15] "ns-2 Network Simulator", http://www. isi.edu/vint/nsnam/, 2000.

A Compatible and Scalable Clock Synchronization Protocol in IEEE 802.11 Ad Hoc Networks

Dong Zhou Ten-Hwang Lai
Department of Computer Science & Engineering
The Ohio State University
{zhoudo, lai}@cse.ohio-state.edu

Abstract

This paper studies the scalability and compatibility problems of clock synchronization in IEEE 802.11 ad hoc networks. The scalability problem of 802.11 timing synchronization has been recognized and studied by researchers in the field, but the proposed solutions are not meeting industry expectation. The compatibility issue is not well investigated by the research community yet. The compatibility issue is very important and practical because of the large deployment base of 802.11 networks. In this paper, we try to address both issues. We propose a simple, compatible protocol without any change of beacon format. The frequency adjustment is proved to be bounded and the maximum clock offset is controlled under $20\mu s$. It is a significant improvement over the current results in the field. The current solutions with similar complexity can only control the maximum clock offset around $125\mu s$ for compatible solutions and $50\mu s$ for non-compatible protocols.
Keywords: IEEE 802.11, ad hoc networks, scalability, compatibility, clock synchronization

1 Introduction

The IEEE 802.11 standards support the peer-to-peer mode Independent Basic Service Set (IBSS), which is an ad hoc network with all its stations within each other's transmission range. Clock synchronization is important for frequency hopping, power management and basic operations of 802.11 networks. IEEE 802.11 standards [1, 2, 3] specify a Timing Synchronization Function (TSF) for the ad hoc mode in the MAC layer.

The scalability problem of 802.11 TSF was first discovered in [4]. The maximum clock offset between stations can be over 4000 μs for a large IBSS running the 802.11 TSF. Several protocols have been proposed during the past few years but the protocol scalability performance is still short of the industry expectation: the maximum clock offset should be under $25\mu s$ for an IBSS of any size. ATSP was proposed in [4] to address the scalability problem. But the protocol has a conflict between mobility handling and scalability of the protocol. The maximum clock offset can be as high as $500\mu s$. Further improvements were proposed in [5]. Two protocols were proposed: TATSF and ABTSF. For TATSF, the maximum clock offset is contained under 125 μs. ABTSF is not compatible with the current 802.11 TSF. ABTSF can control the maximum clock offset under 50 μs. Another solution called ASP was proposed in [6] for a multi-hop network. The maximum clock offset can be controlled around $60\mu s$ if ASP is applied in a single-hop IBSS. But this solution is not compatible with the 802.11 TSF. Due to the design of ASP, the accuracy of ASP degrades quickly if a few stations are running the 802.11 TSF and the rest stations are running ASP. The maximum clock offset can be over 150 μs for ASP in mix mode of operation. The scalability problem is not resolved completely and the compatibility issue still needs to be studied.

In this paper, we first list the requirements for a good clock synchronization protocol. We then propose a new protocol called SATSF to meet all the desirable requirements: simple, scalable, accurate, compatible, bounded and adaptive to station mobility. For SATSF, the maximum clock offset can be controlled within 20 μs with the worst clocks allowed by the standard. In particular, we want to point out that our new protocol is completely compatible with the current 802.11 TSF protocol by keeping the beacon frame format intact. Since beacon frame is one of the most important control frames in 802.11 protocols, a received beacon is validated by the current protocols. A format change may fail these validations and make the TSF protocol fail in a mixed-mode IBSS.

The challenge of our work is to meet the industry expectation of time accuracy (maximum clock offset under $25\mu s$) with a compatible, scalable, mobility-friendly and cheap solution. It is not difficult to satisfy some of the requirements. But it is quite an effort to hit all the targets. Our solution can meet all these challenges.

The rest of the paper is organized as follows. Section 2 reviews 802.11 TSF and related works. Section 3 proposes a new protocol to address the scalability and compatibly problem with all the desirable requirements. Simulation results are discussed in section 4. Section 5 concludes the paper.

2 Overview and Related Works

This section reviews the 802.11 TSF and related works in the field. In 802.11 TSF, clock synchronization is achieved by periodical timing information exchange through beacon frames, which contain timestamps among other parameters.

Each station maintains a TSF timer counting in increments of microseconds (μs). All stations in the IBSS compete for beacon transmission every aBeaconPeriod second. This time period is called a beacon period (BP). At the beginning of each BP, there is a *beacon generation window* consisting of $w + 1$ slots each of length aSlotTime. Each station calculates a random delay uniformly distributed in $[0, w]$ and is scheduled to transmit a beacon when the delay timer expires. If a beacon arrives before the random delay timer has expired, the station cancels the pending beacon transmission and the remaining random delay. Upon receiving a beacon, a station sets its TSF timer to the timestamp of the beacon if the value of the timestamp is later than the station's TSF timer.

Mills [7] proposes a Network Time Protocol (NTP) to synchronize clocks and coordinate time distribution in the Internet system. NTP assumes access to a reliable reference source such as a timecode receiver or a calibrated atomic clock. Most of the 802.11 devices have no access to such devices.

A time synchronism algorithm is proposed in [8] to deal with the partitioning problem in sparse ad hoc networks. This approach targets for sensor networks and is not compatible with the current 802.11 TSF. A different synchronization method called reference broadcast synchronization (RBS) is presented in [9] for broadcast networks, especially for wireless ad hoc networks. A reference broadcast or beacon does not contain an explicit timestamp; instead, its arrival time is used by the receivers as a point of reference for comparing their clocks. RBS uses nontrivial statistical methods such as regression to estimate the clock phase offset and clock frequency offset of any two stations. It cannot be implemented in a compatible fashion under the 802.11 TSF framework.

ATSP was proposed in [4] to solve the scalability problem. The basic idea is to let the fastest station to compete for beacon transmission every beacon period and let other stations to compete only occasionally (every $I_{\max}$ BPs). It takes $O(I_{\max}^2)$ to elect the fastest station. To handle scalability better, the value of $I_{\max}$ should be large. To handle mobility and allow ATSP to select the next fastest station quickly after the fastest station leaves, the value of $I_{\max}$ should be small. It cannot handle both scalability and mobility very well at the same time. The maximum clock offset can be around $500\mu s$ for ATSP.

TATSF and ABTSF are two protocols proposed in [5]. TATSF dynamically classifies the stations into three tiers according to the clock speed. The stations in tier 1 compete for beacon transmission in every beacon period and the stations in tier 2 will compete once in a while and the stations in tier 3 rarely compete. TATSF is compatible with 802.11 TSF but the maximum clock offset is still large (around 125 μs). ABTSF allows clock to move in both directions. It is not compatible with 802.11 TSF. It selects a token holder who is responsible for the beacon transmission. Each station resets its clock after receiving from the beacon holder. The token holder rotated periodically. The accuracy is improved and the maximum clock offset is controlled under 50 μs for ABTSF.

A non-hierarchical network synchronization scheme (mutual synchronization) was proposed in [10]. Even though it can achieve very good accuracy of clocks, however it depends on elaborated schemes. Modeling the dynamics of these networks or even ensuring the stability of the control algorithms can be a very complex task. These types of solutions are very expensive due to the complexity and are applicable only in special cases, e.g. military networks[11]. It violates our requirement for low cost solution.

An interesting adaptive protocol called ASP is proposed in [6] for time synchronization in 802.11-based multi-hop ad hoc networks. The basic idea of the protocol is to let the faster clocks send out beacon more often and adjust clocks' frequencies. But it did not address the scalability problem fully. The maximum clock offset is still over $50\mu s$. Another problem with ASP is the incompatibility with the 802.11 TSF protocol. It changes the beacon format by adding a sequence number in the beacon frame. The timing synchronization function may not work in a mix-mode IBSS where some of the stations are running 802.11 TSF. Suppose some implementations of the 802.11 TSF are flexible enough to understand the extended beacon format, the synchronization accuracy of ASP still degrades quickly when a few stations running the 802.11 TSF join the IBSS. The reason is that ASP trusts the face value of the timestamp of the beacon from the sending station. The result is that the slower station may over-adjust its clock frequency and becomes faster than the original fastest station. This process may keep repeating, the frequencies of the stations are getting faster and faster unnecessarily (i.e. the frequency adjustment is un-bounded). This is very problematic in a mixed-mode IBSS. The time difference between the stations using the new protocol and the ones using 802.11 TSF can be very large. ASP does not address the compatibility issue and the scalability handling of ASP still does not meet the expectation.

3 Our Solution

In this section, we will propose a self-adjusting timing synchronization function (SATSF). First let us briefly analyze the reasons behind the poor scalability of 802.11 TSF.

3.1 Root cause of scalability problem

- Beacon collision: Large number of stations contend for beacon generation within a small contention window.

- Diverse clock frequencies: The IEEE 802.11 specifications only require clock accuracy to be within $\pm 0.01\%$. There are several elements that contribute to the inaccuracy of clocks [11]: starting frequency offset (due to frequency calibration error), frequency drift (due to aging) and oscillator phase noise/offset/drift. Given the typical operating environment and short life span of an IBSS, frequency drift and oscillator phase errors are negligible compared to starting frequency offset.

- Inaccurate timestamp: It takes time for a beacon to travel from the sender's MAC layer (which sets the value of the timestamp on the beacon) to the receiver's MAC layer (which uses the timestamp). Thus, when the receiver synchronizes its clock according to the timestamp's value, the latter is already different from the sending TSF timer's actual value as of that moment. To mitigate this problem, according to the 802.11 standard, a station sending a beacon shall set the value of the beacon's timestamp so that it equals the value of the station's TSF timer at the time that the first bit of the timestamp is transmitted to the PHY plus the transmitting station's delays through its local PHY from the MAC-PHY interface to its interface with the wireless medium. This mechanism maintains the value of the beacon and the value of the sending TSF timer to be within 4 μs plus the maximum propagation delay of the PHY, which adds up to about $\pm 5\mu$s.

3.2 Requirements for TSF Solutions

In our opinion, an acceptable solution to the 802.11 TSF's scalability problem must be accurate, simple, scalable, compatible with the current 802.11 TSF, and able to handle mobility, as elaborated in the following.

- Accurate: the maximum clock offset should be controlled within $25\mu s$ based on the industry expectation.

- Compatible with the current 802.11 TSF: It is important that *the beacon format remains intact*to make sure that stations running the new TSF can seemly form an IBSS with stations using the current 802.11 TSF.

- Highly scalable: An improved TSF should be able to handle a few hundred stations.

- Simple and low cost: Since the 802.11 TSF is typically implemented in hardware, any remedy to the TSF should retain its current simplicity. As 802.11 devices are targeted for mass markets, only inexpensive hardware and software solutions are considered suitable.

- Mobility-tolerant: When new stations join or when old stations leave the network, the protocol's performance should not degrade by too much.

The compatibility requirement entails us to employ only existing fields in the beacon. The scalability and mobility handling are often conflicting. The requirement of simple and low cost solutions excludes complex schemes. As mentioned in the introduction, to meet all these requirements is a challenging task.

3.3 A Scalable Solution for Clock Synchronization: SATSF

Now we are ready to introduce a compatible new scheme to synchronize frequency with bound while satisfying other requirements of clock synchronization for an 802.11 IBSS.

We define the terms and variables related to the new protocol SATSF first, then SATSF itself.

Definition 1 Clock i's *native frequency*, denoted as $f_n(i)$, is the number of ticks the clock accumulates per second driven by its oscillator.

Note that each 802.11 timer has a native frequency within the range of $(1 \pm 0.01\%)$ mega hertz (MHz). (Each timer ticks once per microsecond, but there is an inaccuracy of up to $\pm$ 0.01%.)

Definition 2 Clock i's *frequency adjustment*, denoted as $f_a(i)$, is the number of extra ticks per second that is added to the clock.

Definition 3 The sum $adj\_freq(i) = f_n(i) + f_a(i)$ is the *adjusted frequency* of clock i.

For each station i, we will calculate a frequency adjustment $f_a(i)$, such that $f_n(i) + f_a(i) \approx f_n(fastest\ station)$.

- $T(i)$: TSF timer value of station i.

- $SK(i)$: clock frequency adjustment for station i. The amount $SK(i) * 10^6$ is an estimate of $f_a(i)$, and will be added to $T(i)$ per second.

- $FTT(i)$: this variable controls whether station i should compete for beacon generation. It does iff $FTT(i) = 0$.

- $TS(j)$: the adjusted timestamp value obtained from the beacon sent by j and received by i. It is the sum of the timestamp value in the beacon plus the receiving PHY layer delay and the time since the first bit is received at the receiver's PHY/MAC interface.

- $\pm\delta$: the maximum error that may occur when we estimate the value of $T(j)$ by $TS(j)$. That is, $|T(j) - TS(j)| \leq \delta$ μs when j's beacon arrives at the receiving station's MAC layer.

- $\Delta NT(i)$: the amount of time (native time) since the last time station i received a beacon with a faster timestamp; i.e., the number of ticks according to its native frequency (without frequency adjustment).

- $IND(i)$: station ID (index) of the station from where station i last received a faster beacon.

- $PV(i)$: protocol version of station i, 1 if the station i is running the new protocol (SATSF); 0, otherwise. Protocol version is a 2-bit field in the current 802.11 frame control field. It is an existing field of the current beacon frame.

- $sync\_T^-(i)$: the timer value of station i before being synchronized by a faster beacon.

- $sync\_T^+(i)$: the timer value of station i after being synchronized by a faster beacon.

- $last\_sync\_T^+(i)$: the timer value of station i the last time after being synchronized by a faster beacon.

In this algorithm, we update three variables under the proper conditions to meet our design requirements. We change the TSF timer value of the receiving station i ($T(i)$) when we are sure the clock time difference is out of the margin of error. We modify the FTT timer value to allow or disallow stations to compete for beacon transmission. We reset frequency adjustment (SK) only when we are sure the sender's clock frequency is faster.

When station i receives a beacon from station j, it first checks whether $TS(j) - \delta \geq T(i)$. If that is true, i knows that station j's clock value is larger than its own timer and i will adjust its TSF timer value and records j to $IND(i)$. If the value of $IND(i)$ is j before that, it implies that stations receives beacons from j twice, then the protocol is ready to adjust station i's frequency to be closer to j's frequency. To make sure that j's clock is not reset between these 2 beacons, the protocol further checks whether $(sync\_T^-(i) - last\_sync\_T^+(i)) < \lceil log_2 I_{\max 1} \rceil \times aBeaconPeriod$. We will show in lemma 2 that j is not synchronized by other stations if the check holds. If $sync\_T^+(i) - sync\_T^-(i) \geq 2\delta$, we are sure station j advances faster than station i (we will prove it in theorem 1), then $SK(i)$ is re-calculated. $SK(i)$ reflects the combination of frequency offset and frequency drift. By adding 1 tick every $\lceil 1/SK(i) \rceil$ native time ticks, the frequency of station i is in fact adjusted like a physical frequency change on the clock oscillator. Since it is done through the protocol, no additional hardware is needed. If $SK(i)$ is reset after receiving a beacon from station j, we will say that station i's frequency is synchronized by station j.

SATSF: Self Adjusting Timing Synchronization Function

1. Initially, when station i joins the IBSS, let $SK(i) \leftarrow 0$, $FTT(i) \leftarrow \text{random}(I_{\max 1}, I_{\max 2})$, $IND(i) = -1$. $T(i) \leftarrow 0$ if station i is the initiator of the IBSS; else $T(i) \leftarrow TS(j) - \delta$ if i joins the IBSS by hearing a beacon from station j.
2. If $FTT(i) > 0$, station i will not compete for beacon transmission.
3. If $FTT(i) = 0$, station i is ready to compete.
4. At each TBTT each station that wants to compete for beacon transmission calculates a random delay uniformly distributed in the range $[0, w]$.
5. The station waits for the period of the random delay.
6. When the random delay timer expires, if the medium is idle, the station transmits a beacon with a timestamp; else if it receives a beacon before its random delay timer expiration, it cancels the pending transmission and the remaining random delay.
7. Upon receiving a beacon from station j, a station i performs:

   if $T(i) \leq TS(j) - \delta$ then

   $sync\_T^-(i) \leftarrow T(i)$

   $sync\_T^+(i) \leftarrow T(i) \leftarrow TS(j) - \delta$

   if $[IND(i) = j]$ and $[PV(j) = 1]$ and $[sync\_T^+(i) - sync\_T^-(i) \geq 2\delta]$ and $[sync\_T^-(i) - last\_sync\_T^+(i) < \lceil \log_2 I_{\max 1} \rceil \times aBeaconPeriod]$ then

   $tmp \leftarrow \frac{sync\_T^+(i) - last\_sync\_T^+(i) - \Delta NT(i) - 2\delta}{\Delta NT(i)}$

   $SK(i) \leftarrow \max\{SK(i), tmp\}$

   $IND(i) \leftarrow j$

   $last\_sync\_T^+(i) \leftarrow sync\_T^+(i)$

   $\Delta NT(i) \leftarrow 0$

   $FTT(i) \leftarrow \text{random}(I_{\max 1}, I_{\max 2})$

   if $T(i) \geq TS(j) + \delta$ and $PV(j) = 1$ then

   $FTT(i) \leftarrow \lceil \min(I_{\max 1}, FTT(i))/2 \rceil$
8. If $SK(i) > 0$, station i increments $T(i)$ by 1 every $\lceil 1/SK(i) \rceil$ μs (in terms of station i's native time).
9. At the end of a beacon period,

$$FTT(i) = \begin{cases} 0 & \text{if } FTT(i) = 1 \text{ or } FTT(i) = 0 \\ \lceil FTT(i)/2 \rceil & \text{if the medium was idle for the BP and } FTT(i) > 1 \\ FTT(i) - 1 & \text{otherwise} \end{cases}$$

10. $\Delta NT[i]$ increments by 1 whenever station i's oscillator ticks.

Figure 1: Algorithm SATSF

FTT timer is used to decide whether a station competes for beacon transmission. A station only competes when its *FTT* timer expires. When a station first joins the IBSS, it starts the timer and listens for other beacons.

A station i will reset its *FTT* timer if it receives a beacon from station j with a larger clock value ($TS(j) - \delta \geq T(i)$). This rule is designed to inhibit the beacon transmission from slower stations. Only a small set of stations competes for beacon transmission to avoid the repetitive beacon collisions. The timer is set to half if medium is idle for the whole contention window. Normally, the medium should not be idle. It happens only when the stations that were competing for the beacon transmission (faster stations) left the IBSS all together. By reducing the *FTT* timer by half each time, some of the stations will be able to compete beacon transmission soon. A new set of fast stations will be selected as a result. The $FTT(i)$ timer is set to $\lceil min(I_{\max 1}, FTT(i))/2 \rceil$ after a beacon is received by station i if station i is sure that it has a larger clock value than the station sending the beacon. This scenario happens when a new station with fastest clock joins an IBSS. This rule allows the new fastest station to compete very soon.

We can see that all the variables used in the protocol are either local variables to the station itself or existing fields in the current beacon frame. There is no need to add or change any field of the 802.11 beacon frame. Now we will show that the frequency adjustment is bounded.

Suppose that station i synchronizes its timer, $T(i)$, on receiving another station j's beacon. We show in the following lemma that at the moment right after the synchronization (i.e., when $T(i)$ is updated to $TS(j) - \delta$ in step 7 of the algorithm), the values of the two stations' timers are related by $T(i) \leq T(j) \leq T(i) + 2\delta$.

Lemma 1 *If station i synchronizes its clock with station j, then at the moment right after the synchronization, it holds that $T(i) \leq T(j) \leq T(i) + 2\delta$, or, equivalently, $sync\_T^+(i) \leq T(j) \leq sync\_T^+(i) + 2\delta$.*

Proof. At the moment of synchronization, it is known by assumption (or by the definition of δ) that

$$|T(j) - TS(j)| \leq \delta. \quad (1)$$

During synchronization, station i sets its timer as

$$T(i) := TS(j) - \delta. \quad (2)$$

The lemma follows directly from Eqs. 1 and 2 and the fact that $T(i) = sync\_T^+(i)$ at the moment right after the synchronization. ∎

Lemma 2 *For a station running the new version of TSF, once the station synchronizes its timer with another station, it will not compete for beacon transmission for at least $\lceil \log_2 I_{\max 1} \rceil$ BPs.*

Proof. According to the protocol, whenever a station, say i, synchronizes its timer with some other station, it sets $FTT(i)$ to a value no less than $I_{\max 1}$. After that, as $FTT(i)$ may decrement by no more than 50% per BP (except when $FTT(i) = 1$), it will take at least $\lceil \log_2 I_{\max 1} \rceil$ BPs to reach 0. ∎

Clock frequency adjustment, $f_a(i)$, is defined in Definition 2 as the number of extra ticks per second (in terms of reference time). In the protocol, an extra tick is added to the clock per every $\lceil 1/SK(i) \rceil$ microseconds (in terms of station i's native time). The next lemma establishes the exact relationship between $f_a(i)$ and $SK(i)$, if we ignore the ceiling of $\lceil 1/SK(i) \rceil$.

Lemma 3 *For each station i, $f_a(i) = f_n(i) * SK(i)$ and $adj\_freq(i) = f_n(i) + f_n(i) * SK(i)$.*

Proof. Based on the calculation of $SK(i)$, $SK(i)$ is the adjustment per microsecond in terms of station i's native time. $f_n(i)$ is the number of native microseconds per reference time second. $f_n(i) * SK(i)$ is the number of ticks added per reference time second. Therefore, $f_a(i) = f_n(i) * SK(i)$ and, thus, $adj\_freq(i) = f_n(i) + f_n(i) * SK(i)$. ∎

The following theorem shows that the adjusted frequency of each station is bounded by the frequency of the station with the highest native frequency.

Theorem 1 *For all stations i in the IBSS, $adj\_freq(i)$ is non-decreasing as a function of time. Furthermore, $adj\_freq(i) \leq f_n(s_0)$ for all i, where s_0 is the station with the highest native frequency that has ever joined the IBSS. (Note that s_0 may still be in the IBSS or may have left).*

Proof. Since $SK(i) := \max\{SK(i), ...\}$, $SK(i)$ is obviously non-decreasing as a function of time. It then follows from Lemma 3 that $adj\_freq(i)$ is also non-decreasing.

To establish the bound $adj\_freq(k) \leq f_n(s_0)$ for all k during the life-span of the IBSS, it suffices to show the following: (1) the bound holds at the IBSS's inception, which is obviously true, and (2) if the bound holds up to the time when a station is about to update its SK, then after the update the bound is still valid. To prove the latter statement, consider the event that station i adjusts $SK(i)$ upon receiving a beacon from station j. As the induction hypothesis, assume $adj\_freq(k) \leq f_n(s_0)$ for all k (in particular, $adj\_freq(j) \leq f_n(s_0)$) before the $SK(i)$ update. Since $adj\_freq(j)$ does not change during the event, it is sufficient for us to show $adj\_freq(i) \leq adj\_freq(j)$ after the $SK(i)$ update.

According to the protocol, station i may adjust its SK only if $PV(j) = 1$, i's timer has been synchronized twice in a row by j (through j's beacons) within $\lceil \log_2 I_{\max 1} \rceil$ BPs and

$$sync\_T^+(i) - sync\_T^-(i) \geq 2\delta. \quad (3)$$

Let t_1 be the time (of a reference clock) of the last timing synchronization and t_2 be that of this timing synchronization. Let $T^1(j)$ and $T^2(j)$ be the values of $T(j)$ (j's TSF timer) as of t_1 and t_2, respectively. Let $\Delta t = t_2 - t_1$.

First, we observe that station i's timer does not synchronize with any other station during the interval (t_1, t_2) (except for the two synchronizations in question that occur at t_1 and t_2). This is a result of the mechanism of $IND(i)$, which indicates from whom the station was synchronized for the last time. Second, we claim that during the period (t_1, t_2), station j's clock has never been synchronized by other stations either. This is due to Lemma 2, which indicates that if j's clock is synchronized by any other during (t_1, t_2), it would not have been able send a beacon to trigger the current synchronization to i. Thus, over the period (t_1, t_2), timer $T(j)$ has been ticking at its adjusted frequency, $adj\_freq(j)$, and has advanced from $T^1(j)$ to $T^2(j)$. Therefore,

$$adj\_freq(j) = \frac{T^2(j) - T^1(j)}{\Delta t}. \quad (4)$$

By Lemma 1, $T^2(j) \geq sync\_T^+(i)$ and $T^1(j) \leq last\_sync\_T^+(i) + 2\delta$. Substituting these into Eq. 4 yields

$$adj\_freq(j) \geq \frac{sync\_T^+(i) - last\_sync\_T^+(i) - 2\delta}{\Delta t}. \quad (5)$$

On the other hand, $adj\_freq(i)$ can be computed as follows. Let $\Delta NT(i)$ refer to its value as of time t_2. Then,

$$\begin{aligned} adj\_freq(i) &= \frac{\Delta NT(i) + \Delta NT(i)/(1/\lceil SK(i) \rceil)}{\Delta t} \\ &\leq \frac{\Delta NT(i) + \Delta NT(i) * SK(i)}{\Delta t} \end{aligned} \quad (6)$$

By definition,

$$SK(i) = \frac{sync\_T^+(i) - last\_sync\_T^+(i) - \Delta NT(i) - 2\delta}{\Delta NT(i)}$$

Substituting this into Eq. 6, we obtain

$$adj\_freq(i) \leq \frac{sync\_T^+(i) - last\_sync\_T^+(i) - 2\delta}{\Delta t} \quad (7)$$

Eqs. 5 and 7 together imply $adj\_freq(i) \leq adj\_freq(j)$. ■

Now we want to present an optional feature to the base SATSF protocol. This feature allows a station i to adjust $SK(i)$ if it receives two faster beacons from station j in two consecutive beacon periods while $PV(j) = 0$ and $sync\_T^+(i) - sync\_T^-(i) \geq 2\delta$.

If we assume that a successful beacon will be received by all the stations in the IBSS, then this feature can be turned on safely. SATSF still can maintain the frequency adjustment bound. The reason is that station j's clock cannot be reset by any another station during these two consecutive beacon transmission. According to step 6 of the protocol, a station cancels its timer when it receives a beacon. Only one successful beacon can be sent per beacon period. If this assumption is not always true, the probability that station j's clock is reset in the same beacon period after it sends out a faster beacon is very low. For practical reason, it is still good to turn the feature on.

There are two parameters used in SATSF: $I_{\max1}$ and $I_{\max2}$. $I_{\max1}$ should be small enough to allow other stations to compete when the fastest station leaves the IBSS; it should be large enough to allow the fastest station has the chance to send out two beacons so that other stations can adjust their frequencies of the clocks. Since we use binary close-up procedures, we can set $I_{\max1}$ to 8 or 16.

$I_{\max2}$ is used to spread the stations so that the FTT timers will not expire at the same time when the fastest station leaves. A value close to the number of stations in an IBSS should be a good choice. We can pick $I_{\max2} = 2^{\lfloor log_2^n \rfloor}$

4 Simulation Study on Maximum Clock Offset of 802.11 TSF, ASP and SATSF

In the simulation, we let the clock frequency uniformly distributed in the range of $[-d, d]$. We pick $d = 0.01\%$. It is the worst clock accuracy allowed by the 802.11 standard. The number of slots needed to send a beacon is called beacon length. We run the simulation for OFDM system with bit-rate of 54 Mbps: $w = 30$ and beacon length $b = 4$. The IBSS has n stations. We set the packet error rate to be 0.01%. We run the simulation for 10000 BPs. We let 5% of the stations leave at BP $k * 2000$ ($k > 1$). They return after 500 BPs. The option feature is turned on in the simulation.

802.11 TSF, TATSF, ABTSF

The maximum clock offset can be over $4000\mu s$ when $n = 200$ for 802.11 TSF. It is not scalable. The major reason for the large clock offset is the repeated collision of beacon transmissions. TATSF is compatible with 802.11 TSF, it can control the maximum clock offset under $125\mu s$. It is scalable compared with 802.11 TSF but the accuracy of the protocol is still not as good as the industry expectation. ABTSF is not compatible with 802.11 TSF. It is scalable and it can control the maximum clock offset under $50\mu s$. Again the maximum clock offset is still larger than the expectation. Please refer to [5] for detail simulation results.

ASP

We ran the simulation with $\alpha = 3$ as it is the preferred value by [6]. Fig. 2(a) shows the maximum clock offset during each beacon period for ASP when $n = 200$. We show the maximum clock offset starting from beacon period 50 to ignore the initial clock offset before the protocol stabilizes. It shows good improvement over the 802.11 TSF but it still has large clock

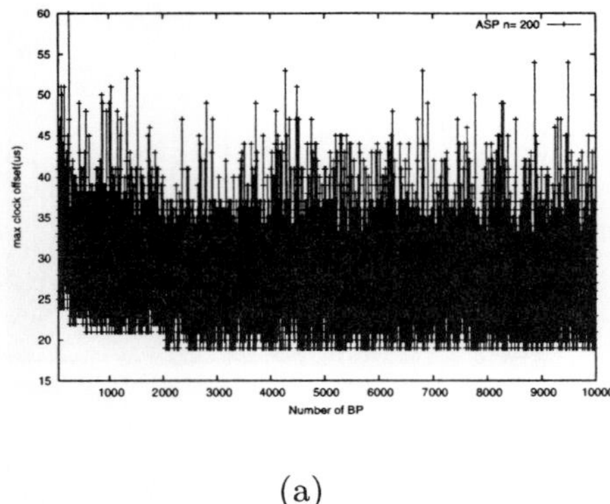

(a)

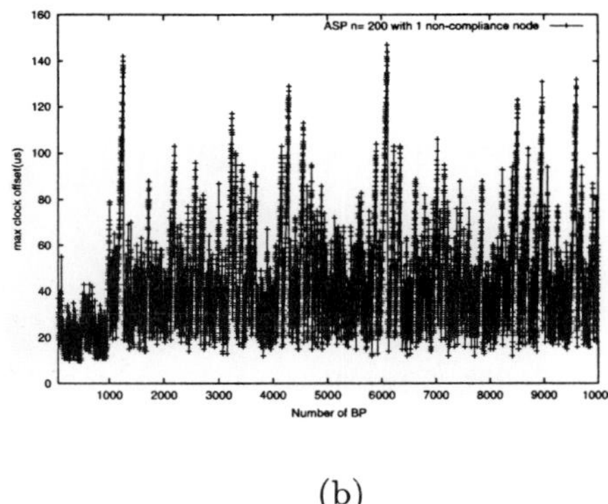

(b)

Figure 2: (a) Maximum clock offset for ASP (b) Maximum clock offset for ASP with one non-compliance station

n	SATSF max offset	ASP max offset
100	12 μs	59 μs
200	10 μs	60 μs
300	11 μs	64 μs
400	10 μs	63 μs
500	11 μs	NC
600	11 μs	NC

Table 1: Maximum and average clock offset of SATSF and ASP

offset. It can be over $50\mu s$. It does not address the scalability issue completely. Fig. 2(b) shows the maximum clock offset during each beacon period for ASP when $n = 200$ and one of the station is running 802.11 TSF. With one non-compliance station, the maximum offset increases about 300%. It can be over 150 μs. Due to the fact of un-bounded frequency adjustment, the clocks can have large offsets in mixed mode.

SATSF

We ran the simulation for our new protocol SATSF with $\delta = 5$, $I_{\max1} = 8$ and $I_{\max2} = 2^{\lfloor log_2^n \rfloor}$.

Fig.3 shows the maximum clock offset for an IBSS with 200 stations. We can see from Fig.3(a) that SATSF can synchronize the clocks very precisely. The maximum clock offset is under $10\mu s$ after the protocol stabilized.

SATSF deals with non-compliance much better than ASP. Fig.3(b) shows the maximum clock offset for 200 stations with one runs on 802.11 TSF. The maximum clock offset is under $18\mu s$. This is a big improvement compared with the maximum clock offset over $150\mu s$ for ASP. The reason behind the improvement is that SATSF's clock frequency adjustment is bounded.

Table 1 shows the maximum clock offset comparison between SATSF and ASP for the number of stations (n) ranging from 100 to 600. For SATSF, The maximum clock offset is well under the industry expectation ($25\mu s$). We can see it scales very well. The maximum clock offset does not go up with the number of stations. The performance of SATSF is good whether the IBSS has 100 stations or 600 stations. ASP can control the maximum clock offset around 60 μs if $n \leq 400$. The maximum clock offset for ASP when $n \leq 400$ is about 300% higher than SATSF. We cannot get a stable maximum clock offset within the simulation periods if $n \geq 500$.

x	SATSF avg max offset	802.11	ASP
1	7 μs	0 μs	31 μs
2	15 μs	20 μs	34 μs
5	24 μs	23 μs	42 μs
10	29 μs	24 μs	50 μs
20	33 μs	32 μs	63 μs
30	38 μs	38 μs	75 μs
40	45 μs	49 μs	87 μs

Table 2: Average maximum clock offset of SATSF and ASP in mixed mode

To further study the compatibility of SATSF, we ran the simulation using SATSF in mixed mode. The total number of stations is 200, where x station(s) our of the 200 are running the 802.11 TSF. We compare the performance against a scenario that there are only x stations and they are running 802.11 TSF. We compare the average maximum clock offsets for the two cases. We ran the simulation with the same setup for ASP.

Table 2 shows the average maximum clock offset for an IBSS running SATSF in mixed mode with x 802.11 TSF stations and $200 - x$ SATSF stations versus the scenario that there are x stations running 802.11 TSF and the case that x stations running 802.11 TSF and $200 - x$ stations running ASP. We can see the SATSF's performance is very close to the 802.11 TSF performance except $x = 1$. If there is only one station running 802.11 TSF, the clock offset is always 0. This result shows that most of the clock offsets is contributed by the stations running 802.11 TSF. SATSF handles compatibility very well.

For ASP, the average maximum offset is about 100% higher than that of SATSF. The reason for the poor performance is that the protocol over-adjusted frequencies in these situations and the offset becomes very

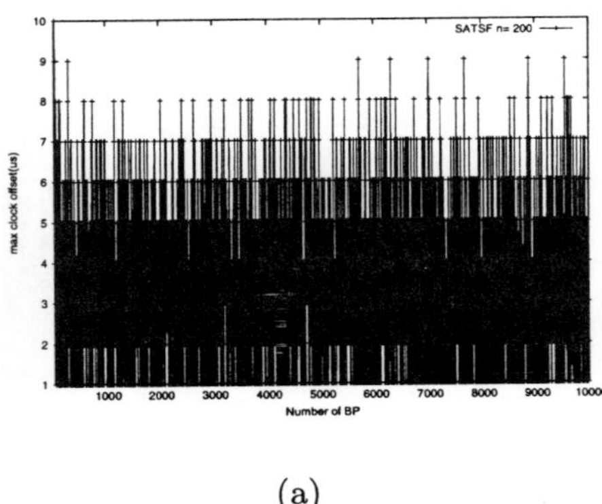

(a)

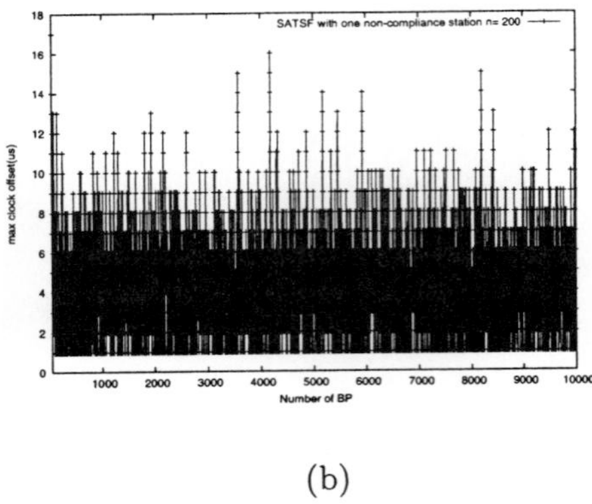

(b)

Figure 3: (a) Maximum clock offset for SATSF (b) Maximum clock offset for SATSF with one non-compliance station

large in the mix mode IBSS.

5 Conclusion

In this paper, we study the scalability and compatibility problems of clock synchronization protocols for 802.11 ad hoc networks. The current solutions to the scalability problem are still short of the industry expectation: the maximum clock offset is around $125\mu s$ for compatible solutions and $50\mu s$ for non-compatible protocols. We propose a simple and compatible protocol called SATSF that can achieve higher accuracy of clock synchronization than any of the current solutions. It can control the maximum clock offset under $20\mu s$. More importantly, SATSF is completely compatible with the 802.11 TSF without any change of beacon format. The frequency adjustment by SATSF is proved to be bounded that further helps the compatibility characteristic of SATSF. SATSF not only improves the clock synchronization accuracy to beat the $25\mu s$ industry expectation, but also resolved the issue of compatibility, which is an important area that the research community has not investigated much yet. The overall performance of the new protocol is a significant improvement over the current results in the field.

References

[1] IEEE Std 802.11. *Wireless LAN Medium Access Control (MAC) and Physical Layer (PHY) specification*, 1999 edition.

[2] IEEE Std 802.11a. *Wireless LAN Medium Access Control (MAC) and Physical Layer (PHY) specification*, 1999 edition.

[3] IEEE Std 802.11b. *Higher-Speed Physical Layer Extension in the 2.4 GHz Band*, 1999 edition.

[4] Lifei Huang, Ten-Hwang Lai. *On the Scalability of IEEE 802.11 Ad Hoc Networks* In *Proceedings of MobiHoc 2002*, pp. 173-182.

[5] Dong Zhou, Ten-Hwang Lai Analysis and Implementation of Scalable Clock Synchronization Protocols in IEEE 802.11 Ad Hoc Networks, the first IEEE international conference on Mobile and Sensor Systems, Oct. 2004.

[6] Jang-Ping Sheu, Chih-Min Chao, Ching-Wen Sun, A Clock Synchronization Algorithm for Multi-Hop Wireless Ad Hoc Networks, pp. 574-581, ICDCS 2004

[7] D. L. Mills. Internet time synchronization: the network time protocol.

In *IEEE Transaction on Communications.* pp. 1482-1493, 1991.

[8] K. Römer and E. Zurich. Time synchronization in ad hoc networks. In *Proceedings of MobiHoc 2001.*

[9] J. Elson, L. Girod, and D. Estrin, Fine-Grained Network Time Synchronization using Reference Broadcasts, Proceedings of the Fifth Symposium on Operating systems Design and Implementation, pp. 147-163, 2002.

[10] C.H. Rentel, T. Kunz, A Non-hierarchical convergent timing synchronization function for real-time QoS support in Wireless LANs: Towards an Autonomous Network Synchronization Algorithm for Wireless Ad Hoc Networks, Wireless World Research Forum, 2004.

[11] S. Bregni, Synchronization of Digital Telecommunications Networks, John Wiley & Sons, 2002.

Single Path Flooding Chain Routing in Ad Hoc Networks

Ming Ma, Chi Ma and Yuanyuan Yang
State University of New York at Stony Brook
Stony Brook, NY 11794, USA

Abstract—**In this paper, we present a new position-based routing algorithm for mobile ad hoc networks. The proposed algorithm minimizes the effect of inaccurate location information on routing, which is caused by periodical updates of the node location information in the network. The algorithm achieves low communication complexity of $O(\sqrt{n})$, compared to other existing position-based algorithms with $O(n)$ complexity, where n is the number of nodes in the network. In addition, unlike some existing routing algorithms, the new algorithm is insensitive to the mobility of mobile nodes and consistently performs well for various mobilities.**

Index Terms—**Mobile ad hoc networks, wireless networks, routing, position-based routing algorithms.**

I. Introduction and Background

In recent years, advanced VLSI and RF technologies accelerate the development and applications of *mobile ad hoc networks* (MANETs). MANETs have played an increasingly important role in both military and civilian applications, such as electronic conference, battlefield surveillance, emergency response and law enforcement. The growing interest in ad hoc networks has resulted in many routing algorithms and protocols proposed for such dynamic, self-organizing and resource-limited networks. Most of work in this area focuses on two types of routing algorithms: *topology-based* routing and *position-based* routing algorithms. Traditional topology-based routing algorithms, which are widely used in wired networks, depend on the link information to make routing decisions. On the other hand, position-based routing algorithms require the physical positions of nodes to perform packet forwarding. In general, the topology of an ad hoc network changes too frequently to be updated timely. Maintaining a routing table at each node introduces a significant amount of network traffic to an ad hoc network. Thus, position-based routing algorithms were proposed to eliminate some limitations of topology-based routing algorithms. In a position-based routing algorithm, there is no need to establish and maintain links, and routing decisions are mainly based on the location information of the destination node and the one-hop neighbors of the current node. Thus the algorithm can avoid the overhead of maintaining global information of the network.

In a position-based routing algorithm, each mobile node in an ad hoc network can obtain its own location information from the *Global Positioning System* (GPS) or some other positioning services [1], [2]. A routing decision at a node is triggered by an incoming packet to the node and is made based on the location information of both the destination node and the one-hop neighbors of the sender. However, it is generally not sufficient to establish routing paths between the source and the destination if all nodes only know their own location information. In most position-based algorithms, each node broadcasts its location information to its one-hop neighbors periodically and requests location information of the destination node by contacting the *location service* [3], [4], [5], [6]. Location services are the mechanisms that provide the location information of a specific node in the network to any node which sends a request to them. Mobile nodes register their location information with the location service. When a node needs the location of a desired node, it contacts the location service to obtain the location of that node. An example of location services is the base station in cellular networks. Each base station is a location server and provides the location information to all mobile nodes in the cell. A survey on location services and position-based algorithms can be found in [7].

When the accurate location information is available, position-based routing algorithms can use local forwarding to achieve global routing tasks. However, the location information may not be always accurate enough for packet forwarding, as the location information is only updated periodically [8], [13]. During each period between two location updates, two connected nodes may become too far to reach each other within their transmission ranges because of the frequent movement of the nodes. Few previously proposed position-based routing algorithms considered this inaccuracy caused by the outdated location information. As will be seen in Section III, our analysis shows that the outdated location information has serious effects on the single path position-based routing algorithm, especially in ad hoc networks with high mobilities.

In this paper, we give a theoretical analysis about the effect of the out-of-date location information on the performance of the single path routing algorithm, and then propose a new position-based routing algorithm for ad hoc networks. As will be seen, the new algorithm achieves much lower communication complexity than the existing flooding-based algorithms, which is measured by the average number of one-hop transmissions required to send a packet from a source node to a destination node, and can consistently perform well for various mobilities. The rest of the paper is organized as follows. In Section II we give a brief overview of some position-based

The research was supported in part by NSF grant numbers CCR-0207999 and ECS-0427345 and ARO grant number W911NF-04-1-0439.

0190-3918/05 $20.00 © 2005 IEEE

routing algorithms. In Section III, we analyze the error probability of the existing single path routing algorithm caused by the location information periodical update. Based on the analysis in Section III, we present in Section IV our new single path flooding chain routing algorithm. Section V contains some simulation results of the algorithm, and finally, Section VI concludes the paper.

II. Related Work

Position-based routing in ad hoc networks has been studied extensively in recent years. Most of proposed work can be divided into *flooding-based* algorithms [8], [9] or *greedy packet forwarding* (single-path based) algorithms [13]. In a flooding-based algorithm, a packet is flooded to the entire or most part of the network. On the other hand, in a greedy packet forwarding algorithm, a packet is transmitted through a single routing path and has only one copy in the network at any time. In this section we discuss some existing flooding-based routing algorithms and greedy packet forwarding algorithms.

A. Flooding-Based Routing Algorithms

The simplest flooding-based routing algorithm in an ad hoc network, called *blind flooding*, is to flood a packet from the source node to all other nodes in the network hop by hop. This approach does not need the location information of the nodes in the network and eliminates the power and bandwidth overhead for exchanging location information. However, this algorithm has a serious scalability problem. Since each packet passes through all nodes in the network, the communication complexity of the blind flooding algorithm is $O(n)$, where n is the number of nodes in the network. In this paper, we say two mobile nodes are *connected* if and only if their distance is less than their transmission radius. Thus there exists a *connected path* between a source node and a destination node if any two adjacent nodes in the path are connected. Although the blind flooding does not require the location information, the high communication complexity prohibits its using in a large ad hoc network.

An improved flooding-based algorithm, *Distance Routing Effect Algorithm For Mobility* (DREAM), was proposed in [8]. In the DREAM algorithm, instead of flooding a packet to the entire network, a source node S floods a packet only to a restricted area which is determined by the *expected region* of the corresponding destination node D. As shown in Figure 1, the circle around node D is its expected region whose radius can be represented by $r = V_{max}(t_1 - t_0)$, where V_{max} is the maximum speed of node D, t_1 is the current time, and t_0 is the time-stamp of node D's location information maintained by S. Since node D locates in the center of its expected region at t_0, it is unlikely to move out of its expected region at t_1, even if it always moves at its maximum speed. Thus in order to cover the expected region of the destination node, the flooding can be restricted only within the angle α, as shown in Figure 1, which is defined

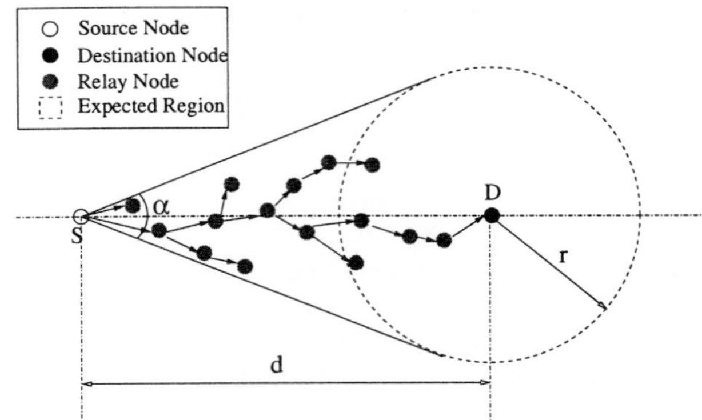

Fig. 1. Illustration of the expected region in the DREAM Algorithm.

by the angle between two tangent lines of the expected region of node D. Compared to the blind flooding algorithm, the DREAM algorithm does not need to flood each packet to all connected nodes. However, though only part of nodes in the network participate in flooding in the DREAM algorithm, as analyzed in [7], the communication complexity of the DREAM algorithm is still $O(n)$. This is because that in the worst case when the distance between the source and the destination node equals to the diameter of the network, each packet covers a sector of the entire network. Furthermore, when the destination node moves too slowly and the distance d between the source and the destination node is too far, the flooding must be constrained in a very small angle α, where $\alpha = 2\sin^{-1}(\frac{(t_1-t_0)V_{max}}{d})$. If all flooding nodes are restricted in such a very narrow area, it is difficult to find a connected path between the source and the destination node. In an extreme case that the destination node is static, the expected region of the destination node becomes a point. Therefore, the packet must be forwarded along the straight line between the source and the destination node. If not all nodes on this line are connected, the DREAM algorithm will fail. Compared to the blind flooding, the DREAM algorithm avoids covering the area outside of the expected region of the destination node, therefore saves a significant amount of power and bandwidth. However, the $O(n)$ communication complexity of the DREAM algorithm affects its scalability in large networks. As can be seen in Section IV, our newly proposed algorithm eliminates a lot of redundancy of the DREAM algorithm while achieving comparable performance by flooding packets in each limited sub-area.

B. Greedy Packet Forwarding Algorithms

A group of more efficient algorithms are *greedy packet forwarding* algorithms [10], [11], [12], [13]. In a greedy packet forwarding algorithm, there is only one routing path between the source node and the destination node, if it exists. Any node that is not contained in the routing path will not participate in forwarding packets. When a packet was forwarded to a node in a routing path at t_1, it can find the next-hop node among its one-hop neighbors by using some strategies, for example, *Most Forward Within R*(MFR) [10], *Nearest with Forward Progress* (NFP) [11] and *Compass Routing* [12]. However, based on the above forwarding strategies, sometimes the greedy packet forwarding algorithm may fail if the current node cannot find the next-hop node in the forwarding direction to the destination node among its neighbors. For instance, in the MFR protocol, if the sender cannot find a node that is closer to the destination node than itself within its transmission range, it will fail. To solve this problem, researchers have proposed some recovery mechanisms, such as the perimeter routing strategy of the *Greedy Perimeter Stateless Routing protocol* (GPSR) [13]. In these algorithms, a packet will be transferred into the recovery mode, when it fails to find a "better" node than itself. Because the communication complexity of forwarding a packet from one node to the other is a linear function of their distance, the communication complexity of the greedy packet forwarding is $O(\sqrt{n})$. It should be pointed out that all algorithms discussed above assume the location information is always accurate. However, since the location information is usually updated periodically, all routing decisions have to be based on the most recent updated location information rather than the current location information. When one node wants to forward a packet to the other node, it thought the other node is still within its transmission range based on the old location information. But the other node may move too far away to be reached after the last location information update. Due to the out-of-date location information and the motion of nodes between two consecutive location information updates, even robust single-path algorithms, such as GPSR [13], may fail to forward the packet successfully. Thus, we say that greedy packet forwarding algorithms are more sensitive to the motion of nodes than flooding-based algorithm. As can be seen from the analysis in Section III and the simulation results in Section V, a single routing path has higher failure probability when nodes move intensively. Thus, greedy packet forwarding algorithms are only suitable to static or low mobility ad hoc networks.

Some researchers try to add some redundancy to enhance the greedy forwarding algorithm. The approach is called *multi-path routing algorithm* [14], in which the source sends several copies of each packet through several separate paths at the same time. The multi-path forwarding algorithm can perform much better than the single path algorithm. The successful packet delivery probability of a multi-path forwarding algorithm $P_{mul} = \sum_k P_k$, where k is the number of multiple paths and P_k is the successful packet delivery probability of the k_{th} path. The equation above can be satisfied only when any two of paths have no dependence. For example, in the case that two paths overlap in some nodes, if any overlapping node dies or moves away, both paths will fail. In order to minimize dependence between any two paths, the source may need to acquire accurate information of the global node distribution to decide several independent paths, whereas single path algorithm only needs the location information of nearby nodes. The overhead of exchanging the global information leads to the tremendous energy and time consumption in large ad hoc networks. As can be seen in section IV, our new algorithm is a kind of "local" algorithm like single path algorithm and improve the performance of the single path algorithm by flooding packets to the nearby area of each forwarding node in the single routing path instead forwarding packets in an arbitrary direction.

III. Path Connectivity Analysis for Greedy Packet Forwarding Algorithms

Before we present our new algorithm, in this section we first analyze the error probability of a routing path caused by the outdated location information. Consider an n-node ad hoc network, where all nodes are located in a two dimensional square and have the same transmission radius R. Each node is able to communicate with its neighbors at most R units away from it. In most position-based routing algorithms, each node broadcasts control packets to update its location information maintained by other nodes in every short period T. The motion trace of a node is recorded by a series of discrete positions which are updated periodically. Since all forwarding decisions are made at these discrete points, it is not necessary to acquire the actual motion curve between any two adjacent points. Moreover, during each short period between two consecutive location information updates, it is very likely for nodes to keep the same direction and the same speed or only change them slightly. For an easy analysis, we assume that each node keeps the same speed and motion direction between two consecutive location information updates. During each location update period, the speed and the motion direction of each node are given randomly according to the uniform distribution in $(0, V_{max})$ and $(0, 2\pi)$, respectively, where V_{max} is the maximum speed of the node. Thus the motion curve of a node can be described by a chain-like curve instead of its actual curve. Also, since the signal transmission time and the computing time of each node has little impact on the performance and the cost of the algorithm compared to the location information update period, we simplify the theoretical analysis and simulations by ignoring these short times.

In an ad hoc network, a routing decision is made based on the most recently updated location information. However, all mobile nodes move from time to time, and as a result, two connected nodes may become disconnected after a short while. There is no guarantee that the packet coming at time t_1 still can pass through the routing path based on the location information at time t_0 (where $t_0 + T > t_1 > t_0$). We define the probability that two connected nodes become disconnected after Δt as q, where $\Delta t = t_1 - t_0$. Assume that there are a total of m hops from the source node to the destination node and the connection status of any two nodes is independent. Then the probability that a routing path determined at time t_0

is still connected at time t_1, P_{path}, can be calculated by

$$P_{path} = (1-q)^m \tag{1}$$

In the following, we calculate the probability q that two connected nodes become disconnected after Δt. Figure 2(a) gives two connected nodes N_1 and N_2 which have absolute velocities $\overrightarrow{V_1}$ and $\overrightarrow{V_2}$, respectively. Let ϕ_1 and ϕ_2 be the motion directions of nodes N_1 and N_2, respectively. To see the upper bound of the error probability, we assume a worst case that both node N_1 and node N_2 move at the maximum speed, that is, $|\overrightarrow{V_1}| = |\overrightarrow{V_2}| = V_{max}$. Without loss of generality, we choose node N_1 as the motion reference object and $\phi_1 = 0$. In this relative motion system, as shown is Figure 2(c), node N_1 becomes the origin of the polar coordinate, and node N_2 is located at (r, θ), where (r, θ) is the position of node N_2 in the polar coordinate. As shown in Figure 2(b), now node N_1 has velocity $\overrightarrow{V_1'} = 0$ and node N_2 has velocity $\overrightarrow{V_2'} = (\overrightarrow{V_2} - \overrightarrow{V_1})$, where the motion direction of $\overrightarrow{V_2'}$, $\phi_2' = \angle\overrightarrow{V_2'} = \frac{\phi_2-\phi_1+\pi}{2} = \frac{\phi_2+\pi}{2}$. We assume that ϕ_1 and ϕ_2 can take any direction within 0 to 2π with the same probability. Thus, ϕ_2' is uniformly distributed in $(\frac{\pi}{2}, \frac{3\pi}{2})$, and the probability mass function of ϕ_2', $f(\phi_2') = \frac{1}{\pi}$. In Figure 2(c), S is defined as the distance from point (r, θ) to the edge of the circle in the direction of ϕ_2', where $S = \sqrt{R^2 - r^2\sin^2(\phi_2' - \theta)} - r\cos(\phi_2' - \theta)$. When $\theta = \phi_2'$, S reaches its minimum value, $S_{min} = (R - r)$. In the relative motion system, if the distance of node N_2 moving in the direction of ϕ_2' during t_0 and t_1 is longer than S, that is, when

$$|\overrightarrow{V_2'}|(t_1 - t_0) > S \tag{2}$$

node N_2 will move out of the transmission range of node N_1. Thus, the probability that the link between nodes N_1 and N_2 becomes disconnected at t_1,

$$q = P_r\{|\overrightarrow{V_2'}|(t_1 - t_0) > S\} \tag{3}$$

Denoting $|\overrightarrow{V_2'}|(t_1 - t_0)$ in (3) as C, we have

$$\begin{aligned} q &= P_r\{C > S\} \leq P_r\{C > S_{min}\} \\ &\leq P_r\{C > R - r\} = P_r\{r > R - C\} \\ &= \int_{\frac{\pi}{2}}^{\frac{3\pi}{2}} \int_0^{2\pi} \int_{R-C}^{R} f(r, \theta, \phi_2') dr d\theta d\phi_2' \end{aligned} \tag{4}$$

We assume mobile nodes are distributed uniformly in the transmission range of node N_1 and the relative motion direction of a node does not depend on its location. Thus,

$$f(r, \theta, \phi_2') = f(r, \theta) f(\phi_2') = \frac{r}{\pi^2 R^2} \tag{5}$$

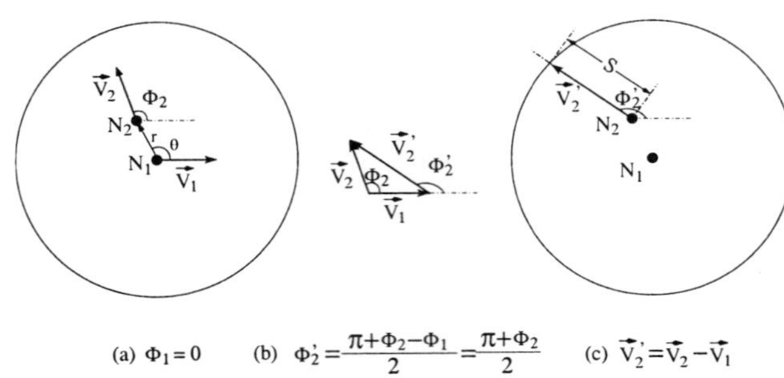

Fig. 2. The motion models of two nodes. (a) Absolute motion model. (b) Velocity composition. (c) Relative motion model.

Plugging (5) into (4), we obtain

$$\begin{aligned} q &\leq \int_{\frac{\pi}{2}}^{\frac{3\pi}{2}} \int_0^{2\pi} \int_{R-C}^{R} \frac{r}{\pi^2 R^2} dr d\theta d\phi_2' \\ &\leq \frac{1}{2\pi^2 R^2} \int_{\frac{\pi}{2}}^{\frac{3\pi}{2}} \int_0^{2\pi} 2RC - C^2 d\theta d\phi_2' \\ &\leq \frac{1}{2\pi^2 R^2} \int_{\frac{\pi}{2}}^{\frac{3\pi}{2}} \int_0^{2\pi} 2RC d\theta d\phi_2' \\ &\leq \frac{2C}{R} \end{aligned} \tag{6}$$

Replacing $C = |\overrightarrow{V_2'}|(t_1 - t_0)$ in (6), we have

$$\begin{aligned} q &\leq \frac{2|\overrightarrow{V_2'}|(t_1 - t_0)}{R} \\ &\leq \frac{2(|\overrightarrow{V_1}| + |\overrightarrow{V_2}|) \times (t_1 - t_0)}{R} \\ &\leq \frac{4V_{max} \times T}{R} \end{aligned} \tag{7}$$

Where T is the location information update period and V_{max} is the maximum speed of a node. When $V_{max} \cdot T \ll R$, $q \to 0$ and $P_{path} = (1-q)^m \to 1$. This means that the routing path based on the location information at t_0 is still connected at t_1 with probability $P_{path} \to 1$. On the other hand, when $\frac{4V_{max} \times T}{R}$ increases, the single routing path between the source node and the destination node becomes increasingly instable. A possible solution to this problem is that after sending a packet to its next-hop node, each node keeps a copy of the packet in the memory until it receives an acknowledgment from the next-hop node. If the next-hop node moves out of the transmission range of the current node, it cannot receive the packet and reply to the current node. If the current node does not receive the acknowledgment within a certain amount of time, it will wait for the next location information update and then look for a new next-hop node based on the new location information. After the current node makes a new forwarding decision, it will re-forward the packet to the new next-hop node. Although this approach can reduce the error probability of a greedy forwarding algorithm, these handshaking messages introduce extra traffic burden to a resource-limited network. Moreover, waiting for the new location information update delays the transmission of packets.

IV. Single Path Flooding Chain Routing Algorithm

As discussed earlier, flooding-based algorithms are more robust than single-path-based routing algorithms. However, they usually have $O(n)$ communication complexity for an n-node ad hoc network, which makes the consumption of energy and bandwidth heavily depend on the number of nodes and affects the scalability of the network. In this section, we propose a new routing algorithm that compromises between flooding-based algorithms and greedy forwarding algorithms. While keeping the low communication complexity, the new algorithm enhances the robustness of single-path-based routing algorithms by flooding the packet only within a limited area near two adjacent nodes in a single routing path.

A. Sub-area Flooding

A packet forwarding decision is usually based on the location information updated earlier than the current time. Thus the next-hop node may move out of the transmission range of the current node and cannot receive the packet. If each node in the single routing path floods the packet within a limited area rather than forwards the packet in an arbitrary direction, it is highly possible for the packet to re-capture the "escaped" next-hop node in constant steps with the help of *relay nodes*. Note that the communication complexity of this approach is $O(\sqrt{n})$, since the flooding only occurs in the nearby nodes of each forwarding node.

Figure 3(a) shows a single routing path along nodes $1 \rightarrow 2 \rightarrow 3 \rightarrow 4 \rightarrow 5 \rightarrow 6 \rightarrow 7$, which is determined by the location information updated at t_0. However, when a packet needs to pass through this path from node 1 to node 7 at t_1, the routing path may become disconnected because of the movement of nodes during t_0 and t_1. For example, in Figure 3(b), node 5 moves out of the transmission range of node 4 at t_1. The link between node 4 and node 5 becomes disconnected. As a result, the packet can no longer reach the destination node 7 along this path.

In Table 1, we give a new position-based algorithm, called *single-path flooding chain algorithm*. Instead of forwarding the packet along a single path, we can choose the "limited flooding area" for each forwarding node in the single path to flood the packet. At the current time t_1, just like the single path routing algorithms, the current forwarding node decides the next-hop node in the single routing path based on the location information updated at t_0. And then it calculates the expected region of its next-hop node, which is the circle around the location of the next-hop node at t_0 with the radius of $r = V_{max}(t_1 - t_0)$. Figure 3(b) shows the expected region of forwarding nodes 1,2,3,4,5,6 and 7. Each sender

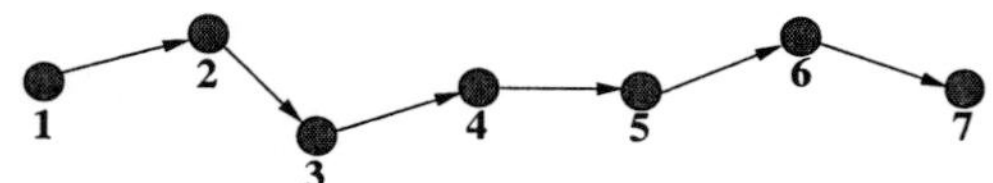

(a) Greedy Packet Forwarding Algorithm:
A single path from 1 to 7 determined by the most recent location information updated at t_0 .

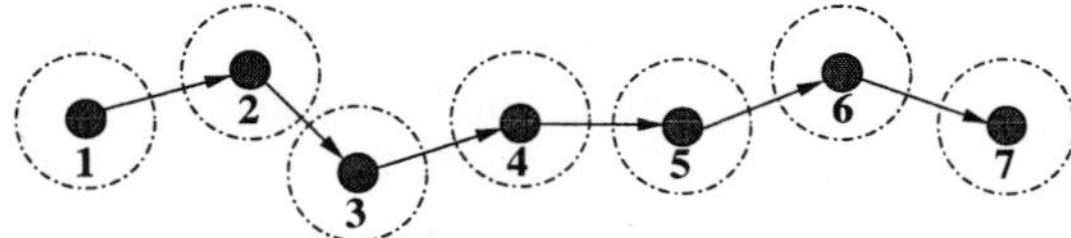

(b) Circles around nodes are their expected regions.

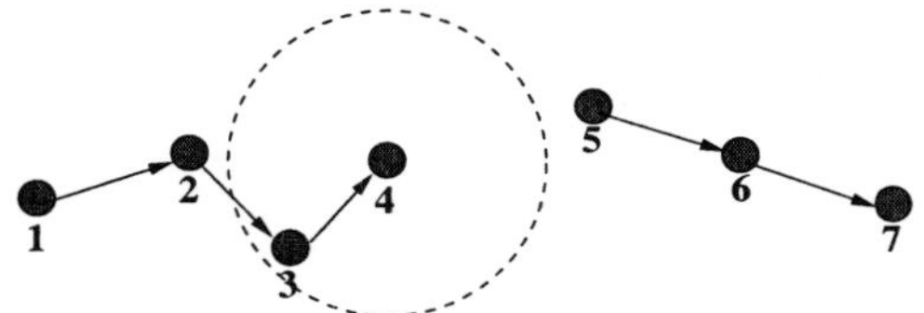

(c) Node 5 runs out of the transmission range of node 4 at t_1
Single routing path becomes disconnected.

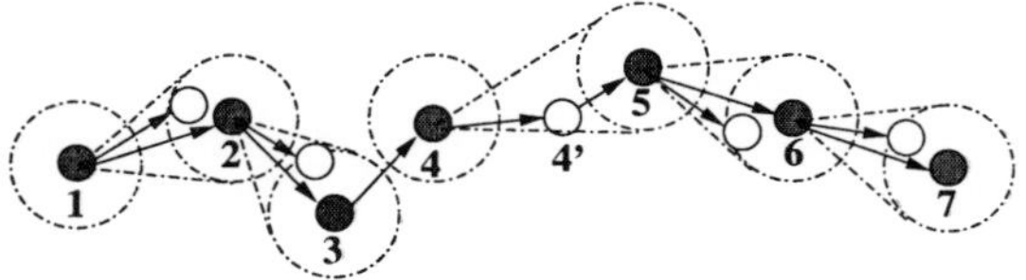

(d) Single Path Flooding Chain Algorithm:
With the relay of node 4', the packet re–capture node 5.

Fig. 3. Examples of greedy packet forwarding and single-path flooding chain algorithms.

in the single routing path tries to cover the expected region of the next-hop node by simply flooding the packet to the nodes within two tangent lines of the expected region of the next-hop node. In Figure 3(d), node 4 can re-capture node 5 through the relay of node $4'$.

B. Communication Complexity

In this subsection, we analyze the communication complexity of the proposed single path flooding chain algorithm. Intuitively, the higher density of an ad hoc network, the more connectivity of the network. Simulation results in [15] showed that six to eight neighbors can make a small size network connected with high probability. Thus in a high density network where each node has more than eight neighbors, routing algorithms may not have a great impact on the performance. Therefore, in order to make a fair comparison on the performance and the complexity of the routing algorithms, we assume that the network has a general density, in which each node has a small constant number of neighbors within its transmission range in average.

In the single path flooding chain algorithm, the packets flooded by a node will cover an area to reach the next-

TABLE I

SINGLE PATH FLOODING CHAIN ALGORITHM

```
Algorithm : Single Path Flooding Chain
for each packet starts from the source node at t1
    current node := source node;
        while current node ≠ destination node
            current node finds the next-hop node based on the location information updated at t0;
            current node calculates the expected region of the next-hop node;
            current node floods the packet to cover the expected region of the next-hop node;
            current node := next-hop node;
        end while;
end for
End
```

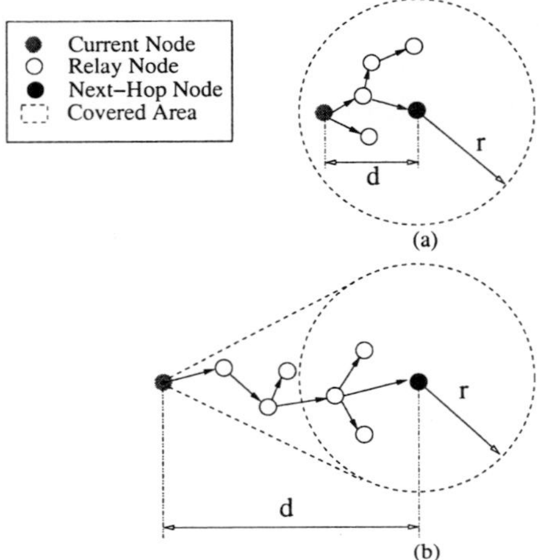

Fig. 4. Covered area of the next hop node. (a) $d < r$. (b) $d > r$.

hop node. We call this area *Covered Area*. The covered area has two possible shapes. As shown in Figure 4(a), when the distance d between the current and the next-hop node is less than the radius r of the expected region (where $r = V_{max}(t_1 - t_0)$), the covered area is bounded by two tangent lines and the arc between two tangent points, which includes the center of the circle. Figure 4(b) is the other case, which shows that when d is longer than r, the covered area is a circle centered at the position of the next-hop node. In both cases, d is less than R, because two adjacent nodes in the single routing path must be in the transmission ranges of each other. r is in fact a measure for the node mobility during the short period between two location information updates. Few existing position-based routing algorithms can perform well in a network with a very high mobility ($r >> R$) except some algorithms which use the flooding strategy, such as the DREAM and the single path flooding chain algorithms. As will be seen in Section V, the greedy packet forwarding algorithm starts to have very poor performance after $\frac{r}{R} > 0.5$. In fact, when r is much larger than R and is similar to the network diameter, the expected region of a node in the DREAM or the single path flooding chain algorithm may cover most nodes in the network. In this case, there is little difference among the DREAM, the single path flooding chain and the blinding flooding algorithms in communication complexity. In order to compare three position-based routing algorithms in a network with a general mobility, we assume that the radius r of the expected region is at most a constant times the transmission radius R. Thus, both r and d can be expressed as a constant times R. Since the size of the covered area is a quadratic function of r and d, it can be represented as $(k \cdot R^2)$, where k is a constant. For given density of nodes, say ρ, each covered area contains a constant number of nodes, which equals $k \cdot \rho \cdot R^2$.

In the algorithm, before the current node floods a packet to the next-hop node, it puts the maximum speed and the location information of the next-hop node into the packet header. When a node receives the packet, it calculates the covered area based on the information in the packet header and its own location, and then checks if it is in the covered area with respect to the packet. If yes, it will act as a "relay node" and floods this packet to its one-hop neighbors in the covered area. Otherwise, the packet will not be forwarded to other nodes. This strategy guarantees that only a constant number of nodes contained in each covered area participate in relaying packets between two adjacent forwarding nodes in a single path. Thus, the complexity of the newly proposed single-path flooding chain algorithm is only a constant factor higher than that of a single-path-based routing algorithm and is still $O(\sqrt{n})$.

V. SIMULATION RESULTS

We have simulated the greedy packet forwarding, DREAM and the single-path flooding chain algorithms and compare their performance and complexities. In the simulations, we use the same node motion model as discussed in Section III. n nodes are placed randomly in a $1 \times 1km^2$ square. Each node has the same transmission range $R = 100m$. Each time the location information is updated, the speed and the direction of each node will change according to the uniform distribution in $(0, V_{max})$ and $(0, 2\pi)$, respectively, where V_{max} is the maximum speed of the node. In both greedy forwarding algorithm and single-path flooding chain algorithm, without loss of generality, MFR [10] strategy is used to decide the next-hop node in the single routing path. In order to analyze the effect of the node mobility, we introduce a metric $\beta = \frac{V_{max}\Delta t}{R}$ to measure the mobility of a mobile node, where Δt is the time between the packet arrival and the last location information update, and R is the transmission radius of the node. We first consider the effect of the node mobility to the *successful packet delivery ratio*, which represents the probability that a packet is sent successfully from a source node to a destination node. We also compare the communication complexities of the algorithms by varying the network size.

A. Successful Packet Delivery Ratio

In this scenario, we compare the successful packet delivery ratios of three algorithms in a network with 400 mobile nodes by ranging β from 0 to 1. For each β, we generate 100 unicast packets between randomly chosen source-destination pairs. Figure 5 shows the relationship between the successful packet delivery ratio P_d and the node mobility metric β. Three curves correspond to the greedy packet forwarding, DREAM and single-path flooding chain algorithms, respectively. As shown in Figure 5, when nodes have very low mobility ($\beta < 0.1$), the P_d of the greedy packet forwarding algorithm is greater than 50%. Since the radius of the expected region is proportional to $V_{max}\Delta t$ in the DREAM algorithm, when $\beta < 0.1$, the P_d of the DREAM algorithm is less than 50%. When β increases, the P_d of the greedy packet forwarding algorithm becomes too low to be acceptable. On the other hand, the successful packet delivery ratio of the DREAM algorithm ascends as β increases and exceeds the single-path flooding chain algorithm slightly when the network has high mobility ($\beta > 0.6$). We can see that unlike other two algorithms, the single-path flooding chain algorithm is not sensitive to the change of the node's speed and can keep a stable high successful packet delivery ratio ($P_d > 75\%$) in both low mobility and high mobility ad hoc networks.

B. Communication Complexity

From Figure 5, we observe that the DREAM algorithm has slightly better successful packet delivery ratio than the single-path flooding chain algorithm when nodes have high mobilities ($\beta > 0.6$). We now compare the communication complexity to see the tradeoff between the DREAM algorithm and the single-path flooding chain algorithm. We analyze the communication complexity by varying the network size from 100 nodes to 1000 nodes, for $\beta = 0.6, 0,7, 0.8$ and 0.9, respectively. We can see from Figure 6 that the successful packet delivery ratios of three algorithms all have an increasing trend when the network size increases from 100 to 1000. In general, the higher network density is, the more

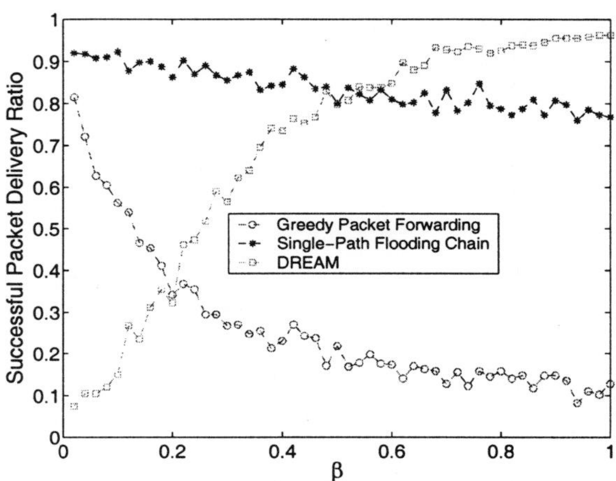

Fig. 5. The successful packet delivery ratio between a randomly chosen source-destination pair.

connectivity of the network has. However, we notice that the difference in the communication complexity between the DREAM algorithm and the single-path flooding chain algorithm becomes larger as the network size increases. Besides the network size, the mobility of the nodes also affects the communication complexity. The faster the node's speed is, the larger the expected region and the higher communication complexity. From Figure 6, we also observe that the DREAM algorithm has higher communication complexity than the single-path flooding chain algorithm when $\beta = 0.9$ than that of $\beta = 0.6, 0,7$ and $0,8$. Thus, the single-path flooding chain algorithm is more scalable than the DREAM algorithm for large size and high mobility ad hoc networks and always has a better successful packet delivery ratio than the greedy packet forwarding algorithm.

VI. Conclusions

In this paper, we have presented a new position-based routing algorithm called single-path flooding chain algorithm for mobile ad hoc networks. Compared to flooding-based routing algorithms with $O(n)$ communication complexity, the newly proposed algorithm reduces the communication complexity to $O(\sqrt{n})$, which is as low as the greedy packet forwarding algorithm. The new algorithm can significantly save the bandwidth and power for resource limited mobile nodes, especially in large networks. In addition, simulation results have showed that single-path flooding chain algorithm consistently performs well for various mobilities and keeps a high successful packet delivery ratio ($> 75\%$), which is insensitive to the change of node's motion speed.

References

[1] E.D. Kaplan, ed., *Understanding GPS – Principles and Applications*, Norwood MA: Artech House, 1996.

[2] S. Capkun, M. Hamdi, J.P. Hubaux, "GPS-free position-

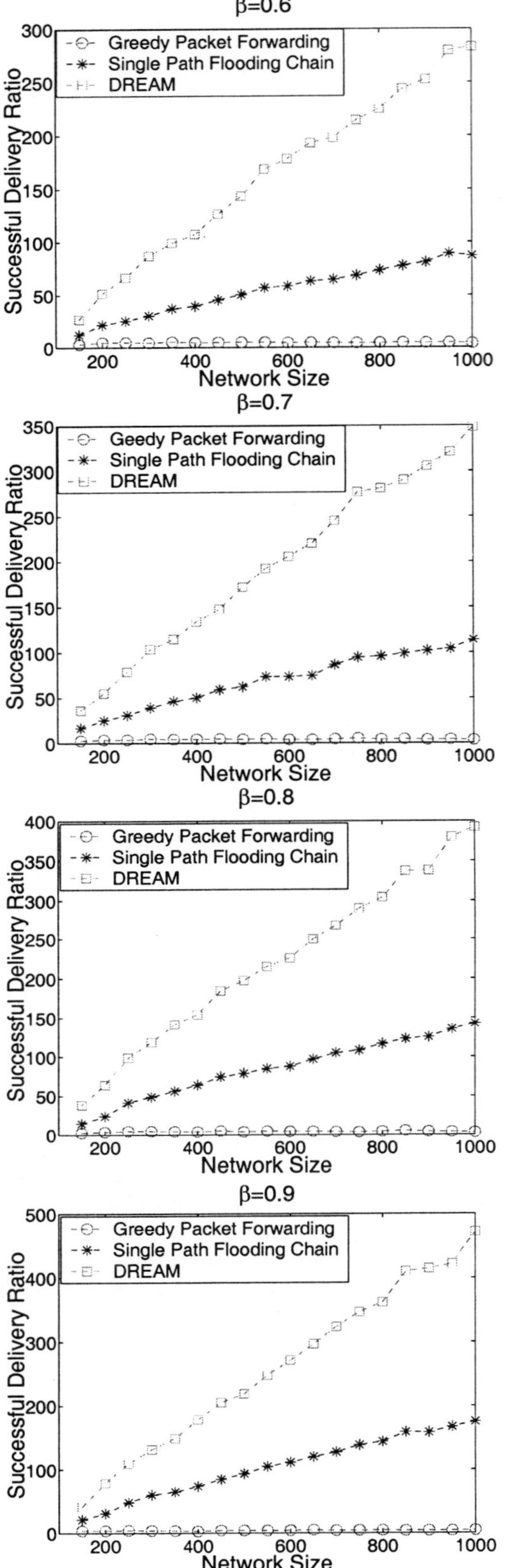

Fig. 6. Communication complexity when $\beta = 0.6, 0.7, 0.8$ and 0.9, respectively.

ing in mobile ad-hoc networks," *Proc. Hawaii Int. Conf. on System Sciences*, Jan. 2001.

[3] Z.J. Haas and B. Liang, "Ad-hoc mobility management with uniform quorum systems," *IEEE/ACM Trans. Networking*, vol. 7, no. 2, pp. 228-240, Apr. 1999.

[4] J. Li, J. Jannotti, D.S.J. De Couto, D.R. Karger and R. Morris, "A scalable location service for geographic ad hoc routing," *Proc. ACM/IEEE MobiCom*, pp. 120-130, Boston, Aug. 2000.

[5] R. Morris, J. Jannotti, F. Kaashoek, J. Li and D. Decouto, "CarNet: A scalable ad hoc wireless network system," *ACM SIGOPS European Workshop*, Kolding, Denmark, Sept. 2000.

[6] S. Giordano and M. Hamidi. "Mobility management: The virtual home region," Technical Report, Oct. 1999.

[7] M. Mauve, J. Widmer, and H. Hartenstein. "A survey on position-based routing in mobile ad hoc networks," *IEEE Network Magazine*, 15(6):30–39, Nov. 2001.

[8] S. Basagni, I. Chlamtac, V.R. Syrotiuk, and B.A. Woodward. "A distance routing effect algorithm for mobility (DREAM)," *Proc. 4th Annual ACM/IEEE International Conference in Mobile Computing and Networking (MobiCom)*, pp. 76-84, 1998.

[9] Y. Ko and N. H. Vaidya, "Location-aided routing (LAR) mobile ad hoc networks," *ACM/IEEE MobiCom'98*, Dallas, TX, 1998.

[10] H. Takagi and L. Kleinrock, "Optimal transmission ranges for randomly distributed packet radio terminals," *IEEE Trans. Communications*, vol. 32, no. 3, pp. 246-257, Mar. 1984.

[11] T.-C. Hou and V.O.K. Li, "Transmission range control in multihop packet radio networks," *IEEE Trans. Communications*, vol. 34, no. 1, pp. 38-44, Jan. 1986.

[12] E. Kranakis, H. Singh, and J. Urrutia, "Compass routing on geometric networks," *Proc. 11th Canadian Conference on Computational Geometry*, Vancouver, Aug. 1999.

[13] B. Karp and and H.T. Kung. "Greedy perimeter stateless routing for wireless networks," *Proc. ACM/IEEE MobiCom*, Boston, MA, Aug. 2000.

[14] D. Ganesan, R. Govindan, S. Shenker, and D. Estrin, "Highly-resilient, energy-efficient multipath routing in wireless sensor networks," *Mobile Computing and Communications Review*, Vol. 4, No. 5, October 2001.

[15] J. Ni and S. Chandler, "Connectivity properties of a random radio network," *Proc. IEE Communications*, vol. 141, pp 289-296, Aug. 1994.

Session 5A: Network Performance and Features

Supporting the Sockets Interface over User-Level Communication Architecture: Design Issues and Performance Comparisons

Jae-Wan Jang
jwjang@camars.kaist.ac.kr

Jin-Soo Kim
jinsoo@cs.kaist.ac.kr

Division of Computer Science
Korea Advanced Institute of Science and Technology (KAIST)

Abstract

Since user-level communication architecture (ULC) provides only primitive operations for application programmers, many high-level communication layers have been developed on top of ULC. One of such high-level communication layers is the sockets interfaces and it can be supported over ULC architectures in several ways. The primary objective of this paper is to identify design issues and trade-offs among these different approaches, and to quantitatively analyze their performance to understand the various costs associated with the communication.

In this paper, we design and implement KSOVIA, a kernel-level sockets layer over VIA, and compare it with the existing approaches such as a user-level sockets layer over VIA and an IP emulation layer over VIA. Our measurement results show that using an IP emulation layer exhibits the worst performance in terms of latency and bandwidth and a user-level sockets layer is useful for latency-sensitive applications. KSOVIA is found to be effective for applications which require high bandwidth or the full compatibility with the sockets interface.

1. Introduction

Cluster systems are becoming attractive as the needs of high performance computing grow rapidly. Since cluster systems are relatively easy to build using commodity off-the-shelf (COTS) components, they show higher performance/price ratio than traditional supercomputers. This makes cluster systems the most common computer architecture seen in the world's fastest TOP500 supercomputer list [1].

One of the main obstacles in constructing a scalable cluster system is the communication performance; as the number of cluster nodes increases, the communication traffic among them also increases inevitably, limiting the overall performance of cluster systems. Recently, many high-speed System Area Networks (SANs), such as Gigabit Ethernet, Myrinet, Quadrics, and InfiniBand Architecture, have appeared supporting raw bandwidth more than one gigabits per second. In spite of the availability of high-speed interconnection hardware, however, it is not easy to deliver the raw transmission speed to end users due to various software overheads involved in communication. Therefore, it is essential to devise an efficient communication architecture which minimizes the communication cost in order to achieve the scalability beyond several tens or hundreds of nodes.

User-level communication (ULC) architectures attempt to accelerate the communication performance by removing the operating system from the critical communication path. It rests on the observation that the traditional communication architecture based on TCP/IP protocol suite suffers from the TCP/IP protocol overhead in the cluster environment. Moreover, ULC architectures perform most of protocol processing in the user space, thus eliminating overheads associated with context switching and data copying between the user and the kernel space.

The Virtual Interface Architecture (VIA) [2] is an early industrial effort to standardize ULC architectures. Recently, InfiniBand Architecture (IBA) [15] has been standardized as one of the next generation interconnection networks borrowing many concepts from VIA. The VIA and IBA define a set of standard application programming interface (API), called VIPL (VI Provider Library) and VAPI (Verbs API), respectively. These APIs provide fully-protected, user-level access to a network hardware, allowing for efficient communication for scalable clusters.

Although VIPL and VAPI enable developers to exploit high performance network at user-level, they are considered to be at too low a level for general network application programming [3]. Hence, many researchers have endeavored to build another portable high-level communication layers over VIA and IBA [11][18][19] that can hide low-level details to end users. Among various popular high-level com-

0190-3918/05 $20.00 © 2005 IEEE

munication layers, one of possible candidates that can be used over ULC architecture is the Berkeley sockets API [4] considering its widespread use and acceptance in distributed environments. The sockets API is a de facto standard for network programming and provides a means for developing applications independent of network hardware or protocols.

There can be several different approaches to supporting the sockets API over ULC architecture. Specifically, we can make the sockets API available for use, either (1) by inserting an IP emulation layer inside the kernel which bridges the gap between IP layer and user-level communication device (e.g. LANEVI for VIA or IPoIB for IBA), (2) by providing a user-level sockets layer, or (3) by providing a kernel-level sockets layer. Both the user-level and the kernel-level sockets layers emulate the sockets API directly over VIA or IBA. However, the user-level sockets layer exists as a library in the user space, while the kernel-level sockets layer resides in the kernel space, which bypasses the TCP/IP protocol stack during data transfer.

Each of the aforementioned approaches reveals different characteristics and design issues, not to mention the communication performance. This urges us to investigate the pros and cons of each approach both qualitatively and quantitatively. Since we have an access to the implementations of the first and second approaches from LANEVI driver of Emulex and our previous work [11], respectively, it is required to have a kernel-level sockets layer over VIA for making the comparison.

Thus, we first design and implement a kernel-level sockets layer, called KSOVIA (Kernel-level Sockets Over VIA), and then compare KSOVIA with other existing approaches. The primary objective of this paper is to identify design issues and trade-offs among different approaches supporting the sockets layer over ULC architecture, and to quantitatively analyze the various factors which affect the resulting communication performance.

The rest of the paper is organized as follows. The next section briefly overviews different approaches to supporting the sockets API over VIA, and presents motivations and contributions of our work. Section 3 compares design issues among different approaches, with emphasis on implementation details of KSOVIA. Section 4 shows experimental results and compares the performance of KSOVIA with other approaches. Section 5 presents related work. Finally, we conclude in section 6.

2. Background

2.1. Virtual interface architecture (VIA)

The organization of VIA is briefly depicted in Figure 1. VIA consists of four basic components: Virtual Interfaces, Completion Queues, VI Provider, and VI Consumer.

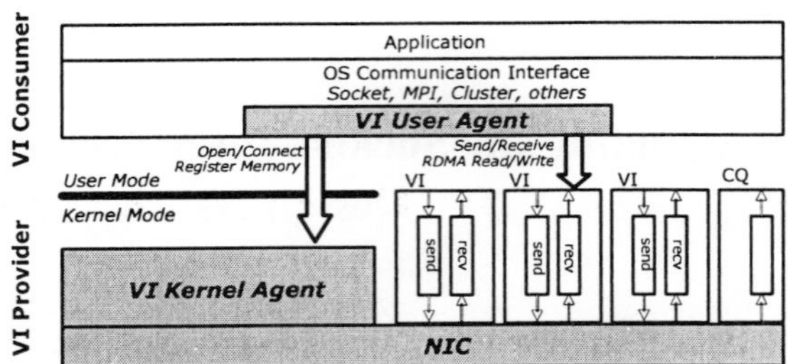

Figure 1. The organization of the Virtual Interface Architecture

VIA provides a consumer process with a protected, directly-accessible interface to a network hardware called Virtual Interface (VI), which is used as a communication endpoint. A VI consists of a pair of work queues: a send queue (SQ) and a receive queue (RQ). VI Provider consists of a physical network adapter and Kernel Agent, while VI Consumer represents the user of a VI.

Sending or receiving data in VIA is comprised of two separate phases, namely the posting phase and the reaping phase. In the posting phase, VI Consumer posts a request on a work queue, in the form of a descriptor which contains all the information to transmit data. When the processing of the descriptor completes, the NIC marks a DONE bit in the status field of the descriptor. Those completed descriptors are identified and then removed from the work queue by VI Consumer in the reaping phase. A Completion Queue (CQ) allows a VI Consumer to coalesce notification of descriptor completions from multiple work queues in a single location. Once this association is established, notification of the completed requests for the work queue is automatically directed to the CQ.

Several VIA implementations are available for Linux platforms. M-VIA [5] emulates the VIA specification by software for legacy Fast Ethernet and Gigabit Ethernet NICs. Berkeley VIA [6], SVIA [7], and MyVIA [8] support the VIA specification on Myrinet by modifying its firmware. Finally, Emulex Corp. (former Giganet Inc.) has developed a proprietary, VIA-aware NIC called cLAN [9]. In this paper, we investigate various issues related to the sockets support on cLAN, as it is one of the most stable VIA implementations.

2.2. Supporting the sockets API over VIA

There can be several different approaches for supporting the sockets interface over VIA, as illustrated in Figure 2. Figure 2(a) shows the traditional communication architecture, in which the sockets layer is located on top of the TCP/IP protocol stack.

A simple way to support the sockets interface on top of VIA is to insert an adaptation layer between IP and VI Kernel Agent, as depicted in Figure 2(b). As the IP layer is

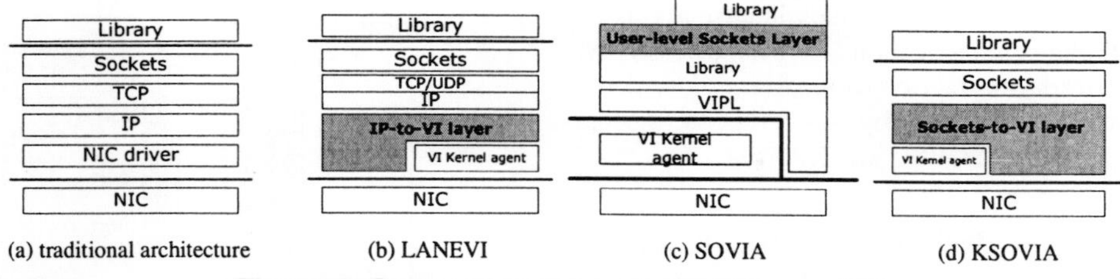

(a) traditional architecture (b) LANEVI (c) SOVIA (d) KSOVIA

Figure 2. Supporting the sockets API over VIA

emulated on VIA, an IP address is assigned to the NIC and the existing IP-based network applications can be run without any modification. The LANEVI (LAN Emulation on VI) [10] driver supplied by Emulex for its cLAN NICs is an example of such layers. Internally, the LANEVI driver relies on a thin layer called kVIPL, which is a kernel-level counterpart to VIPL allowing the kernel to use VIPL-like interfaces to access the NIC. Due to restrictions in the kernel space, however, not all of VIPL interfaces are implemented in kVIPL.

In order to eliminate overheads incurred by the TCP/IP protocol stack and to fully utilize the VIA's user-level data transfer capability, a user-level sockets layer over VIA, such as SOVIA [11], has been proposed. SOVIA is a lightweight and portable communication layer, which aims at providing the sockets interface entirely at user-level without sacrificing the performance of the underlying VIA layer. As Figure 2(c) shows, user-level sockets layers are generally implemented as a user-level library on top of VIPL. It is reported that the SOVIA layer successfully realizes comparable performance to native VIA, while offering the portable sockets semantics to application developers.

User-level sockets layers implemented on top of ULC architectures have been also introduced for Myrinet [12]. Gigabit Ethernet [13], and SCI [14]. However, all of those user-level sockets layers show a compatibility problem in that they hardly support the exec() system call, since sockets-related data structures maintained at the user level are eliminated during exec(). In addition, it is very complicated to share sockets connections between parent and child processes after the fork() system call, which makes it difficult to support concurrent server daemons or "super-server" daemons such as *inetd*. These problems are inherent limitations in any user-level sockets implementations.

Another approach that can solve the compatibility problem of user-level sockets layers is to use a kernel-level sockets layer, which moves the sockets support back into the kernel space, as shown in Figure 2(d). The kernel-level sockets layer supports the sockets API inside the kernel, but still bypasses the TCP/IP protocol stack interacting directly with the VI-aware NIC. It can freely access sockets-related data structures kept inside the kernel and is able to preserve most sockets semantics easily.

2.3. Motivations and Contributions

Our work is motivated by a desire to compare different approaches to supporting the sockets API over ULC architecture, both qualitatively and quantitatively. In order to do that, we first had to develop KSOVIA, a kernel-level sockets layer over VIA, because there was no corresponding implementation that could be used for the comparison.

The KSOVIA layer is intended to behave the same as the existing SOVIA layer as much as possible in terms of protocol processing such as internal state transitions and flow control algorithms, with the only exception being located in the kernel space. There are, however, several cases where some design changes are required in KSOVIA due to intrinsic differences between the user and the kernel space.

The development of KSOVIA enables us to compare three different approaches, LANEVI, SOVIA, and KSOVIA, on the same cLAN-based platform. Because SOVIA and KSOVIA work basically the same way, we can accurately identify the amount of overheads added in the kernel-level implementation (such as context switching overhead) by comparing their performance. Similarly, we can roughly figure out the TCP/IP protocol overhead by comparing the performance of KSOVIA and LANEVI. In the next section, we also describe design differences among LANEVI, SOVIA, and KSOVIA, with respect to data sending, data receiving, connection management, and flow control.

The major contributions of this paper can be summarized as follows.

- We classify different approaches to supporting the sockets interface over ULC architecture such as VIA.
- We design and implement KSOVIA, a kernel-level sockets layer over VIA, in order to perform the comparison with the existing LANEVI and SOVIA layer.
- We examine design and implementation issues in supporting the sockets interface, with paying attention to design differences and trade-offs among LANEVI, SOVIA, and KSOVIA.
- We measure the latency and the bandwidth of LANEVI, SOVIA, KSOVIA, and native VIA, on the same platform to understand their relative performance.

- We quantitatively analyze the individual costs associated with the communication (for example, context switching overhead, data copying overhead, and the TCP/IP protocol overhead) by comparing the performance of LANEVI, SOVIA, and KSOVIA.

3. A comparison of design and implementation issues

In this section, we present the internal workings of KSOVIA, and compare its design and implementation issues with LANEVI and SOVIA. The detailed description on LANEVI has not been published in the literature, and thus it is guessed from the source code. Since we are unable to cover SOVIA completely in this paper due to the space limitation, readers are encouraged to refer to [11] for further details on SOVIA.

3.1. Data receiving

In the traditional TCP/IP-based communication architecture, data receiving is handled by an interrupt handler in a transparent way to user applications. In VIA, however, VI Consumer itself should extract completed descriptors from the receive queue (RQ) and post a new one for each incoming data that is delivered asynchronously.

As the LANEVI driver works at the network device driver level, data receiving is handled similarly to the traditional architecture. First, LANEVI prepares a set of receive descriptors and temporary buffers when it is loaded into the kernel. These descriptors and buffers are registered in advance so that the NIC can access them via DMA operations. When a packet arrives from the peer, an interrupt occurs which enables LANEVI to reap the descriptor after copying received data to a socket buffer. The socket buffer is passed on to the upper layer and processed by the TCP/IP protocol stack.

Whereas LANEVI merely transfers IP packets to and from VIA using the kernel-level interfaces provided by kVIPL, SOVIA emulates the sockets interface directly at user-level using VIPL. Whenever an application calls socket(), SOVIA creates a new VI. All the RQs of VIs are connected to a completion queue (CQ) to get the notification of data arrival in a single location. Usually, the application itself checks the CQ either by polling or by using a blocking VIPL interface, to see if there is any pending data. As in LANEVI, SOVIA also uses temporary buffers to store data sent from the peer.

While SOVIA creates a CQ for each process in the system, KSOVIA uses only one system-wide CQ as it is located in the kernel. KSOVIA also utilizes temporary buffers as SOVIA does, although they are allocated in the kernel

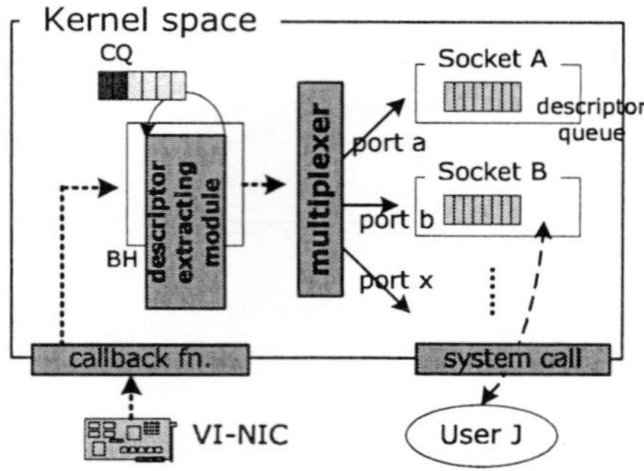

Figure 3. Data receiving in KSOVIA

space in KSOVIA. We elaborate upon the KSOVIA's implementation of recv() in Figure 3. The entire data receiving phase is divided into two sub-phases in KSOVIA. The first phase is to receive data from the peer and the second phase is to multiplex them to a corresponding socket.

When the NIC receives data from the peer, it generates an interrupt which schedules the callback function in KSOVIA. The callback function recognizes the data reception event and delegates the processing to descriptor extracting module (DEM) in the bottom half of the Linux kernel. The DEM obtains a VI handle from the CQ and extracts the completed descriptor from the VI. Since we specify source and destination port numbers in the descriptor, the multiplexer module can enqueue the extracted descriptor to the descriptor queue of the corresponding socket.

As we have seen previously, all of LANEVI, SOVIA, and KSOVIA rely on temporary buffers to satisfy the preposting constraint, because there is excessive synchronization overhead otherwise [11]. As long as we use temporary buffers, one data copy from the temporary buffer to the user buffer is unavoidable. Note that LANEVI experiences one more data copy due to the existence of the kernel socket buffer; one from the temporary buffer to the socket buffer, and the other from the socket buffer to the user buffer.

3.2. Data sending

In LANEVI, sending data via sockets is accomplished with the help of TCP/IP protocols. User data are encapsulated in the socket buffers with TCP and IP headers as they are passed through the TCP/IP protocol stack. Those socket buffers are finally handed over to the LANEVI driver for the transmission. As socket buffers can not be used directly for DMA operations, LANEVI copies the contents of socket buffers to the pre-registered temporary buffers in the kernel. LANEVI also forms send descriptors, and posts them to the SQ.

Unlike LANEVI, SOVIA does not make use of temporary buffers in general. Instead, SOVIA registers the memory region of user data before actual transmission, so that the NIC can access them via DMA operations. This approach avoids the unnecessary data copying and achieves the zero-copy protocol during data sending. However, as users should not modify their data before the NIC finishes the entire sending operation, SOVIA is unable to support the non-blocking mode of send(). For this reason, SOVIA also provides a sending mode that performs one copy from user data to temporary buffers.

In the case of KSOVIA, it is inevitable to use temporary buffers as the user data should be moved into the kernel space first. If users request the send() system call, KSOVIA copies data to temporary buffers located in the kernel, and posts send descriptors to the SQ (the posting phase). After the NIC finishes the sending operation, KSOVIA dequeues them from the SQ (the reaping phase).

3.3. Connection management

Connection management is one of the noticeably different parts among LANEVI, SOVIA, and KSOVIA. In cLAN, when a new node joins, its LANEVI driver automatically connects to every other node in the same cLAN network because VIA is based on the connection-oriented communication model. Establishing a logical connection between two sockets uses special TCP packets and these packets are exchanged through the pre-created VIA connection between two nodes. Thus, when a socket makes a connection with the peer, two separate connection establishments are performed in LANEVI. This mechanism is inefficient, but it is inevitable to emulate connectionless IP services over the connection-oriented VIA.

SOVIA maintains two POSIX threads for connection management. One is the close thread which processes incoming packets after partial close of the connection. The other is the connection thread spawned as a result of the listen() system call. Due to the slight semantic differences in connection models between sockets and VIA, the connection thread is necessary to accept an incoming VI connection request behind the application thread.

KSOVIA does not need a close thread since the kernel is able to receive any incoming packets without resort to the user application. KSOVIA, however, employs a kernel thread to deal with VIA connection requests and replies. As in SOVIA, this kernel thread is created after the listen() system call.

3.4. Flow control

LANEVI has no concern for flow control because flow is mostly managed by the upper TCP layer. Although TCP has many complicated flow control mechanisms, some features of them, such as congestion window, are not necessary in the reliable cluster interconnection networks. Thus, it is required to devise a lightweight flow control mechanism for SOVIA and KSOVIA.

The flow control mechanism used in SOVIA mainly focuses on increasing the bandwidth. SOVIA supports a credit-based flow control which is similar to the TCP's sliding window protocol. It has a notion of windows size w, which denotes the maximum number of data packets the sender is allowed to transmit without waiting for an acknowledgment. When a socket is created, w receive descriptors are pre-posted in the RQ. Whenever the sender transmits a data packet, it decreases w by one to denote that one of the receive descriptors has been consumed. If w reaches zero, the sender stops to transmit data packets until w becomes a positive number. Windows size w is increased by one if an acknowledgement is delivered to the sender. To enhance the bandwidth further, acknowledgements can be delayed and piggybacked to data packets. We have implemented the same flow control algorithm in KSOVIA.

4. Evaluations

4.1. Experimental setup

We have measured the performance of LANEVI, SOVIA and KSOVIA with the Linux kernel 2.4.18 and cLAN driver version 2.0.1. As the original kVIPL supplied by Emulex does not provide connection management APIs, we have slightly extended kVIPL to implement missing interfaces. The hardware platform used for performance evaluation is two Linux servers, each consisting of 1.6GHz Intel Pentium 4 processor, 512KB L2 cache, and 768MB of main memory. Two cLAN1000 network adapters are attached to a 32-bit 33MHz PCI slot of each server without any intermediate switch.

We carry out microbenchmarks which measure the one-way latency and the unidirectional bandwidth. The one-way latency is measured by a half of the round-trip time from several ping-pong tests. The unidirectional bandwidth is obtained by measuring the average time spent for sending 100,000 packets repeatedly. In addition, we use FTP server and client programs to verify the functionality and to evaluate the performance of real sockets applications.

Communication mechanisms evaluated in this paper are summarized in Table 1. The measurement results of VIPL and VIPL_POLL are obtained from microbenchmarks written in VIPL and they are considered as the baseline of other results. Note that SOVIA can be implemented either using non-blocking APIs (SOVIA_POLL) or using blocking APIs (SOVIA). On the contrary, KSOVIA does not use non-blocking APIs because polling is not allowed inside the kernel.

Table 1. Evaluated communication mechanisms

Communication mechanisms	Description
VIPL_POLL	Use VIPL with non-blocking APIs in the user space
VIPL	Use VIPL with blocking APIs in the user space
LANEVI	Use the traditional TCP/IP using the LANEVI driver
SOVIA_POLL	Use a user-level sockets layer over VIA with non-blocking APIs
SOVIA	Use a user-level sockets layer over VIA with blocking APIs
KSOVIA	Use a kernel-level sockets layer over VIA (blocking APIs are used implicitly)

4.2. One-way latency

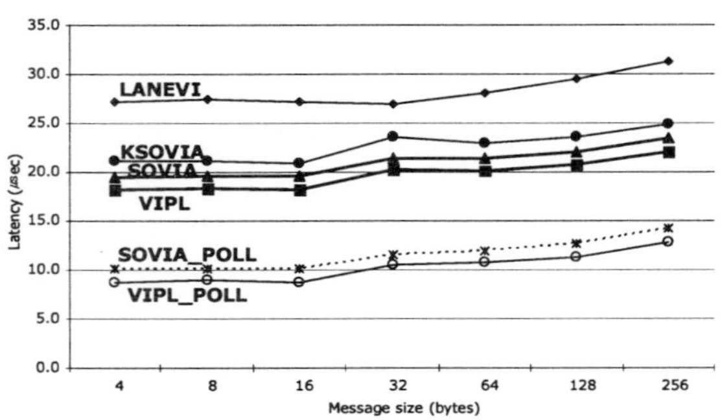

Figure 4. One-way latency for small messages

Figure 4 shows the measured one-way latency when the message size varies from 4 bytes to 256 bytes. As expected, VIPL_POLL shows the smallest latency for all the message sizes. Note that both VIPL_POLL and SOVIA_POLL check the arrival of new data by polling the completion queue. In general, network applications can not use this polling mechanism because it wastes most of CPU times on busy waiting. Thus, these results are only meaningful as the practical lower bound of the one-way latency. Since other communication mechanisms, such as VIPL, SOVIA, KSOVIA, and LANEVI, are based on blocking APIs, they exhibit the higher latency than VIPL_POLL and SOVIA_POLL.

From Figure 4, it can be seen that SOVIA shows the constantly higher latency than VIPL by about 1.3 μsec. It is mainly due to the added complexity in the SOVIA layer to support sockets interface. Figure 4 also illustrates that the latency of KSOVIA is higher than that of SOVIA by 1.7 μsec.

As we have designed KSOVIA to behave the same as SOVIA, the gap between KSOVIA and SOVIA mostly comes from the fact that KSOVIA is located in the kernel. For further analysis on the factors affecting the latency, we measure the time spent for calling a system call (labeled as *send()+recv()*) and for data copy (labeled as *memory copy*). We present the results in Figure 5 in conjunction with the latency of VIPL and SOVIA. Note that *baseline transmission*

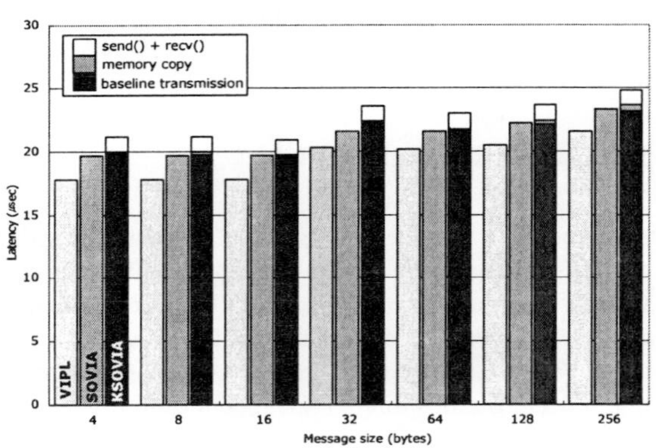

Figure 5. Break down of the one-way latency of KSOVIA for small messages

denotes the latency of KSOVIA except the time for system calls and data copy. We can observe that most of the difference in latency between KSOVIA and SOVIA stems from the context switching overhead between the kernel and the user space around the send() and recv() system calls. The data copying overhead is negligible in Figure 5, as the message size is small.

Compared to KSOVIA, LANEVI has the additional TCP/IP overhead, exhibiting the worst latency in Figure 4. From the difference in latency between LANEVI and KSOVIA, we can roughly conjecture that LANEVI spends 22% of its time (about 6 μsec out of 27.2 μsec) for the TCP/IP protocol processing.

4.3. Unidirectional bandwidth

Figure 6 illustrates the unidirectional bandwidth of each communication mechanism studied in this paper. First, we can see that LANEVI shows the higher bandwidth than any other mechanisms when the message size is less then 2Kbytes. This is because TCP's Nagle algorithm combines small messages together before a packet is transmitted. Although we do not enable this feature for SOVIA and KSOVIA in the measurement, it is already reported in [11] that SOVIA outperforms LANEVI even for the small mes-

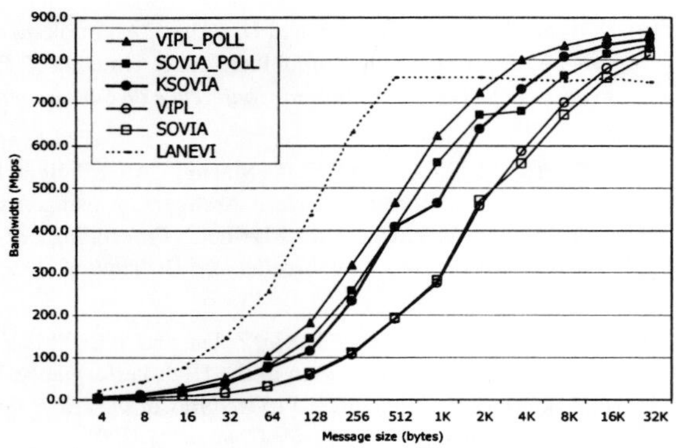

Figure 6. Unidirectional bandwidth

sage sizes if we add the similar ability to SOVIA. The bandwidth of LANEVI is saturated to 760 Mbps at the 512-byte message size and remains the smallest when the message size is larger than 16 Kbytes.

As SOVIA is implemented using VIPL, the performance of SOVIA and SOVIA_POLL are bound to that of VIPL and VIPL_POLL, respectively. The minor difference between SOVIA and VIPL is due to the protocol maintenance overhead in SOVIA.

It is impressive that KSOVIA delivers much higher bandwidth than SOVIA, in spite of the context switching overhead which has increased the latency slightly. SOVIA performs the posting phase and the reaping phase in the same send() system call, while KSOVIA defers the reaping phase to the bottom half in order to process multiple descriptors in a single run. This maximizes the concurrency during data sending in KSOVIA and leads to the bandwidth comparable to SOVIA_POLL. If SOVIA supports this kind of concurrency in sending, the bandwidth of SOVIA is likely to increase further.

4.4. FTP performance

Table 2. FTP bandwdith

	File A		File B	
Size	13,374,187 bytes		168,919,040 bytes	
	sec	MBps	sec	Mbps
LANEVI	0.137	744.80	1.74	740.60
SOVIA	0.134	778.91	1.8	762.57
KSOVIA	0.125	816.30	1.56	826.12
Local copy	0.063	1619.63	1.255	1026.89

We run an FTP server (linux-ftpd-0.17) and client (netkit-ftp-0.17) over different communication mechanisms such as LANEVI, SOVIA, and KSOVIA, in order to verify their functional validity and to measure the performance of real sockets applications. Two files are transferred from the server to the client; one is small (12.75 MB) and the other is rather large (161.1 MB). We have arranged that all the files reside in ram disks to avoid the influence of the disk subsystems. Table 2 summarizes the performance of file transfers. First of all, as the bandwidth of local copy using *cp* command is large enough exceeding 1 Gbps, we can see that the FTP performance is not bounded by the ram disks performance.

Table 2 shows that LANEVI achieves 91.2% (for small file) and 89.6% (for large file) of the bandwidth of KSOVIA. These results are analogous to those obtained from microbenchmarks. As described in the previous section, KSOVIA shows a little higher bandwidth than SOVIA due to several kernel-level optimizations.

5. Related work

The most popular communication layers used in the cluster environments are MPI (Message Passing Interface) and Berkeley sockets interface [4]. Since sockets interface provides more general communication interface, many researches have been performed to support the sockets API on VIA. VIsocket [16] proposed by Itoh et al. is similar to KSOVIA in that it provides sockets functionality below the STREAMS module in Solaris by collapsing internal TCP/IP layers. However, the design and performance details of VIsocket have not been published yet.

Recently, InfiniBand Architecture (IBA) [15] has been standardized by the industry to develop the next generation high-performance interconnection network. As IBA adopts many features from VIA, its software layer is very similar to VIPL. Currently, there are many ongoing research projects to build new convenient layers on top of IBA, such as IPoIB [17] and SDP [17]. IPoIB provides the standardized IP encapsulation over IBA fabrics, whose role is identical to that of LANEVI in a conceptual viewpoint. Sockets Direct Protocol (SDP) defines a standard wire protocol to support stream sockets over IBA bypassing the traditional TCP/IP protocol stack. SDP is essentially a kernel-level sockets layer over IBA and its purpose is the same as that of KSOVIA. Even though some implementations of SDP are availble [17][20][21], there is little publicly available documetation of internal implementation and comparison among several design choices we focus on. Due to many similarities between VIA and IBA, we believe the results obtained in this paper are also useful in developing such layers as IPoIB and SDP.

6. Concluding remarks

This paper compares three different approaches to supporting the sockets interface over ULC architecture. We utilize VIA, one of ULC architectures, for the comparison. We compare LANEVI, SOVIA, and KSOVIA which is developed based on VIA. LANEVI emulates the IP layer on VIA, while SOVIA and KSOVIA represent a user-level and a kernel-level sockets layer over VIA, respectively. Since there is no reference implementation for kernel-level sockets layers, we have designed and implemented the KSOVIA layer in this paper.

From the measurement results, we observe that LANEVI exhibits the worst performance among all the approaches evaluated in this paper. By comparing the latency of LANEVI and KSOVIA, we can roughly conjecture that LANEVI spends 22% of its time (about 6 μsec out of 27.2 μsec) for the TCP/IP protocol processing. It is also identified from the difference in latency between KSOVIA and SOVIA that the context switching overhead is less than 2 μsec. SOVIA or KSOVIA has the added complexity to support sockets interface compared to native VIA, which increases the latency by about 1 μsec.

Putting it all together, we can conclude that there is no reason to use the LANEVI driver for sockets-based applications. It shows the worst performance both in terms of latency and bandwidth, and has the additional overhead in connection management to emulate connectionless IP services on the connection-oriented VIA. On the other hand, SOVIA and KSOVIA have their own pros and cons. Even though SOVIA presents the slightly lower bandwidth than KSOVIA, it is useful when applications are latency-sensitive and do not use fork() or exec() system calls. KSOVIA can be used effectively for applications which require high bandwidth or the full compatibility with the existing sockets interface.

We are going to observe the behavior of the various cluster and Grid applications to see the impact of the different approaches to support sockets interface on real-world applications. Additionally, we plan to extend our work on to the recent InfiniBand Architecture by investigating such layers as IPoIB and SDP.

References

[1] http://www.top500.org, TOP500 Supercomputer sites.

[2] Compaq Corporation, Intel Corporation, and Microsoft Corporation, *Virtual Interface Architecture Specification*, Version 1.0, 1997.

[3] M. Baker, editor, Cluster Computing White Paper (Version 2.0), IEEE Task Force on Cluster Computing, Dec. 2000.

[4] M. K. McKusick, K. Bostic, M. J. Karels and J. S. Quarterman, *The Design and Implementation of the 4.4 BSD Operating System*, Addison-Wesley Publishing Inc., 1996.

[5] P. Bozeman and B. Saphir, "A Modular High Performance Implementation of the Virtual Interface Architecture," *Proceedings of Extreme Linux Conference*, 1999.

[6] P. Buonadonna, A. Geweke, and D. Culler, "An Implementation and Analysis of the Virtual Interface Architecture," *Proceedings of ACM International Conference on Supercomputing*, 1998.

[7] J.-L. Yu, M.-S. Lee and S.-R. Maeng, "An Efficient Implementation of Virtual Interface Architecture using Adaptive Transfer Mechanism on Myrinet," *Proceedings of International Conference on Parallel and Distributed Systems*, 2001.

[8] Y. Chen, X. Wang, Z. Jiao, J. Xie, Z. Du, and S. Li, "MyVIA: A Design and Implementation of the High Performance Virtual Interface Architecture," *Proceedings of the IEEE International Conference on Cluster Computing*, 2002.

[9] http://www.emulex.com/products/legacy/vi/clan1000.html, Emulex Corporation-Products, 2003.

[10] Emulex Inc., cLAN for Linux: Software User's Guide, 2001.

[11] J.-S. Kim, K. Kim, S.-I. Jung, and S. Ha, "Design and Implementation of a User-level Sockets Layer over Virtual Interface Architecture," *Concurrency and Computation: Practice and Experience*, Volume 15, Issue 7-8, 2003.

[12] M. Fischer, "GMSOCKS - A Direct Sockets Implementations on Myrinet," *Proceedings of the IEEE International Conference on Cluster Computing*, 2001.

[13] P. Balaji, P. Shivan, P. Wyckoff, and D. Panda, "High Performance User Level Sockets over Gigabit Ethernet," *Proceedings of the IEEE International Conference on Cluster Computing*, 2002.

[14] F. Seifert and H. Kohmann, "SCI SOCKET - A Fast Socket Implementation over SCI," White paper, Dophin Interconnect Solutions Inc.

[15] http://www.infinibandta.org, InfiniBand Trade Association.

[16] M. Itoh, T. Ishizaki and M. Kishimoto, "Accelerated Socket Communication in System Area Network," *Proceedings of the IEEE International Conference on Cluster Computing*, 2000.

[17] http://infiniband.sourceforge.net, InfiniBand Linux SourceForge Project.

[18] J. Liu, J. Wu, and D. K. Panda, "High Performance RDMA-Based MPI Implementation over InfiniBand," *International Journal of Parallel Programming*, 2004.

[19] http://old-www.nersc.gov/research/FTG/mvich, MVICH - MPI for the Virtual Interface Architecture.

[20] http://www.openib.org, OpenIB.org.

[21] P. Balaji, S. Narravula, K. Vaidyanathan, S. Krishnamoorthy, J. Wu, and D. K. Panda, "Sockets Direct Procotol over InfiniBand in Clusters: Is it Beneficial?," *Proceedings of the IEEE International Symposium on Performance Analysis of Systems and Software*, 2004.

An Empirical Approach for Efficient All-to-All Personalized Communication on Ethernet Switched Clusters *

Ahmad Faraj Xin Yuan
Department of Computer Science, Florida State University, Tallahassee, FL 32306
{faraj, xyuan}@cs.fsu.edu

Abstract

All-to-all personalized communication (AAPC) is one of the most commonly used communication patterns in parallel applications. Developing an efficient AAPC routine is difficult since many system parameters can affect the performance of an AAPC algorithm. In this paper, we investigate an empirical approach for automatically generating efficient AAPC routines for Ethernet switched clusters. This approach applies when the application execution environment is decided, and it allows efficient customized AAPC routines to be created. Experimental results show that the empirical approach generates routines that consistently achieve high performance on clusters with different network topologies. In many cases, the automatically generated routines out-perform conventional AAPC implementations to a large degree.

Keywords: All-to-all personalized communication, Ethernet switched cluster, empirical technique, cluster computing, MPI.
Technical areas: MPI, cluster computing.

1. Introduction

All-to-all personalized communication (AAPC) is one of the most common communication patterns in high performance computing. In AAPC, each node in a system sends a different message of the same size to every other node. The Message Passing Interface (MPI) routine that realizes AAPC is *MPI_Alltoall* [14]. AAPC appears in many high performance applications, including matrix transpose, multi-dimensional convolution, and data redistribution.

Switched Ethernet is the most widely used local-area-network (LAN) technology. Many Ethernet-switched clusters of workstations are used to perform high performance computing. For such clusters to be effective, communications must be carried out as efficiently as possible.

Although a large number of AAPC algorithms have been proposed [1, 5, 8, 9, 12, 16, 18, 21], developing an efficient AAPC routine is still a challenging task. The main challenge comes from the fact that many system parameters can significantly affect the performance of an AAPC algorithm. These system parameters include operating system context switching overheads, the ratio between the network and the processor speeds, the switch design, the amount of buffer memory in switches, and the network topology. These parameters are difficult to model, and it is virtually impossible for the routine developer to make the right choices for different platforms.

The AAPC routines in existing communication libraries such as MPICH [15, 19] and LAM/MPI [11] are implemented before the application execution environment is decided. As a result, these routines do not sufficiently incorporate the knowledge of the system parameters. For example, topology specific algorithms cannot be used since the routines are implemented before the topology is decided. Hence, although these routines correctly carry out the AAPC operation on different platforms, they cannot achieve high performance in many cases.

In this paper, we investigate an empirical approach for automatically generating efficient AAPC routines for Ethernet switched clusters. This approach applies when the application execution environment is decided. Since the AAPC routines are finalized after the execution environment is fixed, architecture specific algorithms can be considered. Furthermore, while it is difficult to model system parameters, the overall impact of the system parameters on AAPC performance can be measured empirically. By utilizing the platform specific information and employing the empirical approach to select the best implementations, it is possible to create an efficient customized AAPC routine for a partic-

* This work is partially supported by NSF grants ANI-0106706, CCR-0208892, and CCF-0342540.

ular platform.

We implemented an empirical based AAPC routine generator for Ethernet switched clusters. The generator includes a module that takes topology information as input and produces topology specific AAPC implementations. In addition, the generator also maintains an extensive set of topology independent AAPC implementations that can potentially achieve high performance in different situations. The implementations in the final customized AAPC routine are selected from the topology independent and topology specific implementations using an empirical approach.

We present AAPC algorithms maintained in the generator and describe the method to generate the customized AAPC routines. We carried out extensive experiments on Ethernet switched clusters with many different network topologies. The results indicate that the generated routines consistently achieve high performance on clusters with different network topologies. In many cases, the generated routines out-perform conventional AAPC implementations, including the ones in LAM/MPI [11] and a recently improved MPICH [19], to a large degree.

The rest of the paper is organized as follows. Section 2 describes the related work. Section 3 discusses the network and performance models. Section 4 presents AAPC algorithms. Section 5 describes the procedure to generate the customized routines. Section 6 reports experimental results. Finally, the conclusions are presented in Section 7.

2. Related Work

AAPC has been extensively studied due to its importance. A large number of optimal AAPC algorithms for different network topologies with different network models were developed. Many of the algorithms were designed for specific network topologies that are used in parallel machines, including hypercube [9, 21], mesh [1, 8, 16, 18], torus [12], k-ary n-cube [21], and fat tree [4]. Topology independent AAPC algorithms were proposed in [8, 19]. Heuristic algorithms were developed for AAPC on irregular topologies [13]. A framework for AAPC that is realized with indirect communications was reported in [10]. Efficient AAPC scheduling schemes for clusters connected by a single switch was proposed in [17]. While the existing AAPC algorithms take some aspects of the architecture into consideration, they may not achieve the best performance in practice since other system parameters may also affect the performance. This paper is not concerned with a particular AAPC algorithm, instead, it focuses on using an empirical approach to obtain customized AAPC routines that are efficient in practice. The empirical technique has been applied successfully to various computational library routines [6, 22]. This approach has also been applied to tune one-to-all and one-to-many types of collective communications [20]. The issues in one-to-all and one-to-many communications are different from those in AAPC.

3. Performance model

We will describe the cost model that we use to estimate the communication performance of the algorithms. Our model reflects the following costs:

1. *Per pair communication time.* The time taken to send a message of size n between any two nodes can be modeled as $\alpha + n\beta$, where α is the startup overhead and β is the per byte transmission time.
2. *Sequentialization overheads.* Some algorithms partition AAPC into a number of phases. A communication in a phase can only start after the completion of some communications in the previous phases. This sequentialization may limit the parallelism in AAPC. We use the notation θ to denote the sequentialization overheads between 2 phases. For an algorithm that realizes AAPC in m phases, the sequentialization overheads is $(m-1)\theta$.
3. *Synchronization overheads.* Many AAPC algorithms introduce synchronization to reduce network contention. There are two types of synchronizations, the system wide synchronization and the light-weight synchronization that ensures that a communication happens before another. The light-weight synchronization, also called *light barrier*, is usually implemented by having one node send a zero byte message to another node. We will use δ_l to denote the cost of a light-weight synchronization. The system wide synchronization is typically implemented with a barrier operation (e.g. *MPI_Barrier* in MPI). We will use δ_h to denote the cost of a system wide synchronization. In most cases, δ_h is larger than δ_l, which in turn, is larger than θ.
4. *Contention overheads.* Contention can happen in three cases: *node contention* when more than one node tries to send messages to the same node, *link contention* when more than one communication uses the same links in the network, and *switch contention* when the amount of data passing a switch is more than what the switch can handle. We will use γ_n to denote node contention, γ_l for link contention, and γ_s for switch contention. We will use

$\gamma = \gamma_n + \gamma_l + \gamma_s$ to denote the sum of all contention costs.

Using this model, the time to complete a collective communication is expressed in five terms: the startup time term that is a multiple of α, the bandwidth term that is a multiple of $n\beta$, the sequentialization costs term that is a multiple of θ, the synchronization costs term that is a multiple of δ_l or δ_h, and the contention costs term that is a combination of γ_n, γ_l, and γ_s. Notice that some parameters in the model such as the sequentialization costs and contention costs can contribute significantly to the overall communication costs; however, they are difficult to quantify. In practice, they cannot be measured accurately since they are non-deterministic in nature. As a result, this cost model is used only to justify the selection of algorithms, but not to accurately predict the performance.

4. AAPC algorithms

This section describes the potential AAPC algorithms, including both topology independent algorithms and topology specific algorithms. We will assume that p is the number of processes and n is the message size.

4.1. Algorithms for small messages

In general, algorithms for AAPC with small messages are concerned about reducing the startup and sequentialization costs while algorithms for large messages usually attempt to reduce the contention and the synchronization costs. Since the startup and sequentialization costs do not depend on the network topology, all algorithms for small messages are topology independent.

Simple. This algorithm basically posts all receives and all sends, starts the communications, and waits for all communications to finish. Let $i \rightarrow j$ denote the communication from node i to node j. The order of communications for node i is $i \rightarrow 0$, $i \rightarrow 1$, ..., $i \rightarrow p-1$. The estimated time is $(p-1)\alpha + (p-1)n\beta + \gamma$. This algorithm does not have sequentialization overheads since all communications are carried out in one phase.

Spreading Simple. This algorithm is similar to the simple algorithm except that the order of communications for node i is $i \rightarrow i+1$, $i \rightarrow i+2$, ..., $i \rightarrow (i+p-1) \bmod p$. By changing the order of communications, node contention may potentially be reduced. The estimated time is the same as that for the simple algorithm except that the γ term might be smaller.

Simple and spreading simple algorithms minimize the sequentialization costs. Another extreme is to minimize the startup costs. The **Bruck**[2] and **recursive doubling** algorithms achieve this by minimizing the number of messages that each node sends at the cost of sending extra data.

Recursive doubling. This algorithm first performs an all-gather operation, which distributes all data in each node to all other nodes, and then copies the right portion of the data to the receiving buffer. Thus, in terms of communication, the recursive doubling algorithm for AAPC is similar to the recursive doubling algorithm for an all-gather operation with a message size of pn. Details about this algorithm can be found in [19]. When the number of nodes is a power of two, the estimated time is $lg(p)\alpha + (p-1)pn\beta + (lg(p)-1)\theta + \gamma$. When the number of processes is not a power of two, the cost almost doubles [19].

Bruck. This is another $lg(p)$-step algorithm that sends a less amount of extra data in comparison to the recursive doubling algorithm. Details can be found in [2, 19]. When the number of processes is a power of two, the estimated time is $lg(p)\alpha + \frac{np}{2}lg(p)\beta + (lg(p)-1)\theta + \gamma$. The startup costs term and the sequentialization costs terms for this algorithm are exactly the same as those for the recursive doubling algorithm. However, the bandwidth term is smaller. This algorithm also works with slightly larger overheads when the number of processes is not a power of two.

Between the two extremes, the generator maintains the **2D mesh** and **3D mesh** algorithms that represent compromises between minimizing the number of messages and minimizing the number of phases. Like the recursive doubling algorithm, both algorithms perform all-gather followed by a copy.

2D mesh. This algorithm applies only when $p = x \times y$ where the processes are organized as a logical $x \times y$ mesh. The algorithm tries to find the factoring such that x and y are close to $\sqrt{p}$. In the worst case, $x = 1$, $y = p$, and this algorithm degenerates to the simple algorithm. Assume that $x = y = \sqrt{p}$, the all-gather operation is first performed in the x dimension with message size equals to pn and then in the y dimension with message size equal to $p\sqrt{p}n$. Thus, the estimated time is $2(\sqrt{p}-1)\alpha + (p-1)pn\beta + \theta + \gamma$. Compared to the simple algorithm, this algorithm sends a smaller number of messages, but more data. The communications in this algorithm are carried out in two phases resulting in a θ term in the estimated time. Compared to the recursive doubling algorithm, this algorithm sends a larger number of messages in a smaller number of phases.

3D mesh. This algorithm applies only when $p = x \times y \times z$ where the processes are organized as a logical $x \times y \times z$ mesh. The algorithm tries to find the factoring such that x, y, and z are close to $\sqrt[3]{p}$. In the worst case, it degenerates to the 2D mesh algorithm or even the simple algorithm. Assume $x = y = z = \sqrt[3]{p}$, the estimated time is $3(\sqrt[3]{p} - 1)\alpha + (p - 1)pn\beta + 2\theta + \gamma$. Compared to the 2D mesh algorithm, this algorithm sends a smaller number of messages, but consists of three phases, which introduce a 2θ sequentialization overhead.

4.2. Algorithms for large messages

To achieve high performance for AAPC with large messages, one of the most important issues is to reduce network contention in the system. However, it must be noted that a contention free AAPC algorithm may not achieve the best performance in practice since most systems can handle a certain degree of contention effectively, which indicates that algorithms that allow a limited degree of contention will likely offer the highest performance. Next, we will describe the AAPC algorithms for large messages.

Ring. This algorithm partitions the all-to-all communication into $p-1$ steps (phases). In step i, node j sends a messages to node $(j + i)$ *mod* p and receives a message from node $(j - i)$ *mod* p. Thus, there is no node contention if all phases execute in a lock-step fashion. Since different nodes may finish a phase and start a new phase at different times, this algorithm only reduces node contention. The ring algorithm does not consider switch contention and link contention. The estimated time is $(p-1)(\alpha + n\beta) + (p-2)\theta + \gamma_n + \gamma_s + \gamma_l$.

Ring with light barrier. In this algorithm, light barriers are added between the communications in different phases to eliminate potential node contention. Note that we assume that node contention happens when more than one node sends large data messages to a receiver and ignore the node contention caused by a large data message and a tiny synchronization message. The estimated time is $(p - 1)(\alpha + n\beta) + (p - 2)\delta_l + \gamma_s + \gamma_l$. Compared to the ring algorithm, this algorithm incurs overheads for the light barriers while reducing the contention overheads.

Ring with MPI barrier. The ring with light barrier algorithm allows the phases to proceed in an asynchronous manner which may cause too many data to be injected into the network. In this algorithm, MPI barriers are added between two phases, which makes the phases execute in a lock-step fashion resulting in a less likely switch contention since the total amount of data in the network at a given time is less than the amount of data transferred in one phase. The estimated time is $(p - 1)(\alpha + n\beta) + (p - 2)\delta_h + \gamma_l$. Compared to the ring with light barrier algorithm, this algorithm increases synchronization overheads while reducing the contention overheads.

Ring with N MPI barriers. Adding a barrier between every two phases may be an over-kill and may result in the network being under-utilized since most networks and processors can effectively handle a certain degree of contention. The ring with N MPI barriers algorithm adds a total of N, $1 \leq N \leq p - 2$, barriers in the whole communication. An MPI barrier is added every $\frac{p-1}{N+1}$ phases. This allows the contention overheads and the synchronization overheads to be compromised. The estimated time for this algorithm is $(p - 1)(\alpha + n\beta) + N\delta_h + \gamma_n + \gamma_s + \gamma_l$. This family of algorithms contains $p-2$ different algorithms (the potential value for N being $1..p - 2$): **Ring with $N = 1$ MPI barriers**, **Ring with $N = 2$ MPI barriers**, ..., **Ring with $N = p - 2$ MPI barriers** algorithms. These algorithms are implemented as one routine with an algorithm parameter N.

Pair. This algorithm only works when the number of processes is a power of two. This algorithm partitions the all-to-all communication into $p - 1$ steps (phases). In step i, node j exchanges a message with node $j \oplus i$ (exclusive or). The estimated time is the same as that for the ring algorithm. However, in the pair algorithm, each node interacts with one other node in each phase compared to two in the ring algorithm. The reduction of the coordination among the nodes may improve the overall communication efficiency. Similar to the ring family algorithms, we have **pair with light barrier**, **pair with MPI barrier**, and **pair with N MPI barriers** algorithms.

The ring family and the pair family algorithms try to remove node contention and indirectly reduce other contention overheads by adding synchronizations to slow down communications. These algorithms are topology independent and may not be sufficient to eliminate link contention since communications in one phase may share the same link in the network. The topology specific algorithm removes link contention by considering the network topology.

Topology specific algorithm. We use a message scheduling algorithm that we developed in [5]. This algorithm finds the optimal message scheduling for a system with any number of Ethernet switches. The idea is to partition the all–to–all communication into phases such that (1) communications within each phase do not have contention, and (2) a minimum number of phases are used to complete the communication. To prevent communications in different phases from affecting each other, light weight barriers are added. Details about this algorithm can be found in [5]. The estimated time for this algorithm depends on the topology.

5. Generating AAPC routines

Armed with the algorithms described in the previous section, the automatic AAPC routine generator uses an empirical approach to determine the best AAPC implementations for a particular platform and for different ranges of message sizes. The generator produces a customized AAPC routine in three steps.

1. The topology specific implementation is generated using the topology information. After this step, the topology specific routine is treated the same as other topology independent routines.
2. The best implementations are determined for a set of message sizes, which includes 1B, 64B, 256B, 1KB, 2KB, 4KB, 8KB, 16KB, 32KB, 64KB, 128KB, and 256KB. For each message size, the best implementation is selected by running all algorithms for the size and empirically measuring the performance. The performance measurement follows the approach in Mpptest [7], which is shown in Figure 1.

```
MPI_Barrier(MPI_COMM_WORLD);
start = MPI_Wtime();
for (count = 0; count < ITER_NUM; count ++) {
  alltoall_simple(...);
}
elapsed_time = MPI_Wtime() - start;
```

Figure 1. Measuring AAPC performance.

3. The exact message sizes that warrant the changes of algorithms are determined in this step. The generator logically partitions message sizes into ranges including $(1B, 64B)$, $(64B, 256B)$, ..., $(128KB, 256KB)$. The system assumes the same algorithm for message sizes $\geq$ 256KB. The system examines each range (s, e). If the same implementation is associated with both s and e, then the implementation is selected for the whole range (s, e). If s and e are associated with different implementations, let I_s be the implementation associated with s and I_e be the implementation associated with e. The generator will determine the size $msize$, $s \leq msize \leq e$, that the algorithm should change from I_s to I_e, that is, I_s is selected for range $(s, msize)$ and I_e is selected for range $(msize, e)$. A binary search algorithm is used to determine $msize$. For each point in the binary search, the performance of both I_s and I_e is measured and compared. Once implementations are decided for the different ranges of message sizes, the generator uses this information to produce the final customized routine.

6. Experiments

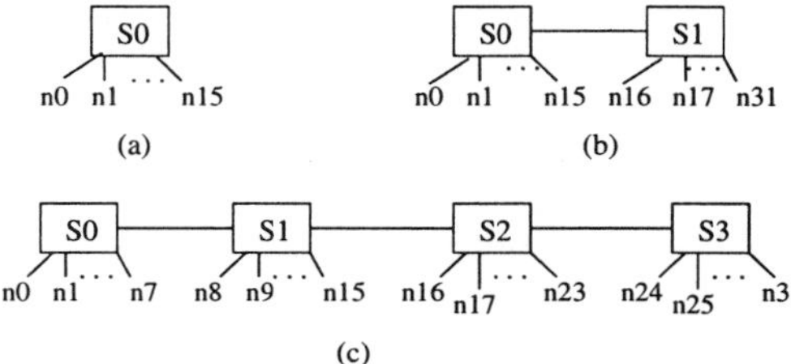

Figure 2. Topologies used in the experiments

The experiments are performed on Ethernet-switched clusters. The nodes in the clusters are Dell Dimension 2400 with a 2.8GHz P4 processor, 128MB of memory, and 40GHz of disk space. All machines run Linux (Fedora) with the 2.6.5-1.358 kernel. The Ethernet card in each machine is Broadcom BCM 5705 with the driver from Broadcom. These machines are connected to Dell Powerconnect 2224 and Dell Powerconnect 2324 100Mbps Ethernet switches.

We conducted experiments on different topologies that are depicted in Figure 2. Figure 2 (a) is a 16-node cluster connected by a single switch. Clusters connected by a single Ethernet switch is common in practice. Figure 2 (b) is a 32-node cluster, connected by 2 switches with 16 nodes on each switch. Part (c) is a 32-node cluster of 4 switches with 8 nodes on each switch. We will refer to these topologies as *topology (a)*, *topology (b)*, and *topology (c)*.

We compare the performance of the generated AAPC routine with *MPI_Alltoall* in LAM/MPI 6.5.9 and a recently improved MPICH 1.2.6 [19]. The generated routines use LAM/MPI point–to–point (send and recv) primitives. We will use the term GENERATED to denote the automatically generated routines. To make a fair comparison, we port the *MPI_Alltoall* routine in MPICH to LAM/MPI and use MPICH-LAM to denote the ported routine.

6.1. The generated routines and generation time

Table 1 shows the algorithms selected in the automatically generated routines for the topologies in Figure 2. For comparison purposes, the algorithms

Table 1. Algorithms in the generated routines

Topo.	Generated AAPC routine
(a)	Simple ($1 \leq n < 8718$) Pair with light barrier ($8718 \leq n < 31718$) Pair w. N=1 MPI barriers ($31718 \leq n < 65532$) Pair w. N=5 MPI barriers ($65532 \leq n < 72032$) Pair w. MPI barrier ($72032 \leq n$)
(b)	Bruck ($1 \leq n < 112$) Simple ($112 \leq n < 29594$) Ring w. light barrier ($29594 \leq n < 144094$) Ring w. N=1 MPI barriers ($144094 \leq n$)
(c)	Bruck ($1 \leq n < 112$) Simple ($112 \leq n < 581$) Ring ($581 \leq n < 8656$) Ring w. light barrier ($8656 \leq n < 65532$) Topology specific ($65532 \leq n$)

Table 2. Algorithms in LAM/MPI and MPICH

LAM/MPI	MPICH
Simple	Bruck ($1 \leq n \leq 256$) Spreading Simple ($257 < n \leq 32K$) Pair ($32K < n$ and p is a power of 2) Ring ($32K < n$ and p is not a power of 2)

in LAM/MPI and MPICH are depicted in Table 2. From Table 1, we can see that for different topologies, the optimal algorithms for AAPC are quite different, which indicates that the one-scheme-fits-all approach in MPICH and LAM cannot achieve good performance for different topologies. As will be shown in the performance study, while the MPICH AAPC algorithms are more sophisticated than the LAM/MPI AAPC algorithm, they perform worse for some topologies. This indicates that, to achieve good AAPC performance, the ability to adapt to the network topology is at least as important as finding good algorithms. The topology specific routine was selected for topology (c). For other topologies, using system wide synchronizations is effective in reducing network contention without knowing the network topology.

The time for generating the tuned routine is 1040 seconds for topology (a), 8913 seconds for topology (b), and 7294 seconds for topology (c). The tuning time depends on many factors such as the number of algorithms, the network topology, and how the performance is measured. The time is in par with that for other empirical approach based systems such as ATLAS [22]. Hence, like other empirical based systems, our approach can be used when the routine tuning time is relatively insignificant, e.g. when the application has a long execution time, or when the application needs to be executed repeatedly on the same system.

6.2. Performance

Figure 1 shows the code segment we use for measuring the performance. The number of iterations in each execution is varied according to the message size: more iterations are used for small message sizes to offset the clock inaccuracy. For the message ranges 1B-3KB, 4KB-12KB, 16KB-96KB, 128KB-384KB, and 512KB-, we use 100, 50, 20, 10, and 5 iterations, respectively. The results are the averages of three executions. We use the *average* time among all nodes as the performance metric. Before we present the results, we will point out two general observations in the experiments. For all example topologies:

1. Ignoring the minor inaccuracy in performance measurement, the generated AAPC routine never performs worse than the best of LAM, MPICH, and MPICH-LAM.
2. There exist some ranges of message sizes such that GENERATED out-performs each of LAM, MPICH-LAM, and MPICH by at least 40%.

Figure 3 shows the performance on topology (a). For small messages ($1 \leq n \leq 256$), both LAM and GENERATED use the simple algorithm, which offers higher performance than the Bruck algorithm used in MPICH. When the message size is 512 bytes, MPICH changes to the spreading simple algorithm, which has similar performance to the simple algorithm. GENERATED, LAM, and MPICH-LAM have similar performance for message sizes in the range from 257 bytes to 9K bytes. As shown in Figure 3 (c), GENERATED significantly out-performs other schemes when the message size is larger than 16KB. For example, when the message size is 128KB, the time for GENERATED is 200.1ms and the time for MPICH (the best among LAM, MPICH, and MPICH-LAM) is 348.2ms, which constitutes a 74% speedup.

The results for topology (b) are shown in Figure 4. For this topology, the simple algorithm in LAM performs reasonably well for medium and large sized messages. In many cases, the simple algorithm performs better than the algorithms used in MPICH. GENERATED and LAM have similar performance for a very wide range of medium and large messages. For small messages, GENERATED offers higher performance than LAM in some cases and MPICH in other cases. For example, for the message size of 1 byte, the time for GENERATED and MPICH-LAM is 0.66ms while the time for LAM is 2.40ms. GENERATED improves over LAM by 264%. For the message size of 256 bytes, the time for GENERATED and LAM is 7.6ms while the time for MPICH-LAM is 11.2ms. GENERATED improves over MPICH-LAM by 47%.

The results for topology (c) are shown in Figure 5. For small messages, the trend is similar to that for topology (b). For medium and large mes-

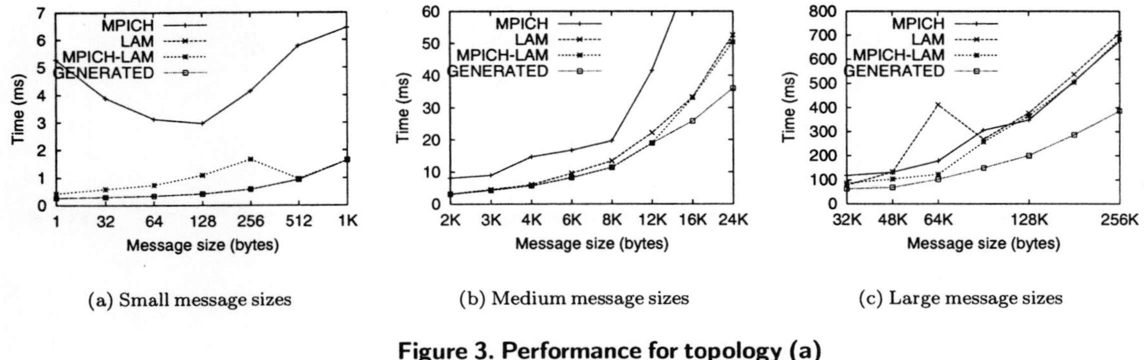

(a) Small message sizes (b) Medium message sizes (c) Large message sizes

Figure 3. Performance for topology (a)

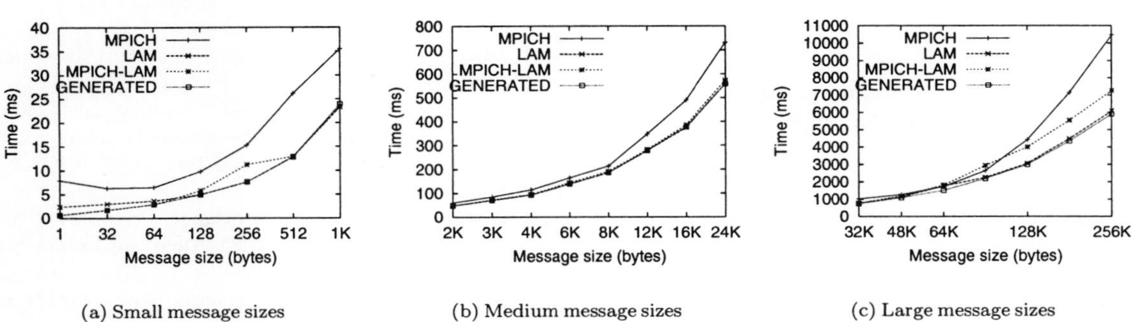

(a) Small message sizes (b) Medium message sizes (c) Large message sizes

Figure 4. Performance for topology (b)

sages, GENERATED performs noticeably better than LAM, MPICH, and MPICH-LAM. For a very wide range of medium and large sized messages, GENERATED is about 10% to 35% faster than the best among LAM, MPICH, and MPICH-LAM. For example, for the message size of 32KB, the time for GENERATED is 842.7ms while the time for LAM (the best among LAM, MPICH, and MPICH-LAM) is 977.2ms: a 16% improvement. For the message size of 128KB, the time for GENERATED is 3451ms while the time for MPICH-LAM is 4590ms: a 33% improvement.

There are some interesting points to be noted in the performance results. First, while MPICH attempts to improve the AAPC performance by using more sophisticated AAPC algorithms, our experimental results do not give clear indications whether the MPICH AAPC routine is better than or worse than the simple AAPC implementation in LAM. This is because an AAPC algorithm achieves good performance only on particular platforms. Hence, to consistently achieve high performance on different platforms, it is essential that different AAPC algorithms are used. Such adaptability cannot be supported in conventional AAPC implementations, but can be provided with an empirical approach. Second, an AAPC implementation that takes into consideration some of the parameters may not be sufficient to yield good performance. MPICH attempts improve AAPC performance by considering some parameters. The AAPC routine in MPICH is able to adapt based on message sizes. However, as shown in the performance study, the performance of the MPICH AAPC routine is far from optimal. To consistently achieve high performance, the aggregated effects of all major system parameters must be considered. This problem is addressed in an empirical approach.

7. Conclusion

Traditional AAPC implementations, such as the ones in MPICH and LAM/MPI, suffer from an inherent limitation: the architecture specific information cannot be fully incorporated. This limitation is due to the fact that the routines are implemented before the program execution environment is decided. An empirical approach overcomes this limitation and can produce AAPC routines that are adaptable to different platforms. We report an automatic AAPC routine generator that is based on an empirical approach and demon-

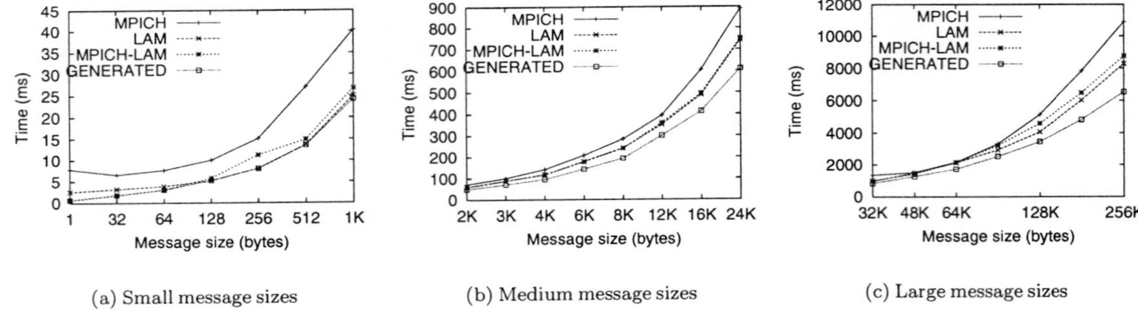

(a) Small message sizes (b) Medium message sizes (c) Large message sizes

Figure 5. Performance for topology (c)

strate that an empirical approach is able to generate AAPC routines that offer higher performance than conventional AAPC implementations. It must be noted that different timing mechanisms can result in very different tuned routines. For the empirical approach to be effective, it is crucial to develop good timing mechanisms that accurately measure the performance.

References

[1] S. Bokhari. Multiphase Complete Exchange: a Theoretical Analysis. *IEEE Trans. on Computers*, 45(2), 1996.

[2] J. Bruck, C. Ho, S. Kipnis, E. Upfal, and D. Weathersby. Efficient Algorithms for All-to-all Communications in Multiport Message-Passing Systems. *IEEE TPDS*, 8(11):1143-1156, Nov. 1997.

[3] H. G. Dietz, T. M. Chung, T. I. Mattox, and T. Muhammad. Purdue's Adapter for Parallel Execution and Rapid Synchronization: The TTL_PAPERS Design. *Technical Report*, Purdue University School of Electrical Engineering, January 1995.

[4] V. V. Dimakopoulos and N.J. Dimopoulos. Communications in Binary Fat Trees. In *IEEE ICDCS*, 1995.

[5] A. Faraj and X. Yuan. Message Scheduling for All–to–all Personalized Communication on Ethernet Switched Clusters. In *IEEE IPDPS*, April 2005.

[6] M. Frigo and S. Johnson. FFTW: An Adaptive Software Architecture for the FFT. In *Proceedings of the International Conference on Acoustics, Speech, and Signal Processing (ICASSP)*, volume 3, page 1381, 1998.

[7] W. Gropp and E. Lusk. Reproducible Measurements of MPI Performance Characteristics. *ANL/MCS-P755-0699*, Argonne National Labratory, June 1999.

[8] S.E. Hambrusch, F. Hameed, and A. A. Khokhar. Communication Operations on Coarse-Grained Mesh Architectures. *Parallel Computing*, Vol. 21, pp. 731-751, 1995.

[9] S. L. Johnsson and C. T. Ho. Optimum Broadcasting and Personalized Communication in Hypercubes. *IEEE Transactions on Computers*, 38(9):1249-1268, Sept. 1989.

[10] L. V. Kale, S. Kumar, K. Varadarajan. A Framework for Collective Personalized Communication. In *IEEE IPDPS*, April, 2003.

[11] LAM/MPI Parallel Computing. http://www.lam-mpi.org/.

[12] C. C. Lam, C. H. Huang, and P. Sadayappan. Optimal Algorithms for All–to–All Personalized Communication on Rings and two dimensional Tori. *JPDC*, 43(1):3-13, 1997.

[13] W. Liu, C. Wang, and K. Prasanna. Portable and Scalable Algorithms for Irregular All–to–all Communication. In *IEEE ICDCS*, 1996.

[14] The MPI Forum. *The MPI-2: Extensions to the Message Passing Interface*, July 1997.

[15] MPICH - A Portable Implementation of MPI. http://www.mcs.anl.gov/mpi/mpich.

[16] N.S. Sundar, D. N. Jayasimha, D. K. Panda, and P. Sadayappan. Hybrid Algorithms for Complete Exchange in 2d Meshes. *International Conference on Supercomputing*, pages 181–188, 1996.

[17] A. Tam and C. Wang. Efficient Scheduling of Complete Exchange on Clusters. In *ISCA PDCS*, Aug. 2000.

[18] R. Thakur and A. Choudhary. All-to-all Communication on Meshes with Wormhole Routing. *8th International Parallel Processing Symposium (IPPS)*, 1994.

[19] R. Thakur, R. Rabenseifner, and W. Gropp. Optimizing of Collective Communication Operations in MPICH. *ANL/MCS-P1140-0304*, Math. and Computer Science Division, Argonne National Laboratory, March 2004.

[20] S. S. Vadhiyar, G. E. Fagg, and J. Dongarra. Automatically Tuned Collective Communications. In *SC'00: High Performance Networking and Computing*, 2000.

[21] E. A. Varvarigos and D. P. Bertsekas. Communication Algorithms for Isotropic Tasks in Hypercubes and Wraparound Meshes. *Parallel Computing*, Volumn 18, pages 1233-1257, 1992.

[22] R. Clint Whaley and Jack Dongarra. Automatically tuned linear algebra software. In *SC'98: High Performance Networking and Computing*, 1998.

Considering the Relative Importance of Network Performance and Network Features

William F. Lawry and Keith D. Underwood
Sandia National Laboratories*
P.O. Box 5800, MS-1110
Albuquerque, NM 87185-1110
{wflawry, kdunder}@sandia.gov

Abstract

Latency and bandwidth are usually considered to be the dominant factor in parallel application performance; however, recent studies have indicated that support for independent progress in MPI can also have a significant impact on application performance. This paper leverages the Cplant system at Sandia National Labs to compare a faster, vendor provided MPI library without independent progress to an internally developed MPI library that sacrifices some performance to provide independent progress. The results are surprising. Although some applications see significant negative impacts from the reduced network performance, others are more sensitive to the presence of independent progress.

1. Introduction

A survey of network marketing literature could easily lead to the conclusion that ping-pong MPI latency and peak ping-pong MPI bandwidth are the dominant factors in application performance. A survey of recent research literature might add a measure of bisection bandwidth, bidirectional bandwidth, and a full bandwidth curve. The most detailed of models, based on LogP[1], LogGP[2], and successors, incorporate further network parameters such as the "gap" between sending messages. Few efforts, however, have considered the relative importance of the set of features available in MPI to making an application perform well. This paper compares two implementations of MPI on a single platform (the Sandia Cplant system) that make two very different design choices. The first (provided by the vendor) delivers the lowest latency and highest bandwidth possible. The second (based on a Portals layer developed at Sandia) sacrifices some bandwidth and significant latency to provide a strict interpretation of the MPI progress rule.

The progress rule in MPI is loosely defined in the MPI standard[1]. A weak interpretation of the progress rule allows an MPI implementation to only make progress toward completing a transfer during application calls to MPI. In contrast, a strong interpretation requires that communications progress independently of calls to MPI. While the weak interpretation is valid, there are potential performance gains from the stronger interpretation.

Recent research[3, 4] has begun to indicate that independent progress can yield significant benefits for applications. To isolate the benefits of independent progress, these studies have attempted to maximize the similarity between the systems under test. Thus, the comparisons have only been done on systems that facilitated the creation of two MPI implementations with different features but matching performance. In contrast, on the Cplant platform, certain aspects of performance (particularly latency) were sacrificed to provide independent progress. The question is: what is more important — latency or independent progress?

To provide insight into this question, this paper presents data from both the NAS parallel benchmark (NPB) suite and some of Sandia's applications. The results are surprising. Although the Portals based implementation sacrifices some performance, the NAS benchmarks (at larger sizes) did not pay a significant penalty. More surprising was the fact that two of the four applications benchmarked show significantly better performance on the Portals based stack. The other two applications were significantly slower due to the difference in latency and bandwidth. Thus, at least in some cases, it is clear that network features can be significantly more important than raw micro-benchmark performance. This raises a fundamental question: are vendors

* Sandia is a multiprogram laboratory operated by Sandia Corporation, a Lockheed Martin Company, for the United States Department of Energy's National Nuclear Security Administration under contract DE-AC04-94AL85000.

1 The original specification was unclear. Since it was not a correctness issue, the MPI-2 forum chose not to strengthen it.

0190-3918/05 $20.00 © 2005 IEEE

making design choices that sacrifice real application performance to enhance micro-benchmark performance?

The next section discusses other studies of network performance. This is followed in Section 3 by a description of the hardware platform and software stack used for this study. The benchmarks and methodology are described in Section 4 and the results are presented in Section 5. The paper closes with conclusions in Section 6.

2. Related Work

The benchmarking of networks is a long-standing practice that ultimately strives to correlate application performance to measurable benchmark performance. Direct comparison of various networks on identical compute platforms is rare due to the difficulties of finding identical processor configurations paired with different networks. In this vein, many efforts have measured application performance and application benchmark performance on various systems and networks[5, 6, 7]. They ultimately attempt to collect micro-benchmark data using ping-pong latency tests[6, 7, 8], bandwidth measures[6, 7, 8, 9], and bisection bandwidth measures[10, 11]. At least two previous efforts have created a benchmark in an attempt to quantify the overlap advantages provided by networks that provide independent progress[12, 5], but the studies were not able to isolate application performance. Furthermore, to our knowledge, there has been no attempt to assess the relative benefits of independent progress and network performance. Similarly, some previous work[13] has presented an in-depth study of application scalability as it relates to the performance of certain aspects of the network, but did not study the issue of overlap or independent progress.

Other efforts have placed a strong focus on extracting deeper measurements of network performance to correlate to application performance. For example, efforts such as the LogP model[1] have decomposed latency into wire latency, host overhead, and network interface gap. Of these parameters, overhead was found to be the most important for many application-like benchmarks followed closely by gap[14]. The work was later extended to include a measure of bandwidth for long messages in the LogGP model[2].

Another type of study that is common is the study of how to create high performing MPI implementations leveraging particularly network features. Recent examples include the specifics of how to map MPI to Infiniband[15, 16, 17, 18]. Other studies include how to improve the MPI infrastructure[19], enhancements to MPI Datatype processing[20, 21] and whether an all eager MPI implementation is beneficial[22]. The issue of independent progress (and its relative importance), has been significantly underrepresented in this set.

The issue of independent progress in MPI has seen much less evaluation than networks in general. The original MPI forums "chose not to choose" a strong definition of the MPI Progress Rule. Since then, many MPI implementations have chosen the weaker interpretation while a few have chosen the stronger. But the question remained: does a strong interpretation of the progress rule matter? Recent research[3, 4] combined with the continued use of an independent progress capability in Quadrics[23] networks and emerging support for independent progress in Myrinet[24, 25] networks would suggest that it does.

The question we begin to consider in this paper has a subtle difference: is independent progress more important than peak bandwidth and minimum latency? The ramifications could be significant as it is the beginning of a series of potential questions regarding whether it is more important to get the MPI feature set right or to hit the minimum latency and maximum bandwidth possible.

3. Experimental Platforms

The experiments presented in this paper were performed on a development version of the Sandia Cplant system[26]. This section describes the hardware used in the experiments as well as the software stacks running on top of them.

3.1. Hardware

The development cluster (*zermatt*) consisted of 132 Compaq XP1000 compute nodes, each having a single Alpha EV6 var 7 500 MHz CPU with a 128 KB L1 cache and a 4 MB off-chip L2 cache. Each compute node had one GB of memory and a Myricom LANai 9 network adapter, except that four compute nodes each had a Myricom LANai 7 adapter. *Zermatt* also had 20 service and IO nodes which were similarly equipped. Nodes were interconnected with Myrinet 16-port SAN/LAN switches.

3.2. Software

Each node ran with the 2.4.18 Linux kernel and the cluster could be configured with one of two communication stacks: a Myricom provided MPICH library ported to their low-level message-passing system (GM) or an MPICH library we ported to our own Portals based communication stack.

The Myricom communication stack consisted of MPICH 1.2.5..10 over Myricom GM version 1.6.5. This stack presents an OS bypass design which avoids the high cost of kernel-to-user context switches and the high cost of interrupts for servicing incoming network traffic. As a result, the Myricom stack provides very low latency and high bandwidth.

In order to avoid performance degrading buffering for message sizes greater than 16 KBs, the Myricom employs a rendezvous protocol. Use of the rendezvous protocol is typical for many message passing implementations including the Portals based stack used in this study. However, since the OS is bypassed in the Myricom communication stack, the rendezvous protocol necessitates additional action by the application in order to fully complete. In other words, a single non-blocking MPI call at each of the sender and the receiver is not sufficient for underlying layers to complete the transfer.

The earliest days of the Cplant project pre-dated the Myricom GM layer. Before the GM layer, the Myricom stack did not provide an end-to-end reliability layer. Furthermore, as Cplant was to be the first Myrinet deployment at almost 2000 processors, there was concern about scalability of the entire system software stack. Thus, the Portals API was ported to Linux and the Myricom network hardware to leverage the existing scalable software base at Sandia and provide the underlying reliability it needed[27].

The Sandia developed communication stack consisted of MPICH 1.2.0 ported to the Portals layer. Portals in turn operates over a Reliable Message Passing Protocol (RMPP) kernel module with a control program running on the Myricom network adapter. Portals is a data movement layer designed to support parallel jobs running on thousands of nodes. A "portal" represents an opening into the address space of a process.

In Portals, a target is not an explicit address. Instead, each message contains a set of match bits that allows the receiver to determine where incoming messages should be placed[27]. This enables Portals to encapsulate the MPI matching semantics, which allows it to provide progress independently of the application. Our implementation is currently based on Portals version 3.0 and supports both one-sided and two-sided communication.

The RMPP [28] kernel module resides in the stack between Portals and the network adapter program and reliably moves the data on a message-by-message basis. RMPP is a message passing protocol designed for large parallel computing systems that implements the basic functionality for interrupt handling and retransmits of messages.

The original implementation of the Portals/RMPP stack was on the Myrinet Lanai 4 with a 33 MHz embedded processor. As such, the original design placed only a very simple packet engine on the Lanai processor. The RMPP kernel module produced and consumed packets on the host while the network adapter program simply transferred packets between the host and the network. This forced an interrupt driven mechanism to enable upper layers of the software stack to handle reliability and perform Portals matching. In favor of stability, this design was maintained into the Lanai 7 and Lanai 9 generations where it continued to pay a penalty in both latency and bandwidth to deliver independent progress.

Recently, the adapter program was revised to implement zero-copy properties for messages greater than 400 bytes as well as to handle messages on the receive side rather than simply handling packets. Additional changes included improved queuing of DMAs between the network adapter and host to streamline progression from individual DMA to individual DMA and to avoid some cycling of the DMA engine between active and idle states. These improvements narrowed the gap between this stack and the Myricom stack in terms of point-to-point bandwidth but did not change small message latency.

Unlike the Myricom communication stack, the improved Portals stack still requires kernel-user context switches and also suffers the cost of interrupts for handling incoming data. However, once the application has identified the message at both the sender and receiver, data movement can progress to completion without further application involvement. As opposed to Myricom's 16 KB threshold, our Portals based stack starts the rendezvous protocol at 8 KB and completion of the rendezvous protocol is fully handled by the RMPP kernel module.

3.3. Known Issues

The software platform, including both communication stacks, was a development version of Cplant which had known issues. For example, under high network traffic (e.g., iterative `MPI_Alltoall` testing) both communication stacks would eventually exhibit corruption as message size increased. The Myricom configuration could handle more stress before failure but it would also eventually fail. One source of corruption in the Portals based communication stack had the appearance of a cache aliasing problem which might also explain the corruption seen with the Myricom stack. The investigation and solution of these issues were not fully completed since it was decided to not release this Cplant version to production use.

Regardless, we performed the study in order to gather as much information as possible given the unique configurability of this development version of Cplant. We attempted to bypass the known issues by dropping from the study those benchmarks/data with erratic timing data, incorrect answers, or inconsistent answers.

Although we could have easily integrated our kernel module and network adapter program improvements into the more stable Cplant version which was previously released to production, that previous Cplant version was not configurable to the Myricom communication stack nor were there plans to implement this.

4. Methodology

To assess each communication stack, we ran standard micro-benchmarks and applied common measurements techniques. We also used the NAS Parallel Benchmarks (NPB) as well as selected parallel applications that are important to *Sandia National Laboratories*. In this section, we discuss these code packages and present the statistical analysis techniques applied to insure the robustness of the measurements taken.

4.1. Micro-benchmarks

A standard MPI based ping-pong micro-benchmark was used to measure the latency and bandwidth provided by each communication stack. In this simple point-to-point benchmark, a single message is sent between two nodes and a reply is returned. The round-trip time is divided by two to obtain the latency and the latency combined with the message size is used to calculate the bandwidth.

The Communication Offload MPI-based Benchmark (COMB) is a self-contained point-to-point micro-benchmark which measures the ability of communication stacks to overlap communication and computation. COMB can also measure communication overhead as experienced at application level while simultaneously measuring bi-directional bandwidth. The details of this benchmark are presented elsewhere[12].

We use this micro-benchmark to generate graphs of host CPU availability versus message size as well as bi-directional bandwidth versus message size. We also use it check for overlap of communication and computation. To check for overlap, non-blocking posts of messages are followed by some amount of simulated work (i.e. loop iterations). After simulated work, the process waits for message completion. Plots of the time spent waiting versus amount of simulated work indicate whether the communication stack can do overlap. This type of overlap equates to the strong interpretation of the progress rule in MPI.

4.2. NAS Benchmarks and Applications

The NAS Parallel Benchmarks (NPB) [29] are a well known collection of 8 programs for assessing parallel computing performance. Theses application benchmarks are derived from computational fluid dynamics (CFD) applications. This study used NPB version 2.3 and its Mops/s performance metric. In addition, three applications specific to Sandia's workload were studied: CTH, ITS, and Trilinos.

CTH CTH is a multi-material, large deformation, strong shock wave, solid mechanics code[30]. CTH has models for multi-phase, elastic viscoplastic, porous and explosive materials. CTH uses second order numerical methods to produce accurate, efficient results. A number of meshes and input data are provided with the CTH package. We use two of the input problems: one provides a two gas scaling study ("2gas") with a non-adaptive mesh and the other input data ("2d-cust4-hs") uses Adaptive Mesh Refinement (AMR). The *2gas* input uses a fixed problem size per node while the AMR input uses a globally fixed problem size regardless of cluster size.

ITS The Integrated TIGER Series (ITS) is a suite of codes to perform Monte Carlo solutions of linear time-independent coupled electron/photon radiation transport problems. It can simulate problems with or without the presence of macroscopic electric and magnetic fields in multi-material, multidimensional geometries. Individual particles are tracked with independent particle histories. We used our Starsat input data and modified the input as needed to maintain a fixed problem size per node.

Trilinos Trilinos[31] is a framework for developing parallel solver algorithms and libraries for the solution of large-scale, complex multi-physics engineering and scientific applications. For our study, we use the Finite Element Interface (FEI) to linear solvers using a "cube3" model problem provided by the Trilinos team. We modified the input data to use a fixed problem size per node.

4.3. Statistical Analysis

A critical product of useful benchmarks is statistically meaningful results. Micro-benchmarks typically have relatively short run-times since they focus on discrete aspects of the system under test and/or involve a limited number of nodes. The short run times allow the averaging of a large number of trials (hundreds to thousands) to arrive at statistically meaningful results. This is the case for the ping-pong and COMB micro-benchmarks used in this study.

On the other had, interesting applications often have significantly longer run times and involve a larger number of nodes. When this is coupled with the otherwise high demand for cycles on large clusters, the accumulated run time for averaging large numbers of application runs becomes prohibitive. For these types of runs we monitored a confidence interval derived from the results of repeated runs.

The confidence interval describes an interval about the average value within which the true population mean likely resides. We decided that an average is statistically significant when the span of the ninety-five percent confidence interval indicates that the sample average is within four percent of the expected population mean. Assuming a normal distribution, we can have some confidence that our metric average is within a few percent of the real but unknown population mean. The selection of the four percent limit is indeed somewhat arbitrary. However, it does exclude widely varying data which may indicate interplay with known issues.

For the application benchmarks and the applications, we only accepted data that met the four percent limit. In the case of CTH, ITS, and Trilinos, the performance metric averages were all within two percent of the anticipated mean. The NAS Parallel Benchmarks were more problematic. Five of the eight programs were omitted from this study due to erratic performance metrics and/or incorrect data. Of the remaining three, all of the NPB results met the four percent limit.

5. Results

Results from the Myricom based network stack and Sandia's Portals based network stack are presented below. The two stacks are compared first on the basis of standard micro-benchmarks. The Myricom stack is a clear winner in all cases except for the amount of overlap available to the application. Application benchmarks and applications are then run to compare the relative importance of the micro-benchmarks.

5.1. Micro-benchmarks

Figure 1 presents typical plots of bandwidth and latency. As discussed in Section 4, these plots represent one-way point-to-point performance. In all cases, the Myricom stack outperforms the Portals based communication stack in this type of performance metric.

Note that the steps in the Sandia line in Figure 1(b) occur at 8 KB intervals which is consistent with the packet size. Likewise, for Myricom there is a smaller step at the 4 KB packet size. The step out at 16 KB is due to a change from the small message protocol to the rendezvous protocol for larger messages.

Figure 2 presents graphs from the COMB micro-benchmark. Figure 2(a) shows Myricom outperforming the Sandia communication stack in point-to-point bi-directional bandwidth by a wider margin than for one-way bandwidth. Also, with respect to CPU availability, Figure 2(b) indicates that Myricom can give the application over four times as many CPU cycles during communication.

The final micro-benchmark examines the ability to allow independent progress without further MPI calls. The benchmark used to generate Figure 3 posts a number of non-blocking receives and then begins simulated work. If a communication stack supports the strong interpretation of the MPI progress rule then, given enough simulated work, the call to `MPI_Wait` to wait for message completion should return almost immediately. The graphs reveal how much communication effort remains after some variable amount of simulated work (i.e. simple loop iterations).

In Figure 3(a), we can see that for short messages, both the Myricom and Sandia stacks support independent progress. These are cases where MPI uses a "short message" protocol. In the case of the Myricom stack, this means that the message is deposited into a system buffer and copied when the `MPI_Wait` is called. The graph also emphasizes Myricom's relatively high performance with small messages.

Switching to a message size that utilizes Myricom's rendezvous protocol, Figure 3(b) shows that Myricom appears to always have the same amount of messaging related work remaining regardless of how much simulated work is accomplished. In actuality, Myricom can accomplish some portion of the rendezvous protocol between MPI calls but this is not enough to result in substantial data movement.

In summary, Figures 1, 2, and 3 show Myricom's communication stack outperforming Sandia's in every case except for independent progress of messages that involve Myricom's rendezvous protocol.

5.2. Application Benchmarks

In light of the micro-benchmark results, the expected result would be that application performance would suffer significantly; however, this does not always seem to be the case. Figure 4 compares the performance of three NAS benchmarks and four applications[2] running each of the network stacks. Each point in the graphs is a "percent improvement" of the Sandia developed Portals based MPI stack over the Myricom developed GM based MPI stack, with positive numbers indicating a win for the Sandia stack and negative numbers indicating a win for the Myricom stack. In the case of the NPB runs, the performance metric was Mops/s and so the relative performance is the difference between Mops/s for the two stacks divided by the result for Myricom. In the case of Sandia's applications, it is essentially the same although the metric is wall clock time and so the difference is reversed from that of the NPB runs (see formula changes in vertical axis labels).

The results in Figure 4 generally show that applications dominated by short messages favor the Myricom network stack. For all of the class A NAS parallel benchmarks, all communications are short and so the Myricom stack is able to provide significant amounts of independent progress and simultaneously has a much lower latency; thus, it has all of the advantages of the Sandia stack without the disadvantages. By the time the applications have scaled to class C,

2 Technically, it is three benchmarks with two input decks on one of the applications; however, one input invokes adaptive mesh refinement (AMR) routines, which creates a more dramatic difference in communication behavior than is seen between many applications.

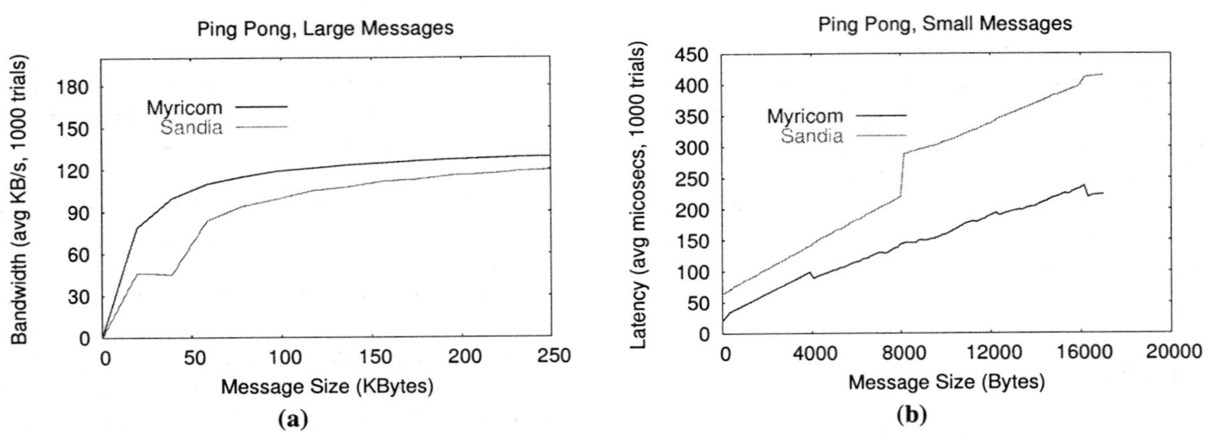

Figure 1: Simple bandwidth and latency performance

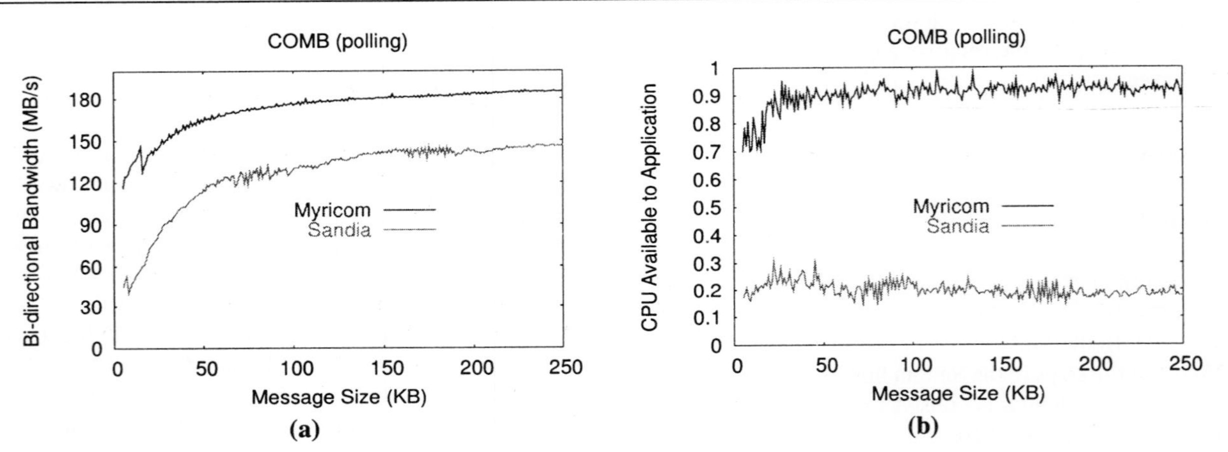

Figure 2: Bi-directional bandwidth with concurrent CPU availability

the performance is much closer to parity for all but the LU benchmark. Previous analysis has indicated that, even with class C problems, the LU benchmark has nothing but short messages, while other benchmarks are much more heavily weighted toward long messages. In the case of BT, the Sandia implementation is able to provide slight advantages in some cases.

Switching to the analysis of applications shown in Figure 4(d) tells a somewhat different story. Two of the applications see a significant advantage from independent progress. As the number of nodes increases, the CTH 2gas problem and the ITS Starsat problem both see dramatic advantages from the Sandia network stack. At 64 nodes, this advantage is 6% and 25% respectively. Thus, in these cases, the advantages of independent progress far outweigh the performance cost associated with this implementation of it.

In contrast, the Trilinos and CTH AMR runs show significant decreases in performance (10% and 20%-60%, respectively) when running the Sandia network stack. Trilinos, being a sparse matrix solver, is hampered by the high latency incurred when making some relatively small transfers. Similarly, the AMR input for CTH is a fixed size problem where the size of the communication continues to decrease as the number of nodes increases and the ratio of communication to computation increases as the number of nodes increases.

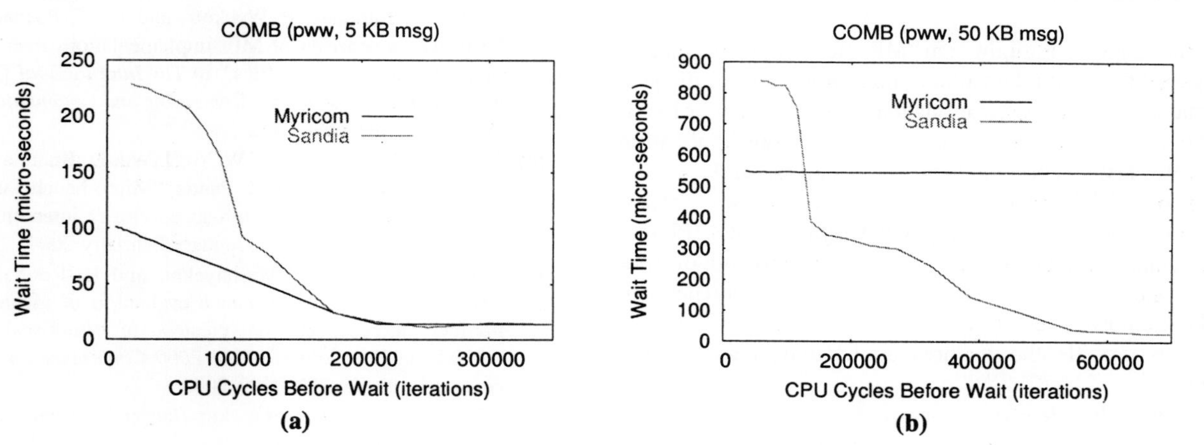

Figure 3: Test for overlap of communication and computation

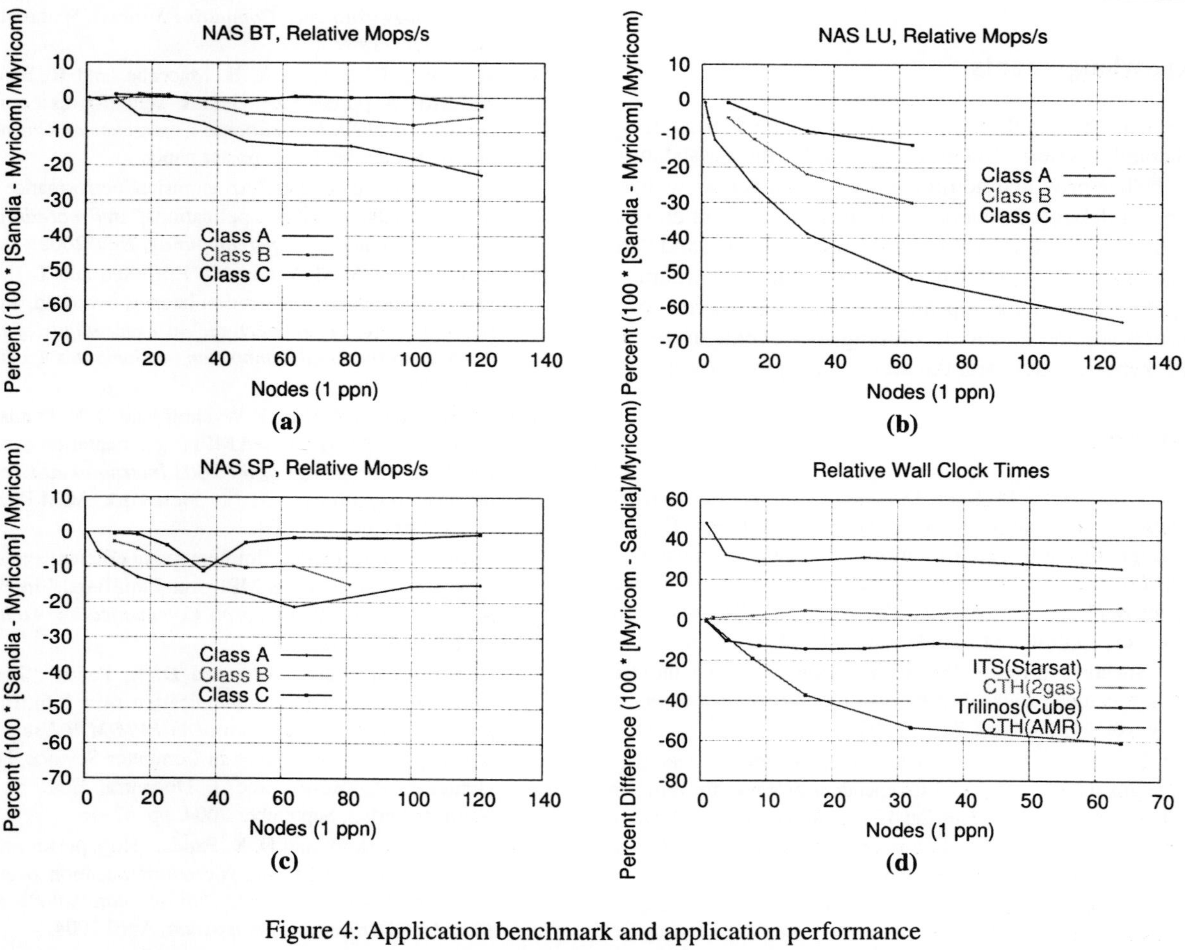

Figure 4: Application benchmark and application performance

6. Conclusions

This paper highlights an MPI feature (independent progress) that is fundamentally more important for the performance of some applications than either latency or bandwidth. Despite a factor of 6 latency penalty, one application is 4-6% faster with independent progress while a second is over 25% faster. Thus, it is clear that, for some cases, it is far more important to get the right set of MPI features than to get the absolute maximum bandwidth or minimum latency. This indicates that vendors may need to make compromises in network performance (if necessary) to provide the features applications need to perform.

What is also clear from this study is that bandwidth and latency are important. The level of performance sacrificed in the Portals implementation on Cplant is clearly a detriment in some cases. Thus, we believe that it is important to continue to drive improvements in both bandwidth and latency, but that such drives must be balanced with robust support for MPI.

Acknowledgements

We want to thank Brice Fisher and Sue Goudy from our Scalable Systems Integration group for their assistance. Brice Fisher provided administrative assistance as well as significant debugging support for our development cluster. Sue Goudy assisted with application build for CTH and ITS. We also want to thank Jeffrey Ogden of our Infrastructures Computing Systems group for maintaining a smaller cluster which supported our developing improvements to the RMPP kernel module and the network adaptor program.

References

[1] D. E. Culler, R. M. Karp, D. A. Patterson, A. Sahay, K. E. Schauser, E. Santos, R. Subramonian, and T. von Eicken, "LogP: Towards a realistic model of parallel computation," in *Proceedings 4th ACM SIGPLAN Symposium on Principles and Practice of Parallel Programming*, 1993, pp. 1–12.

[2] A. Alexandrov, M. F. Ionescu, K. E. Schauser, and C. Sheiman, "LogGP: Incorporating long messages into the LogP model," *Journal of Parallel and Distributed Computing*, vol. 44, no. 1, pp. 71–79, 1997.

[3] R. Brightwell and K. D. Underwood, "An initial analysis of the impact of overlap and independent progress for mpi," in *Recent Advances in Parallel Virtual Machine and Message Passing Interface: 9th European PVM/MPI Users' Group Meeting*, Budapest, Hungary, Sept. 2004.

[4] ——, "An analysis of the impact of overlap and independent progress for MPI," in *Proceedings of the 2004 International Conference on Supercomputing (ICS2004)*, St. Malo, France, June 2004.

[5] J. Liu, B. Chandrasekaran, J. Wu, W. Jiang, S. Kini, W. Yu, D. Buntinas, P. Wyckoff, and D. K. Panda, "Performance comparison of MPI implementations over InfiniBand, Myrinet and Quadrics," in *The International Conference for High Performance Computing and Communications (SC2003)*, November 2003.

[6] J. Liu, B. Chandrasekaran, W. Yu, J. Wu, D. Buntinas, S. P. Kini, P. Wyckoff, and D. K. Panda, "Micro-benchmark performance comparison of high-speed cluster interconnects," *IEEE Micro*, vol. 24, no. 1, January/February 2004.

[7] J. Hsieh, T. Leng, V. Mashayekhi, and R. Rooholamini, "Architectural and performance evaluation of giganet and myrinet interconnects on clusters of small-scale smp servers," in *Proceedings of the 2000 Conference on Supercomputing*, Dallas, TX, Nov. 2000.

[8] *Pallas MPI Benchmarks*, http://http://www.pallas.com/e/products/pmb/index.htm.

[9] *Netperf*, http://www.netperf.org.

[10] *Effective Bandwidth (b_eff) Benchmark*, http://www.hlrs.de/organization/par/services/models/mpi/b_eff/.

[11] K. Solchenbach, "Benchmarking the balance of parallel computers," in *SPEC Workshop on Benchmarking Parallel and High-Performance Computing Systems*, Wuppertal, Germany, Sept. 1999.

[12] W. Lawry, C. Wilson, A. B. Maccabe, and R. Brightwell, "COMB: A portable benchmark suite for assessing MPI overlap," in *IEEE International Conference on Cluster Computing*, September 2002, poster paper.

[13] J. S. Vetter and A. Yoo, "An empirical performance evaluation of scalable scientific applications," in *Proceedings of the 2002 Conference on Supercomputing*, Nov. 2002.

[14] R. P. Martin, A. M. Vahdat, D. E. Culler, and T. E. Anderson, "Effects of communication latency, overhead, and bandwidth in a cluster architecture," in *Proceedings of the 24th Annual International Symposium on Computer Architecture*, June 1997.

[15] J. Liu, J. Wu, S. P. Kini, P. Wyckoff, and D. K. Panda, "High performance RDMA-based MPI implementation over InfiniBand," in *Proceedings of the 2003 International Conference on Supercomputing (ICS-03)*. New York: ACM Press, June 23–26 2003, pp. 295–304.

[16] J. Liu and D. K. Panda, "Implementing efficient and scalable flow control schemes in MPI over InfiniBand," in *Proceedings of the 2004 Workshop on Communication Architecture for Clusters*, April 2004.

[17] G. Santhanaraman, J. Wu, and D. K. Panda, "Zero-copy MPI derived datatype communication over InfiniBand," in *Proceedings of the 11th European PVM/MPI Users' Group Meeting*, ser. Lecture Notes in Computer Science, D. Kranzlmueller, P. Kacsuk, and J. Dongarra, Eds., no. 3241. Springer Verlag, September 2004, pp. 47–56.

[18] J. Wu, P. Wyckoff, and D. K. Panda, "High performance implementation of MPI datatype communication over InfiniBand," in *Proceedings of the 18th International Parallel and Distributed Processing Symposium*, April 2004.

[19] W. Gropp, "MPICH2: A new start for MPI implementations," in *Recent Advances in Parallel Virtual Machine and*

Message Passing Interface: 9th European PVM/MPI Users' Group Meeting, Linz, Austria, ser. Lecture Notes in Computer Science, D. Kranzlmuller, P. Kacsuk, J. Dongarra, and J. Volkert, Eds., vol. 2474. Springer-Verlag, September/October 2002.

[20] S. Byna, X.-H. Sun, W. Gropp, and R. Thakur, "Improving the performance of mpi derived datatypes by optimizing memory-access cost," in *Proceedings 2003 IEEE Conference on Cluster Computing*, December 2003.

[21] R. Ross, N. Miller, and W. Gropp, "Implementing fast and reusable datatype processing," in *Proceedings of EuroPVM/MPI*, September 2003.

[22] R. Brightwell and K. Underwood, "Evaluation of an eager protocol optimization for MPI," in *Proceedings of EuroPVM/MPI*, September 2003.

[23] F. Petrini, W. chun Feng, A. Hoisie, S. Coll, and E. Frachtenberg, "The Quadrics network: High-performance clustering technology," *IEEE Micro*, vol. 22, no. 1, pp. 46–57, January/February 2002.

[24] N. J. Boden, D. Cohen, R. E. F. A. E. Kulawik, C. L. Seitz, J. N. Seizovic, and W.-K. Su, "Myrinet: A gigabit-per-second local area network," *IEEE Micro*, vol. 15, no. 1, pp. 29–36, Feb. 1995.

[25] Myricom, Inc., "Myrinet Express (MX): A high performance, low-level, message-passing interface for Myrinet," July 2003. [Online]. Available: http://www.myri.com/scs/MX/doc/mx.pdf

[26] R. Brightwell, L. A. Fisk, D. S. Greenberg, T. B. Hudson, M. J. Levenhagen, A. B. Maccabe, and R. E. Riesen, "Massively Parallel Computing Using Commodity Components," *Parallel Computing*, vol. 26, no. 2-3, pp. 243–266, February 2000.

[27] R. Brightwell, W. Lawry, A. B. Maccabe, and R. Riesen, "Portals 3.0: Protocol building blocks for low overhead communication," in *Proceedings of the 2002 Workshop on Communication Architecture for Clusters*, April 2002.

[28] R. Riesen, "Message-based, error-correcting protocols for scalable high-performance networks," Ph.D. dissertation, The University of New Mexico, Computer Science Department, Albuquerque, NM 87131, July 2002.

[29] D. Bailey, T. Harris, W. Saphir, R. van der Wijngaart, A. Woo, and M. Yarrow, "The NAS parallel benchmarks 2.0," NASA, Tech. Rep. NAS-95-020, Dec. 1995.

[30] J. E.S. Hertel, R. Bell, M. Elrick, A. Farnsworth, G. Kerley, J. McGlaun, S. Petney, S. Silling, P. Taylor, and L. Yarrington, "CTH: A Software Family for Multi-Dimensional Shock Physics Analysis," in *Proceedings of the 19th International Symposium on Shock Waves, held at Marseille, France*, July 1993, pp. 377–382.

[31] M. Heroux, R. Bartlett, V. H. R. Hoekstra, J. Hu, T. Kolda, R. Lehoucq, K. Long, R. Pawlowski, E. Phipps, A. Salinger, H. Thornquist, R. Tuminaro, J. Willenbring, and A. Williams, "An Overview of Trilinos," Sandia National Laboratories, Tech. Rep. SAND2003-2927, 2003.

Session 5B: Network-Based & Grid Computing

Session-Based Adaptive Overload Control for Secure Dynamic Web Applications

Jordi Guitart, David Carrera, Vicenç Beltran, Jordi Torres and Eduard Ayguadé
European Center for Parallelism of Barcelona (CEPBA)
Computer Architecture Department - Technical University of Catalonia
C/ Jordi Girona 1-3, Campus Nord UPC, Mòdul C6, E-08034 Barcelona (Spain)
{jguitart, dcarrera, vbeltran, torres, eduard}@ac.upc.edu

Abstract

As dynamic web content and security capabilities are becoming popular in current web sites, the performance demand on application servers that host the sites is increasing, leading sometimes these servers to overload. As a result, response times may grow to unacceptable levels and the server may saturate or even crash. In this paper we present a session-based adaptive overload control mechanism based on SSL (Secure Socket Layer) connections differentiation and admission control. The SSL connections differentiation is a key factor because the cost of establishing a new SSL connection is much greater than establishing a resumed SSL connection (it reuses an existing SSL session on server). Considering this big difference, we have implemented an admission control algorithm that prioritizes the resumed SSL connections to maximize performance on session-based environments and limits dynamically the number of new SSL connections accepted depending on the available resources and the current number of connections in the system to avoid server overload. In order to allow the differentiation of resumed SSL connections from new SSL connections we propose a possible extension of the Java Secure Sockets Extension (JSSE) API. Our evaluation on Tomcat server demonstrates the benefit of our proposal for preventing server overload.

1. Introduction

Current web sites have to face three issues to keep clients satisfied. First, the web community is growing day after day, increasing exponentially the load that sites must support. Second, current sites are subject to enormous variations in demand, often in an unpredictable fashion, including flash crowds that cannot be processed. Third, dynamic web content is becoming popular on current sites. At the same time, all information that is confidential or has market value must be carefully protected when transmitted over the open Internet. Security between network nodes over the Internet is traditionally provided using HTTPS [22]. With HTTPS, which is based on using HTTP over SSL (Secure Socket Layer [13]), you can perform mutual authentication of both the sender and receiver of messages and ensure message confidentiality. This process involves X.509 digital certificates that are configured on both sides of the connection. This widespread diffusion of dynamic web content and SSL increases the performance demand on application servers that host the sites, leading sometimes these servers to overload (i.e. the volume of requests for content at a site temporarily exceeds the capacity for serving them and renders the site unusable).

During overload conditions, the response times may grow to unacceptable levels, and exhaustion of resources may cause the server to behave erratically or even crash causing denial of services. In e-commerce applications, which are heavily based on the use of security, such server behavior could translate to sizable revenue losses. For instance, [27] estimates that between 10 and 25% of e-commerce transactions are aborted because of slow response times, which translates to about 1.9 billion dollars in lost revenue.

Overload prevention is a critical issue in order to get a system that remains operational in the presence of overload even when the incoming request rate is several times greater than system capacity, and at the same time is able to serve the maximum the number of requests during such overload, maintaining response times in acceptable levels. With these objectives, several mechanisms have been proposed to face with overload, such as admission control, request scheduling, service differentiation, service degradation or resource management.

Additionally, in many web sites, especially in e-commerce, most of the applications are session-based. A session contains temporally and logically related

0190-3918/05 $20.00 © 2005 IEEE

request sequences from the same client. Session integrity is a critical metric in e-commerce. For an online retailer, the higher the number of sessions completed the higher the amount of revenue that is likely to be generated. The same statement cannot be made about the individual request completions. Sessions that are broken or delayed at some critical stages, like checkout and shipping, could mean loss of revenue to the web site. Sessions have distinguishable features from individual requests that complicate the overload control. For example, admission control on per request basis may lead to a large number of broken or incomplete sessions when the system is overloaded.

In this paper we present an overload control mechanism based on SSL connections differentiation and admission control. First, we propose a possible extension of the Java Secure Sockets Extension (JSSE) API [23], which implements a Java version of the SSL protocol, to allow SSL connections differentiation depending on if the connection will reuse an existing SSL connection on the server or not. This differentiation can be very useful in order to design intelligent overload control policies on server, given the big difference existing on the computational demand of new SSL connections versus resumed SSL connections. Second, we propose a session-based adaptive admission control mechanism for the Tomcat application server. This mechanism will allow the server to avoid throughput degradation and response time increments produced with SSL connections on server saturation. Moreover, the admission control mechanism will maximize the number of sessions completed successfully, allowing to e-commerce sites based on SSL to increase the number of transactions completed, generating higher benefit.

The rest of the paper is organized as follows: Section 2 presents the related work. Section 3 introduces the SSL protocol and its implementation for Java. Sections 4 and 5 detail the implementation of our SSL connections differentiation and SSL admission control mechanisms. Section 6 describes the experimental environment used in our evaluation. Section 7 presents the evaluation results of the overload control mechanism and finally, Section 8 presents the conclusions of this paper.

2. Related Work

The effect of overload on web applications has been covered in several works, applying different perspectives in order to prevent these effects. These different approaches can be resumed on request scheduling, admission control, service differentiation, service degradation, resource management and almost any combination of them.

Request scheduling refers to the order in which concurrent requests should be served. Typically, servers have been left this ordination to the operating system. But, as it is well know from queuing theory that shortest remaining processing time first (SRPT) scheduling minimizes queuing time (and therefore the average response time), some proposals [10][15] implement policies based on this algorithm to prioritize the service of short static content requests in front of long requests. This prioritized scheduling in web servers has been proven effective in providing significantly better response time to high priority requests at relatively low cost to lower priority requests. Although scheduling can improve response times, under extreme overloads other mechanisms become indispensable. Anyway, better scheduling can always be complementary to any other mechanism.

Admission control is based on reducing the amount of work the server accepts when it is faced with overload. Service differentiation is based on differentiating classes of customers so that response times of preferred clients do not suffer in the presence of overload. Admission control and service differentiation have been combined in some works to prevent server overload. ACES [6] attempts to limit the number of admitted requests based on estimated service times, allowing also service prioritization. The evaluation of this approach is done based only on simulation. Other works have considered dynamic web content. An adaptive approach to overload control in the context of the SEDA Web server is described in [26]. SEDA decomposes services into multiple stages, each one of which can perform admission control based on monitoring the response time through the stage. The evaluation includes dynamic content in the form of a web-based email service. In [12], the authors present an admission control mechanism for e-commerce sites that externally observes execution costs of requests, distinguishing different requests types. Yaksha [17] implements a self-tuning proportional integral controller for admission control in multi-tier e-commerce applications using a single queue model.

Some works have integrated the resource management with other approaches as admission control and service differentiation. For example, [3] proposes resource containers as an operating system abstraction that embodies a resource. [25] proposes a resource overbooking based scheme for maximizing revenue generated by the available resources in a shared platform. [5] presents a prototype data center implementation used to study the effectiveness of dynamic resource allocation for handling flash crowds.

Cataclysm [24] performs overload control bringing together admission control, service degradation and dynamic provisioning of platform resources.

Service degradation is based on avoiding refusing clients as a response to overload but reducing the service offered to clients [1][24][26], for example in the form on providing smaller content (e.g. lower resolution images).

On most of the prior work, overload control is performed on per request basis, which may not be adequate for many session-based applications, such as e-commerce applications. A session-based admission control scheme has been reported in [8]. This approach allows sessions to run to completion even under overload, denying all access when the server load exceeds a predefined threshold. Another approach to session-based admission control based on characterization of a commercial web server log, discriminating the scheduling of requests based on the probability of completion of the session that the requests belong to is presented in [7].

Our proposal combines important aspects that previous work has considered in isolation or simply has ignored. First, we consider dynamic web content instead of simpler static web content. Second, we focus on session-based applications considering the particularities of these applications when performing admission control. Third, our proposal is fully adaptive to the available resources and to the number of connections in the server instead of using predefined thresholds. Finally, we consider overload control on secure web applications while none of the above works has covered this issue.

Although none of them has covered overload control, the influence of security on servers scalability has been covered in some works. For example, the performance and architectural impact of SSL on the servers in terms of various parameters such as throughput, utilization, cache sizes and cache miss ratios has been analyzed in [18]. The impact of each individual operation of TLS protocol in the context of web servers has been studied in [9], showing that key exchange is the slowest operation in the protocol.

Servers scalability in secure environments can be also achieved by adding new specialized hardware [19] for processing SSL requests, reducing the processor demand, but increasing the cost of the system.

3. Security for Java Web Applications

3.1 SSL Protocol

The SSL protocol provides communications privacy over the Internet. The protocol allows client/server applications to communicate in a way that is designed to prevent eavesdropping, tampering, or message forgery. To obtain these objectives it uses a combination of public-key and private-key cryptography algorithm and digital certificates (X.509).

The SSL protocol does not introduce a new degree of complexity in web applications structure because it works almost transparently on top of the socket layer. However, SSL increases the computation time necessary to serve a connection remarkably, due to the use of cryptography to achieve their objectives. This increment has a noticeable impact on server performance, which has been evaluated in [14]. This study concludes that the maximum throughput obtained when using SSL connections is 7 times lower than when using normal connections. The study also notices that when the server is attending non-secure connections and saturates, it can maintain the throughput if new clients arrive, while if attending SSL connections, the saturation of the server provokes the degradation of the throughput.

The SSL protocol fundamentally has two phases of operation: SSL handshake and SSL record protocol. We will do an overview of the SSL handshake phase, which is the responsible of most of the computation time required when using SSL. The detailed description of the whole protocol can be found in RFC 2246 [11].

The SSL handshake allows the server to authenticate itself to the client using public-key techniques like RSA, and then allows the client and the server to cooperate in the creation of symmetric keys used for rapid encryption, decryption, and tamper detection during the session that follows. Optionally, the handshake also allows the client to authenticate itself to the server. Two different SSL handshake types can be distinguished: The full SSL handshake and the resumed SSL handshake. The full SSL handshake is negotiated when a client establishes a new SSL connection with the server, and requires the complete negotiation of the SSL handshake, including parts that spend a lot of computation time to be accomplished. We have measured the computational demand of a full SSL handshake in a 1.4 GHz Xeon to be around 175 ms. The SSL resumed handshake is negotiated when a client establishes a new HTTP connection with the server but using an existing SSL connection. As the SSL session ID is reused, part of the SSL handshake negotiation can be avoided, reducing considerably the computation time for performing a resumed SSL handshake. We have measured the computational demand of a resumed SSL handshake in a 1.4 GHz Xeon to be around 2 ms. Notice the big difference between negotiate a full SSL handshake respect to negotiate a resumed SSL handshake (175 ms vs. 2 ms).

Based on these two handshake types, two types of SSL connections can be distinguished: the new SSL connections and the resumed SSL connections. The new SSL connections try to establish a new SSL session and must negotiate a full SSL handshake. The resumed SSL connections can negotiate a resumed SSL handshake because they provide a reusable SSL session ID (they resume an existing SSL session).

3.2 JSSE API Limitations

The Java Secure Socket Extension (JSSE) [23] is a set of packages that enable secure Internet communications. It implements a Java technology version of Secure Sockets Layer (SSL) [13] and Transport Layer Security (TLS) [11] protocols.

The JSSE API provides the `SSLSocket` and `SSLServerSocket` classes, which can be instantiated to create secure channels. The JSSE API supports the initiation of a handshake on a SSL connection in one of three ways. Calling `startHandshake` that explicitly begins handshakes, or any attempt to read or write application data through the connection causes an implicit handshake, or a call to `getSession` tries to set up a session if there is no currently valid session, and an implicit handshake is done. After handshaking has completed, session attributes can be accessed by using the `getSession` method. If handshaking fails for any reason, the `SSLSocket` is closed, and no further communications can be done.

Notice that the JSSE API does not support any way to consult if an incoming SSL connection provides a reusable SSL session ID until the handshake is fully completed. Having this information prior to handshake negotiation could be very useful for example for servers in order to do overload control based on SSL connections differentiation, given the big difference existing on the computational demand of new SSL connections versus resumed SSL connections. It is important to notice that the verification about an incoming SSL connection provides a valid SSL session ID is already performed by the JSSE API prior handshaking in order to negotiate a full SSL handshake or a resumed SSL handshake. Therefore, the addition of a new interface to access this information would not involve additional cost.

4. SSL Connections Differentiation

As we mentioned in the previous section, there is no way in JSSE packages to consult if an incoming SSL connection provides a reusable SSL session ID until the handshake is fully completed. We propose the extension of the JSSE API to allow applications to differentiate new SSL connections from resumed SSL connections prior the handshaking has started.

This new feature can be useful in many scenarios. For example, a connection scheduling policy based on prioritizing the resumed SSL connections (that is, the short connections) will result in a reduction of the average response time, as described in previous works with static web content using the SRPT scheduling [10][15]. Moreover, prioritizing the resumed SSL connections will increase the probability for a client to complete a session, maximizing the number of sessions completed successfully. We have already commented the importance of this metric in e-commerce environments. Remember that the higher the number of sessions completed the higher the amount of revenue that is likely to be generated. In addition, a server could limit the number of new SSL connections that it accepts, in order to avoid throughput degradation produced if server overloads.

In order to evaluate the advantages of being able to differentiate new SSL connections from resumed SSL connections and the convenience of adding this functionality to the standard JSSE API, we have implemented an experimental mechanism that allows this differentiation prior to the handshake negotiation. We have measured that this mechanism does not suppose significant additional cost. The mechanism works at system level and it is based on examining the contents of the first TCP segment received on the server after the connection establishment.

After a new connection is established between the server and a client, the SSL protocol starts a handshake negotiation. The protocol begins with the client sending a SSL ClientHello message (see the RFC 2246 for more details) to the server. This message can include a SSL session ID from a previous connection if the SSL session wants to be reused. This message is sent in the first TCP segment that the client sends to the server. The implemented mechanism checks the value of this SSL message field to decide if the connection is a resumed SSL connection or a new one instead.

The mechanism operation begins when a new incoming connection is accepted by the Tomcat server, and a socket structure is created to represent the connection in the operating system as well as in the JVM. After establishing the connection but prior to the handshake negotiation, the Tomcat server requests to the mechanism the classification of this SSL connection, using a JNI native library that is loaded into the JVM process. The library translates the Java request into a new native system call implemented in the Linux kernel using a Linux kernel module. The implementation of the system call calculates a hash function from the parameters provided by the Tomcat server (local and remote IP address and TCP port) which produces a socket hash code that makes possible to find the socket inside of a connection established socket hash table. When the system `struct sock` that represents the socket is located and in consequence all the received TCP segments for that socket after the connection establishment, the first one of the TCP segments is interpreted as a SSL ClientHello message. If this message contains a SSL session ID with value 0, it can be concluded that the connection tries to establish a new SSL session. If a non-zero SSL session ID is found instead, the connection tries to resume a previous SSL session. The value of this SSL message field is returned by the system call to the JNI native library that, in turn, returns it to the Tomcat server. With this result, the server can decide, for instance, to apply an admission control algorithm in order to decide if the connection should be accepted or rejected.

5. SSL Admission Control

In order to prevent server overload in secure environments, we have incorporated to the Tomcat server a session-oriented adaptive mechanism that performs admission control based on SSL connections differentiation. This mechanism has been developed with two objectives. First, to prioritize the acceptation of client connections that resume an existing SSL session, in order to maximize the number of sessions successfully completed. Second, to limit the massive arrival of new SSL connections to the maximum number acceptable by the server before overloading, depending on the available resources.

To prioritize the resumed SSL connections, the admission control mechanism accepts all the connections that supply a valid SSL session ID. The required verification to differentiate resumed SSL connections from new SSL connections is performed with the mechanism described in Section 4.

To avoid the server throughput degradation and maintain acceptable response times, the admission control mechanism must to avoid the server overload. By keeping the maximum amount of load just below the system capacity, overload is prevented and peak throughput is achieved. For secure web applications, the system capacity depends on the available processors, as it has been demonstrated in [14], due to the great computational demand of this kind of applications. Therefore, if the server can use more processors, it can accept more SSL connections without saturating.

The admission control mechanism calculates periodically, introducing an adaptive behavior, the maximum number of new SSL connections that can be accepted without overloading the server. This maximum depends on the available processors for the server and the computational demand required by the accepted resumed SSL connections. The calculation of this demand is based on the number of accepted resumed SSL connections and the typical computational demand of one of these connections.

After calculating the computational demand required by the accepted resumed SSL connections and with information relative to the available processors for the server, the admission control mechanism can calculate the remaining computational capacity for attending new SSL connections. The admission control mechanism will only accept the maximum number of new SSL connections that do not overload the server (they can be served with the available computational capacity). The rest of new SSL connections arriving at the server will be refused.

Notice that if the number of resumed SSL connections increases, the server has to decrease the number of new SSL connections it accepts, in order to avoid server overload with the available processors and vice versa, if the number of resumed SSL connections decreases, the server can increase the number of new SSL connections that it accepts.

Notice that this constitutes an interesting starting point to develop autonomic computing strategies on the server in a bidirectional fashion. First, the server can restrict the number of new SSL connections it accepts to adapt its behavior to the available resources (i.e. processors) in order to prevent server overload. Second, the server can inform about its resource requirements to a global manager (which will distribute all the available resources among the existing servers following a given policy) depending on the rate of incoming connections (new SSL connections and resumed SSL connections) requesting for service.

6. Experimental Environment

6.1 Tomcat Servlet Container

We use Tomcat v5.0.19 [16] as the application server. Tomcat is an open-source servlet container developed under the Apache license. Its primary goal is to serve as a reference implementation of the Sun Servlet and JSP specifications. Tomcat can work as a standalone server (serving both static and dynamic web content) or as a helper for a web server (serving only dynamic web content). In this paper we use Tomcat as a standalone server.

Tomcat follows a connection service schema where, at a given time, one thread (an HttpProcessor) is responsible of accepting a new incoming connection on the server listening port and assigning to it a socket structure. From this point, this HttpProcessor will be responsible of attending and serving the received requests through the persistent connection established with the client, while another HttpProcessor will continue accepting new connections.

Persistent connections are a feature of HTTP 1.1 that allows serving different requests using the same connection, saving a lot of work and time for the web server, client and the network, considering that establishing and tearing down HTTP connections is an expensive operation. A connection timeout is programmed to close the connection if no more requests are received.

We have configured Tomcat setting the maximum number of HttpProcessors to 100 and the connection persistence timeout to 10 seconds.

6.2 Auction Site Benchmark (RUBiS)

The experimental environment also includes a deployment of the RUBiS (Rice University Bidding System) [2] benchmark servlets version 1.4.2 on Tomcat. RUBiS implements the core functionality of an auction site: selling, browsing and bidding. RUBiS defines 27 interactions. Among the most important ones are browsing items by category or region, bidding, buying or selling items and leaving comments on other users. 5 of the 27 interactions are implemented using static HTML pages. The remaining 22 interactions require data to be generated dynamically. RUBiS supplies implementations using some mechanisms for generating dynamic web content like PHP, Servlets and several kinds of EJB.

The client workload for the experiments was generated using a workload generator and web performance measurement tool called Httperf [20]. This tool, which supports both HTTP and HTTPS protocols, allows the creation of a continuous flow of HTTP/S requests issued from one or more client machines and processed by one server machine. One of the parameters of the tool represents the number of new clients per second initiating an interaction with the server. Each emulated client opens a session with the server. Each session is a persistent HTTP/S connection with the server. Using this connection, the client repeatedly makes a request (the client can also pipeline some requests), parses the server response to the request, and follows a link embedded in the response. The workload distribution generated by Httperf was extracted from the RUBiS client emulator, which uses a Markov model to determine which subsequent link from the response to follow. Each emulated client waits for an amount of time, called the think time, before initiating the next interaction. The think time is generated from a negative exponential distribution with a mean of 7 seconds. Httperf allows also configuring a client timeout. If this timeout is elapsed and no reply has been received from the server, the current persistent connection with the server is discarded, and a new emulated client is initiated. We have configured Httperf setting the client timeout value to 10 seconds. RUBiS defines two workload mixes: a browsing mix made up of only read-only interactions and a bidding mix that includes 15% read-write interactions.

6.3 Hardware & Software Platform

Tomcat runs on a 4-way Intel XEON 1.4 GHz with 2 GB RAM. We use MySQL v4.0.18 [21] as our database server with the MM.MySQL v3.0.8 JDBC driver. MySQL runs on a 2-way Intel XEON 2.4 GHz with 2 GB RAM. We have also a 2-way Intel XEON 2.4 GHz with 2 GB RAM machine running the workload generator (Httperf 0.8). Client machine emulates the configured number of clients performing requests to the server during 10 minutes using the browsing mix (read-only interactions). All the machines are connected through a 1 Gbps Ethernet interface and run the 2.6 Linux kernel. For our experiments we use the Sun JVM 1.4.2 for Linux, using the server JVM instead of the client JVM and setting the initial and the maximum Java heap size to 1024 MB. All the tests are performed with the common RSA-3DES-SHA cipher suit, using 1024 bit RSA key.

7. Evaluation

In this section we present the evaluation comparison of the overload control mechanism on Tomcat server with respect to the original Tomcat.

7.1 Original Tomcat

Figure 1 shows the Tomcat throughput as a function of the number of new clients per second initiating a session with the server when running with different number of processors. Notice that for a given number of processors, the server throughput increases linearly with respect to the input load (the server scales) until a determined number of clients hit the server. At this point, the throughput achieves its maximum value. Notice that running with more processors allows the server to handle more clients before saturating, so the maximum achieved throughput is higher. When the number of clients that overload the server has been

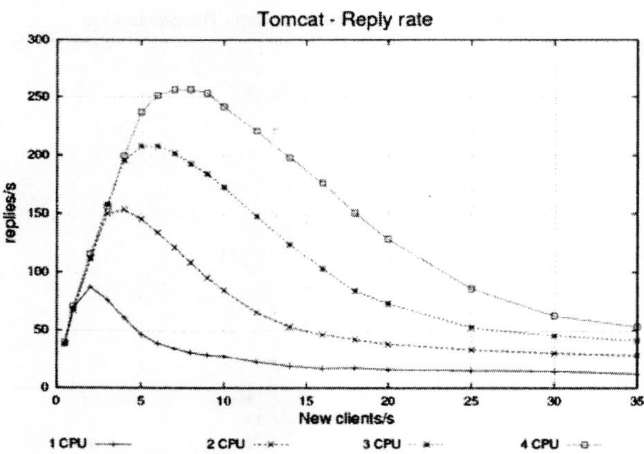

Figure 1. Original Tomcat throughput with different number of processors

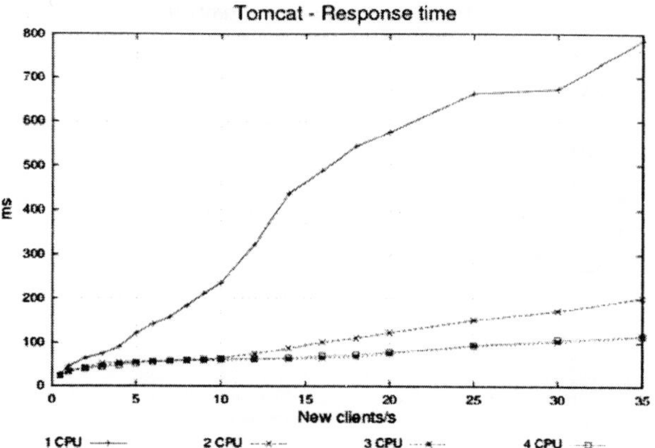

Figure 2. Original Tomcat response time with different number of processors

achieved, the server throughput degrades until approximately the 20% of the maximum achievable throughput while the number of clients increases.

As well as degrading the server throughput, the server overload also affects to the server response time, as shown in Figure 2. This figure shows the server average response time as a function of the number of new clients per second initiating a session with the server when running with different number of processors. Notice that when the server is overloaded the response time increases (especially when running with one processor) while the number of clients increases.

Server overload has another undesirable effect, especially in e-commerce environments where session completion is a key factor. As shown in Figure 3, which shows the number of sessions completed successfully when running with different number of processors, when the server is overloaded only a few sessions can finalize completely. Consider the great revenue lost that this fact can provoke for example in an online store, where only a few clients can finalize the acquisition of a product.

The cause of this great performance degradation on server overload has been analyzed in [14]. They conclude that the server throughput degrades when most of the incoming client connections must negotiate a full SSL handshake instead of resuming an existing SSL connection, requiring a computing capacity that the available processors are unable to supply. This circumstance is produced when the server is overloaded and it cannot handle the incoming requests before the client timeouts expire. In this case, clients with expired timeouts are discarded and new ones are initiated, provoking the arrival of a great amount of new client connections that negotiate of a full SSL handshake, provoking server performance degradation.

Considering the described behavior, it makes sense to apply an admission control mechanism in order to improve server performance in the following way. First, to filter the massive arrival of client connections that need to negotiate a full SSL handshake that will saturate the server, avoiding the server throughput degradation and maintaining a good quality of service (good response time) for already connected clients. Second, to prioritize the acceptation of client connections that resume an existing SSL session, in order to maximize the number of sessions successfully completed.

7.2 Tomcat with Admission Control

Figure 4 shows the Tomcat throughput as a function of the number of new clients per second initiating a session with the server when running with different

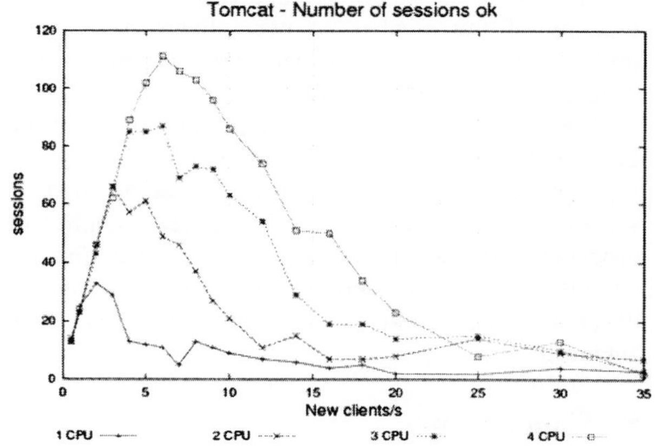

Figure 3. Completed sessions by original Tomcat with different number of processors

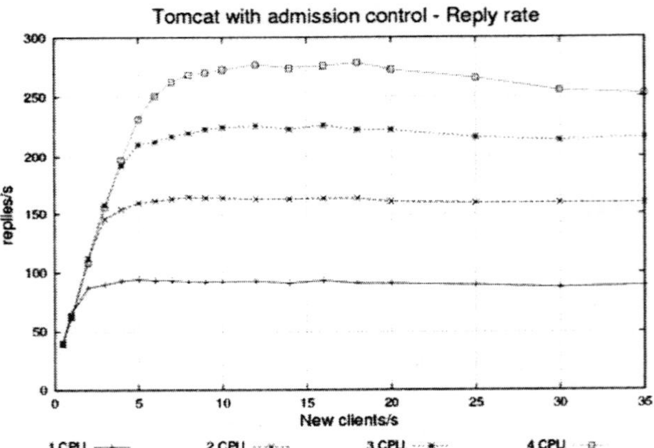

Figure 4. Tomcat with admission control throughput with different number of processors

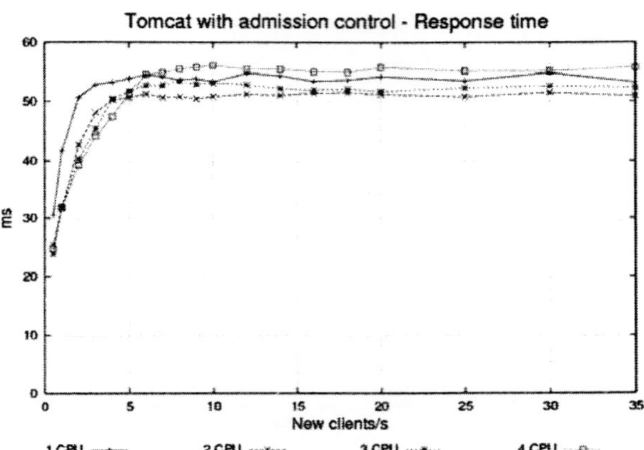

Figure 5. Tomcat with admission control response time with different number of processors

number of processors. Notice that for a given number of processors, the server throughput increases linearly with respect to the input load (the server scales) until a determined number of clients hit the server. At this point, the throughput achieves its maximum value. Until this point, the server with admission control behaves in the same way than the original server. However, when the number of clients that would overload the server has been achieved, the admission control mechanism can avoid the throughput degradation, maintaining it in the maximum achievable throughput, as shown in Figure 5. Notice that running with more processors allows the server to handle more clients, so the maximum achieved throughput is higher.

The admission control mechanism on Tomcat allows also maintaining the response time in levels that guarantee a good quality of service to the clients, even when the number of clients that would overload the server has been achieved, as shown in Figure 5. This figure shows the server average response time as a function of the number of new clients per second initiating a session with the server when running with different number of processors.

Finally, the admission control mechanism has also a beneficial effect for session-based clients. As shown in Figure 6, which shows the number of sessions finalized successfully when running with different number of processors, the number of sessions that can finalize completely does not decrease, even when the number of clients that would overload the server has been achieved.

8. Conclusions

In this paper we have presented a session-based adaptive overload control mechanism based on SSL connections differentiation and admission control. First, we have proposed a possible extension of the JSSE API in order to allow the differentiation of resumed SSL connections (that reuse an existing SSL session on server) from new SSL connections. Second, we have incorporated to the Tomcat server a session-based adaptive admission control mechanism that prioritizes resumed SSL connections to maximize the number of sessions completed successfully (which is a very important metric on e-commerce environments). The admission control also limits dynamically the number of new SSL connections accepted depending on the available resources and the number of resumed SSL connections accepted, in order to avoid server overload.

Our evaluation demonstrates the benefit of our approach on overload prevention for servers on secure environments, and confirms that security must be considered as an important issue that can heavily affect

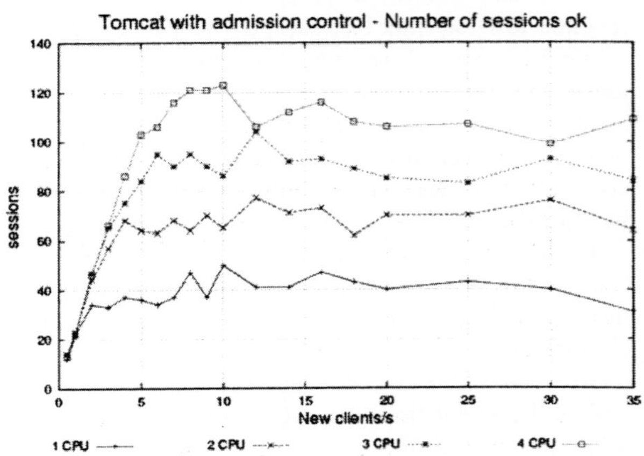

Figure 6. Sessions completed by Tomcat with admission control with different number of processors

the scalability and performance of web applications.

9. Acknowledgments

This work is supported by the Ministry of Science and Technology of Spain and the European Union (FEDER funds) under contract TIN2004-07739-C02-01 and by the CEPBA (European Center for Parallelism of Barcelona). For additional information about the authors, please visit the Barcelona eDragon Research Group web site [4].

10. References

[1] T. Abdelzaher and N. Bhatti. *Web Content Adaptation to Improve Server Overload Behavior*. Computer Networks, Vol. 31 (11-16), pp. 1563-1577, May 1999.

[2] C. Amza, E. Cecchet, A. Chanda, A. Cox, S. Elnikety, R. Gil, J. Marguerite, K. Rajamani and W. Zwaenepoel. *Specification and Implementation of Dynamic Web Site Benchmarks*. IEEE 5th Annual Workshop on Workload Characterization (WWC-5), Austin, Texas, USA. November 25, 2002.

[3] G. Banga, P. Druschel and J. C. Mogul. *Resource Containers: A New Facility for Resource Management in Server Systems*. 3rd Symposium on Operating Systems Design and Implementation (OSDI'99), pp. 45-58, New Orleans, Louisiana, USA. February 22-25, 1999.

[4] Barcelona eDragon Research Group http://www.cepba.upc.es/eDragon

[5] A. Chandra and P. Shenoy. *Effectiveness of Dynamic Resource Allocation for Handling Internet Flash Crowds*. Technical Report TR03-37, Department of Computer Science, University of Massachusetts, USA. November 2003.

[6] X. Chen, H. Chen and P. Mohapatra. *ACES: An Efficient Admission Control Scheme for QoS-Aware Web Servers*. Computer Communications, Vol. 26 (14), pp. 1581-1593. September 2003.

[7] H. Chen and P. Mohapatra. *Overload Control in QoS-aware Web Servers*. Computer Networks, Vol. 42 (1), pp. 119-133. May 2003.

[8] L. Cherkasova and P. Phaal. *Session-Based Admission Control: A Mechanism for Peak Load Management of Commercial Web Sites*. IEEE Transactions on Computers, Vol. 51 (6), pp. 669-685. June 2002.

[9] C. Coarfa, P. Druschel, and D. Wallach. *Performance Analysis of TLS Web Servers*. 9th Network and Distributed System Security Symposium (NDSS'02), San Diego, California, USA. February 6-8, 2002.

[10] M. Crovella, R. Frangioso and M. Harchol-Balter. *Connection Scheduling in Web Servers*. 2nd Symposium on Internet Technologies and Systems (USITS'99), Boulder, Colorado, USA. October 11-14, 1999.

[11] T. Dierks and C. Allen. *The TLS Protocol, Version 1.0*. RFC 2246. January 1999.

[12] S. Elnikety, E. Nahum, J. Tracey and W. Zwaenepoel. *A Method for Transparent Admission Control and Request Scheduling in E-Commerce Web Sites*. 13th International Conference on World Wide Web (WWW'04), pp. 276-286, New York, New York, USA. May 17-22, 2004.

[13] A. O. Freier, P. Karlton, and C. Kocher. *The SSL Protocol, Version 3.0*. November 1996.

[14] J. Guitart, V. Beltran, D. Carrera, J. Torres and E. Ayguadé. *Characterizing Secure Dynamic Web Applications Scalability*. 19th International Parallel and Distributed Symposium (IPDPS'05), Denver, Colorado, USA. April 4-8, 2005.

[15] M. Harchol-Balter, B. Schroeder, N. Bansal and M. Agrawal. *Size-based Scheduling to Improve Web Performance*. ACM Transactions on Computer Systems (TOCS), Vol. 21 (2), pp. 207-233. May 2003.

[16] Jakarta Tomcat Servlet Container http://jakarta.apache.org/tomcat

[17] A. Kamra, V. Misra and E. Nahum. *Yaksha: A Controller for Managing the Performance of 3-Tiered Websites*. 12th International Workshop on Quality of Service (IWQoS 2004), Montreal, Canada. June 7-9, 2004.

[18] K. Kant, R. Iyer, and P. Mohapatra. *Architectural Impact of Secure Socket Layer on Internet Servers*. 2000 IEEE International Conference on Computer Design (ICCD'00), pp. 7-14, Austin, Texas, USA. September 17-20, 2000.

[19] R. Mraz. SecureBlue: An Architecture for a High Volume SSL Internet Server. 17th Annual Computer Security Applications Conference (ACSAC'01), New Orleans, Louisiana, USA. December 10-14, 2001.

[20] D. Mosberger and T. Jin. *httperf: A Tool for Measuring Web Server Performance*. Workshop on Internet Server Performance (WISP'98) (in conjunction with SIGMETRICS'98), pp. 59-67. Madison, Wisconsin, USA. June 23, 1998.

[21] MySQL http://www.mysql.com

[22] E. Rescorla. *HTTP over TLS*. RFC 2818. May 2000.

[23] Sun Microsystems. Java Secure Socket Extension http://java.sun.com/products/jsse/

[24] B. Urgaonkar and P. Shenoy. *Cataclysm: Handling Extreme Overloads in Internet Services*. Technical Report TR03-40, Department of Computer Science, University of Massachusetts, USA. November 2004.

[25] B. Urgaonkar, P. Shenoy and T. Roscoe. *Resource Overbooking and Application Profiling in Shared Hosting Platforms*. 5th Symposium on Operating Systems Design and Implementation (OSDI'02), Boston, Massachusetts, USA. December 9-11, 2002.

[26] M. Welsh and D. Culler. *Adaptive Overload Control for Busy Internet Servers*. 4th Symposium on Internet Technologies and Systems (USITS'03), Seattle, Washington, USA. March 26-28, 2003.

[27] T. Wilson. *E-Biz Bucks Lost under SSL Strain*. Internet Week Online. May 20, 1999. http://www.internetwk.com/lead/lead052099.htm

Efficient Switching Supports of Distributed .NET Remoting with Network Processors

Chung-Kai Chen, Yu-Hao Chang, Cheng-Wei Chen, Yu-Tin Chen,
Chih-Chieh Yang and Jenq-Kuen Lee
Department of Computer Science, National Tsing-Hua University, Taiwan
Email:{ckchen, yhchang, cwchen, ytchen, ccyang}@pllab.cs.nthu.edu.tw
jklee@cs.nthu.edu.tw

Abstract

Distributed object-oriented environments have become important platforms for parallel and distributed service frameworks. Among distributed object-oriented software, .NET Remoting provides a language layer of abstractions for performing parallel and distributed computing in .NET environments. In this paper, we present our methodologies in supporting .NET Remoting over meta-clustered environments. We take the advantage of the programmability of network processors to develop the content-based switch for distributing workloads generated from remote invocations in .NET. Our scheduling mechanisms include stateful supports for .NET Remoting services. In addition, we also propose scheduling policy to incorporate work-flow models as the models are now incorporated in many of tools of grid architectures. Experiments done at clusters with IXP 1200 network processors show that our scheme can significantly enhance the system throughput (up to 55%) compared to NLB method when the traffic is heavy. Our schemes are effective in supporting the switching of .NET Remoting computations over meta-cluster environments.

1. Introduction

Distributed object-oriented environments have become important platforms for parallel and distributed service frameworks. Among distributed object-oriented software, .NET Remoting provides a framework that allows objects to interact with each other across the boundaries. In the .NET Remoting Framework, channels are used to transport messages to and from remote objects, and the .NET Remoting infrastructure provides two types of channels that can be used to provide a transport mechanism for the distributed applications - the TCP channel and HTTP channel. TCP channel is a socket-based transport that utilizes the TCP protocol for transporting the serialized message stream across the .NET Remoting boundaries while HTTP channel utilizes the HTTP protocol for transporting the serialized message stream across the Internet and through firewalls. As other networking applications, such as HTTP, server cluster is deployed for serving tremendous request. To leverage the request load among servers and optimize the cluster utilization, it is necessary to apply a load balancing mechanism in server clusters.

In this paper, we address the issues in supporting .NET Remoting over meta-cluster environments. We take the advantage of the programmability of network processors to develop the content-based switch. Stateful supports for .NET Remoting services are also incorporated. Our work has .NET Remoting applications classified into two separate channels in one application, one is for stateful, and another is for stateless. We then try to dispatch jobs for stateless applications, and also for the scheduling of stateful invocations. In addition, we also incorporate work-flow models for tasks to be scheduled into our frameworks. This is due to many of the tools of grid architectures now are with work-flow model supports [7].

Our experimental platform, Intel IXP1200, contains a StrongARM core of 232 MHz and six programmable 32-bit RISC processors of 232 MHz (a.k.a. microengine). With the benefit of pipeline model, IXP1200 could guarantee wire-speed (up to 622 Mbit/s, OC-12) packet processing performance. The whole system implementation is divided into two parts, one is the control system executed in

[1]The correspondence author is Jenq Kuen Lee. His e-mail is jklee@cs.nthu.edu.tw, phone number is 886-3-5715131 EXT. 3519, FAX number is 886-3-5723694.

[2]The work was supported in part by NSC-93-2213-E-007-025, NSC-93-2220-E-007-020, NSC-94-2752-E-007-004-PAE, MOEA-93-EC-17-A-03-S1-0002, MOEA-94-EC-17-A-01-S1-034, a Microsoft .NET resarch grant (2003-2004), and an Intel research grant for network processors (2003-2005).

0190-3918/05 $20.00 © 2005 IEEE

StrongARM core and the other one is data path system executed in microengines. The control system is implemented in ANSI C code; the system feature includes downloading the microcode to microengine, maintaining the related tables in SRAM and SDRAM, and determining the routing path for new .NET Remoting request. The data path system is implemented in microcode, a kind of assembly codes designed for microengines of Intel network processors. The functionality of data path system includes parsing and rewriting the packet header and delivers the exception packet to StrongARM core. The communication between StrongARM core and microengines was archived by a resource manager and scratch memory. Experiments done on IXP 1200 network processors show that our schemes are effective in supporting .NET Remoting computations over meta-cluster environments.

The rest of this paper is organized as follows. Section 2 presents the frameworks for meta-cluster supports for .NET Remoting with the assistance of IXP network processors. Next, Section 3 presents load-balancing schemes for workflow models. Experimental results are then presented in Section 4. Section 5 describes related works. Finally, Section 6 concludes this paper.

2. Efficient Switching Support for .NET Remoting

For meta-cluster supports with .NET remoting, the workload dispatcher is generally needed. Loading balancing mechanism is divided into centralized [6] [1] and distributed [8] versions. We focus on the centralized version in our work. The centralized mode installs a gateway in front of the cluster. The gateway parses incoming request and makes appropriate routing decisions according to specific request attribute (such as source IP address and URL) and server workload feedbacks. The bottleneck for the .NET remoting dispatchers often occurs in the gateway because it needs high computation power to process a huge number of remoting requests. In addition, if the application is stateful, the gateway will consume additional cost to keep the coherence of sessions. We demonstrate how to distribute workloads of .NET remoting with the assistance of IXP 1200 network processors.

Figure 1 shows the system architecture of our design. The network processor NP serves as the gateway of remoting services hosted on each backend servers. All TCP channel connections of remoting going to the servers are brokered by the network processor. It uses its special hardware architecture to do fast TCP/IP header rewriting for directing packets back and forth. A TCP connection table is maintained in the memory space of the network processor to keep track of the connection information. It includes the IP and port information of the client and the connected server for

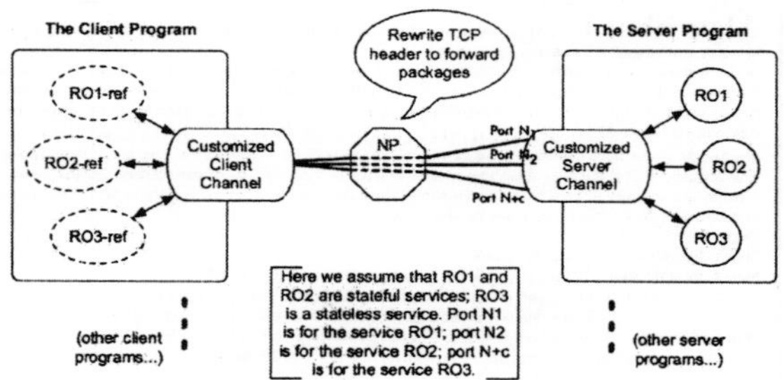

Figure 1. The system architecture of using network processors as the remoting service gateway.

each connection.

As a gateway of the backend servers, the job of NP is to dispatch remoting invocations concerning the load-balancing issues and the session semantics. For stateless remoting services, NP chooses the least load server to dispatch invocations; for stateful remoting services, NP has to make sure that invocations belonging to the same session will be dispatched to the same server. In Figure 1, RO1, RO2 and RO3 are all remoting objects that contain the intended operations for remote invocations. The RO1-ref, RO2-ref and RO3-ref in the client side are the TransparentProxy objects referring to RO1, RO2 and RO3 respectively. Both the proxy object and the remoting object use a channel object to manage network connections for data transportation. In this system, we design and deploy a pair of extended channel objects to automatically distribute remoting invocations into different TCP connection ports according to their service types. By doing this, NP can identify the service types through the examination of the destination port of incoming request packets. On the distribution of services on different ports, we use a map data structure to record the assigned port for each remoting service. All stateless services are bound to the port number large than c, where c is a selected constant. This map information can be a part of the remoting service deployment configurations and is accessible by the clients and the servers. We describe the distribution mechanism done by the channel objects below.

- **Client Channel Object** When the SyncProcessMessage or AsyncProcessMessage method of the client channel object is called in order to start a remoting invocation, it analyzes the parameter IMessage object to fetch the remoting service name. The mapped port for that remoting service is looked up by the map and is used for sending request packets.
- **Server Channel Object** When the server channel object is first instantiated, it looks up the map for all the currently used ports for remoting services. Then it opens corresponding server sockets on these ports to listen to connections.

Algorithm 1 shown in Figure 2 gives the detailed dispatching process done by the network processor. The main effort of this dispatching algorithm is to decide which server

Algorithm 1 **A dispatching algorithm for handling stateless and stateful Remoting invocations by using dedicated TCP channel connections.**

In the context. TCT stands for the TCP connection table that is maintained to track existing TCP connections. Each row in TCT contains four columns: the source IP, the source port, the destination IP and the destination port of one TCP connection. The destination port of each TCP connection is restricted to be within one of the three integer ranges $R_{single-call}$, $R_{singleton}$ and $R_{client-activated}$. They are used to identify the connections dedicated to single-call, singleton or client-activated Remoting invocations, respectively. Another tabie ST is the session table maintained to track existing sessions of stateful services. Each row in ST contains five columns to keep track of information about one session. They are the source IP, the source port, the destination IP, the destination port, and the access time of this session.

Begin
Step 1. Receive a packet from the clients.
Step 2. Read the source IP information in the TCP/IP header into $SrcIP$.
    Read the source port information in the TCP/IP header into $SrcPort$.
    Read the destination port information in the TCP/IP header into $DestPort$.
Step 3. if (there exists a row $Conn$ in TCT that (the source IP of $Conn == SrcIP$)
    && (the source port of $Conn == SrcPort$) && (the destination port of $Conn$
    $== DestPort$))
        Read the destination IP column of $Conn$ into $DestIP$.
        Goto Step 13.
Step 4. if ($DestPort$ is in range $R_{single-call}$)
        Goto Step 7.
Step 5. if ($DestPort$ is in range $R_{singleton}$)
        if (there exists a row $Sess$ in ST that (the destination port of $Sess ==$
        $DestPort$)
            Goto Step 10.
Step 6. if ($DestPort$ is in range $R_{client-activated}$)
        if (there exists a row $Sess$ in ST that (the source IP of $Sess == SrcIP$) &&
        (the source port of $Sess == SrcPort$) && (the destination port of $Sess ==$
        $DestPort$))
            Goto Step 10.
Step 7. Find the least load server and write its IP to S.
Step 8. if ($DestPort$ is in range $R_{single-call}$)
        Goto Step 12.
Step 9. Create a new row $Sess'$.
        Assign $SrcIP$ to the source IP column of $Sess'$.
        Assign $SrcPort$ to the source Port column of $Sess'$.
        Assign $DestPort$ to the destination port column of $Sess'$.
        Assign S to the destination IP column of $Sess'$.
        Assign the current time to the time column cf $Sess'$.
    Insert $Sess'$ to ST
    Goto Step 12.
Step 10. if ((the current time) - (the time column of $Sess$) $>= SESSION\_TIMEOUT$)
        Delete $Sess$ from ST.
        Goto Step 7.
Step 11. Read the destination IP column of $Sess$ into S.
Step 12. Assign S to $DestIP$.
Step 13. Rewrite the TCP/IP header of the packet with $DestIP$ as the destination IP.
Step 14. Send out the packet.
End

Figure 2. The dispatching algorithm for remoting invocations.

a TCP connection is going to be connected with. It is the place where dispatching decisions are made. Once a server is chosen and the connection is constructed, all remoting invocations go through this link are served by this server. Here we can have the channel objects periodically discard connections in purpose for the reconstruction of connections to less load servers. The network processor records the IP and port information of the client and the selected server in the TCP connection table called TCT for each constructed connection. The remoting request packets with the same source IP, the same source port, and the same destination port will be directed to the same destination IP according to TCT. The response packets from the servers are also directed to the correct clients by this connection table. Notice that the destination port mentioned here is used to identify remoting services since we have distributed different services to go on different ports in our customized client channel objects. Step 3 of Algorithm 1 does the checking to see if the incoming packet is already in a TCT entry. In addition, with the destination port plus the IP and port information of the client, we can construct a session table ST. ST is then used to track existing sessions for stateful services.

If the network processor finds that no TCP connection exists for the incoming packet and the destination port shows that it belongs to a stateful service, it will then look up ST to find out the previous assigned server for this service. Step 4 checks if the incoming packet is in the range of stateful services. In addition, State 5 and state 6 checks if the incoming packet is a singleton or a client-activated method. Note that there are three kinds of methods in .Net remoting. Single-call is stateless, and stateful methods include singleton and client-activated methods. Our scheduling policy fully supports these three semanitcs for .Net methods. A time field is also kept in ST to determine the expiration of a session. Step 10 does the checking for the expiration of a session. The network processor can also invalidate the content in TCT and ST on purpose in order to reallocate stateful services to new servers for load-balancing issues, the Remoting proxy in the client side will detect a network failure exception and then can try to construct a new TCP connection to the backend. Step 7 directs the connection construction request to least load servers. Once the least server is found, step 8 checks if the incoming method is indeed a stateful request. A ST will be created if this is a new stateful request. Finally, the algorithm does TCP header rewriting to forward packets to and from the intended server of that connection. This is done between step 11 and step 13.

3. Load Balancing Mechanisms

The key scheduling policy for our algorithm in handling both stateful and stateless services of .NET remoting is shown earlier in Algorithm 1. Step 7 of this dispatching algorithm is to find the least load server for dispatching. Different scheduling methods can be plugged in for this step. In the following, we propose two methods for this purpose. The first method is to schedule tasks to the server minimizing the estimated task time. The second method incorporates work-flow models for task scheduling. This is to exploit the fact that many of the tools of grid architectures are now equipped with work-flow model supports [7].

3.1 ETT Scheduling Methods

According to the characteristics of applications, we propose an algorithm which dispatches the request by referencing cpu computing power and the network bandwidth. The ***Estimated Task Time*** (ETT) model is defined as

$$ETT(n_i, s_j) = \frac{cc(n_i)}{P_j \times (1 - CPU\_load)} + \frac{d(n_i)}{W_j \times (1 - bandwidth\_load)} \tag{1}$$

The $\mathbf{cc}(\mathrm{n}_i)$ is the cycle of task n_i, the $\mathbf{d}(\mathrm{n}_i)$ is the amount of data needed for communications. $\mathbf{P}_j$ is the clock rate of

```
Find_Least_Load_Server(){
    while there is an incoming request n_i do
        for each server s_j do
            Compute ETT(n_i, s_j)
        Assign request n_i to the server s_k that minimizes ETT of request n_i
    end while
}
```

Figure 3. The ETT Load-Balancing Algorithm.

the processor in server s_j. $\mathbf{W}_j$ is the network bandwidth of server s_j. Note that cpu load and network loadings can be gotten from feedbacks of the back-end computing servers, periodically. The characteristics of jobs such as computing time and communication time can also be gotten by profiling schemes of systems. The scheduling algorithm for Step 7 of Algorithm 1 is now given in Figure 3.

3.2. Scheduling Methods with Work-Flow Graphs

We now present a scheduling method which incorporates work-flow models for task scheduling. A work-flow of tasks is represented as directed acyclic graph (DAG). An example of such a graph is shown in Figure 4. Nodes represent application tasks and edges represent data communication. The computation costs and communication costs are stored in a $n \times 1$ and $n \times n$ matrix, respectively. In the example graph, tasks $n_4, n_6, n_8, n_9, n_{10}$ are stateful tasks associating with two different services. The graph also comes with information to mark the stateful tasks when the timeout constraint for expiration is raised. In this case, the successors in the stateful tasks can be redirected to other servers for load balancing. This timeout information is presented as the dotted line of the edge. In our example graph, the edge between tasks n_4 and n_8 is with timeout edge. We assume every server can execute maximum k tasks in parallel. Tasks will be queued until the running tasks are less than k in a server and the computation cost will be n times of the original execution time of a task when there are n tasks executed on a server.

We have defined several attributes for task scheduling. The rank of the tasks represent the priorities of the scheduling order. The $rank(n_i)$ is the approximation of the length of the longest path from the task n_i to the exit task. The rank of task n_i is defined by

$$rank(n_i) = w_i + \max_{n_j \in succ(n_i)} (c_{i,j} + rank(n_j)), \quad (2)$$

where w_i is the computation cost of task n_i, $succ(n_i)$ is the set of the immediate successors of task n_i, $c_{i,j}$ is the communication cost of edge(i, j). According to the rank, we schedule tasks by decreasing order of a rank.

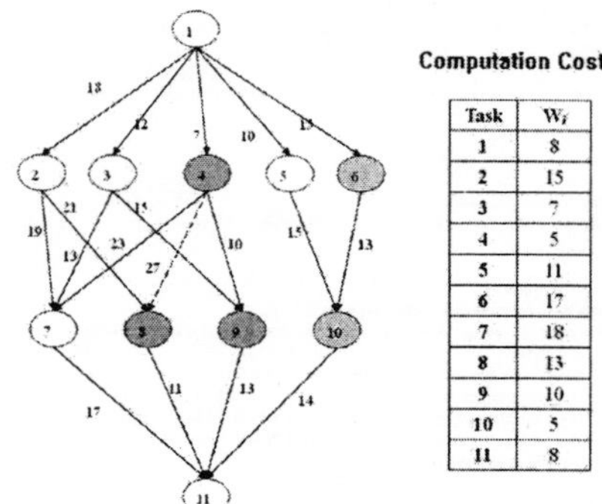

Computation Costs

Task	W_i
1	8
2	15
3	7
4	5
5	11
6	17
7	18
8	13
9	10
10	5
11	8

Figure 4. An example of a task graph with 11 tasks.

Our scheduling algorithm presents a two-phase scheduling policy. In the first phase, we perform a pre-scheduling for all stateful tasks, and then we perform scheduling for stateless tasks in the second phase.

In our first phase, we first mark all the stateful tasks by traversing the graph. If the edge before the task is marked as timeout, all the tasks following the edge will be recognized as a new stateful group. After separating the stateful tasks into different groups, we can then schedule each group one by one. We use the following equation to estimate the load of the stateful tasks which have been scheduled to the server.

$$Load(s_i) = \sum_{\forall g_j \text{ has been scheduled to } s_i} \{ \sum_{\forall n_k \in g_j} R_k \}, \quad (3)$$

where s_i is the i-th server, R_k is the remaining computation time of task n_k, and g_j is the j-th group of the stateful task groups. We also have

$$AddLoad(s_i, g_t) = Load(s_i) + \{ \sum_{\forall n_k \in g_t} R_k \}. \quad (4)$$

In order to balance the group load of the stateful tasks, we use the AddLoad function to calculate the total computation cost of each group when adding a new scheduled group. We then dispatch them to servers by picking up the minimum one. The scheduling algorithm is illustrated in the routine $Phase1\_Stateful\_Scheduler()$ of Figure 5.

After all the stateful tasks have been scheduled, we subsequently schedule the stateless tasks by the order generated by rank. The phase2_stateless_scheduler routine in Figure 5 presents the algorithm for the second phase of the scheduling. When a stateful task leaves the queue and prepare to be executed, we check the timeout value of the stateful group which was separated by the given timeout mark. To see the timeout will happen or not, if not, we will redirect the

```
Algorithm 2 The EFT load-balancing algorithms with work-flow information to handle both
stateful and stateless tasks.

Input: A task graph G with the computation cost, communication costs, and the stateful groups.

Phase1_Stateful_Scheduler(){
    while there is a unscheduled group g_i do
        for each server s_j do
            Compute the AddLoad(s_j, g_i).
        Assign the tasks of g_i to the server s_k that minimizes AddLoad(s_k, g_i).
    end while
}
Phase2_Stateless_Scheduler(){
    while there is a un-scheduled task in the graph do
        Find the highest ranked task among un-scheduled tasks, say n_i, for scheduling
        if task n_i is stateful {
            if(the timeout constraint for expiration is raised for task n_i)
                and ((the current time)-(the time for last done task of this group))<TIMEOUT{
                Assign the tasks of the group to the server which the task of this group has been scheduled.
                Revise this scheduling information to call Phase1_statefull_Scheduler()
                 to re-do remaining stateful tasks.
            }
            else do
                Assign the stateful request to the server assigned at phase one and update the session table.
            end if
        }
        else {/* Schedule stateless tasks */
            for each server s_j do
                Compute EFT(n_i, s_j).
            Assign request n_i to the server s_k that minimizes EFT of request n_i.
        }
        Update the connection table
    end while
}
```

Figure 5. The EFT load-Balancing algorithm for the application with a work-flow graph.

rest stateful tasks to the original server to keep the correctness of the stateful service. In this case, we also indicate the roll-back of the scheduling results for stateful tasks, and re-run the stateful scheduler in the phase one for the remaining stateful tasks. For a stateless task, we use the following function to estimate the finish time of the stateless task executing on the servers.

$$EFT(n_i, s_j) = Exec(w_i, avail[s_j], k) + \max_{n_m \in pred(n_i)} (AFT(n_m) + c_{m,i}), \quad (5)$$

where $pred(n_i)$ is the set of immediate predecessor tasks of task n_i, and $avail[s_j]$ is the earliest time at which server s_j is ready for task execution. AFT(n_m) is the actual finish time of the task n_m. $Exec(w_i, avail[s_j], k)$ is the execution cost of task n_i with computation cost w_i executed on the server s_j which can parallel execute at most k tasks from time $avail[s_j]$. And we choose the server with the minimum EFT to schedule. The last paragraph of the second routine in Figure 5 illustrates this idea.

4 Experiments

The experimental environment includes two clients and two clusters. These two clients each belongs to individual subnet issuing remoting requests to the load balancer. On the other hand, two identical clusters composed of two P4-2GHz servers were employed to run Remoting server applications. In the hardware configuration of NLB experiment,

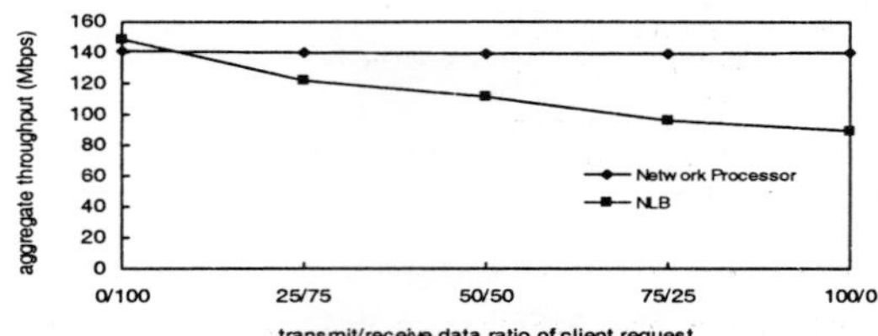

Figure 6. Throughputs with two different load-balancing mechanisms.

we replace IXP1200 with a 4-port 100Mbps switch such that the maximum aggregate throughput from servers could reach to 200Mbps. The throughput is given in Figure 6 where we compare the throughputs of our proposed dispatcher for .NET remoting with that of Microsoft Network Load Balancing (NLB) technology. NLB is a distributed methodology in which each server in the NLB cluster will receive the same copy of packet. Our work is to have .NET remoting framework classified into two separate channels in one application, one is for stateful, and another is for stateless. We then try to dispatch jobs by using the proposed mechanism in Section 3.2.

To measure the throughput, two clients concurrently called a method transferData() which will transmit a piece of data buffer to the server and receive another data buffer back. The ratio between transmitting and receiving buffer size is adjustable. There are totally 128Kbytes exchanged in one method call, that is, a client transmits 128*ratio Kbytes to a server and receives 128*(1-ratio) Kbytes each time transferData() was called. We adjusted the ratio from 0 to 1 progressively and measured the aggregate throughput of two clients. Figure 6 shows the experimental result.

When only the client received data from the server (ratio = 0), the performance of NLB is close to 150Mbps which is 5.4% better than our system. However, the throughput of NLB declined as the ratio increased while our system remained high throughput. When the ratio was raised to 0.08, both two systems have similar performance. The throughput of NLB decreased to 90Mbps when only clients transmitted data to servers. This is because NLB is a distributed methodology in which each server in the NLB cluster will receive the same copy of packet. The NLB driver in front of TCP/IP protocol stack will decide to forward the packet to protocol stack or discard it according to given packet information (ex. TCP/IP header). The aggregate packet received on server side equals the amount of packets transmitted from client side multiplied by the server number of NLB cluster. Consequently, NLB may waste network bandwidth while our system does not.

Next, we compare the scheduling effects with our

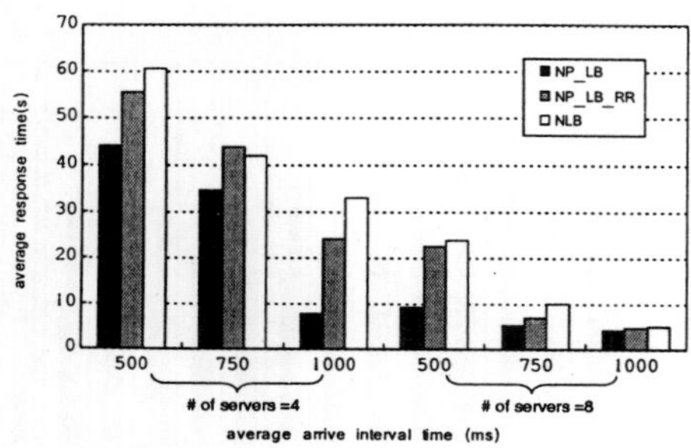

Figure 7. The response time among three load balancing mechanisms with interval time (500, 750, 1000).

	ID	Combination
1	1+1	(Ingress+L2+LB+L3) + (Egress)
2	1+1+1	(Ingress) + (L2+LB+L3) + (Egress)
3	1+4+1	(Ingress) + (L2+LB+L3)*4 + (Egress)
4	1+3+2	(Ingress) + (L2+LB+L3)*3 + (Egress)*2
5	2+3+1	(Ingress)*2 + (L2+LB+L3)*3 + (Egress)
6	2+2+2	(Ingress)*2 + (L2+LB+L3)*2 + (Egress)*2

Figure 8. The effects of microengine allocations.

scheduling policy. In the experiment, we developed a Remoting method getPrimeCount(int X) that could calculate the count of prime number smaller than integer X. (Note that the CPU consumption time of this method is positively proportional to X.) On the client side, the client program invoked the Remoting method repeatedly by an interval time Y (milliseconds). To simulate real environment, we generated Y by an exponential function floor(-log(rand(0,1))* intervalMulti). Similarly, the number X which the client wants to calculate was also generated by an exponential function floor(-log(rand(0,1))* primeRangeMulti). Therefore, the average X and Y are primeRangeMulti and intervalMulti, respectively. According to primeRangeMulti=30K and different intervalMulti values (500, 750 and 1000 ms) for (4, 8) nodes, we generated 3 X-Y distribution samples each with 1000 points. It means the client program will use these samples to call getPrimeCount(X) 1000 times, totally. We measured the response time of each method call in three load balancing mechanisms. The first one is our load balancer (called NP_LB), the second one is also our system but it dispatches jobs in round-robin fashion instead of dispatching by servers' load (called NP_LB_RR). The final one is NLB technology. The results were shown in Figure 7.

We could find out that the average response time of NP_LB is better than NP_LB_RR and NLB in all combinations. When server number is 2 and average arrival interval time is 1 second, NP_LB could reduce 76.1% response latency than NLB. That is because NP_LB dispatches the request according to servers' load rather than the random selection used by NLB or round-robin selection in NB_LB_RR such that it could get better CPU utilization.

In the following we measure the performance factors in microengine allocations of network processors in our implementation. In the experiment, we try different microengine allocation to examine how it affects load balancer. Just like the previous experiment, we measure the aggregate throughput of two clients which invoke transferData() concurrently. There are 6 combinations listed in Table 8. Except for the first combination, the microblocks for layer-2 bridging processing, load balancing processing, and layer-3 forwarding processing (called main processing for short) was allocated together. Take the third combination (1+4+1) as example; it allocates one microengine for packet ingress, one for packet engress, and the other four for the main processing. The result was shown in Figure 9, combination 1 and 2 have the similar performance although the latter activated one more microengine. It explains that the internal packet forwarding from one microengine to another increase the memory access overhead and therefore eliminates the gain of additional microengine computation power. Combination 3 has the best performance because main processing requires most computation power. It was illustrated by combination 4, 5, and 6. We arranged one microengine from main processing to transmit packets in combination 4. Similarly, two microengines were assigned to receive packets in combination 5. These two groups both result about 14% throughput drop compared with the best one. Nevertheless, the last combination which rearranged two microengine for packet ingress, two for main processing and two for packet egress diminish almost quarter throughput. We could summarize that the quantity of computation power for main processing affect the system performance rather than the computation power needed for

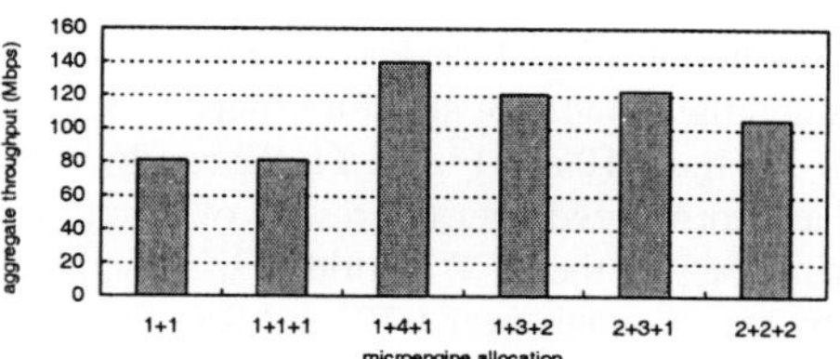

Figure 9. Throughputs with different microengine allocations.

Parameter	Value
V	25, 50, 100, 200, 400
S	1
O	2, 3, 4
CCR	0.3
Stateful groups	2, 4, 8
Stateful task ratio	0.25, 0.5

Table 1. Parameter sets used in Figure 10 and Figure 11

packet input and output.

Finally, we experiment with our workload algorithms EFT by simulations. We have constructed a software simulator that emulates the network processor dispatching behavior for scheduling random tasks. The work-flow graphs of tasks are generated by a general graph generator with several parameters:

- **Number of nodes** v: The number of nodes (tasks) in the graph.
- **Shape of graph** s: We use this parameter to control the shape of graphs. The levels of generated graphs form a normal distribution with the mean value equal to $\sqrt{v}/s$. The nodes of each level also form a normal distribution with the mean value equal to $\sqrt{v} * s$.
- **Out degree** O: Out edges of each node. We use this parameter to control the dependence degrees between two tasks.
- **Communication to computation ratio** CCR: It is the ratio of the communication cost to computation cost. We can generate computation-intensive application graphs by assigning low values to CCR.
- **Number of stateful task groups**: It denotes the number of stateful service groups. We can also control the height of each stateful task group by supplied parameters.

In order to demonstrate the benefits of our ETT algorithm on dealing with stateful tasks, we use the parameters as listed in Table 1. Under the parameter settings in Table 1, we show the performance results of two different stateful task ratio 25% and 50% in Figure 10 and Figure 11, respectively. We use 500 graph instances for evaluating each parameter setttings. The x-axis gives different distribution of task nodes. It includes the amount of tasks and the amount of stateful groups as specified in Table 1. In Figure 10 and Figure 11, the results with ETT and EFT are normalized over the results of Round-robin (RR). We can see that the EFT algorithm has significant performance improvement over ETT and RR. The improvement goes higher with bigger task graph and higher stateful task ratio. While the stateful task ratio is 25%, the improvement of EFT is from 2.76% to 12.63% when compared to ETT and is from 9.31% to 34% when compared to RR; While the stateful task ratio is 50%, the improvement of EFT is from 5% to 21% when compared to ETT and is from 8% to 34% when compared to RR. This phenomenon can be explained by the pre-known knowledge of work-flow graphs and the specific handling of stateful tasks in EFT. In phase 1 of the EFT algorithm, it will first consider the scheduling of stateful task groups. It pre-assigns the stateful groups into back-end servers according to the group computation load. In phase 2, we also provide a mechanism for stateful task groups to timeout and rescheduling. This produces a more fine-grained load-balancing scheduling.

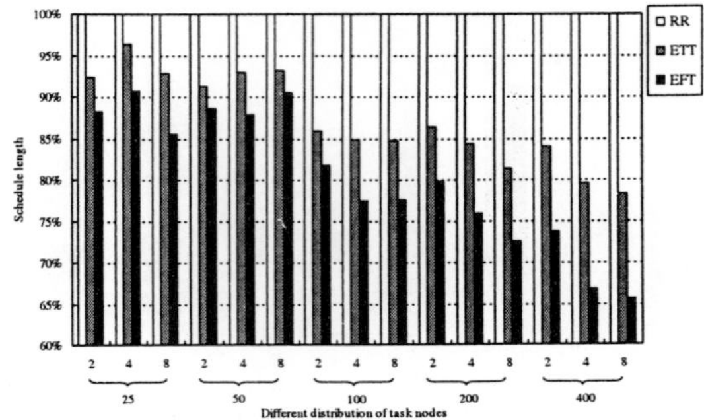

Figure 10. Performance of EFT scheme with work-flow information (25% stateful tasks in each graph).

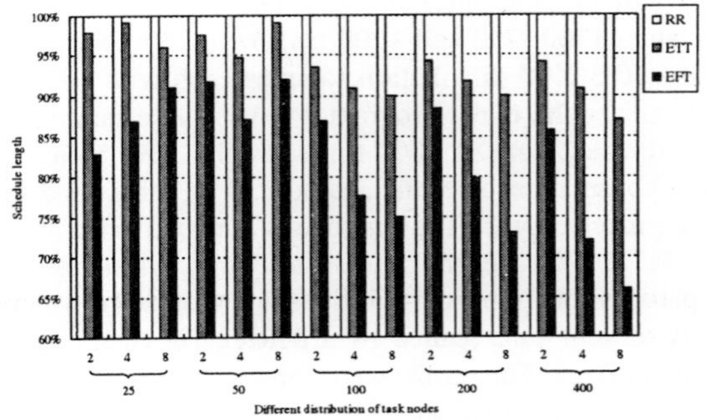

Figure 11. Performance of EFT schemes with work-flow information (50% stateful tasks in each graph).

5. Related Work

Efficient task scheduling algorithms are vital for achieving high performanced from cluster-based computer systems. The task scheduling problem of multiprocessor environments is NP-complete in general forms [9, 10]. Therefore, heuristic solutions are suitable for such problems. There are two models for this problem, static and dynamic model. In static model, task execution time, task type, task dependence, and communication cost should be known in advance. According to foregoing information, tasks are assigned to suitable processors to achieve minimum scheduling length. In the dynamic model, status feedback of each processor, which like CPU utility, bandwidth utility and task distribution, is profiled. Various heuristics were proposed for the task scheduling problem in [11, 12, 13, 14, 15]. Among those work, Wu's work [11] also proposed efficient algorithms HEFT and CPOP to cope with work-flow graph for heterogeneous computing. The HEFT algorithm was used to to find out the Earliest-Finish-Time server to dispatch task, and the CPOP algorithm uses critical path to arrange the dispatch order. Both of two algorithms get good performance and low overhead. In our case, we are dealing with .NET Remoting applications, and we need to handle the schedulings for both the stateful and stateless tasks. In addtion, we allow k tasks to be scheduled in each processor.

6. Conclusion

In this paper, we presented our methodologies in supporting .NET Remoting over meta-clustered environments. Both Stateful and stateless supports for .NET Remoting services are incorporated. Experiments show that our scheme can significantly enhance the system throughput (up to 55%) compared to NLB method when the traffic is heavy. Our work gave a comprehensive study for efficient support of .NET remoting in the presence of advanced network architectures such as IXP network processors. Our proposed scheduling methods include schemes with or without work-flow information of tasks. Further efforts to integrate our scheduling policy with CCA grid environments will be important directions for future research explorations.

References

[1] George Apostolopoulos, David Aubespin, Vinod Peris, Prashant Pradhan, and Debanjan Saha, Design, Implementation and Performance of a Content-Based Switch, in *Proceedings of IEEE Infocom 2000*, Mar. 2000.

[2] Chung-Kai Chen, Cheng-Wei Chen, Jenq Kuen Lee. Specification and Architecture Supports for Component Adaptations on Distributed Environments, *Proceedings of the IPDPS Conference*, Santa Fe, April 2004.

[3] National Science Council(NSC) *Research Excellence Project* http://www.ccrc.nthu.edu.tw/PPAEUII/.

[4] Cheng-Wei Chen, Chung-Kai Chen, Jyh-Cheng Chen, Chien-Tan Ko, Jenq-Kuen Lee, Hong-Wei Lin, Wang-Jer Wu. Efficient Support of Java RMI over Heterogeneous Wireless Networks, *Proceedings of International Conference on Communications (ICC)*, Paris, June 2004.

[5] Patrick Eugster and Sébastien Baehni Abstracting Remote Object Interaction in a Peer-2-Peer Environment. In *Proceedings of Joint ACM Java Grande - ISCOPE 2002 Conference*, pp. 46–55, 2002.

[6] Robert Haas, Lukas Kencl, Andreas Kind, Bernard Metzler, Roman Pletka, Marcel Waldvogel, Laurent Frelechoux, and Patrick Droz, IBM Research Clark Jeffries, IBM Corporation, Creating Advanced Functions on Network Processors: Experience and Perspectives, *IEEE Network*, July/August 2003.

[7] Sriram Krishnan, and Dennis Gannon. XCAT3: A Framework for CCA Components as OGSA Services. In *Proceedings of International Workshop on High-Level Parallel Programming Models and Supportive Environments*, April 2004.

[8] G. Teodoro, T. Tavares, B. Coutinho, W. Meira Jr., and D. Guedes, Load Balancing on Stateful Clustered Web Servers, in *15th Symposium on Computer Architecture and High Performance Computing (SBAC-PAD'03)*, November, 2003.

[9] M.R. Gary and D.S. Johnson, Computers and Intractability: A Guide to the Theory of NP-Completeness. *W.H. Freeman and Co. 1979.*

[10] W.H. Kohler and K. Steiglitz, Characterization and Theoretical Comparison of Branch-and-Bound Algorithms for Permutation Problems, *J.ACM, Vol. 21, no. 1,pp. 140-156*, Jan. 1974.

[11] M. Y. Wu, S. Hariri, and H. Topcuouglu, Performance-Effective and Low-Complexity Task Scheduling forHeterogeneous Computing. IEEE Trans on Parallel and Distributed Systems *IEEE Trans on Parallel and Distributed Systems*,Vol. 13, 260-274, 2002.

[12] Y. Kwok and I. Ahmad,Dynamic Critical-Path Scheduling: An Effective Technique for Allocating Task Graphs to Multiprocessors *IEEE Trans. Parallel and Distributed System*, Vol.7, no.5, pp. 506-521, May 1996.

[13] M. Wu, W. Shu and J. Gu, Local Search for DAG Scheduling and Task Assignment, *Proc. 1997 Int'l Conf. Parallel Processing*, pp. 174-180, 1997.

[14] B. Kruatrachue and T.G. Lewis, "Grain Size Determination for Parallel Processing, *IEEE Software*, PP. 23-32, Jan 1988.

[15] H. El-Rewini, H.H. Ali, and T. Lewis, Task Scheduling in Multiprocessor Systems, *Computer*, pp. 27-37, Dec. 1995.

[16] Intel IXP1200 Network Processor Hardware Reference Manual.

Service Migration in Distributed Virtual Machines for Adaptive Grid Computing

Song Fu and Cheng-Zhong Xu
Department of Electrical and Computer Engineering
Wayne State University, Detroit, Michigan 48202
{oaksong, czxu}@wayne.edu

Abstract

Computational grids can integrate geographically distributed resources into a seamless environment. To facilitate managing these heterogenous resources, the virtual machine technology provides a powerful layer of abstraction and allows multiple applications to multiplex the resources of a grid computer. On the other hand, the grid dynamics requires the virtual machine system be distributed and reconfigurable. However, the existing migration approaches only move the execution entities, such as processes, threads, and mobile agents, among servers and leave the runtime services behind. They are not potent to achieve service reconfiguration in face of server overload or failures. In this paper, we propose a service migration *mechanism, which moves the computational services of a virtual server, for instance a shared array runtime support system, to available servers for adaptive grid computing. In this way, parallel jobs can resume computation on a remote server without requiring service preinstallation. As an illustration of the service migration mechanism, we incorporated it into a Java-compliant distributed virtual machine, DSA, and formed a Mobile DSA (M-DSA) to accommodate adaptive parallel applications in grids. We measured the performance of M-DSA in the execution of applications from the SPLASH-2 benchmark suite on a campus grid. Experimental results show that service migration can achieve system adaptivity effectively.*

1 Introduction

Virtual machine (VM) technology provides a powerful layer of abstraction for resource management in grids [5]. It enables user applications to become strongly decoupled from the system software of the underlying resources and other applications. This property facilitates the development of grid applications by allowing programmers to use well-defined service interfaces. However, the conventional VMs can not efficiently coordinate the resource sharing and scale well in wide area environments, especially across administrative domains. A remedy for these problems is to construct a distributed virtual machine, by factoring virtual machine services into logical components, replicating and distributing them throughout a network [15].

A distributed VM can be viewed as a set of virtual servers running on top of multiple physical servers. It is certainly possible to deploy its components as static computing units. However, when a server running a parallel job is reclaimed by its owner, the remaining processes of the same job have to be stopped. Moreover, the application will terminate when a server failure occurs. Research in [10] shows the CPU availability and host availability are volatile in grids. Adaptivity is fundamental to achieving application performance in such dynamic environments [2]. Therefore, the abstraction layer provided by a distributed virtual machine would not be fully exploited unless it can be instantiated and reconfigured at runtime to tackle the grid dynamics.

The existing approaches to constructing reconfigurable systems, such as process/thread migration [12], have significant limitations. They only move the execution entities among servers and leave the supporting services behind. Their effectiveness is based on two assumptions: (1) there are servers with idle resources; (2) the underlying runtime support system, as a form of grid services, has already been running on the destinations. On the other hand, parallel applications strive to distribute computational jobs evenly among servers. As a result, it is difficult for an overloaded server to steal idle CPU cycles from another one with similar processing capacity. Things become even worse when a server is going to fail. In that case, all of the computational jobs on the failing node will swarm into other existing servers. It will lead to cascaded server overloads and the entire parallel application has to be stopped, if no new servers are added to the system. As to the second assumption, it is not proper to pre-install and execute all possible services on each grid computer, across different administrative domains.

In this paper, we propose a scalable and effective approach, *service migration*, to achieve adaptive grid computing. The semantics of service migration is to suspend the residing execution entities, stop the service programs of a virtual server on the source node, migrate the runtime service data and states along with the execution entities' states to a destination node, initiate a new virtual server with restored services on the destination, and resume application execution. In this way, parallel jobs can continue computation on an available server without requiring service preinstallation, when server overload and/or failures occur. Service migration provides a general approach to service reconfiguration. As a proof of concept, we incorporated service migration into our Distributed Shared Array (DSA) [1] system and designed a Mobile DSA (M-DSA). M-DSA supports a Java-compliant distributed virtual machine to accommodate parallel computation in heterogenous grids. Service migration allows reconfiguring the virtual machine and makes it adaptive to grid dynamics.

Experimental results in a campus grid environment showed that service migration achieved system adaptivity with marginal

0190-3918/05 $20.00 © 2005 IEEE

performance degradation, compared with that in a cluster. Our service migration method is complementary to other migration techniques moving execution entities. A hybrid migration infrastructure will make a system become more adaptive to the changing environment.

The remainder of this paper is organized as follows: Section 2 presents the related work. The overall architecture of M-DSA is given in Section 3. Section 4 describes the service migration design and implementation details. Section 5.1 focuses on the M-DSA interface to Globus service. In Section 6, we present performance results from SPLASH-2 benchmark programs. Conclusions are made in Section 7.

2 Related Work

Our service migration mechanism was inspired by the *capsule* migration in Stanford's Collective project [14]. The Collective capsule encapsulates the complete state of a machine, including the entire operating system as well as applications and running processes. Virtual machine monitors are utilized to capture system state. By transferring a capsule across a network and binding it to a destination computer architecture, a user can resume her work after a commute between home and office. Capsule migration presents the possibility of moving the underlying service components between computers for computation continuity. However, as designed at the OS layer, this migration approach incurs considerable overhead.

Research interests in applying the classical VMs to grid computing are recently revived, with the Denali [19] and DVM [15]. However, these systems are not easily reconfigurable, due to the enormous execution contexts. In contrast, application-level virtual machines can be tuned to become more efficient for specific applications, and it is much easier to migrate these lightweight services in a network. The global object space in JESSICA2 [22], and the DSA [1] in Traveler [21] are such examples.

Figueiredo *et al.* [5] proposed an architecture to provide network-based services in computational grids, based on classical virtual machines. To efficiently manage grid resources, it allows a VM to be created on any computer that has sufficient capacity to support it. Virtual server migration is realized by moving an entire computation environment to a remote virtualized compute server. However, the migration details and associated overheads were not discussed by the authors. With the OS and middleware level support, SODA [9] constructs a distributed VM for an application service on demand. Each virtual service node provides stationary runtime support for grid computation.

Besides, there is a large collection of process/thread migration approaches (see [12] for a good review) for adaptive computation. However, it is difficult to extend them into the heterogenous grids, because of the portability problem of the system software and programming languages that they relied on. JESSICA2 [22] is a distributed JVM supporting multi-threaded Java applications on a set of heterogenous computers. It realized thread migration by transferring the thread states between networked nodes. The success of its thread migration is based on the existence of a global object space, which provides a shared memory for the distributed nodes. As a result, when a node failure occurs, the entire system has to be stopped. HPCM [4] is a middleware supporting process migration in heterogenous environments. However, this is achieved by the scheduler moving pre-processed code to the new destination with a pre-run and machine-specific runtime system. So, process/thread migration alone cannot achieve service reconfiguration and cannot provide adequate adaptivity to the changing environment of wide area computing.

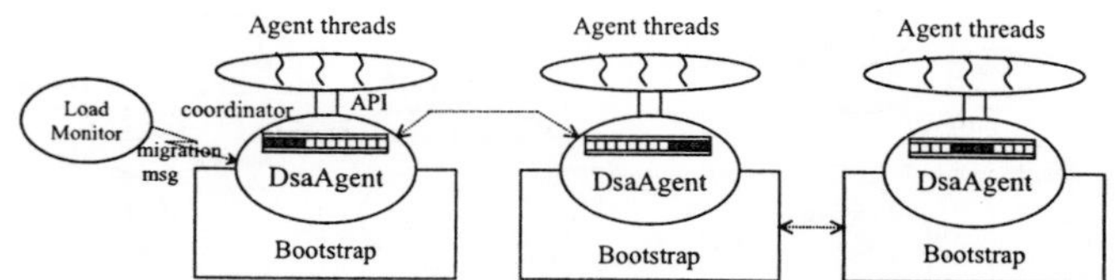

Figure 1. The M-DSA Architecture.

Finally, we note that for adaptive grid computing, the GrADS [8] system applies application migration [17] to manage grid dynamics. Their migration schemes do not move data and states of a runtime support service. Instead, the application's execution environment on a destination node is constructed by a centralized *Rescheduler*. As a result, much global information is maintained by the system, which compromises its scalability.

3 Overview of M-DSA Architecture

Service migration achieves adaptive grid computing by moving runtime support services from an overloaded or failing server to an available one. As an illustration of the service migration concept, we developed M-DSA, which extended a DSA runtime system [1] for virtually shared arrays with mobility support.

3.1 DSA Services

The DSA services provide a single system image across a set of compute nodes for distributed shared arrays. It relieves programmers from runtime scheduling of internode communications and the orchestration of the data distribution. Each DSA virtual server stores a portion of a shared array. Remote data access is supported by the DSA runtime system and transparent to application programs.

The DSA system comprises of a main API component known as the *DsaAgent*. Each virtual server involved in a parallel application has a DsaAgent. The DsaAgents are responsible for local and remote access to shared array elements. Parallel jobs are constructed as computational agents, distributed among the virtual servers. Operations over shared arrays include synchronous and asynchronous read and write. A SCI-like directory-based coherence protocol manages copies of an array block on different virtual servers. Besides, the DSA system provides APIs for barrier synchronization among agent threads. The original DsaAgents are stationary and cannot move between servers. As a result, a parallel application will make little progress or even be terminated, when servers become overloaded or failed.

3.2 Service Migration and M-DSA Architecture

To support service migration, we designed the M-DSA system with an architecture as depicted in Figure 1. The extended

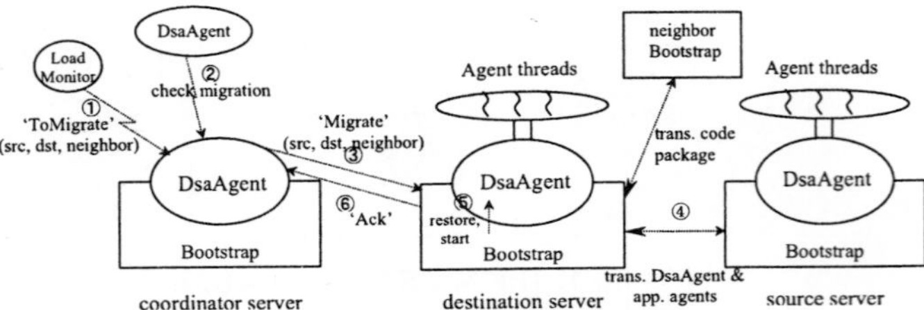

Figure 2. Procedure of Service Migration.

DsaAgents constitute a set of virtual servers in a distributed virtual machine. Migration-enabled methods allow a DsaAgent to perform service migration to transfer DSA services among physical servers. We refer to the DsaAgent on a server that starts a parallel application as the *coordinator*. It is responsible for receiving migration requests from the *LoadMonitor*, and triggering a service migration at some potential migration point. The LoadMonitor makes migration decisions based on the performance information collected by sensors on each virtual server, during the application execution. We discuss the migration decision problem in Section 5.1. The LoadMonitor is an independent Java object that can be run on any server of the distributed virtual machine. To accommodate service images transferred from remote nodes, a *Bootstrap daemon* is pre-run on the destination node. It receives the incoming service image and initiates a new DSA virtual server with the restored services.

Different applications can multiplex a grid computer. This is realized by allowing multiple virtual servers to reside on a physical server. They provide different runtime services and accommodate the corresponding computational agents. The M-DSA runs on top of the JVMs, which facilitate the service migration in heterogeneous environments. We will present the details of service migration in the next section.

4 Service Migration for Adaptive Computation

A service migration involves collecting and packing the states of runtime services and agents, transferring them to a destination node, re-initiating the services and resuming agent execution at the statement prior to migration on the new virtual server. Compared with process/thread migration [12], service migration deals with not only moving the execution context of each process/thread, but also the reconstruction of the execution environment on a remote server. It introduces more technical challenges as a consequence. In this section, we will describe the service migration mechanism for adaptive computation.

4.1 Service Migration Algorithm

As depicted in Figure 2, the service migration mechanism proceeds as follows:

1. When the LoadMonitor detects some server in the system is overloaded or to be unavailable, based on the application performance data collected from execution monitoring sensors, it issues a "ToMigrate" message, along with the addresses of the source and destination servers, and a neighbor server to the coordinator, which will record this message in a message queue.

2. When the parallel computation reaches a synchronization point, the coordinator is requested to perform migration checking, which finds out whether there is a migration request to be served at this synchronization point.

3. If a "ToMigrate" request is found in its queue, the coordinator will send a "Migrate" message to the Bootstrap daemon of the destination server, denoted as $bootstrap_{dst}$, and wait for the acknowledgement of migration completion.

4. Then $\text{bootstrap}_{\text{dst}}$ contacts the Bootstrap daemon on the source server, from which the DSA service pack and agent images will be transmitted to the destination. The related program codes are prefetched from the neighbor server.

5. The $\text{bootstrap}_{\text{dst}}$ loads the retrieved class files and builds the method area in the main memory. The DSA service and agents are reestablished by the restoration procedure. It also starts the DSA service by running the newly-initiated DsaAgent. Computational agents are triggered to resume their parallel jobs at the proper computation phase.

6. As soon as the service migration is successfully completed, the $\text{bootstrap}_{\text{dst}}$ sends an acknowledgement message back to the coordinator.

Next, we will present the details of service migration. Section 4.2 focuses on the monitoring of application performance, which provides crucial information for migration decision. The procedure of wrapping up and restoring the runtime service is described in Section 4.3. As a complement, we briefly discuss the agent migration in Section 4.4.

4.2 Performance Monitoring for Service Migration

The overhead associated with packing, transferring and rebuilding runtime services of a virtual server is relatively high. This requires that agents on a virtual server have sufficient amount of computation and two consecutive service migration points keep distant spans in order to mitigate the impact of migration overhead.

If a distributed virtual machine support a sequential consistency memory model, the system appears like a multiprogrammed uniprocessor and the virtual machine services can be migrated at any point with a guarantee of correctness of resumed execution. However, for better performance, the M-DSA system adopts a relaxed memory model to reduce both the number of messages and amount of data transfers between virtual servers. When the source server performs a service migration to a destination, the shared array partitions managed by the corresponding DsaAgent cannot be accessed during the migration. As a result, the memory consistency is complicated and it is similar to the consistency problem in "partitioned networks" [3]. In such a model, some virtually shared data between two consecutive synchronization points could be in inconsistent states. If agents access such data managed by the migrated DsaAgent, their computation may be incorrect, especially when they are used as input. To ensure correctness, service migration can only be allowed at synchronization points.

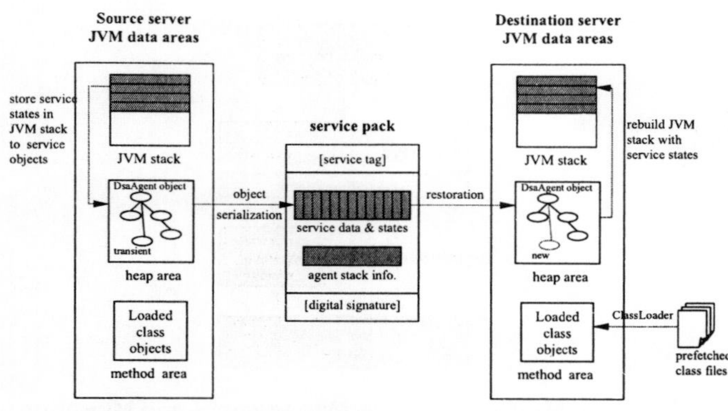

Figure 3. Service wrapping up and restoration in M-DSA service migration.

To exploit the benefits of service migration and minimize the impact of migration overhead, we monitor the dynamic performance of running applications and make migration decisions based on these accurate measurements. The Autopilot [13] toolkit is used to tune the migration timing according to the actual application progress. Each virtual server incorporates an *Autopilot sensor*, which extracts quantitative performance data of the corresponding application. The application program is instrumented with synchronization method calls and the DsaAgents record the execution time of each computation phase at those points. To relieve calculation burden in the *LoadMonitor* and avoid using much global information of the system, we specify an attached function for each sensor to normalize the execution time by the processing speed of a physical server.

When the *LoadMonitor* has collected the performance data from all the sensors, it compares the data with an overload threshold to make migration decisions. This threshold is a positive real number. Its value can be pre-defined or dynamically adjusted to tune to heterogenous systems. When a service migration is decided, we need to find an appropriate destination server to accommodate the migrated virtual server. This involves the resource management in M-DSA. We will present its details along with a rigorous model for migration decision in Section 5.1.

During service migration, the runtime data and states of a virtual server are transferred to a remote physical server. As a consequence, the monitoring infrastructure should be adjusted. This adjustment is small, because there is no direct connections among sensors. A sensor for the new virtual server is instantiated on the destination. Then the Autopilot toolkit registers properties of this sensor to the *Autopilot manager*, which resides on the LoadMonitor and acts as a name server for clients to look up sensors.

4.3 Service Wrapping Up and Restoration

In this section, we discuss the policies for wrapping up and restoring various JVM runtime data structures for service migration. The objective is to minimize the amount of data and states to be captured, while ensuring the correct resumption of services after migration.

The JVM specification [11] defines several data areas that are used during program execution, including the heap, method area, and JVM stack. They together form the execution context of a runtime service on a virtual server. To allow different applications to multiplex resources of a computer, we let the Bootstrap daemon on each node capture the service data and states, and wrap them into an application-independent form, *service pack*. As illustrated in Figure 3, the service pack contains components from the following areas:

The *heap* area for a virtual server stores the dynamically created shared arrays and associated control structures. Since they record the runtime information and contents of the shared arrays, most data structures maintained in the heap area have to be contained in the service pack. An exception is the *locks* for block accesses, because they can be created and initiated on the new virtual server. In M-DSA, we include the shared arrays in service pack instead of in the agent image, because they are allocated in the virtual server address space and accessed by computational agents only via well defined APIs. After the virtual server is restored on a new destination, the agents' references to a shared array will be updated by using the array name to locate the actual array object.

The *method* area stores the per-class structure for each loaded class. It can be rebuilt at the destination when all the referenced classes are loaded. So, we do not include information of the method area in the service pack. To retrieve a remote class file, M-DSA applies a *prefetch* technique to let the new destination server retrieve the virtual server and application program codes in parallel with the transmission of a service pack, from a nearby server. We realize this technique with the aid of *LoadMonitor*. When the *LoadMonitor* triggers a service migration, it selects an existing lightly-loaded physical server that is in the same local area network as the new destination, i.e., their subnet addresses are identical. Then, a migration message containing the network addresses of ⟨class download server, migration source, migration destination⟩ is sent to the Bootstrap daemon of the new destination. The daemon contacts the nearby server for program codes, while waiting for the arrival of service pack from the source.

A *JVM stack* maintains the frames for virtual server method calls. Each virtual server provides the shared array access services to computational agents by defining a set of access methods, and these services will be re-initiated on a new physical server after migration. Therefore, the JVM stack can be rebuilt on the destination without transferring the stack frames. However, there is some control information, such as the shared arrays' names, the number of agents, and their references, that should be kept in a service migration. These control information is well stored in the local variables of the virtual server object when a service migration occurs. Therefore, we transfer the virtual server object containing the necessary control information to the destination, and restore the object there.

If there are multiple virtual servers on a physical server, the Bootstrap daemon wraps them into separate service packs and migrates them one by one. Correspondingly, they will be restored sequentially on the destination server after migration.

4.4 Computational Agent State Capture

A computational agent contains one or a set of threads carrying out parallel jobs. In M-DSA, we transfer the states of computational agents along with the service pack to reduce migration overhead of sequential transmission of service states and agent states. The details are as follows.

Each virtual server contains a data structure recording all its residing agents and having a reference to each agent object. During service packing, as discussed in the preceding subsection, the virtual server object is serialized. As a result, all its referenced non-transient members, including the agent objects, will be included in the service pack. When the service pack is transferred to a new server, the agent thread objects will also be moved there. A challenge in agent movement is how to ensure its threads will resume execution just at the points where they are stopped.

The *program counter* (pc) register, in the per-thread runtime data area, contains the address of the Java instruction currently being executed by a thread. It indicates the starting point of computation after service migration. Since the potential migration points are at the computation phase boundaries, we apply a portable approach to preserve the pc register information. We represent a thread's pc register by a set of integer numbers stored in `phaseNum`. After an agent thread has performed a computation phase, the `phaseNum` is increased by 1 to indicate the index of next phase. Then, a `barrier` method carries out a synchronization operation. It also makes the coordinator DsaAgent check whether there is any service migration request. To let the agent thread locate the right computation phase after migration, a `if` statement is inserted at the beginning of each phase to compare the value of `phaseNum` with the phase index of the following computation. Positive values of `phaseNum` indicate the agent was migrated and has executed on another server.

Unlike service packing, we extract the agent thread execution state stored in the JVM stack frames. We adopt the state capture and restoration approaches proposed in [16] to rebuild thread stack on a server after migration. At the same time, the thread pc register is set according to the value of `phaseNum` and the set of `if` statements. Thus, an agent can resume execution at the correct computation phase after a service migration.

5 Interface to Globus Service

The Globus Toolkit [6] is the de facto standard for grid computing. It provides an infrastructure and tools to manage grid resources. To construct a reconfigurable distributed virtual machine in the grid environment, we developed the interface to Globus in M-DSA for efficient and secure resource management.

5.1 Resource Management and Migration Decision

Resource management is an important component for the system startup and service migration, because we need to select appropriate physical servers to accommodate the DSA services. Figure 4 depicts the resource management architecture of M-DSA. It also presents the components that make the service migration decisions.

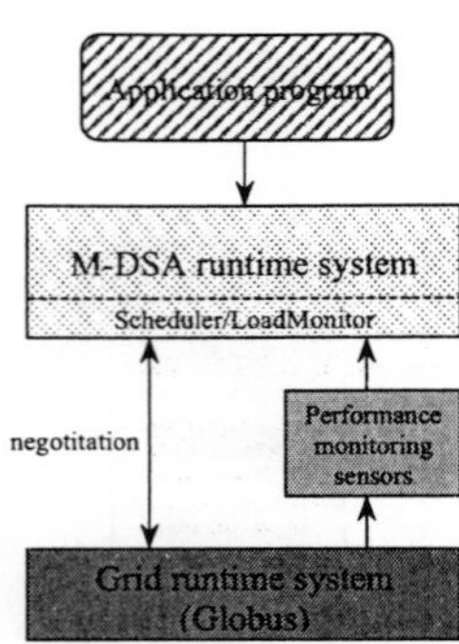

Figure 4. M-DSA Resource Management and Migration Decision Architecture.

When the M-DSA system receives an application program, the *scheduler* will negotiate with the *grid runtime system*, e.g., Globus in our implementation, to obtain a list of available physical servers that have sufficient resources. Then it will broker the allocation and scheduling of application programs on grid resources, or start up the *bootstrap* daemon on the new destination server when a service migration is necessary. This step will also insert sensors to help the *LoadMonitor* control application execution. Next, the scheduler will generate a script file, which specifies the list of servers on which the application programs will be executed; see Figure 5 for a sample script. The Globus Toolkit will startup the application execution by running the script file.

```
( &(resourceManagerContact="node2.grid.wayne.edu")
  (count=1)
  (label="subjob 1")
  (environment=(GLOBUS_DUROC_SUBJOB_INDEX 0))
  (directory=/wsu/home/song/mdsa/app)
  (executable=/usr/java/j2sdk1.4.2_04/bin/java)
  (arguments=-classpath .:../classes:../mdsa.jar
'-Djava.security.policy=mdsa.policy' app.lu.Lu lu/lu.cfg)
)

( &(resourceManagerContact="node8.grid.wayne.edu")
  (count=1)
  (label="subjob 2")
  (environment=(GLOBUS_DUROC_SUBJOB_INDEX 1))
  (directory=/wsu/home/song/mdsa/app)
  (executable=/usr/java/j2sdk1.4.2_04/bin/java)
  (arguments=-classpath .:../classes:../mdsa.jar
'-Djava.security.policy=mdsa.policy' app.lu.Lu lu/lu.cfg)
)
```

Figure 5: A sample script file generated by scheduler.

During program execution, the sensor on each physical server monitors the application performance and reports it to the LoadMonitor, as described in Section 4.2. After LoadMonitor collects the performance data from all the participant sensors, it checks whether there are overloaded servers in the system. If that is the case, service migrations will be triggered, and then the scheduler will modify the resource allocation information. During this process, the scheduler needs to negotiate with the grid runtime system again to find new available resources.

We can see that the *migration decision problem* includes three issues.

- Migration candidate determination, concerning which server should transfer the runtime service and application programs.
- Migration timing, determining when a migration should be performed.
- Destination server selection, selecting a new physical server so that the performance gain from a migration won't be outweighed by its overhead.

In [7], we formulated the migration decision problem as two optimization models and derived the optimal migration policy for distributed and heterogenous systems based on stochastic optimization theories. We summarize the results in the following theorem. Readers are referred to [7] for its proof.

Theorem 1 (Optimal migration timing) *For any server s with capacity c in a distributed virtual machine and a given overload bound R, the optimal service migration timing l^* in phase, is*

$$l^* = \frac{\tilde{c}R - w_0}{\bar{\mu}},$$

where $\tilde{c}$ denotes the ratio of the current server's capacity to that of the original server, w_0 being the initial workload and $\bar{\mu}$ as the average of means of the application components' workload changes.

When a service migration is triggered, we can calculate a lower bound of capacity of candidate servers for destination server selection. Then, the scheduler will negotiate with Globus to find an available server whose capacity equals to or is marginally above the lower bound. Our formal approaches requires the distribution information of application workload changes. We have being proposing a stochastic learning framework to obtain this distribution from the existing application performance data. In this paper, our focus is on the service migration concept and its illustrative example as M-DSA. So, we chose a simplified migration decision scheme based on workload threshold in our experiments.

5.2 Security Protections in M-DSA

The dynamic and multi-domain nature of the grid environments introduces significant security issues [18]. For instance, in a campus grid, clusters of different departments are connected via insecure campus networks. Unauthorized users may dispatch their programs to grid computers, and even try to exhaust grid resources via Denial of Service attacks. Therefore, security protection is a vital issue affecting the feasibility of a system in practice. The Grid Security Infrastructure (GSI) [6] provides authentication and authorization functionality to protect the grid resources. As a runtime support middleware on top of Globus, M-DSA utilizes GSI to ensure secure accesses to the underlying grid resources. In addition, it has its own security measures to protect the communication and service migration between virtual servers.

It is also possible that untrusted users attempt to run their private services on top of the Bootstraps. To tackle this problem, we devised *service tags* to distinguish registered service programs from others. Each Bootstrap daemon on a physical server maintains a list of tags, which map one-to-one to the set of registered services. The tag list is obtained from a trusted server in the system. When a service pack is transmitted to a Bootstrap daemon from a remote server, the daemon checks the tag field of the pack. If the tag matches one in the tag list, the corresponding service program is permitted to be restored and initiated on the server. Otherwise, the service pack will be discarded. To prevent malicious users on a network to extract the tag information from a valid pack, we encrypted its tag field. A digital signature is also included to ensure the pack's integrity. The body of a service pack is not encrypted, due to performance concerns and the observation that a service pack for parallel computation usually does not contain sensitive information.

During the execution of a parallel application, DsaAgents of different servers will contact one another for array accesses. To protect their communication from being tampered by network users, we introduced a *selective signing* approach. That is data, travelling cross two clusters, is appended with a digital signature and the receivers check the digest. However, we assume a cluster is a trusted environment. So intracluster communication is free from digital signature to reduce delay. When a service migration occurs within a cluster, the digital signature of the service pack is also avoided. Our security mechanisms protect system resources from malicious usage, and ensure safe and efficient execution of parallel applications on M-DSA virtual machines.

6 Experiment Results

Our experiment platform was a campus grid in the Wayne State University. The cluster in the Institute of Scientific Computing was composed of eight SUN Enterprise SMP Servers. Five of them were 4-way E3500 with 1024 MB memory and the other three were 4-way E3000 with 512 MB memory. Each processor module had one UltraSPARC II with 400 MHz (E3500) or 336 MHz (E3000), and 4 MB cache. The cluster in the department of Electrical and Computer Engineering had four Dell PowerEdge2400 Servers. Each of them possessed two 733 MHz PentiumIII processor and 256 KB cache. They used the Red Hat Linux8.0 with 2.4.18-14smp kernel. All of the grid nodes ran the Globus Toolkit v3.2 as the grid runtime system. The computers within each cluster were connected through a 100 Mbps Ethernet. The two clusters were located in different buildings and the intercluster connection had a bandwidth of 60 Mbps.

We ported the applications of LU factorization and FFT from the SPLASH-2 [20] benchmark suite to evaluate the performance of service migration on the M-DSA runtime system. All codes were written in Java, compiled in JDK 1.4.1.

6.1 Execution Time of LU and FFT on M-DSA

Figure 6(a) depicts the execution time breakdown of LU, factorizing 2048 x 2048 double matrix. Each virtual server hosts eight computational agents at outset. We changed the block size and measured the costs of computation, synchronization, shared array access and service migration in three different scenarios. In Scenario I, the LU application was executed within the SUN cluster and there was no service migration. The figure shows the overall execution time decreases as block size increases, and it increases after the block size is larger than 64 x 64. It is because

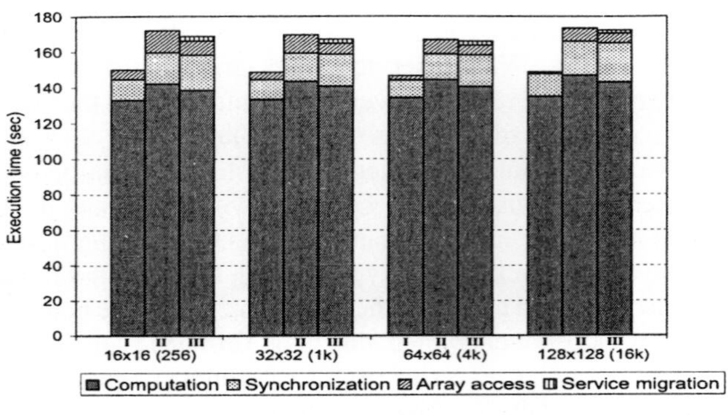

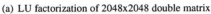

(a) LU factorization of 2048x2048 double matrix

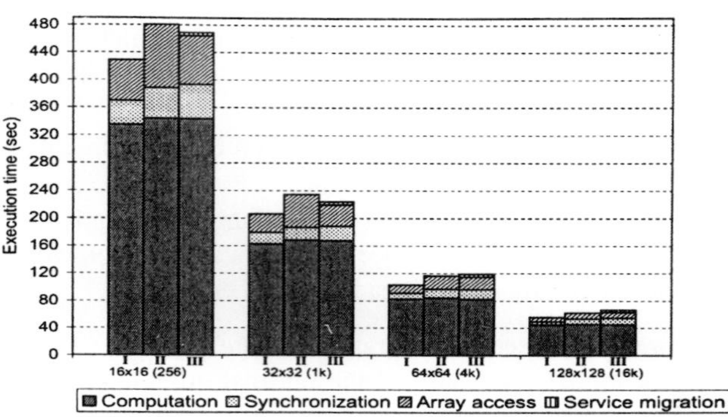

(b) FFT for 2048x2048 double arrays with complex elements

Figure 6. I: execution time in the Sun cluster with no service migration. II: execution time in the campus grid with no service migration. III: execution time in the campus grid with an intercluster service migration.

the data locality can be better exploited with a larger block, but this benefit is compromised by the false sharing when a threshold of block size is exceeded. We also notice the synchronization cost is significant, when the number of agents and computers is large. In Scenario II, we used four SUN E3500 servers and four DELL servers to execute the LU application. In the figure, the computation cost was a little greater than that in Scenario I, due to the relatively slow processing speed of the DELL servers. The intercluster communication leads to more remote access time of the shared array. As a result, the synchronization cost increased by 43.6% to 52.8%. The overall execution time is less than 17% more of that within a cluster. A service migration was occurred in Scenario III, which moved the DSA service from a DELL server to a SUN E3500 server. According to the figure, the computation cost was reduced slightly because of the increased processing speed. However, the synchronization cost was more because the average time waiting for agents to complete a computation phase was increased. The service migration overhead is less than 2.5 seconds, i.e., less than 1.5% of the overall execution time.

The execution time of FFT is shown in Figure 6(b). The execution environment was the same as that for the LU factorization. The inputs were 2048 x 2048 double arrays and each element was a complex number. FFT is a single-writer application with fine-grained access. The intensive shared array access and longer synchronization operations contributed to slow down this application. Its performance in the campus grid degraded, primarily due to the large number of intercluster shared array accesses. The service migration improved the data locality, but introduced more synchronization overheads. The overall execution time of our M-DSA system with service migration was at most 21.4% longer than that within a cluster.

6.2 Service Migration Overhead Breakdown

We measured the overhead breakdown of intracluster and intercluster service migrations with security protections. Figure 7 lists the experiment results in the LU factorization of 2048 x 2048 double matrix with 32 x 32 block size. The distributed virtual machine resided on four SUN E3500 servers and four DELL servers. The intracluster service migration was within the SUN cluster. The intercluster migration was from a DELL server to a SUN E3500 server, with security protection.

	Intra-cluster migration		Inter-cluster migration	
Item	Cost (msec)	Percentage (%)	Cost (msec)	Percentage (%)
Initialization (t_I)	43	2.34	58	2.06
Packing (t_P)	641	34.86	1163	41.23
Service transfer (t_{Tserv})	518	28.17	751	26.61
Code transfer (t_{Tcode})	19	-	19	-
Restoration (t_R)	637	34.63	849	30.10
Total ($C_{service}$)	1839	100.00	2821	100.00

Figure 7. Overhead breakdown of service migration in the campus grid M-DSA.

Given the cost of each category, we can derive the overall service migration cost, $C_{service}$, as,

$$C_{service} = t_I + t_P + max\{t_{Tserv}, t_{Tcode}\} + t_R,$$

where we take the maximum of t_{Tserv} and t_{Tcode} because service pack and codes are transferred in parallel with the prefetch technique. The t_{Tserv} and t_{Tcode} are determined by the sizes of service pack and codes respectively. According to the figure, the service packing and restoration are the most costly operations. This is partially caused by inefficiency of the Java object serialization procedure. The generated service pack is 4.2 MB of size. The security protections contributed 297 ms (25.5%) and 210 ms (24.7%) to the packing and restoration costs in the intercluster service migration. The different processing speed of source and destination computers in the intercluster migration accounts for the difference in packing and restoration time. The measured application performance information from the Autopilot sensors is piggybacked by the synchronization messages. So, the service initialization time is quite small. From the figure, we can see both types of service migration have a total cost less than 1.8% of the overall execution time for the LU application. Compared with stopping a parallel computation when overload and/or failure occur in a distributed environment, service migration is an affordable approach to system adaptivity.

6.3 Security Protection for Intercluster Communication

To evaluate the cost of our security approaches, *selective signing*, for intercluster communication, we measured the execution time for security operations and compared it with a full signing approach, that is to provide a digital signature for all intercomputer communication even within a cluster.

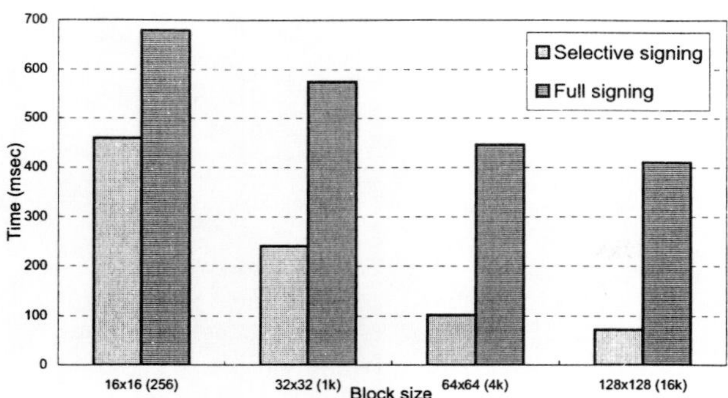

Figure 8. Security protection cost in the campus grid M-DSA.

Figure 8 presents the security protection cost in the LU application for 2048 x 2048 double matrix, using four servers in each cluster. The security operation includes calculating a 128-bit MD5 message digest for the outgoing data and generating a digital signature by the 3DES encryption algorithm. Message integrity is verified by receivers. According to the figure, the selective signing overhead decreased significantly as the block size increased. This is because the number of intercluster array accesses declines with larger blocks. On the other hand, the total array accesses in the entire system reduce at a much slighter rate. So, the full signing cost changed less rapidly, as shown in the figure. Our selective signing approach saved 32.4% to 82.1% of the time for signing all the remote array accesses, and account for less than 3.72% of the overall array access cost and less than 0.27% of the application execution time. Therefore, the selective signing is lightweight.

7 Conclusion and Future Work

In this paper, we have presented a service migration mechanism to move runtime services among networked computers. It allows reconfiguration of a distributed virtual machine for adaptive grid computing. As an illustrative example, we discuss the design and implementation details of service migration in the M-DSA runtime support system for parallel applications. Experiment results in a campus grid environment show that service migration can achieve system adaptivity effectively. Our ongoing work focuses on designing a new underlying runtime system utilizing the data management mechanisms proposed for data grids to achieve high-performance shared data accesses. More real applications will be performed to evaluate the system performance.

Acknowledgment This research was supported in part by U.S. NSF grant ACI-0203592 and NASA grant 03-OBPR-01-0049.

References

[1] R. Basharahil, B. Wims, C.-Z. Xu, and S. Fu. Distributed shared array: An integration of message passing and multithreading on SMP clusters. *Journal of Supercomputing*, 31(2):161–184, 2004.

[2] F. Berman and et al. Adaptive computing on the grid using AppLeS. *IEEE Transactions on Parallel and Distributed Systems*, 14(4):369–382, 2003.

[3] S. B. Davidson, H. Garcia-Molina, and D. Skeen. Consistency in a partitioned network: A survey. *ACM Computing Surveys*, 17(3):341–370, 1985.

[4] C. Du, X.-H. Sun, and K. Chanchio. HPCM: A pre-compiler aided middleware for the mobility of legacy code. In *Proc. of the Int. Conf. on Cluster Computing*, 2003.

[5] R. Figueiredo, P. Dinda, and J. Fortes. A case for grid computing on virtual machines. In *Proc. of the Int. Conf. on Distributed Computing Systems (ICDCS)*, 2003.

[6] I. Foster and C. Kesselman. The globus toolkit. In I. Foster and C. Kesselman, editors, *The Grid: Blueprint for a New Computing Infrastructure*. Morgan Kaufmann, 1998.

[7] S. Fu and C.-Z. Xu. Migration decision for hybrid mobility in reconfigurable distributed virtual machines. In *Proc. of the 33rd Int. Conf. on Parallel Processing (ICPP)*, 2004.

[8] GrADS project homepage. http://nhse2.cs.rice.edu/grads.

[9] X. Jiang and D.-Y. Xu. SODA: A service-on-demand architecture for application service hosting utility platforms. In *Proc. of the Int. Symp. on High Performance Distributed Computing*, 2003.

[10] D. Kondo, M. Taufer, C. Brooks, H. Casanova, and A. Chien. Characterizing and evaluating Desktop Grids: An empirical study. In *Proc. of the 18th Int. IPDPS*, 2004.

[11] T. Lindholm and F. Yellin. *The Java(TM) Virtual Machine Specification*. Addison-Wesley, second edition, 1999.

[12] D. Milojicic, F. Douglis, Y. Panedeine, R. Wheeler, and S. Zhou. Process migration. *ACM Computing Surveys*, 32(3), 2000.

[13] R. L. Ribler, J. S. Vetter, H. Simitci, and D. A. Reed. Autopilot: Adaptive control of distributed applications. In *Proc. of the 7th IEEE High Performance Distributed Computing(HPDC)*, 1998.

[14] C. P. Sapuntzakis, R. Chandra, B. Pfaff, J. Chow, M. S. Lam, and M. Rosenblum. Optimizing the migration of virtual computers. In *Proc. of the 5th OSDI*, pages 377–390, Dec. 2002.

[15] E. G. Sirer, R. Grimm, A. J. Gregory, and B. N. Bershad. Design and implementation of a distributed virtual machine for networked computers. In *Proc. of the 17th ACM SOSP*, Dec. 1999.

[16] E. Truyen, B. Robben, B. Vanhaute, T. Coninx, W. Joosen, and P. Verbaeten. Portable support for transparent thread migration in java. In *Proc. of the 4th Int. Symp. on Mobile Agents*, 2000.

[17] S. Vadhiyar and J. Dongarra. A performance oriented migration framework for the grid. In *Proc. of the 3rd Int. Symp. on Cluster Computing and Grid (CCGrid)*, May 2003.

[18] V. Welch and et al. Security for grid services. In *Proc. of the 12th IEEE HPDC*, June 2003.

[19] A. Whitaker, M. Shaw, and S. Gribble. Denali: Lightweight virtual machines for distributed and networked applications. In *Proc. of the USENIX Technical Conf.*, June 2002.

[20] S. Woo, M. Ohara, E. Torrie, J. Singh, and A. Gupta. The SPLASH-2 programs: Characterization and methodological considerations. In *Proc. of the 22nd Annual Int. Symp. on Computer Architecture*, Jun. 1995.

[21] C.-Z. Xu and B. Wims. A mobile agent based push methodology for global parallel computing. *Concurrency: Practice and Experience*, 14(8):705–726, July 2000.

[22] W. Zhu, C.-L. Wang, and F. C. M. Lau. JESSICA2: A distributed java virtual machine with transparent thread migration support. In *Proc. of the CLUSTER 2002*, September 2002.

Panel Session

Keynote Address 3

Session 5C: Wireless & Mobile Computing

Connected k-Hop Clustering in Ad Hoc Networks *

Shuhui Yang, Jie Wu
Department of Computer Science and Engineering
Florida Atlantic University
Boca Raton, FL 33431
syang1@fau.edu, jie@cse.fau.edu

Jiannong Cao
Department of Computing
Hong Kong Polytechnic University
Hung Hom, KLW, Hong Kong
csjcao@comp.polyu.edu.hk

Abstract

In wireless ad hoc networks, clustering is one of the most important approaches for many applications. A connected k-hop clustering network is formed by electing clusterheads in k-hop neighborhoods and finding gateway nodes to connect clusterheads. Therefore, the number of nodes to be flooded in broadcast related applications could be reduced. In this paper, we study the localized solution for the connectivity issue of clusterheads with less gateway nodes. We develop the adjacency-based neighbor clusterhead selection rule (A-NCR) by extending the "2.5" hops coverage theorem [17] and generalizing it to k-hop clustering. We then design the local minimum spanning tree [9] based gateway algorithm (LMSTGA), which could be applied on the adjacent clusterheads selected by A-NCR to further reduce gateway nodes. In the simulation, we study the performance of the proposed approaches, using different values for parameter k. The results show that the proposed approaches generate a connected k-hop clustering network, and reduce the number of gateway nodes effectively.

1. Introduction

The nature of wireless ad hoc networks (or simply ad hoc networks) makes them different from wireless infrastructure networks. An ad hoc network contains large numbers of hosts that communicate with each other without any centralized management. Scalability is one of the most important issues in large ad hoc networks. Clustering is an important approach to support scalability in many applications. For example, the most reliable method of information propagation in an ad hoc network is flooding, but it demands large overhead and may cause severe collision and contention. If all the hosts are organized into clusters, the information transmission flooding could be confined within each cluster. In an ad hoc network, communication overhead could be reduced by both intra-clustering and inter-clustering [6, 19]. Clustering has also been applied to routing protocols, helping to achieve smaller routing tables and fewer route updates, such as the (α, t) cluster framework [12], the B-protocol [3], and MMWN [15].

The clustering process divides the network into several clusters, and each has a clusterhead and several neighbors of this clusterhead as members. These clusters could be viewed as 1-hop clusters, in which the distance between a clusterhead and any of its members is 1 hop. There are two methods of 1-hop clustering. One is the cluster algorithm, the other is the core algorithm. The main difference between these two are whether clusterheads could be neighbors (as in core), or not (as in cluster). We focus on the first clustering method in this paper.

1-hop clustering could be extended to k-hop clustering. There are two possible extensions. The k-cluster is first defined by Krishna et al [8], in which a k-cluster is a subset of nodes that are mutually reachable by a path of at most k hops. These clusters have no clusterheads and are overlapped. The second is [7, 13], where a k-hop cluster is defined as a set of nodes within k-hop distance from a given node, their clusterhead. The difference between these two extensions is the definition of k hops, whether it is the distance between any pair of members in a cluster or the clusterhead and each member. In our paper, we use the second definition. Within the second definition, we have k-hop cluster [7, 13] (as an extension of 1-hop cluster) and k-hop core [2] (as an extension of 1-hop core). We will focus on k-hop cluster where a clusterhead forms not only a k-hop dominating set (DS) [14], where every node is in the DS or at most k hops away from the DS, but also a k-hop independent set, where clusterheads are at least $k+1$ hops away from each other. By adjusting the parameter k, the number of clusters and clusterheads could be controlled.

In ad hoc networks, clusterheads are in charge of information distribution and collection within clusters. The

*This work was supported in part by NSF grants CCR 0329741, CNS 0422762, CNS 0434533, and EIA 0130806.

0190-3918/05 $20.00 © 2005 IEEE

communication of clusterheads or information aggregation could be accomplished in a multi-hop way. Some gateway nodes, which are non-clusterheads (members), need to be selected to connect clusterheads. To save energy and reduce signal collision, the number of these gateway nodes should be as few as possible.

In this paper, we deal with gateway selection to generate the connected k-hop clustering in ad hoc networks. The approach we use is localized, where each node performs selection based on $(2k+1)$-hop local information. To connect all the clusterheads in a localized way, we divide the process into two phases. Each clusterhead should (1) find some neighbor clusterheads first, and (2) find gateways to connect to these clusterheads. If each clusterhead is connected to every one of its neighbor clusterheads, all the clusterheads in the network are guaranteed to be connected.

We develop an adjacency-based neighbor clusterhead selection rule (A-NCR), which is an extension and generalization of Wu and Lou's "2.5" hops coverage theorem [17], for neighbor clusterhead selection in the first phase. In A-NCR, a small set of neighbor clusterheads (within $2k + 1$ hops) could be found by each clusterhead while ensuring global connectivity of clusterheads. The reduced number of neighbor clusterheads could help to result in fewer gateway nodes. In the second phase for gateway selection, we develop a local minimum spanning tree [9] based gateway algorithm (LMSTGA), which could greatly reduce the gateway nodes selected by the usual mesh-based approach. These two proposed methods could be combined as AC-LMST (where AC stands for adjacent clusterhead) to further reduce the number of resultant gateway nodes. All the approaches proposed in this paper are distributed and localized. At most $2k + 1$ hops broadcasting is needed. The parameter k is tunable, and usually small. This is because in ad hoc networks, network topology changes frequently. Therefore small k may help to construct a combinatorially stable system, in which the propagation of all topology updates is sufficiently fast to reflect the topology change.

The contributions of this paper are as follows. (1) Define the localized gateway node selection issue of connected k-hop clustering in ad hoc networks, and separate this issue into two problems of neighbor clusterhead selection and gateway selection. (2) Design an adjacency-based neighbor clusterhead selection rule (A-NCR) to address the first problem; use the local minimum spanning tree based gateway algorithm (LMSTGA) for the second problem; combine these two into AC-LMST. (3) Perform simulation to evaluate and analyze the performance of these proposed approaches.

The remainder of the paper is organized as follows: Section 2 reviews the related work in the field, including 1-hop clustering and k-hop clustering. Section 3 gives a new heuristic solution for the connected k-hop clustering, and the AC-LMST. A performance study through simulation is conducted in Section 4. The paper concludes in Section 5.

2. Related Work

Organizing a network into a hierarchical structure could make the management efficient. Clustering offers such a structure, and it suits networks with relatively large numbers of nodes. High level clustering, clustering applied recursively over clusterheads, is also feasible and effective in even larger networks.

Clustering is conducted by at first electing clusterheads; then non-clusterheads choose clusters to join and become members. As mentioned above, there are two kinds of clustering algorithms. One is the cluster algorithm [4], and the other is the core algorithm [16]. There are many ways to use different node priorities to select clusterheads. The lowest ID algorithm [10] by Lin and Gerla is widely used. In that algorithm, a node that has the lowest ID among its neighbors that have not joined any clusters will declare itself the clusterhead. Other nodes will select one of the neighboring clusterheads to join and become members. This process is repeated until every node has joined a cluster. In the lowest ID core algorithm, a node u designates the one (including itself) that has the lowest ID in u's 1-hop neighborhood as the clusterhead. Other nodes will select clusters to join. Unlike the cluster algorithm, the core algorithm runs only one round and the resultant clusterheads (also called cores) can be neighbors. Some other node priority can be used instead of node ID for the clusterhead selection, such as node degree [5], node speed, sum of distances to all neighbors, and even random timer [18].

Connectivity among clusterheads is required for most applications such as message broadcasting. Unless extra channels are used [18], all nodes are identical in power supplement; clusterheads do not connect directly with other clusterheads that are at least 2 hops away. Thus the connection between clusterheads should be accomplished in the style of a multi-hop packet relay. That is, some non-clusterheads (members) should be selected as gateway nodes to perform message forwarding between clusterheads. The distance between clusterheads of two neighbor clusters is 2 or 3 hops. One way is to select border nodes as gateways to connect the clusterheads. A *border node* is a member with neighbors in other clusters. Finding gateway nodes to connect all the clusterheads within each other's 3-hop neighborhood is another widely used method. The mesh-based scheme [16] designates a subset of members as gateways so that there is exactly one path by gateways between two neighboring clusterheads. The global tree scheme [1] minimizes the number of gateways by growing a breadth-first search tree via flooding. In [17], Wu and Lou developed the "2.5" hops coverage theorem, in which each clusterhead needs only to connect to all the clusterheads 2 hops away and some of those 3 hops away. They also designed a greedy gateway selection algorithm to connect these clusterheads that are 2.5 hops away.

There are several ways to extend the clustering to support even larger networks. One is to augment the ad hoc network with an overlay network by using a second channel, such as in [18]. The second is to incorporate multiple hierarchies to support aggregation [12]. The third is to use k-hop clustering, as in [2], [7], and [8]. When k is larger than 1, using border nodes as gateways is not enough to make clusterheads connected. Wu and Lou's greedy gateway selection algorithm is not suitable either. One solution is to use a centralized approach to construct a global minimum spanning tree to connect all the clusterheads. Another approach is to use some existing routing algorithms to send messages among clusterheads [5]. To our best knowledge, there is no localized gateway selection algorithm in k-hop clustering networks thus far. Some other detailed information about clustering could be found in [13].

3. A Heuristic Solution for Connected k-Hop Clustering

We use the traditional lowest ID clustering algorithm, and apply it to a k-hop neighborhood. We denote the original connected network after clustering, which has selected clusterheads and classified members, as G. In the clustering algorithm, nodes that have the highest priority within their k-hop neighborhood (including only nodes that have not joined any clusters) declare themselves as clusterheads, and broadcast the clusterhead declaration messages in this neighborhood. Each non-clusterhead collects broadcast messages and selects one cluster to join as a member. Then the same procedure is carried out among nodes that have not joined clusters iteratively until every node joins a cluster. For a non-clusterhead that has received more than one clusterhead declaration message within its k-hop neighborhood, there are several ways for it to decide which cluster to join. (1) ID-based: the node will select the clusterhead with the smallest ID as its clusterhead. (2) Distance-based: the node will select the nearest clusterhead as its clusterhead. (3) Size-based: the decision is made considering the balance of size of clusters. Since each non-clusterhead node selects only one cluster to join, the k-hop clustering algorithm generates non-overlapped clusters.

A *cluster graph* G' is defined as follows.

Definition 1 $G' =< V, E >$. *V is the set of clusterheads; each unidirectional link e ($e \in E$) between node u and v ($u, v \in V$) indicates a path connecting u and v, which consists of gateways only.*

Therefore, our goal is to find a connected G', using as few gateways as possible by a localized solution. We separate it into two phases.

1. **Neighbor clusterhead selection.** Each clusterhead collects information of other clusterheads within its local neighborhood, and designates all/some of them as its neighbor clusterheads. The connectivity of clusterheads should be guaranteed as long as each clusterhead is connected to every one of its neighbor clusterheads.

2. **Gateway selection.** Each clusterhead finds gateways to connect to all its neighbor clusterheads. It can find only gateways to directly connect to some of them, but globally, all the clusterheads are connected.

The challenge in neighbor clusterhead selection is to select as few clusterheads as possible locally, but if each clusterhead finds gateways to collect to every one of its neighbor clusterheads, all clusterheads are connected globally.

3.1. Adjacency-Based Neighbor Clusterhead Selection

Usually, each clusterhead tries to connect to all neighbor clusterheads within $2k + 1$ hops in k-hop clustering to ensure global connectivity among clusterheads. The main result in this subsection is that only a special subset of neighbor clusterheads called adjacent clusterheads needs to be connected to ensure connectivity. *Adjacent clusters* means that there are two neighbor nodes, with one from each cluster. Accordingly, *adjacent clusterheads* are the two clusterheads of adjacent clusters. It is easy to see that in k-hop clustering network G, the distance between every two adjacent clusterheads is m, where $k + 1 \leq m \leq 2k + 1$. If we use sets C_1 and C_2 to denote two clusters, the formal definition of adjacent clusters is as follows.

Definition 2 *Clusters C_1 and C_2 are adjacent clusters if and only if there exist $w_1 \in C_1$, $w_2 \in C_2$, and w_1, w_2 are neighbors in the network G. (w_1, w_2 can be clusterhead, but not both.)*

According to the concept of adjacent clusters, the adjacent cluster graph G'' is defined as follows.

Definition 3 $G'' =< V, E' >$. *V is the set of clusterheads; each link e ($e \in E'$) between nodes u and v ($u, v \in V$) indicates the two clusters with heads u and v are adjacent clusters.*

Theorem 1 *The adjacent cluster graph G'' is connected.*

Proof: Because of the connectivity of graph G, for every pair of vertices u and v in G'', which are clusterheads, there exists a path in G to connect them. We denote the path

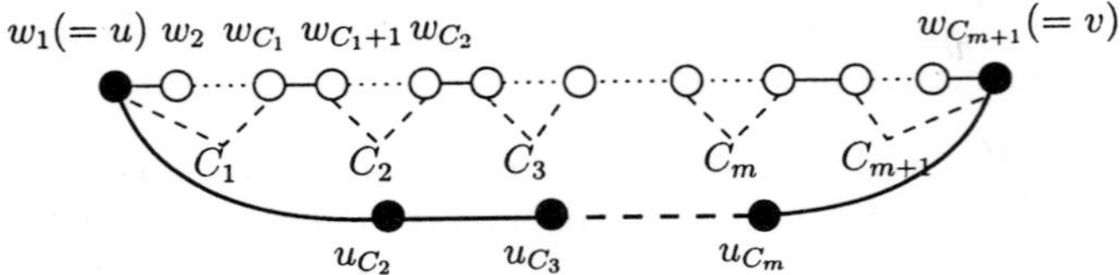

Figure 1. Proof of Theorem 1.

as $w_1(=u), w_2, \ldots, w_{C_1}, w_{C_1+1}, \ldots, w_{C_2}, \ldots, w_{C_{m-1}+1}, \ldots, w_{C_m}, w_{C_m+1}, \ldots, w_{C_{m+1}}(=v)$. The nodes on the path belong to different clusters. We use $C_1, C_2, \ldots, C_m, C_{m+1}$ to denote the clusters, and $u_{C_1}, u_{C_2}, \ldots, u_{C_m}, u_{C_{m+1}}$ as clusterheads of these clusters in sequence, as Figure 1. Nodes w_{C_1} and w_{C_1+1} are neighbors, thus u and u_{C_2} are adjacent clusterheads, and there is a link in G'' between them. In the same way, u_{C_2} is connected to u_{C_3}, u_{C_3} to u_{C_4}, ..., and u_{C_m} to v. Therefore, u and v are connected. G'' is connected. □

Note that a simple and intuitive way to connect all the clusterheads in G is for each clusterhead to select all the clusterheads within $2k+1$ hops as its neighbor clusterheads and find gateways to connect itself and each of them, such as [16] does. We can see that the cluster graph constructed by this simple method is a super graph of G'', therefore it is not efficient enough.

Wu and Lou proposed the 2.5 hops notion for the clusterheads connection [17] when k is 1. That is, clusterheads are connected by carefully selecting non-clusterhead nodes locally at each clusterhead to connect clusterheads within its 2.5 hops. They use the notion of 2.5 hops coverage, where each clusterhead covers clusterheads within its 2 hops neighborhood, and clusterheads within 3 hops that have members within its 2 hop neighborhood. Note that when k is 1, distance between two adjacent clusterheads is either 2 or 3.

Figure 2 is an illustration of their proposed 2.5 hops coverage theorem. (a) is the graph after clustering. (b) uses the simple method to find neighbor when $k = 1$, that is to connect all the clusterheads within 3 hops. (c) is the 2.5 hop connection theory, which can reduce the connections, such as link 2 to 4, 4 to 2, and 1 to 4. Therefore, some unidirectional connections may exist. There are still some redundant connections, such as link 4 to 1, which could be removed. We can see that the directional cluster graph generated by this 2.5 hops coverage theorem is still a super graph of adjacent cluster graph G''. Therefore, it is still not efficient enough, and could be extended to further remove redundant connections among clusterheads, and generalized to k-hop clustering.

Based on Theorem 1, we develop the following neighbor clusterhead selection rule, which is to select only adjacent clusterheads, not all the $2k+1$ neighbor clusterheads to

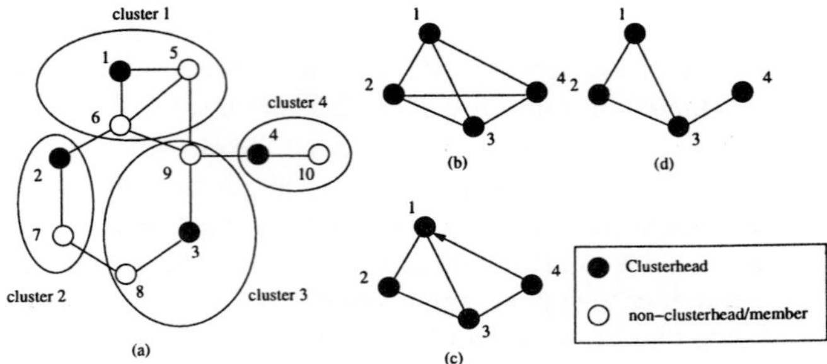

Figure 2. (a) the network G, (b) 3 hops connection, (c) 2.5 hops connection, (d) adjacency-based connection (G'') ($k = 1$).

connect, to reduce redundant connections.

Adjacency-Based Neighbor Clusterhead Selection Rule (A-NCR): *In a k-hop network G which is already clustered, each clusterhead selects the adjacent clusterheads within* $2k+1$ *hops as its neighbor clusterheads to connect.*

The cluster graph G' constructed by A-NCR is exactly the adjacent cluster graph G'', and therefore is efficient.

Wu and Lou's 2.5 hops coverage is a special case of A-NCR, when k is 1. Because if cluster C_2 with clusterhead v has no member within 2 hops of clusterhead u of cluster C_1, these two clusters must be separated by a node, which belongs to neither C_1 nor C_2. We can see that as a result of our method, all the remaining connections between clusterheads are symmetric, therefore the cluster graph G' is still undirected.

3.2. LMST-Based Gateway Algorithm (LMSTGA)

Generally, there are several ways to connect all the clusterheads to form a connected graph. Globally, a minimum spanning tree could be constructed, connecting all the clusterheads via gateways. Note that we use hops between two nodes as the distance separating them. Locally, each clusterhead could find a shortest path to connect to every one of its adjacent clusterheads, and uses the non-clusterheads on the path as gateways. To further reduce the number of gateways, we apply a local minimum spanning tree (LMST) [9] algorithm for connecting to adjacent clusterheads.

Li, Hou, and Sha devised a distributed and localized algorithm (LMST) for the topology control problem starting from a minimum spanning tree. In the network, each node builds its local MST independently based on the location information of its 1-hop neighbors and only keeps links to 1-hop nodes on its local MST in the final topology. The algorithm produces a connected topology. That is, all the links marked together with all the nodes can form a connected

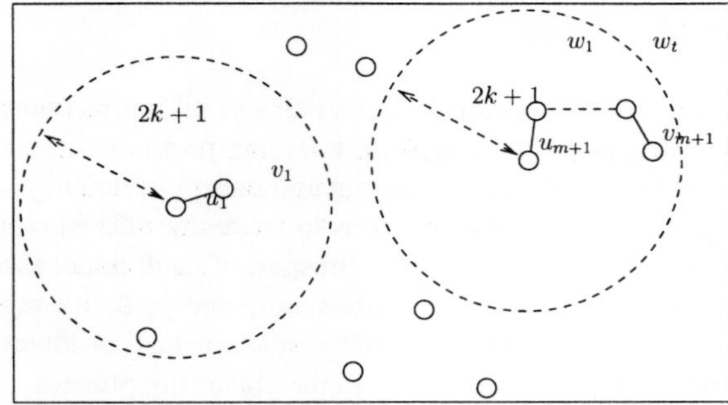

Figure 3. Proof of LMSTGA in G', using A-NCR to select neighbor clusterheads.

graph. An optional phase is provided where the topology is transformed to one with bidirectionl links.

We extend the LMST algorithm, and apply it to our gateway finding procedure. In our extension, we first create "virtual links" among clusterheads. We find a shortest path between every pair of clusterheads if they are adjacent neighbors, and have this path as their "virtual link", using hop count to represent each clusterhead's pairwise "virtual distance". Therefore a global "virtual graph" is formed containing clusterheads and all the virtual links. This virtual graph is the same as the adjacent graph G''. For each clusterhead, all its adjacent clusterheads are viewed as in its virtual "1-hop" neighborhood, although they may be up to $2k+1$ hops away in G. Then, the LMST algorithm is applied on this clusterhead. The IDs of two nodes of a virtual link can be used to break a tie in hop count if needed. When a virtual link is selected in LMST, all nodes on the virtual link are selected as gateways.

LMST-Based gateway algorithm (LMSTGA) : *In a k-hop adjacent cluster graph G'', each clusterhead finds a shortest path to every one of its adjacent clusterheads, and marks it as a virtual link, using hop count as the virtual distance. Each clusterhead constructs a local minimum spanning tree (LMST) among all the adjacent clusterheads rooted at itself, using only virtual links. Then each clusterhead selects the on-tree neighbors (i.e. neighbors on the LMST) to connect to by marking all the intermediate nodes as gateways on the selected virtual links to these neighbors.*

The proof of the following theorem is similar to the one that proves the connectivity of LMST in [9], except for the concept of virtual link and "1-hop" neighborhood.

Theorem 2 *The clusterheads, gateway nodes selected by LMSTGA, using A-NCR to select neighbor clusterheads, and the links among them in the given network G form a connected graph.*

Proof: We have proved that if each clusterhead could be connected to every one of its adjacent clusterheads, the whole cluster graph G' is connected. Therefore, we only need to prove that after applying LMSTGA, there is a path between each clusterhead and every one of its neighbors.

We assume the virtual link between clusterheads u and v denoted as $u \leftrightarrow v$, is selected by LMSTGA, and the virtual distance of the virtual link is $d(u,v)$; if there is a path formed by selected virtual links to connect u and v, say $u \leftrightarrow w_1 \leftrightarrow \ldots \leftrightarrow w_t \leftrightarrow v$, we use $u \Leftrightarrow v$ to denote it. Let us sort all the virtual links in G'', say (u_1,v_1), (u_2,v_2), ..., (u_z,v_z), by increasing distance. We can have the sequence: $d(u_1,v_1) < d(u_2,v_2) < \ldots < d(u_z,v_z)$. Then we use induction to prove that every one of these pairs is connected by those virtual links selected by LMSTGA.

Basic: $m=1$. Since $d(u_1,v_1)$ is the smallest link in the whole graph, it must be the first virtual link selected by u_1. Therefore, we could have $u_1 \leftrightarrow v_1$.

Induction: we assume $u_i \Leftrightarrow v_i$, $i = 1, \ldots m$. Now we prove $u_{m+1} \Leftrightarrow v_{m+1}$. (1) Suppose $u_{m+1} \leftrightarrow v_{m+1}$. That is to say, the virtual link between them is selected by LMSTGA, and $u_{m+1} \Leftrightarrow v_{m+1}$. (2) Suppose a virtual link between them is not selected by LMSTGA. See Figure 3, clusterhead u_{m+1} does not select the virtual link between v_{m+1} and itself. On the LMST rooted at u_{m+1}, there must exist a path to v_{m+1}, say u_{m+1}, w_1, ..., w_t, v_{m+1}. Every virtual link on this path is smaller than $d(u_{m+1}, v_{m+1})$, otherwise it could be replaced by link (u_{m+1}, v_{m+1}) to reduce the weight of the MST. Since we already assume that the virtual link smaller than (u_{m+1}, v_{m+1}) is connected, we could have $u_{m+1} \Leftrightarrow w_1 \Leftrightarrow, \ldots, \Leftrightarrow w_t \Leftrightarrow v_{m+1}$. Therefore, we have $u_{m+1} \Leftrightarrow v_{m+1}$. □

LMSTGA combined with A-NCR is to apply LMST selection on adjacent clusterheads, which is denoted as AC-LMST. The following algorithm is executed on clusterhead u, assuming k-hop clustering has been accomplished.

Algorithm AC-LMST (u)

broadcast within $2k+1$ hops
collect broadcast messages
use A-NCR to find neighbor clusterhead set S
for all $i \in S$
    find a shortest path p_i to i
    designate hop count c_i of p_i as its distance
broadcast set S and distance to every one in S
collect broadcast information
construct an LMST among nodes in S rooted at u
for all $i \in S$ which are also on-tree neighbors
    set nodes on p_i as gateway nodes

End_AC-LMST.

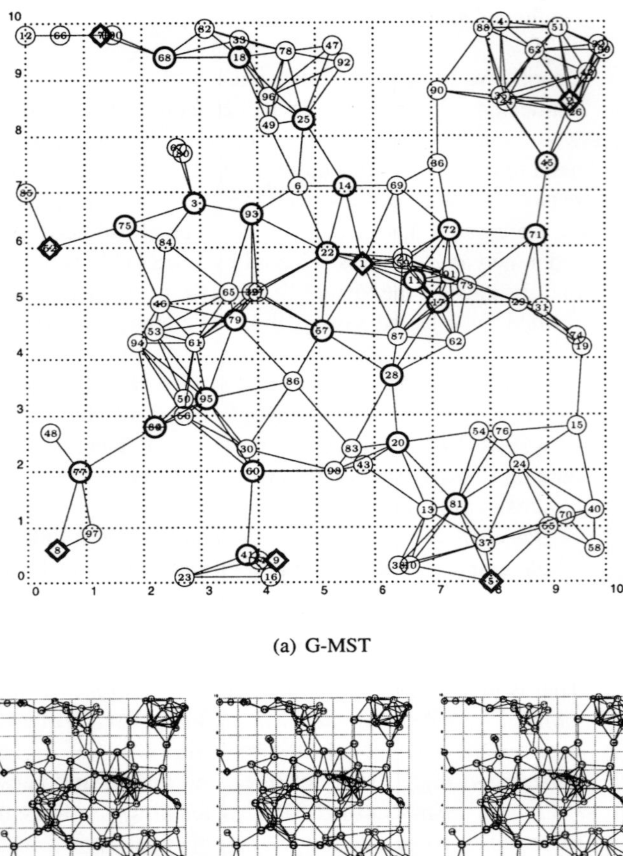

(a) G-MST

(b) NC-Mesh (c) NC-LMST (d) AC-LMST

Figure 4. Example of gateway selection using different algorithms ($N = 100$, $D = 6$, $k = 2$).

Figure 4 is an example of resultant cluster graphs from different gateway selection algorithms. There are 100 nodes in the original network. Lowest ID clustering and ID-based member classification are used. The average degree of each node is 6. k is 3. There are 7 clusterheads (marked by diamonds). (a) shows the result by global minimum spanning tree method (G-MST). There are 23 gateways (bold circles), and they together with the clusterheads form a MST. (b) shows the mesh-based method applied on all the neighbor clusterheads within $2k + 1$ hops (NC-Mesh). There are 35 gateways. (c) is the LMST-based method, applied on all neighbor clusterheads within $2k + 1$ hops (NC-LMST). There are 28 gateways. (d) is AC-LMST, which is LMST applied on adjacent clusterheads. There are 26 gateways.

3.3. Discussion

One of the special characteristics of ad hoc networks is its restricted power supply. Clustering protocols should be oriented towards power-saving and energy-efficiency. One way for power-aware design is to rotate the role of clusterhead to prolong the average lifespan of each node, assuming that a clusterhead consumes more energy than a regular node. Therefore, residual energy level instead of lowest ID can be used as node priority in the clustering process.

k-hop clustering can also easily handle the dynamic situation due to node movement and node switch-on/off operations. Consider a situation when a node "disappears": if it is non-clusterhead and non-gateway, nothing needs to be done with respect to the existing CDS; if it is non-clusterhead but gateway, only the corresponding clusterhead needs to re-run the gateway selection process (to have a local fix); if it is a clusterhead, the clusterhead selection process is applied. Since the number of clusterheads is relatively small, especially for a relatively large constant k, the chance of re-applying the clusterhead selection process is also small.

4. Simulation

This section presents results from our simulation study. The efficiency of the proposed approaches are evaluated and compared with existing ones. All approaches are simulated on a custom simulator, which simulates the k-hop clustering algorithm. For the gateway selection approaches, it simulates neighbor clusterheads (NC) selection, adjacent clusterheads (AC) selection, mesh-based gateway, LMST-based gateway, and also global minimum spanning tree (G-MST) based gateway. Therefore there are four algorithms, NC-Mesh, AC-Mesh, NC-LMST, AC-LMST, in addition to G-MST to be compared. We use G-MST as a lower bound. In fact, G-MST has a constant approximation ratio to the optimal k-hop CDS for a constant k. In 1-hop clustering, the clusterheads and gateway nodes will form a connected dominating set (CDS) to carry out data propagation. Finding a minimum CDS (MCDS) is an NP-complete problem [11]. Clusterheads together with gateways generated by k-hop clustering form a k-hop CDS. Finding a minimum k-hop CDS is also NP-complete.

To generate a random ad hoc network, N nodes are randomly placed in a restricted 100×100 area. In the ad hoc network, we assume all nodes have the same transmission range. We will ignore practical details such as collision and contention, assuming that an ideal MAC layer protocol will take care of them. The tunable parameters in our simulation are as follows. (1) The node number N. We change the number of deployed nodes from 50 to 200 to see the scalability of the algorithms. (2) The average node degree D. We use 6 and 10 as average node degree to see the effect of

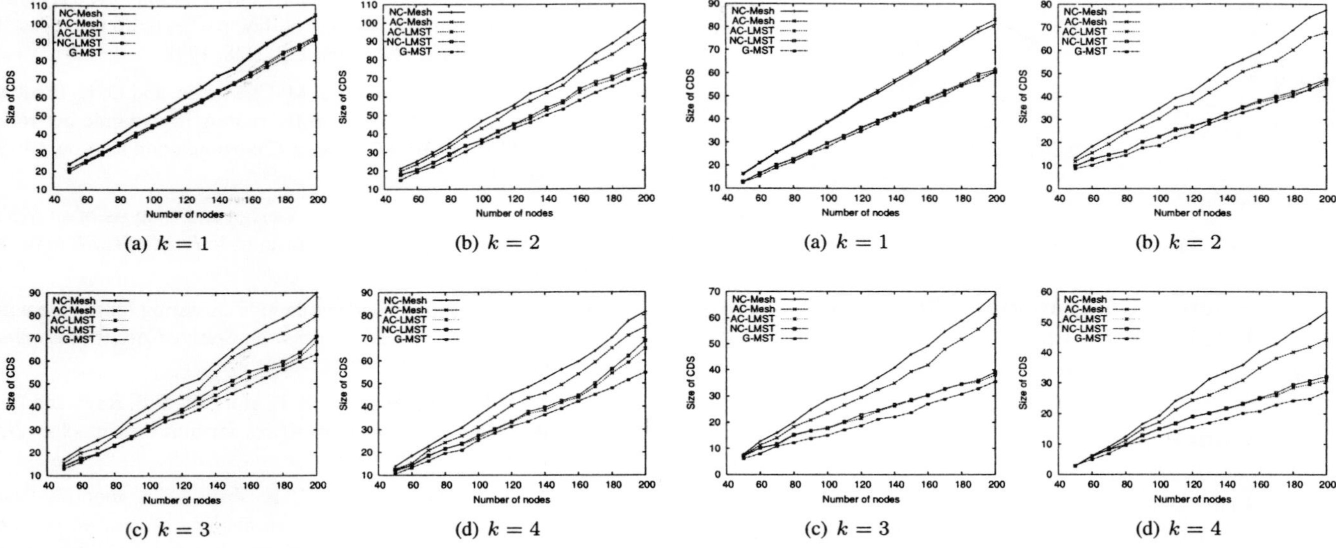

(a) $k = 1$ (b) $k = 2$ (c) $k = 3$ (d) $k = 4$

Figure 5. Comparison of different algorithms in sparse networks ($D = 6$).

(a) $k = 1$ (b) $k = 2$ (c) $k = 3$ (d) $k = 4$

Figure 6. Comparison of different algorithms in dense networks ($D = 10$).

link density on the algorithms. (3) The clustering parameter k. k controls the confines of each cluster, and the number of clusterheads. We use 1, 2, 3 and 4 as its value. The metrics we used to measure the performance of the algorithms are the number of gateway nodes selected, together with clusterheads, and the size of the k-hop CDS. For each tunable parameter, the simulation is repeated 100 times or until the confidence interval is sufficiently small ($\pm 1\%$, for the confidence level of 90%).

Figure 5 is the comparison of the different gateway selection algorithms with average node degree of 6, that is, each node has around 6 nodes as its neighbors, which will result in a relatively sparse graph. Four algorithms are compared. The first is NC-Mesh. The second is AC-Mesh. The third is NC-LMST. In this approach, the LMST algorithm is applied on all the clusterheads within $2k + 1$ hops of the current clusterhead. The last one is AC-LMST, which combines the LMST and A-NCR approaches to make the most of them. We can see that the number of gateway nodes selected is proportional to the number of nodes in the network, and all the approaches have the property of scalability. (a) is for $k = 1$. We can see that AC-Mesh has little advantage over NC-Mesh, as does AC-LMST over NC-LMST. The method of LMST can reduce gateway nodes of Mesh by over 10%. (b) $\sim$ (d) are for $k = 2, 3, 4$. When k is greater than 1, A-NCR works. AC-Mesh reduces gateway nodes of NC-Mesh and AC-LMST reduces gateways of NC-LMST as well. But from the simulation, we can see that the LMST-based approach is more effective than A-NCR. AC-LMST is the most effective one.

Figure 6 is the comparison of these algorithms with average node degree of 10, which will result in a relatively dense graph. Compared with Figure 5, the number of clusterheads and gateway nodes is smaller here. The performance of the four algorithms is similar to that of Figure 5, except that the advantage of AC-LMST over NC-LMST is even less.

Figure 7 shows the effect of the clustering parameter k. AC-LMST is used to find gateways. (a) is the number of clusterheads using different k. The larger the k, the fewer the clusterheads, thus the clusters. (b) is the size of CDS, the number of clusterheads together with gateways. We can see that the size of the resultant CDS becomes smaller with the increase of k, although the number of gateways becomes larger.

Simulation results can be summarized as follows. (1) The proposed A-NCR reduces the number of gateway nodes. (2) The AC-LMST which is a combination of A-NCR and extended LMST could further reduce the number of gateway nodes. (3) The proposed approaches are scalable and suited for both sparse and dense networks. (4) Of these two approaches, LMST is more effective than A-NCR, and AC-LMST has little performance improvement of LMST, especially in dense networks. (5) Larger k results in fewer clusterheads and more gateways, but all together, the size of the final CDS is smaller. (6) AC-LMST has very close performance to G-MST, which is used as a low bound for the number of gateways selected.

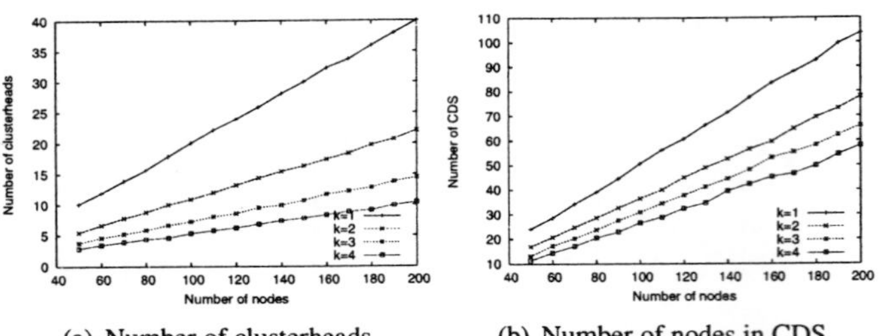

(a) Number of clusterheads (b) Number of nodes in CDS

Figure 7. Comparisons with different k, using LMSTGA ($D = 6$).

5. Conclusion

In this paper, we study the issue of connected k-hop clustering. We separate this problem into two steps in the localized solution. One is neighbor clusterhead selection, the other is gateway node selection. We extend and generalize the 2.5 hops coverage theorem to reduce the neighbor clusterheads to be connected, and develop the A-NCR approach. For the second phase, we extend the LMST algorithm to apply it on the virtual graph abstracted from the given network to select a small number of gateway nodes. AC-LMST is the use of both approaches to find gateway nodes. These two proposed methods could be used separately or together. In the future, we will design a movement-sensitive maintenance policy for the gateway selection algorithm. Communication overhead increases with the growth of the value of k. We will perform some in-depth simulation which should help in analyzing the tradeoff between communication overhead and efficiency of k-hop.

References

[1] K. Alzoubi, P. J. Wan, and O. Frieder. New distributed algorithm for connected dominating set in wireless ad hoc networks. In *Proc. of HICSS*, page 297, 2002.

[2] A. D. Amis, R. Prakash, T. H. P. Vuong, and D. T. Huynh. Max-min d-cluster formation in wireless ad hoc networks. In *Proc. of IEEE Infocom*, 2000.

[3] S. Basagni, D. Turgut, and S. K. Das. Mobility-adaptive protocols for managing large ad hoc networks. In *Proc. of the IEEE International Conference on Communications (ICC)*, page June, 2001.

[4] A. Ephremides, J. E. Wieselthier, and D. J. Baker. A design concept for reliable mobile radio networks with frequency hoping signaling. In *Proc. of IEEE*, pages 56–73, 1987.

[5] M. Gerla and J. T. C. Tsai. Multicluster, mobile, multimedia radio network. *Wireless Networks*, 15(7):255C265, 1995.

[6] V. Kawadia and P. R. Kumar. Power control and clustering in ad hoc networks. In *Proc. of IEEE Infocom*, 2003.

[7] D. Kim, S. Ha, and Y. Choi. k-hop cluster-based dynamic source routing in wireless ad-hoc packet radio networks. In *Proc. of IEEE VTC*, page 224C228, 1998.

[8] P. Krishna, N. N. Vaidya, M. Chatterjee, and D. K. Pradhan. A cluster-based approach for routing in dynamic networks. *ACM SIGCOMM Computer Communication Review*, 49:49–64, 1997.

[9] N. Li, J. Hou, and L. Sha. Design and analysis of an MST-based topology control algorithm. In *Proc. of IEEE Infocom*, 2003.

[10] C. R. Lin and M. Gerla. Adaptive clustering for mobile wireless networks. *IEEE Journal on Selected Areas in Communications*, 15(7):1265C1275, 1997.

[11] M. V. Marathe, H. Breu, H. B. Hunt III, S. S. Ravi, and D. J. Rosenkrantz. Simple heuristics for unit disk graphs. *Networks*, 25:59–68, 1995.

[12] A. B. McDonald and T. F. Znati. A mobility-based framework for adaptive clustering in wireless ad hoc networks. *IEEE Journal on Selected Areas in Communications*, 17(8):1466–87, August 1999.

[13] F. G. Nocetti, J. S. Gonzalez, and I. Stojmenovic. Connectivity based k-hop clustering in wireless networks. *Telecommunication Systems*, 22:1C4, 205C220, 2003.

[14] A. Qayyum, L. Viennot, and A. Laouiti. Multipoint relaying for flooding broadcast message in mobile wireless networks. *Proc. of the 35th Hawaii International Conference on System Science (HICSS-35)*. 2002, (CD-ROM).

[15] R. Ramanathan and M. Steenstrup. Hierarchically-organized, multihop mobile wireless networks for quality-of-service support. *Mobile Networks and Applications*, 3(1):101–19, 1998.

[16] P. Sinha, R. Sivakumar, and V. Bharghavan. Enhancing ad hoc routing with dynamic virtual infrastructures. In *Proc. of IEEE Infocom*, 2001.

[17] J. Wu and W. Lou. Forward node set based broadcast in clustered mobile ad hoc networks. *Wireless Communications and Mobile Computing , a special issue on Algorithmic, Geometric, Graph, Combinatorial, and Vector Aspects of Wireless Networks and Mobile Computing*, 3(2):141–154, March 2003.

[18] K. Xu, X. Hong, and M. Gerla. An ad hoc network with mobile backbones. In *Proc. of the IEEE International Conference on Communications (ICC)*, 2002.

[19] O. Younis and S. Fahmy. Distributed clustering in ad-hoc sensor networks: A hybrid, energy-efficient approach. In *Proc. of IEEE Infocom*, 2004.

Stimulus-based Adaptive Sleeping for Wireless Sensor Networks*

Hoilun Ngan[1], Yanmin Zhu[1], Lionel M. Ni[1] and Renyi Xiao[1,2]

[1]*Department of Computer Science*
Hong Kong University of Science and Technology
Clear Water Bay, Kowloon, Hong Kong

[2]*National Natural Science Foundation of China*
Beijing, China

{cpeglun,zhuym,ni}@cs.ust.hk, xiaory@nsfc.gov.cn

Abstract

Wireless sensor networks have been widely deployed for monitoring environments of interest. The diffusion stimulus (DS) is a very common and important one in real environments, which is characterized by originating at a source spot and continuously spreading outward. DS-based applications are usually time-sensitive and require high accuracy. It is very challenging, however, for sensor networks to monitor a DS when those sensors could usually monitor one point (the sensing range is zero) only. No existing algorithm is effective and energy-efficient for DS monitoring. In this paper, we propose stimulus-based adaptive sleeping (SAS), to tackle this unique challenge. With SAS, each node independently determines its sleep duration based on its local observations on the stimulus. SAS enables sensors near the stimulus boundary to stay alert to accurately capture the stimulus arrival, and those far away from the stimulus to safely sleep longer for energy efficiency.

1. Introduction

With the rapid advancement in wireless communications and microelectromechanical systems (MEMS), wide deployment of large-scale wireless sensor networks (WSN) has been made possible, which promises to revolutionize the way we monitor and control environments of interest [1, 2]. A WSN is a self-organized network consisting of a large number of sensor nodes which are actively interacting with the physical world. A sensor node is a small, inexpensive device that integrates micro-sensing, onboard processing and wireless communication, which enable the node to gather information from the environment and deliver reports to the remote gateway. The gateway is the dedicated node which aggregates and analyzes the reports from sensors, and decides if there are concerned event occurrences. With the development of WSNs, a wide range of attractive applications [3] will come into reality, such as habitat monitoring [4], battlefield surveillance, disaster relief, pollution control and smart environments.

A sensor node is a very resource-constrained device with limited computing power, small memory, and, in particular, short battery lifetime. Sensors are usually intended to be deployed in an unattended or even hostile environment, so it is almost impossible to recharge or replace the battery of these sensors. Applications of sensor networks, on the other hand, desire a robust sensing system with an extended lifetime. Therefore, energy efficiency is a core concern for WSNs. It has been a great research challenge to build a robust, long-lived sensor network with tiny, resource-constrained sensors while maintaining application requirements.

Sensor networks are usually intended to effectively monitor a specific kind of stimulus. There are many different types of stimuli, among which the *diffusion stimulus* (DS) is a very common and important one. A DS is characterized by originating at a source spot and continuously spreading outward. Liquid pollution is an example of the DS. For applications of the DS, which are usually time-sensitive, we want to monitor the dynamics of the DS in real-time, such as how it grows. Although the low per-node cost allows sensor nodes to be densely deployed, it is not feasible to make all sensors constantly active due to power limitation. As discussed above, it is desirable for any sensor network to have a longer lifetime.

The redundancy provided by high density can be exploited to extend the overall system lifetime. The most significant way to conserve power is to put redundant sensors to sleep. Several algorithms [5-9]

* This research was supported in part by Hong Kong RGC Grants HKUST6161/03E and AoE/E-01/99.

have been proposed for conserving energy in sensor networks. To the best of our knowledge, however, no existing algorithm is appropriate for the DS, because they do not take the specific behaviors of stimuli into account. They simply assume an uniform distribution of stimuli across the network and no dynamic growth of the stimuli. Moreover, they make an ideal assumption that the effective sensing area of an individual sensor is an unique disk with non-zero sensing range. It may not be true for some kinds of sensors, such as chemical sensors, which are only able to monitor one point other than a region. Therefore, existing solutions are not suitable for monitoring the DS.

After carefully investigating the unique characteristics of the DS, we propose *stimulus-based adaptive sleeping (SAS)* to enable sensor nodes to sleep adaptively to the dynamics of the DS. With SAS, each node independently determines its sleep durations based on its local observations on the stimulus. This results in energy-efficiency while minimizing event detecting delays. Our algorithm is light-weight and does not require nodes to keep any state information about their individual neighbors. It should be clarified that the role of SAS is a sleeping scheme of sensor nodes to ensure better monitoring of the DS. SAS does not address the data communication problem. The actual delivery of sensed data is carried out by other routing protocols [10-12]. SAS can be implemented as an extension of any energy efficient data communication protocol.

The rest of the paper is organized as follows. In Section 2, we discuss related work of sleeping mechanisms in sensor networks. Section 3 studies the DS and presents two simple solutions for stimulus monitoring. The algorithm design of the SAS is described in detail in Section 4. Section 5 evaluates the performance of our algorithm and presents the simulation results. Finally, we conclude the paper and discuss future work in Section 6.

2. Related work

To the best of our knowledge, no existing work has the same problem coverage as ours. Some researchers have studied sleeping mechanisms which are more relevant to our work. Various algorithms have been proposed to exploit node redundancy to conserve energy in both wireless ad-hoc networks [6, 8, 12] and sensor networks [5, 7, 9, 13]. The algorithms designed for wireless ad-hoc networks are usually not appropriate for sensor networks, because they target at more powerful computing devices which are mobile, but sensors are more resource-constrained and usually remain static after deployment. These algorithms can generally be divided into two categories. One category [5] considers the sensing coverage. And the other category [6-9, 13] does not consider the sensing coverage, but only focuses on network connectivity from the communication perspective. They try to maintain the minimum set of active nodes while meeting the communication requirement, turning off as many other nodes as possible.

GAF [6] divides the whole network into virtual girds. With the location information via GPS or other location services, each node is able to know which grid it resides. In each grid, the nodes are equivalent from the perspective of routing. GAF tries to make only one node active in every grid, and put the remaining into sleep state with a sleep time being a function of the remaining energy of the working node. GAF has mainly laid its efforts on tacking the mobility and failure problems of nodes in an ad-hoc environment.

Greunen et al. [7] proposed an adaptive sleep discipline for energy conservation. They target at applications of opportunistic routing which rely on the existence of equivalent nodes. It is assumed that the application has a delay constraint. The proposed sleep discipline aims to minimize the energy consumption while ensuring that the application constraint is met. Initially, each node computes the optimal wake-up rate. Later, every time a node wakes up, it first estimates the current aggregate wake-up rate by observing the arrivals of packets, and adjusts its next sleep time according to the comparison between the current rate and the optimal rate. One weakness of this algorithm is that it may be difficult to identify the set of equivalent nodes with a given pair of source and destination.

Span [8] is a distributed, randomized algorithm in which each node makes a local decision whether to join the network backbone or not. Each node makes decisions based on an estimation of how many of its neighbors will be benefited from its wake up and the amount of energy available to it. The randomized algorithm rotates the coordinator among the nodes.

In ASCENT [9], most sensors remain in the passive mode in which a node is listening only. When a sink detects high message loss, it signals passive nodes to be active to help forward messages. Once a passive node gets a signal, it decides whether to become active and join the network backbone based on the local situation. An active node is transmitting and receiving messages other than just listening. This work does not evaluate the improvement of energy efficiency. Actually, recent studies [14] have shown that the energy consumed in listening mode is comparable to that in receiving and transmitting mode. If so, the energy savings by putting nodes into listening mode may not be significant.

PEAS [5] tries to conserve energy by putting redundant nodes into sleep while maintaining sufficient sensing coverage. In PEAS, each node is assumed to be able to cover a certain disk region of effective sensing, and also to probe the neighborhood with a certain probing range which is less than the communication range. Given the desired probing rate λ specified by the application, PEAS allows each node to adjust its probing rate adaptively. The weakness of PEAS is that each node is assumed to be able to probe with a certain probing range. Because of the high dynamic nature of radio frequency signals, however, it may be quite difficult to choose a fixed probing range. Moreover, for a sensor, its sensing region may not be a unique disk in practice.

Our work is not intended to deny the usefulness of the aforementioned algorithms. They are effective in certain application scenarios, but not for monitoring the DS. Our work can compensate their weaknesses when the environments of applications are complex.

3. Diffusion stimulus and two simple solutions

In this section, we first study the characteristics of the DS and some key application requirements. Next, we propose two simple solutions: Independent Sleeping (INS) and Blinded Conservative Sleeping (BCS).

3.1 Diffusion stimulus

Diffusion stimuli are very common. For example, a leakage of gas or liquid usually forms a DS. A DS is characterized by two features. First, it originates at a source spot. Second, the stimulus is spreading outward steadily from the source to the nearby environment. The shape of the stimulus is growing and changing over time. What's more, the shape of the stimulus is usually irregular.

Given such a DS, real-time monitoring is crucial. When a stimulus takes place, the system operator wants to have an accurate big picture as well as the real-time dynamics of the stimulus. In particular, it is critical to obtain the accurate information of the moving border. For example, if the stimulus is poisonous and dangerous to the public, it is necessary to take countermeasures before the stimulus border arrives. In general, a sensor could only sense at one point. For accurate monitoring of the stimulus border, more sensors along the border should detect and report the arrival information immediately after the stimulus has just passed over them.

To monitor such a DS, sensor nodes are densely deployed throughout the environment. Due to the extreme power constraint, it is impractical to make all sensors active all the time. Instead, in order to effectively prolong the network lifetime, only a subset of sensors are kept active and the rest are put into sleep. The sleeping nodes wake up from time to time to check whether it needs to become active.

In the following two subsections, we first study two simple solutions to monitoring the DS. These two solutions are ineffective in either energy-efficiency or delay, which trigger our design of SAS.

3.2 Independent sleeping (INS)

With INS, every sensor sleeps from time to time. Each time a node wakes up, it starts to sense. If no stimulus is detected, it computes the duration for next sleep based on a certain probability distribution, and then goes back to sleep. If it detects the presence of the stimulus, it starts to become active and does not go back to sleep any longer.

In this scheme, every sensor independently determines its sleep intervals and interaction with other neighbors may not be required. Therefore, it is very robust and scalable. But it is weak in reducing event detecting delays. It is possible that a sensor is still sleeping while the stimulus has spread over it. In this case, after the sensor has waken up, it detects the stimulus and then reports back to the gateway. However, this report may be significantly delayed, which will result in violating the real-time requirement.

Someone may argue that INS can greatly reduce event detecting delays by shortening the average sleep time of each sensor. By this way, the average delay could be reduced; however, it leads to another serious problem – low energy efficiency. There are notable wakeup overheads in power consumption.

3.3 Blinded conservative sleeping (BCS)

In contrast to INS, BCS adds cooperation between neighboring sensors. With BCS, whenever a sensor wakes up, it broadcasts an ENQUIRE message to all its neighbors, expecting to check if any of its neighbors has detected the presence of the stimulus. When a sensor, which has detected the stimulus and therefore remains active, receives an ENQUIRE message, it immediately replies with an AFFIRMATION message. If the sensor gets an AFFIRMATION reply, it starts to remain active and does not sleep any longer. If a neighbor has detected the stimulus, it implies that the stimulus border will spread to nearby sensors soon. It follows that nearby sensors should stay alert for the potential upcoming arrival of the stimulus. In this way, the sensor having detected the stimulus will soon wake up all its sleeping neighboring sensors.

BCS is expected to have good performance in minimizing event detecting delays. However, it is not energy efficient due to its blindness. Even when a neighboring sensor has detected the stimulus, it is still possible that the stimulus will take a long time to reach some of its neighboring sensors. The worst case is that the stimulus may not spread in a certain direction, which means the stimulus will never reach those sensors in that direction. Consequently, those sensors are simply wasting their energy to stay awake too early.

4. Stimulus-based adaptive sleeping

4.1 Overview

We have the intuition that after the DS arises, the sensors near the stimulus boundary should keep conscious, because the stimulus may spread over them soon. In order to report accurate stimulus arrival time, they should be active before the arrival of stimulus. And for sensors much further away from the boundary, they should sleep to save more power for further operations. It would be the ideal case if we can control their sleep time so they wake up at the right moment just before the arrival of stimulus. In this case, the sensors can capture the accurate arrival of the stimulus while minimizing energy consumption which helps to prolong the network lifetime. But it is impossible to get the ideal case in practice. In this paper, we propose SAS to exploit the previous observations to better monitor DS-like stimuli. The basic idea is that each sensor estimates the arrival time of stimulus boundary, and adaptively adjusts its sleep time. If it takes a long time for the stimulus boundary to reach the sensor, the sensor can safely sleep longer for energy efficiency. Otherwise, the sensor should be cautious. It should sleep shorter or even keep active for the upcoming stimulus. This sleeping time estimation is a localized operation which based on the local observations from the neighbors. The stimulus-based algorithm enables sensors to reduce power consumption while minimizing detection delays.

For applications of environment monitoring, the location information in each sensor is crucial. The location information can be provided by GPS or other location services [15, 16]. Sensors try to detect the stimulus and report the events attached with their respective positions back to the gateway. The gateway will process the data received and generate a global view of the area, for example, the area covered by the stimulus.

4.2 SAS sensor states

We are building a close relationship between sensor's application state and the stimulus. There are three possible application states for the sensors:

- *Covered*: Sensors which have detected the stimulus.
- *Restricted*: Sensors which have not detected the stimulus yet but are being notified by its neighbors that stimulus are approaching. They are usually near the boundary of the stimulus.
- *Non-restricted*: Sensors which have not detected the stimulus yet and have not been notified anything about the stimulus. They are usually far away from the boundary.

Intuitively, *covered* sensors should be active to keep monitoring the area. *Restricted* sensors may sleep but they have to wake up and become active right before the stimulus has arrived. *Non-restricted* sensors may use other sleeping algorithms [5] to control their sleeping behavior. A typical distribution of SAS sensor state is shown in Figure 1.

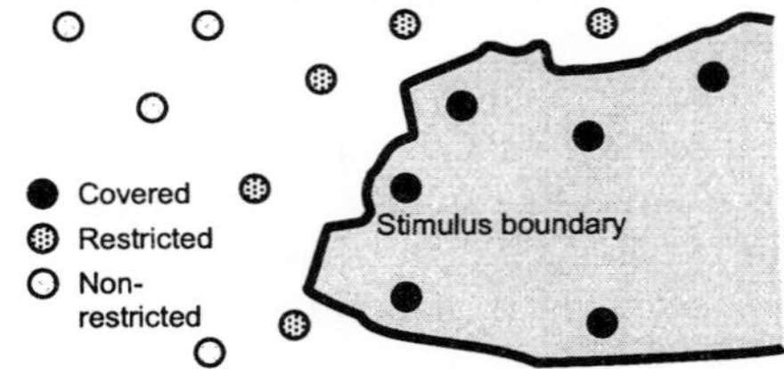

Figure 1: Application states and stimulus

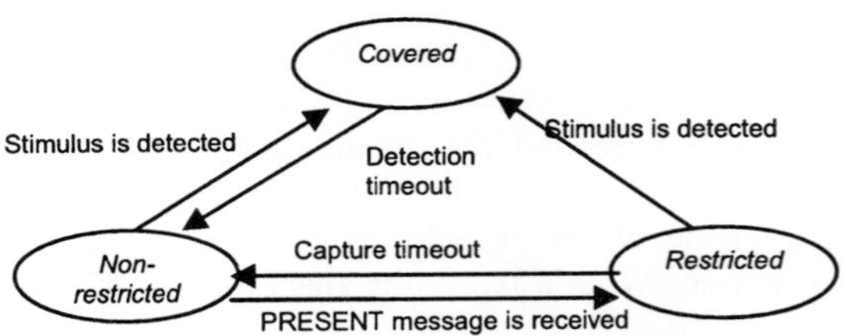

Figure 2: Transition of SAS sensor states

Figure 2 shows the transition of different SAS sensor states. All sensors are initially in *non-restricted* state. The sensor will change from the state of *non-restricted* or *restricted* to *covered* when it has detected the stimulus. *Non-restricted* sensor will change its state to *restricted* when it receives the PRESENT message from a *covered* sensor (to be discussed in Section 4.3). The diagram also shows the transition back to *non-restricted* state when the stimulus has passed away. When the stimulus has left from a *covered* sensor, it will wait for a detection timeout. If there is no detection of stimulus, it returns as a *non-restricted* sensor. If the restricted sensor has not detected the stimulus after a predefined time, it will also change back to *non-restricted* state.

4.3 Message types and operations

SAS has a few messages to be exchanged with sensors in varies operations:

- WAKEUP and PRESENT: Every sensor which has just changed from sleeping to active should broadcast a WAKEUP message with its location information. If *covered* sensors have received the WAKEUP message, they will send back a PRESENT message to indicate that the boundary of stimulus is near to this node. It will then change from the state of *non-restricted* to *restricted.* The message will contain the expected arrival time of the stimulus (to be discussed in section 4.5).
- DETECTION and ELAPSED: When a sensor has just detected the stimulus, it will change its state to the *covered* and broadcast a DETECTION message. All *non-restricted* sensors which have received this message should change the state to *restricted.* These sensors are close to the boundary of the stimulus. All *covered* sensors receiving the DETECTION message should send back the ELAPSED message with elapsed time after their first detection of the stimulus.

4.4 Local velocity estimation

In addition to determining the distance between the boundary and the *restricted* sensors, we need to compute the velocity of the stimulus for calculating the expected arrival time. The velocities vary at different portions of the boundary. We define a local velocity as the spreading speed and the direction between two neighboring sensors A and B which have detected the stimulus already. Speed is the scalar component equal to $\frac{|\overrightarrow{AB}|}{\lambda}$, where $|\overrightarrow{AB}|$ is the distance between sensors *A* and *B*, and λ is the elapsed time between stimulus detection of the two nodes. The direction is equal to drawing an arrow from sensor *A* to sensor *B*.

When sensor *A* has detected the stimulus at time t_0, it starts a timer. When B has detected the stimulus at time $t_0+\lambda$, *B* will broadcast a DETECTION message. Since *A* is a *covered* sensor, *A* will generate and send the ELAPSED message with the elapsed time to *B*. In practice, the elapsed time received is greater than λ because of transmission and processing delays. However, these delays are usually negligibly small compared to the elapsed time between the two nodes. We can safely ignore them in the time estimation without the difficulties in time synchronization.

Location information of the node is also included in the DETECTION message. Therefore, sensor *B* will receive enough information to calculate the velocity $\overrightarrow{AB}$. A sensor usually has more than one neighboring sensors in *covered* state. Thus, a node usually has more than one velocity information. We will show how multiple velocities are useful in estimating the arrival time in the next sub-section.

4.5 Arrival time estimation

After a node has broadcasted its DETECTON message, it will receive elapsed detection times and location information from neighboring *covered* sensors. The node will compute a set of local velocities from different neighbors. The velocity information will be used to estimate the arrival time of stimulus.

Both *restricted* and *non-restricted* sensors do not lie in the region of stimulus. In order to save power, they should sleep most of the time and wake up occasionally to receive latest information around the node. When they awake, they broadcast a WAKEUP message with their location information to their neighbors. *Covered* sensors should respond with a PRESENT message with estimated arrival time of the stimulus. The expected arrival time will be analyzed to decide the next sleeping interval.

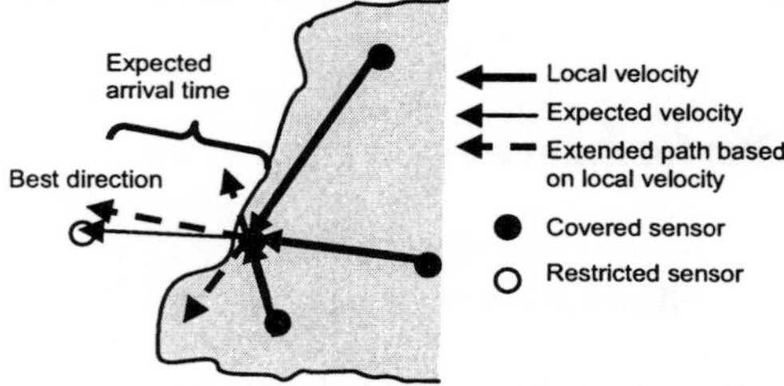

Figure 3: Expected arrival time

The expected arrival time based on different local velocities is illustrated in Figure 3. There will be one expected arrival time for each local velocity. While a *covered* node could have multiple expected arrival time, it will only select and send one to the awaken sensor. The properties of the stimulus suggested that it may not be a wise decision to select the one with the shortest expected arrival time. It will omit the important spatial information of the DS. The one having the closest direction to the *non-restricted* node should be chosen. This local velocity provides more relevant and accurate time for the awaken sensor.

At the same time, the awaken sensor may receive expected arrival time from different *covered* sensors in its transmission range. The sensor will select the smallest one among them.

4.6 Adaptive sleeping

The spreading of the stimulus is non-uniform. The sensors adapt to the localized boundary behaviors and have different sleeping times. The expected arrival time is computed based on the previous knowledge of the stimulus over a nearby region. It may not be an accurate arrival time of the stimulus. If it is used as the sleeping time directly, it is highly probable that the sensor will miss the first detection of stimulus which will result in detection delay. This is because a sensor can only be waken up by its internal timer after it has entered the sleep state. To tackle the problem, a sensor will sleep for a shorter time which is a fraction of the expected arrival time. When it awakes, it broadcasts the WAKEUP message again to receive latest stimulus information and recalculate the next sleeping time. This approach adaptively responses to the dynamics of stimulus which can effectively reduce detection delays.

However, some recent research studies have shown that switching between sleep and active states induces a significant overhead. This implies that the sleeping time should not be divided into too many portions. Our algorithm selects 3 as the number of portions to balance between switching overhead and detection delay. The sleeping time for a *non-restricted* node will be MIN(received expected arrival times) × 1/3.

5. Performance evaluation

5.1 Simulation methodology

We have performed simulation on various algorithms in order to evaluate their effectiveness. In an area with size 50m x 50m, we inject a single spreading DS in the region. A number of sensors are deployed in the region to monitor the DS. Recent researches have shown that power consumptions for transmission, reception and idle in active state have no significant differences. We assume the power consumption for transmission, reception and idle are the same. Based on the measurement of a 1995 AT&T 2Mb/s WaveLAN wireless LAN from Stemm and Katz [14], we use 1.2W and 0.025W as the power consumptions for the active and sleeping sensors, respectively.

Sleeping interval, node density and transmission range will affect the performance of the algorithms. We perform simulations of different combinations of the average sleeping intervals (500, 1000, 2000 and 4000ms), number of nodes (100, 200, 300 and 400) and transmission ranges (5m, 10m, 20m and 40m).

The performance of SAS is compared with two other simple algorithms, BCS and INS, which tend to optimize either one of our performance metrics, average detection delay and average energy consumption.

5.2 Performance metrics

Two performance metrics are used to compare different algorithms. *Average detection delay* is the average elapsed time between the actual arrival time and the moment the sensor has just detected it. We ignore any delays due to hardware and software overhead. If a sensor is active when the stimulus arrives, it will have a zero detection delay. Sleeping sensors will incur detection delay as they will always miss the first arrival time. This is an important measure for the accuracy and usefulness of information.

Average energy consumption is the average energy consumed by each sensor based on the parameters above. The difference in the average energy consumption provides a comparison on the energy efficiency of different algorithms.

5.3 Detection delay

Figure 4 shows the relationship between detection delay and *average sleeping interval* with 100 nodes and transmission range of 40m. Average sleeping interval is the expected time for a node to remain in the sleeping state when the sleeping time is not adaptively determined with stimulus consideration. Average detection delay increases with average sleeping interval for all algorithms. However, the rate for INS is much greater than BCS and SAS as the neighboring nodes are not cooperating with each others. Every node wakes up independently. As the average sleeping in-

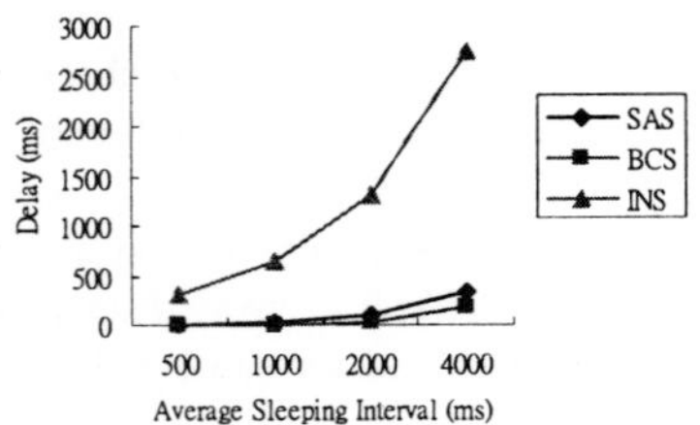

Figure 4: Average detection delay vs. average sleeping interval

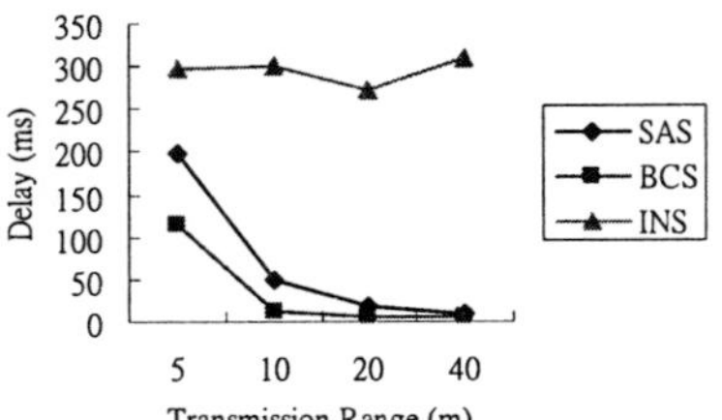

Figure 5: Average detection delay vs. transmission range

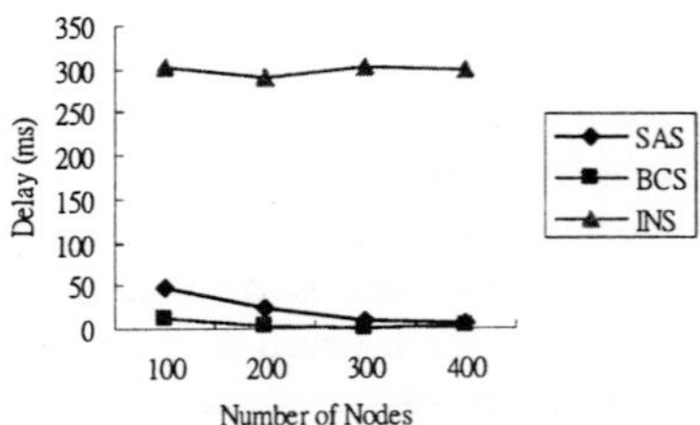

Figure 6: Average detection delay vs. number of nodes

terval increases, nodes will suffer from a greater delay between arrival time and wake up time. In SAS, the sleeping interval is related to the expected arrival time received from neighboring nodes. This effectively reduces the detection delay by constructing the relationship between the stimulus and sleeping interval.

Average detection delay versus transmission range with 100 nodes and sleeping interval of 500ms in the region is shown in Figure 5. Average detection delay of both BCS and SAS decreases while the transmission range increases. INS has a fairly constant delay regardless the transmission range. It is always greater than the other algorithms as it takes no stimulus nor neighbor information to control the sleeping time of the sensors. As a result, the transmission range has no significant effect on it. The nodes using BCS or SAS make use of the stimulus information detected by the neighbors to dynamically adjust the sleeping time. The improvement increases as the transmission range increases. This is because more sensors will receive the detection information and hence most of them are ready to become active nodes before the stimulus arrives.

BCS will always have a smaller delay than the corresponding SAS. With BCS, all its direct neighbors will become active once a sensor has detected the stimulus. On the other hand, SAS will dynamically adjust the sleeping period. They will have slightly greater chances to miss the arrival of stimulus. However, their difference is so small that both are still good choices for applications required to minimize the average detection delay.

Figure 6 shows the average detection delay versus the number of nodes with sleeping interval of 500ms and transmission range of 10m in the network. Given that the region being monitored is fixed, greater number of nodes implies a greater node density in the region. The situation is similar to increasing the transmission range. There will be more direct neighbors for any node. BCS is still the best one as it forces all the neighbors to be active when a node has detected the stimulus. We will look at the drawbacks of making all the direct neighbors active.

5.4 Energy consumption

Figure 7 shows the average energy consumption versus average sleeping interval with 100 nodes and transmission range of 40m. The longer the average sleeping interval, the longer time a node remains in its sleeping state. This results in less energy consumption. Nodes using INS will always sleep using a random time unless it detects the stimulus. In contrast, a node using BCS will activate all its neighbors which will not sleep again. Therefore, INS will always have the lowest average energy consumption while BCS will have the highest. SAS estimates the sleeping period using the information from neighboring nodes and hence they are not necessary to be active all the time. As a result, it operates with average energy consumption between INS and BCS.

The average energy consumption versus transmission range with 100 nodes and sleeping interval of 500ms in the network is shown in Figure 8. The average energy consumption of INS is the lowest and remains nearly constant for different transmission ranges. SAS and BCS will have greater energy consumption.

Sleeping time in INS does not rely on the stimulus. No detection information will be exchanged. This accounts for its fairly constant energy consumption for varies transmission ranges. INS is trading the detection delay for lower energy consumption.

SAS and BCS make use of the neighbors' detection information to adjust the sleeping time. They are designed to allow sensors to wake up before the arrival of stimulus. This design incurs longer active time for the sensors. Instead of keeping all neighbors active and wait in BCS, SAS provides information to neighbors to decide a safe sleeping time. This improves the energy consumptions by suppressing the active time for nodes which are further away from *covered* nodes. As a result, SAS will always have lower energy consumption than BCS.

Figure 9 shows the average energy consumption versus the number of nodes with sleeping interval of 500ms and transmission range of 10m. SAS effec-

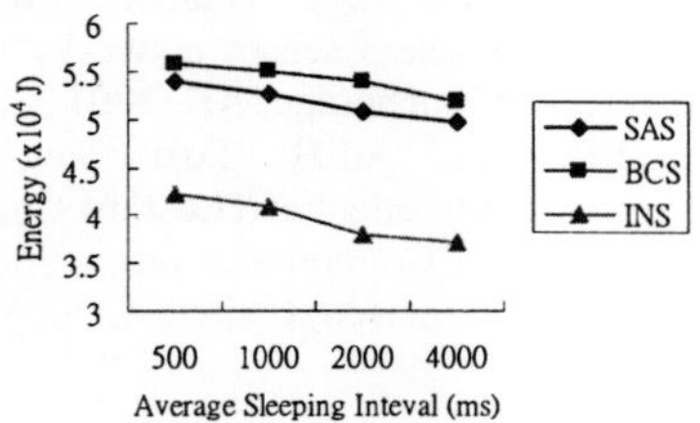

Figure 7: Average energy consumption vs. average sleeping interval

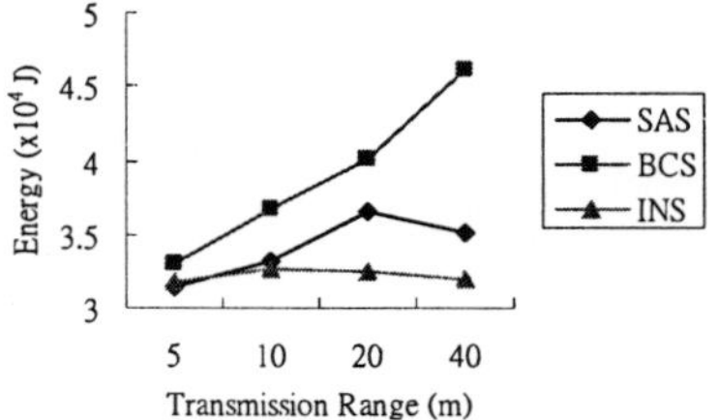

Figure 8: Average energy consumption vs. transmission range

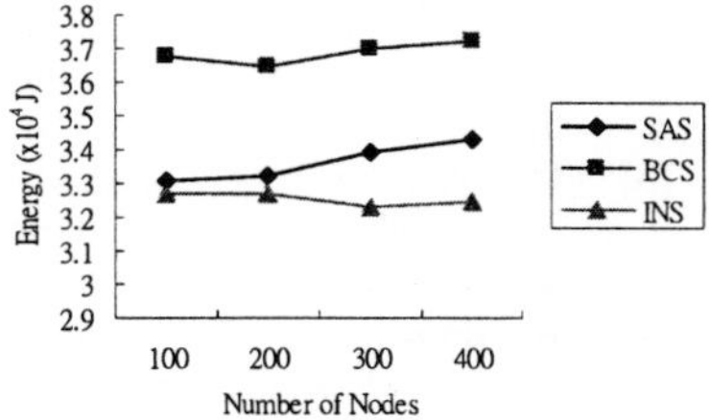

Figure 9: Average energy consumption vs. number of nodes

tively reduces the energy consumption by allowing neighboring nodes in the outer region of transmission range to sleep. It has slightly greater energy consumption than that of INS while providing much smaller average detection delay.

6. Conclusions and future work

Adaptive sleeping is an important technique in sensor networks to reduce operating power consumption and hence lengthen the network lifetime. Apart from traditional criteria like node density, we have identified and analyzed a new criterion, stimulus, in adaptive sleeping design. In applications, like pollution monitoring, which require accurate stimulus detection and location information, stimulus behavior is one of the important factors to reduce power consumption.

We have proposed an algorithm to leverage the energy consumption and the detection delay. Our simulation results have shown that the proposed SAS approach has effectively reduced the detection delay while maintaining low energy consumption. Our algorithm could cooperate with other sleeping algorithms to provide adaptive sleeping based on different criteria of the applications.

In this work, we have the first insight of the importance of the stimulus to the sleeping algorithm. Our work is expected to be effective on multiple sources of stimulus. One of our objectives is to reduce the detection delay. In practice, it is possible for a stimulus to cover the sensor and move to somewhere else after certain period of time. We proposed to change the state to *non-restricted* to save power using a simple timeout mechanism. To further improve the power efficiency, we are going to explore the behavior of the departing stimulus. We intend to study the effect of false alarm and imperfect channel as well.

References

[1] I. F. Akyildiz, W. Su, Y. Sankarasubramaniam, and E. Cayirci, "Wireless Sensor Networks: A Survey" Computer Networks, vol. 38, pp. 393--422, 2002.

[2] G. J. Pottie and W. J. Kaiser, "Wireless integrated network sensors" ACM Communications, vol. 43, pp. 51-58, 2000.

[3] D. Estrin, G. P. L. Girod, and M. Srivastava, "Instrumenting the world with wireless sensor networks" presented at ICASSP, Salt lake City, UT, 2001.

[4] A. Mainwaring, D. Culler, J. Polastre, R. Szewczyk, and J. Anderson, "Wireless sensor networks for habitat monitoring" presented at 1st ACM international workshop on Wireless sensor networks and applications, 2002.

[5] F. Ye, G. Zhong, S. Lu, and L. Zhang, "PEAS: A Robust Energy Conserving Protocol for Long-lived Sensor Networks" presented at The 23rd International Conference on Distributed Computing Systems (ICDCS '03), Rhode Island, 2003.

[6] Y. Xu, J. Heidemann, and D. Estrin, "Geography-informed energy conservation for ad hoc routing" presented at the Seventh Annual ACM/IEEE International Conference on Mobile Computing and Networking (MobiCom'01), Rome, Italy, 2001.

[7] J. V. Greunen, D. Petrovi, A. Bonivento, J. Rabaey, K. Ramchandran, and A. Sangiovanni-Vincentelli, "Adaptive sleep discipline for energy conservation and robustness in dense sensor networks" Paris, 2004.

[8] B. Chen, K. Jamieson, H. Balakrishnan, and R. Morris, "Span: An energy-efficient coordination algorithm for topology maintenance in ad hoc wireless networks" presented at 6th Annual International Conference on Mobile Computing and Networking (Mobicom'01), 2001.

[9] A. Cerpa and D. Estrin, "ASCENT: Adaptive Self-Configuring Sensor Networks Topologies" presented at the Twenty First International Annual Joint Conference of the IEEE Computer and Communications Societies (InfoCom'02), NewYork, NY, USA, 2002.

[10] C. Intanagonwiwat, R. Govindan, D. Estrin, J. S. Heidemann, and F. Silva, "Directed diffusion for wireless sensor networking" IEEE/ACM Transactions on Networking, vol. 11, pp. 2-16, 2003.

[11] M. J. Handy, M. Haase, and D. Timmermann, "Low energy adaptive clustering hierarchy with deterministic cluster-head selection" presented at IEEE International Conference on Mobile and Wireless Communications Networks, Stockholm, 2002.

[12] Y. Xu, J. Heidemann, and D. Estrin, "Adaptive Energy-Conserving Routing for Multihop Ad Hoc Networks" USC/Information Sciences Institute, Technical Report 527 2000.

[13] D. Tian and N. D. Georganas, "A Coverage-Preserving Node Scheduling Scheme for Large Wireless Sensor Networks" presented at ACM Workshop on Wireless Sensor Networks and Applications, Atlanta, 2002.

[14] M. Stemm and R. Katz, "Measuring and reducing energy consumption of network interfaces in handheld devices" Institute of Electronics, Information, and Communication Engineers Transactions on Communications, E80B (8), pp. 125--1131, 1997.

[15] L. Doherty, K. Pister, and L. E. Ghaoui, "Convex position estimation in wireless sensor networks" presented at IEEE Infocom, Anchorage, AK, 2001.

[16] D. Niculescu and B. Nathi, "Ad Hoc Positioning System (APS) using AoA" presented at The 22rd Conference of the IEEE Communications Society (INFOCOM2003), San Francisco, CA, USA, 2003.

A New Service Classification Strategy in Hybrid Scheduling to Support Differentiated QoS in Wireless Data Networks

Navrati Saxena, Kalyan Basu, Sajal K. Das
Comp. Sc. & Engg. Dept.
University of Texas at Arlington
Arlington, Texas, USA
{nsaxena, basu,das}@cse.uta.edu

Cristina M. Pinotti
Maths and Informatics Dept.
University of Perugia
Perugia, Italy
pinotti@unipg.it

Abstract

The wireless telecommunication industry is now slowly shifting the paradigm from circuit-switched voice-alone applications to a new audio-visual world. Diversification of personal communication systems (PCS) and gradual penetration of wireless Internet have generated the need for *differentiated services*. The set of clients (customers) in the wireless PCS networks is generally classified into different categories based on their power and importance. Activities of the customers having higher importance have significant impact on the system and the service providers. The goal of the service providers lies in minimizing the cost associated in the maintenance of the system and reducing the loss incurred from the clients' churn rate. Deployment of such differentiated services calls for efficient scheduling and data transmission strategies. In this paper we have developed a new service classification strategy in hybrid scheduling scheme to support differentiated quality of service (QoS) among the different set of clients. The scheme dynamically computes the data access probabilities and amalgamates the push and pull scheduling schemes to develop the hybrid scheduling framework. While a flat scheduling is used for push system, the major novelty of the work lies in differentiating the clients based on their priority-classes and incorporating the effect of priority in selecting an item from the pull-system. Modeling and analysis of the system is performed to get an average behavior of the QoS parameters like delay in our hybrid scheduling framework. Simulation results points out that the average waiting time for the highest priority clients can be kept very low, while simultaneously minimizing the number of requests dropped by assigning appropriate fraction of available bandwidth. It also demonstrates that by intelligent selection of the cut-off point, used to segregate push and pull systems, the overall cost associated with the system can be minimized.

1 Introduction

Historically, cellular telephone networks were the first radio access networks to be developed and widely deployed. The major objective behind the initial deployment of cellular wireless networks was to provide only an un-interrupted, circuit-switched voice communication. Increasing popularity of hand-held mobile devices, deregulation of wireless services and existence of multiple network operators introduced an era of *competitive* wireless market. This aids in rapid deployment of enhanced wireless communication technologies, thus improving the customer's satisfaction. The gradual deployment of the Internet applications added a new paradigm by introducing the concept of *data services* and *packet technologies*. While the growth in wireless voice communication is almost attaining its saturation, the primary target and attention of competitive service providers is slowly shifting towards the packet-switched, data services in cellular, wireless networks. The popularity of short messaging services (SMS), I-mode (Japan) and *push-to-talk* services over the legacy cellular systems along with the proliferation of IETF (Internet Engineering Task Force) standardized protocols and the speculation behind the deployment of UMTS (Universal Mobile Telecommunications System) is probably the first step of this movement towards wireless data services.

However the most challenging question at this point becomes "what is the level of Quality of Service (QoS) guarantee the wireless systems can provide for these newly introduced data services ?". Recent researches in QoS [8, 11] reveal that the resource (bandwidth) constraints, high bit-error rate, channel fading and interference in wireless channels, along with the hand-off generated from the user-mobility are the major impairments behind meeting the QoS guarantee needed for real-time, wireless services. The inherent asymmetry in wireless systems arising from difference in uplink and downlink channel capacity, number of clients and server, and uplink and downlink message-size makes the problem even more complex and challenging. Hence, in order to meet these stringent QoS requirements of wireless data services, one needs an efficient and scalable data broadcasting and scheduling strategy. Current cellular systems and its data transmission strategies do not differentiate the QoS among the clients, i.e., the sharing and management of resources does not reflect the importance of the clients. A close look into the existing hybrid scheduling strategy for wireless systems reveals that most of the scheduling algorithms aims at minimizing the overall average access time of all the clients. However, we argue that this is not sufficient for future generation cellular wireless systems which will be provid-

0190-3918/05 $20.00 © 2005 IEEE

ing QoS differentiation schemes. The items requested by clients having higher priorities might need to be transmitted in a fast and efficient manner, even if the item has accumulated less number of pending requests. Hence, if a scheduling considers only popularity, the requests of many important (premier) clients' may remain unsatisfied, thereby resulting in dissatisfaction of such clients. As the dissatisfaction crosses the tolerance limit, the clients might switch the service provider. In the anatomy of today's competitive cellular market this is often termed as *churning*. This churning has adverse impacts on the wireless service providers. The more important the client is, the more adverse is the corresponding effect of churning. The data transmission and scheduling strategy for cellular wireless data networks thus needs to consider not only the probability of data items, but also the priorities of the clients.

In this paper, we propose a new service classification strategy for hybrid broadcasting to support the differentiated QoS in wireless data networks. The hybrid scheduling that effectively combines broadcasting of more popular (i.e., push) data and disseminating (upon-request) the less popular (i.e., pull data) in asymmetric (where asymmetry arises because the number of clients is more than the number of servers), heterogeneous (different items have different lengths) environments. At any instance of time, the item to be broadcast is selected by applying a *flat* scheduling. However, the selection strategy for a pull-item is significantly influenced by the influence of the clients and the corresponding service classification scheme. The major novelty of our work lies in separating the clients into different classes and introducing the concept of a new selection criteria, termed as *importance factor*, by combining the clients' priority and the *stretch* (i.e, *max-request min-service-time*) value. The item having the maximum importance factor is selected from the pull queue. We argue that is a more practical and better measure in the system where different clients have different priorities and the items are of variable lengths. The performance of our heterogeneous hybrid scheduler is analyzed using suitable priority queues to derive the expected waiting time. The bandwidth of the wireless channels is distributed among the client-classes to minimize the request-blocking of highest priority clients. The cut-off point, used to segregate the push and pull items is efficiently chosen such that the overall costs associated in the system gets minimized. We argue that the strict guarantee of differentiated QoS, offered by our system, generates client-satisfaction, thereby reducing their churn-rate.

The rest of the paper is organized as follows. Section 2 reviews existing work in the literature of data broadcasting and scheduling. The new hybrid algorithm, which introduces the concept of service classification into hybrid scheduling to provide differentiated QoS is produced in Section 3. A suitable performance model, based on priority queuing, is developed in Section 4 to analyze and estimate the average delay and blocking in the hybrid system. Simulation results in Section 5 supports the performance analysis and points out that the resultant delay and blocking of the highest priority clients can be kept sufficiently low, thereby reducing the overall cost of the system. Finally, Section 6 concludes the paper.

2 Existing Works

A survey into the existing literature reveals the existence of a wide variety of solutions for data broadcasting. However, the solutions can be broadly categorized into two parts: (1) push-based broadcasting and (2) pull-based dissemination. While the *flat, round-robin* scheduling provides the most simple and basic transmission strategy, it always suffers from a fixed average delay, which is half of the sum of the length of all the data items. The work of Acharya and Franklin [1] is perhaps the first attempt to remove this disadvantage by introducing the role of access probability (popularity) in the selection of data items. This problem, better known as the *Broadcast Disk Problem*, groups data items in disks, thus assigning items in the same range of access probabilities to the same disk. The broadcast schedule is then generated by interleaving one item from each disk. The disks having higher access probabilities are of smaller size and have higher rotation speed. This results in the disks having higher access probabilities providing more instances of their data to the broadcast schedule. The Square-Root-Rule (SRR) [5] provides an optimal solution for the uniform-length broadcasting problem. This produces a broadcast schedule, where each data item appears with equally spaced replicas, having frequency directly proportional to the square root of its access probability and inversely proportional to the square root of its length.

A hybrid approach that use the flavors of both push-based and the pull-based scheduling algorithms in one system, appears to be more attractive. Perhaps the first hybrid technique for scheduling and data transmission in asymmetric environment is proposed in [2]. In this work, the server pushes all the data items according to some push-based scheduling, but simultaneously the clients are provided with a limited back-channel capacity to make requests for the items. In our previous work [10], we have developed a hybrid scheduling strategy for transmission of heterogeneous, variable length data items.

A close look into the existing hybrid scheduling strategy reveals that none of the existing works have considered service differentiation and client priorities into account. According to our knowledge, we are the first to develop the new service classification scheme in hybrid scheduling strategy, which is capable of offering differentiated QoS for wireless data networks.

3 Hybrid Scheduling with Service Classification

We assume an environment with a single server serving multiple clients, thus imposing asymmetry. The server-database consists of a total D distinct items, out of which K items are pushed and the remaining $(D-K)$ items are pulled. All the items have variable lengths. The access probability P_i, of an item i is governed by the Zipf's distribution. Every client is also associated with certain priority. These priorities provides the influence and importance of the clients to the service providers. The push-based broadcasting ignores the clients' requests, and uses a *Flat* round-robin scheduling strategy for cyclic broadcasting of popular data items.

The pull-scheduling, on the other hand, is based on a linear combination of the number of clients' requests accumulated and priorities. It should be noted that items with pending requests for higher priority clients should be serviced faster than the items having requests from lower priority clients. However, this scheme might suffer from *un-fairness* to the lower priority clients and also does not consider the number of clients' requests. A data item, requested by many clients having lower importance, might remain in the pull queue for a long time. Eventually, all the pending requests for that item might be lost (blocked). Hence, a better option is to consider both the number of pending requests and the priorities of all clients requesting the particular data item. A close look into the system reveals that, the service time required to serve an item is dependent on the size of that item. The larger the length of an item the higher is its service time. We introduce a new scheduling strategy that combines *stretch optimal or max-request min-service-time first* schedule with the *priority scheduling* to select an item from the pull-queue. Formally if, $\mathcal{S}_i$ represents the stretch associated with item i and $\mathcal{Q}_i$ represents the total clients' priority associated with item i, then the item selected from the pull-queue is determined by the following condition:

$$\gamma_i = \max\left[\alpha\mathcal{S}_i + (1-\alpha)\mathcal{Q}_i\right], \qquad (1)$$

where α is a fraction $0 \leq \alpha \leq 1$, which determines the relative weights between the priority and the stretch value. Clearly, $\alpha = 0$ and $\alpha = 1$ makes the schedule priority-scheduling and stretch-optimal scheduling respectively.

When a client needs an item i, it requests the server for item i and waits until it listens for i on the channel. Note that the behavior of the client is independent of the fact that the requested item belongs to the push-set or the pull-set. Depending on the priorities, the server first classifies the clients into different service classes. The server goes on accumulating the set of requests from the clients. The algorithm starts with a fixed cutoff-point which separates the push and pull set. For any item arrived, it first determines if the item belongs to the push or the pull set. If the request is for a push item, the server simply ignores the request as the item will be pushed according to the online Flat, round-robin algorithm. However, if the request is for a pull item, the server inserts it into the pull queue with the arrival time, and updates its stretch value and total priority of all the clients' requesting that item. After every push, if the pull queue is not empty, the server chooses the item having maximum importance factor (γ_i) from the pull-queue. The bandwidth required by the data item is assumed to follow Poisson's distribution. If the required bandwidth of the data item is less than the bandwidth available for the corresponding service class, then the data item and the corresponding requests are lost. Otherwise, the server assigns the required bandwidth and transmits the item. Once the transmission is complete, the pending requests for that item in the pull-queue is cleared and the bandwidth used is released to update the available bandwidth. Figure 1 provides the pseudo-code of the hybrid scheduling algorithm executing at the server-side. Periodically the algorithm is executed for different cutoff-points and obtains the optimal cutoff-point which minimizes the overall access time (delay).

```
Procedure HYBRID SCHEDULING;
divide the clients among different service-classes;
while true do
      begin
      consider the access/requests arriving;
      ignore the requests for push item;
      append the requests for the pull item in the pull-
      queue with its arrival time and importance-factor;
      take out an item from push part and broadcast it;
      if the pull-queue is not empty then
         extract the item having maximum importance-factor
         (γi) from the pull-queue;
         clear the number of pending requests for that item;
         free the amount of required bandwidth and update
         the amount of available bandwidth;
      end-if
end-while
```

Figure 1: Service Classification in Hybrid Scheduling

4 Delay and Blocking in Differentiated QoS

In this section we study the performance evaluation of our hybrid scheduler system by developing suitable models to analyze its behavior. The prime concern of this analysis is to obtain an estimate of the minimum expected waiting time (delay) of the hybrid system. Since, this waiting time is dependent on the cutoff point K, investigation into the delay dynamics with different values of K is necessary to get the optimal cutoff point. As explained before in Section 3, the selection criteria in the pull system is dependent on both the stretch-value associated with the item and the priority of the clients requesting that particular item. Hence, the performance analysis also needs to consider the clients priority along with the stretch-value associated with every data item. We divide the entire analysis into two parts. In the first part, we consider the system without any role of the client's priority and obtain the expression for average number of items present in the system. In the second part, we introduce the explicit role of priorities in determining the average system performance.

4.1 Average Number of Elements in the System

Assumptions: The arrival rate in the entire system is assumed to obey the Poisson's distribution with mean λ'. The service times of both the push and pull systems are exponentially distributed with mean μ_1 and μ_2, respectively. Let C, D and K respectively represents maximum number of clients, total number of distinct data items and the cut-off point. The server pushes K items and clients pull the rest $(D-K)$ items. Thus, the arrival rate in the pull-system is given by: $\lambda = \sum_{i=K+1}^{D} \mathcal{P}_i \times \lambda'$, where $\mathcal{P}_i$ denotes the access probability of item i. We have assumed that the access probabilities P_i follow the *Zipf's distribution* with *access skew-coefficient* θ, such that $\mathcal{P}_i = \frac{(1/i)^\theta}{\sum_{j=1}^{n}(1/j)^\theta}$.

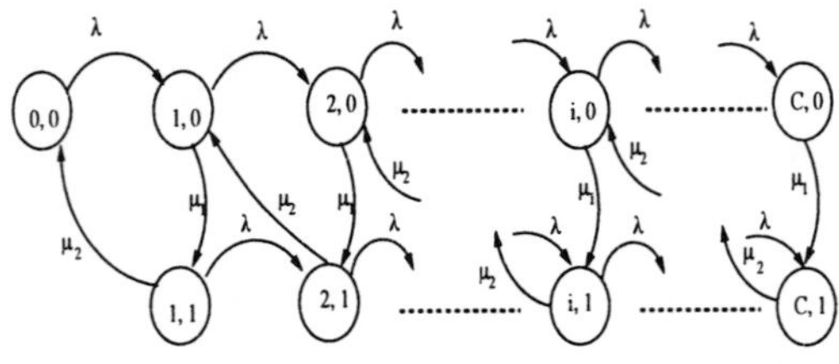

Figure 2: Performance Modelling of Hybrid System

Figure 2 illustrates the birth and death model of our system, where the arrival rate in the pull-system is given by λ. Any state of the overall system is represented by the tuple (i,j), where i represents the number of items in the pull-system and $j = 0$ (or 1) respectively represents whether the push-system (or pull-system) is being served. The arrival of a data item in the pull-system, results in the transition from state (i,j) to state $(i+1,j), \forall i \in [0,C]$ and $\forall j \in [0,1]$. The service of an item in the push system results in transition of the system from state $(i, j=0)$ to state $(i, j=1), \forall i \in [0,C]$. On the other hand, the service of an item in the pull results in transition of the system from state $(i, j=1)$ to the state $(i-1, j=0), \forall i \in [1,C]$. The details of steady-state flow balance equations and their solutions are explained in our previous work [10]. For the sake of clarity, we briefly highlight the major steps here. The steady-state behavior of the system (without considering priority) is represented by the equations given below:

$$p(0,0)\ \lambda = p(1,1)\ \mu_2$$

$$p(i,0)(\lambda+\mu_1) = p(i-1,0)\lambda + p(i+1,1)\mu_2 \quad (2)$$

$$p(i,1)(\lambda+\mu_2) = p(i,0)\mu_1 + p(i-1,1)\lambda \quad (3)$$

where $p(i,j)$ represents the probability of state (i,j). Dividing both sides of Equation (2) by μ_2, letting $\rho = \frac{\lambda}{\mu_2}$, $f = \frac{\mu_1}{\mu_2}$, performing subsequent z-transform and using Equation (2), we get

$$P_2(z) = \rho\, p(0,0) + z(\rho+f)\,[P_1(z) - p(0,0)] - \rho z^2 P_1(z)$$

$$P_2(z) = \frac{f\,[P_1(z) - p(0,0)]}{(1+\rho-\rho z)} \quad (4)$$

Now, estimating the system behavior at the initial condition, we can state that the occupancy of pull and push states is given by: $P_2(1) = \sum_{i=1}^{C} p(i,1) = \rho$ and $P_1(1) = \sum_{i=1}^{C} p(i,0) = (1-\rho)$. Using these two relations in Equation (4), we can obtain the idle probability, $p(0,0)$ as: $p(0,0) = 1 - \rho - \frac{\rho}{f}$. Differentiating both sides of Equation (4) with respect to z at $z=1$, we estimate the expected number of elements in the pull-system ($E[\mathcal{L}_{pull}]$) as follows:

$$\left[\frac{\partial P_2(z)}{\partial z}\right]_{z=1} = E[\mathcal{L}_{pull}] = (\rho+f)\mathcal{N} + (1-\rho) - (\rho+f)\times(1-\rho-\frac{\rho}{f}) - \rho\mathcal{N} \quad (5)$$

where $\left[\frac{\partial P_1(z)}{\partial z}\right]_{z=1} = \mathcal{N}$ represents the average number of elements in the pull queue when a push request is being serviced.

4.2 Priority-based Service Classification

Every client j is associated with a certain priority q_j, which reveals the importance or class of that client. Obviously, this influences the arrival rate associated with every item. The arrival rate associated with i^{th} item for j^{th} priority-client is given by: $\lambda_i = \lambda\, p_i\, q_j$. Now, L_i and R_i represents the length and number of pending requests associated with the ith item, then the stretch-value S_i associated with that item is given by the expression: $S_i = \frac{R_i}{L_i^2}$. If $E[\mathcal{L}_{pull}]$ represents the average length of the pull queue, then average number of ith items present in the queue is given by $E[\mathcal{L}_{pull}]p_i$. Hence, average importance of ith item requested by j^{th} client is given by: $E[\mathcal{L}_{pull}]\,p_i\,q_j$. Representing the influence of the set of clients $\mathcal{S}$ requesting for item i by $\mathcal{Q}_i = \sum_{j=1}^{\mathcal{S}} q_j$, the selection criteria of that element is now given by the following equation:

$$\varrho_i = \left(\alpha \frac{E[\mathcal{L}_{pull}]p_i}{L_i^2} + (1-\alpha)E[\mathcal{L}_{pull}]\,p_i\,\mathcal{Q}_i\right) \quad (6)$$

It should be noted that the above equation actually resembles Equation 1. However, Equation 1 does not consider the number of ith items present in the pull queue. Thus, Equation 6 actually generalizes Equation 1 and boils down to Equation 1, when $E[\mathcal{L}_{pull}]p_i = 1$. This condition provides the position of every item in the priority queue. In order to distinguish this measure with the client priority q_j, we term ϱ_i as the *importance-factor* of item i. We first analyze the system performance with clients belonging to two different classes [4], having two different importance factors. Subsequently, we extend the framework to incorporate clients having multiple importance factors.

4.2.1 Delay Estimation for Two Different Service Classes

Let, λ_1 and λ_2 represents the average arrival rate of the data items having importance factors 1 and 2, i.e., $\lambda = \lambda_1 + \lambda_2$. We also assume that the most important items have the right to get service before the second important item without *preemption*. Now, the probability of every state should incorporate the number of items belonging to both important factors and the class of item currently getting service. We denote it by $p(m,n,r,1)$, such that: $p(m,n,r,1) = Pr[m \, \text{and} \, n$ units of importance factor 1 and 2 are present in the system and a unit of importance factor $r = 1 (or\, 2)$ is in service, the system is in the pull mode]. Proceeding in a similar manner as shown in Section 4.1, we can obtain the steady state balanced equations of the prioritized pull-system as:

$$\begin{aligned}
(\lambda_1+\lambda_2+\mu_2)p(m,n,2,1) &= \lambda_1 p(m-1,n,2,1) \\
&\quad +\lambda_2 p(m,n-1,2,1) \\
(\lambda_1+\lambda_2+\mu_2)p(m,n,1,1) &= \lambda_1 p(m-1,n,2,1) \\
&\quad +\lambda_2 p(m,n-1,2,1) \\
&\quad +\mu_2[p(m+1,n,1,1) \\
&\quad +p(m,n+1,1,1)] \\
(\lambda_1+\lambda_2+\mu_2)p(m,1,2,1) &= \lambda_1 p(m-1,1,2,1) \\
(\lambda_1+\lambda_2+\mu_2)p(1,n,1,1) &= \lambda_2 p(1,n-1,1,1) \\
&\quad +\mu_2[p(2,n,1,1) \\
&\quad +p(1,n+1,2)] \\
(\lambda_1+\lambda_2+\mu_2)p(0,n,2,1) &= \lambda_2 p(0,n-1,2,1) \\
&\quad +\mu_2[p(1,n,1,1) \\
&\quad +p(0,n+1,2,1)] \\
(\lambda_1+\lambda_2+\mu_2)p(m,0,1,1) &= \lambda_1 p(m-1,0,1,1) \\
&\quad +\mu_2[p(m+1,0,1,1) \\
&\quad +p(m,1,2,1)] \\
(\lambda_1+\lambda_2+\mu_2)p(0,1,2,1) &= \lambda_2 p(0,0,0,1) \\
&\quad +\mu_2[p(1,1,1,1) \\
&\quad +p(0,2,2,1)] \\
(\lambda_1+\lambda_2+\mu_2)p(1,0,1,1) &= \lambda_1 p(0,0,0,1) \\
&\quad +\mu_2[p(2,0,1,1) \\
&\quad +p(1,1,2,1)] \\
(\lambda_1+\lambda_2)p(0,0,0,1) &= \mu_2[p(1,0,1,1) \\
+ &\quad p(0,1,2,1)] \qquad (7)
\end{aligned}$$

It should be noted that the probability of the idle state, i.e., $p(0,0,0,0) = p(0,0)$ remains same as before. The reason behind this is that the ordering of service does not affect the probability of idleness; i.e., $p(0,0) = 1 - \rho - \frac{\varrho}{f}$. Now, the occupancy of the pull states is ρ. Hence the fraction of time, the pull-system is busy with type-1 and type-2 items is given by: $\rho\lambda_1/\lambda$ and $\rho\lambda_2/\lambda$. Thus we have,

$$\begin{aligned}
\sum_{m=1}^{C}\sum_{n=0}^{C} p(m,n,1,1) &= \frac{\lambda_1}{\mu} \quad (a) \\
\sum_{m=0}^{C}\sum_{n=1}^{C} p(m,n,2,1) &= \frac{\lambda_2}{\mu} \quad (b) \qquad (8)
\end{aligned}$$

Obtaining a reasonable solution to these set of stationary equations is almost impossible. All we can is to achieve an expected measure of the system performance. We perform two successive z-transforms over the Equations 8 (a)–(b), to get one and two dimensional z-transformed equations in the following way:

$$\begin{aligned}
P_{m1}(z) &= \sum_{n=0}^{\infty} z^n p(m,n,1,1) \\
P_{m2}(z) &= \sum_{n=1}^{\infty} z^n p(m,n,2,1) \qquad (9) \\
H_1(y,z) &= \sum_{m=1}^{\infty} y^m P_{m1}(z) \\
H_2(y,z) &= \sum_{m=1}^{\infty} y^m P_{m2}(z) \qquad (10)
\end{aligned}$$

Combining the above two-dimensional z-transforms we have:

$$\begin{aligned}
H(y,z) &= H_1(y,z) + H_2(y,z) + p(0,0,0,1) \\
&= \sum_{m=1}^{\infty}\sum_{n=1}^{\infty} y^m z^n (p_{m,n,1,1} + p_{m,n,2,1}) \\
&\quad + \sum_{m=1}^{\infty} z^n p(m,0,1,1) \\
&\quad + \sum_{n=1}^{\infty} z^n p(0,n,2,1) + p(0,0,0,1) \qquad (11)
\end{aligned}$$

Solution of the above equations results in:

$$\begin{aligned}
H(y,z) &= H_1(y,z) + H_2(y,z) + p(0,0,0,1) \\
&= \frac{p(0,0,0,1)(1-y)}{1-y-\rho y(1-z-\lambda_1 y/\lambda + \lambda_1 z/\lambda)} \\
&\quad + \frac{(1+\rho-\rho z+\lambda_1 z\mu_2)(z-y)P_{0,2}(z)}{A \times B} \\
A &= z[1+\rho-\lambda_1 y/\mu_2 - \lambda_2 z/\mu_2] \\
B &= [1-y-\rho y(1-z-\lambda_1 y/\lambda + \lambda_1 z/\lambda)] \qquad (12)
\end{aligned}$$

The above equation provides the final solution of the z-transforms associated with the two different priority classes of clients. This equation will help us in obtaining the average performance of both the priority classes and also the overall expected system performance. As discussed earlier in the previous subsection, differentiating this equation will provide the average number of items present in the system. If L_1 and L_2 represents the average number of items for both the classes then,

$$L_1 = \left[\frac{\partial H(y,z)}{\partial y}\right]_{y=z=1} \quad \text{and} \quad L_2 = \left[\frac{\partial H(y,z)}{\partial z}\right]_{y=z=1} \tag{13}$$

The expected waiting time of the data items having two different importance factors now can be easily found by using the Little's formula as: $E[W_1] = L_1/\lambda_1$ and $E[W_2] = L_2/\lambda_2$.

4.2.2 Effect of Multiple Service Classes

The outline of the above procedure however fails to capture the expected system performance when number of importance-factors increase over 2. Thus a better way is to follow a *direct expected value approach* [4]. Considering a non-preemptive system with many importance-factors, let us assume the data items with importance-factor ϱ_j have an arrival rate and service time of λ_j and μ_{2j} respectively. The occupancy arising due to this j^{th} data item is represented by $\rho_j = \frac{\lambda_j}{\mu_{2j}}$ $(1 \le j \le max)$, where max represents maximum possible value of importance-factor. Also let σ_j represents the sum of all occupancy factors ρ_i, i.e., $\sigma_j = \sum_{i=1}^{j} \rho_i$. In the boundary conditions we have, $\sigma_0 = 0$ and $\sigma_{max} = \rho$. If we assume that a data item of importance-factor i arrives at time t_0 and gets serviced at time t_1, then the wait is $t_1 - t_0$. Let at t_0 there are n_j data items present having priorities j. Also let, S_0 be the time required to finish the data item already in service, and S_j be the total time required to serve n_j. During the waiting time of any data item, n'_j new items having higher importance-factor can arrive and go to service before the current item. If S'_j be the total service time required to service all the n'_j items, then the expected waiting time for the ith item will be,

$$E[W_{pull}^{(i)}] = \sum_{j=1}^{i-1} E[S'_j] + \sum_{j=1}^{i} E[S_j] + E[S_0] \tag{14}$$

In order to get a reasonable estimate of $W_{pull}^{(i)}$, three components of Equation 14 needs to individually evaluated.

(i) *Estimating* $E[S_0]$: The random variable S_0 actually represents the remaining time of service, and achieves a value 0 for idle system. Thus, the computation of $E[S_0]$ is performed in the following way:

$$E[S_0] = Pr[\text{Busy-System}].E[S_0|\text{Busy-System}]$$

$$\begin{aligned} &= \rho . \sum_{j=1}^{max} E[S_0|\text{Serving item, importance-factor} = j] \\ &\quad \times Pr[\text{item having importance-factor} = j] \\ &= \rho \times \sum_{j=1}^{max} \frac{\rho_j}{\rho\mu_{2j}} = \sum_{j=1}^{max} \frac{\rho_j}{\mu_{2j}} \end{aligned} \tag{15}$$

(ii) *Estimating* $E[S_j]$: The inherent independence of Poisson's process gives the flexibility to assume the service time $S_j^{(n)}$ of all n_j customers to be independent. Thus, an estimate of $E[S_j]$ can be obtained using the following steps:

$$\begin{aligned} E[S_j] &= E[n_j S_j^{(n)}] = E[n_j]E[S_j^{(n)}] \\ &= \frac{E[n_j]}{\mu_{2j}} = \rho_j E[W_{pull}^{(j)}] \end{aligned} \tag{16}$$

(iii) *Estimating* $E[S'_j]$: Proceeding in a similar way and assuming the uniform property of Poisson's,

$$E[S'_j] = \frac{E[n'_j]}{\mu_{2j}} = \rho_j E[W_{pull}^{(i)}] \tag{17}$$

The solution of Equation 14 can be achieved by combining the results of Equations 15–17 and using Cobham's iterative induction [4]. The expected waiting time of the ith item and the overall expected waiting time of the pull system is given as:

$$\begin{aligned} E[W_{pull}^{(i)}] &= \frac{\sum_{j=1}^{max} \rho_j/\mu_{2j}}{(1-\sigma_{i-1})(1-\sigma_i)} \\ E[W_{pull}^{q}] &= \sum_{i=1}^{max} \frac{\lambda_i E[W_{pull}^{q(i)}]}{\lambda} \end{aligned} \tag{18}$$

The overall expected access time is obtained by combining the time taken to service the push and pull items. Since, the push set contains K items of heterogeneous lengths $L_1, L_2, \ldots, L_K$, the average length of the push (broadcast) cycle is $\frac{1}{2}\sum_{i=1}^{K} L_i \mathcal{P}_i$. Thus, the expected access-time ($E[T_{hyb-acc}]$) of our hybrid system is now given by:

$$E[T_{hyb-acc}] = \frac{1}{2\mu_1} \sum_{i=1}^{K} L_i \mathcal{P}_i + E[W_{pull}^{q}] \sum_{i=k+1}^{D} \mathcal{P}_i, \tag{19}$$

where K is the cutoff-point used to segregate push and pull components of the hybrid system. It should be noted that one major objective of our proposed algorithm is to find out an optimal cutoff-point K such that this delay is minimized. The above expression provides an estimate of the average delay (waiting time) for different class of clients in our hybrid scheduling system. The service providers always try to reduce the delay of the high priority clients, in order to ensure their satisfaction. Apart from this delay, we would like get an estimate of the prioritized cost associated with each class of client. This cost is actually obtained as $q_j \times E[T_{hyb-acc}]$. Intuitively this cost provides an estimate of the client's influence on the service provider and the overall system.

5 Simulation Experiments

In this section we validate the performance analysis of our prioritized hybrid system by performing simulation experiments. We first enumerate the set of assumptions used in our simulation. Subsequently, we provide the series of simulation results obtained.

5.1 Assumptions

1. The simulation experiments are evaluated for a total number of data items $D = 100$.
2. The overall average arrival rate λ' is assumed to be 5. The value of μ_1 and μ_2 is estimated as: $\mu_1 = \sum_{i=1}^{K}(\mathcal{P}_i \times L_i)$ and $\mu_2 = \sum_{i=K+1}^{D}(\mathcal{P}_i \times L_i)$.
3. The length of the data items are varied from 1 to 5, with an average of 2.
4. In order to keep the access probabilities of the items from similar to very skewed, θ is dynamically varied from 0.20 to 1.40. More specifically, we have assumed $\theta = \{0.20, 0.60, 1.0, 1.40\}$.
5. The entire set of clients is divided into three classes: *Class-A, having highest priority, Class-B with medium priority* and *Class-C with lowest priority*. The priorities are taken in the ratio 1 :: 2 :: 3. The fraction α associated in deriving the importance-factor is assumed to be in the range $[0, 1]$, where $\alpha = 1$ indicates the system ignoring the effect of priority and $\alpha = 0$ indicates the system ignoring the effect of stretch.
6. The distribution of clients among different classes is also assumed to obey Zipf's distribution, with lowest number of highest priority (Class-A) clients and highest number of lowest priority clients.

Now we describe the set of simulation results obtained from our simulation experiments.

5.2 Overall Expected Delay

The goal of the first set of experiments is to investigate into the overall delay experienced by each class of clients. Figures 3– 4 demonstrate the dynamics of total delay with the cut-off point experienced by three different classes of clients for $\alpha = \{0, 0.25, 0.50, 0.75, 1.0\}$ respectively. This is performed for different values of access skewness. The delay associated with the Class-A (highest priority) clients is very low (within 5–10 broadcast units). The delay experienced by the Class-B clients remains in the range 20–40 broadcast units. The highest delay (40–70 broadcast units) is experienced by the Class-C clients. However, for all the classes of clients the delay is higher for low values of cut-off point (K). The reason is that for low values of K, the system deviates from the hybrid nature and can not achieve a good balance between push and pull set.

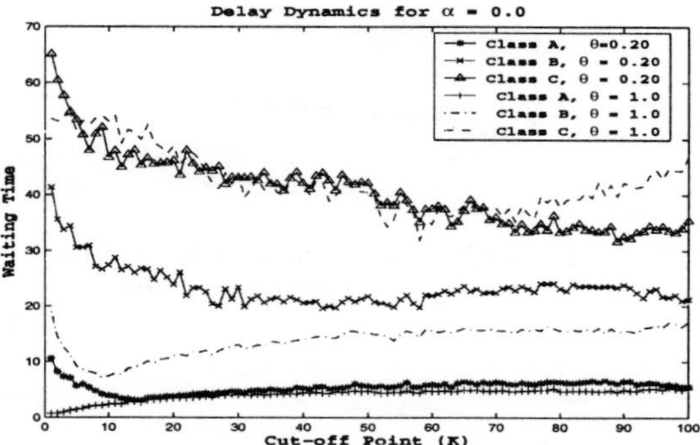

Figure 3: Delay Variation with $\alpha = 0.0$

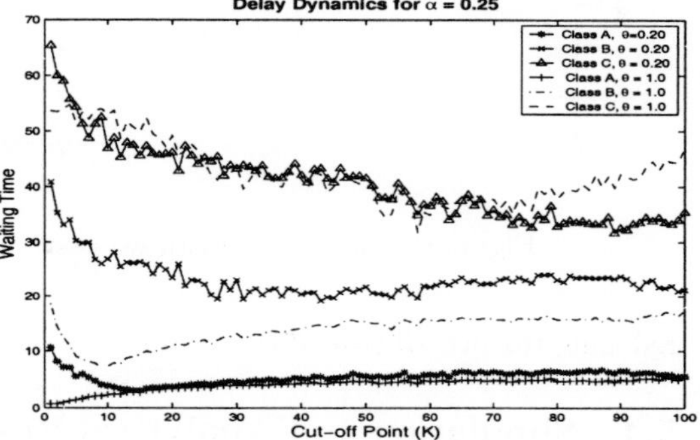

Figure 4: Delay Variation with $\alpha = 1.0$

5.3 Prioritized Costs

The major objective of the second set of experiments is to look into the variation of the prioritized cost associated with each class of clients. As mentioned earlier, the system assigns the costs to each class of clients in proportion to the priority of that particular class. These costs are actually computed by multiplying the priority of the client-class with the expected delay. Figure 5 demonstrates the variation of prioritized costs with the cut-off point, associated with each class of clients for $\alpha = \{0.25, 0.75\}$ and $\theta = 0.60$. The overall objective is to pick up the particular value of cut-off point such that the total prioritized cost is minimized. Figure 6, on the other hand, shows the changes in total optimal prioritized cost of all the client-classes, with different values of α for $\theta = \{0.20, 0.60, 1.40\}$. With decreasing values of α the influence of priority increases and the prioritized cost reduces. The underlying reason is that for lower values of α the increased influence of priority results in serving the important clients first, thereby

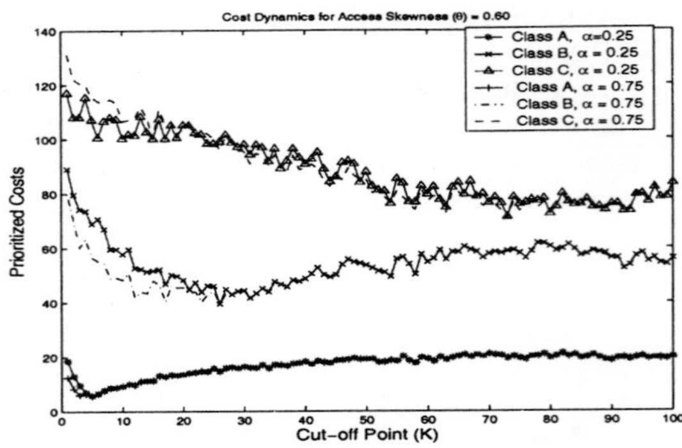

Figure 5: Cost Dynamics for Service Classes

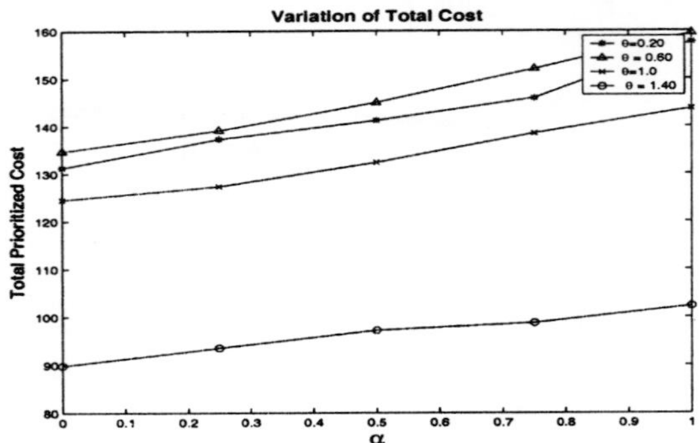

Figure 6: Variation of Prioritized Cost

reducing the overall cost of the system.

5.4 Simulation and Analytical Results

Figure 7 demonstrates the comparison between analytical and simulation results for $\theta = 0.60$ and $\alpha = 0.75$. The analytical results are obtained using the Equation 19. We have chosen the values of α and θ so that these values are almost in the middle of their range. Analytical results closely match simulation results for all the three set of clients, with a minor 10% deviation. The minor deviation is attributed to the memory-less assumption in the system modelling.

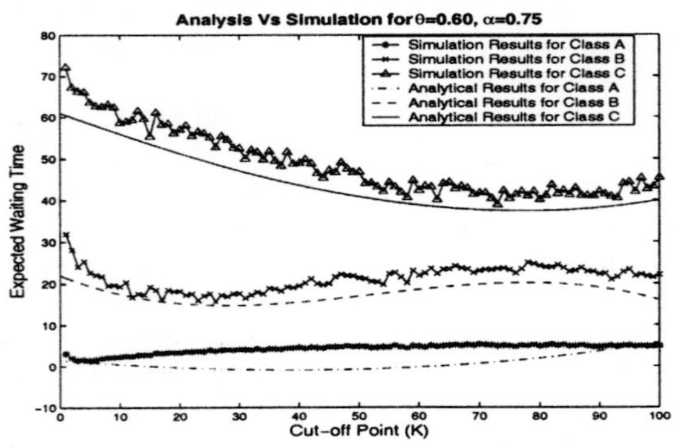

Figure 7: Analytical Vs. Simulation Results

6 Conclusion

In this paper we have proposed a new service classification strategy for hybrid scheduling to support differentiated services in wireless data networks. The hybrid scheduling effectively combines the push and pull systems. The major novelty of the work lies in differentiating the clients into various classes based on their priorities. Subsequently, it uses a linear combination of the clients' priorities and the probabilities of the data items to form a new selection criteria for the pull-system. This is more practical as the system should pay more attention towards the clients having higher importance than the clients having lower importance. By obtaining an optimal cut-off point between the push and pull items the framework minimizes the overall prioritized costs associated to maintain the clients in the system. Performance analysis and simulation results demonstrate that the average waiting time for the premium clients can be significantly reduced, thereby minimizing the total overall cost associated in the system and increasing an overall efficiency of the system and profit of the service providers.

References

[1] S. Acharya, R. Alonso, M. Franklin and S. Zdonik. Braodcast Disks: Data Management for Asymmetric Communication Environments, *Proceedings of ACM SIGMOD Conf.*, pp. 199-210, May 1995.

[2] S. Acharya, M. Franklin, and S. Zdonik. Balancing push and pull for data broadcast. *Proceedings of the ACM SIGMOD Conference*, pp. 183–193, May, 1997.

[3] D. Aksoy and M. Franklin. RxW: A scheduling approach for large scale on-demand data broadcast. *IEEE/ACM Transactions on Networking*, Vol. 7, No. 6, pp. 846-860, Dec. 1999.

[4] D. Gross and C. M. Harris, Fundamentals of Queuing Theory, *John Wiley & Sons Inc.*

[5] S. Hameed and N. H. Vaidya. Efficient algorithms for scheduling data broadcast In *WINET*, Vol. 5, pp. 183-193, 1999.

[6] G. Lee and S. C. Lo. Broadcast Data Allocation for Efficient Access of Multiple Data Items in Mobile Environments. *Mobile Networks and Applications*, Vol. 8, pages 365-375, 2003.

[7] C-W Lin, H. Hu and D-L Lee, "Adaptive Realtime Bandwidth Allocation for Wireless Date Delivery", *ACM/Kluwer Wireless Networks*, (WINET), vol. 10, pp. 103-120, 2004.

[8] M. Mahajan and M. Pashar "Managing QoS for Multimedia Applications in a Differentiated Services Environment", *Active Middleware Services (AMS)*, 2002.

[9] M. C. Pinotti and N. Saxena. Push less and pull the current highest demanded data item to decrease the waiting time in asymmetric communication environments. *4th International Workshop on Distributed and Mobile Computing, Springer-Verlag, (LNCS)*, (IWDC), pp. 203–213, 2002.

[10] N. Saxena, K. Basu and S. K. Das, "Design and Performance Analysis of a Dynamic Hybrid Scheduling for Asymmetric Environment", *IEEE Intl. Workshop on Mobile Adhoc Networks*, WMAN, 2004.

[11] Z. Wu and D. Raichaudhuri, " D-LSMA: Distributed Link Scheduling Multiple Access Protocol for QoS in Ad-Hoc Networks" *Proc. of IEEE GlobeCom*, 2004.

Session 6A: Higher-Level Network Operations

Optimizing Collective Communications on SMP Clusters

Meng-Shiou Wu
Department of Electrical and
Computer Engineering,
Iowa State University
Scalable Computing Laboratory
Ames Laboratory, U.S. DOE
Ames, Iowa 50011, USA
mswu@iastate.edu

Ricky A. Kendall
Scalable Computing Laboratory
Ames Laboratory, U.S. DOE
Department of Computer Science,
Iowa State University
Ames, Iowa 50011, USA
rickyk@scl.ameslab.gov

Kyle Wright
Department of Computer Science,
Iowa State University
Scalable Computing Laboratory
Ames Laboratory, U.S. DOE
Ames, Iowa 50011, USA
kyle@iastate.edu

Abstract

We describe a generic programming model to design collective communications on SMP clusters. The programming model utilizes shared memory for collective communications and overlapping inter-node/intra-node communications, both of which are normally platform specific approaches. Several collective communications are designed based on this model and tested on three SMP clusters of different configurations. The results show that the developed collective communications can, with proper tuning, provide significant performance improvements over existing generic implementations. For example, when broadcasting an 8MB message our implementations outperform the vendor's MPI_Bcast by 35% on an IBM SP system, 51% on a G4 cluster, and 63% on an Intel cluster, the latter two using MPICH's MPI_Bcast. With all-gather operations using 8MB messages, our implementation outperform the vendor's MPI_Allgather by 75% on the IBM SP, 60% on the Intel cluster, and 48% on the G4 cluster.

1 Introduction

Collective communications are important to the performance of many parallel applications, and optimization for collective communications, either generic for different platforms or specific to a particular platform, has been a topic of research interest. Several algorithmic techniques to improve collective communications have been proposed during the last decade [1, 2, 3, 10]. Besides optimizing collective communications through algorithmic techniques, breaking a message into segments and implementing collective communications in a pipeline fashion are also proposed in [5, 8, 9, 15]. Due to the complexity of current parallel architectures, one implementation that performs well on a given platform is not guaranteed to have the same performance on another platform. Thus Fagg *et al.* designed ACCT [5, 15] to automatically tune collective communications for different platforms. The above approaches assume that each node has one processor. When we consider collective communications on clusters consisting of SMP nodes, one question is how to use SMP the architecture to improve the performance of collective communications.

There are two possible optimizations for collective communications on SMP clusters that are not possible on uniprocessor clusters. One optimization is to use concurrent memory access features to design collective communications within an SMP node; this is proposed by Sistare *et al.* [12] on a SUN SMP machine. Another optimization is to overlap inter-node/intra-node communications, proposed by Tipparaju *et al.* [14] on an IBM SP, an SMP cluster. Both proposed approaches are platform specific optimizations. When we want to design an automatic tuning collec-

0190-3918/05 $20.00 © 2005 IEEE

tive communications system for SMP clusters, we must find generic approaches for the two platform specific optimizations so every SMP cluster can take advantage of these two optimizations.

In our previous work [17] we have developed a generic mechanism to design all collective communications within SMP clusters. In this paper we focus on a generic mechanism to overlap inter-node/intra-node communications. Combining these two mechanisms we describe a programming model to develop collective communications on SMP clusters.

2 The Programming Model

Figure 1 outlines the programming model to design collective communications on SMP clusters. There are three layers in this model: the top layer is the inter-node communication layer, the bottom layer is the intra-node communication layer, and the middle layer is the overlapping mechanisms. We listed every possible method on each layer and all possible combinations to design collective communications on SMP clusters in a generic approach.

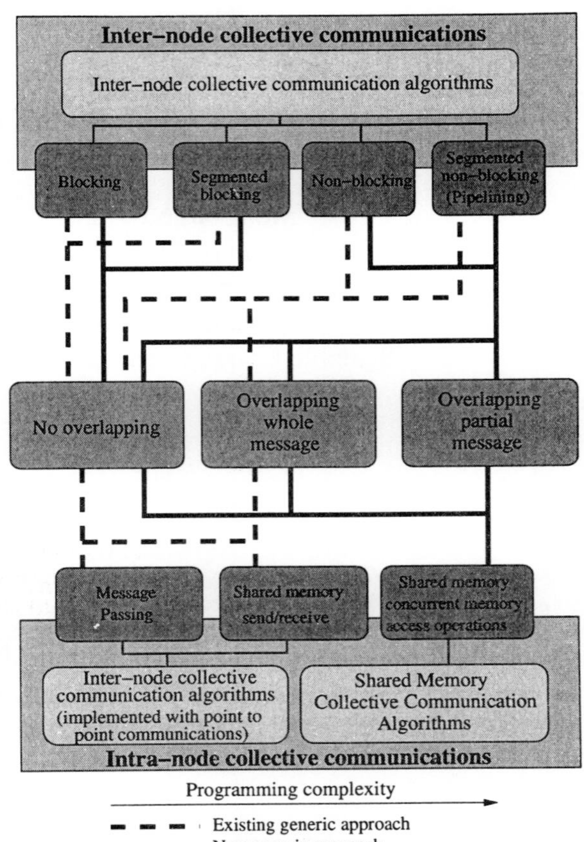

Figure 1. The programming model for designing collective communications on SMP clusters.

2.1 Inter-node communication layer

This is the layer that compute nodes are connected through on a communication network, and the communications between nodes are done through the communication network. On this layer a collective operation can be implemented using different algorithms, and an algorithm can be implemented using different MPI send/receive implementations.

Most MPI implementations, such as MPICH, use blocking send/receive of a whole message to implement a certain collective communication algorithm. An implementation that uses blocking send/receive usually incurs less software overhead than a non-blocking implementation, thus performs well when the communication is latency bound (usually small message) [4].

Segmented non-blocking implementations incur more software overhead, making them difficult to implement and even more difficult to tune to achieve good performance. However, those are the implementations that can utilize pipelining. With proper tuning, a segmented non-blocking implementation usually gives the best performance when the communication is bandwidth bound (usually large messages). Some research projects, such as ACCT [5, 15] or MagPIe [8, 9], use this approach to design their collective communication libraries.

Non-blocking implementations of a whole message and segmented blocking implementations seldom provide good performance; we list them in the model for completeness. Most collective communication algorithms developed during the last decades focus on this top layer with the assumption that each node has one processor. Golebiewski *et al.* [7] and Kielmann *et al.* [8, 9] developed collective communication algorithms for two communication layers, and their algorithms are implemented with point to point communications on both layers.

When implementing our generic, collective communications library, we use only MPI_Send/MPI_Recv for blocking implementations and use MPI_Isend/MPI_Irecv for non-blocking implementations. We did not encounter any problems in porting our implementations to different platforms and overall performance was not impacted by this choice.

2.2 Intra-node communication layer

On the intra-node layer, the communications between processors can be either through the communication network or through shared memory. If the collective communications are implemented with MPI send/receive, they can be used directly on the intra-node layer. Some implementations optimize the data movement via shared memory implementations of the send/recieve. SGI and IBM's MPI and some MPI library implementations [16, 13] use this approach.

A different approach is to use concurrent memory access features of SMP architecture to design collective communications. The basic idea of this approach is that, once a message segment is in the shared memory area, every processor within the same SMP node can access that message segment concurrently. This approach has been used by Steven *et al.* [12] and Tipparaju *et al.* [14] to design broadcast, barrier, and reduce. In our previous work [17] we generalized Steven's approach and categorized concurrent memory access features for collective communications into seven basic shared memory operations. We used those seven basic operations to construct more complex collective communications (such as scatter, gather, and all-to-all) for SMP clusters. Those shared memory operations are implemented with system functions that are available on every UNIX-like system, allowing our shared memory collective communications to be used on a variety of platforms.

Throughout this paper, if an intra-node collective communication is implemented using concurrent memory access features, we call it a shared memory collective communication.

2.3 Inter-node/Intra-node overlapping mechanisms

A novel approach to overlap inter-node/intra-node communications was proposed by Tipparaju *et al.* [14]. The approach uses remote direct memory access (RDMA) to design inter-node collective communications and overlap them with shared memory collective communications. The functions for RDMA are provided by IBM LAPI, and are specific to IBM platforms. Since our final goal is an automatic tuning system for different SMP clusters our first idea was to replace the platform specific RDMA provided by LAPI with existing generic RDMA libraries.

2.3.1 RDMA Functions in other libraries.

There are two libraries that provide generic RDMA functions on different platforms: MPI-2 [6] and the Aggregate Remote Memory Copy Interface (ARMCI) [11]. The MPI-2 standard was first released in 1996, and only recently have the RDMA features been regarded as mature. ARMCI provides similar RDMA functions, but with much simpler rules than the complex rules set by MPI-2 standard.

At the moment, the two generic RDMA approaches pose difficulties for using them to implement generic inter-node layer collective communications. The major reason is that a memory segment must first be registered to be used by RDMA functions. Data in a memory segment which is allocated by *malloc()* or *calloc()* must be copied to a registered memory segment to be accessable to RDMA functions. This means that if we implement non-blocking collective communications using these generic RDMA functions, we would need one extra copy on both the sender and receiver sides. This could lead to performance degradation. Requiring an end-user to allocate memory using the functions provided by these RDMA libraries would be asking them to go through their entire MPI application and make changes accordingly. This is both unrealistic and error-prone. For these reasons, we have chosen not to use RDMA to implement mechanisms for overlapping inter-node/intra-node communications.

2.3.2 Overlapped Inter-node/Intra-node Communications

Another approach is to modify existing non-blocking segmented implementations on the inter-node layer to overlap inter-node/intra-node communications. The idea is very straightforward: within an SMP node one process (group communicator) is in charge of inter-node communications. When processing a collective communication, the group communicator posts non-blocking sends for a message and then starts shared memory collective communications. When a non-blocking receive is posted, shared memory collective operations can be started as soon as a message segment is received. At the same time the communication layer can continue receiving the other message segments. In other words, we can treat shared memory collective communications as computation.

The major difficulty hidden behind this seemly simple strategy is that when using MPI non-blocking calls we cannot merely overlap the entire message segment as in Tipparaju's approach. Let $g(m)$ be the gate value, and $os(m)$ be the send overhead of sending a message of size m as defined in parameterized LogP model [8, 9]. When using non-blocking sends to send a segment, the next segment of size m can not be sent before $g(m)$. The overhead $os(m)$ is usually smaller than $g(m)$, thus the best theoretical interval for overlapping is $g(m) - os(m)$. When we start shared memory collective operations after posting a non-blocking send, it is very possible that the cost of the shared memory collective communications of size m is larger than $g(m) - os(m)$. Simply overlapping a whole segment may delay sending the next message segment. Therefore, when using MPI non-blocking functions to overlap inter-node/intra-node communications we also have to consider overlapping only partial message segment. On the other hand, when communications are latency bound, using

Machine Type	Processors per node	Network type	MPI implementation	Testing MPI tasks
IBM Power3	16	IBM Propriety network	IBM MPI	16x16
Intel Xeon	2	Myrinet	MPICH 1.2.5.2	16x2
Macintosh G4	2	Myrinet	MPICH2 0.97	16x2

Table 1. Three testing platforms.

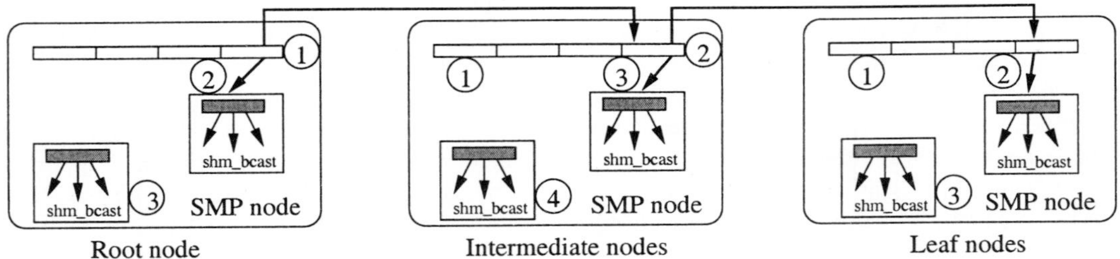

Figure 2. Overlapping inter-node/intra-node communications for broadcast

non-blocking segmented implementations can only make the performance worse since overhead is higher: thus the best approach may be to not overlap at all.

This lead us to construct the programming model outlined in Figure 1. The dashed lines indicate existing generic approaches to design collective communications on SMP clusters. The solid lines are new generic approaches we added. For example, blocking implementations (either whole message or segmented) cannot be combined with any overlapping mechanism, but they can still take advantage of using shared memory collective communications on the intra-node layer to improve overall performance.

The programming complexity of implementing collective communications in Figure 1 is roughly increasing from left to right (with the exception of non-blocking and segmented blocking on the inter-node layer). For a dashed line in Figure 1, inter-node layer collective communications can be used directly on the intra-node layer. For a solid line, new algorithms or implementations are required for good performance.

3 Implementations of Collective Communications and Experimental Results

The most commonly used algorithms for inter-node collective communication are flat-tree, chain-tree, binominal tree and binary tree. Each has strengths and weaknesses under different circumstances; some may even be entirely unsuitable for a given collective communication algorithm. In this section we discuss our optimization of some collective operations on SMP clusters based on the programming model outlined in this paper. Our focus is on how we design overlapping versions of these collective communications.

3.1 Testing Platforms

Three testing clusters are listed in Table 1. The IBM SP system at the National Energy Research Scientific Computing Center is a distributed-memory parallel supercomputer with 380 compute nodes. Each node has 16 POWER3+ processors and at least 16 GBytes of memory, thus at least 1 GByte of memory per processor. Each node has 64 KBytes of L1 data cache and 8192 KBytes of L2 cache. The nodes are interconnected via an IBM proprietary switching network and run IBM's implementation of MPI. The Intel Cluster is located at Iowa State University. It consists of 44 nodes with dual Intel Xeon processors (88 processors). The nodes, running MPICH, are connected with Myrinet. The Macintosh G4 Cluster is located at the Scalable Computing Laboratory at Ames Laboratory. It is a 32-node "Beowulf" style cluster computer consisting of 16 single processor G4s with 512 MB RAM and 16 dual processor G4s with 1 GB RAM, all running Debian Linux. The G4 cluster uses Myrinet for the primary network communication layer. For our testing on the G4 we used only dual processor nodes, running MPICH-GM. Throughout the paper, *A*x*B* denotes that the experiment used *A* nodes, each with *B* MPI tasks.

3.2 Broadcast

Most existing MPI implementations of broadcast use a blocking implementation of a binominal tree algorithm on both layers without overlapping communication at different levels. ACCT uses segmented non-blocking implementation of different algorithms, but only for the inter-node layer. MagPIe measures the difference of the gate value and overhead between two communication layers, and derives a communication tree accordingly. In their overlapping mechanisms, an inter-node point-to-point communication overlaps an intra-node point-to-point communication, so we regard it as a generic overlapping mechanism for a whole message segment.

Our broadcast implementations cover almost every path in the programming model in Figure 1, which covers most of the existing approaches. Our new generic approach is to overlap inter-node communications with shared memory collective communications.

Figure 2 outlines the mechanisms to overlap inter-node/intra-node communications for broadcast. The root node (1) posts a non-blocking send(s) of a segment, starts (2) the shared memory broadcast, and then repeats (1) and (2) until the last segment is processed. The last step (3) is executed if the shared memory broadcast segment size is smaller than the segment size for the inter-node layer broadcast. Intermediate nodes initially (1) post all non-blocking receives. Once a segment is received, it (2) posts a non-blocking send for this segment and then (3) starts a shared memory broadcast. The intermediate nodes repeat (2) and (3) until the last segment is processed and then finish the operation (4) if another shared memory broadcast is required. Leaf nodes operate in the same sequence as intermediate nodes, but without forwarding message segments: thus they (1) post non-blocking receives, (2) wait for a segment to be received and then start the shared memory broadcast, repeating (1) and (2) until the last segment is processed, and (3) process the last shared memory broadcast if necessary. If a node has multiple child nodes (such as in a binominal or binary tree broadcast), it will post all non-blocking sends to all child nodes before starting the shared memory broadcast.

Figure 3 shows the results of different broadcast implementations with an 8 MB message on 3 different platforms. Implementation 1 is a blocking implementation on both layers (most MPI broadcast uses this approach). Implementation 2 is a non-blocking segmented implementation on both layers (the same approach as ACCT and MagPIe). Implementation 3 uses the blocking implementation on the inter-node layer and a shared memory broadcast on the intra-node layer (the same as in our previous work [17]). Implementation 4 uses the segmented non-blocking implementation on the inter-node layer and overlaps with the shared memory broadcast on the intra-node layer. In short, we can look at implementations 1 and 2 as existing generic approaches, while implementations 3 and 4 represent new generic approaches in the programming model.

From Figure 3 we can see that layers of optimization have different effects on different algorithms. Implementation 2 greatly improves performance on all platforms for the chain tree algorithm. Implementation 3 provides good performance improvement only when the number of processes per node is large enough such as on IBM SP (16 processors per node). Implementation 4 provides the best performance across all three platforms. Overlapping for the chain tree broadcast can hide almost all the cost of shared memory broadcast on the IBM SP.

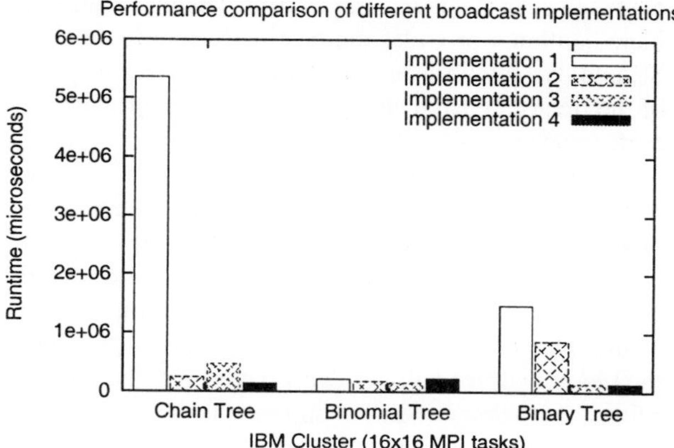

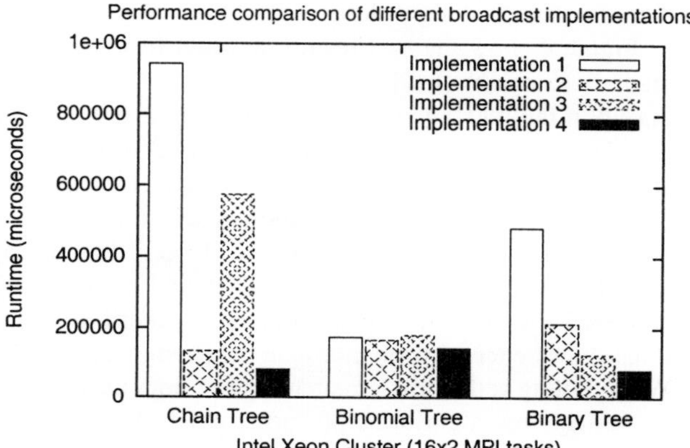

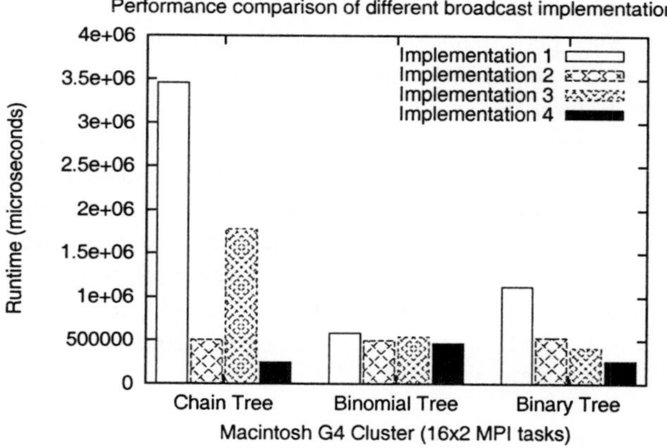

Figure 3. Performance comparison of different broadcast implementations on three platforms, using 8MB messages

For the binary tree algorithm, each layer of optimization

provides a certain degree of performance improvement. Implementation 4 provides the best performance on the IBM SP and the Intel cluster. In fact, the overlapping version of the binary tree and chain tree algorithms provide similar performance on all three platforms.

As for binominal tree algorithm, although implementation 1 provides better performance than the blocking version of the other two algorithms, different optimizations show only very limited performance improvement and sometimes even performance degradation. If our optimization stops at implementation 2 as in existing generic optimizations, the binominal tree still performs better than the other algorithms. However, when we optimize to implementation 4, our binominal tree implementation always performs worse than the other two algorithms.

Figure 4 show the best results selected from our implementations against MPI_Bcast on each platform. Depending upon the message size, the performance improvement is 20% to 46% on the IBM SP; 27% to 63% on the Intel cluster, and 27% to 51% on the G4 cluster. Table 2 shows the details of which implementation is selected for a given message size on the three platforms. Except for message sizes less than 8KB on the G4 cluster and between 1KB and 8KB on the Intel cluster, our new generic optimizations show better performance than the existing approaches. Worth noting is that implementation 4 of both the chain and the binary tree algorithms performs much better than the two stage broadcast (scatter, all-gather) used by MPICH for broadcasting large messages.

The performance of an implementation is a function of {*algorithm, number of nodes, number of processes/processors per node, message size, segment size, and overlapping size*}; to the best of our knowledge there is no such performance model that covers inter-node communications with shared memory collective communications. A new performance model is needed to explain the effects of layers of optimization on different algorithms, and we are currently extending parameterized LogP model and ACCT's performance model to cover shared memory collective communications.

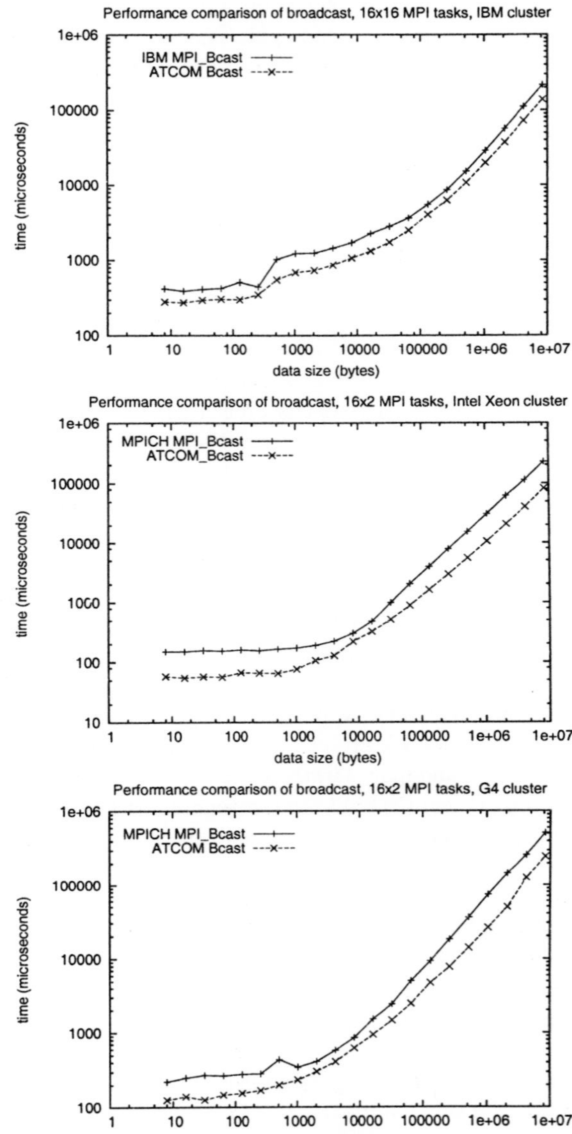

Figure 4. Performance comparison of broadcast on three platforms

3.3 Scatter and Gather

Not all collective operations can take advantage of overlapping inter-node/intra-node communications. When the amount of data for inter-node communications is substantially larger than the intra-node communication data, the performance improvement can be very small. Consider scattering a message of 8M to 4x4 processes: the possible overlapping data size is only 1/15 of the intra-node communication data size. The cost of an intra-node scatter of 512K is almost negligible compared to the cost of sending out 7.5M of data to the inter-node layer. For this reason we did not implement the overlapping version of scatter or gather. However, for scattering or gathering small messages, we can still use concurrent memory access for intra-node scatter or gather to improve the performance since latency can be reduced. The best strategy is to use the blocking implementation for inter-node scatter and shared memory operations for intra-node scatter. We have shown the performance enhancement in our previous work [17].

Message size	IBM SP	Intel Cluster	G4 Cluster
8	*Binominal(b, novp, shm)	*Binominal(b, novp, shm)	Binominal(b, novp, msg)
16	*Binominal(b, novp, shm)	*Binominal(b, novp, shm)	Binominal(b, novp, msg)
32	*Binominal(b, novp, shm)	*Binominal(b, novp, shm)	Binominal(b, novp, msg)
64	*Binominal(b, novp, shm)	*Binominal(b, novp, shm)	Binominal(b, novp, msg)
128	*Binominal(b, novp, shm)	*Binominal(b, novp, shm)	Binominal(b, novp, msg)
256	*Binominal(b, novp, shm)	*Binominal(b, novp, shm)	Binominal(b, novp, msg)
512	*Binominal(b, novp, shm)	*Binominal(b, novp, shm)	Binominal(b, novp, msg)
1024	*Binominal(b, novp, shm)	Binominal(nb, novp, msg)	Binominal(b, novp, msg)
2048	*Binominal(b, novp, shm)	Binominal(nb, novp, msg)	Binominal(b, novp, msg)
4096	*Binominal(b, novp, shm)	Binominal(nb, novp, msg)	Binominal(b, novp, msg)
8192	*Binominal(b, novp, shm)	Binominal(nb, novp, msg)	*Binary(nb, ovp, shm)
16384	*Binary(nb, novp, shm)	*Binary(nb, ovp, shm)	*Binary(nb, ovp, shm)
32768	*Binary(nb, novp, shm)	*Binary(nb, ovp, shm)	*Binary(nb, ovp, shm)
65536	*Binominal(nb, novp, shm)	*Binary(nb, ovp, shm)	*Binary(nb, ovp, shm)
131072	*Binominal(nb, novp, shm)	*Binary(nb, ovp, shm)	*Chain(nb, ovp, shm)
262144	*Binominal(nb, novp, shm)	*Binary(nb, ovp, shm)	*Chain(nb, ovp, shm)
524288	*Binary(nb, novp, shm)	*Binary(nb, ovp, shm)	*Chain(nb, ovp, shm)
1048576	*Binary(nb, novp, shm)	*Binary(nb, ovp, shm)	*Chain(nb, ovp, shm)
2097152	*Binary(nb, novp, shm)	*Binary(nb, ovp, shm)	*Chain(nb, ovp, shm)
4194304	*Binary(nb, ovp, shm)	*Binary(nb, ovp, shm)	*Chain(nb, ovp, shm)
8388608	*Binary(nb, ovp, shm)	*Binary(nb, ovp, shm)	*Chain(nb, ovp, shm)

Table 2. Best implementations for broadcasting different message size on three platforms. The first parameter represents inter-node implementation: nb for non-blocking segmented, b for blocking. The second parameter represents if it overlaps inter-node/intra-node communications. ovp: overlap, novp:no overlap. The third parameter represents use shared memory or message passing for intra-node communication. shm: use shared memory, msg:use message passing. A * means the implementation is provided by new generic approaches.

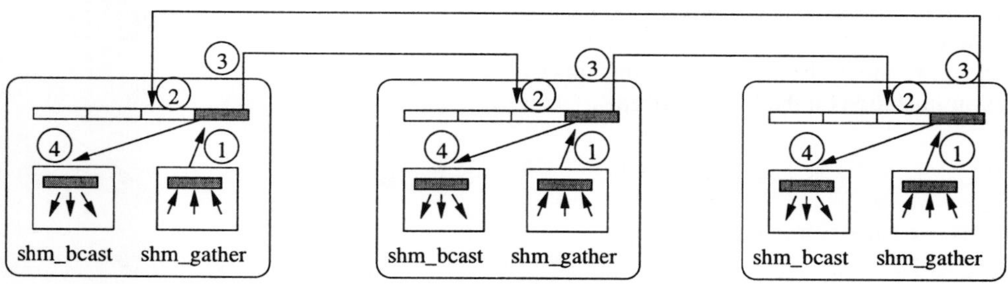

Figure 5. Overlapping inter-node/intra-node communications for all-gather

3.4 All-gather

It is not realistic to implement a collective communication following every path in the programming model in Figure 1. The reason we implemented broadcast following most paths in the programming model is that the results of broadcast can provide basic performance metrics for the other collective communications and give us insight into different algorithms.

Before we optimize a collective communication for SMP clusters we use the existing performance data to evaluate if we can expect improved performance. For example, with the all-gather operation in this section we measured the costs of shared memory gather, shared memory broadcast and intra-node broadcast algorithms. By comparing the performance results of these operations and analyzing the potential performance enhancement we could decide if all-gather should be optimized.

The algorithms for all-gather implemented in MPICH are the binominal tree algorithm for small messages and the ring algorithm for large messages. Tuning is required to determine when to use the ring algorithm and when to use the binominal algorithm. However, through experiments we found that the binominal tree algorithm is used on all three clusters for all message sizes, which leads to very bad performance especially when the message size is large. For example, on the IBM SP, an all-gather of an 8MB message on 16x16 MPI tasks using the default MPI_Allgather implementation is four times slower than MPICH's ring implementation. For this reason the performance comparison in this section is intended to show how much we can improve over the MPICH ring algorithm for all-gather operations on large messages. For small messages we also use the binominal tree algorithm.

MPICH uses MPI_Sendrecv to implement the ring all-gather; the implementation does not allow overlapping so in implementation 2 we replaced the MPI_Sendrecv with an MPI_Isend/MPI_Irecv of the whole message. Implementation 3 of all-gather extends this to the segmented non-blocking approach.

The mechanism to overlap inter-node/intra-node communication are shown in Figure 5. Each node starts with (1) a shared memory gather to the group communicator, (2) posts a non-blocking receive, (3) posts non-blocking send, and (4) starts a shared memory broadcast. It repeats (2)-(3)-(4) until the last segment is received by all processes. This is our implementation 4.

We tested all-gather of message sizes from 512K to 8M and, depending on the message size, the overall performance improvement is 18% to 69% on the IBM SP cluster, 44% to 54% on the Intel cluster, and 11% to 69% on the G4 cluster. Figure 6 shows the performance improvements by adding layers of optimization on the three platforms.

3.5 Summary

From the results, we can observe the following:

1. Existing generic techniques to optimize collective communications do not provide optimal performance on SMP clusters. By taking the SMP architecture into account, the performance of collective communications can be significantly improved by new generic optimizations.

2. Using shared memory collective communications is the key to performance improvememnt on SMP clusters. It reduces the latency and allows overlapping of inter-node/intra-node communications.

4 Conclusion and Future Work

In this paper we have shown that it is possible to design generic implementations of collective operations that

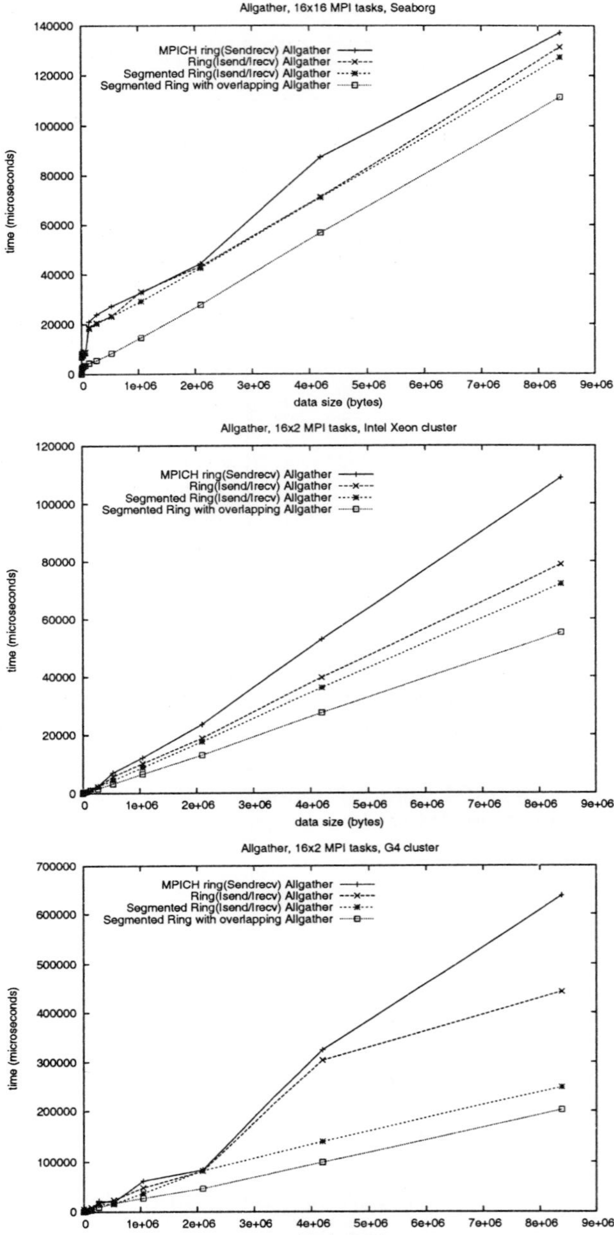

Figure 6. Performance comparison of all-gather on three platforms

take advantage of both shared memory collective communications and overlapping inter-node/intra-node communications. Several collective communications are implemented and our experimental results show that, after proper tuning, the performance improvement over the existing implementations is significant on three different SMP clusters.

While collective communication algorithms on the inter-node layer may be regarded as exhausted, by taking the SMP atchitecture into account and using implementation techniques generically available on all platforms, we still can see impressive performance improvement even if each SMP node has only two processors.

As part of automatic tuning collective communication system for SMP clusters, this project is to explore generic approaches to utilizing the SMP architecture. The price of generic approaches to achieve good performance is that many parameters require tuning. Here we provide a framework to design collective communications on SMP clusters, and leave the tuning job to the automatic tuning mechanisms in our future research.

There are two approaches to reduce the amount of time for tuning. One is to design a good performance model that can predict the run time of a certain implementation. The other one is to use a set of microbenchmarks to minimize the amount of experiments required for tuning. Both are currently under development.

5 Acknowledgements

We thank professor Zhao Zhang for his contribution to the overall undestanding of this work. This work was performed under auspices of the U. S. Department of Energy under contract W-7405-Eng-82 at Ames Laboratory operated by the Iowa State University of Science and Technology. Funding was provided by the Mathematical, Information and Computational Science division of the Office of Advanced Scientific Computing Research. This research used resources of the Scalable Computing Laboratory at Ames Laboratory and the National Energy Research Scientific Computing Center, which is supported by the Office of Science of the U.S. Department of Energy under Contract No. DE-AC03-76SF00098.

References

[1] V. Bala, J. Bruck, R. Cypher, P. Elustondo, A. Ho, C.-T. Ho, S. Kipnis, and M. Snir. A Portable and Tunable Collective Communication Library for Scalable Parallel Computers. *IEEE Transactions on Parallel and Distributed Systems*, pages 154–164, 1995.

[2] M. Barnett, S. Gupta, D. Payne, L. Shuler, R. van de Geijn, and J. Watts. Interprocessor Collective Communication Library (InterCom). In *Scalable High Performance Computing Conference*, pages 357–364, 1994.

[3] M. Barnett, S. Gupta, D. G. Payne, L. Shuler, R. van de Geijn, and J. Watts. Building a HighPerformance Collective Communication Library. In *Proceedings of Supercomputing*, pages 107–116, 1994.

[4] C. Bell, D. Bonachea, Y. Cote, J. Duell, P. Hargrove, P. Husbands, C. Iancu, M. Welcome, and K. A. Yelick. An evaluation of current high-performance networks. In *International Parallel and Distributed Processing Symposium*, page 28, 2003.

[5] G. E. Fagg, S. S. Vadhiyar, and J. J. Dongarra. ACCT: Automatic Collective Communications Tuning. In *EuroPVM/MPI*, 2000.

[6] M. P. I. Forum. MPI-2: Extensions to the Message-Passing Interface. *On the World-Wide Web at http://www.mpi-forum.org/docs/docs.html*, 1997.

[7] M. Golebiewski, R. Hempel, and J. L. Träff. Algorithms for Collective Communication Operations on SMP Clusters. In *The 1999 Workshop on Cluster-Based Computing held in conjunction with 13th ACM-SIGARCH International Conference on Supercomputing*, 1999.

[8] T. Kielmann, H. E. Bal, and S. Gorlatch. Bandwidth-efficient Collective Communication for Clustered Wide Area Systems. In *Proceedings of the International Parallel and Distributed Processing Symposium*. 2000.

[9] T. Kielmann, R. F. H. Hofman, H. E. Bal, A. Plaat, and R. A. F. Bhoedjang. MAGPIE: MPI's Collective Communication Operations for Clustered Wide Area Systems. In *ACM SIGPLAN Symposium on Principles and Proctice of Parallel Programming*. 1999.

[10] P. Mitra, D. Payne, L. Shuler, R. van de Geijn, and J. Watts. Fast Collective Communication Libraries, Please. In *Proceedings of the Intel Supercomputing User's Group Meeting*, 1995.

[11] J. Nieplocha and B. Carpenter. ARMCI: A Portable Remote Memory Copy Library for Distributed Array Libraries and Compiler Run-time Systems. 1998.

[12] S. Sistare, R. van de Vaart, and E. Loh. Optimization of MPI Collectives Clusters of Large-Scale SMP's. In *Proceedings of Supercomputing*, 1999.

[13] T. Takahashi, F. O'Carroll, H. Tezuka, A. Hori, S. Sumimoto, H. Harada, Y. Ishikawa, and P. H. Beckman. Implementation and evaluation of mpi on an smp cluster. In *IPPS/SPDP Workshops*, 1999.

[14] V. Tipparaju, J. Nieplocha, and D. K. Panda. Fast Collective Operations Using Shared and Remote Memory Access Protocols on Clusters. In *International Parallel and Distributed Processing Symposium*, 2003.

[15] S. S. Vadhiyar, G. E. Fagg, and J. Dongarra. Automatically Tuned Collective Communications. In *Proceedings of Supercomputing*, 2000.

[16] B. V.Protopopov and A. Skjellum. Shared-Memory Communication Approaches for an MPI Message-Passing Library. *Concurrency: Practice and Experience*, 2000.

[17] M.-S. Wu, R. A. Kendall, and S. Aluru. A Tunable Collective Communication Framework on Cluster of SMPs. In *Proceeding of the IASTED International Conference on Parallel and Distributed Computing and Networks*, 2004.

Distributed Queue-based Locking using Advanced Network Features

Ananth Devulapalli
Ohio Supercomputer Center
1 South Limestone St., Suite 310
Springfield, OH 45502
ananth@osc.edu

Pete Wyckoff
Ohio Supercomputer Center
1224 Kinnear Road
Columbus, OH 43212
pw@osc.edu

Abstract

A Distributed Lock Manager (DLM) provides advisory locking services to applications such as databases and file systems that run on distributed systems. Lock management at the server is implemented using First-In-First-Out (FIFO) queues. In this paper, we demonstrate a novel way of delegating the lock management to the participating lock-requesting nodes, using advanced network primitives such as Remote Direct Memory Access (RDMA) and Atomic operations. This nicely complements the original idea of DLM, where management of the lock space is distributed. Our implementation achieves better load balancing, reduction in server load and improved throughput over traditional designs.

1 Introduction

Locking is essential for serialization of access to shared resources. In an uniprocessor environment, this is achieved using services such as mutexes, semaphores and monitors [22] that rely on the centralized management provided by the operating system. In shared-memory multiprocessor systems, the architecture frequently provides mechanisms to extend this centralized locking scheme across the domain of the machine. Distributed multiprocessor systems, however, rarely use networks that provide such features and hence resort to using a dedicated process to provide synchronization, called a Distributed Lock Manager (DLM).

DLM is a critical component in many applications that run on distributed systems, such as databases and file systems. Today, many vendors like Oracle [20], IBM [2] and HP [15] provide DLM as an integral component in their systems. Current DLM implementations achieve greater scalability and fault-tolerance over single-site lock serving models by distributing locks among all nodes in the cluster. Each node serves as a server for a subset of locks and as clients for the rest. A server uses FIFO queues for serializing requests for a shared resource.

This work was supported by the US DoE ASC program.

In this paper we show how to further augment load-balancing by distributing the queue-management among the lock-requesting clients. We focus particularly on the use of DLM in non-shared-memory distributed systems and we take advantage of atomicity features provided by modern high-speed communication networks. We start by explaining the current issues that motivate our work in Section 2. In the next section we explain the abstract design of how we distributed the queue-management. Then we explain our implementation of distributed FIFO queue using Remote Direct Memory Access (RDMA) based primitives. In Section 5 we describe the experiments and follow up with their results and analysis.

2 Motivation

In this section we describe traditional DLM designs and advanced capabilities of modern interconnects that motivate our work.

2.1 Locking in distributed systems

In multi-processor distributed systems, processes frequently need to share global resources such as files, memory buffers and access to storage or network devices. One approach to achieve synchronization among these processes is to concentrate the management of locks at a single site. Any node needing to lock a resource sends a request to the centralized manager. While this approach is simple, it suffers from two critical disadvantages, namely the presence of hot spots in the network and a single point of failure at the manager node. In the case of loosely coupled clusters that generally have higher latency networks and low-cost and hence low-reliability nodes, these problems are aggravated. As a result it is difficult to implement high performance shared services like file systems and database servers that rely on this model of centralized lock management.

As an alternative, lock management responsibility can be distributed across multiple nodes in two different fashions: various independent locks can be managed at different nodes, and aspects of the lock management protocol for a single lock can be handled by multiple nodes. The first aspect of spreading the management of multiple locks across

0190-3918/05 $20.00 © 2005 IEEE

nodes has been implemented many times [3, 15, 20, 2]. By distributing lock management among multiple nodes, load is spread throughout the system. The topic of this paper, however, is the second aspect of distributed lock management, namely removing some of the centralized aspect of the management of a *single* lock.

2.2 Advanced interconnects

Within the last decade many new and interesting networking technologies have been implemented. VIA [6], Myrinet [21] and InfiniBand [12] introduced some of the advanced networking primitives that we see today.

2.2.1 Remote Direct Memory Access (RDMA)

RDMA is an efficient means of communication. It is asynchronous, involves minimal operating system overhead, transfers data with zero intermediate copies and consumes fewer CPU cycles, both at the sender and the receiver. To achieve these capabilities, intelligent communication coprocessors are required. Today RDMA appears in a variety of networks [6, 21, 12]. It can be considered analogous to DMA on a peripheral bus such as PCI, in that this capability has been extended to remote node. As DMA absolves the CPU of any involvement in memory transfers, RDMA removes it from the critical path of data transfer, thereby achieving lower latency and higher bandwidth.

2.2.2 Remote atomics

Specialized hardware primitives to assist in the manipulation of concurrent objects in multiprocessor systems have appeared in many different systems and in different forms, either in the processor instruction set [11, 23] or in an associated network component [8]. The classic primitives include atomic registers, *test&set*, *compare&swap*, and *fetch&add*. Algorithms to use these primitives to implement various synchronization have been well studied, for example, simple mutual exclusion, queuing, barriers, and wait-free versions of the same [8, 9, 10].

The interconnect used to perform communications required for concurrent operations is theoretically independent of the operations themselves, and can range from a tightly-coupled bus in a shared memory system to a general purpose wide-area network. Our focus in this work is to consider lock management strategies as implemented using modern networks that provide remote atomic primitives in hardware. In particular, InfiniBand offers both *compare&swap* and *fetch&add* operations with which we construct distributed queue algorithms.

2.3 Traditional DLM architecture

A DLM provides "advisory locking" services to higher level applications [25], meaning applications must cooperate in sharing the resource. Any node interested in locking an entity must first get a lock on a corresponding "lock resource". A lock resource is an abstract entity, identified by a descriptive name and corresponds to exactly one physical entity, for example a file. The management of locks is distributed among the nodes within cluster by distributing the lock namespace.

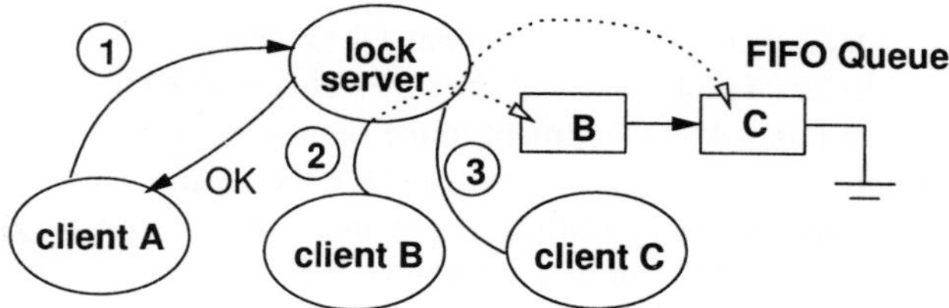

Figure 1. Locking Operation in DLM.

Figure 1 shows the process of locking in DLM. Client A is the first one to request the lock. Since the resource is unlocked, the server grants the lock to A. Then, clients B and C arrive with a request for same lock. But the resource is locked, so the server places them in a FIFO queue of waiting clients. When A is ready to unlock, it sends an unlock message to server, which upon its receipt, de-queues the first client, in this case B, and grants it the lock.

We described a simple version of DLM. Current implementations have many features, like multi-modal locks with conversion between different modes, hierarchical locks and fault-tolerance. But the fundamental concept in all the implementations, is that the lock manager achieves serialization by arranging the nodes in a queue. FIFO queues serialize access to the resource thereby breaking any deadlock cycles. It is important to note that these queues are per lock and queues are not shared among the locks. Also, these data structures are internal to the lock manager.

2.3.1 Critique of the current DLM design

Traditional DLM designs do not take advantage of modern network features, relying only on reliable message delivery with channel semantics. As a result, an active process is always required for lock management, which essentially means handling a queue of blocked processes. Another drawback is that locks are statically distributed, which may not necessarily match the dynamic application load, thereby creating hot-spots during execution. We can solve these problems by delegating the load of lock management to the lock requesting nodes themselves.

The target of our research is the distribution of the FIFO queue, thereby distributing the load. Note that this approach to distribute the data structure (queue), representing the state of a single lock, complements earlier DLM work that successfully distributed the lock space. Our work allows for more concurrency in the locking and unlocking algorithms and decentralizes the work to the lock-requesting clients, improving scalability.

3 Design of distributed FIFO queue

In this section we describe the essential design requirements and an abstract design for distributed FIFO queue based locking mechanism.

3.1 Design requirements

One advantage of traditional DLM designs is that the server has a global view of the state. This enables the server to send an acknowledgment to the requesting process, only when the server is ready to grant the lock. This results in minimum network traffic. Since this luxury is no longer available in the case of a distributed FIFO queue, care must be taken to minimize network traffic.

A FIFO queue by itself guarantees progress, but it does not guarantee freedom from starvation. Any design should try to allocate locks as fairly as possible.

In the case of a distributed FIFO queue, processes will be acting independently, trying to acquire and release locks. Effort must be made to minimize the state communication during each operation.

Since the reason for distributing the management of locks is reduction of server load, this must be achieved. The operation load should be shared among the participating processes. This also means that non-participating processes should be precluded from sharing the burden.

3.2 Distributing the FIFO queue

In the original implementation, which we will refer to as the "Basecase", the server needs to keep information about the current tail and head of the queue. To implement a distributed queue, one can use the fact that it is a *FIFO queue*. Each node in the queue needs information about its predecessor and successor nodes. To release the lock, the owning node sends a message directly to its successor; meanwhile, that node is waiting for a message from its predecessor, and so on down the queue. It is possible for a new node to get the information about its predecessor from the server. But it is not possible for a node to know about its successor beforehand, since there might not be a successor in the first place. The only way a node gets to know about its successor, is when the successor informs it about its presence.

3.2.1 Lock acquisition

For this chaining of the nodes to be possible, the only information that has to be maintained at the lock-server is the current tail of the queue. Figure 2 shows the interactions among three clients in the process of acquiring a single lock from a lock server. In step 1, client *A* queries the server about the current tail on the queue for the lock, and tries to install itself as the new tail. Because the lock is currently not held by any client, this operation succeeds and now *A* owns the lock. Next, client *B* attempts to acquire the lock, setting itself as the current tail at the server, but it must wait until *A* is finished with the lock. To obtain notification when this happens, *B* updates a value in the memory of *A* that declares itself as the next entry in the queue of waiters for the lock. Steps 4 and 5 show a third client also failing to acquire the lock and queuing itself behind the previous last waiting client.

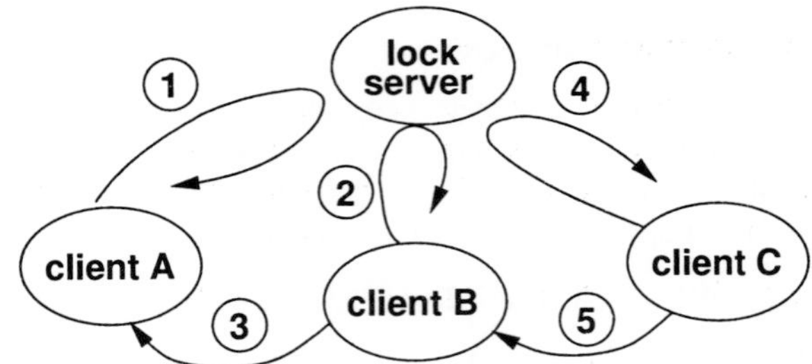

Figure 2. Three clients acquire a lock.

The effect of these operations is that all the processes are serialized in a FIFO queue that is no longer contained and managed at the server. The management load is now distributed among the clients. It is to be noted that only those clients that are participating in the locking process simultaneously are involved in queue management.

3.2.2 Releasing a lock

Figure 3, shows the interactions during a series of unlock operations. Client *A* finds that it has a successor and sends a grant message to it, passing lock ownership to client *B*. Similarly, *B* unlocks by transferring the lock to client *C*. As no other clients are waiting on the lock, *C* has an empty successor field. It updates the tail at the lock server to indicate that the lock is no longer held by any client.

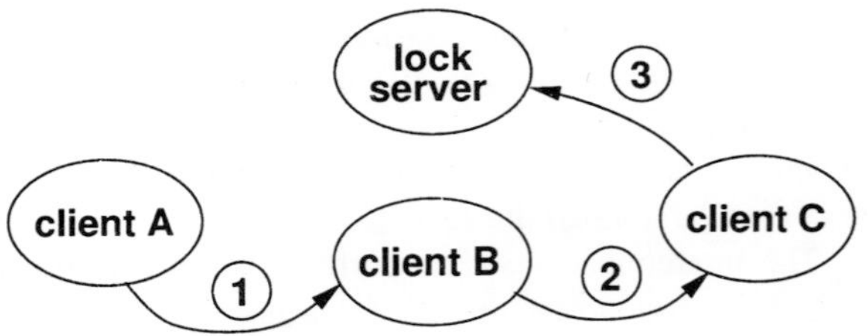

Figure 3. Passing lock ownership.

Compared to the Basecase, by distributing the queue among the processes, we have achieved distribution of the load. Each node takes care of informing the predecessor and successor, if present. The server simply fields requests that read and update the tail. In particular, the server is not involved at all in the unlock phase until the last waiting client has finished with the lock and finally clears the tail at the server.

4 Implementation

In the previous section, we laid out the basic framework for the design of distributed management of a FIFO queue.

In this section we describe the mapping between those abstract ideas and our implementation of FIFO queue based locking.

4.1 Enabling RDMA operations

In Section 3.2.1, we described how the distributed FIFO queue is constructed. By distributing the queue, the load at the server has been effectively reduced by half, since dequeue operations have now been off-loaded to the clients. However, further off-load is possible. This is where the advanced network primitives: RDMA and Remote atomics come into play.

To perform network operations that affect the memory of remote hosts, multiple pieces of information are required to ensure secure operation. In InfiniBand, an RDMA write requires the remote LID, QP number, virtual memory address, and a 32-bit opaque key [12]. These values are, however, static for the lifetime of a particular client, so we employ a caching mechanism at each client to reuse the values after a one-time initial lookup. As each client joins the lock domain, it registers these remote access keys with the lock server that in turn exports them to all other lock clients. If any cached value becomes invalid due to an exiting or initializing client, the network will return an error on the next attempted operation, invalidating the local cache and forcing a full lookup of the new values.

4.2 Lock acquisition

The state information in the tail must include the *identity* of the client that is currently at the tail of the queue. This information is sufficient for a client to know about its predecessor.

For lock acquisition we use atomic RDMA *compare & swap* (*CAS*) primitive. *CAS* [12] takes two 64-bit operands: *compare* and *swap*. The *compare* operand is compared with the value at remote address. Only if they match, the *swap* operand is written to the remote memory location. In either case, the original value at remote address is returned back as the result of the operation.

A client interested in a lock uses *CAS* to swap its identity into the tail atomically. If it succeeds, it has locked the resource. Otherwise, some other client has the lock. This client's identity is returned as a result of *CAS* operation. At this stage, the client does not know whether the current tail is the owner of the lock, or waiting for the lock. In any case, that tail would be this client's most likely predecessor. Therefore, the client tries to swap the current tail with itself. If it succeeds, it has the information about its predecessor. Otherwise it repeats the steps of swapping itself with the tail, until it is successful.

Once a client knows about its predecessor, it sends an alert to it, so that the predecessor is informed about it. It uses RDMA *Write with Immediate* (*RWI*) [12] to signal the predecessor. Since the tail is swapped atomically, each client will have at most one predecessor. Likewise each client will have at most one successor.

4.3 Unlock operation

When a client is ready to unlock, it looks for its successor message. If it finds the message, it sends an alert to the successor using *RWI* thus transferring the lock in the process. Otherwise, since this client does not know about the current state of the tail, it tries to get an update on the tail by swapping itself out with some value that stands for the "unlocked" state. Again, *CAS* is used for this operation. If it succeeds in swapping, it means the resource has been unlocked. For example, in Figure 3, when *B* is ready to unlock, it looks for its successor and finds a message from *C*. *B* then sends an alert using *RWI* to *C*. When *C* is done with the lock, it looks for its successor and finds it empty. Finally, *C* executes *CAS* against the tail and unlocks the resource.

4.3.1 Transient State Race Condition

We need to take care of a transient state during the unlock operation. Again, let us refer to Figure 3, when *B* is ready to unlock. Assume that the moment *B* is looking for its successor, *C* is busy trying to *CAS* the tail. Therefore, *B* thinks it is at the end of the tail and tries to unlock the resource, but finds *C* in the tail instead. Since *B* is no longer at the tail of the queue, it waits for a message from its successor. Also, *B* does not know whether *C* is its successor. The only thing that is certain from *B*'s perspective is that, it is no longer the tail. Therefore, it waits for an alert from its successor. As soon as it gets an alert, it sends an alert back to it, which in this case happens to be *C*.

4.4 Starvation freedom

We have a basic framework for distributing FIFO queue but there is no starvation freedom. The reason for this is *non-atomicity* of lock acquisition. The first client is able to acquire the lock atomically by executing *CAS* against the server. But subsequent clients repeatedly execute *CAS* operations until they are successful. For a slow client, these unbounded attempts can potentially lead to starvation.

We solved this problem, by an approach similar to the bakery algorithm [16]. Each client interested in updating the tail first gets a token from the server. Only when it is the client's turn, it gets a chance to replace the tail. A client interested in updating the tail, gets a number by executing atomic RDMA *fetch & add* (*FA*) against an always-increasing counter. *FA* is similar to *CAS*. *FA* [12] takes one 64-bit operand as its input and executes an unsigned addition with the value at remote location. The new value is stored in the location and the old 64-bit value from the location is returned as the result of this operation.

After executing *FA* against the counter, the client discards the most significant 32 bits of the result and keeps the least significant word as its counter. Since the remote counter is always incremented, this counter will always be changing. Then the client constructs its 64-bit token by appending its *identity*, to its 32-bit counter. It uses this 64-bit token to swap into the tail. Only the client whose counter value is 1 greater than the current tail is allowed to swap into the tail. All other clients, whose counter is further away, will have to wait, for this client to proceed. This serialization ensures that there is no starvation. Every client gets a chance at replacing the tail. But it adds the cost of one additional remote atomic operation to the critical path of locking.

5 Experiments

5.1 Experimental setup

Our experiments were carried out on 32 nodes of Pentium 4 cluster at the Ohio Supercomputer Center. Each node has dual 2.4 GHz Intel P4 Xeon processors, 4 GB of RAM, 80 GB ATA100 hard drives, one 10 Gb/s InfiniBand interface and runs 2.6.6 version of Linux kernel. One of the 32 nodes was designated as lock-server and the rest as clients. For the experiments, we evaluated the following three algorithms:

Basecase: The original implementation of DLM, where the FIFO queue is managed by an active server.

Distributed: Distributed FIFO queue algorithm without starvation-free mechanism.

Starvation-free: Distributed FIFO queue algorithm with starvation-free mechanism.

In Basecase, communication between server and clients was implemented using InfiniBand *Send* and *Receive* primitives. Distributed and Starvation-free used *Send* and *Receive* for an initial look-up for lock information. For all other cases, they used RDMA based primitives as described in Section 4.

5.2 Operation latency

Latency for each primitive was timed in this experiment. Table 1 shows the median, mean and standard deviation of the timings. RDMA CAS, RDMA FA and *Send* were

	Median (μs)	Mean (μs)
RDMA CAS	11.005	11.455 ± 1.652
RDMA FA	11.027	11.467 ± 1.653
RDMA Write Imm	10.997	11.802 ± 2.141
Send	13.453	14.197 ± 2.183

Table 1. Average timings for primitive operations.

measured when a client executed those operations against a server. The size of send message was 100 bytes. RDMA Write Imm was timed between two clients without involving the server, since in distributed FIFO queue, *RWI* was used to send alert messages between clients.

The numbers listed are higher than the numbers others have reported [7]. This is because we implemented each primitive to signal the host upon completion, which adds non-trivial overhead. The DLM application needs message delivery confirmation because of the dependencies of future actions on the past messages. The confirmation of the message delivery triggers the state change in the implementation.

	Lock (μs)	Unlock (μs)
Basecase	34.045 ± 5.388	32.818 ± 3.489
Distributed	11.889 ± 1.720	12.616 ± 1.629
Starvation-free	24.070 ± 3.140	12.350 ± 1.647

Table 2. Mean lock and unlock timings.

	Lock	Unlock
Basecase	$T_{send} + T_{oh} + T_{send}$	$T_{send} + T_{oh} + T_{send}$
Distributed	$T_{cas} + T_{oh}$	$T_{cas} + T_{oh}$
Starvation-free	$T_{fa} + T_{cas} + T_{oh}$	$T_{cas} + T_{oh}$

Table 3. Lock and unlock cost models.

In the second experiment, we measured uncontested, single client, lock and unlock operations against an unloaded server for each algorithm. The timings are shown in Table 2 and the corresponding cost models are listed in Table 3. Basecase uses *Send* for both lock and unlock messages, hence they have equal cost. Distributed uses *CAS* for both lock and unlock operations. Starvation-free also uses *CAS* for unlock, but it has a *FA* in critical path for lock operation. We note that the models explain the observed costs in Table 3, in terms of timings of primitive operations (Table 1).

5.3 Unlock cascade

In the scenario that one client has locked a resource for long enough that others have piled up behind it waiting to do comparatively short operations with the same lock, how long does it take for them to resume once the lock holder releases it? We conducted the experiment by making one client hold onto the lock long enough so that other clients pile up behind it. Next this client starts the timer, releases the lock and immediately sends a lock request. Other clients in the meanwhile are queued up behind this client waiting for their turn at the lock. Upon getting the lock, these clients immediately release the lock. So the lock propagates along the chain of queued processes finally arriving back at the first client, which stops the timer as soon as it gets the lock. The cost of operation, as observed by first client is $T_{cascade} \approx n * T_{transfer}$, where n is the number of clients.

In Basecase, $T_{transfer} \approx 2 * T_{send} + T_{oh}$. One send operation is consumed by an unlocking client and another is consumed by a grant message from the server to the next client. T_{oh} represents the processing cost at the server and clients. In case of Distributed and Starvation-free, $T_{transfer} \approx T_{rdma\_write\_imm} + T_{oh}$, since *RWI* is used to alert the successor. Here, T_{oh} represents the cost of a client looking for its successor's message, the cost of the successor processing an alert from predecessor and the final delivery of message to the user application.

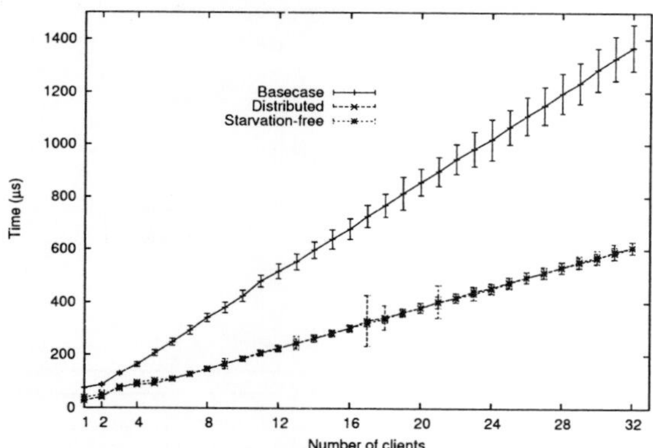

Figure 4. Time to propagate a lock along a queue of waiting clients.

Figure 4 plots the time to propagate the unlock request as the number of clients vary. The curves for Distributed and Starvation-free are overlapped since unlocking steps are similar in both cases. The slope of Basecase is twice that Distributed and Starvation-free, as explained by the cost model of cascade. Also, from the slopes it is evident that in Basecase $T_{oh} \approx 12\mu s$ and in case of Distributed and Starvation-free $T_{oh} \approx 6\mu s$. This experiment demonstrates the effectiveness of load-balancing in our design.

5.4 Throughput under different contention conditions

The scalability of different algorithms under different contention levels was tested under this experiment. Contention is defined as: $Contention = (1 - \frac{L}{N}) * 100$, where L is number of locks and N is number of clients. Three levels of contentions were used: 0%, 50% and 100%. For 0%, $L = N$, for 50%, $L = \frac{N}{2}$ and for 100%, $L = 1$. One node was designated as server, with number of clients varying between 1 and 32. The clients executed lock and unlock operations against server without any work between operations. Figure 5 shows the "cumulative throughput" of all clients for different contention levels and varying number of clients.

For 0% and 50% contention level, all curves reach a plateau. In 0%, Basecase, Distributed and Starvation-free level at 2, 4 and 4 clients respectively. Basecase is server-bound, while others are NIC-bound. In Basecase, the curve

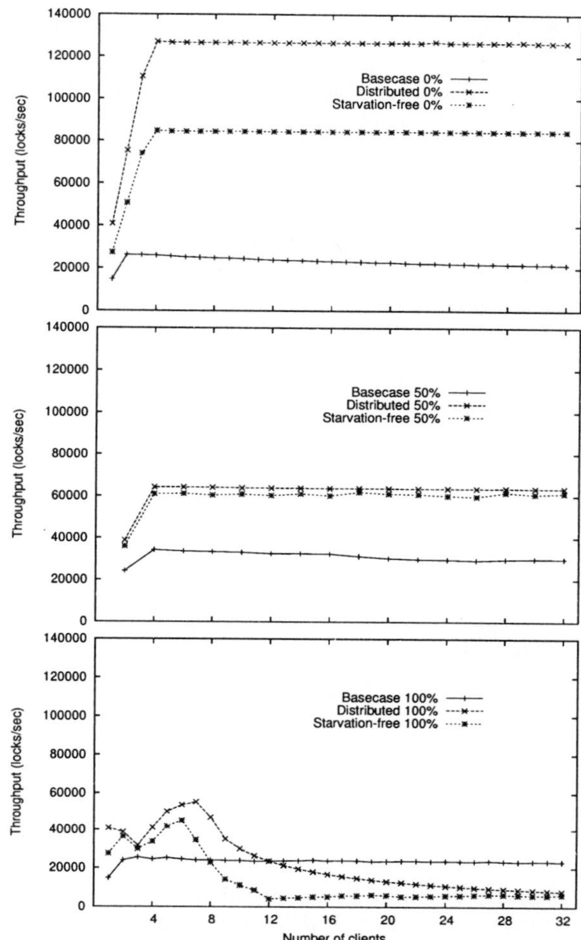

Figure 5. Lock throughput for varying number of clients at three different contention levels.

falls slightly as the number of clients increase due to increase in server processing overhead. Similar trends are also seen in 50% case. In case of Distributed, throughput is approximately *half* of 0% case since only half the attempts are successful. For Starvation-free, throughput drops by 25%. If we refer to cost model in Table 3, compared to 3 operations in 0% case, we have an additional unsuccessful *CAS* due to contention which results in 4 operations. For Basecase, the throughput *increases* relative to 0%, because server is able to overlap acknowledgment of "unlock" and "grant" messages, which was not possible in 0% case.

We observe interesting trends in 100% case. Basecase reaches a plateau and stays there, whereas Distributed and Starvation-free have bell-shaped curves. The curves drop at 3 clients due to an increase in number of unsuccessful *CAS* operations executed by lock-owner due to transient state as discussed in Section 4.3.1. Then with increase in number of clients, the chance for a client to enqueue increases, resulting in increase of successful *CAS* operations. The curves peak and then fall for different reasons. Distributed falls due less per-capita *CAS* operations and an increase in failed *CAS* operations due to increase in transient states. Starvation-free falls more steeply. Since only the successor is allowed to replace the tail, *CAS* operations of remaining clients fail. But in the process they hold back the successor, while the predecessor seeing no successor unlocks the resource. This means there is no chance for queue-formation resulting in serialized lock-unlock operations by individual nodes. Both cases suffer since predecessor releases lock too quickly for successor to queue behind.

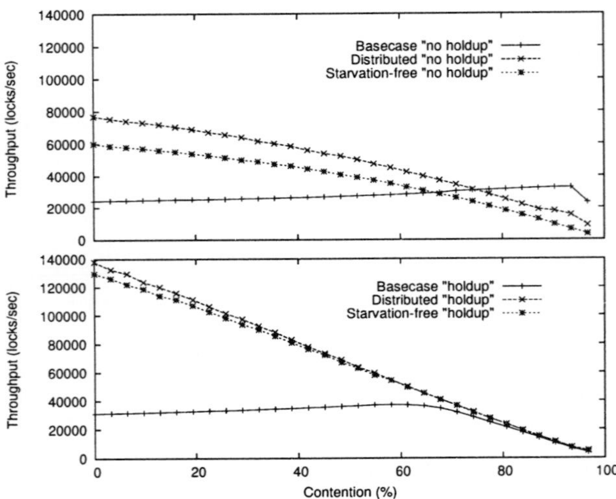

Figure 6. Lock throughput as a function of contention, for two different lock hold times.

To further investigate this issue, we conducted another experiment with some hold time between lock and unlock operations. Figure 6 shows the plot of throughput versus contention. Contention was calculated as in last experiment. Number of clients was fixed at 31 and number of locks was varied between 1 and 31. The top plot shows with no hold-up and the one below it shows when there is $\approx 270\mu s$ hold-up between lock and unlock operations. Distributed and Starvation-free fall below Basecase as contention increases due to failed *CAS* operations. When there is hold-up, throughput of Distributed and Starvation-free reaches the level of 0% case in Figure 5. Both curves stay above Basecase and finally all converge to a point. Basecase falls when contention increases since the lock-owner is not relinquishing locks fast enough to service the waiting clients. But this hold-up enables Distributed and Starvation-free to form queue and take the load from server. In a realistic scenario, one would expect clients to acquire a lock, do some amount of work and then release the lock. If the lock is highly contended, the work gives enough time to other clients to enqueue, thereby taking load off the server. More in-depth analysis of these experiments can be found in [5].

5.5 Loaded throughput

In this experiment, we measured uncontested, single-client, throughput of locks at server, under varying load conditions. Load is quantified by a single cpu-intensive process. Therefore, $load = n$, means there are n cpu-intensive processes running simultaneously with the server. Figure 7 shows two plots. The top plot is of throughput versus load. The plot below it shows the percentage CPU resources available to the server under varying load conditions.

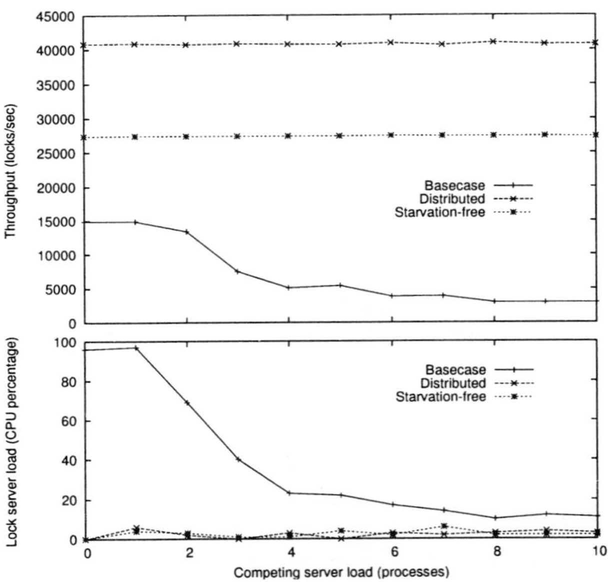

Figure 7. Throughput and utilization at lock-server for different loads.

We observe that Distributed and Starvation-free are agnostic to server-load, but the performance of Basecase takes a hit as the load increases. The reason is Basecase was implemented using polling server, while others were implemented with blocking server using interrupts. One can afford to use interrupts as there is very little involvement of server in the lock/unlock steps. However, in Basecase where server is in critical path, interrupts would have been prohibitively expensive. Even though Distributed and Starvation-free used blocking server, all algorithms used polling clients. We would like to remind that in DLM, each node plays the role of server and client. Therefore in Basecase, we will have two actively polling processes and hence vulnerable to addition of any cpu-intensive process. This experiment conclusively proves our hypothesis that offloading of lock-management to clients in indeed beneficial.

6 Related work

Several DLM alternatives were studied in [14], where they investigated the trade offs between static versus dynamic distribution of locks and gave analytic models for each alternative considered. SSDLM [13] investigated the use of DLM in clustered file-system. A variation of DLM [4], requiring $O(log(N))$ steps has been implemented.

Most of the work on distributed data structures was done in the context of Shared Memory Processors (SMPs). The work was motivated by the architecture of SMPs where cache consistency and coherence costs determined the designs. Basic axioms of lock-free data-structures were laid out by Barnes [1]. Valois [27, 28] further concertized those ideas in several primitive data-structures. Distributed versions of several primitive data-structures like FIFO queue [26, 19], hash-tables [18], priority-queues [24] exist for SMPs, but not for clustered environments, reason being, lack of primitives for efficient remote memory operations. In a related paper [17], Markatos et al. demonstrated the benefit of RDMA operations in building queues. However, the processes enqueued their data at a single site, unlike our implementation, where the queue was distributed.

7 Future Work

Our future work involves investigating ways of reducing unsuccessful *CAS* operations in distributed FIFO queue algorithms. We are also trying to extend our implementation by adding support for multi-modal locks, non-blocking locks and fault-tolerance.

8 Conclusion

In this paper, we presented an implementation of distributed FIFO queue based locking. We demonstrated a starvation-free algorithm which achieves better load-balancing by distributing the lock-management among the clients. Our design provides more throughput while consuming less CPU-resources at the server.

References

[1] G. Barnes. A method for implementing lock-free shared-data structures. In *SPAA '93*, pages 261–270, 1993.

[2] N. S. Bowen. A locking facility for parallel systems. *IBM Systems Journal*, 36(2), 1997.

[3] R. G. Davis. *VAXcluster Principles*. Digital Press, 1993.

[4] N. Desai and F. Mueller. A Log(n) Multi-Mode Locking Protocol for Distributed Systems. In *IPDPS '03*, 2003.

[5] A. Devulapalli and P. Wyckoff. Distributed queue-based locking using advanced network features. http://www.osc.edu/~ananth/papers/icpp05-tech-report.pdf.

[6] D. Dunning et. al. The Virtual Interface Architecture. *IEEE Micro*, 18(2):66–76, 1998.

[7] J. Liu et al. Performance Comparison of MPI Implementations over InfiniBand, Myrinet and Quadrics. In *Supercomputing Conference*, November 2003.

[8] A. Gottlieb, R. Grishman, C. P. Kruskal, K. P. McAuliffe, L. Rudolph, and Snir M. The NYU Ultracomputer—designing a MIMD shared memory parallel computer. *IEEE Transactions on Computers*, 32:175–189, February 1983.

[9] A. Gottlieb, B.D. Lubachevsky, and L. Rudolph. Basic techniques for the efficient coordination of very large numbers of cooperating sequential processors. *Programming Languages and Systems*, 5(2):164–189, 1983.

[10] M. Herlihy. Wait-free synchronization. *ACM TOPLAS*, 11 (1):124–149, January 1991.

[11] IBM Corporation. System/370 principles of operation. Technical Report GA22-7000-8, IBM, 1981.

[12] *InfiniBand Architecture Specification, Release 1.1*. InfiniBand Trade Association, November 2002.

[13] H. Kishida and H. Yamazaki. SSDLM: architecture of a distributed lock manager with high degree of locality for clustered file systems. In *PACRIM '03*, volume 1, pages 9–12, August 2003.

[14] W.J. Knottenbelt, S. Zertal, and P.G. Harrison. Performance analysis of three implementation strategies for distributed lock management. In *Computers and Digital Techniques, IEE Proceedings*, volume 148, pages 176–187, Jul/Sep 2001.

[15] N.P. Kronenberg, H.M. Levy, and W.D. Strecker. VAXcluster: a closely-coupled distributed system. *ACM Trans. Comput. Syst.*, 4(2):130–146, 1986.

[16] L. Lamport. A new solution of Dijkstra's concurrent programming problem. *Comm. ACM*, 17(8), 1974.

[17] E. P. Markatos, M. Katevenis, and P. Vatsolaki. The remote enqueue operation on networks of workstations. In *CANPC '98*, pages 1–14. Springer-Verlag, 1998.

[18] M. M. Michael. High performance dynamic lock-free hash tables and list-based sets. In *SPAA '02*, pages 73–82.

[19] M. M. Michael and M. L. Scott. Simple, fast, and practical non-blocking and blocking concurrent queue algorithms. In *PODC '96*, pages 267–275.

[20] R. Moran. *Oracle8 Parallel Server Concepts & Administration, Release 8.0*. Oracle Corporation, June 1997.

[21] Myricom. Myricom Inc. http://www.myri.com.

[22] A. Silberschatz, P. B. Galvin, and G. Gagne. *Operating System Concepts*. John Wiley & Sons, Inc., sixth edition.

[23] Sparc International. *The SPARC architecture manual, version 9*. Prentice Hall, 1994.

[24] H. Sundell and P. Tsigas. Fast and lock-free concurrent priority queues for multi-thread systems. In *IPDPS '03*, page 84.2, 2003.

[25] K. Thomas. *Programming Locking Applications*. IBM Corporation, 2001.

[26] P. Tsigas and Y. Zhang. A simple, fast and scalable non-blocking concurrent FIFO queue for shared memory multiprocessor systems. In *SPAA '01*, pages 134–143.

[27] J.D. Valois. Lock-free linked lists using compare-and-swap. In *PODC '95*, pages 214–222, 1995.

[28] J.D. Valois. *Lock-free data structures*. PhD thesis, 1996.

Clustered DBMS Scalability under Unified Ethernet Fabric

Krishna Kant
Intel Corporation

Amit Sahoo
Univ. of California, Davis

Abstract

In this paper, we study the performance of a clustered DBMS running an on-line transaction processing (OLTP) workload and using TCP/IP over Ethernet as a "unified fabric" for inter-process communication. The study is based on a comprehensive simulation model of such systems, called DCLUE. It is found that while the protocol overhead has a large impact on performance, the end to end latency has significantly lesser impact. The results suggest that very low-latency protocol offload may not be very beneficial for clustered OLTP workloads, but proper QoS treatment of messages is important.

Key words: Clustered database, TCP/IP, Quality of Service, Latency Impact, Thread switching

1 Introduction

Clustered implementations of traditional SMP applications are becoming popular due to lower cost and technological advancements that allow low-latency and high bandwidth interconnects such as Infiniband architecture (IBA) and HW offloaded TCP/IP over Ethernet [5, 11]. On the software side, there are already solutions available for running applications that do not require painstaking manual partitioning in order to minimize inter-process communication (IPC). A prime example of this is the Oracle 9i/10g database [7]. However, there isn't much information available in the open literature on the performance, scalability and stress behavior of such systems. In particular, although there are studies of clustered system scalability, they are mostly confined to either scientific computation (MPI based) or rather small clusters (8 way). In this paper we provide such an analysis based on a comprehensive simulation model and study the impact of fabric latency and network congestion on scalability.

The primary focus of our study is a cluster using TCP/IP over Ethernet as the "unified" clustering fabric, since we believe that specialized fabrics such as IBA, Myrinet, QS-Net, etc, will remain niche due to huge installed based of TCP/IP/Ethernet systems. In particular, we consider the scenario of a single high speed "pipe" coming into a server that carries all traffic types, which in this case includes inter-process communication (IPC), iSCSI based storage, and normal client-server traffic. Such an approach requires that the unified fabric work almost as well as isolated fabrics under stress conditions. Therefore, understanding the behavior of the clustered application under stress and other abnormal scenarios (e.g., under high latency) is of paramount importance. This paper attempts to contribute to this understanding via a very detailed simulation model of a clustered OLTP server.

The outline of the paper is as follows. Section 2 briefly describes the cluster database architecture and the emulated OLTP workload . Section 3 then provides a high-level overview of the simulation model for such a system. Section 4 then launches into the performance study of the cluster DB and presents a detailed set of results on scalability, latency impact, protocol overhead impact, etc. Section 5 concludes the paper.

2 Clustered Databases

Clustered DBMS implementations cover a wide range in terms of the level of coupling of various nodes. On one extreme, there is the "shared nothing" approach, where each node has its own independent memory and IO subsystem. In this case, the database must necessarily be partitioned among the nodes – either statically or dynamically. A more coupled approach is the "shared IO" approach, where all nodes access a centralized IO subsystem which holds the database. The IO subsystem in this case is invariably a Fiber-channel based SAN (system area network). Here we assume shared IO but with distributed iSCSI based storage. One attraction of such a model is that it allows inexpensive IO system at each node which expands naturally with the cluster size.

In either model, the data cached in the *buffer caches* of various nodes must be kept coherent. This could well be done via MESI or similar protocols used in SMPs [10]. Unfortunately, such a protocol would require substantial inter-process communication (IPC) to accomplish the necessary "snooping" and "invalidation" of copies held by various

0190-3918/05 $20.00 © 2005 IEEE

nodes. Oracle's mechanism, called RAC (real application cluster), attempts to avoid this overhead by exploiting *multi-version concurrency control* (MCC) [1].

The RAC scheme uses a directory based coordination scheme known as *cache fusion* [7] that proceeds as follows. Suppose that a node A experiences a miss on DB block X in its local buffer cache. Node A then determines (via a local table lookup) that some node, say B, holds the directory information for this block. A requests block X from node B, which in turn directs the appropriate data holder C to send the block to A. In case no node holds the data, A obtains block X from the disk (local or remote). Note that it is possible that $A = B$, or $B = C$; in these cases some operations become local and the corresponding messaging is not needed.

The TPC-C benchmark (`www.tpc.org/tpcc`) is a natural choice for an online transaction processing (OLTP) workload because of its popularity and the availability of detailed characterization data. Since TPC-C characteristics are well-known, they will not be repeated here. Some more details on the workload can be found in [4]. A notable characteristic of TPC-C transactions is that they all refer to a single warehouse. This, coupled with the fact that most tables have the number of warehouses as a multiplier, makes TPC-C database trivially partitionable: assign equal blocks of warehouses to each server and direct queries based on the warehouse. For this reason, TPC-C is usually considered an inappropriate workload for clustering studies. We address this weakness by not necessarily directing queries to the right server. Instead, we introduce the notion of *affinity*. An affinity of 1.0 corresponds to the case where a query always goes to the server that hosts the referenced warehouse. An affinity of $\alpha < 1$ means that the query goes to the right server with probability α and to a random server with probability $1 - \alpha$.

3 Overview of Cluster simulation Model

The simulation model called distributed cluster emulator (DCLUE) was developed using the simulation package OPNET (`www.opnet.com`). OPNET provides a fairly complete emulation of the network infrastructure including TCP, IP, and Ethernet MAC layers, QoS support, commercial switches and routers, etc. DCLUE was built on top of the OPNET provided TPAL (transport adaptation layer) which can support multiple transports underneath. This section provides only a brief overview of the model; more details can be found in [4].

Figure 1 shows the DCLUE network model. The network is organized as one or more "subclusters" which we call LATAs (borrowed from telecom). The subclusters are connected via an "outer-router" (or an "outer-switch" if we only want layer 2 switching), at which the clients also home

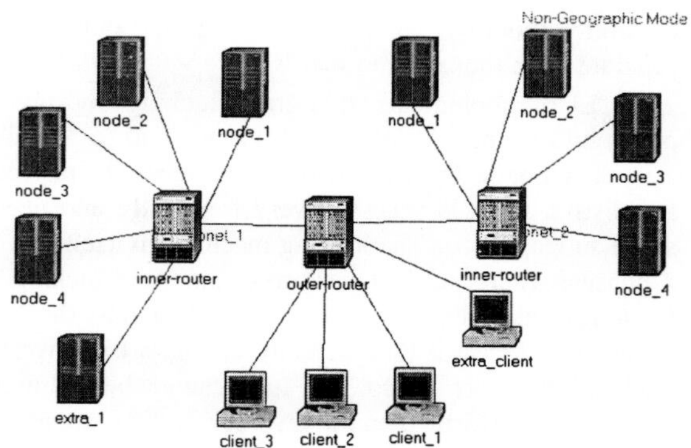

Fig 1. A sample model w/ 2 latas & 4 nodes per lata

in. Each server has internal disk subsystems for normal IO and logging, but not all of them may be used. In the distributed storage configuration, the disks are accessed remotely via the iSCSI protocol and locally via the SCSI protocol.

One of the objectives for the model is to study potential ill effects of running IPC and storage traffic on the normal Ethernet network that carries miscellaneous other types of traffic. For this, the model allows some extra clients and servers to be added to the cluster (distinguished in the model by a different address range). These clients/servers can run some additional applications and cause that traffic to interfere with DBMS traffic on various links and routers. We have a pair of such nodes, marked "extra_client" and "extra_server" in Fig 1.

During initialization, each server establishes 2 TCP connections to every other server: one for IPC messages (data & control) and the other for iSCSI related traffic (command, status, data, etc.). The client-server TCP connections are established dynamically on a per "business transaction" basis. A business transaction consists of the sequence of TPC-C transactions, starting with the new-order, in the appropriate proportions.

DCLUE basically builds the entire TPC-C database in the memory and initializes it according to TPC-C rules. However, the information retained in the tables is only what is essential to interpret and execute queries, which means that DCLUE can use the storage much more efficiently while still retaining the precise row sizes, rows per block, etc. DCLUE also explicitly maintains B^+-tree indices for each table. Since the entire database is sitting in the main memory, buffer cache operations merely change status of the pages in question. Disk IO operations are still simulated in terms of their latency and *path-length*(number of instructions required to execute an operation). Normal disk IO optimizations such as elevator algorithm are implemented on a per table basis. Although the disk writes are lazy and could finish after the transaction is done, the transaction does not commit without writing a log. The logging is done on disks separate from those for normal IO.

DCLUE implements fine-grain locking by dividing pages into subpages. We found that we had to "tune" the size of subpage for each table separately. In particular, the district table is accessed very frequently and needs a small subpage size. The locking mechanism itself involves 2 phases, where phase 1 performs "intention locking" (or *latching*) and brings in any missing data into the buffer cache [9]. Phase 2 then actually attempts to convert the latches into locks. Also, if a lock cannot be acquired, a lock wait is performed on the first lock in the sequence, and later failures result in lock release followed by a delayed retry. The scheme appears to work well even under high contention.

The multiversion concurrency control was implemented using time-stamping mechanism and keeps track of minimum, maximum and current version numbers for a page. Space for versions is allocated from an overflow memory area. If this overflow area runs low, unpinned pages from the buffer cache are "stolen" to replenish it.

The application processing is implemented in detail for each operation (e.g., transaction initiation, table operation, etc.) and so are message sends and receives. The calibration of *path-lengths* for various operations was done based on the NASA report on TPC-C [8] and current TPC-C measurements. The data related to platform characteristics is taken from a long list of comprehensive measurements available internally in Intel. Similarly, data related to IO operations (e.g., accelerated and non-accelerated TCP/IP, RDMA and iSCSI stacks) is taken from available prototypes and measurements [5, 6, 2].

The most crucial aspect of the model is the modeling of threads, thread switching, and its impact on processor caches. Basically, in a transactional workload, latency can be hidden by simply having more concurrent threads. However, given the processor cache size and working set of each thread, only a limited number of threads can be accommodated conveniently. With larger number of threads, the context switch penalty rises very sharply and the cache begins to thrash. Capturing this behavior was essential to properly model the impact of latency on performance. Fortunately, we had available to us a very detailed characterization of this and other OS aspects under Redhat Linux 7.3. This along with internal studies on TPC-C working set size provided us with the requisite data for the modeling of the threads.

The final aspect modeled in detail was the load on the processor bus and memory channels and the corresponding impact on CPU stalls. This again is essential for accurate modeling of the performance of a particular platform. Fortunately, this is one area that is routinely studied in connection with performance projections for various platform configurations (e.g., see [3]). Also, there exists a lot of characterization data based on measurements and cycle-accurate workload simulation of TPC-C. Yet, an accurate projection of MPI as a function of affinity is challenging and is currently based on some heuristics. Address bus, data bus and memory channels are modeled as queuing systems and the resulting memory latency determines CPU stalls via the concept of *blocking factor* (the fraction of latency visible to HW threads). We exploited available data on Intel Pentium 4 to calibrate this aspect of the model.

4 Cluster Performance Studies

In this section we use the DCLUE model to obtain a number of interesting results on scalability, latency sensitivity and impact of cross traffic. As stated earlier, although standard TPC-C specification is exploited heavily in the implementation and model calibration, we are interested in scenarios beyond basic TPC-C particularly in terms of the role of IPC in clustered databases.

4.1 Configurations and database scaling

The configurations that we considered are clusters of Intel Pentium IV class dual-processor (DP) servers. For these systems, unclustered TPC-C measurements and validated platform performance models were readily available and thus allowed detailed result validation at affinity of 1.0. In particular, our baseline server configuration is a 3.2GHz P4 DP system with 1 MB second level cache, 133 MHz bus and 16GB of DDR-266 memory. One such node delivers about 50K (unclustered) tpm-C performance, which amounts to a database with about 4K warehouses. For the network infrastructure, we stuck with the current 1 Gb/s ethernet links and routers primarily because the current processors are unable to drive 10 Gb/s bandwidth except in large clusters. However, in a few cases, 10 Gb/s inter-lata links had to be used since 1 Gb/s links were becoming a bottleneck. The router models used are OPNET supplied 3COM Gigabit routers. Unless stated otherwise, we assume that both TCP and iSCSI have been implemented in hardware.

Unfortunately, a direct simulation of even a small cluster will require long simulation times and huge amounts of memory. The need for $>$ 4GB memory would require the complexity of reworking the simulation to use PSE/AWE on a 32-bit machine. To avoid these problems, we consistently scaled all relevant parameters by a factor of 100x. This includes CPU frequency, processor bus, memory channels, PCI bus, disks, links, routers. Furthermore, all CPU overheads are expressed as "path-lengths" (i.e., number of instructions required to accomplish the operation) or as or path-length equivalents. Thus, a scale back of the obtained results should provide a reasonable estimate of the original performance.

4.2 Performance Scaling vs. Cluster Size

Before studying the impact of latency and traffic, it is important to see how the cluster performance scales with number of nodes. However, since scaling is the net result of many complex activities in the system, we start by examining the latter first.

Figures 2 and 3 show lock waits per transaction and lock wait time as a function of number of nodes. Although both of these parameters vary significantly, they show an unmistakable trend. The same holds for the number of lock failures per transaction (not shown). In the absence of other effects, this aspect will obviously limit the cluster scalability.

Fig. 4 shows the number of IPC control and data messages as a function of number of nodes for 0.8 affinity. The IPC messages are much smaller than data messages (about 250 bytes vs. more than 8KB) but significantly more numerous. The interesting point to note is that the IPC message count rises sharply at first but then "saturates" rather quickly. As a result, number of IPC messages very quickly cease to have any impact on scalability. In other words, no nonlinearity in performance is expected due to the number of IPC messages beyond small cluster sizes.

Let us now examine the scalability. Figure 5 shows this wrt cluster size, with affinity as a parameter. The affinity 1.0 case is shown just as a reference and corresponds to the case of perfect scaling. As expected, the scaling gets progressively poorer as the affinity is decreased. However, the interesting part is an almost linear scaling from 2 or 3 nodes to 10 nodes. For larger clusters, locking and topological issues start to come into effect.

In our experiments we considered 14-port routers/switches, which would be typical fcr a bladed system. Therefore, for cluster larger than 12 nodes (i.e., 16 and 24 node cases shown here), we had to move to a 2-lata scenario. This brings in the latency and queuing impacts of IPC traffic going across latas (through 2 extra links and 2 extra routers). Consequently, there is a change in slope around 12 nodes. However, it is important to note that the increasing lock failures and lock waits also play a substantial role in flattening out the scalability curve. In fact, with affinity of 0.5 or less, the network effectively stops scaling beyond 12 nodes. At 0.8 affinity, the scaling is decent and perhaps could be improved with faster links and routers.

At high affinities, the reason for continued scaling is the lack of any shared bottlenecks in the system. In fact, most resources increase linearly with the cluster size. For example, each new node adds not just CPUs, but also memory, memory channels, processor bus, normal and logging disks, and router links. If the network grows by adding more subnets, the stress on each inner-router also remains unchanged. Even the lock contention per page stays the same since TPC-C mandates that the database size increase linearly with the throughput. For low affinities, the low realized throughput prevents the bus from becoming a bottleneck for moderate cluster sizes, despite a significant increase in the MPI.

Poorer scaling properties can be observed if the linear growth in resources is broken. For example, if the router capacity is limited or the logging is done at a single node, the bottleneck effect pulls down the scaling (not shown for brevity). Fig 6 shows an interesting scenario in this regard, namely a slower growth of DB size as a function of throughput. For this we assumed that for up to 90K tpm-C, the database sizing is according to TPC-C rules (No of warehouses calculated assuming 12.5 tpm-C per warehouse). However, beyond this, the growth rate of warehouses grows as square root of the additional throughput, rather than linearly. With this, the contention for the data increases as the cluster size increases. Consequently, the throughput no longer goes up linearly with the cluster size.

4.3 Protocol Overhead vs. Latency

Compared with specialized fabrics, traditional SW based TCP/IP suffers from two drawbacks: (a) significant overhead of code execution (and associated OS bottlenecks such as interrupt handling), and (b) significantly higher latency. *It is important not to confuse the two.* For example, a significantly better performance achieved with specialized fabrics could well be due to much lower overhead rather than the ultra-low latency. Fig. 7 compares the performance of the following 3 cases for various affinities:

1. Both TCP fast path and iSCSI implemented in HW. This is the normal case considered for most of our experiments. For this, detailed TCP and iSCSI parameters were obtained from current offload prototypes.
2. TCP fast path in HW but iSCSI implemented in SW.
3. Both TCP and iSCSI implemented entirely in SW. The SW TCP assumes single copy for sends and 2 copies for receives.

With affinity 1.0, there is no appreciable difference between the 3 cases. This is because there is hardly any IPC traffic (except for occasional access to item table pages). Also, all disk accesses are local, so iSCSI doesn't come into play at all. The only traffic that benefits from TCP acceleration is client-server. Consequently, the HW TCP performance is slightly better than SW TCP, but not by much.

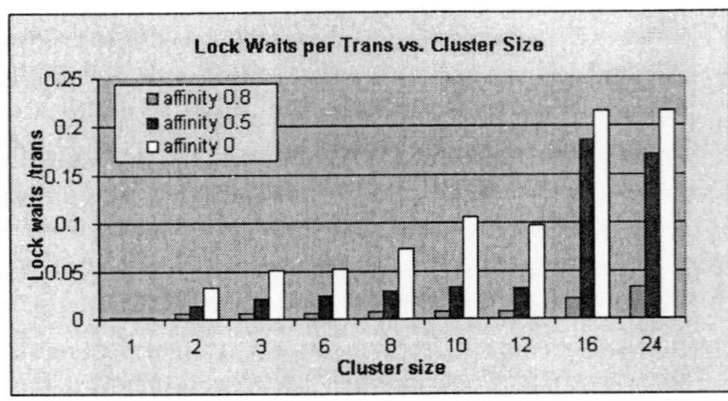

Fig 2. Lock waits/trans vs. #nodes and affinities

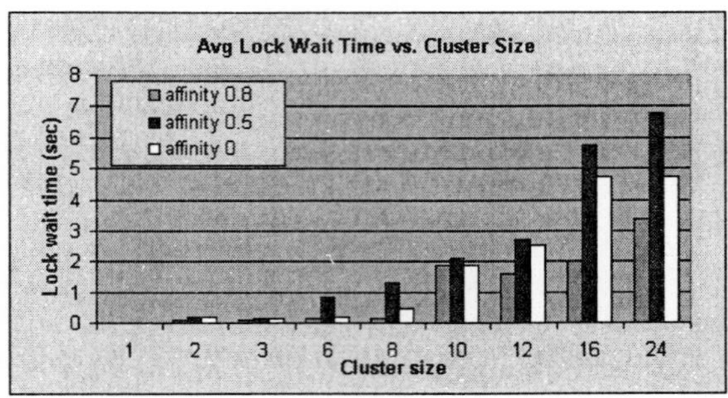

Fig 3. Lock wait time vs. #nodes and affinities

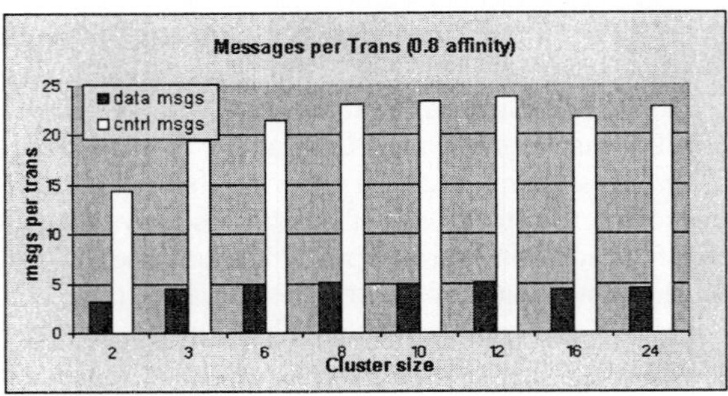

Fig 4. IPC messages per trans for 0.8 affinity

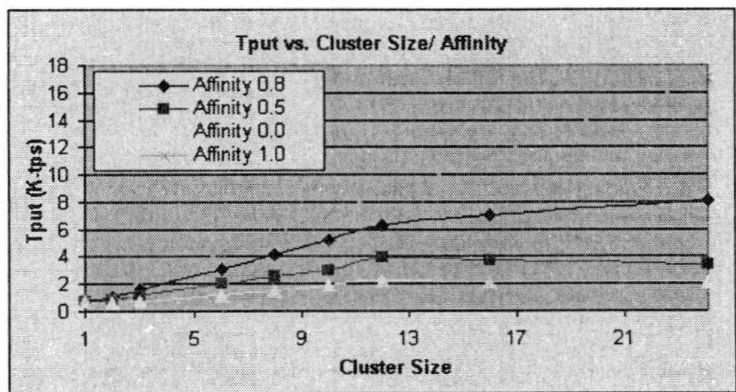

Fig 5. Scaling vs. nodes and affinity

With affinity 0.8, HW TCP provides almost twice as much throughput as SW TCP. This is because the lower overhead and latency of TCP substantially reduces both the workload path-length and stall cycles. However, the difference between SW iSCSI and HW iSCSI is marginal. This is partly due to the fact that disk IO rate is small (since most data comes from other buffer caches). Also, iSCSI implementation path-lengths are small except for the rather large overhead of CRC calculations [2].

Finally, with affinity 0.5, the difference between HW and SW TCP is even wider, but not by much. This result may be surprising since the number of messages per transaction does increase significantly from 0.8 to 0.5 (from 21 control messages per transaction to about 54). However, with 0.5 affinity the major expense in completing a transaction is due to lock failures, and the corresponding path-length increases and CPU stalls. The TCP/IP overhead thus has proportionately smaller impact.

Next we consider the latency impact. High latency tolerance would allow a less expensive implementation and even geographically distributed clusters. We study the impact of latency by simply adjusting the propagation delays of the links. It is important to note that this type of latency introduction is quite different from latencies within the platform (e.g., greater memory access latency or context switch latency) which cause direct CPU stalls. In a transactional workload, the true impact of latency is felt only when the latency cannot be hidden by employing additional threads; therefore, we do not place any bound on the number of threads used. Figure 8 shows the performance of a 2 lata system where each of the two inter-lata links includes one-half of the additional latency shown. The two curves are for 0.8 and 0.5 affinity respectively. It is seen that in both cases, a 1 ms additional delay results in about 3.4% performance drop, whereas a 2 ms delays causes a 6% performance drop. These latencies should be viewed in the context of 1 Gb/sec link. If we were to consider systems capable of driving 10 Gb/sec bandwidth, we might expect similar drops with 1/10th as much latency. That is, we could expect a 100 μs latency to drop the performance by a few percentage points. This is a rather low sensitivity considering the fact that the normal end-to-end delay with HW TCP can easily be brought down to 10-20 us.

We ran the experiment for 0.5 affinity (in addition to 0.8) hoping to see higher latency sensitivity for this case because of much higher IPC messages per transaction. Surprisingly however, the sensitivity is the same in both cases. This situation is a result of worse threading behavior for 0.5 affinity and is discussed more fully in the next subsection.

One reason for the low sensitivity of TPC-C to latency is its huge computational component as indicated by a path-length of 1.5M for the unclustered case, of which only about

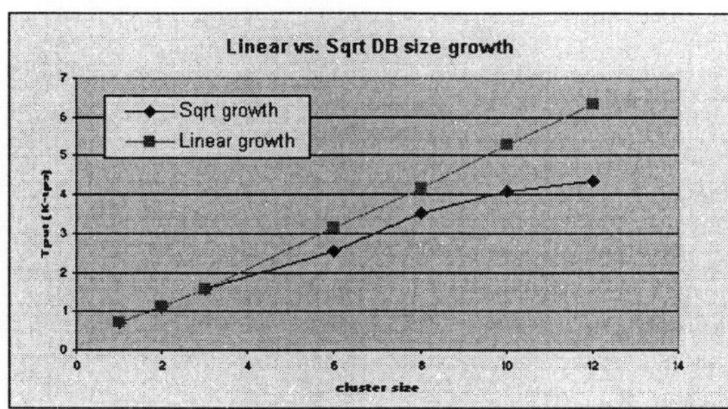

Fig 6. Impact of slower growth in DB size

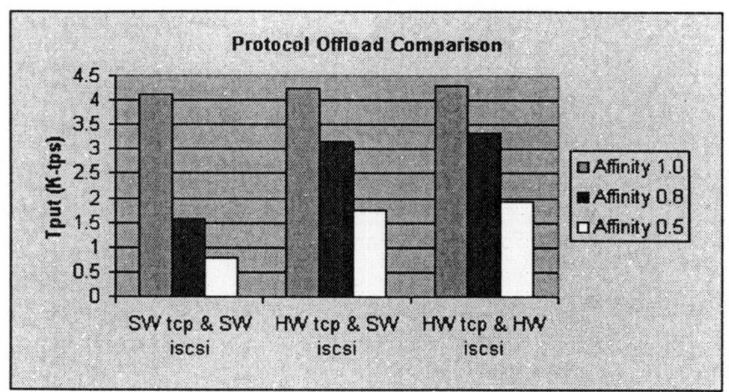

Fig 7. Impact of TCP and iSCSI offload

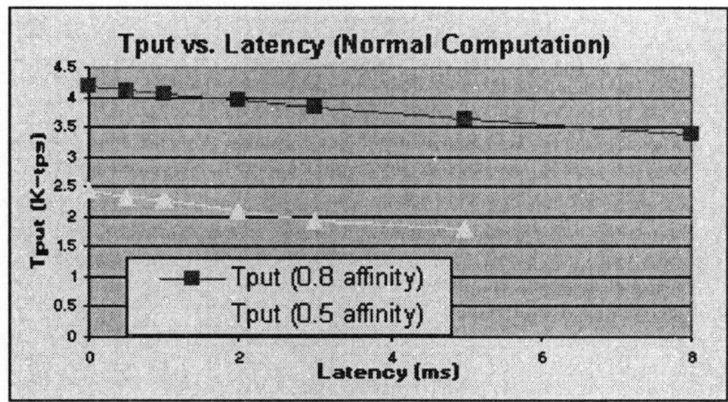

Fig 8. Latency impact: normal comp, 0.5 & 0.8 affinity

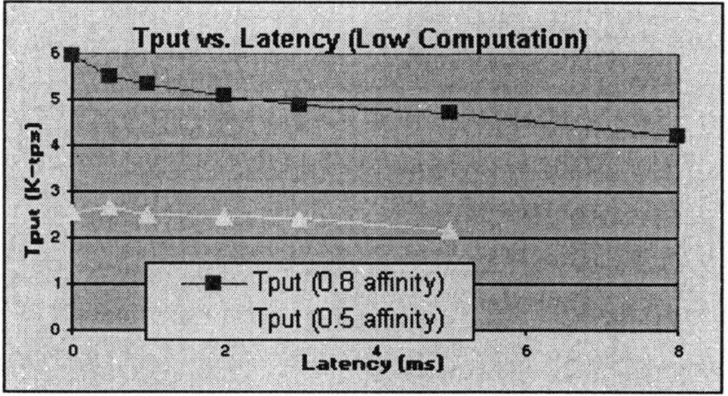

Fig 9. Latency impact: low comp, 0.5 & 0.8 affinity

15% is related to disk IO. Other OLTP workloads are significantly lighter on computation and thus could have higher sensitivity to latency. To investigate this, we simply reduced all computational path lengths by a factor of 4 and the resulting situation is designated as *'low computation'*. (A more realistic method would be to actually make the queries more light-weight, but that requires lot more effort.) Figure 9 shows that the change indeed makes the workload a lot more latency sensitive. In particular, 1 ms of additional latency now results in 10.4% drop in performance.

The results above show that the latency sensitivity is low enough that there is no need for designing ultra-low latency TCP/IP offload or router and switches. Furthermore, if the database characteristics are like TPC-C, it should be possible to geographically separate the subclusters (or latas) on the scale of MAN distances. For example, if we have two subclusters located 50 miles away, the additional 1 ms RTT increase will lower the performance by only a few percent on systems driving 1 Gb/sec bandwidth.

4.4 QoS Impact

In this section, we examine how the IPC and storage traffic is affected by other interfering traffic on the network. The results presented here are for the case where the extra clients/servers run FTP traffic with 100% GETs. As usual, the FTP application sets up new TCP connection for each transfer. This makes the interfering traffic more "stubborn" than the IPC traffic which uses a static connection. In particular, under overload conditions IPC connection may get reset and may have to be re-established. Since connection re-establishment involves a lot of overhead and lost traffic, we have avoided this situation by artificially bumping up the maximum retransmission count to rather high values. While this may not be realistic, we were interested primarily in the effect of cross-traffic as opposed to abnormal conditions created by it. Clearly, some admission control scheme needs to be in place to ensure that unlimited amount of traffic doesn't get into the network and cause connection resets.

We note here that we used FTP traffic here as a generic interfering traffic, and weren't overly concerned with maintaining a real-life file size distribution. In fact, as might be expected, setting the the file sizes too large would punish the FTP connection severely in case of congestion, and thus the traffic will not be able to affect the DBMS traffic that much. On the other hand, with very small transfers, FTP spends most of its effort in setting up/tearing down connections and therefore isn't a good interference candidate. Consequently, we decided to make FTP file sizes similar to the DBMS transfer sizes. DBMS control messages are in the 250 byte range and data messages are 8 KB or larger (because of additional versioning data).

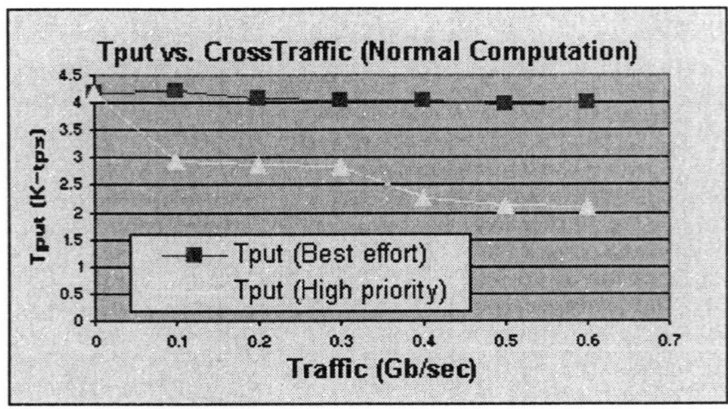

Fig 10. Impact of cross traffic w/ normal computation

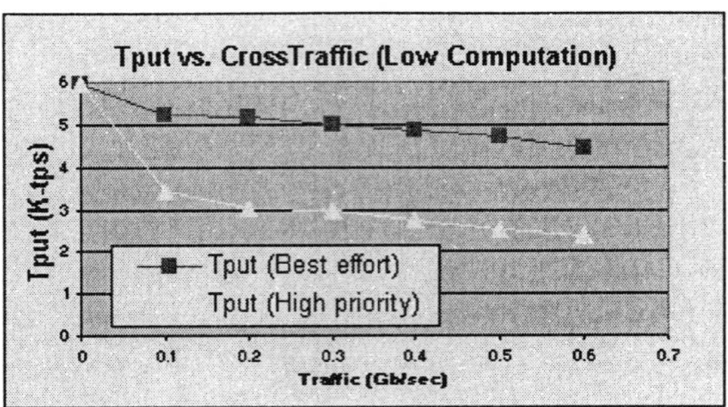

Fig 11. Impact of cross traffic w/ low computation

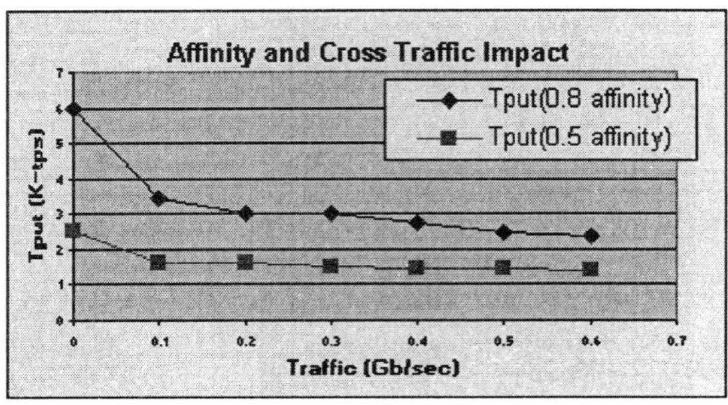

Fig 12. Impact of cross traffic w/ low computation

The scenario studied consisted of two latas, each with 4 nodes and an affinity of 0.8. We considered both normal and low computation cases (see last subsection). In the normal computation case, the combined DBMS traffic on the inter-lata links was about 650 Mb/sec and for low computation case, the traffic was about 920 Mb/sec. The cross traffic (FTP) was varied from 0 Mb/sec to 600 Mb/sec in both cases. It important to note that the *carried* traffic from both DBMS and FTP domains will depend on the interference and QoS setup – the numbers here merely refer to *offered* traffic in isolation.

With respect to QoS setup, we were primarily interested in diff-serv, since int-serv may not be implemented or even needed. The diff-serv space itself is huge and includes a variety of queuing schemes (priority, WFQ, ...), packet drop schemes (tail drop, WRED, FRED, ...), traffic policing/shaping schemes (e.g., leaky bucket), connection admission control, etc. The schemes often involve several hard-to-set tuning parameters thereby making QoS setup a nightmare. In view of this, we concentrate only on rather simplistic scenarios because they are most likely to be found within the data center. In particular, we only report results on the following two cases:

1. Both traffic types are of type *best effort*. This can be described as the "lazy" approach, where the administrator makes no effort to exploit diff-serv mechanisms.
2. DBMS traffic is best effort but the FTP traffic is assigned the DSCP AF21. This scenario represents situations where only certain traffic types use diff-serv for business reasons or because they demand good treatment. Admittedly, FTP isn't a good example of such traffic, but for the purposes of studying intereference, it probably doesn't matter.

In OPNET's default implementation, a higher AF number translates into a larger queue (and hence a lower drop probability) and priority treatment. Note that since the two traffic types don't share a client or server, priority treatment is confined only to the router. Thus, unless the router itself is congested, the priority queuing will not shut out the lower priority traffic under overload. The routers use simple tail-drop (instead of RED, WRED, etc.) and no connection admission control, policing or shaping policies are employed.

Fig 10 shows the results for normal computation for the two QoS arrangements. It is seen that with both traffic types as best-effort, interfering traffic does not make any significant impact on performance. Instead, the performance goes down marginally and at a slower rate as the traffic goes up (until the link really saturates). The explanation is that both DBMS and FTP traffics suffer due to competition and back off. For the DBMS traffic, this simply means a longer wait for the threads and hence more active threads. So long as the thread wait is small enough for the IPC request/response to get through, the performance is not adversely affected.

With FTP traffic given a higher priority, the impact is much more pronounced — a 30% drop in DBMS throughput with only 100 Mb/sec of FTP traffic. The large drop is a result of possible packet losses and increased queuing delay at the routers, which is caused by the priority handling of FTP traffic. In particular, critical IPC control messages such as lock acquire and release are delayed substantially. It was found that not only did the message delays almost double, the lock wait time also went up substantially from about 2 ms to 10 ms.

Surprisingly however, most of the drop happens initially; with more FTP traffic, the performance still goes down but much more slowly. The reason for this phenomenon has to do with caching and context switch behavior of the DBMS traffic. The 100 Mb/sec interfering traffic doubles delays for DBMS IPC traffic, which in turn requires more active threads to keep the CPU busy. In fact, the *average* number of active threads jumps from about 20 to 75. More threads, however, result in more competition for the processor cache since each time a thread is scheduled it needs to bring in its working set. Consequently, the average context switching cost skyrockets – from 17.7K CPU cycles to 69.7K CPU cycles. The result is a significant increase in CPU stalls, which increases the CPI (cycles per instruction) from 11.5 to 16.9 although the path-length does not change much. A larger cross traffic does increase the number of active threads further; however, with cache already almost thrashing, it is harder to afflict significant additional damage.

Fig 11 shows the results for low computation for the two QoS arrangements. As expected, the effect of cross traffic is more pronounced in this case. In particular, with both traffic types as best effort, the throughput drops from 6 K-tps to 5.2 K-tps due to 100 Mb/sec cross traffic, a 13% drop. With high priority traffic, the drop is very severe – down to 3.4 K-tps, or a 43% drop. The greater sensitivity is obviously due to greater dependence of transactions on getting their IPCs completed in a timely manner.

Fig 12 shows the impact of affinity on performance in the presence of cross traffic. For this, we have chosen the low computation case. Since lower affinity leads to more IPC messages per transaction, we might have expected the sensitivity to *increase* as the affinity goes down. In fact, the result is just the opposite. The reason for the apparent anomaly is that lower affinity already requires more threads to keep the CPU busy (because of more communication). Thus further delays due to interference do not degrade the cache performance quite as much. Also, once the cache is on the verge of thrashing, further delays have little chance of degrading the performance further.

5 Conclusions and Future Work

In this paper, we studied the performance of clustered OLTP workloads as a function of a variety of parameters with TCP/IP over Ethernet as a unified fabric. The main result of the modeling appears to be that OLTP workloads are more sensitive to protocol overhead rather than pure end to end latency. The latency sensitivity obviously depends on computation vs. communication, and may be higher for other OLTP workloads that are not so computationally intensive as TPC-C; however, it appears low enough that they may not benefit from *loaded* end-to-end latencies under a few tens of microseconds at 10 Gb/sec. It is worth emphasizing that this conclusion is only for clustered OLTP workloads; HPC and other workloads could well be much more latency sensitive. For example, workloads such as CHARMM [12] with many MPI collectives and a very bursty communication pattern show substantially more latency sensitivity.

In terms of QoS issues, interfering traffic does not adversely affect the DBMS performance so long as all traffic is defaulted to be best effort or the interfering traffic is at a lower priority. However, when competing with higher priority traffic, a substantial increase in queuing delays of crucial IPC messages such as lock acquisition/release could result in significant performance loss. Thus it is important to examine QoS schemes that can minimize inter-application interference and yet provide a good performance for all traffic types.

References

[1] P.A. Bernstein and N. Goodman, "Multiversion concurrency control — theory and algorithms", ACM Trans on Database Systems ., 8(4):465–483, December 1983.

[2] A. Joglekar, "iSCSI Technology Investigation", Intel measurement and evaluation report, Nov 2004.

[3] K. Kant, "An Evaluation of Memory Compression Alternatives", Proc. of CAECW (Computer Architecture Evaluation using Commercial Workloads), Feb 2003, Anaheim, CA.

[4] K. Kant, A. Sahoo and N. Jani, "DCLUE: A Distributed Cluster Emulator", available at http://www.ccwebhost.com/DCLUE.

[5] K. Kant, "TCP offload performance for front-end servers", Proc. of GLOBECOM 2003, Dec 2003, San Francisco, CA.

[6] S.R. King and F.L. Berry, "Software RDMA over TCP/IP on a general purpose CPU", submitted for publication.

[7] T. Lahiri, V. Srihari, et. al., "Cach Fusion: Extending shared disk clusters with shared caches", Proc. 27th VLDB conference, Rome, Italy 2001.

[8] S. Leutenegger and D. Dias, "A modeling study of the TPC-C benchmark", ACM SIGMOD Record archive, Volume 22 , Issue 2 (June 1993), pp22 - 31

[9] E. Rahm, "Concurrency and coherency control in database sharing systems", Technical Report 1993, Institut fr Informatik, Leipzig Germany

[10] T. Shanley, *The unabridged Pentium 4*, Mindshare Inc., 2004.

[11] G. Regnier, S. Makineni, et. al., "TCP onloading for data center servers", Special issue of IEEE Computer on Internet data centers, Nov 2004 (Eds. K. Kant & P. Mohapatra).

[12] M. Taufer, E. Perathoner, et. al., "Performance characterization of molecular dynamics code on PC clusters: Is there an easy parallelism in charmm?", Proc. of IEEE/ACM International Parallel and Distributed Processing Symposium, April 2002, Fort Lauderdale, Florida, USA.

Acknowledgements: Authors are grateful to Nrupal Jani for assistance with simulations reported here.

Session 6B: Services in P2P Systems

Ferry: An Architecture for Content-Based Publish/Subscribe Services on P2P Networks

Yingwu Zhu
Department of ECECS
University of Cincinnati
zhuy@ececs.uc.edu

Yiming Hu
Department of ECECS
University of Cincinnati
yhu@ececs.uc.edu

Abstract

Leveraging DHTs (distributed hash table), we propose Ferry, an architecture for content-based publish/subscribe services. With its novel design in subscription installation, subscription management and event delivery algorithm, Ferry can serve as a scalable platform to host any and many content-based publish/subscribe services: any publish/subscribe service with a unique scheme can run on top of Ferry, and many publish/subscribe services can run together on top of Ferry. For each of the publish/subscribe services running on top of Ferry, Ferry does not need to maintain or dynamically generate any dissemination tree. Instead, it exploits the embedded trees in DHTs such as Chord to deliver events, thereby imposing little overhead. By delivering events along DHT links, Ferry has two main advantages: (1) it eliminates the cost in construction and maintenance of the dissemination trees; (2) it allows further optimization, i.e., the DHT link maintenance messages could be piggybacked onto the event delivery messages to reduce the maintenance cost which is inherent and nontrivial in DHTs. Moreover, Ferry can support a publish/subscribe scheme with a very large number of event attributes.

1. Introduction

Content-based publish/subscribe (pub/sub) is a powerful paradigm for information dissemination from *publishers* to *subscribers* in a large-scale distributed network. In a content-based pub/sub system, subscribers register their interests in future *events* through *subscriptions*. Upon receiving an event (published by a publisher), the system matches the event to the subscriptions which serve as *filters* and deliver the event to the matched subscribers. The major advantage of content-based pub/sub is its high expressiveness in subscriptions, i.e., a subscription is expressed by specifying a set of *predicates* over event attributes [9].

As DHT-based peer-to-peer (P2P) systems [17, 15, 23, 14] attract more and more interests from the research community due to their scalability, fault-tolerance and self-organization, many content-based pub/sub systems [11, 7, 20, 19, 18, 12, 13] have been recently built on top of these DHTs. In such systems, peers cooperate in storing subscriptions and routing events to their subscribers in a fully distributed manner. A big challenge facing a P2P-based pub/sub system is to design a light-weight, efficient, and timely event delivery algorithm. Put in another way, the pub/sub system should impose small overhead on the underlying DHT, and the event delivery should be efficient in terms of bandwidth cost and timely in terms of user-perceived latency.

To this end, we propose an architecture for content-based pub/sub services, called *Ferry*, built on top of Chord [17]. As a platform, Ferry can host *any* and *many* pub/sub services. This is twofold: (1) any pub/sub service with a unique scheme can run on top of Ferry; (2) many pub/sub services can coexist on top of Ferry. For each pub/sub service running on top of Ferry, Ferry does not need to maintain or dynamically generate any dissemination tree to deliver events. Leveraging the embedded trees (formed by DHT links) in the DHT, Ferry aggregates and delivers event messages along DHT links, thereby imposing little overhead. Exploiting DHT links has two major advantages. First, it eliminates the cost in construction and maintenance of dissemination trees used for event delivery. Second, it allows some optimizations. E.g., the DHT link (or routing table) maintenance messages (sent periodically) can be piggybacked onto the event delivery messages to reduce the maintenance cost which is inherent and nontrivial (in terms of bandwidth) in DHTs. To deal with the load balancing issue, Ferry takes three steps. First, it relies on the uniformity of the consistent hash function used in Chord to distribute subscriptions and events across nodes. Second, it proposes a scheme, called *one-hop subscription push* to balance the subscription distribution among neighbor nodes. Finally, it adopts *attribute partitioning* [22] to further improve load

0190-3918/05 $20.00 © 2005 IEEE

balance.

We have built Ferry on top of p2psim [1], a discrete-event packet level simulator. Via detailed simulations, we evaluated Ferry extensively in terms of overlay hops, latency, overhead, and bandwidth cost. The experimental results show that Ferry can deliver events to a large number of subscribers with very small overhead and latency. Moreover, Ferry can support a pub/sub scheme with a very large number of event attributes.

The rest of the paper is structured as follows. Section 2 provides a survey of related work. We present the design of Ferry in Section 3. Section 4 presents experimental setup and results. We conclude this paper in Section 5.

2. Related Work

Due to space constraints, we here just present the most related work. Many distributed content-based pub/sub systems [2, 4, 21, 6, 5, 3] have been proposed by using routing trees to deliver events to the subscribers based on multicast techniques. Among these systems, Ferry is most similar to MEDYM [3]. In MEDYM, each node can be a *matcher* for some subscriptions and events. Upon receiving an event, some matcher responsible for this event matches the event to the subscriptions and obtains a destination list of the matched subscribers. Then, the event delivery message containing the destination list is routed through a dynamically generated dissemination tree with the help of topology knowledge. However, Ferry differs from MEDYM in that it does not need to dynamically generate a dissemination tree on demand and it instead exploits the embedded trees inherent in a DHT to deliver events, thereby imposing little overhead.

DHTs such as Chord [17], Pastry [15], Tapestry [23], and CAN [14] offer an attractive platform to build content-based pub/sub systems due to their scalability, load balance, fault-tolerance, and self-organization. Many attempts have been made in designing a P2P-based pub/sub system [19, 20, 18, 12, 7, 13, 16, 25, 11]. Tam et al. [18] propose a content-based pub/sub system built from Scribe [16]. The problem with their system is that it has some restrictions on the expression of subscriptions. Terpstra et al. [19] propose a content-based pub/sub system built on top of Chord. In order to have the system function correctly, it needs to maintain the invariants for filters in the face of node joins and departures, which is not an easy task. Triantafillou et al. [20] also built their content-based pub/sub system on top of Chord. However, the main drawback is that subscription installation and update may be expensive due to the large number of nodes and messages involved for attribute ranges in subscriptions. Reach [12] and HOMED [7] is a content-based pub/sub system built on top of a P2P overlay which maintains high-level semantic relationships. Both may have a load balancing issue since unevenly distributed subscriptions would cause unevenly distributed nodes in the overlay identifier space. In HOMED, it may be difficult to derive node IDs from their subscriptions while preserving high expressiveness of subscriptions and the change of a node's interests would cause the change of the overlay structure. Meghdoot [11] is based on CAN. Considering skewed distributions of both subscriptions and events in a real application, Meghdoot addresses the load balancing issue by zone splitting and zone replication. The major limitation of Meghdoot is that the overlay's dimension is proportional to the number of event attributes.

Although Ferry is also built on top of a DHT, it differs from existing P2P-based solutions in that it exploits the embedded trees in a DHT to deliver events. Ferry's novel subscription installation and management algorithms allow the event delivery messages to be aggregated as much as possible along the dissemination paths, thereby avoiding redundant messages sent across the DHT identifier space. Moreover, Ferry provides a scalable and efficient platform to run any content-based pub/sub application with a unique scheme. It also supports the application with a very large number of event attributes.

3. System Design

In this section, we present the design of Ferry on top of Chord. However, the techniques discussed here are applicable or easily adaptable to other DHTs such as Pastry and Tapestry. It is worth pointing out that Ferry aims to serve as a platform to host many pub/sub services with unique schemes. For illustration purpose, we base our discussion on a pub/sub scheme $S = \{A_1, A_2, ..., A_n\}$, proposed by Fabret et al. [9]. In this scheme, a subscription is a conjunction of predicates over one or more attributes, and an example subscription is $s = \{(A_1 = v_1) \wedge (v_2 \leq A_3 \leq v_3)\}$. An example event is $e = \{A_1 = c_1, A_2 = c_2, ..., A_n = c_n\}$. In Ferry, each node serves as a rendezvous point (RP) for some subscriptions and events, and also as an intermediate node on the paths of event delivery. Given a scheme $S = \{A_1, A_2, ..., A_n\}$, the RP nodes for its subscriptions and events are the most immediate successors of $k_i = h(A_i)$, where k_i is a key derived from an attribute A_i by using the consistent hash function $h()$ (which is used in Chord to produce node IDs and data keys).

3.1. Subscription Installation

A subscription s is represented by a pair (sid, p), where sid is a subscriber's node ID (*subscriber ID* for short), and p specifies a subscriber's interests in particular events by a conjunction of predicates which define the values or ranges

[1] http://pdos.lcs.mit.edu/p2psim

over one or more attributes in the scheme S. When a user wishes to subscribe for some events, the user first has to register his/her interests to a RP node in the form of a subscription. Due to space constraints, we omit the discussion of *RndRP* algorithm which aims to evenly distribute subscriptions over RP nodes. Please refer to our technical report [24] for more detail.

In this section, we present a more efficient algorithm, called *PredRP*, as outlined in Algorithm 1. The basic idea behind PredRP is that *a subscription s is stored in a RP node whose node ID is equal to or most immediately precedes s's subscriber ID among all the RP nodes of the scheme S.* As shown in Figure 1, r_1 is responsible for the subscriptions from $[r_1, r_2)$, and r_2 is responsible for the subscriptions from $[r_2, r_1)$. PredRP could achieve better performance than RndRP by avoiding sending the redundant messages across the Chord ring space. With RndRP, the event delivery messages from RP nodes r_1 and r_2 may need to traverse the whole Chord ring space since the subscriptions stored on each RP node may come from the subscribers distributed over the whole Chord ring space. However, with PredRP, the event delivery messages from RP nodes r_1 and r_2 only need to traverse a fraction of the Chord ring space due to the fact that each RP node stores only those subscriptions from a contiguous region of the Chord ring space (e.g., $[r_1, r_2)$ and $[r_2, r_1)$) respectively).

Algorithm 1 $install\_subscription$(Subscription s)

1: choose an attribute A_i from S such that $h(A_i)$ either is equal to or most immediately precedes s's subscriber ID among all attributes
2: $k = h(A_i)$
3: store s in a RP node which is an immediate successor node of k

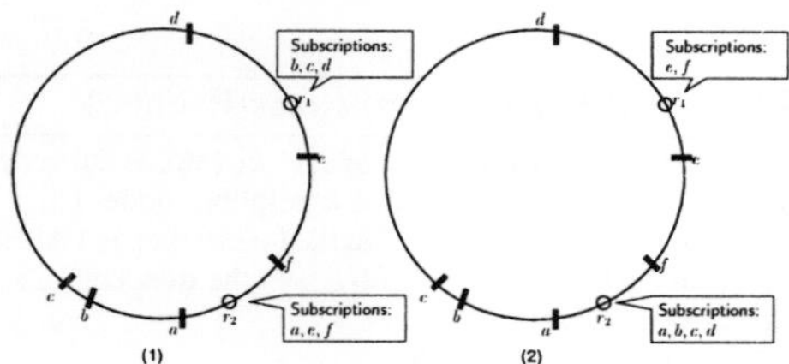

Figure 1. Illustration of RndRP and PredRP. r_1 and r_2 are two RP nodes. a, b, c, d, e, f are subscribers. (1) RndRP (2) PredRP.

When a subscriber leaves the system, he/she may unregister his/her subscriptions installed in the system, by simply requesting the corresponding RP nodes to remove his/her subscriptions. Otherwise, a subscription may have a TTL value. By associating a subscription with a TTL value, a subscriber does not need to unregister his/her subscriptions when leaving. The main drawback is that the subscriber needs to refresh his/her subscriptions periodically. However, the detailed discussion on unsubscribing is not focus of this paper.

3.2. Subscription Management

As discussed in [17], Chord nodes consult their *successor lists* and *finger tables* to route a message with a key k to a destination node whose ID is the successor of k. Consider each subscriber with a unique *sid*. The routing paths from a RP node r to all these *sids* (or subscribers) form a tree rooted at the RP node r, say $EMDTree_r$ (an embedded tree for r) [2]. As will be discussed in Section 3.4, the events will be disseminated along this tree from the RP node to the subscribers. Note that this tree is formed by the underlying DHT links, thereby imposing no additional construction or maintenance cost.

How does a RP node r manage the subscriptions installed by subscribers? Recall that each Chord node's routing table consists of two parts: a *successor list* and a *finger table*. As outlined in Algorithm 2, r manages the subscriptions in a manner that a subscription s is stored according to the entry of a neighbor node (including both successor nodes and finger table nodes) *whose node ID is equal to or most immediately precedes s's sid* [3]. Note that this does not necessary suggest that we put the data structure of subscriptions into r's routing table. We may just keep the metadata of the subscriptions into the entry of its routing table. However, the discussion of how to associate subscriptions with routing table's entries is not focus of this paper.

Algorithm 2 $manage\_subscriptions$(Subscription s)

Require: vector<Subscription> $store[1..k]$ {stores subscriptions in the RP node according to the entry of k neighbor nodes}
1: find the neighbor node n_j whose ID is equal to or most immediately precedes s's sid
2: $store[j].push\_back(s)$

Figure 2 illustrates a RP node r's subscription management (for simplicity of presentation, the subscriptions of subscribers s_2, x, y, z, v and w in r are represented by their *sid*). Subscriber s_2's subscription is stored corresponding to the entry of r's successor node s_2. The subscriptions of subscribers x and y are stored corresponding to the entry of r's finger table node f_2. The subscriptions of subscribers z, w and v are stored corresponding to the entry of r's finger table node f_3. As will be shown later, this novel subscription management can allow a RP node to deliver events by aggregating messages along its DHT links (links to its successor nodes and finger table nodes), thereby reducing the number of messages across the system.

Now consider again Figure 1. PredRP may cause uneven subscription distribution across the RP nodes (r_1 stores less

[2]Other DHTs such as Pastry and Tapestry have similar embedded trees as well.

[3]This manner of subscription management is based on the observation that when routing a message from the RP node r to node s, r will first forward the message to its neighbor node whose ID is equal to or most immediately precedes s's ID.

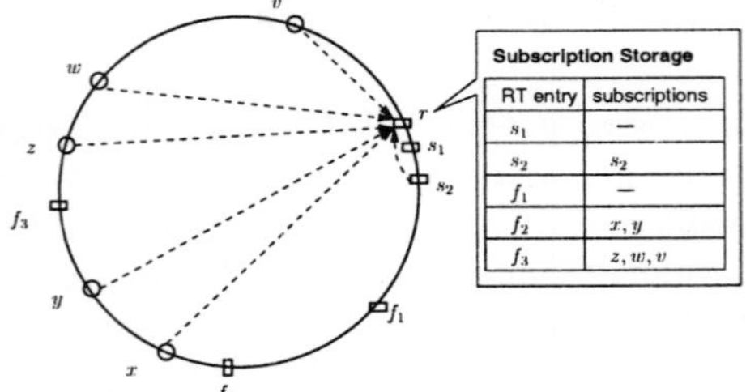

Figure 2. An illustration of a RP node r's subscription management. s_1 and s_2 are r's successors. f_1, f_2, and f_3 are members of r's finger table. s_2, x, y, z, w, and v are subscribers whose subscriptions are stored in r.

subscriptions than r_2). To deal with the load balancing issue, we propose a scheme, called *one-hop subscription push mode* (*one-hop push* for short). The basic idea is that a RP node (say r) may push the subscriptions corresponding to an entry of the finger table to the corresponding finger table node (say n). The RP node r then uses a *summary filter* [4] to represent the subscriptions pushed away. Upon an event e, r matches the event with the summary filter. If it is a match, the RP node r delivers e to the corresponding finger table node n (at this point, no subscriber ID list is carried in the event delivery message), which in turn serves as a RP node for those subscriptions pushed from r and starts delivering e to those matched subscribers.

One-hop push serves two main purposes. The first purpose is to move some of the loads (i.e., subscriptions and thereby subscription matching load) on a RP node to some (or all) of its finger table nodes for load balance. For example, if a RP node r is overloaded by subscriptions, it finds a finger table node f is underloaded or willing to take some subscriptions through the load status piggybacked in the finger table maintenance messages which are sent periodically. Then, r could push those subscriptions corresponding to the entry of f to f. Note that the subscriptions to be pushed could also be piggybacked onto the routing table maintenance messages to reduce the number of messages involved. The second purpose is to reduce the message size from a RP node to its finger table nodes (at this point, no subscriber ID list is carried in the messages) and therefore the bandwidth cost. For more detail of one-hop push, please refer to our technical report [24].

3.3. Event Publication and Matching

When a node wishes to publish an event, the event is first directed to *all* of the RP nodes corresponding to the scheme S. These RP nodes are responsible for matching the event to the subscriptions and starting delivering the event to the matched subscribers. Given an event $e = \{A_1 = c_1, A_2 = c_2, ..., A_n = c_n\}$, Algorithm 3 outlines the process of event publication. It is worth pointing out that the event may be sent to the RP nodes either through the underlying Chord routing protocol, or through the direct point-to-point communication if the event publishing node has already cached the mapping of k_i to the IP address of the RP node. The direct point-to-point communication between the publishing node and the RP nodes is expected to achieve better performance compared to the Chord routing protocol. However, if the number of the RP nodes is large (proportional to the number of attributes in S), either the point-to-point communication model may be inappropriate and impractical, or resorting to the Chord routing protocol may be inefficient (e.g., in terms of bandwidth). We may need to use a more efficient mechanism to publish the event to the RP nodes instead, e.g, multicast techniques. More discussion of this is presented in [24].

Algorithm 3 $publish\_event$(Event e)

for each $A_i \in S$ **do**
  $k_i = h(A_i)$
  send e to a RP node which is an immediate successor node of k_i
end for

When an event e is published to a RP node r, r first needs to find the subscriptions matching the event, and then starts the process of delivering the event to the matched subscribers. Upon an event e, the RP node r needs to match e with the subscriptions it is storing. Algorithm 4 outlines the matching process which returns the list of matched subscribers with respect to the entry of r's k neighbor nodes.

Algorithm 4 $match\_subscriptions$(Event e)

Require: vector<Subscription> $store[1..k]$ {stores subscriptions in the RP node according to the entry of k neighbor nodes}
Require: $is\_match(e, p)$ returns TRUE if e satisfies p, FALSE otherwise
Ensure: vector<ID> $matched\_set[1..k]$ {the matched subscribers' IDs to be returned}
for each neighbor node n_i **do**
  for each subscriptions $s_j = (sid_j, p_j) \in store[i]$ **do**
    if $is\_matched(e, p_j)$ **then**
      $matched\_set[i].push\_back(sid_j)$
    end if
  end for
end for
return $matched\_set$

Note that Algorithm 4 is a linear subscription matching algorithm with respect to the number of subscriptions. To overcome this linear matching inefficiency, we could adopt sublinear matching algorithms based on building a subscription tree that collapses similar subscriptions [1]. However, how to optimize the matching algorithm is not focus of this paper. Algorithm 4 is primarily for illustration purpose.

[4]A summary filter in Ferry corresponds to an entry of the finger table and covers all currently hosted subscriptions for this entry of the finger table by exploiting covering relationships between subscriptions [22].

3.4. Event Delivery

Upon receiving an event, how does a RP node exploit the embedded tree in Chord to deliver events by exploiting the embedded tree $EMDtree_r$? The basic idea behind Ferry's event delivery algorithm is that all the event delivery messages to those subscribers who share common ancestor nodes on the tree $EMDtree_r$ are aggregated into one single message along the path from the root node r to their lowest common ancestor node, thereby minimizing the number of messages. Algorithm 5 and Algorithm 6 outline the event delivery algorithm. The event delivery starts from the RP node r which sends out an event delivery message *carrying a corresponding subscriber ID list* (e.g., $matched\_set[i]$ in Algorithm 4) along its neighbor links (as shown in Figure 3). Upon receiving the message, each neighbor node (e.g., node s_2, f_2, or f_3 in Figure 3) executes $route\_message()$. If there is a subscriber ID matches its own ID, then it delivers the event to its local applications/users. It also partitions the remaining subscriber IDs (if any) in the message according to its own neighbor nodes (i.e., for each subscriber ID, choose a neighbor node whose ID is equal to or most immediately precedes the subscriber ID), and performs $deliver\_event()$ to deliver the messages each of which may carry a corresponding list of subscriber IDs to the remaining subscribers. Note that all RP nodes of the scheme S will perform this event delivery operation in parallel.

This event delivery algorithm is essentially a recursive process where each node along the dissemination paths of $EMDtree_r$ performs $deliver\_event()$ until the event reaches all subscribers. Note that the event delivery algorithm in Ferry has several important features. First, no subscription matching operation is performed along the dissemination path except the RP node, due to the subscriber list contained in the message. Second, unlike MEDYM [3], it does not need to dynamically generate dissemination trees on-demand because it exploits the embedded trees which are inborn and dynamically maintained in Chord. Thirdly, the DHT link (or routing table) maintenance messages could be piggybacked onto the event delivery messages to reduce the maintenance cost which is inherent and nontrivial in DHTs.

Algorithm 5 $deliver\_event$(Event e, vector<ID> $matched\_set[1..k]$)

```
for i = 1 to k do
    if matched_set[i] is not empty then
        Message M ← e + match_set[i] {+ is a concatenation operator}
        send M to the neighbor node n_i, which then calls
        route_message(M) upon receiving M
    end if
end for
```

Algorithm 6 $route\_message$(Message M)

```
vector<ID> matched_set[1..k]
Event e ← extract the event from M
vector<ID> list ← extract the list of subscriber IDs from M
for each sid_i ∈ list do
    if sid_i == this node's ID then
        deliver e to its local applications or users
    else
        find the neighbor node n_j whose node ID is equal to or most
        immediately precedes sid_i
        matched_set[j].push_back(sid_i)
    end if
end for
if matched_set is not empty then
    deliver_event(e, matched_set)
end if
```

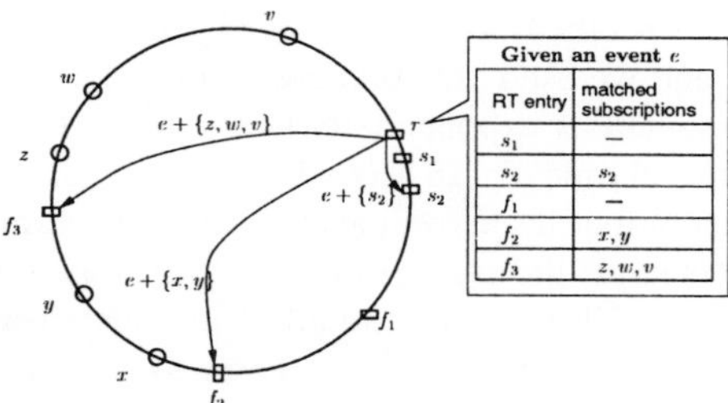

Figure 3. An illustration of the delivery of an event e from a RP node r. s_1 and s_2 are r's successors. f_1, f_2, and f_3 are members of r's finger table. s_2, x, y, z, w, and v are subscribers matching the event e.

4. Evaluation

In this section we evaluate Ferry using a scheme S for stock quotes application proposed by Gupta el al. [11]. We first describe the Ferry simulator, the scheme S for the stock quotes application, the datasets, and the metrics used for evaluation. Then, we present the experimental results.

4.1. Experimental Setup

We implemented Ferry on top of **p2psim** [5], a discrete-event packet level simulator. **p2psim** currently can simulate four P2P systems including Chord. Chord has a configuration named *proximity neighbor selection* (PNS) which allows each Chord node to choose physically close nodes as routing table entries to reduce lookup latency [8]. The simulated network used in our simulations consists of 1024 nodes with inter-node latencies derived from measuring the pairwise latencies of 1024 DNS servers on the Internet using King method [10]. The average round-trip time for the simulated network is 198 milliseconds.

The scheme S we used in our experiments was proposed in Meghdoot [11], and defined as $S = \{[Date : string, 2/Jan/98, 31/Dec/02]$, $[Symbol : string, \text{“aaa”}, \text{“zzzzz”}]$, $[Open : float, 0, 500]$,$[Close : float, 0, 500]$, $[High : float, 0, 500]$, $[Low : float, 0, 500]$,

[5] http://pdos.lcs.mit.edu/p2psim

$[Volume : integer, 0, 310000000]\}$. Specifically, *Symbol* is the stock name. *Open* and *Close* are the opening and closing prices for a stock on a given day. *High* and *Low* are the highest and lowest prices for the stock on that day. *Volume* is the total amount of trade in the stock on that day. Given the scheme S, an example subscription s is $(123456, \{(Symbol = \text{"yhoo"}) \wedge (High > 35.23)\})$, subscribed by a subscriber with $sid = 123456$.

We generated subscriptions by using five template subscriptions suggested in Meghdoot [11] with different probabilities. The number of stocks and subscriptions used in simulations were 100 and 10,000 respectively by default, unless otherwise specified. The events were generated randomly from S and we used 100,000 events in simulations which were modeled as exponentially distributed with an average inter-arrival time of 116 seconds.

We used a set of metrics to evaluate the performance and cost of Ferry: (1) *hops*: the average number of overlay hops taken by Ferry to deliver an event to all of its subscribers; (2) *latency*: the average time taken by Ferry to deliver an event to all of its subscribers; (3) *overhead*: it is defined as the ratio of the number of intermediate nodes involved during the delivery of an event to the number of subscribers for this event. The lower the overhead, the better performance of Ferry; (4) *bandwidth cost*: it is defined as ratio of the total bandwidth cost incurred by an event delivery to the number of nodes involved (including the intermediate nodes and subscriber nodes). The size in bytes of each event delivery message is counted as 20 bytes for headers, 33 bytes for the event, and 4 bytes for each subscriber ID carried in the message.

The results presented next do not include the event publication and we primarily focused our experiments on Ferry's event delivery algorithm. Recall that, in event publication, an event can be either sent directly or routed to the RP nodes from the event publishing node. If the event is directly sent to the RP nodes, the average event publication latency would be average latency between nodes. If the event chooses to be routed to the RP nodes, it can use Ferry's event delivery algorithm to publish the event to the RP nodes by envisioning the RP nodes as the publishing node's subscribers. In this case, the performance and cost of event publication is similar to event delivery.

4.2. Experimental Results

Due to pace constraints, some results are omitted here. Please refer to [24] for more detail. Table 1 shows the performance of Ferry with different configurations for 10,000 subscriptions and 100,000 events, where PNS represents Chord uses proximity neighbor selection (PNS). The average number of subscribers *per event* is 25, about 2.4% of nodes. Note that PredRP outperforms RndRP significantly, and PredRP+PNS performs the best. This is because (1) the

Table 1. Comparison between different Ferry's configurations

scheme	hops	latency(ms)	bw_cost(Bytes/node)	overhead
RndRP	3.94	359.17	53.67	2.51
PredRP	2.64	235.28	52.41	1.20
RndRP+PNS	3.80	154.22	53.56	2.41
PredRP+PNS	2.57	144.34	52.16	1.18

event delivery messages in PredRP traverse shorter ranges of the Chord ring space; and (2) PredRP can avoid sending redundant messages across the Chord ring space.

Figure 4 shows the subscription distribution on 7 RP nodes for RndRP and PredRP. Note that RndRP evenly distributes subscriptions to the RP nodes while PredRP produces a skewed load distribution. This shows one-hop subscription push is very necessary for PredRP to achieve load balance. We also studied the impact of one-hop push on bandwidth cost for RndRP+PNS and PredRP+PNS. One-hop push (here it pushes the corresponding subscriptions of a RP node to its finger table nodes) could reduce the bandwidth cost *per event* for RndRP+PNS from 53.56 to 52.39 Bytes/node, and for PredRP+PNS from 52.16 to 50.34 Bytes/node. The bandwidth cost reduction results from the reduced message sizes from the RP nodes to their finger table nodes (at this point, no subscriber ID list is carried in the messages). Note that the bandwidth cost reduction is per node/event, so a small reduction could result in huge reduction in aggregated bandwidth cost across the system.

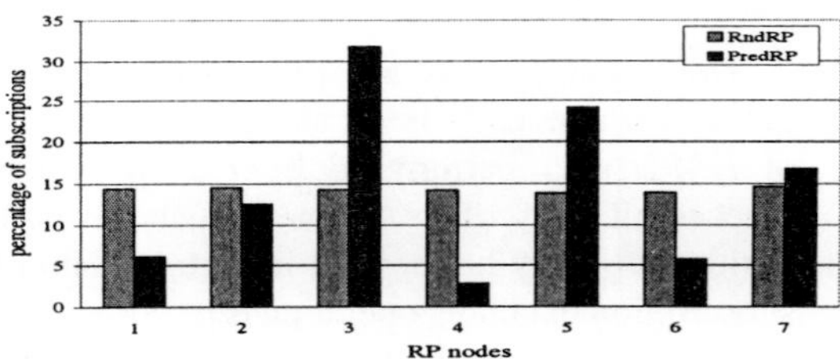

Figure 4. Subscription distribution in RP nodes for RndRP and PredRP.

To explore Ferry's performance (with configuration of PredRP+PNS) for various numbers of subscribers, we each time ran Ferry by delivering 100,000 events each of which has a given number of subscribers randomly chosen from the system. The number of subscribers varied from 2% to 80% of 1024 nodes per event. The results show that, as the number of subscribers increase, the hops and latency almost keep constant at 2.58 hops and 144ms, respectively. The bandwidth cost increases modestly, from 50.99 to 62.69 Bytes/node/event. However, the overhead drops significantly, from 1.36 to 0.02. The results show that Ferry could deliver events to a large number of nodes at very low overhead, involving only a small number of intermediate nodes by the synthesis of its message aggregation and PredRP algorithm.

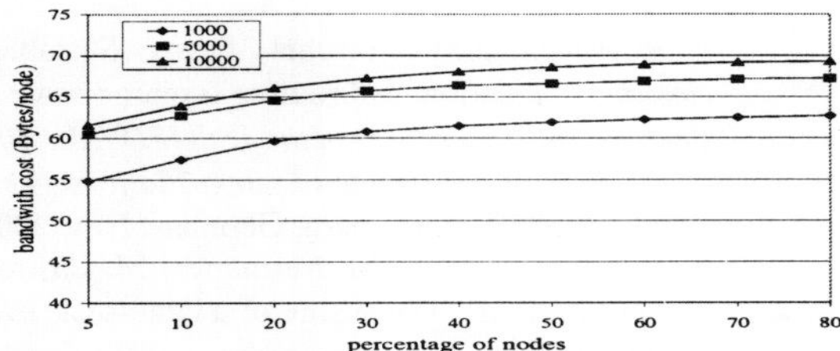

Figure 5. *bandwidth cost* for various network sizes with respect to different percentages of ndoes as subscribers.

We also investigated the performance of Ferry in various network sizes of 1000, 5000, and 10000 nodes. The simulated network of 5000 and 10000 were derived from the the 1024-DNS server measurements. For a give network size, we ran simulations for various percentages of nodes randomly chosen as subscribers (from 5% to 80%). We found the overhead is almost constant for various network sizes with respect to a given percentage of node as subscribers per event, from 0.86 to 0.02 when the number of subscribers varies from 5% to 80% of the system nodes. The number of hops taken by event delivery for network sizes of 1000, 5000, and 10000 are 2.58, 3.82 and 4.21, respectively. As the network size increases, the bandwidth cost incurred by event delivery increases modestly (as shown in Figure 5). This shows that Ferry can scale to a large number of nodes.

5. Conclusions and Future Work

Ferry is essentially a rendezvous network built on top of a DHT to support content-based pub/sub services/applications. Each application/service defines a unique scheme $S = \{A_1, A_2, ..., A_n\}$, and has at most n RP nodes (by hashing its attribute names). Subscriptions are routed to the RP nodes within $O(\log N)$ hops, while events are either directly sent to or routed to the RP nodes. Hence, events are guaranteed to meet all relevant subscriptions in the RP nodes. Ferry has several unique features: (1) Ferry exploits the embedded trees in a DHT to deliver events, thereby incurring little overhead; (2) the subscriptions are managed according to the entry of a RP node's routing table, thereby providing an efficient way to deliver events through aggregated messages; (3) event matching is performed only in the RP nodes (and their neighbor nodes if one-hop push is applied) by encapsulating the subscriber list in the event delivery messages; (4) its novel subscription installation algorithm, PredRP, can avoid sending redundant event delivery messages across the Chord ring space; (5) leveraging the fault-tolerance and self-organizing nature of DHTs, Ferry can reliably deliver events to subscribers and be fault-tolerant to node failures.

In Ferry, each node could be a RP node for some applications/services, and serve as the intermediate node to route events for other RP nodes. Hence, Ferry distributes the onus of event publication, event matching, and subscriptions across all nodes. Load balancing is based on the randomness guarantee of the consistent hashing function used in generating the RP nodes for different pub/sub applications/services (with different Ss). For a pub/sub scheme S with n attributes, the maximum number of RP nodes is n. All subscriptions of S will be stored in and all events will be routed to the n RP nodes. If the application/service corresponding to S is very popular, the subscriptions and events may overload the RP nodes. We therefore propose one-hop push to reduce the load of a RP node by moving part of its subscriptions to its finger table nodes. One-hop push may not work if a RP node's finger table nodes are all overloaded or not willing to take the load. Hence, we could adopt *attribute partitioning* [22] to address this issue. For example, consider a scheme S has an attribute $temperature$ and the value range for $temperature$ is $[0, 100]$. Without partitioning, there is only one RP node. If we partition $temperature$ into several continuous ranges, $[0, 25]$, $(25, 50]$, $(50, 75]$, and $(75, 100]$, we may create 4 RP nodes by hashing the attribute name with a range. Note that with partitioning, we need to adapt the RndRP, PredRP, and event publication algorithms accordingly. Due to space constraints, we do not present the adapted algorithms here. However, the adaptation is very straightforward and simple.

In event publication, an event can be either directly sent or routed (by Chord routing protocol) to the RP nodes. If the number of the RP nodes (which is determined by the number of attributes of a scheme S and also subscription/event partitioning (if applied)) is small, the event publishing node can directly send the event to the RP nodes (by caching the IP addresses of the RP nodes) for better performance. However, if the number of RP nodes is very large, e.g, tens or even hundreds, using point-to-point communication would be impractical and inefficient. This is actually a problem of how to efficiently deliver an event from the publishing node to a large number of RP nodes. Fortunately, Ferry's novel event delivery mechanism has already provided a solution for this problem, by envisioning the RP nodes as the subscribers of the event publishing node. Hence, Ferry can support a pub/sub scheme with a very large number of attributes.

This paper constitutes an initial step to build an efficient and scalable platform for content-based pub/sub. A number of issues need to be explored in our next steps. For instance, we will investigate the reduction of the DHT maintenance cost in terms of bandwidth by piggybacking the DHT link maintenance messages onto the event delivery messages. Another problem we will study is how cooperative P2P nodes have to be in Ferry (e.g., to provide incentive for nodes to cooperate in event delivery).

References

[1] M. K. Aguilera, R. E. Strom, D. C. Sturman, M. Astley, and T. D. Chandra. Matching events in a content-based subscription system. In *Proceedings of the 8th ACM Symposium on Principles of Distributed Computing (PODC)*, pages 53–61, Atlanta, GA, May 1999.

[2] G. Banavar, T. Chandra, B. Mukherjee, J. Nagarajarao, R. E. Strom, and D. C. Sturman. An efficient multicast protocol for content-based publish-subscribe systems. In *Proceedings of the 19th IEEE ICDCS*, pages 262–272, 1999.

[3] F. Cao and J. P. Singh. MEDYM: An architecture for content-based publish-subscribe networks. In *Proceedings of ACM SIGCOMM*, Portland, OG, Aug. 2004.

[4] A. Carzaniga, D. S. Rosenblum, and A. L. Wolf. Design and evaluation of a wide-area event notification service. *ACM Transactions on Computer Systems*, 19(3):332–383, 2001.

[5] A. Carzaniga, M. J. Rutherford, and A. L. Wolf. A routing scheme for content-based networking. In *Proceedings of IEEE INFOCOM*, Hongkong, China, Mar. 2004.

[6] A. Carzaniga and A. L. Wolf. Forwarding in a content-based network. In *Proceedings of ACM SIGCOMM*, pages 163–174, Karlsruhe, Germany, Aug. 2003.

[7] Y. Choi, K. Park, and D. Park. Homed: A peer-to-peer overlay architecture for large-scale content-based publish/subscribe systems. In *Proceedings of the third International Workshop on Distributed Event-Based Systems (DEBS)*, pages 20–25, Edinburgh, Scotland, UK, May 2004.

[8] F. Dabek, J. Li, E. Sit, J. Robertson, M. F. Kaashoek, and R. Morris. Designing a DHT for low latency and high throughput. In *Proceeding of the First Symposium on Networked Systems Design and Implementation (NSDI)*, pages 85–98, San Francisco, CA, Mar. 2004.

[9] F. Fabret, H. A. Jacobsen, F. Llirbat, J. Pereira, K. A. Ross, and D. Shasha. Filtering algorithms and implementation for very fast publish/subscribe systems. In *Proceedings of the 2001 ACM SIGMOD*, volume 30, pages 115–126, Santa Barbara,CA, 2001.

[10] K. P. Gummadi, S. Saroiu, and S. D. Gribble. King: Estimating latency between arbitrary internet end hosts. In *Proceedings of the 2002 SIGCOMM Internet Measurement Workshop*, Marseille, France, Nov. 2002.

[11] A. Gupta, O. D. Sahin, D. Agrawal, and A. E. Abbadi. Meghdoot: Content-based publish/subscribe over p2p networks. In *ACM/IFIP/USENIX 5th International Middleware Conference*, Toronto, Ontario, Canada, Oct. 2004.

[12] G. Perng, C. Wang, and M. K. Reiter. Providing content-based services in a peer-to-peer environment. In *Proceedings of the third International Workshop on Distributed Event-Based Systems (DEBS)*, pages 74–79, Edinburgh, Scotland, UK, May 2004.

[13] P. R. Pietzuch and J. Bacon. Peer-to-peer overlay broker networks in an event-based middleware. In *Proceedings of the Second International Workshop on Distributed Event-Based Systems (DEBS)*, San Diego, CA, June 2003.

[14] S. Ratnasamy, P. Francis, M. Handley, R. Karp, and Shenker. A scalable content-addressable network. In *Proceedings of ACM SIGCOMM*, pages 161–172, San Diego, CA, Aug. 2001.

[15] A. Rowstron and P. Druschel. Pastry: Scalable, decentralized object location, and routing for large-scale peer-to-peer systems. In *Proceedings of the 18th IFIP/ACM International Conference on Distributed System Platforms (Middleware)*, pages 329–350, Heidelberg, Germany, Nov. 2001.

[16] A. I. T. Rowstron, A.-M. Kermarrec, M. Castro, and P. Druschel. SCRIBE: The design of a large-scale event notification infrastructure. In *Proceedings of the 3rd International Networked Group Communication*, pages 30–43, 2001.

[17] I. Stoica, R. Morris, D. Karger, M. Kaashoek, and H. Balakrishnan. Chord: A scalable peer-to-peer lookup service for internet applications. In *Proceedings of ACM SIGCOMM*, pages 149–160, San Diego, CA, Aug. 2001.

[18] D. Tam, R. Azimi, and H.-A. Jacobsen. Building content-based publish/subscribe systems with distributed hash tables. In *Proceedings of the International Workshop on Databases, Information Systems and Peer-to-Peer Computing*, Berlin,Germany, Sept. 2003.

[19] W. W. Terpstra, S. Behnel, L. Fiege, A. Zeidler, and A. P. Buchmann. A peer-to-peer approach to content-based publish/subscribe. In *Proceedings of the Second International Workshop on Distributed Event-Based Systems (DEBS)*, San Diego, CA, June 2003.

[20] P. Triantafillou and I. Aekaterinidis. Content-based publish-subscribe over structured P2P networks. In *Proceedings of the third International Workshop on Distributed Event-Based Systems (DEBS)*, pages 104–109, Edinburgh, Scotland, UK, May 2004.

[21] P. Triantafillou and A. Economides. Subscription summarization: A new paradigm for efficient publish/subscribe systems. In *Proceedings of the 24th IEEE ICDCS*, 2004.

[22] Y.-M. Wang, L. Qiu, D. Achlioptas, G. Das, P. Larson, and H. J. Wang. Subscription partitioning and routing in content-based publish/subscribe systems. In *Proceedings of the 16th International Symposium on Distributed Computing (DISC)*, Toulouse, France, Oct. 2002.

[23] B. Y. Zhao, J. D. Kubiatowicz, and A. D. Joseph. Tapestry: An infrastructure for fault-tolerance wide-area location and routing. Technical Report UCB/CSD-01-1141, Computer Science Division, University of California, Berkeley, Apr. 2001.

[24] Y. Zhu and Y. Hu. Ferry: An architecture for content-based publish/subscribe services on p2p networks. Technical report, Department of ECECS, University of Cincinnati, Oct. 2004.

[25] S. Q. Zhuang, B. Y. Zhao, A. D. Joseph, R. H. Katz, and J. Kubiatowicz. Bayeux: An architecture for scalable and fault-tolerant wide-area data dissemination. In *Proceedings of the Eleventh International Workshop on Network and Operating System Support for Digital Audio and Video (NOSSDAV)*, June 2001.

Distributed Access Control in CROWN Groups

Jinpeng Huai, Yu Zhang, Xianxian Li
Dept. of Computer Science and Technology
Beihang University
Beijing, 100083, P.R.China
huaijp@buaa.edu.cn

Yunhao Liu
Dept. of Computer Science
Hong Kong Univ. of Science and Technology
Clearwater Bay, Kowloon, Hong Kong
liu@cs.ust.hk

Abstract

Security in collaborative groups is an active research topic and has been recognized by many organizations in the past few years. In this paper, we propose a fine-grained and attribute-based access control framework for our key project, CROWN grid. To avoid single point of failure and enhance scalability of the system, we employ a distributed delegation authorization mechanism. We successfully implement our proposed access control in CROWN grid, and evaluate this approach by comprehensive experiments.

Keywords: CROWN group, attribute-based access control, distributed delegation authorization, voting

1. Introduction

The emergence of decentralized and dynamic cooperative applications has recently gained significant attention due to its great potential for sharing a huge amount of resources with millions of users over a wide-area network [6, 7, 9, 15, 20, 21]. A large class of applications including file sharing, grid computing, multi-party conferencing, Internet e-commerce, benefit from a cooperative infrastructure. Collaborative settings may be synchronous or asynchronous, and communication models vary from one-to-many, few-to-many, to any-to-any.

In a complex grid environment, with the rapid growth of cooperation, dynamic peers join/leave and therefore the evolvement of the mesh network is free and uncontrolled. It is of great importance for multiple self-organizing peers with a common set of services aggregated in a controlled manner to accomplish their collective goals. The concept of collaborative peer groups [2, 8, 26] is introduced to refer to such cooperation applications.

The research described in this paper is part of a larger project known as CROWN (**C**hina **R&D** **E**nvironment **O**ver **W**ide-area **N**etwork) [12]. Started in late 2003, CROWN aims to empower in-depth integration of resources and cooperation of researchers nationwide and worldwide. As illustrated in Fig.1, a number of universities and institutes, such as THU (Tsinghua University), PKU (Peking University), CAS (China Academy of Sciences) and BHU (Beihang University) across several cities in China have joined CROWN. Through the Computer Network Information Centre of CAS, CROWN is connected to several popular grid systems including GLORIAD and PRAGMA. Lots of applications in different domains have been deployed into CROWN grid, such as gene comparison in bioinformatics, climate pattern prediction for environment monitoring, etc. The main research objective in this paper is to group home user resources with a robust, scalable, and secure grid middleware infrastructure in a distributed manner.

Consider the following scenario in the CROWN system. Multiple peers from THU, BHU, and CAS, are jointly working on an Air Pollution Monitoring project. These peers construct an APMGroup to share documents and resources. Usually, all peers first negotiate a Collaborative Policy Instance (CPI) to satisfy multiple peers' security requirements. Here we assume the existence of CPI, and the policy negotiation details [22, 28] are beyond the scope of this paper. Four roles are defined in APMGroup, *group authority*, *group member*, *director*, and *researcher*. If a BHU student would like to join the group, the CPI requires at least 40% votes from existing group members, and more than half of those votes must be *yes*. Additionally, large amounts of sensitive experiment data should be stored in a stand alone peer, and the data must be unable to be modified by one single researcher in the group. Thus, an access control framework is needed.

This work was partially supported by Hong Kong RGC DAG 04/05.EG01, NSFC 90412011.

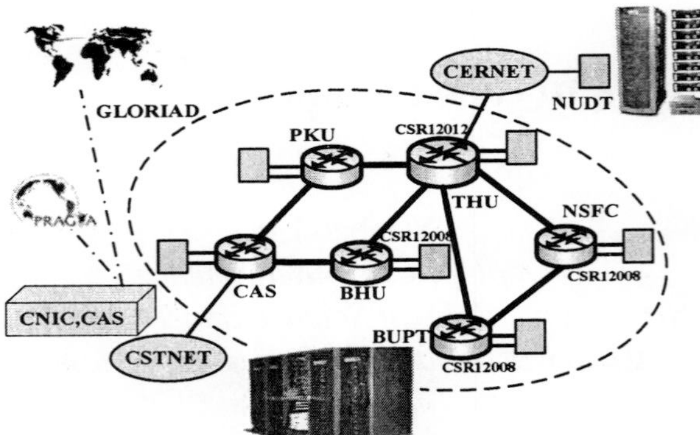

Figure 1. Overview of CROWN Grid

Security in collaborative groups is an active research topic and has been recognized by many organizations in the past few years. Most existing group access control mechanisms adapt centralized architecture, and authorization decisions are made based on requester identities [13]. In a distributed collaborative environment such as CROWN, peers are often dynamic and unknown to each other, which makes centralized and identity based access control less effective. Some trust management systems, granting certain permissions to the subject using credential chains, fail to support distributed environments [5].

In this paper we propose a fine-grained and attribute-based access control framework for CROWN groups. The policy model extends the role-based trust management language RT [16-18] to satisfy security requirements of the CROWN grid. The major contributions of this work are as follows:

1. To avoid single point of failure and enhance scalability of the system, instead of using a centralized model [13], we employ a distributed delegation authorization mechanism. Multiple authorities could exist in this design, reducing both the overhead and the response time of CROWN group authority.

2. Existing approaches fail to deal with the dynamics of the peers. Worse, peers are often unknown to each other, making identity-based approaches ineffective. Our framework addresses the two issues by employing an attribute-based approach. A voting mechanism is also introduced into accepting new members and granting permissions.

3. Sensitive experiment data generated during the collaboration should not be unilaterally modified by any single user. Our framework provides a secure cooperative process for multiple peers.

4. We successfully implement our distributed access control mechanism in CROWN grid. We introduce our implementation experiences and experimental results.

The rest of this paper is organized as follows. Section 2 introduces related work. Section 3 discusses the access control policy model in CROWN groups. We present a formal joint authorization protocol in Section 4. Section 5 describes a secure cooperation process. Section 6 presents performance evaluations. We conclude this work in Section 7.

2. Related work

Many approaches have been taken on security issues in collaborative environments [10, 11, 13, 14, 19, 25, 29]. Gothic [13] provides a security service for IP-Multicast, which considers receiver access control. It employs an external access control server providing authentication and authorization based on PKI certificates. Antigone [10] includes a flexible policy framework for secure group communication and defines policies about re-keying, membership, and application messages. Antigone employs a centralized access control approach in which member access is mediated by a so called Session Leader. However, it is not designed for Grid and P2P systems.

Sconce [14, 25] presents an admission control framework on Gnutella like P2Ps [1]. It proposed three types of admission policy, including access control list APT_ACL, a centralized authority APT_GAUTH, and group members APT_GROUP. A group membership certificate can be issued to a peer under multi-voting schemes. However, Sconce treats peer groups as a flat structure without hierarchy where all peering nodes have identical responsibilities. Lacking the attribute of peers, it cannot simplify authorization in collaborative environments, and is not scalable.

JXTA [2, 8], an open-source project initiated by SUN, recently proposed a security mechanism based on PKI certificate [4]. Intergroup [3] provides access control using an authorization service called Akenti [27], which relies on X.509 identity certificate. All group members register with the authorization service off-line to obtain a membership certificate signed by the Akenti Server. Intergroup provides a coarse granularity for access control.

Spread [19] introduces roles into group. It is a hierarchical client-server architecture where an expensive distributed protocol runs among a set of servers, providing services to the clients. It does not discuss distributed authorization in detail.

Our work focuses on a decentralized model in grid collaborative systems. It is a distributed delegation authorization mechanism. By considering joint authorization and secure cooperation under voting schemes, security for communication and sharing of sensitive data among grouped peers are provided.

3. Access control design overview

In this section, we first introduce roles and permissions in CROWN groups, and then form the access control policy model. An instance is given to illustrate the model.

3.1. Roles and permissions

Many sensitive operations and services need access control [10, 19]. For example, CROWN group has following sensitive services.

- Group Creation Service: to allow a peer to create a CROWN group;
- Content Publishment Service: to allow a peer to publish content within the group;
- Rendezvous Service: to allow a peer to act as a rendezvous within the group;
- Policy Negotiation Service: to allow a peer to negotiate security policy with other peers.

Here we define two kinds of roles: *group role* and *application role*. Group roles are predefined by CROWN groups, and application roles are defined according to different collaborations. Multiple different authority peers may exist in each group, so that the overhead of group authority could be balanced. Group authorities may create or modify group policy template, create or destruct group, and accept or reject new members, etc. Group members may negotiate/modify the group policy, join/leave a group, send/receive messages, and negotiate/access the group key, etc.

3.2. Access control policy model

Before access control is implemented, peers need to be authenticated. General authentication mechanisms include username/password, Kerberos [24], and X.509 [27]. Since peers are often dynamic and unknown to each other , our framework adopts credential in trust management [5, 17] as authentication method. Additionally, what permissions a peer is allowed to carry out depends on the roles and environment factors [23]. To satisfy diverse environments, we introduce the notion of contexts. Group contexts consist of a set of name/value pairs, providing environmental information such as current time and group state.

We propose an access control policy model for grid collaborative systems, which defines the relations of roles and permissions, introduces six credentials from RT, and describes admission and removal policy of roles. Elements of access policy model are as follows.

(1) *C*: Context, defines group contexts, which include variables and their values.

(2) *OBJ*: Object Set, $OBJ=\{obj_1, obj_2, \cdots, obj_n\}$.

(3) *OP*: Operation Set, $OP=\{op_1, op_2, \cdots, op_n\}$.

(4) *P*: Permission Set, $P=OP\times OBJ\times C$, that is, $P=\{<op_i, obj_i, c_i> \mid op_i\in OP, obj_i\in OBJ, c_i\in C\}$.

(5) *RoleTerm*: It is defined as $A.r(h_1, \cdots, h_n)$, where A is entity name(optional), r is role name. A *RoleTerm* may include zero or more restriction parameters h_i. For example, a student of BHU registered after the year of 2000 could be described as BHU.student(since=2000).

(6) *R*: *RoleTerm* Set, $R=SR \cup AR$. *SR* and *AR* are all *RoleTerm* Set, and *SR* is group roles set, while *AR* is application roles set.

(7) *PA*: Relations of *R* and *P*, $PA\subseteq R\times P$.

(8) *Credential*: Our system introduces six kinds of *Credential* from RT [17], each *Credential* has a head part and body part as follows (R_i is *RoleTerm*, *D* is entity).

- $R\leftarrow D$: The body part consists of a simple entity *D*, which means *D* is the member of *R*.
- $R\leftarrow R_1$: The body part consists of a *RoleItem* R_1, which means the principal set of R contains the principal set of R_1.
- $R\leftarrow R_1 \cap\cdots\cap R_k$: The body part consists of an Intersection element, which means the principal set of R contains the principal set of $R_1 \cap\cdots\cap R_k$.
- $R\leftarrow R_1.R_2$: The body part consists of a LinkRole element, which means the principal set of R contains the principal set of $K_B.R_2$, in which K_B is the member of R_1. If R_1 is a manifold role, that is, $\{K_{B_1}, \cdots, K_{B_k}\}$ is the member of R_1, then the principal set of R contains the principal set of $K_{B_1}.R_2\cap\cdots\cap K_{B_k}.R_2$.
- $R\leftarrow R_1 \odot\cdots\odot R_k$: The body part consists of Product element, which means the principal p is the member of R and $p=p_1\cup\cdots\cup p_k$. p_j is the member of R_j.
- $R\leftarrow R_1 \otimes\cdots\otimes R_k$: The body part consists of ExclusiveProduct element, which means the principal p is the member of R and $p=p_1\cup\cdots\cup p_k$. p_j is the member of R_j, especially for each $i\neq j$, $p_i \cap p_j = \varnothing$.

(9) *AP*: Access Policy, each statement has the form of < *ar*, *c*, *vote*>, where *ar* is access rule and similar to *credential*, *c* is group context variable. When a peer requests the role of *ar*'s head part, all policy statements are checked one by one until one of them approve the access. *vote* has one of the following forms:

- *true: vote* is always *true*.
- *fixed* (*r*, *m*, *f*): A voting is called among members of the *r* role. If *k* votes are received and $f\times k$ are yes, then *vote* is *true*(m, $k\in$ integer; $k\geq$m; $f\in[0,1]$).
- *dynamic* (r, f_1, f_2): This is equivalent to *fixed*(r, $m=n\times f_1$, f_2), where the role r has n members(m, $k\in$ integer; $f_1, f_2\in$ [0,1]) .

(10) *RP*: Remove Policy, each statement has the form

< *r*, *c*, *vote*>, in which *r* is role, *c* is context variables. If *c* and *vote* are *true*, then a peer can be removed from the role.

3.3. Collaboration policy instance

According to the above access control policy model, the kernel parts of APMGroup policy is depicted in Table 1.

Table 1. Collaborative policy instance

GroupName: *APMGroup*
C: *day* $\in$ *{MON, ⋯, SUN}*
R: *{group authority, group member, director, researcher}*
PA: *group authority: <create, APMGroup, true> <modify, CPI, true>*
group member: <join, APMGroup, true> <receive, content, true> <access, group key, true>
researcher: <issue, content, true>
director: <update, sensitive data, day=FRI>
AP *:group authority* $\leftarrow$ K_{BHU}*.projectleader, true, true*
group member $\leftarrow$ K_{BHU}*.student(since=2000), true, vote (group member, 0.4, 0.5)*
researcher $\leftarrow$ K_{THU}*.teacher, true, true*
researcher $\leftarrow$ K_{CAS}*.master, true, true*
director $\leftarrow$ *researcher* $\otimes$ *researcher, true, true*
RP: *researcher, true, vote (group authority,2,1)*

The APMGroup defines two application roles, namely *director* and *researcher*. For example, the teacher of THU could apply for the researcher role in APMGroup, which is denoted as *researcher* $\leftarrow$ K_{THU}*.teacher, true, true.* The director role constructed by two different researchers of CROWN group is a manifold role and may update the sensitive data on a given day, such as Friday.

4. Joint authorization

In a distributed environment, peers wish to manage group security by themselves without appealing to a central server or CAs. Joint authorization by multiple peers under voting schemes could satisfy this requirement. Table 2 summarizes the notions used in the rest of this paper.

In the previous example, *group member* $\leftarrow$$K_{BHU}$*.student(since=2000), true, vote (group member, 0.4, 0.5)* represents an event that a BHU student registered after year 2000 is requesting to join the group, and a vote is called among peers. If at least 40% votes are received and half of those votes are *yes*, the requester is allowed to join the group. Specifically, the joint authorization protocol has five phases, which are *group initialization*, *searching group advertisement*, *authorization request*, *voting*, and *CGC issuance*.

Table 2. Notion summary

GA	group authority
M_i	the ith peer within CROWN group
OC_i	organization credential of M_i
CGC_i	CROWN group credential of M_i
SK_i, PK_i	M_i's secret and public keys
$S_i(x)$	signature of message x with SK_i
ID_i	The Peer ID is the fingerprint hash of the CGC_i's public key

1) Group Initialization: The group authority peer initializes the local secure environment by creating a secure CROWN group, and then inserts the secure group advertisement including CPI into the network. The CPI contains the access control policy of CROWN groups and various parameters such as group name, voting type, etc.

2) Searching Group Advertisement: When a new peer wants to join the group, it must obtain the advertisement of its attributive CROWN group first. In this design peers have two ways to get this information. (1) Via some rendezvous points. A rendezvous point could be a special peer which keeps information about the groups, or it could be a public website. (2) To flood a query into the grid system, and get response from other peers.

3) Authorization Request (Step 1 in Fig.2): Having the advertisement message, a new peer may connect with the corresponding authority peer. The new node should provide the related credential OC_{new}, which is obtained offline from its organization. For example, the credential of *YuChu* who is a student of BHU is K_{BHU}*.student*$\leftarrow$*YuChu.* Then the M_{new} will generate a CGC_{new} issuance request containing OC_{new} information about the new node and its desired privileges.

$$M_{new} \rightarrow GA: Role\_REQ,\ S_{new}(Role\_REQ),\ OC_{new}$$

4) Voting (Step 2, 3 in Fig.2): Upon receipt of the authorization request, the authority peer first verifies the signature. In a fully distributed CROWN group, the request is either accepted or rejected by the collective set of current members. The authority peer then propagates the request to call a vote. According to the CPI, multiple peers authenticate the attribute of a requester, vote, and reply with a signed message to approve or reject the authorization request.

$$GA \rightarrow M: Role\_REQ,\ S_{new}(Role\_REQ),\ OC_{new}$$
$$GA \leftarrow M: vote_i,\ CGC_i\ (vote_i = (RES)^{SK_i} \bmod n_i)$$

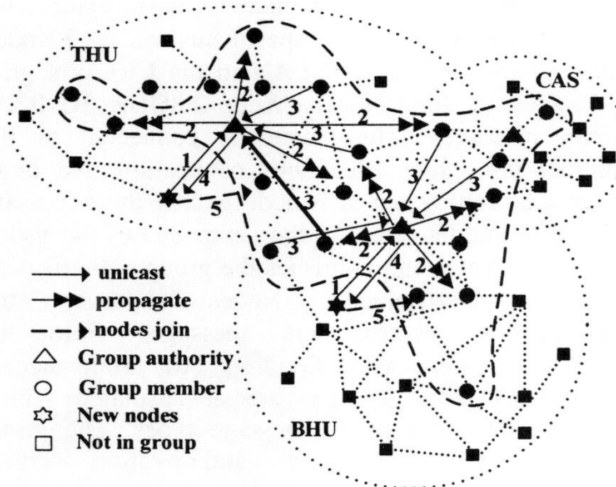

Figure 2. Joint authorization under voting (1 authorization request, 2 propagate request, 3 multiple peers vote, 4 credential issuance, 5 new peer join)

5) CGC Issuance (Step 4, 5 in Fig.2): Once sufficient votes are collected, GA verifies all the votes, and determine whether to accept the new node as a member or not. If the requester is qualified, the authority peer will issue the CGC_{new} to it and update the related CROWN group information. Having the CGC_{new} , the new node can join the secure CROWN group.

$$M_{new} \leftarrow GA: CGC_{new}$$

5. Secure cooperation

Large sensitive data shared by multiple peers will be generated during the whole life cycle of collaboration and should not be modified by any single user. Such resources are usually stored in a stand alone peer. In the APMGroup scenario, the director constructed by two different researcher of the APMGroup is a manifold role and may update the sensitive data on Friday. The policy is described as:

director:<update, sensitive data, day=FRI>
director←researcher ⊗ researcher, true, true

The secure cooperation progress of multiple peers is as follow.

1) Cooperation Request: When a researcher in the APMGroup wants to update the sensitive resource R, it propagates the cooperation request to all researchers.

$$M_{initiator} \rightarrow M_i\text{: } updateR\_REQ, S_{initiator}(updater\_REQ), CGC_{initiator}$$

2) Cooperation Response: Once the request is received, the peers verify the signature, and then the request is either accepted or rejected by the set of current researchers.

$$M_{initiator} \leftarrow M_i\text{: } res_i, CGC_i$$

$$(res_i=(updateR\_RES)^{SK_i} \bmod n)$$

3) Cooperation Implementation: Once enough signed responses are collected, the initiator sends all the signed messages to a stand alone peer M_{server} where sensitive data is stored in. The stand alone peer will approve or reject the request according to the CPI.

$$M_{initiator} \rightarrow M_{server}\text{: } updateR\_REQ, S_{initiator}(updateR\_REQ), CGC_{initiator}, \{(res_1, \cdots, res_t), (CGC_1, \cdots, CGC_t)\}$$

6. Performance evaluation

6.1. CROWN group architecture

We implement the distributed access control in CROWN systems using Java programming language. The cooperation facility among peers is provided by CROWN grid, a fully decentralized grid middleware infrastructure, whose functionalities include file sharing, auctions, distributed computing, and event subscription and publishing.

The system has a three–layer architecture. The bottom layer is the core of CROWN groups. It has building blocks to enable key mechanisms for cooperation applications, including transport, the creation of CROWN groups, and associated security primitives.

Our scheme is implemented in the middle layer, which is built on top of the communication middleware, including security and network services. Examples of network services include searching and indexing, peer discovery, protocol translation, etc. There are three dominant security requirements in CROWN grid systems: confidentiality, integrity, and availability. They actually include functionalities such as authentication, access control, encryption, secure communication, non-repudiation, membership, and group key management. The sequence diagram for CROWN group service design is illustrated in Fig.3.

Generally, to use a service, a peer must present its credential to service providers. We use XML to represent both access control policy and credentials. The credential has the form (issuer ID, owner ID, attribute, issue time, expiration date, peer signature). The credential is signed by the issuer. Delegation credentials should have a short enough lifetime that they are revoked automatically when they expire. Li [16] presents a type system about credentials storage together with algorithms, which ensures chains can be found among distributed credentials storage. The techniques developed in [16] can be used in the CROWN group.

The other component that deserves some words in the middle layer is the policy engine, which acts as the central agent, checking for conformance to the security

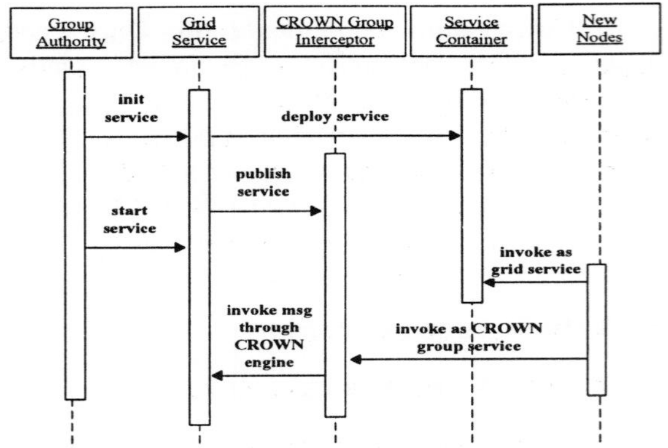

Figure 3. Sequence diagram for CROWN group service

policy. All interpretation of policy occurs within the policy engine, so that multiple policy approaches can be integrated. The enforcement of authentication and access control is performed by the policy engine. Each service is protected by policy. For example, a membership service consults the policy engine when a new node attempts to join the CROWN group. The policy stating the requirements to gain access to the group (i.e., the group contexts and credentials) are stated in the authentication and access control rules, such as *group member* $\leftarrow$ K_{BHU}*.student(since=2000), true, vote* (*group member, 0.4, 0.5*).

Access control policy infrastructures are evolving with the complex environments that they support. Context is used by policy to allow environmental factors to influence how and when policy is enforced. In a grid environment, a context handler mainly collects such information including message context, resource context, and group context, etc.

6.2. Implementation environment

Our proposed access control model is employed by the CROWN grid. To evaluate its performance, we conduct comprehensive experiments on a 32-node cluster with a high-speed LAN in the CROWN grid. All nodes are Intel Nocona Xeon 2.8GHz, 2G RAM Linux machines. The cluster is connected to the Internet through a 100M bps connection. No other tasks are running on each node except the necessary CROWN middleware. As the setup phase, the group authority creates and publishes the group authorization service advertisement. Nodes discover the authorization advertisement messages from the rendezvous peer or by flooding. All group access control protocol messages are encapsulated within standard CROWN group message types. The group authority will refresh the authorization service advertisement after delegating the authority attribute to another group member.

6.3. Experiment results and analysis

6.3.1. Efficiency for concurrent requests

In our first set of experiments, we implement secure CROWN group consisting of 40 members. The access control policy of each node is configured by using XML. We let several new nodes send joint requests concurrently. To better evaluate the CROWN group, we also implement a Gothic [13] like approach , and compare its performance with our design in the prototype system.

In Figures 4, 5 and 6, we plot the accumulated joining ratio against time. There are four curves in the three figures with each represent a different request size, ranging from 10 to 40. Figure 4 plots a Gothic like approach, while Fig. 5 and Fig. 6 adopt our design, having two and three group authorities respectively.

We contrast their performances with 40 new nodes in Fig. 7. We can see that after 20 seconds, the success joining ratios vary from 12.5% for a centralized scheme, 50% for two authorities, to 75% for three auth orities. Figures 8 and 9 show the average joining time

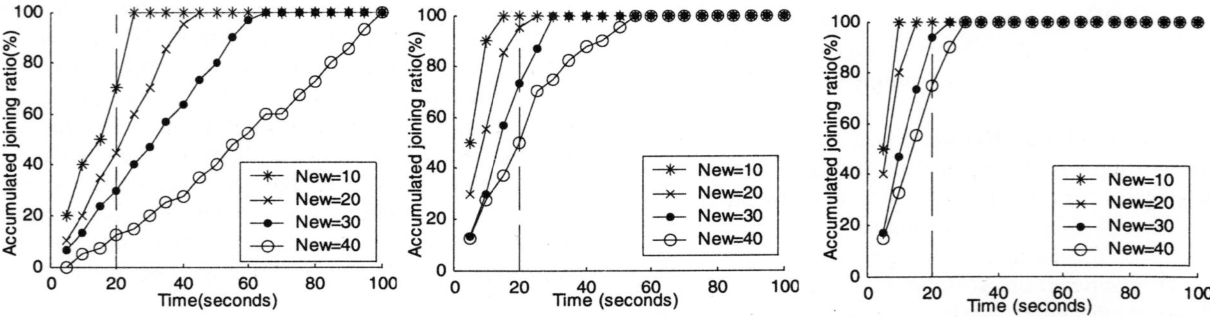

Figure 4. Success ratio in centralized authority

Figure 5. Success ratio in two group authority

Figure 6. Success ratio in three group authority

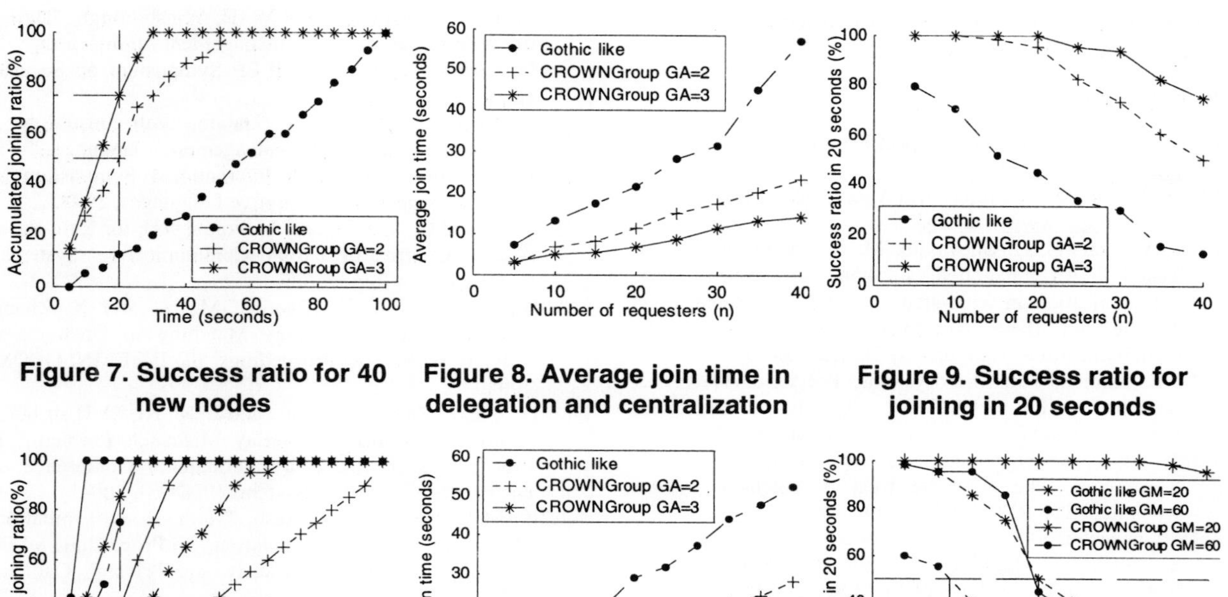

Figure 7. Success ratio for 40 new nodes

Figure 8. Average join time in delegation and centralization

Figure 9. Success ratio for joining in 20 seconds

Figure 10. Success ratio for dynamic group members

Figure 11. Average join time for dynamic group members

Figure 12. Success ratio for dynamic threshold

and the success joining ratio of the CROWN group and the Gothic like scheme by varying the number of concurrent requesters. Clearly, the efficiency of peers concurrently joining is significantly improved by our approach.

6.3.2. Impact of group size and vote threshold

We vary the number of group members from 10 to 100 and plot the accumulated joining ratio versus time in Fig. 10. With a larger group, it takes longer time for new nodes to join. We further show the average joining cost for 20 new nodes when the group size is ranging from 20 to 100 in Fig.11. From both figures we can see our delegation authorization approach provides an effective mechanism to improve the efficiency of a CROWN group, and control the overhead of the group authorities.

We then explore the impact of the vote threshold to the system performance. Figure 12 plots the joining ratio in 20 seconds when 20 new nodes would like to join. In Fig. 12, x-axis represents the vote threshold, and y-axis represents the joining ratio. We can see a CROWN group is more flexible and efficient. For example, as illustrated in Fig. 12, if we want to have half of the new nodes join the group within 20 seconds, the vote threshold must be less than 24% for a Gothic like approach, while it could be 50% for our CROWN group.

7. Conclusion and future work

Our key project, CROWN, holds the main goal to empower integration of resources and co-operation of researchers. To meet security requirements of CROWN, we propose a fine-grained and attribute-based access control framework which extends the role-based trust management language. Our approach employs a distributed delegation authorization mechanism to avoid single point of failure. In order to simplify authorization and access control in collaborations, decisions are made based on authenticated attributes of the peers, which improve flexibility of the system. Furthermore, large sensitive data generated during the collaborations are shared and protected.

This design has been successfully implemented in the CROWN grid environment. We evaluate our proposed approach by comprehensive experiments. We believe that wide deployment of the CROWN group will benefit many grid systems.

Future work leads into investigating trust management in our CROWN group to reduce the spread of malicious content so as to assure reliability as well as availability of services.

8. References

[1]The Gnutella protocol specification 0.6, http://rfc-gnutella.sourceforge.net.

[2]Sun Microsystems Project JXTA v2.0: Java Programmer's Guide, http://www.jxta.org/.

[3]D. A. Agarwal, O. Chevassut, M. R. Thompson, and G. Tsudik, "An integrated solution for secure group communication in wide-area networks," in Proceedings of the 6th IEEE Symposium on Computers and Communications, Hammamet, Tunisia, 2001.

[4]J. E. Altman, Sun Microsystems, Project JXTA : PKI Security for JXTA Overly Networks, http://www.jxta.org/docs/pki-security-for-jxta.pdf.

[5]M. Blaze, J. Feigenbaum, J. Ioannidis, and A. D. Keromytis, "The KeyNote trust management system version2, IETF RFC 2704," 1999.

[6]Y. Chawathe, S. Ratnasamy, L. Breslau, N. Lanham, and S. Shenker, "Making Gnutella-like P2P Systems Scalable," in Proceedings of ACM SIGCOMM, 2003.

[7]I. Foster and A. Iamnitchi, "On Death, Taxes, and the Convergence of Peer-to-Peer and Grid Computing," in Proceedings of the Second International Workshop on Peer-to-Peer Systems (IPTPS), 2003.

[8]L. Gong, Project JXTA: A Technology Overview, http://www.jxta.org/project/www/docs/TechOverview.pdf.

[9]L. Guo, S. Chen, S. Ren, X. Chen, and S. Jiang, "PROP: a Scalable and Reliable P2P Assisted Proxy Streaming System," in Proceedings of the 24th International Conference on Distributed Computing Systems (ICDCS), 2004.

[10]H. Harney, A. Colegrove, and P. McDaniel, "Principles of policy in secure groups," in Proceedings of Network and Distributed Systems Security, San Diego, CA, 2001.

[11]W. Hong, M. Lim, E. Kim, J. Lee, and H. Park, "GAIS: Grid Advanced Information Service based on P2P Mechanism," in Proceedings of the 13th IEEE International Symposium on High Performance Distributed Computing (HPDC-13), 2004.

[12]J. Huai, Y. Liu, X. Li, and C. Hu, "Early Experiences with CROWN Grid," *Technical Report, School of Computer Science,Beihang University*, 2005.

[13]P. Judge and M. Ammar, "Gothic: A group access control architecture for secure multicast and anycast," in Proceedings of INFOCOM, 2002.

[14]Y. Kim, D. Mazzocchi, and G. Tsudik, "Admission control in peer groups," in Proceedings of IEEE International Symposium on Network Computing and Applications (NCA), 2003.

[15]D. Li, X. Lu, and J. Wu, "Fission E: A Scalable Constant Degree and Low Congestion DHT Scheme Based on Kautz Graph," in Proceedings of IEEE INFOCOM, 2005.

[16]N. Li, W. H. Winsborough, and J. C. Mitchell, "Distributed Credential Chain Discovery in Trust Management," in Proceedings of the 8th ACM Conference on Computer and Communications Security, 2001.

[17]N. Li, J. C. Mitchell, and W. H. Winsborough, "Design of a role-based trust management framework," in Proceedings of the 2002 IEEE Symposium on Security and Privacy, 2002.

[18]N. Li and J. C. Mitchell, "Datalog with constraints: A foundation for trust management languages," in Proceedings of the 15th International Symposium on Practical Aspects of Declarative Languages, 2003.

[19]N. Li and C. Nita-Rotaru, "A Framework for Role-Based Access Control in Group Communication Systems," CERIAS Tech Report 2003.

[20]Y. Liu, X. Liu, L. Xiao, L. M. Ni, and X. Zhang, "Location-Aware Topology Matching in Unstructured P2P Systems," in Proceedings of IEEE INFOCOM, 2004.

[21]Y. Liu, Z. Zhuang, L. Xiao, and L. M. Ni, "A Distributed Approach to Solving Overlay Mismatch Problem," in Proceedings of the 24th International Conference on Distributed Computing Systems (ICDCS), 2004.

[22]P. McDaniel and A. Prakash, "Methods and Limitations of Security Policy Reconciliation," in Proceedings of the IEEE Symposium on Security and Privacy, Oakland, California, USA, 2002.

[23]P. McDaniel, "On Context in Authorization Policy," in Proceedings of the 8th ACM Symposium on Access Control Models and Technologies (SACMAT), Como, Italy, 2003.

[24]B. C. Neuman and T. Ts'o, "Kerberos: An authentication service for computer networks," in *IEEE Communications Magazine*, 1994, pp. 33-38.

[25]N. Saxena, G. Tsudik, and J. H. Yi, "Admission Control in Peer-to-Peer:Design and Performance Evaluation," in Proceedings of ACM Workshop on Security of Ad Hoc and Sensor Networks (SASN), Virginia USA, 2003.

[26]V. Sunderam, J. Pascoe, and R. Loader, "Towards a Framework for Collaborative Peer Groups," in Proceedings of the Third IEEE/ACM International Symposium on Cluster Computing and the Grid (CCGRID), 2003.

[27]M. R. Thompson, A. Essiari, and S. Mudumbai, "Certificate-based authorization policy in a PKI environment," *ACM Transactions on Infomation and System Security*, 2003.

[28]V.D.Gligor, H. Khurana, R. Koleva, V. Bharadwaj, and J. Baras, "On the Negotiation of Access Control Policies," in Proceedings of the 9th Security Protocols Workshop, Cambridge, UK, 2001.

[29]L. Xiao, Z. Xu, and X. Zhang, "Low-cost and Reliable Mutual Anonymity Protocols in Peer-to-Peer Networks," *IEEE Transactions on Parallel and Distributed Systems*, 2003.

A peer-to-peer replica magement service for high-throughput Grids

Antony Chazapis, Antonis Zissimos and Nectarios Koziris
National Technical University of Athens
School of Electrical and Computer Engineering
Computing Systems Laboratory
e-mail: {chazapis, azisi, nkoziris}@cslab.ece.ntua.gr

Abstract

Future high-throughput Grids may integrate millions or even billions of processing and data storage nodes. Services provided by the underlying Grid infrastructure may have to be able to scale to capacities not even imaginable today. In this paper we concentrate on one of the core components of the Data Grid architecture - the Replica Location Service - and evaluate a redesign of the system based on a structured peer-to-peer network overlay. We argue that the architecture of the currently most widespread solution for file replica location on the Grid, is biased towards high-performance deployments and can not scale to the future needs of a global Grid. Structured peer-to-peer systems can provide the same functionality, while being much more manageable, scalable and fault-tolerant. However, they are only capable of storing read-only data. To this end, we propose a revised protocol for Distributed Hash Tables that allows data to be changed in a distributed and scalable fashion. Results from a prototype implementation of the system suggest that Grids can truly benefit from the scalability and fault-tolerance properties of such peer-to-peer algorithms.

1 Introduction

The Grid is a wide-area, large-scale distributed computing system, in which remotely located, disjoint and diverse processing and data storage facilities are integrated under a common service-oriented software architecture [11, 12]. A critical component of this infrastructure, commonly referred to as Grid "middleware", is the data management layer. Pioneering Grid efforts [14, 27] were early faced with the problem of managing extremely large-scale datasets - in the order of petabytes - shared among broad and heterogeneous end user communities. It was essential to design a system architecture capable of meeting these advanced requirements in the context of the Grid paradigm. The proposed Data Grid architecture [6] allows the distributed storage and management of a large set of shared data resources, by defining a set of basic data services interacting with one another in order to expose well known, file-like APIs and semantics to end user applications and other higher-level Grid layers.

One of the core building blocks of the Data Grid architecture is the Replica Location Service. The Grid environment may require that data is to be scattered globally due to individual site storage limits, but also remain equally accessible from all participating computing elements. In such cases, it is common to use local caching to reduce the network latencies that would normally add up as a constant overhead of remote data access operations. In Grid terminology, local copies of read-only remote files are called "replicas" [24], while applications running on the Grid request such local file instances through specialized Grid data management services [17]. Data replicas help in improving the performance of applications that require to frequently access remotely placed information. By replicating data closer to the application, the overall access latency is much shorter and the aggregate network usage is reduced. Moreover, through replica-aware algorithms, data movement services can exploit multiple replicas to boost transfer throughput and data recovery tools can reproduce lost original data from their corresponding replicated instances.

Replica Location Service implementations have evolved significantly over the past years. The initial design of a centralized RLS was swiftly put aside in favor of a distributed approach [23]. The most widespread solution currently deployed on the Grid, namely the Giggle Framework [5], follows a multi-tier hierarchical structure, distributing data and queries over global (Grid or VO-wide) and local, site-wide RLS instances. Giggle is currently an integral component of the Globus Toolkit [10] middleware distribution. Nevertheless, all implementations followed so far are optimized for "high-performance" operational environments. Current Grid deployments reside mainly in the scientific area, where hardware crashes and network blackouts are rare exceptions and may be sustained by redundant equipment or special backup systems. However, in future global-scale, "high-throughput" Grids, services like the RLS may have to address these issues. We believe that in order to scale the Grid to these numbers, there is a need to delegate the execution of some of its core services to the edges of its infrastructure. Therefore, service redesigns may benefit from concepts and algorithms used by peer-to-peer overlay networks. Peer-to-peer systems can scale without application and environment specific fine-tuning to billions of simultaneous participants, while their potential grows as more peers join in.

The next section of this paper includes some comments on Giggle's design limitations, while in the following sections, we concentrate on the observation that a special category of peer-to-peer systems, which are tailored for data lookups in a distributed collection of key-value tuples, can effectively address all needs of a truly scale-proof and fault-tolerant RLS infrastructure. However, *structured peer-to-peer networks* or *Distributed Hash Tables* are only capable of storing read-only information. To this end, we analyze the complications associated with supporting update operations in DHTs and propose an algorithm to enable inherent mutable data storage and management in the peer-to-peer network level. In addition, we present how our algorithm can be incorporated into a simple DHT protocol, discuss on the method and evaluate its merits, based on performance results from an early implementation. This paper is concluded with references to related work in the area and thoughts on future work in the same direction.

2 Limitations of the Giggle Framework

As most other preceding RLS designs, the Giggle (GIGa-scale Global Location Engine) Framework constructs a uniform filename namespace of unique per VO identifiers (logical filenames - LFNs) and manages the mappings of these identifiers to physical locations of files (physical filenames - PFNs). LFNs are used by the applications to locate data, while PFNs, which are used by the RLS and other Data Grid services, are structured similar to a URL, describing the access protocol, the site and the path in the site directory structure for a given replica.

In order to distribute the replica location data throughout the Grid, Giggle makes use of two main components, the local replica catalogs (LRCs) and the replica location indices (RLIs). RLIs help in finding which catalogs hold the replica file lists for a given LFN, while LRCs maintain the actual replica location information (LFN to PFN mappings). To meet varying operational requirements, multiple RLIs may be deployed in parallel, providing optional coarse-grain load-balancing and fail-over features to the replica location infrastructure. A standard deployment scenario may include running one LRC per site and a multitude of VO-wide RLIs in a tree-like structure. Each LRC may be linked to multiple RLIs and vice versa. The exact form of the catalog and index hierarchy can be controlled through the definition of a number of deployment parameters. Nevertheless, changes in any LFN's replicas, will all be concentrated at the LRCs responsible for storing the particular mappings. Specific catalogs may get overloaded when very popular LFNs require frequent updates of their associated PFN lists.

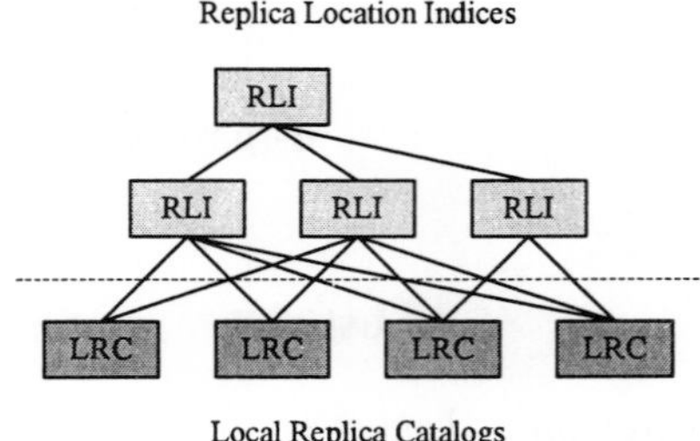

Figure 1. Giggle deployment example

LRCs are required to refresh RLIs, in order to inform them on the latest mapping updates and to prevent them from deleting old mappings because of timeouts. As the update mechanism has to be as efficient as possible, LRCs use soft-state update protocols to inform RLIs of changes. Either full or incremental, updates are asynchronous, so when an add or delete operation occurs, it is not immediately propagated to the appropriate index. Moreover, soft updates can be very demanding on the size of the data involved. To reduce the overhead of such transactions, they are compressed using Bloom filters - a lossy compression scheme. Asynchronous updates and lossy compression of data, may result in clients getting false positive answers. Although the relaxed consistency requirements set by Giggle's designers allow false positives, we believe that the pursuit of scalability has led Giggle to employ complex mechanisms to update data which may in turn limit the system's efficiency on very large networks.

There is also an option to partition mappings among global servers, by defining an LFN namespace segmentation function. Data partitioning can be used to limit the amount of changes that need to be communicated between LRCs and RLIs, but it has to be manually configured. If the RLS has huge data sets to handle and storage requirements change, the participating nodes must manually adapt to the new situation by specifying a new distribution scheme. In general, Giggle's parameters cannot be dynamically changed.

According to the experimental analysis of a prototype implementation [7], compression of the updates induces performance overheads when the filter is initialized and every time a number of hash functions need to be calculated for a filename. In order to reduce the performance loss, the relational database backend is not used when compression is enabled. Instead, there is a need for a customized in-memory data structure and the Giggle code has to support two different methods for the same function. The code becomes more complicated and the logical and organizational advantages of a database backend are lost. On the other hand, although the database backend offers easy modeling and deployment of catalogs and indices, it requires non-trivial fine tuning (e.g. disabling database flush in MySQL or forcing periodic vacuums in PostgreSQL). When database products used are third-party, these modifications may prove even harder to implement. Moreover, the catalogs and indices cannot automatically handle a new addition or deletion of a participating catalog or index. Although the designers have envisioned a membership management service that will allow the system to deal with unplanned LRC and RLI joins and failures, the current static configuration implies that every time a new entity is to be added in the network the whole service may have to be reconfigured.

The number of parameters that have to be tuned in order to deploy and use the RLS, make Giggle difficult to deploy and manage. Moreover, we believe that the distribution approach used may reach its limits, when the number of logical to physical filename mappings or the number of catalogs and indices increase in several orders of magnitude. There are currently no performance results of a very large RLS system serving millions or billions of mappings, so there is no practical way to plead for this hypothesis. Nevertheless, we propose that a Replica Location Service for high-throughput Grid deployments, can be implemented with the help of an already scalable, fault-tolerant and self-configurable peer-to-peer network.

3 Using a peer-to-peer system as the basis of a scalable RLS

Peer-to-peer networks represent a large class of distributed systems that focus on the construction of a scalable and fault-tolerant *overlay* of interconnected *peers*. In peer-to-peer terminology, the terms *network* and *overlay* refer to the mesh of virtual links created between the physical *peers* or *nodes* of the system. The latter can practically be applications, running on actual machines attached to a common lower-level communication infrastructure, like the Internet. By abstracting the underlying network into a higher-level overlay, peers can "encode" application specific semantics in their corresponding links. In general, there are algorithms that can exploit the overlay design in order to provide optimized resource location services.

Recent literature in the field distinguishes peer-to-peer systems into two basic categories, depending on the structure of the overlay network produced when nodes join the system. Unstructured systems like Gnutella leave the peers free to participate in any part of the overlay and the connection graph formed resembles that of a power-law network [22], while structured systems or Distributed Hash Tables (DHTs), such as Kademlia [19], Chord [25] and Tapestry [26], impose a specific virtual structure which accommodates peers in particular slots as they join the network. Each family of systems has its own advantages and disadvantages over the other: In structured systems the lookup procedure is highly deterministic (will almost always return a result if there is such a value in the network) and any operation will almost certainly succeed in a predefined number of steps (usually equal to the logarithm of the number of total participating nodes). On the other hand, unstructured systems, have the ability to handle free-text search queries in very few steps [1], although the procedure is probabilistic and usually requires flooding the network with messages.

An appealing fact is that structured peer-to-peer systems can provide the required mechanisms in order to construct a truly scalable RLS. DHTs try at least to solve the same basic problem as Giggle: Given a unique global identifier, locate in a distributed and scalable way the resource in question [2]. Actually, the idea of using a peer-to-peer lookup system for locating file replicas in a Grid environment is not new. Ian Foster, Adriana Iamnitchi *et al.* in [9, 15], recognize that the peer-to-peer and Grid research communities have much in common and even more to learn one from another. Furthermore, the authors of the Giggle system credit the work being done in peer-to-peer location discovery systems as most relevant to theirs.

3.1 Design

In the context of the Data Grid architecture, the main concern of the RLS is how to locate the physical file names (replica identifiers) that may be available, when knowing the Logical File Name of a resource. LFNs are provided by metadata servers [8] or are hidden in application specific semantics. A DHT can be used to support all needs of a Replica Location Service, if its inherent key-value pairs are correlated to LFN to PFN mappings. In such a system, keys will not be generated by computing the SHA1 hash of the value (as is the common case with DHTs). Keys should correspond to the hash of the logical filename (LFN) of the resource. LFN hashes can then be used as identifiers by the overlay network to route data operations to corresponding PFN lists. A value for a key will actually be a data structure - a list containing the physical locations of replicas (PFNs) for a given LFN. Also, as LFNs are unique per VO identifiers, a single peer-to-peer overlay network must be deployed per VO (a single identifier space). Grid services and end-user applications will access LFN to PFN mappings, by interacting with applications participating in the peer-to-peer overlay, through predefined APIs.

The main problem associated with the usage of a Distributed Hash Table to store file replica locations, lies in the disability of the peer-to-peer network to handle mutable data. DHTs may provide *get* and *set* operations, but there is no straightforward way to update data. When a key-value pair is stored into a DHT it is destined to remain in the overlay unchanged until it expires. These systems are tuned to scale to very large network sizes and adapt to random node behavior. Tracing the nodes responsible for storing a specific data item would require complex and demanding algorithms, so there is no method to determine the exact location(s) of a key-value tuple in any given moment (this is also a prerequisite for peer-to-peer network security [13]). Nevertheless, a data *update* operation is absolutely necessary for serving the needs of the Data Grid's RLS, as PFN mappings for a given LFN could change frequently and there should be a way for propagating the modifications throughout the network as soon as possible.

The ideal solution would be to enable mutable data storage at the level of each individual key-value pair stored at the peer-to-peer system. We argue that this could be done with a very simple addition to the basic DHT algorithm. DHTs may distribute the data in numerous peers of the system, but the only important nodes for every key-value pair are the ones returned by the lookup procedure. If we change the value in these nodes there is a very high probability that upon subsequent queries for the same key, at least one of the updated ones will be contacted. Of course this is not enough, as the network is not a static entity and the nodes responsible for a specific key-value pair storage change over time. DHTs support dynamic node arrivals and departures, so storage relationships between data items and nodes may be altered over time in an unpredictable manner.

As a consequence, every *lookup* should always query all nodes responsible for a specific key-value pair, compare the results based on some predefined version vector (indicating the latest update of the value) and propagate the changes to the nodes it has found responsible for storage but not yet up-to-date with the latest value. This requires that the algorithm for locating data items will not stop when the first value is returned, but continue until all available versions of the pair are present at the initiator. The querying node will then decide which version to keep and send corresponding *store* messages back to the peers that seem to hold older or invalid values. Updates could therefore be implemented through the predefined *set* operation, as version checking would also be done by nodes receiving *store* commands. The latter should check their local storage repositories for an already-present identifier, and if there is a conflict, keep the latest version of the two values in hand. A simple data versioning scheme could be accomplished by using timestamp indicators along every key-value pair.

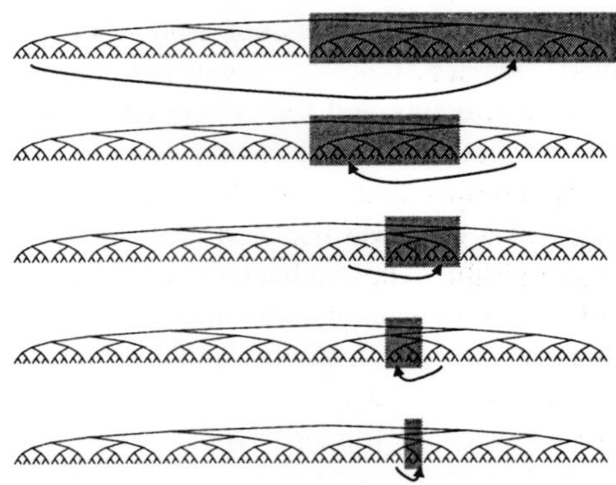

Figure 2. Moving closer towards a key in a Kademlia overlay

3.2 Enabling mutable data storage

With the above design in mind, we have tweaked the Kademlia protocol to support mutable data storage. While these changes could have been applied to any DHT (like Chord or others), we picked Kademlia as it has a simpler routing table structure and uses a consistent algorithm throughout the lookup procedure. Kademlia relies on a XOR operation between identifiers to find which nodes are responsible for storing a specific key-value pair. As in any DHT, Kademlia's peers and data items have identifiers from the same address space. XOR is used as the *distance function*, to indicate which are the closest nodes to a given key. The XOR induced topology is easier to understand if the address space is represented as a binary tree. Nodes and key value pairs are treated as the leaves of the structure, while each node has more routing information for near subtrees and stores items closer to its corresponding leaf (Figure 6).

According to the Kademlia protocol, three RPCs take place in any data storage or retrieval operation: `FIND_NODE`, `FIND_VALUE` and `STORE`. To store a key-value pair, a node will first need to find the closest nodes to the key. Starting with a list of closest nodes from its own routing table, it will send parallel asynchronous `FIND_NODE` commands to the top α nodes of the list. Nodes receiving a `FIND_NODE` RPC should reply with a list of at most κ closest peers to the given ID. The requesting node will collect the results, merge them in the list, sort by distance from the key, and repeat the process. When all κ closest nodes have replied, the key-value pair is copied to the corresponding peers via `STORE` RPCs. The system-wide parameter κ, also specifies the number of copies maintained for each data item and controls the size of routing tables in peers. To retrieve a value from the system, a node will initiate a similar query loop, using `FIND_VALUE` RPCs instead of `FIND_NODE`s. `FIND_VALUE` requests return either a value from the remote node's local repository, or - if no such value is present - a list of at most κ nodes close to the key. In the later case, this information helps the querying node dig deeper into the network, progressing closer towards a node responsible for storing the value at the next step. The procedure stops immediately when a value is returned, or when the κ closest peers have replied and no value is found.

Our modified lookup algorithm works similar to the `FIND_NODE` loop, originally used for storing values in the network. We first find all closest nodes to the requested key-value pair, through `FIND_NODE` RPCs, and then send them `FIND_VALUE` messages. The querying node will check all values returned, find the most recent version and notify the nodes having stale copies of the change. Of course, if a peer replies to the `FIND_VALUE` RPC with a list of nodes it is marked as not up to date. When the top κ nodes have returned a result (either a value or a list of nodes), we send the appropriate `STORE` RPCs. Nodes receiving a `STORE` command should replace their local copy of the key-value pair with its updated version. Storing a new key in the system is done exactly in the same way, with the only difference that the latest version of the data item is provided by the user, so there is no need to send `FIND_VALUE` RPCs to the closest nodes of a key (version checking is done by the remote peers). Moreover, deleting a value equals to updating it to zero length. Deleted data will eventually be removed from the system when it expires.

3.3 Discussion

In the original Kademlia protocol, a *lookup* operation will normally require at most log(N) hops through a network of N peers. If an "early" `FIND_VALUE` RPC returns a result, there is no need to continue with the indirect `FIND_NODE` loop. On the other hand, the changes we propose merge the *lookup* and *store* operations into a common two-step procedure: Find the closest nodes of the given key and propagate the updated value. Cached items are ignored and lookups will continue until finding all nodes responsible for storing the requested data item. The disadvantage is that it is always necessary to follow at least log(N) hops through the overlay to discover an identifier's closest peers.

Nevertheless, the lookup procedure is also used to propagate updated values to the network. So the extra cost in messages is equal to the "price" needed by the infrastructure to support mutable data. There certainly can not be a way to support such a major change in the peer-to-peer system without paying some cost, either in terms of bytes exchanged or in terms of increased latency required for a result (two benchmarking metrics proposed as a common denominator in evaluating peer-to-peer systems [18]). Moreover, the aforementioned drawback in lookup performance could even be accounted as a feature: DHT nodes generally exploit messages exchanged in favor of updating their routing tables. The more the messages, the more fault-tolerant the system gets.

The changes we propose for Kademlia can easily be adopted by other DHTs as well. There is a small number of changes required and most (if not all of them) should happen in the storage and retrieval functions of the protocol. There was no need to change the way Kademlia handles the node join procedure or routing table refreshes. Also, as values are automatically republished on every usage, they is no need to explicitly redistribute key-value pairs every hour. Data items are reseeded only when an hour passes since they were last part of a *store* or *lookup* operation (effectively propagating updates). Nevertheless, there is still a requirement that all tuples expire 24 hours after their last modification. Among other advantages refreshing provides, it is the only way of completely clearing up the ID space of deleted values.

4 Implementation

We implemented the full Kademlia protocol plus our additions in a very lightweight C program. In the core of the implementation lies a custom, asynchronous message handler that forwards incoming UDP packets to a state machine, while outgoing messages are sent directly to the network. Except from the connectionless stream socket, used for communicating with other peers, the message handler also manages local TCP connections that are used by client programs. The program runs as a standard UNIX-like daemon. Client applications willing to retrieve data from the network or store key-value pairs in the overlay, first connect to the daemon through a TCP socket and then issue the appropriate *get* or *set* operations. All items are stored in the local filesystem and the total requirements on memory and processing capacity are minimal.

For our tests we used a cluster of eight SMP nodes, each running multiple peer instances. Another application would generate insert, update and select commands and propagate them to nodes in the peer-to-peer network.

4.1 Performance in a static network

To get some insight on the scalability properties of the underlying DHT, we first measured the mean time needed for the system to complete each type of operation for different amounts of key-value pairs and DHT peers. Kademlia's parameters were set to α=3 and κ=4, as the network size was limited to a few hundred nodes.

Figures 3(a), 3(b) and 3(c) show that the implementation takes less than 2 milliseconds to complete a select operation and an average of 2.5 milliseconds to complete an insert operation in a network of 512 nodes with up to 8K key-value pairs stored in the system. The overall system seems to remain scalable, although there is an evident problem with disk latency if a specific node stores more than 8K key-value pairs as individual files in the filesystem. This is the reason behind the performance degradation of the four node scenario as the amount of mappings increases. As κ has been set to 4, all data items are present at all 4 nodes. When the network has 8K key-value pairs, each node has a copy of all 8K mappings.

Nevertheless, systems larger than 4 nodes behave very well, since the mean time to complete queries does not experience large deviations as the number data items doubles in size. Also, the graphs representing inserts and updates are almost identical. The reason is that both operations are handled in the same way by the protocol. The only functional difference is that inserts are done in an empty overlay, while updates are done after the inserts, so the version checking code has data to evaluate.

4.2 Performance in a dynamic network

Our second goal was to measure the performance of the overlay under high levels of churn (random participant joins and failures), even in a scaled-down scenario. Using the implementation prototype, we constructed a network of 256 peers, storing a total of 2048 key-value pairs, for each of the following experiments. Node and data identifiers were 32 bits long and Kademlia's concurrency and replication parameters were set to α=3 and κ=4 respectively. A small value of κ assures that whatever the distribution of node identifiers, routing tables will always hold a subset of the total population of nodes. Also it guarantees that values will not be over-replicated in this relatively small network.

Each experiment involved node arrivals and departures, as long as item lookups and updates, during a one hour timeframe. Corresponding *startup*, *shutdown*, *get* and *set* commands were generated randomly according to a Poisson distribution, and then issued in parallel to the nodes. We started by setting the item update and lookup rates to 1024 $\frac{operations}{hour}$, while doubling the node arrival and departure rates. Initially 64 new nodes were generated per hour and 64 $\frac{nodes}{hour}$ failed. The arrival and departure rates were kept equal so that the network would neither grow nor shrink. Figure 4 shows the average query completion time during a one minute rolling timeframe for four different node join and fail rates. In the simulation environment there is practically no communication latency between peers. Nevertheless, timeouts were set to 4 seconds.

4.2.1 Handling timeouts

As expected, increasing the number of node failures, caused the total time needed for the completion of each query to scale up. High levels of churn, result in stale routing table entries, so nodes send messages to nonexistent peers and are forced to wait for timeouts before they can continue. Kademlia nodes try to circumvent stale peers in *get* operations, as they take α parallel paths to reach the key in question. It is most likely that at least one of these paths will reach a cached pair, while other paths may be blocked, waiting for replies to timeout. Our protocol additions require that caching is disabled, especially for networks where key-value pairs are frequently updated.

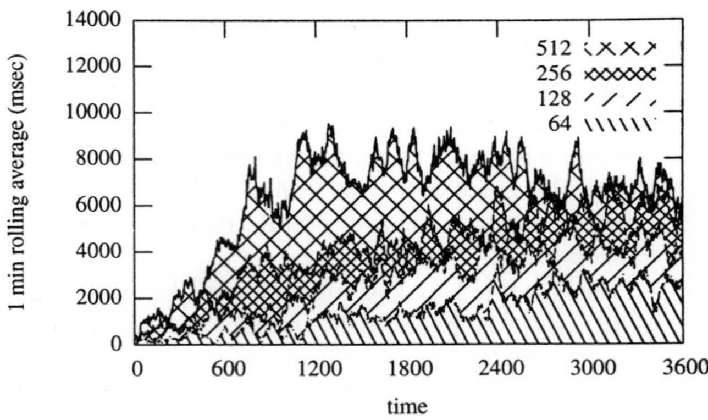

Figure 4. Time to complete queries while increasing node arrival and departure rates

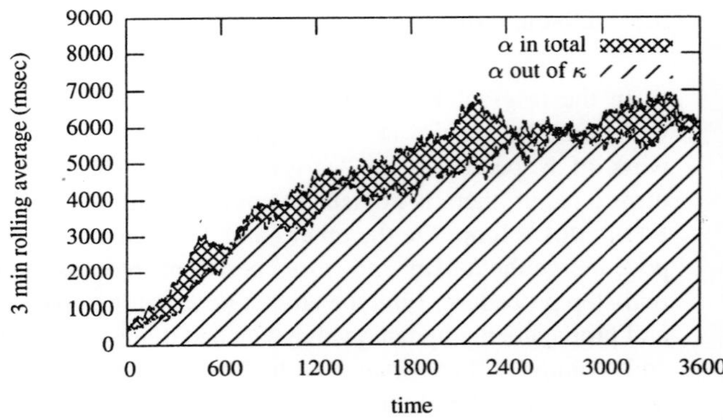

Figure 5. Dynamically adapting α to changes in the lookup list

Instead, we try to lower query completion times by making nodes dynamically adapt their query paths as other peers reply. In the first phase of the *get* operation, where FIND_NODE requests are issued, nodes are instructed to constantly wait for a maximum of α peers to reply from the closest κ. If a reply changes the κ closest node candidates, the requesting node may in turn send more than one com-

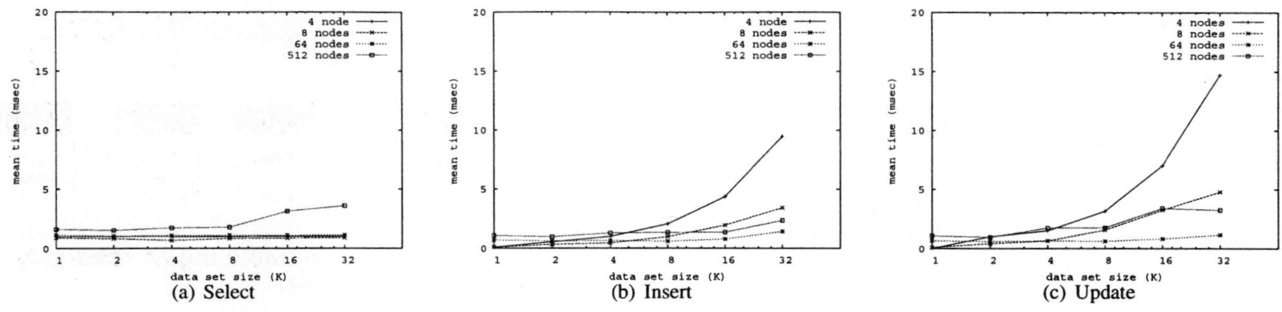

Figure 3. Mean time to complete operations in a static network

mands, thus having more than α requests inflight, in contrast to α in total as proposed by Kademlia. This optimization yields slightly better results in total query completion times, in expense to a small increase in the number of messages. Figure 5 shows a comparison of the two algorithms in a network handling 256 node arrivals and departures per hour.

4.2.2 Handling lookup failures

High levels of churn also lead to increasing lookup failures. Experiment results shown in Table 1 suggest that as the rate of node arrivals and departures doubles, the lookup failure rate grows almost exponentially. In order to prove that the extra messaging cost by our protocol additions can be exploited in favor of overall network fault-tolerance, we reran the worst case scenario (512 node joins and 512 node failures per hour) several times, while doubling the lookup rate from 1024 up to 16384 $\frac{operations}{hour}$. It is evident from the results presented in Table 2, that even in a network with very unreliable peers, a high lookup rate can cause the corresponding failure rate to drop to values less than 1%. This owes to the fact that lookup operations are responsible for propagating key-value pairs to a continuously changing set of closest nodes, while helping peers find and remove stale entries from their routing tables.

Table 1. Increasing node node arrival and departure rates

$\frac{nodes}{hour}$	64	128	256	512
Failures	0	2	32	154
Rate	0.00%	0.19%	3.12%	15.03%

The initial high failure rate is also dependent on the way Kademlia manages routing tables. When a node learns of a new peer, it may send corresponding values for storage, but it is not necessary that it will update its routing table. For small values of κ and networks of this size, routing tables may already be full of other active nodes. As a result, lookups may fail to find the new closest peers to a key. A dominant percentage of lookup failures in our experiments were caused by nodes not being able to identify the latest closest peers of a value. Also, Kademlia's routing tables are designed to favor nodes that stay longer in the network, but the random departure scheme currently used by our simulation environment does not exploit this feature.

Table 2. Increasing the lookup rate

$\frac{operations}{hour}$	1024	2048	4096	8192	16384
Failures	162	106	172	126	84
	131	91	137	80	58
	163	63	145	116	106
	143	61	130	120	87
Rate	15.82%	5.17%	4.19%	1.53%	0.51%
	12.79%	4.44%	3.34%	0.97%	0.35%
	15.91%	3.07%	3.54%	1.41%	0.64%
	13.96%	2.97%	3.17%	1.46%	0.53%

4.3 Results and future work

The prototype implementation behaves very well in terms of scalability and fault-tolerance, which has allowed us to plan future experiments with much larger network sizes and data set populations. We will be focusing on evaluating various aspects of the system, while varying node network characteristics. Nevertheless, scaling the experiments from a few hundred nodes to orders of magnitude upwards is not straightforward, as it requires special considerations regarding the limits of the underlying simulation hardware and software [3].

In future versions of the implementation, we intend on evaluating embedded, lightweight database engines like SQLite for the local storage requirements of each node.

We also plan on adding support for Kademlia's *accelerated lookups* and integrate interfaces to the advanced security services provided by Grid middleware distributions.

A question left open is how to incorporate a caching scheme along our algorithm for distributed mutable data management. If we enable caches there has to be a way of using them without sacrificing the integrity of key-value pairs throughout the network. We are currently investigating various cache management schemes that could fit in as a solution to this problem. There is a need to invalidate caches throughout the network on every data item update. On the other hand, we could just enable caches with small timeouts, especially for replica location environments where *lookups* are much more frequent than *stores* and strict data consistency is not a must.

5 Related work

A solution to the problem of storing mutable data in a DHT is presented by the designers of Ivy [20]. Ivy is a distributed filesystem functioning on top of a structured peer-to-peer network. All operations on files and their contents are stored in a distributed hash table, arranged in a linked list of changes - a log. Each participant of the filesystem knows the identifier of the last data item he put in the system, while each data item contains a list of operations done on the file system and a pointer to the next key-value pair (previous set of changes). By traversing the log from the most recent to the oldest item, the filesystem can "remember" the latest state of each file and directory for a given participant. Nevertheless, there may be a need to go through hundreds of key-value lookups in the DHT in order to find the latest aggregate value, which would incur an intolerable cost in terms of network messages. Even more, Ivy's log records never get deleted as they are needed for recovery in case of network failures and the cost for managing the status of which entries should be deleted could be enormous. An analogous design is followed by OceanStore [16], which implements a file management layer on top of an underlying Tapestry network. The update model used is very similar to the one utilized by Ivy, although updates are handled at the file - not the participant - level. If any of these systems was to be used as the basis for an RLS, there would be a need to maintain an external mutable directory of the latest keys inserted in the peer-to-peer overlay.

Peer-to-peer overlay networks have already been incorporated in other RLS designs. In a recent paper [4], Min Cai *et al.*, have replaced the global indices of Giggle with a Chord network, producing a variant of Giggle called P-RLS. A Chord topology can tolerate random node joins and leaves, but does not provide data fault-tolerance by default. The authors choose to replicate data in the *successor set* of each *root node* (the node responsible for storage of a partic-

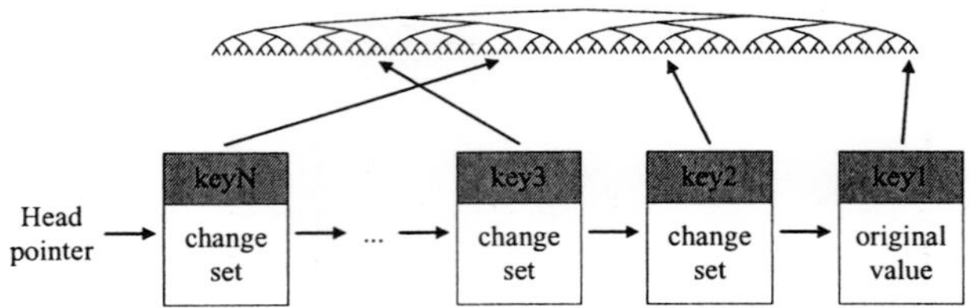

Figure 6. Storing a mutable log of read-only key-value pairs in a DHT

ular mapping), effectively reproducing Kademlia's behavior of replicating data according to the replication parameter κ. In order to update a specific key-value pair, the new value is inserted as usual, by finding the *root node* and replacing the corresponding value stored there and at all nodes in its *successor set*. While there is a great resemblance to this design and the one we propose, there is no support for updating key-value pairs directly in the peer-to-peer protocol layer. It is an open question how the P-RLS design would cope with highly transient nodes. Frequent joins and departures in the Chord layer would require nodes continuously exchanging key-value pairs in order to keep the network balanced and the replicas of a particular mapping in the correct successors. Our design deals with this problem, as the routing tables inside the nodes are immune to participants that stay in the network for a very short amount of time. Moreover, our protocol additions to support mutable data storage are not dependent on node behavior; the integrity of updated data is established only by relevant data operations.

In another variant of an RLS implementation using a peer-to-peer network [21], all replica location information is organized in an unstructured overlay and all nodes gradually store all mappings in a compressed form. This way each node can locally serve a query without forwarding requests. Nevertheless, the amount of data (compressed or not) that has to be updated throughout the network each time, can grow to such a large extent, that the scalability properties of the peer-to-peer overlay are lost.

6 Conclusion

We believe that in future high-throughput Grid deployments, core services - such as the RLS component of the Data Grid architecture - should be distributed to as many resources as possible. To this end, services must use distribution algorithms with unique scalability and fault-tolerance properties - assets already available by peer-to-peer architectures. In this paper, we argue that a truly scalable and fault-tolerant Replica Location Service can be based on a structured peer-to-peer design (a Distributed Hash Table).

Nevertheless, a read-only key-value pair storage facility

is not adequate to store continuously changing replica location mappings. The basic DHT algorithm has to be modified in some way to enable mutable data storage. We have implemented a prototype of a distributed hash table that will allow stored data to be updated through the basic *set* command. Our protocol additions that enable this new operation are very simple and could easily be applied to any analogous peer-to-peer system. We are currently trying to make the initial implementation even more efficient and plan to evaluate its performance in large scale experiments involving close to real-life situations.

The performance of the RLS depends on the effectiveness of its underlying resource lookup algorithm. We do not expect our DHT-based design to outperform the currently deployed system - Giggle, which is based on an hierarchical distribution model. In the contrary, we expect that high-performance Grid deployments will continue to benefit from Giggle's architecture. However, we doubt that Giggle will be able to scale, in order to cover the needs of an extremely large Grid. In contrast to Giggle and other peer-to-peer RLS designs, we envision a service that does not require the use of specialized servers for locating replicas. We believe that a lightweight DHT-enabled RLS peer can run at multiple machines per site or even every machine of the Grid having a public IP address, as the deployment and management requirements are minimal. Furthermore, the architecture of the network will ensure that as more and more nodes join, the replica location infrastructure will scale in storage capacity without significant losses in lookup performance.

References

[1] L. A. Adamic, R. M. Lukose, A. R. Puniyani, and B. A. Huberman. Search in power law networks. *Physical Review E64*, 64:46135–46143, 2001.

[2] H. Balakrishnan, M. F. Kaashoek, D. Karger, R. Morris, and I. Stoica. Looking up data in p2p systems. *Communications of the ACM*, 46(2):43–48, 2003.

[3] E. Buchmann and K. Böhm. How to Run Experiments with Large Peer-to-Peer Data Structures. In *Proc. of IPDPS'04*, Santa Fe, NM.

[4] M. Cai, A. Chervenak, and M. Frank. A peer-to-peer replica location service based on a distributed hash table. In *Proc. of ACM/IEEE Supercomputing'04*, Pittsburgh, PA.

[5] A. Chervenak et al. Giggle: a framework for constructing scalable replica location services. In *Proc. of ACM/IEEE Supercomputing'02*, Baltimore, MD.

[6] A. Chervenak, I. Foster, C. Kesselman, C. Salisbury, and S. Tuecke. The data grid: Towards an architecture for the distributed management and analysis of large scientific datasets. *Journal of Network and Computer Applications*, 23(3):187–200, 2000.

[7] A. Chervenak, N. Palavalli, S. Bharathi, C. Kesselman, and R. Schwartzkopf. Performance and scalability of a replica location service. In *Proc. of HPDC–13'04*, Honolulu, HI.

[8] K. Czajkowski, S. Fitzgerald, I. Foster, and C. Kesselman. Grid information services for distributed resource sharing. In *Proc. of HPDC–10'01*, San Francisco, CA.

[9] I. Foster and A. Iamnitchi. On death, taxes, and the convergence of peer-to-peer and grid computing. In *Proc. of IPTPS'03*, Berkeley, CA.

[10] I. Foster and C. Kesselman. Globus: A metacomputing infrastructure toolkit. *International Journal of High Performance Computing Applications*, 11(2):115–128, 1997.

[11] I. Foster and C. Kesselman, editors. *The Grid: Blueprint for a New Computing Infrastructure*. Morgan-Kaufmann, 1999.

[12] I. Foster, C. Kesselman, and S. Tuecke. The anatomy of the grid: Enabling scalable virtual organizations. *International Journal of High Performance Computing Applications*, 15(3):200–222, 2001.

[13] S. Hazel and B. Wiley. Achord: A variant of the chord lookup service for use in censorship resistant peer-to-peer publishing systems. In *Proc. of IPTPS'02*, Cambridge, MA.

[14] W. Hoschek, J. Jaen-Martinez, A. Samar, H. Stockinger, and K. Stockinger. Data management in an international data grid project. In *Proc. of Grid'00*, Bangalore, India.

[15] A. Iamnitchi, I. Foster, and D. C. Nurmi. A peer-to-peer approach to resource location in grid environments. In *Proc. of HPDC–11'02*, Edinburgh, UK.

[16] J. Kubiatowicz et al. Oceanstore: An architecture for global-scale persistent storage. In *Proc. of ASPLOS–IX'00*, Cambridge, MA.

[17] P. Z. Kunszt, E. Laure, H. Stockinger, and K. Stockinger. Advanced replica management with reptor. In *Proc. of PPAM'03*, Czestochowa, Poland.

[18] J. Li, J. Stribling, T. M. Gil, R. Morris, and M. F. Kaashoek. Comparing the performance of distributed hash tables under churn. In *Proc. of IPTPS'04*, San Diego, CA.

[19] P. Maymounkov and D. Mazières. Kademlia: A peer-to-peer information system based on the xor metric. In *Proc. of IPTPS'02*, Cambridge, MA.

[20] A. Muthitacharoen, R. Morris, T. M. Gil, and B. Chen. Ivy: A read/write peer-to-peer file system. In *Proc. of OSDI'02*, Boston, MA.

[21] M. Ripeanu and I. Foster. A decentralized, adaptive, replica location service. In *Proc. of HPDC–11'02*, Edinburgh, UK.

[22] M. Ripeanu and I. Foster. Mapping the gnutella network: Macroscopic properties of large-scale peer-to-peer systems. In *Proc. of IPTPS'02*, Cambridge, MA.

[23] H. Stockinger and A. Hanushevsky. Http redirection for replica catalogue lookups in data grids. In *Proc. of SAC'02*, Madrid, Spain.

[24] H. Stockinger, A. Samar, K. Holtman, B. Allcock, I. Foster, and B. Tierney. File and object replication in data grids. *Cluster Computing*, 5(3):305–314, 2002.

[25] I. Stoica, R. Morris, D. Karger, M. F. Kaashoek, and H. Balakrishnan. Chord: A scalable peer-to-peer lookup service for internet applications. In *Proc. of SIGCOMM'01*, San Diego, CA.

[26] B. Y. Zhao, L. Huang, J. Stribling, S. C. Rhea, A. D. Joseph, and J. D. Kubiatowicz. Tapestry: A resilient global-scale overlay for service deployment. *IEEE Journal on Selected Areas in Communications*, 22(1):41–53, 2004.

[27] The datagrid project. http://www.eu-datagrid.org/.

Session 6C: Communications Tools

Low Overhead High Performance Runtime Monitoring of Collective Communication

Lars Ailo Bongo, Otto J. Anshus and John Markus Bjørndalen
Department of Computer Science, University of Tromsø, Norway
{larsab, otto, johnm}@cs.uit.no

Abstract

Scalability of parallel applications on clusters and multi-clusters is often limited by communication performance. Message tracing can provide data for understanding bottlenecks, and for performance tuning. However, it requires collecting, storing, analyzing, and transferring potentially gigabytes of data. We have designed the EventSpace system for low overhead and high performance runtime collective communication trace analysis. EventSpace separates the perturbation and performance requirements of data collection, analysis, gathering and visualization. Data collection overhead is low since the minimum amount of data is recorded and stored temporarily in main memory. The recorded data is either discarded or analyzed on demand using available cluster resources. Analysis is distributed for high performance, and coscheduled with the computation and communication system threads for low perturbation. Gathering of analyzed data is done using extensible collective communication operations, which can be tuned to trade off between performance and monitoring overhead. EventSpace was used to do run-time monitoring and analysis of collective communication micro-benchmarks run on clusters, multi-clusters, and multi-clusters with emulated WAN links. Performance data was collected, analyzed and gathered with 0–3% monitoring overhead.

1 Introduction

In Grids rapid changes will be the norm. Hence, it is necessary for applications and the underlying systems to adapt, at run-time, to changes in the availability and performance of resources. An important part of the adaptation will be to reconfigure the point-to-point and collective communication structures used by parallel applications.

On large clusters, a much less dynamic environment than a Grid, communication system performance is important. Of eight scalable scientific application studied in [30], most would benefit from improvements to collective operations, and four would benefit from improvements in point-to-point communication performance. Improved communication performance is essential if Grids are to be used as a high performance computing platform.

Collective operation performance has been shown to improve by using better mappings of computation and data to the clusters in use [16, 24, 26, 27]. In earlier work, we have shown how to tune the mapping based on a performance analysis within the communication system [9]. We found that a global view of the system was needed to detect hotspots and simplify the hotspot analysis. Also, traces of all messages sent in a collective operation spanning tree were needed to understand some performance problems (as the problems described in [21]). Thus, we need to collect, store, analyze, gather, and visualize a large amount of performance data.

Monitoring tools need to collect data with minimal perturbation of the monitored application. For runtime analysis the performance data must be analyzed and often gathered to a single front-end host for use before the data becomes irrelevant. We have built the EventSpace system [8] for low overhead and high performance runtime collective communication trace analysis.

EventSpace is evaluated on clusters, multi-clusters, and multi-cluster with emulated WAN links. We demonstrate how data gathering performance can be tuned to either provide high performance or low perturbation. Our results show that performance data can be collected with less than 1% overhead. The data can be analyzed and gathered with 0–3% overhead, since collective communication intensive applications have low CPU utilization, and since analysis threads can be coscheduled with application and communication system threads.

2 Related Work

Generally performance monitoring tools for MPI programs [19] treats the communication system as a black box

0190-3918/05 $20.00 © 2005 IEEE

and collect data at a layer between the application and the communication system (the MPI profiling layer). To understand why a specific collective operation spanning tree and mapping have better performance than others it is necessary to collect data for analysis inside the communication system, as EventSpace does.

MRNet [23] is the system most similar to EventSpace. Both use collective operations spanning trees to build scalable multi-cast/reduction overlay networks used by performance monitoring tools. MRNet shares the flexible organization and extensibility of EventSpace. In MRNet, communication is only between compute hosts and the front-end host, while EventSpace allows arbitrary communication structures resulting in more flexible and efficient analysis. EventSpace is also more tightly integrated with the underlying communication system, allowing the monitor activity to be coscheduled with the application. Our evaluation differs in that we use EventSpace for a different problem domain than used in [23], and we examine the performance of more complex spanning tree topologies than the balanced trees used in [23]. Another data aggregation tool for Grids is Yggdrasil [4].

PHOTON [28] allows monitoring point-to-point operations used by MPI applications run on large clusters. EventSpace is designed for collective operations, but share the same goals as PHOTON in reducing the monitoring overhead, perturbation and storage requirements of post-mortem trace analysis tools. PHOTON appends information to messages, which requires modifications to the MPI runtime system. This information is sampled and statistics are computed at runtime. Our experience in collective operation analysis [9] is that statistical profiling does not provide the necessary level of detail to understand all performance problems. Hence message tracing is necessary.

NetLogger [25] provides end-to-end application and system level monitoring of high performance distributed systems. It can provide similar performance data as EventSpace does. However, our focus is on how to aggregate and analyze the communication performance of collective operations. This requires monitoring more hosts than the single path usually monitored by NetLogger.

Data stream management systems (for an overview of DSMSs see [3]) have been used to implement network monitors [12]. DSMSs provide a relational/ query interface for the performance analyst. Such an interface could be useful for specifying EventSpace scopes as SQL queries. However, to achieve the desired performance and perturbation, it is still necessary to map, configure and tune the query plan to the clusters in use; as shown in this paper.

Astrolabe [22] is a system for collecting, aggregating and updating large scale system state. Astrolabe is targeted for widely distributed applications and the primary design goal was scalability. EventSpace uses some of the Astrolabe techniques for improving scalability such as hierarchies and aggregation. Other aggregation and filtering systems for Internet are publish-subscribe systems [10], and Grid monitoring and discovery services such as Remos [13]. The filtering and aggregation functions in EventSpace are more specialized towards performance analysis. Also, since Astrolabe and publish-subscribe systems are targeted at widely distributed applications run on the Internet, low latency aggregation is not important.

Cluster monitoring tools such as Ganglia [18], and Grid monitoring tools such as the Network Weather Service [32], does not support the high sample rate necessary for collective operation analysis.

To reduce monitoring overhead, EventSpace coschedule execution of monitoring threads with application and communication system threads. Coscheduling has traditionally been used to schedule communicating processes [1]. Our design is similar to [11], where coscheduling is used to boost the priority of communication threads doing collective communication to improve application performance. However, we do not modify kernel code since coscheduling can be added to the communication system.

Many research projects have optimized MPI collective operations. Some of the approaches used are: (i) using knowledge about the topology hierarchy, going from multi-cluster [16] to individual clusters of SMPs [17,24] and uni-processors. (ii) taking advantage of architecture specific optimizations [24,26], (iii) using a lower-level network protocol [14,26], and (iv) automatically trying different algorithms and buffer sizes [27].

3 Performance Analysis and Optimization

Applications monitored by EventSpace use the PATHS communication system [5], which is an extension to the PastSet structured shared memory system [31]. Threads communicate by reading and writing tuples to shared memory buffers.

The purpose of the analysis is to detect performance problems in a spanning tree and understand how the tree can be reconfigured to improve performance. We briefly describe the metrics computed for the allreduce operation. Other synchronizing collective operations will have similar metrics. For a more detailed description see [9].

Central to the analysis are communication *paths* through the communication system starting from a thread and ending in a PastSet buffer. Each path consists of several *wrappers*; each wrapper has code that is run before and after calling the next wrapper in the path. Wrappers are used to implement communication between hosts and for instrumentation. Also, some wrappers join paths used to implement collective operation spanning trees, and handle the necessary synchronizations. The spanning tree is configured by

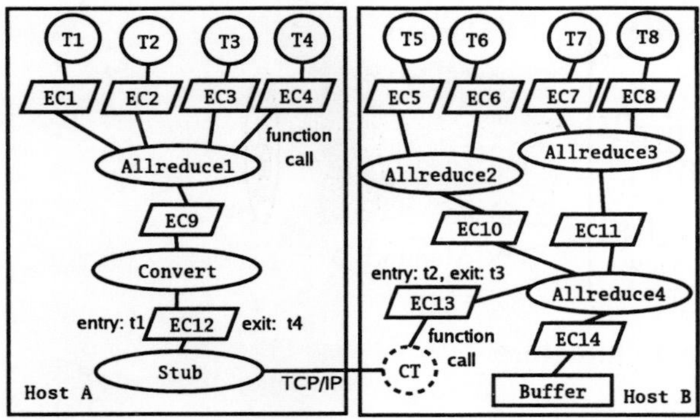

Figure 1. PATHS allreduce spanning tree.

specifying properties of the wrappers and the mapping of wrappers to cluster hosts [5,9].

In summary, we do for the performance analysis the following steps: (i) detect load balance problems, (ii) find paths with similar behavior, (iii) select representative paths for further analysis, (iv) find hotspots by breaking down the cost of a path into several stages, (v) reconfigure the path, and (vi) compare the performance of the new and old configuration.

Figure 1 shows an allreduce spanning tree used by threads T1–T8 instrumented with *event collectors* (EC1–EC14). These collect entry and exit timestamps for each wrapper. The reduced value is stored is a PastSet buffer. CT is a communication thread serving one TCP/IP connection.

For inter-host communication we calculate the two-way TCP/IP latency by $(t_4 - t_1) - (t_3 - t_2)$, where t_1 and t_4 are collected by the event collector before the stub in a path (EC12), and t_2 and t_3 are collected by the first event collector called by the communication thread (EC13).

Allreduce wrappers are called by multiple threads each contributing with a value to be reduced. There is one event collector after the allreduce wrapper, that collects timestamps t_2 and t_3, while the paths from each contributor i have an event collector collecting timestamps $t_{1,i}$ and $t_{4,i}$. For each contributor three latencies are calculated: *down latency* $t_2 - t_{1,i}$, *up latency* $t_{4,i} - t_3$, and *total latency* $(t_{4,i} - t_{1,i}) - (t_3 - t2)$.

Also calculated for each contributor are the *arrival order distribution* and the *departure order distribution*; the number of times the contributor arrived, and departed, at the allreduce wrapper as the first, second, and so on. In addition we calculate: *arrival wait time* $t_{1,l} - t_{1,i}$; how long contributor i had to wait for the last contributor l to arrive, and *departure wait time* $t_{4,i} - t_{4,f}$; elapsed time since the first contributor f departed from the allreduce wrapper, until contributor i departed.

4 EventSpace

The architecture of the EventSpace system is given in figure 2. An application is instrumented by inserting *event collectors* into its communication paths. Each event collector record data about communication operations into a *trace tuple* and stores it in an *event space* consisting of PastSet bounded buffers. Different *views* of the communication behavior can be provided by extracting and combining trace tuples provided by different event collectors. Consumers use an *event scope*, an aggregation/gather network, to do this.

4.1 Design

Runtime monitoring tools need to provide the data necessary for analysis at high performance and without perturbing the monitored application. We describe the design choices made in EventSpace to achieve these goals.

Configurability and extensibility. Being a research tool, EventSpace is designed to be extensible and flexible in order to experiment with different approaches for tuning the trade-off between monitoring performance and perturbation. It is also possible to extend EventSpace by adding other event collectors, and event scopes.

Separation of functional concerns. The tasks of collecting, storing, analyzing, gathering and presenting data are clearly separated in order to allow each part to be implemented and tuned separately. Data is collected by communication system wrappers, and stored using the PastSet structured shared memory system. EventSpace provides mechanisms for distributed analysis and fast collective operations for gathering data from compute hosts to a front-end host, which is responsible for presentation or further analysis of the data.

Low overhead data collection. We expect the number of trace tuple writes to be much larger than the number of reads; hence an event collector only record the minimal information for each communication operation and stores it in binary format in memory using native byte ordering. For heterogeneous environments, the tuple content can be parsed to a common format when it is read. Due to separation of concerns all communication paths are instrumented, and data is recorded for each operation, since event collectors do not know what data monitors need and when they need it.

Temporal trace storage. The challenge for large scale message tracing is the amount of data produced [28]. EventSpace provides temporal storage requiring only a few megabytes of memory (each trace tuple is 28 bytes allowing about 37 450 tuples to be stored in one megabyte of memory). The event scopes used by monitors need to have sufficient performance to read the trace tuples before they

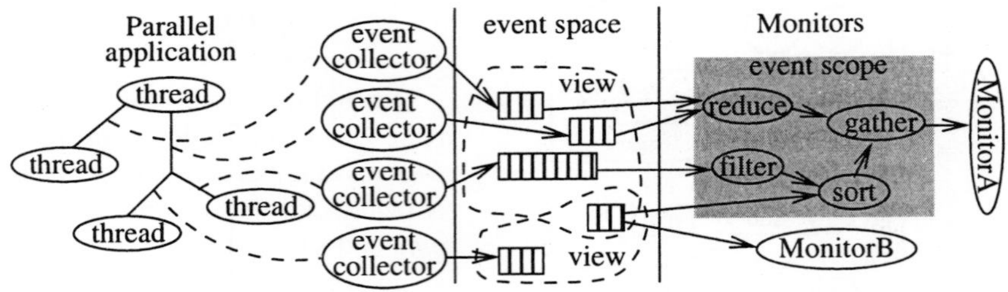

Figure 2. EventSpace architecture.

are discarded. Presently, the amount of tracing can not be dynamically be adjusted as in other monitoring systems (for example NetLogger [25]).

Distributed data analysis. Monitors use event scopes to analyze and gather data from compute hosts. The performance and perturbation of an event scope can be tuned by configuring the collective communication structures used by the event scope, and the mapping of these to the clusters. Data can be reduced or filtered close to the source, to avoid sending all data over a shared resource such as Ethernet, or a slow Internet link. Also some data preprocessing can be done on the compute clusters, thereby reducing the load on the front-end host.

Monitors using distributed analysis can be implemented either as a process on a front-end using an event scope or as a distributed application with several analysis threads. Each analysis thread can read and analyze trace tuples, and stores the result in a PastSet buffer. The results can then be gathered to a front-end for presentation.

Coscheduling. During a synchronizing collective operation all threads on a host must wait for data from other hosts. During the wait-time it is possible to run analysis threads if they are coscheduled with computation, and PATHS/PastSet communication threads. Coscheduling is possible since computation threads are blocked inside the communication system during collective operations and analysis threads also use the communication system for reading trace tuples. Hence, the release order of the different threads can be controlled by releasing all communication threads before computation threads, and finally any blocked analysis threads. No changes to the operating system scheduler are required.

On demand data gathering. Analyzing and gathering performance data comes at a cost. *Computation* is needed for the analysis, *communication* for moving data between hosts, and *storage* for intermediate results. Often these activities use the same resources as the monitored application. Pulling is used by monitors such that shared resources are not used until the data is needed.

Separation of performance concerns. Different parts of the monitoring system have different performance requirements. Event collectors run at the rate the application uses a collective operation. Some analysis threads must also run at this rate, but some lag is allowed due to the trace buffers. With distributed analysis, it is not necessary to gather all intermediate results; hence the gather rate can be lower than the event collecting rate. Further performance relaxation is allowed for presentation to users. The separation of performance concerns also makes it easier to trade-off between monitoring performance and perturbation.

4.2 Implementation

Event Space. An event space is implemented using PastSet buffers. Each trace buffer can have a different size and lifetime. The oldest tuple is automatically discarded when the number of tuples is above a specified threshold.

Event Collectors. An event collector writes a trace tuple to a trace buffer using the blocking PastSet write operation. During the write, the traced communication operation is blocked. As a result it is important to keep the introduced overhead low. The write consist of a mutex lock, a memory copy of 28 bytes, and a mutex unblock (a read is similar). The recorded information is: event collector identifier, PastSet operation type, tuple sequence number, return value, and the start and completion timestamps.

Event scopes. An event scope for a specific monitor is implemented as a spanning tree with PATHS wrappers for: (i) storage, (ii) data manipulation including aggregation, filtering and conversion, (iii) data gathering and scattering, and (iv) inter-host communication. Storage wrappers provide access to PastSet buffers, while inter-host communication wrappers allow setting properties of TCP/IP connections such as socket buffer size. Only the data manipulation wrappers are aware of tuple format and content.

Gather wrappers read tuples from several PastSet buffers, concatenate these and returns one large tuple. Scatter divides and writes a tuple into several PastSet buffers. The gathering and scattering is done in the context of the calling thread. It is also possible to specify that a given number of helper threads should be started for the wrapper. The helper threads allow parallel reads and writes on remote PastSet buffers.

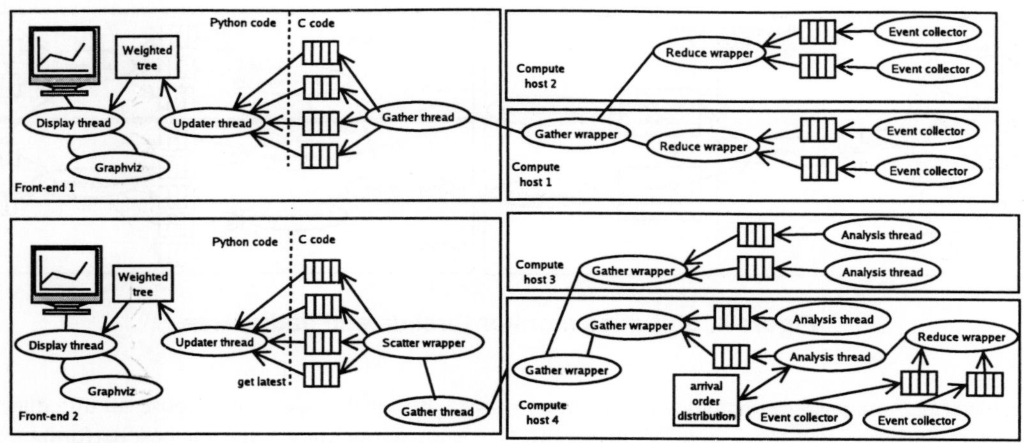

Figure 3. Load-balance monitor with a single event scope (top), and with distributed analysis (bottom).

4.3 Monitors

Load balance monitor. The load balance monitor is used to find load balance problems, which can be caused by workload imbalance, differences in point-to-point communication latency, or the mapping of a spanning tree to clusters. Two implementations are used. The first has a single event scope (figure 3). A gather thread uses the event scope to pull trace tuples produced by the event collectors on each compute host. A reduce wrapper is used to find the tuple with the largest down timestamp. All reduced tuples are then gathered to the front-end where they are scattered to PastSet buffers (one per allreduce wrapper). The tuples contain the number of last arrivals for each participant, and are read by a thread which applies updates to a weighted tree with the number of last arrivals for each participant. This tree is used to generate visualizations.

Distributed analysis reduces communication cost by increasing computation cost, but also complicates the monitor (figure 3). Each host has one analysis thread that counts the last arrivals for each participant by reading and reducing trace tuples as described above. After each read an *intermediate result* tuple is written to a PastSet buffer, containing the number of last arrivals for each participant. The gather thread gathers all intermediate result tuples from the compute hosts and scatters these to the local PastSet buffers. In the visualization we are only interested in the newest state of the system. Hence, not all intermediate result tuples need to be gathered since the arrival order state is maintained by the analysis threads.

Statistics monitor. The statistics monitor (statsm) is used to find paths with similar behavior and to detect hotspots. Computation is offloaded from the front-end by having on each compute host one or more analysis threads computing all statistics for the spanning tree wrappers on the host (figure 4). Our analysis assumes that all trace tuples are read before being discarded.

For each PATHS wrapper, statsm computes mean, minimum, maximum, standard deviation and median (using the sliding window median implementations from NWS [32] with window size set to 100) for the up, down and total latencies. For each wrapper, the results are stored in three 24 byte result tuples and written to three PastSet buffers. In addition, for allreduce wrappers similar results tuples are written for each arrival and departure order wait time. Also, for allreduce wrappers per thread arrival and departure wait time means are computed and stored in a PastSet buffer.

Two gather threads are used. The first gathers all up and down latencies in addition to the arrival and departure wait times. The second gathers per thread statistics (these are not always needed). Results are stored in two buffers at the front-end. These are used by an updater thread that maintains an analysis tree structure with statistics for each wrapper. The analysis tree is used by visualization threads.

5 Methodology

Two micro-benchmarks are monitored. In *Gsum* threads alternate between using two identical allreduce trees to compute a global sum. Gsum is run for 20 000 iterations using 8 byte messages (most scientific applications use small messages in allreduce [29]). *Compute-gsum* alternates between computing (integer sort) and calling allreduce. The benchmark can easily be perturbed since delaying one thread causes all others to wait for it [21]. Compute-gsum is run for either 10 000 or 20 000 iterations, and is tuned to spend 50% of its execution time computing and 50% in allreduce. Both have one computation thread per CPU. Each experiment is repeated at least three times and

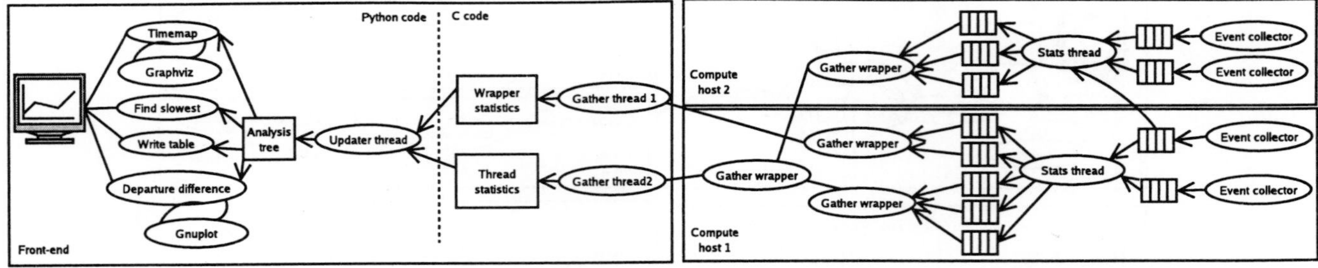

Figure 4. Statistics monitor threads and gather tree.

execution time averages are used to compute monitor overhead. Standard deviation is low (less than 1% of mean). To ensure fairness and experiment repeatability, all event scopes were set up and analysis threads were started before the monitored application.

Four clusters are used: *Copper* 18 dual-CPU Pentium II 300 MHz, 256 MB RAM, *Lead* 10 single-CPU Mobile Pentium III 900 MHz, 1024 MB RAM, *Tin* 51 single-CPU Pentium 4 Hyper-threaded 3.2 GHz, 2 GB RAM, *Iron* 39 singe-CPU Pentium 4 Hyper-threaded 3.2 GHz, 2 GB RAM with EM64T extension.

Copper and Lead share a two-way Pentium II 300 MHz with 256 MB RAM which is used as a gateway and which all communication to/from the cluster goes through. For Tin and Iron one host similar to the compute-hosts is used as gateway. A host outside the clusters, a Pentium 4 1.8 GHz with 2 GB RAM, is used as monitor front-end.

The Tin and Iron clusters have Gigabit Ethernet, while Copper, Lead, and all inter-cluster communication use 100 Mbit Ethernet. The operating system on all clusters is Linux, with the LinuxThreads Pthread library. Iron runs 32-bit code. Hyper-threading was enabled for Tin and Iron. On all TCP/IP connections the Nagle algorithm was disabled and default socket sizes were used.

We emulate WAN links between our clusters using the Longcut WAN emulator [7]. The design of Longcut is similar to the Panda WAN emulator [15]. Tin and Iron are each split into three sub-clusters. For each sub-cluster we select one host to act as a gateway. All communication to the sub-cluster is routed through its gateway, which adds delays to the routed messages to simulate the higher latency and lower bandwidth of a WAN TCP/IP connection. The emulator is implemented using PATHS wrappers.

To calculate the delay added to a message of a given size, we use a latency and bandwidth trace collected by running an instrumented communication intensive application on hosts in Tromsø, Trondheim, Odense and Aalborg. The largest latency is between Tromsø and Aalborg, and is about 36 milliseconds ([7] has additional details about the topology). The sub-clusters are assigned to these sites with two sub-clusters in Tromsø and Odense.

For each cluster we choose an allreduce spanning tree with, to our knowledge, the best performance. For Tin, Iron and Copper this is a hierarchy aware (as in [17,24]), 8-way spanning tree, while for Lead it is a flat tree. For the LAN multi-clusters the cluster spanning trees are connected by adding an inter-cluster allreduce. For WAN multi-clusters the inter-cluster allreduce is replaced by an all-to-all for improved performance (as in MagPIe [16]). The average time per allreduce for the different topologies is about 0.5 ms for Tin with 32 hosts, 0.6 ms for Tin with 49 hosts, 1 ms for a LAN multi-clusters and 65 ms for a WAN multi-cluster (both multi-clusters with 43 Tin hosts and 39 Iron hosts).

6 Experiments

6.1 Data Collection

The overhead added to a PastSet operation by a single event collector is low (1.1 μs on a 3.2 GHz Pentium 4), compared to the hundreds of microseconds per collective operation. Thus, for the gsum and gsum-noise experiments presented below, the overhead due to event collectors range from 0–2%.

The storage requirement for temporal traces is small. For our 8-way allreduce, the hosts with most event collectors (9) stores 252 bytes per call. We use one megabyte memory for trace tuples and one megabyte for intermediate results. Thus, trace buffer size is set to 3750 tuples, and the intermediate result buffers have size set to 5000 tuples.

6.2 Event Scope

To experiment with the performance, perturbation and tuning of an event scope, we instrumented both allreduce trees used by gsum with event collectors, but only monitored one. The allreduce tree for 49 *Tin* hosts has 241 event collectors, but only data from 57 are needed to compute the arrival order at each allreduce wrapper. These are on 8 hosts, and due to the reduce wrapper only 28 bytes need to be gathered from each host. For a single cluster,

Event Scope	Overhead
Event collectors	none–1%
32 Tins, sequential	tuples discarded
32 Tins, parallel	0.4%
LAN multi-cluster, seq.	tuples discarded
LAN multi-cluster, par.	none
WAN multi-cluster, seq.	1%

Table 1. Load balance monitor with single event scope.

Event Scope	Overhead	Gather rate
49 Tins, sequential (gsum)	2%	51%
49 Tins, parallel (gsum)	2%	99%
49 Tins, sequential	1%	65%
49 Tins, parallel	1%	99%
LAN multi-cluster, seq.	none	45%
LAN multi-cluster, par.	3%	100%
WAN multi-cluster, seq.	1%	94%
WAN multi-cluster, par.	3%	100%

Table 2. Load balance monitor with distributed analysis.

the event scope has only one gather wrapper which is run on the cluster gateway. For multi-clusters the event scopes have a gather wrapper on each cluster gateway and a gather wrapper on the monitor front-end gathering from these.

Gsum. Adding event collectors to a 49 *Tin* spanning tree does not introduce a measurable overhead (monitored mean is within one standard deviation of un-monitored mean). Neither does the load balance monitor. To ensure that all trace tuples are read before being discarded, helper threads must be added to the gather wrappers such that data is gathered in parallel. LAN and WAN multi-clusters have similar results.

Compute-gsum. The largest monitoring overhead was for a multi-cluster with emulated WAN links with 49 *Tin*, 18 *Copper* and 10 *Lead* hosts (table 1). However, the overhead is caused by the WAN emulator becoming inaccurate when there are many emulated connections. As for gsum, sequential gathering has often not sufficient performance.

Scalability. For the event scope achieving sufficient performance is harder than keeping the overhead low. The event scope need to be hierarchy aware and do all intra-host reduces before inter-host gathers, and intra-cluster gathers before inter-cluster gathers. Further reconfiguration by for example moving gather wrappers to unused cluster hosts does not improve performance. Also, for the cluster sizes we had available a flat gather tree had sufficient performance. For larger clusters additional levels may be necessary.

Increasing the number of hosts by connecting clusters with LANs or WANs often lowers the performance requirements for the monitor, since the performance of the monitored operation decreases. Also, the event scopes used by monitors such as load balance scale better than allreduce trees, since data is not needed from all hosts.

The higher WAN latency is usually tolerated since the monitored operation is latency bound, and the messages sent by the event scope are small (a few hundred bytes) making them also latency bound. We believe most WAN links have enough bandwidth for concurrent transfers of application and monitor data.

The monitoring scales well with number of monitored spanning trees. Monitoring both spanning trees in gsum and gsum-compute does not increase monitoring overhead or reduce monitoring performance. Similarly modifying gsum to use four spanning trees and monitoring all trees did not increase overhead or reduce performance.

6.3 Distributed Analysis

Load balance monitor. Distributed analysis uses more resources than the single event scope. For each host with allreduce wrappers, 352 bytes are gathered (compared to 224). Also, there is additional computation cost for running the analysis threads, and storage must be allocated for intermediate results. Using distributed analysis increases monitoring overhead from none to about 2% for gsum on a single cluster (table 2). For compute-gsum the monitoring overhead has not changed.

Monitoring cost can be reduced since it is not necessary to gather all intermediate results to the front-end. Hence, the overhead on a LAN multi-cluster can be reduced from 3% to none, by removing the helper threads in all gather wrappers (parallel vs. sequential in table 2). The performance difference between sequential and parallel gather is smallest for the WAN multi-cluster, and largest for the LAN multi-cluster.

6.3.1 Statistics monitor

Gsum. The statistics monitor is a computation and communication intensive monitor; the analysis threads read data from all trace buffers on the host. Some are also read twice; when computing statistics for the wrapper before and after the associated event collector. Also, to compute TCP/IP latencies a trace tuple must be read from another host.

Initially we have one analysis thread per host. Running distributed analysis on a 32 *Tin* host spanning tree, has 9% monitoring overhead. We tried different approaches for reducing the overhead. Removing all statistics computation (but still reading trace tuples) did not reduce the overhead,

Event Scope	Overhead	Wrapper	Thread
Event collectors	none–1%	-	-
Analysis threads	5–9%	-	-
with coscheduling 1	3%	-	-
with coscheduling 2	1%	-	-
32 Tins, sequential	2%	50%	69%
32 Tins, parallel	2%	77%	99%
LAN multi, seq.	see text	43%	68%
LAN multi, par.	+1%	100%	100%
WAN multi, seq.	none	100%	100%

Table 3. Statsm overhead and gather rates.

showing that the slowdown is not caused by computation. Similarly, removing the read and computation of statistics for allreduce wrappers did not reduce the overhead. Thus the problem was not caused by synchronization in the many buffer reads. Removing statistics computation for TCP/IP connections reduced the overhead to 4%, showing that the slowdown was caused by reads on trace buffers on other hosts.

For TCP/IP connections we can choose whether statistics should be computed at the source or destination (the direction of a path is from the thread to a PastSet buffer). Moving the computation from the source to destination host reduced the overhead to 5%. However, the analysis thread was not able to read all trace tuples before they were discarded (since it reads from 8 hosts sequentially). Running two analysis threads on each host allowed reading all tuples, but increased the overhead to 6%.

Finally, we used two coscheduling strategies: (i) analysis threads are blocked until all participating threads have contributed and a message is sent to the next-level host, and (ii) analysis threads are blocked until all participating threads are unblocked. The first strategy tries to do the analysis while the host is idle waiting for the broadcasted reduced value. The second makes sure the broadcast is done before unblocking analysis threads. The first strategy reduced the overhead to 3%, while the second reduced it to 1%. For the remaining experiments the second coscheduling strategy is used.

Adding gathering increased the overhead to 2%. There was no difference in overhead when gather wrappers had helper threads, but with the latter more intermediate results could be gathered (table 3).

The allreduce spanning trees for a LAN multi-cluster with 43 *Tin* hosts and 39 *Iron* hosts had about 20% slower inter-cluster communication than expected. We were not able to reconfigure or remap the spanning tree to remove the problem. However, when data is gathered from the cluster, allreduce operation time *decreases* with up to 18%. Thus we cannot measure the gather overhead for the multi-cluster topology. But we can compare the performance of a gather tree with sequential and parallel gathering. The latter improved wrapper-, and per thread statistics gather rate, but increased monitoring overhead with 1% (table 3).

The larger latency of emulated WAN links hides the performance problem described above. With WAN links, analysis threads introduce a 1% overhead, but data gathering can be done without helper threads, without increasing the overhead, and with sufficient performance to gather all intermediate results.

Compute-gsum. For compute-gsum the execution time variation is larger than for gsum (about 2% of mean), hence we could not see any monitoring overhead. Also, the gather rate is better. Both are probably due to less communication, since compute-gsum has one less allreduce per iteration.

Scalability. Analysis thread performance is independent of cluster size, since each only monitors a subtree. However, the subtree is dependent on the spanning tree shape.

Gather scalability depends on how analysis threads are mapped to the cluster. For example in our initial configuration all hosts had analysis threads which produced intermediate results that had to be gathered, while the final configuration only had analysis threads on the hosts with allreduce wrappers.

Data gathering for multi-cluster with WAN links has better performance, relative to allreduce performance, than for a single-cluster. This could be due to the small cluster sizes used. The largest cluster had only 12 hosts, requiring only 4400 bytes to be sent over a WAN link. For larger clusters the message size would increase, probably decreasing the gather rate.

Monitoring both 32 *Tin* host allreduce spanning trees in gsum, increased the analysis thread overhead to 5%. We were not able to reconfigure the event scope or coschedule the monitoring to reduce it. The overhead is caused by increased communication activity in the monitor. Adding data gathering does not increase the overhead. Neither does increasing the number of allreduce trees to four, since the communication frequency does not increase neither for the benchmark nor the analysis threads. We have similar results for LAN multi-clusters. However, with emulated WAN links monitoring both allreduce trees does not increase the overhead, since the time between each allreduce operation call is larger (due to WAN latency), hence monitoring activity can be scheduled to run during the WAN communication part of the allreduce operation.

We also modified compute-gsum to alternate between using two and four different spanning trees. Monitoring overhead did not increase, since the number of computations, number of allreduce calls, and allreduce call frequency did not change (we reduced the size of all trace and intermediate PastSet buffers to reflect the fewer allreduce calls per spanning tree).

7 Discussion

The low monitoring overhead and high performance of EventSpace suggest that runtime analysis can be incorporated into a communication system for automatically tuning collective operation performance. In earlier work we have shown how our performance analysis approach can be used to improve allreduce performance up to 49% [9].

It is probably easier to reduce monitoring overhead and improve monitoring performance for real applications than the micro-benchmarks we used, which were designed to stress the monitoring system. We believe the benchmarks are representative for the type of applications interesting to monitor with EventSpace, but real applications will have a more complex interaction between computation, communication and I/O providing further challenges for the analysis and tuning of collective operations.

For the load balance monitor we achieved the same performance and scalability when using an aggregation network than with distributed analysis. Due to the increased complexity of distributed analysis aggregation networks should be used. However, for monitors such as the statistics monitor aggregation networks do not have the necessary performance. Event scope performance was tuned by allocating more resources to the collective operations used to implement them. Changing the spanning tree shape or mapping to clusters did not improve performance.

All our clusters use Ethernet for communication. Faster interconnects, such as Myrinet [6], will improve the performance of collective operations. Thus, application with high enough communication ratio to be interesting to monitor with EventSpace will have a higher communication frequency. This requires the analysis computation to be done in a shorter time, but the event scopes will benefit from the improved communication performance.

Even when using Ethernet, communication latency can be improved by using a lower level protocol than TCP. But, we believe it is easier to add distributed analysis than to implement an event scope with a non-reliable lower level protocol.

We have not measured, or focused, on the time to setup and initialize the event scopes (as in [4, 23]). Currently it can take seconds due to the implementation using Python and XML-RPC. A significant performance improvement is possible by using a more efficient implementation.

Coscheduling the computation threads, communication system threads and the analysis threads did reduce perturbation for one benchmark. We believe further reduction could be achieved by priority scheduling all inter-host communication such that the applications messages always had higher priority than EventSpace messages. This would require a reimplementation of the PATHS/PastSet communication system.

8 Conclusions

We have described the EventSpace system for runtime performance monitoring of collective operations within the communication system. EventSpace allows high-performance message tracing without a large perturbation of the monitored application. By combining distributed analysis with fast collective operations to gather and analyze performance data, temporal storage for only a few megabytes of data is required. Separation of performance concerns allows us to tune the different parts of the system to achieve the required monitoring overhead and performance. Close integration with the communication system allows to coschedule analysis activity with the computation and communication of the monitored application.

We evaluated different monitors for collective operation performance analysis. Our findings were as follows: (i) monitor overhead was low, from none to maximum 3%, (ii) for many monitors it is harder to get sufficient performance than low perturbation, (iii) coscheduling allowed to reduce monitoring overhead from 9% to 1% for one benchmark, (iii) the monitoring has good scalability both with regards to the number of cluster hosts, number of clusters, and number of monitored spanning trees, (iv) high performance monitoring of a WAN multi-cluster is often easier than a single cluster, and (v) performance tuning should be done by allocating more threads to a monitor rather than reconfiguring its communication structure.

9 Future Work

Our long term goal is to build automatically reconfigurable collective operations. We will build and evaluate such a system based on the data provided by the monitoring tools in this paper.

Presently we are porting the NAS parallel benchmarks [20] to PATHS/PastSet to be able to use our tools. EventSpace may also be used to monitor other type of communication systems, for example to optimize global work scheduling in distributed work queues [2]. For data Grid applications large data sets are accessed. For such applications communication performance is important, making them interesting to monitor with EventSpace.

Also, important for the usability of EventSpace are graphical tools to simplify the building and tuning of event scopes.

References

[1] A. C. Arpaci-Dusseau. Implicit coscheduling: coordinated scheduling with implicit information in distributed systems. *ACM Transactions on Computer Systems*, 19(3):283–331, 2001.

[2] R. H. Arpaci-Dusseau. Run-time adaptation in River. *ACM Transactions on Computer Systems*, 21(1):36–86, 2003.

[3] B. Babcock, S. Babu, M. Datar, R. Motwani, and J. Widom. Models and issues in data stream systems. In *Proceedings of the twenty-first Symposium on Principles of database systems*, pages 1–16. ACM Press, 2002.

[4] S. M. Balle, J. Bishop, D. LaFrance-Linden, and H. Rifkin. Ygdrasil: Aggregator network toolkit for the grid. In *Proceedings of PARA'04 - Workshop on State-of-the-Art in Scientific Computing*, volume To appear of *Lecture Notes in Computer Science*. Springer, June 2004.

[5] J. M. Bjørndalen. *Improving the Speedup of Parallel and Distributed Applications on Clusters and Multi-Clusters.* PhD thesis, Department of Computer Science, University of Tromsø, 2003.

[6] N. J. Boden, D. Cohen, R. E. Felderman, A. E. Kulawik, C. L. Seitz, J. N. Seizovic, and W.-K. Su. Myrinet: A gigabit-per-second local area network. *IEEE Micro*, 15(1):29–36, 1995.

[7] L. A. Bongo. The Longcut wide area network emulator: Design and evaluation, 2005. Technical Report 2005-53. Dep.of Computer Science, University of Tromsø.

[8] L. A. Bongo, O. Anshus, and J. M. Bjørndalen. EventSpace - Exposing and observing communication behavior of parallel cluster applications. In *Euro-Par*, volume 2790 of *Lecture Notes in Computer Science*, pages 47–56. Springer, 2003.

[9] L. A. Bongo, O. Anshus, and J. M. Bjørndalen. Collective communication performance analysis within the communication system. In *Euro-Par*, volume 3149 of *Lecture Notes in Computer Science*, pages 163–172. Springer, August 2004.

[10] A. Carzaniga, D. S. Rosenblum, and A. L. Wolf. Design and evaluation of a wide-area event notification service. *ACM Trans. Comput. Syst.*, 19(3):332–383, 2001.

[11] G. S. Choi, J.-H. Kim, D. Ersoz, A. B. Yoo, and C. R. Das. Coscheduling in clusters: Is it a viable alternative? In *Proceedings of the 2004 ACM/IEEE conference on Supercomputing*. IEEE Computer Society Press, 2004.

[12] C. Cranor, T. Johnson, O. Spataschek, and V. Shkapenyuk. Gigascope: a stream database for network applications. In *Proceedings of the 2003 ACM SIGMOD international conference on Management of data*, pages 647–651. ACM Press, 2003.

[13] P. Dinda, T. Gross, R. Karrer, B. Lowekamp, N. Miller, P. Steenkiste, and D. Sutherland. The architecture of the Remos system. In *Proc. 10th IEEE Symp. on High Performance Distributed Computing*, 2001.

[14] A. Karwande, X. Yuan, and D. K. Lowenthal. CC-MPI: a compiled communication capable MPI prototype for Ethernet switched clusters. In *Proc. of the ninth ACM SIGPLAN symposium on Principles and practice of parallel programming*, pages 95–106. ACM Press, 2003.

[15] T. Kielmann, H. E. Bal, J. Maassen, R. van Nieuwpoort, L. Eyraud, R. Hofman, and K. Verstoep. Programming environments for high-performance grid computing: the Albatross project. *Future Generation Computer Systems*, 18(8):1113–1125, 2002.

[16] T. Kielmann, R. F. H. Hofman, H. E. Bal, A. Plaat, and R. A. F. Bhoedjang. MagPIe: MPI's collective communication operations for clustered wide area systems. In *Proceedings of the seventh ACM SIGPLAN symposium on Principles and practice of parallel programming*, pages 131–140. ACM Press, 1999.

[17] LAM-MPI homepage. http://www.lam-mpi.org/.

[18] M. Massie, B. Chun, and D. E. Culler. The Ganglia distributed monitoring system: Design, implementation, and experience, 2004.

[19] S. Moore, D.Cronk, K. London, and J.Dongarra. Review of performance analysis tools for MPI parallel programs. In *8th European PVM/MPI Users' Group Meeting, Lecture Notes in Computer Science 2131*. Springer Verlag, 2001.

[20] NASA. NAS Parallel Benchmarks.

[21] F. Petrini, D. J. Kerbyson, and S. Pakin. The case of the missing supercomputer performance: Achieving optimal performance on the 8,192 processors of ASCI Q. In *Proc. of the 2003 ACM/IEEE conference on Supercomputing*, 2003.

[22] R. V. Renesse, K. P. Birman, and W. Vogels. Astrolabe: A robust and scalable technology for distributed system monitoring, management, and data mining. *ACM Transactions on Computer Systems (TOCS)*, 21(2):164–206, 2003.

[23] P. C. Roth, D. C. Arnold, and B. P. Miller. MRNet: A software-based multicast/reduction network for scalable tools. In *Proceedings of the 2003 ACM/IEEE conference on Supercomputing*. IEEE Computer Society Press, 2003.

[24] S. Sistare, R. vandeVaart, and E. Loh. Optimization of MPI collectives on clusters of large-scale SMP's. In *Proceedings of the 1999 ACM/IEEE conference on Supercomputing*. ACM Press, 1999.

[25] B. Tierney, W. E. Johnston, B. Crowley, G. Hoo, C. Brooks, and D. Gunter. The NetLogger methodology for high performance distributed systems performance analysis. In *Proc. 7th IEEE Symp. On High Performance Distributed Computing*, pages 260–267, 1998.

[26] V. Tipparaju, J. Nieplocha, and D. Panda. Fast collective operations using shared and remote memory access protocols on clusters. In *17th Intl. Parallel and Distributed Processing Symp.*, May 2003.

[27] S. S. Vadhiyar, G. E. Fagg, and J. Dongarra. Automatically tuned collective communications. In *Proceedings of the 2000 ACM/IEEE conference on Supercomputing*, 2000.

[28] J. Vetter. Dynamic statistical profiling of communication activity in distributed applications. In *Proceedings of the 2002 ACM SIGMETRICS international conference on Measurement and modeling of computer systems*, pages 240–250. ACM Press, 2002.

[29] J. Vetter and F. Mueller. Communication characteristics of large-scale scientific applications for contemporary cluster architectures. In *16th Intl. Parallel and Distributed Processing Symp.*, May 2002.

[30] J. S. Vetter and A. Yoo. An empirical performance evaluation of scalable scientific applications. In *Proceedings of the 2002 ACM/IEEE conference on Supercomputing*. IEEE Computer Society Press, 2002.

[31] B. Vinter. *PastSet a Structured Distributed Shared Memory System.* PhD thesis, Department of Computer Science, University of Tromsø, 1999.

[32] R. Wolski, N. T. Spring, and J. Hayes. The network weather service: a distributed resource performance forecasting service for metacomputing. *Future Generation Computer Systems*, 15(5–6), 1999.

Automatic Experimental Analysis of Communication Patterns in Virtual Topologies*

Nikhil Bhatia [1], Fengguang Song [1], Felix Wolf [1], Jack Dongarra [1], Bernd Mohr [2], Shirley Moore [1]

[1] University of Tennessee, ICL, 1122 Volunteer Blvd Suite 413, Knoxville, TN 37996-3450, USA
{bhatia, song, fwolf, dongarra, shirley}@cs.utk.edu
[2] Forschungszentrum Jülich, ZAM, 52425 Jülich, Germany
b.mohr@fz-juelich.de

Abstract

Automatic pattern search in event traces is a powerful method to identify performance problems in parallel applications. We demonstrate that knowledge about the virtual topology, which defines logical adjacency relationships between processes, can be exploited to explain the occurrence of inefficiency patterns in terms of the parallelization strategy used in an application. We show correlations between higher-level events related to a parallel wavefront scheme and wait states identified by our pattern analysis. In addition, we visually expose relationships between pattern occurrences and the topological characteristics of the affected processes.

Keywords: performance tools, event tracing, virtual topologies, visualization, wavefront algorithms

1 Introduction

Parallel applications often fail to exploit the full power of the underlying computing hardware. Their optimization, however, is extremely difficult due to the inherent complexity of parallel systems and their communication structures.

In many parallel applications, each process (or thread) communicates only with a limited number of other processes. For example, a simulation modeling the spread of pollutants in the environment might decompose the overall simulation domain into smaller pieces and assign each of them to a single process. Given this distribution, a process would then only communicate with processes owning subdomains adjacent to its own. The mapping of data onto processes and the neighborhood relationship resulting from this mapping is called a *virtual topology*. In general, a virtual topology is specified as a graph. Many applications use Cartesian topologies, such as two- or three-dimensional grids. Virtual topologies can include processes or threads, depending on the programming model being used. Often, the virtual topology also influences the order in which certain computations are performed. For example, wavefront algorithms [7] propagate data along the diagonals of a multi-dimensional grid of processes.

The MPI standard [9] offers a set of API functions to allow for an efficient mapping of virtual topologies onto the physical topology of the underlying machine so that communication speeds between neighbors can be optimized. Beyond that, however, topological knowledge can help identify performance problems more effectively, especially as many parallel algorithms are parametrized in terms of a virtual topology.

In our previous work [14], we demonstrated that searching event traces of parallel applications for patterns of inefficient behavior is a successful method of automatically generating high-level feedback on application performance. This was accomplished by identifying wait states recognizable by temporal displacements between individual events across multiple processes or threads but without utilizing any information on logical adjacency between processes or threads. In this article, we show that enriching the information contained in event traces with topological knowledge allows the occurrence of certain patterns to be explained in the context of the parallelization strategy applied and, thus, significantly raises the abstraction level of the feedback returned. In particular, we demonstrate that topological information allows the following:

1. Detecting higher-level events related to the parallel algorithm, such as the change of the propagation direction in a wavefront scheme.

*This work was supported by the U.S. Department of Energy under Grants DoE DE-FG02-01ER25510 and DoE DE-FC02-01ER25490

2. Linking the occurrence of patterns that represent undesired wait states to such algorithmic higher-level events and, thus, distinguishing wait states by the circumstances causing them.
3. Exposing the correlation of wait states identified by our pattern analysis with the topological characteristics of affected processes by visually mapping their severity onto the virtual topology.

For this purpose, we have developed an easy-to-use extension of the KOJAK toolkit [14]. KOJAK is a post-mortem trace analysis tool that enables application developers to search event traces for the possible occurrence of a large number of execution patterns indicating inefficient behavior. The extension provides a means to record topological information as part of the event trace and to visualize the severity of the analyzed behaviors mapped onto the topology. Moreover, we have enhanced the analysis by specifying additional patterns that exploit topological information to find performance problems related to wavefront algorithms.

The remainder of this article is organized as follows. In Section 2 we give a brief overview of the KOJAK toolkit and its underlying approach of analyzing patterns in event traces. After introducing the extension to record and analyze virtual topologies in Section 3, we demonstrate its usefulness using two practical examples in Section 4. Finally, we consider related work in Section 5 and present our conclusion plus future work in Section 6.

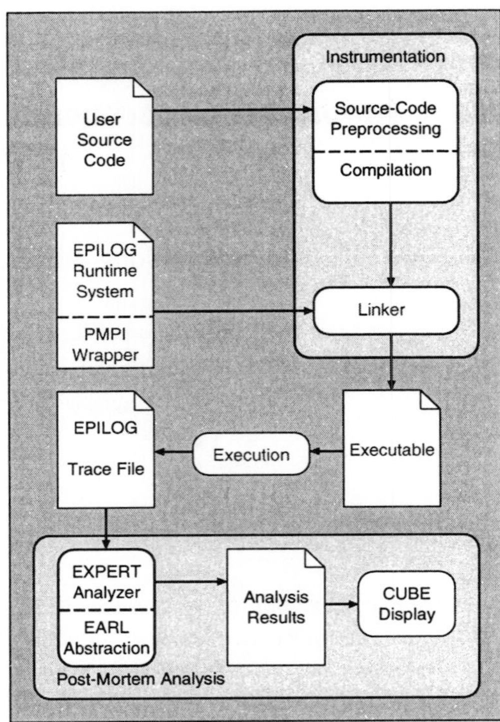

Figure 1. Overall architecture of the KOJAK system.

2 Pattern Analysis in Event Traces

Event tracing is a well-accepted technique for post-mortem performance analysis of parallel applications. Time-stamped events, such as entering a function or sending a message, are recorded at runtime and analyzed offline with the help of software tools. As event traces preserve the temporal and spatial relationships of individual events, they allow a deeper understanding of inter-process communication and an easier identification of wait states associated with it [13]. Since event traces tend to be very large, the coverage of a purely manual analysis is often limited.

KOJAK is an automatic performance evaluation system for parallel applications that relieves the user from the burden of searching large amounts of trace data manually by automatically looking for inefficient communication patterns that force processes into undesired wait states. KOJAK can be used for MPI, OpenMP, and hybrid applications written in C/C++ or Fortran. It includes tools for instrumentation, event-trace generation, and post-processing of event traces plus a generic browser to display the analysis results.

Figure 1 shows the entire process of analyzing an application using KOJAK. Prior to trace generation, the application needs to be instrumented. Depending on the platform, this is done automatically using a combination of source-code preprocessing and compiler-based instrumentation. As a final step, the application is linked with the EPILOG runtime system, which includes a PMPI interposition library that intercepts MPI calls to perform measurements before and after each call. Finally, when the instrumented application is executed, it generates a trace file.

The trace file is written in the EPILOG format [4], which provides event types covering MPI point-to-point and collective communication as well as OpenMP parallelism change, parallel constructs, and synchronization. Also, the trace file may include data from hardware counters.

After program termination, the trace file is analyzed offline using EXPERT [15], which identifies execution patterns indicating low performance and quantifies them according to their severity. These patterns target problems resulting from inefficient communication and synchronization as well as from low CPU and memory performance. The analysis process automatically transforms the traces into a compact call-path profile that includes the time spent in different patterns.

To simplify the analysis, EXPERT accesses the trace

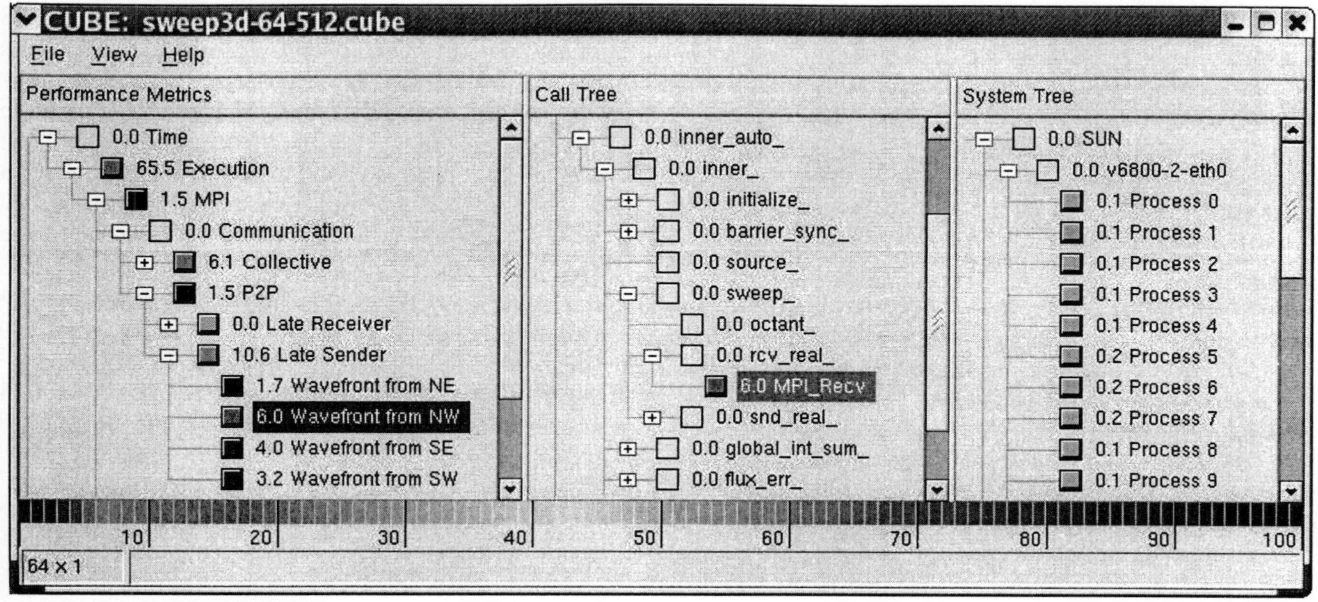

Figure 2. Visualization of performance problems using CUBE.

through the EARL library interface, which provides random access to individual events and precalculated abstractions supporting the search process. EARL is well documented and can be used for a large variety of analysis tasks beyond the analyses performed by EXPERT. The major benefits of using EARL as an intermediate layer between the analysis and the event trace are reduced size and increased readability of the pattern specifications. In EXPERT, patterns are specified separately from the actual analysis process as C++/Python classes [1] This design simplifies a later extension of the predefined pattern base, a feature we exploited here to integrate additional patterns suitable for studying wavefront algorithms.

Finally, the analysis results can be viewed in the CUBE performance browser [11], which is depicted in Figure 2. CUBE shows the distribution of performance problems across the call tree and the parallel system using tree browsers that can be collapsed and expanded to meet the desired level of granularity.

Our analysis will concentrate on a frequently occurring pattern called *late sender*. A process calls a blocking receive operation long before the message was sent and enters a wait state until the message arrives. The situation is depicted in Figure 3. Although this pattern involves two processes, the wait state can be associated with exactly one process, which is process A in this case.

EXPERT recognizes the late-sender situation by maintaining message queues to match corresponding send and

[1] In addition to a C++ version of the analyzer, we also maintain a Python version for prototyping purposes.

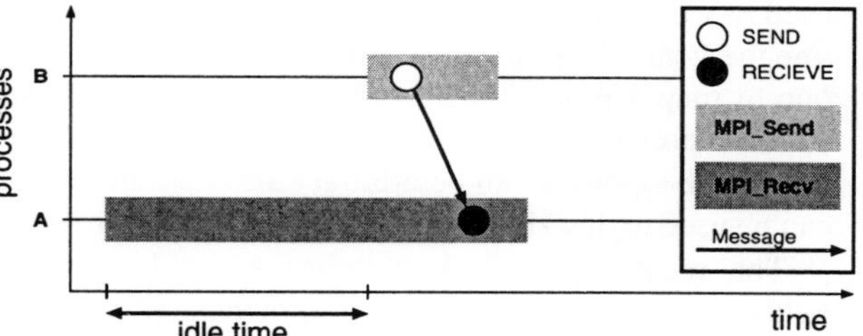

Figure 3. A process waiting for a message that was sent too late.

receive events and by tracking the call tree to associate the respective MPI calls with a call path. While searching the trace file, EXPERT maintains a matrix in which it accumulates the idle times incurred for a particular (call path, process) pair. After completion, the results are stored in an XML file that can be loaded into CUBE for visualization. For example, Figure 2 (left pane) shows that 6.0 % of the execution time was spent in a wait state caused by a special version of late sender called *wavefront from NW*, which is discussed in Section 4.1. The middle tree exposes the affected call path.

3 Virtual Topologies

To make the analysis topology-aware, we extended the following parts of the KOJAK system: (i) trace format, (ii) runtime system, (iii) abstraction layer, (iv) analyzer, and (v) display.

To keep the extension simple, we restricted ourselves to Cartesian topologies as a common case found in many of today's parallel applications. Other topology types, such as general graph topologies, might be included in the future. A Cartesian topology is essentially a multidimensional grid structure characterized by the following parameters:

- Number of dimensions
- Size of each dimension
- Periodicity of each dimension

The periodicity specifies whether the ends of a certain dimension are connected. The periodicity attribute is needed, for example, to specify a torus, a topology often found in physical networks used for point-to-point messaging in systems, such as IBM BlueGene/L. The periodicity attribute, however, is currently not used in our analysis.

Trace format. We added two record types that can be used to specify Cartesian topologies: one record type to define the general layout of a Cartesian topology and another one to map a process or thread onto a particular position within a previously defined topology. Note that the semantics of the topology can be arbitrary and that these records can be used to describe either virtual or physical topologies.

The record type used to define a topology includes fields to specify the number of dimensions, the size in each dimension, and whether a dimension is periodic or not. The record type also contains a field to specify an MPI communicator if the topology was created using the MPI_CART_CREATE function. Using this information, it is possible to filter communication operations by the communicator representing the topology.

The record type used to map a process or thread onto a position within a topology simply specifies a topology identifier and the coordinates of the process or thread within this topology. The mapping does not need to be surjective, that is, not all positions within the topology need to be filled. For example, the topology might represent the physical topology of the machine the application is running on, but without occupying all CPUs.

Runtime system. The runtime system has been extended to support the two new record types. There are two ways of defining a Cartesian topology and writing the corresponding records.

1. Automatically using MPI wrappers
2. Manually using a C/Fortran API

If the application uses MPI_CART_CREATE, the respective topology is automatically recorded as part of the trace file. This feature has been implemented by letting a PMPI wrapper, which is part of the runtime system, intercept the topology attributes and write the topology definition record. After processing the topology outline, the wrapper requests the coordinates of the calling process from the MPI runtime system and writes a corresponding coordinate-definition record.

Unfortunately, MPI topology support is rarely used. For this reason, EPILOG provides a C and Fortran API to perform exactly the steps that would otherwise be the MPI wrapper's responsibility. The API consists of two functions and allows the definition of an up to three-dimensional Cartesian topology. Using the API is fairly simple and requires only minimal effort.

The following example defines a three-dimensional $4 \times 4 \times 4$ topology that is periodic in the first but not in the remaining two dimensions.

```
if (rank .eq. 0) then
  call elgf_cart_create(4,4,4,1,0,0)
endif
call elgf_cart_coords(x,y,z)
```

Every process executing these lines assigns itself coordinates defined through the variables x, y, z, containing values between 0 and 3.

Abstraction layer. The abstraction layer represented by EARL is a high-level interface for reading an event trace. Topology information can now be accessed through EARL's class interface in either C++ or Python and used for a large variety of trace analysis tasks.

Analyzer. The analyzer has been enabled to read the topological information and to pass it on to the visualization component, which performs a general mapping of analysis results onto individual elements of the topology. In addition to this basic capability, four patterns specific to wavefront algorithms have been added to the analyzer. The patterns use topological knowledge to determine the direction of messages and to relate inefficient behavior to certain phases of the wavefront computation. Wavefront algorithms are an important class of algorithms commonly used to solve deterministic particle transport problems. The new patterns along with their implementations are discussed along with an application example in Section 4.1.

Display. A topology view, as depicted in Figures 5 and 6, has been added to the original tree view of processes and threads (Figure 2, right pane). The topology view can be accessed through a menu and shows the distribution of the time lost due to the selected pattern while the program was executing in the selected call path. The view is automatically updated as soon as the user selects another pattern or another call path. In this fashion, the user can study the distribution of a large variety of patterns across virtual topologies.

The topology view can display one-, two-, and three-dimensional Cartesian topologies. Three-dimensional topologies are presented in parallel projection as a collection of grid-like planes arranged on top of each other. To make the display scalable, the user can adjust the size of individual grid cells, the distance between neighboring planes, and the angle used to generate a three-dimensional perspective.

The color assigned to a certain grid cell represents the time spent in a certain pattern. To make differences visible even across a large number of cells, the display is able to utilize the full spectrum of available colors for a single pattern by switching to a high-resolution color mode.

4 Examples

To study how the the virtual topology can be used to classify certain wait states, we applied our tool extension to two example MPI codes, the ASCI SWEEP3D benchmark [1] and an environmental science application called TRACE [5].

4.1 SWEEP3D

The first example shows (i) that topological knowledge can be used to identify higher-level events related to distinct phases of the parallelization scheme used in an application and (ii) how these events influence the severity of certain inefficiency patterns.

The benchmark code SWEEP3D is an MPI program performing the core computation of a real ASCI application. It solves a 1-group time-independent discrete ordinates (Sn) 3D Cartesian geometry neutron transport problem by calculating the flux of neutrons through each cell of a three-dimensional grid (i, j, k) along several possible directions (angles) of travel. The angles are split into eight octants, each corresponding to one of the eight directed diagonals of the grid.

To exploit parallelism, SWEEP3D maps the (i, j) planes of the three-dimensional domain onto a two-dimensional grid of processes. The parallel computation follows a pipelined wavefront process that propagates data along diagonal lines through the grid. Figure 4 shows the data-dependence graph for a 3×3 grid. The long arrows symbolize data dependencies, while diagonal lines cut through algorithmically independent processes and represent the computation as it progresses in the form of "wavefronts" from the lower left to the upper right corner (short arrows). The actual direction of the wavefront is determined by the particular angle or octant being processed at a given moment.

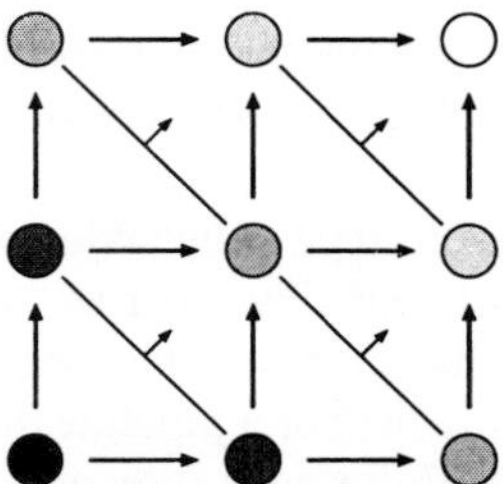

Figure 4. Wavefront propagation of data in SWEEP3D.

Responsible for the wavefront computation in the code is a subroutine called sweep(), which initiates wavefronts from all four corners of the two-dimensional grid of processes. The wavefronts are pipelined to enable multiple wavefronts to follow each other along the same direction simultaneously. Thus, the parallelization in SWEEP3D is based on concurrency among algorithmically independent processes and pipelining among algorithmically dependent processes. The basic code structure of routine sweep() is as follows:

```
DO octants
  DO angles in octant
    DO k planes
      ! block i-inflows
      IF neighbor(E/W) MPI_RECV(E/W)
      ! block j-inflows
      IF neighbor(N/S) MPI_RECV(N/S)
         ... compute grid cell ...
      ! block i-outflows
      IF neighbor(E/W) MPI_SEND(E/W)
      ! block j-outflows
      IF neighbor(N/S) MPI_SEND(N/S)
    END DO k planes
  END DO angles in octant
END DO octants
```

Performance models of wavefront processes, in particular as they appear in SWEEP3D, have been extensively studied [7, 12]. In this article, we analyze the characteristics of wavefront communication from an experimental viewpoint with emphasis on wait states resulting from the data dependencies illustrated in Figure 4.

Although parallel operation in SWEEP3D can be very efficient once the pipeline is filled, the opportunity for parallelism is limited whenever the direction of the wavefront changes and the pipeline has to be refilled, although the algorithm allows for some overlap between pipelines in different directions. As can be seen from the code structure inside routine sweep(), the receive calls are likely to block whenever the pipeline is refilled and the calling process is distant from the pipeline's origin. This phenomenon is a specific instance of the late-sender pattern illustrated in Figure 3.

To investigate this type of behavior, we extended the pattern base normally used by our EXPERT analysis tool and added four patterns describing the occurrence of late-sender instances at the moment of a pipeline direction change (i.e., a refill), one pattern for each direction (i.e., SW, NW, NE, SE). Since these patterns constitute a specialization of late sender, which was already member of the pattern base, their specifications could take advantage of EXPERT's publish/subscribe mechanism [15] through registration for late-sender instances published by the simple late-sender pattern. In this way, only the changes of the pipeline direction needed to be specified, reducing the amount of code necessary to describe the combined situation. As the problem is highly symmetric, we specified the direction change in a parametrized fashion, further decreasing the lines of code needed.

The direction change is recognized by maintaining for every process a FIFO queue that records the directions of messages received. For this purpose, the direction of every message is calculated using topological information. Since the wavefronts propagate along diagonal lines, as depicted in Figure 4, each wavefront direction has a horizontal as well as a vertical component, involving messages in two different orthogonal directions, each of them corresponding to one of the two receive and send statements in routine sweep(). We therefore need to consider two potential wait states at the moment of a direction change, each resulting from one of the two receive statements. Note that the horizontal component is always executed first, limiting the number of cases that need to be considered in order to detect a change.

However, special attention has to be paid to processes located at the border of the grid (Figure 4). Because they have only a limited number of neighbors, their inbound as well as their outbound communication may be restricted to one direction only, depending on their position relative to the wavefront propagation direction. For this reason, our implementation distinguishes between different border areas to which it applies different detection rules. These rules are parametrized in terms of the wavefront origin and the area's horizontal/vertical orientation.

Note that we do not make any assumption about the order in which the different pipeline directions are scheduled, making the detection algorithm more general. To also cover the very first pipeline start, the queue is initially filled with pseudo direction symbols.

To validate our design, we chose a problem size of $512 \times 512 \times 150$ grid points with blocking factors 10 and 3 for k-planes and angles, respectively. We ran the application with 64 processes on a Solaris cluster equipped with UltraSPARC-III 750 MHz processors. MPI was configured to communicate via shared memory within the same node and via Myrinet across different nodes. The instrumentation of user functions in the code was done fully automatically using the platform compiler's profiling interface. As the program does not take advantage of MPI topology support, we recorded the topology by manually inserting the EPILOG API calls described in Section 3 into the module responsible for domain decomposition. Figure 2 shows the output of our analysis as rendered by the original KOJAK GUI. The new patterns appear in the metric tree on the left underneath "Late Sender" and are labeled with the percentage of execution time spent in wait states caused by the pattern. The total time spent in late-sender wait states, which can be obtained by collapsing the late-sender node, was 25.4%. Late sender instances observed simultaneously with a pipeline direction change account for a little less than 60% of the overall late-sender time. The times measured for individual directions vary between 6.0% of total execution time for pipeline refill from North-West and 1.7% for refill from North-East.

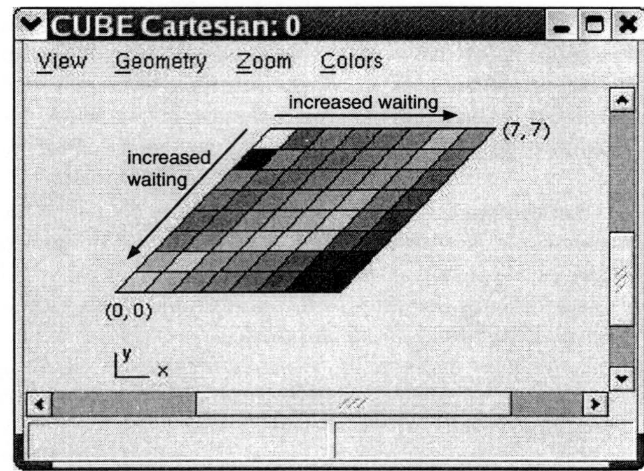

Figure 5. Distribution of late-sender wait states as a result of pipeline refill from North-West.

Figure 5 shows the new topology view rendering the distribution of late-sender times for pipeline refill from North-West (i.e., upper left corner). The colors are assigned relative to the maximum and minimum wait times for this particular pattern. As can be seen, the corner reached by the wavefront last incurs most of the waiting times, whereas processes closer to the origin of the wavefront incur less. Note that the specifications of our patterns do not make any assumption about the specifics of the computation performed, and should therefore be applicable to a broad range of wavefront applications.

Although the current implementation applies to wavefront processes based on a two-dimensional domain decomposition, we assume that it can be easily adapted to a three-dimensional decomposition by considering wavefronts propagating along three orthogonal direction components instead of two.

4.2 TRACE

The second example highlights how visually mapping the results of our pattern analysis onto the virtual topology can help the user identify semantically meaningful clusters of related behavior.

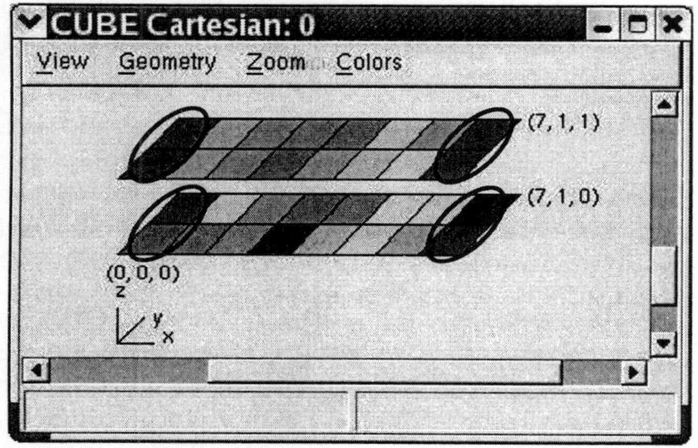

Figure 6. Distribution of wait states caused by inherently synchronizing all-to-all operations.

TRACE simulates the subsurface water flow in variably saturated porous media. It solves the generalized Richards equation in three spatial dimensions. The parallelization is based on a parallelized CG algorithm, which divides the grid into overlapping subgrids and communicates via MPI. The main computation is done in a subroutine called parallelcg(). We executed the application with 32 processes on a Linux cluster with 8 Pentium III Xeon (550 MHz) 4-way nodes. Like in the previous example, MPI was configured to communicate via shared memory within the same node and via Myrinet across different nodes. The resulting topology is a three-dimensional Cartesian $8 \times 2 \times 2$ grid (Figure 6).

The display shows the distribution of wait states in parallelcg() caused by inherently synchronizing all-to-all operations that occur when some processes enter the operation earlier than others. The pattern describing this situation is among the standard patterns included in the EXPERT analyzer.

The figure exhibits clusters of increased waiting times at the corners of the three-dimensional grid that due to their exposed location are assumed to have different computation as well as communication requirements. Without topological knowledge the affected processes would appear as arbitrary processes and the user would be unaware of the correlation between their particular role in the topology and the occurrence of specific inefficiencies.

5 Related Work

Topological information has been used earlier to highlight certain aspects of parallel performance.

Ahn and Vetter mapped counter data onto the virtual topology of the SWEEP3D benchmark to identify clusters of related behavior by statistical means [2]. Müllender visualized different network topologies including four-dimensional hypercubes as well as up to three-dimensional grids and tori using a polygon-like vector representation and mapped certain communication parameters, such as the number of messages, onto their nodes to better observe communication activities in virtual shared memory systems [10].

The three-dimensional topological display developed as part of this work follows in its design the torus view included in TREND [6], a tool for supervising system utilization on the CRAY T3E. However, to accommodate a larger variety of grid sizes ranging from very small to very large, we made additional display parameters adjustable, such as the distance between planes or the angle used to create the three-dimensional perspective.

Topological knowledge has also been used for semantic debugging of parallel applications. Huband and McDonald describe a trace-based debugger called DEPICT that exploits topological information to identify processes with logically similar behavior in traces of MPI applications and to display semantic differences among these groups [8]. The comparison is based on the order and number of events. Also interesting to our work is DEPICT's ability to automatically identify the virtual topology in the trace using graph-distance measures, a mechanism that could render the manual recording exercised in our examples unnecessary.

6 Conclusion and Future Work

Topological knowledge can be used to significantly raise the semantic level of the feedback given by KOJAK's method of scanning event traces for patterns of inefficient behavior.

Using wavefront algorithms as an example, we demonstrated that topological information enables the identification of higher-level events related to a program's parallelization scheme and the correlation of these higher-level events with wait states identified by our previous pattern analysis method. This correlation allowed us to reintroduce a time-dimension into an otherwise timeless data model of analysis results by letting pattern specifications refer to distinct algorithm-specific execution phases. We further showed that visually mapping wait states identified by our pattern analysis onto the topology enables the correlation of these wait states with topological characteristics of the affected processes. To enhance the practical value of these concepts, they have been implemented as an easy-to-use extension of the KOJAK toolkit.

Future work will address the operations of wavefront processes in more detail by (i) studying the overlap between pipelines coming from different directions and (ii) investigating the influence of alternate blocking parameters on the performance behavior observed. We also intend to extend the scope of the underlying principles to other algorithms, such as parallel multi-frontal methods [3]. To further enhance the automatic capabilities of our tool, we will investigate ways to recognize the algorithm in advance so that appropriate analysis patterns can be selected. Options to be considered include adding metadata to the event trace - for example, by instrumenting parallel libraries that are usually aware of the algorithms applied. Another approach would be the automatic detection in the trace itself similar to the automatic topology detection scheme described in [8].

References

[1] Accelerated Strategic Computing Initiative (ASCI). *The ASCI sweep3d Benchmark Code*. `http://www.llnl.gov/asci_benchmarks/`.

[2] D. H. Ahn and J. S. Vetter. Scalable Analysis Techniques for Microprocessor Performance Counter Metrics. In *Proc. of the Conference on Supercomputers (SC2002)*, Baltimore, November 2002.

[3] Iain S. Duff. Parallel implementation of multifrontal schemes. *Parallel Computing*, 3:193–204, 1986.

[4] B. Mohr F. Wolf. EPILOG Binary Trace-Data Format. Technical Report FZJ-ZAM-IB-2004-06, Forschungszentrum Jülich, May 2004.

[5] Forschungszentrum Jülich. *Solute Transport in Heterogeneous Soil-Aquifer Systems*. `http://www.kfa-juelich.de/icg/icg4/Groups/Pollutgeosys/trace_e.html`.

[6] Forschungszentrum Jülich. *TREND - Torus REsources and Node Display*. `http://www.fz-juelich.de/zam/trend/`.

[7] A. Hoisie, O. Lubeck, and H .Wasserman. Performance Analysis of Wavefront Algorithms on Very-Large Scale Distributed Systems. In *Lectures Notes in Control and Information Sciences*, volume 249, page 171, 1999.

[8] S. Huband and C. McDonald. A Preliminary Topological Debugger for MPI Programs. In R. Buyya, G. Mohay, and P. Roe, editors, *Proc. of the First IEEE/ACM International Symposium on Cluster Computing and the Grid*, pages 422–429. IEEE Computer Society, 2001.

[9] Message Passing Interface Forum. *MPI: A Message Passing Interface Standard*, June 1995. `http://www.mpi-forum.org`.

[10] C. Müllender. Visualisierung der Speicheraktivitäten von parallelen Programmen in Systemen mit virtuell gemeinsamen Speicher. Master's thesis, RWTH Aachen, Forschungszentrum Jülich, May 1994.

[11] F. Song, F. Wolf, N. Bhatia, J. Dongarra, and S. Moore. An Algebra for Cross-Experiment Performance Analysis. In *Proc. of the International Conference on Parallel Processing (ICPP)*, Montreal, Canada, August 2004.

[12] D. Sundaram-Stukel and M. K. Vernon. Predictive Analysis of a Wavefront Application Using LogGP. In *Proc. 7th ACM SIGPLAN Symp. on Principles and Practices of Parallel Programming (PPoPP '99)*, pages 141–150, Atlanta, GA, May 1999.

[13] F. Wolf and B. Mohr. Specifying Performance Properties of Parallel Applications Using Compound Events. *Parallel and Distributed Computing Practices*, 4(3):301–317, September 2001. Special Issue on Monitoring Systems and Tool Interoperability.

[14] F. Wolf and B. Mohr. Automatic performance analysis of hybrid MPI/OpenMP applications. *Journal of Systems Architecture*, 49(10-11):421–439, 2003. Special Issue "Evolutions in parallel distributed and network-based processing".

[15] F. Wolf, B. Mohr, J. Dongarra, and S. Moore. Efficient Pattern Search in Large Traces through Successive Refinement. In *Proc. of the European Conference on Parallel Computing (Euro-Par)*, Pisa, Italy, August - September 2004.

Design and Implementation of a Parallel Performance Data Management Framework

Kevin A. Huck, Allen D. Malony, Robert Bell, Alan Morris
Performance Research Laboratory, Department of Computer and Information Science
University of Oregon, Eugene, OR, USA
{khuck,malony,bertie,amorris}@cs.uoregon.edu

Abstract

*Empirical performance evaluation of parallel systems and applications can generate significant amounts of performance data and analysis results from multiple experiments as performance is investigated and problems diagnosed. Hence, the management of performance information is a core component of performance analysis tools. To better support tool integration, portability, and reuse, there is a strong motivation to develop performance data management technology that can provide a common foundation for performance data storage, access, merging, and analysis. This paper presents the design and implementation of the Performance Data Management Framework (*PerfDMF*). PerfDMF addresses objectives of performance tool integration, interoperation, and reuse by providing common data storage, access, and analysis infrastructure for parallel performance profiles. PerfDMF includes an extensible parallel profile data schema and relational database schema, a profile query and analysis programming interface, and an extendible toolkit for profile import/export and standard analysis. We describe the PerfDMF objectives and architecture, give detailed explanation of the major components, and show examples of PerfDMF application.*

1. Introduction

Performance evaluation of parallel programs and systems, whether for purposes of benchmarking or application tuning, requires the analysis of performance data taken from multiple experiments [7, 12, 26]. While sophisticated tools exist for parallel performance profiling and tracing, allowing in-depth analysis of a single execution run, there is significantly less support for the processing and storage of multiple performance datasets generated from a variety of experimentation and evaluation scenarios. It might be expected that each performance tool solve the problem of multi-experiment performance data and results management individually, but one can argue this is neither a reasonable expectation, since resources may be unavailable to build such support for some tool projects, nor a desired one, given the potential for building incompatible solutions. Instead, to promote performance tool integration and analysis portability, and to foster a multi-experiment performance evaluation methodology in general, there is strong motivation to develop open performance data management technology that can provide a common, reusable foundation for performance results storage, access, and sharing. Such technology could offer standard solutions for how to represent types of performance data, how to store performance information in a manageable way, how to interface with the performance storage system in a portable manner, and how to provide performance information services to a broad set of analysis tools and users. A performance data management system built on this technology could serve both as a core module in a performance measurement and analysis system, as well as a central repository of performance information contributed to and shared by several groups.

This paper presents the design and implementation of the *PerfDMF* parallel performance data management framework. The research is motivated by our work in parallel performance analysis and in the development of the TAU parallel performance system [27]. PerfDMF addresses critical requirements in TAU for the storage, maintenance, and processing of multi-experiment performance measurements and results. However, our broader goal with the PerfDMF project is to provide an open, flexible framework that can support common performance management tasks and be extended and re-targeted to enhance performance data integration as well as reuse across performance tools used in the parallel computing community.

The objectives of our performance data manage-

0190-3918/05 $20.00 © 2005 IEEE

ment research and the PerfDMF project are discussed in Section 2. PerfDMF is designed for the management of parallel performance profile data. The PerfDMF architecture consists of four components: profile input/output, profile database, database query and management interface, and profile analysis packages. Section 3 describes the PerfDMF architecture in detail. As performance tool technologists, the implementation of PerfDMF reflects our strong concern for tool integration, reusability, portability, and open software. Implementation choices we have made and API examples are discussed in Section 4. PerfDMF was developed specifically to handle large-scale performance profiles and a large number of profile results. We have integrated PerfDMF into the TAU performance system and include it as part of TAU's distribution. However, PerfDMF provides importers for six common profile formats and could be useful for performance tools other than TAU. Section 5 demonstrates the application of PerfDMF in TAU. Other projects have considered performance databases for different purposes. We contrast PerfDMF with these parallel performance tools in Section 6. We conclude with a summary of the research work and our future PerfDMF plans.

2. Objectives

Research in performance tools for parallel systems is driven by two equally important concerns. The primary purpose of performance tools is, of course, the effective evaluation of performance problems. The creation of powerful techniques for instrumentation, measurement, analysis, and modeling are important for the characterization, understanding, and tuning of parallel performance, particularly for complex scientific applications on large-scale systems. Accomplishments across the performance tools research community attest to the significant advancements being made in performance evaluation methods.

However, unless performance tools can be used in practice, in large-scale and diverse production environments, the advantages of new performance evaluation methods will go largely unnoticed. Performance technology must be built to higher tool engineering standards. Interestingly, the tool technology and engineering requirements that arise in parallel scientific computing pose research problems equally challenging to those in performance evaluation. These include tool portability (e.g., across architectures, computing models, and languages), scalability (e.g., to thousands of threads of execution), robustness (e.g., integrated with compilers, libraries, and runtime systems), and automation. There is also strong present motivation for tool integration, inter-operation, and reuse, and the development of performance technology following an open source methodology. We believe that by addressing these two general concerns – performance tool "science" and tool technology engineering – more sophisticated tools can be realized, built to high software quality standards, and readily assimilated in production environments.

In relation, the PerfDMF project represents primarily research in performance technology engineering. Most empirical parallel performance tools are targeted to the analysis of performance data from a single performance experiment. However, current interest in multi-experiment performance analysis is motivated by several purposes: benchmarking, procurement evaluation, modeling, prediction, and application optimization, to name a few. Indeed, several researchers have demonstrated the importance of multi-experiment methodology and tools [12, 16, 22, 26, 28]. Although there is an obvious degree of overlap in the profile data representation, organization, and basic methods of analysis in these projects, unfortunately, there is little technology sharing. From a tool engineering perspective, if the important profile data management features and functions could be captured in a common framework, performance tools could incorporate the framework in their design and interoperate with other tools that use the framework, resulting in several advantages for both enhancing performance tool capabilities and improving tool deployment.

The PerfDMF research focuses on the design and development of a common, reusable performance data management and analysis framework. The primary objectives of the PerfDMF research work are:

- Import/export of data from/to leading parallel profiling tools.
- Handle large-scale profile data and large numbers of experiments.
- Provide a robust profile data management system that is portable and easily reused.
- Support abstract profile query and analysis API that offers an alternative Data Management System (DMS) programming interface.
- Allow for extension and customization in the performance data schema and analysis API.

The following sections discuss how the PerfDMF design and implementation meets these objectives in more detail. It is important to note that we use the term "framework" to emphasize the intention of PerfDMF to be used as a component in an integrated performance tool environment, one that can be configured and applied for the particular performance analysis purposes. It is the framework concept for performance data management and its representation in PerfDMF that is the primary contribution of our research.

3. PerfDMF Design Architecture

Empirical performance evaluation of parallel and distributed systems or applications often generates significant amounts of performance data and analysis results from multiple experiments and trials as performance is investigated and problems diagnosed. However, the management of performance data from multiple experiments can be logistically difficult, impeding the effective analysis and understanding of performance outcomes. The Performance Data Management Framework (PerfDMF) provides a common foundation for parsing, storing, querying, and analyzing performance data from multiple experiments, application versions, profiling tools and/or platforms. The PerfDMF design architecture is presented in this section. We describe the main components and their interoperation. Attention is also given to the profile database schema as the core of the PerfDMF database support.

3.1. PerfDMF Components

PerfDMF consists of four main components: *profile input/output*, *profile database*, *database query and analysis API*, and *profile analysis toolkit*. Figure 3.1 shows a representation of these four components, and their relationships. PerfDMF is designed to parse parallel profile data from multiple sources. This is done through the use of embedded translators, built with PerfDMF's data utilities and targeting a common, extensible parallel profile representation. Currently supported profile formats include gprof[9], TAU profiles[27], dynaprof[19], mpiP[29], HPMtoolkit (IBM)[6], and Perfsuite (psrun)[20]. (Support for SvPablo [24] is being added.) The profile data is parsed into a common data format. The format specifies profile data by node, context, thread, metric and event. Profile data is organized such that for each combination of these items, an aggregate measurement is recorded. The similarities in the profile performance data gathered by different tools allowed a common organization to be used. Export of profile data is also supported in a common XML representation. In the future, we may also offer exporters to a subset of the formats above.

The profile database component is the center of PerfDMF's persistent data storage. It builds on ro-

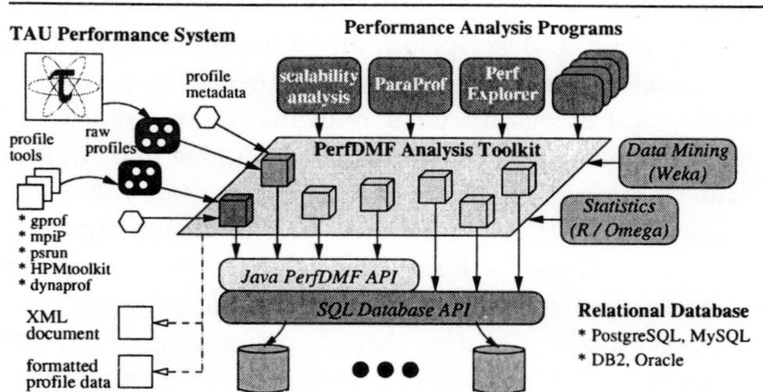

Figure 1. TAU PerfDMF Architecture

bust SQL relational database engines, some of which are freely distributed. The currently supported Relational Database Management Systems (DBMS) are PostgreSQL, MySQL, Oracle and DB2. The database component must be able to handle both large-scale performance profiles, consisting of many events and threads of execution, as well as many profiles from multiple performance experiments. Our tests with large profile data (101 events on 16K processors) showed the framework adequately handled the mass of data.

To facilitate performance analysis development, the PerfDMF architecture includes a well-documented data management API to abstract query and analysis operation into a more programmatic, non-SQL, form. This layer is intended to complement the SQL interface, which is directly accessible by analysis tools, with dynamic data management and higher-level query functions. It is anticipated that many analysis programs will utilize this API for implementation. Access to the SQL interface is provided using the Java Database Connectivity (JDBC) API. Because all supported databases are accessed through a common interface, the tool programmer does not need to worry about vendor-specific SQL syntax.

The last component, the profile analysis toolkit, is an extensible suite of common base analysis routines that can be reused across performance analysis programs. The intention also is to provide a common programming environment in which performance analysis developers can contribute toolkit modules and packages. As will be shown later in Section 5, analysis routines are a useful abstraction for developing profile analysis applications.

3.2. Profile Database Schema

A relational database schema is used to organize the performance data. The top level table, APPLICATION, stores the data relevant to an application, such as name, version, description, etc. The **EXPERIMENT** table contains a foreign key reference to the **APPLICATION** table, and stores all data relevant to an experiment, such as the system information, compiler information, and configuration information. The **TRIAL** table contains a foreign key reference to the **EXPERIMENT** table, and contains information relevant to a trial, such as the date/time, problem definition, node count, contexts per node, and max threads per context. PerfDMF provides a flexible schema for these three tables. The schema requires that the id, name and foreign key reference columns exist in each of these tables, but additional columns may be added to (or removed from) the tables without requiring changes to the Java source code. This ability is provided by the getMetaData() call in JDBC, and provides flexible access to the columns in the database. The schema is designed such that if capturing such data as compiler names and versions, operating system attributes, etc. is important for analysis, then those columns can be added to the database. In addition, the analysis team is free to organize the performance attribute data in any way they like - the compiler information can be stored in the **APPLICATION**, **EXPERIMENT**or **TRIAL** table, or not at all. These features are important for the reusability of PerfDMF.

Some profiling tools, including TAU, collect more than one metric when executing an experiment trial. These metrics can include measurements such as CPU time, data cache misses and floating point operations, as well as derived metrics such as floating point operations per second. Because there can be more than one metric per trial, the schema includes a **METRIC** table, which stores the name of the metric and a foreign key reference to the trial table. Because some analysis tools also generate derived data, derived metrics can be saved with the profile data in the database using the PerfDMF API.

Performance profile instrumentation normally organizes interval data from a profile run according to functions, or as blocks of code given a "function name". Profiling tools can also organize interval data in smaller logical blocks, such as loops, basic blocks or even individual lines of code. The top level interval data table within a trial is the **INTERVAL_EVENT** table. The **INTERVAL_EVENT** table contains the name of the event, an event group (i.e. computation, communication, etc.), and a foreign key reference to the **TRIAL** table, indicating the trial to which it belongs. The **INTERVAL_LOCATION_TABLE** contains the cumulative data for each event, node, context, thread, metric combination. The data captured includes inclusive time, inclusive percentage, exclusive time, exclusive percentage, inclusive time per call, number of calls and number of subroutines. For some profiling tools, the value of one or more of these fields may be undefined. The **INTERVAL_TOTAL_SUMMARY** and **INTERVAL_MEAN_SUMMARY** tables contain the **INTERVAL_LOCATION_TABLE** total and mean values, respectively, across all nodes, contexts and threads.

In addition to the regular instrumented profile data, data from atomic events can be captured in profiles. In TAU, for instance, users can define atomic events at code locations to collect data which varies for each instrumentation call, such as the current application size in memory, or the size of an MPI communication. The **ATOMIC_EVENT** table stores the atomic counter information, such as the name and group name for the counter. The **ATOMIC_LOCATION_PROFILE** table contains a foreign key reference to the **ATOMIC_EVENT** table, as well as the sample count, maximum value, minimum value, mean value and standard deviation for each **ATOMIC_EVENT**, node, context, thread combination.

4. Implementation

Our goals in developing PerfDMF are primarily integration, reusability, and portability. We also wanted an implementation based on robust and open software and protocols. We have decided to use Java, JDBC, XML and ANSI SQL, for portability, standard DBMS connectivity and profile data exchange. There are four main components of PerfDMF, including profile input/output, profile database access, profile management, and the analysis toolkit. All four are self-contained modules, but they share common profile data objects and API. This section discusses the PerfDMF implementation from the perspective of analysis code development. Particular attention is paid to the performance database and the management component.

For historical reasons, there are two methods of data access in PerfDMF. The first method provides an overall data management toolkit, including all of the file parsers and database access for both querying and storing data. The other method provides access for just querying and storing data to the database directly. The nature of the analysis application will determine which method to use. For example, if an analysis application will only be a database client application, and the application developer wants to selectively query the data without having to load entire (possibly large) trials, then the database-only interface should be used. If the analysis application needs to support profile data directly from profiling tools in the form of flat files, and/or doesn't need database support, then the first method should be used. The selection of one method does not preclude the use of the other, and the two are not mutually exclusive.

The two methods logically organize the profile data in the same way. Based on TAU's generalized performance data representation [27], PerfDMF structures its data in a *node*, *context*, and *thread* manner. Each thread then keeps track of a varying number of performance *events*, which associate singleton or aggregate data to named performance elements such as functions, loops or other blocks of code. In addition, for each node, context, thread, event, metric combination, there is an *event profile* object which stores the performance data for that particular combination. This event mapping approach allows an efficient and flexible method of performance data representation. Wrapped around this representation is PerfDMF's API for profile query and management. This API is implemented entirely in Java, and thus provides a completely portable and consistent method of accessing data.

The profile input component is responsible for obtaining performance data from a wide variety of sources, and converting it to PerfDMF's internal representation. It does so by creating a profile `DataSession` object specific to the profile format being imported. The `DataSession` object forms the core abstract object by which interactions with data sources take place. For example, the `GprofDataSession` provides an interface to parse gprof data. Some profiling tools output multiple files, one for each process or thread of execution. In those cases, PerfDMF provides support for parsing a directory of files, or a subset of files in a directory that start with a particular prefix or end with a particular suffix. The profile input component manages the details of parsing the output from the supported profiling tools. There is also support for parsing and managing TAU user-defined events, as mentioned in Section 3.

PerfDMF database access is provided through the use of interface functions that simplify the connection to the database. When building a client, the application developer need not concern herself with the details of database connectivity or with constructing SQL queries if she does not need or want to. It is relatively easy to get a list of `APPLICATION` rows from the database (returned as Java objects), and find an instance of interest. Iterating through the objects is similar to iterating through the the tuples of a SQL query, but with a simpler interface. The profile database component is provided by the `PerfDMFSession` extension of the `DataSession` class. Once the session has been initialized, a call to `getApplicationList()` will return a list of `Application` objects, from which the desired application is selected and set as a filter for subsequent queries. The code is similar for listing and selecting `Experiment`, `Trial`, `IntervalEvent` and `AtomicEvent` objects. Once an object is selected, all further query operations are filtered based on that particular context. For example, if a particular `Trial` has been selected, then any `IntervalEvent` objects that are queried are only those from that particular trial. Alternatively, an application could load an entire performance profile from the database or import from a raw profile dataset into a `DataSession` object (as was mentioned earlier with the gprof example), and then apply selections with the PerfDMF API, setting node, context, and thread parameters. Saving data to the database is also easy, in that the `Application`, `Experiment` and `Trial` objects all have `Save()` methods, which will save the object and all of its related object references to the database. The `Trial` object also has support for adding new, possibly derived, metrics to an existing trial in the database.

PerfDMF also provides an analysis toolkit component. This utilizes API support for application, experiment, and trial access to broaden single-trial profile analysis to multiple experiment datasets. This particular component is only implemented minimally, as the type of analysis done will be is somewhat application specific. However, there are methods for doing rudimentary multi-trial analysis, including performance comparisons and speedup analysis.

5. Application

This section presents some applications of PerfDMF to existing performance tools. We shall consider three applications of PerfDMF: parallel profile analysis and viewing, experiment trial browsing and scalability analysis, and performance data mining. Performance tools for these applications have been developed to use the PerfDMF API. Our ParaProf profile analyzer is particularly enhanced by the ability to parse additional profile formats, and the ability to store data to a database. The other two applications primarily demonstrate the use of analysis interfaces with the database.

5.1. ParaProf

ParaProf[3] is TAU's main profile browser, and is a portable, extensible and scalable tool for parallel performance analysis. ParaProf provides a mature, reliable platform on which to graphically browse parallel performance profile data. It implements graphical displays of all performance analysis results in aggregate and single node/context/thread forms. ParaProf also

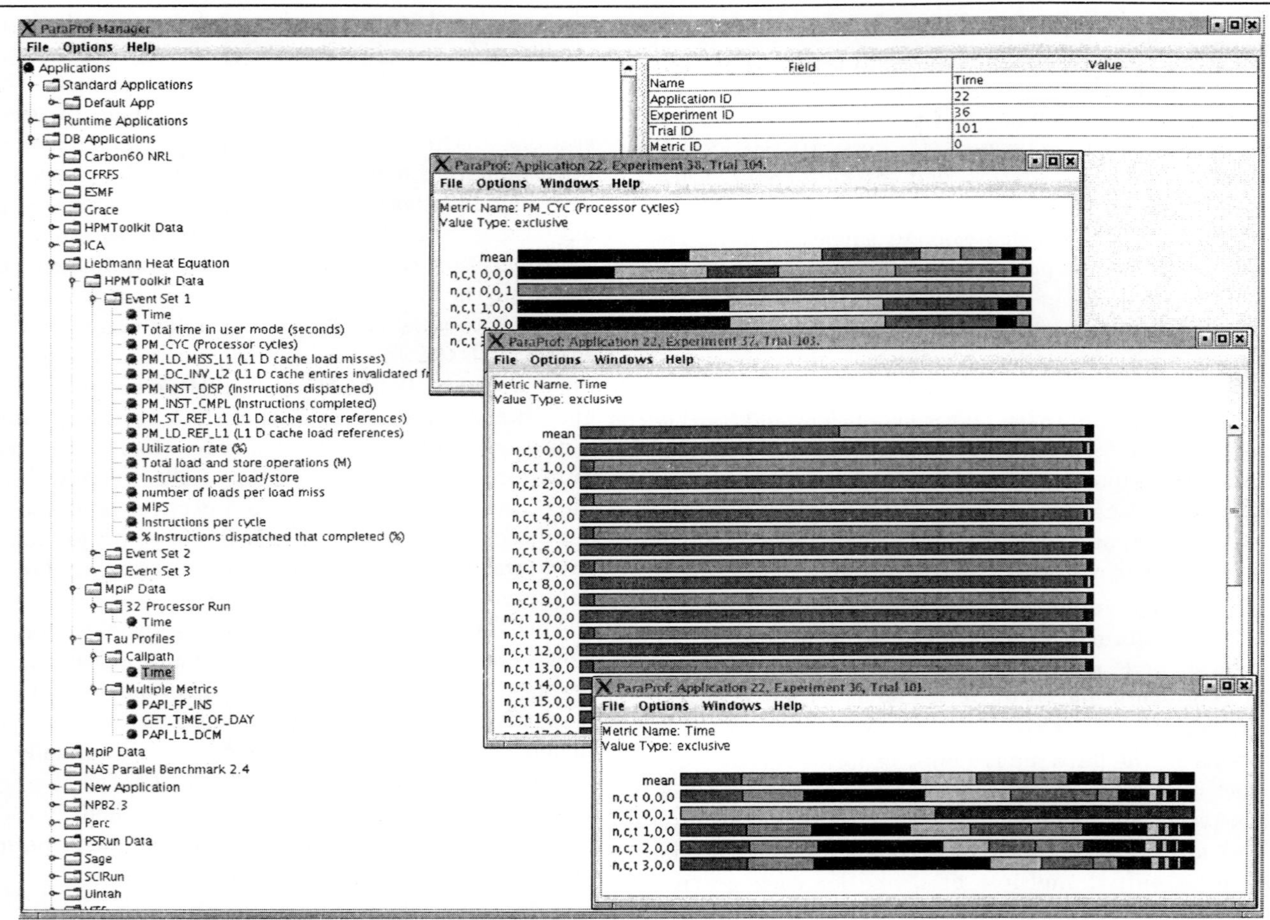

Figure 2. ParaProf with PerfDMF support accessing HPMToolkit, mpiP, and TAU data from a database archive. The top graph window shows the HPMToolkit data, the middle window is mpiP data, and the bottom window is TAU data. ParaProf can also be used to input data into the database.

provides the ability to compare the behavior of one instrumented event across all threads of execution, and offers summary text views of performance data, with various groupings and contextual highlighting. The initial release of ParaProf could only read TAU data from flat files, and though it could generate rudimentary derived data, it had limited methods by which that data could be saved for further analysis. With the addition of PerfDMF, ParaProf is now able to parse profile data from additional profile tools, and has database support for accessing archived profile data and saving derived metric data. ParaProf can also be used by an organization as the primary interface to the performance profile database, providing a graphical user interface which analysts can use to store and view performance profiles in a shared data repository.

Figure 2 shows an example of the enhanced ParaProf using the PerfDMF API to interface with the database. On the left side of the application window is a tree view of the applications, experiments and trials which have been loaded into the database. Three trials shown, all from the same application, have been loaded into the database using the PerfDMF API, and are expanded in the tree. The three trials come from three different profiling tools, specifically HPMToolkit, mpiP and TAU. Additional application profile data is loaded into the database, mostly from TAU data files. This figure is not intended to show comparative analysis between trials, but rather the use of PerfDMF to parse various profile formats and store them in a database archive. This archive could be made available in one physical location for all analysts within an organization. Given

PerfDMF's design, it would be a simple matter to implement access authorization to enforce different policies for performance data security and sharing.

5.2. Trial Browser and Speedup Analyzer

One application we developed to test the PerfDMF API was a trial browser and speedup analyzer. The trial browser exercises a broad subset of the functionality available in the API, and the speedup analyzer demonstrates the need for common analysis capabilities. We applied this tool to study the scalability of the EVH1 benchmark [21]. Given performance data from experiments with varying numbers of processors, the tool automatically calculates the minimum, mean and maximum values for the speedup every profiled routine. The application has access to this data through the PerfDMF API, including requesting standard SQL aggregate operations such as minimum, maximum, mean, standard deviation and others. The fact that the database provides the data in such an organized fashion leaves the application programmer free to develop analysis and visualization code, rather than worry about data management.

5.3. PerfExplorer

The PerfExplorer application is a data mining application for doing parallel performance analysis on very large profile datasets. Because current visualization tools are incapable of displaying thousands of data points with hundreds of dimensions in a meaningful way to a user, statistical analysis methods are used to perform cluster analysis on the data, and then do summarization of the clusters. Additional functionality is currently being added to PerfExplorer to perform additional data mining operations on the data.

PerfExplorer is designed as a client-server system. The client makes requests to an analysis server back end, which is integrated with a performance database, using PerfDMF. Using the PerfExplorer client, the analyst selects a particular trial of interest, sets analysis parameters, and then requests data mining operations on the parallel dataset. Using the PerfDMF API, the analysis server selects the data of interest, gets the relevant profile data and hands it off to an analysis application, R[23]. When R is done with the analysis, the results are saved to the database, using the PerfDMF API. When the analysis is complete, the user can browse the results using the PerfExplorer client. The browse requests are also processed by the PerfExplorer server, using the PerfDMF API.

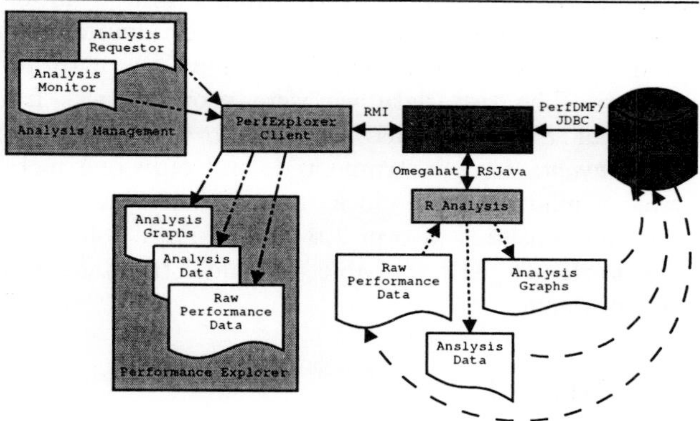

Figure 3. The PerfExplorer high-level design. PerfDMF provides an interface between the DBMS and the PerfExplorer server application.

Figure 3 shows how PerfDMF is integrated into the PerfExplorer application. Because PerfDMF provides database support, the PerfExplorer application developers are left to concern themselves with the user interface and the analysis portions of the application. Because PerfDMF is flexible and extensible, the PerfExplorer developers were able to extend the PerfDMF database API to support saving and retrieving analysis results.

The datasets that the PerfExplorer application have analyzed to date include the ASCI Purple Benchmark[15] applications sPPM, SMG2000 and SPhot and the Miranda[5] application in production at Lawrence Livermore National Laboratory (LLNL). The benchmark applications were run in a number of configurations on large parallel machines available at LLNL. The profile data was generated by a number of profiling tools, including TAU, gprof and in the case of sPPM, self-instrumented data for which a custom parser was written. Up to 1024 threads of execution were available on the resources at LLNL, and up to 7 PAPI[4] hardware counters were collected at a time. PerfDMF was instrumental in organizing the performance data, and providing easy access to the collected data using the PerfDMF API. Analysis results from Ahn and Vetter[1] were reproduced with PerfExplorer, showing interesting floating point operation behavior in the sPPM application. Because targeted data mining analysis of parallel performance data is now available in a reproducable, portable application, more interesting results could be found in other applications by other analysts.

The Miranda application data was provided by

LLNL, in the form of TAU profile data from test runs on Bluegene/L[14], currently in development. When completed, Bluegene/L will have over 64K processors. The test data we were provided was from runs of 8K and 16K processors. Over one hundred events were instrumented, and only one metric was available, wall clock time. The 16K processor run consisted of over 1.6 million data points, and the PerfDMF API was able to handle the data without problems.

6. Related Work

The PerfDMF project inherits from a rich background of research work in the fields of parallel performance benchmarking, performance analysis tools and environments, and performance experiment management systems. The need to manage performance data is a basic requirement of performance benchmarking activities, but is often accomplished in ad hoc ways. Both the Graphical Benchmark Information Service (GBIS) [8] and the more general Performance Database server (PDS) system [13] demonstrate the utility of a high-level access to a performance experiment repository that allows for meaningful queries without user-level knowledge of performance data storage details. With similar goals, PerfDMF intends to provide a common DMS substrate as a robust part of the framework for the development of performance analysis tools.

Directly relevant to PerfDMF are the projects that utilize a performance database as a component of a performance analysis system, particularly for multi-experiment performance analysis. The SIEVE (Spreadsheet-base Interactive Event Visualization Environment) system [25] showed the benefit of a simple table-based structuring of performance data coupled with a programmable analysis engine. More sophisticated performance data models, such as found in Paradyn [18] and CUBE [26], allow a richer analysis algebra to be applied to multi-experiment performance information. Both SIEVE and CUBE would naturally extend to implementation on top of a performance data management system such as PerfDMF.

Similar to PerfDMF, the HPCToolkit [16] targets profile-based performance analysis. It is able to merge data from multiple performance experiments in a database that is correlated with the program source and hyperlinked for analysis and viewing with the HPCView [17] tool. Performance data manipulated by HPCView can come from any source, as long as the profile data can be translated or saved directly to a standard, profile-like input format. To date, the principal sources of input data for HPCView have been sample-based hardware performance counter profiles. In addition to measured performance metrics, HPCView allows the user to define expressions to compute derived metrics as functions of the measured data and of previously-computed derived metrics. In contrast, PerfDMF can work with true parallel profiles from large-scale parallel executions and provides a programmatic interface for building analysis packages, such as those to compute common derived metrics. However, the two systems are complementary in many ways and we will investigate support for importing HPCToolkit profile data into PerfDMF.

The Prophesy system [28] successfully applies a performance database to manage multi-dimensional performance information for parallel analysis and modeling. The database is a core component of the system, implemented using relational DBMS technology and storing detailed information from the Prophesy measurement system and performance modeling processes. The Prophesy architecture has enabled it to be applied to both parallel and grid applications. PerfDMF follows in the spirit of Prophesy, with a specific focus on the performance DMS as a robust, open, and retargetable framework, and on analysis programming. PerfDMF supports the import of profile data from multiple sources and Prophesy's database schema suggests it could be a source of performance data as well. Designed as a framework, PerfDMF would enable open access to the archived performance data and provide a programming interface for building multiple analysis components. This could allow Prophesy's modeling algorithms to be captured as part of a broader analysis library. In this way, several performance tools could benefit from the advanced modeling analysis Prophesy provides.

The PPerfDB project [11] comes closest to sharing the broader objectives as PerfDMF. PPerfDB is developing methods for diagnosing the performance of large-scale applications using data from multiple executions over an application's lifetime. It supports the import of performance data produced from multiple sources and allow performance results to be exchanged and compared across geographically disperse sites. Performance information is related through hierarchical property, resource, and event mappings that enable PPerfDB to support powerful comparison and analysis operations. The PPerfXchange component enables distributed PPerfDB-enabled performance repositories to interoperate (see PPerfGrid [10]). We view PPerfDB and PerfDMF as complementary, rather then competing, systems. The PPerfDB architecture provides the opportunity for the two systems to co-exist in a performance analysis environment. PerfDMF might be used, for instance, to store high-volume TAU performance results for an application suite, while supporting PPerfXchange-compatible interfaces that tie the performance data to a global PPerfDB system. We hope to work with PPerfDB developers on PPerfDB-PerfDMF integration in the coming months.

In [12], multi-experiment performance data is managed to encompass executions from all stages of the lifespan of an application. Here all experiment information is gathered in a *program space* which can be explored with a simple naming mechanisms to answer performance questions that span multiple program instances. With this interface, it is possible to automatically describe differences between two runs of a program, both the structural differences (differences in program source code and the resources used at runtime), and the performance variation (how were the resources used and how did this change from one run to the next). As this work demonstrates, the ability to easily access performance data history and comparatively process the data has high payoff for automating performance diagnosis. Our objectives with PerfDMF to implement necessary performance data management and analysis programming infrastructure are consistent with these aims of automated performance regression analysis and diagnosis. With a extensible programming layer for query and analysis, it is conceivable that higher-level abstract interfaces, such a program space, can be implemented using PerfDMF to offer more sophisticated diagnosis support.

ZENTURIO [22] is another performance experiment management system that incorporates an experiment data repository at the core of its architecture. While ZENTURIO shares features of Prophesy, PPerfDB, and HPCToolkit, it is remarkable for its implementation as a set of services for experimentation and analysis, with a graphical portal for user interaction. In comparison to all of these efforts, PerfDMF is specifically advocating a performance DMS component and analysis programming interface that is flexible for a broad range of applications and is based on open, standard implementations and reusable, pluggable toolkits. We believe PerfDMF could address much of the data management functionality present in these tools.

7. Conclusion and Future Work

The PerfDMF project is developing performance data management infrastructure that we hope will be leveraged by the performance tool community for purposes of tool integration, interoperation, data sharing, and next-generation performance analysis. The utility of PerfDMF is demonstrated in our own TAU parallel performance system, which has fully integrated the framework in its ParaProf profile analysis tool. Additionally, we have developed a performance data mining prototype, PerfExplorer, that incorporates PerfDMF for performance storage and shows how packages such as R can be easily integrated. PerfDMF is being requested by an increasing number of TAU users for application performance analysis as well as systems benchmarking.

We believe the support in PerfDMF for importing common profile data formats and developing reusable and scriptable profile analysis functions will appeal to tools developers and users alike. We hope to work with the University of Tennessee to integrate the CUBE [26] algebra with PerfDMF to implement high-level comparative queries and analysis operations. TAU already supports translation of parallel profiles to CUBE format for presentation with the Expert [30] tool. We also are working with Portland State University (PSU) and LLNL to apply PerfDMF to performance benchmarking for large-scale systems procurement. This work will involve building translational interfaces between PerfDMF and the PPerfDB/PPerfXchange [11] tool suite. Additionally, we hope to began work soon with ORNL on a multi-platform code evaluation study of the PERC benchmarks [21] and PERC performance tools, with PerfDMF being used to store the performance results. These efforts will be important steps forward in linking sophisticated performance technology and tools through open interoperable interfaces and standard data management technology.

Longer term we envision the development of performance profile data and analysis servers that are PerfDMF-compliant and can be easily configured and deployed for specific performance management tasks. The PerfDMF technology will be equally valuable in the creation of shared performance repositories for performance benchmarking purposes as it will for efficiently tracking the performance history of a single application code. We will continue to enhance the features of PerfDMF to address these broader concerns.

8. Acknowledgments

The authors wish to acknowledge the contribution of Li Li, a Ph.D. graduate student in the Department of Computer and Information Science at the University of Oregon, to an earlier design of a parallel performance database that served as a conceptual framework for PerfDMF. This research is supported by the U.S. Department of Energy, Office of Science, under contracts DE-FG03-01ER25501 and DE-FG02-03ER25561.

References

[1] D.H. Ahn and J.S. Vetter., "Scalable Analysis Techniques for Microprocessor Performance Counter Metrics.", Proceedings of Supercomputing, 2002.

[2] APART, IST Working Group on Automatic Performance Analysis: Real Tools. See http://www.fz-juelich.de/.

[3] R. Bell, A. D. Malony and S. Shende, "ParaProf: A Portable, Extensible and Scalable Tool for Parallel Performance Profile Analysis," *Proc. Europar 2003 Conference*, LNCS 2790, Springer, Berlin, pp. 17–26, 2003.

[4] S. Browne, J. Dongarra, N. Garner, G. Ho, and P. Mucci, "A Portable Programming Interface for Performance Evaluation on Modern Processors," *International Journal of High Performance Computing Applications*, **14**(3):189–204, Fall 2000.

[5] W. Cabot, A. Cook and C. Crabb, "Large-Scale Simulations with Miranda on BlueGene BlueGene/L", Presentation from BlueGene/L Workshop, Reno, 14–15 October, 2003.

[6] L. DeRose, "The Hardware Performance Monitor Toolkit," *Euro-Par 2001*, 2001.

[7] T. Fahringer and C. Seragiotto, "Experience with Aksum: A Semi-Automatic Multi-Experiment Performance Analysis Tool for Parallel and Distributed Applications," *Workshop on Performance Analysis and Distributed Computing*, 2002.

[8] Graphical Benchmark Information Service, http://www.netlib.org/parkbench/gbis/html/.

[9] S. Graham, P. Kessler, and M. McKusick, "gprof: A Call Graph Execution Profiler," *SIGPLAN '82 Symposium on Compiler Construction*, pp. 120–126, June 1982.

[10] J. Hoffman, A. Byrd, K. Mohror, and K. Karavanic, "PPerfGrid: A Grid Services-based Tool for the Exchange of Heterogeneous Parallel Performance Data," HIPS-HPGC Joint Workshop on High-Performance Grid Computing and High-Level Parallel Programming Models, in conjunction with IPDPS 2005, April 2005, to appear.

[11] K. Karavanic, PPerfDB. http://www.cs.pdx.edu/~karavan/research.htm.

[12] K. Karavanic and B. Miller, "A Framework for Multi-Execution Performance Tuning," in On-Line Monitoring Systems and Computer Tool Interoperability , Thomas Ludwig and Barton P. Miller, editors, Nova Science Publishers, New York, USA, 2003.

[13] B. LaRose, "The Development and Implementation of a Performance Database Server," M.S. thesis, University of Tennessee, Technical Report CS-93-195, August 1993.

[14] Lawrence Livermore National Laboratory (LLNL), "Bluegene/L", http://www.llnl.gov/asci/platforms/bluegenel/.

[15] Lawrence Livermore National Laboratory (LLNL), "The ASCI sPPM Benchmark Code", http://www.llnl.gov/asci/purple/benchmarks/.

[16] J. Mellor-Crummey, "HPCToolkit: Multi-platform tools for profile-based performance analysis," *5th International Workshop on Automatic Performance Analysis (APART)*, November 2003.

[17] J. Mellor-Crummey, R. Fowler, and G. Marin, "HPCView: A Tool for Top-down Analysis of Node Performance," *The Journal of Supercomputing*, **23**:81–104, 2002.

[18] B. Miller, M. Callaghan, J. Cargille, J. Hollingsworth, R. Irvin, K. Karavanic, K. Kunchithapadam, and T. Newhall, "The Paradyn Parallel Performance Measurement Tool," *IEEE Computer*, **28**(11):37–46, November 1995.

[19] P. Mucci, "Dynaprof." http://www.cs.utk.edu/~mucci/dynaprof/.

[20] National Center for Supercomputing Applications (NCSA), "PerfSuite", http://perfsuite.ncsa.uiuc.edu/, University of Illinois at Urbana-Champaign.

[21] National Energy Research Scientific Computing Center, "Performance Evaluation Research Center (PERC)", http://perc.nersc.gov/.

[22] R. Prodan and T. Fahringer, "On Using ZENTURIO for Performance and Parameter Studies on Cluster and Grid Architectures," *11th EuroMicro Conference on Parallel Distributed and Network-Based Processing (PDP 2003)*, February 2003.

[23] R-Project, "R", http://www.r-project.org/.

[24] D. Reed, L. DeRose, and Y. Zhang, "SvPablo: A Multi-Language Performance Analysis System," *10th International Conference on Performance Tools*, pp. 352–355, September 1998.

[25] S. Sarukkai and D. Gannon, "SIEVE: A Performance Debugging Environment for Parallel Programs," *Journal of Parallel and Distributed Computing*, **18**:147–168, 1993.

[26] F. Song, F. Wolf, N. Bhatia, J. Dongarra and S. Moore, "An Algebra for Cross-Experiment Performance Analysis," International conference on Parallel Processing (ICPP'04), pp. 63–72, August 2004.

[27] TAU (Tuning and Analysis Utilities). http://www.acl.lanl.gov/tau/.

[28] V. Taylor, X. Wu, and R. Stevens,"Prophesy: An Infrastructure for Performance Analysis and Modeling of Parallel and Grid Applications," ACM SIGMETRICS Performance Evaluation Review, **30**(4), pp. 13–18, March 2003.

[29] J. Vetter and C. Chambreau, "mpiP: Lightweight, Scalable MPI Profiling". http://www.llnl.gov/CASC/mpip/.

[30] F. Wolf and B. Mohr, "Automatic Performance Analysis of SMP Cluster Applications," Technical Report IB 2001-05, Research Centre Jülich, 2001.

Session 7A: Network Hardware

PFED: A Prediction-based Fair Active Queue Management Algorithm*

Wenyu GAO, Jianxin WANG, Jianer CHEN, Songqiao CHEN
School of Information Science and Engineering, Central South University, Changsha, China, 410083
gwyy@163.com, jxwang@mail.csu.edu.cn

Abstract

In this paper, we propose a novel active queue management algorithm PFED, which is based on network traffic prediction. The main properties of PFED are: (1) stabilizing queue length at a desirable level with consideration of future traffic, and using a MMSE (Minimum Mean Square Error) predictor to predict future network traffic; (2) imposing effective punishment upon misbehaving flow with a full stateless method; (3) maintaining queue arrival rate bounded by queue service rate through more reasonable calculation of packet drop probability. To verify the performance of PFED, PFED is implemented in NS2 and is compared with RED and CHOKe with respect to different performance metrics. Simulation results show that PFED outperforms RED and CHOKe in stabling instantaneous queue length and in fairness. It is also shown that PFED enables the link capacity to be fully utilized by stabilizing the queue length at a desirable level, while not incurring excessive packet loss ratio.

1. Introduction

A number of active queue management (AQM) algorithms have been proposed since Random Early Detection (RED)[1] was introduced in 1993. RED is the most widely accepted AQM algorithm. However, many studies show that the performance of RED heavily depends on whether or not its parameters are properly tuned. RED is known to be unfair to individual flows, unable to achieve high link utilization and low packet loss rate simultaneously, and exhibit short-term fluctuation in the queue length [2-4]. Thus, many alternative AQM algorithms have been proposed to amend these disadvantages. Unfortunately, few of these algorithms can amend these disadvantages simultaneously.

In this paper, we starting by analyzing a number of well-known AQM algorithms, and discussing their advantages and disadvantages. We then propose a novel AQM algorithm — Prediction-based Fair Early Drop (PFED). The main objects of PFED are (1) to stabilize the queue length at a desirable level through more accurate traffic prediction and more reasonable calculation of packet drop probability, (2) to impose effective punishment upon misbehaving flow, and (3) to maintain queue arrival rate bounded by queue service rate. We implement PFED in NS2 [5] and compare it with a number of well-known AQM algorithms such as RED and CHOKe [6] . The algorithms are examined in terms of stability (i.e., the variance rate of queue length) and fairness, in addition to their complexity. Simulation results show that PFED outperforms RED and CHOKe in stabling instantaneous queue length and in fairness. It is also shown that PFED enables the link capacity to be fully utilized by stabilizing the queue length at a desirable level, while not incurring excessive packet loss ratio.

The reminder of this paper is organized as follows. Section 2 discusses related work (analysis of a few of well-known AQM algorithms). Section 3 is the description of our new PFED algorithm. Section 4 compares PFED with other AQM algorithms in NS2. Finally, section 5 concludes our work.

2. Related works

Active queue management has been extensively studied since early 1990s, and RED is the most widely accepted one. RED detects incipient congestion at network routers in order to promptly notify sources to reduce their rates, punish misbehaving flows without being biased against burst traffic, and avoid global synchronization. RED maintains a long term average of the queue length (buffer occupancy) of the routers to detect incipient congestion, and randomly drops packets in proportion to this buffer occupancy value.

* This work is supported by the Major Research Plan of National Natural Science Foundation of China, Grant No.90304010.

However, RED's performance is extremely sensitive to its parameters. It is difficult to tune the parameters to achieve good performance in different networks.

Furthermore, queue length is only an indirect reflection of traffic load, many studies showed that queue length should not be the only parameter to be observed and controlled.

When mixed traffic types share a link, RED allows unfair bandwidth sharing since RED imposes the same loss rate on all flows regardless of their bandwidths. To remedy this weakness, FRED (Flow RED)[7], proposed in 1997, uses per-active-flow accounting to impose on each flow a loss rate depending on the flow buffer occupancy. Unfortunately, the per-active-flow accounting in FRED suffers from the problem of scalability.

CHOKe [6] is another improved AQM algorithm based on RED, targeting to improve the fairness of RED. The basic idea behind CHOKe is that the contents of the FIFO buffer form a "sufficient statistic" about the incoming traffic and can be used in a simple fashion to penalize misbehaving flows. When a packet arrives at a congested router, CHOKe draws a packet at random from the FIFO buffer and compares it with the arriving packet. If they both belong to the same flow, then they are both dropped, else the randomly chosen packet is left intact and the arriving packet is admitted into the buffer with a probability that depends on the level of congestion (this probability is calculated exactly as in RED). The reason for doing this is that the FIFO buffer is more likely to have packets belonging to a misbehaving flow and hence these packets are more likely to be chosen for comparison. Further, packets belonging to a misbehaving flow arrive more numerously and are more likely to trigger comparison. The intersection of these two high probability events is precisely the event that packets belonging to misbehaving flows are dropped. As a consequence, packets of misbehaving flows will be dropped more often than packets of well-behaved flows.

The main contribution of CHOKe is its fairness over RED. Although CHOKe cannot realize absolute fairness (or max-min fairness), it does punish the misbehaving flows effectively. Moreover, CHOKe does not use per-flow-state, thus maintains the simplicity and scalability of RED. However, CHOKe also inherits the disadvantages of RED, such as instability of instantaneous queue length, and parameter sensitiveness etc.

CSFQ (Core Stateless Fair Queue) [8] is another improved AQM algorithm. The goal of CSFQ is to realize max-min fairness through packet dropping. In CSFQ, a technique named DPS (Dynamic Packet State)[9] is used to relieve core nodes from per-flow-state management, thus improve the scalability of the algorithm.

In CSFQ, network routers are divided into *edges* and *cores*. The edge routers maintain per-flow state, estimate the incoming rate of each flow, and insert a label into each packet based on the estimation. The core routers maintain no per-flow state, but use FIFO packet scheduling augmented by a probabilistic dropping algorithm, which uses the packet labels and an estimate of the aggregate traffic at the router.

Theoretically, CSFQ can achieve more fairness than other AQM algorithms. But in our experimental studies, the fairness of CSFQ is not as good as expected, especially when there are TCP flows.

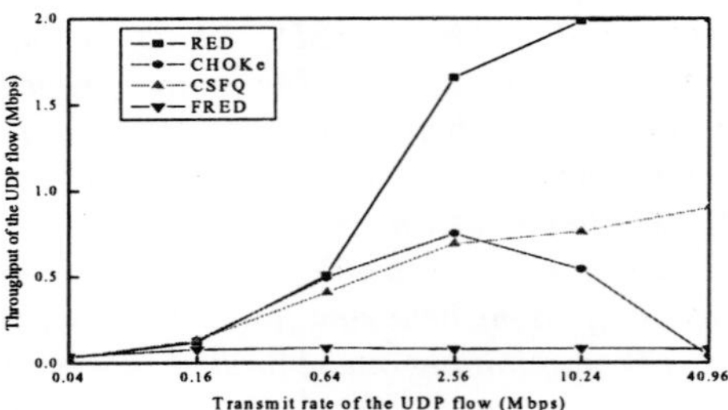

Figure 1. Fairness comparison of AQM algorithms

Fig.1 is the simulation results of several AQM algorithms, aiming to compare their fairness. In this simulation, many TCP flows and a UDP flow compete bandwidth at a bottleneck link (the bandwidth of this bottleneck link is 2Mbps), and the UDP flow's transmit rate increase from 0.04Mbps to 40.96Mbps in this experiment. As shown in Fig.1, the UDP flow gets different bandwidth (throughput) under different algorithms with the increasing of the transmit rate of the UDP flow.

In RED, the UDP flow occupies more and more bandwidth with the increasing of its transmit rate. Finally, it occupies total bandwidth of the bottleneck link. FRED, on the other hand, can achieve good fairness due to its utilization of per-active-flow accounting. The fairness of CSFQ and CHOKe is between that of FRED and RED. With the increasing of the transmit rate of the UDP flow, the UDP flow achieve more and more bandwidth at the bottleneck link, but when the transmit rate of the UDP flow reaches a certain value, the throughput of the UDP flow in CHOKe begins to decrease, while the throughput of the UDP flow in CSFQ still increases steadily, which means that the fairness of CSFQ is even worse than that of CHOKe.

This experiment shows that the fairness of CHOKe is not as good as that of FRED, but it can impose effective punishment on misbehaving flow. Why the fairness of CSFQ is not as good as expected when there are TCP flows? In CSFQ, the fairness is heavily dependent on the measurement of each flow's rate at the edge routers because the rate is used to calculate the drop probability. However, the transmit rate of TCP flows changes so frequently that it cannot be measured accurately by exponential averaging used in CSFQ, which lead to the decline of fairness.

3. PFED

To achieve these goals of PFED, which are described in section 1, we mainly use the following techniques in the PFED algorithm:

(1) Detecting incipient congestion using queue length measurement and traffic prediction (measurement), which uses a simple and effective MMSE (Minimum Mean Square Error)[10] predictor to predict arrival rate in the next interval;

(2) Punishing the misbehaving flow using the method borrowed from CHOKe;

(3) Calculating packet drop probability using load information.

In particular, all of these techniques are very easy to implement, no per-flow state management and no complex computation are involved. The number of parameters needed to be configured is less than that of RED. As a consequence, the proposed PFED algorithm is easy to implement in the current network infrastructures.

3.1. Congestion detection and arrival rate prediction

As described in former sections, using queue length as the only congestion indicator is not sufficient. Queue length is only an indirect reflection of traffic load, thus is just an indirect reflection of network congestion.

In PFED, we use load information, combined with queue length information as the indicator of congestion.

The load information that we use in PFED is the load factor defined as the ratio of periodically measured arrival rate and service rate (service rate is the link bandwidth). The load factor LF is:

$$LF = \frac{r}{C} \tag{1}$$

where r is the arrival rate, and C is the link bandwidth. A high load factor value indicates congestion and a low value indicates link underutilization.

In PFED, we first measure the arrival rate periodically (every τ time), then use MMSE predictor to predict the future arrival rate in the next interval, thus we can calculate the load factor in the next interval. We use the load factor, combined with the measured queue length as the congestion indicator to detect incipient congestion. In detail, when the load factor is larger than 1 (LF >1) and the current queue length is larger than half of the queue buffer size (i.e., $Q_L > Q_S/2$, Q_L is the current queue length, Q_S is the queue buffer size), the congestion is estimated to occur in the next interval.

In the detection of congestion, the most important task is to predict the arrival rate in the next interval. To select a good predictor, we have to consider two criterions: one is the accuracy of the predictor and the other is the simplicity of the predictor, because the predictor will be run online.

We selected MMSE as the predictor of PFED algorithm because MMSE is simple enough to be run online and the accuracy of MMSE is also desirable. We give a detail description of MMSE in the following section.

3.2. MMSE predictor

A number of recent empirical studies of traffic measurements from a variety of working packet networks have convincingly demonstrated that network traffic is self-similar or long-range dependent (LRD) in nature [11-13]. Considering the LRD nature of network traffic, the best traffic predictors are FBM [14] and FARIMA [15]. Unfortunately, FBM and FARIMA include lots of complex calculation, so they are improper for online predictions.

Recently, studies of real traffic traces indicate that the Hurst parameter rarely exceeds 0.85 (Hurst parameter is an indicator of LRD) [11-12,16]. Under this circumstance, the MMSE predictor shows performance as good as FBM or FARIMA. Furthermore, studies in [13] showed that the predictability of aggregate flow is better than that of single flow. In PFED, we only use MMSE to predict aggregate flow rate, not single flow rate, so the prediction accuracy of MMSE is good enough to be used in PFED.

The following is the description of MMSE.

Let $\{X_t\}$ denote a linear stochastic process and suppose that the next value of $\{X_{t+1}\}$ can be expressed as a linear combination of the current and previous observations. That is:

$$X_{t+1} = WX^t + \varepsilon_t$$

Where

$$W = (w_m, w_{m-1}, \ldots, w_1)$$
$$X = (X_t, X_{t-1}, \ldots, X_{t-m+1})$$

m is the order of regression.

Let $\hat{W}$ denote the estimated weight vector, and $\hat{X}_{t+1}$ denote the predicted value of X_{t+1}. While minimizing the mean square error, i.e., minimizing $E[e_t^2] = E[(X_{t+1} - \hat{X}_{t+1})^2]$, we get

$$\hat{W} = [\rho_m \quad \cdots \quad \rho_1] \times \begin{bmatrix} \rho_0 & \rho_1 & \cdots & \rho_{m-1} \\ \rho_1 & \rho_0 & \cdots & \rho_{m-2} \\ \cdots & \cdots & \cdots & \cdots \\ \rho_{m-1} & \rho_{m-2} & \cdots & \rho_0 \end{bmatrix}^{-1}$$

Where $\rho_k = \frac{1}{m} \sum_{t=k+1}^{m} X_t X_{t-k}$

The benefit of using MMSE is the simplicity of implementation. There are only some matrix manipulations that can readily be implemented in hardware and software at a very high speed. Moreover, there are approximation approaches called NMMSE (Normalized MMSE)[17-18] for computing the weight vector $\hat{W}$,- which eliminates matrix inversion and autocorrelation computations by adaptive and recursive solutions. That is

$$\hat{W}_{t+1} = \hat{W}_t + \mu \frac{\mathrm{X}}{\|\mathrm{X}\|^2} e_t$$

where $\theta \psi is \psi the \psi$adaptation constant and determines the convergence speed. NMMSE is convergent in the mean square error sense if θ satisfies the condition 0 < $\theta \psi < \psi 2$.

3.3. Punishing misbehaving flow

In order to impose effective punishment on misbehaving flow, we borrow the method used in CHOKe. When a packet arrives at a congested router, PFED draws a packet at random from the FIFO buffer and compares it with the arriving packet. If they both belong to the same flow, then they are both dropped, else the randomly chosen packet is left intact and the arriving packet is dropped with a probability that depends on the level of congestion, the drop probability Pdrop is calculated as shown in the next subsection

3.4. Calculating drop probability

In PFED, load factor and queue length are combined to calculate the packet drop probability P_{drop}.

$$P_{drop} = (\frac{r-C}{r})\frac{Q_L}{Q_S} = (1-\frac{C}{r})\frac{Q_L}{Q_S} = (1-\frac{1}{LF})\frac{Q_L}{Q_S} \qquad (2)$$

Where LF is the load factor, r is the arrival rate, C is the link bandwidth, Q_L is the current queue length, and Q_S is the queue buffer size.

Using load factor to calculate drop probability can keep the queue arrival rate at or below the queue service rate. This is also helpful for improving the stability of queue length.

3.5. Pseudo code of PFED algorithm

For completeness, we give the pseudo code of PFED algorithm in Fig. 2.

```
on receiving packet p
if (interval> τ ) {
  calculate the arrival rate in last interval;
  use MMSE to predict the arrival rate in the
next interval;
  calculate LF using equation (1);
}
if ((LF >1) && (Q_L> Q_S/2)) {
  draw a packet at random from the queue;
  if (both packets from the same flow) {
    drop both packets;
  } else {
    calculate P_drop using equation (2);
    if (random(0,1)< P_drop)
      drop packet p;
    else
      enque (p);
  }
} else {
  enque (p);
}
```

Fig. 2. Pseudo code of PFED

4. Simulation results and analysis

To verify the performance of PFED, we implement PFED along with RED and CHOKe in NS2 [5], and conducted a simulation study to compare the performance of PFED with other AQM algorithms. We examine the behavior of these algorithms in a variety of network topologies and traffic sources. Due to the space limitation, we only report on a small set of the simulations that we believe is the most representative.

The parameter used in PFED is: $\tau = 0.02s$ (measurement and prediction interval). The parameters of RED are set as w_p=0.002, min_{th}=20, max_{th}=70. The parameters of CHOKe are set the same as RED. Queue buffer capacity (Q_S) is set to 100 packets in all experiments.

4.1. Single bottleneck topology

Firstly, we compare the stability and other properties of PFED with RED and CHOKe in single bottleneck topology. The topology of the simulation is shown in Fig. 3, the bandwidth of the bottleneck link is 2Mbps, and the delay is 1ms.

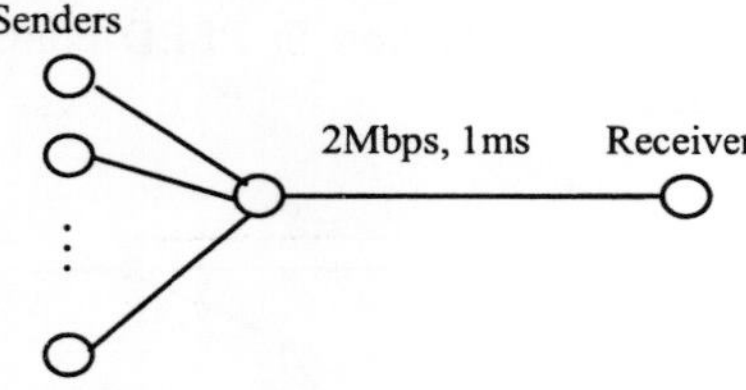

Fig. 3. The single bottleneck topology

In this experiment, *k* TCP connections are established over the single bottleneck link, where *k* varies from 50 to 100.

Fig. 4(a) gives the standard deviation of instantaneous queue length under different algorithms where the number of connections varies from 50 to 100. Fig. 4(b) gives the packet loss ratio under different algorithms. Fig. 4(c) gives the link utilization under different algorithms.

From Fig. 4, we can see that the instantaneous queue length of PFED is much more stable than that of RED and CHOKe, the packet loss ratio of PFED is less than that of RED and CHOKe, and the link utilization of these three algorithms are close.

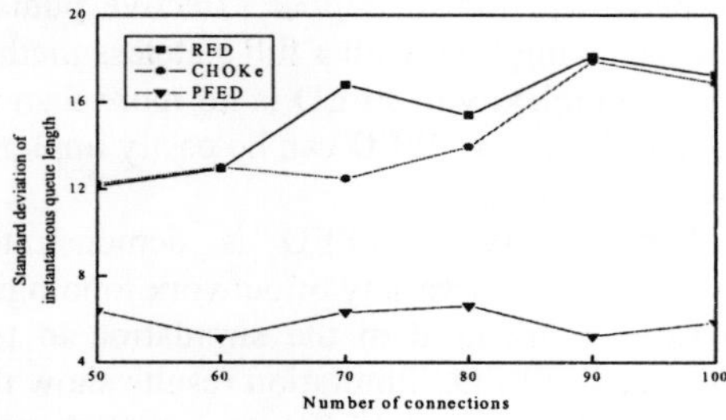

(a) Standard deviation of instantaneous queue length

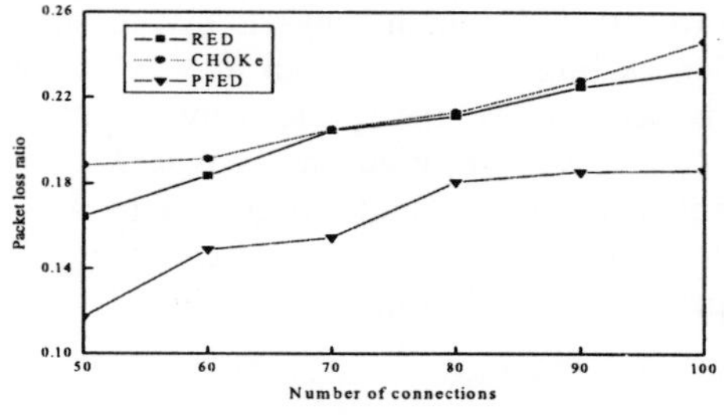

(b)Packet loss ratio

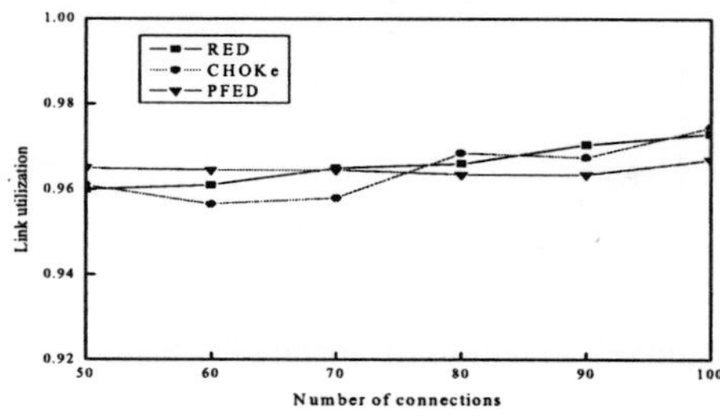

(c)Link utilization

Fig. 4. Comparisons of different algorithms in single bottleneck topology

4.2. Multiple bottlenecks topology

We repeat the same experiment in a network with multiple bottlenecks, as shown in Fig. 5. The bandwidth of all bottleneck links is 2Mbps, and the delay is 1ms. There are 5 queues (Q1, Q2, Q3, Q4, Q5) among which Q2 and Q4 are shared with cross traffic of 30 TCP connections. We also establish *k* TCP connections with the senders at the left hand side and the receivers at the right hand side, where *k* varies from 50 to 100.

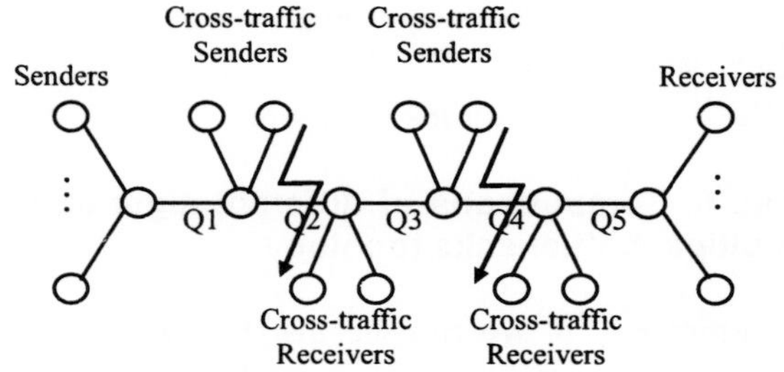

Fig. 5. The multiple bottlenecks topology

Simulation results show that the queue length at Q5 is always 0 or 1, which suggests that the link is not a bottleneck link. The other four queues exhibit similar trends as far as the performance comparison is concerned. So we give the standard deviation of instantaneous queue length of Q4, the packet loss ratio of Q4, and the link utilization of Q4 in Fig. 6 to show the performance of different algorithms.

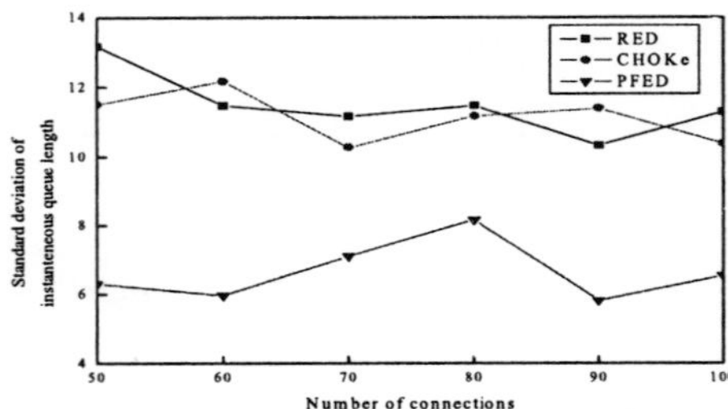

(a)Standard deviation of instantaneous queue length

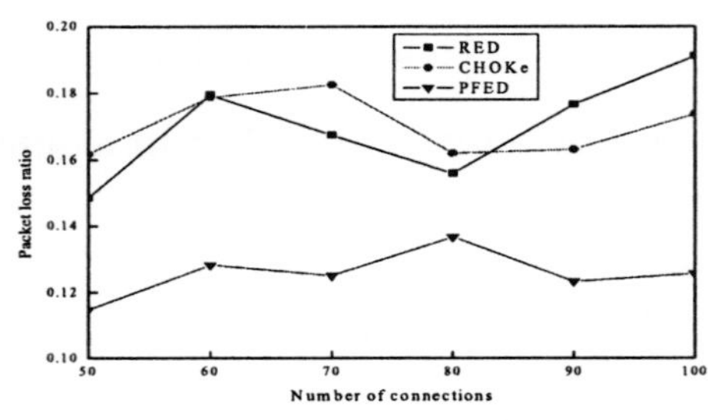

(b)Packet loss ratio

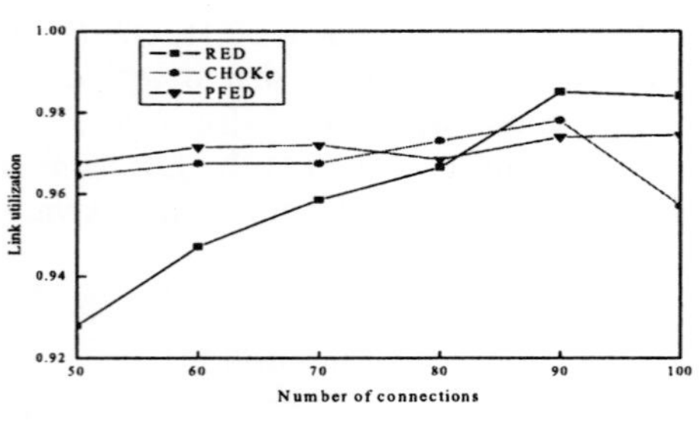

(c)Link utilization

Fig. 6. Comparisons of different algorithms in multiple bottlenecks topology

From Fig. 6, we can see that PFED outperforms RED and CHOKe with respect to stability of instantaneous queue length and packet loss ratio, but the link utilization of these three algorithms are close.

4.3. Fairness comparison

To show the effectiveness of punishment for misbehaving flow with different algorithms, we do this experiment in the topology shown in Fig. 3. We establish 49 TCP flows and 1 UDP flow, and the transmit rate of the UDP flow increases from 0.04Mbps to 40.96Mbps.

As shown in Fig.7, the UDP flow gets different bandwidth (throughput) under different algorithms with the increasing of the transmit rate of the UDP flow. The throughput of the UDP flow in PFED is much less than that in RED, and a little less than that in CHOKe, which means the fairness of PFED is better than that of RED and CHOKe.

In fact, the method of punishing misbehaving flow in PFED is the same as that in CHOKe, but the more accurate congestion detection in PFED contributes to its better fairness.

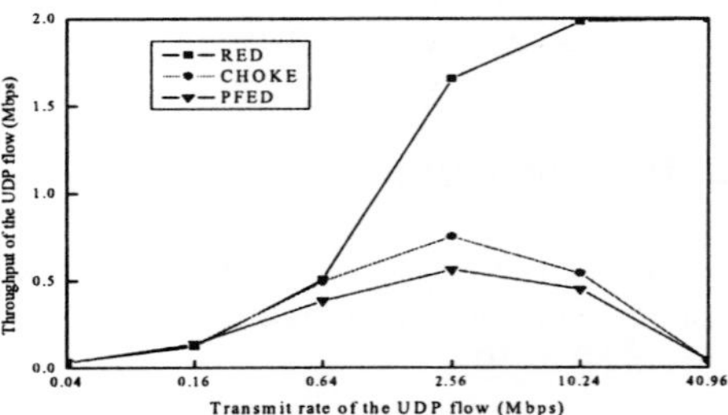

Fig. 7. Fairness comparison of different AQM algorithms

5. Conclusions

1) A novel AQM algorithm PFED is proposed, the main objectives of PFED are to stabilize the queue length at a desirable level with consideration of future traffic and with more reasonable calculation of packet drop probability; and to impose effective punishment upon misbehaving flow with a full stateless method.

2) The complexity of PFED is no more than that of RED and CHOKe, so PFED can be easily implemented in current networks.

3) The validity of PFED is demonstrated by simulation on NS2, a variety of network topologies and traffic sources are used in the simulation to test the performance of PFED. Simulation results show that the stability and fairness of PFED are much better than those of RED and CHOKe.

4) Through the simulation, it is also shown that by stabilizing the queue length at a desirable level, PFED enables the link capacity to be fully utilized, while not incurring excessive packet loss ratio.

References

[1] S. Floyd, V. Jacobson. Random early detection gateways for congestion avoidance. IEEE/ACM Transactions on Networking, 1993,1(4),397-413

[2] Floyd S. A report on some recent development in TCP congestion control. IEEE Communication Magazine, 2001

[3] Christiansen M, Jeffay K, Ott D et al. Tuning RED for Web traffic. ACM SIGCOMM'00, Sweden, 2000. 139- 150

[4] Firoiu V, Borden M. A study of active queue management for congestion control. IEEE INFOCOM'00, Israel, 2000. 1435- 1444

[5] VINT Project U. C. Berkeley/LBNL , NS2: network simulator. http://www.isi.edu/nsnam/ns, 2004

[6] R. Pan, B. Prabhakar, K. Psounis. CHOKe, A stateless active queue management scheme for approximating fair bandwidth allocation. IEEE INFOCOM'00, Mar. 2000

[7] D.Lin, R.Morris. Dynamics of random early detection. ACM SIGCOMM'97, 127-137, 1997

[8] Core-stateless fair queue: Achieving approximately fair bandwidth allocations in high speed networks. IEEE/ACM Transactions on Networking, 2003,11(1):33-46

[9] I. Stoica, and H. Zhang. Providing guaranteed services without per flow management. ACM SIGCOMM'99, 1999

[10] P. Whittle. Prediction and regulation by linear least-square methods, University of Minnesota Press, 1983

[11] M. E. Crovella and A. Bestavros. Self-similarity in world wide web traffic: Evidence and possible causes. IEEE/ACM Transactions on Networking. 1997,5(6): 835–846.

[12] R. Ramachandran and V. R. Bhethanabotla. Generalized autoregressive moving average modeling of the Bellcore data[A]. IEEE LCN'00, Tampa, USA, Nov. 2000, pp. 654–661.

[13] A. Sang, S. Li. A predictability analysis of network traffic. Computer Networks, 2002,39(2-3): 329-345

[14] P.J. Brockwell, and R.A. Davis. Time series: Theory and methods, Springer-Verlag, 1991

[15] Y. Shu, L. Wang, L. Zhang. Internet traffic modeling and predict ion using FARIMA models. Chinese Journal of computers, 2001, 24(1): 46-54

[16] W. Willinger, M. S. Taqqu, R. Sherman, and D. V. Wilson. Self-similarity through high-variability: Statistical analysis of Ethernet LAN traffic at the source level. IEEE/ACM Transactions on Networking, 1997,5(1): 71–86.

[17] S. Haykin, Adaptive Filter Theory, 4th ed. Prentice Hall, 2002.

[18] P. S. R. Diniz. Adaptive filtering: Algorithms and Practical Implementation, 2nd Edition, Kluwer academic publishers. 2002

Toward Effective NIC Caching: A Hierarchical Data Cache Architecture for iSCSI Storage Servers *

Xiaoyu Yao and Jun Wang
Department of Computer Science and Engineering
University of Nebraska-Lincoln, Lincoln, NE 68588-0115
{xyao,wang}@cse.unl.edu

Abstract

In this paper, we present a hierarchical Data Cache Architecture called DCA to effectively slash local interconnect traffic and thus boost the storage server performance. DCA is composed of a read cache in NIC card called NIC cache and a read/write unify cache in host memory called Helper cache. NIC cache services most portion of read requests without fetching data via PCI bus, while Helper cache 1) supplies some portions of read requests given partial NIC cache hits; 2) directs cache placement for NIC cache and 3) absorbs most transient writes locally. We developed a novel State Locality Aware cache Placement algorithm called SLAP to improve NIC cache hit ratio for mixed read and write workloads. To demonstrate the effectiveness of DCA, we developed a DCA prototype system and evaluated it with open source iSCSI implementation under representative storage server workloads. Experimental results showed that DCA can boost iSCSI storage server throughput by up to 121% and slash the PCI traffic by up to 74% compared with an iSCSI target without DCA.

1. Introduction

The iSCSI [8] technique has been gradually pushing current networked storage systems evolving from Storage Area Network (SAN) [10] and Network Attached System (NAS) [6] to economic SAN built over the mature TCP/IP network infrastructure. As playing a core role in the economic SAN, the iSCSI-based IP storage servers determine the overall performance of storage system.

In an iSCSI storage server, both volume storage traffic and network traffic travel across the local interconnect bus and easily overwhelm the bus. Today, many storage servers typically employ a 32 bits, 33 MHz PCI bus, which can only support 133 MB/sec of maximum raw bandwidth. This speed is only half of the bandwidth of a full-duplex Gigabit Ethernet. In recent years, new local interconnects such as PCI-X and PCI-Express have been proposed to mitigate the PCI bus bottleneck, but none of them can solve all the problems. First, the aggregate I/O traffic resulting from link aggregation with the usage of multiple high-speed I/O devices can easily saturate the local interconnect bandwidth. Second, the improvement pace of networking speed and storage bandwidth have exceeded that of local interconnect bus bandwidth. Recently, Feng *et al.* found that the peak bandwidth of a 133 MHz, 64-bit PCI-X bus in a PC is 8.5 Gb/s, which is less than half the 20.6 Gb/s bidirectional data rate that the Intel 10 GbE adapter can support [5]. As a result, the traffic burden on local interconnect will be even worse. Based on the above observations, solving the local interconnect bottleneck becomes a pressing problem today.

Orthogonal to the aggressive PCI bus innovations, few work have been done on reducing local interconnect traffic through an effective caching approach. Kim *et al.* in reference [9] first proposed adopting a small read cache in programmable Ethernet NIC to reduce PCI traffic in a web server. The results showed that a single NIC cache can work efficiently in a read dominant web server with a small working set and good locality. However, the mixed read and write traffic in a storage server is much more intensive. More importantly, the locality of the block-level I/O accesses in a storage server is typically poor as most locality has already been filtered by multiple higher level buffer caches. Therefore, a simple NIC cache for web server cannot work well in storage environment.

Zhang and Yang developed a novel bottom-up cache structure called BUCS in a networked HBA card [12]. They used synthetic read-exclusive, write-exclusive traces and a TPC-C (99% read ratio) trace in the experiments. Their experimental results showed that the response time and system throughput can be improved by up to a factor of three. However, BUCS requires a hardware IOP board to process both storage and network I/Os. The internal PCI bus and

*This research is sponsored in part by NSF under grant #CCF-0429995 and University of Nebraska-Lincoln Layman Fund.

0190-3918/05 $20.00 © 2005 IEEE

processor on IOP board may become a new bottleneck in a storage server. In addition, it is unclear whether the performance gain derives from the IOP hardware or from the cache structure itself.

In this paper, we present a hierarchical *Data Cache Architecture* called *DCA* to boost the iSCSI Storage server performance through effective NIC caching. It is notable that a large body of previous research in storage servers focus on hierarchical cache collaboration [11, 4, 7] between clients and servers to reduce much unnecessary network traffic. Effective NIC caching by DCA essentially extends the benefit of network traffic reduction between clients and servers to the local interconnect bus within a storage server.

DCA employs a read cache at NIC side called *NIC cache* to reduce traffic between host system and Ethernet NIC. To make NIC cache work effectively, a unify read and write cache called *Helper Cache* is adopted at host side to assist the placement of NIC cache and absorb transient writes. A novel *State Locality Aware Placement (SLAP)* algorithm is developed to effectively direct placement and replacement of NIC cache, and efficiently maintain cache coherency. To realize a near-optimal NIC cache hit ratio with good implementation efficiency, the algorithm defines a new locality metric named *state locality distance*. The idea is to utilize both the block access state and access frequency to effectively predict the locality.

We developed a DCA prototype system based on an Intel [2] iSCSI target under Linux kernel 2.4.20. We used two real-world block-level storage server traces (cello99 and TPC-D) to conduct experiments. The results show that DCA can significantly boost storage server performance.

2. Architecture Overview

In a storage server cache, the locality distance [4] is usually longer than that of a higher level cache. This is because multi-level storage caches deployed on client-side and application server have already filtered out most of application locality. As a consequence, the PCI bus traffic in a storage server is more intensive than that of application servers such as Web server. We have simulated single-level LRU based NIC cache proposed in reference [9] with a set of configurations ranging from 2 MB to 128 MB under representative storage server traces, resulting in only negligible NIC hit rate and local interconnect traffic reduction. This motivates us to explore new cache architecture that can best exploit the block-level locality and NIC cache space for an iSCSI based storage server.

Figure 1 illustrates the two-level DCA caching architecture in a typical iSCSI storage server. In this figure, memory is connected to CPU via MCH (Memory Control Hub) and network interface is connected to ICH (I/O Control Hub) via PCI bus. A read-only *NIC Cache* works on the NIC side to

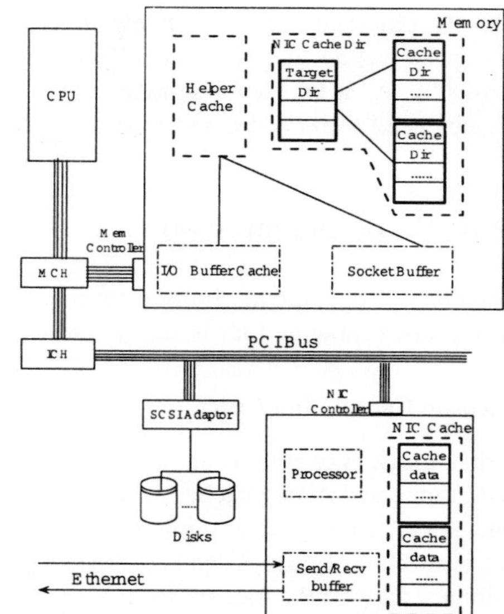

Figure 1. DCA Architecture Illustration

reduce PCI traffic between memory and network interface. In an iSCSI storage server, multiple iSCSI target modules are usually setup to provide various data services in parallel. Therefore, the on-board NIC cache space is usually shared by multiple iSCSI targets. To efficiently manage the NIC cache space for all iSCSI targets, in DCA, a *target directory* for the whole NIC cache and its per target *cache directories* are maintained by the host system. Because the host system is the only place to decapsulate iSCSI packets, it is good to maintain these NIC cache meta-data in host memory to significantly reduce the PCI traffic resulting from the NIC cache lookup and maintenance operations.

For the consideration of compatibility, we design a unify read and write cache called *Helper Cache* at iSCSI application level instead of being merged with kernel level socket buffer or disk I/O buffer cache that have already been optimally implemented for different purposes. The size of a helper cache is larger than that of NIC cache. It is used to assist NIC cache in making placement decision and absorb transient writes by employing a write-back policy with periodical flushes.

3 Design Issues

In DCA, the PCI traffic reduction is largely determined by three factors: the NIC cache hit ratio, helper cache hit ratio and cache coherency overhead between NIC cache and helper cache. As an on-board cache, NIC cache has a limited memory space. Our initial experimental results indicated that current separate NIC cache and system I/O buffer cache solutions cannot deal with mixed read and write traffic well. To efficiently and effectively utilize the limited memory space, we developed a new effective NIC caching solution-DCA. As a two level storage cache architecture, more issues need to be addressed than a single level NIC cache.

3.1 NIC Cache Organization

To efficiently organize the limited space on NIC cache, we consider the following four issues in our design.

3.1.1 Basic Cache Line Unit

Single disk block is chosen as an atomic cache line unit in both NIC cache and helper cache for the following considerations. A block-level cache implementation using single block as basic cache line unit can take advantage of the partial hit to best capture the locality in storage servers. Given part of the requested blocks are found in NIC cache, DCA only sends the remaining blocks from helper cache to NIC. After that, NIC combines both parts together into a complete package and send it out. By this way, every block cached at NIC is effectively utilized. More importantly, there are no alignment problem and extra overhead involved here at all.

Although client-informed application-level hints can also be utilized to effectively capture the locality in lower-level storage cache [11, 7], it is expensive and sometime prohibitive to modify the client-side software to provide such hints. As a result, it is imperative to employ single block as a basic cache line unit to best capture locality and make DCA be compatible with current applications.

3.1.2 Managing Cache Space

Even given a NIC cache in the several hundreds of megabytes, without a good organization, the hit rate could still be very low because the interleaved volume iSCSI data traffic with multiple targets and poor locality. A flat NIC cache space allocation scheme may work well in a Web server environment with a small working set. For an iSCSI based storage server, a simple flat cache space shared by multiple targets can be easily polluted by capacity misses. To solve the problem, we organize the space of NIC cache into a hierarchical structure. As shown in Figure 1, at the first level, we use a *target directory* to maintain per iSCSI target related information such as basic block size, maximum LBA address and cache space currently allocated for the specific target. Each entry in target directory is indexed by a unique pair of IP address and TCP port. At the second level, we save the cache data and related meta-data (i.e., cache directory) separately for each target. We maintain the first level target directory and second level per target cache directory in host system to reduce the PCI traffic due to cache lookup, leaving real data blocks in the NIC cache. In this way, the NIC cache space is exclusively utilized for data caching.

3.1.3 Inclusive vs. Exclusive

Previous research in multi-level cache architectures between storage server and application server tells us that the exclusive cache property is preferred because their size and price are usually commensurable [11, 4]. In this environment, an inclusive cache architecture would waste half of the cache space in storing redundant data. Given an exclusive cache architecture, no data would be saved in different level caches at the same time. However, exclusive cache does not fit well for DCA in that the DEMOTE and Reload operations [11, 4] overhead itself may overwhelm the local interconnect. The reload overhead here over PCI bus can not be avoided by applying techniques proposed in reference work [4]. In addition, the size of the NIC cache is quite precious and relatively small compared with the cheaper and larger host memory. We make helper cache and NIC cache to be inclusive so that NIC cache can take the advantage of volume helper cache space as a backup reservoir upon a miss. The write-back policy in helper cache also makes the blocks stay at host memory for a longer time so that more block information can be used to make better NIC cache placement decision.

3.1.4 Cache Coherency

For multi-level inclusive caches, maintaining the coherence property of multiple data copies is an important problem. *Aggressive update* scheme can easily overwhelm the PCI bus due to the heavy update traffic between helper cache and NIC cache. *Conservative invalidate* scheme usually keeps the blocks of helper cache and NIC cache in an inconsistent state. To strike a good tradeoff, we choose a hybrid policy combining the advantages of both aggressive update and conservative invalidate schemes.

3.2 NIC Cache Placement

Since a simple access-based placement algorithm for NIC cache cannot work well with mixed read and write traffic, we need to develop a new algorithm which can identify the blocks which access frequency exceeds a pre-defined threshold but still have high possibility of future reads. We call these blocks as *hot blocks*. The objective of our cache placement algorithm is to cache most hot blocks in NIC cache, save *warm blocks* as reservoir in helper cache and kick *cold blocks* out of cache.

A large body of research work [11, 4, 7] have been done in client-oriented hierarchical cache architecture in storage environment. Their experimental results showed that cache hit rate can be significantly improved by collaborative placement. Inspired by their work, DCA hands over the NIC cache placement decision to the helper cache instead of simply caching every recently accessed block.

Although DCA shares some similarities with hierarchical cache architecture, there exists significant differences between DCA and previous work. First, DCA cache placement decision is made within a storage server and transparent to the clients while current approaches collaborate with storage client. Second, DCA maintains inclusive property between helper cache and NIC cache. Third, current hierarchical cache architecture solutions aim to improve hit rate at a higher level and reduce demotion overhead over the wide area network. But DCA aims to maximize the lower-level NIC cache hit rate, thus slashing local interconnect traffic. To the best of our knowledge, this work is among the first to develop the hierarchical cache placement algorithm to effectively reduce PCI traffic within storage servers.

3.2.1 Off-line Analysis

We define a new metric called *State Locality Distance* to measure the locality in storage traffic, namely, RR (Read after Read) distance, WR (Read after Write) distance, WW (Write after Write) distance and RW (Write after Read) distance. Taking both access type and distance into consideration, the new metric indicates how many correlated read and write patterns exist in a block reference sequence.

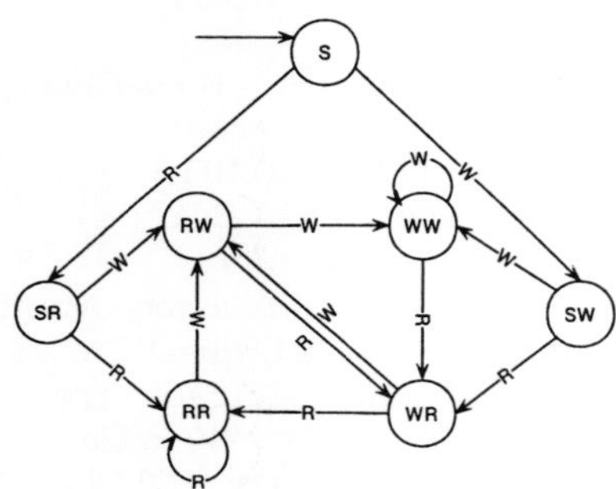

Figure 2. Finite State Machine for Cache Blocks

Figure 2 illustrates a seven-state finite state machine that models the state transition of a cacheline in DCA, namely S (Start), SR (Single Read), SW (Single Write), RR (Read after Read), RW (Write after Read), WR (Read after Write) and WW (Write after Write). In the diagram, any block begins with the start state S. Given current request type as input, the state of a block is changed according to the transition arrows shown in Figure 2.

To detect the typical access patterns in storage traffic, we conduct an off-line analysis on representative storage server traces (cello96, cello99, and TPC-D) at block level, mining clues on the strength of locality with the help of state locality distance and finite state machine model.

Figure 3 draws the histogram of RR distance, WR distance, WW distance, and RW distance distribution in an one-hour cello99 trace segment (one of the busiest hour between 03:00AM and 04:00AM on April, 29, 1999). The X-axis shows the length of state locality distance. The Y-axis denotes the number of occurrences that corresponds to a specific length of state locality distance. To derive the state locality distance from the traces, each request is decomposed into a unique block access event and assigned a new sequence number. The state locality distance is calculated based on the access type (r/w) and difference between sequence number of last two accesses on the same block.

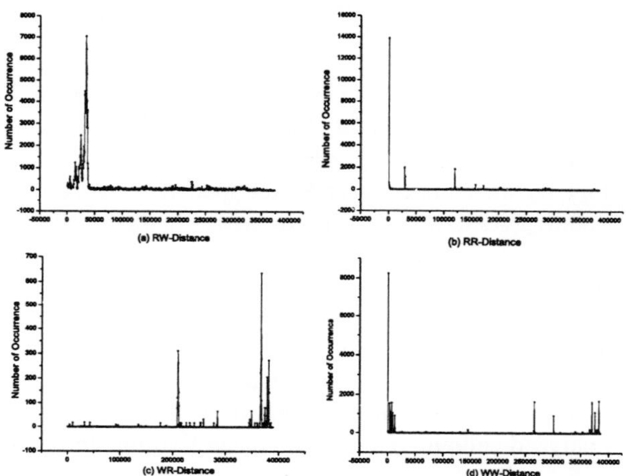

Figure 3. Categorized Cello99 Trace Reference Distance Histogram

As seen in Figure 3 (c), the read after write distance is clustered at about 220,000, 360,000 and 380,000, which implies the weakest locality among the four types of state locality. The number of read after write cases is 4306, which only accounts for 2% of overall re-visited blocks. Therefore, this type of state locality may be considered as low priority to be cached in NIC cache.

Figure 3 (d) shows that there is a strong locality of transient write as evident by the fact that most of WW distance is less than 10,000. In other words, a block is often written and then overwritten instead of being visited by another read in between. Combined with the fact that WW pattern accounts for 15% of all re-visited blocks, it is wise to cache transient write in helper cache rather than NIC cache without discrimination.

For read access, strong locality strength does exist for Read after Read as evidenced by the fact that 45.1% of RR distance is less than 450 as shown in Figure 3 (b). Com-

Table 1. *Statistics of State Locality Distance in Cello99*

Category	*RR*	*RW*	*WR*	*WW*
$TotalNumberofCases$	34935	120171	4306	28130
$AverageLocalityDistance$	85827.5	71736.6	318230.4	128695.5

paring the number of cases that fall into the four categories of state locality shown in Table 1, we can conclude that the block reference pattern that matches RR and RW sequence has more cases and shorter average locality distance than those of WR. WW is not considered here since only read-related access pattern is exploited by a read-only NIC cache. As a result, we need to distinguish the the state locality of RR from that of RW in order to enforce effective PCI traffic reduction. However, it may be too expensive to maintain the state locality distance for all cache blocks at runtime. We need to seek an efficient way to track the four types of locality distance.

It is noticed that in a LRU based cache, the longer the locality distance, the higher the possibility one block will be kicked out. Therefore, for those blocks with strong RR state locality, the number of reads on a specific block (called read count) always exceeds that of writes (called write count). The reason is that given either RW or WR as subsequence, the read count and write count on a given block do not change. Only RR and WW break the tie of read count and write count on the block. However, WW is more likely to have longer state locality distance and fewer occurrences than RR as shown in both Figure 3 (d) and Table 1. We analyzed cello96 and TPC-D traces and got similar observations. Due to space limitation, we do not present these results here. We use these observations as a basis to develop a new heuristic *State Locality-Aware cache Placement* algorithm called *SLAP*, which will be discussed in the next section.

3.2.2 Online Algorithm

Based on the off-line analysis, we develop a heuristic placement algorithm that can 1) reduce the cold misses as well as capacity misses with an modest NIC cache size and 2) lower the overhead of cache coherency. The main idea is to use the difference between the read count and write count on a block as hints of state locality strength. The blocks that currently have more reads than writes are identified as hot blocks and are placed in NIC cache. By this way, not only the block-level locality is captured, but also the runtime overhead is minimized. Before describing the SLAP algorithm, we introduce four interfaces between NIC cache and Helper cache.

- `search_nic_cache()` Determine whether a block is cached in the NIC cache or not by searching the target directory.
- `mov_nic_cache()` Notify the NIC cache to move blocks from NIC send buffer to a specific target's portion of NIC cache. It may be noted that this operation does not introduce additional traffic over host PCI bus as any requested data have to pass the NIC anyway.
- `update_nic_cache()` Duplicate newly written blocks from helper cache to NIC cache. DCA is conservative on this operation because it introduces extra data block transfers over PCI bus.
- `invalidate_nic_cache()` Invalidate the corresponding cache block in NIC cache. Compared with update_nic_cache(), this operation does not involve block data transfer over PCI bus.

```
/*The algorithm runs on each block b in a request req*/
  Update R/W count and state of block b;
  if (req.type = DCA_READ)
    if (NIL!=search_nic_cache(b))
      return NIC_READ_HIT; //b is in NIC Cache
    else if (b not in Helper Cache)
      Add b to disk read pending list;
      return HELP_READ_MISS;
    else{
      if (ReadCount(x) > WriteCount(x))
        mov_nic_cache(req);
      return HELP_READ_HIT;}
  else if (req.type = DCA_WRITE)
    if (b in Helper Cache){
      //hcache_entry is the directory entry of b in helper cache
      if (hcache_entry.last_type = DCA_WRITE)
        invalidate_nic_cache(req);
      if (ReadCount(b) > WriteCount(b)) &&
          (ReadCount(b) > MOV_THRESHOLD)
        update_nic_cache(req);
      return HELP_WRITE_HIT;}
    else{
      allocate new cache_entry in helper cache;
      set dirty bit;
      return HELP_WRITE_MISS;}
```

Figure 4. SLAP Algorithm in Pseudo-code

The SLAP algorithm is detailed in Figure 4. To predict future accesses more accurately, a placement policy based on a larger history window of state locality distance may be used. However, the maintenance overhead associated with each cacheline involves an O(n) time operation upon each block access. To strike a good trade-off, SLAP algorithm selectively chooses hot blocks based on state and access frequency, which requires only O(1) time to make the NIC cache placement decision.

4 Implementation

Considering different iSCSI target implementations [2, 3], we have several ways to implement DCA. The helper cache can be implemented in non-pageable host memory area with interfaces to both iSCSI target and NIC cache. The NIC cache resides in NIC on-board memory and accepts placement direction from Helper cache via driver interfaces. The target directory and per target cache directory information of NIC cache are maintained by NIC driver in host system. We initially attempted to use common programmable NIC card with firmware source code available. However, most of them provide up to 2 MB on-board memory which may only be applicable for higher-level caching such as static web pages. For storage servers, some latest NIC cards provide on-board memory extension such as Adaptec 7211c card [1] that supports 512 MB memory and is priced less than 500$. However, its firmware source code is not publicly available for modification as some programmable NIC cards. In addition, its memory space is either used as an I/O buffer or simple cache without interaction with higher level caches.

Therefore, we choose to adopt a non-programmable NIC to emulate DCA prototype system based on open source software of iSCSI target provided from Intel [2]. We implement DCA software components by modifying the request process flow of the iSCSI target module and integrate it with helper cache and NIC cache management modules. To truly replay the data traffic over the PCI bus, given any NIC cache hit (including partial hit), we forward those blocks that miss in NIC cache along with corresponding iSCSI response headers to the NIC card. The NIC card only sends out the data from the host system, leaving the blocks that hit in the NIC cache unsent. By this scheme, the data traffic over PCI is unchanged. Since we use a non-programmable NIC in experiments, the the traffic over Ethernet is changed because the blocks that hit in NIC cache are not composed and sent to the network. We believe that this would lead to trivial impact on our results for the following reasons: 1) all the results are collected at iSCSI target side which are not affected by the modified network traffic any way; 2) current full-duplex Gigabit Ethernet is not the system bottleneck compared with PCI bus that services both network and storage I/Os; 3) the CPUs in a storage server are powerful enough to deal with both I/O requests and DCA cache management.

5 Performance Evaluation

5.1 Experimental Methodology

To evaluate the performance of DCA, we setup an iSCSI based storage system testbed. Two commodity PCs act as an iSCSI client (or initiator) and an iSCSI storage server (or target) respectively. They are connected to a NetGear GS105 Gigabit Ethernet switch by two Intel Pro 1000/MT Gigabit Ethernet cards. Both machines have 1 GB DDR PC2700 RAM and run Linux kernel 2.4.20. The machine running as iSCSI storage server is installed with an Adaptec 39160 SCSI adaptor and a 73 GB Maxtor Atlas10K4 Ultra 320 SCSI disk. And the iSCSI client machine uses a Western Digital IDE disk with 200 GB capacity.

The current DCA prototype system has been developed based on open source software iSCSI implementation from Intel [2], with about 700 lines of the iSCSI target code and 500 lines of iSCSI initiator code modified. On iSCSI target side, two-level DCA cache management and the SLAP algorithm module are integrated into the user-space iSCSI target module. To run real-world workloads for performance evaluation, we developed a trace generator by modifying the iSCSI initiator module code. The modified iSCSI initiator fetches requests from real-life block-level storage server traces and sends them to the iSCSI target via Ethernet. The performance results in terms of cache hit/miss ratio and PCI traffic along with iSCSI storage server throughput were all collected at iSCSI target side.

Two real-world storage server traces cello99 and TPC-D provided by HP were chosen to drive the experiments as they represent modern file server and decision-making database server applications. Both contain mixed read and write requests with different read-to-write ratio from multiple users, which fits well with iSCSI applications. Cello99 trace segment has a 1,203 MB data set with 57.3% reads (collected between 02:00AM and 03:00AM on May, 02, 1999) while the TPC-D trace segment we use is collected during Q10 benchmark with a 105, 075 MB data set in total with an read ratio of 82.5%.

5.2 Results and Analysis

5.2.1 PCI Traffic Reduction

To evaluate the DCA performance, we conducted a comprehensive set of experiments, varying the NIC cache size from 8 MB to 128 MB and helper cache size from 128 MB to 512 MB. The maximum size of helper cache in experiments is set to be 512 MB due to the physical memory limitation on the iSCSI Target server. The amount of PCI traffic is collected by summarizing all the data (i.e., block transfers, movements and updates from helper cache to NIC cache) and control messages (i.e., iSCSI headers) that pass the PCI

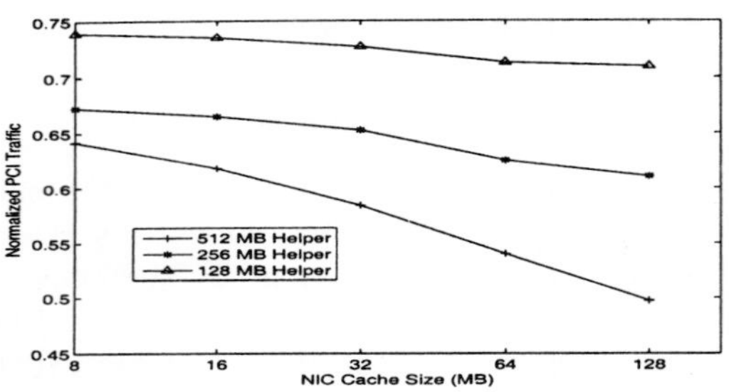

Figure 5. Normalized PCI Traffic of Cello99

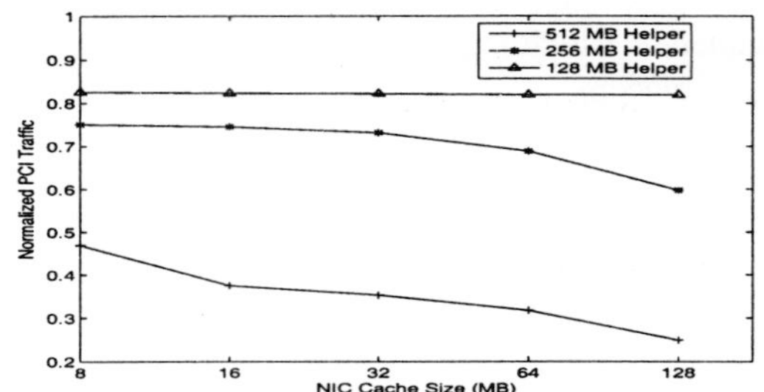

Figure 6. Normalized PCI Traffic of TPC-D

bus. We present the results for cello99 and TPC-D in Figure 5 and Figure 6 respectively. All the numbers shown in Y-axis are PCI traffic normalized to that of a standard iSCSI storage server without DCA support, namely a baseline system. Although DCA has a large helper cache, we believe that the comparison here is fair because current Linux 2.4 kernel adopts an aggressive I/O buffer allocation policy. As a result, the size of I/O buffer cache in baseline system is always commensurate to the sum of the helper cache size and I/O buffer cache size in DCA prototype system during our experiments.

Given a DCA with a 128 MB helper cache, the percentage of the PCI traffic reduction remains at 27% for cello99 and 18% for TPC-D. However, given a DCA with a 512 MB helper cache, increasing the NIC cache size from 8 MB to 128 MB results in remarkable PCI traffic reduction, as seen from the fact that the normalized PCI traffic curve drops sharply from 64% to 51% for cello99. The same trend can be observed conspicuously in TPC-D workload, which changes from 53% to 26% when increasing the NIC cache size from 8 MB to 128 MB, given a 512 MB helper cache.

Based on the above results, we conclude that DCA matches our conjectures of effective PCI traffic reduction. DCA always beats the kernel-level I/O buffer cache scheme (i.e., baseline system) and the separate NIC cache solution in terms of PCI traffic reduction because the LRU algorithm cannot work well for a storage server workload with long locality distances. To have a further insight look at PCI traffic reduction, we analyze the cache Hit/Miss ratio next.

5.2.2 Anatomy of Cache Hit/Miss Ratio

We first decompose the cache hits in DCA into three categories, namely NRH (NIC Read Hit), HRH (Helper Read Hit) and HWH (Helper Write Hit). Since NIC cache only serves read requests, we interchangeably use NIC hit and NRH in the rest of this paper. In DCA, both read and write misses eventually resort to the helper cache, which leads to either HRM (Helper Read Miss) or HWM (Helper Write Miss). Figure 7 and Figure 8 present the anatomy of cello99 and TPC-D experimental results with different DCA configurations. In both figures, X-axis denotes the NIC cache size and Y-axis denotes the stacked ratio of NRH, HRH, HWH, HRM and HWM in a bottom-up order. The left, middle and right sub-graphs of each figure show the results of a 128 MB, 256 MB and 512 MB helper cache respectively.

As seen in Figure 7, the larger the NIC cache, the higher the NIC cache hit ratio. However, Figure 7.b shows that the highest hit ratio of NIC cache with a 128 MB helper cache is always lower than 7.2%, even when the NIC cache size is increased to 128 MB. This indicates that a helper cache with less than 128 MB is not large enough to mine useful hints for NIC cache and thus resulting in a limited hit ratio gain. For simple NIC cache schemes (if there is no helper cache), the mixed read and write traffic can easily pollute the NIC cache space by indiscriminately filling it up with all blocks accessed recently. When the helper cache is enlarged to 512 MB, we observe that the increase of NIC cache size is much more productive than both 128 MB and 256 MB helper cache cases. The hit ratio of NIC cache increases from 4.4% to 19.7% when the cache size changes from 8 MB to 128 MB.

For TPC-D, we get similar results as in cello99 with a 128 MB helper cache. Although TPC-D represents a typical read-dominant decision making database workload, the amount of PCI traffic reduction is insensitive to the NIC cache size, given a 128 MB helper cache. This implies that simple NIC cache cannot work efficiently even for some read-dominant workloads. This is because LRU algorithm cannot work well for block-level caches, especially when the locality distance is larger than the LRU stack length. As seen from Figure 8.b, a 256 MB helper cache can effectively assist NIC cache in choosing real hot blocks for caching, peaking NIC hit ratio at 18.6% with a 128 MB NIC cache. Compared with Figure 8.a, the NIC hit ratio with the same NIC cache size is only 5.5%. We can obtain more than three times improvement on NIC cache hit ratio by applying SLAP algorithm to an appropriate helper cache

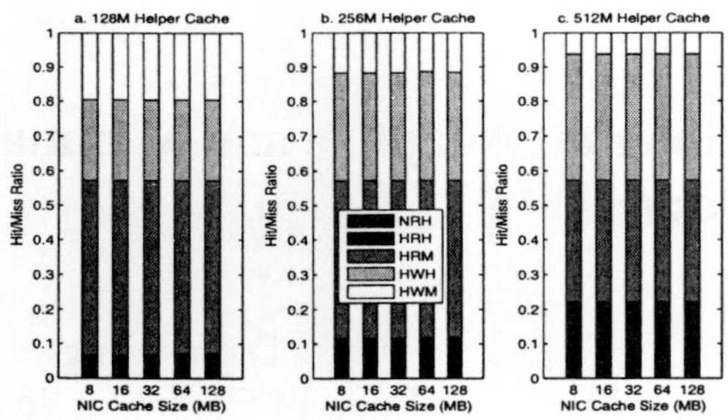

Figure 7. Hit/Miss Rate of cello99

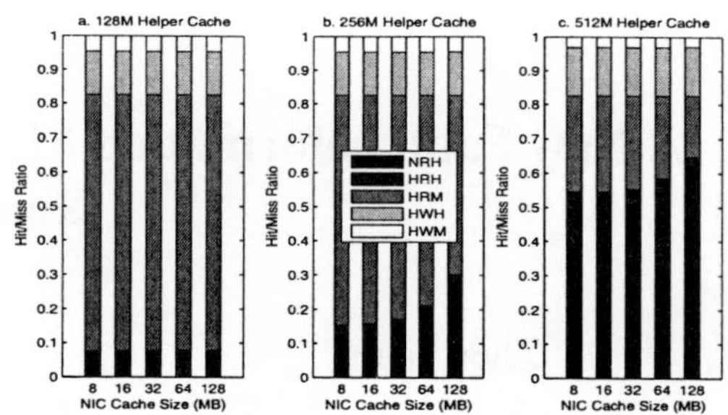

Figure 8. Hit/Miss Rate of TPC-D

size. As seen from Figure 8.b, the NRH ratio increases from 12% to 27% when the NIC cache size increases from 8 MB to 128 MB. Given a 512 MB helper cache, the maximum NIC cache hit ratio reaches 52% with a 128 MB NIC cache. Combined with the write hits at helper cache, the above anatomy results explain how DCA is able to slash the PCI traffic by up to 73%.

5.2.3 Server Performance Improvement

Due to the space limitation, we only present the results of a 512 MB helper cache and a 128 MB NIC cache. The result of cello99 shows that the server throughput has been improved by 76.9%, increasing from 4.95 MB/s to 8.76 MB/s. The result of TPC-D realizes a 121% server throughput improvement compared to an iSCSI storage server without DCA support. These numbers further prove our conjectures of DCA design. For TPC-D, the NIC cache hit ratio reaches 61.5% and thus delivers a much better overall performance than that of cello99.

6 Conclusion

In this paper, we have developed a novel Data Cache Architecture called DCA to effectively reduce local interconnect traffic. In DCA, a moderate-size NIC cache serves most read requests without fetching data from the host system via local interconnect while a large read/write unify helper cache employs a SLAP algorithm to direct cache placement for NIC cache. The proposed DCA architecture exhibits an extreme flexibility, as it can work either for a single server with multiple iSCSI targets, or a group of servers with multiple iSCSI targets (such as clustered storage servers). Our comprehensive experiments with representative real-life storage server workloads prove that DCA can effectively slash the PCI traffic by up to 74% and boost iSCSI storage server throughput by 121% compared with an iSCSI target without DCA support.

7 Acknowledgments

We thank Peng Gu for his participation and discussion in the early stage of this project. We also would like to thank Hewlett-Packard Labs for providing storage traces including cello99 and TPC-D.

References

[1] Adaptec iscsi card7211c data sheet. http://graphics.adaptec.com/pdfs/iscsi_7211_datasheet.pdf.

[2] Intel iSCSI Reference Implementation. http://sourceforge.net/projects/intel-iscsi/.

[3] UNH-iSCSI project. http://unh-iscsi.sourceforge.net/.

[4] Z. Chen, Y. Zhou, and K. Li. Eviction-based cache placement for storage caches. In *USENIX Annual Technical Conference, General Track 2003*, pages 269–281, 2003.

[5] W. chun Feng, Justin, Hurwitz, H. B. Newman, S. Ravot, R. L. Cottrell, O. Martin, F. Coccetti, C. Jin, D. Wei, and S. Low. Optimizing 10-gigabit Ethernet in networks of workstations, clusters, and grids: A case study. In *Proc. Of ACM/IEEE Supercomputing 2003: High-Performance Networking and Computing Conference*, 2003.

[6] G. Gibson and R. Meter. Network attached storage architecture. *Communications of ACM*, 43(11):37–45, November 2000.

[7] S. Jiang and X. Zhang. ULC: A file block placement and replacement protocol to effectively exploit hierarchical locality in multi-level buffer caches. In *Proceedings of the 24nd International Conference on Distributed Computing Systems (ICDCS'04)*, pages 168–177, Tokyo, Japan, March 2004.

[8] J.Satran, K.Meth, C. Sapuntzakis, and M. Chadalapaka. Internet Engineering Task Force, RFC 3720:Internet Small Computer System Interface (iSCSI). RFC 3720.

[9] H. Kim, V. Pai, and S. Rixner. Increasing web server throughput with network interface data caching. In *International Conference on Architectural Support for Programming Languages and Operating Systems (ASPLOS'02)*, San Jose, CA, October 2002.

[10] B. Phillips. Have storage area networks come of age? *IEEE Computer*, 31(7):10–12, July 1998.

[11] T. M. Wong and J. Wilkes. My cache or yours? making storage more exclusive. In *USENIX Annual Technical Conference, General Track 2002*, pages 161–175, 2002.

[12] M. Zhang and Q. Yang. BUCS a bottom-up cache structure for networked storage servers. In *Proc. Of the 2004 International Conference on Parallel Processing (ICPP'04)*, pages 310–317, Montreal, Quebec, Canada, August 2004.

A New Fault Information Model for Fault-Tolerant Adaptive and Minimal Routing in 3-D Meshes *

Zhen Jiang
Dept. of Computer Science
Information Assurance Center
West Chester University
West Chester, PA 19383
zjiang@wcupa.edu

Jie Wu
Dept. of Computer Sci. & Eng.
Florida Atlantic University
Boca Raton, FL 33431
jie@cse.fau.edu

Dajin Wang
Dept. of Computer Science
Montclair State University
Upper Montclair, NJ 07043
wang@pegasus.montclair.edu

Abstract

In this paper we rewrite Wang's Minimal-Connected-Component (MCC) model [7] in 2-D meshes without using global information so that not only the existence of a minimal path can be ensured at the source, but also such a path can be formed by routing decisions at intermediate nodes along the path. We extend this MCC model and the corresponding routing in 2-D meshes to 3-D meshes. It is based on our early work on fault tolerant adaptive and minimal routing [9] and the boundary information model [8] in 3-D meshes. We study fault tolerant adaptive and minimal routing from the source and the destination and consider the positions of the source and destination when the new faulty components are constructed. Specifically, all faulty nodes will be contained in some disjoint faulty components and a healthy node will be included in a faulty component only if using it in the routing will definitely cause a non-minimal routing path. A sufficient and necessary condition is proposed for the existence of the minimal routing path in the presence of our faulty components. Based on such a condition, the corresponding routing will guarantee a minimal path whenever it exists.

Index Terms: Adaptive routing, fault information models, fault tolerance, minimal routing, 3-D meshes.

1 Introduction

The *mesh-connected topology* is one of the most thoroughly investigated network topologies for multicomputer systems. Like 2-dimensional (2-D) meshes, 3-D meshes are lower dimensional meshes that have been commonly discussed due to structural regularity for easy construction and high potential of legibility of various algorithms. Some multicomputers were built based on the 3-D meshes [1, 5]. The performance of such a multicomputer system is highly dependent on the node-to-node communication cost. It is necessary to present a *minimal routing* (i.e., a shortest path routing) in mesh networks. We focus here on achieving fault tolerance using the inherent redundancy present in 3-D meshes, without adding spare nodes and/or links.

Most existing literature [2, 3, 6, 10] uses the simplest orthogonal convex region to model node faults (link faults can be treated as node faults by disabling the corresponding adjacent nodes). Wu provided a node labelling scheme in [8] that identifies nodes (faulty and non-faulty) that cause routing detours in 2-D meshes and such nodes are called unsafe nodes. Connected unsafe nodes form a rectangular region, also called a rectangular faulty block. In [8], the information of rectangular faulty blocks is distributed to a limited number of nodes at the boundary lines to prevent a routing message from entering a detour area. By using this so-called limited global fault information at boundary lines in 2-D meshes, Wu's fully adaptive routing proposed in [8] can easily find a minimal path. To reduce the number of non-faulty nodes contained in rectangular faulty blocks, Wang [7] proposed the minimal connected component (MCC) model as a refinement of the rectangular faulty block model by considering the relative locations of source and destination nodes. The original idea is that a node will be included in an MCC only if using it in a routing will definitely make the route non-minimal. It turns out that each MCC is of the rectilinear monotone polygonal shape and is the absolutely minimal fault region in 2-D meshes.

In this paper, we provide a boundary construction for MCCs in 2-D meshes through message exchanges among neighboring nodes. With the information of MCCs at the boundary lines, Wang's sufficient and necessary condition

*The work was supported in part by NSF grants ANI 0083836, CCR 9900646, CNS 0422762, CNS 0434533, and EIA 0130806.

0190-3918/05 $20.00 © 2005 IEEE

of the existence of the minimal routing can be re-written so that not only a minimal routing can be ensured at the source node but also a minimal path can be formed by routing decisions at intermediate nodes along the path. After that, the MCC model and its boundary construction will be extended to 3-D meshes. A sufficient and necessary condition is proposed for the existence of the minimal routing in 3-D meshes. Based on this condition, a new (fully) adaptive routing is provided to build a minimal path between source and destination nodes whenever such a minimal path exists. Extensive simulation has been done to determine the number of non-faulty nodes included in MCCs in 3-D meshes and the rate of success minimal routing under MCC model. The result obtained is compared with the best existing known result. Due to the space limit, these simulation results are not shown. Details can be found in [4].

The challenge here is not only to conduct a theoretical study on the MCC model in 3-D meshes and its corresponding sufficient and necessary condition for existence of minimal routing, but also to search for a practical and efficient implementation in a system where each node knows only the status of its neighbors. First, after each non-faulty node in an MCC is labelled, the whole 3-D fault region should be identified. Then, the identified information of this MCC will be propagated in two dimensions along some 2-D surfaces (also called boundaries) to avoid the routing entering the detour area. Finally, a new routing with two phases is proposed. In phase one, the boundary information of any MCC that may block the routing message is collected and used to build the assurance of minimal routing at the source node. The routing process at the source will be activated only if a minimal path exists. In phase two, the routing process at each intermediate node between source and destination nodes will forward the message to the next node along the path. It uses the boundary information to avoid sending the message to the detour area and to keep the routing path minimal. It is noted that all these are implemented through the message transmission (including information messages and routing messages) between two neighboring nodes along one of those three dimensions X, Y and Z. Throughout the paper, proofs to theorems are omitted. Details can be found in [4].

2 Preliminary

A k-ary n-dimensional mesh with k^n nodes has an interior node degree of $2n$ and the network diameter is $(k-1)n$. Each node u has an address $(u_1, u_2, ..., u_n)$, where $0 \leq u_i \leq k-1$. Two nodes $(v_1, v_2, ..., v_n)$ and $(u_1, u_2, ..., u_n)$ are neighbors if their addresses differ in one and only one dimension, say dimension i; moreover, $|v_i - u_i| = 1$. Basically, nodes along each dimension are connected as a linear array. In a 2-D mesh, each node u is labelled as (x_u, y_u) and

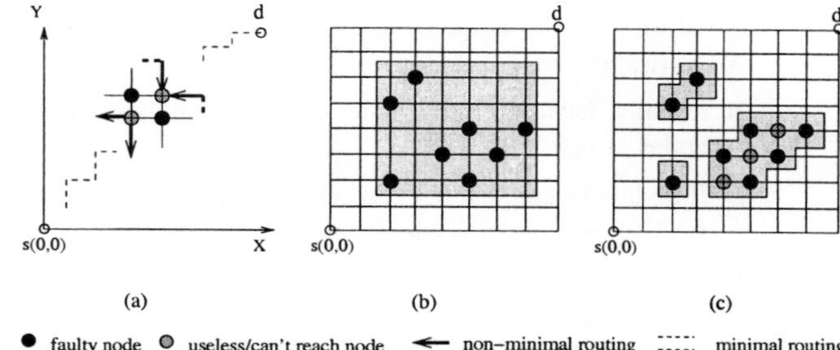

Figure 1. (a) Definition of useless and can't-reach nodes. (b) Sample of rectangular faulty block. (c) The corresponding MCCs.

the distance between two nodes u and v, $D(u, v)$, is equal to $| x_v - x_u | + | y_v - y_u |$. For a node $u(x_u, y_u)$, node $v(x_u + 1, y_u)$ is called the $+X$ neighbor of u. Respectively, $(x_u - 1, y_u)$, $(x_u, y_u - 1)$, and $(x_u, y_u + 1)$ are $-X$, $-Y$ and $+Y$ neighbors of node u in a 2-D mesh. When node v is a neighbor of node u, v is called a *preferred neighbor* if $D(v, d) < D(u, d)$ where d is the destination; otherwise, it is called a *spare neighbor*. Respectively, the corresponding connecting directions are called *preferred direction* and *spare direction*. Without loss of generality, assume node $s(0, 0)$ is source node and node $d(x_d, y_d)$ $(x_d, y_d \geq 0)$ is the destination node. A routing process is *minimal* if the length of the routing path from source node s to destination node d is equal to $D(s, d)$. Similarly, in a 3-D mesh, $(0, 0, 0)$ is the source node, $u(x_u, y_u, z_u)$ is the current node, $d(x_d, y_d, z_d)$ $(x_d, y_d, z_d \geq 0)$ is the destination node, and the distance between two nodes u and v, $D(u, v)$, is equal to $| x_v - x_u |$ $+ | y_v - y_u | + | z_v - z_u |$. $(x_u + 1, y_u, z_u)$, $(x_u - 1, y_u, z_u)$, $(x_u, y_u + 1, z_u)$, $(x_u, y_u - 1, z_u)$, $(x_u, y_u, z_u + 1)$ and $(x_u, y_u, z_u - 1)$ are $+X$, $-X$, $+Y$, $-Y$, $+Z$, and $-Z$ neighbors of node u.

The formation of MCC in 2-D meshes [7] is based on the notions of *useless* and *can't-reach* nodes (see in Figure 1 (a)): A node labelled useless is such a node that once a routing from $(0, 0)$ to (x_d, y_d) $(x_d, y_d \geq 0)$ enters it, the next move must take either $-X$ or $-Y$ direction, making the routing non-minimal. A node labelled can't-reach is such a node that for a routing to enter it, a $-X$ or $-Y$ direction move must be taken, making the routing non-minimal. The node status (non-faulty, faulty, useless, and can't-reach) can be determined through a labelling procedure. All faulty, useless, and can't-reach nodes are also called unsafe nodes. The labelling procedure is given in Algorithm 1. Only the affected nodes update their status. Figure 1 (a) shows the idea of the definition of useless and can't-reach nodes. Figure 1 (c) shows some samples of MCCs for the routing from

Algorithm 1: Labelling procedure of MCC for the routing from $(0,0)$ to (x_d, y_d) $(x_d, y_d \geq 0)$

1. Initially, label all faulty nodes as *faulty* and all non-faulty nodes as *safe*.
2. If node u is safe, but its $+X$ neighbor and $+Y$ neighbor are faulty or useless, u is labelled *useless*.
3. If node u is safe, but its $-X$ neighbor and $-Y$ neighbor are faulty or can't-reach, u is labelled *can't-reach*.
4. The nodes are recursively labelled until there is no new useless or can't-reach node. All faulty, useless, and can't-reach nodes (other than safe nodes) are also called *unsafe* nodes.

$(0,0)$ to (x_d, y_d) $(x_d, y_d \geq 0)$.

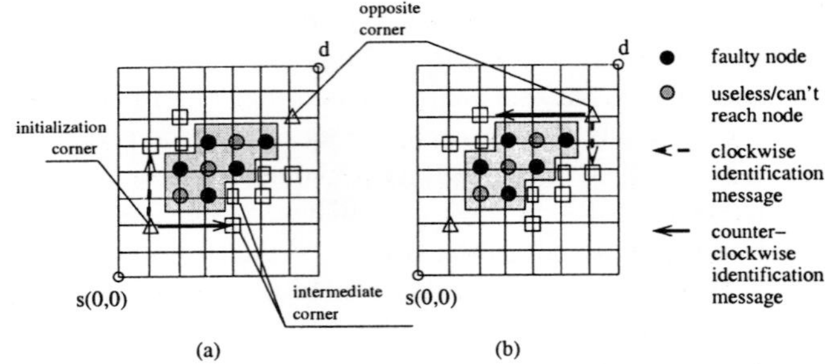

Figure 2. (a) Identification process activated at the initialization corner. (b) Identified information re-sending.

3 Boundary information in 2-D meshes

In this section, we provide a distributed process to collect the information of each MCC and distribute it along the boundaries. Based on such information, the new routing process provided in this section can form a minimal path from the source to destination nodes whenever this path exists.

Corner and boundary of MCC . To collect the information of all MCCs for routing process, each MCC needs to identify its fault region. Any node inside fault region MCC is called an unsafe node. Otherwise, it is called a safe node. Any safe node with an unsafe neighbor in an MCC is called an *edge* node of that MCC. A *corner* is a safe node with two edge nodes of the same MCC in different dimensions or a safe node with two unsafe node of the same MCC in different dimensions. After the labelling procedure, the identification process starts from an *initialization corner*. The initialization corner is a corner with two edge nodes of the same MCC in the $+X$ and $+Y$ dimensions. A safe node with two edge nodes of the same MCC in the $-X$ and $-Y$ dimensions is called its *opposite corner*.

From that initialization corner, two identification messages, one clockwise and one counter-clockwise, are initiated. Each message carries partial region information: First, they will be sent to these two edge neighbors. Such propagation will continue along the edges until the messages reach the opposite corner. When the clockwise message passes through any intermediate corner u, node information (x_u, y_u) will be attached to the message and be used at the opposite corner to form the shape of this MCC. Similarly, the counter-clockwise message will also bring the node information of every intermediate corner it passed through to the opposite corner. After these two messages meet at the opposite corner, the propagation will continue and bring the shape information back to the initialization corner. This time, no new intermediate corner needs to be identified and no new information will be added into each message. Figure 2 shows a sample of the identification process.

An MCC has only one initialization corner $c(x_c, y_c)$ and one opposite corner $c'(x_{c'}, y_{c'})$. If two identification messages cannot meet at that opposite corner, or if any of them finds the change of shape when it is sent back to c, it suggests that this MCC is not stable. The message is discarded to avoid generating incorrect MCC boundary information. If only one message is received at the initialization corner, the other has been discarded in the propagation procedure and this message should also be discarded. Normally, a TTL (time-to-live) is associated with each identification message and the corresponding message will be discarded once the time expires.

In 2-D meshes, an MCC with the initialization corner c is noted by $M(c)$. A routing message should be forbidden to enter the region right below it if the destination is right above it. The first region is also called the *forbidden region*, noted by $Q_Y(c)$. The corresponding region right above $M(c)$ is called *critical region*, noted by $Q'_Y(c)$. Similarly, the routing message should avoid entering the forbidden region $Q_X(c)$ on the left side of $M(c)$ if the destination is in the critical region $Q_X(c)$ on the right side of $M(c)$. To guide the routing process, two boundary messages will be initiated when two identification messages are both received at node c. One boundary message (also called Y boundary) will carry the information $M(c)$, $Q_Y(c)$, and $Q'_Y(c)$ and propagate to all the nodes along the boundary line $x = x_c$ in the $-Y$ direction until it reaches the edge of this 2-D mesh. When this boundary line intersects with another MCC ($M(v)$), a turn in the $-X$ direction is made. After that, it will go along the edges of $M(v)$ to join the same boundary of $M(v)$ at the initialization corner v. At that corner v, $Q_Y(v)$ merges into $Q_Y(c)$ ($Q_Y(c) = Q_Y(c) \cup Q_Y(v)$) (see in Figure 3 (a)). Similarly, another boundary propagation (construction of

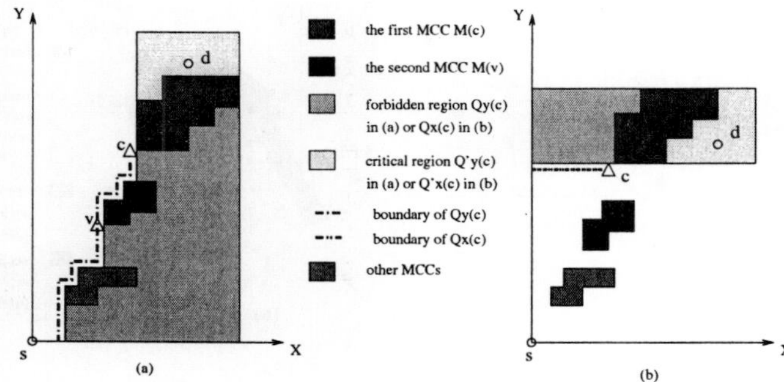

Figure 3. Samples of boundary construction under MCC model in 2-D meshes.

X boundary) carrying $M(c)$, $Q_X(c)$, and $Q'_X(c)$ will go along $y = y_c$ in the $-X$ direction and make a turn in the $-Y$ direction if necessary (see in Figure 3 (b)). The whole procedure is shown in Algorithm 2.

Algorithm 2: Identifi cation process and boundary construction

1. Identifi cation of edge nodes, the initialization corner c, intermediate corners, and the opposite corner c'.
2. Identifi cation process of MCC $M(c)$: (a) From node c, two identifi cation message (one clockwise and one counter-clockwise) are sent along the edge nodes of $M(c)$ until they reach node c'. (b) Node information of all corners is transferred to form the shape of $M(c)$ at node c'. (c) After they meet at node c', the propagation will continue until the shape information reaches back to node c. (d) The stable shape of $M(c)$ can be ensured at node c once two identifi cation messages are both received. Meanwhile, the critical and forbidden regions ($Q_X(c)$, $Q_Y(c)$, $Q'_X(c)$, $Q'_Y(c)$) are identifi ed.
3. X / Y boundary construction of $M(c)$: A boundary construction is activated at node c after it receives two identifi-cation messages. The information of $M(c)$, $Q_X(c)$ / $Q_Y(c)$, and $Q'_X(c)$ / $Q'_Y(c)$ is propagated along the boundary line $y = y_c$ / $x = x_c$. When the propagation intersects another MCC ($M(v)$), it will go along the edges of $M(v)$ and join the same boundary of $M(v)$. Since then, the area information of forbidden region of $M(v)$ ($Q_X(v)$ / $Q_Y(v)$) will merge into that of $M(c)$: $Q_X(c)$ / $Q_Y(c)$.

Sufficient and necessary condition for the existence of minimal routing. The MCC model includes much fewer non-faulty nodes in its fault region than the conventional rectangular model in 2-D meshes. Many non-faulty nodes that would have been included in rectangular faulty blocks now can become candidate routing nodes. As a matter of fact, MCC is the "ultimate" minimal fault region; that is, no non-faulty node contained in an MCC will be useful in a minimal routing. A routing that enters a non-faulty node in the MCC would force a step that violates the requirement for a minimal routing. If there exists no minimal routing under the MCC model, there will be absolutely no minimal routing. In [7], a sufficient and necessary condition was provided for the existence of minimal routing. This can be rewritten as the following:

Lemma 1: *A routing does not have a minimal path if and only if there exists an MCC $M(c)$ in which (a) $s \in Q_X(C) \wedge d \in Q'_X(c)$, or (b) $s \in Q_Y(C) \wedge d \in Q'_Y(c)$.*

Theorem 1: *A routing does not have a minimal path if and only if there exists an MCC in which (a) $d \in Q'_X(c)$ and its X boundary does not intersect with the segment $[0:0, 0:y_d]$, or (b) $d \in Q'_Y$ and its Y boundary does not intersect with the segment $[0:x_d, 0:0]$.*

Boundary-information-based routing. Wu proposed a minimal and adaptive routing in 3-D meshes in [9]. It can easily be extended to a routing in 2-D meshes under the MCC model (see in Algorithm 3). In this routing, at the source node s, a detection is activated to check if there exists a minimal path. First, node s will play the role as the destination in Theorem 1. It sends two detection messages, one along $+Y$ direction and one along $+X$ direction. If the first one cannot reach the segment $[0:x_d, y_d:y_d]$, a minimal path is impossible (return "No"). If it intersects with another MCC, make a turn to the $+X$ direction, and then, turn back to the $+Y$ direction as soon as possible. Similarly, the second one is to check if the segment $[x_d:x_d, 0:y_d]$ can be reached. If the source s knows both segments can be reached, based on Theorem 1, a minimal path exists from d to s (i.e., a minimal routing is feasible from s to d).

Algorithm 3: Routing from $s(0,0)$ to $d(x_d, y_d)$ ($x_d, y_d \geq 0$)

1. Feasibility check: At source s, send two detection messages (the fi rst along the $+Y$ direction and the second along $+X$ direction) until they reach the line $x = x_d$ or line $y = y_d$. If the fi rst / second message intersects with another MCC, make a turn to $+X$ / $+Y$ direction, and then, turn back to the $+Y$ / $+X$ direction as soon as possible. If it intersects with the segment $[0:x_d, y_d:y_d]$ / $[x_d:x_d, 0:y_d]$, return YES to node s; otherwise, return NO. If any return is No, stop the routing since there is no minimal path.
2. Routing decision and message sending at the current node u, including node s, (a) add all the preferred directions into the set of candidates of forwarding directions F and fi nd all the records of MCCs, (b) for each MCC found, exclude a direction from F if the destination is in the critical region and the neighbor of u along this direction is inside forbidden region, (c) apply any fully adaptive and minimal routing process to pick up a forwarding direction from set F, and (d) forward the routing message along the selected forwarding direction to the next node.

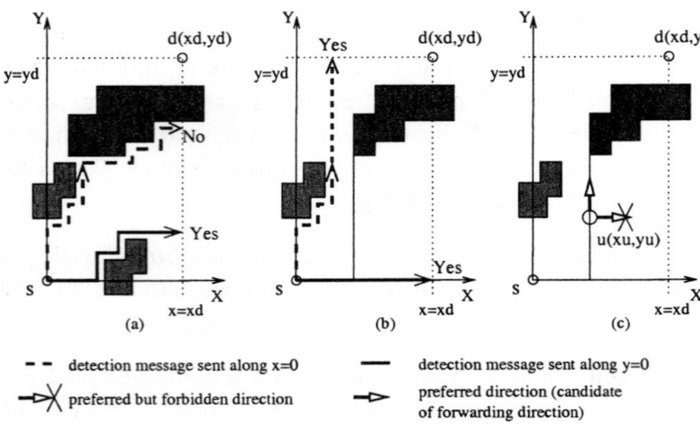

Figure 4. (a) Feasibility check for a case without minimal routing path. (b) Feasibility check to ensure the existence of minimal routing path. (c) Routing decisions in routing process to construct a minimal routing path.

After the detection, at each node along the routing path, including the source node s, the routing process basically has two preferred directions: $+X$ and $+Y$ directions. The boundary information of an MCC with the destination in the critical region will help the routing process avoid entering the forbidden region by excluding the corresponding preferred direction from the candidates for forwarding direction. Any fully adaptive and minimal routing process could be applied to pick up the forwarding direction and forward the routing message along this direction to the corresponding neighbor. The procedure of feasibility check and routing decision can also be seen in the samples in Figure 4.

4 MCC model in 3-D meshes

In this section, we present our distributed solution for constructing MCCs and propagating the region information in 3-D meshes. First, the status of each node is identified in a labelling process. Then, each 2-D section of a 3-D fault region and its neighboring sections are identified in an identification process. After that, the information of 2-D sections of a fault region are collected along the edges of this fault region in the edge construction. With this information, the region is identified as an MCC and the information of its shape, forbidden region, and critical region are formed. Finally, in boundary construction, this information will be propagated along the boundary of this MCC to avoid the routing entering its forbidden region.

Labelling process. For a non-faulty node u in 3-D meshes, if it has only two useless or faulty neighbors in $+X$ and $+Y$ directions, the routing message can take the $+Z$ direction and route around the fault region. Therefore, a non-faulty node is useless in 3-D meshes if and only if it has three useless or faulty neighbors in $+X$, $+Y$, and $+Z$ directions. Similarly, a non-faulty node is can't-reach if and only if it has three can't-reach or faulty neighbors in $-X$, $-Y$, and $-Z$ directions. The corresponding labelling scheme is shown in Algorithm 4.

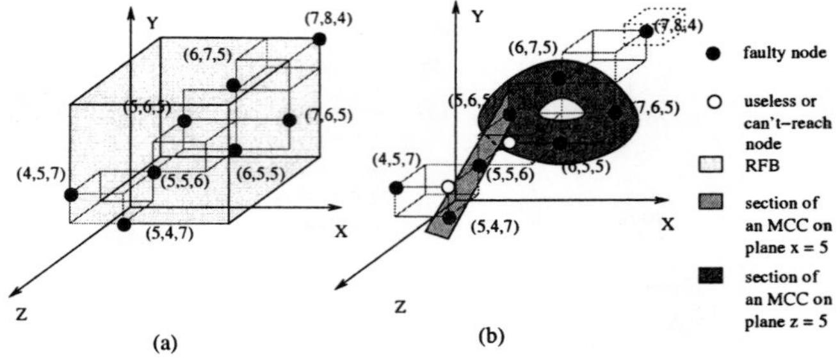

Figure 5. (a) Sample rectangular faulty block in 3-D meshes. (b) The corresponding MCCs.

Algorithm 4: Labelling procedure of MCC in 3-D meshes

1. Initially, label all faulty nodes as *faulty* and all non-faulty nodes as *safe*.
2. If node u is safe, but its $+X$, $+Y$, and $+Z$ neighbors are faulty or useless, u is labelled *useless*.
3. If node u is safe, but its $-X$, $-Y$, and $-Z$ neighbors are faulty or can't-reach, u is labelled *can't-reach*.
4. The nodes are recursively labelled until there is no new useless or can't-reach node. All faulty, useless, and can't-reach nodes are also called *unsafe* nodes.

Figure 5 (b) shows two sample MCCs in 3-D meshes. One MCC contains only one faulty node $(7, 8, 4)$ and the other MCC contains all the other unsafe nodes, including the faulty nodes: $(5, 5, 6)$, $(6, 5, 5)$, $(5, 6, 5)$, $(6, 7, 5)$, $(7, 6, 5)$, $(5, 4, 7)$, and $(4, 5, 7)$. $(5, 5, 5)$ becomes useless and $(5, 5, 7)$ becomes can't-reach in our labelling process. Usually, a 2-D section of the MCC parallel to plane $x = 0$, plane $y = 0$, or plane $z = 0$ is not a *convex polygon*. A convex polygon has been defined as a polygon P for which a line segment connecting any two points in P lies entirely within P. A section of the second MCC on the plane $z = 5$ shows a hole at $(6, 6, 5)$ in the MCC region.

Identification process. The identification process for an MCC in 3-D meshes is based on the one in 2-D meshes. It starts from the identification of each 2-D section on the XY plane, YZ plane, and XZ plane simultaneously. Simply, we call these sections XY sections, YZ sections, and XZ sections. For each 2-D section, for example, a XY

section, a two-head-on message identification process in algorithm 2 is activated at a corner c. This XY section may have several corners. The one with the minimum coordinate along the X dimension of those which have the maximum coordinate along Y dimension is called $(+Y-X)$-corner of this section. Respectively, we have $(+X-Y)$-corner of the same XY section, $(+X-Z)$- and $(+Z-X)$-corners of a XZ section, and $(+Y-Z)$- and $(+Z-Y)$-corners of a YZ section. Each XY / YZ / XZ section will be identified by a similar process initialize from its $(+Y-X)$- / $(+Z-Y)$- / $(+X-Z)$-corner. It is noted that these two identification messages may meet at any edge node of the 2-D section, not necessary a corner node.

After section identification, six kinds of edges of each MCC are identified for the boundary construction: $(+Y-X)$-edge, $(+Y-Z)$-edge, $(+X-Y)$-edge, $(+X-Z)$-edge, $(+Z-Y)$-edge and $(+Z-X)$-edge. Any of these edges is defined by all of its edge nodes and each edge node is the corresponding corner in its 2-D section. The identification process starts from each of these corners and has three phases. It is to find a path to link each pair of the preceding node and its succeeding node along the edge so that the whole edge can be formed. In phase one, a message will be initiated at the start corner and route around its 2-D section to find a path to the neighboring section. In phase two, this message will be propagated along that path to the neighboring section. In phase three, it will route around that neighboring section to reach its corresponding start corner. Once this message reaches that corner, those same type corners in neighboring sections are identified as preceding and succeeding edge nodes and the path between them will be used for future edge construction.

For example, the $(+Y-X)$-edge of an MCC is defined by the $(+Y-X)$-corners of all XY sections of this MCC. In phase one, from a $(+Y-X)$-corner $c(x_c, y_c, z_c)$ in the XY section $z = z_c$ in Figure 6 (a), a message will be sent to route around this section. When such a message passes through a node $u(x_u, y_u, z_c)$ with an unsafe neighbor in the $-Y$ dimension, the identified information of the YZ section on the plane $x = x_u$ is used to find a neighboring section on plane $z = z_c + 1$. In phase two, the message will go around the corresponding YZ section to the neighboring XY section (seen in Figure 6 (a)). In phase three, once the message arrives at a node of the neighboring XY section, a two-head-on message propagation will be initiated to go around that section (one clockwise and one counter-clockwise) to reach its corresponding $(+Y-X)$-corner u' (seen in Figure 6 (b)). At node u', c is identified as its succeeding node along the edge and the information of the path to node c (see in Figure 6 (c)) is saved for future information propagation.

Edge construction. If the neighboring section cannot be found in phase one in the above identification process, that start corner is identified as one end of this edge and the corresponding section is identified as the surface of this MCC (see corner c' in Figure 6 (a)). In phase three of the above identification process, a concave region of the MCC containing the start corner can be identified if there is another 2-D section in the same plane. For example, in Figure 6 (b), at node u'', the second section is found. Once such a concave region is found, the start corner (corner c'' in the example in Figure 6 (b)) will be identified as one end of another edge (an inner edge of this MCC towards a concave area).

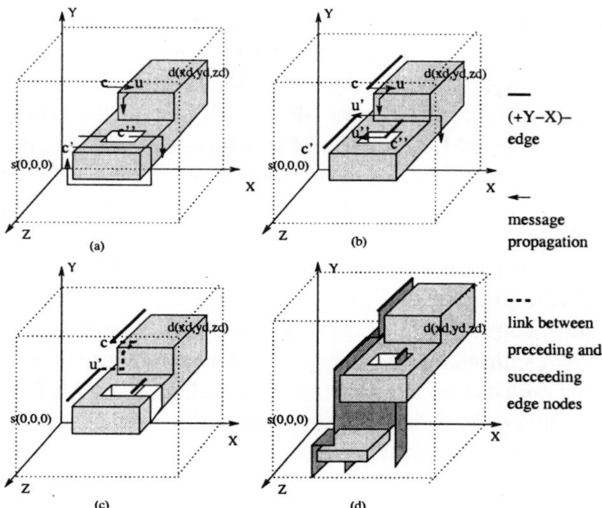

Figure 6. (a) Section identification. (b) Edge Identification. (c) Edge construction. (d) Boundary construction.

Starting from an identified end node u , the entire edge will form by collecting all the links between preceding and succeeding nodes along this edge. From u, a message is sent along the path to its succeeding node and such propagation will continue until it reaches the other end (an edge node without any succeeding node). At each edge node v it passes through, the section information is collected and the previously saved information is used to form a part of this MCC, $M(v)$. This $M(v)$ includes the MCC area from the current node v to the end node u. With the information of $M(v)$, the information of forbidden region $Q(v)$ and the critical region $Q'(v)$ can also be formed at node v (see in the example in Figure 6 (c)).

Boundary construction. At each edge node u, say along a $(+Y-X)$-edge, after $M(u)$ is formed, the information of $M(u)$, $Q_Y(u)$, and $Q'_Y(u)$ will be propagated along the boundary (also called $(+Y-X)$-boundary) to block the routing from entering the detour area $Q_Y(u)$ in the $+X$ dimension if the destination is inside the critical region $Q'_Y(u)$. Initially, a message carrying the information is sent from node u along the $-Y$ dimension. Once this message intersects with another MCC at node u', the boundary of node u will make a $-X$ turn and route around the XY section of the latter MCC until it joins the boundary of the latter MCC from v. Meanwhile, the forbidden region of node v ($Q_Y(v)$) will be merged into $Q_Y(u)$ ($Q_Y(u) = Q_Y(v) \cup Q_Y(u)$). If node u is the $(-Z)$-most edge node (the edge node without any succeeding node), at node u', a copy of the message will be sent to node v. From node v, it will go along that $(+Y - X)$-edge and reach the $(-Z)$-most edge node of the latter MCC. At each edge node v' it passes through, a boundary is constructed for node u with the information of $M(u)$, $Q'_Y(u)$, and $Q_Y(u) \cup Q_Y(v')$. A sample of boundary construction is shown in Figure 6 (d). The whole procedure is shown in Algorithm 5.

Algorithm 5: Identifi cation and boundary construction of an MCC in 3-D meshes

1. Identifi cation of each 2-D section (see in Algorithm 2).
2. Identifi cation of each edge: (a) a message is sent along each XY, YZ, or XZ section from its start corner to fi nd the neighboring section; (b) the message reaches the neighboring section in one hop; (c) an identifi cation process in algorithm 2 is applied to reach the corresponding corner in this neighboring section, the preceding node of that start corner.
3. Edge construction: If no neighboring section is found or there is another section in the same plane, the start corner will be identifi ed as an end node without a preceding node. From this end node, a message is sent to the succeeding node along the edge and the propagation will continue until it reaches the other end edge node. It will collect the section information at each edge node c and the previously saved information will be used to form the concerning MCC part $M(c)$, the forbidden region $Q(c)$, and the critical region $Q'(c)$.
4. Boundary construction: After $M(u)$, $Q(u)$, and $Q'(u)$ is formed at an edge node u, say along the $(+Y - X)$-edge, the information will be propagated along its $(+Y - X)$-boundary in the $-Y$ direction. If it intersects with another MCC, $M(v)$, it will join the boundary of the "nose" part of $M(v)$ and merge $Q_Y(v)$ into $Q_Y(u)$.

---

5 Suffi cient and necessary condition for the existence of minimal routing in 3-D meshes

After the boundary construction, a boundary node will have the region information $M(c)$, the forbidden region information $Q(c)$ ($Q_X(c)$, $Q_Y(c)$, or $Q_Z(c)$), and the critical region information $Q'(c)$ ($Q'_X(c)$, $Q'_Y(c)$, or $Q'_Z(c)$). When a routing enters this node and its destination d is inside the critical region, the boundary line can be used as a part of the routing path to route around the $M(c)$ and avoid detours. We have the following sufficient and necessary condition for the existence of minimal routing in 3-D meshes:

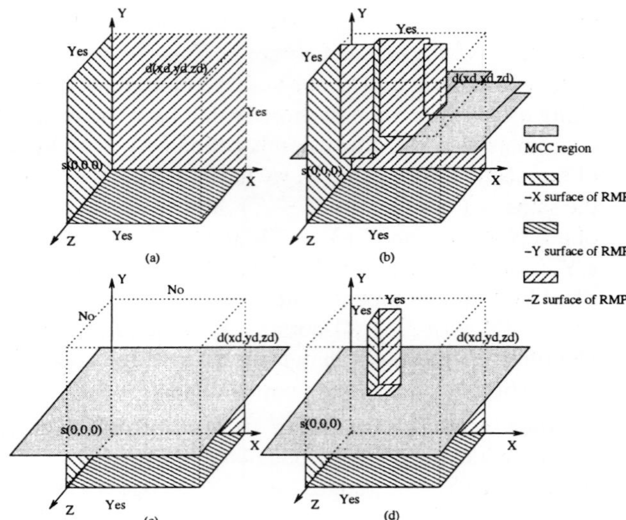

Figure 7. Samples of feasibility check.

Theorem 2: *A routing does not have a minimal path if and only if there exists an MCC for which (a) $d \in Q'_X$ and neither its $(+X-Y)$-boundary nor its $(+X-Z)$-boundary intersects with the surface $[0:0, 0:y_d, 0:z_d]$, (b) $d \in Q'_Y$ and neither its $(+Y - X)$-boundary nor its $(+Y - Z)$-boundary intersects with the surface $[0:x_d, 0:0, 0:z_d]$, or (c) $d \in Q'_Z$ and neither its $(+Z - X)$-boundary nor its $(+Z - Y)$-boundary intersects with the surface $[0:x_d, 0:y_d, 0:0]$.*

6 Boundary-information-based routing under MCC model in 3-D meshes

Based on Theorem 2, Wu's routing in [9] in 3-D meshes is extended to a routing under the MCC model (see in Algorithm 6). Such a routing can find a minimal path from the source and destination nodes whenever this path exists.

Algorithm 6: Routing process.

1. Feasibility check at s: Send detection messages along three surfaces of RMP, which includes all the intermediate nodes along the shortest path from s to d: $(-X)$-surface on the $-X$ side, $(-Y)$-surface on the $-Y$ side, and $(-Z)$-surface on the $-Z$ side. Any message on $(-X)$-surface reaches the surface $[0:x_d, y_d:y_d, 0:z_d]$, it will return the result back to s. Similarly, the propagation on the $(-Y)$- or $(-Z)$-surface is to see if the surface $[0:x_d, 0:y_d, z_d:z_d]$ or $[x_d:x_d, 0:y_d, 0:z_d]$ can be reached. If any surface

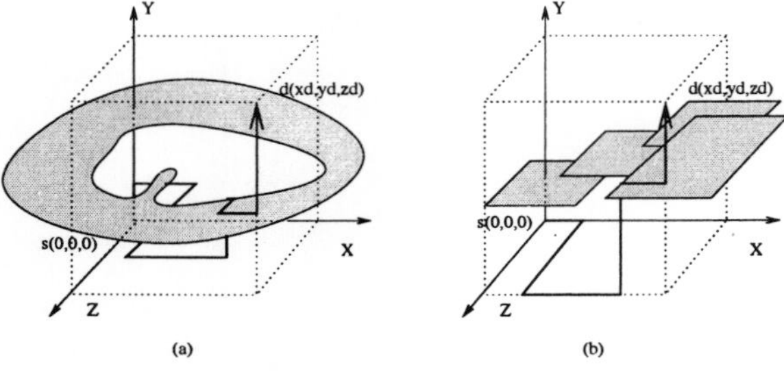

Figure 8. Samples of routing.

cannot be reached, stop the routing since there is no minimal path.

2. Routing decision and message sending at the current node u, including node s: same as step 2 in Algorithm 3.

Similar to the routing in 2-D meshes, at the source node s a detection is first activated to make sure if there exists a minimal path. The source node s will play the role of the destination in Theorem 2 and three detection messages will be sent from s along each surface of the region of minimal path (RMP): $(-Y)$-surface on the $-Y$ side, $(-Z)$-surface on the $-Z$ side, and $(-X)$-surface on the $-X$ side. The RMP includes each node along the shortest path from s to d. For each surface, say the $(-X)$-surface, a message will first propagate to the neighbors of s in the $+Y$ and $+Z$ directions. After that, at each node u that receives it, this message will continue to propagate to u's $+Y$ neighbor and $+Z$ neighbor. If any propagation in one of $+Y$ or $+Z$ directions intersects with another MCC, it will make a $+X$ turn until it can go back to the original direction. The propagation along $+Y$ and $+Z$ direction will continue from that new node. If the message can reach the surfaces $[0 : x_d, y_d : y_d, 0 : z_d]$, it will return this information back to s. The propagation of detection messages on other surfaces is similar. If the source s can know all the surfaces $[x_d : x_d, 0 : y_d, 0 : z_d]$, $[0 : x_d, y_d : y_d, 0 : z_d]$, and $[0 : x_d, 0 : y_d, z_d : z_d]$ can be reached, based on the sufficient and necessary condition for the existence of minimal path in Theorem 2, a minimal routing is feasible from d to s (i.e., a minimal routing from s to d). Figure 7 shows some samples of this feasibility check.

After the feasibility check, the routing process considering three preferred directions: the $+X$, $+Y$, and $+Z$ is similar to that in 2-D meshes which only considers $+X$ and $+Y$ directions. Figure 8 shows some samples of routing under our MCC model in 3-D meshes.

7 Conclusion

In summary, the contributions of this paper are listed as the following: (a) We have rewritten the MCC model in 2-D meshes without using global information so that the shape information at our boundaries can be used not only to ensure the existence of a minimal path, but also to form a minimal routing by routing decisions at intermediate nodes along the path. This routing will find a minimal path from source s to destination d whenever it exists. (b) We have extended the MCC model in 2-D meshes to 3-D meshes. The labelling process, edge identification process, edge construction, and boundary construction are presented to collect and distribute the MCC information for minimal routing. (c) Based on the information collected in the above limited-global-information model, a new minimal routing in 3-D meshes has been provided. It will find a minimal path from s to d whenever it exists. In our future work, we will extend our results to dynamic networks in which all the faulty components can occur during the routing process. Also, our results will be extended to higher dimension networks.

References

[1] F. Allen et al. Blue gene: A vision for protein science using a petaflop supercomputer. *IBM Systems Journal*. 40, 2001, 310-327.

[2] R. V. Boppana and S. Chalasani. Fault tolerant wormhole routing algorithms for mesh networks. *IEEE Transactions on Computers*. Vol. 44, No. 7, July 1995, 848-864.

[3] Y. M. Boura and C. R. Das. Fault-tolerant routing in mesh networks. *Proc. of 1995 International Conference on Parallel Processing*. August 1995, I 106- I 109.

[4] Z. Jiang, J. Wu, and D. Wang. A new fault information model for fault-tolerant adaptive and minimal routing in 3-d meshes. Technical Report, West Chester University, 2004, available at http://www.cs.wcupa.edu/ zjiang/3d.pdf.

[5] R. K. Koeninger, M. Furtney, and M. Walker. A shared memory MPP from Cray research. *Digital Technical Journal*. Vol. 6, No. 2, Spring 1994, 8-21.

[6] C. C. Su and K. G. Shin. Adaptive fault-tolerant deadlock-free routing in meshes and hypercubes. *IEEE Transactions on Computers*. 45, (6), June 1996, 672-683.

[7] D. Wang. A rectilinear-monotone polygonal fault block model for fault-tolerant minimal routing in meshes. *IEEE Transactions on Computers*. Vol. 52, No. 3, March 2003.

[8] J. Wu. Fault-tolerant adaptive and minimal routing in mesh-connected multicomputers using extended safety levels. *IEEE Trans. on Parallel and Distributed Systems*. 11, (2), Feb. 2000, 149-159.

[9] J. Wu. A simple fault-tolerant adaptive and minimal routing approach in 3-d meshes. *Journal of Computer Science and Technology*. Vol. 18, No. 1, 2003, 1-13.

[10] J. Zhou and F. Lau. Fault-tolerant wormhole routing algorithm in 2d meshes without virtual channels. *Proc. of ISPA'2004*. 2004, pp. 688-697.

Session 7B: Peer-to-Peer Technology

PeerWindow: An Efficient, Heterogeneous, and Autonomic Node Collection Protocol

Jinfeng Hu, Ming Li, Hongliang Yu, Haitao Dong and Weimin Zheng
Department of Computer Science and Technology, Tsinghua University, P. R. China
hujinfeng00@mails.tsinghua.edu.cn, mingli@cs.umass.edu, hlyu@tsinghua.edu.cn, dht02@mails.tsinghua.edu.cn, zwm-dcs@tsinghua.edu.cn

Abstract

Nodes in peer-to-peer systems need to know the information about others to optimize neighbor selection, resource exchanging, replica placement, load balancing, query optimization, and other collaborative operations. However, how to collect this information effectively is still an open issue. In this paper, we propose a novel information collection protocol, PeerWindow, with which each node can collect a large amount of pointers to other nodes at a very low cost. Compared to existing protocols, PeerWindow is 1) efficient, the cost of collecting 1,000 pointers being less than 1kbps in a common system environment, 2) heterogeneous, nodes with different capacities collecting different amounts of information, and 3) autonomic, nodes determining their bandwidth cost for node collection by themselves and adjusting it dynamically. PeerWindow can be used in many existing peer-to-peer systems and has tremendous potential for future expansions.

1. Introduction

Peer-to-peer nodes need to know the information about others. However, in most cases they have too limited knowledge about the outside world (sometimes they only hold a small routing table that contains no more than 100 pointers). In peer-to-peer backup systems, nodes need to find partners with similar [4] or different [10] operating systems, to reduce redundant data storing or to guard against simultaneous virus attack. In resource trading systems [5], nodes need to find adequate bargainers in terms of capacity, availability, physical location, bidding price, etc. In load balancing algorithms [6], heavily-loaded nodes need to find lightly-loaded ones to transfer the overload. In range query protocols [1], nodes need to gather other nodes' information for query optimization. In file sharing protocol of GUESS [19], nodes need to collect a large amount of pointers to other nodes to increase the local hit rate of submitted queries.

All these examples indicate that nodes in peer-to-peer systems have a desire to know others' information. However, cost-effective information-collection method is still an open issue. For the lack of general solutions, most projects design their own methods on top of an existing overlay. For example, Pastiche modifies Pastry, Mercury uses random walk on a small-world overlay, and GUESS piggybacks node pointers upon response messages within a Gnutella-like unstructured overlay.

The goal of our work is to propose a more general solution for node collection, which can be used in existing and future peer-to-peer systems. To be adaptive to the peer-to-peer environment, the protocol must hold following properties:

1. *Efficiency.* Nodes are able to collect a large amount of pointers (a *pointer* means a piece of information about another node) at a low cost. We believe efficiency is the most significant property for a node collection protocol because obviously the more pointers a node collects, the more satisfactory partners it may find locally when desired.

2. *Heterogeneity.* For the inevitable heterogeneity of peer-to-peer systems [13], nodes with different capacities should be allowed to collect different amounts of pointers (at different bandwidth cost). Heterogeneity makes it possible for the weak nodes to participate in the system, and also prevents those powerful nodes from being restricted by the weak ones.

3. *Autonomy.* We should let every node determine its cost for node collection (and thereby the amount of collected pointers) independently and be able to adjust it dynamically. This is accordant with the autonomy

This work is supported by National Science Foundation of China under contract 60433040.

0190-3918/05 $20.00 © 2005 IEEE

spirit of "peer-to-peer" and makes the protocol adaptive to the environment changes.

The most critical problem in designing such a protocol is the maintenance of pointers: when a node joins or leaves the system, all the related nodes should update their pointers timely. There are two common ways for pointer maintenance: explicit probing (send heartbeat messages to all the neighbors[1] periodically) and multicasting (when a node joins or leaves, multicast the event to all the related nodes). Explicitly probing is not efficient because most probes get active response, and therefore have no positive effects on pointer-state updating. For example, assuming that the nodes' average lifetime[2] is about 2 hours [13] and a node probes all its neighbors every 30 seconds, then $239/240 \approx 99.58\%$ of the probes would return positively, indicating that the corresponding neighbors are still alive. Actually, these messages can be seen as a waste. If the node uses 10kbps for pointer maintenance, it can only maintain 600 pointers (assuming each heartbeat message is 500-bit in size). Compared to the scale of the whole system (perhaps comprising millions of nodes), this amount is very small.

In contrast, multicasting is more efficient because a node only receives messages when its neighbors change their state (joining or leaving). In another word, all the received messages are useful for pointer-state updating. While multicasting can achieve high efficiency, it faces another critical problem: given a heterogeneous system, how to determine which nodes hold pointers to a given node? Obviously, such information cannot be stored explicitly, because 1) it greatly complicates the protocol; 2) it is hard to determine where to place it and how to keep it available and reliable; and 3) even if we can obtain such information when needed, efficient multicast algorithm is still a hard problem.

In this paper, we propose *PeerWindow*, a novel node collection protocol that solves this maintenance problem and hence holds the above three properties (efficiency, heterogeneity and autonomy) simultaneously. Each PeerWindow node has a nodeId and a self-determined attribute *level*. A node at level l keeps about $N/2^l$ pointers (where N is the total number of the nodes). Then nodes with different capacities run at different levels. PeerWindow sets a smart mapping between a node's identifier and the pointers it should maintain, which makes it possible to judge whether a node keeps a pointer to another node by simply looking at their identifiers and levels. In this way, when a node joins or leaves, PeerWindow can figure out which nodes need to know the event without additional information storing. Furthermore, PeerWindow devises a tree-based multicast protocol that disseminates the event efficiently. PeerWindow nodes are allowed to adjust their levels dynamically to tune their bandwidth cost, which makes PeerWindow more adaptive than previous protocols.

In the following, we will first outline the PeerWindow protocol in section 2, and then discuss how to use PeerWindow in some existing peer-to-peer systems in section 3. Protocol details are presented in section 4. After reporting the experiment results in section 5, we introduce related works in section 6 and make final conclusion in section 7.

2. System Overview

Every node in PeerWindow keeps a large list of pointers to other nodes, called *peer list*. PeerWindow uses multicast to maintain the peer lists: a state-changing event, e.g., a node's joining, leaving or information changing, will be multicast to all the nodes who are interested in the changing node, in another word, whose peer list contains (or should contain) a pointer to the changing node. As discussed in the introduction, the most challenging problem is to determine which nodes keep, or should keep, such pointers. PeerWindow solves it by setting a novel mapping between a node and its peer list.

Each PeerWindow node has a unique identifier *nodeId* that is 128-bit-long, commonly the result of consistent hashing of its public key or IP address. Thereby, nodes should be evenly distributed in the nodeId space. Additionally, every node has another self-determined attribute *level*, which can be 0, 1, 2, and so on. It is demanded that the peer list of an l-level node should contain pointers to all the nodes whose nodeId's first l bits are the same with the local one.

Figure 1 shows a 10-node PeerWindow example, in which nodeIds are 4-bit long. The first l bits of an l-level node are called the node's *eigenstring*, which is underlined in figure 1. It can be seen that 0-level nodes have blank eigenstrings, 1-level nodes can be classified into two categories according to their different eigenstrings, 2-level nodes into four categories (only three of them are not empty in the example, nodes with eigenstring "11" being absent) and so on. In general, l-level nodes can be classified at most into 2^l categories with different eigenstrings. A pointer consists of the corresponding node's IP address, nodeId, level, and a

[1] If node A keeps a pointer to node B, then say B is a neighbor of A.

[2] Lifetime means the period from the time when a node joins system to the time when it leaves.

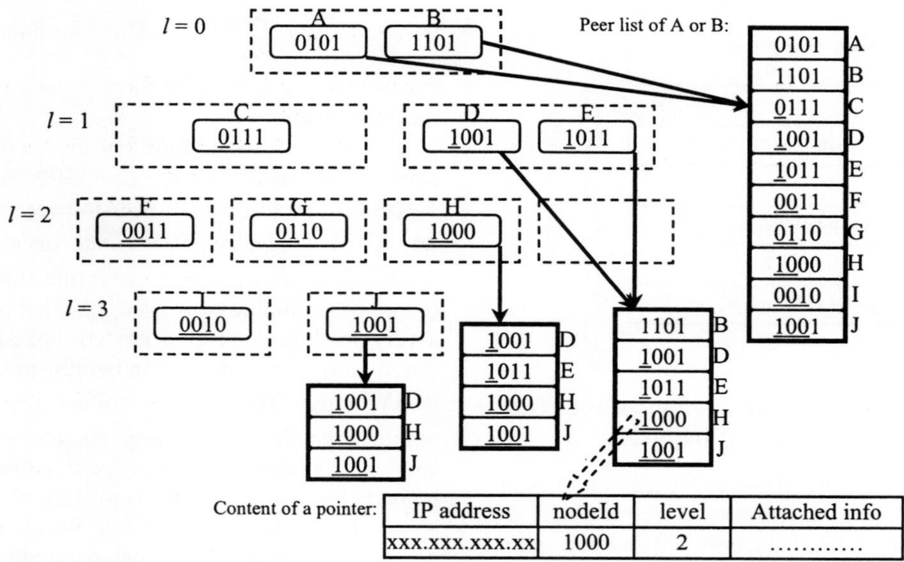

Figure 1. A PeerWindow example with 10 nodes. NodeIds are 4-bit long and eigenstrings are underlined. Peer lists of nodes C, F, G, and I are not shown for the neat of the figure

piece of attached info that can be specified by upper applications.

Peer list has the following properties:

1. Nodes with the same eigenstring must have the same peer list, e.g., nodes D and E in figure 1.

2. If a node's eigenstring is a prefix of another node's (e.g., nodes E and H), the former's peer list must completely cover the latter's. We call the former is *stronger* than the latter, in another word, the latter is *weaker* than the former.

3. A 0-level node's peer list covers the whole system, e.g. node A.

4. Two nodes at the same level, but with different eigenstrings must have entirely different peer lists, e.g., nodes C and E.

5. All nodes with the same eigenstring are fully connected through their peer lists ("fully connected" means that within a set of nodes, everyone keeps pointers to all the others), e.g., all the nodes with eigenstring "1", i.e. nodes D and E.

Attention should be paid to a special scenario where there is no 0-level node in the whole system (i.e., removing node A and B from figure 1). In this case, the system will split into two parts that are wholly unrelated to each other (nodes CFGI and nodes DEHJ). PeerWindow protocol does not rely on 0-level nodes and is able to work well in each part of a split system. To be convenient for statement, in this paper we first assume that there are 0-level nodes in the system and call them *top nodes*, and then discuss the special handling for a split system in section 4.4.

All the nodes whose peer list contains a pointer to a given node form a set, called the node's *audience set*. As discussed above, when a node changes its state, including joining, leaving, shifting its level and changing the attached info, all the nodes in its audience set must be informed. PeerWindow does not store audience sets explicitly, because they can be recognized simply by looking at the related nodes' nodeIds and levels.

For example, in figure 1, node E's audience set consists of these nodes: node A and B at level 0; node D and E at level 1 with eigenstring "1"; and node H at level 2 with eigenstring "10". That is to say, the audience set contains all the nodes whose eigenstring is a prefix of E's nodeId (1011).

Generally, the audience set of a node with nodeId "$N_0N_1N_2N_3$…" comprises all the nodes with eigenstrings of "" (blank string), "N_0", "N_0N_1", "$N_0N_1N_2$", and so on, as illustrated in figure 2. Therefore, a node in the audience set can directly judge whether another node is also in the set, by checking the node's eigenstring. In this way, a top node in an audience set can easily find out the whole set, whilst an arbitrary node in the set can find out those nodes (also in the set) at the same level or at lower levels. For example, in figure 2, 0-level nodes know the whole audience set, 1-level nodes know those at level 1, 2

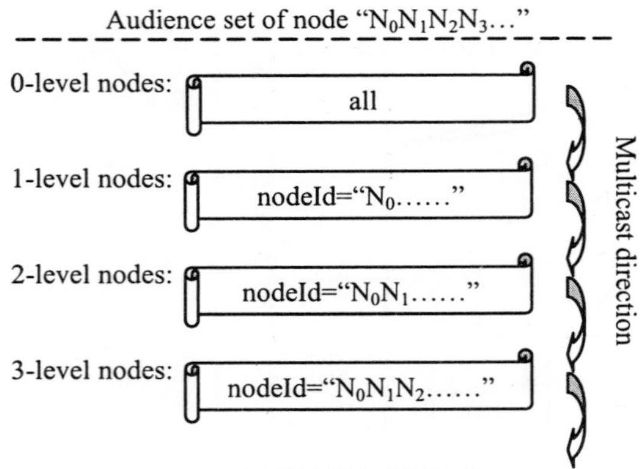

Figure 2. Composition of an audience set. The changing node's nodeId is "$N_0N_1N_2N_3$..."

and 3, 2-level nodes know those at level 2 and 3, and so on.

This leads to a useful deduction: when a top node gets a node's state-changing event, it has sufficient information to multicast it around the audience set of the changing node, as long as the message strictly flows from stronger nodes to weaker nodes during the multicast process, as illustrated in figure 2. A simple manner is by gossip: the top node first initiates a gossip around all the top nodes, and then sends the event message to a level-1 node L_1; L_1 then initiates a gossip around all the level-1 nodes, and then sends the message to a level-2 node. This process continues until all the nodes in the audience set receive the message. Here we emphasize the *feasibility* of the multicast design. Various multicast protocols can be devised in this environment, with different efficiency, reliability, and redundancy. In section 4.2, we will propose a tree-based multicast as the basic design of PeerWindow.

Noting that a multicast is always originated by a top node, a changing event must firstly be sent to a top node before being multicast around the audience set. To enable this, every PeerWindow node also keeps another list, i.e., *top-node list*, which contains pointers to *t* top nodes. Commonly we set $t = 8$.

Before turning to the protocol details, we first estimate PeerWindow's performance.

Assuming that nodes' average lifetime is *L* seconds, each node changes its state *m* times during the lifetime (including the joining and the leaving), and the multicast protocol has *r*-degree redundancy (i.e., a node receives *r* messages for each event), then a node will receive $\frac{m \times r}{L}$ messages per second on average for maintaining one pointer. Assuming that the average message size is *i* bits and a node would like to spend *W* bps bandwidth on node collection, the number of pointers it can collect (namely, the size of its peer list) is about $p = \frac{W \times L}{m \times r \times i}$. This formula shows that PeerWindow achieves the three properties proposed in the introduction:

1. *Efficiency*. Assuming that in a common peer-to-peer environment where $L = 3600$ (less than the measured result of real peer-to-peer systems [13]), $m = 3$ (a node changes its state once per lifetime), $i = 1000$ (sufficient for most applications) and $r = 1$ (a tree-based multicast is used, like that in section 4.2), a very weak node (e.g., a modem-linked node) would spend only 10% of its bandwidth, about 5kbps, on PeerWindow. Then, it can collect about $p = 6000$ pointers, which is a very large amount. For those high-bandwidth nodes, it is very easy to collect much more pointers by spending more bandwidth.

2. *Heterogeneity*. A PeerWindow node can determine its bandwidth cost on node collection by itself. Thus powerful nodes will never be restricted by the limit of the low bandwidth of those weak nodes.

3. *Autonomy*. Nodes can adjust their levels to be adaptive to the changing environment. Essentially, this is because of the direct proportion between peer list size *p* and nodes' lifetime *L*: peer lists will automatically expand when the system turns stable gradually. For instance, in a given PeerWindow system, a modem node sets an upper bandwidth threshold 5kbps, collecting about 6000 pointers, at level *l*. Then the system gradually turns stable (i.e., the average lifetime *L* increases), resulting in fewer events and less bandwidth cost. Once the bandwidth cost drops to a value below 2.5kbps, the node will automatically shift the level to $l-1$ and the peer list will inflate accordingly. Thereafter, the bandwidth cost returns to 5kbps, with about 12000 pointers in the peer list.

3. Usage

PeerWindow endows every node with a large number of pointers to other nodes, which can facilitate upper applications in many ways. In this section, we present a brief discussion on how to utilize PeerWindow to serve different requirements.

Looking at the level value for powerful nodes. A simple and direct way is finding powerful nodes by looking at the level value in the pointers. Practical experience shows that nodes with higher bandwidth (at high levels[3] in PeerWindow) also tend to stay longer and contribute more resources [15].

[3] "Higher level" means smaller level value, i.e., 0 is the highest level.

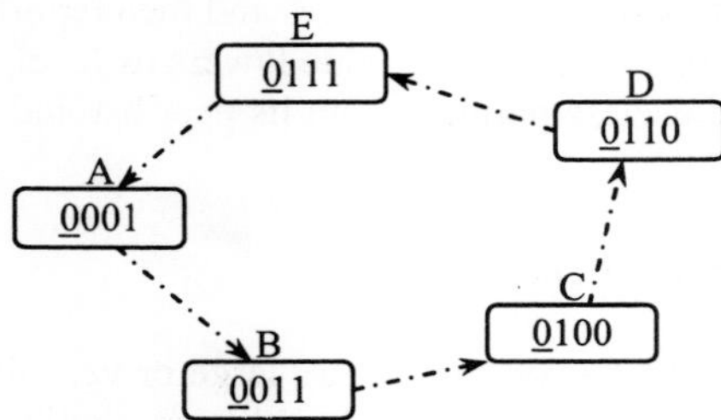

Figure 3. illustration of failure detection

Directly using the attached info. Some applications need to exchange some brief information among the nodes. They can directly attach the information into the pointers. For example, GUESS [19] protocol can attach the number of shared files to the pointers. Backup systems [4][10] can attach operating system versions. Range-query systems [1] can attach load distribution, node-count distribution, and query selectivity. Bidding systems [5] can attach nodes' basic status, such as storage space, bandwidth, availability, software/hardware summary, approximate bid, etc.

Using compression techniques to express more info. PeerWindow pointers should be kept small, because large pointers will finally deflate the peer lists. Therefore, if nodes need to express much about their status, some compressing techniques should be combined. For example, Pastiche [4] can attach the content abstracts into the pointers. LOCKSS [11] can use bloom filter [2] to indicate whether a node contains a given digital document and attach the filter results into the pointers.

4. Protocol Details

4.1 Failure Detection

Peer-to-peer nodes can leave the system without notification. Therefore, leaving events must be detected by some means (then multicast around the audience set).

Recall that PeerWindow nodes can be divided into multiple groups according to their different eigenstrings. Nodes in each group are fully connected through their peer lists. Thus, all the nodes in a given group can be seen as a circle based on their nodeIds. It is demanded that a PeerWindow node always probe its right neighbor in the circle ("right" means the direction from small to large). Figure 3 shows an example, in which there are five nodes with eigenstring "0" and every node sends heartbeat messages to the node whose nodeId is just larger than it.

```
rcv_event(nodeId=M, event_type=et, step=s)
            //receive change event of node M at step s.
(1)   adjustList(list, et, M)
            //adjust the peer list according to the event.
(2)   Rs = getAudience(list, M)
            //get M's audience set from the peer list.
      for i := s + 1 to 64 do
(3)     Rn := getSuffix(Rs, localID, i − 1)
            //get all pointers to the nodes whose
            //nodeIds are the same with the local
            //at the first i−1 bits, but different at the ith.
(4)     if Rn = null then
          continue
        fi
(5)     P := getHighestLevel(Rn)
            //get the pointer with the highest level from
            //Rn. If more than one pointers are of the
            //same (highest) level, randomly pick one.
(6)     send_event(P, M, et, i)
          //send the event to P, tagged as step i.
      od
```

Figure 4. Pseudocde of multicast

Once a node detects the failure of its right neighbor, it immediately reports the event to a top node, randomly chosen from its top-node list, and redirects its probing to the next neighbor. Note that such detection mechanism is resilient to concurrent failures. For instance, node B and C concurrently leave the system in figure 3. Then node A will first detect B's failure and report it to a top node. After that it removes B from its peer list and redirects its probing to node C, and then immediately detects C's failure and reports it.

4.2 Tree-based Multicast

As mentioned in section 2, multicast protocol can be designed in many ways. In this subsection we present a tree-based method as PeerWindow's basic design, the pseudocode of which is shown in figure 4.

The fundamental principle of the protocol is as follows. When a top node starts to multicast an event, it first sends the event to a node whose nodeId's first bit is different with the local one. Thus there will be two nodes having received the event, with different first bits in their nodeIds. After that, each of these two nodes sends the event to another node whose nodeId has the same first bit but different second bit with the local one. Then, all the four informed nodes have different first two bits with each other in their nodeIds. In general, at step s, every informed node sends the event to another node whose nodeId has the same first s bits and different (s+1)th bit (see figure 4(3)). This process continues until no more appropriate node can be found (see figure 4(4)).

It must be noted that at each step the local node always chooses a target node with the highest level from all possible nodes, as shown in figure 4(5).

The multicast protocol has four major properties:

1. Event messages always flow from the stronger nodes to the weaker nodes.

2. Different nodes have different out-degrees. Stronger nodes have more out-degrees than weaker ones. The root node of the multicast tree has approximately $\log_2 N$ out-degrees.

3. An event message can reach all the nodes in the audience set through about $\log_2 N$ steps.

4. The multicast tree is not pre-determined. Every node dynamically chooses the next target in the multicast tree at runtime (see figure 4(5)).

To guard against stale pointers in the peer lists, acknowledgement is required for all the multicast messages. When a message gets no response after three continuous attempts, the corresponding pointer will be removed from the peer list and the message will be redirected to a new target node (i.e., turn back to the line (3) in figure 4).

4.3 Joining Process and Level Shifting

A new node contacts a bootstrap node that is already in the system for joining. Four steps are needed: 1) finding out a top node, 2) determining the joining node's level, 3) downloading the peer list and top-node list, and 4) multicasting its joining event around its audience set. The key problem here is how to determine which level is suitable for its capacity before practical running. The estimation is by this way: the top node tells the new node its own level l_T, as well as its current bandwidth cost W_T that is dynamically measured. Then the new node estimates its level l_X based on these two values, as well as its own permitted bandwidth cost W_X: $l_X = \left\lceil l_T + \log_2 \frac{W_T}{W_X} \right\rceil$. More detailed description of these four steps can be found in [8].

A new node can also first set a low level so as to start working in a relatively short period, and then ask stronger nodes for a larger peer list. After completing the background downloading, it raises it level and reports the state-changing event to a top node. We call this process *warm-up*.

A node can adjust its level at runtime due to the change of the system environment or the upper bandwidth threshold set by the user. When a node raises its level, it should first download those required pointers from stronger nodes and then reports the event to a top node. When a node lowers its level, it removes those useless pointers from its peer list and reports the event.

4.4 Split PeerWindow

When the system is very large or very dynamic, no node can afford the bandwidth cost running at level 0. In this circumstance, the system will split into two parts, one comprising all the nodes whose nodeId starts with "0" and the other comprising all the nodes whose nodeId starts with "1". It can be easily seen that these two parts are wholly independent to each other (a node in one part must keep no pointer to any node of the other part) and each one is a complete PeerWindow (all the protocols proposed above in this paper are still suitable for each part).

To be general, PeerWindow is made up of several parts that are independent to one another. The highest-level nodes in each part are called *top nodes*. Every node maintains t pointers (in its top-node list) to the top nodes in its part. When a node changes its state or detects failure of another node, it reports the event to a top node, which will then multicast the event around the changing node's audience set, using the tree-based multicast protocol presented in section 4.2.

A top node's top-node list does not contain pointers to top nodes of its own part. Instead, it contains pointers to some top nodes of other parts, t pointers for each part. When a joining node X and its bootstrap node Y are not in the same part, X needs to find a top node of its own part first (step 1 of the joining process, seeing section 4.3). X accomplishes this by asking a top node in Y's part, say Z. Z's top-node list must contain t top nodes of X's part.

4.5 Top-node List Maintenance

Top-node lists are maintained in a lazy manner. When a node M reports an event to a top node, the top node should return a response, piggybacking $t-1$ pointers to top nodes, which will help M refresh its top-node list. If the report does not get a response, M will redirect the report to another top node within its top-node list. If all the top nodes in its top-node list are unavailable, it will then ask another node in its peer list for his top-node list as a substitution.

A top node's top-node list is maintained similarly. When a top node T works for another node's joining process, it chooses a live pointer from its top-node list and asks the corresponding node for $t-1$ pointers to top nodes of that part. If all the pointers in T's top-node list are stale, it will ask another top node of its own part for help.

4.6 Accuracy Improvement

Because of the Internet asynchrony, the multicast protocol can never be absolutely reliable. Therefore, there must be some errors in the peer lists, which fall into two types: absent pointers and stale pointers. Both of them are only of a very small fraction and do no substantial harm. An absent pointer would be automatically revised when the corresponding node leaves the system, while a stale pointer would be removed when being used during multicast procedure and getting no response. But these errors would accumulate before being revised, from the view of whole system.

To guard against this accumulation, PeerWindow devises a refreshing mechanism. Every node measures the lifetime of all the nodes in its peer list, and calculates the average lifetime of each level, noted LT_i, where *i* denotes the level. An *l*-level node multicasts its state around its audience set every $2 \cdot LT_l$ (by reporting to a top node). An *m*-level pointer that has not been refreshed for a period of $3 \cdot LT_m$ will be directly removed from the peer list, without explicit probing. This mechanism can limit the accumulation of both absent pointers and stale pointers, and make the error fraction of peer list convergent. In practice, most nodes never perform such refreshing multicast because their lifetimes are much shorter than twice the average lifetime.

5. Experiment Results

Our basic experiment goal is to simulate a 100,000-node PeerWindow in a common environment, where the distributions of node capacity and lifetime are both accordant with the measurement result of Gnutella in [13], and the Internet topology is generated by the Transit-Stub model [20]. After that, we examine PeerWindow's scalability and adaptivity, i.e., how PeerWindow varies when the system scale or the nodes' lifetime changes.

To make large-scale experiments possible, we first developed ONSP [17], a general platform for large-scale overlay simulation on a homogeneous cluster. ONSP is based on parallel discrete events and uses MPI for machine communication. Transit-Stub model is naturally integrated into ONSP as its network topology.

Considering that PeerWindow nodes with the same eigenstring would have the same peer list, we record all the correct peer lists in a centralized data structure, and only record erroneous items in nodes' individual data structures. This method has two advantages: making it possible to run the whole experiment in memory and facilitating the calculation of the error rate of the peer lists. Meanwhile, it does not harm the validity of the experiment results.

Based on ONSP, our experiment program comprises 1,600 lines of C++ code and is performed on a 16-server cluster that is connected by 2Gbps Myrinet. Each server has four 700MHz Xeon CPUs and 1GB memories, running an operating system of Linux Redhat 7.3.

5.1 Common PeerWindow

We simulate a common PeerWindow with 100,000 nodes. That is to say, we first create 100,000 nodes on the ONSP platform and then let new nodes join and existing nodes leave, with almost the identical joining and leaving rates. In this experiment, the following characteristics are hold:

- Distribution of nodes' lifetime meets the measurement results of Gnutella (figure 6 of [13]), in which the average lifetime is about 135 minutes.
- Distribution of nodes' available bandwidth meets the measurement results of Gnutella (figure 3 of [13]).
- The user-set upper (input) bandwidth threshold is 1% of the node's total bandwidth, but cannot be less than 500bps (a small value that is affordable even for modem-linked nodes).
- The Transit-Stub network model is generated by the tool of GT-ITM [20], in which there are 120 transit domains, each containing 4 transit nodes. Every transit node has 5 stub domains, each containing 2 stub nodes. Thus, there are totally 4800 stub nodes. To reach the required 100,000-node scale, each stub node is assigned with about 20 PeerWindow nodes. Common latency parameters are set as follows: transit-to-transit latency is 100ms; transit-to-stub is 20ms; stub-to-stub is 5ms; and node-to-node is 1ms.
- Nodes join the system in a Poisson process, with the expectation of the time interval of two successive node joining events is 100,000/135 minutes.
- The event message size is 1,000 bits.
- During the multicast procedure, every medium node delays the message for 1 second that is spent on receiving, calculating and sending.

Figure 5 plots the distribution of the nodes at different levels. Somewhat surprisingly, there are more

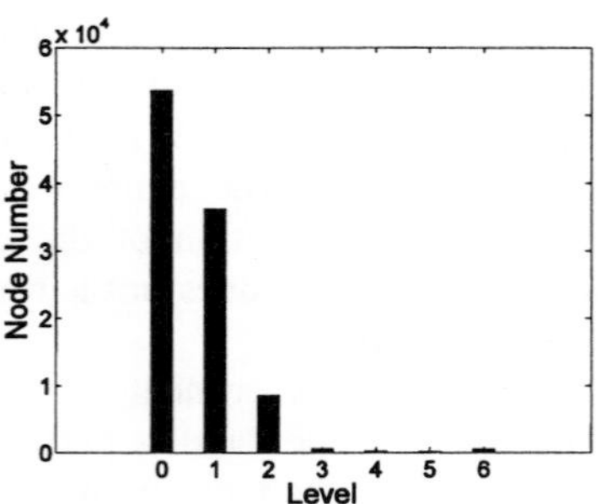

Figure 5. Node distribution in common PeerWindow

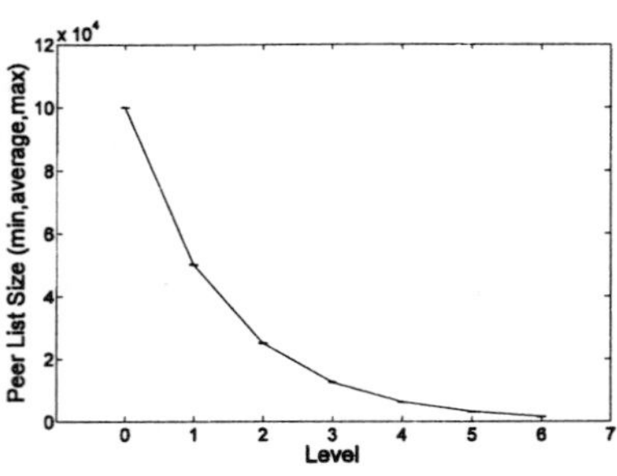

Figure 6. Size of peer lists at different levels

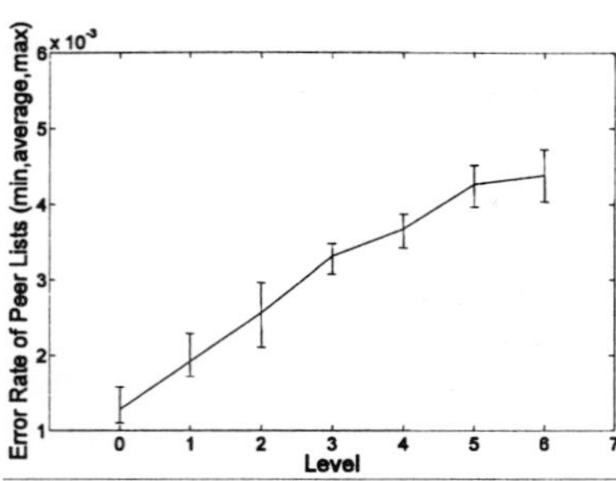

Figure7. Error rate of the peer lists at different levels

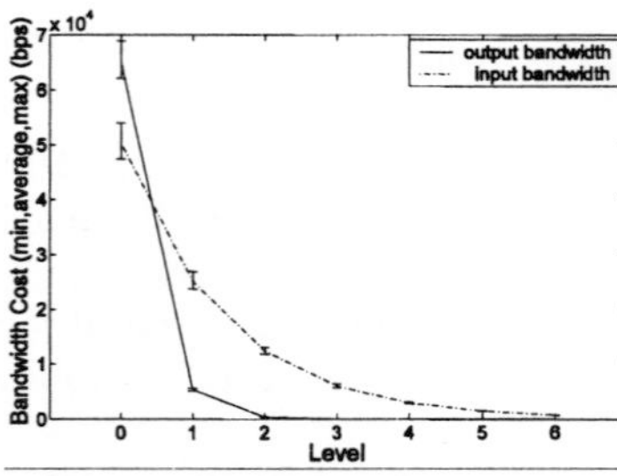

Figure 8. bandwidth cost at different levels

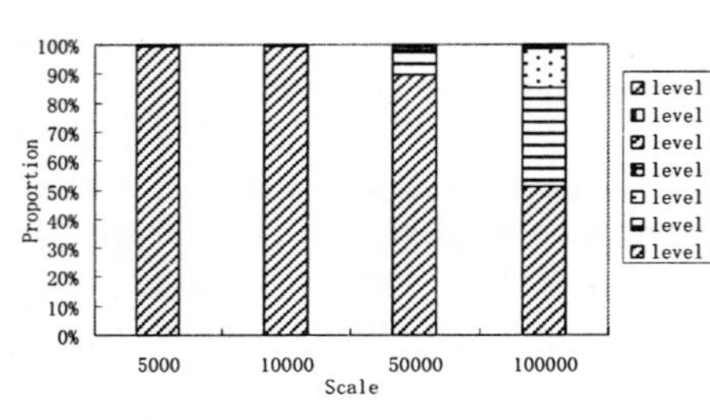

Figure 9. Node distribution in different system scales

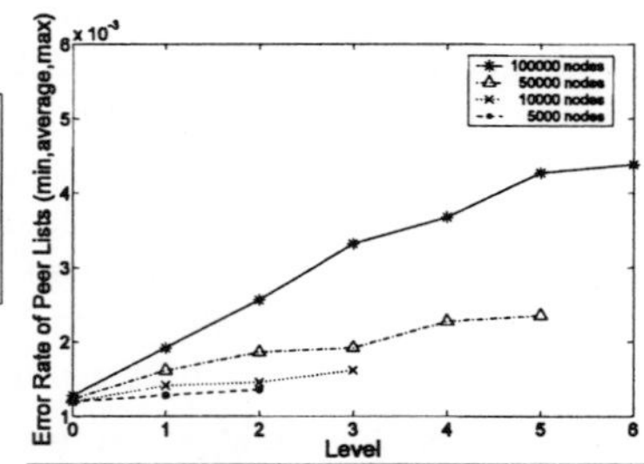

Figure 10. Average peer list error rate in different scales

than half of the nodes running at level 0. It seems quite a lot. However, it is really consistent with the measurement result of real peer-to-peer systems (seeing figure 3 of [13]) in which only 20% nodes' available bandwidth is less than 1Mbps. Perhaps our intuition that a large portion of Internet nodes are weak ones is somewhat questionable.

Figure 6 shows the size of the peer lists of the nodes at different levels. According to the PeerWindow protocol, an l-level node collects the pointers to all the nodes whose nodeId has an l-bit common prefix with the local nodeId. Because nodes are evenly distributed in the nodeId space, the peer lists of the nodes at a given level are almost of the same size. (Figure 6 plots the maximum and the minimum values, but they are hard to be distinguished.)

Although the peer lists are large, they have very few errors. As figure 7 shows, the error rate is less than 0.5%. This is because a changing event will be reported to the top node immediately when it is detected and multicast around the audience set without delay. The multicast needs $\log_2 100{,}000 \approx 16.6$ steps. Assuming that each step costs 500ms on average, all the nodes in the audience set will receive the event within $(1+0.5)\times 16.6 = 24.9s$, that is to say, a point will be kept stale for no longer than 25 seconds. Compared to the average lifetime of the nodes (135 minutes), the error rate will be no more than $25/(135\times 60) \approx 0.0035$, which is accordant with the experiment result.

Higher-level nodes have peer lists with fewer errors than lower-level nodes. This is because the multicast process ensures the higher-to-lower direction of the message flow, which indicates that higher-level nodes can revise their peer lists earlier than lower-level ones.

Figure 8 shows the input and output bandwidth for the peer list maintenance. As participated, the input bandwidth is in proportion to the peer list size. The input-bandwidth cost for every 1000 pointers is about 500bps. As discussed in section 4.2, higher-level nodes will have larger output-bandwidth cost. In this case, almost all the messages are sent from 0-level or 1-level nodes. But their output cost is only a little more than the input, also very light for these powerful nodes.

5.2 Scalability

The main impacts of the system scale are the distribution of the nodes and the error rate of the peer lists. Figure 9 depicts the variation of the percentage of the nodes at each level when the system scale changes, using different figure patterns for different levels. In a 5000-node PeerWindow, all the nodes run at level 0. When the system expands, there comes out more levels and more nodes tend to work at lower levels. This is because those weak nodes cannot afford the bandwidth

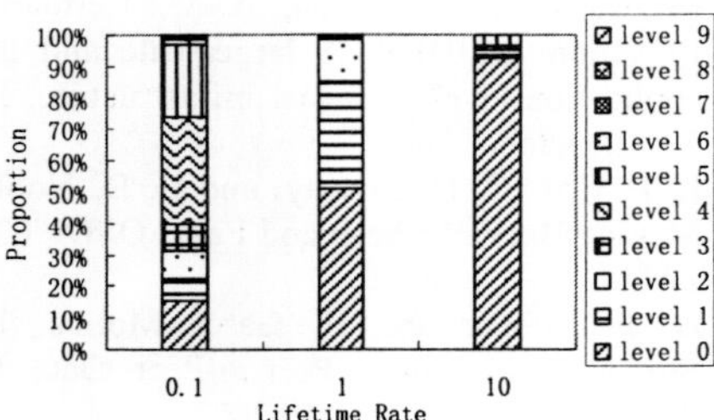

Figure 11. Nodes distribution with different lifetime rate (to the common PeerWindow)

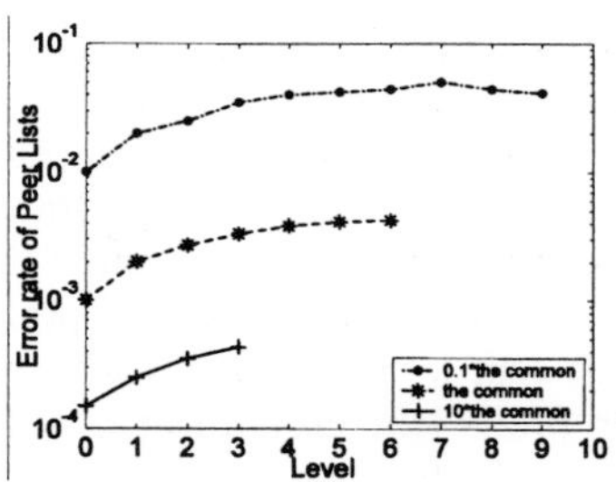

Figure 12. Average peer list error rate in the systems with different lifetime rates

cost at high levels in a large system. The error rate of the peer lists also rises (seeing figure 10), because multicast needs longer time and the errors in the peer lists are revised less timely. But the change is very slight.

5.3 Adaptivity

Nodes in different peer-to-peer systems will have different lifetimes, which are essentially determined by the usage model. Even in a given system, the nodes' lifetime may vary along with time. We assume that nodes' lifetimes are *Lifetime_Rate* times of that in the common case (section 5.1). The node distribution and the error rate of peer list at different *Lifetime_Rate* are shown in figures 11 and 12, respectively. Note that figure 12 uses the logarithmic scale on the y-axis.

When the *Lifetime_Rate* is 0.1 (this means that the average lifetime is 13.5 minutes) there comes out 10 levels and only about 15% 0-level nodes. This is because when the lifetime turns short, more state-changing events will occur in a given time interval. Therefore, a node can only maintain a small peer list and run at a low level.

Figure 12 shows that the peer lists' error rate also increases when lifetime turns shorter. This is because the error rate is proximately determined by the formula $error\_rate = multicast\_delay / lifetime$. Since the system scale does not change, the number of multicast hops ($\log_2 N$) also does not change. Thus the lifetime will be approximately in inverse proportion to the average error rate. As shown in figure 12, in a system with $Lifetime\_Rate = 0.1$, the average peer list error rate is about 10 times of that in the common case ($Lifetime\_Rate = 1$), which is between 1% and 5%. However, such a result can hardly turn to the reality because of its very short average lifetime.

6. Related Work

Most previous projects devised their node collection protocol based on some existing overlay structures.

RanSub [9] is based on an application-level multicast tree. Using information collection and distribution, RanSub offers every node O(log*N*) pointers. By explicit probes through these pointers, every node changes it parent node dynamically. In this way, the multicast tree is optimized piece by piece. GUESS [19] is based on a Gnutella-like unstructured overlay. By piggybacking some known pointers on the response of a ping or query message, every node can collect a large number of pointers, which are used for non-forwarding search. Pastiche [4] uses a modified Pastry to collect pointers to those nodes who are storing similar data with the local node. Mercury [1] is built on top of a small-world overlay. To optimize the attribute-base query and load balancing, Mercury deploys random walk upon the overlay to collect other nodes' information, including load distribution, node-count distribution, and query selectivity. Compared to these previous protocols, PeerWindow is not based on any existing overlays and simultaneously holds the properties of efficiency, heterogeneity, and autonomy. We believe PeerWindow can also be used in the above systems and works well.

Another peer-to-peer system in which nodes collect a large amount of pointers is the one-hop DHT [7], compared to PeerWindow, one-hop DHT treats almost all the nodes as homogeneous peers and costs too much for weak nodes when the system is very large and dynamic or some application-specified information should be attached into the pointers.

There are also some previous works aiming at peer-to-peer node information *aggregation* (not collection), such as SOMO [21], SDIMS [18] and Willow [12]. The main difference between these protocols and PeerWindow is that they summarize the state of the whole system (e.g. the total load of the current system), while PeerWindow simply presents individual nodes' information to others.

PeerWindow uses a prefix-based multicast for event notification. Prefix-based multicast has been proposed for a long time [16] and was also introduced into the global multicast service recently [14]. However, the multicast in PeerWindow has a substantial difference with previous protocols. In previous protocols, a message must be sent to all the nodes whose nodeIds have a common prefix (the groupId in I3 [14]), while in PeerWindow all the nodes receiving a given message do not have a common prefix, but their eigenstrings must be prefix of a given identifier (the changing node's nodeId).

Also there are some application-level multicast protocols that use prefix-based relationship to construct a multicast tree, e.g., Scribe [3]. In them, every node within a group needs to maintain the states of its parent node and children nodes, which is not desired in PeerWindow's multicast protocol.

7. Conclusion

The spirit of peer-to-peer system is collaboration, intercommunion, and resource exchanging among different nodes. All these operations are based on mutual understanding of the nodes. Therefore, letting peer-to-peer nodes know each other is very important. In this paper, we propose a novel node collection protocol PeerWindow that simultaneously holds the fine properties of efficiency, heterogeneity, autonomy, dynamical adjustability, self-organizing, and adaptivity. PeerWindow can be used in many existing peer-to-peer systems and we believe it can also serve well for future peer-to-peer system constructions.

Acknowledgement

We thank Professor Jie Wu for some valuable suggestions on the paper. We thank the anonymous reviewers for their useful comments. We thank Zheng Zhang, Ben Y. Zhao, Xuezheng Liu, Shuming Shi and Yun Mao for their discussion with us on the basic idea of PeerWindow. We also thank Yinghui Wu for his ONSP platform that simplifies our experiment significantly.

References

[1] A. R. Bharambe, M. Agrawal, and S. Seshan. Mercury: Supporting Scalable Multi-Attribute Range Queries. SIGCOMM 2004. August 2004.

[2] B. Bloom. Space/time trade-offs in hash coding with allowable errors. Communications of the ACM, 13(7), pages 422–426, July 1970.

[3] M. Castro, P. Druschel, A.-M. Kermarrec, and A. Rowstron. SCRIBE: A large-scale and decentralized application-level multicast infrastructure. IEEE JSAC, 20(8), October 2002.

[4] L. P. Cox, C. D. Murray, and B. D. Noble. Pastiche: Making Backup Cheap and Easy. OSDI '02. December 2002.

[5] B. F. Cooper and H. Garcia-Molina. Bidding for Storage Space in a Peer-to-Peer Data Preservation System. ICDCS '02. Junly 2002.

[6] B. Godfrey, K. Lakshminarayanan, S. Surana, R. Karp, and I. Stoica. Load Balancing in Dynamic Structured P2P Systems. INFOCOM 2004. March 2004.

[7] A. Gupta, B. Liskov, and R. Rodrigues. One Hop Lookups for Peer-to-Peer Overlays. HOTOS IX. May 2003.

[8] J. Hu, M. Li, H. Dong, and W. Zheng. PeerWindow: An Efficient, Heterogeneous, and Autonomic Node Collection Protocol. Full report, available at http://hpc.cs.tsinghua.edu.cn/granary/.

[9] D. Kostic, A. Rodriguez, J. Albrecht, A. Bhirud, and A. Vahdat. Using Random Subsets to Build Scalable Network Services. USITS '03. March 2003.

[10] M. Lillibridge, S. Elnikety, A. Birrell, M. Burrows, and M. Isard. A Cooperative Internet Backup Scheme. USNIX '03. June 2003.

[11] P. Maniatis, M. Roussopoulos, T. Giuli, D. S. H. Rosenthal, M. Baker, and Y. Muliadi. Preserving Peer Replicas By Rate-Limited Sampled Voting. SOSP '03. October 2003.

[12] R. van Renesse and A. Bozdog. Willow: DHT, Aggregation, and Publish/Subscribe in One Protocol. IPTPS '04. February 2004.

[13] S. Saroiu, P. K. Gummadi, and S. D. Gribble. A Measurement Study of Peer-to-Peer File Sharing Systems. MMCN '02. January 2002.

[14] I. Stoica, D. Adkins, S. Zhuang, S. Shenker, and S. Surana. Internet Indirection Infrastructure. SIGCOMM 2002. August 2002.

[15] B. Wilcox-O'Hearn. Experiences Deploying a Large-Scale Emergent Network. IPTPS '02. March 2002.

[16] J. Wu and L. Sheng. Deadlock-Free Routing in Irregular Networks Using Prefix Routing. PDCS '99. Auguest 1999.

[17] Y. Wu, M. Li, and W. Zheng. ONSP: Parallel Overlay Network Simulation Platform. PDPTA '04. June 2004.

[18] P. Yalagandula and M. Dahlin. A Scalable Distributed Information Management System. SIGCOMM 2004. August 2004.

[19] B. Yang, P. Vinograd, and H. Garcia-Molina. Evaluating GUESS and Non-Forwarding Peer-to-Peer Search. ICDCS '04. March 2004.

[20] E. Zegura, K. Calvert, and S. Bhattacharjee. How to Model an Internetwork. INFOCOM 1996. June 1996.

[21] Z. Zhang, S. Shi, and J. Zhu. SOMO: Self-organized Metadata Overlay for Resource Management in P2P DHT. IPTPS '03. November 2003.

Caching Routing Indices in Structured P2P Overlays *

Hailong Cai, Jun Wang
Department of Computer Science and Engineering
University of Nebraska, Lincoln
{hcai,wang}@cse.unl.edu

Abstract

Because of the omnipresence of node dynamic activities, large scale P2P systems built on structured overlays suffer high maintenance overhead and compromised routing performance. In this paper, we study the characteristics of P2P node dynamic behaviors and present a novel routing indices caching scheme, called SORIC, which solves this problem by fully exploiting the round-trip pattern in node dynamic behaviors and heterogeneity among peers in the system. SORIC selectively caches routing indices of transient departed nodes in other relatively stable and capable nodes for two purposes. First, rejoin of the cached nodes is drastically simplified to $O(1)$ complexity, thus cutting off a large portion of system maintenance overhead. Second, caching routing indices of departed nodes minimizes the negative effects of node departures and rejoins, and thus enables the system to sustain an uninterruptedly high quality routing service.

1. Introduction

Compared with Gnutella-like unstructured P2P systems, structured overlays (or called DHTs) offer a logarithmically bounded lookup efficiency and good scalability, but may suffer high maintenance overhead and compromised routing performance, especially in a highly dynamic environment. Unfortunately, a significant feature of P2P systems is the omnipresence of node dynamic activities. As we will show by trace studies in Section 2, there are many instances of node departure and arrival back activities undergoing at a given time. While some peers (possibly, with a high-speed network connection like cable modem) stay in the system for a long time, many other peers leave and rejoin the system very often, especially when low bandwidth connections are used. This is reasonable because these nodes do not have enough bandwidth to stay online for a long time.

*This work is supported in part by NSF under grant #CCF-0429995 and a University of Nebraska Lincoln Layman Fund.

However, current structured overlays do not take the *round-trip* (a round-trip activity is defined as a node's departure and its next arrival back) rhythm into consideration, though some new systems have been proposed to deal with node churn [6]. By studying current DHT systems, we notice that no matter what kind of routing geometry is formed, or routing algorithm adopted, all the query messages are forwarded by looking up some kind of routing indices that are initialized by an expensive node join procedure. Unfortunately, when a node departs or fails, its valuable routing information is also lost, and has to be setup from scratch when the node comes back to the system. While it is inevitable to run the join procedure for a brand new node, doing this for round-trip nodes that are regularly coming back incurs a lot of maintenance overhead [5, 7, 10] that could be actually avoided. Furthermore, before the node departure/failure is detected and the recovery algorithm finishes, all the paths through this peer are invalid, thus compromising the routing quality and resulting in poor static resilience [3].

The above observations suggest that caching the routing indices of departed nodes could be helpful in both routing performance and system maintenance. A simple idea is to cache the routing indices in each node's local buffer when the node leaves the system. When the node comes back, the cached routing indices are restored from the local disk instantly rather than initialized by a lengthy node join process. Unfortunately, this scheme incurs two major problems. First, the cached routing indices are likely to be out-of-date when the node comes back, especially in a highly dynamic environment. The cost to repair these routing indices may offset or even outweigh the benefits obtained from the scheme. Second, the cached routing information of departed nodes is of no use to the system before the nodes come back. In short, this local caching scheme does not help much on system maintenance and routing performance. To develop an effective routing indices caching scheme, we have to 1) keep the cached routing indices up-to-date; and 2) be able to use them to facilitate query routing during the node absent periods.

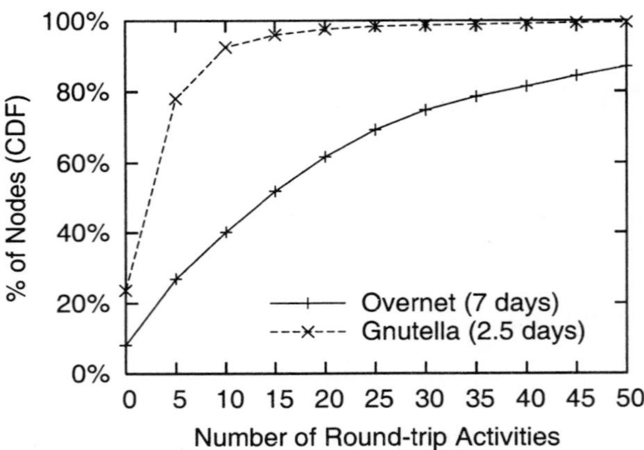

Figure 1. The CDF of the number of round-trip activities experienced by the nodes probed in the Overnet and Gnutella traces.

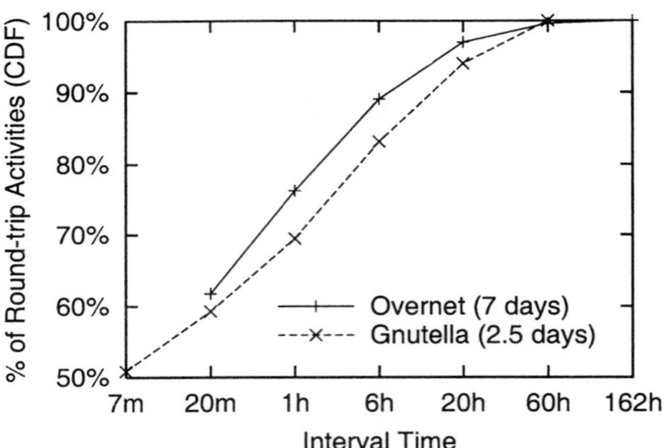

Figure 2. The CDF of the interval times of the round-trip activities in the Overnet and Gnutella traces.

Another fact motivates us to develop a mature solution by taking advantage of node heterogeneity. The measurement study of Saroiu *et al.* [8] has shown that the node capacities may vary up to five orders of magnitude across the peers in the P2P system. It is recommended to exploit the heterogeneity to improve system performance. Some researchers [11, 13] suggested using super-peers, which are supposed to form a secondary overlay, and forward/receive all the messages to/from the peers in each cluster. This approach is effective in reducing query hops, but complicates the design and implementation for the two-layer system architecture. Moreover, since super-peers have to forward much more messages than other nodes, they tend to become the network bottleneck or a point of failure for a whole group of peers.

By elegantly utilizing node dynamic activity patterns and node heterogeneities, we propose a lightweight routing indices caching scheme called SORIC (Structured Overlay with Routing Indices Caching) to address the above-mentioned problems. SORIC selectively saves and maintains the routing indices of departed nodes on other live and relatively stable nodes during node departures, and the departed nodes may reclaim their cached routing indices upon arrival back. The cached routing indices can be used to uninterruptedly serve related queries on behalf of the departed nodes, thus sustaining a high quality routing service. In addition, when the departed nodes arrive back, they can quickly join the system by reclaiming their fresh routing indices. Notice that the selected caching host nodes do not have to be very powerful since they only perform additional indices caching and message forwarding for departed nodes. Our simulation results show that SORIC drastically reduces the maintenance overhead and boosts the routing performance compared to current structured P2P systems.

2. Node dynamic activities in DHTs

A lot of measurement studies have shown the presence of many node dynamic activities in P2P systems [1, 8, 9]. We get the Overnet trace from University of California, San Diego [1] and the Gnutella trace from University of Washington [8] and study the characteristics of node behaviors in current P2P systems.

The Overnet trace monitors 2,400 nodes in the network by probing them every 20 minutes and recording their arrival and departure events over a period of one week. This trace contains 27,151 node joins, among which 25,964, more than 95% are due to arrival back of nodes that have ever joined the system at least once. From the Gnutella trace collected by probing 17,125 peers every 7 minutes for a period of 60 hours, we derive 39,001 node arrivals, among which 31,399, over 80% result from node rejoins. Due to limitation of the peer probing method, we are able to derive a node join event by its liveness and a node leave event by its unreachability, but can not tell a node leave is a graceful departure or unexpected node failure.

Figure 1 shows the cumulative distribution of the number of round-trip activities experienced by the nodes in both traces. It can be seen that over 92% Overnet nodes leave and rejoin the system at least once, and around 60% experience 10 or more round-trips within one week. In the Gnutella trace, while more than 77% peers have at least one rejoins, nearly 8% experience 10 or more round-trips within two and a half days. Both traces exhibit an obvious round-trip pattern among the participating nodes, while the Overnet trace sees more such activities than the Gnutella trace because of its smaller number of probed nodes and longer period of trace time. This also implies that in a typical P2P system, a majority of nodes will have more and more round-trip activities over time. Additionally, we plot the cumulative distribution of interval times of round-trip activities in these two traces, as shown in Figure 2. The interval time is calculated as the time elapsed between a node departure and its next arrival back. From this figure we can see that more than 61% Overnet round-trips are done within 20 minutes, and nearly 76% in 1 hour. In contrast, over 50% Gnutella round-trips complete within 7 minutes, and around 70% within 1 hour.

The results indicate a large number of round-trip activities undergoing on many peers within a short time. This will result in extremely high system overhead because of the $O(logN)$ complexity in DHT maintenance. Such workload may easily overwhelm those nodes with low bandwidth connections as well as apparent round-trip patterns. Furthermore, the routing performance may be seriously compromised if all of these node departures and rejoins are to be handled by conventional maintenance procedures used in current DHTs [3, 4].

3. SORIC preliminaries

Current DHTs discard the routing indices any time a node leaves the system, and have to run the lengthy node join process (including bootstrapping) when the same node arrives back. Instead of this, SORIC selectively caches the routing indices of departed nodes with frequent round-trip patterns in order to reduce the system maintenance overhead and improve the routing performance.

SORIC classifies participating node into three categories: *RICH (routing indices caching host) nodes*, *RICC (routing indices caching client) nodes* and *open nodes*. RICH nodes are peers ready to provide caching service to nodes in their service areas, while a RICC node refers to a client that may request the service from the RICH node to which it has registered. Those peers out of service areas of any RICHs are called open nodes. The service area of a RICH node is determined by service size and service radius. The service size defines the maximum number of RICC nodes a RICH can serve, and the service radius limits the maximum distance between a RICH node and its RICC nodes. Both parameters are used to avoid overloading RICH nodes and ensure good network proximity.

The three types of nodes have different characteristics as follows. In order to provide the caching service, RICH nodes have to be relatively stable and capable for this duty. It is expected that stable nodes in P2P systems tend to be relatively powerful, because otherwise they would not stay in the system for a long time concerning resource consumption. Although each RICC is serviced by a RICH node, it may be qualified to be a RICH candidate by itself or not. When the original RICH leaves or fails, a qualified candidate will take the responsibility and retain the service. The open nodes are not qualified to be RICH nodes because otherwise a qualified open node will work as a new RICH node itself. To determine the qualification of a node to be a RICH, we define a RICH candidacy factor for each node according to its availability and capacity. To be a RICH candidate, a node must have a RICH candidacy factor larger than a predefined threshold.

When departing the P2P system, a RICC node always sends its routing indices to its RICH node, asking for a caching service. If possible, the routing indices will be saved and maintained by the RICH node. When the same RICC node rejoins some time later, it may reclaim its fresh routing indices from the RICH and finish its join process in $O(1)$ time, rather than running an $O(\log N)$ join procedure as in most DHTs. During its absence, the RICH node maintains the cached routing indices and provides additional routing service to other nodes using the cached routing information, as if the departed RICC node is still alive. Furthermore, since the cached routing information is still available to be accessed, there is no need for other nodes to repair corresponding routing index entries that refer to this node. As a result, the negative affects of node round-trip activities are diminished by maintaining and utilizing the up-to-date routing indices of departed RICC nodes.

For the indices caching service, SORIC introduces several new data structures. Each RICH node maintains a *routing indices cache*, and a *client list*. The routing indices cache is the block of memory where routing index records of departed RICC nodes are cached. The client list contains some information for the live and cached RICC nodes in the RICH's service area, including the node status (live or cached), node RICH candidacy and estimated offline period (EOP) for those cached clients. To implement SORIC on top of structured overlays, for each routing table entry node N, we add the IP address of N's RICH node in addition to N's own IP address. A query message whose next hop is supposed to be node N will be redirected to N's RICH when node N is gone, as explained in later sections.

In addition to the above data structures, we define some new types of messages here. We explain more details in later related sections.

RICH Contact When departing and rejoining the system, a client node will contact the RICH by sending a "RICH Contact" message to get its routing indices cached and reloaded respectively.

Live Refresh These messages are sent from RICC nodes to their RICHs periodically, to keep the client lists on the RICHs up to date. A timer is attached to each item in a client list. Initially the timer is set to a slightly larger value than the "Live Refresh" cycle time. To keep the list up to date, each live RICC node sends "Live Refresh" messages to its RICH periodically. When receiving a refresh message, RICH node updates the corresponding item in the list and resets the timer. At the same time, the RICH node replies the refresh message instantly, so that a RICH failure can be quickly detected by its client nodes through an acknowledgement timeout.

RICH Change When a departed RICH node is replaced, the new RICH node that inherits the client list will send a "RICH Change" message to the clients.

RICH Ready When a RICH is replaced, the new RICH may broadcast a "RICH Ready" message within its service radius to cover open nodes until there is no reachable open nodes or the service size is reached.

Reverse Update The RICH information integrated into the routing entries may be stale if the RICH of that node is changed. We employ a lazy *reverse update* mechanism to solve the problem during normal query routings.

4. SORIC algorithms

In this section, we first present the self-organization algorithms in SORIC, and then propose an enhanced routing procedure that exploits the cached routing indices to sustain a high quality routing service.

4.1. RICH selection

When a RICH candidate enters the system, it becomes a new RICH if it can not find an existing RICH node nearby that can provide caching service for it. After becoming a new RICH node, it broadcasts a "RICH Ready" message within service radius. All open nodes that receive this message will reply with positive ACKs. Based on the replies, the RICH accepts RICC nodes with a first-come-first-serve policy until the service size is reached.

When the RICH is on a planned leave, it will try to pick up the next most qualified node among its live RICC nodes to become the new RICH node. If no RICH candidate is found in the list, all the live RICC nodes will become open nodes consequently. If such a candidate is found successfully, this node becomes the new RICH and inherits the client list. However, the cached routing index records and corresponding items in the client list are both discarded since these nodes can not find the new RICH node when they come back. After that, the new RICH sends a "RICH Change" message to the live RICC nodes, which will change their RICH addresses accordingly. If the service size is not reached, the new RICH will then broadcast a "RICH Ready" message to cover open nodes nearby.

In case of a RICH failure, as indicated by an acknowledgement timeout of a "Live Refresh" message from a RICC node, there is no chance for the failed RICH to pick a new one. If the client that detects the failure is not a RICH candidate, it simply becomes an open node. If it is a candidate, it will become a new RICH and broadcast a "RICH Change" message along with the old RICH IP within its service radius. Upon receiving this message, each live RICC node compares its RICH IP with the one in the message, and if they are the same, switches to the new RICH node after being acknowledged by the new RICH. In addition, the open nodes in this service area will also be covered by this RICH node similarly.

However, this strategy may lead to multiple RICH nodes rising up after a RICH failure. Suppose R_1 is the first RICH candidate to detect the RICH failure event, if another RICH candidate also detects the RICH failure by a refresh acknowledgement timeout before it receives the "RICH Change" message from R_1, it may become a new RICH node unnecessarily. Fortunately, the probability of this case is very low. Let T be the cycle time of "Live Refresh" messages. Assume a RICH serving a number of RICC nodes, X of which are qualified to be RICH, and at time t RICH candidate R_1 firstly detects the RICH failure event. To claim a new RICH, R_1 sends out the "RICH Change" messages within the service radius r. These messages will reach all potential RICC nodes of this new RICH node within time r. Suppose the start time for each RICC node to send next refresh message is randomly distributed, the probability for i nodes to detect the RICH failure simultaneously (i.e. from time t to time $t+r$) is

$$p_i = \binom{X-1}{i-1}\left(\frac{r}{T}\right)^{i-1}\left(1-\frac{r}{T}\right)^{X-i}.$$

Suppose the service size is 40, service radius is $r = 30$ ms, and the cycle time for refresh messages is $T = 10$ minutes. Even if all live clients are RICH candidates, i.e., $X = 40$, the maximum probability of initializing two RICHs ($i = 2$) is calculated as $p_2 = \binom{40-1}{2-1}\left(\frac{30ms}{10min}\right)^{2-1}\left(1-\frac{30ms}{10min}\right)^{40-2} = 0.1946\%$. Considering all possible scenarios, the total probability for two or more nodes to become RICH nodes is

$$\begin{aligned} p_{all} &= \sum_{i=2}^{X} p_i = 1 - p_1 = 1 - \left(1-\frac{r}{T}\right)^{X-1} \\ &= 1 - \left(1-\frac{30ms}{10min}\right)^{40-1} = 0.1948\%. \end{aligned}$$

Since the propagated latency within a service radius is much shorter than a refresh cycle, the live RICC nodes are very likely to see the "RICH Change" message from R_1 before they find the RICH failure. In most cases, most live RICC nodes in the old service area will successfully migrate to the service ares of new RICH R_1 that is the first RICH candidate to detect the RICH failure.

4.2. Node join, departure and failure

When joining the system, a new node P that doesn't have a RICH IP address in its local buffer still has to run the DHT bootstrapping and join procedure to collect its routing information. After this, node P contacts its neighbors to see if any RICH node is available. These neighbors will reply with their RICH IP addresses if they have. Then node P sends contact messages to these RICHs requesting for service coverage. On receiving a positive reply from a RICH node, node P successfully becomes a client of that RICH node. Following replies are simply ignored. However, in case of no RICH to contact or positive replies, node P may become a new RICH node if it is qualified, or otherwise stay as an open node.

Having RICH IP address in local buffer, a rejoining node firstly tries to contact the RICH node and reclaim its routing indices. If the node successfully gets back its routing indices from the RICH node, this process is called a *fast rejoin* done instantly. At the same time, its node status, EOP value and RICH candidacy are updated on the RICH node accordingly. However, if the reclaim fails for some reasons (the RICH has changed, or the cached routing index has been replaced), this node has to run a *slow rejoin* process, which is the same as a new node join.

In the simplest case, open nodes depart the system autonomously. For a live RICC node to depart or fail, we have the following three cases.

First, a live client departs the system intentionally, and its routing indices are not cached because the cache is full and no victim entry is found. This implies that the departing node is not likely to arrive back in near future, so the RICH node simply removes it from the client list.

Second, a live client departs the system intentionally, and its routing indices are successfully cached (its status is changed in the RICH's client list accordingly). Because a cached node can not send refresh messages, its timer is changed to a slightly larger value than its EOP. This is straightforward since the cached node is expected to rejoin the system within its EOP.

Third, a node fails silently. If the timer of a live client expires before RICH receives a refresh message from it, this node is assumed to have failed. In this case, SORIC simply removes the corresponding item from the client list. When coming back, this node will be regarded as a new node. With a more aggressive caching scheme, live RICC nodes can send routing indices to their RICH nodes periodically (e.g. along with the refresh messages), such that routing indices of these nodes may be successfully cached on their RICH nodes before failures.

4.3. Routing indices cache replacement

If the cache is full when a RICC node departs, then we have to decide whether to discard this node's routing information or free a space in the cache. An approximately LRU replacement algorithm is developed to manage the routing indices caches so that RICC nodes most likely to come back sooner will get cached. To do this, we design an Estimated Offline Period field (EOP for short) for each node to indicate its offline period before its coming back next time. Each node is assigned a default value of EOP when it joins in the system for the first time, and updated each time the node rejoins the system by the formula $EOP_{new} = EOP_{old} \times \alpha + OP \times \beta$, where $\alpha + \beta = 1$, and OP is the offline period since the node's last departure. The values of α and β indicate how much the node's latest round-trip activity affects its EOP. Typically we set $\alpha = 0.2$, $\beta = 0.8$, as suggested by our experiments, but they may be adjusted according to the amount of node round-trip activities observed.

When a RICH node receives a caching request from a departing RICC node, it checks if the cache is full or not. If it is full (if not, no replacement is needed), the RICH will examine the cache content seeking for a victim. If an "expired" record or an item of a node whose remaining offline time is larger than the departing node's EOP is found, this record becomes the victim for replacement. A node's remaining offline time is calculated by subtracting the elapsed offline time from its EOP value. The elapsed offline time can be obtained from the corresponding timer in the routing indices cache. If no such item is found, however, no replacement occurs as the departing node has the least probability to arrive back in the near future.

4.4. SORIC routing

When a peer leaves the system, SORIC tries to cache its routing indices. The cached information can still provide routing service on behalf of the departed nodes, making the offline node virtually online to the rest of the system. Unless the query is asking for an object stored on the departed node, the departure of a node whose routing indices are cached seems transparent to the query initiator and no routing indices repair is needed, *i.e.*, its negative impact is minimized. Notice that the cached routing indices are continuously maintained by the RICH in a similar way to the query processes. A maintenance message may be directed to a RICH if the next hop node is cached in that RICH. The idea is to keep the routing information fresh until it is claimed by the rejoining node.

During the query lookup process, if the next hop node N is not alive, the previous node will set a "Cache Fetch" flag in the query message and send it to N's RICH node specified in this routing entry (if not null). Upon receiving this "Cache Fetch" tagged query message, the RICH node looks up in its cache for the corresponding nodeId and routing indices. If the information is found (cache hit), the query message simply bypasses the offline node and still goes through the optimal route. If the routing information is not found

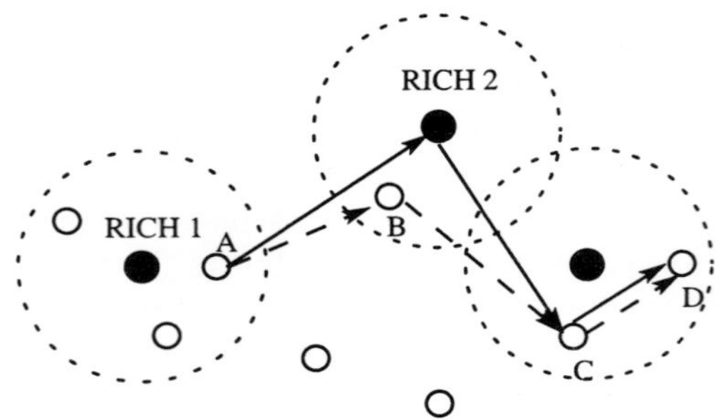

Figure 3. Routing of a query message from node A to node D. Dashed lines show the route when node B is online. Solid lines show the route when node B is offline but its routing indices are cached in RICH 2.

in the cache (cache miss), this route fails and traces back to the last step. Our experiment results have shown a more than 90% cache hit rate when replaying both Overnet and Gnutella traces.

An example of the enhanced routing in SORIC is shown in Figure 3. Supposing node A issues a query with a key closest to node D's nodeId, and the optimal route is from A to B to C to D. When node B leaves, its routing information is saved in the routing indices cache of RICH 2, assuming it is cached successfully. Now suppose the same query message is sent from node A again. According to the lookup protocol, the next hop is node B, which is now offline. Instead of trying another sub-optimal route, the message is sent to RICH 2. By looking up in the cache, RICH 2 finds node B's routing indices in the cache and routes the message to the next hop, node C.

When a RICH node is replaced, the RICH address in some other nodes' routing entries may become stale. We apply a lazy *reverse update* mechanism to solve this problem in the process of query routings. When forwarding a lookup message to the next hop node N, the previous node always piggybacks N's RICH information to the message. On receiving this message, node N checks whether the attached RICH information is fresh or not. If not, it sends a "Reverse Update" message to the previous node on the route, which will make necessary corrections accordingly. Taking the same example above, suppose that RICH 2 is replaced by another candidate RICH 3, but B's RICH address in node A's routing table still refers to RICH 2. This inconsistency is resolved by our *reverse update*: when forwarding a query to node B, node A appends B's currently known RICH address in the message. Upon reception, B discovers this inconsistency and sends a "Reverse Update" message back to node A, and A can update the routing table entry immediately. Experimental results show that this scheme only leads to minor overhead.

Table 1. Maintenance overhead of Pastry and SORIC when running the two traces.

Trace	msg/(node×minute)		Overhead reduction	Rejoin hit rate
	Pastry	SORIC		
Overnet	1.1891	0.2133	82.06%	85%
Gnutella	0.9008	0.3441	61.78%	84%

5. Evaluation

We developed a SORIC system simulator based on a representative DHT, Pastry and its latest prototype, FreePastry 1.3 [2]. Then we conduct trace-driven simulations to evaluate its benefits by replaying two real-world P2P traces, Overnet and Gnutella as mentioned in Section 2.

We built the simulator over a large-scale, physical network topology using the GT-ITM [12] model with 100,000 physical machines arranged hierarchically, from which P2P nodes were randomly selected as required by the Overnet and Gnutella trace. In all the experiments, we set the Pastry parameters as $b = 4$, $|L| = 16$ and $|M| = 32$. The default values for SORIC system parameters are set as follows: the cache size is set to 20, service size 40, and service radius 30 ms. The default EOP is set to 6 hours so that most round-trip activities can benefit from our SORIC caching scheme. The prototype was written in Java.

5.1. Maintenance overhead reduction

In order to measure the overall maintenance efficiency of SORIC, we use two specific metrics on maintenance overhead hereafter: *overhead reduction* and *rejoin hit rate*. The overhead reduction is calculated as the percentage reduction in total maintenance cost. The rejoin hit rate is the percentage of fast rejoins among all the rejoin events, and tells how well the routing indices cache replacement algorithm works. In experiments, we replay the Overnet and Gnutella traces using Pastry and SORIC algorithms, and collect the total number of maintenance messages and the number of fast rejoins and slow rejoins. Then we calculate the average number of maintenance messages per node per minute, the overall maintenance overhead reduction and the rejoin hit rates, as shown in Table 1. It shows that SORIC drastically reduces the system maintenance overhead by nearly 82% for Overnet, and 62% for Gnutella. The rejoin hit rate is around 85% and 84% respectively. The results also indicate that more benefit can be achieved as in the Overnet trace where nodes involve more round-trip activities. The reason is that SORIC has more chances to cache routing indices for departed nodes with more round-trip activities.

To examine the workload on different type of nodes, we collect the detailed numbers of messages used to process

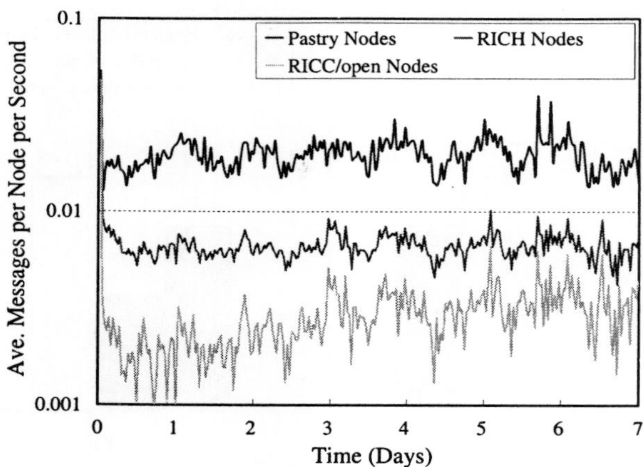

Figure 4. Maintenance overhead in average number of messages per node per second when replaying Overnet trace.

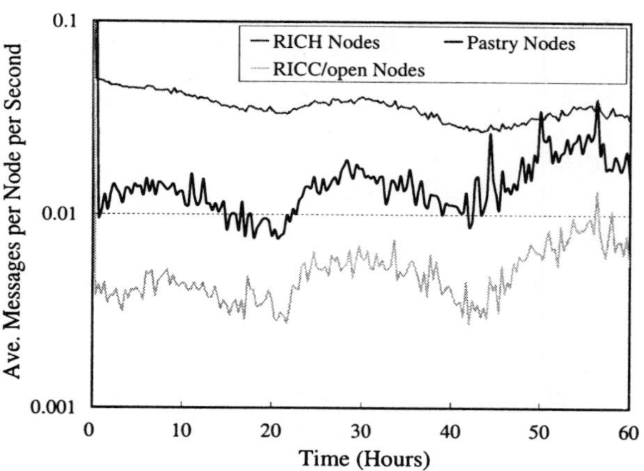

Figure 5. Maintenance overhead in average number of messages per node per second when replaying Gnutella trace.

each node join and departure request in both traces, and plot the workload distribution among SORIC nodes compared to Pastry nodes over time, as shown in Figure 4 and Figure 5, respectively. The results demonstrate running SORIC on the Gnutella trace reduces the maintenance overhead for RICC and open nodes by a factor of 4, while only increasing load on a small number of RICH nodes. This load increase is not significant with regarding to the bigger node capacity of RICH nodes over other nodes. For the Overnet trace, however, the workloads on *both* RICH and RICC/open nodes are significantly reduced, because there are much more beneficial round-trip activities involved in this trace so that maintenance overhead is substantially reduced on all participating nodes. This also implies that the more extensively peers conduct dynamic activities, the more maintenance overhead can be reduced by SORIC. This helps improve the system scalability in terms of the number of nodes leaving the network and joining back. Another easy observation is that the RICH nodes deal with more workload than RICC and open nodes. This skew of workload distribution approximately conforms to the heterogeneity among participating nodes, since the RICH nodes are supposed to be relatively stable and capable.

In the next experiment, we study the SORIC self-organization efficiency when some nodes fail unexpectedly rather than depart intentionally. Since failed nodes do not have a chance to be cached, the performance is expected to degrade, as is shown in Figure 6. Notice that when all node departures are changed to node failures, SORIC degrades to the baseline system and shows no improvement. In a system with failure rate less than 10%, SORIC reduces the system maintenance overhead by more than 70% when running the Overnet trace and 53% when running the Gnutella trace.

5.2. Routing performance improvements

The routing performance is measured in terms of three metrics: *propagated latency*, *logical hop* and *relative distance*. We studied the routing performance of SORIC compared to Pastry by running lookup tests on several selected time instants during the trace-replay period. Specifically, we run 10,000 lookups for every 10,000 events in each trace consumed (i.e., replayed) by Pastry and SORIC. Then we collect the routing performance gains on *propagated latency*, *routing hops* and *relative distance* at each selected time instant, and calculate the averages for them.

As shown in Figure 7, SORIC offers substantial improvement on routing quality for both traces. This stems from the different approaches in Pastry and SORIC dealing with a query that passes an offline node on its optimal routing path. In Pastry as well as other DHTs, the query will be traced back to the last step. But in SORIC, the query will typically be forwarded to a RICH with "Cache Fetch" tag. If this request is satisfied (a routing cache hit), the query is further forwarded along the optimal route. Since a larger portion of nodes involve round-trip activities and have their routing indices cached with the Overnet trace, we can see more routing performance gains than Gnutella. Another metric to measure routing performance gains is the routing cache hit ratio, which tells how well the routing indices cached in RICH nodes answer the cache fetch requests for query messages. In the experiments, we obtain the number of routing cache hits and misses, and figure out a cache hit ratio of around 90% for both traces (not shown in the graphs for space limitation). This high hit ratio also implies a much improved fault resilience [3] due to more valid routing information maintained in the whole system.

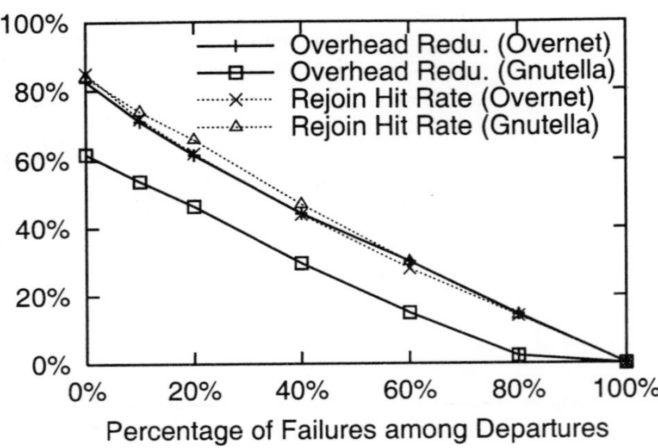

Figure 6. Maintenance overhead reduction and rejoin hit rate of SORIC with node failures.

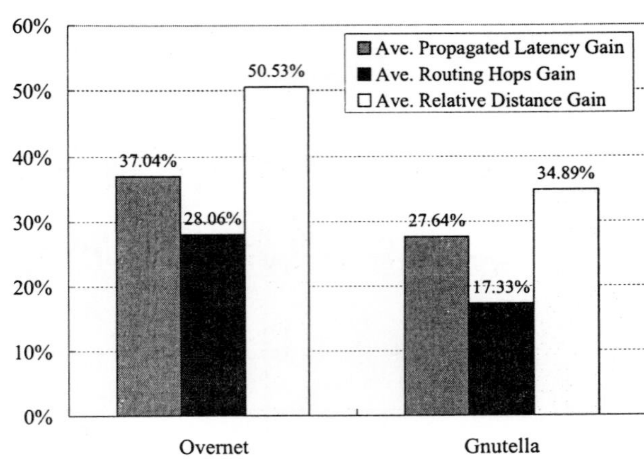

Figure 7. SORIC Routing performance gains compared with Pastry when running lookups.

6. Conclusions and future work

In this paper, we design and implement SORIC, a novel routing indices caching system that significantly reduces system maintenance overhead and improves routing performance for structured P2P systems in a dynamic environment. We advocate exploiting both node heterogeneity so as to assign different responsibilities to nodes with diverse capabilities, and the round-trip characteristics of dynamic activities in P2P systems by saving and maintaining routing indices for departed round-trip nodes. We find that SORIC drastically reduces the maintenance overhead by up to 82% while simultaneously boosting the routing quality when deployed on top of current structured P2P systems. In the future work, we will enhance our scheme in handling node failures, and implement it on top of other DHTs such as Chord and CAN and study its effectiveness and efficiency.

References

[1] R. Bhagwan, S. Savage, and G. Voelker. Understanding availability. In *Proceedings of the 2nd International Workshop on Peer-to-Peer Systems (IPTPS)*, Berkeley, CA, Feb. 2003.

[2] FreePastry. http://freepastry.rice.edu.

[3] K. Gummadi, R. Gummadi, S. Gribble, S. Ratnasamy, S. Shenker, and I. Stoica. The impact of DHT routing geometry on resilience and proximity. In *Proceedings of ACM SIGCOMM'03*, pages 381–394, Karlsruhe, Germany, August 2003.

[4] D. Liben-Nowell, H. Balakrishnan, and D. Karger. Analysis of the evolution of peer-to-peer systems. In *Proceedings of 21st ACM Symposium on Principles of Distributed Computing (PODC 2002)*, pages 233–242, Monterey, CA, USA, July 2002.

[5] S. Ratnasamy, P. Francis, M. Handley, R. Karp, and S. Shenker. A scalable content-addressable network. In *Proceedings of the ACM SIGCOMM 2001*, pages 161–172, San Diego, CA, USA, August 2001.

[6] S. Rhea, D. Geels, T. Roscoe, and J. Kubiatowicz. Handling churn in a DHT. In *Proceedings of the USENIX Annual Technical Conference*, pages 127–140, Boston, MA, USA, June 2004.

[7] A. Rowstron and P. Druschel. Pastry: Scalable, decentralized object location, and routing for large-scale peer-to-peer systems. In *Proceedings of the 18th IFIP/ACM International Conference on Distributed Systems Platforms (Middleware)*, pages 329–350, Heidelberg, Germany, Nov. 2001.

[8] S. Saroiu, P. Gummadi, and S. Gribble. A measurement study of peer-to-peer file sharing systems. In *Proceedings of Multimedia Computing and Networking (MMCN)*, San Jones, CA, Jan. 2002.

[9] S. Sen and J. Wong. Analyzing peer-to-peer traffic across large networks. In *Proceedings of Second Annual ACM Internet Measurement Workshop*, November 2002.

[10] I. Stoica, R. Morris, D. Karger, F. Kaashoek, and H. Balakrishnan. Chord: A scalable peer-to-peer lookup service for Internet applications. In *Proceedings of the ACM SIGCOMM 2001*, pages 149–160, San Diego, USA, August 2001.

[11] B. Yang and H. Garcia-Molina. Designing a super-peer network. In *Proceedings of the 19th International Conference on Data Engineering (ICDE)*, pages 49–60, Bangalore, India, March 2003.

[12] E. Zegura, K. Calvert, and S. Bhattacharjee. How to model an internetwork. In *Proceedings of the IEEE Conference on Computer Communication*, pages 594–602, San Francisco, CA, Mar. 1996.

[13] B. Zhao, Y. Duan, L. Huang, A. Joseph, and J. Kubiatowicz. Brocade:landmark routing on overlay networks. In *Proceedings of the 1st International Workshop on Peer-to-Peer Systems (IPTPS)*, Cambridge, MA, March 2002.

Locality-Aware Randomized Load Balancing Algorithms for DHT Networks

Haiying Shen and Cheng-Zhong Xu
Department of Electrical & Computer Engineering
Wayne State University, Detroit, MI 48202
{shy,czxu}@ece.eng.wayne.edu

Abstract

Structured P2P overlay networks based on a consistent hashing function have an aftermath load balance problem that needs to be dealt with. A load balancing method should take into account both proximity and dynamic features of DHTs. Randomized matching between heavily loaded nodes with lightly loaded nodes can deal with the dynamic feature. But current randomized methods are unable to consider physical proximity of the node simultaneously. There are locality-aware methods that rely on an additional logical network to capture the physical locality in load balancing. Due to the cost for network construction and maintenance, these locality-aware algorithms can hardly deal with DHTs with churn. This paper presents a locality-aware randomized load balancing algorithm to deal with both of the proximity and dynamic features of DHTs. We introduce a factor of randomness in the probing process in a range of proximity to deal with the DHT churn. We further improve the randomized load balancing efficiency by d-way probing. Simulation results show the superiority of a locality-aware 2-way randomized load balancing in DHTs, in comparison with other pure random policies and locality-aware sequential algorithms. In DHTs with churn, it performs no worse than the best churn resilient algorithm.

1 Introduction

Over the past years, the immerse popularity of peer-to-peer (P2P) resource sharing services has produced a significant stimulus to content-delivery overlay network research. An important class of the overlay networks is distributed hash tables (DHTs) [7, 11, 8, 10] that map keys to the nodes of a network based on a consistent hashing function. However, consistent hashing [3] produces a bound of $O(\log n)$ imbalance of keys between nodes, where n is the number of nodes in the system. Load balancing algorithm is to avoid load imbalance by distributing application load among the nodes in proportional to node capacities. The design of a load balancing algorithm should take into account DHT proximity feature to minimize load balancing cost and dynamic feature to handle churn — a situation where a great number of nodes join, leave and fail continually and rapidly.

In the past, numerous load balancing algorithms were proposed with different characteristics [11, 6, 2, 16, 4]. However, few of them are able to deal with both the dynamism and proximity. In general, the dynamic feature of DHTs should be dealt with by randomized matching between heavily loaded nodes with lightly loaded nodes. Rao and Godfrey *et al.* [6, 2] proposed randomized load balancing algorithms for dynamic DHTs with churn. The algorithms treat all nodes equally in random probing, without consideration of node proximity information in load balancing. Zhu and Hu presented a proximity-aware algorithm to take into account the node proximity information in load balancing [16]. The algorithm is based on an additional network constructed on top of DHTs. Although the network is self-organized, the load balancing algorithm is hardly applicable to DHTs with churn.

In this paper, we present novel locality-aware randomized (LAR) load balancing algorithms to deal with both the proximity and dynamic features of DHTs. The algorithms take advantage of the proximity information of the DHTs in node probing and distribute application load among the nodes according to their capacities. We introduce a factor of randomness in the probing process in a range of proximity so as to make the load balancing algorithm resilient enough to deal with the dynamic feature of DHTs. We further improve the efficiency of the random probing process by d-way probing. The algorithms are implemented in Cycloid [10], based on a concept of "moving item" for retaining DHTs' network efficiency and scalability. We evaluated the performance of the LAR load balancing algorithms via comprehensive simulations. Simulation results demonstrate the superiority of a locality-aware 2-way randomized load balancing algorithm in DHTs, in comparison with other pure random approaches and locality-aware sequential algorithms. In DHTs with churn, it performs no worse than the best churn resilient algorithm.

The rest of this paper is structured as follows. Section 2 presents a concise review of representative load balancing approaches for structured P2P systems. Section 3 details a load balancing framework. Section 4 presents the LAR load balancing algorithms. Section 5 shows the performance of the approaches in terms of a variety of metrics in DHTs

0190-3918/05 $20.00 © 2005 IEEE

with and without churn. Section 6 concludes this paper with remarks on possible future work.

2 Related Work

Load balance is an aftermath problem in any DHTs based on consistent hashing functions. Karger *et al.* proved that the consistent hashing function in chord [11] leads to a bound of $O(\log n)$ imbalance of keys between the nodes. Stoica *et al.* proposed an abstraction of "virtual servers" for Chord load balancing. This abstraction simplifies the treatment of load balancing problem at the cost of higher space overhead and lookup efficiency compromise. The original concept of "virtual servers" ignored the file size and node heterogeneity. Later on, Rao *et al.* [6] proposed three algorithms to rearrange load based on nodes' different capacities. Their basic idea is to move load from heavy nodes to light nodes so that each node's load does not exceed its capacity. Most recently, Godfrey *et al.* [2] extended this work for dynamic P2P systems. This is, if a node's capacity utilization exceeds a predetermined threshold, its excess virtual servers will be moved to a light one immediately without waiting for next periodic balancing. The algorithms assumes a goal of minimizing the amount of load moved. They neglects the effect of proximity information. With proximity consideration, load transferring and communication are between physically close heavy nodes and light nodes. One of the first work to utilize the proximity information to guide load balancing is due to Zhu *et al.* [16]. The authors suggested to build a K-nary tree (KT) structure on top of a DHT overlay. The KT tree helps to use proximity information to move load between physically close heavy and light nodes. However, the construction and maintenance of KT are costly, especially in churn. Besides, when a parent fails or leaves, the load imbalance of some of its children in the subtree cannot be solved before its recovery. Most recently, Karger and Ruhl [4] proved that the "virtual servers" method could not be guaranteed to handle item distributions in a certain condition. As a remedy, they proposed two schemes with provable features: *moving items* and *moving nodes* to achieve equal load between a pair of nodes, and then a system-wide load balance state.

This paper presents LAR algorithms to take into account proximity information in load balancing and deal with network churn meanwhile and a first implementation of item movement based load balancing algorithms though it is also suitable for "virtual servers".

3 Load Balancing Framework

Cycloid is a lookup efficient constant-degree DHT with $n{=}d \cdot 2^d$ nodes, where d is dimension. Each Cycloid node has $O(1)$ neighbors and is represented by a pair of indices $(k, a_{d-1}a_{d-2}\dots a_0)$, where k is a cyclic index and

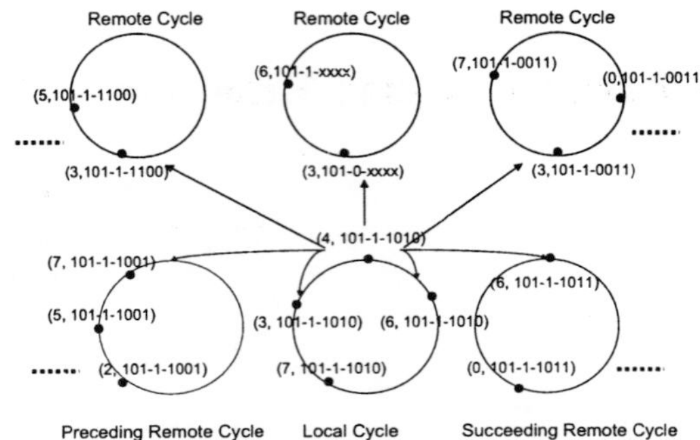

Figure 1. Cycloid node routing links state.

$a_{d-1}a_{d-2}.....a_0$ is a cubical index. The cyclic index is an integer, ranging from 0 to $d-1$ and the cubical index is a binary number between 0 and $2^d - 1$. The nodes with the same cubical index are ordered by their cyclic index mod d on a *local cycle*. The largest cyclic index node in a local cycle is called the *primary node* of the nodes at the same local cycle. All local cycles are ordered by their cubical index mod 2^d on a *large cycle*. Figure 1 shows the routing links of a Cycloid node (4,10111010). They include the node's predecessor and successor in the local cycle, two primary nodes of the preceding and the succeeding remote cycles, one *cubical neighbor* and two *cyclic neighbors*. For more information about Cycloid, please refer to [10].

In the following, we will present a framework for load balancing based on "moving item" on Cycloid. It takes advantage of the Cycloid's topological properties and conduct a load balancing process in two steps: *local load balancing* within a cluster and *global load balancing* between clusters.

A general load balancing approach with consideration of node heterogeneity is to partition nodes into a super node with high capacity and a class of regular nodes with low capacity [14]. Each super node, together with a group of regular nodes, forms a cluster in which the super node operates as a server to the others and all the super nodes operate as equal nodes. Super-peer network strikes a balance between the inherent efficiency of centralization and distribution, and takes advantage of capacity heterogeneity, as well. Since Cycloid consists of cycles with a primary node in each cycle, we build a Cycloid super-peer network by assigning each primary node as a super node in its cycle/cluster. The neighborhood construction mechanism in [12] can be used to construct super-peer networks in other DHTs such as Chord, Pastry, etc.

Let L_i represent the *actual load* of a real server i. It is the sum of the load of the items it stores: $L_i = \sum_{k=1}^{m_i} L_{i,k}$, assuming the node has m_i items. Let C_i be the capacity of node i and T_i its pre-defined target load in a percentage of the node capacity. We refer to the node whose actual load is no larger than its target load (*i.e.* $L_i \leq T_i$) as a *light node*; otherwise a heavy node. We define *node utilization* NU_i as the fraction of its target capacity that is used: $NU_i =$

L_i/T_i. A *system utilization* is the fraction of the system's total target capacity.

Each node contains a list of data items, labelled as ID_k $(k = 1, 2, \ldots)$. To reduce the workload of a heavy node, the items chosen to transfer are called *excess items*. Each primary node has a pair of donating sorted list (DSL) and starving sorted (SSL) list which store the load information of all nodes in its cluster. A DSL is for light nodes and a SSL is for heavy nodes. The *free capacity* of light node i, $\triangle L_i$, is defined as $\triangle L_i = T_i - L_i$. *Load information* of a heavy node i is expressed as $<L_{i,1}, ID_{i,1}, ip\_addr(i)>$, $<L_{i,k}, ID_{i,k}, ip\_addr(i)>$, $\ldots$, $<L_{i,m}, ID_{i,m}, ip\_addr(i)>$, in which $ip\_addr(i)$ denotes the IP address of node i. Load information of a light node j is expressed as $<\triangle L_j, ip\_addr(j)>$. A SSL is sorted in a descending order of $L_{i,k}$. A DSL is sorted in an ascending order of $\triangle L_j$. Load rearrangement is executed between a pair of DSL and SSL, as shown in Algorithm 1. This scheme guarantees that heavier items have high priorities to be reassigned to a light node, which means faster convergence to a system-wide load balance state.

Algorithm 1 Primary node performs load rearrangement periodically between a pair of DSL and SSL.

for each item k in SSL **do**
  for each item j in DSL **do**
    if $L_{i,k} <= \triangle L_j$ **then**
      item k is arranged to be transferred from i to j
      if $\triangle L_j - L_{i,k} > 0$ **then**
        put $< (\triangle L_i - L_{i,k}), ip\_addr(i) >$ back to DSL
      end if
    end if
  end for
end for

We use a centralized method for local load balancing, and a decentralized method for global load balancing. Periodically, each node reports its load information to its primary node. A primary node with nonempty starving list (PNS) first performs local load rearrangement between its DSL and SSL. It then probes other primary nodes' DSLs for global load rearrangement until its SSL becomes empty. This scheme can be extended to perform load rearrangement between one SSL and multiple DSLs for improvement.

4 Locality-Aware Randomized Load Balancing Algorithms

The load balancing framework presented in the preceding section facilitates the development of load balancing algorithms with different characteristics. The key difference between the algorithms is, for a PNS, how to choose another primary node for a global load rearrangement between their SSL and DSL. It affects the efficiency and overhead to reach a system-wide load balance state.

4.1 D-way Randomized Probing

In a randomized probing policy, each PNS probes other primary nodes randomly for load rearrangement. A simple form is one-way probing, in which a PNS, say node i, probes other primary nodes one by one to execute load rearrangement between SSL_i and DSL_j, where j is a probed node.

The randomized probing in our load balancing framework is similar to load balancing problem in other contexts: *competitive online load balancing* and *supermarket model*. Competitive online load balancing is to assign each task to a server on-line with the objective of minimizing the maximum load on any server, given a set of servers and a sequence of task arrivals and departures. Azar *et al.* [1] proved that in competitive online load balancing, allowing each task to have two server choices to choose a less loaded server instead of just one choice can exponentially minimize the maximum server load and result in a more balanced load distribution. Supermarket model is to allocate each randomly incoming task modelled as a customer with service requirements, to a processor (or server) with the objective of reducing the time each customer spends in the system. Mitzenmacher *et al.* [5] proved that allowing a task two server choices and to be served at the server with less workload instead of just one choice leads to exponential improvements in the expected execution time of each task. But a poll size larger than two gains much less substantial extra improvement.

The randomized probing in our load balancing framework can be represented by the above models if we regard SSLs as tasks, and DSLs as servers. As to the problem of the same capacity for each server in those models, we treat the condition that different DSLs have different total free capacity in the same way as that those DSLs are already assigned some tasks and with different free capacity left; that is, in the middle way of task assignment with a same very large total target capacity for each of DSLs. We generalize the one-way random probing policy to a d-way probing, denoted by R_d ($d \geq 1$), in which d primary nodes are probed at a time, and the primary node with the most total free capacity in its DSL is chosen for load rearrangement. We expect that 2-way probing could achieve a more balanced load distribution with faster speed even in churn, but d (>2)-way probing may not result in much additional improvement.

4.2 Locality-Aware Probing

One goal of load balancing is to keep each node's utilization below one with minimum overhead and time. Proximity is one of the most important performance factors. We integrate proximity-neighbor selection and topologically-aware overlay construction techniques [13] into Cycloid to build a topology-aware Cycloid. That is, a node selects the routing table entries pointing to the topologically nearest among all nodes with nodeId in the desired portion of the Id space, and each node Id is represented by its Hilbert number so that physically close primary nodes are close to each other in the large cycle. As a result, the primary nodes of a node's neighbors are closer to the node than randomly chosen primary nodes in the entire network, such that the cost for communication and load movement can be reduced if a primary node contacts its primary node neighbors or primary nodes of its neighbors. There are two methods for locality-aware probing: *randomized* and *sequential* method. In locality-aware randomized probing, each PNS contacts its primary node neighbors or primary nodes of its neighbors. After all neighbors have been tried, if the PNS's SSL is still nonempty, global random probing is started in the entire Id space. In locality-aware sequential probing, denoted by Lseq, each PNS contacts its successor, *Successor(PNS)*. After load rearrangement, if its SSL is still nonempty, *Successor(Successor(PNS))* is tried. This process is repeated, until that SSL becomes empty.

5 Performance Evaluation

We designed and implemented a simulator in Java for evaluation of the load balancing algorithms on topology-aware Cycloid. We selected 15 nodes as landmark nodes to generate the landmark vector and a Hilbert number [13] for each node Id. We use two transit-stub topologies generated by GT-ITM [15]: "ts5k-large" and "ts5k-small". "ts5k-large" has 5 transit domains, 3 transit nodes per transit domain, 5 stub domains attached to each transit node, and 60 nodes in each stub domain on average. "ts5k-small" has 120 transit domains, 5 transit nodes per transit domain, 4 stub domains attached to each transit node, and 2 nodes in each stub domain on average. "ts5k-large" is used to represent a situation in which Cycloid overlay consists of nodes from several big stub domains, while "ts5k-small" represents a situation in which Cycloid overlay consists of nodes scattered in the entire Internet and only few nodes from the same edge network join the overlay. To account for the fact that interdomain routes have higher latency, each interdomain hop counts as 3 hops of units of latency while each intradomain hop counts as 1 hop of unit of latency. Table 1 lists the parameters of the simulation and their default values. Pareto distribution reflects real world where there are machines with capacities that vary by different orders of magnitude. We will compare the different load balancing algorithms in Cycloid without churn in terms of the following performance metrics; performance of the LAR in Cycloid with churn will be evaluated in Section 5.4.

(1) *Load movement factor*, defined as the total load transferred due to load balancing divided by the system actual load. It represents load movement cost for load balance.

(2) *Total time of probings*, defined as the time spent for primary node probing assuming that probing one node takes 1 time unit, and probing n nodes simultaneously also takes 1 time unit. It represents the speed of probing phrase in load balancing to achieve a system-wide load balance state.

(3) *Total number of load rearrangements*, defined as the total number of load rearrangement between a pair of SSL and DSL.

(4) *Total probing bandwidth*, defined as the sum of the bandwidth consumed by all probings. A probing's bandwidth is the sum of the bandwidth of all communication, each of which is message size times physical path length of the message travelled. It is assumed that the size of a message asking and replying for information is 1 unit. It represents the traffic burden caused by probings.

(5) *Moved load distribution*, defined as the cummulative distribution function (CDF) of the percentage of moved load versus moving distance. It represents the load movement cost for load balance. The more load moved along the shorter distances, the less load balancing costs.

Table 1. Simulation settings and algorithm parameters.

Environment Parameter	Default value
Object arrival location	Uniform over Id space
Number of nodes	4096
Node capacity	Bounded Pareto: shape 2 lower bound:2500, upper bound: 2500*10
Number of items	20480
Existing item load	Bounded Pareto: shape: 2, lower bound: mean item actual load/2 upper bound: mean item actual load/2*10

Because metrics (2) and (3) are not affected by topology, we will only show results of them in "ts5k-large".

5.1 Effectiveness of LAR Algorithms

In this section, we will show the effectiveness of LAR load balancing algorithms. First, we present the impact of LAR algorithm on the alignment of the skews in load distribution and node capacity when the system is fully loaded. From Figure 2(a) and (b), we can see that many nodes are overloaded before load balancing and after load balancing they become light by transferring excess items to light nodes. Figure 2(c) shows the scatterplot of loads according to node capacity. These figures show that the load balancing frame assigns load to nodes based on their capacity with the consideration of node heterogeneity.

We measured the load movement factors due to different load balancing algorithms: one-way random (R_1), two-way random (R_2), LAR_1, LAR_2, and Lseq, on systems of utilization from 0.5 to 1, with 0.05 increase in each step. The simulation results showed that the algorithms require the same

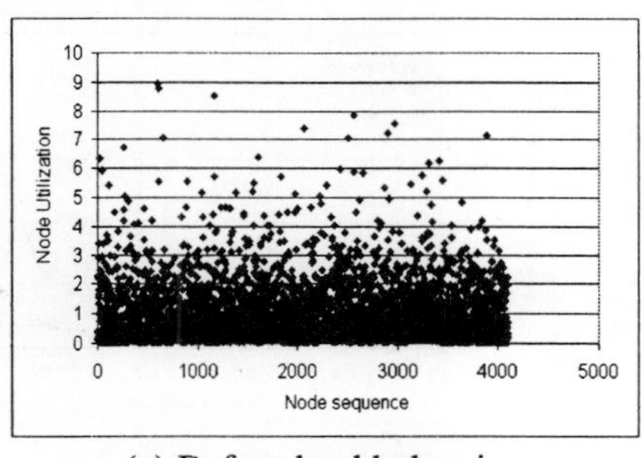

(a) Before load balancing

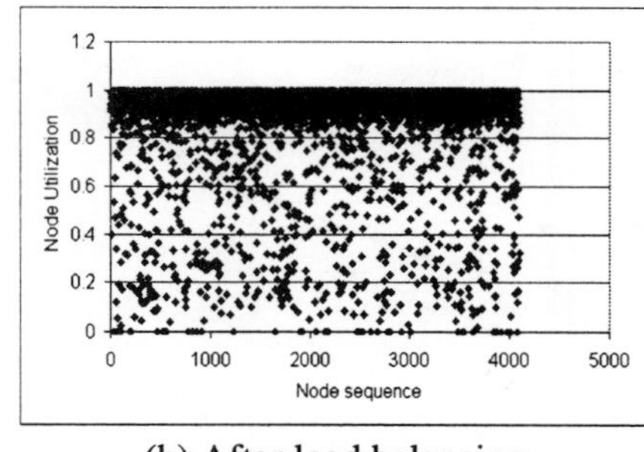

(b) After load balancing

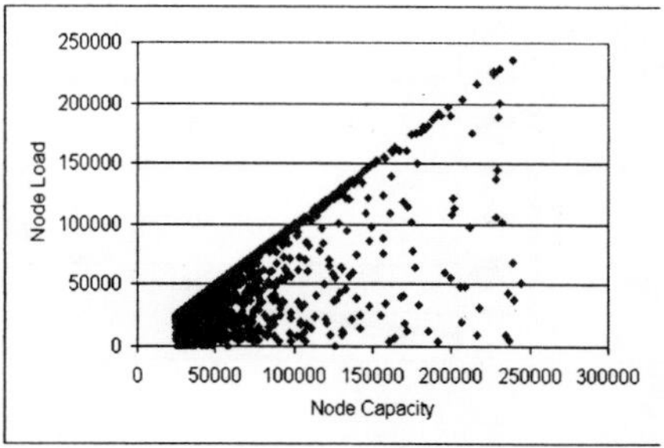

(c) Utilization of nodes after load balancing

Figure 2. Effect of load balancing

amount of load movement in total for load balance. This is in consistent with the observations by Rao, *et al.* [6] that the load moved depends only on distribution of loads, the target to be achieved and not on load balancing algorithms. This result suggests that a better load balancing algorithm should explore how to move the same amount of load along shorter distance to reduce item transfer cost; in another word, how to achieve locality-aware load balancing. In the following, we will examine the performance of various load balancing algorithms in terms of other performance metrics.

5.2 Comparison Between Different Algorithms

Figure 3(a) shows the probing time of Lseq is much more than R_1 and LAR_1. This result implies that random algorithm is better than sequential algorithm in probing efficiency. Figure 3(b) shows that the rearrangement number of those three methods are almost the same. This implies that these three algorithms need almost the same number of primary nodes for load rearrangement to achieve load balance. However, more probing time of Lseq suggests that Lseq is not as efficient as random probing. It is consistent with the observation of Mitzenmacher in [5] that simple randomized load balancing schemes can balance load effectively although it is often difficult to analyze such schemes.

Figure 3(c) and (d) show the performance of the algorithms in "ts5k-large". From Figure 3(c), we can observe that bandwidth for probings of R_1, LAR_1 and Lseq are almost the same in lightly loaded system with utilization no more than 0.6. When system utilization is greater than 0.6, this bandwidth of R_1 is more than LAR_1 and Lseq, and the performance gap increases as the system load increases. It is because that much less number of probings is needed in lightly loaded system compared with that in heavily loaded system. Such that, probing distance has less effect in bandwidth consumption in lightly load system. The bandwidth results of LAR and Lseq are almost the same when system utilization is no more than 0.9, and when system utilization is more than 0.9, the bandwidth of LAR is more than Lseq's. This is due to the fact that in more heavily loaded system, more randomly chosen nodes from entire Id space need to be probed, which have longer distances to probing nodes than sequential nodes, resulting in more probing bandwidth consumption. Figure 3(d) shows the moved load distribution in global load balancing with system utilization approaches to 1. We can see that LAR_1 and Lseq are able to transfer about 60% of total moved load within 10 hops, while R_1 transfers only about 15% within 10 hops. That's because R_1 is locality-oblivious while LAR_1 and Lseq are locality-aware.

Figure 3(e) and (f) show the performance of algorithms in "ts5k-small". These results also confirm that LAR_1 and Lseq achieve better locality-aware performance than R_1, although the improvement is not so significant as that in "ts5k-large". It is because that in "ts5k-small" topology, nodes are scattered in the entire network. In this case, the neighbors of a primary node may not be physically closer than other nodes.

In summary, these results suggest that the randomized algorithm is more efficient than the sequential algorithm in the probing process. The locality-aware approaches can effectively assign and transfer loads between neighboring nodes first, thereby reduce network traffic and improve load balancing efficiency. The LAR algorithm performs best among the three algorithms.

Figures 4 and 5 show the breakdown of total probed nodes in percentage of the probed nodes got from neighbors or from randomly choosing in entire Id space in LAR_1 and LAR_2 respectively. Label "one neighbor and one random" in Figure 5 represents the condition when there's only one neighbor in routing table, then another probed node is chosen randomly from Id space. We can see that the percentage of neighbor primary node constitutes the most part. With system utilization increases, the percentage of neighbor primary node decreases because the neighbors' DSLs don't have enough free capacity for a larger number of excess items. Therefore, neighbors can support most of system excess items in load balancing, and randomly chosen primary nodes must be resorted to for excess items that cannot be supported by neighbors.

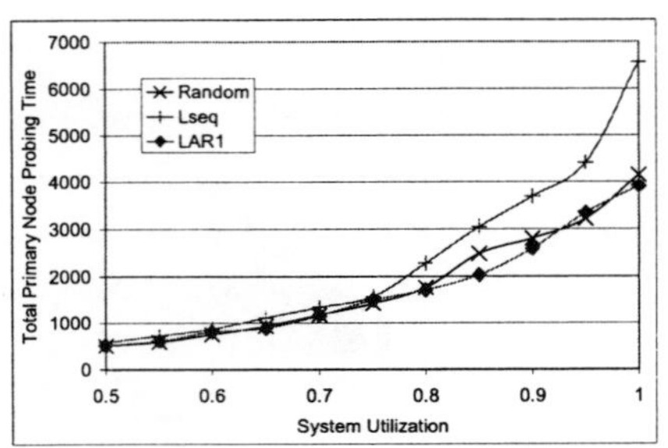

(a) Total primary node probing time "ts5k-large"

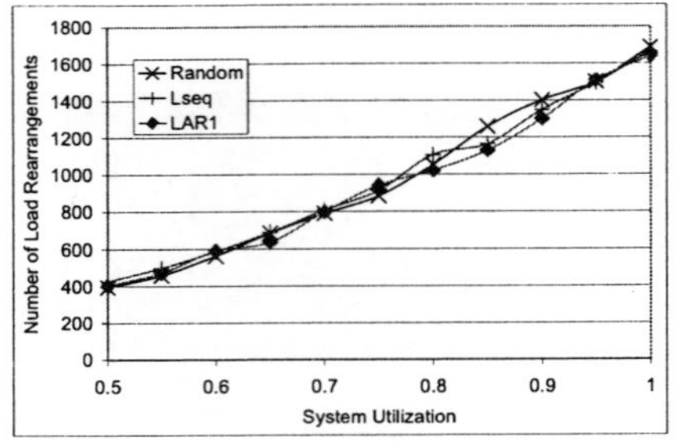

(b) Total number of load rearrangements "ts5k-large"

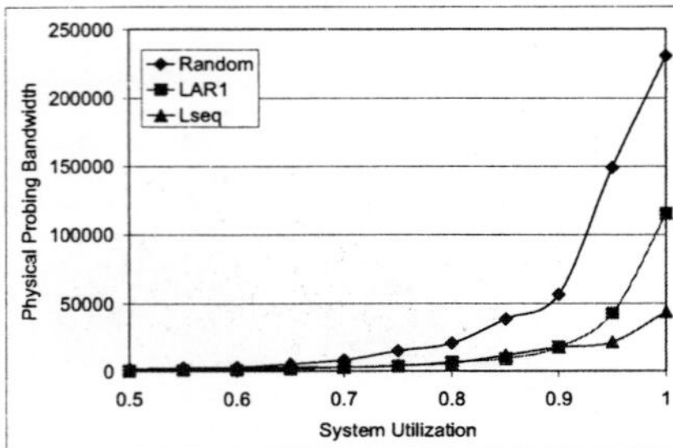

(c) Total bandwidth of probings in "ts5k-large"

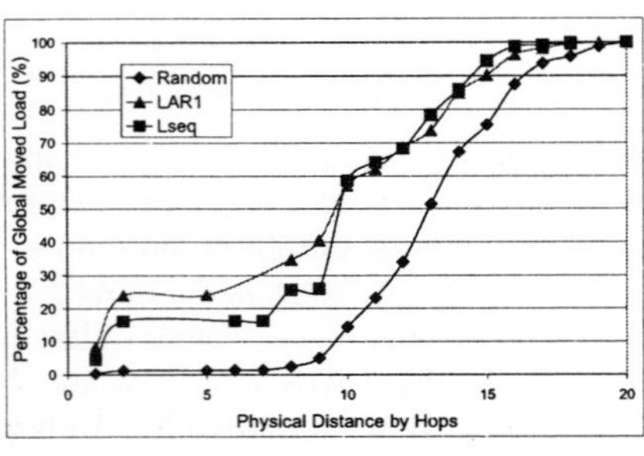

(d) CDF of moved load distribution in "ts5k-large"

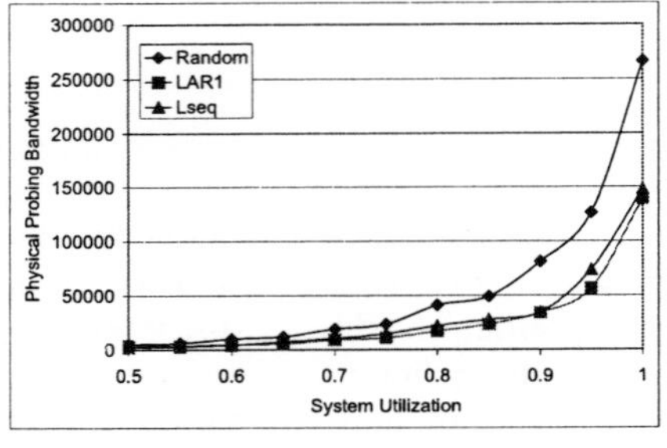

(e) Total bandwidth of probings in "ts5k-small"

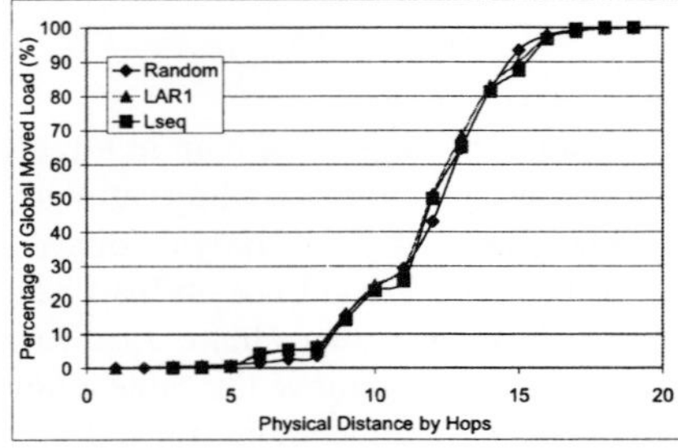

(f) CDF of moved load distribution in "ts5k-small"

Figure 3. Effect of load balancing due to different probing algorithms

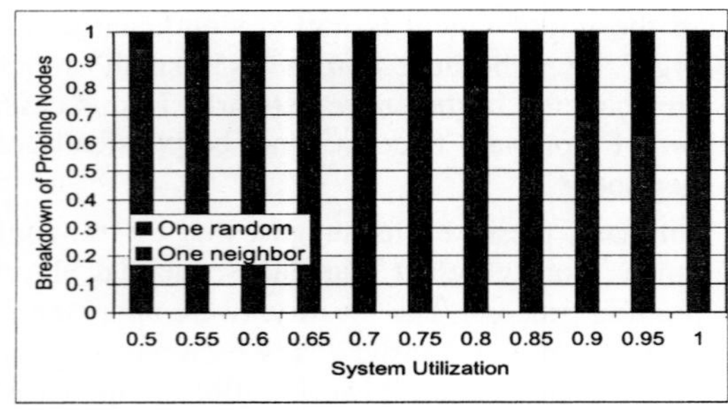

Figure 4. Breakdown of probed nodes of LAR$_1$

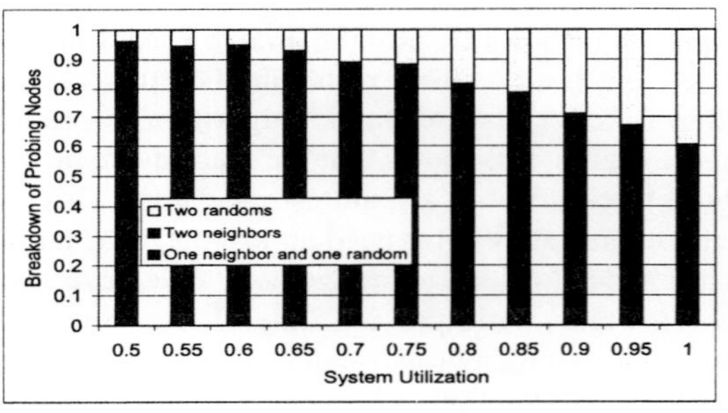

Figure 5. Breakdown of probed nodes of LAR$_2$

5.3 Effect of D-Way Random Probing

We tested the performance of the LAR$_d$ algorithms with different concurrency degree d. Figure 6(a) shows that LAR$_2$ has much less probing time than LAR$_1$. It implies that LAR$_2$ reduces the probing time of LAR$_1$ at the cost of more number of probings. Unlike LAR$_1$, in LAR$_2$, a probing node only sends its SSL to a node with more total free capacity in its DSL between two probed nodes. The more item transfers in one load rearrangement, the less probing time. It leads to less number of SSL sending operation of LAR$_2$ than LAR$_1$, resulting in less number of load rearrangements as shown in Figure 6(b). Therefore, simultaneous probings to get a node with more total free capacity in its DSL can save load balancing time and reduce network traffic load.

From Figure 6(a) and (b), we can observe that the probing efficiency of LAR$_d$ (d>2) is almost the same as LAR$_2$, though they need to probe more nodes than LAR$_2$. Our results are almost in consistent with the observations of randomized algorithms in parallel computing that a two-way probing method leads to an exponential improvement over one-way probing, but a d-way (d>2) probing leads to much less substantial additional improvement [5]. In the following, we will show whether the improvement of LAR$_d$ ($d \geq 2$) over LAR$_1$ is at the cost of more bandwidth consumption or locality-aware performance degradation. Figure 6(c) and (d) show experiment results in "ts5k-large". We can see from Figure 6(c) that the probing bandwidth of LAR_2 is almost the same as LAR_1. Figure 6(d) shows the moved load distribution in global load balancing of each algorithm. We can see that the distribution of LAR_2 is proximately the same as LAR_1, and their performance is better than that of LAR_4 and LAR_6, which are almost the same. This is caused by the fact that the more simultaneous probed nodes, the less possibility that the best primary node is a close neighbor node. Based on these results, we can conclude that LAR_2 improves on LAR_1 at no cost of bandwidth consumption. It retains the advantage of locality-aware probing.

Figure 6(e) and (f) show the performance of each algorithm "ts5k-small". The nodes in "ts5k-small" are scattered all over the network. This feature leads to less significant result in Figure 6(f). However, we can get the same conclusions as those in "ts5k-large".

5.4 Load Balancing in Systems with Churn

In practice, nodes and items continually join and leave P2P systems. It is hard to achieve load balance with churn because of two facts. First, before a node leaves, it transfers all its items to its neighbor, which becomes overloaded if it cannot provide sufficient capacity for those items. Second, continuous and fast file joins increase the probability of overloaded nodes generation. These require an load balancing algorithm to find nodes with sufficient free capacity for excess items quickly in order to keep load balance condition in churn.

We evaluated the efficiency of the LAR algorithms in dynamic situations with respect to a number of performance factors. Experiment results verified the superiority of the algorithm in DHTs with churn, in comparison with a churn resilient algorithm (CRA) proposed in [2]. Due to space constrains, we present a summary of experimental results in this section; more details can be found in [9]. In this experiment, We run each trial of the simulation for 20T simulated seconds, where T is a parameterized load balancing period, and it was set to 60 seconds in our test. The item join/departure rate was modelled by a Poisson process with a rate of 0.4; that is, there were one item join and one item departure every 2.5 seconds. The system utilization of system was set to 0.8. We adopted the same metrics as in [2]:

(1) *99.9th percentile node utilization (99.9th NU).* We measure the maximum 99.9th percentile of the utilizations of the nodes after each load balancing period T in simulation and take the average of those results over a 20T period as the 99.9th NU.
(2) *Load movement factor*, defined as the load moved movement factor corresponding to the 99.9th NU.
(3) *Load moved/DHT load moved (L/DHT-L)*, defined as the total load moved incurred due to load balancing divided by the total load of items moved due to node joins and departures in the system.

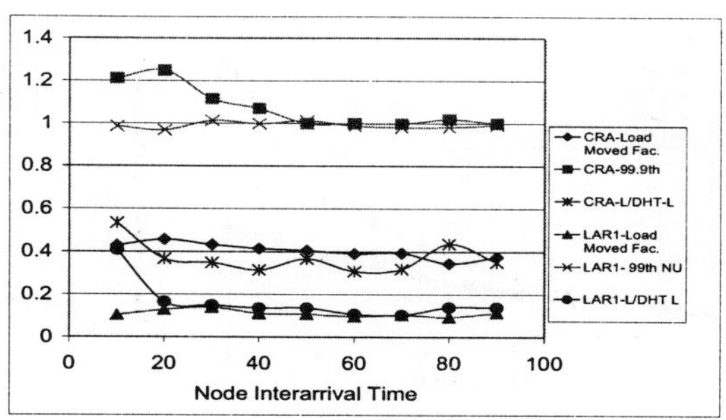

Figure 7. Effect of load balancing with churn

Figure 7 plots the performance due to LAR_1 and CRA versus node interarrival time. By comparing results of LAR_1 and CRA, we can have a number of observations. First, the 99.9th NUs of LAR_1 and CRA are kept no more than 1 and 1.25 respectively. This implies that on average, LAR_1 can achieve the load balancing goal in churn. Second, LAR_1 moves up to 20% and CRA moves up to 45% of the system load to achieve load balance for system utilization as high as 80%. Third, the load moved due to load balancing is very small compared with the load moved due to node joins and departures and it is up to 0.4 for LAR_1 and 0.53 for CRA. When the node interarrival time is 10, the L/DHT-L is the highest. It is because faster node joins and departures generate much higher degree of load imbalance, such that more load transferred is needed to achieve load balance. The fact that the results of LAR_1 are comparable to CRA implies that LAR algorithm is as efficient as CRA to handle churn. In summary, in the face of rapid arrivals and departures of items of widely varying load and nodes of widely varying capacity, LAR algorithm achieves load balance while moving up to 20% of the load that arrives into the system, and up to 40% of the load the underlying DHT moves due to node arrivals and departures. It ensures a load balance condition even in churn.

6 Conclusions

This paper presents LAR load balancing algorithms to deal with both of the proximity and dynamic features of DHTs. The algorithms distribute application load among the nodes by "moving items" according to node capacities, as well as node proximity information in topology-aware DHTs. We introduce a factor of randomness in the probing process in a range of proximity to deal with DHT churn. We further improve the randomized load balancing efficiency by d-way probing. Simulation results show the superiority of a locality-aware 2-way randomized load balancing in DHTs with and without churn.

We note that the load balancing algorithms work for key distribution load balancing. In file sharing P2P systems,

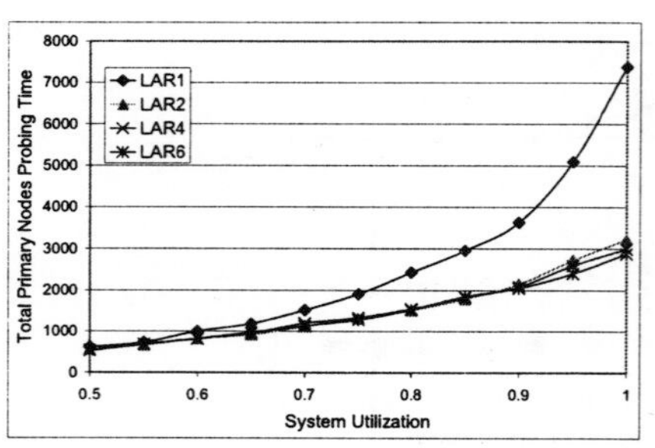

(a) Total primary node probing time "ts5k-large"

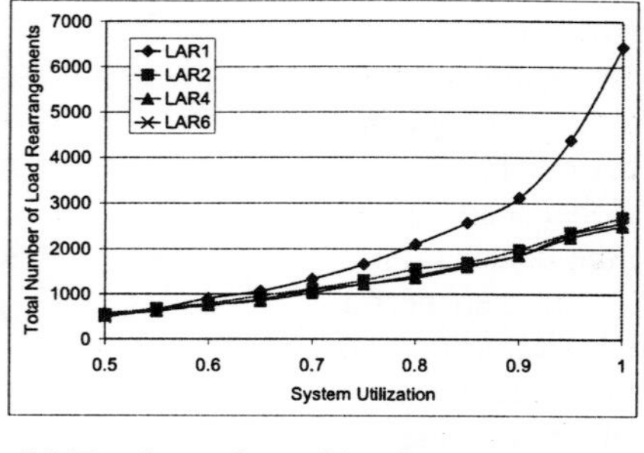

(b) Total number of load rearrangements "ts5k-large"

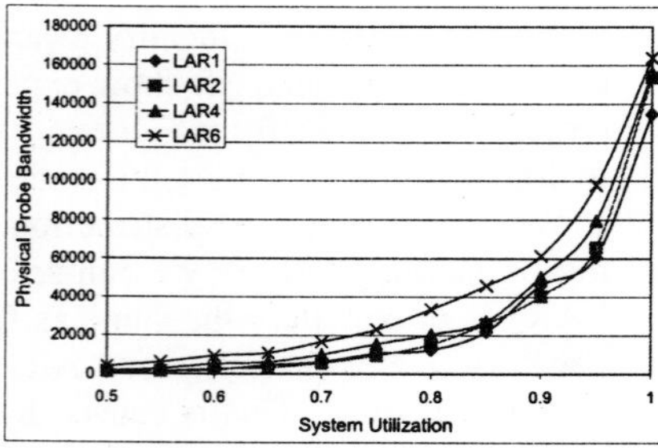

(c) Total bandwidth of probings in "ts5k-large"

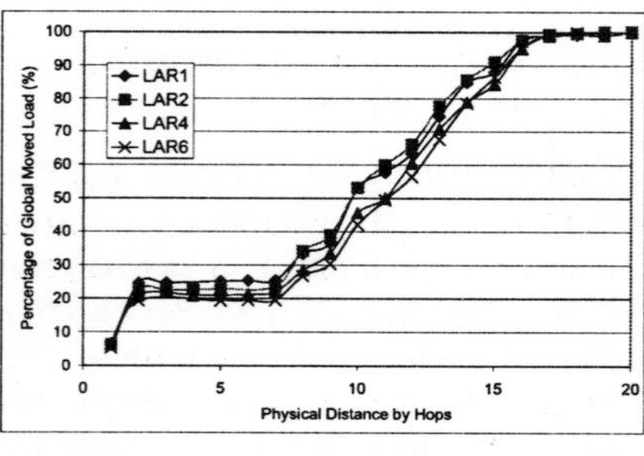

(d) CDF of moved load distribution in "ts5k-large"

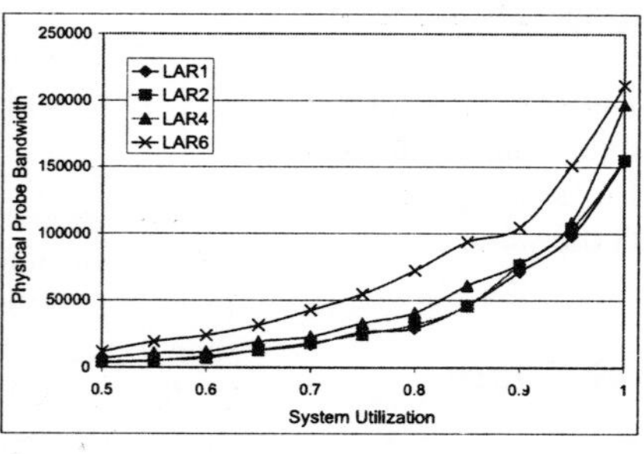

(e) Total bandwidth of probings in "ts5k-small"

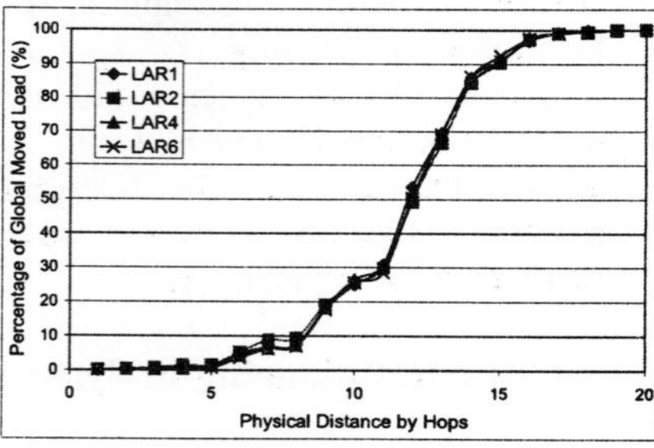

(f) CDF of moved load distribution in "ts5k-small"

Figure 6. Effect of load balancing due to different LAR algorithms

a main function of nodes is to handle key location query. Query load balancing is a critical part of P2P load balancing; that is, the number of queries that nodes receive, handle and forward is based on their different capacities accordingly. We will explore methods for this.

Acknowledgments

This research was supported in part by U.S. NSF grant ACI-0203592 and NASA grant 03-OBPR-01-0049.

References

[1] Y. Azar, A. Broder, A. Karlin, and E. Upfal. Balanced allocations. In *Proc. of ACM STOC*, pages 593–602, 1994.

[2] B. Godfrey, K. Lakshminarayanan, S. Surana, R. Karp, and I. Stoica. Load balancing in dynamic structured p2p systems. In *Proc. of IEEE INFOCOM*, 2004.

[3] D. Karger, E. Lehman, T. Leighton, M. Levine, D. Lewin, and P. R. Consistent hashing and random trees: Distributed caching protocols for relieving hot spots on the World Wide Web. In *Proc. of STOC*, pages 654–663, 1997.

[4] D. R. Karger and M. Ruhl. Simple efficient load balancing algorithms for peer-to-peer systems. In *Proc. of IPTPS*, 2004.

[5] M. Mitzenmacher. On the analysis of randomized load balancing schemes. In *Proc. of the 9th ACM SPAA*, pages 292–301, 1997.

[6] A. Rao, K. Lakshminarayanan, S. Surana, R. Karp, and I. Stoica. Load balancing in structured p2p systems. In *Proc. of IPTPS*, 2003.

[7] S. Ratnasamy, P. Francis, M. Handley, R. Karp, and S. Shenker. A scalable content-addressable network. In *Proc. of ACM SIGCOMM*, pages 329–350, 2001.

[8] A. Rowstron and P. Druschel. Pastry: Scalable, decentralized object location and routing for large-scale peer-to-peer systems. In *Proc. of IFIP/ACM Middleware*, 2001.

[9] H. Shen and C. Xu. Locality-aware randomized load balancing algorithms for structured p2p systems. Technical report, ECE Department, Wayne State University, 2004.

[10] H. Shen, C. Xu, and G. Chen. Cycloid: A scalable constant-degree p2p overlay network. *Performance Evaluation*, 2005.

[11] I. Stoica, R. Morris, D. Liben-Nowell, D. R. Karger, M. F. Kaashoek, F. Dabek, and H. Balakrishnan. Chord: A scalable peer-to-peer lookup protocol for Internet applications. *IEEE/ACM Transactions on Networking*, 1(1):17–32.

[12] K. Whitehouse, C. Sharp, E. Brewer, and D. Culler. Hood: A neighborhood abstraction for sensor networks. In *Proc. of MOBISYS*, 2004.

[13] Z. Xu, C. Tang, and Z. Zhang. Building topology-aware overlays using global soft-state. In *Proc. of ICDCS*, 2003.

[14] B. Yang and H. Garcia-Molina. Designing a super-peer network. In *Proc. of ICDE*, 2003.

[15] E. Zegura, K. Calvert, and S. Bhattacharjee. How to model an internetwork. In *Proc. of IEEE INFOCOM*, 1996.

[16] Y. Zhu and Y. Hu. Towards efficient load balancing in structured p2p systems. In *Proc. of IPDPS*, 2004.

Session 7C: Algorithms & Applications

Filter Decomposition for Supporting Coarse-Grained Pipelined Parallelism

Wei Du Gagan Agrawal
Department of Computer Science and Engineering, Ohio State University, Columbus OH 43210
duw@cse.ohio-state.edu, agrawal@cse.ohio-state.edu

ABSTRACT

We consider the *filter decomposition* problem in supporting coarse-grained pipelined parallelism. This form of parallelism is suitable for data-driven applications in scenarios where the data is available on a repository or a data collection site on the internet, and the final results are required on a user's desktop. A filter decomposition algorithm takes an application divided into a sequence of *atomic filters*, and maps them into a given number of *filters*.

We propose three polynomial time algorithms for this problem. Dynamic programming algorithm MIN_ONETRIP optimizes the one trip cost for a packet passing through the pipeline. MIN_BOTTLENECK is also a dynamic programming algorithm, which minimizes the time spent on the bottleneck stage. Finally, MIN_TOTAL is an approximate greedy algorithm which tries to minimize the total execution time.

The results show that our heuristic algorithms work quite well in practice, with the possible exception of MIN_ONETRIP when the number of packets is large. However, the relative performance of the algorithms is not always what we would expect, because of the certain limitations in how we model the problem.

1. INTRODUCTION

The work presented in this paper is in the context of *coarse-grained pipelined parallelism*. Two recent trends are making this form of parallelism feasible and desirable. The first one is the advent of grid computing. A grid environment facilitates better sharing of data and compute resources. Particularly, the availability of data repositories and access to data collection instruments and sensors is creating a new scenario for execution of many applications [23, 21].

The second trend is the proliferation of a new class of data-driven or data-intensive applications. Processing and analyzing large volumes of data plays an increasingly important role in many domains of scientific research, including scientific data analysis, data mining, data visualization, and image analysis [17, 27, 24, 18, 20, 15, 19, 1, 10]. Business decisions today are also largely driven by analysis of data. Various data mining and On Line Analytical Processing (OLAP) techniques are used in decision support systems. One example is the creation of *virtual organizations*, which comprise a large body of institutions or entities sharing and analyzing information [11]. These applications are typically both compute and data intensive, and require fast or interactive response time.

A coarse-grained pipelined execution model provides a good solution for executing such data-intensive applications in scenarios where the data is available on a repository or a data collection site on the internet, and the final results are required on a user's desktop. It is usually not possible to perform all analysis at the site hosting such a shared data repository or a data collection instrument. Similarly, networking and storage limitations make it impractical to download all data at a single site before the actual processing. Thus, the application needs to be broken into several stages, with one stage residing on the site hosting or collecting the data, one or more stages executing on clusters or SMP machines, and a final stage sitting on the user's local machine.

Many research groups have developed runtime support and scheduling techniques for this class of applications [3, 25, 28]. In recent work, we have developed language and compiler support for this form of parallelism [9], and also have addressed issues in optimizing packet size [8].

In this paper, we focus on an important issue arising in any runtime or compilation system that supports such an execution, which is *filter decomposition*. Simply put, it is the problem of partitioning a given application into a set of stages, so as to achieve the best performance. More technically, we have an application divided into a sequence of *atomic filters*. We need to map these atomic filters into *filters*, such that the number of filters equals the number of stages in the pipeline. The total execution time for pipelined execution is roughly the sum of the time taken by one packet to traverse the pipeline, and the time taken by all packets at the *bottleneck* stage. This complicates the problem of performing filter decomposition to achieve the minimum execution time.

We consider this problem in the context of a runtime system or a profile-driven compilation system. In such an environment, the amount of computation in each atomic filter and the volume of communication between consecutive atomic filters are given. Similarly, the computing power for each stage and the available communication bandwidth between consecutive stages are known. Given such information, we can predict the execution time for a certain decomposition. However, there are an exponential number of possible decomposition choices. Therefore, enumerating all choices and finding an optimal one is extremely expensive.

We propose three polynomial time algorithms for this problem. Dynamic programming algorithm MIN_ONETRIP optimizes the one trip cost for a packet passing through the pipeline. MIN_BOTTLENECK is also a dynamic programming algorithm, which minimizes the time spent on the bottleneck stage. Finally, MIN_TOTAL is an approximate greedy algorithm which tries to minimize the total execution time.

We have evaluated these algorithms with three applications and different configurations. As the results, these heuristic algorithms work quite well in practice, with the possible exception of MIN_ONETRIP when the number of packets is large. However, the relative performance of the algorithms is not always what we would expect, because of certain limitations in modeling the problem.

Our work is being implemented and evaluated using DataCutter, which is an existing runtime system for supporting pipelined parallelism in a grid environment [5, 3]. Specifically, DataCutter supports a *filter-stream* model of execution. Typically, one filter executes one stage of the pipeline, using one or more input *streams*. The results of the processing are packed and sent as one or more output *streams*.

The rest of the paper is organized as follows. The filter decomposition problem is formally defined in Section 2, followed by our proposed three algorithms in Section 3. Section 4 focuses on the experimental evaluation of our algorithms. We compare our work with related research efforts in Section 5 and conclude in Section 6.

2. FILTER DECOMPOSITION PROBLEM

To execute an application in the coarse-grained pipelined fashion, an important initial step is to decompose the application into filters. The number of these filters needs to be equal to the number of stages in the environment available for execution. In performing

0190-3918/05 $20.00 © 2005 IEEE

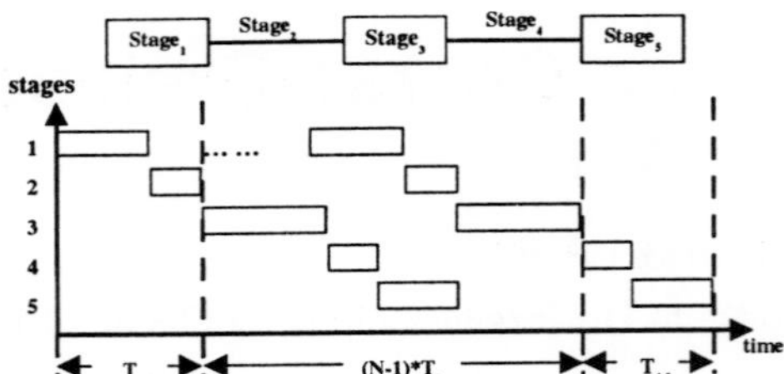

Figure 1: Execution Time-line of a Pipeline with Three Computation Stages and Two Communication Stages. $Stage_3$ is the bottleneck stage.

the decomposition, our goal is to minimize the overall execution time. This execution time depends on the the amount of computation in each filter and the volume of communication between consecutive filters.

The input to our filter decomposition algorithms is a program that is divided into a sequence of *atomic filters*. Typically, the number of such atomic filters is much larger than the number of stages in the execution environment, or the number of filters we need to generate. In our earlier work, we had described how our compiler could obtain the sequence of atomic filters from a data parallel program [9]. Alternatively, an application developer may also specify such atomic filters. We are assuming that filter decomposition decisions are made at runtime or in a profile-driven compiler. Therefore, in such a scenario, the amount of computation in each atomic filter and the volume of communication between consecutive atomic filters are known. Similarly, the computing power for each stage and the available communication bandwidth between consecutive stages are known.

In this section, we define the filter decomposition problem formally. Initially, we state the cost model we use for comparing different filter decompositions.

2.1 Cost Model

Consider a pipeline of m computing units, denoted by $C_1, \ldots, C_m$, and let the connection between units C_i and C_{i+1} be denoted by L_i. In total, there are $2 * m - 1$ stages in the pipeline. Suppose N packets are to be processed on the pipeline. We want to calculate the total execution time.

For simplicity, we assume that each packet is of the same size, the computing power at a given computation stage remains unchanged during the execution, and similarly, bandwidth offered by a given communication stage remains unchanged. Further, we assume that processing time is independent of the data. Thus, each packet takes the same amount of time on a given computing or communication stage.

The expression for execution time is based upon the notion of *bottleneck stage*. This is the stage whose processing rate is the slowest, and therefore, is always busy since the first packet is received, and before the last packet exits. We denote the *bottleneck stage* as b^{th} stage in the pipeline.

The total execution time comprises two components, the time taken by one packet to reach from the start of the pipeline to the end, and the time spent by all but one packet at the bottleneck. Let the time spent by one packet at $stage_i$ be denoted by T_i. Then, the total execution time is

$$T = \sum_{i=1}^{2*m-1} T_i + (N-1) \times T_b \qquad (1)$$

Figure 1 shows the execution time-line of a pipeline consisting of three computing stages and two communication stages.

2.2 Filter Decomposition Problem

Let the application comprise n atomic filters, $f_1, \ldots, f_n$. Then, we can denote the application as a two-tuple

$$Appl = (Comp, Comm),$$

where,

- $Comp$ is a vector characterizing the computation workload of each atomic filter.
  $$Comp = < Comp_{f_1}, \ldots, Comp_{f_n} > .$$
  The term $Comp_{f_i}$ represents the computation workload of the ith atomic filter f_i.
- Similarly, $Comm$ is a vector describing the communication amount between two consecutive atomic filters.
  $$Comm = < Comm_{f_1}, \ldots, Comm_{f_n} > .$$
  The term $Comp_{f_i}$ denotes the communication volume from the atomic filter f_i to f_{i+1}. Note that the term $Comm_{f_n}$ represents the amount of data to be transfered by the atomic filter f_n, if f_n is not placed on the last stage of the pipeline.

As we stated previously, we have m computing units in a pipeline $C_1, \ldots, C_m$, which are connected by $m-1$ communication links $L_1, \ldots, L_{m-1}$. For the computing unit C_i, the computing power is denoted by $P(C_i)$, and for the communication link L_i, the available network bandwidth is denoted by $B(L_i)$. Note that some of the computing units in our pipeline can be parallel machines, like a cluster or an SMP machine. In our description, such a possibility is captured by associating a higher computing power with the unit.

Now, we want to choose a placement for these n atomic filters over the m computing units, such that the total execution time for the pipeline is minimal. Let $\wp(f_1, \ldots, f_n)$ be a placement, then

$$\wp(f_1, \ldots, f_n) = (\mathcal{F}_1, \ldots, \mathcal{F}_m)$$

where

$$\mathcal{F}_i = f_{i_1, i_1+1, \ldots, i_k}$$

i.e., atomic filters $f_{i_1}, f_{i_1+1}, \ldots, f_{i_k}$ are merged together, and placed on computing unit C_i, for $1 \leq i_1, i_k \leq n$. Thus, by Equation 1, the total execution time for placement $\wp(f_1, \ldots, f_n)$ can be expressed as

$$\begin{aligned} T_{\wp(f_1,\ldots,f_n)} &= \sum_{i=1}^{2*m-1} T_i + (N-1) \times T_b \\ &= \sum_{i=1}^{m} Cost\_comp(P(C_i), Comp_{\mathcal{F}_i}) + \\ &\quad \sum_{i=1}^{m-1} Cost\_comm(B(L_i), Comm_{\mathcal{F}_i}) + \\ &\quad (N-1) \times T_b \qquad (2) \end{aligned}$$

where,

$$\begin{aligned} T_b &= max\{\max_{i=1,\ldots,m} Cost\_comp(P(C_i), Comp_{\mathcal{F}_i}), \\ &\quad \max_{i=1,\ldots,m-1} Cost\_comm(B(L_i), Comm_{\mathcal{F}_i})\}. \qquad (3) \end{aligned}$$

Here, the function *Cost_comp* takes the power of a computing unit and the computation task of a filter as inputs, and returns the time of execution. The function *Cost_comm* takes bandwidth of a communication link and the communication volume as parameters, and outputs the time of communication. The term T_b represents the execution time of the bottleneck stage, which is the most time-consuming stage among all the computation and communication stages.

Our goal is to find a placement $\overline{\wp}(f_1, \ldots, f_n)$, such that $T_{\overline{\wp}(f_1,\ldots,f_n)}$ is, or is very close to, the minimal execution time.

3. ALGORITHMS FOR FILTER DECOMPOSITION

This section presents several algorithms for the filter decomposition problem, as defined in the previous section.

Recall that we need to group n atomic filters into m stages. Alternatively, the problem can be viewed as of inserting $m-1$ boundaries between $n-1$ candidate boundaries. An exhaustive search will involve considering C_{m-1}^{n+m-1} placements. This term is exponential in the value of m. To avoid such an exhaustive search, we present three algorithms in the following subsections. These three algorithms are:

- MIN_ONETRIP is a dynamic programming algorithm that minimizes the time taken by one packet to traverse the pipeline. Therefore, it assumes that the time spent on the bottleneck stage is not dominant. The time complexity for this algorithm is $O(nm)$.
- MIN_BOTTLENECK is also a dynamic programming algorithm that minimizes the time spent by all packets at the bottleneck stage. Therefore, it assumes that the time spent by one packet to traverse the pipeline is not dominant. The time complexity for this algorithm is $O(n^2m)$.
- MIN_TOTAL is a heuristic greedy algorithm that minimizes the overall execution time, with time complexity is $O(nm)$.

3.1 MIN_ONETRIP Algorithm

The focus of this algorithm is on optimizing the single trip cost, that is, the cost for one packet passing through the entire pipeline. In the context of Equation 2, we optimize the sum of the first two terms. We can formulate the problem as following:

Problem: We are given an application

$$Appl = (Comp, Comm),$$

and a pipeline of m computing resources, which are connected by $m-1$ communication links. We want to find a placement $\overline{\wp}(f_1, \dots, f_n) = (\mathcal{F}_1, \dots, \mathcal{F}_m)$, such that $\sum_{i=1}^{2*m-1} T_i$ is optimal, where

$$T_i = Cost\_comp(P(C_i), Comp_{\mathcal{F}_i})$$

for a computation stage, or

$$T_i = Cost\_comm(B(L_i), Comm_{\mathcal{F}_i})$$

for a communication stage.

We present a dynamic programming algorithm which can minimize this cost. The algorithm is based on the following observation. To get the final results on the last computing unit C_m, we can either put the last atomic filter f_n on it, or we can finish all the computations in the first $m-1$ computing units and then transmit the final results to C_m. Similarly, after determining the placement of the filter f_n, say on C_m, we can either put filter f_{n-1} on C_m, or we can finish all the work from f_1 to f_{n-1} before the computation reaches C_m, and then forward the results of f_{n-1} to C_m.

Let $T[i,j]$ denote the minimum cost of doing computations up to f_i on computing units $C_1, \dots, C_j$, while the results of f_i are on C_j. Thus, the lowest cost of completing all n filters on m computing units would be $T[n,m]$.

We can define $T[i,j]$ recursively as follows. The atomic filter f_i can either be placed on C_j while all computations up to f_{i-1} are completed before it, or it can be finished on previous $j-1$ computing units and the results are forwarded to C_j. So, we have

$$T[i,j] = min \begin{cases} T[i-1,j] + Cost\_comp(P(C_j), Comp_{f_i}) \\ T[i,j-1] + Cost\_comm(B(L_{j-1}), Comm_{f_i}) \end{cases}$$

Our algorithm is outlined in Figure 2. To calculate $T[n,m]$, the algorithm needs to fill in all cells in the $(n+1) \times (m+1)$ matrix E. Since it takes $O(1)$ time to compute each cell, the total execution time of the algorithm is $O(mn)$.

Even though we use a $(n+1) \times (m+1)$ matrix to record E in the algorithm, we only need to consider the values in $E[i-1,j]$ and $E[i,j-1]$ for computing $E[i,j]$. Also, we can write back $E[i,j]$ in the cell used by $E[i-1,j]$, after $E[i,j]$ is computed. Thus, the algorithm only has a space complexity of $O(m)$.

```
GetPlacement(Sol)
local Array map;
{*start from Sol[n,m], fill the array map*}
while ! (the first row or first column of Sol)
    if Sol[i,j] == 2
        set current element of map to i;
        i - -;
    else
        set current element of map to "|";
        j - -;
output ( the inverse of array map);
```

Figure 3: GetPlacement Procedure for Outputting the Placement from MIN_ONETRIP Algorithm

To get the placement leading to the lowest cost, we use an array Sol, as shown in Figure 2. The element $Sol[i,j]$ notes which one of the two terms, $E[i-1,j]$ or $E[i,j-1]$, is chosen when computing the value of $E[i,j]$. If $E[i,j-1]$ is chosen, $Sol[i,j]$ is set to 2, which means atomic filter f_i and f_{i+1} will not be placed on the same computing unit. On the other hand, if $E[i-1,j]$ is chosen, $Sol[i,j]$ is set to 1. Based on the information stored in array Sol, we can extract the optimal placement. This is described by the psuedo-code in Figure 3. The procedure utilizes an extra array map. It starts from $Sol[n,m]$, and sets values for elements in map one by one. Here, "|" denotes a separation between atomic filters f_i and f_{i+1}.

We use the following example to illustrate the algorithm.

Example 1: We are given an application $AppE$ with six atomic filters,

$$AppE = (< 200, 500, 800, 400, 200, 300 >, \\ < 100, 500, 1500, 200, 200, 500 >)$$

and a pipeline of three computing resources, which are connected by two communication links. It is required that f_1 must be placed on C_1, since we always assume the pipeline starts from the site hosting datasets. Here the $Comp$ and $Comm$ are the execution time of atomic filters on a particular machine C, or the data transmission time on a particular link L, in μs. Then, the power of computing units and the bandwidth of communication links on the pipeline are specified in terms of machine C and link L. Suppose the power of the computing units, relative to C, are 2, 3, and 1, respectively. And the bandwidth of the connection links are 1 and 0.6, with respect to L.

Following the MIN_ONETRIP algorithm in Figure 2, suppose we already have the matrix E, such that,

$$E = \begin{pmatrix} \infty & 0 & 0 & 0 \\ \infty & 100 & 200 & 366.667 \\ \infty & 350 & \ddots & \\ \vdots & \vdots & & \ddots \end{pmatrix}$$

We want to calculate $E[2,2]$, that is the minimum cost for executing atomic filters f_1 and f_2 over computing units C_1 and C_2. For this purpose, we need to consider two conditions: 1) both f_1 and f_2 are on C_1; and 2) f_1 on C_1, f_2 on C_2. The latter case is covered by $E[1,2]$, and the first is by $E[2,1]$. So,

$$E[2,2] = min\{350 + 500/1, 200 + 500/3\} = 366.667\mu s$$

After executing the algorithm, we get the placement

$$\overline{\wp}(f_1, \dots, f_n) = (f_1, f_{2-5}, f_6).$$

```
MIN_ONETRIP {
  Inputs:
    An application Appl, Appl = (Comp, Comm)
    A sequence of m computing units C_1, ..., C_m with computing powers P(C_1), ..., P(C_m)
    A sequence of m − 1 network links L_1, ..., L_{m−1} with bandwidths B(L_1), ..., B(L_{m−1})
  Goal:
    E[n, m]

  Array E[0···n, 0···m];
  {* init *}
  for j ← 0 to m { E[0, j] = 0; }
  for i ← 0 to n { E[i, 0] = ∞; }
  E[1, 1] = Cost_comp(P(C_1), Comp_{f_1});
  Sol[1, 1] = 2;
  {* compute E[1,j], j = 2, ..., m *}
  for j ← 2 to m
    E[1, j] = min{E[1, j − 1] + Cost_comm(B(L_{j−1}), Comm_{f_1}), E[0, j] + Cost_comp(P(C_j), Comp_{f_1})};
    Sol[1, j] = 1;
  {* compute E[i,j], i = 2, ..., n,  j = 1, ..., m *}
  for i ← 2 to n
    for j ← 1 to m
      E[i, j] = min{E[i, j − 1] + Cost_comm(B(L_{j−1}), Comm_{f_i}), E[i − 1, j] + Cost_comp(P(C_j), Comp_{f_i})};
      Sol[i, j] = which_min{E[i, j − 1] + Cost_comm(B(L_{j−1}), Comm_{f_i}), E[i − 1, j] + Cost_comp(P(C_j), Comp_{f_i})};
}
```

Figure 2: MIN_ONETRIP Algorithm for Filter Decomposition

$$N[i,j] = min\begin{cases} max\{N[i,j-1], Cost\_comm(B(L_{j-1}), Comm_{f_i})\} \\ max\{N[i-1,j-1], Cost\_comm(B(L_{j-1}), Comm_{f_{i-1}}), Cost\_comp(P(C_j), Comp_{f_i})\} \\ max\{N[i-2,j-1], Cost\_comm(B(L_{j-1}), Comm_{f_{i-2}}), Cost\_comp(P(C_j), Comp_{f_{i-1}} + Comp_{f_i})\} \\ \vdots \\ max\{N[1,j-1], Cost\_comm(B(L_{j-1}), Comm_{f_1}), Cost\_comp(P(C_j), Comp_{f_2} + \cdots + Comp_{f_i})\} \end{cases}$$

$$= min\begin{cases} max\{N[i,j-1], Cost\_comm(B(L_{j-1}), Comm_{f_i})\} \\ \max_{k=1,\ldots,i-1}\{N[i-k,j-1], Cost\_comm(B(L_{j-1}), Comm_{f_{i-k}}), \sum_{l=i-k+1}^{i} Cost\_comp(P(C_j), Comp_{f_l})\} \end{cases}$$

Figure 4: Recursive Definition of $N[i, j]$

3.2 MIN_BOTTLENECK Algorithm

This algorithm minimizes the time spent by all the packets at the bottleneck stage. Formally, we can describe the problem as follows.

Problem: We are given an application

$$Appl = (Comp, Comm),$$

and a pipeline of m computing resources, which are connected by $m-1$ communication links. We want to find a placement $\wp(f_1, \ldots, f_n) = (\mathcal{F}_1, \ldots, \mathcal{F}_m)$, such that T_b is optimal, where T_b is defined in Equation 3.

MIN_BOTTLENECK is also a dynamic programming algorithm which minimizes the time spent at the bottleneck stage. To see the approach, let us consider the placement of the final atomic filter, f_n. We have the following two options:

Option 1: The filters $f_1, \ldots, f_n$ are all placed on computing units C_1 through C_{m-1}, then the final results need to be transfered to C_m.

Option 2: The filter f_n is placed on the last computing unit of the pipeline, C_m.

To find a placement which gives the minimum cost of the bth stage, with Option 1, we only need to compare the communication cost on the last link with the bottleneck stage cost of placing $f_1, \ldots, f_n$ over $C_1, \ldots, C_{m-1}$. However, more attention should be paid when dealing with the second option. When f_n is assigned to C_m, it is possible that no other filter is on C_m. It is also possible that before assigning f_n, atomic filter f_{n-1} is already on C_m. Still, it is possible that atomic filters f_{n-2} and f_{n-1} are on C_m already. Following this pattern, we need to consider $n-1$ possibilities.

Let $N[i, j]$ denote the minimum cost of the bth stage for computing atomic filters $f_1, \ldots, f_i$ over computation pipeline $C_1, \ldots, C_j$, with the results of f_i on C_j. Hence, the lowest cost of the bottleneck stage for completing the application *Appl* will be $N[n, m]$.

Now, we can recursively define $N[i, j]$ as follows. The atomic filter f_i could be computed before the computation reaches C_j, with the resulting data being forwarded to C_j. The other choices include f_i being placed on C_j alone, f_i being placed together with f_{i-1} on C_j, f_i being placed together with f_{i-1} and f_{i-2} on C_j, and so on. Formally, we can state this as a mathematical expression, as shown in Figure 4.

The MIN_BOTTLENECK algorithm is presented in Figure 5. In order to compute $N[n, m]$, an array H of size $(n+1) \times m$ is used. As can be seen, to calculate $H[i, j]$, we always need to do i comparisons. Since each comparison can be done in $O(1)$ time, it takes $O(n)$ time to compute one element in the array H. Therefore, the total execution time of this algorithm is $O(n^2 m)$.

Although a $(n+1) \times m$ array was used for presenting the algorithm, in the actual implementation, we only need a $2 \times (n+1)$ array to store H. When computing $H[i, j]$, only $H[1, j-1], \ldots, H[i, j-1]$ are required, so after filling up the jth column, we can reuse the space taken by the $(j-1)^{th}$ column to store the $(j+1)^{th}$ column. Thus, the space complexity of the algorithm is $O(n)$.

For extracting the optimal placement, we also use an auxiliary array Sol. The element $Sol[i, j]$ records the largest numbered filter on unit C_j. That is, if we let $k = Sol[i, j]$, then filters $f_{Sol[k,j-1]+1}, \ldots, f_k$ are placed together on computing node C_j.

Running this algorithm on Example 1, we reach the placement

$$\wp(f_1, \ldots, f_n) = (f_{1-2}, f_{3-4}, f_{5-6}).$$

```
MIN_BOTTLENECK {
  Inputs:
    An application Appl, Appl = (Comp, Comm)
    A sequence of m computing units C_1, ..., C_m with computing powers P(C_1), ..., P(C_m)
    A sequence of m - 1 network links L_1, ..., L_{m-1} with bandwidths B(L_1), ..., B(L_{m-1})
  Goal:
    H[n, m - 1]

  Array H[0 ... n, 0 ... m - 1];
  {* init *}
  for j <- 0 to m - 1 { H[0,j] = 0; }
  {* compute H[i,0], i = 1, ..., n *}
  for i <- 1 to n { H[i,0] = Cost_comp(P(C_1), Σ_{k=1}^{i} Comp_{f_k}); }
  {* compute H[i,j], i = 1, ..., n,  j = 1, ..., m *}
  for j <- 1 to m - 1
    for i <- 1 to n
      H[i,j] = min{max{H[i, j - 1], Cost_comm(B(L_{j-1}), Comm_{f_i})},
                   max_{k=1,...,i-1}{H[i - k, j - 1], Cost_comm(B(L_{j-1}), Comm_{f_{i-k}}),
                   Σ_{l=i-k+1}^{i} Cost_comp(P(C_{j+1}), Comp_{f_l})}}
      Sol[i,j] = which_min{max{H[i, j - 1], Cost_comm(B(L_{j-1}), Comm_{f_i})},
                   max_{k=1,...,i-1}{H[i - k, j - 1], Cost_comm(B(L_{j-1}), Comm_{f_{i-k}}),
                   Σ_{l=i-k+1}^{i} Cost_comp(P(C_{j+1}), Comp_{f_l})}}
}
```

Figure 5: MIN_BOTTLENECK **Algorithm for Filter Decomposition**

3.3 MIN_TOTAL **Algorithm**

The previous two algorithms target different portion of the cost exposed in Equation 2. This algorithm uses a greedy heuristic to minimize the overall cost.

Our approach is as follows. Starting from the beginning of the pipeline, we successively decide the filter assignment for each of the computing unit. Our algorithm is presented in Figure 6.

The algorithm iterates to choose the filters placed on computing units C_1 through C_{m-1}. The variable $Current\_pos$ denotes the first atomic filter which has not been assigned to any computing hosts. Initially, its value is 1. For choosing filters placed on C_i, we consider all options ranging from $f_{Current\_pos}$ only to $f_{Current\_pos}, \ldots, f_n$. We estimate the execution time associated with each choice, and keep the one with the minimum value.

However, it is not possible to accurately estimate the execution time without knowing the placement of the following atomic filters. For this purpose, we take an approximation. The term $Aggregate\_Power(i)$ denotes the aggregate power of all computing units from $i+1$ to m. To estimate the cost associated with placing atomic filters $f_{Current\_pos}, \ldots, f_j$ ($j = Current\_pos, \ldots, n$) on C_i, we assume that the ith computing unit is connected with a single computing unit which has the power $Aggregate\_Power(i)$. The function $Evaluate$ uses this approximation, along with the actual computing power $P(C_i)$ and the network bandwidth $B(L_i)$.

Clearly, it is easy to get the final placement from array min_pos, since $min\_pos[i]$ actually identifies the number of the last atomic filter on C_i.

Applying the MIN_TOTAL algorithm on Example 1 in Section 3.1, assuming there are 4500 packets, we get the array $min\_pos[2] = \{2, 5\}$. Converting it to the placement, we have

$$\overline{p}(f_1, \ldots, f_n) = (f_{1-2}, f_{3-5}, f_6).$$

To summarize, the placements selected by our three algorithms for Example 1 are all among the top four most efficient ones. In fact, the MIN_ONETRIP algorithm is more suitable when we have a small number of packets. Therefore, it is not suprising that it does not produce the best results when we have 4500 packets. In contrast, the algorithm MIN_BOTTLENECK is more appropriate when the number of packets is large. The placement chosen by this algorithm is within 0.01% of the optimal. MIN_TOTAL finds the best results in this example.

4. EXPERIMENTAL RESULTS

In this section, we report results from a series of experiments conducted with the following two goals: 1) demonstrating the effectiveness of our algorithms on real applications, and 2) understanding the limitations of our current work to direct our future efforts. Before discussing the results, we first describe the experimental setting and the applications we have used.

4.1 Experimental Setting and Applications

In the long run, we expect that pipelined parallelism can be exploited in wide-area networks. Recent trends are clearly pointing in this direction, as seen by the National Lambda Rail (NLR) effort and the Optiputer project. However, for our study, we did not have access to a wide-area network that gave high bandwidth and allowed repeatable experiments. Therefore, all our experiments were conducted within a single cluster. The cluster we used had 1 GHz Pentium machines connected through Gigabit Ethernet.

We deployed three applications on a pipeline of 3 computing units connected through 2 communication links. Three configurations were simulated to represent various relative communication bandwidths at different links and varying computing power at the stages. These are shown in Table 1. The numbers on the top line of each configuration represent the relative power of the computing unit, and those on the bottom denote the relative communication bandwidth. The value 1 denotes the computing power of the 1 GHz machines or the bandwidth available in a cluster with a Gigabit Ethernet. Lower computing power was simulated by putting more work on the computing processors, and lower communication bandwidth was simulated by delaying packets on the links.

We briefly explain the rationale behind the choice of these configurations. `Config 1` is the default configuration. `Config 2` has lower and uneven communication bandwidths, and corresponds to the environment where the remote data repository is severely bandwidth limited. `Config 3` emulates the situation where both data repository and the intermediate processing unit have extremely fast processing speed and high bandwidth interconnect, relative to the user's desktop. `Config 4` shows the scenario where intermediate processing unit has the highest processing power, followed by the remote repository, and then the user's desktop.

The first application we use is Virtual Microscope. This is an emulation of a microscope which allows users to view part of the

MIN_TOTAL {
Inputs:
An application $Appl$, $Appl = (Comp, Comm)$
A sequence of m computing units $C_1, \ldots, C_m$ with computing powers $P(C_1), \ldots, P(C_m)$
A sequence of $m-1$ network links $L_1, \ldots, L_{m-1}$ with bandwidths $B(L_1), \ldots, B(L_{m-1})$

$Current\_pos = 1$
For $i = 1$ to $m-1$ do {
{ * *Place the filter boundary* i *}
$min\_cost(i) = Infinite$
$Aggregate\_Power(i) = \sum_{k=i+1}^{m} P(C_k)$
For $j = Current\_pos$ to n do {
{ * *Evaluate the cost of placing boundary* i *at candidate* j *}
$Exec\_time(i,j) =$ Evaluate($j, P(C_i), B(L_i), Aggregate\_Power(i)$)
If ($Exec\_time(i,j) < min\_cost(i)$) {
$min\_cost(i) = Exec\_time(i,j)$
$min\_pos(i) = j$
}
}
Place the boundary i at the candidate $min\_pos(i)$
$Current\_pos = min\_pos(i)$
}
}

Figure 6: MIN_TOTAL **Algorithm for Filter Decomposition**

Config 1:	1——1——1 1 1
Config 2:	1——1——1 0.1 0.5
Config 3:	1——1——0.01 1 0.001
Config 4:	0.1——1——0.01 1 0.001

Table 1: Configurations Used for Our Experiments

original image with numerous resolutions [1]. A query specifies a rectangular region and a value for the *subsampling factor* for the desired output. This application have 5 atomic filters, which are for reading original JPEG image from the disk-resident dataset, decompressing the image to RGB format, clipping the image with the user specified range, zooming the image according to the user desired resolution, and viewing the image.

Two other applications both implement isosurface rendering. They are, z-buffer based isosurface rendering and active pixels based rendering, referred to as ZBUF and ACTP, respectively. Isosurface rendering is a key visualization problem. The inputs to the problem include a three-dimensional grid, a scalar isosurface value, and a two-dimensional viewing screen associated with an angle. The goal is to view a surface, as seen from the given viewing angle, which captures the points in the grid where the scalar value matches the given isosurface value. For this application, there are 7 atomic filters in total, to fulfill the tasks ranging from reading the original images from disk, organizing them as cubes, extracting triangles out of the cubes, rastering the triangles, and finally rendering.

Note that in our implementation of different versions, we have one major difference from the cost model we have used. If two atomic filters are put together at one site, we actually merge them into one filter, saving the cost of copying between buffers. As we will observe later, this will have some impact on the effectiveness of our algorithms.

4.2 Experiments with Virtual Microscope

We use a 800 MB image for this application, which corresponds to a 29328×28800 region. We considered 3 queries on the image, which are denoted as $Q1$, $Q2$, and $Q3$, respectively. The corresponding number of packets processed in these three queries is 1, 4, and 4500. Here, one packet always contains a region of size 256×256.

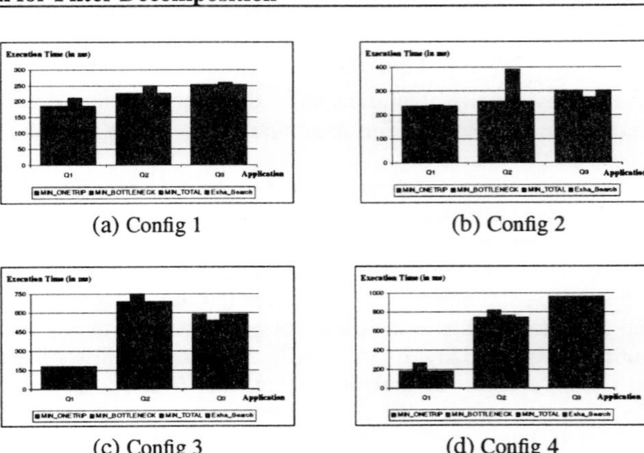

(a) Config 1 (b) Config 2 (c) Config 3 (d) Config 4

Figure 7: Execution Time for Virtual Microscope

In Table 2, we summarize the placements generated by different algorithms under four configurations for the above three queries. Besides the three algorithms we presented in the previous section, we have also shown the results obtained from the exponential exhaustive search algorithm, denoted as Exhaustive_Search.

Figures 7(a), 7(b), 7(c), and 7(d) show the actual execution times. The execution times from $Q3$ are always normalized, so that they could be shown on the same chart with other values.

Two sets of observations can be made from these results. First, the performance variance between different algorithms is very small. This helps to show the effectiveness of our heuristic polynomial-time algorithms. Second, these experiments show some limitations of our modeling of the problem, that is, the relative performance of the algorithms is not what one would expect. The Exhaustive_Search algorithm does not always perform best.

There are two major limitations of how we have modelled the problem that come into play here. We only use the execution time from one packet for each atomic filter as the input to our algorithm, assuming that it remains the same for different packets. In practice, the amount of computation in a particular atomic filter may vary from packet to packet. Also, in our cost model, when we put two atomic filters f_1 and f_2 on the same computing unit C_1, the new execution time on C_1 is calculated as the sum of execution time of each individual filter. However, in our actual implementation, we

Query	Algorithm	Config 1			Config 2			Config 3			Config 4		
		C_1	C_2	C_3	C_1	C_2	C_3	C_1	C_2	C_3	C_1	C_2	C_3
Q1	MIN_ONETRIP	f_{1-4}		f_5	f_{1-4}		f_5	f_{1-4}	f_5		f_1	f_{2-5}	
	MIN_BOTTLENECK	f_{1-4}		f_5	f_{1-4}		f_5	f_{1-4}		f_5	f_1	f_{2-4}	f_5
	MIN_TOTAL	f_{1-4}	f_5		f_{1-4}	f_5		f_{1-4}	f_5		f_1	f_{2-5}	
	Exhaustive_Search	f_{1-4}		f_5	f_{1-4}		f_5	f_{1-4}	f_5		f_1	f_{2-5}	
Q2	MIN_ONETRIP	f_{1-3}		f_{4-5}	f_{1-3}		f_{4-5}	f_{1-3}	f_{4-5}		f_{1-3}	f_{4-5}	
	MIN_BOTTLENECK	f_{1-3}		f_{4-5}	f_{1-3}		f_{4-5}	f_{1-3}		f_{4-5}	f_1	f_{2-3}	f_{4-5}
	MIN_TOTAL	f_{1-3}	f_4	f_5	f_{1-3}	f_{4-5}		f_{1-3}	f_{4-5}		f_1	f_{2-5}	
	Exhaustive_Search	f_{1-3}		f_{4-5}	f_{1-3}		f_{4-5}	f_{1-3}	f_{4-5}		f_{1-3}	f_{4-5}	
Q3	MIN_ONETRIP	f_{1-4}		f_5	f_{1-4}		f_5	f_{1-4}	f_5		f_{1-4}	f_5	
	MIN_BOTTLENECK	f_{1-4}		f_5	f_{1-4}		f_5	f_{1-4}		f_5	f_1	f_{2-4}	f_5
	MIN_TOTAL	f_{1-4}	f_5		f_{1-4}	f_5		f_{1-4}	f_5		f_1	f_{2-5}	
	Exhaustive_Search	f_{1-4}		f_5	f_{1-4}		f_5	f_{1-4}	f_5		f_1	f_{2-5}	

Table 2: Placements Generated by Different Algorithms: Virtual Microscope

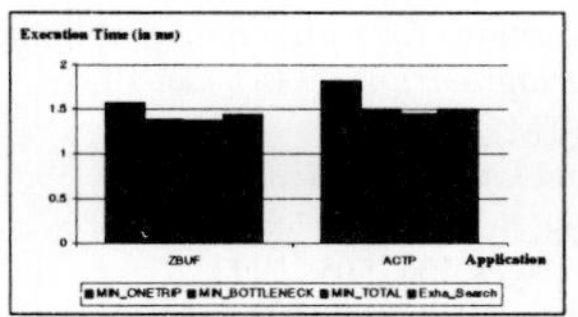

(a) Small Dataset

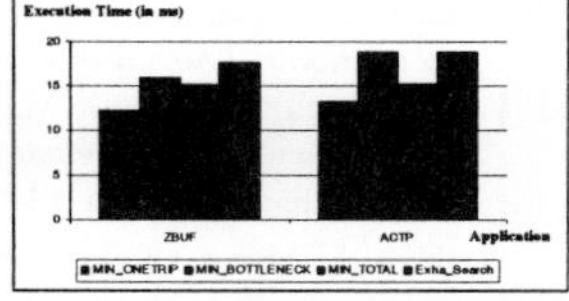

(b) Large Dataset

Figure 8: Execution Time of ZBUF and ACTP

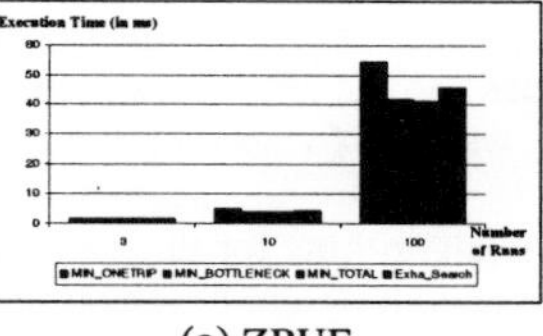

(a) ZBUF

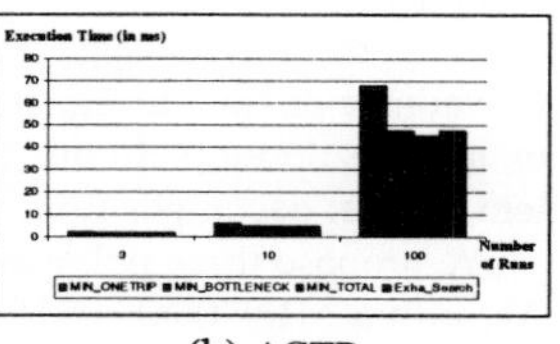

(b) ACTP

Figure 9: Execution Time for Multiple Runs with the Same Packet

generate a new filter that avoids the copying between the buffers. Therefore, the time taken by the new filter is less than the time required by f_1 plus the time required by f_2.

4.3 Experiments with Iso-Surface

There are two datasets we used for this set of experiments, which were generated by an environmental simulator ParSSim [2] and were previously used in earlier studies also [4, 9, 8]. These datasets comprised grid data for 10 time-steps, and were 1.5 GB and 6 GB, respectively. The two datasets are referred to as `small` and `large` datasets. We report experiments on processing a single time-step, the data corresponding to which is 150 MB and 600 MB for these two datasets. The number of packets involved in the processing of `small` dataset is 3, and that for the `large` dataset is 47. For Iso-surface, we only report results from `Config 1`, as the trends from all configurations were very similar.

Query	Algorithm	Placement		
		C_1	C_2	C_3
ZBUF	MIN_ONETRIP	f_1		f_{2-7}
	MIN_BOTTLENECK	f_{1-2}	f_{3-4}	f_{5-7}
	MIN_TOTAL	f_{1-3}	f_4	f_{5-7}
	Exhaustive_Search	f_1	f_{2-4}	f_{5-7}
ACTP	MIN_ONETRIP	f_1		f_{2-7}
	MIN_BOTTLENECK	f_{1-4}	f_5	f_{6-7}
	MIN_TOTAL	f_{1-3}	f_4	f_{5-7}
	Exhaustive_Search	f_{1-4}	f_5	f_{6-7}

Table 3: Placements Generated by Different Algorithms: Iso-Surface Rendering, Config 1

In Table 3, we list the placements generated by different algorithms for the two versions of Iso-surface, `ZBUF` and `ACTP`. Figures 8(a) and 8(b) plot the actual execution time of the application on two datasets, with the placement selected by our algorithms.

As we can see, the difference in the performance of the algorithms is limited. The MIN_TOTAL algorithm always finds a placement which performs best for the `small` dataset, while the algorithm MIN_ONETRIP provides the best performance for the `large` dataset. In both the cases, the exhaustive search algorithm does not generate the most efficient placement. The main reason is that the Iso-surface rendering application is very data dependent, which introduces more variance for different packets.

To further understand the impact of data dependence, we performed additional experiments. Figures 9(a) and 9(b) show the execution time when the same packet is processed multiple times, based on the placements generated by our algorithms. As we can see, the results are much closer to our expectations. The performance of the exhaustive search algorithm is either the best, or very close to the best. Because MIN_ONETRIP models only a small part of the cost when the number of packets is large, its performance is the worst with 100 runs with the same packet. The performance of both MIN_TOTAL and MIN_BOTTLENECK is very similar to the exhaustive search one.

4.4 Discussion

On the positive side, our results have shown that our heuristic algorithms can perform quite well in practice. However, our results have also shown limitations of our model. So, in our future work, we will try to model the following two aspects of the applications:

- Estimate of the performance change resulting from combining several atomic filters and avoiding the cost of copying between the buffers.
- Estimate of the impact of data dependence on the performance for each atomic filter.

Clearly, these characteristics can be very application dependent and hard to model. For example, we could try to limit the data impact by using the average execution time of all packets on a certain atomic filter. Still, our model may not be accurate, especially if there is a large variance in the processing time for each packet. Further, we need to experiment with applications having a larger number of atomic filters and/or configurations with more stages, to gain additional insights about these algorithms.

5. RELATED WORK

We are not aware of any previous work on filter decomposition with the same cost model as we have considered. However, the component of the cost model that is minimized by our MIN_BOTTLENECK algorithm has been used as the cost function by several other efforts. Bokhari *et al.* initially provided a $O(n^3m)$ solution to this problem [6, 7]. This was subsequently improved to

$O(n^2m)$ by Hansen [12] and Nicol [22]. Our MIN_BOTTLENECK algorithm has the same complexity. Our main contribution in this work is the overall treatment of the problem and the other algorithms we have presented, as well as experimental evaluation of each of these algorithms. Also, many researchers have considered somewhat different versions of the problem. A faster but approximate algorithm for the same problem was developed by Iqbal [14]. Sheu and Chiang considered a generalization [26], whereas, Hsu presented an algorithm having a merge phase and an assignment phase [13]. Chan and Young even answered the *decision* version of the problem and found the optimal solution with minimal number of processors [16, 29].

6. CONCLUSIONS

The work presented here has been in the context of coarse-grained pipelined execution model. This model is very suitable for the execution of data-driven applications in an environment where the data is available on remote data repositories and the results are desirable on a user's desktop. In this context, we have focused on the problem of filter decomposition.

We propose three polynomial time algorithms for this problem. Algorithm MIN_ONETRIP is a dynamic programming algorithm that optimizes the one trip cost for a packet passing through the pipeline. Algorithm MIN_BOTTLENECK is also a dynamic programming algorithm, which minimizes the time spent on the bottleneck stage. Finally, MIN_TOTAL is an approximate greedy algorithm which tries to minimize the total execution time.

We have evaluated these three algorithms using three applications and many different configurations. Our results show that our heuristic algorithms work quite well in practice, with the possible exception of MIN_ONETRIP when the number of packets is large. However, the relative performance of the algorithms is not always what we would expect, because of the certain limitations in how we model the problem.

7. REFERENCES

[1] Asmara Afework, Michael D. Beynon, Fabian Bustamante, Angelo Demarzo, Renato Ferreira, Robert Miller, Mark Silberman, Joel Saltz, Alan Sussman, and Hubert Tsang. Digital dynamic telepathology - the Virtual Microscope. In *Proceedings of the 1998 AMIA Annual Fall Symposium*. American Medical Informatics Association, November 1998.

[2] T. Arbogast, S. Bryant, C. Dawson, and M. F. Wheeler. Parssim: The parallel subsurface simulator, single phase. *http://www.ticam.utexas.edu/~arbogast/parssim*.

[3] Michael D. Beynon, Tahsin Kurc, Umit Catalyurek, Chialin Chang, Alan Sussman, and Joel Saltz. Distributed processing of very large datasets with DataCutter. *Parallel Computing*, 27(11):1457–1478, October 2001.

[4] Michael D. Beynon, Tahsin Kurc, Umit Catalyurek, Alan Sussman, and Joel Saltz. A component-based implementation of iso-surface rendering for visualizing large datasets. Technical Report CS-TR-4249 and UMIACS-TR-2001-34, University of Maryland, Department of Computer Science and UMIACS, May 2001.

[5] Michael D. Beynon, Tahsin Kurc, Alan Sussman, and Joel Saltz. Optimizing execution of component-based applications using group instances. In *Proceedings of the Conference on Cluster Computing and the Grid (CCGRID)*, pages 56–63. IEEE Computer Society Press, May 2001.

[6] S. H. Bokhari. *Assignment Problems in Parallel and Distributed Computing*. New York: Kluwer, 1987.

[7] S. H. Bokhari. Partitioning problems in parallel, pipeline, and distributed computing. *IEEE Trans. Comput.*, 37(1):48–57, 1988.

[8] Wei Du and Gagan Agrawal. Packet Size Optimization for Supporting Coarse-Grained Pipelined Parallelism. In *Proceedings of the International Conference on Parallel Processing (ICPP)*, August 2004.

[9] Wei Du, Renato Ferreira, and Gagan Agrawal. Compiler Support for Exploiting Coarse-Grained Pipelined Parallelism. In *Proceedings of Supercomputing 2003*, November 2003.

[10] R. Ferreira, B. Moon, J. Humphries, A. Sussman, J. Saltz, R. Miller, and A. Demarzo. The Virtual Microscope. In *Proceedings of the 1997 AMIA Annual Fall Symposium*, pages 449–453. American Medical Informatics Association, Hanley and Belfus, Inc., October 1997. Also available as University of Maryland Technical Report CS-TR-3777 and UMIACS-TR-97-35.

[11] Ian Foster, Carl Kesselman, and Steven Tuecke. The Anatomy of Grid: Enabling Scalable Virtual Organizations. *International Journal of Supercomputing Applications*, 2001.

[12] Pierre Hansen and Keh-Wei Lih. Improved algorithms for partitioning problems in parallel, pipelined, and distributed computing. *IEEE Trans. Comput.*, 41(6):769–771, 1992.

[13] C. C. Hsu. A two-phase approach for the optimal assignment of a chain-like task on a chain-like network computer. Technical report, National Taiwan Institute of Technology, 1993.

[14] M. Ashraf Iqbal. Approximate algorithms for partitioning problems. *International Journal of Parallel Programming*, 20(5), Oct 1991.

[15] Land Satellite Thematic Mapper (TM). *http://edcwww.cr.usgs.gov/nsdi/html/landsat_tm/ landsat_tm*.

[16] Chi lok Chan and Gilbert H. Young. Scheduling algorithms for a chain-like task system. In *ISAAC*, pages 496–505, 1993.

[17] Richard A. Luettich, Johannes J. Westerink, and Norman W. Scheffner. *ADCIRC*: An advanced three-dimensional circulation model for shelves, coasts, and estuaries. Technical Report 1, Department of the Army, U.S. Army Corps of Engineers, Washington, D.C. 20314-1000, December 1991.

[18] Kwan-Liu Ma and Z.C. Zheng. 3D visualization of unsteady 2D airplane wake vortices. In *Proceedings of Visualization'94*, pages 124–31, Oct 1994.

[19] The Moderate Resolution Imaging Spectrometer. *http://ltpwww.gsfc.nasa.gov/MODIS/MODIS.html*.

[20] NASA Goddard Distributed Active Archive Center (DAAC). Advanced Very High Resolution Radiometer Global Area Coverage (AVHRR GAC) data. *http://daac.gsfc.nasa.gov/CAMPAIGN_DOCS/ LAND_BIO/origins.html*.

[21] Grid Physics Network. GriPhyN. http://www.griphyn.org.

[22] David M. Nicol and David R. O'Hallaron. Improved algorithms for mapping pipelined and parallel computations. *IEEE Trans. Comput.*, 40(3):295–306, 1991.

[23] Ron Oldfield. Summary of existing and developing data grids. White paper, Remote Data Access Group, Global Grid Forum, available from http://www.sdsc.edu/GridForum/RemoteData/Papers/papers.html.

[24] G. Patnaik, K. Kailasnath, and E.S. Oran. Effect of gravity on flame instabilities in premixed gases. *AIAA Journal*, 29(12):2141–8, Dec 1991.

[25] U. Ramachandran, R. S. Nikhil, N. Harel, J. M. Rehg, and K. Knobe. Space-Time Memory: A Parallel Programming Abstraction for Interactive Multimedia Applications. In *Proceedings of the Conference on Principles and Practices of Parallel Programming (PPoPP)*, pages 183–192. ACM Press, May 1999.

[26] Jang-Ping Sheu and Zen-Fu Chiang. Efficient allocation of chain-like task on chain-like network computers. *Inf. Process. Lett.*, 36(5):241–245, 1990.

[27] T. Tanaka. Configurations of the solar wind flow and magnetic field around the planets with no magnetic field: calculation by a new MHD. *Jounal of Geophysical Research*, 98(A10):17251–62, Oct 1993.

[28] M. T. Yang, R. Kasturi, and A. Sivasubramaniam. An Automatic Scheduler for Real-Time Vision Applications. In *Proceedings of the International Parallel and Distributed Processing Symposium (IPDPS)*, 2001.

[29] Gilbert H. Young and Chi lok Chan. Efficient algorithms for assigning chain-like tasks on a chain-like network computer. In *ISAAC*, pages 607–615, 1994.

On the Architectural Requirements for Efficient Execution of Graph Algorithms

David A. Bader*
Department of Electrical and Computer Engineering
University of New Mexico
dbader@ece.unm.edu

Guojing Cong
IBM T.J. Watson Research Center
Yorktown Heights, NY
gcong@us.ibm.com

John Feo
Cray, Inc.
feo@sdsc.edu

Abstract

Combinatorial problems such as those from graph theory pose serious challenges for parallel machines due to non-contiguous, concurrent accesses to global data structures with low degrees of locality. The hierarchical memory systems of symmetric multiprocessor (SMP) clusters optimize for local, contiguous memory accesses, and so are inefficient platforms for such algorithms. Few parallel graph algorithms outperform their best sequential implementation on SMP clusters due to long memory latencies and high synchronization costs. In this paper, we consider the performance and scalability of two graph algorithms, list ranking and connected components, on two classes of shared-memory computers: symmetric multiprocessors such as the Sun Enterprise servers and multithreaded architectures (MTA) such as the Cray MTA-2. While previous studies have shown that parallel graph algorithms can speedup on SMPs, the systems' reliance on cache microprocessors limits performance. The MTA's latency tolerant processors and hardware support for fine-grain synchronization makes performance a function of parallelism. Since parallel graph algorithms have an abundance of parallelism, they perform and scale significantly better on the MTA. We describe and give a performance model for each architecture. We analyze the performance of the two algorithms and discuss how the features of each architecture affects algorithm development, ease of programming, performance, and scalability.

Keywords: List ranking, Connected Components, Graph Algorithms, Shared Memory, Multithreading.

*This work was supported in part by NSF Grants CAREER ACI-00-93039, ITR ACI-00-81404, DEB-99-10123, ITR EIA-01-21377, Biocomplexity DEB-01-20709, DBI-0420513, ITR EF/BIO 03-31654; and DARPA Contract NBCH30390004.

1. Introduction

The enormous increase in processor speed over the last decade from approximately 300 MHz to over 3 GHz has far out-paced the speed of the hardware components responsible for delivering data to processors. For many large-scale applications, performance is no longer a function of how many operations a processor can perform per second, but rather the rate at which the memory system can deliver bytes of data. The conventional approach to ameliorating the memory bottleneck is to build hierarchical memory systems consisting of several levels of cache and local and remote memory modules. The first level cache can usually keep pace with the processor; but, fetching data from more remote memory causes the processor to stall. Since data is moved to the L1 cache in lines, reading data in sequence (i.e., with spatial locality) maximizes performance.

Combinatorial problems such as those from graph theory pose serious challenges for parallel machines due to non-contiguous, concurrent accesses to global data structures with low degrees of locality. The hierarchical memory systems of clusters are inefficient platforms for such algorithms. In fact, few parallel graph algorithms outperform their best sequential implementation on clusters due to long memory latencies and high synchronization costs.

A parallel, shared memory system is a more supportive platform. These systems typically have higher-bandwidth, lower-latency networks than clusters, and direct access to all memory locations avoids the overhead of message passing. Fast parallel algorithms for graph problems have been developed for such systems. List ranking [11, 31, 32, 23] is a key technique often needed in efficient parallel algorithms for solving many graph-theoretic problems; for example, computing the centroid of a tree, expression evaluation, minimum spanning forest, connected components, and planarity testing. Helman and JáJá [19, 20] present an efficient list ranking algorithm with implementation on SMP servers that achieves significant parallel speedup. Using this implementation of list ranking, Bader *et al.* have designed fast parallel algorithms and demonstrated speedups compared with the best sequential implementation for graph-theoretic problems such as ear decomposition [2], tree contraction and expression evaluation [3], spanning tree [4], rooted spanning tree [13], and minimum spanning forest [5]. Many of these algorithms achieve good speedups due to algorithmic techniques for efficient design and better cache performance. For some of the instances, e.g., arbitrary, sparse graphs, while we may be able to improve the cache performance to a certain degree, there are no known general techniques for cache performance optimization because the memory access pattern is largely determined by the structure of the graph.

In this paper, we discuss the architectural features necessary for efficient execution of graph algorithms by investigating the performance of two graph algorithms, list ranking and connected components, on two classes of shared memory systems: symmetric multiprocessors (SMP) such as the Sun Enterprise servers and multithreaded architectures (MTA) such as the Cray MTA-2. While our SMP results confirm the results of previous studies, we find the systems' reliance on cache microprocessors limits performance. For the MTA, we find its latency tolerant processors and hardware support for fine-grain synchronization make performance primarily a function of parallelism. Since graph algorithms often have an abundance of parallelism, these architectural features lead to superior performance and scalability.

The next section presents a brief overview of SMPs and a detailed description of the Cray MTA-2. We give a performance cost model for each machine. Sections 3 and 4 present SMP and MTA algorithms for list ranking and connected components, respectively. The SMP algorithms minimize non-contiguous memory accesses, whereas, the MTA algorithms maximize concurrent operations. Section 5 compares the performance and scalability of the implementations. In the final section, we present our conclusions and ideas for future work. In particular, we summarize how different architectural features affect algorithmic development, ease of programming, performance, and scalability.

2. Shared-Memory Architectures

In this section, we give a brief overview of two types of modern shared-memory architectures: symmetric multiprocessors and multithreaded architectures. While both allow parallel programs to access large globally-shared memories, they differ in significant ways as we discuss next.

2.1. Symmetric Multiprocessors (SMPs)

Symmetric multiprocessor (SMP) architectures, in which several processors operate in a true, hardware-based, shared-memory environment and are packaged as a single machine, are commonplace in scientific computing. Indeed, most high-performance computers are clusters of SMPs having from 2 to over 100 processors per node. Moreover, as supercomputers increasingly use SMP clusters, SMP computations play a significant and increasing role in supercomputing and computational science.

The generic SMP processor is a four-way super-scalar microprocessor, 32 to 64 hardware registers, and two levels of cache. The L1 cache is small (64 to 128 KB) and on chip. It can issue as many words per cycle as the processor can fetch and latency is a few cycles. The size of the L2 cache can vary widely from 256 KB to 8 MB. Bandwidth to the processor is typically 8 to 12 GB per second and latency is 20 to 30 cycles. The processors are connected to a large shared memory (4 to 8 GB per processor) by a high-speed bus, crossbar, or a low-degree network. The bandwidth to main memory falls off to 1 to 2 GB per second and latency increases to hundreds of cycles.

Caching and prefetching are two hardware techniques often used to hide memory latency. Caching takes advantage of spatial and temporal locality, while prefetching mechanisms use data address history to predict memory access patterns and perform reads early. If a high percentage of read/write operations are to L1 cache, the processor stays busy sustaining a high execution rate; otherwise, it starves for data. Prefetching may substantially increase the memory bandwidth used, and shows limited or no improvement in cache hits for irregular codes where the access patterns cannot be predicted, as is often the case in graph algorithms. Moreover, there is no hardware support for synchronization operations. Locks and barriers are typically implemented in software either by the user or via system calls. (Some newer systems do provide atomic memory operations such as compare-and-swap that may be used to build these features.) While an SMP is a shared-memory architecture, it is by no means the PRAM used in theoretical work — synchronization cannot be taken for granted, memory bandwidth is limited, and performance requires a high degree of locality. The significant features of SMPs are that the input can be held in the shared memory without having to be partitioned and they provide much faster access to their shared-memory (an order of magnitude or more) than an equivalent message-based architecture. As such SMPs provide a reasonable execution platform for graph algorithms. As noted above, parallel graph algorithms that execute faster than sequential algorithms do exist for this class of architecture.

To analyze SMP performance, we use a complexity model similar to that of Helman and JáJá [20] which has been shown to provide a good cost model for shared-memory algorithms on current symmetric multiprocessors [19, 20, 2, 3]. The model uses two parameters: the problem's input size n, and the number p of processors. For instance, for list ranking, n is the number of elements in the list, and for connected components, n is the number of vertices in the input graph. Running time $T(n,p)$ is measured by the triplet $\langle T_M(n,p)\ ;\ T_C(n,p)\ ;\ B(n,p)\rangle$, where $T_M(n,p)$ is the maximum number of non-contiguous main memory accesses required by any processor, $T_C(n,p)$ is an upper bound on the maximum local computational complexity of any of the processors, and $B(n,p)$ is the number of barrier synchronizations. This model, unlike the idealistic PRAM, is more realistic in that it penalizes algorithms with non-contiguous memory accesses that often result in cache misses and algorithms with more synchronization events.

We tested our SMP implementations in this paper on the Sun E4500, a uniform-memory-access (UMA) shared memory parallel machine with 14 UltraSPARC II 400MHz processors and 14 GB of memory. Each processor has 16 Kbytes of direct-mapped data (L1) cache and 4 Mbytes of external (L2) cache. We implement the algorithms using POSIX threads and software-based barriers.

2.2. Multithreaded Architectures (MTAs)

The Cray MTA is a flat, shared-memory multiprocessor system. All memory is accessible and equidistant from all processors. There is no local memory and no data caches. Parallelism, and not caches, is used to tolerate memory and synchronization latencies.

An MTA processor consists of 128 hardware streams and one instruction pipeline. The processor speed is 220 MHz. A stream is a set of 32 registers, a status word, and space in the instruction cache. An instruction is three-wide: a memory operation, a fused multiply-add, and a floating point add or control operation. Each stream can have up to 8 outstanding memory operations. Threads from the same or different programs are mapped to the streams by the runtime system. A processor switches among its streams every cycle, executing instructions from non-blocked streams in a fair manner. As long as one stream has a ready instruction, the processor remains fully utilized.

The interconnection network is a partially connected 3-D torus capable of delivering one word per processor per cycle. The system has 4 GBytes of memory per processor. Logical memory addresses are hashed across physical memory to avoid stride-induced hotspots. Each memory word is 68 bits: 64 data bits and 4 tag bits. One tag bit (the full-and-empty bit) is used to implement synchronous load/store operations. A synchronous load/store operation retries until it succeeds or traps. The thread that issued the load or store remains blocked until the operation completes; but the processor that issued the operation continues to issue instructions from non-blocked streams.

Since the MTA is a shared-memory system with no data cache and no local memory, it is comparable to an SMP where all memory reference are remote. Thus, the cost model presented in the previous section can be applied to the MTA with the difference that the magnitudes of $T_M(n,p)$ and $B(n,p)$ are reduced via multithreading. In fact, if sufficient parallelism exists, these costs are reduced to zero and performance is a function of only $T_C(n,p)$. Execution time is then a product of the number of instructions and the cycle time.

The number of threads needed to reduce $T_M(n,p)$ to zero is a function of the memory latency of the machine, about 100 cycles. Usually a thread can issue two or three instructions before it must wait for a previous memory operation to complete; thus, 40 to 80 threads per processor are usually sufficient to reduce $T_M(n,p)$ to zero. The number of threads needed to reduce $B(n,p)$ to zero is a function of intra-thread synchronization. Typically, it is zero and no additional threads are needed; however, hotspots can occur. Usually these can be worked around in software, but they do occasionally impact performance.

The MTA is close to a theoretical PRAM machine. Its latency tolerant processors, high bandwidth network, and shared memory, enable any processor to execute any operation and access any word. Execution time can reduce to the product of the number of instructions and the machine's cycle time. Since the MTA uses parallelism to tolerate latency, algorithms must often be parallelized at very fine levels to expose sufficient parallelism to hide the latencies. Fine levels of parallelism require fine grain synchronization that would cripple performance without some near zero-cost synchronization mechanism, such as the MTA's full-and-empty bits.

3. List Ranking

List ranking and other prefix computations on linked lists are basic operations that occur in many graph-based algorithms. The operations are difficult to parallelize because of the non-contiguous structure of lists and asynchronous access of shared data by concurrent tasks. Unlike arrays, there is no obvious way to divide the list into even, disjoint, continuous sublists without first computing the rank of each node. Moreover, concurrent tasks may visit or pass through the same node by different paths, requiring synchronization to ensure correctness.

List ranking is an instance of the more general prefix problem. Let X be an array of n elements stored in arbitrary order. For each element i, let $X(i)$.*value* be its value and $X(i)$.*next* be the index of its successor. Then for any binary associative operator $\oplus$, compute $X(i)$.*prefix* such that $X(\textit{head})$.*prefix* $=$ $X(\textit{head})$.*value* and $X(i)$.*prefix* $=$ $X(i)$.*value*$\oplus X(\textit{predecessor})$.*prefix*, where *head* is the first element of the list, i is not equal to *head*, and *predecessor* is the node preceding i in the list. If all values are 1 and the associative operation is addition, then prefix reduces to list ranking.

Our SMP implementation uses the Helman and JáJá list ranking algorithm [19] that performs the following main steps:

1. Find the head h of the list which is given by $h = (n(n-1)/2 - Z)$ where Z is the sum of successor indices of all the nodes in the list and n is the number of elements in the list.

2. Partition the input list into s sublists by randomly choosing one node from each memory block of $n/(s-1)$ nodes, where s is $\Omega(p \log n)$ and p is the number of processors. Create the array *Sublists* of size s. (Our implementation uses $s = 8p$.)

3. Traverse each sublist computing the prefix sum of each node within the sublists. Each node records its sublist index. The input value of a node in the *Sublists* array is the sublist prefix sum of the last node in the previous *Sublists*.

4. The prefix sums of the records in the *Sublists* array are then calculated.

5. Each node adds its current prefix sum value (value of a node within a sublist) and the prefix sum of its corresponding *Sublists* record to get its final prefix sums value. This prefix sum value is the required label of the leaves.

For $n > p^2 \ln n$, we would expect in practice the SMP list ranking to take $T(n,p) = (M_M(n,p); T_C(n,p)) = \left(\frac{n}{p}, O\left(\frac{n}{p}\right)\right)$. For a detailed description of the above steps refer to [19].

Our MTA implementation (described in high-level in the following four steps and also given in detail in Alg. 1) is similar to the Helman and JáJá algorithm.

1. Choose NWALK nodes (including the head node) and mark them. This step divides the list into NWALK sublists and is similar to steps 1 and 2 of the SMP algorithm.

2. Traverse each sublist computing the prefix sum of each node within the sublist (similar to step 3 of the SMP algorithm).

3. Compute the rank of each marked node (similar to step 4 of the SMP algorithm).

```
int list[NLIST+1], rank[NLIST+1];

void RankList(list, rank)
  int *list, *rank;
{ int i, first;
  int tmp1[NWALK+1], tmp2[NWALK+1];
  int head[NWALK+1], tail[NWALK+1], lnth[NWALK+1], next[NWALK+1];

#pragma mta assert noalias *rank, head, tail, lnth, next, tmp1, tmp2


  first = 0;
#pragma mta use 100 streams
  for (i = 1; i <= NLIST; i++) first += list[i];

  first = ((NLIST * NLIST + NLIST) / 2) - first;

  head[0] = 0; head[1]      = first;
  tail[0] = 0; tail[1]      = 0;
  lnth[0] = 0; lnth[1]      = 0;
  rank[0] = 0; rank[first] = 1;

  for (i = 2; i <= NWALK; i++) {
      int node = i * (NLIST / NWALK);
      head[i]     = node;
      tail[i]     = 0;
      lnth[i]     = 0;
      rank[node] = i;
  }

#pragma mta use 100 streams
#pragma mta assert no dependence lnth
  for (i = 1; i <= NWALK; i++) {
      int j, count, next_walk;

         count = 0;
         j     = head[i];
         do {count++; j = list[j];} while (rank[j] == -1);

         next_walk = rank[j];

         tail[i]          = j;
         lnth[next_walk] = count;
         next[i]          = next_walk;
  }

  while (next[1] != 0) {

#pragma mta assert no dependence tmp1
      for (i = 1; i <= NWALK; i++) {
          int n    = next[i];
          tmp1[n] = lnth[i];
          tmp2[i] = next[n];
      }

      for (i = 1; i <= NWALK; i++) {
          lnth[i] += tmp1[i];
          next[i]  = tmp2[i];
          tmp1[i]  = 0;
  }   }

#pragma mta use 100 streams
#pragma mta assert no dependence *rank
  for (i = 1; i <= NWALK; i++) {
      int j, k, count;
      j      = head[i];
      k      = tail[i];
      count = NLIST - lnth[i];
      while (j != k) {
        rank[j] = count; count--; j = list[j];
      }
  }
}
```

Algorithm 1: The MTA list ranking code.

4. Re-traverse the sublists incrementing the local rank of each node by the rank of the marked node at the head of the sublist (similar to step 5 of the SMP algorithm).

The first and third steps are O(n). They consist of an outer loop of O(NWALK) and an inner loop of O(*length of the sublist*). Since the lengths of the local walks can vary, the work done by each thread will vary. We discuss load balancing issues below. The second step is also O(NWALKS) and can be parallelized using any one of the many parallel array prefix methods. In summary, the MTA algorithm has three parallel steps with NWALKS parallelism. Our studies show that by using 100 streams per processor and approximately 10 list nodes per walk, we achieve almost 100% utilization—so a linked list of length $1000p$ fully utilizes an MTA system with p processors.

Since the lengths of the walks are different, the amount of work done by each thread is different. If threads are assigned to streams in blocks, the work per stream will not be balanced. Since the MTA is a shared memory machine, any stream can access any memory location in equal time; thus, it is irrelevant which stream executes which walk. To avoid load imbalances, we instruct the compiler via a pragma to dynamically schedule the iterations of the outer loop. Each stream gets one walk at a time; when it finishes its current walk, it increments the loop counter and executes the next walk. A machine instruction, *int_fetch_add*, is used to increment the shared loop counter. The instruction adds one to a counter in memory and returns the old value. The instruction takes one cycle.

Alg. 1 gives our new source code for the MTA list ranking algorithm. **The fully-documented source codes for the SMP and MTA implementations of list ranking are freely-available from the web by visiting `http://www.ece.unm.edu/~dbader` and clicking on the *Software* tab.**

4. Connected Components

Let $G = (V, E)$ be an undirected graph with $|V| = n$ and $|E| = m$. Two vertices u and v are *connected* if there exists a path between u and v in G. This is an equivalence relation on V and partitions V into equivalence classes, i.e., connected components. Connectivity is a fundamental graph problem with a range of applications and can be building blocks for higher-level algorithms. The research community has produced a rich collection of theoretic deterministic [28, 21, 30, 26, 8, 9, 7, 18, 24, 34, 1, 12, 14] and randomized [17, 29] parallel algorithms for connected components. Yet for implementations and experimental studies, although several fast PRAM algorithms exist, to our knowledge there is no parallel implementation of connected components (other than our own [4, 6]) that achieves significant parallel speedup on sparse, irregular graphs when compared against the best sequential implementation.

Prior experimental studies of connected components implement the Shiloach-Vishkin algorithm [16, 22, 25, 15] due to its simplicity and efficiency. However, these parallel implementations of the Shiloach-Vishkin algorithm do not achieve any parallel speedups over arbitrary, sparse graphs against the best sequential implementation. Greiner [16] implemented several connected components algorithms (Shiloach-Vishkin, Awerbuch-Shiloach, "random-mating" based on the work of Reif [33] and Phillips [30], and a hybrid of the previous three) using NESL on the Cray Y-MP/C90 and TMC CM-2. On random graphs Greiner reports a maximum speedup of 3.5 using the hybrid algorithm when compared with a depth-first search on a DEC Alpha processor. Hsu, Ramachandran, and Dean [22] also implemented several parallel algorithms for connected components. They report that their parallel code runs 30 times slower on a MasPar MP-1 than Greiner's results on the Cray, but Hsu *et al.*'s implementation uses one-fourth of the total memory used by Greiner's hybrid approach. Krishnamurthy *et al.* [25] implemented a connected components algorithm (based on Shiloach-Vishkin) for distributed memory machines. Their code achieved a speedup of 20 using a 32-processor TMC CM-5 on graphs with underlying 2D and 3D regular mesh topologies, but virtually no speedup on sparse random graphs. Goddard, Kumar, and Prins [15] implemented a connected components algorithm (motived by Shiloach-Vishkin) for a mesh-connected SIMD parallel computer, the 8192-processor MasPar MP-1. They achieve a maximum parallel speedup of less than two on a random graph with 4096 vertices and about one-million edges. For a random graph with 4096 vertices and fewer than a half-million edges, the parallel implementation was slower than the sequential code.

In this paper, we compare implementations of Shiloach-Vishkin's connected components algorithm (denoted as SV) on both SMP and MTA systems. We chose this algorithm because it is representative of the memory access patterns and data structures in graph-theoretic problems. SV starts with n isolated vertices and m PRAM processors. Each processor P_i (for $1 \leq i \leq m$) grafts a tree rooted at vertex v_i (represented by v_i, in the beginning, the tree contains only a single vertex) to the tree that contains one of its neighbors u under the constraints $u < v_i$ or the tree represented by v_i is only one level deep. Grafting creates $k \geq 1$ connected subgraphs, and each of the k subgraphs is then shortcut so that the depth of the trees reduce at least by half. The approach continues to graft and shortcut on the reduced graphs until no more grafting is possible. As a result, each supervertex represents a connected graph. SV runs on an arbitrary CRCW PRAM in O($\log n$) time with O(m) processors. The formal description of SV can be found in Alg. 2.

Input: 1. A set of m edges (i, j) given in arbitrary order
2. Array $D[1..n]$ with $D[i] = i$

Output: Array $D[1..n]$ with $D[i]$ being the component to which vertex i belongs

begin
  while *true* **do**
    1.**for** $(i, j) \in E$ *in parallel* **do**
      if *D[i]=D[D[i]] and D[j]<D[i]* **then**
        $D[D[i]] = D[j]$;
    2.**for** $(i, j) \in E$ *in parallel* **do**
      if *i belongs to a star and D[j]≠D[i]* **then**
        $D[D[i]] = D[j]$;
    3.**if** *all vertices are in rooted stars* **then** exit;
    for *all i in parallel* **do**
      $D[i] = D[D[i]]$
end

Algorithm 2: The Shiloach-Vishkin algorithm for connected components.

```
while (graft) {
   graft = 0;
#pragma mta assert parallel
   1. for (i=0; i<2*m; i++) {
         u = E[i].v1;
         v = E[i].v2;
         if (D[u]<D[v] && D[v]==D[D[v]]) {
           D[D[v]] = D[u];
           graft = 1;
         }
      }
#pragma mta assert parallel
   2. for(i=0; i<n; i++)
        while (D[i] != D[D[i]]) D[i]=D[D[i]];
}
```

Algorithm 3: SV on MTA. `E` is the edge list, with each element having two fields, `v1` and `v2`, representing the two endpoints.

SV can be implemented on SMPs and MTA, and the two implementations have very different performance characteristics on the two architectures, demonstrating that algorithms should be designed with the target architecture in consideration. For SMPs, we use appropriate optimizations described by Greiner [16], Chung and Condon [10], Krishnamurthy *et al.* [25], and Hsu *et al.* [22]. SV is sensitive to the labeling of vertices. For the same graph, different labeling of vertices may incur different numbers of iterations to terminate the algorithm. For the best case, one iteration of the algorithm may be sufficient, and the running time of the algorithm will be $O(\log n)$. Whereas for an arbitrary labeling of the same graph, the number of iterations needed will be from one to $\log n$. We refer the reader to our previous work [4] for more details on the SMP connectivity algorithm and its analysis (presented next).

In the first "graft-and-shortcut" step of SV, there are two non-contiguous memory accesses per edge, for reading $D[j]$ and $D[D[i]]$. Thus, first step costs $T(n,p) = \langle T_M(n,p) \,;\, T_C(n,p) \,;\, B(n,p)\rangle = \left\langle 2\frac{m}{p} + 1 \,;\, O\!\left(\frac{n+m}{p}\right) \,;\, 1\right\rangle$. In the second step, the grafting is performed and requires one non-contiguous access per edge to set the parent, with cost $T(n,p) = \left\langle \frac{m}{p} + 1 \,;\, O\!\left(\frac{n+m}{p}\right) \,;\, 1\right\rangle$. The final step of each iteration runs pointer jumping to form rooted stars to ensure that a tree is not grafted onto itself, with cost $T(n,p) = \left\langle \frac{n\log n}{p} \,;\, O\!\left(\frac{n \log n}{p}\right) \,;\, 1\right\rangle$. In general, SV needs multiple iterations to terminate. Assuming the worst-case of $\log n$ iterations, the total complexity for SV is $T(n,p) = \langle T_M(n,p) \,;\, T_C(n,p) \,;\, B(n,p)\rangle \leq \left\langle \frac{n\log^2 n}{p} + \left(3\frac{m}{p} + 2\right)\log n \,;\, O\!\left(\frac{n\log^2 n + m\log n}{p}\right) \,;\, 4\log n\right\rangle$.

On the other hand, programming the MTA is unlike programming for SMPs, and code for the MTA looks much closer to the original PRAM algorithm. The programmer no longer specifies which processor works on which data partitions, instead, his/her job is to discover the finest grain of parallelism of the program and pass the information to the compiler using directives. Otherwise the compiler relies on the information from dependence analysis to parallelize the program. The implementation of SV on MTA is a direct translation of the PRAM algorithm, and the C source code is shown in Alg. 3. Alg. 3 is slightly different from the description of SV given in Alg. 2. In Alg. 3 the trees are shortcut into supervertices in each iteration, so that step 2 of Alg. 2 can be eliminated, and we no longer need to check whether a vertex belongs to a star which involves a significant amount of computation and memory accesses. Alg. 3 runs in $O(\log^2 n)$, and the bound is not tight. The directives in Alg. 3 are self-explanatory, and they are crucial for the compiler to parallelize the program as there is obvious data dependence in each step of the program.

5. Performance Results and Analysis

This section summarizes the experimental results of our implementations for list ranking and connected components on the SMP and MTA shared-memory systems.

For list ranking, we use two classes of list to test our algorithms: **Ordered** and **Random**. Ordered places each element in the array according to its rank; thus, node i is the ith position of the array and its successor is the node at position $(i + 1)$. Random places successive elements randomly in the array. Since the MTA maps contiguous logical

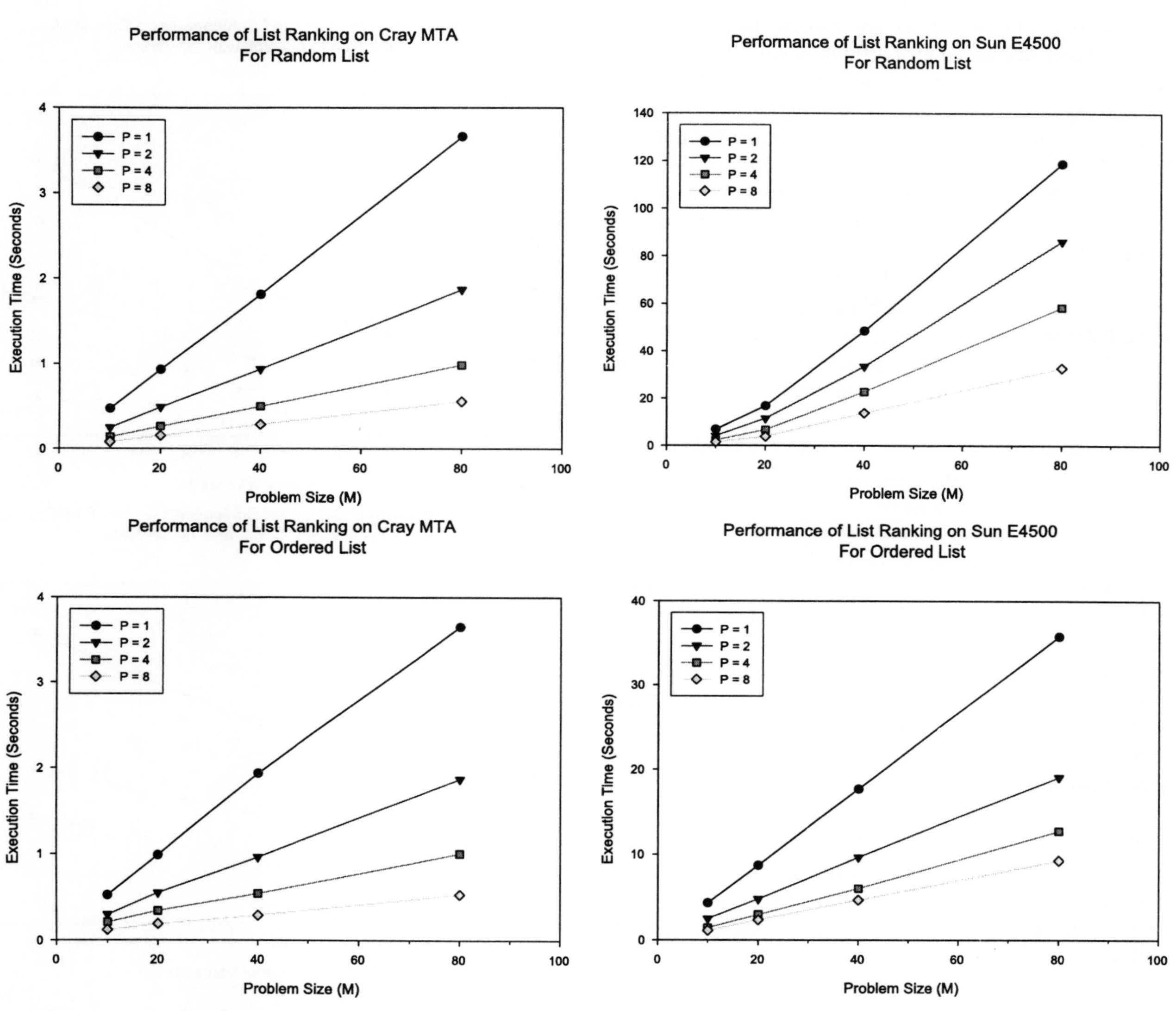

Figure 1. Running Times for List Ranking on the Cray MTA (left) and Sun SMP (right) for $p = 1, 2, 4$ and 8 processors.

addresses to random physical addresses the layout in physical memory for both classes is similar. We expect, and in fact see, that performance on the MTA is independent of order. This is in sharp contrast to SMP machines which rank Ordered lists much faster than Random lists. The running times for list ranking on the SMP and MTA are given in Fig. 1. First, all of the implementations scaled well with problem size and number of processors. In all cases, the running times decreased proportionally with the number of processors, quite a remarkable result on a problem such as list ranking whose efficient implementation has been considered a "holy grail" of parallel computing. On the Cray MTA, the performance is nearly identical for random or ordered lists, demonstrating that locality of memory accesses is a non-issue; first, since memory latency is tolerated, and second, since the logical addresses are randomly assigned to the physical memory. On the SMP, there is a factor of 3 to 4 difference in performance between the best case (an ordered list) and the worst case (a randomly-ordered list). On the ordered lists, the MTA is an order of magnitude faster than this SMP, while on the random list, the MTA is approximately 35 times faster.

For connected components, we create a random graph of n vertices and m edges by randomly adding m unique edges to the vertex set. Several software packages generate random graphs this way, including LEDA [27]. The running times for connected components on the SMP and MTA are given in Fig. 2 for a random graph with $n = 1M$ vertices and from $m = 4M$ to $20M$ edges. (Note that throughout this paper $M = 2^{20}$.) Similar to the list ranking results, we see that both shared-memory systems scale with problem size and number of processors for finding the connected components of a sparse, random graph. This is also a truly remarkable result noting that no previous parallel implementations have exhibited parallel speedup on arbitrary, sparse graphs for the connected components problem. (Note that we give speedup results for the SMP approach in [4, 6].) In comparison, the MTA implementation is 5 to 6 times faster than the SMP implementation of SV connected components, and the code for the MTA is quite simple and similar to the PRAM algorithm, unlike the more complex code required for the SMP to achieve this performance.

Number of Processors	List Ranking: Random List	List Ranking: Ordered List	Connected Components
1	98%	97%	99%
4	90%	85%	93%
8	82%	80%	91%

Table 1. Processor Utilization for List Ranking and Connected Components on the Cray MTA.

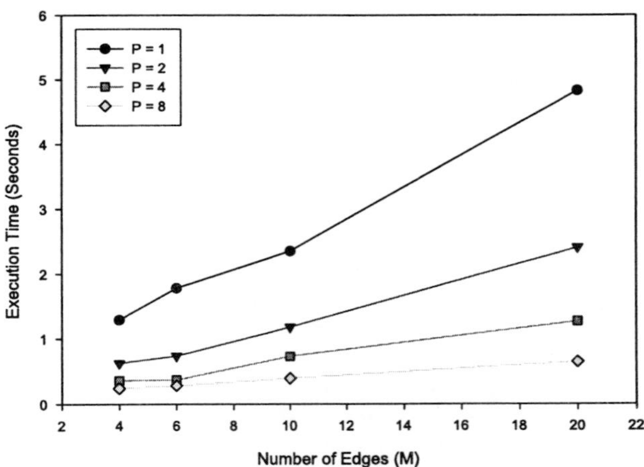

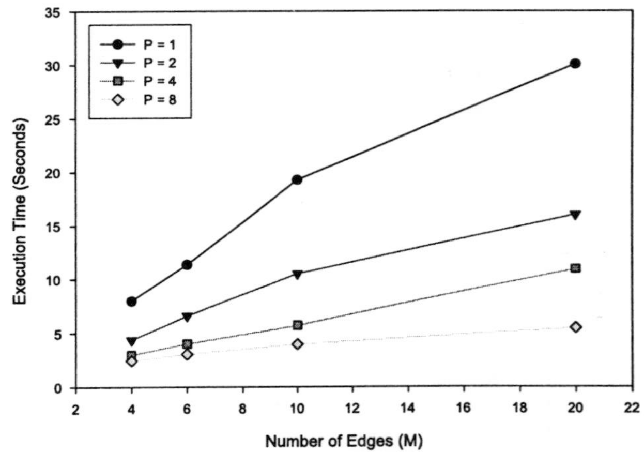

Figure 2. Running Times for Connected Components on the Cray MTA (left) and Sun SMP (right) for $p = 1, 2, 4$ and 8 processors.

On the Cray MTA, we achieve high-percentages of processor utilization. In Table 1 we give the utilizations achieved for the MTA on List Ranking of a $20M$-node list, and Connected Components with $n = 1M$ vertices and $m = 20M(\approx n \log n)$ edges.

6. Conclusions

In summary, we show that fast, parallel implementations of graph-theoretic problems such as list ranking and connected components are well-suited to shared-memory computer systems. We confirm the results of previous SMP studies and present the first results for multithreaded architectures. The latter highlights the benefits of latency-tolerant processors and hardware support for synchronization. In our experiments, the Cray MTA achieved high utilization rates for performing both list ranking and connected components. In addition, the MTA, because of its randomization between logical and physical memory addresses, and its multithreaded execution techniques for latency hiding, performed extremely well on the list ranking problem, no matter the spatial locality of the list.

Although both are shared memory machines, the programming model presented to the user by the two machines is different. The Cray MTA allows the programmer to focus on the concurrency in the problem, while the SMP server forces the programmer to optimize for locality and cache. We find the latter results in longer, more complex programs that embody both parallelism and locality.

We are currently developing additional graph algorithms for the MTA. In particularly, we are investigating whether the technique used in the list ranking program is a general technique. In that program, we first compacted the list to a list of super nodes, performed list ranking on the compacted list, and then expanded the super nodes to compute the rank of the original nodes. The compaction and expansion steps are parallel, O(n), and require little synchronization; thus, they increase parallelism while decreasing overhead.

In 2005, Cray will build a third generation multithreaded architecture. To reduce costs, this system will incorporate commodity parts. In particular, the memory system will not be as flat as in the MTA-2. We will reconduct our studies on this architecture as soon as it is available.

References

[1] B. Awerbuch and Y. Shiloach. New connectivity and MSF algorithms for shuffle-exchange network and PRAM. *IEEE Transactions on Computers*, C-36(10):1258–1263, 1987.

[2] D. Bader, A. Illendula, B. M. Moret, and N. Weisse-Bernstein. Using PRAM algorithms on a uniform-memory-access shared-memory architecture. In G. Brodal, D. Frigioni, and A. Marchetti-Spaccamela, editors, *Proc. 5th Int'l Workshop on Algorithm Engineering (WAE 2001)*, volume 2141 of *Lecture Notes in Computer Science*, pages 129–144, Århus, Denmark, 2001. Springer-Verlag.

[3] D. Bader, S. Sreshta, and N. Weisse-Bernstein. Evaluating arithmetic expressions using tree contraction: A fast and scalable parallel implementation for symmetric multiprocessors (SMPs). In S. Sahni, V. Prasanna, and U. Shukla, editors, *Proc. 9th Int'l Conf. on High Performance Computing (HiPC 2002)*, volume 2552 of *Lecture Notes in Computer Science*, pages 63–75, Bangalore, India, Dec. 2002. Springer-Verlag.

[4] D. A. Bader and G. Cong. A fast, parallel spanning tree algorithm for symmetric multiprocessors (SMPs). In *Proc. Int'l Parallel and Distributed Processing Symp. (IPDPS 2004)*, Santa Fe, NM, Apr. 2004.

[5] D. A. Bader and G. Cong. Fast shared-memory algorithms for computing the minimum spanning forest of sparse graphs. In *Proc. Int'l Parallel and Distributed Processing Symp. (IPDPS 2004)*, Santa Fe, NM, Apr. 2004.

[6] D. A. Bader and G. Cong. A fast, parallel spanning tree algorithm for symmetric multiprocessors (SMPs). *Journal of Parallel and Distributed Computing*, 2005. to appear.

[7] F. Y. Chin, J. Lam, and I.-N. Chen. Efficient parallel algorithms for some graph problems. *Commununications of the ACM*, 25(9):659–665, 1982.

[8] K. Chong and T. Lam. Finding connected components in $O(\log n \log \log n)$ time on the EREW PRAM. *J. Algorithms*, 18:378–402, 1995.

[9] K. W. Chong, Y. Han, and T. W. Lam. Concurrent threads and optimal parallel minimum spanning tree algorithm. *Journal of the ACM*, 48:297–323, 2001.

[10] S. Chung and A. Condon. Parallel implementation of Borůvka's minimum spanning tree algorithm. In *Proc. 10th Int'l Parallel Processing Symp. (IPPS'96)*, pages 302–315, Apr. 1996.

[11] R. Cole and U. Vishkin. Faster optimal prefix sums and list ranking. *Information and Computation*, 81(3):344–352, 1989.

[12] R. Cole and U. Vishkin. Approximate parallel scheduling. part II: applications to logarithmic-time optimal graph algorithms. *Information and Computation*, 92:1–47, 1991.

[13] G. Cong and D. A. Bader. The Euler tour technique and parallel rooted spanning tree. In *Proc. Int'l Conf. on Parallel Processing (ICPP)*, pages 448–457, Montreal, Canada, Aug. 2004.

[14] H. Gazit. An optimal randomized parallel algorithm for finding connected components in a graph. *SIAM J. Comput.*, 20(6):1046–1067, 1991.

[15] S. Goddard, S. Kumar, and J. Prins. Connected components algorithms for mesh-connected parallel computers. In S. N. Bhatt, editor, *Parallel Algorithms: 3rd DIMACS Implementation Challenge October 17-19, 1994*, volume 30 of *DIMACS Series in Discrete Mathematics and Theoretical Computer Science*, pages 43–58. American Mathematical Society, 1997.

[16] J. Greiner. A comparison of data-parallel algorithms for connected components. In *Proc. 6th Ann. Symp. Parallel Algorithms and Architectures (SPAA-94)*, pages 16–25, Cape May, NJ, June 1994.

[17] S. Halperin and U. Zwick. An optimal randomised logarithmic time connectivity algorithm for the EREW PRAM. In *Proc. 7th Ann. Symp. Discrete Algorithms (SODA-96)*, pages 438–447, 1996. Also published in J. Comput. Syst. Sci., 53(3):395–416, 1996.

[18] Y. Han and R. A. Wagner. An efficient and fast parallel-connected component algorithm. *Journal of the ACM*, 37(3):626–642, 1990.

[19] D. R. Helman and J. JáJá. Designing practical efficient algorithms for symmetric multiprocessors. In *Algorithm Engineering and Experimentation (ALENEX'99)*, volume 1619 of *Lecture Notes in Computer Science*, pages 37–56, Baltimore, MD, Jan. 1999. Springer-Verlag.

[20] D. R. Helman and J. JáJá. Prefix computations on symmetric multiprocessors. *Journal of Parallel and Distributed Computing*, 61(2):265–278, 2001.

[21] D. S. Hirschberg, A. K. Chandra, and D. V. Sarwate. Computing connected components on parallel computers. *Commununications of the ACM*, 22(8):461–464, 1979.

[22] T.-S. Hsu, V. Ramachandran, and N. Dean. Parallel implementation of algorithms for finding connected components in graphs. In S. N. Bhatt, editor, *Parallel Algorithms: 3rd DIMACS Implementation Challenge October 17-19, 1994*, volume 30 of *DIMACS Series in Discrete Mathematics and Theoretical Computer Science*, pages 23–41. American Mathematical Society, 1997.

[23] J. JáJá. *An Introduction to Parallel Algorithms*. Addison-Wesley Publishing Company, New York, 1992.

[24] D. Johnson and P. Metaxas. Connected components in $O(\log^{3/2}|v|)$ parallel time for the CREW PRAM. In *Proc. of the 32nd Ann. IEEE Symp. on Foundations of Computer Science*, pages 688–697, San Juan, Puerto Rico, 1991.

[25] A. Krishnamurthy, S. S. Lumetta, D. E. Culler, and K. Yelick. Connected components on distributed memory machines. In S. N. Bhatt, editor, *Parallel Algorithms: 3rd DIMACS Implementation Challenge October 17-19, 1994*, volume 30 of *DIMACS Series in Discrete Mathematics and Theoretical Computer Science*, pages 1–21. American Mathematical Society, 1997.

[26] C. Kruskal, L. Rudolph, and M. Snir. Efficient parallel algorithms for graph problems. *Algorithmica*, 5(1):43–64, 1990.

[27] K. Mehlhorn and S. Näher. *The LEDA Platform of Combinatorial and Geometric Computing*. Cambridge University Press, 1999.

[28] D. Nash and S. Maheshwari. Parallel algorithms for the connected components and minimal spanning trees. *Information Processing Letters*, 14(1):7–11, 1982.

[29] S. Pettie and V. Ramachandran. A randomized time-work optimal parallel algorithm for finding a minimum spanning forest. *SIAM J. Comput.*, 31(6):1879–1895, 2002.

[30] C. Phillips. Parallel graph contraction. In *Proc. 1st Ann. Symp. Parallel Algorithms and Architectures (SPAA-89)*, pages 148–157. ACM, 1989.

[31] M. Reid-Miller. List ranking and list scan on the Cray C-90. In *Proc. 6th Ann. Symp. Parallel Algorithms and Architectures (SPAA-94)*, pages 104–113, Cape May, NJ, June 1994.

[32] M. Reid-Miller. List ranking and list scan on the Cray C-90. *J. Comput. Syst. Sci.*, 53(3):344–356, Dec. 1996.

[33] J. Reif. Optimal parallel algorithms for integer sorting and graph connectivity. Technical Report TR-08-85, Harvard Univ., Boston, MA, Mar. 1985.

[34] Y. Shiloach and U. Vishkin. An $O(\log n)$ parallel connectivity algorithm. *J. Algs.*, 3(1):57–67, 1982.

Scalability of Heterogeneous Computing

Xian-He Sun, Yong Chen, Ming Wu
Department of Computer Science
Illinois Institute of Technology
{sun, chenyon1, wuming}@iit.edu

Abstract

Scalability is a key factor of the design of distributed systems and parallel algorithms and machines. However, conventional scalabilities are designed for homogeneous parallel processing. There is no suitable and commonly accepted definition of scalability metric for heterogeneous systems. Isospeed scalability is a well-defined metric for homogeneous computing. This study extends the isospeed scalability metric to general heterogeneous computing systems. The proposed isospeed-efficiency metric is suitable for both homogeneous and heterogeneous computing. Through theoretical analysis, we derive methodologies of scalability measurement and prediction for heterogeneous systems. Experimental results verify the analytical results and confirm that the proposed isospeed-efficiency scalability works well in both homogeneous and heterogeneous environments.

1. Introduction

Scalability is an essential factor for performance evaluation and optimization of parallel and distributed systems. It has been used widely for describing how the system size and problem size will influence the performance of parallel computers and algorithms. It measures the ability of parallel architectures to support parallel processing at different machine ensemble sizes, and measures the inherent parallelism of parallel algorithms.

Although scalability is important for parallel and distributed systems, most of current research is focused on homogeneous environments. As computing environments evolving, understanding scalability of heterogeneous environments becomes timely important and necessary. In this paper, we propose an isospeed-efficiency method for general heterogeneous computing, based on the isospeed metric proposed in [10]. Analytical and experimental studies are conducted to confirm the correctness and effect of the newly proposed scalability metric. Results show that the isospeed-efficiency metric is practical and effective.

The following of this paper is organized as follows: Section 2 reviews related work. Section 3 presents the proposed isospeed-efficiency scalability metric. The analytical results of the proposed scalability metric are provided in Section 4. Section 5 presents experimental results that match the analytical results well. Finally, we summarize our current work and discuss future work.

2. Related work

Several metrics are proposed to measure the scalability of algorithms and parallel machines[3][5][7][8][9][10], but most of these metrics are designed for homogeneous environments. They cannot readily be applied to heterogeneous environments. In [10], Sun and Rover proposed the isospeed scalability metric to describe the scalability of an algorithm-machine combination in homogenous environments. An algorithm-machine combination is defined to be scalable if the achieved average unit speed of the algorithm on the given machine can remain constant with increasing number of processors, provided the problem size can be increased with the system size. By this definition, a scalability function can be defined as

$$\psi(p, p') = \frac{p'W}{pW'}$$

where p and p' are the initial and scaled number of processors of the system respectively, and W and W' are the initial and scaled work (problem size) respectively. The isospeed scalability works well in homogeneous environment and is well cited in scholarly publications, including several widely used textbooks [2][4][7].

There is another well-known scalability metric, isoefficiency scalability[3]. The isoefficiency scalability is defined as the ability of parallel machine to keep the parallel efficiency constant when the system and problem size increases, where the parallel efficiency is defined as speedup over the number of processors. Speedup, in turn, is defined as the ratio of sequential execution time and parallel execution time. In theoretical analysis, the requirement of sequential execution time does not appear to be a problem. In practice, to measure the execution time of large applications on a single node is problematic, if not impossible. Scalability is to measure the ability of parallel systems at different system and problem sizes. It does not need to refer single-node sequential execution time of large scale computing. Isoefficiency scalability may have some difficulty to extend to general heterogeneous environments directly.

Isospeed scalability uses average unit speed as efficiency and does not refer to sequential execution time. It is practical. However, similar to isoefficiency scalability, it is based on the assumption that the underlying parallel machine is homogeneous. This assumption becomes too restricted for modern computing systems. It is necessary to extend the isospeed scalability metric to general parallel computing environments. In this study, we combine the merits of both isospeed and isoefficiency scalability to propose the isospeed-efficiency scalability for heterogeneous computing.

There are some recent attempts to generalized scalability metrics. Jogalekar and Woodside proposed a strategy-based scalability metric for general distributed systems[5]. The scalability is based on productivity which is defined as the value delivered by the system divided by its cost (money charge) per unit time. A system is scalable if productivity keeps pace with cost. Their scalability metric measures the worthiness of renting a service. However, commercial charge varies from customer to customer, based on business considerations, and does not necessarily reflect the inherent scalability of the underlying computing system. Pastor and Bosque proposed a heterogeneous efficiency function to define the heterogeneous scalability[7]. Their work tries to extend the homogeneous isoefficiency scalability model to heterogeneous computing and, therefore, inherits the limitation of parallel speedup, requiring the measurement of solving large-scale problem on single node as we analyzed for homogeneous isoefficiency scalability.

3. Isospeed-efficiency scalability

3.1 The marked speed

In order to fully describe the characteristic of a given algorithm-system combination in a heterogeneous environment, we need to describe all the computing features of the system. These features include the computing power, memory capacity and memory speed, network bandwidth, I/O speed and other features of the system. In engineering practice, however, we cannot get into all the details; otherwise, the scalability model will be too complex to use. We need to balance the simplicity and effectiveness. For this reason, we introduce a new concept, 'marked speed', to describe the combined computing power of a general distributed system. First, we give a definition of 'marked speed of a computing node'.

Definition 1 The marked speed of a computing node is a (benchmarked) sustained speed of that node.

Marked speed can be calculated based on hardware peak performance, which in general is much higher than an actual delivered performance. In practice, we can use benchmarks to measure the "power" or marked speed of each node. Standard benchmarks can be selected for different applications, for instance Linpack or NPB for scientific computing or appropriate benchmark from the Perfect benchmarks suite. Once the marked speed of a computing node is measured, it should be used as a constant parameter. Let C_i denote the marked speed of node i. In a heterogeneous environment, C_i may be different from each other due to the heterogeneity of the nodes. In homogeneous environment, all C_i are the same.

Definition 2 The marked speed of a computing system is the sum of the marked speed of each node that composes the computing system.

Let C stand for the marked speed of a computing system. According to definition, we have $C = \sum_{i=1}^{p} C_i$ in a general parallel computing environment with p nodes.

3.2 Definition of isospeed-efficiency scalability

Let S denote the actual achieved speed, which is defined as work divided by execution time, of a computing system. Let W denote work and T denote execution time. So we have $S = W / T$.

Marked speed describes the computational capability of a computing system, which is a constant for a study. The achieved speed of an application may not be the same as the benchmarked marked speed given by Definition 2, especially for distributed/parallel computing where the marked speed does not consider the communication cost. Achieved speed describes the actual computational performance when the system tries to solve users' applications. It varies with the system and problem size.

Definition 3 The speed-efficiency of a computing system is defined as the achieved speed divided by the marked speed of the computing system.

The speed-efficiency reflects the performance gain of an algorithm-system combination. Let E_s denote the speed-efficiency. So we have $E_s = \frac{S}{C} = \frac{W}{TC}$.

Based on previous definitions and discussion, we propose the following isospeed-efficiency scalability for any algorithm-system combination on a general distributed computing system.

Definition 4 Isospeed-efficiency Scalability An algorithm-system combination is scalable if the achieved speed-efficiency of the combination can remain constant with increasing system ensemble size, provided the problem size can be increased with the system size.

In this isospeed-efficiency scalability definition, the computing system can be either a homogeneous or heterogeneous system. The method for increasing system size includes increasing nodes, increasing the number of processors in one or more nodes, or upgrading to more powerful nodes. The approach to increase problem size depends on the algorithm.

3.3 Isospeed-efficiency scalability function

For a scalable algorithm or application, its communication requirement should increase slower than its computation requirement. So we can increase the problem size to keep the speed-efficiency constant when the system size is increased. The increment of problem size depends on the underlying algorithm and computing system. This variation provides a quantitative measurement of scalability.

Let *C*, *W* and *T* be the initial system size (we call a system with marked speed *C* as a system with system size *C* in the rest of this study), problem size and execution time. Let C' be the increased system size, W' be the increased problem size, and T' be the new execution time for the scaled problem size. Then, we have the isospeed-efficiency condition:

$$\frac{W}{TC} = \frac{W'}{T'C'},$$

This condition is to constrain the new problem size W'.

We define the **isospeed-efficiency scalability function** as:

$$\psi(C,C') = \frac{C'W}{CW'}$$

In the ideal situation, $W' = C'W/C$ and $\psi(C,C') = 1$. Generally, $W' > C'W/C$ and $\psi(C,C') < 1$.

When we apply the isospeed-efficiency scalability to a homogeneous environment, because all C_i are equal, we have $C = pC_i$, and $C' = p'C_i$. Thus, the scalability function is

$$\psi(C,C') = \frac{C'W}{CW'} = \frac{p'W}{pW'}$$

This shows that the original homogeneous isospeed scalability metric is a special case of isospeed-efficiency scalability metric.

3.4 Theoretical studies

The following theoretical results are important for scalability study.

Theorem 1: Let an algorithm has a balanced workload on each node and the sequential portion (which cannot be parallelized) of the algorithm is α, if we can find a problem size to keep the speed-efficiency constant when the system size is increased, then the system is scalable and the scalability is

$$\psi(C,C') = \frac{t_0 + T_o}{t_0' + T_o'}$$

where t_0 and t_0' are the execution time of the sequential portion, T_o and T_o' are the communication overhead of system C and C' separately.

Proof: The parallel execution time can be divided into two parts, $T = T_c + T_o$, where T_c is the computation time, and T_o is the total overhead spent on communication, synchronization and other overhead. If computing system C is used to compute a problem with size W, and W' is the increased problem size to satisfy the isospeed-efficiency condition when the computing system is increased to C', we have

$$\frac{W}{(T_c + T_o)C} = \frac{W'}{(T_c' + T_o')C'}$$

Since the algorithm is evenly load balanced and the sequential portion of the algorithm is α, we have

$$W_i = (1-\alpha)W\frac{C_i}{C}$$

where W_i is the workload assigned on node *i*, so,

$$T_c = \frac{W_i}{C_i} + t_0 = \frac{(1-\alpha)W}{C} + t_0$$

where $t_0 = \frac{\alpha W}{C_i}$, which represents the execution time of the sequential portion of algorithm hence,

$$\frac{W}{\left[(\frac{(1-\alpha)W}{C}+t_0)+T_o\right]C}=\frac{W'}{\left[(\frac{(1-\alpha)W'}{C'}+t_0')+T_o'\right]C'}$$

Thus, the increased problem size W' is

$$W'=\frac{C't_0'+C'T_o'}{Ct_0+CT_o}\cdot W=\frac{C'(t_0'+T_o')}{C(t_0+T_o)}\cdot W$$

Therefore, the computing system is scalable and the scalability is

$$\psi(C,C')=\frac{C'W}{CW'}=\frac{C'W}{C\cdot\frac{C'(t_0'+T_o')}{C(t_0+T_o)}\cdot W}=\frac{t_0+T_o}{t_0'+T_o'}\quad\blacksquare$$

Theorem 1 not only provides a method to calculate the scalability of an algorithm-system combination, but also shows a meaningful and significant understanding for scalability. It reflects that the scalability is decided by both the sequential portion of the work and the communication overhead. When the problem size is increased to keep the speed-efficiency constant, the sequential portion of work might be increased because the problem size is increased, and the communication overhead is increased too because the system size is increased. So in practice, the scalability is likely to be smaller than 1.

Corollary 1: If an algorithm can be parallelized perfectly and has a balanced workload on each node, and if the communication overhead is constant for any problem size and system size, then the algorithm-system combination is scalable and the scalability is perfect with a constant value 1.

Proof: According to theorem 1, we have

$$\psi(C,C')=\frac{t_0+T_o}{t_0'+T_o'}$$

In an ideal case, the algorithm can be parallelized perfectly, which means $\alpha=0$. Thus, $t_0=t_0'=0$.

If the communication overhead is constant at any problem size and system size, we have $T_o=T_o'$.

Therefore, the scalability is 1. ■

Corollary 1 shows the scalability of an ideal case. According to previous analysis of the isospeed-efficiency scalability, the scalability of an ideal case is 1.

Corollary 2: If an algorithm can be parallelized perfectly and has a balanced workload on each node, and if we can find a problem size to keep the speed-efficiency constant when the system size is increased, then the algorithm-system combination is scalable and the scalability is

$$\psi(C,C')=\frac{T_o}{T_o'}$$

Proof: Similar to the proof in Corollary 1, if the algorithm can be parallelized perfectly, we have $\alpha=0$ and $t_0=t_0'=0$. According to theorem 1, the scalability is

$$\psi(C,C')=\frac{t_0+T_o}{t_0'+T_o'}=\frac{T_o}{T_o'}\quad\blacksquare$$

Corollary 2 demonstrates that if an algorithm can be parallelized perfectly and has a balanced workload on each node, then the scalability will only be decided by the total overhead at different problem and system size.

These theorems and corollaries show that if we are able to analyze the total overhead at system C and C', and the sequential ratio of the algorithm, we can calculate and predict the scalability of system with size C' based on the system with size C. We will show this method in experiments.

3.5 Calculation of isospeed-efficiency scalability

The isospeed-efficiency scalability can be obtained in many ways. The most straightforward one is to compute the scalability. This method is to measure the execution time at different system and problem sizes and calculate the scalability by using isospeed-efficiency scalability definition.

Another approach is to analyze and predict the scalability. This method is to analyze the computational part and communicational part of the algorithm and the communication latency of the machine, and then use derived theoretical results to calculate the scalability. This method can also be used to verify the computed scalability or predict the scalability.

The following experiments will show how we can compute or predict the isospeed-efficiency scalability.

4. Experimental results and analyses

Experimental testing has been conducted to verify the correctness of the isospeed-efficiency and the associated analytical results and to show the isospeed-efficiency is practically applicable.

4.1 Algorithm and implementation

Two classical algorithms, Gaussian Elimination algorithm and Matrix Multiplication algorithm, are selected for testing. Both of them are used widely in scientific computing.

4.1.1 Gaussian Elimination (GE). GE algorithm solves dense linear equations $Ax=b$, where A is a known matrix of size $N \times N$, x is the required solution vector, and b is a known vector of size N. The algorithm has two stages:

(1) Gaussian elimination stage: the original system of equations is reduced to an upper triangular form $Ux = y$, where U is a matrix of size $N \times N$ in which all elements below the diagonal are zeros and the diagonal elements have the value 1. The vector y is the modified version of vector b.

(2) Back substitution stage: the new system of equations is solved to obtain the value of x.

The parallel GE algorithm used in experiments is described as following.

(1) Process 0 distributes the data of matrix A and vector b proportionally to other nodes according to their marked speeds by using row-based heterogeneous cyclic distribution[6]

(2) All processes compute concurrently:

(2.1) For ($i = 0$; $i < N - 1$; i++)

(2.1.1) The process which owns the pivot row broadcasts the pivot row to all processes

(2.1.2) For ($j = i + 1$; $j < N$; j++)

(a) Each process judges if row j belongs to itself or not

(b) If yes, then conducts Gaussian elimination on this row

(2.2) Synchronize all processes due to data dependence

(3) Process 0 collects temporary results from other processes and conducts the back substitution stage

Through analyzing the algorithm, the workload of this algorithm is,

$$W(N) = \frac{2}{3}N^3 - \frac{1}{2}N^2 - 3\frac{1}{6}N + 3$$

This polynomial is used to calculate the workload in our experiments.

4.1.2 Matrix Multiplication (MM). MM algorithm calculates the product of two matrices, $C = A \times B$. For simplicity, we restrict matrix A and B to be square $N \times N$ matrices. [1] conducted a thorough research for matrix multiplication optimization on heterogeneous platform. It stated that the matrix multiplication optimization problem on heterogeneous platform is the problem to balance the workload with different speed resources and minimize the communication overhead. Unfortunately, this problem has been proved to be a NP-Complete problem. A polynomial heuristic algorithm called Optimal Column-based Tiling was thus proposed and proved to be a good solution for heterogeneous platforms in [1].

Our experiments are designed to verify the proposed scalability metric. There is no intent to introduce new algorithms on heterogeneous platforms. We have implemented a simple row-based heuristic algorithm. Our algorithm adopts the HoHe strategy proposed in [6]. The HoHe strategy distributes homogeneous processes over different speed processors with each process running on a separate processor, while distribution of matrices over the processes is heterogeneous block cyclic pattern. In our algorithm, first, process 0 distributes matrix A by using a row-based heterogeneous block distribution, which means A is distributed proportionally into other nodes according to these nodes' marked speeds. Then process 0 distributes matrix B to other nodes. After data distribution, each node computes part of the matrix multiplication on its own data. Finally, process 0 collects all results from other processes. Since there is no communication during computation, communication only occurs in data distribution and collection. This algorithm is not a perfect algorithm, but this algorithm does balance the workload between different speed resources, since each node will work on $N \times C_i / C$ rows of data and the workload of each node is $2 \times N^3 \times C_i / C$. The total workload of our algorithm is $W(N) = 2 \times N^3$. The implementation of this algorithm follows HoHe strategy, which generates the same number of processes as the number of processors and distributes each process on a separate processor.

4.2 Experimental platform

The experimental platform is the Sunwulf cluster in the Scalable Computing Software (SCS) laboratory at Illinois Institute of Technology. Sunwulf is composed of one SunFire server node (sunwulf node), 64 SunBlade compute nodes (hpc-1 to hpc-64) and 20 SunFire V210 compute nodes (hpc-65 to hpc-84). The server node has four CPUs and 4GB memory. Each CPU is 480 MHz. The SunBlade compute node has one 500-MHz CPU and 128M memory. The SunFire V210 compute node has two 1GHz CPUs and 2GB memory. The network connecting all these nodes is 100M Ethernet. The software platform includes SunOS 5.8 and MPICH 1.2.5 release version.

4.3 Measuring the marked speed

In our experiments, we use NASA Parallel Benchmark to measure the marked speed. We run each benchmark, including LU, FT, BT, and etc., on each node and take the average speed on each node as its marked speed. Table 1 gives the measured marked speed of the server node with one CPU, the SunBlade compute node and the SunFire V210 compute node. Once the marked speed of each node is measured, the marked speed of a whole computing system can be calculated according to Definition 2. For example, if we choose the following nodes to participate computation: Server node with 1 CPU, one SunBlade compute node and two SunFire compute nodes with 1 CPU, the marked speed of this computing system is:

$$20.88 + 20.29 + 2 \times 36.45 = 114.07 \text{ (Mflops)}$$

Table 1 Marked speed of Sunwulf nodes (Mflops)

Node	Server Node (1 CPU)	SunBlade	SunFire V210 (1 CPU)
Marked Speed	20.88	20.29	36.45

4.4 Experimental results and analyses

4.4.1 GE experimental results. Experiments have been conducted to analyze the proposed scalability metric for GE algorithm with different system configurations. We start with two nodes of Sunwulf, one SunBlade node and one server node. In this case, server node uses two CPUs. From Table 1, we can calculate the marked speed of this environment.

$$C_2 = 20.88 \times 2 + 20.29 = 62.05 \text{ (Mflops)}$$

Table 2 shows the workload, execution time, achieved speed and speed-efficiency of GE at different matrix sizes on two nodes. The speed-efficiency is calculated according to Definition 4.

Table 2 Experimental results on two nodes

Rank N	Workload W	Execution Time T	Achieved Speed	Speed-efficiency
100	661353	260.770	2.536	0.041
200	5312703	473.786	11.213	0.181
300	17954053	925.242	19.405	0.313
400	42585403	1587.725	26.822	0.432
500	83206753	2657.918	31.305	0.505

Based on the experimental results, we show the relationship between speed-efficiency and matrix size in Fig. 1. Since the function between speed-efficiency and matrix size is polynomial, we use a polynomial trend line to approach the sample results. From the polynomial trend line, we can read the approximate value of speed-efficiency at any matrix size or read the approximate required matrix size to obtain a specified speed-efficiency. For example, if we want to obtain a speed-efficiency of 0.3, the required matrix size should be around 310. We measured the speed-efficiency when matrix size is 310 and the result is 0.312, which is shown with a light gray dot in Fig. 1. This verifies the method that we can read the required matrix size for a specified speed-efficiency from trend line works.

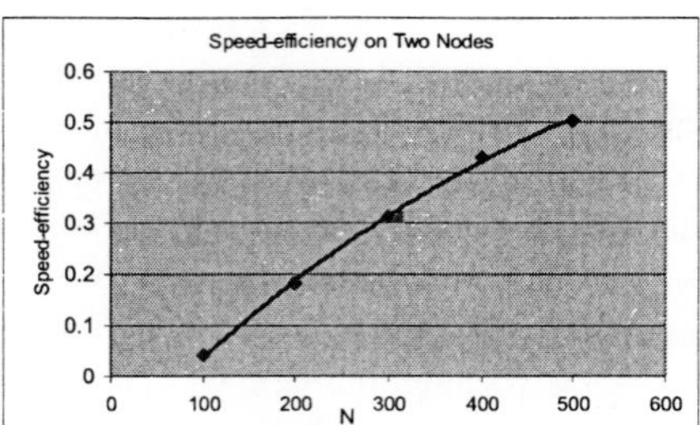

Fig. 1 Speed-efficiency on two nodes

Now, we increase the system size to four nodes and the configuration of four nodes has also changed. The new computing system is composed of hpc-40, hpc-41, hpc-42 and server node with two CPUs. Similar to the analysis in the case of two nodes, we calculate the workload and marked speed, then calculate the speed-efficiency. In this case, the marked speed is C_4 = 102.63Mflops. The required matrix size to obtain a 0.3 speed-efficiency is around 480.

Based on these results, we use the first method in Section 3.5 to calculate the scalability when system size increases from two nodes to four nodes. We select the speed-efficiency at 0.3. The required matrix size will be around 310 in the case of two nodes and 480 in the case of four nodes. According to the scalability function definition, we have

$$\psi(C_2, C_4) = \frac{C_4 \cdot W(N)}{C_2 \cdot W(N')} = 0.445$$

Similar to the previous analysis, we obtain the results of the case of 8 nodes, 16 nodes and 32 nodes. In each case, one node is server node and the rest nodes are SunBlade compute nodes. We select speed-efficiency at 0.3 and read the required matrix size from all those figures. The result is shown in **Table 3**.

Table 3 Required rank to obtain 0.3 speed-efficiency

System Configuration	Rank N	Workload W	Marked Speed(Mflops)
2 Nodes, C_2	310	1819093	62.05
4 Nodes, C_4	480	11682713	102.63
8 Nodes, C_8	1000	6.66E+08	183.79
16 Nodes, C_{16}	1700	3.27E+09	346.11
32 Nodes, C_{32}	3200	2.18E+10	670.75

The measured scalability of GE algorithm on Sunwulf is shown in following table.

Table 4 Measured scalability of GE on Sunwulf

$\psi(C_2, C_4)$	$\psi(C_4, C_8)$	$\psi(C_8, C_{16})$	$\psi(C_{16}, C_{32})$
0.445	0.198	0.383	0.290

4.4.2 MM experimental results. Another experiment we have conducted to analyze the proposed scalability metric is MM algorithm. We have tested the MM algorithm on 2, 4, 8, 16 and 32 nodes of Sunwulf cluster. In each case, half nodes are SunBlade compute nodes and the other half nodes are SunFire V210 nodes except one node is server node. For example, in the case of 8 nodes, the computing system is composed of one server node, three SunBlade compute nodes and four SunFire V210 compute nodes. The marked speed of the computing system in each case is different with previous experiment due to different system configuration. For instance, in the case of 8 nodes, the marked speed is:

$C_8' = 20.88 + 3 \times 20.29 + 4 \times 36.45 = 227.55$ (Mflops)

The experiment is similar to the previous experiment. The details are omitted here. The speed-efficiency of MM algorithm at different system configurations is given in Fig. 2.

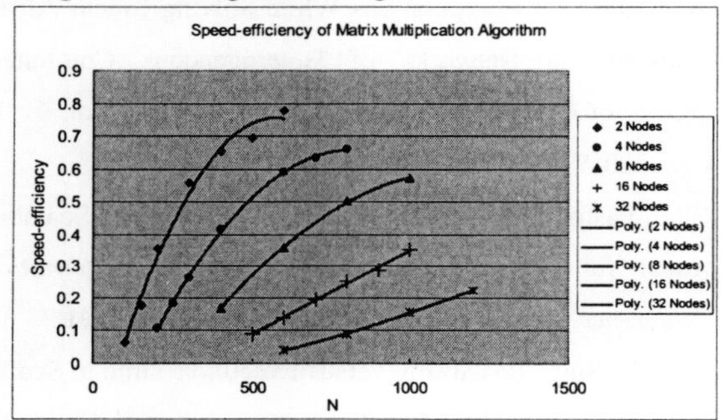

Fig. 2 Speed-efficiency of MM on Sunwulf

Similarly to the analysis in the GE experiment, we use the first method in Section 3.5 to calculate the scalability when system size changes. If the given speed-efficiency is 0.2, we read the required matrix size at different system configurations from Fig. 2. Then, we calculate the isospeed-efficiency scalability for the MM algorithm on Sunwulf as following.

Table 5 Scalability of MM on Sunwulf

$\psi(C_2', C_4')$	$\psi(C_4', C_8')$	$\psi(C_8', C_{16}')$	$\psi(C_{16}', C_{32}')$
0.539	0.416	0.443	0.470

4.4.3 Comparison of two experimental results. The above two experiments are actually two different algorithm-system combinations. Although both of them are conducted on a series of different system configurations of the Sunwulf cluster, the machine parameters, such as machine latency, are the same. By using the proposed isospeed-efficiency scalability metric, we are able to quantify the scalability of these two different combinations.

Compared with the scalability of GE-Sunwulf combination given in Table 6, we find the scalability of MM-Sunwulf combination is higher. This indicates that the MM-Sunwulf combination is more scalable than the GE-Sunwulf combination. The GE algorithm has a sequential portion and has more communications than that of the MM algorithm. Its scalability should be smaller than the scalability of the latter. Our experiment verifies this fact and presents actual quantified scalability advantage of the MM algorithm on Sunwulf cluster.

4.5 Scalability prediction

As we proved in Section 3, if we are able to analyze the sequential ratio and measure the communication latency of the machine, we can predict the scalability. We use the GE-Sunwulf combination to illustrate how scalability can be predicted.

According to the parallel GE algorithm in Section 4.1.1, the sequential ratio of this algorithm is $\alpha = O(1/N)$. When N is large enough, we treat $\alpha \approx 0$. The total communication overhead is

$$T_o = T_{broadcast} + 2 \times (p-1) \times (T_{send} + T_{recv}) + N \times (2 \times T_{broadcast} + T_{barrier})$$

where p is the number of processes. We have measured the parameters in the above equation on Sunwulf,

$$T_{boradcast} \approx 0.12 + p \times 0.23(ms)$$

$$T_{send} = T_{recv} \approx 0.08 + (0.00003 \times N)(ms)$$

$$T_{barrier} \approx p \times 0.39(ms)$$

The computation time can be written as

$$T_c = \frac{W(N) \times t_c}{p}$$

where t_c is the time of one unit computation, we have measured $t_c \approx 3.1 \times 10^{-5}(ms)$. Based on these analyses and parameters, according to Corollary 2, we predict the scalability is $\psi(C, C') = T_o / T_o'$, where N is constrained by the isospeed-efficiency condition.

Based on the case of two nodes, our prediction result for the required N to keep constant speed-efficiency at 0.3 is as following,

Table 6 Predicted required rank

Nodes	4	8	16	32
N (predicition)	492	928	1683	3226

Thus, the predicted scalability is

Table 7 Predicted scalability of GE on Sunwulf

$\psi(C_2, C_4)$	$\psi(C_4, C_8)$	$\psi(C_8, C_{16})$	$\psi(C_{16}, C_{32})$
0.413	0.267	0.316	0.275

We can see that the predicted scalability is close to our measured scalability, which also verifies the isospeed-efficiency scalability metric works well.

5. Conclusion and future work

In this study, we propose an isospeed-efficiency scalability metric for general distributed environment. The proposed metric contains the homogenous isospeed scalability[10] as a special case. We first introduce a new concept of marked speed to describe the computational capability of computing systems. Based on the marked speed concept, we present the isospeed-efficiency scalability for heterogeneous computing. We then analyze the new scalability metric in theory and derive useful formulas for calculating and predicting this scalability. We have conducted experiments to verify these formulae in a heterogeneous computing environment. These results match the analytical results well and show that the proposed isospeed-efficiency scalability metric is appropriate for a general scalable computing environment, homogeneous or heterogeneous, tightly coupled or widely distributed.

Marked speed is a simple but effective metric to reflect the computational capability of general distributed systems. In future, we plan to extend the single parameter marked speed to multi-parameter marked performance that has several parameters to describe the full capability of a computing system, to provide users more options for their needs.

We have demonstrated that the scalability can be predicted based on derived formulas. We plan to explore the possibility of extending the prediction of scalability into system support so that the scalability can be predicted automatically or semi-automatically.

6. Acknowledgements

This research was supported in part by national science foundation under NSF grant SCI-0504291, CNS-0406328, ACI-0305355, EIA-0224377, and ANI-0123930.

7. References

[1] O. Beaumont, V. Boudet, F. Rastello and Y. Robert, "Matrix Multiplication on Heterogeneous Platforms", *IEEE Trans. Parallel Distributed Systems*, Vol. 12, No. 10, pp.1033-1051, 2001.

[2] D. Culler, J. Singh and A. Gupta, *Parallel Computer Architecture: A Hardware/Software Approach*, Morgan Kaufmann Publishers, 1999.

[3] V. Kumar, A. Grama, A. Gupta and G. Karypis, *Introduction to Parallel Computing: Design and Analysis of Parallel Algorithms*, 1994.

[4] K. Hwang and Z. Xu, *Scalable Parallel Computing*, McGraw - Hill, 1998.

[5] P.P. Jogalekar and C.M. Woodside, "Evaluating the Scalability of Distributed Systems", *IEEE Trans. on Parallel and Distributed Systems*, Vol. 11, No. 6, pp.589-603, 2000.

[6] A. Kalinov and A. Lastovetsky, "Heterogeneous Distribution of Computations While Solving Linear Algebra Problems on Networks of Heterogeneous Computers", *Journal of Parallel and Distributed Computing*, Vol. 61, No. 4, pp.520-535, 2001.

[7] L. Pastor and J.L. Bosque, "An Efficiency and Scalability Model for Heterogeneous Clusters". *IEEE International Conference on Cluster Computing*, pp.427-434, 2001.

[8] X.H. Sun, "Scalability versus Execution Time in Scalable Systems", *Journal of Parallel and Distributed Computing*, Vol. 62, No. 2, pp.173 - 192, 2002.

[9] X.H. Sun and L.M. Ni, "Scalable Problems and Memory-Bounded Speedup", *Journal of Parallel and Distributed Computing*, Vol. 19, pp.27-37, 1993.

[10] X.H. Sun and D. Rover, "Scalability of Parallel Algorithm - Machine Combinations", *IEEE Trans. Parallel Distributed Systems*, Vol. 5, pp.599 - 613, 1994.

Session 8A: Interconnection Networks

VLAN-based Minimal Paths in PC Cluster with Ethernet on Mesh and Torus

Tomohiro Otsuka Michihiro Koibuchi* Akiya Jouraku Hideharu Amano
Department of Information and Computer Science, Keio University
3-14-1, Hiyoshi, Kohoku-ku, Yokohama, 223-8522 Japan
{terry,koibuchi,jouraku,hunga}@am.ics.keio.ac.jp

Abstract

In a PC cluster with Ethernet, well-distributed multiple paths among hosts can be obtained by applying VLAN technology. In this paper, we propose VLAN topology sets and path assignment methods in mesh and torus. The proposed VLAN-based methods on mesh require N^{M-1} and $\lfloor N^{M-1}/2 \rfloor + 1$ VLANs to provide balanced minimal paths and partially balanced ones respectively, where N is the number of switches per dimension and M is the number of dimensions. Similarly, those on torus require $2N^{M-1}$ and $N^{M-1}+2$ VLANs respectively. Simulation results show that the proposed methods improve up to 902% and 706% of throughput respectively.

1. Introduction

Ethernet has been used to connect hosts in PC clusters, because of its high performance per cost. Unlike the early Beowulf clusters, recent PC clusters employ system software[6][7] which enables zero- or one-copy communication used in system area networks (SANs)[2][3]. In background of enabling the simplified software stack at hosts to provide low-latency and high-bandwidth communication, high-throughput switching fabrics are recently implemented; indeed, a packet is not often discarded. In addition, link bandwidth of Ethernet is rapidly increased, such as GbE or 10GbE standardization, as CPU computation power is increased. Thus, Ethernet has become an alternative network for high-performance PC clusters, and Ethernet topology and its routing paths will become one of crucial components to build a large-scale system.

However, most of PC clusters using Ethernet have employed simple tree-based topologies, since the spanning tree protocol (STP) logically requires acyclic topologies for dynamic host configuration. This is because Ethernet technology is not originally designed for high-performance computing or parallel computing.

Thus, even when building a typical topology for parallel computers, such as a torus, PC clusters with Ethernet must accept non-minimal embedded-tree paths, and links which do not belong to a spanning tree cannot be used. That is, well-distributed minimal paths, such as the dimension-order routing[1] studied for parallel computers and SANs cannot be applied. We consider that this is the reason why various topologies for parallel processing have not been focused in research field of PC clusters with Ethernet.

Kudoh et al. proposed to apply VLAN technology to PC clusters with Ethernet so as to employ multiple paths between switches under various topologies including fat-tree, mesh and hyper crossbar[4][5]. They also showed that VLAN-based routing made the best use of link bandwidth under well-distributed paths.

VLAN technology is originally not for increasing network throughput, but for partitioning hosts into multiple groups. However, VLAN can also be used to provide multiple paths between hosts to increase throughput as follows: all VLAN groups are extended to include all hosts, and different link sets are assigned to each VLAN topology. In this case, all pairs of hosts can communicate via any VLAN group. Thus, multiple paths which include different links are available between each pair of hosts.

Although each VLAN topology is logically a tree, by introducing multiple VLANs each of which consists of a different set of links, a flexible physical path set including all links can be employed. For example, Figure 1 shows three examples of VLAN topologies, which include all hosts and different link sets. As shown in this figure, minimal paths can be taken by selecting a suitable VLAN topology from (b), (c) and (d) at a source host.

Note that each path is assigned into a single VLAN, and each source host must indicate a VLAN number corresponding to a path. Thus, Ethernet physical topology is free from tree-based structures with VLAN technology. VLAN-based routing can be conducted by L2 Ethernet[5], and it is likely to be supported by the low-level communication library in PC clusters[6].

*Presently with National Institute of Informatics, koibuchi@nii.ac.jp

0190-3918/05 $20.00 © 2005 IEEE

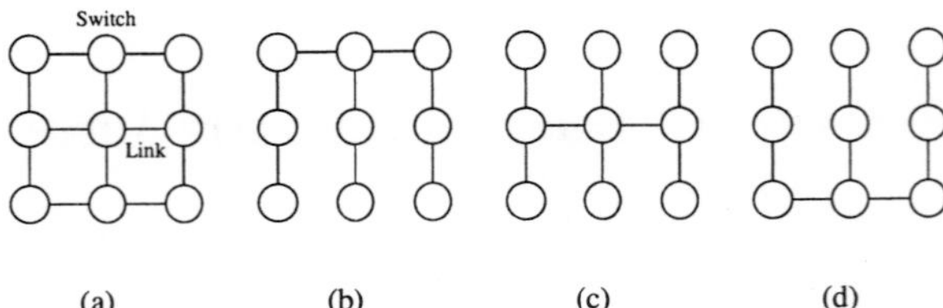

Figure 1. Examples of VLAN topologies for 3×3 2-D mesh

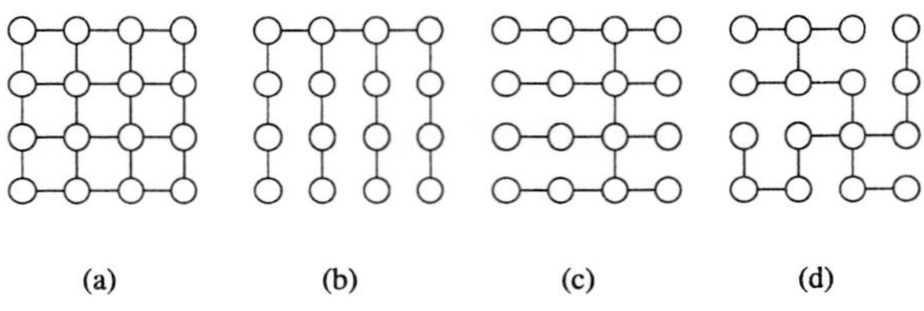

Figure 2. 4×4 2-D mesh and examples of its VLAN topologies

Although IEEE 802.1Q VLAN tag field can identify 4,094 ($2^{12}-2$) VLANs, commercial cost-effective Ethernet switches support only a limited number of VLANs, which would be a limiting factor in an implementation and extension of PC clusters. Since balanced minimal paths, which decrease packet collisions, are essential to improve performance in PC clusters, an efficient strategy to employ VLAN topologies is required for PC clusters with Ethernet.

In this paper, we propose VLAN topology sets and path assignment methods to them in mesh and torus. The rest of this paper is organized as follows. In Section 2, we show VLAN topology sets and path assignment methods in mesh, and we also show them in torus in Section 3. In Section 4, evaluation results of VLAN-based paths and the STP-based paths are shown, and in Section 5, the conclusion is presented.

2. VLAN-based Minimal Paths on Mesh

In this section, we show two VLAN-based methods to take balanced or partially balanced minimal paths. The first one ensures minimal and well-distributed paths, which are the same as those of the dimension-order routing (DOR)[1], which is known as a method to make well-distributed paths. In the dimension-order routing on two-dimensional (2-D) mesh, packets are forwarded to x-direction with required hops first, and then forwarded to y-direction. The second method guarantees minimal paths with a slight loss of path uniformity, while the number of required VLANs is about a half of that in the first method.

2.1. Preliminary

Figure 2 shows 4×4 2-D mesh and three examples of VLAN topologies for it. In the figure, each vertex and arc represents Ethernet switch and link respectively. Although it is possible that some hosts are connected to each switch, they are omitted here.

Definition 2.1 (2-D mesh) *Assign a number with a two-dimensional coordinate (x, y) where $0 \leq x < N$ and $0 \leq y < N$ to each switch. By connecting vertex (x, y) with vertexes $(x+1, y)$, $(x-1, y)$, $(x, y+1)$ and $(x, y-1)$, if $x+1 < N$, $x-1 \geq 0$, $y+1 < N$ and $y-1 \geq 0$ respectively, an $N \times N$ two-dimensional mesh is formed.* □

Two-dimensional mesh treated here is commonly defined as an N-ary 2-cube, and its numbering is as follows:

$$\begin{array}{cccc} (0,0) & (1,0) & \cdots & (N-1,0) \\ (0,1) & (1,1) & \cdots & (N-1,1) \\ \vdots & \vdots & \ddots & \vdots \\ (0,N-1) & (1,N-1) & \cdots & (N-1,N-1) \end{array}$$

Each of VLAN topologies in Figure 2 is a spanning tree of physical network (a), and consists of N^2 switches and N^2-1 links. As shown in Figure 2, there are various alternative VLAN topologies (trees) in mesh. However, it is difficult to establish a simple minimal-path set using trees with low regularity, such as (d), in combination with other VLAN topologies. Therefore, VLAN topologies in the proposed methods are based on simple topologies similar to (b) or (c). In order to identify each VLAN topology used in the proposed methods, we use the following notation.

Definition 2.2 (linear connection in 2-D mesh) *A vertical connection in 2-D mesh is represented as $l(x, -)$. That is, vertex (x, y) is connected with vertexes $(x, y+1)$ and $(x, y-1)$, if $y+1 < N$ and $y > 0$ respectively, in the connection. Similarly, a horizontal connection in 2-D mesh is represented as $l(-, y)$. That is, vertex (x, y) is connected with $(x+1, y)$ and $(x-1, y)$, if $x+1 < N$ and $x > 0$ respectively.* □

A VLAN topology can be formed by a single linear connection in a dimension and all linear connections in the opposite dimension. For example, the VLAN (b) in Figure 2 consists of connections $l(0, -)$, $l(1, -)$, $l(2, -)$, $l(3, -)$ and $l(-, 0)$, while the VLAN (c) consists of connections $l(2, -)$, $l(-, 0)$, $l(-, 1)$, $l(-, 2)$ and $l(-, 3)$. Such a VLAN topology is represented as the following notation.

Definition 2.3 (VLAN topology in 2-D mesh) *Each of the VLAN* $\mathrm{VL}(-, y_0)$ *and* $\mathrm{VL}(x_0, -)$ *consists of all switches (vertexes) and the following set of linear connections:*

$$\begin{aligned} \mathrm{VL}(-, y_0): & \quad \{l(x, -) \mid 0 \le x < N\} \cup \{l(-, y_0)\} \\ \mathrm{VL}(x_0, -): & \quad \{l(-, y) \mid 0 \le y < N\} \cup \{l(x_0, -)\} \end{aligned}$$

□

2.2. Minimal Paths for the DOR in 2-D Mesh

Definition 2.4 (DOR VLANs in 2-D mesh) *The DOR VLAN set consists of the following* N *VLANs in* $N \times N$ *mesh:*

$$\{\mathrm{VL}(-, y) \mid 0 \le y < N\}$$

□

A path from a source switch (x_S, y_S) is assigned into the VLAN $\mathrm{VL}(-, y_S)$. An example of the DOR VLANs is shown in Figure 3. Figure 3 shows that four VLANs, $\mathrm{VL}(-,0)$, $\mathrm{VL}(-,1)$, $\mathrm{VL}(-,2)$ and $\mathrm{VL}(-,3)$, are employed to take the DOR paths in 4×4 2-D mesh.

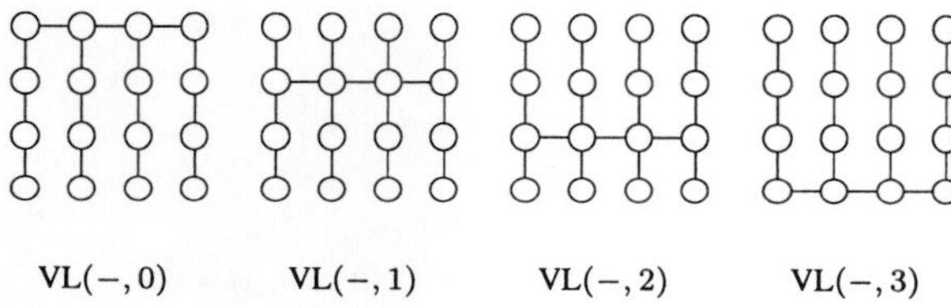

Figure 3. The DOR VLANs in 4×4 2-D mesh

Theorem 2.1 *The DOR VLANs provide the same minimal-path set as that of the dimension-order routing in 2-D mesh.*

Proof A VLAN $\mathrm{VL}(-, y_S)$ consists of a horizontal connection $l(-, y_S)$ and all of N vertical connections. Thus, on $\mathrm{VL}(-, y_S)$, all paths from a source switch (x_S, y_S) are minimal along the dimension-order routing. Since there are N VLANs $\{\mathrm{VL}(-, y) \mid 0 \le y < N\}$, paths from a source switch (x_S, y_S) on $\mathrm{VL}(-, y_S)$ are the same as that of the dimension-order routing. □

Note that an Ethernet switch does not have dedicated channel buffers and flow control mechanism for VLANs, unlike virtual channels in interconnection networks for parallel computers. Thus, the path distribution among VLANs hardly affects network performance, and VLAN selection for minimal paths from a source switch (x_S, y_S) to a destination switch (x_D, y_D), which can be assigned to different VLANs, is trivial.

2.3. Minimal Paths with Partial DOR (PDOR) in 2-D Mesh

We show the second method whose path set is similar to that of the dimension-order routing.

Definition 2.5 (PDOR VLANs in 2-D mesh) *The PDOR VLAN set consists of the following* $\lfloor N/2 \rfloor + 1$ *VLANs in* $N \times N$ *mesh:*

$$\{\mathrm{VL}(-, 2i+1) \mid 0 \le i < \lfloor N/2 \rfloor\} \cup \{\mathrm{VL}(x_0, -)\}$$

□

Figure 4 shows an example of the PDOR VLANs in 4×4 2-D mesh. This method employs only three VLANs, $\mathrm{VL}(-,1)$, $\mathrm{VL}(-,3)$ and $\mathrm{VL}(1,-)$, by taking different minimal-path set from that of the DOR. The selection of the value x_0 is trivial, because links of the vertical connection in $\mathrm{VL}(x_0, -)$ are never used by paths.

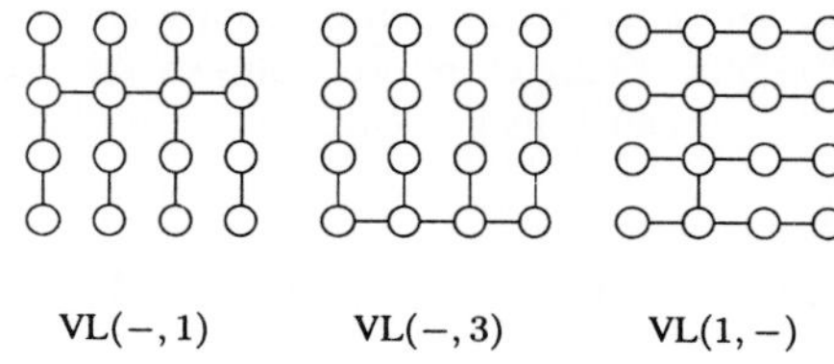

Figure 4. The PDOR VLANs in 4×4 2-D mesh

Compared with the DOR VLANs, $\lfloor (N+1)/2 \rfloor$ VLANs $\{\mathrm{VL}(-, 2i) \mid 0 \le i < \lfloor (N+1)/2 \rfloor\}$ are deleted, and $\mathrm{VL}(x_0, -)$ is newly employed.

As illustrated in $\mathrm{VL}(-,1)$ and $\mathrm{VL}(-,3)$ in Figure 4, on the VLAN $\mathrm{VL}(-, 2i+1)$, all paths from a switch $(x, 2i+1)$ to all destination switches take minimal paths along the dimension-order routing. On the other hand, paths from a switch $(x, 2i)$ cannot be along the dimension-order routing for all destinations, because of lack of the VLAN $\mathrm{VL}(-, 2i)$. Thus, in order to take minimal paths, each source switch (x_S, y_S) uses one of appropriate VLANs selected by the following procedure for a destination switch (x_D, y_D).

if y_S **mod** $2 = 1$ **then** use $\mathrm{VL}(-, y_S)$;
else if $y_D < y_S$ **then** use $\mathrm{VL}(-, y_S - 1)$;
else if $y_D > y_S$ **then** use $\mathrm{VL}(-, y_S + 1)$;
else $\{y_D = y_S\}$ use $\mathrm{VL}(x_0, -)$;

Theorem 2.2 *The PDOR VLANs provide a minimal-path set in 2-D mesh.*

Proof Since $\mathrm{VL}(x_0, -)$ has all horizontal connections, paths from a source switch $(x_S, 2i)$ to a destination switch

$(x, 2i)$ on $\mathrm{VL}(x_0, -)$ are minimal along one of the horizontal connections. For other destinations, paths from a source switch $(x_S, 2i)$ are minimal via switch $(x_S, 2i+1)$ on $\mathrm{VL}(-, 2i+1)$ for $y_D > y_S$, and those are minimal via switch $(x_S, 2i-1)$ on $\mathrm{VL}(-, 2i-1)$ for $y_D < y_S$.

On the other hand, according to Theorem 2.1, paths from a source switch $(x_S, 2i+1)$ on $\mathrm{VL}(-, 2i+1)$ are minimal. Since both $(x_S, 2i+1)$ and $(x_S, 2i-1)$ belong to $\{(x_S, 2i{+}1) \mid 0 \le i < \lfloor N/2 \rfloor\}$, the PDOR VLANs provide a minimal-path set in 2-D mesh. □

For example, assuming that the source switch is $(0, 0)$ and the destination switch is $(3, 2)$ in Figure 4, the path is along the following order using $\mathrm{VL}(-, 1)$.

$$(0,0) \to (0,1) \to (1,1) \to (2,1) \to (3,1) \to (3,2)$$

With this method, the path set is slightly different from that of the dimension-order routing, since it differs from the dimension-order routing only when a source switch is $(x_S, 2i)$. However, the difference is only for the first step toward y-dimension. Therefore, paths of this method are still well-distributed. Its influence will be evaluated in Section 4.

2.4. Generalization (M-dimensional Mesh)

We simply show a generalization of the VLAN-based minimal paths for N^M M-dimensional mesh.

By extending Definition 2.1, we assign an M-dimensional coordinate $(x_0, x_1, \ldots, x_{M-1})$ to each switch, where $0 \le x_0, x_1, \ldots, x_{M-1} < N$.

Similarly, by simply extending Definition 2.2, $l(x_0, x_1, \ldots, x_{i-1}, -, x_{i+1}, \ldots, x_{M-1})$ is stated as a linear connection which is parallel with i-th axis and has N vertexes $\{(x_0, x_1, \ldots, x_i, \ldots, x_{M-1}) \mid 0 \le x_i < N\}$.

A VLAN

$$\mathrm{VL}\big(x_0, x_1, \ldots, x_{i_0-1}, -, x_{i_0+1}, \ldots, x_{M-1} \mid (i_0, i_1, \ldots, i_{M-1})\big)$$
$$\big(i_0, i_1, \ldots, i_{M-1} \in \{0, 1, \ldots, M-1\},\ i_j \ne i_k\ (j \ne k)\big)$$

consists of the following $(N^M - 1)/(N-1)$ connections (one parallel with i_0-th axis, N connections parallel with i_1-th axis, and so on).

$$\begin{aligned}
&\{l(x_0, x_1, \ldots, x_{i_0-1}, -, x_{i_0+1}, \ldots, x_{M-1})\} \\
\cup\ &\{l(x_0, x_1, \ldots, x_{i_1-1}, -, x_{i_1+1}, \ldots, x_{M-1}) \mid 0 \le x_{i_0} < N\} \\
\cup\ &\{l(x_0, x_1, \ldots, x_{i_2-1}, -, x_{i_2+1}, \ldots, x_{M-1}) \mid 0 \le x_{i_0}, x_{i_1} < N\} \\
&\quad \vdots \\
\cup\ &\{l(x_0, x_1, \ldots, x_{i_{M-1}-1}, -, x_{i_{M-1}+1}, \ldots, x_{M-1}) \mid 0 \le x_{i_0}, x_{i_1}, \ldots, x_{i_{M-2}} < N\}
\end{aligned}$$

Definition 2.6 (DOR VLANs in M-dimensional mesh) *The DOR VLAN set consists of the following N^{M-1} VLANs in N^M M-dimensional mesh:*

$$\{\mathrm{VL}(-, x_1, x_2, \ldots, x_{M-1} \mid A) \mid 0 \le x_1, x_2, \ldots, x_{M-1} < N\}$$
$$(A = (0, 1, \ldots, M-1))$$

□

All paths from a source switch $(x_{0_S}, x_{1_S}, \ldots, x_{(M-1)_S})$ are along the dimension-order routing on a VLAN $\mathrm{VL}(-, x_{1_S}, x_{2_S}, \ldots, x_{(M-1)_S} \mid A)$. It is a simple extension of the case in the two-dimensional mesh.

Next, we shift to the second method whose path set is similar to that of the dimension-order routing.

Definition 2.7 (PDOR VLANs in M-dimensional mesh) *The PDOR VLAN set consists of the following $\lfloor N^{M-1}/2 \rfloor + 1$ VLANs in N^M M-dimensional mesh:*

$$\Big\{\mathrm{VL}(-, x_1, x_2, \ldots, x_{M-1} \mid A) \ \Big|\ 0 \le x_1, x_2, \ldots, x_{M-1} < N, \ \sum_{k=1}^{M-1} x_k \equiv 1 \bmod 2\Big\}$$
$$\cup\ \{\mathrm{VL}(x_0, x_1, \ldots, x_{M-2}, - \mid B)\}$$
$$\big(A = (0, 1, \ldots, M-1),\ B = (M-1, M-2, \ldots, 0)\big)$$

□

All paths from a source switch $(x_{0_S}, x_{1_S}, \ldots, x_{(M-1)_S})$ to a destination switch $(x_{0_D}, x_{1_D}, \ldots, x_{(M-1)_D})$ are minimal using one of appropriate VLANs selected by the following procedure.

```
if Σ_{k=1}^{M-1} x_{k_S} mod 2 = 1 then
  use VL(−, x_{1_S}, x_{2_S}, ..., x_{(M-1)_S} | A) ;
else begin
  selected := false ;
  for i := 1 to M−1 do
    if x_{i_D} > x_{i_S} then begin
      use VL(−, x_{1_S}, x_{2_S}, ..., x_{(i-1)_S},
              x_{i_S}+1, x_{(i+1)_S}, ..., x_{(M-1)_S} | A) ;
      selected := true ; break ;
    end else if x_{i_D} < x_{i_S} then begin
      use VL(−, x_{1_S}, x_{2_S}, ..., x_{(i-1)_S},
              x_{i_S}−1, x_{(i+1)_S}, ..., x_{(M-1)_S} | A) ;
      selected := true ; break ;
    end
  end
  if selected ≠ true then
    use VL(x_0, x_1, ..., x_{M-2}, − | B) ;
end
```

Note that the VLAN $\mathrm{VL}(x_0, x_1, \ldots, x_{M-2}, - \mid B)$ is selected only if the following condition is held:

$$\sum_{k=1}^{M-1} x_{k_S} \equiv 0 \bmod 2, \quad x_{i_S} = x_{i_D} \quad (1 \le i < M)$$

3. VLAN-based Minimal Paths on Torus

In this section, we show the two VLAN-based methods (DOR and PDOR) on torus. Although the number of VLANs in the PDOR VLAN set is about a half of that in the DOR VLAN set as well as in mesh, it is not the minimum number of VLANs to take minimal paths in torus. However, the method for the minimum number of VLANs causes traffic imbalance, and not treated here.

3.1. Preliminary

In this subsection, we state some notations to represent VLAN topologies in torus. Figure 5 shows 4 × 4 2-D torus (a) and three examples of its VLAN topologies, (b), (c) and (d). Unlike a mesh, there are wrap-around links in a torus (snipped off in this figure, however these two lines are actually linked).

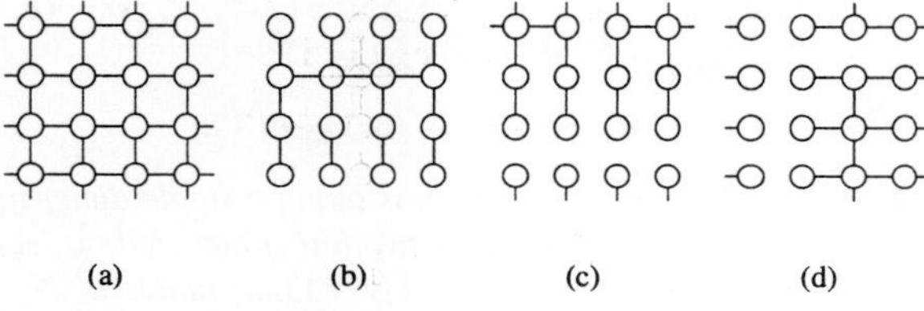

Figure 5. 4×4 **2-D torus and examples of its VLAN topologies**

Definition 3.1 (2-D torus) *Assign a number with a two-dimensional coordinate* (x, y) *where* $0 \le x < N$ *and* $0 \le y < N$ *to each switch. By connecting vertex* (x, y) *with four vertexes* $\big((x \pm 1{+}N) \bmod N,\ y\big)$ *and* $\big(x,\ (y \pm 1{+}N) \bmod N\big)$, *an* $N \times N$ *two-dimensional torus is formed.* □

Two-dimensional torus treated here is commonly defined as an N-ary 2-cube, and its numbering is the same as that of the mesh.

The VLAN (b) in Figure 5 is the identical with a VLAN $\mathrm{VL}(-, 1)$ used in the previous section. However, the VLAN (c) and (d) cannot be represented by the notation of VLAN topologies for a mesh (see Section 2.1). Thus, we state the notation of VLAN topologies for a torus.

As shown in Figure 5(a), there are N links including a wrap-around link in each dimension, and they form a loop. Therefore, one of these N links must be cut off in a VLAN topology.

Definition 3.2 (linear connection in 2-D torus) *A vertical connection, which consists of* N *vertexes and* $N-1$ *links, is represented as* $l(x_0, - : y_0)$ *in 2-D torus. That is, vertex* (x, y) *is connected with the neighboring two vertexes* $\big(x,\ (y{\pm}1{+}N) \bmod N\big)$, *except for a (cutting off) link between vertexes* (x_0, y_r) *and* $\big(x_0,\ (y_r{+}1) \bmod N\big)$, *where* $y_r = (y_0{+}\lfloor N/2 \rfloor) \bmod N$.

Similarly, a horizontal connection, which consists of N *vertexes and* $N-1$ *links, is represented as* $l(- : x_0, y_0)$ *in 2-D torus. That is, vertex* (x, y) *is connected with the neighboring two vertexes* $\big((x \pm 1{+}N) \bmod N,\ y\big)$, *except for a link between vertexes* (x_r, y_0) *and* $\big((x_r{+}1) \bmod N,\ y_0\big)$, *where* $x_r = (x_0{+}\lfloor N/2 \rfloor) \bmod N$. □

As shown in Figure 6, the vertex (x_0, y_0) is centered in each horizontal connection.

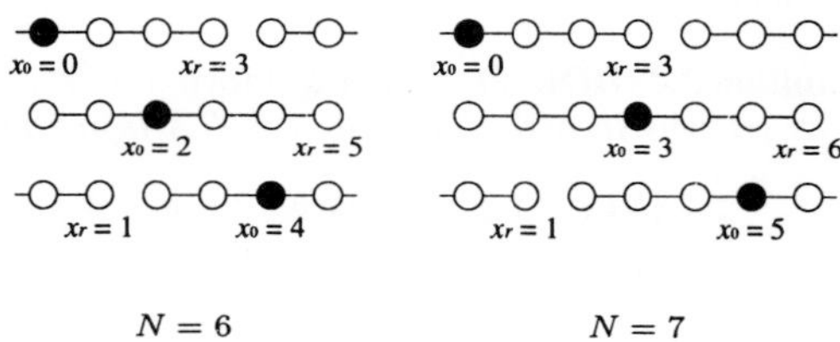

Figure 6. Examples of horizontal connections in 2-D torus

According to Definition 3.2, the VLAN (b) in Figure 5 consists of connections $l(0, - : 1)$, $l(1, - : 1)$, $l(2, - : 1)$, $l(3, - : 1)$ and $l(- : 1, 1)$, while the VLAN (c) consists of connections $l(0, - : 0)$, $l(1, - : 0)$, $l(2, - : 0)$, $l(3, - : 0)$ and $l(- : 3, 0)$, and the VLAN (d) consists of connections $l(2, - : 2)$, $l(- : 2, 0)$, $l(- : 2, 1)$, $l(- : 2, 2)$ and $l(- : 2, 3)$.

Definition 3.3 (VLAN topology in 2-D torus) *Each of the VLAN* $\mathrm{VL}(- : x_0, y_0)$ *and* $\mathrm{VL}(x_0, - : y_0)$ *consists of all switches and the following set of linear connections:*

$$\begin{aligned}
&\mathrm{VL}(- : x_0, y_0) : \\
&\quad \big\{ l(x, - : y_0) \mid 0 \le x < N \big\} \cup \big\{ l(- : x_0, y_0) \big\} \\
&\mathrm{VL}(x_0, - : y_0) : \\
&\quad \big\{ l(- : x_0, y) \mid 0 \le y < N \big\} \cup \big\{ l(x_0, - : y_0) \big\}
\end{aligned}$$

□

According to Definition 3.3, VLANs (b), (c) and (d) in Figure 5 are represented as $\mathrm{VL}(-:1,1)$, $\mathrm{VL}(-:3,0)$ and $\mathrm{VL}(2,-:2)$, respectively.

In addition, we use two kinds of term "distance" from a source switch (x_S, y_S) to a destination switch (x_D, y_D) on each x- or y-coordinate as follows.

$$d^+(x_S, x_D) = (x_D - x_S + N) \bmod N$$
$$d^-(x_S, x_D) = (x_S - x_D + N) \bmod N$$

Each of $d^+(x_S, x_D)$ and $d^+(y_S, y_D)$ is the distance on positive direction of x- or y-axis, while each of $d^-(x_S, x_D)$ and $d^-(y_S, y_D)$ is the distance on negative direction. For example, distances from switch $(0, 3)$ to switch $(3, 1)$ on 4×4 torus are as follows:

$$d^+(x_S, x_D) = 3, \quad d^-(x_S, x_D) = 1,$$
$$d^+(y_S, y_D) = 2, \quad d^-(y_S, y_D) = 2$$

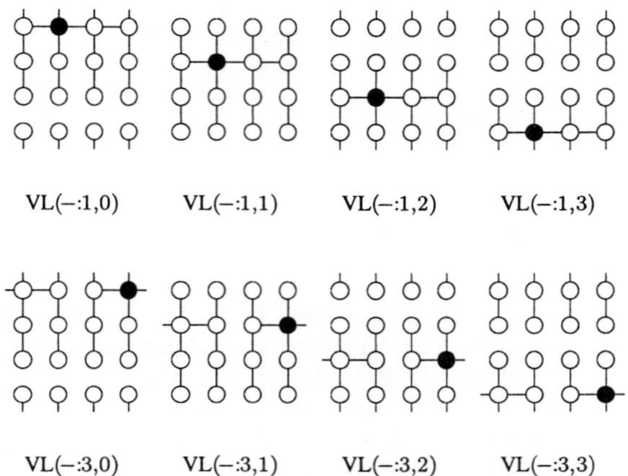

Figure 7. The DOR VLANs in 4×4 2-D torus

3.2. Minimal Paths for the DOR in 2-D Torus

In this subsection, we show VLANs based paths along the dimension-order routing in 2-D torus.

Definition 3.4 (DOR VLANs in 2-D torus) *The DOR VLAN set consists of the following $2N$ VLANs in 2-D torus:*

$$\{\mathrm{VL}(-:x, y) \mid x = a, b, \ 0 \leq y < N\}$$
$$(a = \lfloor (N-1)/2 \rfloor, \ b = N-1)$$

□

This method is similar to that on the mesh, however, a larger number of VLANs is used due to wrap-around links. An example of the DOR VLANs is shown in Figure 7. Figure 7 shows that eight VLANs, $\mathrm{VL}(-:1,0)$, $\mathrm{VL}(-:1,1)$, $\mathrm{VL}(-:1,2)$, $\mathrm{VL}(-:1,3)$, $\mathrm{VL}(-:3,0)$, $\mathrm{VL}(-:3,1)$, $\mathrm{VL}(-:3,2)$ and $\mathrm{VL}(-:3,3)$, are employed to take the DOR paths in 4×4 2-D torus.

In this method, paths from a switch (x_S, y_S) take one of two VLANs $\mathrm{VL}(-:a, y_S)$ and $\mathrm{VL}(-:b, y_S)$. For example, in Figure 7, all paths from the switch $(0, 0)$ use $\mathrm{VL}(-:1,0)$ for the destination switch $(1, y_D)$ ($y_D \in \{0,1,2,3\}$), while they use $\mathrm{VL}(-:3,0)$ for the destination switch $(3, y_D)$.

Assuming that a source switch is (x_S, y_S) and a destination switch is (x_D, y_D), the procedure for selecting an appropriate VLAN is described as follows.

```
function select_ab (s, d, N : integer) : integer
begin
  if d+(s,d) ≤ d-(s,d) then begin
    if s < ⌊N/2⌋ then select_ab := a ;
    else select_ab := b ;
  end else {d+(s,d) > d-(s,d)} begin
    if s < ⌊N/2⌋ then select_ab := b ;
    else select_ab := a ;
  end
end
use VL(− : select_ab (xS, xD, N), yS) ;
```

For example, if the source switch is $(0, 0)$ and the destination switch is $(3, 2)$ in Figure 7, the path is along the following order using VLAN $\mathrm{VL}(-:3,0)$. ($b = 3$, $d^+(x_S, x_D) = 3$, $d^-(x_S, x_D) = 1$)

$$(0,0) \to (3,0) \to (3,1) \to (3,2)$$

Lemma 3.1 *As long as a path is along a single dimension in a torus, it can be formed by two linear connections, each of which is centered on $a = \lfloor (N-1)/2 \rfloor$ and $b = N-1$ respectively.*

Proof Assume that the path is along x-dimension and two linear connections are $l(-:a, y_0)$ and $l(-:b, y_0)$. $l(-:a, y_0)$ lacks just the wrap-around link between $(N-1, y_0)$ and $(0, y_0)$. Since the maximum distance within x-dimension (the small one of $d^+(x_S, x_D)$ and $d^-(x_S, x_D)$) on the torus is $\lfloor N/2 \rfloor$, the minimal-path set which cannot be covered by $l(-:a, y_0)$ is across the following vertex set.

$$\{(x, y_0) \mid x = x_1, x_1+1, \ldots, N-1, \ 0, 1, \ldots, x_2\}$$
$$(x_1 = N - \lfloor N/2 \rfloor, \ x_2 = (N-1+\lfloor N/2 \rfloor) \bmod N)$$

Note that $x_1 > x_2$ is held. $l(-:b, y_0)$ includes the above vertex set, since $x_r = (b + \lfloor N/2 \rfloor) \bmod N = x_2$. Therefore, the two linear connections $l(-:a, y_0)$ and $l(-:b, y_0)$ are sufficient for minimal paths for all pairs of a source switch and a destination switch among $\{(x, y_0) \mid 0 \leq x < N\}$. □

Theorem 3.1 *The DOR VLANs provide the same minimal-path set as that of the dimension-order routing in 2-D torus.*

Proof Each of VLANs VL($-:a, y_S$) and VL($-:b, y_S$) consists of a horizontal linear connection $l(-:a, y_S)$ or $l(-:b, y_S)$ and N vertical linear connections $\{l(x, y_S) \mid 0 \leq x < N\}$. According to Lemma 3.1, a path between each pair of switches among $\{(x, y_S) \mid 0 \leq x < N\}$ is minimal along the horizontal linear connection. In each vertical linear connections, all paths from (x, y_S) to (x, y) $(0 \leq y < N)$ are minimal, because (x, y_S) is the center of the vertical linear connection. Thus, by selecting an appropriate VLAN of VL($-:a, y_S$) and VL($-:b, y_S$), all paths from a source switch (x_S, y_S) are minimal. Since there are $2N$ VLANs $\{\text{VL}(-:x, y) \mid x = a, b,\ 0 \leq y < N\}$, paths from a source switch (x_S, y_S) using an appropriate one of VL($-:a, y_S$) and VL($-:b, y_S$) are the same as that of the dimension-order routing. □

3.3. Minimal Paths with Partial DOR (PDOR) in 2-D Torus

The second method for the PDOR VLAN set in the torus is also similar to that in the mesh.

Definition 3.5 (PDOR VLANs in 2-D torus) *The PDOR VLAN set consists of the following* $2\lfloor(N+1)/2\rfloor+2$ *VLANs in* $N \times N$ *torus:*

$$\{\text{VL}(-:x, 2i) \mid x = a, b,\ 0 \leq i < \lfloor(N+1)/2\rfloor\}$$
$$\cup\ \{\text{VL}(a, -:y_a),\ \text{VL}(b, -:y_b)\}$$
$$(a = \lfloor(N-1)/2\rfloor,\ b = N-1)$$

□

Figure 8 shows an example of the PDOR VLANs in 4×4 2-D torus. This method employs only six VLANs, VL($-:1, 0$), VL($-:1, 2$), VL($-:3, 0$), VL($-:3, 2$), VL($1, -:1$) and VL($3, -:3$).

Compared with the DOR VLANs, VL($-:1, 2i+1$) and VL($-:3, 2i+1$) ($i = 0, 1, \ldots$) are deleted, and VL($1, -:y_a$) and VL($3, -:y_b$) are newly employed. The selection of the values y_a and y_b is trivial, because links of the vertical connections in VL($1, -:y_a$) and VL($3, -:y_b$) are never used by paths.

In this method, paths from switch $(x_S, 2i)$ $(0 \leq i < \lfloor N/2\rfloor)$ are along the dimension-order routing for all destination switches using one of two VLANs VL($-:a, 2i$) and VL($-:b, 2i$) in the same way in the first (DOR) method. On the other hand, minimal paths from switch $(x_S, 2i+1)$ are achieved by using one of appropriate VLANs, VL($-:a, 2i$), VL($-:b, 2i$), VL($-:a, (2i+2) \bmod N$), VL($-:b, (2i+2) \bmod N$), VL($a, -:y_a$) and VL($b, -:y_b$).

Assuming that a source switch is (x_S, y_S) and a destination switch is (x_D, y_D), the procedure for selecting an appropriate VLAN for this method is described as follows (function *select_ab* was described in Section 3.2).

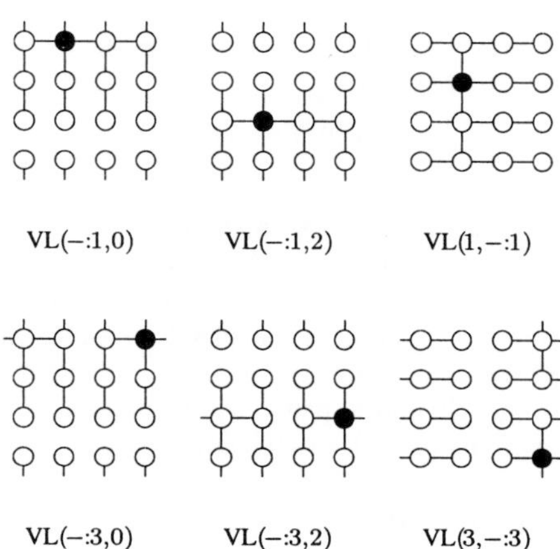

Figure 8. The PDOR VLANs in 4×4 2-D torus

```
ab := select_ab (xS, xD, N) ;
if yS mod 2 = 0 then use VL(−:ab, yS) ;
else begin
  if yD = yS then use VL(ab, −:yab) ;
  else if d+(yS, yD) ≤ d−(yS, yD) then
    use VL(−:ab, (yS+1) mod N) ;
  else {d+(yS, yD) > d−(yS, yD)}
    use VL(−:ab, yS−1) ;
end
```

Theorem 3.2 *The PDOR VLANs provide a minimal-path set in 2-D torus.*

Proof Since VL($a, -:y_a$) and VL($b, -:y_b$) have N horizontal linear connections $\{l(-:a, y) \mid 0 \leq y < N\}$ and $\{l(-:b, y) \mid 0 \leq y < N\}$ respectively, paths from a source switch $(x_S, 2i+1)$ to a destination switch $(x, 2i+1)$ $(0 \leq x < N)$ on an appropriate one of VL($a, -:y_a$) and VL($b, -:y_b$) are minimal (according to Lemma 3.1). For other destinations, paths from a source switch $(x_S, 2i+1)$ are via the switch $(x_S, (2i+2) \bmod N)$ with VL($-:a, (2i+2) \bmod N$)) or VL($-:b, (2i+2) \bmod N$)) for $d^+(y_S, y_D) \leq d^-(y_S, y_D)$, or those are via the switch $(x_S, 2i)$ with VL($-:a, 2i$) or VL($-:b, 2i$) for $d^+(y_S, y_D) > d^-(y_S, y_D)$.

On the other hand, according to Theorem 3.1, paths from a source switch $(x_S, 2i)$ using appropriate one of VL($-:a, 2i$) and VL($-:b, 2i$) are minimal. Since both $(x_S, (2i+2) \bmod N)$ and $(x_S, 2i)$ belong to $\{(x_S, 2i) \mid 0 \leq i < \lfloor(N+1)/2\rfloor\}$, the PDOR VLANs provide minimal-path set in 2-D torus. □

For example, if the source switch is $(0, 3)$ and the destination switch is $(1, 1)$ in Figure 8, the path is along the following order using VLAN VL$(- : 1,0)$. ($a = 1$, $d^+(x_S, x_D) = 1$, $d^-(x_S, x_D) = 3$, $d^+(y_S, y_D) = 2$, $d^-(y_S, y_D) = 2$)

$$(0,3) \to (0,0) \to (1,0) \to (1,1)$$

With this method, the path set is slightly different from that of the DOR VLANs, since it differs from the dimension-order routing when the source switch is $(x_S, 2i+1)$. However, as well as the PDOR VLANs on a mesh, the difference is possible only for the first step toward y-dimension. Therefore, paths of this method are still well-distributed. Its influence will be evaluated in Section 4.

3.4. Generalization (M-dimensional Torus)

We simply show a generalization of the VLAN-based minimal paths for N^M M-dimensional torus.

By extending Definition 3.1, we assign an M-dimensional coordinate $(x_0, x_1, \ldots, x_{M-1})$ to each switch, where $0 \leq x_0, x_1, \ldots, x_{M-1} < N$.

Similarly, by simply extending Definition 3.2, $l(x_0, x_1, \ldots, x_{i-1}, - : x_i, x_{i+1}, \ldots, x_{M-1})$ is stated as a connection which is parallel with i-th axis and is centered on vertex $(x_0, x_1, \ldots, x_{M-1})$.

A VLAN

$$\mathrm{VL}\big(x_0, x_1, \ldots, x_{i_0-1}, - : x_{i_0}, x_{i_0+1}, \ldots, x_{M-1} \;\big|\; (i_0, i_1, \ldots, i_{M-1})\big)$$

$$\big(i_0, i_1, \ldots, i_{M-1} \in \{0, 1, \ldots, M-1\},\; i_j \neq i_k \; (j \neq k)\big)$$

consists of following $\left(N^M - 1\right)/(N-1)$ connections (one parallel with i_0-th axis, N connections parallel with i_1-th axis, and so on).

$$\begin{aligned}
&\big\{l(x_0, x_1, \ldots, x_{i_0-1}, - : x_{i_0}, x_{i_0+1}, \ldots, x_{M-1})\big\} \\
\cup\; &\big\{l(x_0, x_1, \ldots, x_{i_1-1}, - : x_{i_1}, x_{i_1+1}, \ldots, x_{M-1}) \;\big|\; 0 \leq x_{i_0} < N\big\} \\
\cup\; &\big\{l(x_0, x_1, \ldots, x_{i_2-1}, - : x_{i_2}, x_{i_2+1}, \ldots, x_{M-1}) \;\big|\; 0 \leq x_{i_0}, x_{i_1} < N\big\} \\
&\vdots \\
\cup\; &\big\{l(x_0, x_1, \ldots, x_{i_{M-1}-1}, - : x_{i_{M-1}}, x_{i_{M-1}+1}, \ldots, x_{M-1}) \;\big|\; 0 \leq x_{i_0}, x_{i_1}, \ldots, x_{i_{M-2}} < N\big\}
\end{aligned}$$

Definition 3.6 (DOR VLANs in M-dimensional torus) *The DOR VLAN set consists of the following $2N^{M-1}$ VLANs in N^M M-dimensional torus:*

$$\begin{aligned}
&\big\{\mathrm{VL}(- : x_0, x_1, x_2, \ldots, x_{M-1} \mid A) \;\big|\; x_0 = a, b,\; 0 \leq x_1, x_2, \ldots, x_{M-1} < N\big\} \\
&\big(A = (0, 1, \ldots, M-1),\; a = \lfloor (N-1)/2 \rfloor,\; b = N-1\big)
\end{aligned}$$

$\square$

All paths from a source switch $(x_{0_S}, x_{1_S}, \ldots, x_{(M-1)_S})$ to a destination switch $(x_{0_D}, x_{1_D}, \ldots, x_{(M-1)_D})$ are minimal along the dimension-order routing using (function *select_ab* was described in Section 3.2):

$$\mathrm{VL}(- : \mathit{select\_ab}\,(x_{0_S}, x_{0_D}, N),\; x_{1_S}, x_{2_S}, \ldots, x_{(M-1)_S} \mid A)$$

If N is an odd number, the PDOR VLAN set becomes complicated and is similar to the case of an even number $N+1$ due to wrap-around links. Here we show the PDOR VLAN set only in the case that N is an even number.

Definition 3.7 (PDOR VLANs in M-dimensional torus) *The PDOR VLAN set consists of the following $N^{M-1} + 2$ VLANs in N^M M-dimensional torus:*

$$\begin{aligned}
&\Big\{\mathrm{VL}(- : x_0, x_1, x_2, \ldots, x_{M-1} \mid A) \;\Big|\; x_0 = a, b,\; 0 \leq x_1, x_2, \ldots, x_{M-1} < N,\; \sum_{k=1}^{M-1} x_k \equiv 0 \bmod 2\Big\} \\
\cup\; &\big\{\mathrm{VL}(x_0, x_1, \ldots, x_{M-2}, - : x_{M-1} \mid B) \;\big|\; x_0 = a, b\big\} \\
&\big(A = (0, 1, \ldots, M-1),\; B = (M-1, M-2, \ldots, 0),\; a = \lfloor (N-1)/2 \rfloor,\; b = N-1\big)
\end{aligned}$$

All paths from a source switch $(x_{0_S}, x_{1_S}, \ldots, x_{M-1_S})$ to a destination switch $(x_{0_D}, x_{1_D}, \ldots, x_{M-1_D})$ are minimal using one of appropriate VLANs selected by the following procedure.

```
ab := select_ab (x0S, x0D, N) ;
if Σ_{k=1}^{M-1} xkS mod 2 = 0 then
   use VL(− : ab, x1S, x2S, ..., x(M−1)S | A) ;
else begin
   selected := false ;
   for i := 1 to M − 1 do
      if xiS = xiD then continue ;
      else if d+(xiS, xiD) ≤ d−(xiS, xiD) then begin
         use VL(− : ab, x1S, x2S, ..., x(i−1)S,
                  (xiS + 1) mod N,
                  x(i+1)S, ..., x(M−1)S | A) ;
         selected := true ; break ;
      end else {d+(xiS, xiD) > d−(xiS, xiD)} begin
         use VL(− : ab, x1S, x2S, ..., x(i−1)S,
                  (xiS − 1 + N) mod N,
                  x(i+1)S, ..., x(M−1)S | A) ;
         selected := true ; break ;
      end
   end
   if selected ≠ true then
      use VL(ab, x1, x2, ..., xM−2, − : xM−1 | B) ;
end
```

The VLAN $\mathrm{VL}(ab, x_1, x_2, \ldots, x_{M-2}, - : x_{M-1} \mid B)$ is selected only if the following condition is held:

$$\sum_{k=1}^{M-1} x_{k_S} \equiv 1 \bmod 2, \quad x_{i_S} = x_{i_D} \quad (1 \leq i < M)$$

4. Performance Evaluation

In this section, we evaluate the performance of the proposed two VLAN-based methods by software simulation.

4.1. Simulation Condition

The following three methods are evaluated: the DOR VLANs based routing (DOR_VB), the PDOR VLANs based routing (PDOR_VB) and the STP-based routing (STP_B). For the comparison, we also evaluate the STP-based method, which uses only one VLAN providing the minimum average path hops among available ones. Thus, its topology is equal to a single spanning tree.

The following six topologies are employed: 4×4 2-D mesh/torus, 8×8 2-D mesh/torus, and $4 \times 4 \times 4$ 3-D mesh/torus. Uniform traffic, in which a host sends a packet to the randomly selected host, is used as a traffic pattern.

We have used a generic flit-level network simulator written in C++. A switch-based Ethernet with point-to-point links is employed. In the network, adjacent switches are connected with just one link each other, and one host is attached to each switch. Every switch uses cut-through as the switching technology, and hosts inject a frame independently of each other.

A simple model consisting of channel buffers, a crossbar, link controllers, a routing table and control circuits is used for the switching fabric. As timing parameters, at least ten clock cycles are required for routing and crossbar set in each switch, and five clock cycles are consumed for link delay (transferring a flit to the next switch or host). We set the frame header size to 6 flits, and payload size to 128 flits. In the simulator, we assume that each flit size is 4 bytes. Thus, total frame size is 536 bytes (134 flits). The simulation time is set to 100,000 clock cycles ignoring the first 10,000 clock cycles.

We use accepted traffic and latency as performance measures. Accepted traffic is the flit reception rate. We define throughput as the maximum accepted traffic. Whereas, latency is the elapsed time in clock cycles after the generation of a frame at a source host until it is delivered at a destination host.

4.2. Simulation Results

Figure 9 shows the latency versus the accepted traffic of three routing methods in each topology.

First, we focus on evaluation results on the mesh (Figure 9(a)(b)(c)). They clearly demonstrate that both of proposed methods improve throughput as compared with the STP-based routing. The improvement is enhanced as the number of dimensions and switches are increased. In particular, Figure 9(c) shows the DOR VLANs based routing improves throughput up to 753% as compared with the STP-based routing. The reason is that the STP-based routing uses only links in a spanning tree, increasing non-minimal paths and traffic concentration due to the non-uniform path distribution. It can be said that the proposed methods for minimal paths are quite efficient to improve network performance. In all conditions, the DOR VLANs based routing achieves higher throughput than the PDOR VLANs based routing up to 75%. The reason is that the PDOR VLANs based routing is different from the DOR VLANs based routing in some paths, leading non-uniform path distribution which increases traffic concentration.

Next, we focus on evaluation results on the torus (Figure 9(d)(e)(f)). As well as results on the mesh, They demonstrate that the proposed methods achieve higher throughput than the STP-based routing, and the DOR VLANs based routing achieves the highest throughput in all conditions. In addition, the improvement on throughput by the proposed methods increases than that in the mesh topologies. In particular, Figure 9(f) shows the DOR VLANs based routing increases throughput up to 902% as compared with the STP-based routing. The reason is explained as follows: since a torus is a symmetric topology due to its wrap-around links, the number of minimal paths of the proposed methods increases, and the paths are distributed more uniformly than that in the mesh. However, the number of minimal paths and the path distribution of the STP-based routing are almost the same in the mesh and the torus, because the STP-based routing can use only links in a spanning tree. As a result, the improvement of the proposed methods in the torus increases as compared with that in the mesh.

On the other hand, the performance gap between the two proposed methods becomes smaller than that in the mesh. The reason is that the difference of the path distribution is smaller than that in the mesh due to the symmetric property of torus.

To sum up, the proposed methods drastically improve throughput as compared with the STP-based routing in all conditions, and the DOR VLANs based routing achieves the highest throughput. The throughput is strongly affected by not only the number of minimal paths but also the uniformity of path distribution.

5. Conclusions

Ethernet has been used to connect hosts in PC clusters by employing system software which enables zero- or one-

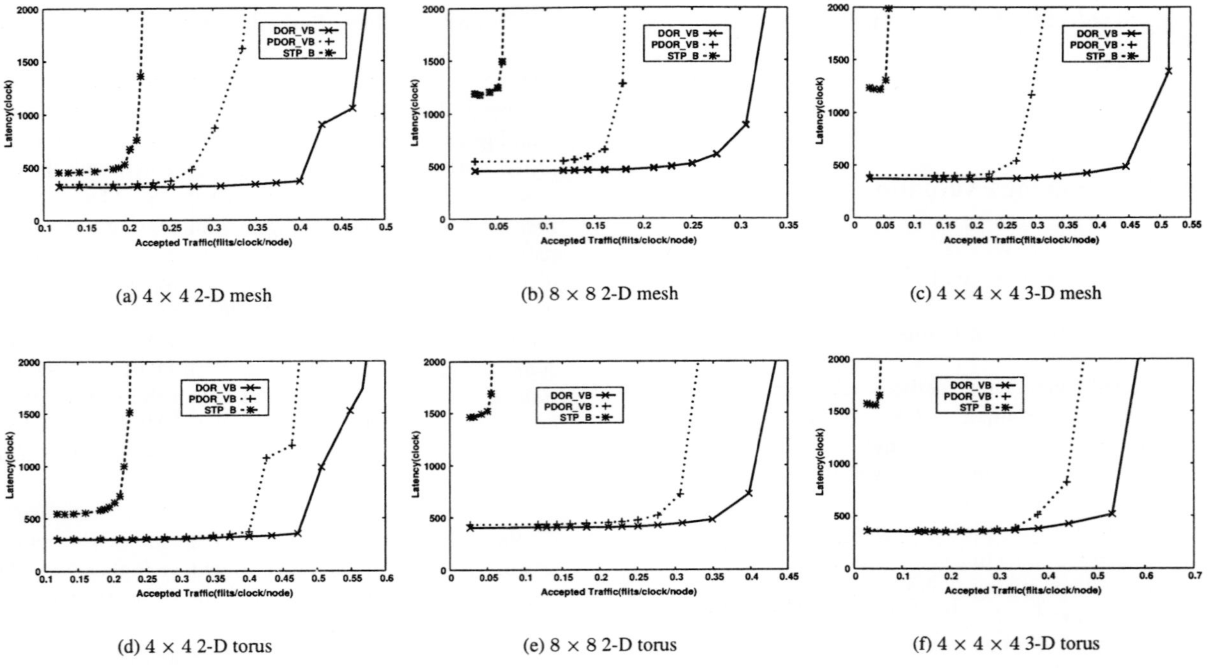

(a) 4×4 2-D mesh (b) 8×8 2-D mesh (c) $4 \times 4 \times 4$ 3-D mesh

(d) 4×4 2-D torus (e) 8×8 2-D torus (f) $4 \times 4 \times 4$ 3-D torus

Figure 9. Accepted traffic and latency under each topology

copy communication. Unlike interconnection networks in parallel computers, links which do not belong to a spanning tree cannot be used for routing due to the limitation of the spanning tree protocol (STP), and simple tree-based topologies have been employed. Thus, even when building a typical topology, such as a torus, clusters with Ethernet must accept non-minimal embedded-tree paths. However, by applying VLAN technology, all links in a cluster with Ethernet can be used to take minimal and/or balanced paths.

In this paper, we proposed VLAN topology sets and path assignment methods to them. The proposed VLAN topology sets on mesh require N^{M-1} and $\lfloor N^{M-1}/2 \rfloor + 1$ VLANs to provide balanced minimal paths and partially balanced ones respectively, where N is the number of switches per dimension and M is the number of dimensions. Similarly, those on torus require $2N^{M-1}$ and $N^{M-1}+2$ VLANs respectively. Simulation results show that the proposed balanced minimal paths improve up to 902% of throughput compared with the STP-based paths, and the proposed partially balanced minimal paths with a slight loss of path uniformity still improve up to 706% of throughput. We are currently planning to evaluate the proposed VLAN-based minimal paths and the STP-based paths on a real PC cluster with 16- or 64-switch Gigabit Ethernet.

References

[1] W. J. Dally and C. L. Seitz. Deadlock-Free Message Routing in Multiprocessor Interconnection Networks. *IEEE Trans. Comput.*, 36(5):547–553, May 1987.

[2] I.T.Association. Infiniband architecture. specification volume 1,release 1.0.a. *available from the InfiniBand Trade Association, http://www.infinibandta.com*, June 2001.

[3] Myricom, Inc. `http://www.pccluster.org/`.

[4] T.Kudoh, H.Tezuka, M.Matsuda, Y.Kodama, O.Tatebe, and S.Sekiguchi. VLAN-based Routing: Multi-path L2 Ethernet Network for HPC Clusters. In *Proceedings of 2004 IEEE International Conference on Cluster Computing (Cluster'2004)*, 2004.

[5] T.Kudoh, M.Matsuda, H.Tezuka, T.Shimizu, Y.Kodama, O.Tatebe, and S.Sekiguchi. VLAN-based Multi-path L2 Ethernet Network for Clusters. *IPSJ Transactions on Advanced Computing System*, 45(SIG 6):35–43, May 2004 (in Japanese).

[6] T.Takahashi, S.Sumimoto, A.Hori, H.Harada, and Y.Ishikawa. PM2: High Performance Communication Middleware for Heterogeneous Network Environment. In *SC2000*, pages 52–53, Nov. 2000.

[7] Y.Ishikawa, H.Tezuka, A.Hori, S.Sumimoto, T. Takahashi, F. O'Carroll, and H. Harada. RWC PC Cluster II and SCore Cluster System Software – High Performance Linux Cluster. In *5th Annual Linux Expo*, pages 55–62, May 1999.

Fault-Tolerant Routing in Meshes/Tori Using Planarly Constructed Fault Blocks

Dong Xiang, Jia-Guang Sun, Jie Wu, and Krishnaiyan Thulasiraman

Abstract

A few faulty nodes can make an n-dimensional mesh or torus network unsafe for fault-tolerant routing methods based on the block fault model, where the whole system ($n-$dimensional space) forms a fault block. A new concept, called extended local safety information in meshes or tori, is proposed to guide fault-tolerant routing, and classifies fault-free nodes inside $2-$dimensional planes. Many nodes globally marked as unsafe become locally enabled inside $2-$dimensional planes. A fault-tolerant routing algorithm based on extended local safety information is proposed for $k-$ary $n-$dimensional meshes/tori. Our method does not need to disable any fault-free nodes, unlike many previous methods, and this enhances the computational power of the system and improves performance of the routing algorithm greatly. All fault blocks are constructed inside 2-dimensional planes rather than in the whole system. Extensive simulation results are presented and compared with the previous methods.

Index Terms: Computational power, fault-tolerant routing, extended local safety, unsafe systems, mesh/torus.

1 Introduction

Torus and mesh-connected networks have been widely used in recent experimental or commercial multicomputers [1]. The performance of such multicomputers is highly dependent on the node-to-node communication cost. It is necessary to present an effective fault-tolerant routing algorithm in a mesh/torus.

Dong Xiang and Jia-Guang Sun are with the School of Software, Tsinghua University, Beijing 100084, P. R. China. Jie Wu is with the Department of Computer Science and Engineering, Florida Atlantic University, Boca Raton, FL 33431, USA. Krishnaiyan Thulasiraman is with the School of Computer Science, the University of Oklahoma, Norman, OK 73019, USA. Work in this paper is supported in part by the NSF of China under grants 60373009 and 60425203 and the NSF of USA under grants CNS0422762 and CNS0434533.

The block fault model is the most popular fault model. Some fault-free nodes must be disabled when faults are arbitrarily shaped to form fault blocks. A fault-free node is marked unsafe according to previous methods [2,4,6,15,16] if it has two faulty or unsafe neighbors along different dimensions. Since an unsafe node is disabled, a few faulty nodes can disable a large number of fault-free nodes or even disable all fault-free nodes based on the block fault model, especially for higher dimensional meshes/tori. As shown in Fig. 1, only 7 faulty nodes make all fault-free nodes disabled in the 5x5x5 mesh. All previous methods [2,4,6,15,16] can handle only the case in which both the source and destination are outside of a fault block.

The proposed method constructs fault blocks inside 2D planes, where many unsafe nodes become safe in separate planes. All resources related to the disabled nodes can still be used to route a message. Each fault-free node keeps its status in separate planes based on the safety measure to be introduced in this paper. Safety information kept in each fault-free node is about three times as that of the extended safety levels [16] in a 3D mesh/torus and n times in an n-dimensional mesh/torus because each fault-free node needs to keep its safety information inside $((n-1)\cdot n/2)$ 2-dimensional planes and the proposed safety measure in the whole system.

Note that fault blocks may be conjointed. Connected fault blocks may not maintain the convexity property. Therefore, a message may have to be routed around a non-convex fault block that may result in substantial backtracks for the whole message in a wormhole-routed network. Backtracking the whole message in a network can greatly influence performance of a fault-tolerant routing algorithm, especially when the network contains enough faulty nodes or the load of the system is large enough. This also indicates the necessity to construct fault blocks planarly and establish a path before sending a message, as in pipelined-circuit-switching [9].

The main work of this paper is: (1) A new limited-global safety-based measure called the extended local safety information is proposed to guide fault-tolerant

0190-3918/05 $20.00 © 2005 IEEE

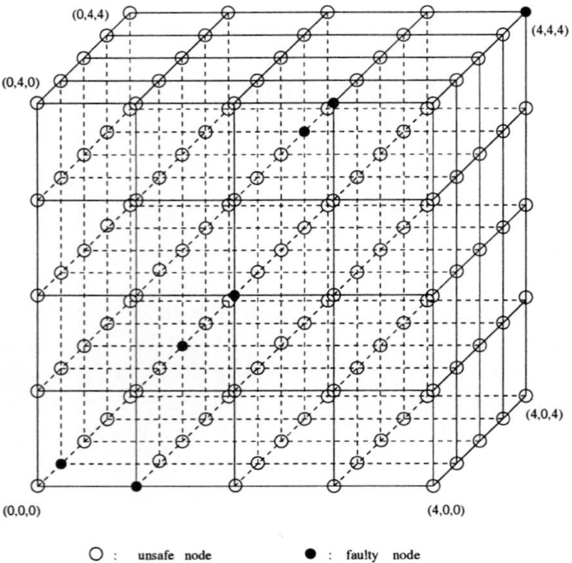

Figure 1: An unsafe 5−ary 3D mesh.

routing, based on which a new path set-up scheme is proposed. (2) Fault blocks are constructed inside separate planes, where many unsafe nodes can be activated. This can significantly improve the computational power of the system and enhance the performance of the fault-tolerant routing algorithm greatly. (3) A new fault-tolerant routing algorithm based on the extended local safety information is presented with a new virtual subnetwork partitioning scheme to avoid deadlocks.

The number of virtual channels required by the proposed method is linearly proportional to the number of dimensions of the network. This number is acceptable for a practical mesh/torus network according to [3,7], where the number of virtual channels is not the main factor that contributes to the cost of a router in a network. Unlike PCS [9,10], the proposed path set-up scheme does not need to reserve any resource of the network, which returns only the path. This scheme can save a lot of bandwidth compared to PCS while still presenting the same reliable path establishment. Certainly, a new deadlock avoidance technique is necessary. The proposed method works better when the number of faults in the network and the load of the network are not very low.

2 Related Work

Bruck *et al.* [5] proposed a method to partition a hypercube into small subcubes, each of which has a small number of faults. It was guaranteed that most of the fault-free nodes form a fault-free connected component. These kinds of connected components can be used to implement various fault-tolerant algorithms in hypercubes. Xiang [17] routed a message by localizing safety inside some safe subcubes even though the whole hypercube is unsafe. Safety information inside subcubes called local safety information was used to guide fault-tolerant routing effectively. This idea is also used in this paper to construct fault blocks inside separate 2D submeshes (called planes).

Fault-tolerant routing in direct networks has been studied extensively. Xiang and Chen in [18] proposed a fault-tolerant routing scheme for 2D meshes/tori based on local safety. Local safety is an improved safety measure of extended safety levels [15,16]. The method does not need to disable any fault-free node to form fault blocks. Gomez *et al.* proposed techniques for fault-tolerant routing in 3D meshes/tori without disabling any fault-free nodes in [11].

Linder and Harden [12] extended the concept of virtual channel to multiple virtual interconnection networks that provide adaptivity, deadlock-freedom, and fault-tolerance. Chien and Kim [6] proposed a planar-adaptive routing algorithm that limits routing freedom and makes it possible to prevent deadlocks with only a fixed number of virtual channels (three) independent of network dimension. Judicious extension of the proposed algorithm can efficiently handle routing inside faulty nD meshes. Boppana and Chalasani [2] developed fault-tolerant routing algorithms for mesh-connected networks based on the $e-$cube routing algorithm and the block fault model. At most four virtual channels are sufficient to make fully-adaptive algorithms tolerant to multiple fault blocks in $n-$dimensional meshes. A deadlock-free fault-tolerant routing algorithm for $n-$dimensional meshes was proposed in Boura and Das [4] using three virtual channels per physical channel. Fault regions were converted into rectangular regions by a node labeling scheme. However, the above methods [2,4,6] must disable some fault-free nodes to construct the fault blocks, which can result in a great loss of computational power for 3D or higher dimensional networks. Recently, Wang [14] proposed a rectilinear-monotone polygonal fault block model to do fault-tolerant routing in 2D meshes by disabling fewer fault-free nodes. Most recently, Puente, Gregorio, Vallejo, and Beivide [13] proposed a fault-tolerant routing mechanism for the 2D torus, which can handle any number of faults if the network is connected. The method [13] must build multiple routing tables.

Path set-up was used first by circuit switching that needs to reserve a physical path before routing a message without any further deadlock avoidance technique, but can waste bandwidth and increase message latency. The pipelined-circuit-switching (PCS) [9,10] establishes a path by reserving a virtual channel path before sending a message, which can tolerate dynamic faults and simplify deadlock-free design. Wu [15,16] proposed an adaptive and deadlock-free fault-tolerant routing method based on extended safety levels. The method needs to establish a region of minimal paths before sending a message, which is the first known fault-tolerant routing scheme based on a limited-global safety measure.

3 Preliminaries

A mesh has k^n nodes, in which each dimension has k nodes. Two nodes $(a_n a_{n-1} \dots a_2 a_1)$ and $(b_n b_{n-1} \dots b_2 b_1)$ in a $k-$ary $n-$dimensional torus network are connected if they differ at exactly one bit i with $a_i = (b_i + 1) \mathrm{mod} k$. Two nodes in a $k-$ary $n-$dimensional mesh $(a_n a_{n-1} \dots a_2 a_1)$ and $(b_n b_{n-1} \dots b_2\ b_1)$ are connected if they differ at exactly one bit i $(a_i \neq b_i)$, where $|a_i - b_i| = 1$, and $a_i, b_i \in \{0, 1, 2, \dots, k-1\}$.

A rectangular fault block contains all the connected faulty and unsafe nodes. Some unsafe nodes can still be locally enabled in one or more planes. In this paper, we say a message is sent from a source s to a destination d along a *minimum feasible path* if the length of the path equals the number of hops that s and d differ, where all nodes in the path are fault-free.

Faults and unsafe nodes in 2D meshes can form rectangular shapes. A set of faults or unsafe nodes F in a 2D mesh (or torus) are block faults if there is one or more rectangles such that: (1) There are no faults on the boundary of each rectangle. (2) The interior of the rectangle includes all faults and unsafe nodes in F. (3) The interior of the rectangle contains no node or link that is not presented in F. Fault blocks in a 3D mesh/torus or n-dimensional mesh/torus can be formed like [2,6]. The only difference is that no fault-free node is disabled. Local safety was introduced to guide fault-tolerant routing in $2D$ torus and mesh-connected networks [18]. Assume the system contains rectangular fault blocks, in which the distance between any two fault blocks is at least two. For each fault-free node v in a mesh/torus network, the local safety of v is defined as follows:

Definition 1 *The local safety of a safe node v in an nD mesh (or torus) network is defined as a $2n-$element tuple $(v_1, v_2, \dots, v_{2n})$, where $v_1, v_2, \dots, v_{2n}$ are each defined as the length of the longest feasible path (not entering a fault block) from v along all $2n$ different directions, respectively.*

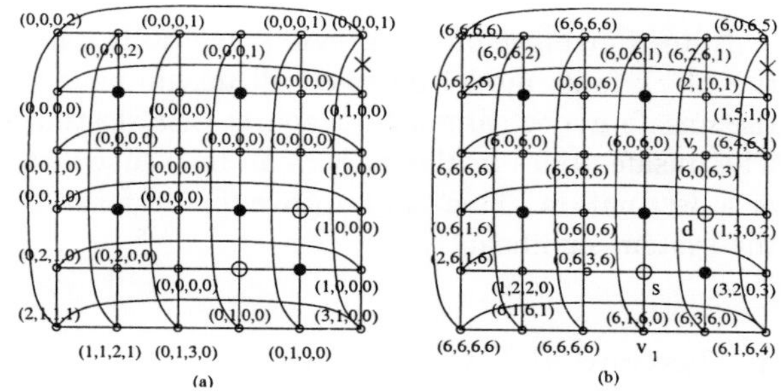

Figure 2: Extended safety level and the local safety: (a) extended safety level [15], and (b) local safety [18].

An element of the extended safety levels is defined as the distance from the node along the corresponding direction to a fault block [15,16]. Figs. 2(a) and 2(b) show the extended safety level and the local safety of all enabled fault-free nodes [18] in the 6−ary 2−cube. Let (E, S, W, N) and (v_e, v_s, v_w, v_n) be the extended safety level and the local safety of a node along directions east, south, west, and north, respectively. It is clear that the local safety of a fault-free node is never less than the extended safety level of that node.

Consider node (0,0) at the southwestern corner of the 6x6 torus as shown in Fig. 2. The eastward path from the node touches a fault block after 2 hops, therefore, $E = 2$. The westward, northward, and southward paths from the node reach the boundaries of three fault blocks after one hop. So, $W = S = N = 1$. As for the local safety of the same node, the length of the longest feasible paths from the node to east, south, west, and north are all 6.

Intermediate nodes must be found like [18] when either the source or the destination is inside a fault block. As shown in Fig. 2(b), consider sending a message from s to d. It is necessary to find two enabled nodes near to s and d. As shown in Fig. 2(b), v_1 and v_2 are selected as intermediate nodes of s and d, respectively.

Definition 2 *Nodes in a mesh (or torus) network can be classified as faulty, unsafe, and enabled. A fault-free node is called an unsafe node if it has two faulty or unsafe neighbors along different dimensions; otherwise, it is an enabled node. A system is called unsafe if fault-free nodes in the system are all unsafe.*

Note that most of the previous methods based on the block fault model disabled all unsafe nodes, and the unsafe nodes cannot be a source or a destination. The unsafe nodes in this paper can be either a source or a destination. This can improve the performance of the system significantly.

4 Extended Local Safety

Only a few faults can make a 3D or n-dimensional mesh/torus unsafe. However, reliable message routing can still be conducted inside many submeshes in a mesh/torus in many cases although the system is unsafe. Let two dimensions form a 2D submesh called a plane. Let us check the 5−ary $3D$ mesh as shown in Fig. 1 again. All fault-free nodes are enabled in each plane except (0,0,0) and (1,0,1) in the plane (*,0,*). Actually, a message between any pair of fault-free nodes can be completed reliably. The following definition needs to be presented first.

Definition 3 *Fault-free nodes inside a faulty nD mesh (or torus) system are classified with respect to a specific 2D plane: a fault-free node is a locally unsafe node with respect to the submesh if it has at least two faulty or locally unsafe neighbors inside the submesh; otherwise, a fault-free node is a locally enabled node with respect to the plane.*

We consider safety of all fault-free nodes inside various 2D submeshes (planes) in this paper, which can also be extended to any other submeshes. Many nodes become safe inside different planes although they are unsafe in the whole system. Consider node $(0,0,0)$ in the faulty 5−ary 3D mesh. All fault-free nodes are unsafe in the whole system, but all of them except (0,0,0) and (1,0,1) are locally enabled in all planes. Nodes (0,0,0) and (1,0,1) are locally unsafe in the plane (*,0,*) because they have two faulty neighbors inside the submesh. Influences of faults can be limited inside the corresponding subnetworks when the local safety information is considered.

Definition 4 *The extended local safety of a fault-free node v in a $k-ary$ nD mesh can be defined as a $2n-tuple$ $(v_1, v_2, \dots, v_{2n})$; each v_i $(1 \leq i \leq 2n)$ is obtained by*

$$v_i = min_j\{v_{ij}\}, \tag{1}$$

where v_{ij} is the corresponding value of the local safety of the node along direction i inside the plane formed by dimensions i and j, and v is locally enabled inside the plane.

Procedure *extended-local-safety()*
repeat
For each fault-free node v in the system, parallel do
local-class(v);
parallel end.
until stable states have been obtained.

local-class(i)

1. Node i gets its states in different planes that contain it;
2. if i has at least two faulty or locally unsafe neighbors along different dimensions in a plane, set state of v in that plane as locally unsafe.

The extended local safety information of a system can be updated if necessary. It should also be noted that the extended local safety information is not prepared to route one message. It is kept by each fault-free node to guide fault-tolerant routing until new faults occur. The effort to capture the extended local safety information should be comparable to that required to form the rectangular fault blocks [2,4,6,15,16,18], or to obtain the extended safety levels [15,16] and the local safety [19]. The amount of safety information stored in each node should be at most as n times as that in [16], which should be acceptable for practical networks. The extra information stored in each node should include: (1) safety information of the node in $n \cdot (n-1)/2$ different planes that contain it, and (2) the extended local safety information of the node, which is a 2n-tuple. Consider a 3D mesh/torus: the amount of the extended local safety information stored in each fault-free node is at most 3 times as much as that of the extended safety levels [16], which is acceptable.

The method in [18] presents a fault-tolerant routing algorithm only in 2D meshes or tori. Compared with the safety measure in [18], the proposed method can improve the adaptivity and performance of the algorithm because all fault-free nodes inside a fault-block can be the intermediate node of a message from a source inside or outside of the fault block. The resources with respect to globally unsafe nodes can thus be used by the messages.

Let the extended local safety of a fault-free node in a $k-$ary 3D mesh be represented as (E, S, F, W, N, B), where E, W, F, S, N, and B represent the extended local safety values of the node along directions east, west, front, south, north, and behind, respectively. As shown in Fig. 1, the extended local safety of nodes (0,1,0) and (3,2,2) is $(1, 2, -, -, 2, 4)$

and $(1,2,2,3,2,2)$, respectively, where "-" stands for don't care. We consider safety of fault-free nodes inside each plane.

The size of the safe node set based on the planarly constructed fault blocks should be no less than that of the one based on the conventional fault block model. The extended local safety information can always present more information for fault-tolerant routing. As shown in Fig. 1, the extended local safety of nodes (0,3,0), (4,3,4), and (2,0,2) are (4,3,-,-,1,4), (-,3,4,4,0,-), and (2,-,2,2,4,2), respectively, where "-" is don't care. We consider safety inside planes; therefore, our method is presented based on the extended local safety information with respect to each plane. However, the extended safety level [16], the planar adaptive routing method [6] and Boppana's routing protocol [1] can do nothing on the 3D mesh because the network is unsafe.

5 Virtual Subnetwork Partitioning for Deadlock Avoidance

A 3D mesh can be partitioned into eight different virtual subnetworks: x+y+z+, x+y+z-, x+y-z+, x+y-z-, x-y+z+, x-y+z-, x-y-z+, and x-y-z-. All eight virtual subnetworks can be combined into 4 different virtual subnetworks: x+y+z* (c_1+,c_1+,c_1), x-y*z+ (c_2-,c_2,c_2+), x-y*z- (c_1-,c_3,c_2-) and x+y-z* (c_2+,c_1-,c_3). Labels in the brackets show virtual channel assignments of all virtual subnetworks. Messages are classified based on the relative locations of the source and destination. For example, a message to be sent from (0,1,0) to (3,0,3) falls into the 4th class of messages.

Let both the source and destination be safe in any plane. Only one additional virtual channel is enough to support non-minimal routing and avoid deadlocks because no turn is generated by the additional virtual channels in these cases. Let at least one of source and destination be unsafe inside at least one plane. Turns may be formed by the extra virtual channel. Two additional virtual channels are required in this case. A deroute message should use c_4 first. A turn from a lower label dimension to a higher label dimension should use c_4, and a turn from a higher label dimension to a lower label dimension should use extra virtual channel c_5. No cyclic dependency among the extra virtual channels forms.

As for 3D torus networks, possible cyclic dependency generated by the wraparound links must be eliminated. Linder and Harden [12] used another virtual network after traversing a wraparound link, which needs $O(n \cdot 2^n)$ virtual channels for each physical channel. In our method, techniques similar to those for meshes are adopted. All messages are partitioned into 4 different classes in a 3D torus. Virtual network partitioning is still utilized like 3D meshes. A message uses the regular virtual channels assigned to the corresponding virtual network along a specific dimension with "+") if the label of the current node with respect to the dimension is less than that of the destination. And the message uses an extra virtual channel c_4 or c_5 if the label of the current node with respect to the dimension is greater than that of the destination. A message uses the regular virtual channels assigned to the corresponding virtual network along a specific dimension with "−" if the label of the current node with respect to the dimension is greater than that of the destination. And the message uses an extra virtual channel c_4 or c_5 if the label of the current node with respect to the dimension is less than that of the destination. When a message is routed along a dimension with "*", virtual channels are utilized like a dimension with "+" if the label of the destination along the dimension is greater than that of the source; otherwise, virtual channels are assigned like a dimension with "−".

The potential cyclic dependency among the wraparound links must also be avoided. As mentioned earlier, a message, when it uses a regular virtual channel for the first wraparound link to a higher label dimension wraparound link, uses virtual channel c_4, while a turn from a higher dimension label wraparound link to a lower dimension wraparound link utilizes extra virtual channel c_5. This scheme can successfully eliminate the cyclic dependency among the wraparound links. It is clear that no cycle exists in any virtual subnetwork and among virtual subnetworks [12,8,16]. Also, the derouted messages cannot form any cycles if the network is not disconnected. Virtual channels c_4 and c_5 should be idle in most cases. Our method utilizes the idle virtual channels and assigns them as any virtual channels when necessary. The label of the virtual channel can be relabeled as the previous number after the message has been sent [7]. The technique can improve performance of the system in most cases. Unlike [16], the proposed method does not partition each virtual subnetwork into a sequence of planes when sending a message. A message can be routed to any minimum hop via the assigned virtual channel inside the specified virtual subnetwork, which can enhance adaptivity and performance of the algorithm compared with [16].

6 Routing Algorithm Based on the Extended Local Safety

The routing algorithm might be approximately described as follows: take a step in the direction most likely to meet fault blockage; repeat until the destination is reached. In the case of blockage at the final step, deroute along an unblocked path and continue. A heuristic based on the extended local safety information as presented in Equation (2) is used to avoid fault blocks. In Equation (2), $L_i(s,d)$ is the number of hops that s and d differ along dimension i, and d_i is the extended local safety information of the source with respect to dimension i as defined in Definition 4. Only the extended safety information of the source is necessary to compute the heuristic function.

$$h_i = \begin{cases} 0 & \text{if } d_i \geq L_i(s,d), \\ d_i - L_i(s,d) & \text{otherwise.} \end{cases} \quad (2)$$

The PCS [9,10] and circuit switching need to reserve some resources of the network before sending a message, which may waste some bandwidth. We would like to propose a scheme without reserving any resource. However, path set-up is still used. Assume the source does not have knowledge of the extended local safety of the destination. Each message falls into a unique virtual subnetwork. A feasible path leading to the destination is established inside the selected virtual subnetwork until reaching the destination. The message is derouted along the additional virtual channels if necessary, and returns to the virtual subnetwork as soon as possible. The above process continues until a feasible path has been set up. The set-up path can be stored in the header.

In the rest of this section, procedure *route-message-in-nD-mesh*() sends a message from s to d in a $k-$ary n-dimensional mesh. Procedure *select-path*() completes the path set-up from the destination d to the source s, and the procedure *send-message*() sends the message from the source s to the destination d based on the extended local safety information of the destination and location of the current node if a minimum feasible path is not found in the first two stages.

route-message-in-nD-mesh()

1. Keep the extended local safety of the source s. Find a path from the source leading to the destination inside the assigned virtual subnetwork.
2. If a minimum feasible path from s to d has been set up at the destination d, send a signal from d to s along the setup path. The source s sends the message along the setup minimum feasible path. Otherwise (3).
3. Try to set up a minimum feasible path from d to s inside the corresponding virtual subnetwork. If s and d differ in only one dimension and there exists a feasible path from the destination to the source, a minimum feasible path has been set up. Otherwise call *select-path*().
4. If a minimum feasible path has been found, send the message from s along the selected path. Otherwise, call *send-message*().

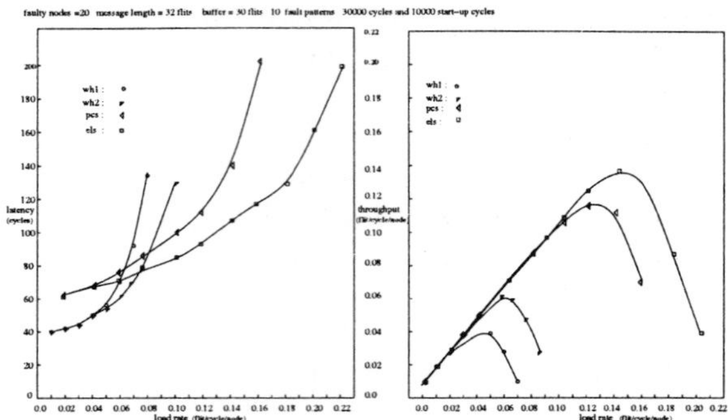

Figure 3: Performance comparison with PCS and the wormhole routing techniques in 8x8x8 meshes.

select-path()

1. Go along dimension t, where the source s has the least heuristic h_t corresponding to location of the current node v and the extended local safety information of the source if a possible path along dimension t is available, otherwise (2).
2. Go along another dimension among the remaining ones with the least heuristic based on Equation (2) if the selected next hop is inside a fault block in all planes that d and s differ.
3. Continue the above process until reaching a point where s and d differ only in one dimension. A feasible path has been set up if a feasible path from the node to s is available. Otherwise (4).
4. Deroute the signal to a node, where s has the most extended local safety along that dimension. Go along a minimum hop if possible. Continue the above process until reaching the source s.

send-message()

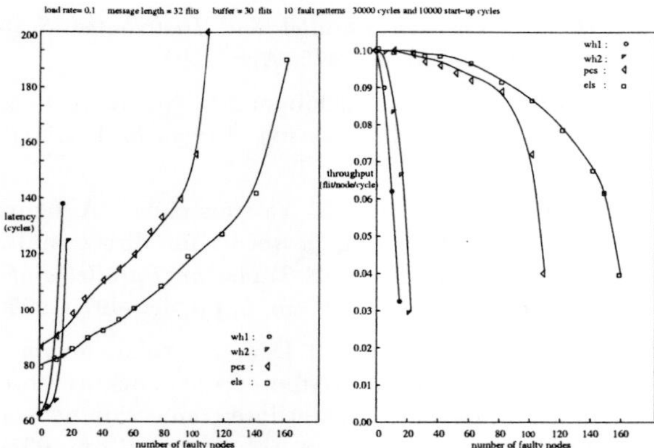

Figure 4: Performance comparison in 8x8x8 meshes with fixed load rate.

1. Send the message along dimension t, where d has the least heuristic h_t with respect to the extended local safety information of the destination and location of the current node if the node is fault-free and not in a fault block in one plane, otherwise (2).
2. Pass the message along another dimension, where the destination d has the least heuristic among the remaining dimensions and the next node is not in a fault block in at least one plane.
3. Continue the above process until reaching a node that differs from the destination in one dimension.
4. If there exists a minimum feasible path from the node to the destination, pass the message along the feasible path; otherwise, deroute the message to a fault-free neighbor until a fault-free neighbor in a minimum path from the current node to the destination along another dimension is available.
5. Continue the above process until the destination is reached.

7 Simulation Results

A flit-level simulator has been implemented to evaluate the proposed extended-local-safety-information-based fault-tolerant routing algorithm (*els*). Flit-level simulators on the planar adaptive routing algorithm (*wh1*) [6], the wormhole-routing-based algorithm proposed by Boppana and Chalasani (*wh2*) [2], and the pipelined-circuit-switching-based algorithm (*pcs*) [9] have also been implemented to compare with the proposed algorithm. All results in the following figures present the average of 10 different fault patterns.

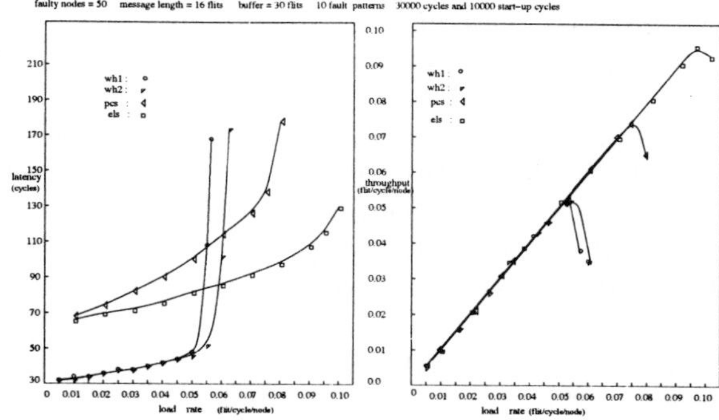

Figure 5: Performance comparison in 16x16x16 meshes.

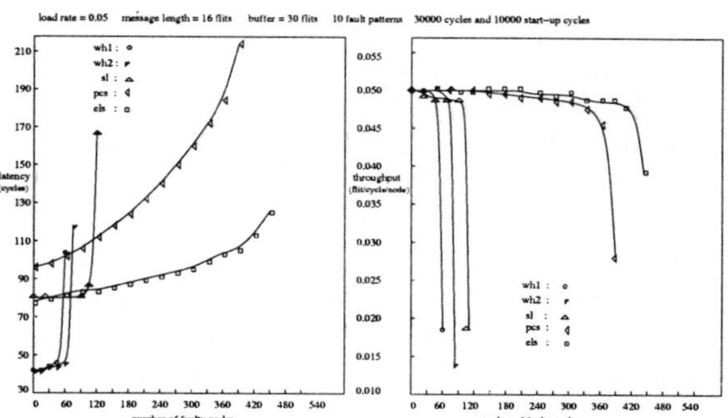

Figure 6: Performance comparison in 16x16x16 meshes with fixed load rate.

Faults are randomly inserted. The simulation results are presented only for static faulty nodes, which can be extended to link failure easily. The proposed method can also be extended to dynamic faults easily like PCS [9]. It is shown that *wh2* always works a little better than *wh1*. The most important reason can be that *wh1* always makes messages routed inside 2D planes and also *wh2* uses four virtual channels, but *wh1* uses only three virtual channels for each physical channel. Two important metrics, latency (the number of cycles required to deliver a message) and throughput (flit/node/cycle), are evaluated. The message length and buffer size of each node in 8x8x8 meshes are set as 32 flits and 30 flits, respectively.

Fig. 3 presents performance comparison of all four methods when the system has different load rates and the 8x8x8 mesh contains 20 faulty nodes. Fig. 4 presents performance comparison of the four methods when the load rate of the 8x8x8 mesh system is set as 0.10. Figs. 5 and 6 present performance comparisons of the proposed extended local safety information with the previous methods. Fig. 5 presents performance comparison of the four methods when the 16x16x16 mesh contain 50 faulty nodes. Latency and throughput comparisons of *wh1*, *wh2*, *pcs*, and *els* are presented when load rate of the system is set as 0.01−0.10. Fig. 6 demonstrates performance comparison of the proposed method with five previous methods on the 16x16x16 meshes when the load rate of the system is fixed as 0.05. The extended safety level (*sl*) [15,16] is implemented for 16x16x16 meshes.

8 Conclusions

Extended local safety was utilized to guide fault-tolerant routing in an n-dimensional mesh/torus, which calculates safety information by forming fault blocks inside each plane. The extended local safety considers safety of a mesh/torus inside each plane instead of in the whole system. This technique can make numerous unsafe nodes in the whole system locally enabled in the 2D planes. The proposed method did not disable any fault-free nodes, and any fault-free nodes inside a fault block in a plane can still be a source or a destination. Extensive simulation results were presented by comparing with previous methods.

References

[1] F. Allen, *et al.*, "Blue gene: A vision for protein science using a petaflop supercomputer," *IBM Systems Journal*, vol. 40, pp. 310-327, 2001.

[2] R. V. Boppana and S. Chalasani, "Fault-tolerant wormhole routing algorithms for mesh networks," *IEEE Trans. Computers*, vol. 44, no. 7, pp. 848-864, 1995.

[3] R. V. Boppana and S. Chalasani, "A framework for designing deadlock-free wormhole routing algorithms," *IEEE Trans. on Parallel and Distributed Systems*, vol. 7, no. 2, pp. 169-183, 1996.

[4] Y. M. Boura and C. R. Das, "Fault-tolerant routing in mesh networks," Proc. of *IEEE Int. Conf. on Parallel Processing*, I106-I109, 1995.

[5] J. Bruck, R. Cypher, and D. Soroker, "Tolerating faults in hypercubes using subcube partitioning," *IEEE Trans. on Computers*, vol. 41, no. 5, pp. 599-605, 1992.

[6] A. A. Chien and J. H. Kim, "Planar adaptive routing: Low-cost adaptive networks for multiprocessors," *J. of ACM*, vol. 42, no. 1, pp. 91-123, 1995.

[7] W. J. Dally and Aoki, "Deadlock-free adaptive routing multicomputer networks using virtual channels," *IEEE Trans. on Parallel and Distributed Systems*, vol. 4, no. 4, pp. 466-475, Apr. 1993.

[8] J. Duato, S. Yalamanchili, and L. Ni, *Interconnection Networks: An Engineering Approach*, IEEE Press, 1997.

[9] P. T. Gaughan and S. Yalamanchili, "A family of fault-tolerant routing protocols for direct multiprocessor networks," *IEEE Trans. on Parallel and Distributed Systems*, vol. 6, no. 5, pp. 482-497, 1995.

[10] P. T. Gaughan, B. V. Dao, S. Yalamanchili, and D. E. Schimmel, "Distributed, deadlock-free routing in faulty, pipelined, direct interconnection networks," *IEEE Trans. Computers*, vol. 45, no. 6, pp. 651-665, 1996.

[11] M. E. Gomez, J. Flich, P. Lopez, A. Robles, J. Duato, N. A. Nordbotten, O. Lysne, and T. Skeie, "An effective fault-tolerant routing methodology for direct networks," Proc. of *IEEE Int. Conference on Parallel Processing*, pp. 222-231, 2004.

[12] D. H. Linder and J. C. Harden, "An adaptive and fault-tolerant wormhole routing strategy for $k-$ary $n-$cube," *IEEE Trans. Computers*, Vol. 40, no. 1, pp. 2-12, 1991.

[13] V. Puente, J. A. Gregorio, F. Vallejo, and R. Beivide, "Immunet: A cheap and robust fault-tolerant packet routing mechanism," Proc. of *ACM/IEEE Int. Symp. on Computer Architecture*, pp. 198-209, 2004.

[14] D. Wang, "A rectilinear-monotone polygonal fault block model for fault-tolerant minimal routing in mesh," *IEEE Trans. on Computers*, vol. 52, no. 3, pp. 310-320, 2003.

[15] J. Wu, "Fault-tolerant adaptive and minimal routing in mesh-connected multicomputers using extended safety levels," *IEEE Trans. Parallel and Distributed Systems*, vol. 11, no. 2, pp. 149-159, 2000.

[16] J. Wu, "A fault-tolerant adaptive and minimal routing approach in nD meshes," Proc. of *IEEE Int. Conf. Parallel Processing*, Aug., pp. 431-438, 2000.

[17] D. Xiang, "Fault-tolerant routing in hypercube multicomputers using local safety information," *IEEE Trans. on Parallel and Distributed Systems*, vol. 12, no. 9, pp. 942-951, 2001.

[18] D. Xiang and A. Chen, "Fault-tolerant routing in 2D tori or meshes using limited-global-safety information," Proc. of *IEEE Int. Conf. on Parallel Processing*, pp. 231-238, Vancouver, Aug., 2002.

[19] J. Zhou and F. C. M. Lau, "Adaptive fault-tolerant wormhole routing in 2D meshes," Proc. of 15-th *IEEE Int. Parallel and Distributed Processing Symp.*, pp. 249-256, 2001.

Peak Power Control for a QoS Capable On-Chip Network

Yuho Jin[1], Eun Jung Kim[1], Ki Hwan Yum[2]
[1]*Texas A&M University* [2]*University of Texas at San Antonio*
{yuho,ejkim}@cs.tamu.edu *yum@cs.utsa.edu*

Abstract

In recent years integrating multiprocessors in a single chip is emerging for supporting various scientific and commercial applications, with diverse demands to the underlying on-chip networks. Communication traffic of these applications makes routers greedy to acquire more power such that the total consumed power of the network may exceed the supplied power and cause reliability problems. To ensure high performance and power constraint satisfaction, the on-chip network must have a peak power control mechanism. In this paper, we propose a credit-based peak power control scheme to assure power consumption to be under the given peak power constraint, without performance degradation. The peak power control scheme efficiently regulates each flow's injection rate at the sender to minimize performance penalty. We have two different throttling schemes for real-time traffic and best-effort traffic; a rate-based throttling and an energy-budget based throttling, respectively. The simulation results on mesh networks show that the credit-based peak power control effectively prevents performance degradation and meets the peak power constraint.

1. Introduction

Integrating multiple components in a single chip by the help of the network leverages modular design, layered protocols, and high performance, instead of global dedicated wiring between processing components [1]. As the number of components increases, the simple broadcast bus-based network is not favored any more, since it lacks performance, energy efficiency, and scalability [2]. For example, one request in bus-based interconnects monopolizes the ownership and induces high latency due to the centralized arbitration. Moreover, broadcast data transmission incurs unnecessary energy consumption at every receiver and the sharing of a bus limits the connectivity. However, a switch-based network can overcome these problems, structure components into tiles, and borrow many efficient techniques used in the interconnection network connecting multiple chips.

It is definitely true that the on-chip network has area and power constraints, since it must incorporate many processing components in a single chip. Planarity of a chip prefers 2-dimensional network topology. The reduced on-chip network area for switches and wires makes room for more transistors of processing components. The satisfaction of peak power consumption in a single chip is essential to maintaining supply voltage levels, to supporting reliability, to limiting capacity of heat sinks and to meeting affordable packaging costs [3]. Since the total power supplied to a chip is distributed to all the units of a chip, each unit should keep its power consumption below a preset upper limit. With the increasing demand for interconnect bandwidth, an on-chip network becomes the major power consumer in a chip. The power model of on-chip networks, Orion [5, 6], showed the significant power dissipation on the on-chip networks of two chip multiprocessors (CMPs): MIT Raw [7] and UT Austin TRIPS [8].

Multimedia applications on a System-on-Chip (SoC) are extensively being studied for bandwidth requirements over heterogeneous components of the network [10]. However, we are focusing on the QoS environment in the homogenous network such as chip multiprocessors. An on-chip network must support guarantee for the delivery of multimedia data (real-time traffic) as well as the normal message-oriented communication (best-effort traffic).

One of the approaches that provide QoS support in a communication network is to supply admission and congestion control to regulate the number of active connections and the number of injected packets in those connections [4]. Admission control determines the acceptance of a new connection in the network, based on the requirement of the new connection and the current resource capacity. If the acceptance of the new connection jeopardizes QoS guarantees of already established connections, admission control denies the new connection setup. Congestion control typically monitors the network load and intervenes when the network load reaches a certain threshold value indicating network congestion. A congestion control mechanism regulates traffic injection into a network to avoid network saturation, which may lead to performance degradation.

0190-3918/05 $20.00 © 2005 IEEE

In this paper, we propose a credit-based peak power control to meet pre-specified power constraints while maintaining the service quality, by regulating injection of packets. We take different approaches for different traffic types. For real-time traffic, instead of throttling the injection of packets of already established connections, our scheme works by determining the acceptance of a new connection based on the requirement of the consumed power and the available power budget as in the case of admission control. We also show how to calculate the expected power consumption of a connection from its bandwidth requirement. For best-effort traffic, we calculate the required power of a packet based on the distance from its source to the destination. If the expected power consumption exceeds the power budget, we throttle the injection of the packet such as the congestion control. We compare our scheme with the existing peak power control scheme (PowerHerd [21]). Our evaluation on mesh networks shows that, even though PowerHerd is very efficient to satisfy peak power constraints, it incurs significant performance degradation in all ranges of workload. We also show that the proposed credit-based peak power control outperforms PowerHerd in terms of the average packet latency, while it satisfies peak power constraints as PowerHerd does.

This paper is organized as follows. In the next section, a brief review of the related work is presented. Section 3 explains the basic architectures of an on-chip network including routers and Injection Throttle Logic (ITL), and also the power models are discussed. The proposed credit-based peak power control technique is discussed in Section 4. Experimental results are shown in Section 5, while the last section summarizes the conclusions of the paper.

2. Related Work

Due to the pivotal role of the on-chip networks in both CMPs and SoCs, several power models have been proposed to analyze the behavior of power consumption. Patel, et al. first proposed the analytical power model for interconnection networks based on transistor counts [16]. Orion model presented a micro-architectural power model to estimate the average and the maximum power of on-chip networks [5]. Dynamic power consumption model with bit-level accuracy was explored in different switch fabrics in [17]. A common observation in the related research literature is that the buffers in a router are the main power consumers followed by the links.

Energy management and low power design on an on-chip network is still an ongoing research area. Recent techniques for energy efficiency in SoCs are summarized in [18]. The application-specific constrained design is another direction in SoCs. Mapping components onto a network and structuring interconnects are explored in terms of energy efficiency [19], bandwidth requirement [10], and high resource utilization [20].

However, since it seems difficult to adapt chip multiprocessor design for a specific application, reconfiguration or control mechanism are required to overcome constraints. Recently, PowerHerd is proposed to dynamically regulate each router's power consumption by throttling packet flow through a flow distribution mechanism to satisfy the given peak power constraint in the network [21]. In this scheme, each router estimates its power consumption, predicts the future demand, and shares its power budget with neighboring routers. In the MIT Raw chip targeting seamless integration of 1024 processors, each tile has one static router and two dynamic routers for different application traffic demands and properties [7].

3. System Architecture

In this section we describe the on-chip network that includes the QoS capable wormhole router architecture and the Injection Throttle Logic (ITL) regulating the traffic pushed into the injection channel in Figure 1. The router is connected to neighbor routers through 4 physical links, to ITL through an injection link, and to the processor core through an ejection link on the mesh network architecture of a CMP. The energy model implemented in the on-chip network is also described.

3.1. QoS Capable Router Architecture

The fundamental function of a router is to receive flits through links from its attached hosts or neighboring routers and to forward the received flits to the adjacent routers according to the routing information stored in the header flits [14]. In Figure 1(b), Stage 1 synchronizes the incoming flits and demultiplexes them so that they can go to the proper Virtual Channel (VC) buffer to be subsequently decoded. For a header flit, routing decision and arbitration for the correct crossbar output is executed in the Stages 2 and 3. On the other hand, both middle and tail flits bypass these two stages. Flits get routed to the correct crossbar output in Stage 4. Finally, Stage 5 does buffering for flits flowing out of the crossbar, multiplexes the physical channel bandwidth amongst multiple VCs. Unlike traditional routers that use a FIFO scheduler, the QoS capable router used in this paper has a WRR (Weighted Round Robin) scheduler at the input ports of the crossbar in Figure 1(b) [11-14]. This 5-stage pipelined router outperforms the traditional routers especially when handling different types of traffic.

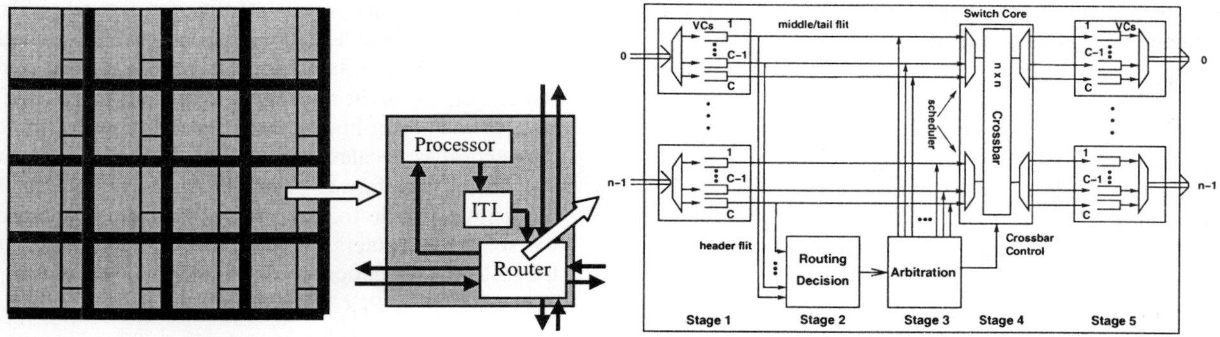

(a) On-chip network (b) 5-stage pipelined router architecture

Figure 1. Tile-based on-chip network architecture of a CMP

It is noted that the buffer size in wormhole switching does not affect the performance severely. Thus we can exploit small buffers in the router to reduce power dissipation.

3.2. Injection Throttle Logic

The Injection Throttle Logic (ITL) regulates the injection rate of each traffic type, attached to each core (the processor), in order to meet the peak power constraint in Figure 1(a). To provide the separate regulation of two kinds of traffic, the ITL has the power budget register and the router has the bandwidth register. In addition, the unit of control is different for each type of traffic. First, the maximum power budget of the best-effort traffic for each router is initially stored to the budget register in the ITL. The ITL allows a best-effort traffic packet to enter into the network only when its power budget register has sufficient power. On the other hand, the bandwidth register of the router has the maximum bandwidth corresponding to the sustainable power of the real-time traffic. The ITL checks the bandwidth registers of the routers along the path at the connection establishment stage. Only does the ITL permit a new connection (instead of a unit of packet) if all of the relevant routers agree to make a room for it in their bandwidth budgets. In other words, ITL monitors its power budget register for best-effort traffic, while checking the routers' bandwidth budget registers on the delivery path for real-time traffic.

3.3. Energy Model

The main components of the router are FIFO buffers, routing logic, crossbar and output port arbiter. We obtained the energy parameters of the router components from the HSPICE simulation in 180 nm technology under a supply voltage 1.8V. Each router has 16 VCs of 10-flit buffers for each input/output port and one flit is 256 bits long. In wormhole switching, the buffer size can be smaller than the packet size and, thus, the wormhole router can have the smaller power requirement than the packet switching router. We assume that the link operates with 1GHz clock and its power consumption follows the model proposed in [23]. The main energy parameters are summarized in Table 1. In addition, the leakage power of both the router and the link is fairly smaller than the switching power.

Table 1. Energy parameters of router and link

Component	Status	Energy (pJ)
Input/Output Buffer	Read	76.41
	Write	79.62
Arbitration	Active	6.10
Routing	Active	310.00
Crossbar	Active	83.00
Link (per bit)	Active	5.52

4. Credit-Based Peak Power Control

In this section, we propose a credit-based peak power control that regulates the injection of packets in the router and the ITL. Fundamentally, before sending a packet or establishing a connection, we check the power budget availability (power credit) for the packet or the connection. Only packets/connections that earn power credits can enter the network.

The peak power constraint is given to the network, when the system designer divides the total power budget for each part of the system to keep away from the detrimental thermal impact. It is required for the reliable communication between the routers to operate safely. Since the routers try to consume more power to maximize their performance, the router circuit can get burned or have malfunctions without the peak power control [21].

Therefore, in order to maintain power consumption of the on-chip network under the specified power limit, we regulate the injection rate in the ITL. As shown in Figure 2, we can observe that the power consumption is proportional to the network load, which is, in turn, determined by the integral input load among all routers. Note that, if we successfully control the peak input load that corresponds to the peak power, the network can be sustained without any malfunctions.

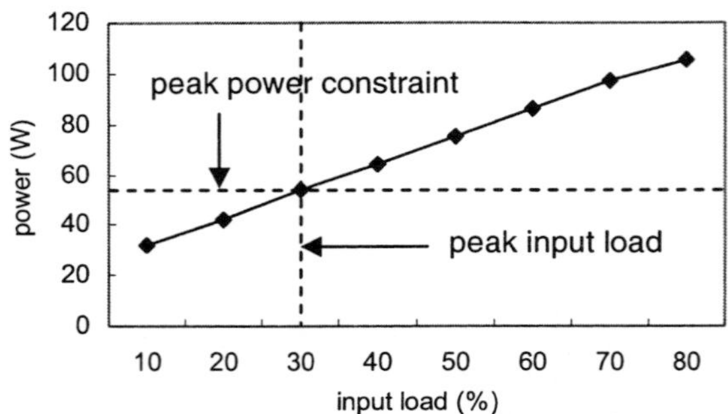

Figure 2. Relationship of input load and peak power (simulation on a 4x4 mesh network using a mixed traffic workload)

Our goal is to maintain the service quality while controlling the peak power consumption. We can categorize network traffic into two classes; connection-based (real-time traffic) and connectionless (best-effort traffic). Connection-based traffic usually requires QoS guarantees, which means that once a connection is established, we need to provide a certain service level. On the other hand, connectionless traffic does not have such a strict demand of performance. Thus, we should take different approaches to handle each traffic type. To apply different schemes for each traffic type, the total power budget (P_{total}) is divided and distributed to each traffic class by its ratio.

$$P_{total} = P_{RT} + P_{BE} \leq P_{peak}$$

where P_{RT} is power consumption for real-time traffic and P_{BE} is power consumption for best-effort traffic.

Real-time traffic control: Since each flow of real-time traffic has its bandwidth requirement and the requirement should be guaranteed, we cannot throttle packet injection of the admitted connection to control power consumption. Thus we can only restrict the number of connections/flows to be admitted in the network so as to meet the peak power constraint. This scheme can be regarded as an extension of admission control. For admission control, we only check the bandwidth availability. In the credit-based peak power control, we check the power budget as well as bandwidth availability.

Before a new connection is established in the network, the probe message checks whether the routers on the path from the source to the destination have both sufficient bandwidth and sufficient power budget for this new connection to guarantee QoS and to meet the power constraints, respectively. If all the routers have both sufficient bandwidth and sufficient power budget, this connection can be established in the network. Otherwise, it gets rejected.

The bandwidth of the connection determines the power required for that connection. The real-time traffic, whose bandwidth is r bps, injects r/f flits per second, where f is the flit size in bits. The energy consumed for a single flit in a router (E_{router}), is obtained from our power model of the router. So a flit consumes $E_{router} \times r/f$ Watts at each router. The power budget of each router on the path of the connection is recalculated by subtracting the consumed power from the former power budget of the router. It can be denoted by the following formula. For each router i in the set of the routers on the path, the budget changes by the following equation:

$$P_{RT}(i) = P_{RT}(i) - E_{router} \times r / f$$

where $P_{RT}(i)$ is the power budget for router i. The bandwidth of router i, having the updated power budget, becomes equivalent to the available bandwidth that can be assigned to a new real-time connection in the router.

When we set the peak input load to k (which is equal to the peak power constraint), the allocated power budget of the router i for real-time traffic is designated as $E_{router} \times k(R/f)$, where R is the maximum bandwidth. The sum of all routers' power budgets is equal to the total power budget of real-time traffic (P_{RT}).

Best-effort traffic control: Since best-effort traffic has no bandwidth requirement and no connection setup, it is impossible to satisfy the peak power constraint by controlling the admission of connections. So our method estimates the consumed energy for a best-effort packet and its traversal time in the network, and regulates the injection of the packet in the ITL. The ITL updates its energy estimate register at both the packet departure and the expected arrival by subtracting and adding the packet's energy value. If the ITL does not have enough energy budget for a new packet to inject, the packet will be throttled. To achieve this, we need to convert the power budget (P_{BE}) into the energy budget (E_{BE}). The power budget is converted into the energy budget for every short period of time, T (Note that $E_{BE} = P_{BE} \cdot T$) [21]. The total amount of best-effort power budget (P_{BE}) is equally divided and assigned to each ITL.

We need to estimate how much energy and time are required for a single packet delivery on a certain path. The wormhole switching requires the switching energy (E_{packet}) and the time (T_{packet}) to send a packet from a given source to a destination as shown in the following formulae assuming one packet consists of N flits:

$$E_{packet} = [E_{router} \cdot D + E_{link} \cdot (D+1)] \cdot N \,,$$

$$T_{packet} = [D \cdot C_{router} + (D+1) \cdot C_{link} + N\,] \cdot T_{cycle} + W_{ITL}$$

where E_{router} and E_{link} are energy values consumed by routers and links, respectively. D is the distance between source and destination or the number of routers traversed by a packet through the network. A packet traverses (1 + the number of routers) links, taking into account injection and ejection links. C_{router} and C_{link} is the number of cycles for router and link to handle one flit. T_{cycle} is the clock cycle time. W_{ITL} denotes the average waiting time in the

ITL that models the network contention and it is estimated from the queue operations. However, when we consider the micro-architecture of a router, the routing and arbitration activities are necessary only for head flits and the expected energy consumption of a single packet can be expressed in the following detailed formula:

$E_{packet} = [(2E_{rd} + 2E_{wr} + E_{xb}) \cdot D + E_{link} \cdot (D+1)] \cdot N + (E_{route} + E_{arb}) \cdot D$

where E_{rd}, E_{wr}, E_{xb}, E_{route}, and E_{arb} are energy consumption parameters for reading from the buffer, writing to the buffer, traversing the crossbar, routing, and arbitration, respectively.

Before a packet departs from the ITL, the estimate of E_{packet} is subtracted from the energy budget of the ITL if it has a sufficient energy budget. After T_{packet} time, the estimated energy is restored to the budget register of the ITL. Since the ITL does not inject a best-effort packet when it has insufficient energy budget, the sum of all energy budgets in the ITLs is less than or equal to P_{BE}. Therefore, the total allocated energy budget for best-effort traffic can be satisfied by monitoring the energy budget and regulating the injection rate inside the ITL.

5. Experimental Results

5.1. Simulation Platform

For our experiment, we used a 4x4 mesh network with 6-port routers as a base configuration. The router has four links for interconnecting neighboring routers, one for an injection link, and one for an ejection link. Each router has 16 VCs and 10-flit buffers for wormhole switching. The flit size is 256 bits and each packet has 40 flits except control packets, which are 10-flit long. To avoid the initial warm-up effect of the simulation, we measure the consumed power and the latency after injecting 10,000 packets.

Network traffic consists of real-time traffic, best-effort traffic, and control traffic as proposed in [4]. We used ON/OFF real-time traffic by producing a stream of messages according to the given injection rate. Best-effort traffic is generated from the Poisson distribution, whereas the destination of each packet is determined by a uniform distribution. Control traffic is typically used for network configuration, congestion control, and transfer of other information. It has the highest priority, but it consumes only a very small portion of the total bandwidth. Therefore, we don't have any power control scheme for control traffic.

5.2. Peak Power Control Results

We compare our credit-based peak power control with the dynamic peak power controller (PowerHerd [21]) in terms of power consumption and performance. The same peak power value is used for comparison between our method and PowerHerd. The different mixed ratios of real-time traffic and best-effort traffic are used to show peak power satisfaction of two types of traffic. Figure 3 shows the consumed power and the latency in three kinds of workloads: 50% real-time and 50% best-effort traffic (mixed workload), 100% best-effort traffic, and 100% real-time traffic. The basic QoS router, the QoS router with the credit-based peak power control, and PowerHerd are indicated by **none**, **PC**, and **PH**. To set a power constraint for an on-chip network, we use the average consumed power at 30% input load in these workloads. The peak power values are 53.9W (mixed workload), 52.8W (100% best-effort workload), and 53.6W (100% real-time workload). Although the system designer can choose other values, the peak input load associated with the peak power constraint should not incur saturation of the network.

We observe that power consumption in the basic QoS router configuration exceeds the peak power constraint over 30% input load of each workload, since the input load is related with power consumption. Beyond the peak power constraint, the dissipated heat can overrun the cooling capacity and induces the electronic failures. This harmful phenomenon that threatens reliability and safety of the on-chip network can be prevented with the peak power control. Moreover, the power constraint can prevent the over-provisioned design and the remaining power can be supplied to computation components.

The credit-based peak power control and PowerHerd satisfy the peak power constraint for all three workloads. For example, Figure 3(a) shows that 60% input load consumes 69.7% of the total power budget with the peak power control in the mixed traffic workload. In case of single type workloads, we can observe that each mechanism is effective to control of each traffic type to meet the constraint as shown in Figure 3(b) and 3(c). Moreover, the best-effort traffic control uses, on the average, 84% of the total power budget, utilizing its budget better than the real-time traffic control (70% of the total budget), since it controls the unit of a packet rather than a flow.

The latency graphs in Figure 3 show that the credit-based peak power control has graceful performance slowdown as the input load increases, although this latency increase is hard to notice because the latency is represented exponentially. It implies that the additional effect of the peak power control is preventing the network congestion since it throttles the traffic injection into the

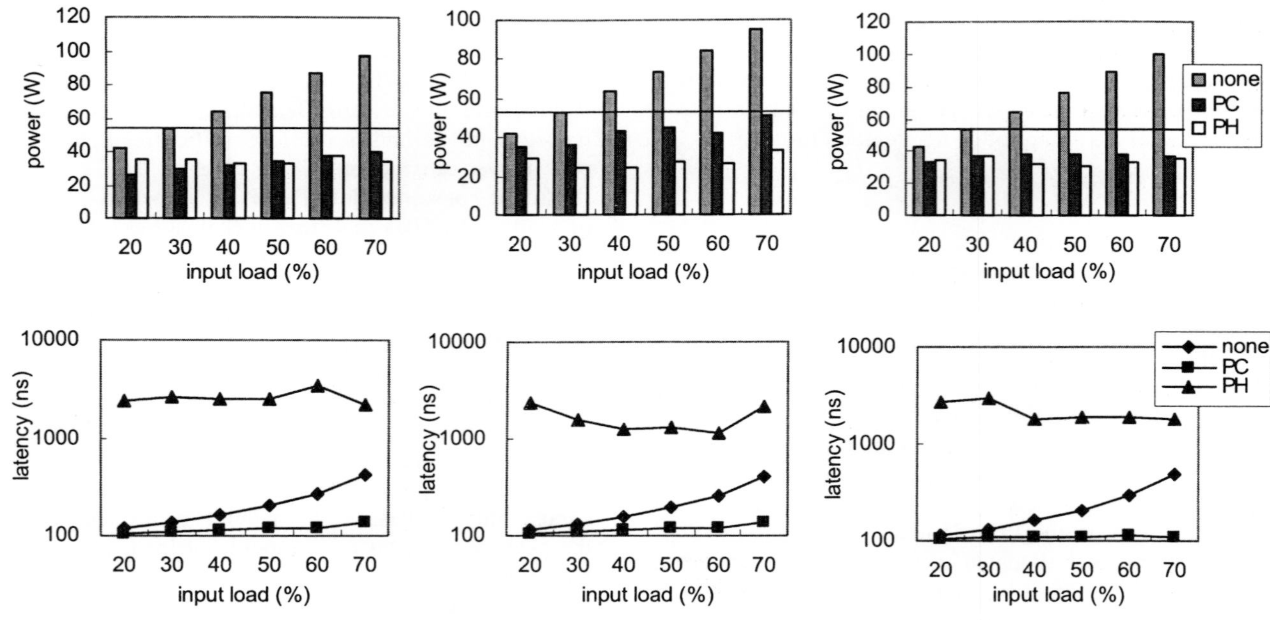

Figure 3. Power consumption and packet delivery latency in a 4x4 mesh network for various workloads

network. As expected, PowerHerd shows very high latency over all the ranges of the input load since it controls the flow in the middle of network to satisfy the router's local power budget. In other words, the dynamic flow control in PowerHerd, adaptively finding less power-hungry routers in the path, incurs significant performance degradation. Another reason for the big difference is that the small buffer size in wormhole switching aggravates the latency problem. Therefore, the peak power control in PowerHerd does not avert congestion and it even worsens the latency due to the throttling logic of the crossbar inside the router.

In the mixed workload, two types of traffic compete with each other for the shared resources such as physical channels, buffer schedulers, and crossbars. The increasing rate of the latency in best-effort traffic without the peak power control is greater than that of real-time traffic at the high input loads, since real-time traffic has higher priority to be transferred than best-effort traffic in the QoS router. It suggests that controlling the injection rate of best-effort traffic is difficult in the mixed workload.

Next, we measure the average power consumption every 500 cycles (500 ns) to show the validity of runtime peak power satisfaction, since one of the needs for the peak power control is the thermal management. The period is assumed to be much smaller than the thermal RC constant (product of thermal resistance and thermal capacitance driven from the duality between heat transfer and electrical phenomena) to localize the heatsink temporally [22]. Figure 4 shows power consumption of each period under the peak power constraint (53.9 W) in the mixed workload. Power consumption is fluctuating below the peak power along the time and may not cause any harmful thermal effect.

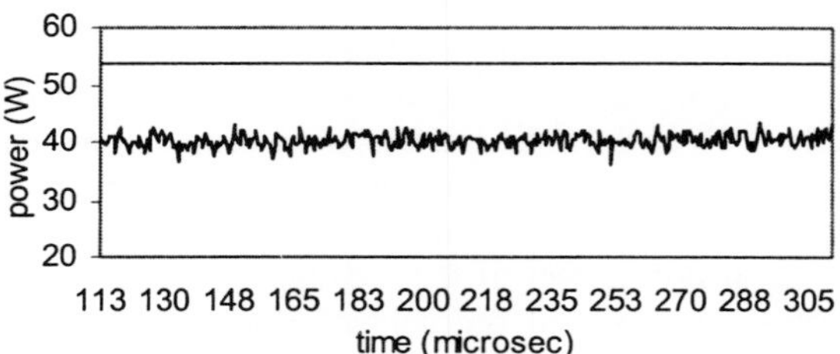

Figure 4. Runtime power consumption for 70% input load of mixed traffic in a 4x4 mesh network

5.3. Effectiveness of Credit-Based Peak Power Control

Theoretically, the credit-based peak power control should scale well with other workloads that are different from the test workload, since the scheme has the ability to manage each kind of traffic independently and divide the total power budget into each budget of traffic type with respect to its ratio in the workload. Furthermore, it does not suffer from the latency problem like PowerHerd, and has a property of congestion avoidance by regulating the injection rate for high input load.

By observing the behavior of power consumption without any peak power control (**none**) in Figure 3, we can tell that power consumption of each workload shows a similar pattern. It implies that it has little relationships with the mixed ratio of each traffic type, but it has close relationships with the input load, assuming that both of them try to make use of the network. The next experiments are conducted for different percentages of two traffic types (best-effort: 10% ~ 90%, real-time: 90% ~ 10%) with the same peak power constraint (53.9W) of 50% best-effort and 50% real-time traffic. Figure 5 shows power consumption of two cases (50% and 70% input loads) in a 4x4 mesh network with the credit-based peak power control. Note that each traffic type has its own power budget that is the product of its ratio of workload and the total power budget. The results in Figure 5 illustrate that the given power constraint is satisfied in all the cases except 40% best-effort traffic workload of 70% input load with the credit-based peak power control.

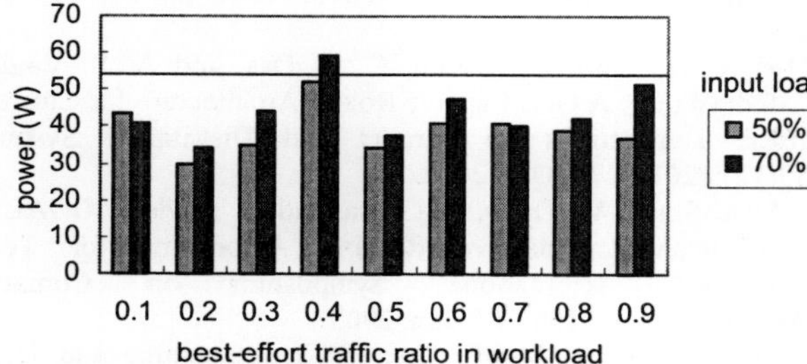

Figure 5. Effectiveness to various mixed ratio of traffic in a 4x4 mesh network (The ratio of real-time traffic decreases 0.9 to 0.1 on x-axis.)

Next, we experiment the effectiveness of the credit-based peak power control with 4 different traffic patterns, which are usually used to show performance of the adaptive routing algorithms in [15]. Two traffic patterns, NN (nearest neighbor) and UR (uniformly distributed), are benign, since they have the load balancing and good throughput properties. Next two patterns, TP (transpose) and TOR (tornado), are adversarial ones that cause load imbalance and make hot spots. The peak power constraint of the UR pattern in the equally mixed workload is used to assess the effectiveness of peak power control in other traffic patterns.

In the QoS capable network without a peak power constraint, the latency graph tends to be convex in benign patterns, while the adversarial patterns draw the concave graph as shown in Figure 6(a). Load imbalance patterns cause network saturation for a relatively low input load and show the highly increasing rate of the latency over benign patterns. Figure 6(b) shows satisfaction of peak power constraint in hot spot traffic patterns as well as a benign pattern of NN, and TOR pattern shows less power consumption than others since it does not use vertical links.

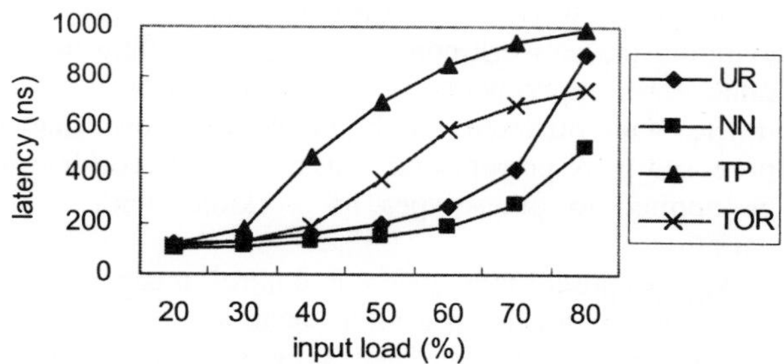

(a) Average latency without peak power control

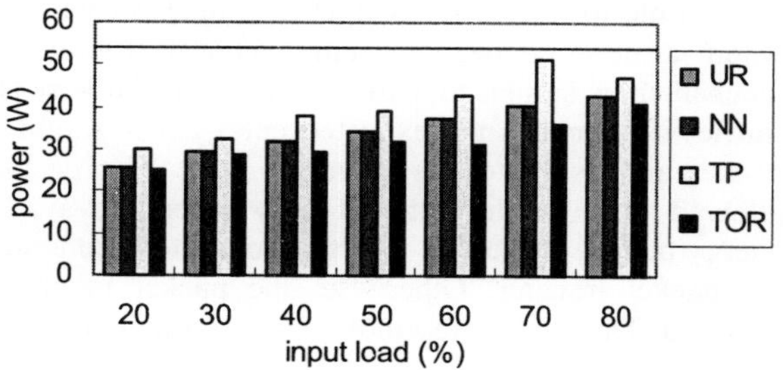

(b) Power consumption with peak power control

Figure 6. Comparison of peak power control for various traffic patterns in a 4x4 mesh network

Finally, we conduct the experiments for the different network size. Figure 7 shows power consumption for the different size of networks using a uniform distribution for message destinations. The behavior of controlling power and satisfaction of peak power constraint of larger network is similar to that of 4x4 mesh network. The used peak power constraints are power consumption for 30% input load of each network. These values are 93.2W (5x5), 146.7W (6x6), 216.3W (7x7), and 306.7W (8x8). The gap between the peak constraint and the consumed power increases as the network size grows.

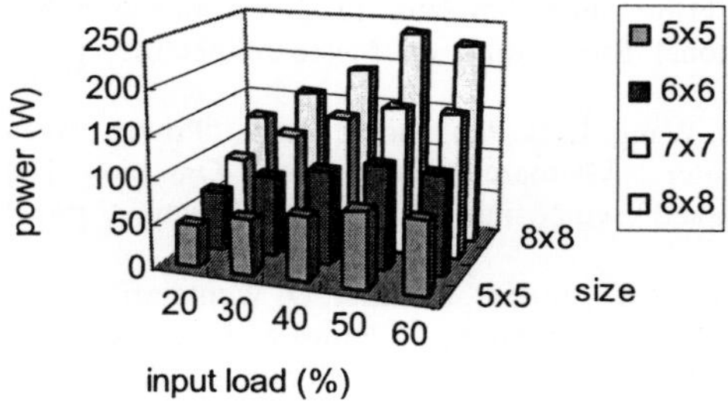

Figure 7. Effectiveness of various network size

6. Conclusions

The proposed credit-based peak power control aims for the management of peak power consumption in the QoS capable on-chip networks. It turns out that the credit-based peak power control outperforms the prior technique, PowerHerd, in terms of packet latency, while avoiding the network congestion by controlling injection rates. The experiments with different mixed ratio of traffic and different mesh networks show that the proposed peak power control in a specific workload can be applied to other types of workload with a small variation.

We proposed two different control mechanisms for two types of traffic in a QoS capable on-chip network. For real-time traffic, the peak power control administers the admission of a new real-time traffic connection by considering the sustainable bandwidth that can be convertible to the power budget assigned to each router, when a new connection setup request arrives. This mechanism is similar to admission control. For best-effort traffic, it computes the expected energy dissipation of a packet and estimates its traversal time. The packet is allowed to enter the network only when the available energy budget of the ITL is large enough to accommodate the packet transfer. Otherwise, the packet injection is throttled. This feature resembles congestion control.

References

[1] W. Dally and B. Towles, "Route Packets, Not Wires: On-chip Interconnection Networks", Design Automation Conference, pp. 684-689, 2001.

[2] L. Benini and G. De Micheli., "Networks on Chips: A New SoC Paradigm", IEEE Micro, pp. 70-77, 2002.

[3] D. Singh, J. M. Rabaey, M. Pedram, F. Catthoor, S. Rajgopal, N.Sehgal, and T.J.Mozdan, "Power conscious cad tools and methodologies: A perspective" Proceedings of the IEEE, 83(4):570-594, Apr. 1995.

[4] K. H. Yum, E. J. Kim, C. R. Das, M. Yousif, and J. Duato "Integrated Admission and Congestion Control for QoS Support in Clusters," International Conference on Cluster Computing, pp. 325-332, 2002.

[5] H.-S. Wang, X. Zhu, L.-S. Peh, and S. Malik, "Orion: A Power-Performance Simulator for Interconnection Networks," International Symposium on Microarchitecture, pp. 294-305, 2002.

[6] H.-S. Wang, L.-S. Peh, and S. Malik, "Power-driven Design of Router Microarchitectures in On-chip Networks," International Symposium on Microarchitecture, pp. 105-116, 2003.

[7] M. B. Taylor, J. Kim, J. Miller, D. Wentzlaff, F. Ghodrat, B. Greenwald, H. Hoffmann, P. Johnson, J.-W. Lee, W. Lee, A. Ma, A. Saraf, M. Seneski, N. Shnidman, V. Strumpen, M. Frank, S. Amarasinghe and A. Agarwal, "The Raw Microprocessor: A computational fabrics for software circuits and general-purpose programs", IEEE Micro, 22(2):25-35, 2002.

[8] K. Sankaralingam, R. Nagarajan, H. Liu, C. Kim, J. Huh, D. Burger, S. W. Keckler, and C. R. Moore, "Exploiting ILP, TLP, and DLP with the polymorphous TRIPS architecture", International Symposium on Computer Architecture, pp. 422-433, 2003.

[9] E. J. Kim, K. H. Yum, G. M. Link, N. Vijaykrishnan, M. Kandemir, M. J. Irwin, M. Yousif, and C. R. Das, "Energy Optimization Techniques in Cluster Interconnects," International Symposium on Low Power Electronics and Design, pp. 459-464, 2003.

[10] S. Murali and G. De Micheli, "Bandwidth-Constrained Mapping of Cores onto NoC Architectures", Design, Automation and Test in Europe, pp. 896-903, 2004.

[11] J. H. Kim and A. A. Chien, "Rotating Combined Queuing (RCQ): Bandwidth and Latency Guarantees in Low-Cost, High-Performance Networks," International Symposium on Computer Architecture, pp. 226-236, May 1996.

[12] J.-P. Li and M. Mutka, "Priority Based Real-Time Communication for Large Scale Wormhole Networks," International Parallel Processing Symposium, pp. 433-438, May 1994.

[13] J. Duato, S. Yalamanchili, M. B. Caminero, D. Love, and F. J. Quiles, "MMR: A High-Performance Multimedia Router Architecture and Design Tradeoffs," International Symposium on High Performance Computer Architecture, pp. 300-309, Jan. 1999.

[14] K. H. Yum, E. J. Kim, C. R. Das, and A. S. Vaidya, "MediaWorm: A QoS Capable Router Architecture for Cluster," IEEE Transactions on Parallel and Distributed Systems, 13(12):1261-1274, Dec. 2002.

[15] A. Singh, W. Dally, A. Gupta, and B. Towles, "GOAL: A Load-Balanced Adaptive Routing Algorithms for Torus Networks", International Symposium on Computer Architecture, pp. 194-205, Jun. 2003.

[16] C. S. Patel, S. M. Chai, S. Yalamanchili, and D. E. Schimmel, "Power Constrained Design of Multiprocessor Interconnection Networks," International Conference on Computer Design, pp. 408-416, 1997.

[17] T. T. Ye, L. Benini, and G. De Micheli, "Analysis of Power Consumption on Switch Fabrics in Network Routers," Design Automation Conference, pp. 524-529, 2002.

[18] V. Raghunathan, M. B. Srivastava, and R. K. Gupta, "A Survey of Techniques for Energy Efficient On-chip Communication", Design Automation Conference, pp. 900-905, 2003.

[19] J. Hu, and R. Marculescu, "Exploiting the Routing Flexibility for Energy/Performance Aware Mapping of Regular NoC Architectures", Design, Automation and Test in Europe, pp. 10688-10693, 2003.

[20] W. H. Ho, and T. M. Pinkston, "A Methodology for Designing Efficient On-Chip Interconnects on Well-Behaved Communication Patterns", International Symposium on High Performance Computer Architecture, pp. 377-, 2003.

[21] L. Shang, L.-S. Peh, and N. K. Jha, "PowerHerd: Dynamic Satisfaction of Peak Power Constraints in Interconnection Networks," International Conference on Supercomputing, pp. 98-108, 2003.

[22] K. Skadron, T. Abdelzaher, and M. R. Stan, "Control-theoretic techniques and thermal-RC modeling for accurate and localized dynamic thermal management", International Symposium on High Performance Computer Architecture, pp. 17–28, Feb. 2002.

[23] X. Chen and L.-S. Peh, "Leakage Power Modeling and Optimization in Interconnection Networks", International Symposium on Low Power Electronics and Design, 2003.

Session 8B: Cross-Node Clustering

Impact of Exploiting Load Imbalance on Coscheduling in Workstation Clusters

Jung-Lok Yu[†] Driss Azougagh[†] Jin-Soo Kim[‡] Seung-Ryoul Maeng[†]
Division of Computer Science, Department of EECS
Korea Advanced Institute of Science and Technology (KAIST), South Korea
[†]{jlyu,driss,maeng}@calab.kaist.ac.kr [‡]jinsoo@cs.kaist.ac.kr

Abstract

Implicit coscheduling is known to be an effective technique to improve the performance of parallel workloads in time-sharing clusters. However, implicit coscheduling still does not take into consideration the system behavior like load imbalance that severely affects cluster utilization. In this paper, we propose the use of global information to enhance the existing implicit coscheduling schemes. We also introduce a novel coscheduling approach - named PROC (Process ReOrdering-based Coscheduling) - based on process reordering exploiting global load imbalance information to coordinate communicating processes. The results obtained from an in-depth simulation study show that our approach significantly outperforms previous ones (by up to 38.4%) by reducing the idle time (by up to 86.9%) and spin time (by up to 36.2%) caused by the load imbalance.

1 Introduction

Workstation clusters are emerging as a platform for the execution of general-purpose workloads [1, 2]. For the successful use of clusters in domains such as scientific applications, databases, web servers and multimedia, etc., scheduling techniques are required that can effectively handle workloads with diverse demanding characteristics [1, 2, 4, 6, 15]. For those workloads, time-sharing approaches are particulary attractive because they provide good response times for interactive jobs and good throughput for I/O-intensive jobs. Unfortunately, time-sharing can be very inefficient for running parallel jobs that need process synchronization due to the lack of coordination among local schedulers [13, 15].

Over the years, two main strategies to coordinate individual local schedulers have been proposed in the literature: *explicit coscheduling* [3, 5] and *implicit coscheduling* [1, 7, 6, 13]. Explicit coscheduling [3, 5] uses explicit global knowledge constructed a *priori* and performs simultaneous global context switch to coschedule parallel processes across all CPUs. While it has been shown to be essential for fine-grained parallel applications, explicit coscheduling doesn't seem to be viable option for a cluster environment in that it suffers from high global synchronization overhead. Recently, another class of coscheduling schemes such as Demand-based Coscheduling (DCS) [7], Spin Block (SB) [6, 13] and Periodic Boost (PB) [1] have been proposed for cluster systems. These implicit coscheduling schemes use communication events - message arrival and response time - of parallel processes to guide the local schedulers toward coscheduled execution whenever needed. For example, on a message arrival (or fast response), the implication is that the sender (or corresponding) process is currently scheduled. Therefore, it will benefit to schedule, or keep scheduled the receiver process. Compared to explicit coscheduling, these schemes are easier to implement on cluster environments, and have better scalability and reliability.

From the above discussion, we raise two important questions. (i) *how optimal previous implicit coscheduling schemes are in terms of performance?* (ii) *if not, what are the missing factors that limit the system utilization?* We observe that most implicit coscheduling schemes rely only on the locally available information (message arrival and response time). We also realize that there is crucial global information, for example, load imbalance, representing the behavior of the system, which can be exploited to optimize the system utilization.

We argue that global load imbalance information are critical to implicit coscheduling in a cluster. Load imbalance is one of the major factors to interfere with the efficient utilization of clusters. Load imbalance has three main sources: 1) uneven load (computation, I/O, and communication) distribution to equally powerful computing nodes, 2) heterogeneity in cluster hardware resources, and 3) the presence of the local jobs and background (or daemon) jobs (multiprogramming) [4]. Since this load imbalance results in the increment of the idle time on CPU resources and the waiting time on communicating processes, it has a marked detrimental effect on cluster utilization. Therefore, exploiting globalized load imbalance can be the key point to implicit coscheduling to improve the performance of cluster. This paper presents a novel coscheduling approach that exploits both local and global information to answer above questions. At the best of our knowledge, no previous study has exhaustively investigated this issue in the context of implicit coscheduling on a cluster environment.

In view of this, we present an innovative coscheduling scheme, called **Process ReOrdering-based Coscheduling (PROC)**, based on process reordering which exploits global runtime information as well as the limited knowledge available locally to coordinate the communicating processes across all CPUs. We realize that the combination of the average CPU time spent by each process and the expected number of processes ready to be executed before the current process is rescheduled, represents the global load imbalance (and synchronization) information in the system. PROC measures these values dynamically at run-time, and exchanges the information by piggybacking them with normal messages. Based on the load imbalance information, the local scheduler can then make better coscheduling decisions by reordering processes with pending messages. Through an in-depth simulation study, we show that our approach significantly outperforms previous implicit coscheduling schemes by reducing the idle time and the spinning time caused by the load imbalance, thus improves cluster utilization.

The rest of the paper is organized as follows. In Section 2, we present the overview of the implicit coscheduling strategies proposed in the literature. Section 3 discusses the proposed PROC approach in details. Section 4 describes the simulation methodology and Section 5 discusses the results obtained from our experiments. Finally, Section 6 concludes the paper.

2 Related Work

As described in [13], implicit coscheduling are classified by two components: *message waiting action* taken by processes waiting for a message and *message handling action* performed by the kernel when a message arrives, as summarized in Table 1.

LOCAL is the most straightforward coscheduling technique. A receiving process is just spinning until the message arrives, and becomes coscheduled with the sender process only if the message arrives while it is spinning.

The next straightforward one is **Immediate Block (IB)**. In IB, the process blocks immediately if the message has not arrived yet, and is waken up by the kernel when the message eventually arrives. **Spin Block (SB)** [6, 13] is a compromise between LOCAL and IB. Here a process spins on a message arrival for a fixed amount of time, as referred to *spin time*, before blocking itself (called *two-phased spin blocking*). The underlying rationale is that a process waiting for a message should receive it within the spin time if the sender process is also currently scheduled. Consequently, if the message arrives within the spin time, the receiver process should hold onto the CPU to be coscheduled with the sender process. Otherwise, it should block in order not to waste the CPU resource. On subsequent message arrival, the network interface cards (NIC) raises an interrupt, which is serviced by the kernel to wake up the process and give a priority boost to the awaken process. As a variant of SB, Agarwal et al. proposed **Co-ordinated Coscheduling (CC)** [16], which performs sender-side optimization to coschedule parallel jobs. In the CC scheme, a sender spins for a fixed amount of time to wait for a send complete event. If a send is not completed within this time, it is implicitly inferred that the outstanding message queue at the NIC is long and hence, it is better to block and let another process use the CPU. However, these blocking-based schemes (IB, SB and CC) still have the limitation that they can not eliminate or reduce the idle time caused by load imbalance.

Table 1. Implicit coscheduling schemes

Scheme	Msg. Waiting Action		Msg. Handling Action
	Sender	Receiver	
LOCAL	Spin-Only	Spin-Only	Nothing
IB	Spin-Only	Imme. Block	Interrupt & Boost
SB (CC)	Spin-Only(-Block)	Spin-Block	Interrupt & Boost
DCS	Spin-Only	Spin-Only	Interrupt & Boost
PB	Spin-Only	Spin-Only	Periodic Boost

Demand-based CoScheduling (DCS) [7] uses an incoming message as an indication that the sending process is currently scheduled on the sender node. In DCS, a receiving process performs busy-waiting. Periodically, NIC finds out which process is currently running on its host CPU. On message arrival, the NIC checks whether the message destination process is currently executing or not. If there is a mismatch, an interrupt is raised. The interrupt service routine (ISR) boosts the priority of the destination process to coschedule it with the sending process. **Periodic Boost (PB)**, proposed in [1, 15], is an alternative coscheduling scheme to avoid expensive interrupt cost. In PB, the receiving process is busy-waiting like DCS. However, in this scheme, rather than raising an interrupt for each incoming message, a periodically invoked kernel thread examines message queues of each process, and boosts the priority of a process with pending messages based on some selection criteria. Whenever the scheduler is invoked in the near future, it would preempt the current process and schedule the boosted process. Obviously, these spinning-based schemes (DCS and PB) suffer from the time wasted by processes while spinning for messages to arrive. This problem can become more harmful when processes are highly imbalanced in the cluster.

From the above description, we realize that the exploitation of global information (like ready-queue size in remote nodes) might solve most of those limitations. To exploit the global information, a new novel coscheduling scheme to efficiently reduce the idle time and the spinning time, is required. In this research, we introduce a coscheduling scheme based on reordering technique as an example to prove the importance of exploiting global load imbalance information.

3 Proposed Coscheduling Scheme

Exploiting the global load imbalance information has a major impact on the performance of cluster systems. Figure 1 shows the example of scheduling sequence performed by priority boost (and preemption) in each node. Note that normally, there are multiple incoming messages destined to distinct processes during a single scheduling quantum, and as a result of it, multiple processes are boosted (or waken up) until the next context switch. In this figure, we assume that N_1 and N_3 are the nodes with low load, and N_2 is heavily loaded (load(N_1) < load(N_3) < load(N_2)). In spinning-based schemes, N_1 and N_3 suffer from the spinning time if N_2 schedules the processes with pending messages without considering the load status of N_1 and N_3 (see Fig. 1(a.1)). As depicted in Fig. 1(a.2), P_1 and P_3 can be scheduled in advance in N_2 if N_2 realized that N_1 and N_3 have the lower load than other remote nodes. Similarly, in blocking-based schemes, N_1 and N_3 suffer from the idle time if N_2 schedules the awaken processes regardless of the loads of N_1 and N_3 (see Fig. 1(b.1)). As shown in Fig. 1(b.2), using load imbalance information from N_1 and N_3, N_2 can schedule P_1 and P_3 at time t and t' to reduce the idle time in N_1 and N_3. Therefore, by scheduling in advance a process whose corresponding processes will be scheduled sooner in remote nodes, we are able to decrease the spinning time and the idle time. This allows parallel processes to achieve better progress.

As described above, although the load imbalance has a marked detrimental effect on cluster's utilization, most implicit coscheduling strategies described in Section 2 take no account of the load imbalance to coordinate communicating processes. To address this concern, **PROC (Process ReOrdering-based Coscheduling)** measures the load imbalance information dynamically at run-time, and exchanges the information by piggybacking them with normal messages. Based on the load imbalance information, the local scheduler can then make better coscheduling decisions by reordering processes with pending message(s).

Then, the next question is how to measure the load imbalance information. In fact, it is very difficult to correctly measure the degree of load imbalance with a little overhead.

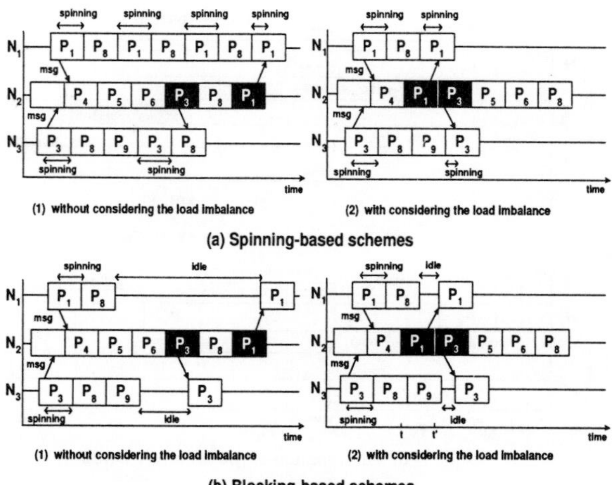

Figure 1. Effect of load imbalance in (a) spinning-based schemes and (b) blocking-based schemes

In order to minimize the overhead for measuring the degree of load imbalance, we use a heuristic algorithm as follows.

At any time, each node has a current process that uses a CPU. Each node N_i can compute: (a) the average CPU time spent by each process (averaged time difference between consecutive context switches) (TS_i), and (b) the expected number of processes ready to be executed (ENP_i) before the current process is scheduled again. In this paper, ENP_i is calculated to the summation of: (1) the number of processes with ready-to-run state (or with pending messages) in the highest-level ready queue on N_i and (2) the average number of processes to be additionally waken(or boosted) up by I/O completion and message arrival during the time interval ($TS_i \times$ the number of processes obtained from (1)).

Let us assume that there is a system with N nodes where each node N_i contains P processes. Each node N_i piggybacks TS_i and ENP_i in every outgoing messages as the load imbalance information of N_i. When a process P_k in N_j receives a message from N_i at time t, we define the followings:

- $\boldsymbol{TS_{ijk}} \leftarrow TS_i$, $\boldsymbol{ENP_{ijk}} \leftarrow ENP_i$
- $\boldsymbol{T_{ijk}}$: the latest time a process P_k in N_j receives a message from N_i ($T_{ijk} \leftarrow t$)
- $\boldsymbol{T_{ij}}$: the time of the last received message by N_j from N_i ($T_{ij} = \max_k(T_{ijk})$)
- $\boldsymbol{TS_{ij}}$: the most recent TS_i of N_i received by N_j

Each time N_j receives a new message from N_i, NIC updates a data structure (in scheduling layer) related to

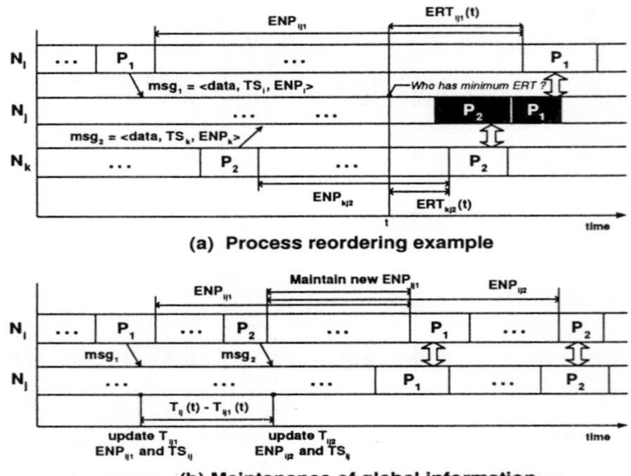

Figure 2. Process reordering example and maintenance of global information

the load imbalance information (ENP_{ijk}, T_{ijk}, TS_{ij}, and T_{ij}) of the remote node N_i based on TS_i and ENP_i extracted from the message. As each process with pending message(s) contains a list of the most recent load imbalance information of remote nodes, our reordering algorithm makes a new order among processes in N_j by sorting local processes mainly based on the Expected Remaining Time (ERT) to schedule the corresponding processes in remote nodes (see Fig. 2(a)). Our reordering algorithm is shown in the Algorithm 1.

The ERT_{ijk} represents the expected remaining time to schedule the corresponding process of local process P_k in the remote node N_i. It is updated by extracting the time spent in N_j from the total expected remaining time required to reschedule the corresponding process in N_i, as shown in line 14 in the algorithm. In line 15, we determine ERT_{jk} which represents the minimum ERT_{ijk} among all remote nodes. Based on the ERT_{jk}, our reordering algorithm computes the least Expected Reordering Factor (ERF) in N_j (ERF_j) among all processes with pending message(s). The Candidate Set of the Preferable processes (CSP) in N_j contains all processes with ERT_{jk} equal to the least ERF_j (see from line 18 to 22 in the algorithm). It represents the set of the most urgent processes which should be scheduled first. Note that when the queue has less than two processes with pending messages, this reordering procedure is not invoked. For the simplicity reason, the scheduler randomly selects one candidate process from the set CSP to be scheduled next. Before computing the CSP, processes receiving messages from the same remote node, they can share load imbalance information and maintain their information as shown from line 9 to 12 in the algorithm (see also Fig. 2(b)).

Algorithm 1: Process reordering algorithm

```
1  Reordering Procedure (node N_j, current time t, CSP) {
2    CSP = null;
3    ERF_j = infinite;
4    for each process P_k with pending message(s) in N_j {
5      ERT_jk = infinite;
6      for each message m of P_k {
7        i = sender node of message m;
8        // maintain the load imbalance information
9        if ( T_ijk < T_ij ) {
10         ENP_ijk = ENP_ijk - ((T_ij - T_ijk) / TS_ij);
11         T_ijk = T_ij;
12       }
13       // determine minimum ERT value in a process
14       ERT_ijk = (TS_ij * ENP_ijk) - (t - T_ijk);
15       if ( ERT_jk > ERT_ijk ) ERT_jk = ERT_ijk;
16     }
17     // determine a process set with minimum ERF value
18     if ( ERF_j > ERT_jk ) {
19       ERF_j = ERT_jk;
20       CSP = { k };
21     }
22     else if ( ERF_j == ERT_jk ) CSP = CSP + { k };
23   }
24 }
```

For experimental purpose, SB and PB are selected as two case studies since they represent the most successful and rich strategies among others. In SB, our reordering algorithm can be applied at each scheduler invocation by determining the process with minimum ERT value. In contrast to SB, PB needs to apply the reordering algorithm at each PB kernel thread invocation ($\sim$ 1ms). For the convenience, we call the former case **SB+PROC**, and the latter **PB+PROC**.

4 Experimental Methodology

Simulator. We used a detailed, process-oriented event-driven simulator, named ClusterSchedSim [17] built on CSIM19 [19] package, and added our proposed scheme onto it. As depicted in Fig. 3(a), each workstation com-

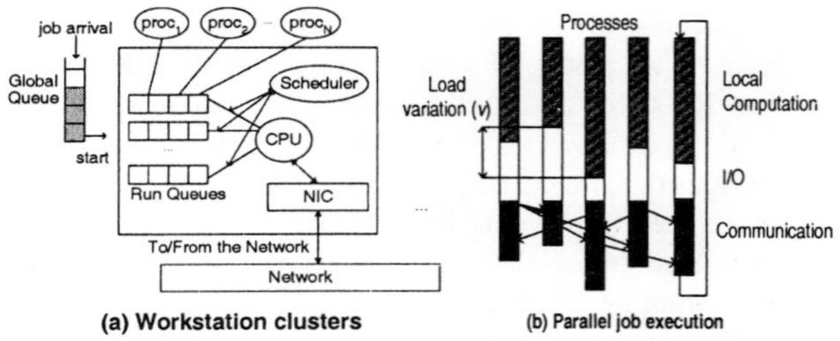

Figure 3. Simulation model of workstation cluster and parallel job execution

Table 2. Workloads characteristics

	Comp.	I/O	Comm.		
J1	70	5	25	*WL1*	a set of J1
J2	48	5	47	*WL2*	a set of J2
J3	25	5	70	*WL3*	a set of J3
				WL4	equal mix of J1,J2,J3

(a) Synthetic Workloads

	Pattern	Comm.	Msg. Size (bytes)
LU	NN (four)	11.5%	320, 640 (48.3%) 40,960, 81,920 (1.56%)
CG	NN (six)	63.4%	8 (59%), 16 (1%) 14,000(40%)
IS	AA, Barrier	30.1%	4 (50%) 32,768 (50%)
FT	AA	56.3%	128KB (50%) 256KB (50%)

(b) Realistic Workloads

Table 3. Simulation parameters and values

Parameters	Value(s)
System size	32
MPL(Multi-Programming Level)	5, 10
Communication patterns	NN, AA
Message size	32 KB
One-way latency	187.97 μs
Variance (v)	0.5, 1.5
Context switching cost	100 μs
Interrupt processing cost	30 μs
Check an endpoint	2 μs
Download (or upload) of global info.	2 μs
Change the position in scheduling queue	2 μs

prises a NIC, OS scheduler, and a set of user processes. The NIC module models the interactions between user processes (or scheduler) and the network. Whenever a message is received from the network, the NIC delivers it into a user buffer and raises an interrupt. Similarly, the NIC waits for outgoing messages and enqueues them into the network module. This form of operation is typical of user-level communication approach [8]. Costs for these operations have been obtained from microbenchmarks performed on a cluster of Pentium III-800 MHz workstations connected by Myrinet [9]. The scheduler module emulates Solaris scheduler [10] and is responsible for manipulating a priority-based multi-level feedback queue (60 queues) on which ready-to-run processes are placed. Each workstation may run an arbitrary number of user processes, whose executions are expressed by a simple language that allows the specification of computations, disk I/O and communication operations. For the global scheduler, we adopt FIFO.

The periodic boost mechanism used in PB and PB+PROC becomes active every one millisecond. For SB and SB+PROC, we set the *spin time* for a message to be the expected one-way latency. In both SB+PROC and PB+PROC, costs for downloading (or uploading) the global information to NIC (or to scheduling layer), calculating and comparing the ERT values, and changing the position in the scheduling queue are modeled in the simulator.

Workloads. We consider two types of workloads: synthetic and realistic. Synthetic workloads are generated from San Diego Supercomputer Center (SDSC) SP2 traces, which are widely used in scheduling studies [11, 12]. During the synthetic workload generation, job arrival time, execution time, and size information are characterized to fit a mathematical model called Hyper-Erlang distribution of common order [14]. Each job in the workload requires 32 processes and iterates phases of local computation, disk I/O, and interprocess communication. We consider two different communication patterns: Nearest Neighbor (NN) and All-to-All (AA), which are commonly used in many parallel scientific applications. We assume that both communication patterns use a fixed message size of 32KB. By fixing the end-to-end one-way latency of a message, the computation and I/O time per iteration can be calculated. By multiplying the computation and I/O time by a value uniformly selected in $(1 + unif(-v/2, v/2))$ and by varying the load variance (v), we model the load imbalance across CPUs (see Fig. 3(b)).

In order to obtain realistic workloads, four parallel applications (LU, IS, CG, and FT) have been directly derived from the NAS Parallel Benchmarks (NPB) 2.4 suite [18]. More specifically, these applications have been obtained by translating their source codes in NPB into the language accepted by the ClusterSchedSim, without changing their execution flow, communication topology, and message sizes. The duration of sequential parts of these parallel application codes have been determined from measurements performed by running the corresponding NPB applications on a cluster of Pentium III-800MHz workstations. The characteristics of workloads and the simulation parameters used in our experiments are summarized in Table 2 and Table 3, respectively.

5 Experimental Results

5.1 Benefit Analysis of PROC

Here, we examine the results concerning the impact of workload characteristics (different proportions of computation, I/O, and communication) and communication patterns on the performance of different coscheduling schemes. *WL1*, *WL2*, and *WL3* represent computation-intensive, well-balanced, and communication-intensive workload, respectively. For this experiment, we limit the maximum Multi-Programming Level (MPL) to five and set the load variance factor (v) to 0.5. Figure 4 shows the average job response

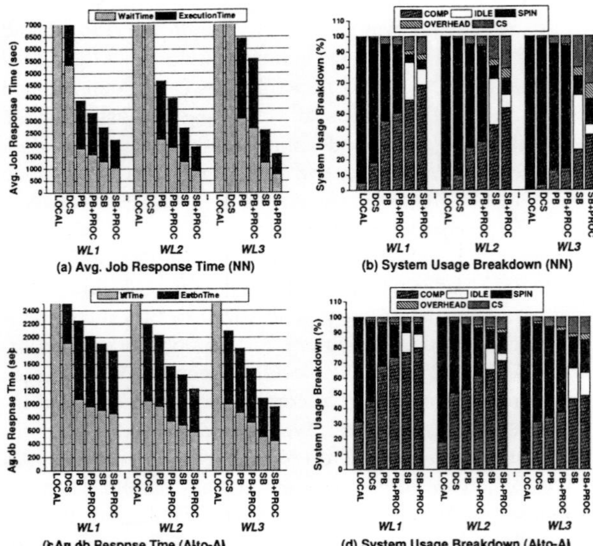

Figure 4. Impact of workload characteristics and communication patterns (MPL = 5, v = 0.5)

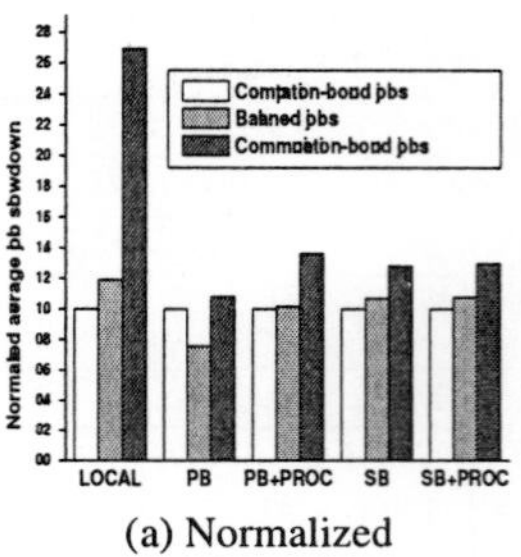

(a) Normalized avg. job slowdown

scheme	coeff. of variation
LOCAL	0.456
PB	0.157
PB+PROC	0.165
SB	0.107
SB+PROC	0.111

(b) Coefficient of variation of slowdown

Figure 5. Fairness (*WL4* with NN, MPL=5, v=0.0)

time and the system usage breakdown of our interesting six coscheduling schemes for these three workloads with Nearest Neighbor and All-to-All communication patterns.

The most striking observation in these figures is that the proposed coscheduling schemes, PB+PROC and SB+PROC, achieve better performance than PB and SB, respectively. We also note that SB+PROC has the lowest average job response time among all scheduling schemes. PB+PROC scheme reduces the average job response time by up to 23.1% compared to PB, and SB+PROC scheme by up to 38.4% compared to SB. The main reason the reordering-based schemes outperform prior coschedulings is that they avoid the unnecessary spinning time or idle time of previous schemes occurred by load imbalance. In DCS and SB, the boost sequence of a parallel process is determined by message arrival, and in PB by simple round-robin fashion. In contrast, PB+PROC and SB+PROC reorder the boost sequence of a parallel process according to the global load imbalance (by boosting a process with minimum ERT as described in Section 3), trying to reduce the unnecessarily wasted time. From Fig. 4(b) and 4(d), we can see that PB+PROC reduces the spinning time of PB by up to 36.2% and SB+PROC reduces the idle time of SB by up to 86.9%. When reordering is applied, the overhead is increased due to the cost for the maintenance and appliance of load imbalance information described in Section 3, and the context switch is increased since the process reordering makes the probability of scheduling appropriate (or urgent) processes high. However, these additional costs do little affect the overall benefit. Across all workloads, we also find that the blocking-based schemes (SB and SB+PROC) show better performance than the spinning-based schemes (LOCAL, DCS, PB and PB+PROC). This is because blocking technique allows processes of other applications to proceed in their computations, thus improving the response time.

Next, to evaluate the fairness, we calculate the coefficient of variation of slowdown over three different types of jobs in *WL4* with NN[1] (see Fig. 5). As depicted in Fig. 5, our scheme has almost the same fairness value as previous schemes. We also notice that blocking-based schemes are more fair than spinning-based schemes.

5.2 Effect of Load Imbalance and Multi-Programming Level (MPL)

In this section, we examine the effect of the load imbalance and Multi-Programming Level (MPL) on the performance of the considered different coscheduling approaches. In this experiment, we exclude LOCAL and DCS because there is no point to show their performance. We consider two extreme scenarios that have less communication (*WL1* with NN communication pattern) and intensive communication (*WL3* with AA) to analyze the behavior of reordering in relation with the load variance and MPL.

Figure 6 shows the average job response time and the system usage breakdown for these workloads with two different load variance values (0.5 and 1.5) and two different MPL values (5 and 10). All obtained results show that even with highly imbalanced load (or with larger MPL), applying reordering (PB+PROC and SB+PROC) enhances the performance of the previous schemes.

In Fig. 6 (right two groups of bars of each graph), since the higher load imbalance makes the probability of mismatch of communicating processes high, we observe that the response time increases with a larger load vari-

[1]The results for *WL4* with AA are omitted due to space limitation.

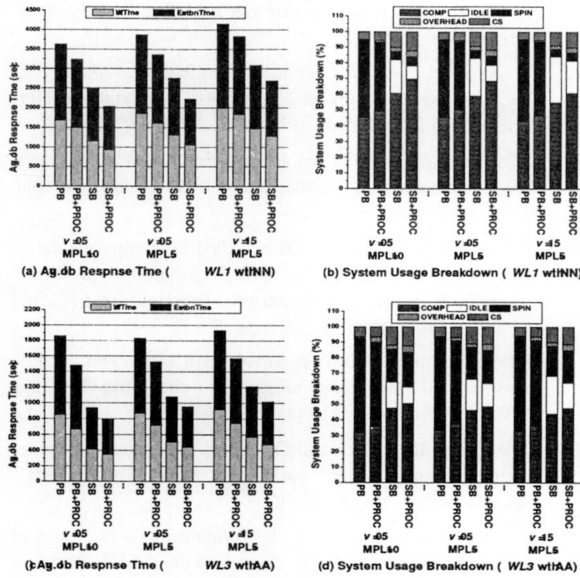

(a) Avg. Job Response Time (*WL1* with NN) (b) System Usage Breakdown (*WL1* with NN)

(c) Avg. Job Response Time (*WL3* with AA) (d) System Usage Breakdown (*WL3* with AA)

Figure 6. Impact of load imbalance and MPL

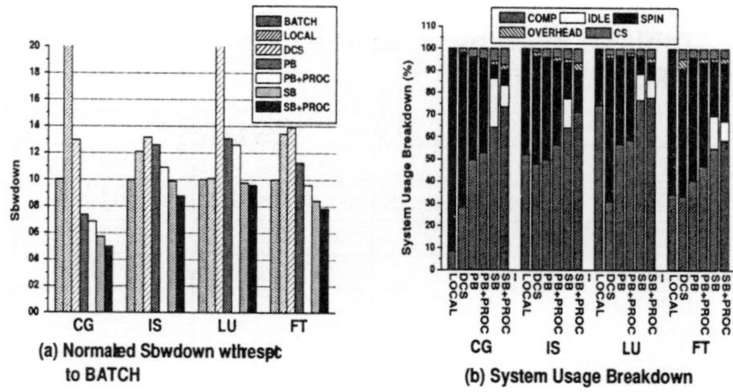

(a) Normalized Slowdown with respect to BATCH (b) System Usage Breakdown

Figure 7. Realistic workloads performance (MPL = 5)

ance value. This increment is mainly affected by the spinning time increase for the spinning-based approaches (PB and PB+PROC) and the idle time increase for the blocking-based approaches (SB and SB+PROC). From Fig. 6(a) and 6(c), we know that the effect of load imbalance (the increment of job response time) can be better hidden in AA than in NN due to the overlapping between communication and computation.

5.3 Realistic Workloads Performance

Finally, we consider four realistic workloads (CG, IS, LU, and FT) as described in Table 2(b). In each experiment, all jobs require 32 nodes, and are started simultaneously. Figure 7 reports the slowdown of implicit coscheduling schemes relative to BATCH (estimated as the ratio of the last job completion time divided by the sum of the execution times of the all applications run in isolation) and the system usage breakdown for these four realistic workloads.

In Fig. 7, it is clearly shown that with the use of global load imbalance information and reordering, PB+PROC and SB+PROC significantly outperform PB and SB, respectively, for all realistic workloads. Again, SB+PROC performs the best across all realistic workloads, and consistently shows speedup compared to BATCH. It is observed that for the application with low communication intensity like LU, there is hardly any need for coscheduling (note that in LU case, spinning-based schemes perform even worse than LOCAL). However, as the communication intensity increases (LU $<$ IS $<$ FT $<$ CG), the impact of implicit coscheduling becomes prominent. In CG, which has the highest communication intensity, PB+PROC shows about 30% speedup compared to BATCH, and SB+PROC gets at least 50% speedup. Also, the observation in this experiment reconfirms the fact that blocking-based schemes perform better than spinning-based schemes.

5.4 Discussion

From the previous results, applying the reordering mechanism substantially enhances the performance of PB and SB. Using the global load imbalance information, our reordering scheme tries to avoid the unnecessary spinning time or idle time of previous schemes occurred by load imbalance. This makes the exploitation of global load imbalance information as a main key point for our reordering scheme as well as any future coming reordering variants in clusters. Accordingly, in this section, we introduce the results of average message pending time for more analysis.

Table 4 shows the average message pending time (MSG_PENDING_TIME) of previous and proposed schemes for NN communication pattern [2] with different communication intensity. MSG_PENDI-NG_TIME is defined by the average time spent when messages arrive until they are consumed. Since implicit coscheduling schemes record small MSG_PENDING_TIME compared to LOCAL, the employment of implicit coscheduling onto workstation clusters is strongly recommended. We also notice that a considerable MSG_PENDING_TIME difference between spinning-based schemes (DCS, PB and PB+PROC) and blocking-based schemes (SB and SB+PROC) proportionally reflects the performance achieved in terms of average job response time in all previous results. MSG_PENDING_TIME is reduced by up to

[2]The results with AA are omitted because the overall trend of MSG_PENDING_TIME with AA is the same as with NN.

Table 4. Average message pending time (NN, MPL = 5, v = 0.5)

	MSG_PENDING_TIME		
	WL1	*WL2*	*WL3*
LOCAL	94.590 msec	88.875 msec	98.494 msec
DCS	19.039	15.958	20.959
PB	6.909	5.912	5.916
PB+PROC	6.202	5.587	5.641
SB	4.762	2.913	2.115
SB+PROC	3.726	2.039	1.347

10% in PB+PROC compared to PB and 36% in SB+PROC compared to SB. This reduction represents one of the key point of our reordering scheme. Our reordering algorithm favorites urgent processes that have high expectation to achieve synchronization with their corresponding ones in remote nodes in the near future. This fact reduces the MSG_PENDING_TIME, and consequently allows a process in average to consume its messages quicker and proceed for further executions.

6 Conclusion and Future Work

In this paper, we proposed the use of global information to address the main limitation of existing implicit coscheduling schemes - less accurate decision on who to boost to be coscheduled without regard to the load imbalance. We also presented a novel coscheduling approach based on process reordering exploiting global load imbalance information to coordinate the local schedulers.

We used the synthetic and realistic workloads to evaluate PROC compared to other schemes. We performed various experiments to analyze how the exploitation of global information using our reordering technique impacts on the performance of implicit coscheduling. The results reported in this paper show that our approach clearly provides better performance by reducing the idle time and the spinning time, thus improving the utilization of clusters. In PB+PROC, we achieved the improvement in terms of average job response time by up to 23.1%, while in SB+PROC, by up to 38.4%.

We plan to explore more global information that affects the coordination among communicating processes such as message frequency, queue size in NIC, etc. We also plan to extend our work by considering sequential and interactive jobs, and to implement PROC in a Linux cluster.

References

[1] Y. Zhang, A. Sivasubramaniam et al., Impact of Workload and System Parameters on Next Generation Cluster Scheduling, *IEEE Transactions on Parallel and Distributed System*, 2001, 12-9, pp. 967-985

[2] C. Anglano, A Comparative Evaluation of Implicit Coscheduling Strategies for Networks of Workstations, High Performance Distributed Computing, 2000, pp. 221-228

[3] J. Ousterhouw, Scheduling techniques for concurrent systems, 3rd International Conference on Distributed Computing Systems, 1982, pp. 22-30

[4] U. Rencuzogullari and S. Dwarkadas, Dynamic adaptation to Available Resources for Parallel Computing in an Autonomous Network of Workstations, Principles and Practice of Parallel Programming, 2001, pp. 72-81

[5] D. Feitelson and M. Jette, Improved Utilization and Responsiveness with Gang Scheduling, Job Scheduling Strategies for Parallel Processing, 1997, pp. 238-261

[6] A. Dusseau, R. Arpaci and D. Culler, Effective Distributed Scheduling of Parallel Workloads, ACM SIGMETRICS Conf. MMCS, 1996, pp. 25-36

[7] P. Sobalvarro, S. Pakin, et al., Dynamic Coscheduling on Workstation Clusters, IPPS Workshop on JSSPP, 1998, pp. 231-256

[8] D. Dunning et al., The Virtual Interface Architecture, *IEEE Micro*, 1998, pp. 66-75

[9] N. Borden et al., Myrinet: A Gigabit-per-second Local Area Network, *IEEE Micro*, 1995, 15, pp. 29-36

[10] SUN Microsystems Inc., Solaris 2.6 Software Developer Collection, 1997, Available from http://www.sun.com/

[11] G. Sabin, R. Kettimuthu, et al., Scheduling of Parallel Jobs in a Heterogeneous Multi-Site Environment, JSSPP, 2003, pp. 87-104

[12] D. Feitelson, Metric and Workload Effects on Computer Systems Evaluation, *Computer*, 2003, pp. 18-25

[13] S. Nagar, A. Banerjee, et al., Alternatives to Coscheduling a Network of Workstations, *Journal of Parallel and Distributed Computing*, 1999, 59-2, pp. 302-327

[14] H. Franke, J. Jann, et al., Evaluation of Parallel Job Scheduling for ASCI Blue-Pacific, Supercomuting, 1999.

[15] S. Nagar, A. Banerjee, et al., A Closer Look at Coscheduling Approaches for a Network of Workstations, ACM Symp. Parallel Algorithms and Architectures, 1999, pp. 96-105

[16] S. Agarwal, G. S. Choi, et al., Coordinated Coscheduling in Clusters through a Generic Framework, Cluster Computing, 2003, pp. 84-91

[17] Y. Zhang and A. Sivasubramaniam, ClusterSchedSim: A Unifying Simulation Framework for Cluster Scheduling Strategies, *SIMULATION: Transactions of the Society for Modeling and Simulation*, May 2004, pp. 191-206

[18] NAS division., The NAS parallel benchmarks Available from http://www.nas.nasa.gov/Software/NPB/

[19] H. D. Schwetman, CSIM19: a powerful tool for building system models, 2001 Winter Simulation Conference, 2001, pp. 250-255

Push-Pull: Guided Search DAG Scheduling for Heterogeneous Clusters[†]

Sang Cheol Kim and Sunggu Lee
Dept. of Electrical Engineering
Pohang University of Science and Technology (POSTECH)
San 31 Hyoja Dong, Pohang 790-784, South Korea
{ksc, slee}@postech.ac.kr

Abstract

Consider a heterogeneous cluster system, consisting of processors with varying processing capabilities and network links with varying bandwidths. Given a DAG application to be scheduled on such a system, the search space of possible task schedules is immense. *One possible approach for this type of NP-complete problem, which has been proposed by previous researchers, starts with the best task schedule found by a fast deterministic task scheduling algorithm, and then iteratively improves the task schedule using a random search method such as genetic algorithm search. However, such an approach can lead to extremely long search times, and the solutions found are sometimes not significantly better than those found by the original deterministic task scheduling algorithm. In this paper, we propose an alternative strategy, termed* Push-Pull, *which starts with the best task schedule found by a fast deterministic task scheduling algorithm, and then iteratively attempts to improve the current best solution using a deterministic guided search method. Our simulation results show that this new method performs quite well, executing faster and finding better solutions than a genetic algorithm-based method, which in turn has been shown to perform better than previous algorithms.*

1. Introduction

In parallel and distributed computing, development of an efficient static task scheduling algorithm for directed acyclic graph (DAG) applications is an important problem. The static task scheduling problem is NP-complete in its general form [1]. Although optimal solutions are known for restricted cases of this problem [2, 3, 4], such restrictions prevent the static task scheduling problem from being applicable to general computing environments. For this reason, there has been considerable research into heuristic static task scheduling algorithms [5]. Since such heuristic methods do not find the optimal solution, there is always room for improvement. Thus, if a solution (referred to as the "initial solution") is generated by one of the existing heuristic algorithms (referred to as the "baseline algorithm" [6]) and it is not yet an optimal solution, there is a possibility of improving it through additional search operations.

This paper proposes a new deterministic guided search strategy for heterogeneous cluster systems. The type of heterogeneous system considered is a system in which there are a collection of independent cluster systems that are connected by a wide area network. Each of these cluster systems consist of a set of heterogeneous processors and a local area network, which typically has higher bandwidth than the wide area network. This kind of cluster-of-clusters system, which can be considered as a type of grid computer, has become more popular in recent years. However, since this type of system has both processor heterogeneity and network heterogeneity, the search space of task scheduling solutions becomes extremely large and the task scheduling problem becomes more complicated.

In the proposed approach, obtaining a high quality solution consists of two steps. The first step is to generate a good solution using a baseline algorithm. As the baseline algorithm, list-based heuristics are widely used due to their high performance and low time complexity [7, 5]. However, these methods leave a lot of room for improvement, especially when they are used in specialized heterogeneous environments such as heterogeneous cluster systems. This is because these methods were developed for fast execution on general heterogeneous environments. Thus, in the second step, the initial solution found by the baseline algorithm is improved using a guided search strategy. The *Push-Pull algorithm* has been proposed for this purpose.

Two technical schemes are included in the Push-Pull algorithm in order to improve the initial solution. The first in-

† This research was supported in part by the POSTECH Information Research Laboratory (PIRL).

volves finding all feasible holes (the idle gaps in processor time between two assigned tasks) of the given schedule and checking if there is a possibility that a group of tasks can be inserted into these holes. Successful insertion of tasks to holes can significantly reduce the *makespan*, defined as the overall execution time of all tasks in the given DAG application. The second scheme involves finding the critical path and trying to reduce the makespan by moving tasks to other processors and thereby decreasing the assigned start time of the critical tasks. These two schemes, termed the "pull" and "push" procedures, respectively, are iteratively executed until there is no further improvement in the search solution.

2. Preliminaries and Definitions

2.1. DAG, Heterogeneous Clusters System and Scheduling Problem

An application is represented by a DAG $G = (T, E)$, where T is a set of N_T tasks and E is a set of N_E edges. Each edge $e_{i,j} = (t_i, t_j) \in E$ represents a precedence constraint that indicates that task t_i should complete executing before task t_j can start. A task t_i has a weight $\tau_i (1 \leq i \leq N_T)$, corresponding to the execution time of task t_i on a baseline processor platform, and an edge $e_{i,j} (1 \leq i,j \leq N_T)$ has a weight $\epsilon_{i,j}$, corresponding to the amount of data to be transmitted from p_i to p_j [17]. $PRED(t_i)$ is the set of predecessor tasks of the task t_i.

The target heterogeneous cluster system can be represented hierarchically by an undirected graph $HC = (C, L_W)$, where $C = \{C_k | 1 \leq k \leq N_C\}$ corresponds to a set of N_C clusters and $L_W = \{l_{C_i C_j} | C_i, C_j \in C\}$ corresponds to a set of wide area network (WAN) links between clusters, Each cluster, $C_k = (P(k), L(k))$, contains a set $P(k)$ of processors and a set $L(k)$ of local area network (LAN) links used for communicating among the processors in $P(k)$.

For the purposes of task scheduling, a heterogeneous cluster system can also be represented by a nonhierarchical graph $NHC = (P, L)$, where $P = \cup_{k=1}^{N_C} P(k) = \{p_1, ..., p_{N_P}\}$ and $L = L_W \bigcup (\cup_{k=1}^{N_C} L(k)) = \{l_{p_i p_j} | p_i, p_j \in P\}$. In this representation, given a link $l_{p_i p_j}$, if both p_i and p_j belong to the kth cluster $C(k)$, then the link corresponds to a LAN link in $L(k)$. Otherwise, link $l_{p_i p_j}$ is a WAN link in L_W. Each processor p_q has a (relative) computing power factor w_q; it takes $\tau_i \cdot w_q$ time-units to execute the task t_i on the processor p_q. Likewise, we let $\lambda_{p_q p_r}$ denote the inverse of the bandwidth of the link between p_q and p_r, so that $\epsilon_{i,j} \cdot \lambda_{p_q p_r}$ time-units are required to send $\epsilon_{i,j}$ from p_q to p_r [8].

Given a DAG G and a heterogeneous cluster NHC, the problem addressed in this paper is to find a task *schedule*, a mapping of G onto NHC. The quality of a solution is determined by the *makespan*, the total length of the resulting schedule.

2.2. A Schedule as a Problem Solution

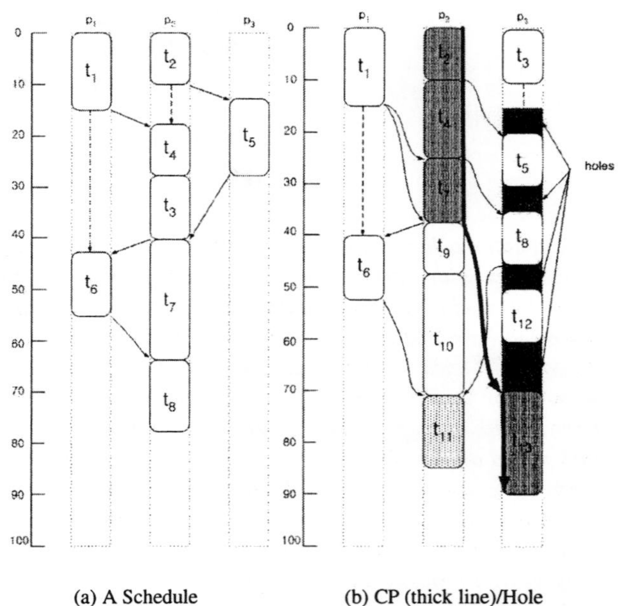

(a) A Schedule (b) CP (thick line)/Hole

Figure 1. Examples for a Schedule/CP/Hole

A schedule $\psi = (\phi, \chi)$ (refer to Fig. 1) consists of two information components, a *task assignment* $\phi : T \rightarrow P$ and a *task ordering* $\chi = \{\chi_i | 1 \leq i \leq N_P\}$, where χ_i is an ordered list of tasks assigned to processor p_i. The list χ_i is of the form $(t_{j_1}, t_{j_2}, ..., t_{j_{r_i}})$, where $t_{j_{r_i}}$ is the r_i^{th} task to be executed on processor p_i. The task $t_{j_{r_i}}$ in χ_i, with *rank* r_i, is the r_i^{th} task to be executed on processor p_i. The symbol '$\prec$' is used to represent an execution ordering. For example, if a task $t_{j_l} \in \chi_i$ has a smaller rank (executes earlier) than another task $t_{j_m} \in \chi_i$, then $t_{j_l} \prec t_{j_m}$. In particular, when the ranks differ by one, we can use the notation '$\overset{1}{\prec}$' instead of '$\prec$'. Other definitions related to a task schedule are given below.

- $[t_{j_l} :: t_{j_m}]$ is a set of t_{j_k} tasks such that $l \leq k \leq m$, where $\phi(t_{j_l}) = \phi(t_{j_m}) = \phi(t_{j_k})$.
- $BITS(t_i)$ is a set of t_{j_k} tasks that are independent of the task t_i, where $t_{j_k} \prec t_i$ and $\phi(t_{j_k}) = \phi(t_i)$. All the tasks in $BITS(t_i)$ must have no DAG precedence re-

lationship with the task t_i and have smaller execution ranks than the task t_i as well.

2.3. Evaluation of a Schedule

Given a schedule $\psi = (\phi, \chi)$, it can be evaluated using the list heuristic method introduced by Correa *et. al.* [9]. After a schedule is evaluated, it is possible to determine $AST(t_i)$ and $AFT(t_i)$, which are the *assigned start time* and *assigned finish time*, respectively, of the task t_i. $T_{data}(t_i)$ is the time required to receive all the data from the predecessors of task t_i executing on processor $\phi(t_i)$, and $T_{avail}[\phi(t_i)]$ is the time when processor $\phi(t_i)$ is available. Then $AST(t_i) = \max[T_{avail}[\phi(t_i)], T_{data}(t_i)]$ and $AFT(t_i) = AST(t_i) + comp(t_i, \phi(t_i))$, where $comp(t_i, \phi(t_i))$ is the computational cost of the task t_i on the processor $\phi(t_i)$. Other definitions related to the evaluation of a schedule are shown below.

- $cpt(t_i)$ is a critical predecessor task of task t_i. $T_{data}(t_i)$ is determined by the predecessor tasks of the task t_i. The predecessor task that provides data to task t_i at the latest time, among all predecessor tasks of t_i, is $cpt(t_i)$.
- CP is the critical path of a schedule, consisting of a path of tasks and edges leading to the minimum completion time for that schedule. Tasks in CP are referred to as *critical tasks.*
- The *makespan* of a schedule is the length of CP.
- $\sum exec(N, p_j)$ is the sum of computational costs for a task set, $N = [t_{j_l} :: t_{j_m}]$, on a processor p_j; This can be computed as $\sum_{i=l}^{m} \tau_{j_i} \cdot w_j$.
- $hole(p_j)$ is an empty space in the execution time for a processor p_j within a given schedule. No tasks are assigned to p_j during $hole(p_j)$.
- $\sum_{\sigma_s}^{\sigma_e} hole(p_j)$ is the sum of holes on a processor p_j from σ_s to σ_e.

Figure 1 shows an example of a critical path $t_2 t_4 t_7 e_{7,13} t_{13}$ using a thick solid line. If we assume $N = [t_5 :: t_{12}] = \{t_5, t_8, t_{12}\}$, then $\sum exec(N, p_3) = 30$ and $\sum_{15}^{75} hole(p_3) = 25$.

2.4. Modification of a Schedule

In search-based scheduling algorithms, a commonly-used technique involves attempting to find an improved task schedule by modifying the current best task schedule, and then testing if the new schedule is better than the current schedule. If the new schedule is better, it is taken as the current best schedule during the next iteration. In our algorithm design, a new schedule is accepted as long as the new schedule is not worse than the current best schedule. In this case, it is said that the new schedule is *acceptable*.

This "modify-and-test" scheme gives us the possibility of finding successively better task schedules with each iteration. However, there must be a method of generating new schedules that searches the space of possible solutions in an effective manner. In addition, the new schedule generated must have a valid representation. We present two functions for this purpose as follows.

• $\psi' = Reassign(N \rightarrow p_j|\psi)$ changes the schedule ψ by reassigning all of the tasks in a set N to the processor p_j with the following steps (where N is a set of tasks assigned on the same processor under ψ). **Step 1.** Whenever a pair of tasks $(t_{j_k}, t_{j_{k+1}})$ under schedule ψ is not an element of E, add the pair as a zero-weighted pseudo-edge into the DAG. **Step 2.** Sort the resulting DAG in topological order and construct a string which contains a series of matching pairs of the form (t_i, p_j). Such a matching implies that the task t_i is mapped to processor p_j. **Step 3.** Replace the processor portion of the matching for p_j; that is, use $(t_k, \phi(t_k))$ instead of (t_k, p_j) for $t_k \in N$. **Step 4.** Construct a new schedule based on the topological ordering and the matching used in the modified string.

• $\psi' = Reorder(t_{n2} \overset{1}{\prec} t_{n1}|\psi)$ changes the schedule ψ by placing t_{n2} immediately prior to t_{n1}, given two independent tasks t_{n1} and t_{n2}, $t_{n1} \overset{1}{\prec} t_{n2}$ and $\phi(t_{n1}) = \phi(t_{n2})$.

3. Related Work

There have been many previous research works that use an iterative method to improve upon a baseline scheduling solution. Most of these works use a random guided search strategy [9, 10, 6, 11, 12]. This strategy uses the knowledge of the problem to guide the solution toward a more promising region in a somewhat random manner (in order to avoid getting trapped in local minima regions). Genetic algorithms (GAs) [9, 10, 6] are known as the most popular and widely used random guided search technique for many types of combinatorial problems. One problem with the random guided search strategy is that this "randomness" prevents the search from proceeding in the proper search direction quickly. Another problem with the random guided search based strategy is that it typically requires a large number of control parameters, which need to be determined by experiments. This is a serious limitation because good experiments, which reflect the actual execution environments, are crucial to obtaining good solutions [13].

Another type of scheduling approach uses deterministic instead of random search. Such an approach, referred to deterministic guided search, involves starting with a baseline scheduling solution and then attempting to improve upon that solution in a non-random iterative manner, using the knowledge of the problem to guide the search. Wu *et. al.* [14] used a deterministic guided search strategy for static task scheduling on multiprocessor systems. The scheduling problem for multiprocessor systems is simpler than that for heterogeneous cluster systems.

4. Proposed Algorithm : Push-Pull

Algorithm Push-Pull

```
Generate schedule ψ using a baseline algorithm
Repeat
    Create new schedule ψ' using pull procedure
    Create new schedule ψ'' using push procedure
    ψ ← schedule with best makespan among {ψ,ψ',ψ''}
Until (no change in ψ for T iterations)
Return ψ (the current best schedule)
```

Figure 2. Pseudocode description of the Push-Pull algorithm.

4.1. Push-Pull Algorithm

The overall description of the proposed deterministic guided search strategy, referred to as the *Push-Pull algorithm*, is given in Fig. 2. Initially, it obtains a schedule ψ using a baseline algorithm (e.g. list-based heuristic). Next, it repeats the pull and push procedures until the quality of the solution is not improved for T iterations. T is the unique control parameter in the Push-Pull algorithm (typically set to a small value such as $T = 4$ or 5). When the algorithm terminates, it returns the best schedule found thus far.

The Push-Pull algorithm is a guided search algorithm that uses two main methods in its search: the *push procedure* and the *pull procedure*. Each procedure consists of a series of smaller-unit operations, referred to as *pull* and *push* operations. An important point is that the algorithm has been designed so as to alternate between the push and pull procedures one after the other. The push procedure has the effect of stretching the schedule while the pull procedure contracts the schedule. The push procedure scatters tasks originally assigned on one processor onto many processors while the pull procedure gathers tasks spread over many processors into one processor. By alternating between these two procedures, dramatic changes in the structure of the schedule can result, with the overall goal of finding a schedule with a small makespan. The push procedure pursues parallelism by scattering tasks while the pull procedure removes heavy communication costs between tasks.

4.2. Pull and Push Operations

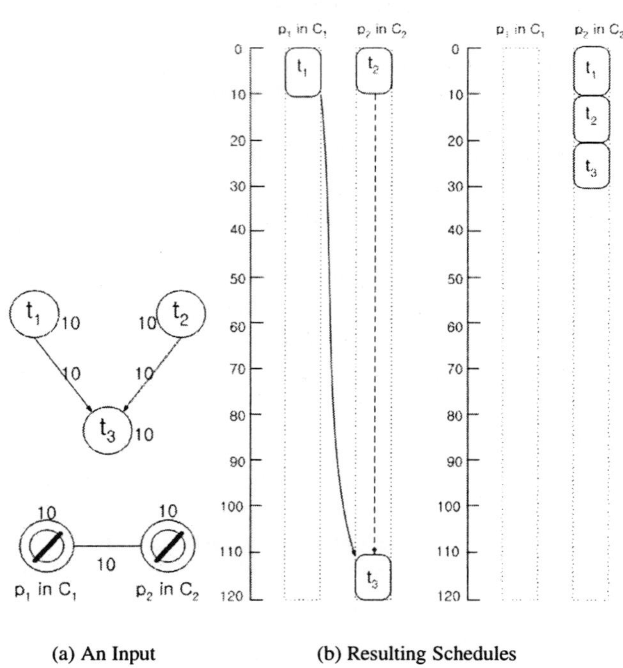

(a) An Input

(b) Resulting Schedules

Figure 3. Problematic list scheduling result.

The pull operation was motivated by a major problem that occurs when an up-to-date list scheduling algorithm, such as HEFT (Heterogeneous Earliest Finish-Time) [5] or HCPT (Heterogeneous Critical Parent Trees) [15], is used with a heterogeneous cluster as the target system. Since such algorithms use the earliest-finish-time-first scheduling policy, they may not consider large communication costs, such as those incurred by wide area network links, effectively. To explain the problem, let us consider a simple DAG and a simple heterogeneous cluster system, with only a single processor per cluster and parameter values set to 10 as shown in Fig. 3(a). Assuming the HEFT algorithm is used, the resulting schedule is shown on the left half of Fig. 3(b). This algorithm forms a sequence of tasks (t_1, t_2, t_3) according to their priorities and then assigns them to processors one by one in that order. t_1 and t_2 will be evenly distributed into two processors, p_1 and p_2 because of the earliest finish time scheduling policy of the algorithm. As a result, the resulting schedule has a makespan of $10+10\times 10+10 = 120$ regardless of the processor on which the task t_3 is assigned. From this example, it can be seen that large communication costs can significantly increase the makespan. Note, however, that if the task t_1 is simply reassigned to processor p_2, the makespan can be decreased to 30 as shown in the right half of Fig. 3(b).

Given two tasks, connected with a DAG edge but assigned to different processors such as in this example, if one task "pulls" the other task, then the pulled task is attracted to the processor on which the pulling task is assigned. This is referred to as a *pull operation*. The pulling task is referred to as the *trigger task* and the pulled task is referred to as the *target task*. In the pull operation, the condition when the two tasks t_i and $cpt(t_i)$ (the critical predecessor task of t_i) are assigned on different processors is referred to as the *pull condition*. Therefore, the trigger task is t_i and the target task is $cpt(t_i)$. As a result of the pull operation, a target task will be reassigned to the processor on which a trigger task is assigned. This makes the two tasks execute on the same processor, thereby eliminating the communication cost between them.

There is another problem that can arise when a target task is pulled. Suppose that a target task t_k and $cpt(t_k)$ are assigned to the same processor. If a trigger task t_i pulls the target task t_k, it does not remove the communication cost between t_k and $cpt(t_k)$, although it may remove the communication cost between t_i and t_k. The same situation exists if $cpt(cpt(t_k))$ resides on the same processor as $cpt(t_k)$.

One solution for this problem is to consider an entire chain of critical predecessor tasks (assigned on one processor) as the set of target tasks. Let N be the set of target tasks. The set N can be constructed as a stack in which the top element is the last target task and the the bottom element is the first target task. N can be expressed as $[t_{j_l} :: t_{j_m}]$, where t_{j_l} and t_{j_m} are the top and bottom elements, respectively, of the stack.

In the pull operation, all target tasks in N will be considered to be pulled. Thus, all of the tasks in N will be reassigned by this operation. This pull operation can be expressed in a mathematical form (when a trigger task t_i pulls N) as $\mathbf{Pull}(t_i, N) \equiv Reassign(N \rightarrow \phi(t_i))$.

Unlike the pull condition, consider the situation in which two independent tasks are assigned to the same processor. If one task "pushes" the other task, the pushed task will be repelled from the processor on which it is currently assigned. This is referred to as a *push operation*. The pushing task is referred to as the *trigger task* and the pushed task is referred to as the *target task*. Given a task t_i and $BITS(t_i)$ (the set of independent predecessor tasks of t_i assigned to the same processor as t_i), the trigger task is t_i and the target tasks are the tasks in $BITS(t_i)$.

The Push operation can lower the execution rank of a trigger task by pushing away target tasks. This enables a trigger task to be executed earlier. Since the push operation actually reassigns a target task to one of the other processors, a push operation in which a task t_i pushes a task t_j can be expressed as $\mathbf{Push}(t_i, t_j \rightarrow p_j) \equiv Reassign(\{t_j\} \rightarrow p_j)$, where p_j is one of the other processors, not yet specified.

4.3. Pull and Push Procedures

In the *pull procedure*, a trigger task and the corresponding target tasks need to be determined. The tasks in T are inspected in topological order. If a task being inspected and the corresponding target task satisfy the pull condition, they become the trigger and target tasks, respectively. The target task t_k is then expanded into a set of target tasks N that include $cpt(t_k)$, $cpt(cpt(t_k))$, etc., if they reside on the same processor. The pull procedure ends when all of the tasks in T have been inspected.

Pulling all of the tasks in N may not always be beneficial. This is because the pull operation can increase the makespan if the processor on which target tasks need to be assigned does not have enough space for the target tasks. Thus, the following *feasibility check* is used to consider this possibility.

- **Feasibility Check** Given a stack $S = [t_{j_l} :: t_{j_m}]$ and a processor p_j on which a trigger task is assigned, the insertion of S into processor p_j is *feasible* if and only if $\sum exec(S, p_j) \leq \sum_{\sigma_s}^{\sigma_e} hole(p_j)$ where $\sigma_s = AST(t_{j_l})$ and $\sigma_e = AFT(t_{j_m})$.

In the pull procedure, a pull operation is performed only if the feasibility check is passed and the new schedule is acceptable (not worse than the current best schedule). If the feasibility and acceptability checks fail for the current stack S, then the pull procedure removes the top of the stack S and repeats the process until either the checks are passed or the stack becomes empty. The overall procedure is shown in Fig. 4.

Procedure Pull-Procedure

```
 1: T' ← topologically sorted list of tasks in T
 2: while T' is not empty do
 3:     select the first trigger task t_k from T'
 4:     if t_k satisfies the pull condition
 5:         create S, a set of target tasks for t_k
 6:         repeat
 7:             if insertion of S is feasible, then
 8:                 ψ' ← Pull(t_k, S|ψ)
10:                 if ψ' is acceptable for ψ then
11:                     ψ ← ψ' and go to Step 14
12:             remove top of S
13:         until S = ∅
14:     T' ← T' − {t_k}
15: end while
```

Figure 4. The pull procedure.

In the *push procedure*, a trigger task t_c needs to be determined. Once t_c is determined, all of the tasks in $BITS(t_c)$ automatically become target tasks. Critical tasks can be regarded as good candidates for trigger tasks because since such tasks contribute directly to the makespan. Thus, the algorithm considers the tasks in CT, which are the set of critical tasks, in topological order.

Before proceeding with the push operation for a trigger task, the *reordering procedure* is performed. This procedure attempts to improve the makespan by reordering the trigger task before other tasks with lower execution rank. This can be done by repeating the function $\psi' = Reorder(t_c \overset{1}{\prec} t_k|\psi)$, where t_c is a trigger task and t_k is the task with the largest execution rank among the tasks in $BITS(t_c)$. The reordering procedure ends when a new schedule ψ' found by reordering is determined to not be acceptable. The overall procedure is shown in Fig. 5. After this procedure ends, the size of $BITS(t_c)$ may be decreased due to the reordering operation.

Procedure Reordering-Procedure(t_c); t_c is a trigger task

obtain $BITS(t_c)$
repeat
    $t_r \leftarrow$ task w/ largest execution rank in $BITS(t_c)$
    $\psi' \leftarrow Reorder(t_c \overset{1}{\prec} t_r|\psi)$
    if ψ' is acceptable then
        $\psi \leftarrow \psi'$
        $BITS(t_c) \leftarrow BITS(t_c) - \{t_r\}$
until ψ' is not acceptable

Figure 5. The reordering procedure.

The push procedure begins by pushing out each of the tasks in $BITS(t_c)$ for a given trigger task t_c. Each task to be pushed must be reassigned to one of the other processors. But since there are a large number of processors in a typical heterogeneous cluster environment, it is desirable limit the set of processors to be considered. Thus, whenever a target task is selected, only the following processors are considered as *candidate processors*: (1) processors on which at least one task is assigned and (2) the fastest processor (with the lowest w_q) among the processors on which no tasks are assigned in each cluster. While attempting to assign a target task to the set of candidate processors, the innermost loop is exited when the new schedule is found to be acceptable. The push procedure ends when CT becomes empty. The entire push procedure is shown in Fig. 6

Procedure Push-Procedure

$CT \leftarrow$ topologically ordered list of critical tasks
while CT is not empty
    $t_c \leftarrow$ first task in CT
    $BITS(t_c) \leftarrow$ Reordering-Procedure(t_c)
    repeat
        $t_r \leftarrow$ task w/ largest execution rank in $BITS(t_c)$
        $PS \leftarrow$ candidate processors
        repeat
            select a processor p_j from PS
            $\psi' \leftarrow \mathbf{Push}(t_c, t_r \rightarrow p_j|\psi)$
            if ψ' is acceptable then
                $\psi \leftarrow \psi'$
                $PS \leftarrow PS - \{p_j\}$
        until ψ' is acceptable
        $BITS(t_c) \leftarrow BITS(t_c) - \{t_r\}$
    until $BITS(t_c)$ is empty
    $CT \leftarrow CT - \{t_c\}$
end while

Figure 6. The push procedure.

5. Performance Study

Simulation studies were used to compare the performance of the Push-Pull algorithm with a GA(Genetic Algorithm)-based task scheduling algorithm, which has been shown to perform better than previous random guided scheduling algorithms [6]. Two list-based heuristic algorithms, HEFT [5] and HCPT [15], were used as our baseline algorithms because these are two of the best-performing algorithms proposed thus far for heterogeneous clusters.

For our experiments, a variety of synthetic DAGs and heterogeneous cluster systems were generated using a random graph generator and a random heterogeneous cluster system generator. The method and parameters used for the generation of these random graphs were similar to those used by Topcuoglu *et. al.* [5]. The generation of a random DAG requires five parameter inputs: the number of tasks (N_T), out-degree of a task, shape, deviation of task size and data size. The task size was randomly selected from the values between 1 and $X \cdot 10^3$ and the data size was randomly set to a value between 1 and 100. The random heterogeneous cluster generator produces a random computing environment based on three parameters: $alpha$ (network heterogeneity), $beta$ (processor heterogeneity) and $nclusters$ (the number of clusters). The sets of parameter values used in our experiments are shown in Fig. 7. All combinations of the parameter value sets, a total of 31680 cases, were used to create the application DAGs G and heterogeneous cluster graphs HC.

Simple parameter value settings were used for the two task scheduling algorithms compared in this study. The T parameter used by the Push-Pull algorithm was set to the constant 5. The parameter values used for the GA algorithm were the same as those used by Wang *et. al.* [6].

$SET_{N_T} = \{15, 16, 39, 45, 56, 81, 82, 102, 157, 173, 217\}$
$SET_{out-degree} = \{1, 2, 3, 4, 5\}$
$SET_{shape} = \{0.5, 1.0, 2.0\}$
$SET_X = \{1, 10, 100\}$
$SET_{alpha} = \{10, 20, 50, 100\}$
$SET_{beta} = \{10, 20, 50, 100\}$
$SET_{nclusters} = \{4(100), 6(150), 8(200), 10(270)\}$
$(x(y) \rightarrow x$ clusters with y processors per cluster)

Figure 7. Parameter values used in the simulations.

5.1. Performance Metric

The SLR (schedule length relative to the minimum critical path) is a common performance metric used for the evaluation of DAG scheduling algorithms [5]. However, since the Push-Pull algorithm was designed to *improve* the makespan of the schedule generated by a baseline algorithm, another performance metric, *SLR improvement*, was used for the evaluation of the scheduling algorithms considered. If SLR_{BA} is the SLR of the schedule produced by the baseline algorithm and SLR_{GSA} is the SLR of the schedule produced by the guided search algorithm used, then SLR improvement(%) $= (SLR_{BA} - SLR_{GSA})/SLR_{BA} \times 100$.

Besides the quality of the solution produced by a scheduling algorithm, the overhead of the algorithm used can also be an important consideration. Thus, the *running time* of the scheduling algorithms used were measured on a common computing platform, a dual-CPU Intel Xeon (3.0 GHz) PC. Finally, for the Push-Pull algorithm, the *Push/Pull contribution* was measured to determine which of these two operations was more useful in improving the makespan.

5.2. Simulation Results

In the figures for the simulation results, the searching strategy used is indicated in the form (Baseline Algorithm)+(Search Algorithm). Thus, for example, "HEFT+GA" indicates that the GA algorithm was used with an initial (baseline) solution generated by the HEFT algorithm.

Fig. 8 shows the average SLR improvement and average running time as the number of tasks is varied. With a small N_T, both GA and Push-Pull improve the HEFT or HCPT schedule greatly (up to 27%). The large improvements for small N_T values is due to the small problem solution space. In this case, both search algorithms find the optimal or the near-optimal solution. However, the SLR improvement approaches zero for GA as the number of tasks

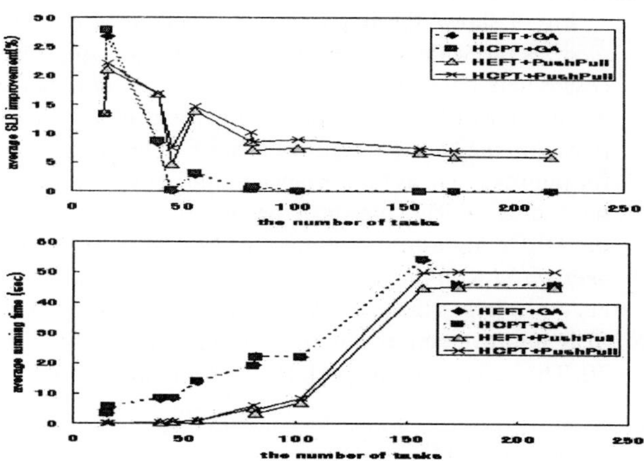

Figure 8. Average SLR improvement and running time as a function of the number of tasks.

is increased, while the SLR improvement remains above approximately 7% for Push-Pull.

With respect to the running time, Fig. 8 shows that the Push-Pull algorithm is, on average, faster than GA. Since GA is a random search algorithm, its execution time varies during each run and is dependent on the parameter values used. However, even when more time was expended, on average, for the GA algorithm, its performance was found to be inferior to that of the Push-Pull algorithm.

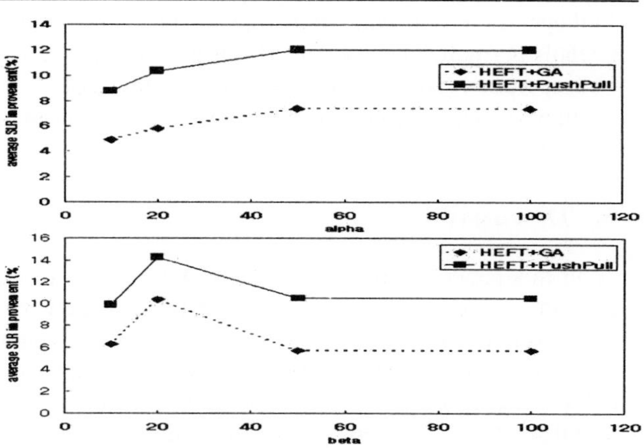

Figure 9. Average SLR improvement a function of alpha and beta.

Fig. 9 shows the impact on the average SLR improvement as the wide area link heterogeneity ($alpha$) and processor heterogeneity ($beta$) are varied. As $alpha$ increases, the average SLR improvement increases gradually. This implies that the baseline algorithm (HEFT) leaves more room for improvement as the variance in the network link capacities increases. This is to be expected from the problem with the HEFT algorithm presented in Fig. 3(b). However, the average SLR improvement appears to saturate when $alpha$ becomes larger than 50. With respect to $beta$, the average SLR improvement is almost constant except when $beta$ is 20. The reason for this peak is still being investigated.

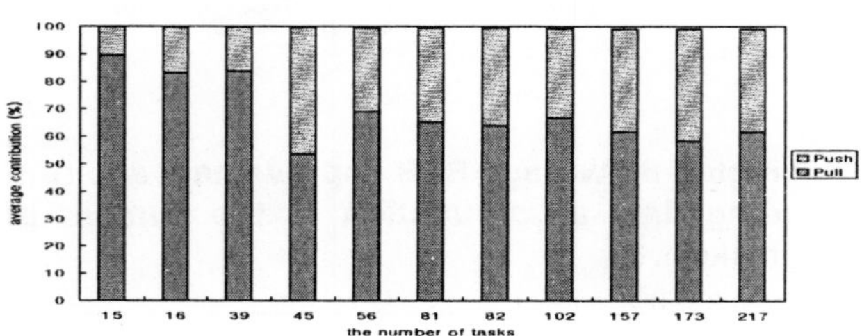

Figure 10. Average contribution of push and pull operations towards increasing the makespan as the number of tasks is increased.

In Fig. 10, the average contributions (towards SLR improvement) of the Push and Pull operations are shown. The Pull operation contributes more than the Push operation, especially at small values of N_T. This is probably because the pull operation fixes a major weakness of the HEFT algorithm when applied to networks with large variations in link capacities.

6. Discussion

In this paper, we presented a new static scheduling algorithm based on a deterministic guided search strategy, termed Push-Pull, for heterogeneous cluster systems (in particular, cluster-of-clusters systems). This algorithm searches for an improved solution starting from the initial solution generated by a baseline algorithm. By pushing or pulling tasks in a given schedule, we can significantly improve the initial solution. In particular, because the pull operation fixes a major shortcoming of list scheduling algorithms, we found that large schedule length improvements were possible even with modestly large communication-to-computation ratios. According to our experiments, the *makespan*, the total DAG application execution time, was improved significantly, over both the baseline algorithms and random guided search methods, when the Push-Pull algorithm was used.

References

[1] M. R. Garey and D. S. Johnson, *A Guide to the Theory of NP-Completeness*. W.H.Freeman & Co., 1979.

[2] J. R. Coffman, *Computer and Job-Shop Scheduling Theory*. John Wiley & Sons, 1976.

[3] H. El-Rewini, T. G. Lewis, and H. H. Ali, *Task Scheduling in Parallel and Distributed Systems*. W.H.Freeman & Co., 1979.

[4] R. L. Graham, E. L. Lawler, J. Lenstra, and A. R. Kan, "Optimization and approximation in deterministic sequencing and scheduling," *A Survey, Annals of Discrete Math.*, vol. 5, pp. 287–326, 1979.

[5] H. Topcuoglu, S. Harir, and M.-Y. Wu, "Performance-effective and low-complexity task scheduling for heterogeneous computing," *IEEE Trans. on Parallel and Distributed Systems*, vol. 13, pp. 260–274, Mar. 2002.

[6] L. Wang, H. J. Siegel, V. P. Roychowdhury, and A. A. Maciejewski, "Task matching and scheduling in heterogeneous computing environments using a genetic-algorithm-based approach," *Journal of Parallel and Distributed Computing*, vol. 47, pp. 8–22, 1997.

[7] T. L. Adam, K. M. Chandy, and J. R. Dickson, "A comparison of list schedules for parallel processing systems," *Communication of ACM*, vol. 17, pp. 685–690, Dec. 1974.

[8] A. Giersch, Y. Robert, and F. Vivien, "Scheduling tasks sharing files on heterogeneous clusters," tech. rep., Ecole Normale Superieure de Lion, May 2003.

[9] R. C. Correa, A. Ferreira, and P. Rebreyend, "Scheduling multiprocessor tasks with genetic algorithms," *IEEE Trans. Parallel and Distributed Systems*, vol. 10, pp. 825–837, Aug. 1999.

[10] H. Singh and A. Youssef, "Mapping and scheduling heterogeneous task graphs using genetic algorithms," in *Proc. Heterogeneous Computing Workshop*, pp. 86–97, 1996.

[11] S. Kirkpatrick, C. D. Gelatt, and M. P. Vecchi, "Optimization by simulated annealing," *Science, Number 4598, 13 May 1983*, vol. 220, 4598, pp. 671–680, 1983.

[12] H. Barada, S. M. Sait, and N. Baig, "Task matching and scheduling in heterogeneous systems using simulated evolution," in *Proceedings of the 15th Int'l Prallel and Distributed Processing Symposium*, 2001.

[13] Y. G. ssab and V. B. Rao, "Combinatorial optimization by stochastic evolution," *IEEE Transactions on Computer-Aided Design*, vol. 10, pp. 525–535, Oct. 1999.

[14] M.-Y. Wu, W. Shu, and J. Gu, "Efficient local search for dag scheduling," *IEEE Transaction on Parallel and Distributed Systems*, vol. 12, June 2001.

[15] T. Hagras and J. Janecek, "A simple scheduling heuristic for heterogeneous computing environments," in *Proceedings of the 2nd Int'l Symposium on Parallel and Distributed Computing*, 2003.

Incremental Parallelization Using Navigational Programming: A Case Study

Lei Pan, Wenhui Zhang, Arthur Asuncion, Ming Kin Lai, Michael B. Dillencourt, and Lubomir F. Bic *
Donald Bren School of Information & Computer Sciences
University of California, Irvine, CA 92697-3425, USA
{pan,wzhang,aasuncio,mingl,dillenco,bic}@ics.uci.edu

Abstract

We show how a series of transformations can be applied to incrementally parallelize sequential programs. Our Navigational Programming (NavP) methodology is based on the principle of self-migrating computations and is truly incremental, in that each step represents a functioning program and every intermediate program is an improvement over its predecessor. The transformations are mechanical and straightforward to apply. We illustrate our methodology in the context of matrix multiplication. Our final stage is similar to the classical Gentleman's Algorithm. The NavP methodology is conducive to new ways of thinking that lead to ease of programming and high performance.

Keywords: *programming methodologies, incremental parallelization, navigational programming (NavP), program transformation, matrix multiplication, Gentleman's Algorithm, Cannon's Algorithm*

1. Introduction

In this paper, we show how a series of transformations can be applied to a sequential algorithm to obtain programs that represent incremental steps in exploiting parallelism in the original algorithm. The transformations are provided in Navigational Programming (NavP).

In NavP, migrating computations are the composing elements of a distributed parallel program. The code transformations in NavP – distributing the data and inserting corresponding navigational commands, pipelining, and phase shifting – can be used to incrementally turn a sequential program to a distributed sequential computing (DSC) program, and later to a distributed parallel computing (DPC) program. These transformations can be applied repeatedly, or in a hierarchical fashion. The benefits of the NavP incremental parallelization include: (1) Every program is a result of applying the mechanics of one of the transformations and is a natural and incremental step from its predecessor. As a result, no abrupt change in code will happen between any consecutive steps; (2) Every intermediate program is an improvement from its predecessor. If program development is limited by time or resources, any one of the intermediate programs can be taken as production code; (3) The transformations are highly mechanical and straightforward to use, and yet, as illustrated here, the resulting parallel programs can be elegant and efficient. The NavP methodology is conducive to different ways of thinking that lead to ease of programming and high performance.

We will briefly describe the NavP methodology in Section 2 and apply NavP to the classical problem of matrix multiplication in Section 3. The well-known message-passing solution to the same problem, i.e., Gentleman's Algorithm, is presented in Section 4. Section 5 contains performance data, followed by a brief comparison of the two implementations. Our final section includes a brief survey and comparison of some competing approaches.

2. Navigational programming

Navigational Programming (NavP) is a methodology for distributed parallel programming based on the use of self-migrating computations. In NavP code, a programmer inserts navigational commands, i.e., `hop()` statements, to migrate the computation locus in order to access remotely distributed data and spread out computations. Small data is carried by the moving computation in "agent variables," which are private to a computation thread and available to the thread wherever it migrates. Large data that stays on a computer is held in "node variables" that are resident on a particular PE (processing element) and are shared by all computation threads currently on that PE. The cost of a `hop()` is essentially the cost of moving the data stored in agent variables plus a small amount of state data. Although the state of the computation is moved on each hop, the code is not moved. The synchronization among different migrating computations is done through "events"

*The authors gratefully acknowledge the support of The U.S. Department of Education GAANN Fellowship.

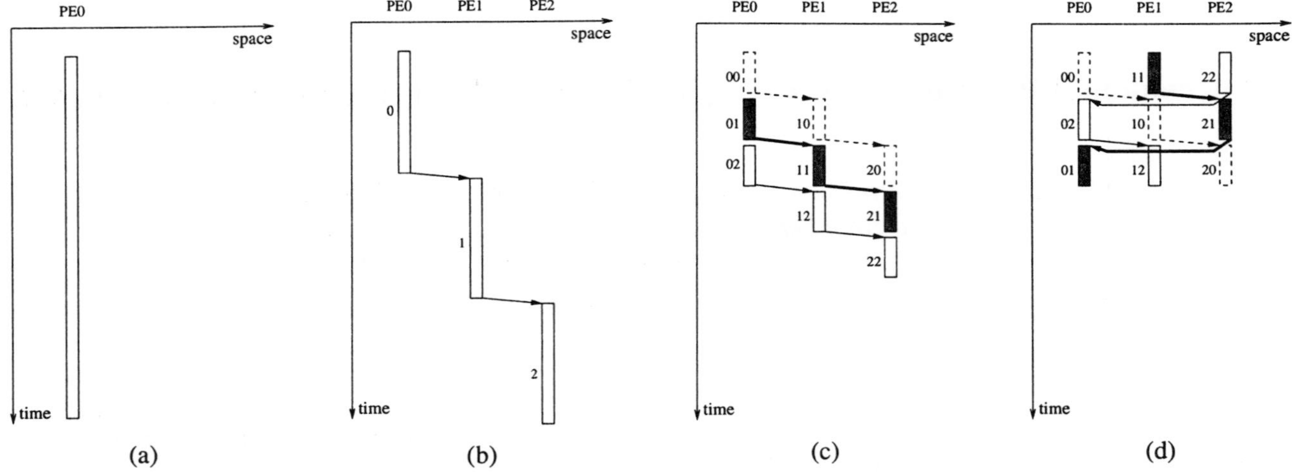

Figure 1. The code transformations in NavP. (a) Sequential. (b) DSC. (c) Pipelining. (d) Phase shifting.

(`signalEvent()` and `waitEvent()`). A programmer can "inject," or spawn, a migrating thread at command line. The injection of a thread can also be done by another thread, called a "spawner." All injections happen locally (i.e., a thread can spawn another thread only on the node on which it currently resides). Details of the underlying system of NavP, MESSENGERS, can be found online at `http://www.ics.uci.edu/~bic/messengers`.

NavP provides a different view of distributed computation from the classical SPMD (Single Program Multiple Data) view [14]. The SPMD view describes distributed computations at stationary locations, while the NavP view describes a computation following the movement of its locus. The NavP view changes the way distributed parallel programs are composed and provides some new benefits.

The three transformations under the NavP view are depicted in Figure 1. The arrows indicate `hop()` operations. The basic idea behind the transformations is to spread out computations using self-migrating computation threads as soon as possible without violating any dependency conditions. **(1) DSC Transformation**: Large data is distributed among the PEs, and `hop()` statements are inserted into the sequential code in order for the computation to "chase" large data while carrying small data. The DSC Transformation is schematically depicted by Figures 1(a) and (b). The resulting program performs distributed sequential computing. The immediate benefit of DSC is that, with a small amount of work, a sequential program can efficiently solve large problems that cannot fit in the main memory of one computer. By using a network of workstations, the DSC program removes paging overhead by trading it against a modest amount of network communication [13]. DSC also serves as the starting point of parallel program development in NavP. **(2) Pipelining Transformation**: This transformation is depicted by Figures 1(b) and (c). The basic idea is to overlap the execution of multiple DSC threads by staggering their starting times. Synchronization may be necessary to ensure that the data dependencies among the DSC threads are not violated. **(3) Phase-shifting Transformation**: Sometimes the dependency among different computations allows different DSC threads to enter the pipeline from different PEs. In these situations, we can phase shift the DSC threads to achieve full parallelism, as depicted in Figures 1(c) and (d).

The NavP transformations can be systematically applied repeatedly or hierarchically in different dimensions of a network of PEs, as will be shown with matrix multiplication later in this paper. At each step, we have a fully functional implementation that is an improvement over the previous step. The result of the final step has a resemblance to the classical Gentleman's Algorithm, but there are important differences as described briefly in Section 5.

3. Incremental parallelization of matrix multiplication

Matrix multiplication is a fundamental operation of many numerical algorithms. We show how the transformations of Section 2 can be repeatedly applied to incrementally parallelize matrix multiplication. Pseudocode for sequential matrix multiplication is listed in Figure 2. Throughout the paper, we assume `N` is the order of the square matrices.

It is clear that the computation of each entry of the matrix `C` is independent of all other entries of `C`, and therefore there are N^2 updatings that can be done in parallel. Nevertheless, exploiting the abundant parallelism in matrix mul-

```
do i=0,N-1
  do j=0,N-1
    t = 0.0
    do k=0,N-1
      t += A(i,k) * B(k,j)
    end do
    C(i,j) = t
  end do
end do
```

Figure 2. Sequential pseudocode.

```
doall i=0,N-1
  doall j=0,N-1
    C(i,j) = 0.0
    do k=0,N-1
      C(i,j) += A(i,k) * B(k,j)
    end do
  end doall
end doall
```

Figure 3. Parallel pseudocode using `doall`.

tiplication is not as straightforward as one might think. If we parallelize the two outer loops using the popular `doall` notation, as shown in Figure 3, contention could happen as multiple PEs request the same entries at the same time. On the other hand, if we cache multiple copies of the same entry on the PEs that require it, we have a non-scalable solution. Gentleman conducted research into the data movement required for matrix multiplication, and his analysis confirmed that data movement – and not arithmetic operations – is often the limiting factor in the performance of algorithms [9, 12].

Throughout this paper, we describe the problem and our solution at a fine granularity level for simplicity. That is, we assume $N == P$, where P is either the number of PEs in a one-dimensional (1D) processor network or the order of a two-dimensional (2D) processor network. To extend our solution to a coarser level, we simply need to take each and every element (e.g., C01 or A21) as a sub-matrix block, instead of an entry of the matrix.

3.1. From sequential to DSC

We first apply DSC Transformation to sequential matrix multiplication, as depicted in Figure 4 where we assume $N = 3$. This DSC transformation essentially distributes the computation in the j dimension. The PE network is 1D in which each PE has a unique identifier $\texttt{HnodeID} = 0, 1, ..., N-1$ from west to east. Again, the arrows represent hop() operations. Thick boxes contain node variables on different machines, and thin boxes carry agent variables. All PEs are assumed to be fully connected via a collision-free switch, rather than being connected as a ring. This assumption is true for most modern hardware environments, and it makes the initial staggering (i.e., moving the entries of the three matrices to the right places before any computation begins) faster, because each matrix entry can be shipped to any destination directly instead of having to go stepwise through a number of intermediate PEs.

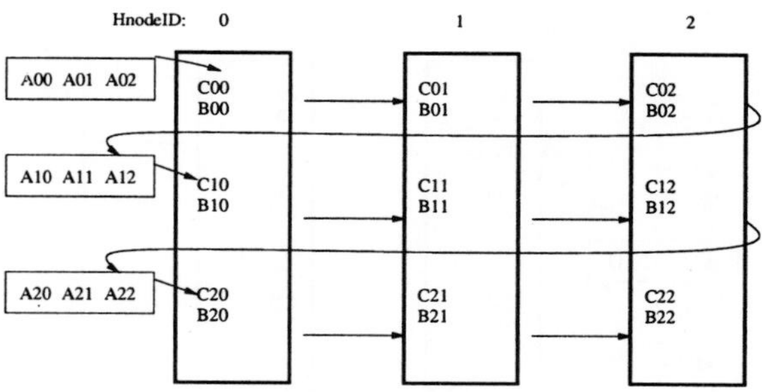

Figure 4. DSC.

Pseudocode for DSC matrix multiplication is listed in Figure 5. In the pseudocode hereafter, A and B indicate node variables, whereas mA and mB represent agent variables. [1] Matrix A is loaded into agent variable mA and carried by the migrating thread.

In Figure 4, matrix A is initially put on the PE with $\texttt{HnodeID} = 0$, and the columns of matrices B and C are distributed such that B(∗,j) and C(∗,j) are on the PE with $\texttt{HnodeID} = \texttt{j}$. In Figure 5, node(j) maps to the PE that hosts column j of matrices B and C. Every time the computation thread hops back to node(0), it will pick up a different row of matrix A for the computation of the loop over j.

```
hop(node(0))
inject(RowCarrier)

RowCarrier
  do mi=0,N-1
    do mj=0,N-1
      hop(node(mj))
      if(mj=0) mA(*) = A(mi,*)
      t = 0.0
      do k=0,N-1
        t += mA(k) * B(k)
      end do
      C(mi) = t
    end do
  end do
end
```

Figure 5. Pseudocode for DSC.

[1] In our NavP programs, we adapt a naming convention of starting an agent variable's name with a lowercase m.

3.2. DSC pipelining

We apply our Pipelining Transformation to the DSC code obtained from the previous step. The result of this transformation is depicted in Figure 6. Each row of matrix A is assigned to a different computation thread. Injected into the PE pipeline in order, these threads follow each other in the network to compute the corresponding C entries.

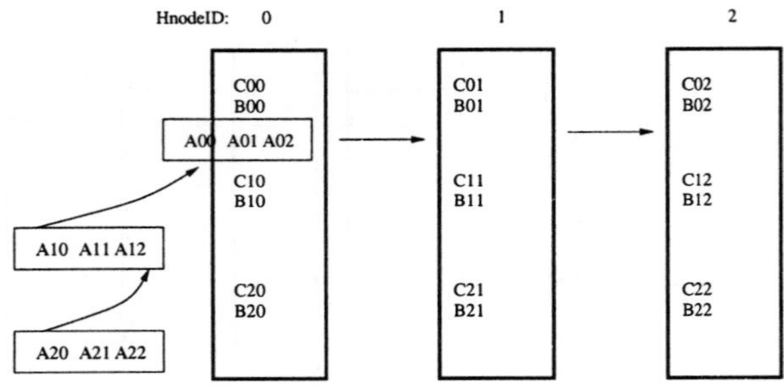

Figure 6. DSC with pipelining.

Pseudocode for pipelined DSC matrix multiplication is listed in Figure 7. The matrix A is initially put on the PE with $\mathtt{HnodeID} = 0$, and the columns of matrices B and C are distributed such that $\mathtt{B}(*, \mathtt{j})$ and $\mathtt{C}(*, \mathtt{j})$ are on the PE with $\mathtt{HnodeID} = \mathtt{j}$.

```
hop(node(0))
do i=0,N-1
  inject(RowCarrier(i))
end do

RowCarrier(int mi)
  mA(*) = A(mi,*)
  do mj=0,N-1
    hop(node(mj))
    t = 0.0
    do k=0,N-1
      t += mA(k) * B(k)
    end do
    C(mi) = t
  end do
end
```

Figure 7. Pseudocode for pipelined DSC.

3.3. From DSC to full DPC

We apply our Phase-shifting Transformation to achieve a full DPC, as depicted in Figure 8. This is possible because each row of A, though needed on all three PEs, can start its computation from any PE.

Pseudocode for phase-shifted DPC matrix multiplication is listed in Figure 9. Rows of matrix A are carried by the corresponding agent variables mA.

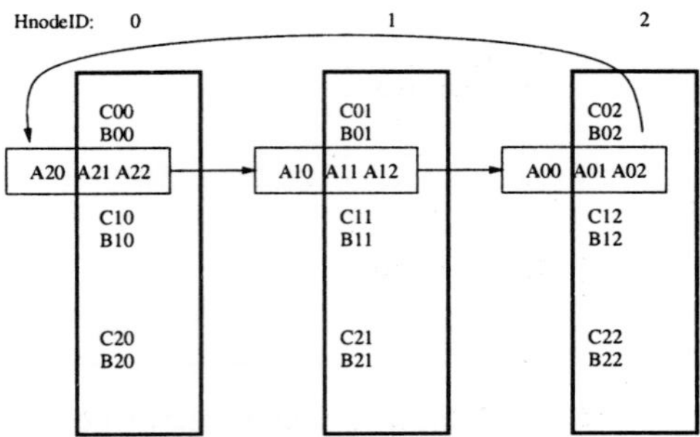

Figure 8. Full DPC through phase shifting.

In this full DPC implementation, matrix A is initially distributed such that $\mathtt{A}(\mathtt{i}, *)$ is on the PE with $\mathtt{HnodeID} = \mathtt{i}$, and the columns of matrices B and C are distributed such that $\mathtt{B}(*, \mathtt{j})$ and $\mathtt{C}(*, \mathtt{j})$ are on the PE with $\mathtt{HnodeID} = \mathtt{j}$.

```
do mi=0,N-1
  hop(node(mi))
  inject(RowCarrier(mi))
end do

RowCarrier(int mi)
  mA(*) = A(*)
  do mj=0,N-1
    hop(node((N-1-mi+mj)%N))
    t = 0.0
    do k=0,N-1
      t += mA(k) * B(k)
    end do
    C(mi) = t
  end do
end
```

Figure 9. Pseudocode for phase-shifted DPC.

3.4. DSC in the second dimension

What we have achieved so far (Figure 8) is a 1D DPC consisting of phase-shifted pipelined computations in which the rows move through the pipeline. What we will do in the next three steps is achieve further parallelization by introducing a second dimension, effectively letting each entry of each row move through a pipeline.

The first step is to introduce a 2D network in which each PE has a unique 2D identifier ($\mathtt{HnodeID}, \mathtt{VnodeID}$), where $\mathtt{HnodeID} = 0, 1, ..., \mathtt{N} - 1$ from west to east, and $\mathtt{VnodeID} = 0, 1, ..., \mathtt{N} - 1$ from north to south. Then the DSC Transformation is applied in the second dimension, as depicted in Figure 10. Essentially, this DSC transformation further distributes the computations in the i dimension.

Pseudocode for DSC in the second dimension is listed in Figure 11. The rows of matrix A and columns of ma-

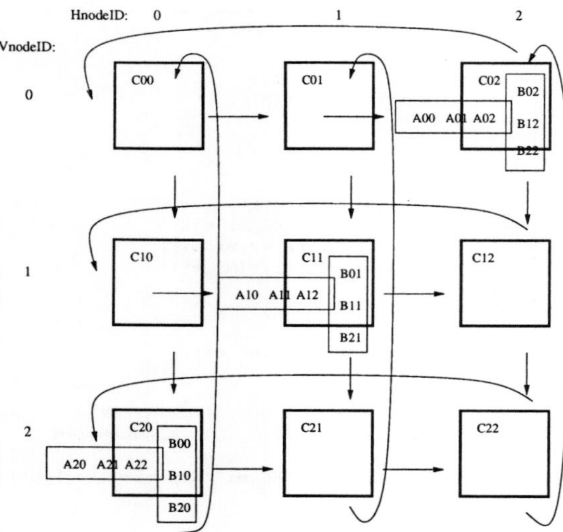

Figure 10. DSC in the second dimension.

```
do ml=0,N-1
  hop(node(N-1-ml,ml))
  inject(RowCarrier(N-1-ml))
  inject(ColCarrier(ml))
end do

RowCarrier(int mi)
  mA(*) = A(*)
  do mj=0,N-1
    hop(node(mi,(N-1-mi+mj)%N)
    waitEvent(EP(mi,(N-1-mi+mj)%N))
    do k=0,N-1
      C += mA(k) * B(k)
    end do
  end do
end

ColCarrier(int mj)
  mB(*) = B(*)
  do mi=0,N-1
    hop(node((N-1-mj+mi)%N,mj))
    B(*) = mB(*)
    signalEvent(EP((N-1-mj+mi)%N,mj))
  end do
end
```

Figure 11. Pseudocode for DSC in the 2nd dimension.

trix B are carried in their corresponding agent variables mA and mB, respectively. The ColCarriers ship the B columns, and the RowCarriers use these B columns to compute with the A rows that they carry. The events are necessary because the consumers, i.e., the RowCarriers, need to hold on their computations until the producers, i.e., the ColCarriers, finish putting the columns of B in place.

The matrices are initially distributed, as shown in Figure 10, such that $\mathtt{A(N-1-1,*)}$ and $\mathtt{B(*,1)}$ are on $\mathtt{node(N-1-1,1)}$, and $\mathtt{C(i,j)}$ (initialized to 0) is on $\mathtt{node(i,j)}$, where $\mathtt{node(i,j)}$ maps to the PE that hosts entry $\mathtt{(i,j)}$ of matrix C.

3.5. DSC with pipelining in both dimensions

We apply our Pipelining Transformation in both dimensions, as depicted in Figure 12. Basically, a pair of A and B entries can move on along their pipelines respectively as soon as they finish computing and contributing the corresponding C entry. A producer BCarrier needs to make sure that the B entry produced by its predecessor in the pipeline is consumed before it puts the B entry it carries in place. This is the reason for a second event EC(.,.).

Pseudocode for DSC with pipelining in both dimensions is listed in Figure 13. The entries of matrices A and B are carried in their corresponding agent variables mA and mB, respectively.

The matrices are initially distributed, as shown in Figure 12, such that $\mathtt{A(N-1-1,*)}$ and $\mathtt{B(*,1)}$ are on $\mathtt{node(N-1-1,1)}$, and $\mathtt{C(i,j)}$ (initialized to 0) is on $\mathtt{node(i,j)}$. An event $\mathtt{EC(i,j)}$ is signaled on $\mathtt{node(i,j)}$ for all values of i, j initially.

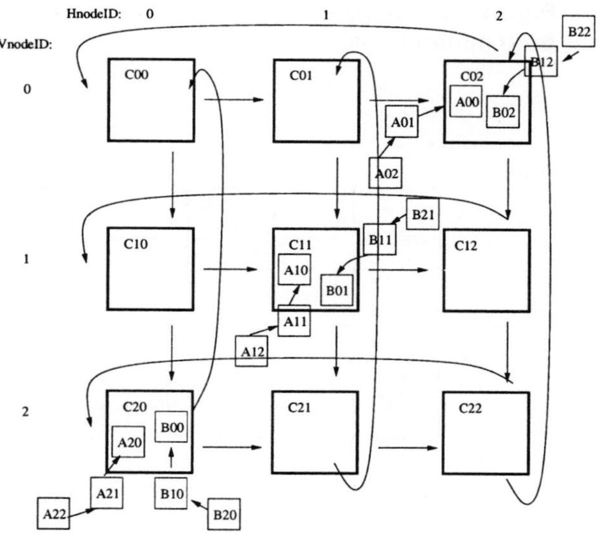

Figure 12. DSC pipelining in both dimensions.

3.6. Full DPC in both dimensions

We apply our Phase-shifting Transformation in both dimensions to achieve full parallelization, as depicted Figure 14.

Pseudocode for DPC in both dimensions is listed in Figure 15. The entries of matrices A and B are carried in their

```
do ml=0,N-1
  hop(node(N-1-ml,ml))
  inject(spawner(ml))
end do

spawner(int ml)
  do mk=0,N-1
    inject(ACarrier(N-1-ml,mk))
    inject(BCarrier(mk,ml))
  end do
end

ACarrier(int mi, int mk)
  mA=A(mk)
  do mj=0,N-1
    hop(node(mi,(N-1-mi+mj)%N))
    waitEvent(EP(mi,(N-1-mi+mj)%N))
    C += mA * B
    signalEvent(EC(mi,(N-1-mi+mj)%N))
  end do
end

BCarrier(int mk, int mj)
  mB=B(mk)
  do mi=0,N-1
    hop(node((N-1-mj+mi)%N,mj))
    waitEvent(EC((N-1-mj+mi)%N,mj))
    B = mB
    signalEvent(EP((N-1-mj+mi)%N,mj))
  end do
end
```

Figure 13. Pseudocode for DSC pipelining in both dimensions.

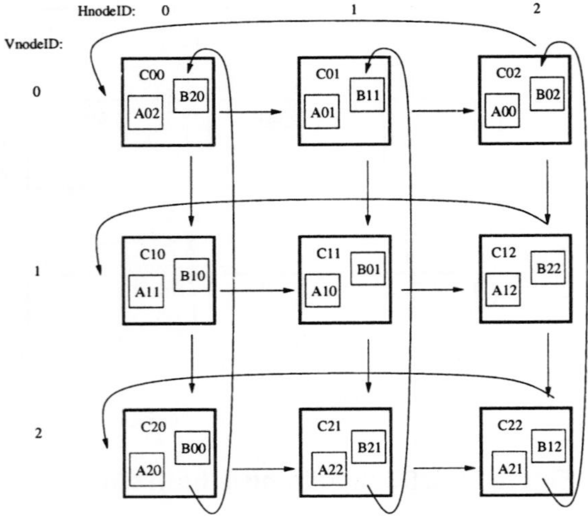

Figure 14. Phase shifting in both dimensions.

corresponding agent variables mA and mB, respectively.

The matrices are initially distributed such that A(i, j), B(i, j) and C(i, j) (initialized to 0) are on node(i, j).

In the above figures such as Figure 14, each sub-matrix

```
do mj=0,N-1
  hop(node(0,mj))
  inject(spawner(mj))
end do

spawner(int mj)
  do mi=0,N-1
    hop(node(mi,mj))
    signalEvent(EC(mi,mj))
    inject(ACarrier(mi,mj))
    inject(BCarrier(mi,mj))
  end do
end

ACarrier(int mi, int mk)
  mA = A
  do mj=0,N-1
    hop(node(mi,(N-1-mi-mk+mj)%N)
    waitEvent(EP(mi,(N-1-mi-mk+mj)%N))
    C += mA * B
    signalEvent(EC(mi,(N-1-mi-mk+mj)%N))
  end do
end

BCarrier(int mk, int mj)
  mB = B
  do mi=0,N-1
    hop(node((N-1-mj-mk+mi)%N,mj))
    waitEvent(EC((N-1-mj-mk+mi)%N,mj))
    B = mB
    signalEvent(EP((N-1-mj-mk+mi)%N,mj))
  end do
end
```

Figure 15. Pseudocode for full DPC in both dimensions.

block, e.g., A10 or C11, is called a "distribution block" in our implementation, as it is a basic unit of data distribution on a PE. To achieve better performance from a block algorithm, a further level of matrix decomposition is used [16]. A distribution block is decomposed into "algorithmic blocks," and each algorithmic block of A or B is carried by a migrating thread (i.e., ACarrier or BCarrier). Our sequential and MPI (Message Passing Interface) implementations described below use algorithmic blocks as well.

4. Gentleman's Algorithm

Gentleman's Algorithm [9, 19] is a classical SPMD algorithm for parallel matrix multiplication. The pseudocode is listed in Figure 16, in which an arrow represents a combination of receive and send among remote PEs. During initial staggering, each entry of matrix A will stagger i times to the west, where i is the entry's row number, and each entry in matrix B will stagger j times to the north, where j is the entry's column number. An entry can be either a single value or a sub-matrix. Thus, a skewed transformation of matrices A and B results. Like the NavP pseudocode, our MPI implementation assumes a fully connected

```
do k=0,N-2
  doall node(i,j) where 0<=i,j<=N-1
    if i>k then
      A ← east(A)
    end if
    if j>k then
      B ← south(B)
    end if
  end do
end do

doall node(i,j) where 0<=i,j<=N-1
  C = A * B
end do
do k=0,N-2
  doall node(i,j) where 0<=i,j<=N-1
    A ← east(A)
    B ← south(B)
    C += A * B
  end do
end do
```

Figure 16. Pseudocode for Gentleman's Alg.

network, and matrix staggering is accomplished in a single step (not shown in Figure 16) rather than in a series of steps. Throughout the entirety of Gentleman's Algorithm, matrix C remains stationary.

Once the initial staggering completes, matrices A and B are multiplied and the results are placed in matrix C. For $N - 1$ iterations, matrix A shifts its columns one step to the west and matrix B shifts its rows one step to the north, and A and B are multiplied with the results added to the C matrix.

In our implementation, non-blocking receives (i.e., `MPI_Irecv()`) are used in conjunction with blocking sends to prevent deadlocking. `MPI_Wait()`, which blocks until the incoming matrix has been received, assists in providing synchronization between PEs.

As a result of using algorithmic blocks, many blocks are shifted from a PE to itself during the computation. Instead of sending an algorithmic block to a PE itself, or copying an algorithmic block from a local memory, we use pointer swapping to shift an algorithmic block locally.

5. Performance data

We have implemented parallel matrix multiplication using both NavP and message passing. The NavP system used was MESSENGERS (Version 1.2.05 Beta) developed in Donald Bren School of Information & Computer Sciences, University of California Irvine. The message passing system used was LAM 7.0.6 from Indiana University [3]. The ScaLAPACK used was version 1.7 from University of Tennessee, Knoxville and Oak Ridge National Laboratory [2]. The C compiler used was GNU gcc-3.2.2, and the Fortran compiler used was GNU g77-3.2.2. The performance data was obtained from SUN workstations (SUN Blade 100, CPU: 502 MHz SUNW,UltraSPARC-IIe, OS: SunOS Release 5.8) with 256MB of main memory, 1GB of virtual memory, and 100Mbps of Ethernet connection. These workstations have a shared file system (NFS).

When the working set of a sequential program exceeds the physical memory on a PE, thrashing happens and the performance degrades. In a distributed program, however, the data of a sub-problem may fit in the memory of a machine completely even if the entire problem is too large. In order to obtain fair speedup numbers, we calculate sequential timing for large problems using least squared curve fitting with a polynomial of order 3 using performance numbers collected with small problems.

Table 1 lists the performance data for NavP and ScaLAPACK on a 1D PE network of three machines. It can be seen that the performance improves as we go from NavP DSC to NavP pipelining and then to NavP phase shifting. For small problems, NavP 1D DSC is only marginally slower than the corresponding sequential execution; however, as the problem size grows, NavP 1D DSC becomes faster, as indicated by the data from actual runs (not curve-fitted data). Table 2 indicates that with several networked computers DSC performs almost as fast as the sequential program running with enough main memory, and it is significantly faster than the sequential program paging using virtual memory. With $N = 9216$, the total memory usage is about 1GB, but our machines each have only 256MB of main memory.

Tables 3 and 4 list the performance data for MPI, NavP, and ScaLAPACK on a 2D PE network of nine machines. Again, performance improves as we hierarchically apply the three NavP transformations in the second dimension.

In both 1D and 2D cases, our DSC and pipelining programs achieve high performance. This can be attributed to the use of algorithmic blocks. The `RowCarriers` or `ACarriers`, each of which responsible for the computation of a row of algorithmic blocks or an algorithmic block, can spread out their computations to the entire network earlier than if a full distribution block on a PE has to be computed before these carriers can hop out.

The MPI implementation used for the comparison was Gentleman's Algorithm modified to use block partitioning of matrices; moreover, pointer swapping was used in order to avoid unnecessary local data copying. ScaLAPACK uses a logical LCM hybrid algorithmic blocking technique [16], so the block orders in the tables do not apply to the ScaLAPACK numbers.

The performance data indicates that the NavP implementation achieves a higher speedup than the MPI implementation. Some differences between these two implementations are discussed briefly below. More details can be found in our full-length technical report [15].

1. **Communication.** We use block algorithms for better cache and communication performance. The algo-

Table 1. Performance on 3 PEs

		Sequential		NavP (1D DSC)		NavP (1D pipeline)		NavP (1D phase)		ScaLAPACK(#)	
Matrix order	Block order	Time (s)	Speed up	Time (s)	Speed up	Time (s)	Speed up	Time (s)	Speed up	Time (s)	Speed up
1536	128	65.44	1.00	67.22	0.97	27.72	2.36	24.55	2.67	26.80	2.44
2304	128	219.71	1.00	229.45	0.96	91.03	2.41	81.23	2.70	82.83	2.65
3072	128	520.30	1.00	543.91	0.96	205.87	2.53	189.50	2.75	211.45	2.46
4608	128	1934.73 (1745.94*)	1.00	1809.73	0.96	688.18	2.54	653.64	2.67	767.91	2.27
5376	128	3033.92 (2735.69*)	1.00	2926.24	0.93	1151.07	2.38	990.05	2.76	1173.46	2.33
6144	256	5055.93 (4268.16*)	1.00	4697.32	0.91	1811.77	2.36	1554.99	2.74	1984.18	2.15

(*) Obtained from least squared curve fitting and used in calculating speedup.
(#) ScaLAPACK uses a logical LCM hybrid algorithmic blocking technique, not controlled by users [16].

Table 2. Performance on 8 PEs

		Sequential		NavP (1D DSC)	
Matrix order	Block order	Time (s)	Speed up	Time (s)	Speed up
9216	128	36534.49 (13921.50*)	1.00	14959.42	0.93

(*) Obtained from least squared curve fitting and used in calculating speedup.

rithmic blocks of C on a PE can be updated in different orders. In the case of NavP, the order is not predefined and the CPU cycles are thus efficiently utilized in computations as the data they need arrives. An efficient run-time task scheduling, handled by the queuing mechanisms built into the MESSENGERS daemon, is provided to the NavP programmers. As a result, NavP programmers only need to concern themselves with the two event handling commands as the interface to the queuing mechanisms that are otherwise hidden at the system level. It is the NavP view that allows us to focus on describing the application level computations following their movement and to factor out the functionality associated with scheduling – code that describes behaviors at fixed locations. In MPI, the situation is quite different. The straightforward way to program the block implementation is to have a loop over all the algorithmic blocks of C on a PE. The loop introduces an artificial sequential order to the communications and computations even though they are actually independent of each other and hence may result in slower performance. Possible ways to remove the artificial sequencing are proposed [15], but they all require significantly more programming work.

2. **Cache performance.** The NavP and the sequential programs have a similar cache performance because in both cases during the execution there is an algorithmic block (of C for the sequential program and of A for the NavP program, respectively) that would stay in the cache for the duration of computation using other two algorithmic blocks. In contrast, in the block-oriented MPI program, triplets of A B C blocks are frequently fresh in the cache, which leads to less efficient cache use. A simple analysis shows that this cache performance of NavP can account for as much as a 4% improvement over MPI [15].

3. **Initial staggering.** The NavP program uses "reverse staggering" for matrices A and B. That is, the "chain" of a row or a column is both shifted and reverse-ordered. In contrast, both Gentleman's Algorithm and Cannon's Algorithm [4, 17] use "forward staggering," which only shifts the positions of the entries without reversing the order. It is shown [15] that reverse staggering never requires more than two communication phases, while forward staggering often requires three communication phases.

It would be possible to improve the performance of the MPI code by subtle fine-tuning at a cost of considerably more programming effort. Nevertheless, the data makes it clear that the NavP program is faster than a straightforward implementation of Gentleman's Algorithm and competitive with a highly tuned version.

6. Final remarks

In incremental parallelization, a programmer uses sequential code as the starting point and introduces parallelism in a step by step fashion, until satisfactory performance is achieved or a time/resource constraint is reached. Oftentimes, programmers begin with the performance critical "hot spots" in a program and gradually parallelize other parts of the program.

Shared-memory programming is believed to be more programmable and more amenable to incremental parallelization [11]. The reason is that data need not be distributed among the processors (in the case of DSM (Distributed Shared Memory) [18] or HPF (High Performance Fortran) [20], data is distributed but a logical single address space is provided). Shared-memory programs are similar to the familiar sequential original codes, and therefore the transition is easier for programmers. Some programming languages (e.g., HPF or UPC(Unified Parallel C) [7]) provide special language constructs such as `doall` or `!HPF$ INDEPENDENT`, so ideally parallelization is as simple as changing `do` loops to `doall` loops. In OpenMP [5], parallel directives (e.g., `!$ OMP PARALLEL`)

Table 3. Performance on 2×2 PEs

		Sequential		MPI (Gentleman)		NavP (2D DSC)		NavP (2D pipeline)		NavP (2D phase)		ScaLAPACK(#)	
Matrix order	Block order	Time (s)	Speed up	Time (s)	Speed up	Time (s)	Speed up	Time (s)	Speed up	Time (s)	Speed up	Time (s)	Speed up
1024	128	19.49	1.00	6.02	3.24	7.63	2.55	5.88	3.31	5.54	3.52	5.23	3.73
2048	128	158.51	1.00	50.99	3.11	50.59	3.13	42.61	3.72	41.54	3.82	45.53	3.48
3072	128	520.30	1.00	157.53	3.30	158.06	3.29	144.09	3.61	137.39	3.79	156.27	3.33
4096	128	1281.58 (1238.21*)	1.00	367.04	3.37	362.73	3.41	328.98	3.76	321.70	3.85	417.83	2.96
5120	128	2727.86 (2373.32*)	1.00	733.91	3.23	792.23	3.00	757.67	3.13	624.87	3.80	907.16	2.62

(*) Obtained from least squared curve fitting and used in calculating speedup.
(#) ScaLAPACK uses a logical LCM hybrid algorithmic blocking technique, not controlled by users [16].

Table 4. Performance on 3×3 PEs

		Sequential		MPI (Gentleman)		NavP (2D DSC)		NavP (2D pipeline)		NavP (2D phase)		ScaLAPACK(#)	
Matrix order	Block order	Time (s)	Speed up	Time (s)	Speed up	Time (s)	Speed up	Time (s)	Speed up	Time (s)	Speed up	Time (s)	Speed up
1536	128	65.44	1.00	10.97	5.97	13.66	4.79	9.18	7.13	8.21	7.97	8.08	8.10
2304	128	219.71	1.00	29.95	7.34	39.53	5.56	29.93	7.34	26.74	8.22	29.39	7.48
3072	128	520.30	1.00	82.25	6.33	86.52	6.01	66.94	7.77	62.36	8.34	70.92	7.34
4608	128	1934.73 (1745.94*)	1.00	241.92	7.22	268.41	6.50	220.28	7.93	205.68	8.49	255.87	6.82
5376	128	3033.92 (2735.69*)	1.00	437.27	6.26	421.78	6.49	360.77	7.58	323.67	8.45	398.50	6.86
6144	256	5055.93 (4268.16*)	1.00	637.79	6.69	745.18	5.73	584.85	7.30	510.29	8.36	635.36	6.72

(*) Obtained from least squared curve fitting and used in calculating speedup.
(#) ScaLAPACK uses a logical LCM hybrid algorithmic blocking technique, not controlled by users [16].

can be used to parallelize any program segment (called "parallel region") that the programmer chooses. Unfortunately, although changing do's to doall's or using OpenMP parallel regions in matrix multiplication does exploit parallelism in the algorithm, both of these methods will cause communication contention for a "zero-inventory" implementation, as pointed out in Section 3.

For better performance, programmers must take care of data distribution explicitly (e.g., HPF or UPC provides such mechanism), and hence the advantage of not needing explicit data distribution on shared-memory is weakened. OpenMP is targeted mainly at SMP (Symmetric MultiProcessor) architectures, and therefore does not provide the opportunity for its programmers to specify data distribution. Consequently, the OpenMP implementations on distributed memory (with an underlying DSM system such as TreadMarks [1]) have seen less satisfying performance. The reported speedups on SMP clusters for OpenMP are within 7-30% of those of MPI implementations [10].

Message passing programming is less amenable to incremental parallelization. Transforming a sequential program into a message-passing one is an abrupt break, since data must be distributed and code structure is often dramatically changed. This is seen in the matrix multiplication example – one either gets no parallelism at all with the sequential code, or one gets all parallelism with Gentleman's Algorithm. Going directly from the sequential code to a parallel algorithm such as Gentleman's Algorithm requires considerable ingenuity. Nevertheless, message passing programming usually leads to good performance. This phenomenon can be attributed to the message passing programmers' explicit control of data distribution and careful avoidance of communication contention and extra data movement.

In NavP, the DSC Transformation involves data distribution and insertion of migration statements (i.e., hop()). The other two code transformations exploit parallelism by decomposing the long DSC threads and properly managing the synchronization among the shorter threads. The programmability of NavP is similar to that of HPF in that they both require explicit control of data distribution and explicit synchronization (through the use of barriers, events, critical regions, etc. in HPF, and events in NavP). Similar to HPF, synchronization errors are more likely to happen in NavP than in message passing. Unlike HPF, NavP requires its programmers to handle details in communication by using agent variables to carry data around. As a result, the NavP programmers know exactly how much is communicated to where at what time. NavP composes parallel code from shorter DSC threads, and the parallel code is structurally the same as the original sequential code. This property of NavP is referred to as Algorithmic Integrity [13].

Our NavP matrix multiplication implementation is faster than our MPI code. This is mainly because the NavP code successfully hides some of the communication overhead using an efficient but transparent run-time scheduling. This task scheduling functionality is factored out from the application code under the NavP view and put into the MESSENGERS daemon. Although it is entirely possible to achieve better task scheduling in the MPI code, with the MPI environment available today, the code that implements this will have to be developed for each and every application and will be interleaved with the application code. In this sense, message passing is harder to use than NavP.

A hybrid use of MPI and OpenMP [6, 21], with

OpenMP's multi-threading capability used for the computation on a computer node, is another way of introducing efficient run-time scheduling. Traditionally, multi-threading and message passing are significantly different methods rooted in two different architectures – shared-memory and message-passing architectures. Recent years have seen a trend of merging these two different styles of parallel programming in order to efficiently program the next generation supercomputers: cluster of multi-processor systems. Some examples include a thread-compliant implementation of MPI supporting `MPI_THREAD_MULTIPLE` in LAM/Open MPI [8] and a hybrid use of MPI and OpenMP. NavP is a uniform methodology that conveniently provides the combined functionalities of message passing and multi-threading, using navigational commands and synchronization commands.

Our NavP methodology uses highly mechanical and incremental steps to guide programmers in achieving elegant implementations with superior performance. The NavP transformations are at least partially automatable. Building tools to automate them is part of our future work.

Acknowledgements

The authors wish to thank Koji Noguchi for his great help with MESSENGERS and valuable discussions.

References

[1] C. Amza, A. L. Cox, S. Dwarkadas, P. Keleher, H. Lu, R. Rajamony, W. Yu, and W. Zwaenepoel. TreadMarks: Shared memory computing on networks of workstations. *IEEE Computer*, 29(2):18–28, Feb. 1996.

[2] L. S. Blackford, J. Choi, A. Cleary, E. D'Azevedo, J. Demmel, I. Dhillon, J. Dongarra, S. Hammarling, G. Henry, A. Petitet, K. Stanley, D. Walker, and R. C. Whaley. *ScaLAPACK Users' Guide*. Society for Industrial and Applied Mathematics, Philadelphia, Pa., 1997.

[3] G. Burns, R. Daoud, and J. Vaigl. LAM: An Open Cluster Environment for MPI. In *Proceedings of Supercomputing Symposium*, pages 379–386, 1994.

[4] L. E. Cannon. *A cellular computer to implement the Kalman Filter Algorithm*. PhD thesis, Montana State University, 1969.

[5] R. Chandra, L. Dagum, D. Kohr, D. Maydan, J. McDonald, and R. Menon. *Parallel Programming in OpenMP*. Morgan Kaufmann Publishers, San Francisco, Calif., 2001.

[6] E. Chow and D. Hysom. Assessing performance of hybrid MPI/OpenMP programs on SMP clusters. Technical Report UCRL-JC-143957, Lawrence Livermore National Laboratory, Livermore, Ca., 2001.

[7] T. El-Ghazawi and S. Chauvin. UPC benchmarking issues. In L. M. Ni and M. Valero, editors, *Proceedings of the 2001 International Conference on Parallel Processing (ICPP 2001)*, pages 365–372, Los Alamitos, Calif., Sept. 2001. IEEE Computer Society.

[8] E. Gabriel, G. E. Fagg, G. Bosilca, T. Angskun, J. J. Dongarra, J. M. Squyres, V. Sahay, P. Kambadur, B. Barrett, A. Lumsdaine, R. H. Castain, D. J. Daniel, R. L. Graham, and T. S. Woodall. Open MPI: Goals, concept, and design of a next generation MPI implementation. In *Proceedings, 11th European PVM/MPI Users' Group Meeting*, Budapest, Hungary, 2004.

[9] W. M. Gentleman. Some complexity results for matrix computations on parallel computers. *Journal of the ACM*, 25(1):112–115, Jan. 1978.

[10] Y. C. Hu, H. Lu, A. L. Cox, and W. Zwaenepoel. OpenMP for networks of SMPs. In *Proceedings IPPS/SPDP*, pages 302–310. IEEE Computer Society Press, 1999.

[11] C. Leopold. *Parallel and Distributed Computing: A Survey of Models, Paradigms, and Approaches*. John Wiley & Sons, New York, 2001.

[12] J. J. Modi. *Parallel algorithms and matrix computation*. Clarendon Press, Oxford, 1988.

[13] L. Pan, L. F. Bic, and M. B. Dillencourt. Distributed sequential computing using mobile code: Moving computation to data. In L. M. Ni and M. Valero, editors, *Proceedings of the 2001 International Conference on Parallel Processing (ICPP 2001)*, pages 77–84, Los Alamitos, Calif., Sept. 2001. IEEE Computer Society.

[14] L. Pan, L. F. Bic, M. B. Dillencourt, and M. K. Lai. NavP versus SPMD: Two views of distributed computation. In T. Gonzalez, editor, *Proceedings of the Fifteenth IASTED International Conference on Parallel and Distributed Computing and Systems (PDCS 2003)*, volume 2, Algorithms, pages 666–673, Anaheim, Calif., Nov. 2003. ACTA Press.

[15] L. Pan, W. Zhang, A. Asuncion, M. K. Lai, M. B. Dillencourt, and L. F. Bic. Incremental parallelization using navigational programming: A case study. School of Information & Computer Sciences Technical Report TR# 05-04, University of California, Irvine, Irvine, CA, Mar. 2005.

[16] A. P. Petitet and J. J. Dongarra. Algorithmic redistribution methods for block-cyclic decompositions. *IEEE Transactions on Parallel and Distributed Systems*, 10(12):1201–1216, 1999.

[17] N. Petkov. *Systolic Parallel Processing*. Elsevier Science Publishers, Amsterdam, North-Holland, 1993.

[18] J. Protic, M. Tomasevic, and V. Milutinovic, editors. *Distributed Shared Memory: Concepts and Systems*. IEEE Computer Society, Los Alamitos, CA, 1998.

[19] M. J. Quinn. *Parallel computing theory and practice*. McGraw-Hill, 1994.

[20] R. S. Schreiber. An introduction to HPF. *Lecture Notes in Computer Science*, 1132:27–44, 1996.

[21] L. Smith and M. Bull. Development of mixed mode MPI/OpenMP applications. *Scientific Programming*, 9(2–3):83–98, Spring–Summer 2001.

Session 8C: Scheduling

An ACO-based Approach for Scheduling Task Graphs with Communication Costs

Markus Bank Udo Hönig Wolfram Schiffmann
FernUniversität Hagen
Lehrgebiet Rechnerarchitektur
58084 Hagen, Germany
{Markus.Bank, Udo.Hoenig, Wolfram.Schiffmann}@FernUni-Hagen.de

Abstract

In this paper we introduce a new algorithm for computing near optimal schedules for task graph scheduling problems. In contrast to conventional approaches for solving those scheduling problems, our algorithm is based on the same principles that ants use to find shortest paths between their nest and food sources. Like their natural counterparts, artificial ants cooperate by means of pheromone trails where information about the quality of the possible solution's building blocks is stored. Based on this common communication structure, new solutions emerge by means of cooperative interaction between the ants. In the paper we demonstrate how this basic principle can be adapted to solve scheduling problems. We also evaluated the performance of the proposed ANTLS-algorithm (Ant List Scheduler) by means of a comprehensive test bench with more than 30,000 test cases. Compared to two conventional and two other nature-inspired approaches it performed very well.

1. Introduction

The number of networked computers world wide is steadily increasing. If one has to conduct complex computations it is therefore useful to distribute the working load over multiple computers. In this way one can not only accelerate the computation but also improve the usage of the available computers. To solve a specific problem, we need a parallel algorithm whose components will be executed on a homogeneous or heterogeneous network of more or less spatial distributed computers (e.g. cluster or grid computers, respectively).

Dependencies between the parts of a parallel algorithm can be described by means of a directed acyclic graph (DAG), also known as *task graph*. In general, the nodes and edges of a task graph are weighted. The work load of a specific task i is indicated by the node's weight w_i. It corresponds to the time needed by a task to compute new outputs using the results of preceding tasks as inputs. The cost of communication between two tasks i and j is specified by an edge weight c_{ij}. This cost must be considered only if the communicating tasks will be mapped to different processing elements.

If we want to execute an algorithm which is specified by a task graph on a parallel machine like a cluster or grid computer, we have to find a schedule that determines both, optimal sequencing and optimal mapping of the tasks to the available processing elements. Most often, the objective of solving this *task graph scheduling problem* is to minimize the overall computing time by making efficient use of the parallel processing elements. In this paper, we suppose a homogeneous computing environment. Despite the restriction to identical processing elements, the problem to determine an optimal schedule – apart from some restrained cases – has been proven to be NP-complete [1]. Thus, most researchers use heuristic approaches to solve the problem for reasonable sizes of the task graph. Three categories can be distinguished: list–based, clustering–based and duplication–based heuristics. List–based heuristics assign priority levels to the tasks and map the highest priority task to the best fitting processing element [2]. Clustering–based heuristics embrace heavily communicating tasks and assign them on the same processing element, in order to reduce the overall communication overhead [3]. Duplication-based heuristics also decrease the amount of communication while simultaneously the amount of (redundant) computation will be increased. It has been combined with both list-based [4] and cluster-based approaches [5].

In this paper we will introduce a list-based approach that concentrates on finding a near optimal sequence for the tasks. The mapping subproblem is solved by a so called *greedy mapper* that simply assigns the next task to be sched-

0190-3918/05 $20.00 © 2005 IEEE

uled to that processing element where it can be started as soon as possible. In order to find a nearly optimal sequence, we use a quite new approach that models the behavior of ant colonies.

In contrast to other list-based heuristics, our algorithm mimics the successful strategies of ants in finding solutions to the complex routing problems the ants are faced with in real life. We compare the results found by this so called *Ant Colony Optimization* (ACO) approach with the performance of other well known conventional and also nature-inspired heuristics. This comparison is based on a comprehensive test bench of task graph problems that provides the actual *optimal* solutions to a collection of various task graph problems [6]. By means of this test bench we can easily evaluate and analyze the strengths and drawbacks of the proposed ACO-approach. Even though the ACO-approach has been applied to various optimization problems, e.g. the Traveling Salesman Problem (TSP), in this contribution it has been for the first time applied to task graph scheduling. By the introduction of problem dependent rules for computing the pheromone concentrations, the stability of the algorithm and the quality of its results could be improved.

The paper is organized as follows: In the next section the ACO-metaheuristic will be described. Then, we introduce into the details of our ant list scheduler algorithm (ANTLS) for computing near optimal sequences to a given task graph scheduling problem by means of the ACO-metaheuristic. Then, we compare the results achieved by ANTLS with those of two conventional and two nature-inspired approaches. We also analyze the influence of different parameter settings and the size of the task graphs to the achieved performance.

2. The Ant Colony Optimization Metaheuristic

As a result of the considered task graph scheduling problem's NP-completeness, researchers developed a large number of deterministic and stochastic heuristics in order to find near optimal schedules in reasonable time, many of them basing on metaheuristics (e.g. [7, 8]). A *metaheuristic* is a generic algorithm, that guides the processing of at least one subordinated (local) heuristic which is specialized in the given problem. A detailed description of general metaheuristics' characteristics as well as a survey of the currently most popular methods can be found in [9]. Some metaheuristics imitate natural processes and are therefore called *nature-inspired*. Among Simulated Annealing, Genetic Algorithms and many others, the class of metaheuristics also comprises a method called *Ant Colony Optimization* (ACO)[10, 11].

ACO is inspired by the indirect communication of a foraging ant swarm. By means of this communication behavior, the swarm is enabled to find shortest paths between food sources and the nest. While moving, every ant deposits a trail of a chemical substance, called *pheromone*, on its way. The more ants pass by, the higher is the pheromone concentration at a location. Although every ant selects its direction at random, a path's probability of being chosen raises with its pheromone concentration. Since every ant leaves a pheromone trail at the selected path, it reinforces the already deposited pheromone and therefore raises the path's attractiveness for later ants. Without any limitation mechanism, this positive feedback would lead to a soon convergence and the selection of a probably poor path. In nature, this limitation is achieved by *evaporation* which reduces the pheromone concentration by-and-by, if the path is not frequently used. This way, an ant colony will 'forget' a path if it is of no further use.

The ACO metaheuristic applies the described behavior of natural ants to optimize constructive search processes for combinatorial problems. By using *artificial pheromone* trails, a swarm of independent agents, the *artificial ants*, is guided through the investigated search space. The general structure of the ACO metaheuristic, including some of the later described optional extensions is shown in Figure 1. While a problem dependent termination criterion is not satisfied, the following steps are conducted: Firstly, every ant constructs a solution to the given problem. Next, the found solutions are evaluated and the artificial pheromone trails are updated. The third step is optional and deals with so-called *daemon actions* which are centralized actions that need global knowledge.

```
while termination criterion is not satisfied{
1.      ants construct solutions
2.      pheromone trail update
                online delayed pheromone update (opt.)
                evaporation
3.      daemon actions (opt.)
                elitism (opt.)
                offline pheromone update (opt.)
}
```

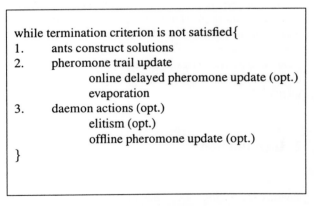

Figure 1. The ACO-metaheuristic.

The termination criterion is usually a combination of a demand on the found solution's quality and an upper bound of allowed loop iterations. If the search gets stuck in a local extremum, this bounding ensures that ACO terminates within a reasonable period of time.

An artificial ant performs its walk through the search space by incrementally completing a solution of the given problem. In every construction step, the ant has to select a building block that should be integrated in its current partial solution next. This decision problem corresponds to the problem of natural ants to select a suitable direction. Like their natural counterparts, artificial ants can use the pheromone trails of preceding ants as a guideline for this decision. In addition, a local heuristic provides further information that can be used to guide each ant.

To fulfill its task, every artifical ant is equipped with enough memory to remember its path through the search space. This information can be required to find a valid solution, to evaluate the found solution or to deposit the ant's pheromone trail afterwards.

In contrast to nature, where every moving ant deposits a continuous and constant pheromone trail, ACO permits several alternative ways. The trail update can either be conducted by the ant itself (*online update*) or a daemon process (*offline update*). In case of an online update, the ant can deposit the pheromone immediately at every construction step (*online step-by-step pheromone update*) or after finishing the whole construction process (*online delayed pheromone update*). A delayed trail generation enables the consideration of a solution's quality when selecting the amount of pheromone to deposit. This way, the further search can be biased more strongly to promising areas of the search space.

Like in nature, without any appropriate protection mechanism the artificial ants' positive feedback would lead to an early convergence of the algorithm with possibly bad results. For this reason, ACO-algorithms usually implement some kind of *evaporation*, allowing the artificial ants to 'forget' and therefore favoring the exploration of new search space areas.

Many ACO-algorithms implement an 'elitism'-function. Among plenty of possible alternatives, elitism can – for example – be realized by considering only the best solution of every run for the trail update [12], or by means of an daemon action, that deposits an extra amount of pheromone upon the global best ant's path every run [13].

3. ANTLS (Ant List Scheduling)

In ANTLS, ants build sequences of tasks by visiting the nodes of a DAG in a topological order. The scheduling lists are used as an input of a greedy list scheduler which maps the tasks to the processors. The length of the resulting schedule is then used as a quality measure of the generated solution.

Building a scheduling list for a DAG requires the consideration of the predefined precedence constraints. If they are not taken into account, it is most likely that the mapper can not create a feasible schedule. This does not only limit the set of starting nodes, but also the set of nodes that are allowed to be scheduled at each step. In order to create feasible scheduling lists, every ant's memory has to store the following information:

- The current node the ant is. This is the last scheduled node.
- A set of nodes, the so-called *free* nodes, which are ready for scheduling. This set will be updated after every step.
- The number of unscheduled predecessors for each node. This is used by the ant to detect when a node becomes ready for being processed. The ant needs to keep track of this information because a node must not be scheduled if it has unscheduled predecessors.
- The scheduling list which is build by the ant.

At the beginning, the set of free nodes will be preset with the entry nodes. The ant will be placed at a pseudo node $v_0 \notin V$, V denoting the set of the DAG's nodes, which will not be scheduled. The purpose of this pseudo node is to let the ants decide which entry node should be scheduled first. The number of unscheduled predecessors for each node will be initialized and the ants scheduling list is empty.

We now define the relationship between pheromone and scheduling lists. For that purpose we introduce a pheromone value $\tau(v, w)$ that represents the benefit of scheduling a node w directly after node v, where $v, w \in V$. If a scheduling list which schedules a node w directly after a node v results in a short schedule, this fact should be saved for succeeding ants by depositing some pheromone between v and w. Later ants will then be attracted to schedule the nodes in an order that resulted in a short schedule. The initial amount of pheromone at the start of the algorithm will be initialized to $\tau(v, w) = \tau_0$ for each pair of nodes (v, w), so at the beginning there will be no guidance by pheromone.

Additionally, the ants use a local heuristic, supporting them to build good scheduling lists. At each step an ant has to decide between several nodes to schedule next. Classical task scheduling heuristics, such as HLFET [14] and MCP [15] are making such a decision by assigning priorities to the nodes. These priorities are often based on levels implied by the structure of the DAG, for example:

- $blevel(v)$ which is the length of the longest path from v to an exit node, excluding the weight of node v.
- $sblevel(v)$ which is the same as $blevel(v)$ but without considering edge weights.

We compared the results of using $sblevel$ and $blevel$ ordering and found that scheduling nodes in descending $sblevel$-order gives slightly better results than scheduling in $blevel$-order. For this reason, we define a local heuristic to schedule a node w directly after a node v (which is in fact independent of v) as:

$$\eta(v, w) = sblevel(w) \tag{1}$$

We will now describe, how an ant k selects the next node to be scheduled. Assume the ant is at node Pos_k and its set of free nodes is denoted as $Free_k$. At first, the ant decides between the exploitation of a known good scheduling order or the exploration of different orderings. The balance of exploitation and exploration is controlled by a parameter $q_0 \in [0, 1]$ which indicates the probability that an ant decides to exploit a good order and schedules the node with the highest attractiveness. This is the one, which possesses the best combination of a high *sblevel* and a large amount of pheromone.

$$Next_k = \underset{u \in Free_k}{argmax} \{\tau(Pos_k, u) \cdot \eta^\beta(Pos_k, u)\} \quad (2)$$

where β is a parameter that controls the influence of the local heuristic. If the currently considered ant decided to explore, it selects one node $w \in Free_k$ by using a so called *random-proportional* decision rule. The probability the ant selects node w is:

$$p(w) = \frac{\tau(Pos_k, w) \cdot \eta^\beta(Pos_k, w)}{\sum\limits_{u \in Free_k} \tau(Pos_k, u) \cdot \eta^\beta(Pos_k, u)} \quad (3)$$

After the ant has selected a node $Next_k$, it moves to this node and updates its set of free nodes by decrementing the number of unscheduled predecessors for each successor of $Next_k$. If a successor's number of unscheduled predecessors reaches zero, it is added to the set of free nodes. After maintaining its internal state, every ant immediately applies a local pheromone update using the following rule:

$$\tau(Pos_k, Next_k) \leftarrow (1-\rho) \cdot \tau(Pos_k, Next_k) + \rho \cdot \tau_0 \quad (4)$$

In the above rule, the parameter $\rho \in [0, 1]$ controls the ratio of pheromone evaporation and reinforcement. Unlike other ant algorithms, e.g. *Ant Colony System* (ACS) for the TSP [13], we decided to update the pheromone directly after an ant made its step. Since all ants start at the same pseudo node and therefore the set of allowed nodes to schedule is the same for all ants at the start of an iteration, without an immediate update the probability that all ants choose the same node would be quite high, leading to a soon convergence.

After all ants have built their scheduling lists, these lists are evaluated by mapping the nodes to the processors. We used a greedy mapper which maps a node to the processor that allows its earliest starting time. The ant whose scheduling list resulted in the shortest schedule is called the *iteration best ant*. Analogous we keep a *global best ant*, which is the best ant over all iterations.

At the end of an iteration, a global pheromone update is applied by allowing the global best ant to deposit some extra pheromone between the nodes it has visited. This will attract ants in later iterations to schedule the nodes in a similar order which might also result in a short schedule. Let $(v_{i_1}, \ldots, v_{i_n})$ be the global best ant's scheduling list. Pheromone will be updated for each $j \in \{1, \ldots, n-1\}$ by means of the following rule:

$$\tau(v_{i_j}, v_{i_{j+1}}) \leftarrow (1-\alpha) \cdot \tau(v_{i_j}, v_{i_{j+1}}) + \alpha \cdot \Delta_\tau \quad (5)$$

Similar to the local pheromone update, a parameter $\alpha \in [0, 1]$ controls the ratio of evaporation and reinforcement. In [13] the amount of reinforcement is determined by ${L_{gb}}^{-1}$, where L_{gb} is the global best ant's tour length. In ANTLS we chose a different approach to compute the reinforcement. In order to formalize this approach, we have to introduce a lower bound of an optimal schedule length first.

Assume scheduling a DAG on an unbounded number of processors. Then, the length of a critical path without considering communication costs CP_{len} will be a first lower bound of an optimal schedule length which is implied by the structure of the DAG. A second lower bound can be achieved by assuming scheduling the nodes to a bounded number of processors p. If all nodes are equally distributed to all processors and there are no idle times, the schedule length is bounded by:

$$SL_{min} = \left\lceil \frac{\sum\limits_{v \in V} w(v)}{p} \right\rceil \quad (6)$$

By using these two bounds, we get a lower bound SL_{lb} of an optimal schedule length by:

$$SL_{lb} = \max\{CP_{len}, SL_{min}\} \quad (7)$$

Now, let SL_{gb} be the length of the global best ant's schedule. We define the amount of reinforcement as:

$$\Delta_\tau = \frac{1}{SL_{gb} - SL_{lb} + 1} \quad (8)$$

Subtracting the lower bound SL_{lb} makes the reinforcement independent of the actual DAG. Assume an optimal schedule has length SL_{opt}. If $SL_{opt} = SL_{lb}$, the reinforcement of an ant that created an optimal scheduling list will always be 1.

As a consequence, the amount of pheromone deposited by the global best ant will be much higher as if a reinforcement of ${SL_{gb}}^{-1}$ was used. This needs to be considered when computing the initial amount of pheromone τ_0 at the start of the algorithm. In ANTLS we therefore initially deposit

$$\tau_0 = \frac{1}{|V|} \quad (9)$$

between each pair of nodes (v, w).

4. Results

In order to conduct an unbiased analysis of our algorithm, we used the test bench proposed in [6] as test set. This test bench comprises 36000 task scheduling problems with task graphs ranging from 7 to 24 nodes and target architectures ranging from 2 to 32 parallel computers. Since the optimal schedules comprised by this test bench are not yet available for all test cases, the interim version used for the presented analysis is limited to 30511 task graphs with known optimal solutions. To our knowledge there exists no comparable test bench for the evaluation of heuristic scheduling algorithms. Although in [16] a test bench for task graphs with up to 5000 tasks is provided these task graphs do not take communication overhead into account. Also, it is not guaranteed that the minimum schedule length is given for every task graph problem, because of the NP-completeness the run time of the search algorithm was limited to 10 minutes. In [17] a performance study of 15 heuristic scheduling algorithms is presented. In contrast to the test set used, the number of task graphs is much lower (≈ 350) and for most of the investigated task graphs (250) the optimal schedules are not known.

Like other metaheuristics, ACO allows for a wide range of alternative options for several parameters. Our first investigation was therefore to find a setting, enabling the algorithm to find as many optimal schedules as possible. Since ACS performed well considering the Traveling-Salesman-Problem, we decided to realize an ACS-like implementation (see fig. 2(A)) as starting point for our search. The number of iterations was set to 60, with an iteration-size of 17 ants, totaling 1020 ants. We selected

- the local heuristic,
- the amount of reinforcement Δ_τ,
- the initial amount of pheromone τ_0 and
- the timing of the pheromone update's conduction

for variation. Figure 2 can show only some of the obtained results. Implementations using the *sblevel* as local heuristic are slightly superior to those using the *blevel* (fig. 2(A) and (B)). Increasing Δ_τ from ACS's default to $\Delta_\tau = \frac{1}{SL_{gb} - SL_{lb} + 1}$ produces worse results if the initial amount of pheromone (τ_0) is unchanged (see fig. 2(C)). In combination with an increased initial amount of pheromone ($\tau_0 = \frac{1}{|V|}$), this value for Δ_τ achieves much better results (fig. 2(D)). In comparison to ACS's pheromone update, an early pheromone update after every single ant's move shows no observable difference as can be seen in figure 2, (D) and (E). This way, we found the implementation described in section 3, which will be further analyzed.

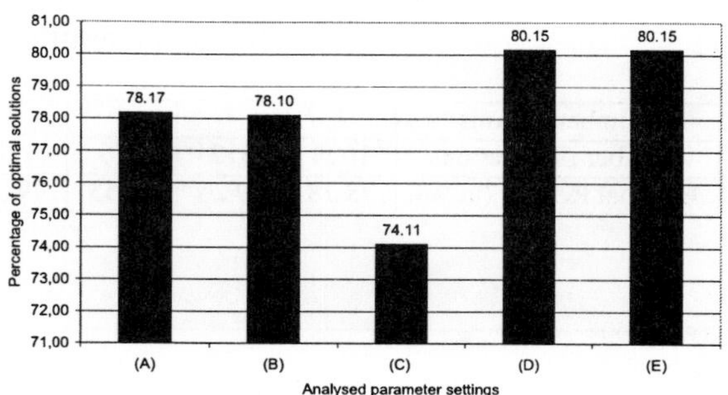

Figure 2. Results of several variations of our ACO-algorithm.

Our next aim is to investigate the influence of the ant/iteration-ratio on the quality of the achieved results. The number of total ants is fixed to a value of about 1024. As can be seen in table 1, the results of different ant/iteration-ratios differ by a maximum of only 1,47%. Although the results of [13] are approximately confirmed, at least for small task graphs our algorithm seems to be quite stable here.

While the ratio of ants and iterations is of minor importance considering the test set used, the number of ants that move accumulated over all iterations has a strong influence on the quality of ANTLS's results. For a closer investigation, we varied this parameter within a range of 1 and 2048 ants and analyzed the effects with respect to several task graph properties. Exemplarily, we will now focus on the task graphs' sizes. Figure 3 shows the achieved results for task graphs consisting of 7, 15 and 24 tasks as well as the overall test set with all task graph sizes. It is obvious that the algorithm finds the optimal schedules more often, the smaller the considered task graphs are. Independent of the task graphs' size, the benefit of adding more ants to the search process declines soon and finally reaches a level where it is almost zero. The bigger the task graph, the more ants are required to reach this level.

The compared heuristics were originally all designed for static scheduling. Although the runtime of an algorithm is less important in static scheduling environments, a too extensive overhead would make it inapplicable for larger task graphs. For this reason, we investigated the scaling behavior of our ANTLS algorithm and compared the obtained results with those of other heuristics. The experiment was conducted upon a PC with an Athlon-1000 MHz processor. Figure 4 shows the runtimes of the considered nature inspired heuristics. The deterministic algorithms are not considered since their runtimes are all within a few seconds and would therefore appear as flat lines only. ANTLS, SA and GA obtain similar results, with the GA performing the best and ANTLS the worst. Although this overhead prevents

Table 1. Results of different ant/iteration-ratios

Number of Ants	1	2	4	8	16	21	32	64	128	256	512	1024
Number of Iterations	1024	512	256	128	64	49	32	16	8	4	2	1
Optimal Results (in %)	78.78	79.26	79.55	79.91	80.11	80.25	80.09	80.15	79.86	79.45	79.21	79.03

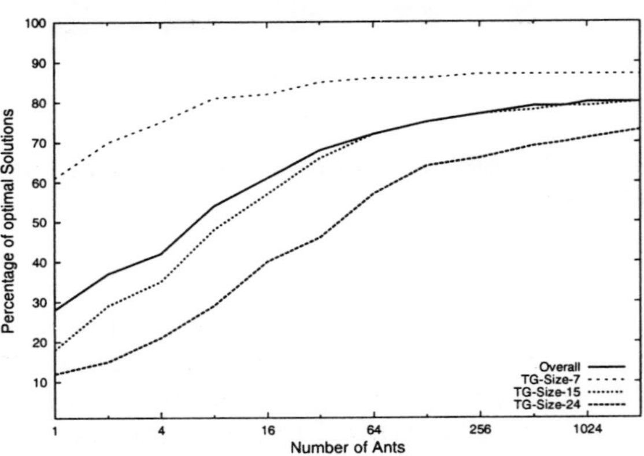

Figure 3. Influence of the number of ants involved in the search process.

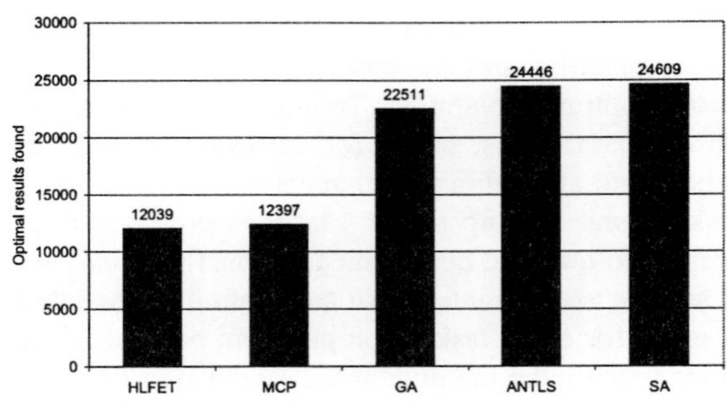

Figure 5. Comparison of several scheduling heuristics.

these heuristics from being applied in dynamic scheduling environments, the shown performance is sufficient for static scheduling and analysis purposes.

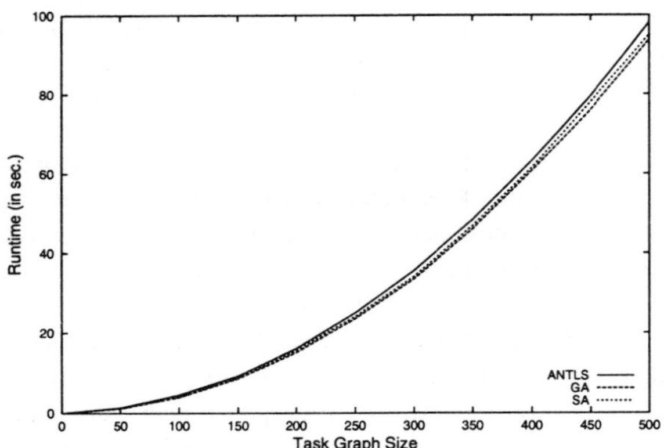

Figure 4. Comparison of the nature inspired algorithms' scalability.

ANTLS achieves promising results when being compared to other nature-inspired stochastic as well as to deterministic scheduling heuristics. As can be seen in figure 5, it performs best with exception of Simulated Annealing (SA). In general, the nature-inspired stochastic algorithms perform much better than the deterministic ones.

These observations hold to a large extend, when considering larger task graphs with a maximum of 250 tasks. ANTLS is still the second best after SA. The better deterministic algorithms close up to the Genetic Algorithm (GA) but are far-off to SA and ACO. A more detailed comparison can be found in [18]. Although our algorithm's current version already provides good results, we nevertheless expect a further improvement when exchanging our algorithm's greedy mapping heuristic by an ACO-based mapping.

5. Conclusion and future work

In this paper we demonstrated how the emergent behavior of cooperating ants can be simulated to solve task graph scheduling problems. We proposed the ANTLS-algorithm and evaluated its performance by means of a comprehensive test bench with over 30,000 test cases. By the introduction of problem dependent rules for computing the pheromone concentrations, the stability of the algorithm and the quality of its results have been improved. ANTLS performs very well compared to several other investigated nature-inspired as well as conventional approaches. We plan for the future work to improve the greedy mapping part of the ANTLS-algorithm. Especially, it would be interesting to investigate if this component can also be realized by an integrated ACO-based approach.

References

[1] Kwok, Y.-K., Ahmad, I.: Static scheduling algorithms for allocating directed task graphs to multiprocessors, ACM Computing Surveys, Vol. 31, No. 4, 1999, pp. 406–471

[2] Radulescu, A., van Gemund, J.C.:Low-Cost Task Scheduling for Distributed-Memory Machines, IEEE Transactions on Parallel and Distributed Systems, Vol. 13, No. 6, June 2002

[3] Aguilar, J., Gelenbe E.: Task Assignment and Transaction Clustering Heuristics for Distributed Systems, Information Sciences, Vol. 97, No. 1& 2, pp. 199–219, 1997

[4] Bansal, S., Kumar, P., Singh, K.: An improved duplication strategy for scheduling precedence constrained graphs in multiprocessor systems, IEEE Transactions on Parallel and Distributed Systems, Vol. 14, No. 6, June 2003

[5] Park, C.-I., Choe, T.Y.: An optimal scheduling algorithm based on task duplication, IEEE Transactions on Computers, Vol. 51, No. 4, April 2002

[6] Hönig, U., Schiffmann, W.: A comprehensive Test Bench of optimal Schedules for the Evaluation of Scheduling Heuristics, Proceedings of the sixteenth IASTED International Conference on Parallel and Distributed Computing and Systems (PDCS 2004), Cambridge, U.S.A., 2004

[7] Greenwood, G.W., Gupta, A., McSweeney, K.: Scheduling Tasks in Multiprocesor Systems Using Evolutionary Strategies, International Conference on Evolutionary Computation, pp. 345–349, 1994

[8] Kwok, Y.-K., Ahmad, I.: Efficient Scheduling of Arbitrary Task Graphs to Multiprocessors Using a Parallel Genetic Algorithm, Journal of Parallel and Distributed Computing, Vol. 47, No. 1, pp. 58–77, 1997

[9] Blum, C., Roli, A.: Metaheuristics in Combinatorial Optimization: Overview and Conceptual Comparison, ACM Computing Surveys, Vol. 35, No. 3, 2003, pp. 268–308

[10] Dorigo, M., Maniezzo, V., Colorni, A.: Ant System: Optimization by a colony of cooperating Agents, IEEE Transactions on Systems, Man and Cybernetics, Part B, Vol. 26, No. 1, 1996, pp.1–13

[11] Dorigo, M., Stützle, T.: The Ant Colony Optimization Metaheuristic: Algorithms, Applications and Advances, In F. Glover and G. Kochenberger (Eds.), Handbook of Metaheuristics, volume 57 of International Series in Operations Research & Management Science, pp. 251–285, Kluwer Academic Publishers, Norwell, MA, 2002

[12] Stützle, T.: An Ant Approach to the Flow Shop Problem, Proceedings of the 6th European Congress on Intelligent Techniques & Soft Computing (EUFIT'98), 1998, Vol. 3, pp. 1560–1564

[13] Dorigo, M., Gambardella, L. M.: Ant Colony System: A Cooperative Learning Approach to the Traveling Salesman Problem, IEEE Transactions on Evolutionary Computation, Vol. 1, No. 1, pp. 53–66, 1997

[14] Adam, T. L., Chandy, K. M., Dickson, J. R.: A comparison of list schedules for parallel processing systems, Communications of the ACM, Vol. 17, No. 12, pp. 685–690, 1974

[15] Wu, M.Y., Gajski, D. D.: Hypertool: A Programming Aid for Message-passing Systems, IEEE Transactions on Parallel and Distributed Systems, Vol. 1, No. 3, pp 330-343, 1990

[16] Kasahara Laboratory, http://www.kasahara.elec.waseda.ac.jp/schedule/index.html, 2004

[17] Y.-K. Kwok, I. Ahmad, Benchmarking the Task Graph Scheduling Algorithms, *Proceedings of the 12th International Parallel Processing Symposium*, Orlando, U.S.A., 1998, 531-537

[18] Hönig, U., Schiffmann, W.: Comparison of nature inspired and deterministic scheduling heuristics considering optimal schedules, In B. Ribeiro et al. (Eds.), Adaptive and Natural Computing Algorithms, ISBN 3-211-24934-6, Springer-Verlag, 2005

A Task Duplication Based Scheduling Algorithm Using Partial Schedules*

Doruk Bozdağ[†], Füsun Özgüner[†], Eylem Ekici[†], Umit Catalyurek[‡]
[†] Department of Electrical and Computer Engineering
[‡] Department of Biomedical Informatics
The Ohio State University
{bozdagd,ozguner,ekici}@ece.osu.edu, umit@bmi.osu.edu

Abstract

We propose a novel replication-based two-phase scheduling algorithm designed to achieve DAG scheduling with small makespans and high efficiency. In the first phase, the schedule length of the application is minimized using a novel approach that utilizes partial schedules. *In the second phase, the number of processors required is minimized by eliminating and merging these partial schedules. Experimental results on random DAGs show that the makespans generated by the proposed algorithm are slightly better than those generated by the well known CPFD algorithm whereas the number of processors used is less than half of what is needed by CPFD solutions.*

1 Introduction

Low cost, high performance commodity computing and network hardware turned the distributed memory multiprocessor systems (DMMS) into viable alternatives to the traditional supercomputers. In order to achieve high performance with a DMMS, efficient task partitioning of the application and scheduling of those tasks onto parallel processors is of utmost importance. Assuming that the application has already been partitioned into tasks and the task dependencies are represented as a *directed acyclic graph (DAG)*, the goal of scheduling is to minimize the execution time, also referred to as *schedule length* or *makespan*, of the application by allocating tasks on DMMS such that the precedence constraints are preserved [2]. DAG scheduling problem is shown to be an NP-complete problem in its general form [7]. Optimal polynomial solutions exist only for limited cases where either the cost or the shape of the DAG is restricted [6, 14]. In general, proposed heuristic algorithms offer trade-offs between the quality and the complexity of the solutions. Besides the schedule length, various cost criteria such as the number of processors used are also taken into account in many cases.

Task duplication is a relatively new approach for DAG scheduling [1, 3, 6, 14, 15, 17]. This kind of scheduling is also an NP-complete problem [13]. Performance of the duplication based algorithms are superior to non-duplication based ones in terms of generating smaller schedule lengths. However, this is usually achieved at the expense of higher time complexity and larger number of processors.

In this work, we propose a novel two-phase duplication-based scheduling algorithm, called *DUPS*. The first phase, called *minSL*, aims to minimize the schedule length by minimizing the earliest finish time of each task on a new processor. The schedule on the processor associated with a task is called the *partial schedule* of that task. In the second phase, called *minNP*, the required number of processors is minimized by eliminating and merging the partial schedules without increasing the schedule length found in the first phase. A nice feature of *minNP* is that, with small modifications, it can be applied to the output of the existing scheduling algorithms to improve their efficiency. Performance evaluation of DUPS is presented in comparison to the CPFD algorithm which is shown to be a superior algorithm compared to other related scheduling algorithms in terms of producing the smallest schedule length with requiring a moderate amount of processors [1, 4, 8].

2 Related Work

An excellent survey and taxonomy of task scheduling algorithms and some benchmarking techniques are presented in [11, 12]. DAG scheduling algorithms can be divided into two with respect to whether they allow task duplication or not. Non-duplication based algorithms aim to keep the number of processors required minimal

*This research was supported in part by the National Science Foundation under Grants #CCF-0342615, #ACI-0203846, #ANI-0330612, #CNS-0426241, NIH NIBIB BISTI #P20EB000591, Ohio Board of Regents BRTTC #BRTT02-0003, Sandia National Laboratories under Doc.No: 283793.

0190-3918/05 $20.00 © 2005 IEEE

and to achieve low-complexity scheduling without allowing any task duplication. In task duplication based algorithms, on the other hand, some tasks are duplicated on more than one processor to eliminate the interprocessor communication cost.

Two common approaches in non-duplication based scheduling are list scheduling and cluster-based scheduling. In list scheduling [16, 18], each task in a DAG is first assigned a priority. Then the tasks are considered in non-ascending order of priorities for scheduling on a set of available processors. Despite the fact that the quality of their schedules is usually worse than that of other algorithm classes, low complexity of the list-based algorithms still make them attractive alternatives.

In cluster-based scheduling, processors are treated as clusters and the completion time is minimized by moving tasks among clusters [10, 18]. At the end of clustering, heavily communicating tasks are assigned to the same processor, reducing the interprocessor communication. However, after clustering is completed, merging the clusters to fit into a smaller number of processors without degrading the schedule is usually the bottleneck for this class of algorithms.

The proposed algorithm is a duplication-based static scheduling algorithm and it differs from the previous algorithms by addressing the minimization of the schedule length and the number of processors used as separate problems to be optimized in two distinct phases.

3 Preliminaries

A DAG $\mathcal{G} = (\mathcal{N}, \mathcal{E})$ consists of a set of nodes $\mathcal{N}$ representing the tasks and a set of directed edges $\mathcal{E}$ representing dependencies among tasks. The edge set $\mathcal{E}$ contains edges $(n_p, n_j) \in \mathcal{E}$ for each task n_p that n_j depends on. The task n_p, from which the directed edge originates, is called the *parent task* and the task n_j, to which the directed edge points, is called the *child task*. A child task depends on its parent tasks such that the execution of a child task cannot start before it receives data from all of its parents. A task having no parents is called an *entry task* whereas a task having no children is called an *exit task*. A *non-join task* and a *join task* are defined as tasks having a single and multiple parents, respectively.

The weight w_j of a node n_j represents the computational weight associated with the respective task, whereas the cost $c_{p,j}$ of a directed edge (n_p, n_j) represents the communication cost between tasks n_p and n_j. In the DAG scheduling problem, if a task scheduled on one processor depends on a task scheduled on another processor, an interprocessor communication is required between those processors. However, if both of the tasks are assigned to same processor, the communication requirement is considered negligible. In the DAG shown in Figure 1(a), the numbers in the circles represent the computational weights of the respective nodes and the numbers on the edges represent the communication costs. In literature, several methods exist to make good estimations of computational weights and communication costs in a DAG [9, 18].

Earliest start time $est(n_j, P_\ell)$ of a task $n_j \in \mathcal{N}$ for a processor $P_\ell \in \mathcal{P}$ denotes the earliest time that n_j can start execution on P_ℓ, where $\mathcal{P}$ represents the set of homogeneous processors. Since a task can only start execution when all of its inputs are ready on a processor, $est(n_j, P_\ell)$ can be computed as $max\{min\{ft(n_p, P_\ell), ft(n_p, P_k) + c_{p,j}\}\}$ for each parent n_p of n_j and $P_k \neq P_\ell$ where $ft(n_p, P_k)$ denotes the *finish time* of task n_p on processor P_k. If n_p is not copied on P_k, $ft(n_p, P_k)$ is considered to be infinity. Please note that, we assume all links in the interprocessor network are contention free and processors can compute and communicate simultaneously. Execution of a task does not necessarily start at its *est* since another task may be scheduled to execute at that time slot on the same processor. For a task n_j scheduled on processor P_ℓ, $st(n_j, P_\ell)$ denotes the *start time* of n_j on P_ℓ. Note that, with non-preemptive execution of tasks, $ft(n_j, P_\ell) = st(n_j, P_\ell) + w_j$. If $est(n_j, P_\ell)$ is lower bounded due to a parent n_p of n_j which is not scheduled on P_ℓ to finish before $st(n_j, P_\ell)$, that parent is called the *critical parent* of n_j for processor P_ℓ.

Schedule length (SL) is the most important performance indicator of scheduling algorithms. It is defined as $SL = max_{n_j \in \mathcal{N}, P_\ell \in \mathcal{P}}\{ft(n_j, P_\ell)\}$. A widely used metric to evaluate the schedule length is the *normalized schedule length (NSL)* [1]. NSL is defined as the ratio of the parallel schedule length to the sum of the computational weights along the critical path, where *critical path* is defined as the path from an entry task to an exit task, along which the sum of the computational weights and communication costs is maximum. Another metric is the number of processors required by the generated parallel schedules. This metric measures how efficiently an algorithm utilizes the processors in scheduling the tasks.

4 The Algorithm

In the following subsections, the two main phases of the Duplication-based Scheduling Algorithm Using Partial Schedules (DUPS) and their relationship are described in more detail.

4.1 minSL: Minimizing the Schedule Length

The *minSL* algorithm exploits the assumption that an infinite number of processors are available, by creating a minimized partial schedule for each task on a separate processor. Basically, each task is first scheduled on a

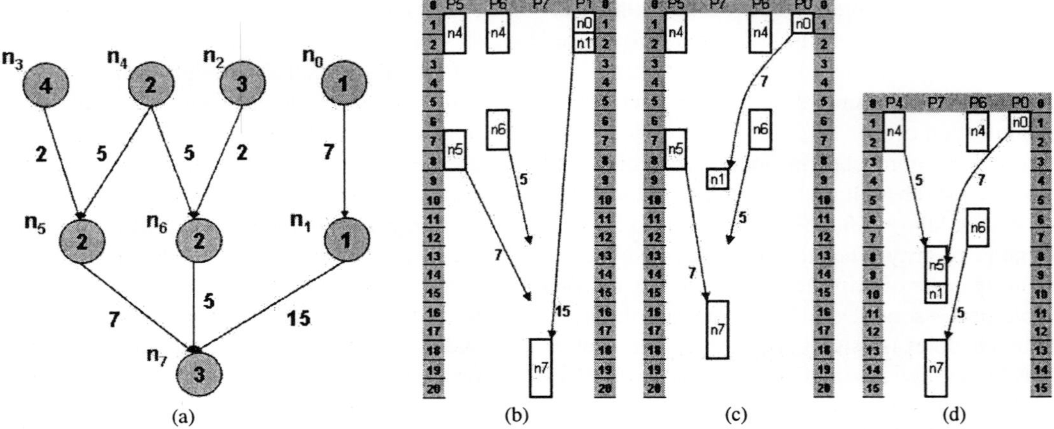

Figure 1. (a) DAG (b) Initializing n_7 (c) Duplicating n_1 on P_7. (d) Duplicating n_5 on P_7.

Algorithm 1 minSL

1: schedule each entry task n_s on a new processor P_s with $st(n_s, P_s) \leftarrow 0$
2: **while** there are unscheduled tasks **do**
3: $n_t \leftarrow$ a randomly chosen task whose parents' partial schedules have been determined
4: **if** n_t is a non-join task **then**
5: copy its parent's (n_p) partial schedule to P_t and set $st(n_t, P_t) \leftarrow ft(n_p, P_t)$
6: **else**
7: $st(n_t, P_t) \leftarrow est(n_t, P_t)$
8: $n_i \leftarrow n_t$ and $n_c \leftarrow$ critical parent of n_i
9: **while** n_c exists **and** ($SL_{t,current}-$ idle time on $P_t) + w_c < SL_{t,best}$ **do**
10: compute $est(n_c, P_t)$ and schedule n_c on P_t
11: put tasks scheduled after n_c into *rList*
12: sort tasks in the *rList* and reschedule on P_t
13: **if** $SL_{t,current} < SL_{t,best}$ **then**
14: $P_{t,best} \leftarrow P_{t,current}$
15: find the critical child n_i and critical task n_c

new processor, then its parents (and parents of parents etc.) are duplicated on that processor one by one until there is no potential improvement by further duplication. Since each task n_j's partial schedule will be constructed on a new processor P_j, we will also use P_j to denote the partial schedule of n_j. Although this scheme requires as many processors as the number of tasks, the second phase of the *DUPS* algorithm will minimize the processor requirement by maintaining the achieved SL at this phase.

minSL algorithm (Algorithm 1) starts with scheduling each of the entry tasks on a new processor. Then, the partial schedules of the remaining tasks are constructed one by one. In step 3, one of tasks whose parents have already been scheduled is randomly selected as the *target task* (n_t), which is the task whose partial schedule will be constructed next. If n_t is a non-join task, the best partial schedule can be obtained by duplicating its parent's partial schedule onto a new processor P_t, called the *target processor*, and scheduling n_t to start immediately after its parent (step 5).

If the target task is a join task, first it is scheduled on a new processor P_t to start at its *est* in step 7. Then n_t's partial schedule is tried to be improved by duplicating tasks onto P_t (steps 9-15). The next task to be duplicated on P_t is called the *critical task* n_c, which is the critical parent of the *critical child* n_i, chosen among the tasks scheduled on P_t. In step 8, we set n_i to n_t and n_c becomes the critical parent of n_t. Please note that at the current moment the only way to improve the partial schedule P_t is duplicating critical parent of n_t on P_t.

Duplication of n_c onto P_t can create a potential improvement (step 9) only if the sum of the computational weights on P_t after duplication is smaller than the smallest partial schedule length obtained so far. If this is the case, n_c is scheduled to start either at the first idle slot after $est(n_c, P_t)$ or at $st(n_i, P_t)$, whichever is earlier (step 10). After n_c is scheduled, all tasks that were scheduled to start after its start time, including n_i, are pushed into the *rList* for rescheduling in order to avoid any overlaps and to utilize the idle slots better (step 11). Since n_c may also be the critical parent of some tasks scheduled on P_t other than n_i, those tasks may now start earlier as well. Sometimes such tasks can start earlier than the tasks scheduled to start before themselves in the previous iteration. Therefore, in step 12, the tasks in the *rList* are sorted with respect to their est's on P_t to allow each task to start as early as possible. While doing that the precedence of each previous n_c to its n_i is preserved to make sure that they will not again become a critical child and parent pair for the same partial schedule. Furthermore, any duplicate of n_c in the *rList* is removed. This situation only occurs if current n_c was also the critical task for a previous critical child and hence it had been duplicated on P_t; but it had been scheduled to start after current n_i. Since n_c will be scheduled before current n_i in the current iteration, that copy of n_c becomes redundant.

Tasks in the *rList* are rescheduled on P_t such that if a task's est on P_t is earlier than the finish time of the task scheduled just before itself, it is scheduled at the finish time of that task; otherwise, it is scheduled at its est. If the duplication results in a better partial schedule than the best obtained so far, it is saved as the best partial schedule in step 14.

After the first pass of the loop in steps 9-15, partial schedule P_t may be improved by duplicating the critical parent of a task scheduled on P_t. Here, *minSL* chooses the critical child (n_i) as the latest starting task on P_t that starts at its est and has a critical parent. The rationale behind this choice is that the tasks scheduled to start after the critical child n_i start later than their est, and they can start earlier if an idle time slot can be created just before their start time. However, since n_i already starts at its est, it cannot start earlier on P_t and blocks those tasks unless its critical parent is duplicated on P_t to improve its est. Clearly, the choice of the task to be replicated is an heuristic decision. We have also experimented duplicating the critical parents of non-critical children and observed that it usually did not improve or slightly improved the schedule.

For the sample DAG displayed in Figure 1(a), consider the scheduling of task n_7. Since n_7 is a join task, at step 7 of Algorithm 1, it is initialized to start at its est, which is 17, on a new processor P_7 (Figure 1(b)). Since the sum of current computational weights and the computational weight of the critical task n_1 ($SL_{t,current}-$ idle time on $P_7 + w_1$ = 4) is less than the best schedule length so far (20); there is a potential to improve the schedule. Hence n_7's critical parent n_1 is duplicated on P_7 (Figure 1(c)). Since n_7 is the only task after n_1 on P_7, it is inserted into the *rList* and rescheduled, resulting a new best schedule length of 18. Then, n_7 and n_5 become the next critical child and the critical task respectively (step 15). n_5 is duplicated on P_7 to start its est (7) and both n_1 and n_7 are inserted into the *rList*. Finally they are rescheduled on P_7 resulting a new best partial schedule of length 15 (Figure 1(d)).

In the next iteration, n_c becomes n_6 with an est of 7. However, task n_5 is already scheduled to start at that time on P_7, therefore, n_6 is scheduled at the first idle slot after its est (Figure 2(a)). Note that at the end of this iteration SL did not improve. However, the algorithm does not stop here, since the schedule can still potentially be improved as it will be in the next iteration when n_4 becomes n_c and its duplication result in a new best partial schedule of length 13 (Figure 2(b)). Please note that after the duplication and sorting, n_6 was able to start before n_5 which allowed SL to improve by 1 compared to the case where n_5 is forced to start before n_6. After this point, duplication of the next critical task n_3 would not improve SL and the schedule on P_7 is stored as the partial schedule of task n_7. Note that although *minSL* stops here, as mentioned earlier it is possible to improve the schedule by duplicating a parent (n_0) of a non-critical child (n_1), as displayed in Figure 2(c). Our algorithm chooses not to search for such cases, because the high runtime cost do not amortize the negligible improvements.

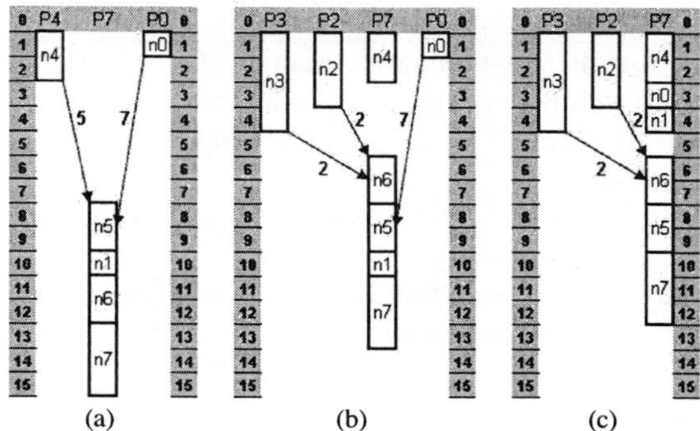

Figure 2. (a) Duplicating n_6 on P_7 (b) Duplicating n_4 on P_7 (c) Partial schedule on P_7 if n_0 is duplicated

4.2 minNP: Minimizing the Number of Processors Used

The *minNP* algorithm tries to minimize the number of processors required by the schedule generated by *minSL* without degrading the achieved schedule length. *minNP* consists of subsequent calls to two subroutines. First, redundant partial schedules are discarded by *elimProcs*, then the remaining ones are merged, as much as possible, by *mergeSchedules*.

elimProcs (Algorithm 2) checks whether a task is duplicated on a partial schedule other than its own to finish early enough such that it can fulfill the dependency requirements of its children. If it is, task's partial schedule is discarded and its duplicates on other partial schedules are shifted to later idle slots as much as possible to relax the *latest finish time* (lft) constraints of the task's parents. lft of a task is defined as the time that at least one of its duplicates should finish execution so that its children will receive data before their start time.

In *elimProcs*, all processors are considered one by

Algorithm 2 elimProcs

1: **for all** P_t with non-increasing SL_t order **do**
2: **if** target task n_t on P_t is an exit task **then**
3: $lft(n_t) \leftarrow SL; \quad fixed(n_t) \leftarrow P_t$
4: **else**
5: $\mathcal{D}_t = \{P_\ell | (n_t, n_d) \in \mathcal{E}$ and $ft(n_t, P_\ell) > st(n_d, P_\ell)\}$
6: $t_k \leftarrow$ start time of the next task after n_t on P_k
7: **if** $\mathcal{D}_t = \emptyset$ **then**
8: $\mathcal{P} \leftarrow \mathcal{P} - \{P_t\}$
9: **else**
10: $lft(n_t) \leftarrow min_{P_\ell \in \mathcal{D}_t}\{st(n_d, P_\ell) - c_{t,d}\}$
11: **if** $lft(n_t) \geq ft(n_t, P_\ell)$ for $P_\ell \in \mathcal{P}$ such that $SL_\ell > SL_t$ **and** $min_{P_k \in (\mathcal{P} - \{P_t\})}\{t_k - ft(n_t, P_k)\} = t_\ell - ft(n_t, P_\ell)$ **then**
12: $P_c \leftarrow P_\ell; \quad \mathcal{P} \leftarrow \mathcal{P} - \{P_t\}$
13: **else**
14: $P_c \leftarrow P_t$
15: $fixed(n_t) \leftarrow P_c$
16: $ft(n_t, P_k) \leftarrow t_k$ for all $P_k \in \mathcal{P} - \{P_c\}$
17: $ft(n_t, P_c) \leftarrow min\{t_c, lft(n_t)\}$

one in non-increasing partial schedule length in order to ensure that a task is always considered after its children. One duplicate of each task finishing no later than the lft is fixed on the processor it is scheduled and not allowed to finish later than its lft. Each task is fixed on at most one processor, and array *fixed* is used to keep track of the processors where each task is fixed. There is no lft restriction on the remaining duplicates.

If the target task n_t, the task that its partial schedule is created on the processor P_t, is an exit task, it is scheduled to finish at SL and *fixed* on P_t (step 3). For a non-exit n_t on the other hand, first the processors hosting its dependent children are found in step 5. If there is no such child, P_t is no longer needed (step 8). Otherwise, $lft(n_t)$ is calculated considering all dependent children n_d. Then, it is checked whether a duplicate of n_t on $P_\ell \neq P_t$ starts before $lft(n_t)$. In such a case, P_ℓ is labeled as the *candidate processor* P_c. If there are more than one such duplicates, ties are broken by choosing the processor on which the idle time immediately after n_t is the smallest. If no P_c is found, P_t is labeled as P_c. In step 15, n_t is fixed on P_c so that it cannot be scheduled to finish after $lft(n_t)$ on P_c in later steps.

In step 16, all duplicates of n_t except the one on P_c are shifted to finish at the start time of the next task after each of them. The duplicate on P_c is scheduled to finish at the smaller of $lft(n_t)$ and the start time of the next task on P_c.

An example DAG and the partial schedules after

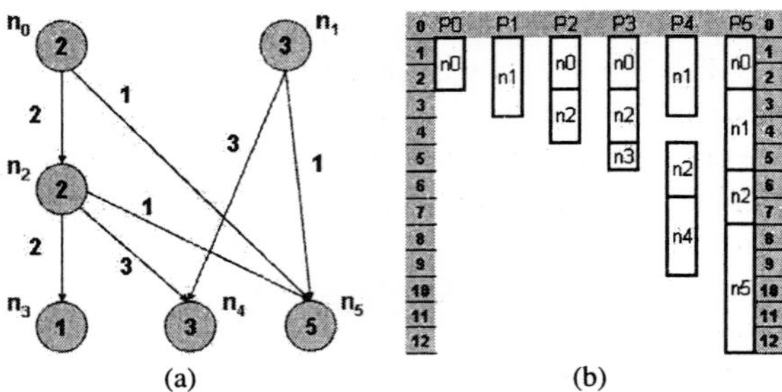

Figure 3. (a) DAG (b) Partial schedules after the *minSL* algorithm

minSL is given in Figure 3. *minNP* starts with considering P_5 which is the longest partial schedule. Since n_5 and similarly n_4 and n_3 are exit tasks, they are simply shifted to finish at SL. For the next longest partial schedule, P_2, it is checked if there is a dependent child that requires the partial schedule of n_2. In this example, n_2 is duplicated before its children on all relevant processors, therefore it has no dependent child and P_2 is discarded. The duplicates of n_2 are shifted to later slots as shown in Figure 4(a). By the same argument, partial schedule of n_1 is also discarded (Figure 4(b)).

The situation is different for n_0 since n_2 on P_4 is a dependent child of n_0 and $lft(n_0)$ is 5 due to this child. Out of the two duplicates of n_0 on processors P_3 and P_5 both of which finish earlier than $lft(n_0)$, the one on P_5 is chosen as the candidate since the idle time following n_0 is the smallest on P_5. As a result, n_0 is fixed on P_5 and P_0 is discarded. The resulting schedule is shown in Figure 4(c).

Further reduction in the number of processors can be achieved by merging the partial schedules by utilizing the idle slots. The *mergeSchedules* subroutine (Algorithm 3) designed for this purpose considers two processors at a time in non-increasing SL order and tries to merge the tasks on these processors without violating any dependency constraints. Before merging begins, *data send time* (dst), the time that all children of a task finishes receiving data from the task is calculated. dst will be used to remove redundant duplicates during merging.

Out of the two processors being considered, the one having the longer (shorter) SL is labeled as $P_\ell(P_s)$. A merged schedule is constructed on a temporary processor P_m, which is filled back to front, by considering tasks one by one. To keep track of the start time of the last scheduled task, a counter t is initialized to SL in step 4. Next, the latest starting unconsidered non-redundant (with a dst larger than t) task from P_ℓ or P_s is picked as the next task to be merged (n_m) by the *pickTask* subroutine. If P_m becomes infeasible at any

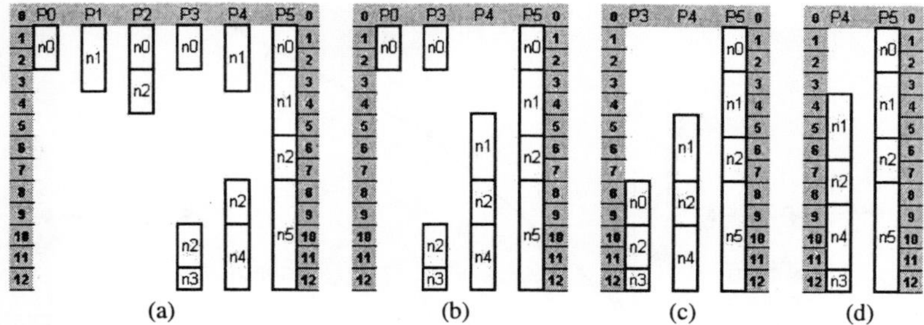

Figure 4. (a) Shifting n_2 (b) Shifting n_1 (c) After *elimProcs* (d) After *mergeSchedules*

Algorithm 3 mergeSchedules

1: $dst(n_i) \leftarrow lft(n_i) + max_{n_j}\{c_{i,j}\}\ \forall(n_i, n_j) \in \mathcal{E}$
2: **for all** P_ℓ with non-increasing SL_ℓ order **do**
3:   **for all** P_s starting from the one after P_ℓ in non-increasing SL_s order **do**
4:     $t \leftarrow SL$
5:     **while** $n_m \leftarrow$ pickTask(P_ℓ, P_s) **do**
6:       **if** n_m is fixed on P_ℓ or P_s **then**
7:         $ft(n_m, P_m) \leftarrow min\{lft(n_m), t\}$
8:       **else**
9:         $ft(n_m, P_m) \leftarrow t$
10:       $t \leftarrow st(n_m, P_m) \leftarrow ft(n_m, P_m) - w_m$
11:       **if** $t < 0$ **then**
12:         merge is not feasible; skip P_s
13:       **else**
14:         **for all** parents n_p of n_m which has no unconsidered duplicate on P_ℓ or P_s **do**
15:           **if** $st(n_m, P_m) < lft(n_p) + c_{p,m}$ **then**
16:             merge is not feasible; skip P_s
17:     $P_\ell \leftarrow P_m$; $\mathcal{P} \leftarrow \mathcal{P} - \{P_s\}$
18:     fix tasks previously fixed on P_s on P_ℓ

---

point, merging the current processor pair is canceled and the next pair is considered. If two schedules are merged without any dependency problems, P_m is stored as P_ℓ and P_s is discarded (step 17). Moreover, any task that was previously fixed on P_s is fixed on P_ℓ. In the example displayed in Figure 4, partial schedules P_3 and P_4 are merged and the resulting schedule is stored as P_4 whereas P_3 is discarded (Figure 4(d)).

After n_m is selected, it is tentatively scheduled on P_m and the feasibility of the schedule is checked. If n_m is fixed on P_ℓ or P_s, it is scheduled to finish at the minimum of $lft(n_m)$ and t (step 7). Otherwise, it is scheduled to finish at t. If this makes the start time of n_m negative then schedule is infeasible (step 12). We also need to verify if $st(n_m, P_m)$ is larger than $est(n_m, P_m)$. Here, when computing the est, we do not consider the parents duplicated on P_ℓ or P_s and have not been scheduled onto P_m yet. Clearly such parents will be scheduled before n_m on P_m (recall that we are filling P_m back-to-front). However, if data from any of the parents that will not be duplicated on P_m arrives after the scheduled start time of n_m, again P_m becomes infeasible (steps 14-16).

minNP algorithm can be used to increase the efficiency of other scheduling algorithms with some modification in *elimProcs*. In the current form, *elimProcs* exploits the structure of the partial schedules generated by *minSL*, and it discards a processor P_i if a duplicate of n_i on another processor can provide n_i's output to its dependent children in a timely manner. Since schedules generated by other algorithms are not guaranteed to have such a structure, *elimProcs* should be altered. In the modified *minNP* algorithm, *MminNP*, *elimProcs* is changed such that the lft calculation and task shifting steps are done in separate loops for a more accurate lft computation. The duplicate of each task starting closest to its lft is *fixed*, and non-fixed tasks are shifted to later slots on the other processors. The *mergeSchedules* subroutine is used without any modification.

5 Experimental Results

We evaluated the performance of the proposed DUPS algorithm on random DAGs and compared to the CPFD algorithm [1]. We also applied *MminNP*, to the output of CPFD to investigate the reduction in the number of processors used. This version of CPFD is called *CPFD+MminNP*.

The parameters of interest are the number of tasks (N), *communication to computation ratio (CCR)*, and the number of parent tasks (p) to control the number of dependencies. In the generated DAGs, N varies between 50 and 550, CCR between 0.1 and 10, and p between 2 and 10. For each parameter set 14 random DAGs are generated, resulting in 2520 DAGs. We have implemented both DUPS and CPFD using C++ and compiled using GNU gcc 3.2. All experiments are carried out on a Linux box equipped with 2.8GHz Pentium IV CPU and 512MB memory.

Due to lack of space we are only presenting the aver-

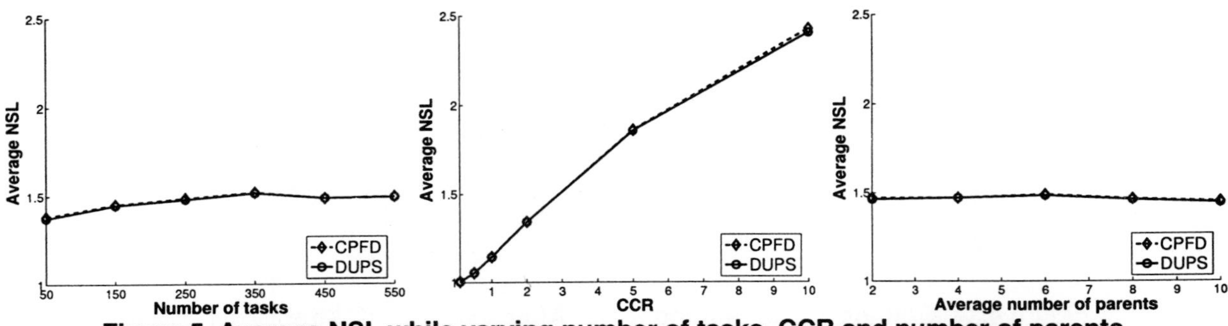

Figure 5. Average NSL while varying number of tasks, CCR and number of parents.

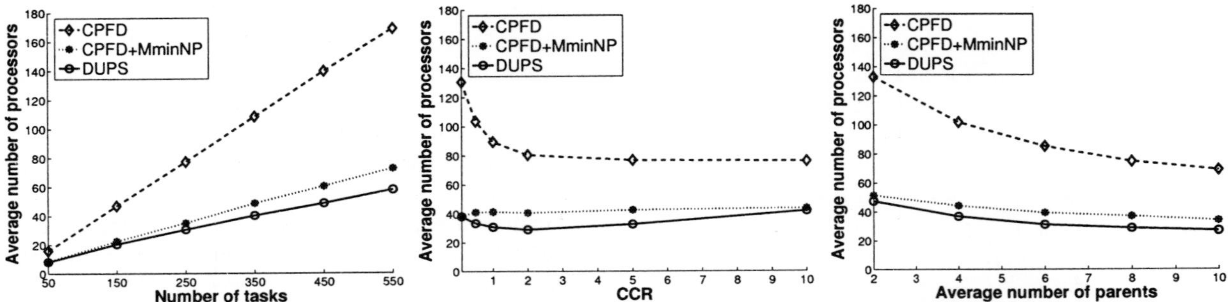

Figure 6. Average number of processors while varying number of tasks, CCR and number of parents.

age performance results in this paper. Detailed results for different values of DAG parameters can be found in [5]. NSL and the processor requirement of the schedules generated by DUPS, CPFD and CPFD+MminNP algorithms are presented in Figures 5-6. The results indicate that, the NSL of the schedules by DUPS and CPFD are very close to each other where DUPS is marginally (0.34%) better. Furthermore, the number of processors required by DUPS is only 37% of what is required by CPFD. Similarly, the processor requirement of CPFD+MminNP is 45% of CPFD. It is expected that as N increases, SL would also increase. However it is important that SL scale well with the change in N. Results illustrate that DUPS scales well both in terms of NSL and the number of processors used.

CCR is defined as the ratio of the average communication cost to the average computation cost in a DAG. The larger the CCR, the more important the communication costs become in scheduling. If on the average, communication takes considerably larger amount of time than computation, i.e. if CCR is large, the processors tend to be idle for a larger amount of time. The reason is that the child tasks have to wait until all the data from their parents are communicated before their execution can start. Therefore scheduling algorithms usually suffer more with larger CCR. Figure 6 displays that both CPFD and DUPS suffer with large CCR and the performance improvement of DUPS over CPFD is not significant in terms of NSL. The difference in the number of processors used for DUPS and CPFD+MminNP is the largest when CCR is around 1.0 to 5.0 and it is relatively smaller at the extreme cases of CCR (0.1 and 10.0).

The final parameter of interest is the average number of parents of the tasks. Let E be number of edges in the DAG. Then p can be computed as $p = \frac{E}{N}$. As E increases for a constant N, each task will depend on a larger number of tasks which may complicate the scheduling problem. The effect of this parameter has not been investigated thoroughly in previous related studies. Our experiments demonstrated that NSL does not change considerably with p. This result can be interpreted as the change in SL is highly correlated with the change in the sum of the computation costs along the critical path, therefore increase in SL with p is proportional to this sum. On the other hand, the processor requirement decreases slightly as the number of dependencies increase. The reason is that, increasing SL with p, results in larger time slots to be utilized on the processors. Thus, tasks can fit on a smaller number of processors. Please also refer to [5] for detailed experimental results.

The run time comparison of DUPS and CPFD as well as the run time of DUPS phases and MminNP are shown in Figure 7. Please note that we have coded both algorithms for correct functionality but did not optimize them for run time. The results show that DUPS has a

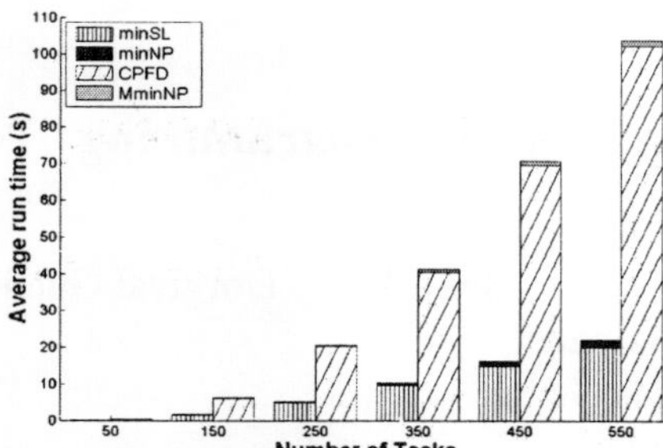

Figure 7. Runtime comparison of CPFD+MminNP and DUPS

smaller run time although both algorithms have the same time complexity of $O(N^4)$. CPFD schedules each task on all processors that contain any of its parents before choosing the best processor to schedule the task. On the contrary, in DUPS, only a single partial schedule is constructed for each task, thus avoiding several scheduling attempts to find the best choice.

6 Conclusion and Future Work

The schedules produced by the proposed DUPS algorithm has been shown to require only 37% of the number of processors required by the well known CPFD algorithm while achieving the same schedule length on the average. We also applied the second phase of the proposed algorithm after CPFD. The results showed that we were able to reduce the processor requirement of CPFD to its 45%, however, still considerably larger than that of DUPS.

Testing DUPS on real world applications and comparing it with algorithms that aim to optimize different metrics are included in our future work plan. We also plan to generalize the algorithm to suit for problems with tighter constraints.

References

[1] I. Ahmad and Y.-K. Kwok. On exploiting task duplication in parallel program scheduling. *IEEE Transactions on Parallel and Distributed Systems*, 9(9):872–892, September 1998.

[2] I. Ahmad and Y.-K. Kwok. On parallelizing the multiprocessor scheduling problem. *IEEE Transactions on Parallel and Distributed Systems*, 10(4):414–432, April 1999.

[3] S. Bansal, P. Kumar, and K. Singh. An improved duplication strategy for scheduling precedence constrained graphs in multiprocessor systems. *IEEE Transactions on Parallel and Distributed Systems*, 14(6):533–544, June 2003.

[4] C. Boeres and V. Robello. Cluster-based static scheduling: Theory and practice. *Proceedings of the 14th Symposium on Computer Architecture and High Performance Computing*, pages 133–140, October 2002.

[5] D. Bozdağ. A task duplication based scheduling algorithm using partial schedules. Master's thesis, The Ohio State University, 2005.

[6] S. Darbha and D. Agrawal. Optimal scheduling algorithm for distributed memory machines. *IEEE Transactions on Parallel and Distributed Systems*, 9(1):87–95, January 1998.

[7] M. Garey and D. Johnson. *Computers and Intractability, A Guide to the Theory of NP Completeness.* W.H. Freeman and Co., 1979.

[8] L. Guodong, C. Daoxu, W. Daming, and Z. Defu. Task clustering and scheduling to multiprocessors with duplication. *Proceedings of the International Parallel and Distributed Processing Symposium*, April 2003.

[9] M. Iverson, F. Özgüner, and L. Potter. Statistical prediction of task execution times through analytical benchmarking for scheduling in a heterogeneous environment. *IEEE Transactions on Computers*, 48(12):1374–1379, December 1999.

[10] Y.-K. Kwok and I. Ahmad. Dynamic critical path scheduling: An effective technique for allocating task graphs to multiprocessors. *IEEE Transactions on Parallel and Distributed Systems*, 7(5):506–521, May 1996.

[11] Y.-K. Kwok and I. Ahmad. Benchmarking and comparison of the task graph scheduling algorithms. *Journal of Parallel and Distributed Computing*, 59(3):381–422, December 1999.

[12] Y.-K. Kwok and I. Ahmad. Static scheduling algorithms for allocating directed task graphs to multiprocessors. *ACM Computing Surveys*, 31(4):406–471, December 1999.

[13] C. Papadimitriou and M. Yannakakis. Towards an architecture independent analysis of parallel algorithms. *SIAM Journal of Computing*, 19:322–328, April 1990.

[14] C. Park and T. Choe. An optimal scheduling algorithm based on task duplication. *IEEE Transactions on Computers*, 51(4):444–448, April 2002.

[15] G. Park, B. Shirazi, and J. Marquis. Mapping of parallel tasks to multiprocessors with duplication. *Proceedings of the 31st Annual Hawaii International Conference on System Sciences*, 7:96–105, January 1998.

[16] A. Radulescu and A. van Gemund. Low-cost task scheduling for distributed-memory machines. *IEEE Transactions on Parallel and Distributed Systems*, 13(6):648–658, June 2002.

[17] M. Wu, W. Shu, and J. Gu. Efficient local search for dag scheduling. *IEEE Transactions on Parallel and Distributed Systems*, 12(6):617–627, June 2001.

[18] M.-Y. Wu and D. Gajski. Hypertool: A programming aid for message-passing systems. *IEEE Transactions on Parallel and Distributed Systems*, 1(3):330–343, July 1990.

Scheduling Data Flow Applications Using Linear Programming

Luiz Thomaz do Nascimento Renato A. Ferreira Wagner Meira Jr. Dorgival Guedes
Department of Computer Science
Universidade Federal de Minas Gerais
Belo Horizonte, MG, Brazil
{lthomaz,renato,meira,dorgival}@dcc.ufmg.br

Abstract

Grid environments are becoming cost-effective substitutes to supercomputers. Datacutter is one of several initiatives in creating mechanisms for applications to efficiently exploit the vast computation power of such environments. In Datacutter, applications are modeled as a set of communicating filters that may run on several nodes of a Computational Grid. To achieve high performance, a number of transparent copies of each of the filters that comprise the application need to be appropriately placed on different nodes of the grid. Such task is carried out by a scheduler which is the focus of this work. We present LPSched, a scheduler for Datacutter applications which uses linear programming to make decisions about the number of copies of each filter as well as the placement of each of the copies across the nodes. LPSched bases its decisions upon the performance behavior of each filter as well as the resources currently available on the Grid.

1 Introduction

Grid computing has emerged as a cost effective alternative to large supercomputers. As a computing grid, a vast collection of heterogeneous computational resources connected through wide area networks might be effectively used for high performance applications. A lot of effort is currently going towards building infrastructure that enables application developers to easily take advantage of the enormous computation power available on the Grid [10, 2].

One particular technology that has been used effectively for building Grid enabled applications is Datacutter [4]. This environment is based on the data-flow model, and assumes that applications are decomposed into filters that communicate using streams. These filters can be instantiated on several machines across the Grid and the system takes care of connecting the streams appropriately. Multiple instances of the same filter are allowed to balance the different computational requirements of different filters, and to achieve high performance.

In this paper we present LPSched, a scheduling mechanism for Datacutter, based on linear programming. The idea is to create a linear programming problem [3] based on collected information about the execution environment and the application. Upon the solution of the problem, LPSched is able to determine the number of copies for each filter as well as an appropriate host where each copy should run. Our experiments have shown that LPSched is able to effectively produce schedules that achieve good performance while being conservative about host allocation.

This paper is organized as follows. In the next section we describe the basics on Datacutter and the application model it implements. The following section goes into the details of LPSched and the linear programming problem it generates to produce an efficient schedule. Section 4 presents some experimental results and in Section 5 we conclude the work and present some future directions.

2 Datacutter

In this section we describe the user-level middle-ware called Datacutter [5], which has been developed at the University of Maryland and the Ohio State University. Datacutter supports the filter-stream programming model, where an application executes over distributed, heterogeneous environments by allowing decomposition of application-specific data processing operations into a set of filters that communicate exclusively via streams.

The specification of a filter consists of an initialization function (init), a processing function (process), and a finalization function (finalize). A stream is an abstraction used for all filter communication, and specifies how filters are logically connected. All transfers to and from streams are through a provided buffer abstraction. Streams transfer data in these fixed size buffers. Filter operations progress as a sequence of cycles, with each cycle handling a single application defined unit-of-work. A work cycle starts when the filtering service calls the filter init function, which is where any required resources such as memory or disk

0190-3918/05 $20.00 © 2005 IEEE

scratch space are pre-allocated. Next the process function is called to continually read data arriving on the input streams in buffers from the sending filters. The finalize function is called after all processing is finished for the current unit-of-work, to allow the release of allocated resources.

The use of Datacutter relieves programmers from several low-level tasks, such as process initiation and interprocess communication, as well as it provides flexible shared memory or distributed memory parallelization associated with its support for transparent copies. Transparent copies allow a finer level of parallelism via multiple copies of a single filter. The filter run-time system maintains the illusion of a single logical point-to-point stream for communication between a logical producer filter and a logical consumer filter. When the logical producer or logical consumer is transparently copied, the system decides for each producer which copy to send a stream buffer to. Schemes like round-robin allocation are used to achieve load balancing.

To execute a Datacutter application, the user needs to specify the filter connectivity as well as a placement for each filter copy on the available hosts. This information is read by the run-time system from a configuration file which can be generated by an automatic scheduler.

3 Linear programming scheduler (LPSched)

In this Section we present LPSched, our scheduler based on Linear Programming. The idea behind LPSched is that it uses information about the application being scheduled and the available computational resources to create a Linear Programming Problem (LPP). Upon the solution of this problem, a Datacutter schedule can be generated.

The main idea behind our approach is to consider Datacutter as running in steady state, meaning, the filters are receiving data at a given rate, processing that data, and then producing an output at a particular rate. In such framework, filters can be thought of as consumers and producers of data, and the problem becomes that of balancing the data-flows coming in and out of each filter. Such problems can be modeled very conveniently using the Linear Programming methodology.

We now describe the information LPSched uses to produce its LPP. Then we present how this LPP is generated. The problem is very similar to the classical flow optimization problem described in the theory of Linear Programming [3], in particular, we generate a Mixed Integer Linear Programming Problem, and it can be solved using a Simplex solver associated with branch-and-bound techniques. Finally, we show that a schedule can be generated from the solution to the corresponding LPP.

3.1 Problem parameters

LPSched models the platform as a set of clusters connected using wide area networks. Each cluster is composed of a number of machines that are connected through switches. The information required for the network connections is the communication bandwidth. For the nodes, LPSched needs some information to be able to compare different nodes on an heterogenous environment. This is provided by a number that gives the processing capability of the node as perceived by a Datacutter filter. The larger the number, the faster the filter will execute on that node.

Figure 1 shows an example of an infrastructure available for Datacutter to execute applications. There are three clusters ($C1, C2, C3$ in the picture), all connected using some WAN. The network bandwidth available between the clusters are represented by $BW[C_i, C_j]$. The other two parameters, not shown in the picture, are $BW[C_i]$, the bandwidth available within C_i and the performance indicator $P[h_i]$ for each host h_i available.

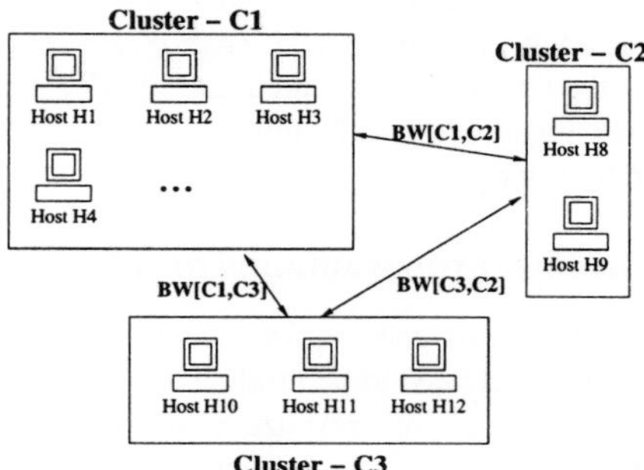

Figure 1. Available computational resources.

The applications modeled in LPSched are similar to the one presented in Figure 2. The current implementation considers only applications that can be decomposed as a pipeline of filters. The nodes on the graph represent the filters that comprise the application. In our example, there are 3 filters. The first one, R, is the Read filter. This is the filter that retrieves the application data from disk and starts the data flow. Read filters are special in any Datacutter application for it is the source of the data for the remaining filters. It is specially marked and recognized by LPSched. The second filter, T, receives data chunks from the first and performs some transformation on the data. The last filter, V, is the visualization filter, which receives the transformed data and creates the output. The edges represent the streams. There are two edges shown in the picture, connecting R to T and connecting T to V.

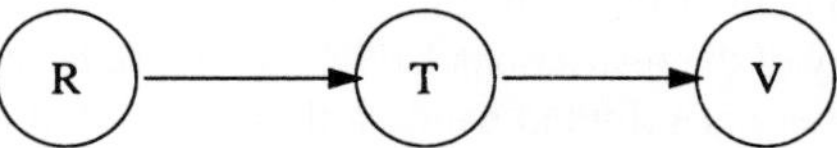

Figure 2. Sample application graph.

In addition to the application graph described above, LPSched needs some additional information about the application. First, it needs to know which nodes in the computation infrastructure contain portions of the input data. LPSched handles each group of nodes that contain a complete replica of the input data as a separate input data configuration set. Each set i is represented by two variables, $X_R[h,i]$ and $V_R[h,i]$. The first is a boolean and tells whether there should be a Read filter on host h for data source configuration i. The second variable represents the amount of data available on host h for option i as a percentage of the total input. These two variables are related and are provided by the application programmer in a configuration file. The decision of which source to use is up to LPSched.

Also, LPSched relies on information collected during a controlled execution of the application where there is one single instance of each filter, running on a separate, unloaded host. It is assumed that the load to which the system is submitted on this trial run is representative of the load during the real execution. The following information is collected for each filter in the trial run: $P[f]$, the processing power of the host which executed filter f, $V[f]$, the volume of data produced by filter f, and $T[f]$, the processing time required by filter f.

3.2 The linear programming problem

As any LPP, this one requires a set of variables which are the values that need to be produced by the solver. These must be such that will optimize some objective function while, at the same time, satisfying a set of restrictions posed to the problem. To create an LPP is, therefore, to create these three pieces of information (variables, objective function, and restrictions).

Variables. The values that LPSched must produce constitute the execution schedule, the information about which filter replica should be run in each node, if any. One assumption we make is that there will be only one instance of any filter running on any node. This is so that we avoid multiple filter instances competing for the node at execution time. We call these variables $vX[f,h]$ which are boolean values indicating the presence of filter f in processor h. The solution to the LPP will assign values 0 or 1 to these variables and from that information a schedule can be produced in a straight forward way.

The second set of values is related to the amount of data transfered to and from each node. This is not actually an output for the scheduler, but a fundamental piece of information in the LPP itself. In particular, these values are used in many of the restrictions LPSched impose to the problem, since there is a limited bandwidth in and out of every node of the system. These variables, $vF[f_p, f_c, h_p, h_c]$, represent the volume of data communicated from the instance of filter f_p running on host h_p to the instance of filter f_c running on host h_c. The values are real numbers given in Megabytes per Second.

Figure 3 shows a representation of the scheduling graph of our example application assuming there are 12 hosts available to execute the application. The variables of the LPP are represented in the figure.

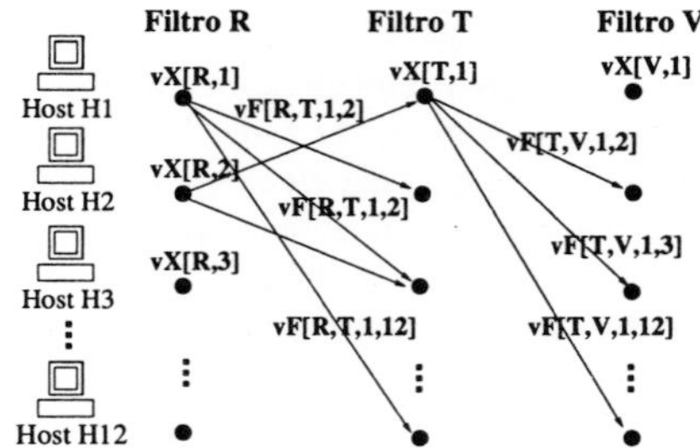

Figure 3. Scheduling graph.

A third set of variables for the LPP, which is not represented in Figure 3, is related to the choices available for the input data source configuration set. A boolean variable $vOP[i]$ is used to tell whether or not configuration set i is chosen as the input data source

Objective function. A Linear Programming Solver will assign values to the variables of the problem in such a way as to optimize a given objective function. In the context of LPSched, an optimal schedule can be thought of in two ways.

First, an optimal schedule is such that the application runs as fast as possible. If we consider that filters operate on the information that flows through them, the faster the filters communicate, the faster the output is produced and the computation finishes. To achieve that, LPSched should maximize the flow of data between filters. The equation below computes the total data-flow. We introduce one additional parameter here, which is a weight for cross-cluster communication, a function $W_C(C_i, C_j)$ where C_i and C_j are any two clusters ($i = j$ is a possibility). Additionally, $Cl(h)$ is a function that returns the cluster to which host h belongs.

$$S1 = \sum_{\substack{(fp,\, fc) \in filters \\ (hp,\, hc) \in hosts}} W_C(Cl(hp), Cl(hc)) \times vF[fp, fc, hp, hc] \quad (1)$$

On the other hand, a good scheduler should consume the minimum of the available resources necessary for each application. Grids are thought of as collaborative shared resources, therefore LPSched should be conservative about using nodes, and place filters only on as many nodes as it consider useful. The total number of processors used for any given schedule is given by the equation below. We introduce another additional weight here, W_X, which is a cost that should be paid for every additional node LPSched chooses to use.

$$S2 = \sum_{\substack{f \in filters \\ h \in hosts}} W_X \times vX[f, h] \quad (2)$$

The objective function adopted in LPSched is, then, to maximize $(S1 - S2)$.

The weights introduced previously in this section can be used as knobs for fine tuning of the scheduler. For instance, the user can use W_C to favor certain cluster over others. W_X can also be seen as a nice way to represent a tradeoff between additional nodes and extra MB/s.

Restrictions. These are used in Linear Programming to provide bounds to the values of the variables, and to relate different aspects of the problem. The restrictions are a set of inequalities on the problem variables and any viable solution to the problem must satisfy all of them.

The first restriction is related to the **choice of input data source**. The restriction is used to guarantee that for every schedule produced, one and only one input data set is used. This situation can be modeled by the formula below.

$$\sum_{i \in options} vOP[i] = 1 \tag{3}$$

Once we guarantee that a choice is made, we have to make sure that the **Read filters are correctly placed**.

$$\forall h \in hosts, \quad vX[R, h] = \sum_{i \in choices} (vOP[i] \times X_R[h, i]) \tag{4}$$

LPSched can easily compute the data flow produced by a Read filter on any host h available to the application. It does that by using information from the trial run. In that run, a single Read filter that read the entire dataset ran on a single processor. The flow for that filter is given by $V[R]/T[R]$. For a different host h, the flow is $F_{out}[R, h] = V[R]/T[R] \times P[h]/P[R]$. Notice that $P[R]$ is the performance index for the host in which the filter R ran during the trial run, while $P[h]$ is the performance index for host h. With that information, LPSched produces another set of restrictions that will **create values for the variables** $vF[h]$ for the host h where the Read filters might run. Notice the filter f in the equations. That is the filter that follows R in the pipeline. In the case of the example shown in Figure 2, it would be the filter T.

$$\forall h \in hosts, \quad \sum_{h' \in hosts - \{h\}} vF[R, f, h, h'] = \sum_{i \in choices} vOP[i] \times X_R[h, i] \times F_{out}[R, h] \tag{5}$$

Next, LPSched generates a set of equations to guarantee that **at least a copy of each filter exists** in any viable schedule.

$$\forall f \in filter, \quad \sum_{h \in hosts} vX[f, h] \geq 1 \tag{6}$$

Going back to the data flows, we showed how $F_{out}[R, h]$ could be computed for filter R on host h. For any choice of input data source, multiple hosts can be used to read data. Therefore, the notion of an aggregate flow exists and consists of $F_{tot}[R, i] = \sum_{h \in hosts} (X_R[h, i] \times F_{out}[R, h])$, the total aggregate data flow for filter R if option i is taken for input data source. The data produced by a filter is the data consumed on the following filter. From the trial run we know the volume of data produced on each filter. For our example application, we have from the trial run that the data produced by filter R is $V[R]$. The next filter is T, and the data produced by it is $V[T]$. So we know that filter T produces $V[T]/V[R]$ data for every byte it receives. Therefore we can extend the notion of the total aggregate flow beyond the Read filter. LPSched uses that computation to provide restrictions that will create an upper bound on the data flow. These restrictions will limit the total data flow between two filters so that **no more communications than necessary** will be generated.

$$\forall edges(f_p, f_c) \in \text{application graph}, \quad \sum_{h_p, h_c \in hosts} vF[f_p, f_c, h_p, h_c] \leq F_{tot}[f_p, i] \tag{7}$$

Based on that same information, another set of restrictions need to be generated to **guarantee that every filter will receive all the data it requires, and will also produce all the data it needs to**.

$$\forall h \in hosts, \ \forall \text{pairs of edges}(f1, f), (f, f2), \quad \sum_{hp \in hosts} vF[f1, f, hp, h] = \frac{V[f1]}{V[f]} \times \sum_{hc \in hosts} vF[f, f2, h, hc] \tag{8}$$

For every filter f in the application, we can compute $F_{out}[f, h]$ from the information of the trial run. We have used that same computation for the Read filter (R) above to compute the maximum flow a given choice of input data source can produce. This value also represents the processing capacity for a given filter on a given node. Another set of restrictions generated by LPSched was designed to prevent **overloading of certain processors**. These restrictions will limit the flow into any filter on any host to its maximum capacity on that host.

$$\forall h \in hosts, \ \forall edges(f_p, f) \in \text{application graph}, \quad \sum_{h_p \in hosts} vF[f_p, f, h_p, h] \leq F_{out}[f, h] \tag{9}$$

The next set of restrictions are generated to limit the **number of filters a schedule produces**. In the equations below, we see that the second summation corresponds to the maximum computation rate available for a given filter. The first summation is the demand. The inequality guarantees that there will be enough computing power to consume the incoming data. Yet another fine tuning knob is provided in this equation, in the form of the parameter W_F. This value is a percentage of extra capacity that is forced on the schedule.

$$\forall edges(f_p, f_c), \quad (1 + W_F) \times \sum_{i \in options} F_{tot}[f_p, i] \times vOP[i] \leq \sum_{h \in hosts} vX[f_c, h] \times F_{out}[f_c, h] \tag{10}$$

Another set of restrictions need to be created to **limit network bandwidth**. The schedule should not try to push more data through a connection than its capacity. For the switched LAN, LPSched restricts the solutions so that no connection between two machines on the same cluster exceeds the capacity of the switch.

$$\forall pairs(h_p, h_c) on same cluster, \quad \sum_{f_p, f_c \in filters} vF[f_p, f_c, h_p, h_c] \leq BW[c] \tag{11}$$

For WANs, LPSched considers two different models: in the first one, the network connections is considered to be shared, meaning that the sum of all data flowing into that cluster need to be added up and the summation cannot be greater than the total. The other case, the connections are not shared, and therefore only the specific data flows need to be limited by the network bandwidth. The equations are very similar to Equation 11 and are omitted here.

The final set of restrictions are the ones **relating the variables vF and vX**. As mentioned earlier, the former represents the data flow between two instances of filters, while the latter indicates the existence of a copy of a given filter on a given host. These two variables are related in the sense that the existence of a flow in or out of a filter in a particular host indicates the presence of that filter running on that host. We introduce yet another parameter here, $W_{MIN}[f]$ which represents the minimum flow produced by a given filter on any host running that filter. From that parameter we compute a minimum flow, or capacity of a given filter at a given node as $F_{min}[f, h] = W_{MIM}[f] \times MIN(F_{out}[f, h], MAX(F_{tot}[f_c, i]))$. These variables are generated for every f and every h.

$$vF \times vX: \quad \forall h \in hosts, \ \forall edge(f_p, f_c) \in application\ graph, \quad \frac{\sum_{h_p \in hosts} vF[f_p, f_c, h_p, h]}{MAX(F_{tot}[f_c, i])} \leq vX[f_c, h] \tag{12}$$

$$vX \times vF: \quad \forall h \in hosts, \ \forall edge(f_p, f_c) \in application\ graph, \quad \frac{\sum_{h_p \in hosts} vF[f_p, f_c, h_p, h]}{F_{min}[f, h]} \geq vX[f_c, h] \tag{13}$$

With these restrictions, it is not hard to realize that if one of the variables is zero, the other one will be forced to zero, and if one of them is not zero, the other is not either. In particular, vF will be greater than $F_{min}[h, p]$ if vX is 1.

3.3 Implementation

A version of LPSched has been implemented for testing and validation purposes. It is currently integrated with Datacutter original API and users can benefit from it by simply informing Datacutter that the placement of the filters will be determined by LPSched. The configuration files are all in INI file format, as are the original Datacutter configuration files. The information on the trial runs are generated by the original profiling information output by Datacutter.

One important feature of LPSched implementation is that it probes the computational environment for current loads on the machines, and therefore it is capable of generating schedules adapted to the current status of the Grid. It does that by consulting an infrastructure built on top of the Network Weather Service (NWS) [8] which monitors current and past activity on the hosts and estimates future loads. LPSched then modifies all the information from the trial runs and the hardware capabilities to reflect the estimated load on the system.

With that information, LPSched creates a set of equations that define the LPP. These equations are generated by LPSched and submitted to CPLEX, a sophisticated Simplex solver. The problem is then solved and the solution (the values of the variables) are retrieved to produce the optimal schedule. It is important to mention that CPLEX has capabilities to solve the problem for integer variables. It uses some branch-and-bound based techniques to compute the optimal solutions internally. The integer values of the variables $vX[f, h]$ correspond directly to the schedule.

Also, a few relaxations were implemented to the proposed model. The restrictions that were discussed earlier consider that there is enough computation power and network bandwidth to meet the demand. If that is not the case, the LPSched relaxes some of the restrictions so that a sub-optimal schedule can still be generated. We omit this discussion here due to space constraint. A more comprehensive description of the entire model is available in [6].

4 Experimental results

In this section we discuss experimental results of the application of LPSched to several scenarios, where we are able to evaluate the actual behavior of the scheduler, and its impact in terms of both execution time and computational resource usage.

We compare LPSched to two scheduling strategies. The first strategy, which we call trivial, allocates a single processing node to each filter. The second strategy is similar, but it uses all processing nodes available, dividing them among the filters evenly. The comparison between LPSched and these strategies allows us to verify how LPSched reacts to load imbalance among filters, in terms of creating copies for the filters that perform more computation and exploiting the available resources more effectively. We believe that these two strategies, although very simple, represent ad-hoc approaches that are commonly employed.

4.1 Experimental setup

The experiments presented in this section were performed using three geographically distributed clusters of machines, located at Universidade Federal de Minas Gerais (UFMG), Brazil, at University of Maryland, College Park, and at Ohio Supercomputer Center. These machines were organized in several configurations depending on the purpose of the evaluation and they were also running NWS to gather information about current load from other applications. We used up to 19 nodes from UFMG, which are divided into 3 clusters. The first cluster comprises 8 machines that provide 1.4745 processing units each. The second and third clusters comprise 4 and 7 machines, respectively, and each machine in those clusters provides 0.9912 processing units. We also used up to 48 machines from the University of Maryland, each with 1.29105 processing units. Finally, we used up to 24 machines from the Ohio Supercomputer Center with 1.85466 processing units each. All clusters are connected internally by dedicated Fast Ethernet switches.

We used two different applications to experiment with LPSched. The first application is a modified version of the *GridArrayAverager*, a little three filter application. A text input file is read by filter *ArrayReader* and the numbers read are grouped in blocks and sent to filter *ArrayAdder*, which sums the numbers in each block. Each sum is sent to filter *ArrayAverager* that calculates the average of all numbers. This is a toy application but it is simple enough to allow us to change computational requirements on each filter so that we can experiment with different aspects of LPSched. The second application is the virtual microscope [1, 4], a popular application in the Datacutter domain. It is implemented using 5 filters: *Reader*, *Decompress*, *Clip*, *Zoom* and *View*.

4.2 Scenarios

During the experiments described in the next sections, we evaluate two popular metrics: execution time and resource utilization. The results presented are the average over three executions. There were not significant variations among the executions. As mentioned, we evaluate the effectiveness of LPSched regarding five criteria in the following sections: load balancing, multiprogramming, variable I/O throughput, intra- and inter-cluster connectivity. The average time to schedule is shown on each figure. Notice however, that once an application is scheduled to run, it can run for a very long time with the same configuration. In our experiments, we run the application for only a single iteration.

Load balancing. The first set of experiments demonstrates the effectiveness of LPSched in determining the proper amount of computational resources for applications that are composed of filters that impose diverse processing demands. We employed the modified GridArrayAverager and varied the demand posed by the *Array Adder*. We used seventeen of the nineteen machines available in UFMG, excluding two of the faster ones.

We adjust the application so that the *ArrayAdder* demands five times more processing than the other filters (1 x 5 x 1). We also vary the input data size ranging from 2 to 32MB, for all three scheduling strategies. The results of these experiments are presented in Figure 4. LPSched allocated seven machines for these executions. The first observation is that the gains of LPSched over the Trivial scheduling are significant, running almost 5 times faster. LPSched was also able to recognize the filters that demand more processing, and allocate the most powerful processors to the *ArrayAdder* and *ArrayReader* tasks, while the *ArrayAverager*, which is less computationally intensive, gets executed on a slower machine. LPSched runs slightly faster than Total, which can be explained by the smaller amount of traffic generated and its choice of faster machines.

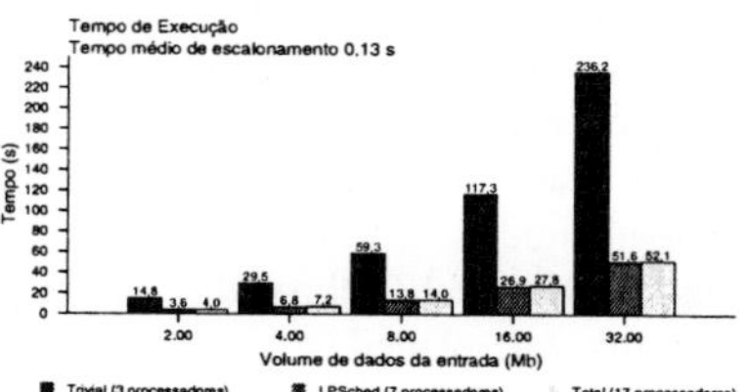

Figure 4. Execution time of the Modified GridArrayAverager — 1 x 5 x 1

Multiprogramming. The goal of this experiment is to evaluate the use of LPSched in multiprogrammed environments. We used all machines from UFMG and placed an external load of 50% in some of the machines. We them compared the scheduling generated by LPSched to the Total scheduling for a modified *GridArrayAverager* with a load imbalance factor of 7, that is, the *ArrayAdder* filter demands 7 times more processing than the other filters. LPSched used 12 of the 19 processors available, and achieved better performance for all input sizes, as shown in Figure 5. The performance gains may be explained by the fact that LPSched allocated load proportional to the availability of each machine, while the Total scheduling does it in a round-robin fashion.

Variable I/O throughput. The experiments presented in this section evaluate the ability of LPSched to generate good assignments considering the I/O configuration and data distribution of the input data. In these experiments we employed all 19 machines from UFMG, and the modified *GridArrayAverager* with an imbalance factor of 5, using an input data file of 32 MB. Regarding input data source, we used two different types of machines, one being 3 times more powerful than the other considering their I/O speeds and processing power.

In the first experiment, LPSched chose between two input data source configurations: (1) whole data in one of

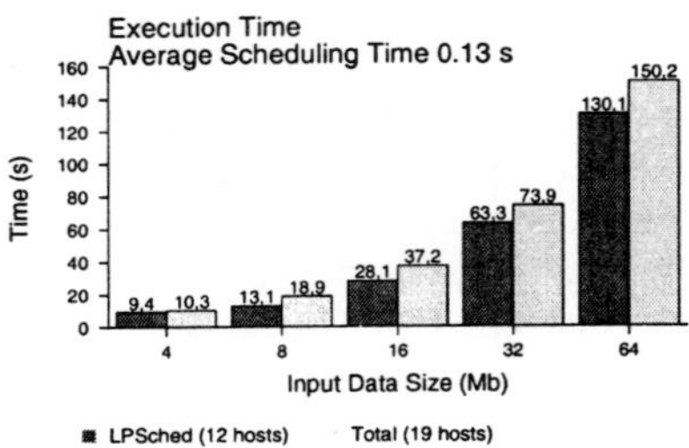

Figure 5. Execution time of the Modified Grid Array Averager using the NWS — 1 x 7 x 1

the fast machines, and (2) evenly divided among two of the slow machines. LPSched chose the first option, as expected, resulting in a overall execution time of 53.2 seconds. In our second experiment, we changed the second configuration, dividing the data evenly among four of the slow machines. In this case, LPSched chose the later, resulting in an execution time of 41.7 seconds, an improvement of 22%.

We then evaluated the ability of LPSched to handle both multiprogramming and I/O throughput. We repeated the first experiment, but placed an external load of 50% in MG1. In this case, LPSched chose the second option, resulting in an execution time of 81.2 seconds. We also repeated the second experiment, but placing an external load of 50% in each of the slow machines. when the single fast machine was chosen by LPSched. These experiments showed not only the ability of LPSched to take into consideration the I/O throughput of machines, but also to generate good schedules considering tradeoffs in more than one dimension, in particular multiprogramming and I/O throughput.

Intra-cluster connectivity. This set of experiments demonstrates the ability of LPSched to handle connectivity restrictions among machines that belong to a cluster. We employed the machines from the University of Maryland and the virtual microscope application, which is remarkable because of its I/O demands. The *Decompress* filter generates a large amount of data, while the filters *Clip*, *Zoom*, and *View* perform a small amount of processing compared to the communication time, making it a good application for evaluating the impact of communication constraints. We employed the three scheduling strategies and all data is located in a single node, which also runs the *Reader* filter in all cases. The Trivial scheduling chose just 5 machines, one for each filter. The Total scheduling allocates machines according to the expected load for each filter, that is, 35 machines run the *Decompress* filter, 6 machines run the *Clip* filter, 5 machines run the *Zoom* filter, and one machine runs the *View* filter. Finally, LPSched allocated 45 machines, using 31 machines for the *Decompress* filter, 7 machines for the *Clip* filter, 5 machines for the *Zoom* filter, and 1 machine for the *View Filter*.

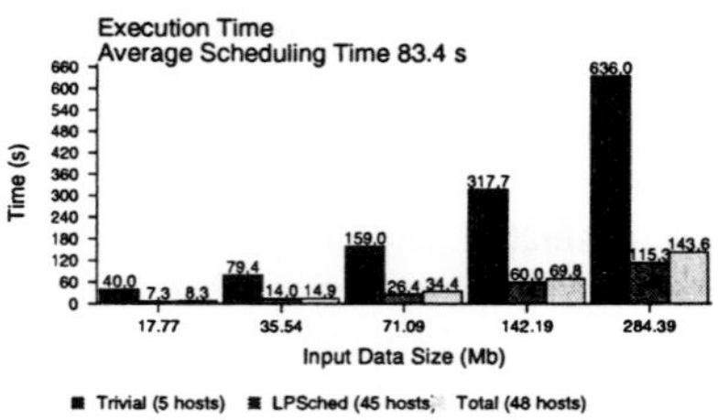

Figure 6. Intra-cluster network connectivity restrictions — Virtual Microscope Application

The execution times for all experiments are shown in Figure 6. As expected, both Total and LPSched resulted in better performance than Trivial, and LPSched outperformed Total, improving the execution time up to 25% despite the fact it uses 3 fewer machines.

Inter-cluster connectivity. The goal of the last set of experiments is to demonstrate the ability of LPSched to determine good schedules considering the connectivity inter clusters of machines. For this evaluation we use again the virtual microscope because of the amount of communication it performs. We used the clusters from the University of Maryland and from the Ohio Supercomputer Center. Again, we employed the three scheduling strategies: Trivial, Total, and LPSched. The trivial scheduling allocates one machine per filter, all of them in the MD cluster. The total scheduling allocates one for the *Reader* filter, 47 MD machines and 8 OH machines to the *Decompress* filter, 10 OH machines to the *Clip* filter, 5 OH machines to the Zoom filter, and the filter *View* is allocated to a single machine at OH. We also set the minimum machine utilization to 70% and kept all other parameters from the intra-cluster experiment.

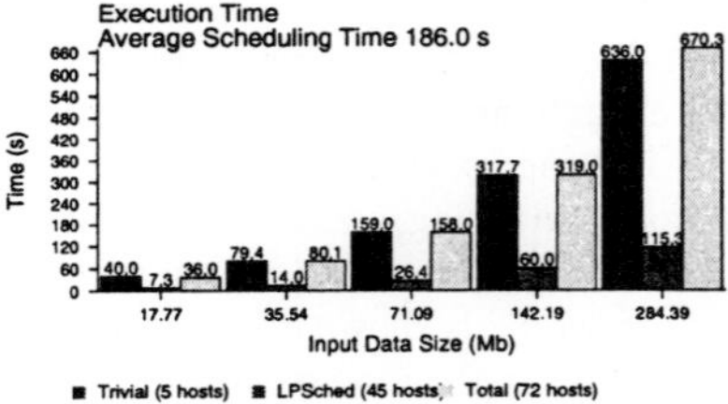

Figure 7. Inter-cluster network connectivity restrictions — Virtual Microscope Application

The results are presented in Figure 7 where we can see that the Total scheduling is the worst option for larger input data, as a consequence of the utilization of the OH machines, which increased the delays due to the inter-cluster traffic. LPSched indicated the same allocation of the intra-cluster experiment, since it considered that it was not worth communicating through the shared link between the two clusters. The results show that the use of all machines is as bad as using just one machine per filter, that is, the machine contention of the Trivial scheduling results in the same performance of a shared long-distance connection between a large number of machines. Further, LPSched was able to recognize such problem and decided not to use all computational resources available. In this case, the placement of the initial data and the minimum utilization restriction were the reasons behind the utilization of the MD machines.

5 Conclusions and future work

We presented LPSched, a linear programming based scheduler that is capable of generating good schedules for Datacutter applications. Datacutter is a filter-stream based run-time framework that allows execution applications on heterogeneous distributed environments. Applications in Datacutter are broken into filters which are the basic computation blocks communicating through streams. A critical portion of achieving high performance in Datacutter applications is by making good choices about how many copies of each filter to create and where to run them.

Such scheduling can be modeled with classical strategies [11, 9, 12], where the problem is modeled as a graph of tasks that must be scheduled (each task is a filter) and a heuristic is used to map them to the available processors. Such strategies focus just on the processing demands and frequently do not consider communication demands. They differ regarding the decision criteria used on allocating tasks to processors. Some strategies use clustering [7], others employ scheduling lists [4], and there are some that employ a combination of both. The strategies vary significantly and are often specific to a given environment.

We have shown that LPSched is capable of generating schedules that achieve good performance, while being conservative about allocating system resources. Such property is desirable in any shared environment such as the Grid. Moreover, over-allocating resources may actually hinder performance by producing extra communication across slow networks. LPSched is also capable of adapting to current observed loads on the environment and will produce good schedules for a dynamic environments.

Our extensive experimentation have shown a good compromise between performance and rationalization of resources. When comparing LPSched to other schedulers in the literature, we see that it presents some improvements to the classic scheduling algorithms. While the latter are often based on heuristics that cannot guarantee optimality, LPSched is based on Linear Programming and it does generate optimum schedules that satisfy all the restrictions of the system.

Two things jump to mind as possible extensions of the current work:

1. More general application graphs. The model may be extended to include, for example, graphs with loops and different fan-ins and fan-outs.

2. While LPSched outputs what the optimal data-flow should be across filters, right now Datacutter does not have any mechanisms to use that information. This can lead to sub-optimal executions of optimal plans.

References

[1] A. Afework, M. Beynon, F. Bustamante, A. Demarzo, R. Ferreira, R. Miller, M. Silberman, J. Saltz, A. Sussman, and H. Tsang. Digital dynamic telepathology - the virtual microscope. In *Proceedings of the 1998 AMIA Annual Fall Symposium. American Medical Informatics Association*, Nov 1998.

[2] N. Andrade, W. Cirne, F. Brasileiro, and P. Roisenberg. Ourgrid: An approach to easily assemble grids with equitable resource sharing. In *Proceedings of the 9th Workshop on Job Scheduling Strategies for Parallel Processing (JSSPP)*, June 2003.

[3] J. J. Bazaraa M. and S. H.D. Linear programming and network flows. Book-Second Edition, John Wiley and Sons, 1990.

[4] M. Beynon. Supporting data intensive applications in a heterogeneous environment. In *Phd Thesis 2001 University of Maryland at College Park*, 2001.

[5] M. Beynon, C. Chang, U. atalyrek, T. Kur, A. Sussman, H. Andrade, R. Ferreira, and J. Saltz. Processing large-scale multi-dimensional data in parallel and distributed environments. *Parallel Computing*, 28(5):827–859, 2002.

[6] L. T. do Nascimento. Escalonamento de aplicações de fluxo de dados. Master's thesis, Universidade Federal de Minas Gerais, 2004. (in Portuguese).

[7] T. K. and C. A. A heuristic algorithm for mapping communicating tasks on heterogeneous resources. In *Proceedings of the Heterogeneous Computing Workshop 2000*, University of California, 2000.

[8] NWS. Network weather service. http://nws.cs.ucsb.edu, 2004.

[9] Su A., Casanova H. and Berman F. Utilizing DAG Scheduling Algorithms for Entity-Level Simulations. In *Proceedings of HPC 2002*, San Diego, CA, april 2002.

[10] D. Thain, T. Tannenbaum, and M. Livny. Distributed computing in practice: The condor experience. *Concurrency and Computation: Practice and Experience*, 2004.

[11] Yang Y. And Casanova H. UMR a multi-round algorithm for scheduling divisible workloads. In *Proceedings of the International Parallel and Distributed processing Symposium (IPDPS'03)*, Nice, France, april 2003.

[12] A. YarKhan and J. Dongarra. Experiments with scheduling using simulated annealing in a grid environment. In *Proceedings of the Third International Workshop on Grid Computing*, pages 232–242. Springer-Verlag, 2002.

Author Index

Press Operating Committee

Chair
Roger U. Fujii
Vice President
Northrop Grumman Mission Systems

Editor-in-Chief
Donald F. Shafer
Chief Technology Officer
Athens Group, Inc.

Board Members

Mark J. Christensen, *Independent Consultant*
Richard Thayer, *Professor Emeritus, California State University, Sacramento*
Ted Lewis, *Professor Computer Science, Naval Postgraduate School*
Linda Shafer, *Professor Emeritus, University of Texas at Austin*
James Conrad, *Associate Professor, UNC-Charlotte*
John Horch, *Independent Consultant*
Deborah Plummer, *Manager, Authored Books*
Thomas Baldwin, *Manager, Conference Publishing Services (CPS)*

IEEE Computer Society Executive Staff

David Hennage, *Executive Director*
Angela Burgess, *Publisher*

IEEE Computer Society Publications

The world-renowned IEEE Computer Society publishes, promotes, and distributes a wide variety of authoritative computer science and engineering texts. These books are available from most retail outlets. Visit the CS Store at *http://computer.org/cspress* for a list of products.

IEEE Computer Society *Conference Publishing Services* (CPS)

The IEEE Computer Society produces and actively promotes conference publications for more than 175 acclaimed international conferences each year in a variety of formats, including soft-cover books, hard-cover books, CD-ROMs, video, and on-line publications. For information about the IEEE Computer Society's *Conference Publishing Services* (CPS), please e-mail tbaldwin@computer.org or write to Proceedings, IEEE Computer Society, P.O. Box 3014, 10662 Los Vaqueros Circle, Los Alamitos, CA 90720-1314. Telephone +1-714-821-8380. Fax +1-714-761-1784. Additional information about the IEEE Computer Society's *Conference Publishing Services* (CPS) can be accessed from our web site at: *http://www.computer.org/proceedings/.*

IEEE Computer Society / Wiley Partnership

The IEEE Computer Society and Wiley partnership allows the CS Press authored book program to produce a number of exciting new titles in areas of computer science and engineering with a special focus on software engineering. IEEE Computer Society members continue to receive a 15% discount on these titles when purchased through Wiley or at: *http://wiley.com/ieeecs*. To submit questions about the program or send proposals, please e-mail dplummer@computer.org or write to Books, IEEE Computer Society, 10662 Los Vaqueros Circle, Los Alamitos, CA 90720-1314. Telephone +1-714-821-8380. Additional information regarding the Computer Society's authored book program can also be accessed from our web site at: *http://computer.org/cspress.*

Revised: 03 January 2005